Twenty Best

EUROPEAN PLAYS

on the

AMERICAN STAGE.

edited with an introduction by

JOHN GASSNER

CROWN PUBLISHERS, INC. · NEW YORK

DRAMA -- COLLECTIONS.

Fifth Printing, June, 1966

CONTENTS

* The plays as printed are so much the work of the adapters that the main authorship is theirs.
** A free German adaptation of Ben Jonson's *Volpone* (1606).

To the Memory

of

HELEN GOALWIN

(December 26, 1895—August 30, 1954)

who combined the graces of the Old World

with the good will of the New

PREFACE

Explanations do not alter the character of a book, but they may be useful in defining its limits. The present anthology is not an attempt to *represent* the modern European drama. Instead, it *presents* that drama as an element or factor in American professional stage production that my Crown anthologies of contemporary American plays have hitherto neglected.

The neglect was intentional in my "Best American Plays" collections, which presented, and will continue to present, exclusively *American* playwriting. Readers of these compilations would have formed confused impressions of the qualities of American playwriting if European plays had been included for the sake of swelling my periodic chronicle of the American stage. It was long apparent, however, that the chronicle would be flagrantly incomplete unless it were supplemented by one or more volumes of European plays.

The present volume is my first effort to enlarge the record of American stage production since World War I, and the character of the anthology may well explain why I postponed publishing it. The conventional compilations of plays from the time of Ibsen to the time of Sartre would not serve my purpose. These books — and I compiled one of them, *A Treasury of the Theatre*, myself — are intended for the study of the European or the modern drama. The present anthology is intended primarily for the study of the American stage, as will any sequel to this volume that may appear later. I say "study," because a comparison between the plays printed here and their original form will instruct the careful reader about Broadway's way of dealing with its imports. It may also dismay him at times, and that can be instructive, too. But it would be disingenuous for me to say that in preparing this anthology I hoped to instruct the general reader instead of merely interesting him. At most I wanted to show him another face of the American theatre, even if, in many instances, it may turn out to be the same face that some of us adore and others deplore. I could not have convinced my publishers to print so large a volume in so inflationary a period if I had been unable to offer a bounty to the public that takes its pleasure wherever it can find it.

Many of the plays afforded pleasure to a large number of playgoers in the recent or not too remote past; and a number of these pieces also deservedly won a measure of regard even in the austerest critical circles that look askance at Broadway adaptations. Several of the plays — most notably *Tiger at the Gates* — brought French wisdom and wit into our theatre. Several — especially the plays by Turgenev and Chekhov — contributed depth of emotion and high artistry to realistic theatre. Other plays, mostly from Central Europe, introduced dramatic experimentation into our theatre as well as a note of vexation with the drift of modern society. One thing is certain: there was no lack of variety in the dramatic literature we imported from continental Europe, not always knowing why and not always knowing what to do with the plays once we had acquired them.

In our haphazard proceedings, moreover, we managed to make the acquaintance of many of the writers who gave the European stage substantial claims to distinction. It has been possible therefore to bring plays by such contemporary playwrights as Giraudoux, Anouilh, Sartre, Werfel, Pirandello, and Molnar into this volume. And it is even possible that readers will be curious to examine what English and American writers (I include both, since both have made translations and adaptations for our stage), what experts in our own tongue such as Christopher Fry, Ashley Dukes,

Emlyn Williams, P. G. Wodehouse, S. N. Behrman, Sidney Howard, and Lillian Hellman, have done with the work of their foreign colleagues. We have in this anthology indeed a double galaxy of playwrights, the original ones and their translators and adapters. The latters' contribution also falls within the province of this chronicle and anthology, sometimes quite importantly when a Sidney Howard, for instance, domesticates a play by a little known French writer and produces *The Late Christopher Bean*.

But it is surely unnecessary, if not indeed inappropriate, for the anthologist to advertise his wares when they are so glaringly evident. It is the omissions that require explanation. It should be evident, for instance, that no attempt has been made to cover the course of European drama from Ibsen's time to our own. I have not included any plays by Ibsen and Strindberg because these have already been anthologized with great frequency for the past three decades and more, and no new translations by these pioneers of modernism have recently made the impact on our theatre that Stark Young's Chekhov translations have made since the Lunts appeared in his translation of *The Sea Gull* in the 1937-38 season. Arthur Miller's earnest adaptation of *An Enemy of the People* has been the sole exception, and its effect on Broadway was too slight to give Ibsen a position of dominance in our theatre such as Miller's original exercises in Judgment Day drama had indirectly assured him. New translations of Strindberg have been printed in recent years (by Elizabeth Sprigge, Arvid Paulson, and Walter Johnson) and more will follow. But even the 1950 centenary of Strindberg failed to bring to Broadway more than a run-of-the-mill production of *The Father*. Nor could a more recent effort to revive *Miss Julie* be set down as particularly successful. Luck in our theatre has been all on the side of the pre-Soviet Russians ever since Arthur Hopkins presented John Barrymore in Tolstoy's *The Living Corpse* under the title of *Redemption* in 1918 — a fact represented here by the inclusion of that play, the Stark Young translation of *The Sea Gull*, and the Emlyn Williams version of Turgenev's *A Month in the Country*, a play twice successful on our stage. It may also be observed that another imbalance in our collection arises from Broadway's partiality for the French drama and for one Parisian dramatist in particular — Jean Giraudoux, three of whose plays are included in this book. But the modern German drama has had a rather erratic career in our theatre, and at neither of its chronological extremes, as represented by Hauptmann and Brecht, has it had successful representation on Broadway during the period of this survey from World War I to the season of 1955-56. The one exception, an off-Broadway one, has been the long run of Marc Blitzstein's adaptation of *The Threepenny Opera* at the Theatre de Lys in Greenwich Village, and this version could not be printed for reasons of litigation.

The other omissions for which an explanation will not be obvious to experts or unnecessary for more fortunate mortals fall into one of two categories. There are plays which could not be cleared for this anthology in time for publication, although an entire year was consumed in trying to secure clearances. And at this point I could a tale unfold that would make each particular hair stand up, if fellow anthologists have any left after similar experiences with the foreign rights and the claims and counter-claims of producers, agents, authors, translators, and legatees. There are also plays I could mention only too easily available for a consideration. They are among their authors' very best work, they had long runs, and they made a strong impression on Broadway and its satellite theatres. But there would have been no point in reproducing such pieces as *Cyrano de Bergerac*, *Liliom*, *R.U.R.* and *The Cradle Song* in our volume, unless they had been successfully re-translated or re-adapted. They have long appeared in standard anthologies that serve another, if by no means less justifiable, purpose. There are, besides, many worthy European plays that have thus far made little headway in our professional precincts, which it is no longer necessary to introduce in print at least, since that important task has been executed by Mr. Eric Bentley. All these plays and others that I hope to present in a supplementary volume belong to a history of European drama. But they do not necessarily belong in the present volume.

Perhaps mention should also be made here — but then, again, mention should not be made — of continental plays omitted because of my unwillingness to do the original authors the injustice of perpetuating their work in unreadable, if more or less accurate, translations or in more or less readable but flagrantly distorted versions. Some free adaptations have been admitted into this anthology for one reason or another which will be evident, I hope. But even a tolerant, if not indeed overindulgent, anthologist will draw the line somewhere between more or less understandable modifications of the original text and downright incompetence or mayhem. The theatre has invited protests against high-handed appropriation and distortion of play material ever since Roman playwrights helped themselves to Greek comedies in the third and second centuries B.C. The fellowship of sinners has had branches in every theatrical capital in every age, and Broadway since World War I has actually been less culpable than in previous periods. Yet the massacre of innocent European scripts continues with seasonal regularity.

We are inveterate empirics all — that is, all of us who are in showbusiness or try to get into it. And the fun really starts when Broadway empiricism proves howlingly disastrous, which is likely to be the case if the European play already adapted by a British cousin is adapted again by an American hack and that adaptation of an adaptation is further adapted by the Broadway producer and his director before, during, and after rehearsals. That is when showbusiness really becomes showbusiness and everybody loses money as well as face. It is one of the traditions of Broadway, from which departures are as rare as they are praiseworthy, never to let a play alone until ministering hands have squeezed it as dry as an overworked lemon. The reader of this anthology has been spared the most mutilated bodies of plays that had a shapely existence in their original habitat. And this just about exhausts the summary of qualifications, if it is also understood that the "modern" European play in this collection may be as old as *A Month in the Country*, completed by Turgenev at the midpoint of the last century, provided it found a haven here after World War I, which is the wavering boundary-line between our old theatre and our new.

This much for those who will scrutinize the selections. For other, and probably happier mortals, the table of contents will speak for itself. The selections appear in reversed chronological order, from the most recent productions to the oldest. Among the first plays in the volume are several which represent the noteworthy revival of French dramatic writing since the early 1930's. In the rest of the book will be found examples of the kinds of dramatic writing that won our attention especially in the "sophisticated" and "experimental" nineteen-twenties. The selections exhibit Central European sophistication in the Molnar vein that once entranced Broadway and can still beguile it, as *The Play's The Thing* proved in its second Broadway production during the 1948-1949 season; expressionistic fancies in the mood of Kaiser and the Capek brothers which were paralleled by native works such as O'Neill's *The Hairy Ape* and Elmer Rice's *The Adding Machine;* and a variety of realistic or critical works from the Continent that our still somewhat virginal stage before World War I would have considered too earnest, too raw, or too irreverent.

JOHN GASSNER

ACKNOWLEDGMENTS

To the persons who made this collection possible, the present writer is immensely grateful. I am particularly sensible of indebtedness to the following individuals, as well as to the publishers and owners of the plays: To Marta Abba for making Pirandello's *As You Desire Me* available to me and for translating the play, which had been available to English readers only in a translation that the late Samuel Putnam had made without regard to any stage production. To Robert Simon, one of Crown's publishers, for his special guidance· and help. To Leah Salisbury, the agent for

Christopher Fry, and Oxford University Press for the very special permission to anthologize *Tiger at the Gates*. To Lillian Hellman and to Donald Klopfer of Random House for the permission to include *The Lark*, and to Miss Marjorie Currey and Random House for the release of the adaptations of *The Madwoman of Chaillot* and *Ondine* and *My Three Angels*. To the publishing firm of Charles Scribner's Sons for the release of *The Passion Flower* and the Stark Young translation of *The Sea Gull*. To Viking Press for a somewhat complicated clearance of *Volpone*, a somewhat complicated "property" since it is by Austrian Stefan Zweig out of Ben Jonson's original *Volpone*. To Liveright Publishing Corporation for *The Dybbuk*. To Alfred A. Knopf and to Hamish Hamilton, Ltd. for *No Exit*. To A. D. Peters of London for facilitating clearance on Ashley Dukes' version of Georg Kaiser's *From Morn to Midnight* and to Mr. Dukes himself, a master of the English language, for his granting of the permission. To Dr. Edmond Pauker, the Molnar Estate, and Paramount Pictures Corporation for *The Play's the Thing*. To Mr. William Koppelmann of Brandt and Brandt for his strenuous efforts in clearing *Jacobowsky and the Colonel* and the Emlyn Williams version of *A Month in the Country*, and to Mr. Williams himself for his favorable response to my interest while he was busily engaged in production. To Arthur Wilmurt for his ready consent to the inclusion of his version of *Noah*. I am, finally, greatly indebted to Mr. M. Abbott van Nostrand of Samuel French for his kind co-operation in making *The Late Christopher Bean*, *The World We Live In* and *The Good Hope* available to me. Indeed, the co-operation of the above-mentioned individuals and organizations was generous enough to supply me with plays which could form the beginnings of a second volume. Finally, I am grateful for editorial help to Herbert Michelman of Crown Publishers and to my wife Mollie Gassner, who must be getting tired of seeing her name in her husband's books but who has only herself to blame, since it is her fabulous proficiency that deprives her of anonymity.

J.G.

Introduction

EUROPEAN DRAMA IN THE AMERICAN THEATRE

By John Gassner

I.

We, in a new country, were ever borrowers, although we were resisters, too. We started to resist European influence soon after the Declaration of Independence, and for the next three quarters of a century our stage abounded in local personalities while our plays were filled with native wood-notes wild of Yankee dialect. We created the stage-Yankee, upright and shrewd, to maintain New World wholesomeness against aristocratic pretense and Old World decadence. And in our effort to make the most of what was our own or took to be our own, we even established the Indian as a stage hero. Having glorified the outspoken paleface we went on to discover the great-hearted redskin. The noble savage Metamora, Carabasset, or Tecumseh joined the grease-paint company of such "true blue sons of liberty" as Jonathan Postfree, Lot Sap Sago, and the Adam Trueman whom Mrs. Mowatt's *Fashion* presented as the natural enemy of European-infiltrated American life. Our resistance to subversion from alien shores was not so consistent, however, that we did not even then accept the foreign play and the American, or British, adaptation as a staple of showbusiness.

Our first professional dramatist, William Dunlap, made a thriving trade of skewering French and German plays for American consumption. The vogue of Kotzebue delicatessen was strong in the land, for Europe had developed a taste for romantic melodrama and so had we. Even without borrowings from the British Isles, our foreign debt mounted in the last century. Our obligations to the European continent grew even when the nominal creditor was an English or Irish playwright, since the British theatre itself was now a heavy importer of continental goods. Many of the one hundred and fifty or more plays turned out by Dionysius Lardner Boucicault, for example, were translations or near-translations from the French. By the time of his death in 1890, in the palmy days before an international copyright agreement, this actor-dramatist of Irish extraction, less colorfully known as Dion Boucicault, had acquitted himself at least as well as his American cousins in the business of picking up unconsidered trifles from the European stage. (Later, he became a citizen of our theatre, too, for he started to divide his time between America and England.) A case that may challenge Hollywood's supremacy in the multiple-authorship derby has been dug up by me from what I hope are reliable sources. The case is that of the early American playwright John Howard Payne's adaptation of Kotzebue's *Das Kind der Liebe* under the title of *Lovers' Vows* after the original piece had already been adapted in England and America by Mrs. Inchbald, Benjamin Thompson, Anne Plumptre, and William Dunlap. Since Augustus Friedrich Ferdinand Kotzebue, who wrote over two hundred now unregarded plays but was assassinated in 1819 for political rather than artistic reasons, was a German who worked for a time in Austria, then directed the Court theatre in Russia, then went to Weimar, and finally became Russian consul-general in Prussia, a translation such as *Lovers' Vows* may be considered less a play than an international incident.

I am not aware that there were any audible protests against this early U.N. or UNESCO manifestation. The virus of xenophobia actually struck our stage people only with the coming of Ibsen. The arrival of *A Doll's House* was tame enough. It reached us under the title of *Thora*, for Nora had become Thora, and the role of the incipient "free woman" was played by the disarmingly attractive Polish actress Helena Modjeska, who had emigrated with her husband to California in 1876. Moreover, the play that

had exploded on the European stage to the accompaniment of groans from conserva-
tives had acquired a happy ending in transit. A reviewer for *The Louisville Courier-
Journal* reported on December 6, 1883 that after the disillusioned wife dons a street
dress with the intention of leaving her husband, the latter "argues and pleads in vain,
but finally, through the medium of the children, some indefinite talk about 'religion,'
there is a reunion, a rushing together and a falling curtain on a happy family tableau."
The reviewer, as indifferent to Ibsen's intentions as the anonymous adapter had been,
thought that a more consistent ending to the play would have been Nora's — that is,
Thora's — death. But his was a mild reservation. Opposition to the subversive Ibsen
was to come not from this first viewing of *A Doll's House*, but from the accumulating
evidence of a growing number of published plays that Ibsenism, as the dean of dramatic criticism at the turn of the century put it, was "rank, deadly pessimism," a
commodity for which Americans had never been known to have any use. The *doyen*,
William Winter, who admitted he could not forgive even "the despondent, hysterical,
inflammatory Jeremiah in the Bible," summed up the case against Ibsen in choice
remonstrances: Ibsen's views, once adopted, "would disrupt society." The Norwegian
playwright was one of those "who murder to dissect," and a reformer like Ibsen,
"who calls you to crawl with him into a sewer, merely to see and breathe its feculence,
is a pest."

It is difficult to say when the resistance to Ibsen began to give way. It would be
better to say perhaps that despite William Winter's strenuous objections there was no
widespread resistance to Ibsen if for no other reason than that there was also no great
passion for his work in our land and he had no doughty turn-of-the-century champions
comparable to William Archer and Bernard Shaw in England. Ibsen, it may be said,
was both quietly accepted and quietly ignored by us before World War I. And his
Swedish colleague Strindberg also encountered little opposition from us, if for no
other reason than that he won no particular victories. It was the old-fashioned "well-
built" problem play, developed by the French two or three decades before the appearance of *A Doll's House* in 1879, that really had some vogue in pre-war America. Muck-
raking journalism, trust-busting, and rising liberal sentiment favored the melodramatic
or sentimental treatment of a social problem such as municipal corruption far more
than it promoted either Ibsenism or the European brand of naturalism represented by
Hauptmann's *The Weavers* or Gorki's *The Lower Depths*. In sum, the pre-modern European drama had long flourished here while the pioneer playwrights from Scandinavia,
like their British compeer Shaw, had, astonishingly, come and gone with little fanfare
before the end of the first World War. As Joseph Wood Krutch noted so accurately
in his *American Drama Since 1918*, Ibsen and Shaw were known on our stage by isolated
successes, and even less may be said for the playwright both held in awe, the disconcerting August Strindberg. "Indeed," wrote Mr. Krutch, "these foreign masters
were beginning to be almost passé as literature without having exerted a very profound
influence on the native stage . . . By 1915 new thought was no longer so very new."

It remained for the "new theatre" movement of the second decade of our century
really to discover the modern European drama for America. Although a few critics
and travelers, among whom James Huneker had been the most articulate, had called
attention to the leading playwrights of the continent, only stage productions could
give their plays some measure of importance as living theatre. By now many plays once
associated with the advancing theatre have lost their aura for us, and very few indeed
have any value as literature. But they were distinctly important to progress-making
and progress-shouting stalwarts. Nor was it the dramatic work of Ibsen and other
European realists or naturalists that entranced the "art-theatre" groups that were
making theatrical history in America after 1910. They constituted the first "art-
theatre" movement we had ever known in the United States — previously, we had
known only stock companies and touring English and American stars of the first and

second magnitude. And *art* was now more likely to be associated with poetic than with realistic playwriting.

Considerably symptomatic was the vogue of Maurice Maeterlinck, still the prophet of a new dispensation when the Washington Square Players, the most European-oriented of the amateurs, began operations in 1916. Maeterlinck, who had made an impression in the theatre a quarter of a century before, still represented progress as the exponent of dramatic symbolism, atmosphere, and "style," for he had made much of nuance and suggestion in contrast to the sharp outlines and the concreteness of realistic drama. His short pieces, vintage 1890-95, were examples of so-called static drama and were still considered ultra-modern experiments. It was progress for us to forego the dramatic contrivances of the "well-made play" at about the same time that modern fiction was being liberated from the machinery of plot. When the present writer got to know the youthful Theatre Guild, the Broadway successor of the Washington Square Players, the quality in a play that invited instant condemnation was contrivance. To dismiss a new play from consideration by the Guild it was necessary only to call it "contrived." A symbolical or expressionist play, however was not called contrived, nor was a drama charged however vertiginously with so-called modern thought.

Maeterlinck's little poetic masterpiece of the year 1894, *L'Intérieure*, was a special favorite. The Washington Square Players rarely omitted *Interior* or some other piece by Maeterlinck (such as *The Miracle of St. Anthony*, and *The Death of Tintagiles*) from their programs of one-acters. And if Maeterlinck engrossed our early, if fickle, interest (we soon tired of "Maeterlinckèd sweetness"), so did his Russian symbolist disciple Leonid Andreyev. The Washington Square Players approved the latter's one-act plunge into profound pessimism, *Love of One's Neighbor*, and his even more cheerless full-length allegory, *The Life of Man*. They staged the latter in 1917, and when they reorganized themselves in 1919 as The Theatre Guild, they waited only two seasons before presenting the only slightly less pessimistic and symbolist *He Who Gets Slapped* — this time, however, reaping a Broadway bonanza with their fidelity to the author. Kissing cousins of Maeterlinck and Andreyev were also made welcome by the young Guild when the group presented Nicholas Evreinov's *The Chief Thing*, Emile Verhaeren's *The Cloister*, Paul Claudel's *The Tidings Brought to Mary*, and Benavente's *commedia dell' arte* social fantasy *Los interes creados*. The last-mentioned, presented on April 9, 1919, under the title of *The Bonds of Interest* was, in fact, the Guild's very first production. It is worth noting, too, that the Theatre Guild's first Molnar production, *Liliom*, was a symbolic fantasy, as was its first Shaw production, *Heartbreak House*. Both plays were given in the Guild's third year, in the season of 1920-21.

Even when the advance-guard took heed of Ibsen, it was mainly the romantic and symbol-favoring playwright that attracted them. *Peer Gynt* was unsuccessfully presented by the Theatre Guild in its fifth season, early in 1923, and *The Wild Duck* was ably produced by The Actors' Company in the season of 1924-25. And favored at Eva Le Gallienne's Civic Repertory Theatre during the nineteen-twenties were the more or less symbolist dramas *The Master Builder* and *John Gabriel Borkman*. Ibsen's masterpiece of realistic drama, *Hedda Gabler*, naturally attracted Broadway-minded managements, too, but chiefly because it contained the star part of Hedda. There was true magnificence in the role when the stunning Emily Stevens, Mrs. Fiske's tall and exotic blonde niece, played it on Broadway. And the role was an obvious choice for other outstanding American actresses such as Mrs. Fiske herself, Nance O'Neil, Alla Nazimova, and Eva Le Gallienne. As a matter of fact, Hedda was first played in London, in 1891, by an American actress — Elizabeth Robins — and she, too, gave a performance that was considered remarkable. Perhaps Hedda should have been an American woman from the start.

Ghosts, to which the Washington Square Players condescended with a production in May 1917, may be put down as another exception to the rule that our advanced groups favored the non-realistic side of Ibsen's career. But it has long been evident that a mechanically realistic view of this work results in a boring production. One pedestrian production, given in the 1935-36 season, was indeed redeemed by the luminous performance of Mrs. Alving by Alla Nazimova, but Nazimovas are as rare as dull dramatic productions are numerous. *Ghosts*, with its symbolic action and *Fall of the House of Usher* atmosphere, could commend itself to venturesome groups as a work of the imagination rather than as an outdated exposé of life in late nineteenth-century Norway — or as the kind of clinical play that the discovery of salvarsan had deprived of its terrors.

And much the same thing can be said concerning that other founding father of modernism, August Strindberg. In his case, too, it was less the formidable naturalist than the innovator of imaginative dramaturgy who prevailed, except that his psychological tremors attracted the intellectuals of an age callowly fascinated by the revelations of Havelock Ellis and Sigmund Freud. The Theatre Guild was less than two years old when it took a reckless plunge with one of Strindberg's most devastating dramas of sexual conflict *The Dance of Death*. This production came in the second season, on May 9, 1920, a few months after the Guild had produced Tolstoy's powerful sex tragedy *The Power of Darkness*. But the Strindberg play was not selected for production as an orthodox piece of naturalism; O'Neill's view, given in the Provincetown Playbill of January 3, 1924, was the prevailing one for art-theatre devotees: "He [Strindberg] carried naturalism to a logical attainment of such intensity that if the work of any other playwright is to be called 'naturalism,' we must classify a play like *The Dance of Death* as 'super-naturalism,' and place it in a class by itself . . ." And the Washington Square Players in producing the psychological oddity of *Pariah* as early as May 1917, and the Provincetown Players, as late as 1924, in presenting *The Spook Sonata* (now more accurately titled *The Ghost Sonata*), paid homage to the Strindberg the art-theatre movement really admired as a playwright rather than as an oracle of the sex-duel. That is, the Strindberg who, in addition to taking the drama into a dense forest of symbols, churned up time and space, reality and dream, violently enough to become the originator of expressionism more than a decade before it became an advanced art neurosis in Central Europe.

It was for the playbill printed in connection with that last-mentioned production of the Provincetown's season of 1923-1924 that O'Neill wrote a celebrated tribute to Strindberg, whom he considered greater than Ibsen and to whom he paid the tribute of imitation. The American playwright's monologue *Before Breakfast*, written in 1916, recalls Strindberg's *tour de force*, *The Stronger*, and his full-length play of the season of 1923-1924, *Welded*, is a typical, if less than successful, Strindbergian sex-drama. More importantly, the influence of Strindberg, openly acknowledged by O'Neill at the same time that he rejected the imputation of influence by the German expressionists, was apparent in the imaginative dramaturgy of *The Emperor Jones* and *The Hairy Ape* which the Provincetown produced in the fall of 1920 and the spring of 1922 respectively. The production of *The Spook Sonata*, which was directed by Robert Edmond Jones and James Light and had Clare Eames, Mary Blair, Mary Morris, and Walter Abel in the cast, was an ambitious one. It did not succeed and it did not reach Broadway. But it indicated the direction in which young theatre people looked then as now. The Provincetown Players, indeed, looked again in the same direction, though without making any greater impression on the American public, when they opened a production of Strindberg's symbolic fantasy *The Dream Play*, the next season, in January 1925. It is indeed curious that at the present writing, more than forty years after the beginning of the American "art" or "little" theatre movement, a strongly stylized art of theatre — whatever the label under which it reaches us — is and almost has to be the rallying cause of the new progressive groups.

In the note on *The Spook Sonata*, O'Neill spoke not only for himself, but also to a considerable degree for our art theatre movement, especially for his production associates, the critic Kenneth Macgowan and the designer Robert Edmond Jones. (The trio produced *Welded*, *The Fountain*, and *The Great God Brown* together.) In praising this "behind-life" drama, he maintained that the "old" naturalism or realism no longer "applies." He described it as an earlier generation's "daring aspirations toward self-recognition by holding the family kodak up to ill-nature." "But to us," he declared, "their old audacity is *blague*" and "we have endured too much from the banality of surfaces." Protesting against "fourth-wall" technique in drama he announced, "We are ashamed of having peeked through so many keyhoes, squinting always at heavy, uninspired bodies — the fat facts," and he added confidently that "we have been sick with appearances and are convalescing."

There would come a time, after the stockmarket crash of 1929, when a departure from dramatic realism was more likely to be denounced as retrograde than acclaimed as advanced. It would be scorned as irresponsible estheticism unless the non-realistic technique was tied to the kite of left-wing social convictions, as in the case of *Waiting for Lefty* and *Bury the Dead*. But O'Neill was speaking for the advanced elements of the earlier generation coming to maturity during the prosperous and sophisticated nineteen-twenties. And the "banality of surfaces" was the very trademark of the commercial managements the little art theatre groups had sprung up to defy and, if possible, to destroy. They could entertain some respect only for the early Theatre Guild created by former members of the Washington Square Players, and for a few Broadway managers such as Winthrop Ames, the producer of Maeterlinck's successful *Blue Bird* in 1910, and Arthur Hopkins, with whom even so advanced an artist as Robert Edmond Jones was able to collaborate in designing such an imaginative production as the famous *Macbeth* of 1921. And, characteristically, when these managements produced a play it, too, was likely to be something romantic like Sem Benelli's *The Jest*, the drama of a Renaissance esthete's fine Italian revenge on a philistine bully,* which Hopkins produced with great success in 1919. When the better managements did give Broadway a strong naturalistic work such as Jacinto Benavente's *La Malquerida* or *The Passion Flower*, produced in 1920, the effect was not considered commonplace owing to the extraordinary intensity of this story of illicit passion and owing to the esoteric effect of Spanish peasant tragedy. Peasant drama, even when noted for its uncompromising realism, has usually had some poetic quality, if nothing more than that produced by primitivism in the environment and by manifestations of elemental passion and conflict. And peasant dialect has also been usually accounted an approximation of poetry, even when the language has fallen short of Synge's prose-poetry. It was probably a poetry of primitiveness that led Arthur Hopkins to produce Gerhart Hauptmann's naturalistic story of lust and infanticide, *Rose Bernd*, with Ethel Barrymore in the title role, and to win the approval of advanced circles in 1922, although the play was, like other pungent European imports, a Broadway failure.

Usually, European realism and naturalism fared poorly here. Thus *Thérèse Raquin*, Zola's celebrated naturalistic showpiece of the year 1873, had to wait until the 1940's before it was seen as a full-fledged Broadway production in an adaptation by Thomas Job. Sam Shubert presented Becque's *La Parisienne* as early as 1904, but with Réjane, in French, for only three performances; and Anne Nichols was barely able to squeeze four performances out of this celebrated naturalistic comedy with the assistance of Mme. Simone. The same author's formidable drama *Les Corbeaux*, known in English as *The Vultures*, never even reached Broadway—not even in French, since it has no stellar role for an actress. So far as I have been able to determine, New Yorkers never saw a full-fledged production of it in English until Erwin Piscator staged it at the New School for Social Research in the nineteen-forties, with Elaine Stritch playing the

---

* I should have liked to present this play here. But the Edward Sheldon version used by Hopkins was apparently never published and the English version now available, only as a typed copy distributed by the Walter H. Baker Company of Boston, is the joint work of Benelli and a Dr. Royce Emerson. And the latter is listed under a 1939 copyright as sole author since Benelli's death in 1949.

youngest daughter. Hauptmann's naturalistic social drama *The Weavers* was only moderately successful when staged by Augustin Duncan, Isadora's brother, on December 14, 1915. Helped by the rising tide of socialist or, at least, pro-labor sentiment at that time, the production had 87 performances, surely a modest run by comparison with the 377 performances rolled up by Avery Hopwood's now forgotten *Fair and Warmer* which had opened some five weeks earlier. And even so titillating a play as Arthur Schnitzler's *Affairs of Anatol* ran only 72 performances in the fall of 1912 with a cast that included John Barrymore and Doris Keane. One of the most powerful pieces of Central European naturalism, *The She-Devil* by Karl Schoenherr, met with complete indifference, as did other noteworthy realistic dramas, such as the same author's *Children's Tragedy* and the grim "tragedies of sex" by the mordant Frank Wedekind. The Washington Square Players staged his brilliant one-actor *The Tenor*, but when the group became the Theatre Guild it abandoned this gifted, if demanding, author.

There is little point, however, in multiplying the evidence that the first revolution in the modern European theatre, that of realism and of the so-called free theatres, won less adherence from us and especially from our advanced circles than did the second revolution. That revolution was "romantic" (and one should cite here the most strikingly popular instances — the interest in *Cyrano de Bergerac* and *The Miracle*), "symbolist," and vaguely or violently anti-realistic. When our commercially disposed theatre favored realism, it did not rely so much on imports from the Continental stage as upon home-made and British products which were closer and more congenial to us. And when we began to turn to a more challenging brand of realism in the turbulent nineteen-thirties, the new *avant-garde* of a more or less leftist persuasion tended to dismiss the realistic European drama as rather bourgeois and démodé. By then the realistic masterpieces were already "old," and they seemed even older than they were because their emphasis was patently "reformist" rather than "revolutionary." *The Weavers* came to be regarded as a confused and misleading play because the action rose to a climax with the weavers' frantic destruction, rather than Marxian seizure, of "the means of production." Even native topical plays of such recent origin as the nineteen-twenties had become *passé;* how, then, could European plays written as early as 1890, 1900, or 1910 possess a viable "social significance?"

2.

Nevertheless, it would be inaccurate to say that dramatic realism had entirely ceased to be a progressive cause for writers and producers of 1915. Even the realistic plays that won some measure of success from 1915 to 1930 — plays such as *Redemption* and *The Passion Flower*, included in the present volume — once represented somewhat bold ventures for their American producers.

Arthur Hopkins was considered an imprudent adventurer among the Broadway managers not merely when he staged his Poësque *Macbeth* with Robert Edmond Jones's non-representational black hangings, silvery masks, and sets of arches, but also when he presented Tolstoy's social drama *The Living Corpse* under the somewhat sentimental title of *Redemption*. Its problem-play aspects, as a protest against the marriage laws of Russia under the Czars, were hardly startling to Broadway in 1919. Enoch Arden complications — that is, the hero Fedya's pretended suicide in his effort to free his wife for a better marriage than she has had with him — were not as such strange to Hopkins' public. But the picture of Fedya's sordid life as roué and tramp, and the relentless course of the action that carries Fedya to a real suicide after the faked one instead of culminating in a reconciliation with his wife — all this was still an alien pessimism in 1919.

I possess a crumbling copy of the New York *Tribune* review of April 5, 1919, in which a reviewer declares that Tolstoy's play is an "unfortunate choice" for the American stage. The curious wording of the impeachment against naturalism or, indeed, naturalness in playwriting follows: "In spite of the fact that he has given us people like ourselves — selfish, sentimental persons, desiring and creating love, persons moving according to their own definite characteristics and unaffected by the attempted and forced happiness — his lesson is obscured by their very naturalness. Then how can people like ourselves teach us anything." And in the next sentence the American public is urged to "call to itself an American Tolstoy who can present the identical theme of 'Redemption' and by his very understanding of our essential national idealism dispel the clouds which rise of necessity between us and a Russian idealism . . . and . . . instruct us where the Russian 'genius' merely makes us titter." The reference to "idealism" is, I take it, mainly a reference to Fedya's redeeming himself with the sacrifice of his life when the law, discovering that he is alive, threatens to destroy the happiness of his wife, who has remarried since his disappearance. Following this endeavor to direct our gaze toward ideals, the reviewer becomes lyrical and promises us, through "an American Fedya," the attainment of "beauty so exquisite that what poor man can achieve seems worse than nothing." After these bizarre statements it will be evident that Hopkins was not "playing safe" with The Living Corpse although he appears to have smoothed out its wrinkles in offering Redemption to the American public.

There was risk, too, in an American production of Jacinto Benavente's most powerful realistic drama La Malquerida, a work which this Nobel Prize author of more than 170 plays wrote in 1912 while he was Spain's most progressive writer of drama. Staged under the title of The Passion Flower in 1920, it owed more than a little of its popular success (it had 866 performances in New York and on tour) to the intense performance of Nance O'Neil. It was the most successful of Benavente's or, despite the popularity of Martínez Sierra's The Cradle Song, any other Spanish playwright's work in America. It also had the benefit of a modern psychological approach to a tragedy of love since Benavente traced the growth of an illicit passion between a peasant girl and her stepfather. It was a passion hemmed in by convention and, more than that, by the dread of incest that the popularization of Freudian teachings was making known in America. Everything favored the popularity of a play that deserved success as one of the few genuine tragedies of the realistic stage but could easily have missed it under less favorable circumstances. The Passion Flower rode the crest of a wave of anti-puritanical candor in the literature of the twenties, and the elemental passion that sweeps the characters from their conventional moorings and lifts them beyond the commonplaces of desire was impressively dramatic. But, for all that, the play was not a "safe" choice for producers in 1920.

Not the least obvious choice for an American repertoire in the twenties, too, was The Good Hope, a play by a little known Dutch spokesman for social conscience in the theatre, Herman Heijermans. He was hardly three years dead and all but completely forgotten, if indeed he had ever been known, in our world when Eva Le Gallienne presented The Good Hope at her Civic Repertory Theatre in the fall of 1927. Moreover, the subject of criminal negligence in Dutch shipping at the turn of the century was hardly shattering enough to command interest beyond the Netherlands a quarter of a century after the original production of the play. But as Brooks Atkinson noted, it was evident that Heijermans "loved life more intensely than theses." With its vital characterization and vigorous picturing of common life, The Good Hope managed to escape the numbness that besets most problem-playwriting. The play did not thrust forth claims to importance such as were advanced by The Weavers; or by Gorki's The Lower Depths, a masterpiece of Russian naturalism that, like Hauptmann's drama, had no particular public in our twenties and was, curiously, also ignored even by social-minded theatres in the next decade. (Arthur Hopkins had presented the Russian work in December, 1919, without making any dent in the American theatre with it. The late Burns Mantle did not even see fit to include Gorki's drama in a "Best Plays of 1919-20" list which contained such "best plays" as James Forbes's *The Famous Mrs. Fair*, Salisbury Field's *Wedding Bells*, and Rachel Barton Butler's *Mamma's Affair* . . .) Still, in receiving a well-attended stage production from Eva Le Gallienne and winning the regard of responsible reviewers, *The Good Hope* helped to give European realism some respectable representation in the New York theatre.

Our theatre, however, was to become familiar with still more distinguished realistic artistry when it interested itself in the work of the Russian playwrights after staging Tolstoy's *Redemption*. The stock of Turgenev and Chekhov has risen higher, decade after decade, while Ibsen's realistic stock has tended, on the whole, to decline almost steadily and Strindberg's was almost wholly ignored before the centenary of his birth in 1949. (Since then, Broadway and its tributary stages in Manhattan have had productions, if not particularly successful ones, of *The Father, Creditors, Miss Julie*, and *Comrades*. But we have yet to do justice to this remarkably difficult dramatist on the American stage.) The most rapid rise was registered by Chekhov, who has indeed come to be regarded in both the English and the American theatre as the most attractive and perdurable playwright of continental Europe. But an earlier "Chekhovian" playwright, a master of characterization and dramatic nuance, also won some share of recognition. Russia's second great novelist, Ivan Turgenev (the first was surely Nikolai Gogol), who never dreamed of acquiring a place in the theatre even in his native country, made an enviable impression in New York twice within about a quarter of a century with an almost accidental *chef d'oeuvre*, *A Month in the Country*, written as far back as 1849. The first impression was made by the Theatre Guild production of the 1929 1930 season. Nazimova played the part of the provincial lady whose passion for her son's tutor exploded tragicomic complications in the static world of country life. The cast included, in addition to Mme. Nazimova, Dudley Digges, Henry Travers, Alexander Kirkland, and Eunice Stoddard. "As perfect a performance as any American group of players could be expected to give," was the verdict of Arthur Ruhl in the New York *Herald Tribune*, and many other reviewers concurred. The second impressive occasion was a production of the season of 1955-1956 by the young Phoenix Theatre. Uta Hagen gave a glowing performance in Nazimova's part and Michael Redgrave, who had performed in *A Month in the Country* in London, staged the play with uncommon skill. The director of the first-mentioned production, Rouben Mamoulian, used his own adaptation of the standard translation by M. S. Mandell; the Phoenix used an admirable adaptation Emlyn Williams had prepared a dozen years before for a British production. It is this adaptation that is presented in this anthology through the courtesy of Mr. Williams.

Whether in these adaptations or in unadapted form, *A Month in the Country*—"an entrancing cotillion of love, no less endearing because it is desperate," Redgrave has called it—is a beautiful play; and it is gratifying to know that New York has been able to respond to its excellence when given an opportunity to view it in adequate productions. It is transparently a work of the best kind of realism there is — *inner realism*, because the author was primarily interested in his characters, remaining notably close to most of them while maintaining the objectivity of a cool observer. "What do I care whether a woman perspires in the middle of her back or under her arms?" wrote Turgenev. "I do not care how or where she sweats; I want to know how she thinks." Turgenev's manner in his hundred-year-old play, moreover, is one of extraordinary naturalness. The plot seems almost an inadvertence, as if the action, mostly a flurry of unwonted feelings, were an intrusion into an otherwise placid round of existence. Yet several lives have been strongly affected by a restive woman's infatuation with her child's unresponsive tutor. Half a century before Chekhov, Turgenev had evolved an art of chiaroscuro, of half-lights and sudden illuminations, as well as a type of drama neither tragic nor predominantly comic, which provides an introduction to the complexities of human nature.

And if American reviewers and playgoers could take to Turgenev, they were bound to respond even more fully to Chekhov. One need only compare the earlier author's masterpiece with Chekhov's major plays to discover that the nineteenth century has vanished and that we are in a world of unrest verging on the inner and outer upheavals we associate with our own century. Stanislavsky could declare with some degree of accuracy that *A Month in the Country* was "built on the most delicate curves of love experience," but there is more weighty and far-reaching matter in *The Cherry Orchard*, "where," as Michael Redgrave put it, "the trees fall one by one under the axe of social change." And surely Mr. Redgrave is correct in pointing out that Chekhov's predecessor was less Turgenev than the social realist Ostrovsky, who at this writing still remains to be discovered for Broadway even though the Moscow Art Theatre introduced him here about three decades ago with one of its productions. In the nine-teen-tens, Chekhov was virtually unknown on the New York stage save for productions of his little "vaudeville" *The Boor*, given under the title of *A Bear* by the Washington Square Players in 1915 and 1917, and a brief venture by the same group with *The Sea Gull* in 1916. It is not surprising that the Washington Square Players' successor, the Theatre Guild, should have given Chekhov his most memorable production on Broadway some twenty years later with the same play in preference to Chekhov's other masterpieces, which thus far have failed to reach Broadway proper in Stark Young's distinguished translations.

The many productions on Broadway, whatever their actual merit — usually consider-able, yet rarely as just to the author as the Theatre Guild's *Sea Gull*—and the off-Broadway David Ross productions of other Chekhov plays in the mid-fifties—confirmed a mounting reputation. During the last quarter of a century it seemed indeed that the Russian playwright, rather than Ibsen, was the founder of our century's realistic art. Our numerous tributes to Chekhov's artistry, whatever snares he may have unin-tentionally set for imitators, are entirely deserved. We don't want to give up realism, yet we would willingly discard the demonstrations without subtlety and the arid characterizations without nuance that we have so often had to accept along with realism of environment and a sociological point of view. Chekhov, more than any of the old masters of modern drama, showed, apparently without strain, that our wishes are not unrealizable. His example has been dangerous only in the one respect that a writer cannot will himself into writing like Chekhov. An author would first have to be Chekhov, and there could be only one such individual. Chekhov's work has pointed in certain directions for English and American writers, but they have had to go it alone — as O'Casey did in *Juno and the Paycock*, as Odets did in *Awake and Sing*, and as Enid Bagnold has done, more recently and, to my mind, less impressively, in *The Chalk Garden*. And Chekhov himself could have taught American and English playwrights this lesson of productive individuality: for all his affinities to other Russian novelists and playwrights, he did not write as a member of any school.

"Beautiful, fragmentary, elliptical" . . . "It was not the speech of the character that interested him, but the motive for the speech" . . . "the little gray moth-like theme of man's pursuit of the unattainable" . . . "the wonderful range of these characters" — such statements, as well as the epigram, "Chekhov will always remain, to the boob *Art*, and, to the enlightened, *entertainment*," represented one effort to define Chekhovian drama for us. (The effort was Rose Caylor's in her Introduction to *Uncle Vanya* as "Translated and Adapted" for the Jed Harris Broadway production of 1930.) There have been many other expressions to fit one aspect or another of Chekhov's work. But it is unnecessary to proceed further here. It is al-together evident that the European realism that made the most favorable impression upon us after World War I was *not realism at all, in the ordinary sense of the term* but a sublimated realism not sharply distinguishable from a poetry of the plateaus — a "poetry of plateaus," that is, if we are to distinguish it from the great poetic drama of the Attic and Elizabethan past. Our general avoidance of direct clinical and social drama from the European stages, except in cases of sensational subject matter such as Edmond Bourdet's study of inverted sexuality, *The Captive*, was indeed curious in view of the fact that our own theatre tended to continue its wonted drudgery in the bleak valleys of commonplace derisions and assertions.

Perhaps our domestic surfeit deterred us from importing the same kind of drama from abroad. And especially remarkable was it that our diffidence was strong even after 1930 when European conflicts came to concern us with increasing intensity. European anti-Nazi plays, as well as war plays, made little impression here. We sympathized with the author's cause but not with his playwriting. Before and after Hitler's ascendancy, the European theatre was replete with dramas of social conflict. But among these perhaps only Friedrich Wolf's play, *The Sailors of Cattaro*, as produced by the Theatre Union in the mid-thirties, won some regard — and this work was largely historical rather than journalistically topical with its account of the mutiny of the Austrian fleet during World War I. We did not even respond favorably to so gifted a playwright as Carl Zuckmayer when he wrote his famous satire on Prussianism, *The Captain of Köpenick*, in 1930 and when he collaborated a decade later with the actor Fritz Kortner in composing the French Resistance drama, *Somewhere in France*, during World War II.

Both Zuckmayer and Kortner were then living in the United States, and their mischances were chronic among the distinguished European writers who found a haven in our land. The arduous Ferdinand Bruckner could not get his plays beyond the precincts of downtown New York, where Erwin Piscator produced a new version of *Criminals* at the New School. (I would note parenthetically that departures from realism did not help either. Bertolt Brecht, whose *Threepenny Opera* had been fabulously successful in Central Europe but had suffered a quick demise on Broadway before his exile from Germany, had only a haphazard and "epically" fulsome production in New York during World War II for his powerful chronicle *The Private Life of the Master Race* and, a few years after the war, an off-Broadway production of his *Galileo* which won no converts to Brechtian "epic theatre." The noble poet-playwright Ernst Toller, whom the Theatre Guild had introduced to New York in 1924 with the stirring expressionist drama of social conflict *Masse-Mensch* under the title of *Man and the Masses*, endured suffocation here as a writer before he extinguished his life in a New York hotel.) The Dutch writer Jan de Hartog—although he employed realistic playwriting—had a distinctly qualified success in 1947-48 with his earnest and ethical *Skipper Next to God*, the drama of some Jewish refugees' effort to reach Palestine through the British blockade. Only Franz Werfel succeeded in getting the voice of liberal Europe a proper hearing in our theatre. Having taken an oblique approach to the European crisis, he was able to dramatize the fall of France and the joint flight of a humble Jewish merchant and a fiery Polish nobleman in comic terms in *Jacobowsky and the Colonel*. The humor was enriched by our best writer of comic dialogue S. N. Behrman for one of the better war-time Theatre Guild productions, directed by Elia Kazan with a fine cast that included Louis Calhern and Oscar Karlweis. They gave each other a spirited fight on the stage as strange and at best only tentatively reconciled bedfellows. They are beyond all contention now, having both died in the year 1956 within less than four months of each other. But their mock contentions of the year 1944 brightened and deepened our theatre of the war years.

With the exception of *Jacobowsky and the Colonel*, presented in the present anthology as the one successful war play written by a European (a powerful *The Devil's General* by Zuckmayer never came to Broadway), the European record in our theatre was a bleak one during the years of crisis between 1930 and 1945. The European theatre failed us (others would say that we failed the European theatre) precisely when its realism should have been able to speak most powerfully to our playgoers. At a time when our local stages were trying to outdo each other in singing "songs of social significance," as the saying went in the embattled thirties, "social drama" fared especially poorly with us when we got it from foreign writers even in the familiar mode of realism. We were not dramatically enriched even when we got it from a theoretically reliable source — namely, the theatre of Soviet Russia. Our indifference to Soviet realism in playmaking could not have been greater if it had been the result of principle rather than of our sense of remoteness or of unpremeditated and unprincipled boredom. An early political melodrama such as Tretyakov's *Roar China*, which pitted the Chinese coolie against British "imperialists," failed to excite our interest despite the exciting staging possibilities made manifest in Lee Simonson's brilliantly devised stage setting. The best plays of Afinogenov, an author of some promise who rubbed Soviet literary bureaucracy the wrong way at times, and Michael Bulgakov's *Days of the Turbins*, the best because the most just and character-rooted drama about the Civil War in Russia after 1917, did not achieve Broadway production. Katayev's comedy of Soviet manners *Squaring the Circle* did and was found moderately attractive and entertaining. Konstantin Simonov, the white hope of the Soviet stage during World War II, had his war-drama *The Russian People* presented in Manhattan, but Broadway critics and playgoers found his patriotism more evident than his talent. And so it runs — the record of the European drama of social and political reference in our theatre after 1930.

3.

Fortunately we were sooner or later fairly well supplied throughout the four decades of this survey with fancy, romance, theatricality (if it was less exacting than Brecht's style), and comic sophistication. Although we overlooked or misjudged many imaginative and stylized works or mistreated them with our adaptations and stage productions, we nevertheless managed to enrich our theatrical seasons. Within limits that cannot be defined here without detailed examples, such as our failure as late as 1956 to give Broadway production to Cocteau's *The Infernal Machine*, we even took an interest in several varieties of poetic or quizzical work from the Continent. In each area of theatre we had the good sense or good luck to encounter the better European plays as well as the worse, although I wish I could be as confident that we always took to the *best* as I am sure that we courted many of the worst. Still, it is true that our enterprise in importing stage-pieces covered enough territory to bring us to works of beauty and power or of gaiety and urbanity.

Fancy interested us early, since, as noted before, our little art theatres sprang into being while poetic and symbolic theatre was in favor across the Atlantic. (We made our own mild contribution to it, too, with such pieces as Percy MacKaye's *The Scarecrow*, Josephine Preston Peabody's *The Piper* in 1910, and George C. Hazelton and Benrimo's pseudo-Chinese play *The Yellow Jacket* in 1912.) Amid the inevitable ineptitude that fancy invites there was, fortunately, material of pith and point in a number of the works we received. Plainly the most durable of these was *The Dybbuk*, Ansky's stirring piece of folk-drama first written in the Yiddish language, then adapted into the Russian at the suggestion of Stanislavsky (he also suggested the introduction of "The Messenger" into the play), and then translated into classical Hebrew by the great poet Bialik. The career of this play also established its international character. It had a great production in Russian when it was staged for the Hebrew-language Habimah Theatre in Moscow by none other than Eugene Vakhtangov, Stanislavsky's favorite pupil, the short-lived Soviet stage director to whom everybody attributed genius. Then the Habimah players, who moved permanently to Palestine in 1931 and have been the classical Hebrew theatre of Israel ever since, made *The Dybbuk* the chief work in their repertory. Moreover, they not only toured with the play throughout a large part of the Western world, but brought it to New York, for the first time in 1926 and for a second time in the spring of 1948. The Yiddish version was the first production of

Maurice Schwartz's Jewish Art Theatre in New York for the 1921-22 season. And as translated into English by H. G. Alsberg and Winifred Katzin it not only made theatrical history in 1926 at the Neighborhood Playhouse in New York, but reached the Leeds Civic Playhouse and the Royalty Theatre in London a year later. It is a reasonable conclusion, one supposes, that there could be international agreement at least on the theatrical merits of The Dybbuk, if on nothing else. We participated in this agreement, even if it cannot be claimed that the play rocked Broadway with its popularity. At least we recognized a really good story when we came across one, we were affected by the atmospheric enchantments of a play in which a realistic picture of the East-European environment is also a poetic reality, and we were moved by a mystical tale of passion and death. The Dybbuk may be the greatest love poem we have had from the modern European stage. In an older period it would have been written in verse. But even in prose, it is evocative beyond the ordinary effects of prose. It is true, at the same time, that The Dybbuk has remained a rarity in our theatre. Plays of this nature are scarce on any stage, and for us its atmospheric intensity and its dark rapture, qualities most apparent in the Habimah players' performance, could not become a theatrical staple.

We should have derived gratification, too, from several of the Spanish poet Lorca's folk-dramas. It is a pity that Blood Wedding did not thrive in the climate of our theatre or that D'Annunzio's wild folk-drama The Daughter of Jorio could not take root in our soil earlier. But Latin emotionalism proved too exacting for our actors and playgoers whenever it reached the white heat of poetry within the environs of alien provincial life.

After The Dybbuk, reprinted in this volume, almost any other fantasy that we did produce was likely to prove mild, although for that reason alone it was not necessarily less successful here. On the contrary, the much milder fantasy of Casella's Death Takes a Holiday, as presented by the Shuberts (from whose grasp it could not be extracted by the present anthologist), proved decidedly more popular. And amidst other conceits of varying interest, André Obey's philosophical comedy Noah is the most substantial while remaining congenial to a cosmopolitan theatre public. Although produced under distinctly limited auspices, Noah came to be cherished as an affecting work all the more attractive because created with spontaneous theatricality yet not without rueful comment on human nature and the human condition — this by implication and exposition, however, rather than by preachment. And with Noah there came to our stage a breath, however rarified in transit, from one of the most cherished sources of theatrical art in Europe. For Noah was written for production by a company of actors, the Compagnie des Quinze, that had been carefully trained in the best traditions of Jacques Copeau, the apostle of "the theatre theatrical" movement in France. Working as a philosopher-poet on the implications of the story of Noah and his family during the Deluge, Obey also worked as a theatrician bent upon making ample use of the histrionic art of the Compagnie des Quinze. In discussing his play, the author said with simple but telling truthfulness — "telling" and "truthful," of course, only because so many modern writers have labored to restrain or conceal the theatricality of their playwriting: "I thought of the stage and that was enough."

Nearly fifteen years after the New York production, which brought Pierre Fresnay from Paris for the role of the patriarch, the scholar-critic Francis Fergusson was moved to devote a little section of his book The Idea of a Theatre to Obey's play. "The stage itself is accepted . . . for what it is:" he wrote, "illusion is dispensed with, or playfully accepted as such." And he rightly pointed to the attendant merits of Obey's writing—to the "lightness and economical directness," the irony, and the alert willingness to see a joke. The playwright had made a thing of the theatre out of myth, and he had made it carry a heavy burden of reality, too—but lightly, wistfully, gingerly. Maintaining what Mr. Fergusson calls "the fiction of its literal reality," the play made its appeal "to the full poetic or histrionic sensibility rather than to the mind." That is, of course, a limitation of the play, which is also perhaps too arch at times to take significant command of the stage. For all that, however, the play belongs in this record and in our anthology not merely as a lovely thing but as an example of the aspirations of devotees of a modern poetic theatre.

At the other end of the spectrum of fantasy, there have been somber works charged with anger and dismay. In these works the European theatre found a way of mediating between social drama and the need for imaginative art. Three examples appear in this book, *From Morn to Midnight*, *The World We Live In*, and *No Exit*, although some more familiar examples suggest themselves here as well as a few less familiar ones such as Toller's *Man and the Masses* and Werfel's *The Goat Song*. Even a limited success on Broadway was important, since some of these works exerted an influence or had a life on our stage in excess of their run on Broadway. It is probable that the style of *From Morn to Midnight* influenced playwriting, although our writers were not necessarily conscious of indebtedness to Kaiser and his expressionist colleagues of the Central European theatre.

Among the three European fantasies of protest in this volume, Kaiser's *From Morn to Midnight*, a Theatre Guild offering of the year 1922, was the most pessimistic in content. It left the world no shred of decency with which to cover its naked meretriciousness. The play was one of those products of the expressionist movement in Germany which started in violence just before World War I and ended in hysteria just a few years after it. Since Kaiser worked in a variety of veins and had many stage productions, he also possessed the greatest skill among the writers who endeavored to employ expressionism in the theatre. *From Morn to Midnight*, the most controlled of his expressionist plays to come to our attention, also possessed the greatest variety of events — this as a result of its author's intention to expose the hollowness of many aspects of German life under the monarchy. (The play was composed in 1916, less than two years before the end of the German monarchy with the defeat of Germany.) If Theatre Guild directors expected that Americans in 1922 would like to look at themselves in the mirror of this chronicle of a little man's escape from his teller's cage into the great outside world of nothingness, they were surely mistaken. It may even be true that better playwriting would have silvered the glass so that it would have reflected images of our humanity more convincingly. Yet it was important for us to become acquainted with Kaiser's and his colleagues' technique of expressive distortion, of passionate imaginativeness, of an art harsh, violent, and intense.

Among other imported plays of the same or similar constitution, one piece, Josef and Karel Capek's *The World We Live In*, possessed a distinctly wider appeal. Arriving on Broadway in the same year of 1922, it had a good press and a long run. Although slightly worse for wear after some thirty-five years, it possessed a colorful theatricality capable of captivating audiences at least on a first encounter. Produced in the same year and season as Karl Capek's more concentrated fantasy on the mechanization of modern life, *R.U.R.*, it raised the stock of Central European theatre. We began to look to it for more imports and expected from it a new and fruitful dispensation which turned out to be no dispensation after a few more years. The Theatre Guild, for instance, continued to be hopeful and presented such off-beat dramas as Ernst Toller's *Man and the Masses* and Franz Werfel's *The Goat Song* in its sixth and eighth seasons, but discovered that Central Europe could supply a far more marketable supply of comedies such as Molnar's *The Guardsman*, Ernest Vajda's *Fata Morgana*, Sil-Vara's *Caprice*, and Frantisek Langer's *The Camel Through the Needle's Eye*. On one memorable earlier occasion, the production of Molnar's *Liliom* in 1921, the Guild and the American public discovered that a deft reconciliation of fantasy and comedy could pay theatrical dividends. And these dividends were multiplied in the fourth decade when Molnar's play underwent its musical transformation into *Carousel*.

Yet neither the bite nor the bile was wholly extracted from European fantastication. From Italy, for example, there arrived a series of provocative pieces from its so-called "school of the grotesque" headed by Luigi Pirandello, a writer of undoubted genius. He fascinated us, even if it is a historian's duty to add that our theatre was rarely able to do his works justice with our Broadway translations and stage productions. Except for some off-Broadway endeavors — the most successful of which was the only half-Pirandellian Tyrone Guthrie adaptation of *Six Characters in Search of an Author* at the Phoenix Theatre in 1955 — ventures into Pirandellian drama usually looked like ventures into a jungle of confusions. Pirandello's deepest dramas, *Six Characters in Search of an Author* and *Henry IV* (the latter presented on Broadway under the title of *The Living Mask*) were produced here with scanty results. He did, however, have one genuinely successful production in 1931 with *As You Desire Me*, included in the present anthology. He was fortunate in his cast. The main role, that of an intensely suffering woman who craves a saving identity and requires it vainly from others, was played by Judith Anderson, our ablest tragedienne and perhaps our only genuine one. *As You Desire Me*, above all, had the advantage of the powerful story directly told. We did not quite know how to "take" the sleight-of-hand artist in such engrossing pieces as *Right You Are, If You Think You Are* (The Theatre Guild's 1927 title for Pirandello's finest comedy) and *Six Characters in Search of an Author*. There is no blinking the fact that some kinds of so-called intellectual drama were too elusive for Broadway's impatient clientele. But we were able to accept *As You Desire Me*, a success on the stage here and also a film vehicle for the great Garbo, since the Pirandellian premise of the relativity of human identity in this work could be experienced as a tragic reality.

Pirandello died in 1936, and there was no one to challenge our minds from the European continent for a decade except the largely overlooked Bertolt Brecht. But imaginative drama began to reach us with revived provocativeness shortly after World War II, this time from France, where a renovation of dramatic art was apparent even before 1939 and began to display new vigor even under the German occupation of Paris. The Parisian theatre sent us Jean-Paul Sartre's bitter existentialist drama *No Exit*, along with other formidable contributions to the theme of disaster such as the same author's *The Flies* and Jean Anouilh's *Antigone*, as well as his Joan of Arc drama *The Lark*, which is a harsher work in the original than in the Lillian Hellman adaptation that flourished in our 1955-56 season. Since the years 1955 and 1956 also brought New York productions of Samuel Beckett's devastating *Waiting for Godot* (originally written in French and produced in Paris, though by an Irish author who had affinities to James Joyce and should not be considered a French writer at all) and Jean Genet's acrimonious drama of frustration *The Maids*, one could surmise that our theatre was not wholly immune to the mood of disenchantment that hovered over the European stage. And that opinion could be further sustained in the 1955-56 season by "off-Broadway" productions of Andreyev's *He Who Gets Slapped*, Cocteau's *The Telephone*, Brecht's *Life of the Master Race*, and Sartre's *No Exit*.

In 1946 this last-mentioned work of the imagination — an imagination truly in want of more than an ounce of civet — had been presented in New York with loving care and a professional cast calculated to impress the Broadway public. Broadway, abetted if not indeed incited by the reviewers, failed to be greatly impressed and the production closed after thirty-one performances. Yet *No Exit* was one existentialist nightmare that could not be banished for long. It returned to one off-Broadway house, The Cherry Lane, about half a year later, and won some credit there. And finally, it won genuine applause in another off-Broadway production and gained a new public in 1956. This belated victory for *No Exit*, it is curious to note, occurred in one of the most prosperous and ostensibly optimistic years of American society.

That human behavior can be nauseous is information that the author of a pre-war novel entitled *Nausea* pressed home in his first play, *No Exit*, as if it were a new truth instead of an old half-truth. That the ultimate punishment is imprisonment in the prison of other people's opinion was the central image of this existentialist fantasy. It happened to be urged upon us with an animus born less of the author's philosophical study than of national humiliation in the war, underground resistance after the fall of Paris, and redemption in blood and fire. And it was this animus that gave Sartre's plays, as well as the plays of other existentialist authors, their special tension and dramatic pulsation. Theatrical craftsmanship was not always ready at hand for the existentialist writer, and Sartre himself was often too strained and talkative for our theatre. (I suppose it is true that we have a low saturation point where discussion is concerned — unless the discussion has been conducted by Shaw.) Yet Sartre managed to engage our reluctant interest with his abhorence of human weakness. With his drama about a Southern lynching-spree, *The Respectful Prostitute*, as adapted for the New Stages experimental company, he even became a popular author on our stage. But the play succeeded more for the sensationalism of its sexual and racial matter than for its existentialist critique and acrid irony. Sartre gave us a more honestly charged work and an admirably concentrated one in *No Exit*. The play may have barely skirted— and, for some playgoers, failed to skirt — the fringes of a psychological and cerebral grand-guignol. But we needed this reminder that all was not fluff in the war-shattered theatre of Western Europe.

4.

It is necessary, finally, to take notice of the brands of Continental romance and so-called sophisticated comedy upon which we drew avidly. But to recall our importations would burst the seams of this essay. Here it may be necessary to remember only those that rose conspicuously above the ordinary level and dubious status of such entertainments.

Romantic drama, for instance, never really vanished from the European capitals. And even as late as the nineteen-fifties the Continental theatres produced, and we borrowed, romances although the species was supposed to have disappeared with the victories of Ibsen and the blasts against Sardoodledom Shaw had sounded more than half a century ago. In one instance, Jean Cocteau's *The Eagle Has Two Heads*, the Ruritanian confection even arrived with advance trumpetings from the intellectual corners of criticism. Although we promptly signified our rejection of this import, not to mention other plays less augustly endorsed and unsupported by the formidable talents of Tallulah Bankhead, we were as susceptible as other mortals to good romantic drama. We have not failed to give our plaudits to *Cyrano de Bergerac* with becoming regularity ever since Richard Mansfield opened in it on October 3, 1898, with Margaret Anglin playing Roxane while Augustin Daly presented another version with Ada Rehan in the same part on the same memorable evening. And the triumphs of Hampden and Ferrer as Cyrano are of course inscribed in the latter-day annals of the American stage. We received some of Rostand's other pieces with regard, too, if with no vast enthusiasm, and, as noted earlier, we gave Sem Benelli's turbulent piece *La Cena delle Beffe*, produced by Hopkins under the title of *The Jest*, a rousing reception.

Nevertheless, latter-day European romanticism was not altogether congenial to us. We preferred our own brand when Edwin Justus Mayer provided his Cellini play *The Firebrand* and Maxwell Anderson his Elizabethan dramas, starting with *Elizabeth the Queen* in 1930. It was European sophistication, chiefly in the form of light (sometimes sentimental, sometimes cynical) comedy, that won us over, and we were particularly captivated by it in the blithe and breezy nineteen-twenties. The stock of European bohemian and modish attitudes rose as high as the stock of our more materialistic enterprises and dropped only with the advent of the Depression, although more slowly than the national income. We were not to be outdone in the twenties by the gay world across the Atlantic, and we even produced our own styles in sophistication when the Kaufman school of so-called debunkers took the ''bunk'' out of our popular culture and specialized in nose-thumbing entertainment. It was also at that time, however, that the index of importations from the European markets rose highest. An especially thriving market was the Hungarian. It flourished so well indeed that Hollywood caught on to this fact too, as did the Hungarian theatrical fraternity, so that our celluloid capital became full of Magyar literati. Was it not once rumored that it had become necessary to post a notice at the entrance to MGM's writers' building admonishing applicants that it was not enough to be a Hungarian?

Some lovely and still remembered wares came from Budapest. The present writer, for one, affectionately recalls Vajda's comedy of adolescence, *Fata Morgana*, staged for the Theatre Guild by the best director of comedy in the twenties, the scintillating Philip Moeller. This production came toward the end of the 1923-24 season, and the Guild opened its next season with Molnar's *The Guardsman* and the season after that with the same Danubian expert's quizzical romance *The Glass Slipper*. Molnar also accounted for Gilbert Miller's production of *The Good Fairy*, in which the youthful Helen Hayes played a blithe Miss Fix-It, and for the same producer's presentation of *The Play's the Thing*, a semi-Pirandellian piece of impudence in which humor takes liberties not only with the folk and folklore of the theatre but with dramatic structure as well. Among several plays that are about equally representative of a vanished Mittel-Europa, *The Play's the Thing* is perhaps the most durable next to Molnar's familiar masterpiece *Liliom*.

To take the human species lightly and to take its faith and works somewhat lightly, too, was indeed the best kind of instruction the Austrian-Hungarian theatre could give us. In view of our traditional Calvinism, which had and still has odd ways of reasserting itself in our precincts, this enfranchising instruction was quite in order. This was evident even in the *commedia dell' arte* improvisation that the Austrian writer Stefan Zweig made out of Ben Jonson's *Volpone*. The production of this Viennese *Volpone* on Broadway is also an example of the odd way in which we sometimes get texts for the stage. It may be recalled that the *Jedermann* production Reinhardt brought over from Austria was Hugo von Hofmannsthal's adaptation of the English morality-play *Everyman*, itself apparently an adaptation from an earlier Dutch allegory *Elckerlijc*. Admittedly, there is considerable oddity in English classics reaching us through Austrian versions, and purists may demur at so cavalier an attitude toward one of the English masterpieces. But protests on this score would not have troubled the insouciant Theatre Guild of the twenties. When the production opened in New York in the spring of 1928 with Alfred Lunt playing Mosca to the Volpone of Dudley Digges, there was a brightness upon the stage that would be remembered by those who saw the production. There were not many who did, for the play was chiefly entertainment for the cognoscenti of subscription audiences. But is is not only interesting to present this work to students, who will compare it with Jonson's play and perhaps carp at its transformation because it was beyond Herr Zweig and his translator to prevail with crackling Jonsonian language, but also pleasurable to display this *Volpone* as a theatrician's *tour de force*. And here it is embalmed in our anthology like a fly in amber, a fly that while it flew had a lovely color and a lively buzz.

Inevitably more practical for Broadway production, of course, was a translation or moderate adaptation from a foreign language, on the one hand, or a complete domestication of a comedy. The predatoriness of the human animal was a favorite theme of the twenties and, in view of the disrepute of business enterprise during the Depression, it remained a popular subject in the thirties. Not surprisingly there were many European treatments to which we could have helped ourselves, and we turned to several of them in addition to *Volpone*. One of the lightest and, to my mind, best of these, Jules Romains' *Dr. Knock*, proved a weak entry here, perhaps because the producer of the Granville-Barker adaptation, the American Laboratory Theatre, was not particularly potent in the market place. (The production ran for twenty-three performances early in 1928, and the cast included young actors who would later make their way in such opposite worlds as the academic and the cinematic — Francis Fergusson in the former and Harold Hecht in the latter.) But *Topaze*, Marcel Pagnol's demonstration of the prevalence of unscrupulous worldly conduct and a schoolmaster's discovery of its abundant rewards, had in Benn Levy's British adaptation a thriving career in 1930 under Lee Shubert's auspices. And an even greater, as well as more lasting success (*Topaze*, later on, failed twice on Broadway after having rolled up 215 performances in 1930) rewarded Sidney Howard's domestication of René Fauchois' comedy *Prenez garde à la peinture* under the title of *The Late Christopher Bean*. Gilbert Miller presented it brilliantly in New York in the season of 1932-33 with an excellent cast headed by Pauline Lord, Walter Connolly, and Beulah Bondi. Sidney Howard, who had had much experience in preparing European plays for the American stage, brought all his mastery of local color and play-structure to the job of giving this exposé of avarice a native habitation. In its transformed state the play came so close to American genre painting and folk idiom that it is arguable whether *The Late Christopher Bean* is European drama at all. That, however, is precisely the point of my including it in this anthology. The play represents a rare instance of our successfully incorporating a European work into the corpus of American drama.

Efforts to attain the same objective rarely turned out half as well, and other adept adapters such as Robert Sherwood and Sam and Bella Spewack, when they turned out Jacques Deval's *Tovarich* and Albert Husson's *My Three Angels* respectively, had the wisdom to leave the foreign play in its original setting. In the last-mentioned instance, skill and tact on the part of the adapters combined with fortunate casting to make a Broadway success out of a minor play, *La Cuisine des Anges*, by a minor French writer. The adapters, whose *savoir-faire* had proved its edge in previous assignments with sophisticated comedy, maintained a deft and detached humor in their adaptation as well as a profitable balance between amorality and sentimentality. *My Three Angels* may stand in the present volume as the most recent example of rapport between our theatre and that of the Continent in respect to the business of entertainment. It was not the first time, of course, that a rapport had been achieved, and it might have been established even more steadily if plays such as André Roussin's *The Little Hut* had fallen into the right hands. With a good translator and producer inconsequential plays, which are nonetheless as entertaining as *My Three Angels* proved to be, have traveled from country to country with more luck in transit than important masterpieces have had. Between 1915 and 1955 we got tremendous hits from Central European authors not one of whom was called Goethe, Schiller, Kleist, Hebbel, Hauptmann, or Schnitzler.

Since World War II, however, we have enjoyed the experience of genial re-cognition in the case of one European writer who combined an urbane spirit with a reflective one. Somewhat belatedly, we have discovered or rediscovered Jean Girau-doux after having rejected his first serious play *Siegfried* in 1930 and delighted too lightly in his *Amphitryon 38* as a Lunt vehicle in a trim S. N. Behrman adaptation in which the by-play of Giraudoux's intellect could be only faintly detected. We have now (that is, by 1956) made the partial acquaintance of the Giraudoux who summed up in his work some of the best qualities of the French stage that grew out of the efforts of Copeau, Dullin and Jouvet to retheatricalize the theatre without cheapening it and without depriving it of thought, feeling, and general literary excellence. The tragic and near-tragic Giraudoux, it is true, has remained largely unknown, since we have had no professional productions of his *Electra* and *Judith*. And the comic Giraudoux has remained only partially known, since Maurice Valency's adaptations of *The Mad-woman of Chaillot* and *Intermezzo* (called *The Enchanted* on Broadway) tempered Girau-doux' celebrated baroque style—a fine burst of eloquence, much nuance, imagery, and wit—to Broadway ears. Nor did we quite get a right view of his *Ondine* in 1954 through an operatic production chiefly redeemed by the beauty of Audrey Hepburn's person and performance. Only in the Christopher Fry translation of *La Guerre de Troie n'aura pas lieu* under the title of *Tiger at the Gates* for Harold Clurman's production of the season of 1955-56 did Giraudoux's talent remain intact on Broadway.

All the Giraudoux pieces that reached Broadway after 1930 had the same nimbleness of spirit that has been considered too elusive for American playgoers. Their response to *Tiger at the Gates* was not so niggardly as to suggest that they had to be spared mental exercise from Giraudoux's teeming brain in the other productions. But one cannot be sure either that a straight translation would not have militated against Giraudoux on Broadway in the case of so complex a play as *The Madwoman of Chaillot*. What one can be sure of is the enrichment the American theatre derived from its meeting up with the work of Giraudoux, who died in 1944 shortly after the composition of the last-mentioned play and about a decade after the writing of the work that under the title of *Tiger at the Gates* won an almost reverential reception from the press in New York.

Giraudoux's junior colleague, Jean Anouilh, another nimble craftsman, found our reviewers and playgoers less responsive, and on occasion outspokenly hostile. It seemed for several years that after having been overrated in England, he was fated to be under-rated in America. He had, however, some near-misses such as *Ring Round the Moon*, his London success of 1950 adapted by Fry, and *Mademoiselle Colombe*, adapted by Louis Kronenberger. And he received compliments for an early effort, *The Thieves' Carnival*, when it was produced in the off-Broadway Cherry Lane theatre in 1955. Anouilh, the master of entertainments that had the spice of imagination in their composition, found Broadway reluctant to acknowledge the savoriness of his condiments. But by 1955 it was the heavier, if not necessarily more gifted, Anouilh of tragic pretensions who had forged ahead in the race for recognition. His Joan of Arc drama *The Lark* was staged here with stunning impact on a public that had rejected his *Legend for Lovers*, unsatisfactorily adapted from his *Eurydice*, and, despite Katherine Cornell's services, his *Antigone*, a drama of close reasoning and nihilistic intensity that had made an impression abroad. Undoubtedly the American production of *The Lark* owed much of its success to Julie Harris, as vibrant an actress as we have had within memory. And regardless of any complaints lodged against the addition of romantic elements and the subtraction of cynical ones by Lillian Hellman, *The Lark* was a Hellman success as well as an Anouilh one. *The Lark* was not the play the author's advocates would have chosen for the purpose of forwarding his reputation. Still, with the arrival of both *Tiger at the Gates* and *The Lark* on Broadway in the season of 1955-56, relations between New York and Paris appeared to be quite satisfactory.

5.

This brings us to the conclusion of a discourse that could have been more satisfactory if it had been either much briefer or much longer. Briefer or longer, however, it would still have had to take notice of some further points. One of these would refer to our sources of European drama, especially for practical purposes. The Scandinavian countries from which the stream of dramatic modernism had poured down abundantly before 1900 sent us only a trickle, and Russia stopped feeding our reservoirs of drama after the Bolshevik revolution. We evinced high regard for the Soviet theatre in the twenties and early thirties as a seedbed of experimentation in production style but could not work up any enthusiasm for the new Russian plays. The emphasis in them was on utility rather than art, and both their content and form were adversely affected by the growing blight of a dictatorship that did not spare the arts. The German theatre fascinated us mostly with its expressionistic phase of the twenties and with the plays produced under that influence, and this was also true of plays written in the neighboring lands, especially in Czechoslovakia. We had similar difficulty with the dramas of the Italian school of the grotesque, headed by Pirandello, although we were aware that the Italian theatre was bustling with imaginative activity. Spain gave us only a few touching plays and one truly exciting one, *The Passion Flower*, until the mid-thirties. On the European contintent the most ample sources of our theatre were Central European and French. Historical events, moreover, affected our supply throughout the continent. Germany, indeed all of Central Europe, dried up as a source with the advent of Hitler, as Russia did with the advent of Stalin; and two decades of Mussolini were also unfavorable to the burgeoning of theatre despite the Duce's own dabblings in playwriting. Somehow only French dramatic art weathered the political climate throughout the decades — this even under the German occupation. It is a curious fact that the French managed not only to write but to produce plays as challenging as Sartre's *The Flies* and *No Exit* right under the noses of the German occupation authorities.

Men as well as nations belong to this summary, for it was the vogue of individual playwrights that counted heavily with our importers, the Broadway play agents and producers. As previously noted, the greatest vogue was that of Chekhov — not that he became a popular writer, but that he was the one "old" master who left a really deep impression upon our playwrights and critics. But while Chekhov beckoned to us from the shades, Molnar kept us close company for a decade. No commanding figure could be discerned by us during the European crisis from the rise of Hitler until the day of his debacle. But no sooner had that been accomplished than we began to be intrigued, if not exactly overwhelmed, by Sartre and entranced, in the main, with Giraudoux. And since Giraudoux will write no more plays and few of his best works remain to be professionally produced, it may be Anouilh who will occupy the horizon in the next ten years. There is in this traffic with dramatic material a problem of criticism, of course, that has yet to be resolved in the case of recent writers and that has already been almost closed in the case of the older playwrights who followed Ibsen and Strindberg. Concerning the latter I should be deceiving the reader if I maintained that there was more than one great playwright among them — namely Chekhov — or that among the recent writers there were any who gave evidence of attaining the stature of Chekhov. But we cannot keep our eyes constantly fixed on literary stature in matters theatrical, for the theatre is a quotidian affair when it is a living one.

To worry over the possibility of our overrating so gifted a writer as Pirandello or Giraudoux would certainly lead to neurotic anxiety when much of the author's work still needs to be assimilated in our theatre. And also when our general problem remains one of making more, rather than less, use of talented writers. Aside from the work of minor playwrights we have thus far ignored or mismanaged, I have in mind plays by Strindberg, Wedekind, and Pirandello; poetic dramas by Lorca, to whom we have thus far been unable to do much justice, and by Paul Claudel, whose majestic work we have evaded ever since the young Theatre Guild presented *The Tidings Brought to Mary* in 1922; plays by Henry de Montherlant, a dramatist whose talent is as formidable as his reputation in America is negligible; and, surely, plays by Bertolt Brecht, who died in his fifty-eighth year in the summer of 1956 without having had a single production on Broadway except an unsuccessful one of his collaboration with the composer Kurt Weill, *The Threepenny Opera*, about a quarter of a century before. In downtown New York, an adaptation by Marc Blitzstein of the aforementioned work had been running for two seasons, and plans had been drawn by the Phoenix Theatre for producing his incisive fable *The Good Woman of Setzuan*, a play I had hoped to get produced at the Theatre Guild about a dozen years before. It seemed possible, at this time, that Brecht was on the verge of a career long denied him, although it would now have to a posthumous one. There are, besides, cases of minor default too numerous to mention and the misfortunes of less than towering authors for whom some of us would have liked a better reception than they got — for instance, Lenormand, whose extraordinary drama of deteriorating human relations, *Les Ratés*, was staged by Stark Young for the Theatre Guild in 1923 under the title of *The Failures*. It is, finally, also true that many of our translations and adaptations, some indeed in the very volume for which I have made myself responsible, have left something to be desired. The problem of translation has been a vexing one ever since theatres throughout the world began to produce foreign as well as native plays.*

But it is not to lodge complaints in behalf of foreign authors that I have written the above paragraphs. It is rather to show that the European drama has had more to give than we have been willing or able to take. In view of the great variety of the European theatres and their long history, it would be surprising indeed if there were no more available to us than we have displayed on our professional stages. Fortunately, even this much has been large enough to give us a small library of American-produced European plays, and the twenty included in the present volume could easily be doubled if one were to add others already available in other collections or omitted for one reason or another. We, on the other hand, started exporting plays in the nineteen-twenties (those of O'Neill found a brisk market quite quickly) and the demand for our dramas and musicals grew steadily again after World War II. It would appear then that the theatre has provided an active means of international exchange. The exchange has entailed loss as well as profit and dismay as well as delight, but it has fortunately occupied us with commodities over which the battles we wage are fought with expletives rather than explosives.

* To this by no means negligible matter the *Hudson Review* recently devoted an article full of acute observations and fine fury by William Becker.

The Plays and the Playwrights

TIGER AT THE GATES

Tiger at the Gates was a miracle in our theatre — an effective piece of theatre that could also qualify as a literary masterpiece, and a European one that had not been diluted for the purpose of successful presentation on Broadway. As for the excellence of the original play of Jean Giraudoux, chief luminary of the French avant-garde stage, much could be said without exhausting the subject. Many words flowed in its praise after the Harold Clurman production opened on Broadway, soon after the same deft director's London production. The wit and passion of the work could easily be noted, as could the throb of essential action in the midst of the sparkling discursiveness of the writing. For the most part, that discursiveness happened to be intrinsic action, too — action of the mind, combined with the dramatic suspense of awaiting doom in the very act of talking about it. And a good deal of the discourse, superbly written and therefore forceful in itself, gained added pulsation from the context of irony throughout this drama of foredoomed disaster that bore the ironic title of *La Guerre de Troie n'aura pas lieu* — *The Trojan War Will Not Take Place*.

It was furthermore fortunate that the American producers secured the services of Christopher Fry, the English theatre's ablest stylist, as Giraudoux's translator. The English version is a complete and faithful translation. Two short scenes were omitted from the French play by the time the production reached Broadway. (The omissions are indicated in the complete text reprinted in this anthology.) In the opinion of the present editor the omissions are not at all regrettable; they improved the work by overcoming a tendency toward *lycée* cleverness from which Giraudoux was not always free.

The piece was first produced in 1935 by Louis Jouvet, with Jouvet playing the part of Hector. But its arrival in the American theatre was long delayed — although credit should go to Professor John Reich of Columbia University for making a translation and endeavoring to get a production for the play a number of years before the Broadway premiere.* Giraudoux's drama may have struck us as too fatalistic before the outbreak of World War II and too obvious as well as painful in its irony once the war was in progress, while in the early post-war years the theme may have seemed *passé*. One way or another, we managed to postpone professional production of this brilliantly written play for two decades.

The play indeed was conceived in a mode strange in our theatre, whereas the retelling and reinterpretation of classic subject-matter has been traditional on the French stage since the neo-classic age of Corneille and Racine. And Giraudoux had followed their example in writing an *Electra* and an *Amphitryon 38* — the latter so numbered because the author surmised that his was the thirty-eighth treatment of the classic triangle of Alkmena, Amphitryon, and Zeus. *The Trojan War Will Not Take Place* was, of course, something more than just another academic exercise. It was the culmination of its author's concern for the state of the Western world, a state with which he was professionally occupied as a member of the French diplomatic service until his death and with which he had occupied himself as a writer ever since publishing his novel *Siegfried et le Limousin* in 1922 and basing the play *Siegfried* on it. A provocative drama which had a very successful Jouvet production in 1928, *Siegfried* was a failure on the

---

* Apparently at least one other translation prior to Fry's, which was commmissioned by the New York producer Robert Joseph, in 1954 or 1955, circulated in America. It was made by Marcel Reboussin and was staged by Althea Hunt at the College at William and Mary, Williamsburg, Virginia on March 11 and 12, 1953. It may have had other productions.

American stage, but our reception of Giraudoux's later anti-war drama in 1955 was wholly admiring. It was evident that the response of our critics and ordinary playgoers to the play renamed *Tiger at the Gates*, a title in some respects better than *La Guerre de Troie n'aura pas lieu*, was a response to a dramatist who had attained complete maturity as a thinker and dramatist and as a poet and satirist.

And in *Tiger at the Gates*, never distant from the approach of the thinker and the writer — the writer of plays notably literary in texture — is the talent of the man of the theatre. It is perhaps the last thing one would ordinarily expect in a man who served many years in the French foreign ministry, heading the Press Bureau at the Quai d'Orsay in 1924, who became a cabinet minister in 1939, and did not have a play produced until he was forty-six years old. He was nevertheless a true man of the theatre — a *Theatermensch*, as Giraudoux, who had taken a university degree in German literature, would have called himself. Or, rather, he became one as a result of close collaboration with Louis Jouvet ever since the latter's production of *Siegfried*. Giraudoux became one of those modern playwrights, as fortunate as they are rare, who have a theatrical company to write for and to count on, who know almost always for whom they are shaping a part, who create a dramatic character and a playing part simultaneously. In this particular case, moreover, the playwright, for whom characterization was not actually an overriding interest (his characters were well described by Maurice Valency as persons who "express themselves with the precision of trained conversationalists, all voluble, all witty, all a bit precious — all Giraudoux"), also knew that he had a producer in Jouvet who would welcome a fanciful bent of mind. In consequence, Giraudoux was as theatrical in his language as in his dramatic action, and his inclination to write complex speeches or cerebral arias at great length proved more of an advantage than a detriment. For *Tiger at the Gates*, a largely intellectual drama in which the author and his characters are primarily thinking and talking about war instead of waging it, Giraudoux the showman was as essential as Giraudoux the man of letters. Few modern plays indeed start off with so many disadvantages for the stage and end up with so many advantages as this fascinating and heartbreaking discussion drama. Its interest never flags, its tension or excitement rarely ebbs. If Giraudoux failed to resolve any political problems, he surely managed to resolve some difficult dramatic ones.

A statement by Harold Clurman, who staged *Tiger at the Gates*, first in London in June 1955, and then in New York, is significant. Mr. Clurman, contributing a pre-premiere article to *The New York Times* of October 2, 1955, declared that his purpose was "to shape the acting into elements so dynamic in their physical and emotional thrusts that the play's balance of strong action, explosive feeling, sparkle and dignity of expression might be rendered palpable . . ." For this purpose he believed that well-spoken actors "experienced in poetic drama — both classic and contemporary — were essential." That was a chief reason why the production, which was projected by American producers, was first presented in London with an all-English cast. Most members of that cast were brought over from England for the American presentation of *Tiger at the Gates*.

The dates of the first performances of the plays of Jean Giraudoux in Paris follow:
Siegfried — May 3, 1928
Amphitryon 38 — November 8, 1929
Judith — November 4, 1931
Intermezzo (The Enchanted in America) — February 27, 1933
La Guerre de Troie n'aura pas lieu (Tiger at the Gates in England and America) — November 21, 1935
Electra — May 13, 1937
Cantique des Cantiques (The Song of Songs, as yet unproduced on Broadway) — October 12, 1938

Ondine — May 3, 1939
L'Apollon de Marsac (later called *L'Apollon de Bellac*, adapted by Maurice Valency under
the title of *The Apollo of Bellac)* — June 6, 1942
Sodome et Gomorrhe (as yet unproduced on Broadway) — October 11, 1943
La Folle de Chaillot (The Madwoman of Chaillot) — December 21, 1945
Pour Lucrèce (For Lucretia, as yet [1956] unproduced in the United States) — November
5, 1953

THE LARK

The passage of time may reverse our verdict on the plays of Anouilh which we
rejected so brusquely when they were presented on Broadway, for it may have been
the adaptations and the productions that put us off in the case of *Eurydice*, renamed
Legend for Lovers, and the seemingly loathsome *Cry of the Peacock*. In time, we may also
reverse our judgment of Anouilh's *L'Alouette* and conclude that we overrated that
work, which is surely inferior to *Saint Joan* and somewhat akin to *Joan of Lorraine*. It may
turn out that the vast enthusiasm that greeted *The Lark* on Broadway was engendered by
the combined contribution of Lillian Hellman and Julie Harris as adapter and star-
actress respectively. Indeed, many articulate New Yorkers were apt to say so from the
start of the play's run, although there was more agreement concerning the star's
contribution than the adapter's; for there were hardy readers who, resorting to the
French text or to Christopher Fry's straight translation which Oxford University Press
published, compared the original play and the adaptation.

Not all of these were partial to the former even while deprecating the latter. Alice
Griffin in the May 1956 issue of *Theatre Arts* magazine summarized the views of the
prosecution. Noting that the adaptation was shorter than the original by a third, she
declared that it lacked "the spirit and tone of Anouilh's original." She added that
"Miss Hellman's version . . . is romantic while Fry's, like Anouilh's, is ironic and
witty; the latter appeals to the head, while Miss Hellman appeals to the heart."
To which, a proper rejoinder might be that it isn't much of a head that Anouilh
appealed to in the first place, and that irony in a retelling of Joan's story is by now a
shopworn article.

And it may be maintained that for all the cynical pinpricks of Anouilh's original
treatment, its core is as romantic as any believer in the glory of men and women
would have it. As the author of the first English book on him, Edward Owen Marsh, has
declared, Anouilh's plays so far "have the attitude of youth clothed in the observation
of age" and "are in fact the product of an obsession with an idealist's problems, not
of a reasoning out of them."* In *The Lark*, the romanticism, for example, is surely
apparent when Anouilh makes a character comment on the final coronation scene,
that "the real end of Joan's story . . . isn't the powerful and miserable end of the
cornered animal caught at Rouen, but the lark singing in the open sky." Miss Hellman's making Joan exclaim at the end of the coronation scene that she wanted the
Dauphin Charles crowned "because I wanted my country back . . . And God gave
it to us on this Coronation Day" actually gives substance to the romantic afflatus of the
coronation scene. It introduces sense rather than a new romantic element into the
play — and there are times when the present writer is delighted to see Anouilh pinned
down to something concrete. The French writer's *Antigone*, for instance, would not
have been the futile, nihilistic piece and the decadent variation of Sophocles' tragedy
that it is, if Anouilh had pinned himself down more to reality.

There have been areas of evasiveness in Anouilh's general outlook which have
produced great charm for amateur theatricals and for a theatre of civilized diversion

* *Jean Anouilh: Poet of Pierrot and Pantaloon* (London, W. H. Allen & Co., 1953), pp. 198, 198-99.

in some of his "rosy" comedies or so-called *pièces roses*. His poetic farce *The Thieves'* *Carnival (Le Bal des Voleurs)* will probably be a favorite piece for amateurs for a long time precisely because its semi-fantastic world of three grossly inefficient thieves and some scrambled members of aristocratic and middle-class society evokes the spirit of play in the playgoer as well as in the player. (The latter is indeed in danger of performing in this piece as if he were extraordinarily pleased with himself because he is so charming.) And in England especially, Anouilh's charade-like comedy *L'Invitation au* *Château*, which Christopher Fry adapted under the title of *Ring Round the Moon*, won a rapturous reception in 1950. It had its occasions of penetration into character, but its action moved dreamily through a world of mistaken identities and tenuous threads of pretense. Anouilh was able to resolve his shadowy conflicts here with a blithe arbitrariness that was not objectionable in view of the fantastication of the work. It was a different matter, however, whenever Anouilh, turning to his favorite theme of the corruption of society and the individual, wrote his "darker" plays, the so-called *pièces noires*. In such pieces, ranging from a drama of disenchantment such as *Mademoiselle Colombe* to a drama of tragic temper such as *Antigone*, Anouilh has tended to produce puzzling and sometimes frustrating variations on the bankruptcy of the human spirit. The American production of *The Lark* in the 1955-56 season may have given Anouilh his first real success, after seven successive Broadway fiascoes in the United States, largely owing to the fact that Lillian Hellman gave the play some directness and affirmativeness. It is far from certain that when Anouilh engages himself to a tragic theme his ambivalences and nihilism — the qualities a German publication, the *Tagesspiegel*, aptly called his *"melancholische Skepsis"* — are assets.

Among continental European plays professionally produced here, *The Lark*, as trimmed and tightened or, shall we say, "tautened," by Lillian Hellman, is neither characteristic of Anouilh's playwriting nor of Miss Hellman's. The amalgam, however, proved intensely effective on the stage. "What results," Richard Watts, Jr. wrote in the *New York Post*, "is a compassionate, admiring and yet steadily realistic and believable portrait . . ." And Walter Kerr, in the *New York Herald Tribune*, expressed the relief of playgoers who had dreaded seeing another story of Joan when he declared that "the familiar events seem freshly lived." Our response was, not strangely, similar to the German reception of the play when it was staged by Leo Mittler in Berlin on December 30, 1953. One review, in the Bremer *Nachrichten*, actually called *Die Lerche (The Lark)* Anouilh's strongest and best play.

We may add, however, that we did not greatly examine our responses. Curiously, few reviewers took note of the unique organization of the drama, which, both in the original and in Miss Hellman's adaptation, starts with the theatrical assumption that the characters in Joan's drama want to reenact Joan's story, proceeds by means of flashbacks toward the climax of her execution, and then cuts back to the scene in which Joan managed to get Charles crowned King of France. The use of a climax *after* the climax was also a bold stroke of imaginative theatricality. It was evident in our response to *The Lark*, as to *The Madwoman of Chaillot*, that the art of imaginative theatre, brought to a peak in France by Copeau's successors Dullin and Jouvet, had begun at long last to make inroads into our predominantly realistic theatre.

Anouilh, who started out with a theatrical background, having been born on June 23, 1910, in Bordeaux to a mother who played the violin at performances of numerous operettas he was allowed to attend as a child (at least up to the first intermission), came directly from the tradition of these renovators of the stage. And at the age of twenty-two, after a year and a half at law school and two years in an advertising company, Anouilh became secretary to Louis Jouvet's company—from which he borrowed the scenery of Giraudoux's *Siegfried* in order to start housekeeping with a young actress wife. Such other leaders of the French movement to "retheatricalize the theatre" as Pierre Fresnay and George Pitoëff also played an important part in Anouilh's career, the latter having given him his first real financial success in 1937. Thereafter an

Anouilh play was produced almost every season at the advanced Théâtre de L'Atelier. It is theatricality of a literary and philosophical nature that has been most characteristic of Anouilh's work. So much so that he has been adept in using character types, in exaggerating characters stagily, and in contriving and resolving events "improbably." He believed, as he declared to the press as early as 1936, "that the dramatist could and should *play with* his characters, with their passions, and their actions." And he added that to "play" with a subject — and he has done so occasionally, as in *The Waltz of the Toreadors*, in such a way that his farce veers on tragedy and his humor on painful irony — is "to create a new world of conventions and surround it with spells and a magic of their own."* Peter Brook, who staged *Ring Round the Moon* in London, was quite correct in saying of Anouilh that "He is a poet, but not a poet of words: he is a poet of words-acted, of scenes-set, of players-performing." (Preface to *Ring Round the Moon*, Methuen & Co., Ltd., 1950.)

Still, it is possible to wonder whether Anouilh did not "play" too much with his subject in making the characters in *The Lark* "real" yet also actor-characters who have been reenacting the story of Joan and who can cut back to any episode and in any sequence at will. (The Hellman adaptation tries to glide over this arbitrary theatricalization of the action, just as it omits the ironical last speech of Joan's unpleasant father who tells her little brother just before the coronation tableau to take his fingers away from his nose — *"Et tire tes doigts de ton nez"* — and observe the honor that has come to Joan who, he had always said, had a future: *"J'avais toujours dit moi, que cette petite avait de l'avenir"* — a detail omitted in both the Fry and Hellman versions. Thereupon the coronation scene is formally enacted in broad pantomime and the curtain slowly descends on a picture-book tableau — *"Le rideau tombe lentement sur cette belle image de livre de prix,"* rendered by Fry as "The Curtain slowly descends on this beautiful illustration from a school prize" and ignored by Miss Hellman, whose version ends with the solemn singing of the "Gloria" of the Mass. Indeed, the last dozen speeches in her version are entirely her own, so that the text I have included in this book affords an excellent example of the ways of adaptation. The reasons for Miss Hellman's alterations and changes are apparent; they supply the exaltation the American playgoer expects from the story of Joan. But there are losses, too, even if one need not be particularly impressed with the whole of Anouilh's original ending. The Inquisitor's last line in the original is superb. With his eyes averted from the scene of execution, he has asked whether Joan was flinching and has been told that she wasn't; he has asked whether there was a smile on her lips and has been told that there was. Thereupon, with his head bowed, he says sorrowfully, *"Je ne le vaincrai jamais"* — "I shall never be able to master him," meaning the Devil. In the American adaptation he merely says, "I have seen it all before."

In conclusion, the reader should perhaps be referred to Anouilh's own statement of his view of *The Lark* as printed in the program of the French production which opened at the Théâtre Montparnasse Gaston Baty on October 14, 1953, with Suzanne Flon in the part of Joan. In this explanation, Anouilh dismissed rational analysis of Joan's career, "the mystery of Joan." She could not be explained "any more than you can explain the tiniest flower growing by the wayside." For him there was "just the phenomenon of Joan, as there is a phenomenon of a daisy or of the sky or of a bird." Shaw, in writing *Saint Joan*, wanted to know and show more than that. Anouilh exclaimed, "What pretentious creatures men are, if that's not enough for them" and claimed to have presented Joan without knowing more about the secret of her inspiration than a child imitating a bird-song knows about ornithology.

* See *Jean Anouilh*, by Edward Owen Marsh (London: W. H. Allen & Co., 1953), p. 189.

A MONTH IN THE COUNTRY

Ivan Turgenev (1818-1883) is too well known as a novelist to be discussed here, especially since his playwriting was a divagation, if an unusually inspired one, into an essentially alien field. In addition to writing some amusing one-act pieces, he composed several studies of character noteworthy for their subtlety. Turgenev had a talent for the exposition of feelings his characters tried to conceal or did not fully comprehend, as well as for affecting contrasts between his characters' dreams and their failure to fulfill them. Especially appealing are the one-acters *The Lady from the Provinces* and *Where It is Thin, There It Breaks*, the study of a provincial Hamlet and a sensitive but resolute girl who tires of his irresolution as a lover. Effective, too, are *A Poor Gentleman*, a study in failure and irony, and *The Bachelor*, a quiet comedy about a gentleman and his young ward which is the ideal counterpart to Molière's *The School for Wives*, since the bachelor-guardian is a wonderfully sympathetic character and is rewarded with the girl's love.

But Turgenev's masterpiece is, without question, *A Month in the Country*, written in 1849, and it was, besides, a Chekhovian masterpiece long before Chekhov began to write for the stage. "Had this play been written by a contemporary playwright," declared Allardyce Nicoll in his *World Drama*, "it would have been made into a drama of the grand passion" — which it obviously isn't in Turgenev's treatment. The young man, the tutor loved by two women, would have been the hero of the play rather than an indifferent and unromantic character. "In a French play, too," Professor Nicoll, thinking of the French "well-made" play formula, continued, "the 'intrigue' would have been concentrated and made economic with respect to means," whereas Turgenev "not only introduces numerous scenes of no importance for the development of the plot, but brings in lengthy speeches entirely unrelated, except by emotional implication, to the main story," a fact which may not be altogether evident in the abbreviated version made — and made quite well — by Emlyn Williams.

Although Turgenev did not expect his play to reach the stage, it did get a production some twenty years after it was written, by which time the author had long ago renounced all intentions of writing plays. (These were all products of his youth; he stopped trying to write for the theatre at the age of thirty-three.) Production apparently gave him no reason to revise his decision. But, a quarter of a century after his death, in 1909, the Moscow Art Theatre ended his exile from the theatre by successfully staging *A Month in the Country*. And it was especially appropriate that the part of Natalia, the love-sick provincial wife, should have been played in this production by Chekhov's widow, the celebrated Olga Knipper.

It should be added that the Emlyn Williams version used by our Phoenix Theatre was first presented in London on February 11, 1943 at the St. James' Theatre, with Valerie Taylor in the role of the distressed lady Natalie Petrovna, and Michael Redgrave, who staged the 1956 Phoenix Theatre production, in the part of the platonic lover Rakitin. This version was produced again by the Old Vic in 1950 with direction by Michel Saint-Denis.

Since *A Month in the Country* is a novelist's play it is perhaps necessary to remind ourselves that, except for its length, which caused even the Moscow Art Theatre to abbreviate its dialogue drastically (as did Emlyn Williams in the version printed here), this is a highly theatrical work. Audiences of the Theatre Guild and Phoenix Theatre productions had no difficulty in sensing that it was. Literary critics may have found it more difficult to arrive at this realization, especially if they were impressed by the association of realism with the work of both Turgenev and the Moscow Art Theatre. It is true, nevertheless, that Turgenev instinctively satisfied the requirements of good theatre without violating realism of characterization and viewpoint. He created a number of good acting parts and several excellent ones in his play, and one virtuoso role in the character of Natalia. The characters convince us of their reality, but they also belong to the theatre through the vividness of their conduct and the intensity of their concentration upon whatever they happen to be doing or feeling. Turgenev, furthermore, created great playing scenes such as those singled out by Michael Redgrave from his experience with the play to prove that at its core "is the gold of pure theatre". In an introduction to the English adaptation, Mr. Redgrave called attention to the scene "where Natalia lays bare Vera's heart; the scenes where Rakitin and Natalia — she needing his help and he ready to give it — turn against each other; the Doctor's courtship of Lizaveta; Vera's challenge to Natalia; the parting scene of Islaev [Natalia's husband] and Rakitin and the whole glorious, gay and yet autumnal ending . . ."

Superbly "theatre" yet movingly real as well — and complexly so — are the soliloquies that reveal the characters. (Soliloquies, we will recall, were to be banished from the theatre by dogmatic naturalism within several decades of the composition of *A Month in the Country.*) And, finally, one can have nothing but admiration for the tact with which Turgenev avoided a maudlin presentation of Natalia's and Vera's emotional state and gave the play as a whole a basically anti-romantic, comic quality by gently exposing the theatricality of his lovelorn heroine and other characters.

Mr. Redgrave has reminded us of the importance of the fact that Natalia is only twenty-nine, so that her situation is not that "of an aging woman suffering from . . . the humiliation of a desperate last fling." If she believes that her infatuation with the young tutor is a last fling "we should know from the look of her that it is not" and we should smile when she refers to herself and her thirty-year-old platonic lover Rakitin as "We old people." And Rakitin himself, although surely not a subject for vulgar laughter because he cannot "make" his friends' wife, is nevertheless a comic character. He is caught in an attachment more disconcerting than overpowering. He is a man whose keen intelligence is as much of a disadvantage to him as a lover as are his good breeding and sense of honor. Moreover, Rakitin, a role originally played by Stanislavsky himself, is rather acutely aware of his situation and dramatizes it to himself and to Natalia. Turgenev's theatrical treatment of these and several other self-dramatizing characters (except Vera, the girl who suddenly acquires womanly stature in the course of events) is one of affectionate mockery.

A Month in the Country owes its fascination indeed to a multi-faceted reality and theatricality not easily exhausted in a single reading. It challenged its professional producers, and it will long remain a challenge to actors and directors in English. Fortunately, the potential results are extraordinarily rewarding, as both the Theatre Guild and the Phoenix Theatre productions proved in New York.

MY THREE ANGELS

No one will mistake *My Three Angels* for anything but the entertainment it is. Nor will anyone who knows the New York stage be amazed that the essentially amoral, or shall we say amoral-sentimental, comedy of a hitherto unknown French writer (the original *La Cuisine des Anges* was Albert Husson's first play to be performed on the Parisian professional stage) should have been successfully re-created by Sam and Bella Spewack. The married couple, both born in the same year, 1899, are Russian and Hungarian respectively. Sam Spewack had enjoyed European connections ever since he had covered the Geneva Conference in 1922 — he was even press attaché for our embassy in Moscow in 1943. Bella Spewack had served as a press agent for *The Miracle*, the *Chauve Souris*, and the visiting musical studio of the Moscow Art Theatre during the twenties. This playwriting team, which had proved proficiency in farce-comedy with *Boy Meets Girl* and with the "book" for *Kiss Me Kate*, possessed the *savoir faire* for improving relations with European farceurs and contrivers of amoral comedy who can convert even penal-colony convicts into companionable fellows. And our international relations on this level had long needed improving. Most of our favors had been lavished on confectionery for which the eighteenth-century French term of tearful comedy or *comédie larmoyante* remains an apt definition, unless we should adopt the even apter one of *Kitsch* from the German language. *Kitsch*, a trumpery quality, might indeed have vitiated a play in which innocence is protected by soft-hearted swindlers and murderers but for the tactful ministrations of the adapters who brought a becoming *insouciance* to the subject matter.

As a result of the combined efforts of the Spewacks and Monsieur Husson, *La Cuisine des Anges*, literally "Angels' Cooking," possessed a fine icing of paradox and irony more frequent in European theatres than in our own. And, fortunately, the irony of criminals doing the work of angels in defending goodness against villainy, was casual and genial, so that the confection was not too tart for our playgoing public. The writing was farcical rather than sardonic, whimsically impudent rather than acidulous; and homicide in this piece could be considered no more outrageous than the triumph of virtue could be considered uplifting. In short, the play, escaping the disabilities of some superior Continental comedies for production on our stage — of, shall we say, Becque's *La Parisienne* and Wedekind's *The Marquis of Keith* — was inviolably popular in its ingredients. In Paris, Albert Husson, whose next New York production — *Les Pavés de Ciel* (Heaven's Paving-stones) adapted as *The Heavenly Twins* — was a disaster, won the 1952 Tristan Bernard prize for *La Cuisine des Anges*. In New York, the Spewacks won no prizes to speak of, but their adaptation, *My Three Angels*, won the material reward of a long Broadway run.

ONDINE

Ondine, with its medieval setting and supernatural element, may have been an effort on Giraudoux's part to escape for a while from the pressures of events that were coming to a head in a war that had seemed inevitable to the author while writing his ironic forecast, *The Trojan War Will Not Take Place*, several years earlier. A year or so before the outbreak of World War II, Giraudoux, then active in the French diplomatic service, turned to a story about a water-sprite or *ondine* lost in the human world, a fairy tale that had been told more than a century before by a German descendant of French Huguenots, La Motte Fouqué, in his *Undine*. Giraudoux, in any case, did not consider his interest in his new play *Ondine* incompatible with his concern over the international situation. Perhaps it is symbolic of his dual life as artist and public official that he should have left a copy of *Ondine* with Miss Helburn and me while he was on a diplomatic mission. His rueful fairy-tale, in which a mortal gains an ideal love only to betray it in the end, may be regarded as a sublimation through art of the disenchantment of Giraudoux the political observer and social thinker. Nor did the writing of *Ondine* represent a radically new tendency in the literary career of a playwright whose bent had always been toward poetry and fantasy, and whose dialogue had always had a much richer texture than the dialogue of most of his contemporaries.

Ondine was intended by Giraudoux for the imaginative, non-realistic theatre — "the theatre theatrical" — for which his producer Louis Jouvet had become renowned along with other disciples of the path-breaking Jacques Copeau. Jouvet staged the play in Paris in the spring of 1939 with himself in the role of Hans, the inadequate mortal husband of a water-spirit, and with Madeleine Ozeray playing the hapless Ondine. There was considerable delay, however, in transplanting the play to Manhattan. Schuyler Watts had made a translation that did not get beyond the stage of receiving an amateur production on May 19, 1949, at the little theatre in the Barbizon-Plaza hotel from which few plays graduate to Broadway. Some time then elapsed before Maurice Valency, who had successfully adapted *The Madwoman of Chaillot* by the same author, could be prevailed upon to prepare a new English version for Broadway, and the preparation of a production was no easy matter until the services of the greatly sought-after Audrey Hepburn were acquired.

When the play was finally staged — and it was staged rather more operatically than some of Giraudoux' admirers could approve — it was apparent that the play did not fit snugly into our theatre. It was a pathetic story rather than a profound or keen drama, yet it hinted at profundity; explication could arrive at profundity, but common sense would easily dissipate it. The play, besides, required sympathy from the playgoer, yet kept him at some distance because the lovers were a supernatural creature that cannot be destroyed and a man who cannot be awakened to either ecstasy or tragic pain. A man who is, as Mr. Valency put it in some comments on the play, "a social being tied to the mundane by a thousand living threads" and a hero whose despair "plumbs no depths beyond wretchedness." With limitations such as these, *Ondine* is probably difficult to stage with complete success under any circumstances. It is significant, for example, that fault was found with the playing of Hans whether it was Hollywood's Mel Ferrer or the Parisian theatre's great actor Jouvet who played the part.

By comparison with a drama truly rooted in folk-tradition such as *The Dybbuk*, Giraudoux's urbanely written, if still touching and rueful, play cannot be said to come alive as myth; and by the same token it cannot come wholly alive as reality. *Ondine* derives from a "literary" fairy-tale and the work of the playwright was a redaction and interpretation of something that was already literature. Yet it does not seem right to complain that a work of disenchantment lacks spontaneity and that a play which makes a point of man's inability to give himself up completely to the wonder in life is deficient in magic. ("There is the side [in Hans, the typical man] that yearns for the infinite," Mr. Valency has written. "There is the side that yearns for its dinner . . . His soul longs for beauty, for the absolute, the transcendental; when he attains it he has no use for it; it oppresses him." Mr. Valency further volunteered the opinion that the story of *Ondine*, with its knight's wavering between the unworldly sprite and the all-too-human fleshly Bertha is "the story of marriage.") Even so, a suitably ethereal spirit in the characterization of *Ondine* was brought to the stage in Audrey Hepburn's playing, and some magic survived the worldliness and irony of the treatment in the text. *Ondine*, whatever its patent limitations, was a rare experience for American playgoers accustomed to mundane realism. It came to many of them not only as a *tour de force* of the imagination but as a wistful statement on mankind's eternal fluctuation between dream and reality.

THE MADWOMAN OF CHAILLOT

With the Alfred de Liagre production of *La Folle de Chaillot* or *The Madwoman of Chaillot* on December 27, 1948, Giraudoux acquired the status of a major playwright in the United States that had already been granted him for some time across the Atlantic. By then, however, the career of Giraudoux had ended: born in 1882, he had died in 1944, and *The Madwoman of Chaillot* was a posthumous work that brought honor to its author in America that had not been extended to him for previous productions. Eva Le Gallienne's presentation of his early post-war drama *Siegfried* at her Civic Repertory Theatre had only succeeded in puzzling her public and the Theatre Guild presentation of his classic comedy *Amphitryon 38*, a huge success with the Lunts in 1938, was welcomed in S. N. Behrman's neat abbreviation and adaptation more as a bedroom farce than as the complex comedy it was in the original with its philosophical overtones and its opulent pile of literary dialogue.

Giraudoux first won a reputation in France with novels little known in America. But one of these, which dealt with the amnesia of a French soldier who believes himself to be a German, brought him into the theatre. *Siegfried*, the title of both the novel and the play, was an attention-arresting work, especially on the stage, because it dealt with the problem of Franco-German relations that might well agitate playgoers whose memories of the holocaust of World War I were still quite fresh. The play was a plea for international understanding and expressed the convictions of Giraudoux the citizen and the civil servant. But its message was so imaginatively projected and expressed with such subtle dialogue that *Siegfried*, regardless of its faults of contrivance and overlengthy discussions, also introduced Giraudoux as a potential master of poetic meditation and argument. The same promise was also apparent in his unsuccessful biblical drama *Judith* (1931), a wry and penetrative dramatization of the conflict between complex personal motivation and the single-tracked demands of national interest. His treatment of the Oresteian theme in his *Electra* (first staged by Louis Jouvet in 1937) again combined the social and the poetic prepossessions of the author, the theme being the error and evil of vengefulness even when the cause is just. It was memorable for its imaginative theatrical action and dazzlingly embroidered dialogue and monologue. *Judith* and *Electra* evidenced their author's endeavor to effectuate himself as a tragic poet, and it may yet be that adequate stage productions will reveal a facet of Giraudoux's talent still unknown to the American playgoing public.

Still, it was the Giraudoux of ultra-modern comic art who won both a national and international reputation. It is an art that is at once witty and poetic, wonderfully clear at the edges and fascinatingly ambiguous at the core. This may be said of even so popular a play as his *Amphitryon 38* in the original, and of his *Intermezzo*, called *The Enchanted* in the Maurice Valency adaptation that rather befuddled and only intermittently interested Broadway playgoers. In *Intermezzo*, indeed, the author's comic fancy was brilliantly theatrical and, at the same time, hauntingly poetic, although the interest was somewhat intermittent and the mingling of the human and the supernatural in the play was somewhat disturbing to a public accustomed to simpler dramaturgy from most of its native playwrights. And, finally, the humorous and serious sides of Giraudoux's talent and his joint aptitudes for comedy of manners and imaginative extravaganza whipped up that most delightful, as well as most mentally nourishing, of modern soufflés, *La Folle de Chaillot*.

If *The Madwoman of Chaillot*, written just before the playwright's death, in 1943, is not perhaps the very best of Giraudoux' plays—strong claims may be pressed for *Tiger at the Gates* and perhaps for *Electra*—it is certainly the final distillation of his art of dramatic poetry and social satire, which may have led *Theatre Arts* magazine to define the play as "one part fantasy, two parts reason." The definition would indeed be an acceptable one if it were understood that the fantasy functions in the service of the author's critical reason and that Giraudoux's reasoning is so poetic in discourse and so inventive that it is fantastic. *The Madwoman of Chaillot* exemplifies reason-charged fantasy and fantastic reason. It is, in short, the dream of a complex and ultra-civilized man. That the man should have become the spokesman of the complex and ultra-civilized French nation in his native theatre is understandable. That he should have also won an appreciative hearing in our own theatre is a marvel that remains to be accounted for.

He did not win it without assistance from his American producer and stage director Mr. Alfred de Liagre, and his American adapter, however much critics might cavil. Mr. De Liagre was decorated by the French government for his part in Giraudoux's triumph on our stage after *The Madwoman* was awarded the New York Critics Circle prize as the best foreign play of the year. Mr. Valency, a popular professor of comparative literature at Columbia University, received commissions to adapt such other Giraudoux fables as *Intermezzo* and *Ondine*. And his success as an adapter was an indirect reward for years of frustration as an interesting playwright in his own right. One of his plays, an original version of the *Alcestis* under the title of *The Thracian Horses*, had been frequently slated for a Broadway production which somehow never materialized.

It is true that the Giraudoux composition that reached American playgoers — after

an earlier and fuller yet quite cumbersome translation had gone the rounds on Broadway — was a thinned-out one. The geyser of Giraudoux's language had been reduced
to a manageable English stream. The adapter admitted as much, and for all the finger-
pointing of George Jean Nathan as well as the tongue-lashing Professor Valency was to
receive in literary quarterlies, some points could be raised in extenuation of his
procedure. It could be argued that half a loaf of Giraudoux's yeasty commodity was
better than none, and that in the case of so bizarre and "baroque" a work as *The
Madwoman* (a grotesque work by comparison with the classic contours, if by no means
classic spirit, of the earlier-written *Tiger at the Gates*, which Broadway presented in a
translation rather than an adaptation seven years later) there would have been none at
all but for Valency's moderating services. Something, moreover, could be said amid
all the tributes to Giraudoux that would acknowledge the limitations of the original
play. And something was later said, very aptly indeed, by Eric Bentley in the *New
Republic* of March 8, 1954, in connection with the production of the author's earlier-
written *Ondine*. Mr. Bentley, while granting that Giraudoux was "a first-rank man of
letters consecrating his maturity to the theatre" and that his plays "constitute a claim
to vast originality," offered the qualification that in his work "thought is more important than action" and "words are more important than thought." If all the words
in *The Madwoman*—the words that give it so rich a vitality in French—had been left
intact, they might not indeed have buried the thought (the "thought" that is surely
nothing very profound whether considered as philosophy or social criticism) but they
might have buried the American playgoer. And for all the emphasis that is properly
put on the verbal texture of Giraudoux' plays, his effectiveness as a dramatic poet, even
perhaps in French but surely in English, is mainly in the invention of the action (very
apparent in the mad noblewoman's plot to destroy the French nation's speculators,
which sustains the drama) and in the zany characterizations—tender in the case of the
"madwoman" and her friends— which are at their best an *action* too. These considerations, however, have not been intended for the praise or defense of the American
adaptation. They are intended instead to express a view of Giraudoux, undoubtedly
the most gifted foreign playwright to be taken by us at something like his true worth,
if hardly in complete measure, after the second World War.

John Mason Brown called *The Madwoman* "one of the most interesting and rewarding
plays to have been written within the last twenty years," and Brooks Atkinson referred
to it as "pure gold, with no base metal." George Jean Nathan hailed it in the *New
York Journal-American* issue of August 25, 1947, more than a year prior to its Broadway
debut, as a work endowed with "an enveloping and irresistible humor," with "all
kinds of little imaginative touches," and with a social theme developed in an ironic
direction that saved the play from the boredom attendant upon most message-plays.
For the sake of accuracy it is necessary to report, however, that Mr. Nathan was
considerably less enthusiastic about the production he saw at the Belasco Theatre and
about the adaptation, to which he attributed "a frosty air of classroom precision." He
would have preferred a more exuberant production and a more effusive translation.

A fanciful exuberance and much effusiveness, as well as a general impression of improvisation (evident, for example, in the prose-poem at the end of the first act, pared
down in English), were indeed essential to *The Madwoman*. Some of the original
long passages abbreviated in the adaptation and some of the extravagance of personality
moderated by the Broadway cast had obviously been intended for the theatrically
heightened acting Giraudoux could expect from Louis Jouvet's company. Giraudoux
had discussed the play with Jouvet and started writing it in 1942. And Jouvet, who
also played the role of the ragpicker performed in New York rather mutedly by John
Carradine, presented *The Madwoman* at his theatre on December 19, 1945, with all the
affectionate care he had given to previous Giraudoux productions. It does not follow,
however, that there was only one way of staging this elusive comic fantasy. Nor is it
certain that Giraudoux attained a really final form for his play — which he did not live

to see produced, even if individual scenes, such as the mad tea-party, could hardly be improved. As Jouvet himself reported in *The New York Times* in 1949, Jean Giraudoux "wrote three versions of *The Madwoman of Chaillot*, of which two were entirely different." It is not at all certain that the play, written by Giraudoux in a time of troubles, reached completeness even in the final version. Fortunately, however, even an imperfect *Madwoman*, the product of a truly original mind as well as compassionate spirit, is beyond doubt a notably ingratiating achievement.

NO EXIT

Jean-Paul Sartre, ex-schoolmaster and former Sorbonne professor, was active in the French underground struggle during World War II while writing *Huis Clos* or *No Exit*, and the play was produced in Paris about a month before D-day in 1944. Sartre was also a philosopher, the leading exponent indeed of atheistic and nihilistic Existentialism which he had just formulated at formidable length in his treatise on "being and non-being," *L'Être et le néant*. Some five years earlier he had also given imaginative versions of his view of the "nothingness" of life in two works of fiction, the novel *Nausea* and a collection of short stories entitled *The Wall*. By 1943, however, his view of man's condition and potentialities in a godless and pointless universe had acquired a moral, indeed puritanical, slant from the positive character of the patriotism in the French underground movement.

Sartre began to stress man's responsibility to himself in consequence of his so-called freedom — that is, his freedom from a supernatural power capable of determining his fate. Bravely and tragically, in loneliness and in anguish, the existentialist hero was to be entirely on his own. Man was compelled indeed to create his own existence; he made himself because what he was as a person—his "existence," so to say—was the product of his decisions and deeds. Having called upon men to reject bondage to a supernatural ruler, Sartre also urged them to spurn bondage to convention and dependency upon the opinions of others — a view expressed in *No Exit* when a character is made to say, "*L'enfer c'est les autres*" — hell is other people. Thus through a self-reliance that recalls the Emersonian ideal, though without any Emersonian faith or *mystique*, Sartre called for liberation from self-deception and moral cowardice—in effect, for integrity of character in a country which many believed to have collapsed in 1940 mainly for want of integrity.

In *The Flies*, a retelling of the classical Electra-Orestes story, which appeared in 1943, Sartre showed how this integrity could be won and secured against the pressures and deceptions of political and religious despotisms—the despotisms of the guilty couple, Queen Clytemnestra and King Aegistheus, and of Zeus. In *No Exit*, concentrating on characters who are precisely what the lives they led has made them, Sartre exposed the lack of integrity, the moral cowardice and self-deception, he found prevalent in the modern world. And he symbolically represented the condign punishment of his "sinners" as incarceration with others of their kind upon whose opinion, owing to their lack of inner freedom, they are eternally dependent. Hell in *No Exit* (also known in a 1946 British production as *Vicious Circle*), is, indeed, this dependency —"hell is other people." It is all the more that since in Sartre's inferno the characters are stripped of their evasions in front of each other.

Sartre, while becoming the head of a briefly fashionable cult in Paris and becoming involved in both literary and political conflicts, went on to write other plays, the latest and most ambitious being *Le Diable et le Bon Dieu (God and the Devil)* which opened in Paris in June 1951. Those that have won some attention from us thus far have been a sardonic and wildly implausible play about our deep South, *La putain respectueuse* (1946) or *The Respectful Prostitute*, which enjoyed a moderate success here; an existentialist Resistance melodrama, *Morts sans sépulture* (1946), adapted by Thornton

Wilder and called *The Victors* in a good New York production that was too gruesome for popularity; and a play full of political ambivalences, *Les mains sales* (1948), called for inscrutable reasons *Red Gloves* in America instead of "Dirty Hands" (meaning as Sartre declared to the press, "that no one who lives and acts can avoid dirty hands") and given a confusing production despite excellent playing by Charles Boyer and others. *No Exit*, however, remains the most concentrated expression of Sartre's pristine talent for the drama — a talent which while by no means unflawed by discursiveness and grand-guignol sensationalism had, in its first manifestations of the 1943-44 period, moral passion, if not compassion, and bold, if not altogether original, inventiveness. These characteristics appear especially in the situation, well described by Lynton Hudson in *Life and the Theatre:* "In this room without mirrors in which to see themselves and unable to close their eyes, for their eyelids have disappeared—*il faut vivre les yeux ouverts . . . pour toujours*—they can only read their judgment in one another's eyes, and the other always judges by results, by what he sees, not by the conflicting motives, the noble aspirations, that lie beneath the surface."

JACOBOWSKY AND THE COLONEL

Among refugees from the holocaust Hitler's hordes were spreading over Europe, Franz Werfel, who was born in Prague in 1890 and died in Beverly Hills in 1945, had the good fortune of bringing with him a dual talent — a triple talent, indeed, if we include one for writing disinguished poetry. He was a playwright and novelist of long-standing reputation. But, until the success of *Jacobowsky and the Colonel* in 1944, it was as a novelist that he was really known in the United States, where *The Forty Days of Musa Dagh* (1934) and *The Song of Bernadette* (1942) gave him a popular reputation and a good livelihood. His plays, like his short masterpiece in the field of fiction, *Class Reunion*, had been slighted here, and he had apparently resigned himself to permanent exile from our theatre after the poor reception of the Theatre Guild's productions of *The Goat Song* and *Juarez and Maximilian* in 1926 and the debacle of his epic on the mission and burden of the Jewish people, *The Eternal Road*, in New York in 1936. The fall of France stirred Werfel to return to the theatre and to bring to the treatment of this catastrophe his familiar sympathy and romantic flair for the celebration of courage and the noble gesture, as well as his knowledge of European class distinctions.

It was also fortunate for the career of the new play *Jacobowsky and the Colonel* that the Theatre Guild prevailed upon the vivacious Elia Kazan to stage it and upon S. N. Behrman to give it the benefit of a tart comic style. In the final form of *Jacobowsky and the Colonel*, Werfel and Behrman wrung affirmative humor from the depression that had oppressed the free world when Paris fell. And more than that, the joint work of Werfel and Behrman introduced in our war-time theatre a rare spirit of urbanity without the irresponsibleness of indifference or cynicism. Even the unavoidable topicality of the subject matter was somewhat modified, since the contrasts between the Jewish refugee Jacobowsky and the Polish Colonel were presented as eternal within the larger unity of human nature.

There was hokum, too, in the play, but it was consonant with the flamboyance of one of Pilsudsky's flashiest officers and one of the Diaspora's most resourceful citizens. Playing the roles of Don Quixote and Sancho Panza or of Don Giovanni and Leporello to each other and to a lady companion who had become a veritable symbol of *la belle France* to them, they were even conscious at times — Jacobowsky all the time and the Colonel occasionally — that they were actors in some grotesque tragicomedy requiring large gestures from them. The flummery of the play, especially as embodied in the personalities projected by Louis Calhern and Oscar Karlweis, helped to endear this odd comedy to its audiences. There was also some understandable sentimentality in the play, but it happily escaped mawkishness on virtually every occasion when the writing seemed to be succumbing to it. And even the melodrama of the next to the last scene—a product of Broadway opportunism—was not actually inapposite under the circumstances. Chiefly, however, the work was saved by its various manifestations of candor, and the American stage was saved by Werfel, late in the course of World War II, from the ignominy of not having been able to sustain a single European play on the subject of the crisis of the age.

Jacobowsky and the Colonel, Werfel's last play, may be considered a climax in his career even though this stage piece did not attain the success of *Forty Days of Musa Dagh* and *The Song of Bernadette*. Werfel, who was born on September 10, 1890, in Prague to Jewish parents with a German background, had received an Austrian-German education, had attended the University at Leipzig after studying at the University of Prague, had also lectured at the University of Leipzig, and then served in the Austrian army from 1915 to 1917 on the Russian front. After World War I, he settled in Vienna, where his success as a novelist and dramatist brought him wealth as well as leadership in advanced literary circles. His standing in Germany was just as high as it was in Austria, and he was made a member of the Prussian Academy of Art. But he became a marked man when the Nazis came to power because of his religion and his liberalism. He was expelled from the Prussian Academy of Art in 1933 and his books were banned a year later. Werfel prudently moved his residence from Vienna to Paris, but when Paris, too, fell to Hitler's forces, Werfel became a full-fledged refugee like his Jacobowsky. He fled with Alma Maria Mahler (his wife, the widow of the composer Gustav Mahler) to the Côte d'Azur and, soon after, to Marseilles. He tried to cross over into Spain, but was turned back at the border and found a temporary refuge at Lourdes, where upon hearing for the first time the story of Bernadette, he vowed to "sing her song" if he succeeded in escaping capture by the Nazis. He managed to elude them and get to Lisbon, and from Portugal got to the United States in the fall of 1940. "Jacobowsky" had managed to survive and lived on to fight for humanity with his pen in accordance with his credo which he defined as "My only political credo . . . to search for humanity everywhere and to avoid barbarism." He kept his promise to write the "song" of Bernadette in 1942, and a year or so later wrote his first draft of *Jacobowsky and the Colonel*.

THE SEA GULL

When *The Sea Gull* was first performed at the Alexandrinsky Theatre in St. Petersburg in 1896—in the then customary and still half-tolerated manner of ham-theatricality and pseudo-realism—Chekhov was denounced for having created characters who were "mere idiots." He was also castigated for ignoring "the laws of drama" by writing a story instead of a play. The one person in the audience who conspicuously entertained a different opinion was a prize-winning playwright, Nemirovitch-Dantchenko, soon to become co-founder, with Stanislavski, of the Moscow Art Theatre. He seriously considered turning down his "best-play-of-the-year" prize as a tribute to Chekhov who, in turn, was resolved to renounce the theatre entirely after the fiasco of *The Sea Gull*. Fortunately, that fiasco was erased within two years by the triumphant Moscow Art Theatre production, and the estimate of Chekhov's contribution to the stage came to be sharply revised with that production.

After having seen *The Sea Gull* with the Lunts in 1938, John Mason Brown wrote that "Although Treplev is thinking in terms of dramatic abstractions when he condemns realism . . ., there can be no denying Chekhov managed to turn realism itself into a new form of expression when he wrote this play." *The Sea Gull* was indeed a turning point not merely for Chekhov but for the course of realism, even if one could not have realized that this would be so several decades before the advent of such dramas as *Juno and the Paycock*, *Awake and Sing*, and *The Chalk Garden*, as well as several years before his own *Uncle Vanya*, *The Three Sisters* and *The Cherry Orchard*. Mr. Brown, in his review of March 29, 1938, went on to praise, with no claim to discovery of course but still with characteristic justness and wit, Chekhov's genius for letting characters seem to speak for themselves, for turning them into "geysers of autobiography" yet "transforming their prattle into significant revelation," and for "putting inconsequentials to a large purpose."

Other critics have pin-pointed Chekhov's ability to imagine characters to the details of dress and idiosyncrasies, at one extreme, and his lyricism at the other; his sympathy and elegiac mood, on the one hand, and his objective and vital humor, on the other. Many efforts have been made indeed, to reconcile the seeming contradictions of Chekhov's artistry. But since his American translator, Stark Young, who prepared the translation for the Lunt production, also happened to be one of our most distinguished theatrical critics, his views are the most reliable: The lyricism, Mr. Young observed, is intrinsic to the vitality of the characters instead of being superimposed on the characterization. The characters *excite* Chekhov, and "there is a curious kind of singing life" in the play. It arises from the characters' "passionate will and desire" — and, I would add, from a rebelliousness that vibrates variously in different characters. Their rebellion, however diffuse or vaguely directed, achieves, at times, a solo exaltation and, at other times, an orchestration of laughter and grief, wild confessionals and singing silence. There is also wit in *The Sea Gull*, and Mr. Young rightly calls it "an elusive but wholly robust wit proceeding from within a gentle nature and therefore not inhuman or cruel; pervading all; and giving a vibrant proportion to the whole."

From all this there finally arises a mixed type of drama that transcends academic categories and makes *The Sea Gull*, as well as the later Chekhov plays, especially modern in tone and in the quality of the approach to life. And Mr. Young, in his noteworthy preface, "Translating *The Sea Gull*," wisely turned to his colleague Joseph Wood Krutch's attempt to describe the special nature of this species of drama. Mr. Krutch, reviewing the Lunt production in *The Nation*, maintained that *The Sea Gull* is "not a mixture of comedy and tragedy" because "Neither the spirit of tragedy nor the spirit of comedy could include all the variety of incident and character which the play presents." Mr. Krutch maintained that the elements of the play "can only be included within some mood less downright than that of tragedy and comedy, and one of Chekhov's originalities was just his success in creating such a mood." Which does not remove the fact that in its totality, *The Sea Gull* is neither a mist nor a mood, but a clearly outlined and compelling play. And despite the overpublicized "*Chekhovskoe nastromnie*" or "Chekhovian melancholic" state of mind, it is the work of a buoyant intelligence and wholesome spirit, from which one could expect such a recommendation of self-respect and confidence as his telling us somewhere to rejoice that we are "not a drayhorse, a bacillus, a pig, an ass, a bear led by a gypsy, or a bug . . ." It is obvious that Chekhov was the observer and not the victim of the individual debilitation he recorded or of the stagnant provincial society he memorialized. Chekhov meant business in his work instead of being content to spin loose threads and leave his plays entangled in them. It was Chekhov, the master of moods, who wanted us to remember that "those writers we call eternal, or simply good, and who intoxicate us, have one common and very important characteristic: they get somewhere and they summon you there."

Anton Chekhov's distinguished place in the fields of drama and short fiction—whether he excelled more as a playwright than as a short-story writer is as unnecessary to decide as it would be difficult—invites a detailed essay rather than a brief note such as can be given here. The son of a former slave, and a tyrannical one at that, Chekhov (1860-1904) made his way through medical school with the help of his gift for narration. He first made himself a tidy living and a reputation as the author of light and brief fiction, the analogue to which is the series of little plays, nearly or actually "skits," that he called his "vaudevilles." (Later, he wrote deeply stirring stories and short novels that rank with the greatest in world literature, and it is equally as a writer of fiction and as a playwright that Chekhov possesses stature in our century.) He expressed fondness for his light pieces, all written between 1888 and 1894, and his partiality has been shared by the many amateur groups that have staged his *Proposal*, *The Anniversary*, *The Wedding*, and especially the earliest of these, *The Bear (Medved)* also known as *The Boor*. In these playlets he also evinced his humorous way of looking fondly askance at humanity, his talent for comedy which he was loath to see suppressed in his major dramas even by Stanislavsky and the Moscow Art Theatre which first gave him success on the stage and a commanding position in Western theatre. Hence his tendency to insist that his major works be considered comedies rather than gloom-drenched dramas, although his opinion should receive qualified rather than literal acceptance.

Coming after the depressing *Ivanov*, usually considered an artistic failure, and *The Wood Demon*, a discarded draft of *Uncle Vanya*, *The Sea Gull* (the Russian title *Chaika* simply means *The Gull)* was Chekhov's third full-length drama and his first fully realized one. *The Sea Gull* called for the kind of poetic and "inner" realistic staging that first began to appear after the founding of the Moscow Art Theatre in 1897. Indeed, even Stanislavksy, its co-founder and the master-director of Chekhovian theatre who staged *The Sea Gull*, admitted that at first he had not understood "the essence, the aroma, the beauty" of this piece for the writing of which there were (and are) neither rules nor extra-artistic justifications.

The Moscow Art Theatre made theatrical history with its production of the play, became uniquely the theatre of Chekhov at the turn of the century, and adopted a sea gull for its symbol and trademark. And Chekhov got started on a career that made him one of the half-dozen master-dramatists of modernity. It was a career abbreviated by the untimely death of the long consumptive writer in 1904. But *Uncle Vanya* in 1899, *The Three Sisters* in 1901, and *The Cherry Orchard* in 1904 were all noteworthy successors to *The Sea Gull*.

NOAH

André Obey (1892-   ), one of the most talented practitioners of non-boulevard theatre in France, has been a cause more than a playwright in the United States. American actors, playwrights, and even a critic or two have labored with no great success to advance his standing with the American public. They came closest to succeeding with his gentle but acute biblical play *Noah* which ran first on Broadway for forty-five performances in 1935, in Arthur Wilmurt's standard American version which I have reprinted here, and then a year later, for another forty-five performances, in an adaptation by Carlton Moss, with music by Jean Stor, when produced by the Negro Theatre unit of the Federal Theatre. Obey's play has continued to be serviceable ever since on the "off-Broadway" stage. Among this playwrights' other plays, *Le Viol de Lucrece*, 1931, based on Shakespeare's poem *The Rape of Lucrece*, had the benefit of an adaptation by Thornton Wilder, a musical score by Deems Taylor, and a production by Katharine Cornell, who inevitably played Lucrece. Even with such doughty support, this play, which had won acclaim a year before at the Vieux-Colombier in Paris, could achieve only a short run of thirty-one performances at the Belasco Theatre. It may be noted, too, that New York had had an opportunity to become familiar with the author's work ever since the fall of 1921 when the Theatre Guild presented *The Wife with the Smile*, originally *La Souriante Mme. Beudet*, a dazzling Parisian success of the spring of 1921 on which he had collaborated with Denys Amiel, a specialist in feminine and feminist drama.

Noah was adapted for the Broadway production by Arthur Wilmurt (1906-   ), who had studied playwriting at Yale University under George Pierce Baker, had taught at Yale for a while, and is now a professor of drama at the Carnegie Institute of Technology. He had his first play, *The Guest Room*, produced in New York in 1931 after a production at the Yale University Theatre staged by the distinguished university director Alexander Dean. Mr. Wilmurt made his translation of *Noah* in the same year for an avant-garde group at the Princess Theatre. The group disbanded, but the play was later picked up by one of its members, Jerome Mayer, who prevailed upon Pierre Fresnay, playing in Noel Coward's *Conversation Piece* in 1934, to fill the part of Noah which that great actor had previously played in Paris. The same version was staged in London at the New Theatre by Copeau's nephew Michel Saint-Denis with John Gielgud in the role of Noah and Alec Guinness in the part of "The Wolf."

Mr. Wilmurt's comments in June, 1956, to me deserve to be placed on record: "On the basis of the critical reaction here, Obey made quite extensive revisions of the second, third, and fourth Scenes. I translated these revisions and John Gielgud played that version in London through the summer of 1935. It still seems popular all over the Commonwealth: within the past two years I've heard of, among other productions, a radio broadcast from Singapore and a TV broadcast in Australia. The 'American version' seems more popular in colleges than anywhere. The Kraft Theatre did it on TV in 1950." Mr. Wilmurt and the producers of the "American version" of this flagrantly uncommercial philosophical folk-piece can take reminiscent pleasure in their 1934 press notices. Especially encouraging were the *New York World-Telegram* plea, "Please see *Noah* if not for Heaven's sake, for the sake of your theatre-going soul" and the assurance extended by the *New York American* that "Some of this *Noah* has the taste of dew from Heaven and some of it the tang of Attic salt."

Compliments of this character were particularly welcome for a work that was not destined — or, for that matter, not intended — for success on the Great White Way or on the boulevards of Paris. Obey had written the piece between 1929 and 1930 for a company, *La Compagnie des Quinze*, which he had first seen performing in Lyons — a company of young actors who had been working together for nine years, trying to realize Copeau's ideals of a retheatricalized art. They followed Copeau in turning his back, as Saint-Denis put it in an Introduction to the British edition of *Noah*, "on the theatre of the rationalists, of the psychologists who had made the stage into either a platform for discussing political, social and even medical problems, or into a laboratory for the study of special cases."

Obey had views on the drama that accorded with the animating principle of the *Compagnie des Quinze*. "My theory," he wrote, "is that a play is a *thing* of the theatre so strictly—and yet, at the same time, so freely—invented for the stage, composed and developed on the stage, subjected to the stage to such an extent that the life, the reality and the rhythm of the drama are there before the words which express it." The *Compagnie des Quinze* could help the author to realize these principles of play-writing on the stage. "We were actors," says Saint-Denis, "capable of showing life rather than explaining it, relying more on sound and physical movement than on talking, used to singing and dancing, able to build up from choral work to the invention of simple, clearly defined characters." Neither New York nor London was able to provide such an acting company for *Noah*, whereas it was precisely what Obey required for the complete realization of a play that is fable and parable in one, that represents typical humanity with broad and simple strokes of the brush, and that employs two choruses — a group of animals and a group of children expected to give, through the art of the mime, form to the meaning and rhythm to the movement of the action. If, as Francis Fergusson declares, Copeau "was interested in the histrionic as a means of revivifying play-writing," he succeeded in this one instance, whatever the limitations of the play, through the mediacy of the young company for which *Noah* was written.

VOLPONE

Ben Jonson's *Volpone*, one of the major masterpieces of Elizabethan comedy, should not need any introduction to English readers. And perhaps Stefan Zweig's free version of Jonson's comedy of parasites should not need any either, since this Viennese author was not primarily a playwright. He was chiefly a novelist, biographer, and essayist of distinction, renowned especially for such non-fiction works as *Three Masters* (Balzac, Dickens, and Dostoevski), *Joseph Fouché*, and *Mental Healers*. But before he died in 1942, in a suicide pact in Brazil, a refugee from his beloved Vienna where he had been born to Jewish parents in 1881, Zweig had also written six or seven plays. And two of these won considerable attention.

The earlier was the biblical poetic drama *Jeremiah*, written as a protest against the World War in 1917 and first produced in Zurich, where Zweig had been working for peace in close collaboration with other European intellectuals. Zweig presented his hero Jeremiah as the prototype of all who have struggled tragically against the folly and evil of the war-makers. (The play was subsequently produced by the Theatre Guild on the eve of a second World War, in 1938, in a version made for the Guild by Worthington Miner and the present writer which got greatly mangled during the last desperate rehearsals.) The second play, in 1926, was Zweig's adaptation of the Ben Jonson comedy, a work which was followed in 1933 by the adaptation of another Jonson comedy, *Epicene, or The Silent Woman* which Zweig prepared as a libretto for an opera by Richard Strauss under the German title of *Die schweigsame Frau*.

If the reader will compare Zweig's *Volpone* with the original English play, he will be able to draw all pertinent deductions for himself. There is no reason to draw them for him. There may also be no great impulse to do anything at all on the part of the general reader. He may well be content to simply enjoy the intrigue and satire, the rich variations on "the motive of chicane" Harry Levin mentions in his Random House edition of Jonson's *Selected Works*. These are to be found in both Zweig's comedy and the original play.

THE LATE CHRISTOPHER BEAN

René Fauchois was an old hand at manufacturing Parisian entertainments when he composed *Prenez garde à la peinture*, a play inspired by the last years of Vincent van Gogh that somehow caught the fancy of the English-speaking stage, so that Emlyn Williams adapted it for England and Sidney Howard based the New England comedy *The Late Christopher Bean* on it. Born in 1882, Fauchois had first won some repute as the author of verse plays, and one of these, *Beethoven*, first staged at the Odéon in 1909, had been presented in New York in 1910. He turned to the writing of comedies after the failure in 1911 of another verse drama *Rivoli*, a play that explained Napoleon's military prowess as compensation for Josephine's betrayal of him with a handsome hussar. One of the comedies, *Le Singe qui parle*, produced in Paris in 1924, was presented the next year in New York for a moderate run under the title of *The Monkey Talks*. The production featured Philip Merivale in the role of an aristocrat who, after falling in love with an equestrienne, loses his social position and joins a circus with a talking-monkey act. Fauchois, like his junior colleague Jacques Deval (1893—   ), whose *Tovarich* was successfully adapted by Robert Sherwood in 1936, became one of those busy contrivers of facile French comedy who generally won more success at home and abroad than more incisive playwrights such as Salacrou, Savoir, and Crommelynck.

Fauchois, like Deval, owed his longest run in New York and an ample reception in the rest of the country to an adapter. Sidney Howard (1891-1939), who transplanted Fauchois' action and turned *The Late Christopher Bean* into an authentic American comedy with some New England grit in the payload of sentiment, was an old hand at adapting plays. He had also won a respectable success as a playwright in his own right with such work as the Pulitzer Prize comedy *They Knew What They Wanted* in 1924 and *Ned McCobb's Daughter* in 1926. The last-mentioned piece may have actually set the tone for *The Late Christopher Bean*, which Gilbert Miller produced in 1932. Both plays have their main action in New England and provide contrasts between small town and big city life. In both, the heroine is a sympathetic countrywoman whose simplicity is more than a match for the guile of city slickers. In both pieces, besides, there is a bracing air of wintry comedy. As refurbished by Sidney Howard, who had been servicing European drama satisfactorily ever since his adaptations of Charles Vildrac's sensitive plays *S.S. Tenacity* and *Michel Auclair* between 1922 and 1925, Fauchois' comedy contained a keen sense of character, as well as some pardonable sentiment. "Pungency under the surface and surprise around the edges" was the friendly verdict of the *New York Sun*, and there was mainly agreement with this opinion in the nation's press.

THE PLAY'S THE THING

In 1925, Ferenc Molnar, the wit and genial master-conversationalist of Budapest café society, as well as a busy playwright for all Europe, summed up his career with a brevity rare among autobiographers:

"1878, I was born in Budapest. [He was the son of a well-known Jewish physician.]
"1896, I became a law student at Geneva.
"1896, I became a journalist in Budapest. [He contributed a series of weekly articles to a newspaper.]
"1897, I wrote a short story.
"1900, I wrote a novel. [It was the celebrated story of juvenile gang warfare, *The Paul Street Boys*.]
"1902, I became a playwright at home. [He wrote his first play, and a successful one too, *The Lawyer*, at the request of the Royal National Theatre.]
"1914, I became a war correspondent.
"1916, I became a playwright once more.
"1918, my hair turned snow white.
"1925, I should like to be a law student in Geneva once more."
Instead, he proceeded to get *The Play's the Thing* produced in Budapest and later in New York, a city already well disposed toward him, which became his second home in 1940 when Nazism came to his native country.

He had been an expert contriver of plays ever since the writing of *The Devil* in 1907, and he convinced two continents that this facility was beyond question when in 1910 he contrived *The Guardsman*, with which the Theatre Guild and the gay Lunts romped to success in 1924. He had charmed audiences with the romantic sentiment and corrective, if gentle, realism of *The Swan* in 1920. In 1924 he had also scored a success with the Cinderella-fantasy of a romantic Budapest servant *The Glass Slipper*, which the Guild presented in the fall of 1925. And he had exhibited deeper insights with an even greater flair for theatricality when he wrote *Liliom* (in a famous café) as early as 1909, although it became an international success only after 1921 when the then still struggling Theatre Guild in its third season produced the play—to be exact, on April 20, 1921. The Budapest première had been more or less of a fiasco, and in later years his friendly enemies or hostile friends in Budapest liked to say that Molnar had vowed after the première never to write another play like *Liliom* and that this was one promise Molnar had kept . . .

The Play's the Thing—the original title was *The Play in the Castle*—was then the ripe result of a great familiarity with the devices of play-craft, a familiarity as evident to the American playgoer as to the European since New York produced seventeen of his plays after the great success of *The Devil* there in 1908. *The Play's the Thing*, a play about the theatre as gay and irreverent and ingenious as only Molnar could make it, enjoyed the services of a fellow-wit and sophisticate, P. G. Wodehouse, who adapted the original play. And not inappropriately this version was tried out in Great Neck, Long Island, not yet then the common man's preserves that it has been since the great ex-urbanite migrations after World War II. A run of 244 performances on Broadway alone after the première on November 3, 1926, attested the popularity of this theatrical work, which recalls the gayety of play-making for its own rather than for conscience's sake that Budapest playwrights tried to preserve as long as it was possible to do so, if not indeed longer.

There came a time after 1930 when even Molnar found it difficult to sustain the tradition of theatrical insouciance with fresh success, though he managed to win one more triumph with a new play, *The Good Fairy*, in 1931 and 1932. But he remained a great gentleman of the world and wit to the end of his days (he died in his seventy-fourth year on April 1, 1952), and the fact that his buoyancy of invention could still be appreciated after a second World War was attested to in the United States by a success-ful revival of *The Play's the Thing* which opened in New York on April 28, 1948, with jaunty performances by Louis Calhern, Ernest Cossart, Arthur Margetson, and Faye Emerson. All had evidently learned a lesson from the author whose rule for successful theatre, he said, was "you must do some swindling." Wrote Joseph Wood Krutch in *The Nation* of May 15, 1948: "Its most ardent admirers never claimed for it importance of any possible sort, but it is just as fresh and just as funny as it was twenty-two years ago." And Mr. Krutch rightly gave it special praise because "it is a satire on itself" and because "the author—who has shown in other works that he can be senti-mental enough on occasion—keeps his tongue firmly planted in his cheek." The plain truth is that *The Play's the Thing* is a miracle of gay and worldly-wise virtuosity and theatrical dexterity.

AS YOU DESIRE ME

Luigi Pirandello, who was born in 1867, introduced a "Pirandellian" situation as early as 1904 in a novel, *The Late Mattia Pascal*, and he gave full rein to his quizzical view of reality in a play as early as 1915 in *Cap and Bells*, if not indeed even earlier. *As You Desire Me*, published in Milan in 1930, is one of the later plays of Pirandello, and it is one of the most personalized treatments of his characteristic subject—the nature of identity. The play bears directly upon this theme with a comparatively simple story, although one that starts on an assumption that may be regarded as far-fetched or contrived. Actually Pirandello's plot was very similar to a case of mistaken identity that had been publicized in Italian newspapers a year before. The contrast between appearance and reality, between the "mask" and the "face," moreover had been insisted upon in a variety of ways in Pirandello's earlier pieces. The misunder-standings in *As You Desire Me* were plainly the result of philosophical and literary intentions rather than of addiction to plot-contrivance. These intentions had already occasioned much rueful legerdemain on his part in such plays as *Cosi e (se vi pare)* or *Right You Are—If You Think You Are*, *Six Characters in Search of An Author*, and the power-ful melodrama *Henry IV*, ruined by Broadway under the title of *The Living Mask*.

As he multiplied his plays and as his reputation grew, Pirandello's themes became almost monotonously familiar without the plays really being understood in the United States, although many writers, even a few Americans, appear to have leaned heavily on him in some of their work. Personality is something we self-deceivingly invent for ourselves, or that others invent for us. "Facts" about human reality are not actually facts at all, but now they look one way and now another. "Truth is the representation each of us makes of it," declares a character in *Right You Are*. What seems to be reality may be pretense, and what seems pretense may be reality — relative reality, of course, for absolute reality is beyond our penetration, if indeed it exists at all. And as Pirandello once declared directly, "each of us believes himself to be one, but that is a false assumption: each of us is so many, so many, as many as are all the potentialities of being that are in us . . ."

Pirandello could sometimes make one's head whirl with these intellectual capers while he cut them into comic and emotional patterns of dramatic complication. In *As You Desire Me*, however, he anchored speculation in a story elementary as well as subtle, pathetic as well as reflective. In addition, he irradiated this drama with passionate idealism through the character of his heroine, significantly called the "Unknown," who, after a sordid life, would like to know herself, as well as be known by others, in the soul of an ideal, vanished woman. The inevitable doom of such an ambition in a world of sullying materialism, accommodation, and doubt could only intensify the play, justifying the Pirandello scholar Domenico Vittorini's reference to it as "a play of absolute exasperated, irrational idealism, indicting modern life with its ambiguity, its lust, its commercialized sensuality . . ." Vittorini (to whose book *The Drama of Luigi Pirandello*, 1935, Pirandello himself wrote a Foreword) declared that "in the avowed intention of the author," the play is "the story of the soul that has tried to live on this earth and could not"—and there is much in the piece to justify so pessimistic a conclusion.

By the same token, it is less certain that the work attains "the grandeur of tragedy" Professor Vittorini claimed for it. Nor was it necessary to press that claim, since the play, which is not altogether free from sentimental theatricality (while *Six Characters* and *Henry IV* are completely free), had proved quite satisfactory on less exalted levels. *As You Desire Me* is a provocative enough drama of the isolation of individuals from each other and the division of their souls, which they endeavor to heal with the illusions they cherish in a world of hypocrisies and pettiness. As a moving play about one person's search for a valid life in the midst of corruption, *As You Desire Me*—with or probably without all the Pirandellian ingredients that make even this "simple" piece anything but simple—won a larger audience than the author's other works. It had 142 performances in New York alone, and it acquired a very much larger public when it was translated, how faithfully I do not know, into a motion picture for Greta Garbo.

It may also be of interest to the reader to know that the main role, played on Broadway by Judith Anderson, was originally performed in Italy by the great Pirandellian actress Marta Abba who has made the translation of *Come tu mi vuoi* used in this book. The emotional conviction of *As You Desire Me* and its freedom from a cold abstractness often charged against the author may be credited in part to Miss Abba. Pirandello undoubtedly had her in mind for the part when he created the mystifying but intensely human heroine around whom the grotesque action revolves.

THE GOOD HOPE

Herman Heijermans (1864-1924) was the leader of a new, realistic and socially engaged theatre in the Netherlands at a time when the entire European theatre was undergoing modernization. As a journalist, novelist, short-story writer (a remarkably prolific one), and dramatist, this descendant of old Dutch Jewry played a major role in the cultural renaissance of his country between 1880 and 1920. The revival of Dutch literature gained momentum in the eighteen-eighties, so that the movement Heijermans headed with the poet Albert Verwey and the novelist Frederik van Eeden came to be known as the Movement of Eighty. Heijermans brought its fruits to the theatre of Germany, England, and America as well as to the Dutch stage.

Heijermans won his first success on the stage under a Russian pseudonym with the one-act play *Ahasuerus* in 1893. He strengthed his position in the theatre with such plays as *The Ghetto* (1898), a vivid picture of Jewish life but also a liberal's criticism of fanatical orthodoxy, and *The Seventh Commandment* (1899), an exposé of middle-class narrowness in general. These and other products of critical realism such as *The Maid* and *Eva Bonheur*, studies in souls warped by the lives they have led, made their author the outstanding Dutch playwright.

The dramatic piece with which Heijermans won an international reputation is *Op Hoop van Zegen*, known in English as *The Good Hope*, which appeared in 1901 and was soon translated into many European languages. Doubtless its social content, the plight of underprivileged fishing crews sent out in unseaworthy vessels, promoted the success of the play in the early years of our century. *The Good Hope* indeed was credited with having inspired long-needed reforms in Holland's fishery trade in 1909, and the men of the Dutch merchant marine had occasion to express their gratitude when they raised a fund for the support of Heijermans' widow and two children when he died on December 3, 1924, in a less than affluent state after the bankruptcy of a theatrical company he had founded in Holland. But it is Heijermans' vivid and compasionate artistry that gave his play its durability.

Counting on its durability as art, Eva Le Gallienne staged the play at her Civic Repertory Theatre in the fall of 1927, and *The Good Hope* was indeed one of the few social dramas that made a strong impression before "social significance" became a slogan in our theatre after the Wall Street stockmarket crash. Brooks Atkinson, in a foreword to the English translation, expressed the prevailing appreciative view when he wrote: "In the final analysis the ideals of art and human life are one; when they blend perfectly, may we not regard their expression in a play as noble, majestic — as luminously true?" And he rightly praised its excellent characterization and "its deep tonal values of a Dutch painting."

Ellen Terry brought *The Good Hope* to America in 1906 along with *Captain Brassbound's Conversion* in repertory, and we may speculate as to what Fabian influence had strengthened Heijermans' spell over that very middle-class actress whom Shaw adored and endeavored to instruct. But she must have been affected, too, by the intense life in this play. Certainly Max Beerbohm was not the man to be taken with a play simply because its author had social sympathies. Yet he declared as early as 1903 that it was a pity that other dramatists could not "through their coldly observant eyes, see life half so clearly and steadily as it is seen through the somewhat flashing eyes of Heijermans."[*]

Joseph Wood Krutch, who would not have allowed social sentiment to stand in the way of his critical judgment, was also sufficiently stirred to say in his review of the 1927 Le Gallienne production that *The Good Hope* "will not take its place quietly upon the shelf." (If it nevertheless did soon after, the reason was probably that the conflicts that began to shake the United States and Europe within a few years favored more turbulent treatments of capital and labor.) As A. J. Barnow pointed out in a 1925 issue of *Theatre Arts Monthly*, "The playgoer of today sees in the shipowner not the embodiment of a wicked system, but a wicked man as there are wicked men among his victims. And it is this triumph of the author's creation of a living character over the symbol that he intended his creature to be which lifts this play from the mass of timely propaganda into the realms of timeless art."

THE WORLD WE LIVE IN

Karel Capek[**] (1890-1938) and his artist-brother Josef (1887-1945) were the most distinguished playwrights of the Czechoslovakian republic, which had been established by the Versailles Peace Treaty under the presidency of Thomas Masaryk, their friend. But the distinction of being the new nation's leading writers would not have in itself

---

[*] See Seymour Flaxman's *Herman Heijermans and His Dramas*, published in The Hague in 1954.
[**] Capek should be pronounced as through the C were Ch.

impressed other countries, especially ours. The Capek brothers won an international reputation in consequence of the international character of their concern with broad issues such as the implications of longevity in *The Makropoulos Secret* and of the growing mechanization of the Western World in *R.U.R.* The last-mentioned work, published in 1921, was the *chef d'oeuvre* of Karel Capek and in the same year he collaborated with his brother on *Ze zivota hmyzu, The Insect Comedy* or *The Life of the Insects*, in which the whole life of man was reviewed in allegorical scenes. Here, too, the state of the modern world—a world to which the authors imputed much folly and rapacity—was the frame of reference. And here, as in *R.U.R.*, the dim outlook was transcended by a last-minute affirmativeness.

Unlike *R.U.R.*, this piece, which was first known in New York under the title of the Broadway adaptation *The World We Live In*, is not a compact drama. It may be described as a philosophical revue in the expressionist manner much in vogue in Central Europe immediately after World War I. It was a decidedly more expressionist and symbolic work than *R.U.R.* and impressed us in the early twenties as the more venturesome presentation. It required a European background or a distinctly fastidious taste in a critic to protest that the symbolism was too transparent. The authors indeed put much trust in the parallels to the human situation suggested to them by the French entomo- logist Fabre's *La Vie des Insectes* and *Souvenirs Entomologiques*. They dutifully explained the parallel with unintentionally comic results in a preface written in less than im- peccable English. As given in the Samuel French acting edition, their comment over- explains a work that surely needs no explication.

Owen Davis, a veteran of our "pre-modern" stage with many a facile melodrama, signalized his reformation by doing a stint of adaptation on "the insect comedy" for the producer of the Capek fantasy, William Brady, who was duly complimented for his "courage in producing a play so difficult and unusual" by none other than David Belasco. For a time it seemed that all the bastions of our theatrical conservatism were falling. The reviewer for the *New York Sun* declared that the production had given him the "greatest thrill we ever had" and a *New York Times* critic declared, "No theatre- goer who wants to see the bold, brave things which the young folks *(sic)* are up to can afford to miss this play," while the *New York Telegram* solemnly told its readers that "no household should be content until its members have seen how their daily life is patterned after insects." There was indeed more buzzing about this production than the most optimistic progressives could have anticipated when they first gazed at theatrical horizons in Washington Square Park half a dozen years before.

THE DYBBUK

The Dybbuk is the play with which it is most usual to identify Jewish drama in the English-speaking theatre, as well as in the European theatres. One might question the justification of this all-too-exclusive identification. Drama in the Yiddish and Hebrew languages has been extensive since 1900 and has engaged writers of considerable distinction such as David Pinski, Sholem Asch, Isaac Loeb Peretz, the great humorist Sholom Aleichem, Peretz Hirschbein, and H. Leivick, whose folk-drama *The Golem* is known on two continents. However, only Pinski's moralistic drama of greed *The Treasure*, first produced in German by Max Reinhardt in 1910 and later in English by the Theatre Guild, rivals *The Dybbuk*—and this without actually possessing half the merit of *The Dybbuk*. Yet its author S. Ansky—we derive the name from Sh. An-sky, the pen-name of Solomon Z. Rapaport (1863-1920)—would have been little known but for this play. It was the outgrowth of his main occupation, for he was primarily a student of Russian and Jewish folklore rather than a dramatist.

He wrote the play in 1914 and succeeded in interesting Stanislavsky. The latter considered it for production by the Moscow Art Theatre and suggested the introduction of a new character, the mystic Messenger, into the work. However, the play was not staged until December 9, 1920 when the Vilna Troupe, a Jewish acting company founded in Vilna, Poland, during World War I, produced it as a memorial to the author, who had died a month before. An instant sensation, this play, which combined realism of environment and fantasy of plot, came to be regarded not merely as a folk-drama, but as universal love-tragedy.

The folk-character of this work has been ably explicated by Mr. Samuel J. Citron in *A History of Modern Drama*, edited by Barrett H. Clark and George Freedley: "Even the death of Honon [Channon in our text] cannot extinguish that love, and his spirit enters the body of Leah as a 'dybbuk,' an additional soul . . . The Great Anathema pronounced upon the dybbuk-Honon finally forces him to leave the maiden. But even anathemas cannot overcome the preordained love of the pair. Leah dies and her soul is fused with the soul of Honon in eternal love."

The romanticism of the work is apparent. The dark splendor of this macabre play attracted many imaginative directors, such as the talented Stanislavsky disciple Eugene Vakhtangov whose ideal of combining reality of emotion with theatrical stylization was realized in the text of *The Dybbuk*. In addition to all its other values, the play had the value of exemplifying a rewarding synthesis of realistic and theatrical art. It was a synthesis especially possible in the context of myth and tradition.

FROM MORN TO MIDNIGHT

Georg Kaiser was one of the most prominent as well as controversial figures of the European theatre in the decade between 1914 and 1924. He was the most consequential member of the so-called expressionist movement which had its center in Germany, Austria, and Czechoslovakia. Born in 1878 to a well-to-do merchant in Magdeburg, Germany, he first turned to a business career which carried him as far as Buenos Aires. He returned to Germany and became a writer only after he had found the climate uncongenial, but he was still drawn to business enterprise in a curious fashion. His most dramatic experience indeed stemmed from this inclination when he was tried for embezzlement of funds. His plea—an unsuccessful one, I understand—was, nevertheless, that of a writer rather than of a businessman, since he declared that he was too exceptional a person to be expected to abide by the civil code. (Ironically, however, it was as a professional writer, and not as a businessman that he finally found a respectable place in society.) And, when he defended himself in court, he could have even used Oscar Wilde's claim that nature imitates art. Years before his differences with the law, Kaiser had actually made a case of embezzlement the springboard of one of his best-known plays, *From Morn to Midnight*, which was written in 1916.

Kaiser started to write as early as 1905, but his first published play, a satirical version of the story of Judith under the title of *The Jewish Widow (Die jüdische Witwe)*, appeared in 1911. Shortly thereafter he became a key figure of the German theatrical world; so much so, indeed, that twenty-six of his plays were staged in Central Europe between 1914 and 1924. Subsequently, his importance waned with that of expressionism, but he continued to turn out plays long after 1924. As late as 1933, he wrote a fable about wealth and poverty called *Silbersee (Silver Lake)*, worth noting if only because Kurt Weill wrote the music for it; earlier, Kaiser had furnished two librettos for Weill, in 1924 and 1926 respectively, *Der Protagonist* and *Der Zar lässt sich photographieren*. Kaiser was an irrepressible worker and continued to write in Switzerland, in exile from Nazi Germany, throughout the war years, right up to his death in 1945. One of his latter-day works was a novel *Villa Aurea* which was translated into English as *A Villa in Sicily*. He also continued to write plays. There must have been more than a few of these, since the present writer recalls receiving several from Kaiser. One, *Klawitter*, was an ironic account of subterfuges and deceptions in Nazi

Germany; another, *The Soldier Tanaka*, was a severe indictment of the Japanese military machine and concerned the plight of a common soldier.

Kaiser's most impressive work came in the heyday of expressionism during the Central European crisis from 1914 to about 1924. *The Burghers of Calais*, with its idealistic theme of self-sacrifice, won considerable respect in 1917. Particularly impressive was Kaiser's trilogy about the tensions and fears of the Machine Age which also exercised the imagination of other expressionists such as Karel Capek, in *R.U.R.*, and Ernst Toller, in *Die Maschinenstürmer* or *The Machine Wreckers*. The trilogy consisted of *The Coral* (1917), *Gas I* (1918), and *Gas II* (1920). The high point of the fable comes in *Gas I* with the explosion of an idealistic capitalist's super-plant which manufactures a new gas for servicing technical progress, a disaster that is followed in *Gas II* with pictures of mass-destruction and chaos. Kaiser himself thought he was writing plays of ideas or *Denkspiele* (literally, thought-plays), and he declared, in fact, that "to write a drama is to follow a thought to its conclusion." But the "ideas" were not incorporated in psychologically revealed, truly dimensioned characters, so that Kaiser's work, like that of his expressionist colleagues, was often as barren as it was bizarre. A "thought-play" by Kaiser was certainly abstract by comparison with character-rooted "plays of ideas" written by Ibsen and Shaw.

Kaiser's epic trilogy did not receive any particular attention from us. *Gas I* had its première in English on November 24, 1923 at Birmingham, England, when the Birmingham Repertory Theatre Company presented the work with Cedric Hardwicke playing the idealistic capitalist who tries to forestall disaster by starting a back-to-the-land movement among his workers. Another striking production of *Gas* was given in Amsterdam in 1928. Our own theatrical world was more favorably inclined toward Kaiser's earlier written *From Morn to Midnight*, a drama of disillusionment consequent to a little man's search for happiness in a world conspicuously hollow and corrupt. It proved to be one of the early Theatre Guild's most experimental offerings, received high praise, and had, after four special performances, a run of fifty-two performances, first at the Garrick and then at the larger Frazee Theatre.

Some of the credit for the Guild's text, reprinted here, must go to the English adapter, Ashley Dukes, a contributing critic to *Theatre Arts* magazine in the twenties and a leader of a little art theatre movement in London, as well as the author of an imaginative drama, *The Man With a Load of Mischief*. Considerable credit for the impression made by the work also belonged to the imaginative settings by the Guild's distinguished scene designer, Lee Simonson, who picked the seven swift scenes of the play out of a surrounding and haunting darkness. And the production also owed much to the stage direction by Frank Reicher, a son of the famous German actor who directed the Jewish Art Theatre and had staged the first production of Hauptmann's *The Weavers* in English. What was, perhaps, most stirring in the production, wrote Walter Prichard Eaton in 1929 in *The Theatre Guild: The First Ten Years*, "was the driving pace at which Frank Reicher sent it along, like scenes shaping, dissolving, in a tortured mind."

Von Morgens bis Mitternachts or *From Morn to Midnight*, which had its première in Berlin in 1919 under Max Reinhardt's direction at the Deutsches Theater, was first produced in New York by the Theatre Guild on May 21, 1922, at the end of the season that brought playgoers O'Neill's expressionist drama *The Hairy Ape*. The play has been favored by experimental groups ever since for its imaginative technique, although it could also arouse violent dislike, as when in reviewing an off-Broadway production Brooks Atkinson denounced the play in *The New York Times* in December 1948 as "gibberish out of a period of romantic despair that fortunately is now finished." One may well wonder whether the play is gibberish and whether the period of romantic or any other kind of despair is actually finished, although the faults of Kaiser's dramatic nightmare are transparent enough in the text and can be exaggerated in inexpert stage productions. The style, which alternates between passionate speeches

and staccato phrases like telegrams, and the use of depersonalized, mechanical characters are intended to convey the disorder of contemporary society and the dis-
orientation of the individual. We may balance against the detractions the play invites,
the views of another distinguished man, the adapter, who maintained in his introduction to the published play that a need was felt for "an art which consists in a series
of graphic gestures, like a vigorous clenching of the smooth palm of actuality." Ashley
Dukes, who may have overlooked Strindberg's late plays and minimized their influence, held that Kaiser had brought "a new method" into the theatre. "To the most
unfriendly gaze," he added, "Georg Kaiser will appear to be a link between the three-
dimensional stage and the screen, and a portent therefore not to be despised. But
others who look deeper will read in the movement of his nameless hurrying throng of
characters the poet's reflection of a universal gesture, and in their faces his image
of a common unrest."

THE PASSION FLOWER

The Passion Flower was first produced in Spanish under the title of *La Malquerida*
in Madrid in 1913. The role of Raimunda was filled by the celebrated Maria Guerrero,
who also played this part in a Spanish production given in New York in May 1926.

Jacinto Benavente y Martínez was born in Madrid on August 12, 1866, the son of a
famous pediatrician. He turned to acting instead of following the legal profession he
was expected to pursue. He became a prolific writer after 1892 and was soon recognized as a master of the craft of playwriting. The first decade of the twentieth-
century theatre in Spain used to be called "the Benavente period" because he was its
dominant figure, and he was without doubt the leading Spanish playwright since
Calderón of the seventeenth century. Until the poet Federico García Lorca turned
to playwriting after 1930, Benavente was also modern Spain's most talented dramatist.
Like the playwrights of the Spanish classic age, he wrote a vast number of pieces of all
kinds (including bread-and-butter melodramas and vaudevilles), and he also translated
and adapted foreign plays. An active man of the theatre, he became the director the
Spanish National Theatre, the *Teatro Español*, in 1920 and also developed an "Art
Theatre" and a children's theatre. He won the Nobel Prize for literature in 1923.

In one respect, Benavente reflected his upbringing in the home of a distinguished
physician. He responded with sympathy to the scientific and liberal spirit that
had gained ascendancy in European countries more industrialized than his own. He
brought the modernity of Ibsen and Shaw into the Spanish theatre with many of
his social dramas, so that he came to be called the "Bernard Shaw of Spain." He
was also interested in the new psychology of the century, Freudianism; and a product
of that interest, in combination with vivid observation of the Spanish countryside, was
La Malquerida or *The Passion Flower*. It is to be noted, however, that this play, like his
favorite drama of jealousy *Señora Ama* (1908), was a less characteristic product of his
career than many other pieces, such as *The Field of Ermine* (1916), a social drama based
on the conflict between aristocratic family-pride and human love, and *The Bonds of
Interest* (1907), an amalgam of satire and tenderness notably theatrical. (It was a
comedy highly attractive to advanced theatre groups even as late as 1919, when the
Theatre Guild made this play its first presentation.) *The Passion Flower*, however, was
the most powerful example of that fusion of Spanish genre painting with the modern
naturalistic and psychological spirit that was necessary before the twentieth-century
Spanish theatre could achieve more than sentimental appeal abroad or more than local
importance.

REDEMPTION

Lev or Leo Tolstoy (1828-1910) is too well known a figure to be introduced here. He was first and foremost a novelist. Nevertheless, he also proved himself a powerful writer for the theatre, for which he wrote, in addition to some short pieces such as the little pro-temperance comedy *The First Distiller* (1887), the overpowering peasant tragedy *The Power of Darkness* (1889). This late product of his genius was followed by the incisive comedy *The Fruits of Enlightenment* (1891), a picture of the deterioration of Russia's landed gentry that anticipated Chekhov's treatment of the same theme in *The Cherry Orchard* by more than a decade. For a long period, Tolstoy completed no other play. In 1892, he even declared that he would have written more plays "with great pleasure," that he felt "a special need to express myself in that way; but I felt the Censor would not pass my plays . . ." But in 1900 he wrote *Zhivoi trup* or *The Living Corpse*, which Arthur Hopkins produced under the title of *Redemption*. This work has also been translated as *The Live Corpse* and *The Man Who Was Dead*. It was his last play except for the remarkable antobiographical drama of idealism and its all-too human contradictions, *The Light That Shines in Darkness*, of which the last act exists only in outline.

In writing *Redemption* Tolstoy was motivated by the fact that the laws of Czarist Russia prohibited divorce. The play was based on a real case supplied to Tolstoy by a friend, a judge and lecturer on criminal law at Moscow University. The subject of the case had actually been convicted and imprisoned. He had returned to Moscow and given up drinking, the cause of his marital misfortunes, when he learned that the great author was writing about him. He visited Tolstoy, who learned facts about him that the law-case did not contain. But when Tolstoy reworked the first draft of the play on the basis of his acquaintance with the man, he nevertheless invented for *Redemption* a new tragic ending. Tolstoy was first concerned with the legal problem, but soon became concerned, as usual, with an individual human being. In the final draft, the characterization and the action of the play are placed on a higher level of interest, are permeated with Tolstoyan compassion, and culminate in a demonstration of the Christian gospel of self-sacrifice for the sake of others. Partly in consequence of John Barrymore's superb playing of Fedya, the Broadway production of the play duplicated the success it had had in the theatres of Western Europe, which had earlier used Tolstoy's *The Power of Darkness* as an opening barrage in the then progressive struggle for naturalism.

JEAN GIRAUDOUX's

Tiger at the Gates

(La Guerre de Troie N'Aura Pas Lieu)

In the translation by CHRISTOPHER FRY

The Robert L. Joseph production first presented by The Playwrights' Company, in association with Henry M. Margolis, on October 3, 1955, at the Plymouth Theatre, New York, with the following cast*:

ANDROMACHE .... Barbara Jefford	POLYXENE .... Ellen Christopher
CASSANDRA .... Leueen MacGrath	HELEN .... Diane Cilento
LAUNDRESS .... Judith Braun	MESSENGER .... Ernest Graves
HECTOR .... Michael Redgrave	TROILUS......................... Peter Kerr
PARIS .... Leo Ciceri	ABNEOS......................Howard Caine
FIRST OLD MAN .... Howard Caine	BUSIRIS..................... Wyndham Goldie
SECOND OLD MAN .... Jack Bittner	AJAX..........................Felix Munso
PRIAM..................... Morris Carnovsky	ULYSSES .... Walter Fitzgerald
DEMOKOS....................... John Laurie	A TOPMAN .... Nehemiah Persoff
HECUBA .... Catherine Lacey	OLPIDES .... Jack Bittner
MATHEMATICIAN................. Milton Selzer	SENATOR .... Tom McDermott
LADY IN WAITING .... Jacqueline Brookes	SAILOR........................ Louis Criss

* Characters omitted in this production—PEACE, IRIS

Directed by Harold Clurman
Settings and costumes designed by Loudon Sainthill
(New York production supervising designer: Paul Morrison)
Incidental music by Lennox Berkeley
Stage Manager: Louis Criss

The action takes place in and around the Palace of Troy
just prior to the outbreak of the Trojan War.

ACT ONE

ANDROMACHE. There's not going to be a Trojan War, Cassandra!

CASSANDRA. I shall take that bet, Andromache.

ANDROMACHE. The Greeks are quite right to protest. We are going to receive their ambassador very civilly. We shall wrap up his little Helen and give her back to him.

CASSANDRA. We shall receive him atrociously. We shall refuse to give Helen back. And there *will* be a Trojan War.

ANDROMACHE. Yes, if Hector were not here. But he is here, Cassandra, he is home again. You can hear the trumpets. At this moment he is marching into the city, victorious. And Hector is certainly going to have something to say. When he left, three months ago, he promised me this war would be the last.

CASSANDRA. It is the last. The next is still ahead of him.

ANDROMACHE. Doesn't it ever tire you to see and prophesy only disasters?

CASSANDRA. I see nothing. I prophesy nothing. All I ever do is to take account of two great stupidities: the stupidity of men, and the wild stupidity of the elements.

ANDROMACHE. Why should there be a war? Paris and Helen don't care for each other any longer.

CASSANDRA. Do you think it will matter if Paris and Helen don't care for each other any longer? Has destiny ever been interested in whether things were still true ot not?

ANDROMACHE. I don't know what destiny is.

CASSANDRA. I'll tell you. It is simply the relentless logic of each day we live.

ANDROMACHE. I don't understand abstractions.

CASSANDRA. Never mind. We can try a metaphor. Imagine a tiger. You can understand that? It's a nice, easy metaphor. A sleeping tiger.

ANDROMACHE. Let it sleep.

CASSANDRA. There's nothing I should like better. But certain cocksure statements have been prodding him out of his sleep. For some considerable time Troy has been full of them.

ANDROMACHE. Full of what?

CASSANDRA. Of cocksure statements, a confident belief that the world, and the supervision of the world, is the province of mankind in general, and Trojan men and women in particular.

ANDROMACHE. I don't follow you.

CASSANDRA. Hector at this very moment is marching into Troy?

ANDROMACHE. Yes. Hector at this very moment has come home to his wife.

CASSANDRA. And Hector's wife is going to have a child?

ANDROMACHE. Yes; I am going to have a child.

CASSANDRA. Don't you call these statements a little overconfident?

ANDROMACHE. Don't frighten me, Cassandra.

(A Young Laundress goes past with an armful of linen.)

LAUNDRESS. What a beautiful day, miss!

CASSANDRA. Does it seem so, indeed?

LAUNDRESS. It's the most beautiful spring day Troy has seen this year. *(Exit)*

CASSANDRA. Even the laundrymaid is confident!

ANDROMACHE. And so she should be, Cassandra. How can you talk of a war on a day like this? Happiness is falling on us out of the sky.

CASSANDRA. Like a blanket of snow.

ANDROMACHE. And beauty, as well. Look at the sunshine. It is finding more mother-of-pearl on the rooftops of Troy than was ever dragged up from the bed of the sea. And do you hear the sound coming up from the fishermen's houses, and the movement of the trees, like the murmuring of sea shells? If ever there were a chance to see men finding a way to live in peace, it is today. To live in peace, in humility. And to be immortal.

CASSANDRA. Yes, I am sure those cripples who have been carried out to lie in their doorways feel how immortal they are.

ANDROMACHE. And to be good. Do you see that horseman, in the advance-guard, leaning from his saddle to stroke a cat on the battlements? Perhaps this is also going to be the first day of true fellowship between men and the animals.

CASSANDRA. You talk too much. Destiny, the tiger, is getting restive, Andromache!

ANDROMACHE. Restive, maybe, in young girls looking for husbands; but not otherwise.

CASSANDRA. You are wrong. Hector has come home in triumph to the wife he adores. The tiger begins to rouse, and opens one eye. The incurables lie out on their benches in the sun and feel immortal. The tiger stretches himself. Today is the chance for peace to enthrone herself over all the world. The tiger licks his lips. And Andromache is going to have a son! And the horsemen have started leaning from their saddles to stroke tomcats on the battlements! The tiger starts to prowl.

ANDROMACHE. Be quiet!

CASSANDRA. He climbs noiselessly up the palace steps. He pushes open the doors with his snout. And here he is, here he is!

(Hector's voice: Andromache!)

ANDROMACHE. You are lying! It is Hector!

CASSANDRA. Whoever said it was not?

(Enter Hector.)

ANDROMACHE. Hector!

HECTOR. Andromache!

(They embrace.)

And good morning to you, too, Cassandra. Ask Paris to come to me, if you will. As soon as he can.

(Cassandra lingers.)

Have you something to tell me?

ANDROMACHE. Don't listen to her! Some catastrophe or other!

HECTOR. Tell me.

CASSANDRA. Your wife is going to have a child. (Exit Cassandra)

(Hector takes Andromache in his arms, leads her to a stone bench, and sits beside her. A short pause.)

HECTOR. Will it be a son or a daughter?

ANDROMACHE. Which did you want to create when you called it into life?

HECTOR. A thousand boys. A thousand girls.

ANDROMACHE. Why? Because it would give you a thousand women to hold in your arms? You are going to be disappointed. It will be a son, one single son.

HECTOR. That may very well be. Usually more boys are born than girls at the end of a war.

ANDROMACHE. And before a war? Which, before a war?

HECTOR. Forget wars, Andromache, even this war. It's over. It lost you a father and a brother, but it gave you back a husband.

ANDROMACHE. It has been too kind. It may think better of it presently.

HECTOR. Don't wory. We won't give it the chance. Directly I leave you I shall go into the square, and formally close the Gates of War. They will never open again.

ANDROMACHE. Close them, then. But they will open again.

HECTOR. You can even tell me the day, perhaps?

ANDROMACHE. I can even tell you the day: the day when the cornfields are heavy and golden, when the vines are stooping, ready for harvest, and every house is sheltering a contented couple.

HECTOR. And peace, no doubt, at its very height?

ANDROMACHE. Yes. And my son is strong and glowing with life. (Hector embraces her)

HECTOR. Perhaps your son will be a coward. That's one possible safeguard.

ANDROMACHE. He won't be a coward. But perhaps I shall have cut off the index finger of his right hand.

HECTOR. If every mother cut off her son's right-hand index finger, the armies of the world would fight without index fingers. And if they cut off their sons' right legs, the armies would be one-legged. And if they put out their eyes, the armies would be blind, but there would still be armies: blind armies groping to find the fatal place in the enemy's groin, or to get at his throat.

ANDROMACHE. I would rather kill him.

HECTOR. There's a truly maternal solution to war!

ANDROMACHE. Don't laugh. I can still kill him before he is born.

HECTOR. Don't you want to see him at all, not even for a moment? After that, you would think again. Do you mean never to see your son?

ANDROMACHE. It is your son that interests me. Hector, it's because he is yours, because he is you, that I'm so afraid. You don't know how like you he is. Even in this no-man's-land where he is waiting, he already has everything, all those qualities you brought to this life we live together. He has your tenderness, your silences. If you love war, he will love it. Do you love war?

HECTOR. Why ask such a question?

ANDROMACHE. Admit, sometimes you love it.

HECTOR. If a man can love what takes away hope, and happiness, and all those nearest to his heart.

ANDROMACHE. And you know it can be so. Men do love it.

HECTOR. If they let themselves be fooled by that little burst of divinity the gods give them at the moment of attack.

ANDROMACHE. Ah, there, you see! At the moment of attack you feel like a god.

HECTOR. More often not as much as a man. But sometimes, on certain mornings, you get up from the ground feeling lighter, astonished, altered. Your whole body, and the armour on your back, have a different weight, they seem to be made of a different metal. You are invulnerable. A tenderness comes over you, submerging you, a kind of tenderness of battle: you are tender because you are pitiless; what, in fact, the tenderness of the gods must be. You advance towards the enemy slowly, almost absent-mindedly, but lovingly. And you try not to crush a beetle crossing your path. You brush off the mosquito without hurting it. You never at any time had more respect for the life you meet on your way.

ANDROMACHE. And then the enemy comes?

HECTOR. Then the enemy comes, frothing at the mouth. You pity him; you can see him there, behind the swollen veins and the whites of his eyes, the helpless, willing little man of business, the well-meaning husband and son-in-law who likes to grow his own vegetables. You feel a sort of love for him. You love the wart on his cheeck and the cast in his eye. You love him. But he comes on; he is insistent. Then you kill him.

ANDROMACHE. And you bend over the wretched corpse as though you are a god; but you are not a god; you can't give back his life again.

HECTOR. You don't wait to bend over him. There are too many more waiting for you, frothing at the mouth and howling hate. Too many more unassuming, law-abiding family men.

ANDROMACHE. Then you kill them.

HECTOR. You kill them. Such is war.

ANDROMACHE. All of them: you kill them all?

HECTOR. This time we killed them all. Quite deliberately. They belonged to an incorrigibly warlike race, the reason why wars go on and multiply in Asia. Only one of them escaped.

ANDROMACHE. In a thousand years time, there the warlike race will be again, descended from that one man. His escape made all that slaughter futile after all. My son is going to love war, just as you do.

HECTOR. I think, now that I've lost my love for it, I hate it.

ANDROMACHE. How do you come to hate what you once worshipped?

HECTOR. You know what it's like when you find out a friend is a liar? Whatever he says, after that, sounds false, however true it may be. And strangely enough, war used to promise me many kinds of virtue: goodness, generosity, and a contempt for anything base and mean. I felt I owed it all my strength and zest for life, even my private happiness, you, Andromache. And until this last compaign there was no enemy I haven't loved.

ANDROMACHE. Very soon you will say you only kill what you love.

HECTOR. It's hard to explain how all the sounds of war combined to make me think it was something noble. The galloping of horse in the night, the clatter of bowls and dishes where the cooks were moving in and out of the firelight, the brush of silk and metal against your tent as the night-patrol went past, and the cry of the falcon wheeling high above the sleeping army and their unsleeping captain: it all seemed then so right, marvellously right.

ANDROMACHE. But not this time: this time war had no music for you?

HECTOR. Why was that? Because I am older? Or was it just the kind of weariness with your job which, for instance, a carpenter will be suddenly seized by, with a table half finished, as I was seized one morning, over an adversary of my own age, about to put an end to him? Up to that time, a man I was going to kill had always seemed my direct opposite. This time I was kneeling on a mirror, the death I was going to give was a kind of suicide. I don't know what the carpenter does at such a time, whether he throws away his hammer and plane, or goes on with it. I went on with it. But after that nothing remained of the perfect trumpet note of war. The spear as it slid against my shield rang suddenly false; so did the shock of the killed against the ground, and, some hours later, the palace crumbling into ruin. And, moreover, war knew that I understood, and gave up any pretence of shame. The cries of the dying sounded false. I had come to that.

ANDROMACHE. But it all still sounded right for the rest of them.

HECTOR. The rest of them heard it as I did. The army I brought back hates war.

ANDROMACHE. An army with poor hearing.

HECTOR. No. When we first came in sight of Troy, an hour ago, you can't imagine how everything in that moment sounded true for them. There wasn't a regiment which didn't halt, racked to the heart by this sense of returning music. So much so, we were afraid to march boldly in through the gates: we broke up into groups outside the walls. It feels like the only job worthy of a good army, laying peaceful siege to the open cities of your own country.

ANDROMACHE. You haven't understood, this is where things are falser than anywhere. War is here, in Troy, Hector.

That is what welcomed you at the gates.

HECTOR. What do you mean?

ANDROMACHE. You haven't heard that Paris has carried off Helen?

HECTOR. They told me so. What else?

ANDROMACHE. Did you know that the Greeks are demanding her back? And their ambassador arrives today? And if we don't give her up, it means war.

HECTOR. Why shouldn't we give her up? I shall give her back to them myself.

ANDROMACHE. Paris will never agree to it.

HECTOR. Paris will agree, and very soon. Cassandra is bringing him to me.

ANDROMACHE. But Paris can't agree. His honour, as you all call it, won't let him. Nor his love either, he may tell you.

HECTOR. Well, we shall see. Run and ask Priam if he will let me speak to him at once. And set your heart at rest. All the Trojans who have been fighting, or who can fight, are against a war.

ANDROMACHE. There are still the others, remember. (*As Andromache goes . . . Cassandra enters with Paris*)

CASSANDRA. Here is Paris.

HECTOR. Congratulations, Paris. I hear you have been very well occupied while we were away.

PARIS. Not badly. Thank you.

HECTOR. What is this story they tell me about Helen?

PARIS. Helen is a very charming person. Isn't she, Cassandra?

CASSANDRA. Fairly charming.

PARIS. Why these reservations today? It was only yesterday you said you thought she was extremely pretty.

CASSANDRA. She is extremely pretty, and fairly charming.

PARIS. Hasn't she the ways of a young, gentle gazelle?

CASSANDRA. No.

PARIS. But you were the one who first said she was like a gazelle.

CASSANDRA. I made a mistake. Since then I have seen a gazelle again.

HECTOR. To hell with gazelles! Doesn't she look any more like a woman than that?

PARIS. She isn't the type of woman we know here, obviously.

CASSANDRA. What is the type of woman we know here?

PARIS. Your type, my dear sister. The fearfully unremote sort of woman.

CASSANDRA. When your Greek makes love she is a long way off, I suppose?

PARIS. You know perfectly well what I'm trying to say. I have had enough of Asiatic women. They hold you in their arms as though they were glued there, their kisses are like battering-rams, their words chew right into you. The more they undress the more elaborate they seem, until when they're naked they are more overdressed than ever. And they paint their faces to look as though they mean to imprint themselves on you. And they do imprint themselves on you. In short, you are definitely *with* them. But Helen is far away from me, even held in my arms.

HECTOR. Very interesting! But, one wonders, is it really worth a war, to allow Paris to make love at a distance?

CASSANDRA. With distance. He loves women to be distant but right under his nose.

PARIS. To have Helen with you not with you is worth anything in the world.

HECTOR. How did you fetch her away? Willingly, or did you compel her?

PARIS. Listen, Hector! You know women as well as I do. They are only willing when you compel them, but after that they're as enthusiastic as you are.

HECTOR. On horseback, in the usual style of seducers, leaving a heap of horse manure under the windows.

PARIS. Is this a court of enquiry?

HECTOR. Yes, it is. Try for once to answer precisely and accurately. Have you insulted her husband's house, or the Greek earth?

PARIS. The Greek water, a little. She was bathing.

CASSANDRA. She is born of the foam, is she? This cold one is born of the foam, like Venus.

HECTOR. You haven't disfigured the walls of the palace with offensive drawings, as you usually do? You didn't shout to the echoes any word which they would at once repeat to the betrayed husband?

PARIS. No. Menelaus was naked on the river bank, busy removing a crab from his big toe. He watched my boat sail past as if the wind were carrying his clothes away.

HECTOR. Looking furious?

PARIS. The face of a king being nipped by a crab isn't likely to look beatific.

HECTOR. No onlookers?

PARIS. My crew.

HECTOR. Perfect!

PARIS. Why perfect? What are you getting at?

HECTOR. I say perfect, because you have done nothing irrevocable. In other words: she was undressed, so neither her clothes nor her belongings have been insulted. Nothing except her body, which is negligible. I've enough acquaintance with the Greeks to know they will concoct a divine adventure out of it, to their own glory, the story of this little Greek queen who goes down into the sea, and quietly comes up again a few months later, with a look on her face of perfect innocence.

CASSANDRA. We can be quite sure of the look on her face.

PARIS. You think that I'm going to take Helen back to Menelaus?

HECTOR. We don't ask so much of you, or of her. The Greek ambassador will take care of it. He will put her back in the sea himself, like a gardener planting water-lilies, at a particulier chosen spot. You will give her into his hands this evening.

PARIS. I don't know whether you are allowing yourself to notice how monstrous you are being, to suppose that a man who has the prospect of a night with Helen will agree to giving it up.

CASSANDRA. You still have an afternoon with Helen. Surely that's more Greek?

HECTOR. Don't be obstinate. We know you of old. This isn't the first separation you've accepted.

PARIS. My dear Hector, that's true enough. Up to now I have always accepted separations fairly cheerfully. Parting from a woman, however well you love her, induces a most pleasant state of mind, which I know how to value as well as anybody. You come out of her arms and take your first lonely walk through the town, and, the first little dressmaker you meet, you notice with a shock of surprise how fresh and unconcerned she looks, after that last sight you have had of the dear face you parted from, her nose red with weeping. Because you have come away from such broken, despairing farewells, the laundrygirls and the fruitsellers laughing their heads off, more than make up for whatever you've lost in the parting. By losing one person your life has become entirely re-peopled. All the women in the world have been created for you afresh; they are all your own, in the liberty, honour, and peace of your conscience. Yes, you're quite right: when a love-affair is broken off it reaches its highest point of exaltation. Which is why I shall never be parted from Helen, because with Helen I feel as though I had broken with every other woman in the world, and that gives me the sensation of being free a thousand times over instead of once.

HECTOR. Because she doesn't love you. Everything you say proves it.

PARIS. If you like. But, if I had to choose one out of all the possible ways of passion, I would choose the way Helen doesn't love me.

HECTOR. I'm extremely sorry. But you will give her up.

PARIS. You are not the master here.

HECTOR. I am your elder brother, and the future master.

PARIS. Then order me about in the future. For the present, I obey my father.

HECTOR. That's all I want! You're willing that we should put this to Priam and accept his judgment?

PARIS. Perfectly willing.

HECTOR. On your solemn word? We both swear to accept that?

CASSANDRA. Mind what you're doing, Hector! Priam is mad for Helen. He would rather give up his daughters.

HECTOR. What nonsense is this?

PARIS. For once she is telling the thrut about the present instead of the future.

CASSANDRA. And all our brothers, and all our uncles, and all our great-great uncles! Helen has a guard-of-honour which includes every old man in the city. Look there. It is time for her walk. Do you see, there's a fringe of white beards draped all along the battlements?

HECTOR. A beautiful sight. The beards are white, and the faces red.

CASSANDRA. Yes; it's the blood pressure. They should be waiting at the Scamander Gate, to welcome the victorious troops. But no; they are all at the Sceean Gate, waiting for Helen.

HECTOR. Look at them, all leaning forward as one man, like storks when they see a rat going by.

CASSANDRA. The rat is Helen.

PARIS. Is it?

CASSANDRA. There she is: on the second terrace, standing to adjust her sandal, and giving careful thought to the crossing of her legs.

HECTOR. Incredible. All the old men of Troy are there looking down at her.

CASSANDRA. Not all. There are certain crafty ones looking up at her.

(Cries offstage: Long live Beauty!)

HECTOR. What are they shouting?

PARIS. They're shouting 'Long live Beauty!'

CASSANDRA. I quite agree with them, if they mean that they themselves should die as quickly as possible.

(Cries offstage: Long live Venus!)

HECTOR. And what now?

CASSANDRA. 'Long live Venus.' They are shouting only words without R's in them because of their lack of teeth. Long live Beauty, long live Venus, long live Helen. At least they imagine they're shouting, though, as you can hear, all they are doing is simply increasing a mumble to its highest power.

HECTOR. What has Venus to do with it?

CASSANDRA. They imagine it was Venus who gave us Helen. To show her gratitude to Paris for awarding her the apple on first sight.

HECTOR. That was another brilliant stroke of yours.

PARIS. Stop playing the elder brother!

(Enter two old men.)

1st OLD MAN. Down there we see her better.

2nd OLD MAN. We had a very good view.

1ST OLD MAN. But she can hear us better from up here. Come on. One, two, three!

BOTH. Long live Helen!

2ND OLD MAN. It's a little tiring, at our age, to have to climb up and down these impossible steps all the time, according to whether we want to look at her or to cheer her.

1ST OLD MAN. Would you like us to alternate? One day we will cheer her? Another day we will look at her?

2ND OLD MAN. You are mad! One day without looking at Helen, indeed! Goodness me, think what we've seen of her today! One, two, three!

BOTH. Long live Helen!

1ST OLD MAN. And now down we go again!

(They run off.)

CASSANDRA. You see what they're like, Hector. I don't know how their poor lungs are going to stand it.

HECTOR. But our father can't be like this.

PARIS. Hector, before we have this out in front of my father, I suppose you wouldn't like to take just one look at Helen.

HECTOR. I don't care a fig about Helen. Ah: greetings to you, father!

(Priam enters, with Hecuba, Andromache, the poet Demokos and another old man. Hecuba leads by the hand little Polyxene.)

PRIAM. What was it you said?

HECTOR. I said that we should make haste to shut the Gates of War, father, see them bolted and padlocked, so that not even a gnat can get between them.

PRIAM. I thought what you said was somewhat shorter.

DEMOKOS. He said he didn't care a fig about Helen.

PRIAM. Look over here.

(Hector obeys)
Do you see her?

HECUBA. Indeed he sees her. Who, I ask myself, doesn't see her, or hasn't seen her? She takes the road which goes the whole way round the city.

DEMOKOS. It is Beauty's perfect circle.

PRIAM. Do you see her?

HECTOR. Yes, I see her. What of it?

DEMOKOS. Priam is asking you what you see.

HECTOR. I see a young woman adjusting her sandal.

CASSANDRA. She takes some time to adjust her sandal.

PARIS. I carried her off naked; she left her clothes in Greece. Those are your sandals, Cassandra. They're a bit big for her.

CASSANDRA. Anything's too big for these little women.

HECTOR. I see two charming buttocks.

HECUBA. He sees what all of you see.

PRIAM. I'm sorry for you!

HECTOR. Why?

PRIAM. I had no idea that the young men of Troy had come to this.

HECTOR. What have they come to?

PRIAM. To being impervious to beauty.

DEMOKOS. And, consequently, ignorant of love. And, consequently, unrealistic. To us who are poets reality is love or nothing.

HECTOR. But the old men, you think, can appreciate love and beauty?

HECUBA. But of course. If you make love, or if you are beautiful, you don't need to understand these things.

HECTOR. You come across beauty, father, at every street corner. I'm not alluding to Helen, though at the moment she condescends to walk our streets.

PRIAM. You are being unfair, Hector. Surely there have been occasions in your life when a woman has seemed to be more than merely herself, as though a radiance of thoughts and feelings glowed from her flesh, taking a special brillance from it.

DEMOKOS. As a ruby represents blood.

HECTOR. Not to those who have seen blood. I have just come back from a close acquaintance with it.

DEMOKOS. A symbol, you understand. Soldier though you are, you have surely heard of symbolism! Surely you have come across women who as soon as you saw them seemed to you to personify intelligence, harmony, gentleness, whatever it might be?

HECTOR. It has happened.

DEMOKOS. And what did you do?

HECTOR. I went closer, and that was the end of it. And what does this we see here personify?

DEMOKOS. We have told you before: Beauty.

HECUBA. Then send her quickly back to the Greeks if you want her to personify that for long. Blonde beauty doesn't usually last for ever.

DEMOKOS. It's impossible to talk to these women!

HECUBA. Then don't talk *about* women. You're not showing much gallantry, I might say; nor patriotism either. All other races choose one of their own women as their symbol, even if they have flat noses and lips like two fishes on a plate. It's only you who have to go outside your own country to find it.

HECTOR. Listen, father: we are just back from a war, and we have come home exhausted. We have made quite certain of peace on our continent for ever. From now on we mean to live in happiness, and we mean our wives to be able to love us without anxiety, and to bear our children.

DEMOKOS. Wise principles, but war has never prevented wives from having children.

HECTOR. So explain to me why we have come back to find the city transformed all because of Helen? Explain to me what you think she has given to us, worth a quarrel with the Greeks?

MATHEMATICIAN. Anybody will tell you! I can tell you myself!

HECUBA. Listen to the mathematician!

MATHEMATICIAN. Yes, listen to the mathematician! And don't think that mathematicians have no concern with women! We're the land-surveyors of your personal landscape. I can't tell you how we mathematicians suffer to see any slight disproportion of the flesh, on the chin or the thigh, any infringement of your geometrical desirability. Well now, until this day mathematicians have never been satisfied with the countryside surrounding Troy. The line linking the plain with the hills seemed to us too slack: the line from the hills to the mountains too taut. Now, since Helen came, the country has taken on meaning and vigour.

And, what is particularly evident to true mathematicians, space and volume have now found in Helen a common denominator. We can abolish all the instruments we have invented to reduce the universe to a manageable equation. There are no more feet and inches, ounces, pounds, milligrams or leagues. There is only the weight of Helen's footfall, the length of Helen's arm, the range of Helen's look or voice; and the movement of the air as she goes past is the measure of the winds. That is what the mathematicians will tell you.

HECUBA. The old fool is crying.

PRIAM. My dear son, you have only to look at this crowd, and you will understand what Helen is. She is a kind of absolution. To each one of these old men, whom you can see now like a frieze of grotesque heads all round the city walls: to the old swindler, the old thief, the old pandar, to all the old failures, she has shown they always had a secret longing to rediscover the beauty they had lost. If throughout their lives beauty had always been as close at hand as Helen is today, they would never have tricked their friends, or sold their daughters, or drunk away their inheritance. Helen is like a pardon to them: a new beginning for them, their whole future.

HECTOR. These old men's ancient futures are no concern of mine.

DEMOKOS. Hector, as a poet I approach things by the way of poetry. Imagine if beauty, never, at any time, touched our language. Imagine there being no such word as 'delight'.

HECTOR. We should get on well enough without it. I get on without it already. 'Delight' is a word I use only when I'm absolutely driven to it.

DEMOKOS. Well, then the word 'desirable': you could get on without that as well, I suppose?

HECTOR. If it could be bought only at the cost of war, yes, I could get on without the word 'desirable'.

DEMOKOS. One of the most beautiful words there are was found only at the cost of war: the word 'courage'.

HECTOR. It has been well paid for.

HECUBA. And the word 'cowardice' was inevitably found at the same time.

PRIAM. My son, why do you so deliberately not understand us?

HECTOR. I understand you very well. With the help of a quibble, by pretending to persuade us to fight for beauty you want to get us to fight for a woman.

PRIAM. Would you never go to war for any woman?

HECTOR. Certainly not!

HECUBA. And he would be unchivalrously right.

CASSANDRA. If there were only one woman, then perhaps he would go to war for her. But we have exceeded that number, quite extravagantly.

DEMOKOS. Wouldn't you go to war to rescue Andromache?

HECTOR. Andromache and I have already made our secret plans for escaping from any prison in the world, and finding our way back to each other again.

DEMOKOS. Even if there's no hope of it on earth?

HECTOR. Even then.

HECUBA. You have done well to unmask them, Hector. They want you to make war for the sake of a woman; it's the kind of lovemaking men believe in who are past making love in any other way.

DEMOKOS. And doesn't that make you all the more valuable?

HECUBA. Ah yes! You may say so!

DEMOKOS. Excuse me, but I can't agree with you. The sex which gave me my mother will always have my respect, even its least worthy representatives.

HECUBA. We know that. You have, as we know, shown your respect for instance to ——

(The servants who have stood by to hear the argument burst out laughing.)

PRIAM. Hecuba! Daughters! What can this mean? Why on earth are you all so up in arms? The Council are considering giving the city a public holiday in honour of one of your sex.

ANDROMACHE. I know of only one humiliation for a woman: injustice.

DEMOKOS. It's painful to say so, but there's no one knows less what a woman is than a woman.

(The young servant, passing: Oh, dear! dear!)

HECUBA. We know perfectly well. I will tell you myself what a woman is.

DEMOKOS. Don't let them talk, Priam. You never know what they might say.

HECUBA. They might tell the truth.

PRIAM. I have only to think of one of you, my dears, to know what a woman is.

DEMOKOS. In the first place, she is the source of our energy. You know that, Hector. The soldiers who haven't a portrait of a woman in their kit aren't worth anything.

CASSANDRA. The source of your pride, yes, I agree.

HECUBA. Of your vices.

ANDROMACHE. She is a poor bundle of uncertainty, a poor mass of fears, who detests whatever is difficult, and adores whatever is vulgar and easy.

HECTOR. Dear Andromache!

HECUBA. It's very simple. I have been a woman for fifty years, and I've never yet been able to discover precisely what it is I am.

DEMOKOS. Secondly, whether she likes it or not, she's the only reward for courage. Ask any soldier. To kill a man is to merit a woman.

ANDROMACHE. She loves cowards and libertines. If Hector were a coward or a libertine I shouldn't love him less; I might even love him more.

PRIAM. Don't go too far, Andromache. You will prove the very opposite of what you want to prove.

POLYXENE. She is greedy. She tells lies.

DEMOKOS. So we're to say nothing of her fidelity, her purity: we are not to mention them?

THE SERVANT. Oh, dear! dear!

DEMOKOS. What did you say?

THE SERVANT. I said 'Oh, dear! dear!' I say what I think.

POLYXENE. She breaks her toys. She puts them headfirst into boiling water.

HECUBA. The older we women grow, the more clearly we see what men really are: hypocrites, boasters, he-goats. The older men grow, the more they doll us up with every perfection. There isn't a slut you've hugged behind a wall who isn't transformed in your memories into a loved and lovely creature.

PRIAM. Have you ever deceived me, Hecuba?

HECUBA. Only with yourself; scores of time with yourself.

DEMOKOS. Has Andromache ever deceived Hector?

HECUBA. You can leave Andromache out of this. There is nothing she could recognize in the sad histories of erring women.

ANDROMACHE. But I know if Hector were not my husband, if he were a club-footed, bandy-legged fisherman I should run after him and find him in his hovel, and lie down on the pile of oyster-shells and seaweed, and give him a son in adultery.

POLYXENE. She pretends to go to sleep at night, but she's really playing games in her head with her eyes shut.

HECUBA (to Polyxene). You may well say so! It's dreadful! You know how I scold you for it!

THE SERVANT. The only thing worse than a woman is a man; there are no words to describe him.

DEMOKOS. Then more's the pity if a woman deceives us! More's the pity if she scorns her own value and dignity! If she can't be true to a pattern of perfection which would save her from the ravages of conscience, we have to do it for her.

THE SERVANT. Oh, the kind guardian angel!

PARIS. One thing they've forgotten to say of themselves: they are never jealous.

PRIAM. My dear daughters, the fact that you're so furious is a proof in itself that we are right. I can't conceive of any greater unselfishness than the way you now fight for peace, when peace will give you idle, feeble, chicken-hearted husbands, and war would turn them into men.

DEMOKOS. Into heroes.

HECUBA. Yes, we know the jargon. In war-time a man is called a hero. It doesn't make him any braver, and he runs for his life. But at least it's a hero who is running away.

ANDROMACHE. Father, I must beg you to listen. If you have such a fondness for women, listen to what they have to say to you, for I can promise I speak for all the women in the world. Let us keep our husbands as they are. The gods took care to see they were surrounded with enough obstacles and dangers to keep them brave and vigourous. Quite enough if they had nothing to cope with except floods and storms! Or only wild animals! The small game, foxes and hares and pheasants, which a woman can scarcely distinguish from the heather they hide in, prove a man's quickness of eye far better than this target you propose: the enemy's heart hiding in flesh and metal. Whenever I have seen a man kill a stag or an eagle, I have offered up thanks to them. I know they died for Hector. Why should you want me to owe Hector to the deaths of other men?

PRIAM. I don't want it, my dear child. But why do you think you are here now, all looking so beautiful, and valiantly demanding peace? Why: because your husbands and your fathers, and their fathers, and theirs, were fighting men. If they had been too lazy and self-indulgent to spring to arms, if they hadn't known how this dull and stupid business we call life suddenly leaps into flame and justifies itself through the scorn men have for it, you would find you were the cowards now, and you would be clamouring for war. A man has only one way of being immortal on this earth: he has to forget he is mortal.

ANDROMACHE. Why, exactly so, father you're only too right. The brave men die in war. It takes great luck or judgment not to be killed. Once at least the head has to bow and the knee has to bend to danger. The soldiers who march back under the triumphal arches are death's deserters. How can a country increase in strength and honour by sending them both to their graves?

PRIAM. Daughter, the first sign of cowardice in a people is their first moment of decay.

ANDROMACHE. But which is the worse cowardice? To appear cowardly to others, and make sure of peace? Or to be cowardly in your own eyes, and let loose a war?

DEMOKOS. Cowardice is not to prefer death on every hand rather than the death of one's native land.

HECUBA. I was expecting poetry at this point. It never lets us down.

ANDROMACHE. Everyone always dies for his country. If you have lived in it, well and wisely and actively, you die for it too.

HECUBA. It would be better if only the old men fought the wars. Every country is the country of youth. When its youth dies it dies with them.

DEMOKOS. All this nonsense about youth! In thirty years time youth is nothing but these old men you talk about.

CASSANDRA. Wrong.

HECUBA. Wrong! When a grown man reaches forty we change him for an old one. He has completely disappeared. There's only the most superficial resemblance between the two of them. Nothing is handed on from one to the other.

DEMOKOS. I still take a serious concern in my fame as a poet.

HECUBA. Yes, that's quite true. And your rheumatism.

(Another outburst of laughter from the servants.)

HECTOR. And you can listen to all this without saying a word, Paris? Can you still not decide to give up an adventure to save us from years of unhappiness and massacre?

PARIS. What do you want me to say? My case is an international problem.

HECTOR. Are you really in love with Helen, Paris?

CASSANDRA. They've become now a kind of symbol of love's devotion. They don't still have to love each other.

PARIS. I worship Helen.

CASSANDRA (at the rampart). Here she is.

HECTOR. If I persuade her to set sail, will you agree?

PARIS. Yes, I'll agree.

HECTOR. Father, if Helen is willing to go back to Greece, will you hold her here by force?

PRIAM. Why discuss the impossible?

HECTOR. Do you call it impossible? If women are a tenth of what you say they are, Helen will go of her own free will.

PARIS. Father, now I'm going to ask you to let him do what he wants. You have seen what it's like. As soon as the question of Helen cropped up, this whole tribe royal turned itself into a family conclave of all the poor girl's sisters-in-law, mother- and father-in-law, brother-in-law, worthy of the best middle-class tradition. I doubt if there's anything more humiliating than to be cast for the part of the seducer son in a large family. I've had quite enough of their insinuations. I accept Hector's challenge.

DEMOKOS. Helen's not only yours, Paris. She belongs to the city. She belongs to our country.

MATHEMATICIAN. She belongs to the landscape.

HECUBA. You be quiet, mathematician.

CASSANDRA. Here's Helen; here she is.

HECTOR. Father, I must ask you to let me handle this. Listen; they are calling us to go to the ceremony, to close the Gates of War. Leave this to me. I'll join you soon.

PRIAM. Do you really agree to this, Paris?

PARIS. I'm eager for it.

PRIAM. Very well, then, let it be so. Come along, the rest of you; we will see that the Gates of War are made ready.

CASSANDRA. Those poor gates. They need more oil to shut them than to open them.

(Paris and the rest withdraw. Demokos stays.)

HECTOR. What are you waiting for?

DEMOKOS. The visitation of my genius.

HECTOR. Say that again?

DEMOKOS. Every time Helen walks my way I am thrown into a transport of inspiration. I shake all over, break into sweat, and improvise. Good heavens, here it is! (He declaims:)

Beautiful Helen, Helen of Sparta,
    Singular as the evening star,
The gods forbid that we should part a
    Pair as fair as you and Paris are.

HECTOR. Your line-endings give me a headache.

DEMOKOS. It's an invention of mine. I can obtain effects even more surprising. Listen: (declaims)

Face the great Hector with no qualm,
    Troy's glory though he be, and the
        world's terror;
He is the storm, and you the after-calm,
    Yours is the right, and his the
        boist'rous error.

HECTOR. Get out!

DEMOKOS. What are you glaring at? You look as though you have as little liking for poetry as you have for war.

HECTOR. They make a pretty couple! Now vanish.

(Exit Demokos. Enter Cassandra.)

CASSANDRA. Helen!

(Enter Helen and Paris.)

PARIS. Here he is, Helen darling; this is Hector. He has a proposition to make to you, a perfectly simple proposition. He wants to hand you over to the Greeks, and prove to you that you don't love me. Tell me you do love me, before I leave you with him. Tell me in your own words.

HELEN. I adore you, my sweet.

PARIS. Tell me how beautiful the wave was which swept you away from Greece.

HELEN. Magnificent! A magnificent wave! Where did you see a wave? The sea was so calm.

PARIS. Tell me you hate Menelaus.

HELEN. Menelaus? I hate him.

PARIS. You haven't finished yet. I shall never again return to Greece. Say that.

HELEN. You will never again return to Greece.

PARIS. No, no, this is about you, my darling.

HELEN. Oh, of course! How silly I am! I shall never again return to Greece.

PARIS. I didn't make her say it. — Now it's up to you. *(He goes off)*

HECTOR. Is Greece a beautiful country?

HELEN. Paris found it ravishing.

HECTOR. I meant is Greece itself beautiful, apart from Helen?

HELEN. How very charming of you.

HECTOR. I was simply wondering what it is really like.

HELEN. Well, there are quite a great many kings, and a great many goats, dotted about on marble.

HECTOR. If the kings are in gold, and the goats angora, that would look pretty well when the sun was rising.

HELEN. I don't get up very early.

HECTOR. And a great many gods as well, I believe? Paris tells me the sky is crawling with them; he tells me you can see the legs of goddesses hanging down from the clouds.

HELEN. Paris always goes about with his nose in the air. He may have seen them.

HECTOR. But you haven't?

HELEN. I am not gifted that way. I will look out for them when I go back there again.

HECTOR. You were telling Paris you would never be going back there.

HELEN. He asked me to tell him so. I adore doing what Paris wants me to do.

HECTOR. I see. Is that also true of what you said about Menelaus? Do you not, after all, hate him?

HELEN. Why should I hate him?

HECTOR. For the one reason which might certainly make for hate. You have seen too much of him.

HELEN. Menelaus? Oh, no! I have never seen Menelaus. On the contrary.

HECTOR. You have never seen your husband?

HELEN. There are some things, and certain people, that stand out in bright colours for me. They are the ones I can see. I believe in them. I have never been able to see Menelaus.

HECTOR. Though I suppose he must have come very close to you sometimes.

HELEN. I have been able to touch him. But I can't honestly tell you I saw him.

HECTOR. They say he never left your side.

HELEN. Apparently. I must have walked across him a great many times without knowing it.

HECTOR. Whereas you have seen Paris.

HELEN. Vividly; in the clearest outline against the sky and the sun.

HECTOR. Does he still stand out as vividly as he did? Look down there: leaning against the rampart.

HELEN. Are you sure that's Paris, down there?

HECTOR. He is waiting for you.

HELEN. Good gracious! He's not nearly as clear as usual!

HECTOR. And yet the wall is freshly whitewashed. Look again: there he is in profile.

HELEN. It's odd how people waiting for you stand out far less clearly than people you are waiting for.

HECTOR. Are you sure that Paris loves you?

HELEN. I don't like knowing about other people's feelings. There is nothing more embarrassing. Just as when you play cards and you see your opponent's hand. You are sure to lose.

HECTOR. What about yourself? Do you love him?

HELEN. I don't much like knowing my own feelings either.

HECTOR. But, listen: when you make love with Paris, when he sleeps in your arms, when you are circled round with Paris, overwhelmed with Paris, haven't you any thoughts about is?

HELEN. My part is over. I leave any thinking to the universe. It does it much better than I do.

HECTOR. Have there been many others before Paris?

HELEN. Some.

HECTOR. And there will be others after him, wouldn't you say, as long as they stand out in clear relief against the sky, or the white sheets on the bed? It is just as I thought it was. You don't love Paris particularly, Helen; you love men.

HELEN. I don't dislike them. They're as pleasant as soap and a sponge and warm water; you feel cleansed and refreshed by them.

HECTOR. Cassandra! Cassandra!

CASSANDRA (entering). What do you want?

HECTOR. Cassandra, Helen is going back this evening with the Greek ambassador.

HELEN. I? What makes you think so.

HECTOR. Weren't you telling me that you didn't love Paris particularly?

HELEN. That was your interpretation. Still, if you like.

HECTOR. I quote my authority. You have the same liking for men as you have for a cake of soap.

HELEN. Yes; or pumice stone perhaps is better. What about it?

HECTOR. Well, then, you're not going to hesitate in your choice between going back to Greece, which you don't mind, and a catastrophe as terrible as war?

HELEN. You don't understand me at all, Hector. Of course I'm not hesitating. It would be very easy to say 'I will do this or that, so that this can happen or that can happen.' You've discovered my weakness and you are overjoyed. The man who discovers a woman's weakness is like the huntsman in the heat of the day who finds a cool spring. He wallows in it. But you mustn't think, because you have convinced me, you've convinced the future, too. Merely by making children behave as you want them to, you don't alter the course of destiny.

HECTOR. I don't follow your Greek shades and subtleties.

HELEN. It's not a question of shades and subtleties. It's no less than a question of monsters and pyramids.

HECTOR. Do you choose to leave here, yes or no?

HELEN. Don't bully me. I choose what happens in the way I choose men, or anything else. I choose whatever is not indefinite and vague. I choose what I see.

HECTOR. I know, you said that: what you see in the brightest colours. And you don't see yourself returning to Menelaus in a few day's time?

HELEN. No. It's very difficult.

HECTOR. We could no doubt persuade your husband to dress with great brilliance for your return.

HELEN. All the purple dye from all the murex shells in the sea wouldn't make him visible to me.

HECTOR. Here you have a rival, Cassandra. Helen can read the future, too.

HELEN. No, I can't read the future. But when I imagine the future some of the pictures I see are coloured, and some are dull and drab. And up to now it has always been the coloured scenes which have happened in the end.

HECTOR. We are going to give you back to the Greeks at high noon, on the blinding sand, between the violet sea and the ochre-coloured wall. We shall all be in golden armour with red skirts; and my sisters, dressed in green and standing between my white stallion and Priam's black mare, will return you to the Greek ambassador, over whose silver helmet I can imagine tall purple plumes. You see that, I think?

HELEN. No, none of it. It is all quite sombre.

HECTOR. You are mocking me, aren't you?

HELEN. Why should I mock you? Very well, then. Let us go, if you like! Let us go and get ready to return me to the Greeks. We shall see what happens.

HECTOR. Do you realize how you insult humanity, or is it unconscious?

HELEN. I don't know what you mean.

HECTOR. You realize that your coloured picture-book is holding the world up to ridicule? While we are all battling and making sacrifices to bring about a time we can call our own, there are you, looking at your pictures which nothing in all eternity can alter. What's wrong? Which one has made you stop and stare at it with those blind eyes? I don't doubt it's the one where you are standing here on the ramparts, watching the battle going on below. Is it the battle you see?

HELEN. Yes.

HECTOR. And the city is in ruins or burning, isn't that so?

HELEN. Yes. It's a vivid red.

HECTOR. And what about Paris? You are seeing his body dragged behind a chariot?

HELEN. Oh, do you think that is Paris? I see what looks like a flash of sunlight in the dust. A diamond sparkling on his hand Yes, it is! Often I don't recognize faces, but I always recognize the jewellery. It's his ring, I'm quite certain.

HECTOR. Exactly. Do I dare to ask you about Andromache, and myself, the scene of Andromache and Hector? You are looking at us. Don't deny it. How do you see us? Happy, grown old, bathed in light?

HELEN. I am not trying to see it.

HECTOR. The scene of Andromache weeping over the body of Hector, does that shine clearer?

HELEN. You seem to know. But sometimes I see things shining, brilliantly shining, and they never happen. No one is infallible.

HECTOR. You needn't go on. I understand. There is a son between the weeping mother and the father stretched on the ground?

HELEN. Yes. He is playing with his father's tangled hair. He is a sweet boy.

HECTOR. And these scenes are there in your eyes, down in the depths of them. Could I see them there?

HELEN. I don't know. Look.

HECTOR. Nothing. Nothing except the ashes of all those fires, the gold and the emerald in dust. How innocent it is, this crystal where the future is waiting. But there should be tears bathing it, and where are they? Would you cry, Helen, if you were going to be killed?

HELEN. I don't know. But I should scream. And I feel I shall scream if you go on at me like this, Hector. I am going to scream.

HECTOR. You will leave for Greece this evening, Helen, otherwise I shall kill you.

HELEN. But I want to leave! I'm prepared to leave. All that I'm trying to tell is that I simply can't manage to distinguish the ship that is going to carry me there. Nothing is shining in the least, neither the metal on the mast, nor the ring in the captain's nose, nor the cabin-boy's eyes, nor anything.

HECTOR. You will go back on a grey sea under a grey sun. But we must have peace.

HELEN. I cannot see peace.

HECTOR. Ask Cassandra to make her appear for you. Cassandra is a sorceress. She can summon up shapes and spirits.

A MESSENGER (entering). Hector, Priam is asking for you. The priests are opposed to our shutting the Gates of War. They say the gods will consider it an insult.

HECTOR. It is curious how the gods can never speak for themselves in these difficult matters.

MESSINGER. They have spoken for themselves. A thunderbolt has fallen on the temple, several men have been killed, the entrails of the victims have been consulted, and they are unanimously against Helen's return to Greece.

HECTOR. I would give a good deal to be able to consult the entrails of the priests . . . I'll follow you.

(The messenger goes.)

Well, now, Helen, do we agree about this?

HELEN. Yes.

HECTOR. From now on you will say what I tell you to say? You will do what I tell you to do?

HELEN. Yes.

HECTOR. When we come in front of Ulysses you won't contradict me, you will bear out everything I say?

HELEN. Yes.

HECTOR. Do you hear this, Cassandra? Listen to this solid wall of negation which says Yes! They have all given in to me. Paris has given in to me, Priam has given in to me, Helen has given in to me. And yet I can't help feeling that in each of these apparent victories I have been defeated. You set out, thinking you are going to have to wrestle with giants; you brace yourself to conquer them, and you find yourself wrestling with something inflexible reflected in a woman's eye. You have said yes beautifully, Helen, and you're brimful of a stubborn determination to defy me!

HELEN. That's possible. But how can I help it? It isn't my own determination.

HECTOR. By what peculiar vagary did the world choose to place its mirror in this obtuse head?

HELEN. It's most regrettable, obviously. But can you see any way of defeating the obstinacy of a mirror?

HECTOR. Yes. I've been considering that for the past several minutes.

ANOTHER MESSENGER (entering). Hector, make haste. They are in a turmoil of revolt down on the beach. The Greek ships have been sighted, and they have hoisted their flag not masthead but hatchway. The honour of our navy is at stake. Priam is afraid the ambassador may be murdered as soon as he lands.

HECTOR. I leave you in charge of Helen, Cassandra. I must go and give my orders.

HELEN. If you break the mirror, will what is reflected in it cease to exist?

HECTOR. That is the whole question.
(Exit Hector.)

*CASSANDRA. I never see anything at all, you know, either coloured or not. But I can feel the weight on me of every person who comes towards me. I know what is in store for them by the sensation of suffering which flows into my veins.

* The following portion of the act was omitted in the Broadway production.

HELEN. Is it true that you are a sorceress? Could you really make Peace take shape and appear for us?

CASSANDRA. Peace? Very easily. She is always standing in her beggarly way on every threshold. Wait . . . you will see her now.
(Peace appears.)

HELEN. Oh, how pretty she is!

PEACE. Come to my rescue, Helen: help me!

HELEN. But how pale and wan she is.

PEACE. Pale and wan? What do you mean? Don't you see the gold shining in my hair?

HELEN. Gold? Well, perhaps a golden grey. It's very original.

PEACE. Golden grey? Is my gold now grey?
(She disappears.)

CASSANDRA. I think she means to make herself clearer.
(Peace re-appears, outrageously painted.)

PEACE. Is that better now?

HELEN. I don't see her as well as I did before.

PEACE. Is that better?

CASSANDRA. Helen doesn't see you as well as she did.

PEACE. But you can see me: you are speaking to me.

CASSANDRA. It's my speciality to speak to the invisible.

PEACE. What is going on, then? Why are all the men in the city and along the beach making such a pandemonium?

CASSANDRA. Apparently their gods are insulted, and their honour is at stake.

PEACE. Their gods! Their honour!

CASSANDRA. Yes . . . You are ill!

THE CURTAIN FALLS

ACT TWO

A palace enclosure. At each corner a view of the sea. In the middle a monument, the Gates of War. They are wide open.

HELEN. You, you, hey! You down there! Yes, it's you I'm calling. Come here.

TROILUS. No.

HELEN. What is your name?

TROILUS. Troilus.

HELEN. Come here.

TROILUS. No.

HELEN. Come here, Troilus!

(Troilus draws near.)

That's the way. You obey when you're called by your name: you are still very like a puppy. It's rather beguiling. Do you know you have made me call out to a man for the first time in my life. They keep so close to my side I have only usually to move my lips. I have called out to seagulls, to dogs, to the echoes, but never before to a man. You will pay for that. What's the matter? Are you trembling?

TROILUS. No, I'm not.

HELEN. You tremble, Troilus.

TROILUS. Yes, I do.

HELEN. Why are you always just behind me? If I walk with my back to the sun and suddenly stop, the head of your shadow stubs itself against my feet. That doesn't matter, as long as it doesn't overshoot them. Tell me what you want.

TROILUS. I don't want anything.

HELEN. Tell me what you want, Troilus!

TROILUS. Everything! I want everything!

HELEN. You want everything. The moon?

TROILUS. Everything! Everything and more!

HELEN. You're beginning to talk like a real man already; you want to kiss me!

TROILUS. No!

HELEN. You want to kiss me, isn't that it, Troilus?

TROILUS. I would kill myself directly afterwards!

HELEN. Come nearer. How old are you?

TROILUS. Fifteen. Alas!

HELEN. Bravo that alas. Have you kissed girls of your own age?

TROILUS. I hate them.

HELEN. But you have kissed them?

TROILUS. Well, yes, you're bound to kiss them, you kiss them all. I would give my life not to have kissed any of them.

HELEN. You seem prepared to get rid of quite a number of lives. Why haven't you said to me frankly: Helen, I want to kiss you! I don't see anything wrong in your kissing me. Kiss me.

TROILUS. Never.

HELEN. And then, when the day came to an end, you would have come quietly to where I was sitting on the battlements watching the sun go down over the islands, and you would have turned my head towards you with your hands—from golden it would have become dark, only shadow now, you would hardly have been able to see me—and you would have kissed me, and I should have been very happy. Why this is Troilus, I should have said to myself: young Troilus is kissing me! Kiss me.

TROILUS. Never.

HELEN. I see. You think, once you have kissed me, you would hate me?

TROILUS. Oh! Older men have all the luck, knowing how to say what they want to!

HELEN. You say it well enough.

(Enter Paris.)

PARIS. Take care Helen, Troilus is a dangerous fellow.

HELEN. On the contrary. He wants to kiss me.

PARIS. Troilus, you know that if you kiss Helen, I shall kill you?

HELEN. Dying means nothing to him; no matter how often.

PARIS. What's the matter with him? Is he crouching to spring? Is he going to take a leap at you? He's too nice a boy. Kiss Helen, Troilus. I'll let you.

HELEN. If you can make up his mind to it you're cleverer than I am.

(Troilus who was about to hurl himself on Helen immediately draws back.)

PARIS. Listen, Troilus! Here's a committee of our revered elders coming to shut the Gates of War. Kiss Helen in front of them; it will make you famous. You want to be famous, don't you, later on in life?

TROILUS. No. I want nobody to have heard of me.

PARIS. You don't want to be famous? You don't want to be rich and powerful?

TROILUS. No. Poor. Ugly.

PARIS. Let me finish! So that you can have all the women you want.

TROILUS. I don't want any, none at all, none.

PARIS. Here come the senators! Now

you can choose: either you kiss Helen in front of them, or I shall kiss her in front of you. Would you rather I did it? All right! Look!... Why, this was a new version of kiss you gave me, Helen. What was it?

HELEN. The kiss I had ready for Troilus.

PARIS. You don't know what you're missing, my boy! Are you leaving us? Goodbye, then.

HELEN. We shall kiss one another, Troilus. I'll answer for that.

(*Troilus goes.*)

Troilus!

PARIS (*slightly unnerved*). You called very loudly, Helen.

(*Enter Demokos.*)

DEMOKOS. Helen, one moment! Look me full in the face. I've got here in my hand a magnificent bird which I'm going to set free. Are you looking? Here it is. Smooth back your hair, and smile a beautiful smile

PARIS. I don't see how the bird will fly any better if Helen smooths her hair and gives a beautiful smile.

HELEN. It can't do me any harm, anyway.

DEMOKOS. Don't move. One! Two! Three! It's all over, you can go now.

HELEN. Where was the bird?

DEMOKOS. It's a bird who knows how to make himself invisible.

HELEN. Ask him next time to tell you how he does it.

(*She goes.*)

PARIS. What is this nonsense?

DEMOKOS. I am writing a song on the subject of Helen's face. I needed to look at it closely, to engrave it, smiling, on my memory.

(*Enter Hecuba, Polyxene, Abneos, the Mathematician, and some old men.*)

HECUBA. Well, are you going to shut these Gates for us?

DEMOKOS. Certainly not. We might well have to open them again this very evening.

HECUBA. It is Hector's wish. And Hector will persuade Priam.

DEMOKOS. That is as we shall see. And what's more I have a surprise in store for Hector.

POLYXENE. Where do the Gates lead to, mama?

ABNEOS. To war, my child. When they are open it means there is war.

DEMOKOS. My friends...

HECUBA. War or not, it's an absurd symbolism, your Gateway, and those two great doors always left open look very unsightly. All the dogs stop there.

MATHEMATICIAN. This is no domestic matter. It concerns war and the Gods.

HECUBA. Which is just as I said: the Gods never remember to shut their doors.

POLYXENE. I remember to shut them very well, don't I, mama?

PARIS. And you even include your fingers in them, don't you, my pretty one?

DEMOKOS. May I ask for a moment of silence, Paris? Abneos, and you, Mathematician, and you, my friends: I asked you to meet here earlier than the time fixed for the ceremony so that we could hold our first council. And it promises well that this first council of war should be, not a council of generals, but a council of intellectuals. For it isn't enough in war-time to have our soldiers drilled, well-armed, and spectacular. It is absolutely necessary to bring their enthusiasm up to fever pitch. The physical intoxication which their officers will get from them by a generous allowance of cheap wine supplied at the right moment, will still be ineffective against the Greeks, unless it is reinforced by the spiritual and moral intoxication which the poets can pour into them. If we are too old to fight we can at least make sure that the fighting is savage. I see you have something to say on the subject, Abneos.

ABNEOS. Yes. We must make a war-song.

DEMOKOS. Very proper. A war requires a war-song.

PARIS. We have done without one up to now.

HECUBA. War itself sings quite loud enough.

ABNEOS. We have done without one because up to now we were fighting only barbarians. It was nothing more than a hunt, and the hunting horn was all we needed. But now with the Greeks we're entering a different region of war altogether.

DEMOKOS. Exactly so, Abneos. The Greeks don't fight with everybody.

PARIS. We already have a national anthem.

ABNEOS. Yes. But it's a song of peace.

PARIS. If you sing a song of peace with enough gestures and grimaces it becomes a war song. What are the words we have already?

ABNEOS. You know them perfectly well. There's no spirit in them:

'We cut and bind the harvest,
We tread the vineyard's blood.'

DEMOKOS. At the very most it's a war-song against farm produce. You won't frighten the Spartans by threatening a wheatfield.

PARIS. Sing it with a spear in your hand, and a dead body at your feet, you will be surprised.

HECUBA. It includes the word 'blood', there's always that.

PARIS. The word 'harvest' as well. War rather approves of the word 'harvest'.

ABNEOS. Why discuss it, when Demokos can invent an entirely new one in a couple of hours.

DEMOKOS. A couple of hours is rather short.

HECUBA. Don't be afraid; it's more than you need for it. And after the song will come the hymn, and after the hymn the cantata. As soon as war is declared it will be impossible to hold the poets back. Rhyme is still the most effective drum.

DEMOKOS. And the most useful, Hecuba; you don't know how wisely you speak. I know war. As long as war isn't with us, and the Gates are shut, each of us is free to insult it and execrate it as we will. But once war comes, its pride and autocracy is huge. You can gain its goodwill only by flattery and adoration. So the mission of those who understand how to speak and write is to compliment and praise war ceaselessly and indiscriminately, otherwise we shut ourselves out from his favour.

PARIS. Have you got an idea for your song already?

DEMOKOS. A marvellous idea, which no one will understand better than you.

War must be tired of the mask we always give it, of Medusa's venomous hair and a Gorgon's lips. I have had the notion to compare War's face with Helen's. It will be enchanted by the comparison.

POLYXENE. What does War look like, mama?

HECUBA. Like your Aunt Helen.

POLYXENE. She is very pretty.

DEMOKOS. Then the discussion is closed. You can expect the war-song. Why are you looking worried, Mathematician?

MATHEMATICIAN. Because there are other things far more urgent than this war-song, far more urgent!

DEMOKOS. You think we should discuss the question of medals, false information, atrocity stories, and so on?

MATHEMATICIAN. I think we should discuss the insulting epithets.

HECUBA. The insulting epithets?

MATHEMATICIAN. Before they hurl their spears the Greek fighting-men hurl insults. You third cousin of a toad, they yell! You son of a sow! — They insult each other, like that! And they have a good reason for it. They know that the body is more vulnerable when self-respect has fled. Soldiers famous for their composure lose it immediately when they're treated as warts or maggots. We Trojans suffer from a grave shortage of insults.

DEMOKOS. The Mathematician is quite right. We are the only race in the world which doesn't insult its enemies before it kills them.

PARIS. You don't think it's enough that the civilians insult the enemy civilians?

MATHEMATICIAN. The armies have to show the same hatred the civilians do. You know what dissemblers armies can be in this way. Leave them to themselves and they spend their time admiring each other. Their front lines very soon become the only ranks of real brotherhood in the world. So naturally, when the theatre of war is so full of mutual consideration, hatred is driven back on to the schools, the salons, the tradespeople. If our soldiers aren't at least equal to the Greeks in the fury of their epithets, they will lose all taste for insults and calumny, and as a natural consequence all taste for war.

DEMOKOS. Suggestion adopted! We will organize a cursing parade this evening.

PARIS. I should have thought they're big enough to find their own curses.

DEMOKOS. What a mistake! Could you, adroit as you are, find your own effective curses?

PARIS. I believe so.

DEMOKOS. You fool yourself. Come and stand face to face with Abneos and begin.

PARIS. Why Abneos?

DEMOKOS. Because he lends himself to this sort of thing, with his corpulence and one thing and another.

ABNEOS. Come on, then, speak up, you piece of pie-crust!

PARIS. No, Abneos doesn't inspire me. I'll start with you, if you don't mind.

DEMOKOS. With me? Certainly. You can let fly at ten paces. There we are. Begin.

HECUBA. Take a good look at him. You will be inspired.

PARIS. You old parasite! You filthy-footed iambic pentameter!

DEMOKOS. Just one second. To avoid any mistake you had better say who it is you're addressing.

PARIS. You're quite right! Demokos! Bloodshot bullock's eye! You fungus-ridden plum-tree!

DEMOKOS. Grammatically reasonable, but very naive. What is there in a fungus-ridden plum-tree to make me rise up foaming at the lips?

HECUBA. He also called you a bloodshot bullock's eye.

DEMOKOS. Bloodshot bullock's eye is better. But you see how you flounder, Paris? Search for something that can strike home to me. What are my faults, in your opinion?

PARIS. You are cowardly; your breath smells, and you have no talent.

DEMOKOS. You're asking for trouble!

PARIS. I was trying to please you.

POLYXENE. Why are we scolding Uncle Demokos, mama?

HECUBA. Because he is a cuckoo, dearest!

DEMOKOS. What did you say, Hecuba?

HECUBA. I was saying that you're a cuckoo, Demokos. If cuckoos had the absurdity, the affectation, the ugliness and the stench of vultures, you would be a cuckoo.

DEMOKOS. Wait a bit, Paris! Your mother is better at this than you are. Model yourselves on her. One hour's exercise each day for each soldier, and Hecuba has given us the superiority in insults which we badly need. As for the war-song, I'm not sure it wouldn't be wiser to entrust that to her as well.

HECUBA. If you like. But if so, I shouldn't say that war looks like Helen.

DEMOKOS. What would you say it looks like, in your opinion?

HECUBA. I will tell you when the Gates have been shut.

(Enter Priam, Hector, Andromache, and presently Helen. During the closing of the Gates, Andromache takes little Polyxene aside and whispers a secret or an errand to her.)

HECTOR. As they nearly are.

DEMOKOS. One moment, Hector!

HECTOR. Aren't we ready to begin the ceremony?

HECUBA. Surely? The hinges are swimming in oil.

HECTOR. Well, then.

PRIAM. What our friends want you to understand, Hector, is that war is ready, too. Consider carefully. They're not mistaken. If you shut these Gates, in a minute we may have to open them again.

HECUBA. Even one minute of peace is worth taking.

HECTOR. Father, you should know what peace means to men who have been fighting for months. It's like solid ground to someone who was drowning or sinking in the quicksands. Do let us get our feet on to a few inches of peace, touch it, if only with the tips of our toes.

PRIAM. Hector: consider: inflicting the word peace on to the city today is as ruthless as though you gave it poison. You will take her off her guard, undermine her iron determination, debase, with the word peace, the accepted values of memory, affection, and hope. The soldiers will rush to buy the bread of peace, to drink the wine of peace, to hold in their arms the woman of peace, and in an hour you will put them back to face a war.

HECTOR. The war will never take place!

(The sound of clamour near the Gates.)

DEMOKOS. No? Listen!

HECTOR. Shut the Gates. This is where we shall meet the Greeks. Conversation will be bitter enough as it is. We must receive them in peace.

PRIAM. My son, are we even sure we should let the Greeks disembark?

HECTOR. Disembark they shall. This meeting with Ulysses is our last chance of peace.

DEMOKOS. Disembark they shall not. Our honour is at stake. We shall be the laughing-stock of the whole world.

HECTOR. And you're taking it upon yourself to recommend to the Senate an action which would certainly mean war?

DEMOKOS. Upon myself? No, not at all. Will you come forward now, Busiris. This is where your mission begins.

HECTOR. Who is this stranger?

DEMOKOS. He is the greatest living expert on the rights of nations. It's a lucky chance he should be passing through Troy today. You can't say that he's a biased witness. He is neutral. Our Senate is willing to abide by his decision, a decision which all other nations will agree with tomorrow.

HECTOR. And what is your opinion?

BUSIRIS. My opinion, Princes, based on my own observation and further enquiry, is that the Greeks, in relation to Troy, are guilty of three breaches of international law. If you give them permission to disembark you will have sacrificed your position as the aggrieved party, and so lost the universal sympathy which would certainly have been yours in the conflict to follow.

HECTOR. Explain yourself.

BUSIRIS. Firstly, they have hoisted their flag hatchway and not masthead. A ship of war, my dear Princes and colleagues, hoists its flag hatchway only when replying to a salute from a boat carrying cattle. Clearly, then, so to salute a city and a city's population is an insult. As it happens, we have a precedent. Last year the Greeks hoisted their flag hatchway when they were entering the port of Orphea. The reply was incisive. Orphea declared war.

HECTOR. And what happened?

BUSIRIS. Orphea was beaten. Orphea no longer exists, nor the Orpheans either.

HECUBA. Perfect.

BUSIRIS. But the annihilation of a people doesn't alter in the least their superior moral position.

HECTOR. Go on.

BUSIRIS. Secondly, on entering your territorial waters the Greeks adopted the formation known as frontal. At the last congress there was some talk of including this formation in the paragraph of measures called defensive-aggressive. I was very happy to be able to get it restored under its proper heading of aggressive-defensive: so without doubt it is now one of the subtle forms of naval manœuvre which is a disguised form of blockade: that is to say, it constitutes a fault of the first degree! We have a precedent for this, as well. Five years ago the Greek navy adopted the frontal formation when they anchored outside Magnesia. Magnesia at once declared war.

HECTOR. Did they win it?

BUSIRIS. They lost it. There's not one stone of Magnesia still standing on another. But my redraft of the paragraph is still standing.

HECUBA. I congratulate you. We were beginning to be anxious.

HECTOR. Go on.

BUSIRIS. The third fault is not so serious. One of the Greek triremes has crept close in to shore without permission. Its captain, Ajax, the most unruly and impossible man among the Greeks, is climbing up towards the city, shouting scandal and provocation, and swearing he would like to kill Paris. But this is a very minor matter, from the international point of view; because it isn't, in any way, a formal breach of the law.

DEMOKOS. You have your information. The situation can only be resolved in one of two ways. To swallow an outrage, or return it. Choose.

HECTOR. Oneah, go and find Ajax. Head him off in this direction.

PARIS. I'm waiting here for him.

HECTOR. You will be good enough to

stay in the palace until I call for you. As for you, Busiris, you must understand that our city has no intention of being insulted by the Greeks.

BUSIRIS. I am not suprised. Troy's incorruptible pride is a legend all the world over.

HECTOR. You are going to provide me, here and now, with an argument which will allow our Senate to say that there has been no fault whatever on the part of our visitors, and with our pride untouched we welcome them here as our guests.

DEMOKOS. What nonsense is this?

BUSIRIS. It isn't in keeping with the facts, Hector.

HECTOR. My dear Busiris, all of us here know there's no better way of exercising the imagination than the study of law. No poet ever interpreted nature as freely as a lawyer interprets truth.

BUSIRIS. The Senate asked me for an opinion: I gave it.

HECTOR. And I ask you for an interpretation. An even subtler point of law.

BUSIRIS. It goes against my conscience.

HECTOR. Your conscience has seen Orphea destroyed, Magnesia destroyed: is it now contemplating, just as light-heartedly, the destruction of Troy?

HECUBA. Yes. He comes from Syracuse.

HECTOR. I do beg of you, Busiris. The lives two countries depend on this. Help us.

BUSIRIS. Truth is the only help I can give you.

HECTOR. Precisely. Discover a truth which saves us. What is the use of justice if it doesn't hammer out a shield for innocent people? Forge us a truth. If you can't, there is one thing I can tell you, quite simply: we shall hold you here for as long as the war goes on.

BUSIRIS. What are you saying?

DEMOKOS. You're abusing your position, Hector!

HECUBA. During war we imprison the rights of man. There seems no reason why we shouldn't imprison a lawyer.

HECTOR. I mean what I say, Busiris. I've never failed yet to keep my promises, or my threats. And now either these guards are going to take you off to prison for a year or two, or else you leave here,

this evening, heaped with gold. With this in mind, you can dispassionately examine the evidence once again.

BUSIRIS. Actually there are certain mitigating arguments.

HECTOR. I was sure there were.

BUSIRIS. In the case of the first fault, for instance, when the cattle-boat salute is given in certain seas where the shores are fertile, it could be interpreted as a salute from the sailors to the farmers.

HECTOR. That would be, in fact, the logical interpretation. The salute of the sea to the earth.

BUSIRIS. Not to mention that the cargo of cattle might easily be a cargo of bulls. In that case the homage would verge on flattery.

HECTOR. There you are. You've understood what I meant. We've arrived at our point of view.

BUSIRIS. And as to the frontal formation, that could as easily mean a promise as a provocation. Women wanting children give themselves not from the side but face to face.

HECTOR. Decisive argument.

BUSIRIS. Then, again, the Greek ships have huge carved nymphs for figureheads. A woman who comes towards you naked and open-armed is not a threat but an offer. An offer to talk, at any rate.

HECTOR. So there we have our honour safe and sound, Demokos. The next step is to make this consulation with Busiris public. Meanwhile, Minos, tell the port authorities to let Ulysses disembark without any loss of time.

DEMOKOS. It's no use even trying to discuss honour with these fighting men. They trade on the fact that you can't treat them as cowards.

MATHEMATICIAN. At any rate, Hector, deliver the Oration for the Dead. That will make you think again.

HECTOR. There's not going to be an Oration for the Dead.

PRIAM. But it's a part of the ceremony. The victorious general must always speak in honour of the dead when the Gates are closed.

HECTOR. An Oration for the Dead of a war is a hypocritical speech in defence of the living, a plea for acquittal. I am not so sure of my innocence.

DEMOKOS. The High Command is not responsible.

HECTOR. Alas, no one is: nor the Gods either. Besides, I have given my oration for the dead already. I gave it to them in their last minute of life, when they were lying on the battlefield, on a little slope of olive-trees, while they could still attend me with what was left of their sight and hearing. I can tell you what I said to them. There was one, disembowelled, already turning up the whites of his eyes, and I said to him: 'It's not so bad, you know, it's not so bad; you will do all right, old man.' And one with his skull split in two; I said: 'You look pretty comical with that broken nose.' And my little equerry, with his left arm hanging useless and his last blood flowing out of him; and I said, 'It's a good thing for you it's the left arm you've splintered.' I am happy I gave them one final swig of life; it was all they asked for; they died drinking it. And there's nothing else to be said. Shut the Gates.

POLYXENE. Did the little equerry die, as well?

HECTOR. Yes, puss-cat. He died. He stretched out his right arm. Someone I couldn't see took him by his perfect hand. And then he died.

DEMOKOS. Our general seems to confuse remarks made to the dying with the Oration for the Dead.

PRIAM. Why must you be so stubborn, Hector?

HECTOR. Very well: you shall have the Oration. (He takes a position below the gates) — You who cannot hear us, who cannot see us, listen to these words, look at those who come to honour you. We have won the war. I know that's of no moment to you. You are the victors, too. But we are victorious, and still live. That's where the difference is between us and why I'm ashamed. I don't know whether, among the crowd of the dead, any privilege is given to men who died victorious. But the living, whether victorious or not, have privilege enough. We have our eyes. We see the sun. We do what all men do under the sun. We eat. We drink. By the

moon, we sleep with our wives. And with yours, now you have gone.

DEMOKOS. You insult the dead!

HECTOR. Do you think so?

DEMOKOS. Either the dead or the living.

HECTOR. There is a distinction.

PRIAM. Come to the peroration, Hector. The Greeks are coming ashore.

HECTOR. I will come to it now . . . Breathe in this incense, touch these offerings, you who can neither smell nor touch. And understand, since I speak to you sincerely, I haven't an equal tenderness and respect for all of you. Though all of you are the dead, with you as with us who survive there are men of courage and men of fear, and you can't make me confuse, for the sake of a ceremony, the dead I admire with those I can't admire. But what I have to say to you today is that war seems to me the most sordid, hypocritical way of making all men equal: and I accept death neither as a punishment or expiation for the coward, nor as a reward to the living. So, whatever you may be, absent, forgotten, purposeless, unresting, without existence, one thing is certain when we close these Gates: we must ask you to forgive us, we, the deserters who survive you, who feel we have stolen two great privileges, I hope the sound of their names will never reach you: the warmth of the living body, and the sky.

POLYXENE. The gates are shutting, mama!

HECUBA. Yes, darling.

POLYXENE. The dead men are pushing them shut.

HECUBA. They help, a little.

POLYXENE. They're helping quite a lot, especially over on the right.

HECTOR. Is it done? Are they shut?

GUARD. Tight as a clam.

HECTOR. We're at peace, father, we're at peace.

HECUBA. We're at peace!

POLYXENE. It feels much better, doesn't it, mama?

HECTOR. Indeed it does.

POLYXENE. I feel much better, anyway. (The sound of the Greeks' music.)

A MESSENGER. The Greeks have landed, Priam!

DEMOKOS. What music! What frightful music! It's the most anti-Trojan music there could possible be! Let's go and give them a welcome to match it.

HECTOR. Receive them royally, bring them here safely. You are responsible.

MATHEMATICIAN. At any rate we ought to counter with some Trojan music. Hector, if we can't be indignant any other way, you can authorize a battle of music.

CROWD. The Greeks! The Greeks!

MESSENGER. Ulysses is on the landing-stage, Priam. Where are we to take him?

PRIAM. Conduct him here. Send word to us in the palace when he comes. Keep with us, Paris. We don't want you too much in evidence just yet.

HECTOR. Let's go and prepare what we shall say to the Greeks, father.

DEMOKOS. You'd better prepare it somewhat better than your speech for the dead; you're likely to meet more contradiction.

(Exeunt Priam and his sons.)

If you are going with them, tell us before you go, Hecuba, what it is you think war looks like.

HECUBA. You insist on knowing?

DEMOKOS. If you've seen what it looks like, tell us.

HECUBA. Like the bottom of a baboon. When the baboon is up in a tree, with its hind end facing us, there is the face of war exactly: scarlet, scaley, glazed, framed in a clotted, filthy wig.

DEMOKOS. So he has two faces: this you describe, and Helen's. *(Exit)*

ANDROMACHE. Here is Helen now. Polyxene, you remember what you have to say to her?

POLYXENE. Yes.

ANDROMACHE. Go to her, then.

(Enter Helen.)

HELEN. Do you want to talk to me, darling?

POLYXENE. Yes, Aunt Helen.

HELEN. It must be important, you're so very tense.

POLYXENE. Yes, Aunt Helen.

HELEN. Is it something you can't tell me without standing so stiffly?

POLYXENE. No, Aunt Helen.

HELEN. Do tell me, then; you make me feel terrible when you stand there like a little stick.

POLYXENE. Aunt Helen, if you love anyone, please go away.

HELEN. Why should I go away, darling?

POLYXENE. Because of the war.

HELEN. Do you know about war already, then?

POLYXENE. I don't exactly know about it. I think it means we have to die.

HELEN. And do you know what dying is?

POLYXENE. I don't exactly. I think it means we don't feel anything any more.

HELEN. What exactly was it that Andromache told you to ask me?

POLYXENE. If you love us at all, please to go away.

HELEN. That doesn't seem to me very logical. If you loved someone you wouldn't leave them?

POLYXENE. Oh, no! Never!

HELEN. Which would you rather do: go right away from Hecuba, or never feel anything any more?

POLYXENE. Oh, never feel anything! I would rather stay, and never feel anything any more.

HELEN. You see how badly you put things to me. If I'm to leave you, I mustn't love you. Would you rather I didn't love you?

POLYXENE. Oh, no! I want you to love me.

HELEN. In other words, you didn't know what you were saying, did you?

POLYXENE. No.

HECUBA *(offstage)*. Polyxene!

(Enter Hecuba.)

Are you deaf, Polyxene? Why did you shut your eyes when you saw me? Are you playing at being a statue? Come with me.

HELEN. She is teaching herself not to feel anything. But she has no gift for it.

HECUBA. Can you hear me, Polyxene? And see me?

POLYXENE. Yes, I can hear you. I can see you, too.

HECUBA. Why are you crying? Don't you like to see and hear me?

POLYXENE. If I do, you will go away.

HECUBA. I think it would be better, Helen, if you left Polyxene alone. She is too sensitive to touch the insensitive, even through your beautiful dress and your beautiful voice.

HELEN. I quite agree with you. I advise Andromache to carry her own messages. Kiss me, Polyxene. I shall go away this evening, since that is what you would like.

POLYXENE. Don't go! Don't go!

HELEN. Bravo! You are quite loosened up again!

HECUBA. Are you coming with us, Andromache?

ANDROMACHE. No: I shall wait here. *(Exeunt Hecuba and Polyxene.)*

HELEN. You want an explanation?

ANDROMACHE. I believe it's necessary.

HELEN. Listen to the way they're shouting and arguing down below. Isn't that enough? Do you and I have to have explanations, since I'm leaving here anyway?

ANDROMACHE. Whether you go or stay isn't any longer the problem.

HELEN. Tell Hector that. You will make his day easier.

ANDROMACHE. Yes, Hector is obsessed by the thought of getting you away. All men are the same. They take no notice of the stag in the thicket because they're already chasing the hare. Perhaps men can hunt like that. But not the gods.

HELEN. If you have discovered what the gods are after in this affair, I congratulate you.

ANDROMACHE. I don't know that the gods are after anything. But there is something the universe is after. Ever since this morning, it seems to me, everything has begged and cried out for it, men, animals, even the leaves on the trees and my own child, not yet born.

HELEN. Cried out for what?

ANDROMACHE. That you should love Paris.

HELEN. If they know so certainly that I don't love Paris, they are better informed than I am.

ANDROMACHE. But you don't love him! You could love him, perhaps. But, at present, you are both living in a misunderstanding.

HELEN. I live with him happily, amicably, in complete agreement. We understand each other so well, I don't really see how this can be called a misunderstanding.

ANDROMACHE. Agreement is never reached in love. The life of a wife and husband who love each other is never at rest. Whether the marriage is true or false, the marriage portion is the same: elemental discord. Hector is my absolute opposite. He shares none of my tastes. We pass our days either getting the better of one another, or sacrificing ourselves. There is no tranquillity for lovers.

HELEN. And if I went pale whenever I saw Paris: and my eyes filled with tears, and the palms of my hands were moist, you think Menelaus would be delighted, and the Greeks pleased and quite satisfied?

ANDROMACHE. It wouldn't much matter then what the Greeks tought.

HELEN. And the war would never happen?

ANDROMACHE. Perhaps, indeed, it would never happen. Perhaps if you loved him, love would call to the rescue one of its own equals: generosity or intelligence. No one, not even destiny itself, attacks devotion lightheartedly. And even if the war did happen, why, I think even then ———

HELEN. Then it wouldn't be the same war, I suppose.

ANDROMACHE. Oh, no, Helen! You know what this struggle is going to be. Fate would never take so many precautions for an ordinary quarrel. It means to build the future on this war, the future of our countries and our peoples, and our ways of thinking. It won't be so bad if our thoughts and our future are built on the story of a man and a woman who truly love each other. But fate hasn't noticed yet that you are lovers only on paper, officially. To think that we're going to suffer and die only for a pair of theoretical lovers: and the splendour and calamity of the age to come will be founded on a trivial adventure between two people who don't love each other—that's what is so horrible.

HELEN. If everybody thinks that we love each other, it comes to the same thing.

ANDROMACHE. They don't think so. But no one will admit that he doesn't.

Everyone, when there's war in the air, learns to live in a new element: falsehood. Everybody lies. Our old men don't worship beauty: they worship themselves, they worship ugliness. And this indignation the Greeks are showing us is a lie. God knows, they're amused enough at what you can do with Paris! Their boats, in the bay, with their patriotic anthems and their streamers flying, are a falsehood of the sea. And Hector's life and my son's life, too, are going to be played out in hypocrisy and pretence.

HELEN. So?

ANDROMACHE. I beg of you, Helen. You see how I'm pressed against you as though I were begging you to love me. Love Paris! Or tell me that I'm mistaken! Tell me that you would kill yourself if Paris were to die! Tell me that you would even let yourself be disfigured if it would keep him alive. Then the war will only be a scourge, not an injustice.

HELEN. You are being very difficult. I don't think my way of loving is as bad as all that. Certainly I don't get upset and ill when Paris leaves me to play bowls or go fishing for eels. But I do feel commanded by him, magnetically attracted. Magnetism is a kind of love, as much as devotion. And it's an old and fruitful passion in its own way, as desperate devotion and passionate weeping are in theirs. I'm as content in this love as a star in a constellation. It's my own centre of gravity; I shine there; it's the way I breathe, and the way I take life in my arms. And it's easy to see what sons this love can produce: tall, clear-cut boys, of great distinction, with fine fingers and short noses. What will it all become if I fill it with jealousy, with emotion, and anxiety? The world is nervous enough already: look at yourself!

ANDROMACHE. Fill it with pity, Helen. That's the only help the world needs.

HELEN. There we are; I knew it would come; the word has been said.

ANDROMACHE. What word?

HELEN. The word 'pity'. You must talk to someone else. I'm afraid I'm not very good at pity.

ANDROMACHE. Because you don't know unhappiness.

HELEN. Maybe. It could also be that I think of unhappy people as my equals, I accept them, and I don't think of my health and my position and beauty as any better than their misery. It's a sense of brotherhood I have.

ANDROMACHE. You're blaspheming, Helen.

HELEN. I am sure people pity others to the same extent that they would pity themselves. Unhappiness and ugliness are mirrors they can't bear to look into. I haven't any pity for myself. You will see, if war breaks out. I'll put up with hunger and pain better than you will. And insults, too. Do you think I don't hear what the Trojan women say when I'm going past them? They treat me like a slut. They say that the morning light shows me up for what they think me. It may be true, or it may not be. It doesn't matter to me, one way or the other.

ANDROMACHE. Stop, Helen!

HELEN. And of course I can see, in what your husband called the coloured picture-book in my head, pictures of Helen grown old, flabby, toothless, sitting hunched-up in the kitchen, sucking sweets. I can see the white enamel I've plastered over my wrinkles, and the bright colours the sweets are, very clearly. But it leaves me completely indifferent.

ANDROMACHE. I am lost.

HELEN. Why? If you're content with one perfect couple to make the war acceptable, there is always you and Hector, Andromache.

(Enter Ajax, then Hector.)

AJAX. Where is he? Where's he hiding himself? A coward! A typical Trojan!

HECTOR. Who are you looking for?

AJAX. I'm looking for Paris.

HECTOR. I am his brother.

AJAX. Beautiful family! I am Ajax! What's your name?

HECTOR. My name's Hector.

AJAX. It ought to be pimp!

HECTOR. I see that Greece has sent over her diplomats. What do you want?

AJAX. War.

HECTOR. Not a hope. Why do you want it?

AJAX. Your brother carried off Helen.

HECTOR. I am told she was willing.

AJAX. A Greek woman can do what

she likes. She doesn't have to ask permission from you. He carried her off. It's a reason for war.

HECTOR. We can offer our apologies.

AJAX. What's a Trojan apology? We're not leaving here without your declaration of war.

HECTOR. Declare it yourselves.

AJAX. All right, we will. As from this evening.

HECTOR. That's a lie. You won't declare war. There isn't an island in the archipelego that will back you if we aren't in any way responsible. And we don't intend to be.

AJAX. Will you declare it yourself, personally, if I call you a coward?

HECTOR. That is a name I accept.

AJAX. I've never known such unmilitary reaction! Suppose I tell you what the people of Greece thinks of Troy, that Troy is a cess-pit of vice and stupidity?

HECTOR. Troy is obstinate. You won't get your war.

AJAX. Suppose I spit on her?

HECTOR. Spit.

AJAX. Suppose I strike you, you, one of her princes?

HECTOR. Try it.

AJAX. Suppose I slap your face, you disgusting example of Troy's conceit and her spurious honour?

HECTOR. Strike.

AJAX (*striking him*). There. If this lady's your wife she must be proud of you.

HECTOR. I know her. She is proud. (*Enter Demokos.*)

DEMOKOS. What's all the noise about? What does this drunkard want, Hector?

HECTOR. He has got what he wants.

DEMOKOS. What is going on, Andromache?

ANDROMACHE. Nothing.

AJAX. Two times nothing. A Greek hits Hector, and Hector puts up with it.

DEMOKOS. Is this true, Hector?

HECTOR. Completely false, isn't it, Helen?

HELEN. The Greeks are great liars. Greek men, I mean.

AJAX. Is it natural for him to have one cheek redder than the other?

HECTOR. Yes. I am healthier on that side.

DEMOKOS. Tell the truth, Hector. Has he dared to raise his hand against you?

HECTOR. That is my concern.

DEMOKOS. It's the concern of war. You are the figurehead of Troy.

HECTOR. Exactly. No one is going to slap a figurehead.

DEMOKOS. Who are you, you brute? I am Demokos, second son of Achichaos!

AJAX. The second son of Achichaos? How do you do? Tell me: is it as serious to slap a second son of Achichaos as to strike Hector?

DEMOKOS. Quite as serious, you drunk. I am the head of the Senate. If you want war, war to the death, you have only to try.

AJAX. All right. I'll try. (*He slaps Demokos*)

DEMOKOS. Trojans! Soldiers! To the rescue!

HECTOR. Be quiet, Demokos!

DEMOKOS. To arms! Troy's been insulted! Vengeance!

HECTOR. Be quiet, I tell you.

DEMOKOS. I *will* shout! I'll rouse the city!

HECTOR. Be quiet! If you won't, I shall hit you, too!

DEMOKOS. Priam! Anchises! Come and see the shame of Troy burning on Hector's face!

(*Hector strikes Demokos. Ajax laughs. During the scene, Priam and his lords group themselves ready to receive Ulysses.*)

PRIAM. What are you shouting for, Demokos?

DEMOKOS. I have been struck.

AJAX. Go and complain to Achichaos!

PRIAM. Who struck you?

DEMOKOS. Hector! Ajax! Ajax! Hector!

PARIS. What is he talking about? He's mad!

HECTOR. Nobody struck him, did they, Helen?

HELEN. I was watching most carefully, and I didn't notice anything.

AJAX. Both his cheeks are the same colour.

PARIS. Poets often get upset for no reason. It's what they call their inspiration.

We shall get a new national anthem out of it.

DEMOKOS. You will pay for this, Hector.

VOICES. Ulysses! Here is Ulysses!

(Ajax goes amicably to Hector.)

AJAX. Well done. Plenty of pluck. Noble adversary. A beautiful hit.

HECTOR. I did my best.

AJAX. Excellent method, too. Straight elbow. The wrist on an angle. Safe position for the carpus and metacarpus. Your slap must be stronger than mine is.

HECTOR. I doubt it.

AJAX. You must be able to throw a javelin magnificently with this iron fore-arm and this shoulder-bone for a pivot.

HECTOR. Eighty yards.

AJAX. My deepest respect! My dear Hector, forgive me. I withdraw my threats, I take back my slap. We have enemies in common, in the sons of Achichaos. I won't fight with anybody who shares with me an enmity for the sons of Achichaos. Not another mention of war. I don't know what Ulysses has got in mind, but count on me to arrange the whole thing.

(He goes towards Ulysses and comes back with him.)

ANDROMACHE. I love you, Hector.

HECTOR *(showing his cheek)*. Yes; but don't kiss me just yet.

ANDROMACHE. You have won this round, as well. Be confident.

HECTOR. I win every round. But still with each victory the prize escapes me.

ULYSSES. Priam and Hector?

PRIAM. Yes. And behind us, Troy, and the suburbs of Troy, and the land of Troy, and the Hellespont.

ULYSSES. I am Ulysses.

PRIAM. This is Anchises.

ULYSSES. There are many people here for a diplomatic conversation.

PRIAM. And here is Helen.

ULYSSES. Good morning, my queen.

HELEN. I've grown younger here, Ulysses. I've become a princess again.

PRIAM. We are ready to listen to you.

AJAX. Ulysses, you speak to Priam. I will speak to Hector.

ULYSSES. Priam, we have come to take Helen home again.

AJAX. You do understand, don't you, Hector? We can't have things happening like this.

ULYSSES. Greece and Menelaus cry out for vengeance.

AJAX. If deceived husbands can't cry out for vengeance, what can they do?

ULYSSES. Deliver Helen over to us within an hour. Otherwise it means war.

HECTOR. But if we give Helen back to you give us your assurance there will be peace.

AJAX. Utter tranquillity.

HECTOR. If she goes on board within an hour, the matter is closed.

AJAX. And all is forgotten.

HECTOR. I think there's no doubt we can come to an understanding, can we not, Helen?

HELEN. Yes, no doubt.

ULYSSES. You don't mean to say that Helen is being given back to us?

HECTOR. Exactly that. She is ready.

AJAX. What about her baggage? She is sure to have more to take back than when she came.

HECTOR. We return her to you, bag and baggage, and you guarantee peace. No reprisals, no vengeance!

AJAX. A woman is lost, a woman is found, and we're back where we were. Perfect! Isn't it, Ulysses?

ULYSSES. Just wait a moment. I guarantee nothing. Before we say there are going to be no reprisals we have to be sure there has been no cause for reprisals. We have to make sure that Menelaus will find Helen exactly as she was when she was taken from him.

HECTOR. How is he going to discover any difference?

ULYSSES. A husband is very perceptive when a world-wide scandal has put him on his guard. Paris will have had to have respected Helen. And if that isn't so . . .

CROWD. Oh, no! It isn't so!

ONE VOICE. Not exactly!

HECTOR. And if it is so?

ULYSSES. Where is this leading us, Hector?

HECTOR. Paris has not touched Helen. They have both taken me into their confidence.

ULYSSES. What is this absurd story?

HECTOR. The true story, isn't it, Helen?

HELEN. Why does it seem to you so extraordinary?

A VOICE. It's terrible! It puts us to shame!

HECTOR. Why do you have to smile, Ulysses? Do you see the slightest indication in Helen that she has failed in her duty?

ULYSSES. I'm not looking for one. Water leaves less mark on a duck's back than dishonour does on a woman.

PARIS. You're speaking to a queen.

ULYSSES. Present queens excepted, naturally. So, Paris, you have carried off this queen, carried her off naked; and I imagine that you didn't go into the water wearing all your armour; and yet you weren't seized by any taste or desire for her?

PARIS. A naked queen is dressed in her dignity.

HELEN. She has only to remember to keep it on.

ULYSSES. How long did the voyage last? I took three days with my ships, which are faster than yours.

VOICES. What are these intolerable insults to the Trojan navy?

A VOICE. Your winds are faster! Not your ships!

ULYSSES. Let us say three days, if you like. Where was the queen during those three days?

PARIS. Lying down on the deck.

ULYSSES. And Paris was where? In the crow's nest?

HELEN. Lying beside me.

ULYSSES. Was he reading as he lay beside you? Or fishing for goldfish?

HELEN. Sometimes he fanned me.

ULYSSES. Without ever touching you?

HELEN. One day, the second day, I think it was, he kissed my hand.

ULYSSES. Your hand! I see. An outbreak of the animal in him.

HELEN. I thought it was more dignified to take no notice.

ULYSSES. The rolling of the ship didn't throw you towards each other? I don't think it's an insult to the Trojan navy to suggest that its ships roll?

A VOICE. They roll much less than the Greek ships pitch!

AJAX. Pitch? Our Greek ships? If they seem to be pitching it's because of their high prows and their scooped-out sterns!

A VOICE. Oh, yes! The arrogant face and the flat behind, that's Greek all right.

ULYSSES. And what about the three nights you were sailing? The stars appeared and vanished again three times over the pair of you. Do you remember nothing of those three nights?

HELEN. I don't know. Oh, yes! I'd forgotten. I learnt a lot more about the stars.

ULYSSES. While you were asleep, perhaps, he might have taken you . . .

HELEN. A mosquito can wake me.

HECTOR. They will both swear to you, if you like, by our goddess Aphrodite.

ULYSSES. We can do without that. I know what Aphrodite is. Her favourite oath is a perjury.—It's a curious story you're telling me; and it will certainly destroy the idea that the rest of the Archipelego has always had of the Trojans.

PARIS. Why, what do they think of us in the Archipelego?

ULYSSES. You're thought of as less accomplished at trading than we are, but handsome and irresistible. Go on with your story, Paris. It's an interesting contribution to the study of human behaviour. What good reason could you have possibly had for respecting Helen when you had her at your mercy?

PARIS. I . . . I loved her.

HELEN. If you don't know what love is, Ulysses, I shouldn't venture on the subject.

ULYSSES. You must admit, Helen, you would never have followed him if you had known the Trojans were impotent.

VOICES. Shame! Muzzle him! Bring your women here, and you'll soon see! And your grandmother!

ULYSSES. I expressed myself badly. I meant that Paris, the handsome Paris, is impotent.

A VOICE. Why don't you say something, Paris? Are you going to make us the laughing-stock of the world?

PARIS. Hector, you can see, this is a most unpleasant situation for me!

HECTOR. You have to put up with it only a few minutes longer. Goodbye, Helen. And I hope your virtue will become as proverbial as your frailty might have done.

HELEN. That doesn't worry me. The centuries always give us the recognition we deserve.

ULYSSES. Paris the impotent, that's a very good surname! If you care to, Helen, you can kiss him for once.

PARIS. Hector!

FIRST TOPMAN. Are you going to tolerate this farce, commander?

HECTOR. Be quiet! I am in charge here!

TOPMAN. And a rotten job you make of it! We've stood quite enough. We'll tell you, we, Paris's own seamen, we'll tell you what he did with your queen!

VOICES. Bravo! Tell him!

TOPMAN. He's sacrificing himself on his brother's orders. I was an officer on board his ship. I saw everything.

HECTOR. You were quite wrong.

TOPMAN. Do you think a Trojan sailor doesn't know what he sees? I can tell the sex of a seagull thirty yards off. Come over here, Olpides. Olpides was up in the crow's nest. He saw everything from on top. I was standing on the stairs in the hatchway. My head was exactly on a level with them, like a cat on the end of a bed. Shall I tell him, Trojans?

HECTOR. Silence!

VOICES. Tell him! Go on and tell him!

TOPMAN. And they hadn't been on board more than two minutes, wasn't that true, Olpides?

OLPIDES. Only time enough for the queen to dry herself, being just come up out of the water, and to comb the parting into her hair again. I could see her parting, from her forehead over to the nape of her neck, from where I was.

TOPMAN. And he sent us all down into the hold, except the two of us who he couldn't see.

OLPIDES. And without a pilot, the ship drifted due north. There was no wind, and yet the sails were bellied out full.

TOPMAN. And when I looked out from where I was hiding, what I should have seen was the outline of one body, but what I did see was in the shape of two, like a wheaten loaf and rye bread, baking in the oven together.

OLPIDES. But from up where I was, I more often saw one body than two, but sometimes it was white, and sometimes it was golden brown.

TOPMAN. So much for impotence! And as for respectful, inexpressive love, and unspoken affection, you tell him, Olpides, what you heard from your ledge up there! Women's voices carry upwards, men's voice stay on the ground. I shall tell you what Paris said.

OLPIDES. She called him her ladybird, her little ewe-lamb.

TOPMAN. And he called her his lion, his panther. They reversed the sexes. Because they were being so affectionate. It's not unusual.

OLPIDES. . And then she said: 'You are my darling oak-tree, I put my arms round you as if you were an oak-tree.' When you're at sea you think about trees, I suppose.

TOPMAN. And he called her his birch-tree: 'My trembling silver birch-tree!' I remember the word birch-tree very well. It's a Russian tree.

OLPIDES. And I had to stay up in the crow's nest all night. You don't half get thirsty up there, and hungry, and everything else.

TOPMAN. And when at last they got up from the deck to go to bed they swayed on their feet. And that's how your wife Penelope would have got on with Trojan impotence.

VOICES. Bravo! Bravo!

A WOMAN'S VOICE. All praise to Paris.

A JOVIAL MAN. Render to Paris what belongs to Paris!

HECTOR. This is a pack of lies, isn't it, Helen?

ULYSSES. Helen is listening enraptured.

HELEN. I forgot they were talking about me. They sound so wonderfully convincing.

ULYSSES. Do you dare to say they are lying, Paris?

PARIS. In some of the particulars, yes, I think they are.

TOPMAN. We're not lying, either in the general or the particular. Are we, Olpides? Do you deny the expressions of love you used? Do you deny the word panther?

PARIS. Not especially the word panther.

TOPMAN. Well, birch-tree, then? I see. It's the phrase 'trembling silver birch-tree' that embarrasses you. Well, like it or not, you used it. I swear you used it, and anyway what is there to blush about in the word 'birch-tree'? I have seen these silver birch-trees trembling against the snow in wintertime, by the shores of the Caspian, with their rings of black bark apparently separated by rings of space, so that you wondered what was carrying the branches. And I've seen them at the height of summer, beside the canal at Astrakhan, with their white rings like fresh mushrooms. And the leaves talked and made signs to me. To see them quivering, gold above and silver underneath, it makes your heart melt! I could have wept like a woman, isn't that true, Olpides? That's how I feel about the birch-tree.

CROWD. Bravo! Bravo!

ANOTHER SAILOR. And it wasn't only the topman and Olpides who saw them, Priam. The crew came wriggling up through the hatches and peering under the handrails. The whole ship was one great spy-glass.

THIRD SAILOR. Spying out love.

ULYSSES. There you have it, Hector!

*HECTOR. Be quiet, the lot of you.

TOPMAN. Well, keep this quiet, if you can!

(Iris appears in the sky.)

PEOPLE. Iris! Iris!

PARIS. Has Aphrodite sent you?

IRIS. Yes, Aphrodite sent me, and told me that I should say to you that love is the world's chief law. Whatever strengthens love becomes in itself sacred, even falsehood, avarice, or luxury. She takes all lovers under her protection, from the king to the goat-herd. And she forbids both of you, Hector and Ulysses, to separate Paris from Helen. Or else there will be war.

PARIS AND THE OLD MEN. Thank you, Iris.

HECTOR. Is there any message from Pallas Athene?

IRIS. Yes; Pallas Athene told me that I should say to you that reason is the chief law of the world. All who are lovers, she wishes me to say, are out of their minds. She would like you to tell her quite frankly what is more ridiculous than the mating of cooks with hens or flies. And she orders both of you, Hector, and Ulysses, to separate Helen from this Paris of the curly hair. Or else there will be war.

HECTOR AND THE WOMEN. Thank you, Iris!

PRIAM. Oh, my son, it isn't Aphrodite nor Pallas Athene who rules the world. What is it Zeus commands us to do in this time of uncertainty?

IRIS. Zeus, the master of the Gods, told me that I should say to you that those who see in the world nothing but love are as foolish as those who cannot see it at all. It is wise, Zeus, master of the Gods informs you, it is wise sometimes to make love, and at other times not to make love. The decision he gives to Hector and Ulysses, is to separate Helen and Paris without separating them. He orders all the rest of you to go away and leave the negotiators to face each other. And let them so arrange matters that there will be no war. Or else—he swears to you: he swears there will be war.

(Exit Iris)

HECTOR. At your service, Ulysses!

ULYSSES. At your service.

(All withdraw. A great rainbow is seen in the sky.)

HELEN. How very like Iris to leave her scarf behind.

HECTOR. Now we come to the real tussle, Ulysses.

ULYSSES. Yes: out of which either war or peace is going to come.

HECTOR. Will war come of it?

ULYSSES. We shall know in five minutes time.

*Omitted from the Broadway production, but used in the stage version at the Apollo Theatre in London. At this point in the Broadway production Hector requested the populace to leave Ulysses and him alone together.

HECTOR. If it's to be a battle of words, my chances are small.

ULYSSES. I believe it will be more a battle of weight. It's as though we were one on each side of a pair of scales. How we weigh in the balance will be what counts in the end.

HECTOR. How we weigh in the balance? And what is my weight, Ulysses? My weight is a young man, a young woman, an unborn child. Joy of life, belief in life, a response to whatever's natural and good.

ULYSSES. And my weight is the mature man, the wife thirty-five years old, the son whose height I measure each month with notches against the doorpost of the palace. My weight is the pleasures of living, and a mistrust of life.

HECTOR. Hunting, courage, loyalty, love.

ULYSSES. Circumspection in the presence of the gods, of men, and everything else.

HECTOR. The Phrygian oak-tree, all the leafy, thick-set oak-trees that grow on our hills with our curly-coated oxen.

ULYSSES. The power and wisdom of the olive-tree.

HECTOR. I weigh the hawk, I look straight into the sun.

ULYSSES. I weigh the owl.

HECTOR. I weigh the whole race of humble peasants, hard-working craftsmen, thousands of ploughs and looms, forges and anvils . . . Why is it, when I put all these in the scale in front of you, all at once they seem to me to weigh so light?

ULYSSES. I am the weight of this incorruptible, unpitying air of these coasts and islands.

HECTOR. Why go on? The scales have tipped.

ULYSSES. To my side? Yes, I think so.

HECTOR. And you want war?

ULYSSES. I don't want it. But I'm less sure whether war may not want us.

HECTOR. Our peoples have brought us together to prevent it. Our meeting itself shows that there is still some hope.

ULYSSES. You are young, Hector! It's usual on the eve of every war, for the two leaders of the peoples concerned to meet privately at some innocent village, on a terrace in a garden overlooking a lake. And they decide together that war is the world's worst scourge, and as they watch the rippling reflections in the water, with magnolia petals dropping on to their shoulders, they are both of them peace-loving, modest and friendly. They study one another. They look into each other's eyes. And, warmed by the sun and mellowed by the claret, they can't find anything in the other man's face to justify hatred, nothing, indeed, which doesn't inspire human affection, nothing incompatible in their languages any more, or in their particular way of scratching the nose or drinking wine. They really are exuding peace, and the world's desire for peace. And when their meeting is over, they shake hands in a most sincere brotherly fashion, and turn to smile and wave as they drive away. And the next day war breaks out. And so it is with us both at this moment. Our peoples, who have drawn aside, saying nothing while we have this interview, are not expecting us to win a victory over the inevitable. They have merely given us full powers, isolated here together, to stand above the catastrophe and taste the essential brotherhood of enemies. Taste it. It's a rare dish. Savour it. But that is all. One of the privileges of the great is to witness catastrophes from a terrace.

HECTOR. Do you think this is a conversation between enemies we are having?

ULYSSES. I should say a duet before the full orchestra. Because we have been created sensible and courteous, we can talk to each other, an hour or so before the war, in the way we shall talk to each other long after it's over, like old antagonists. We are merely having our reconciliation before the struggle instead of after it. That may be unwise. If one day one of us should have to kill the other, it might be as well if it wasn't a friend's face we recognized as the body dropped to the ground. But, as the universe well knows, we are going to fight each other.

HECTOR. The universe might be mistaken. One way to recognize error is the fact that it's universal.

ULYSSES. Let's hope so. But when destiny has brought up two nations, as for years it has brought up yours and mine, to a future of similar invention and authority, and given to each a different scale of values (as you and I saw just now, when we weighed pleasure against pleasure, conscience against conscience, even nature itself against nature): when the nation's architects and poets and painters have created for them opposing kingdoms of sound, and form, and subtlety, when we have a Trojan tile roof, a Theban arch, Phrygian red, Greek blue: the universe knows that destiny wasn't preparing alternative ways for civilization to flower. It was contriving the dance of death, letting loose the brutality and human folly which is all that the gods are really contented by. It's a mean way to contrive things, I agree. But we are Heads of State, you and I; we can say this between ourselves: it is Destiny's way of contriving things, inevitably.

HECTOR. And this time it has chosen to match Greece with Troy?

ULYSSES. This morning I was still in doubt. As soon as I stepped on to your landing stage I was certain of it.

HECTOR. You mean you felt yourself on enemy soil?

ULYSSES. Why will you always harp on the word enemy? Born enemies don't fight. Nations you would say were designed to go to war against each other—by their skins, their language, their smell: always jealous of each other, always hating each other—they're not the ones who fight. You will find the real antagonists in nations fate has groomed and made ready for the same war.

HECTOR. And you think we have been made ready for the Greek war?

ULYSSES. To an astonishing extent. Just as nature, when she foresees a struggle between two kinds of insects, equips them with weaknesses and weapons which correspond, so we, living well apart, unknown to ourselves, not even suspecting it, have both been gradually raised up to the level where war begins. All our weapons and habits correspond with each other and balance against each other like the beams of a gable. No other women in the world excite less brutality in us, or less desire, than your wives and daughters do; they give us a joy and an anguish of

heart which is a sure sign of impending war between us. Doom has transfigured everything here with the colour of storm: your grave buildings shaking with shadow and fire, the neighing horses, figures disappearing into the dark of a colonnade: the future has never impressed me before with such startling clarity. There is nothing to be done. You're already living in the light of the Greek war.

HECTOR. And do the rest of the Greeks think this?

ULYSSES. What they think is no more reassuring. The rest of the Greeks think Troy is wealthy, her warehouses bulging, her soil prolific. They think that they, on the other hand, are living cramped on a rock. And your golden temples and golden wheatfields flashed from your promontories a signal our ships will never forget. It isn't very wise to have such golden gods and vegetables.

HECTOR. This is more like the truth, at last. Greece has chosen Troy for her prey. Then why a declaration of war? It would have been simpler to have taken Troy by surprise when I was away with the army. You would have had her without striking a blow.

ULYSSES. There's a kind of permission for war which can be given only by the world's mood and atmosphere, the feel of its pulse. It would have been madness to undertake a war without that permission. We didn't have it.

HECTOR. But you have it now.

ULYSSES. I think we do.

HECTOR. But why against us? Troy is famous for her arts, her justice, her humanity.

ULYSSES. A nation doesn't put itself at odds with its destiny by its crimes, but by its faults. Its army may be strong, its treasury well filled, its poets at the height of inspiration. But one day, why it is no one knows, because of some simple event, such as the citizens wantonly cutting down the trees, or their prince wickedly making off with a woman, or the children getting out of hand, the nation is suddenly lost. Nations, like men, die by imperceptible disorders. We recognize a doomed people by the way they sneeze or pare their nails.

There's no doubt you carried off Helen badly.

HECTOR. What fairness of proportion can you see between the rape of one woman, and the possible destruction of a whole people, yours or mine, in war?

ULYSSES. We are speaking of Helen. You and Paris have made a great mistake about Helen. I've known her fifteen years, and watched her carefully. There's no doubt about it: she is one of the rare creatures destiny puts on the earth for its own personal use. They're apparently quite unimportant. It might be not even a person, but a small town, or a village: a little queen, or a child; but if you lay hands on them, watch out! It's very hard to know how to recognize one of these hostages of fate among all the other people and places. You haven't recognized it. You could have laid hands with impunity on our great admirals or one of our kings. Paris could have let himself go with perfect safety in a Spartan bed, or a Theban bed, with generous returns twenty times over; but he chose the shallowest brain, the hardest heart, the narrowest understanding of sex. And so you are lost.

HECTOR. We are giving Helen back to you.

ULYSSES. The insult to destiny can't be taken back.

HECTOR. What are we discussing, then? I'm beginning to see what is really behind your words. Admit it. You want our wealth! You had Helen carried off to give you an honourable pretext for war! I blush for Greece. She will be responsible and ashamed for the rest of time.

ULYSSES. Responsible and ashamed? Do you think so? The two words hardly agree. Even if we believed we were responsible for the war, all our generation would have to do would be to deny it, and lie, to appease the conscience of future generations. And we shall lie. We'll make that sacrifice.

HECTOR. Ah, well, the die is cast, Ulysses. On with the war! The more I hate it, the more I find growing in me an irresistible need to kill. If you won't help me, it were better you should leave here.

ULYSSES. Understand me, Hector; you have my help. Don't ask me to interpret fate. All I have tried to do is to read the world's hand, in the great lines of desert caravans, the wake of ships, and the track of migrant birds and wandering peoples. Give me your hand. There are lines there, too. We won't search to see if their lesson tells the same story. We'll suppose that these three little lines at the base of Hector's hand contradict the waves, the wings, and the furrows. I am inquisitive by nature, and not easily frightened. I'm quite willing to join issue with fate. I accept your offer of Helen. I will take her back to Menelaus. I've more than enough eloquence to convince a husband of his wife's virtue. I will even persuade Helen to believe it herself. And I'll leave at once, to avoid any chance of disturbance. Once back on my ship perhaps we can take the risk of running war on to the rocks.

HECTOR. Is this part of Ulysses' cunning, or his greatness?

ULYSSES. In this particular instance, I'm using my cunning against destiny, not against you. It's my first attempt, so I deserve some credit for it. I am sincere, Hector. If I wanted war, I should have asked for a ransom more precious to you than Helen. I am going now. But I can't shake off the feeling that the road from here to my ship is a long way.

HECTOR. My guard will escort you.

ULYSSES. As long as the road of a visiting king, when he knows there has been a threat against his life. Where are the assassins hiding? We're lucky if it's not in the heavens themselves. And the distance from here to the corner of the palace is a long way. A long way, taking this first step. Where is it going to carry me among all these perils? Am I going to slip and kill myself? Will part of the cornice fall down on me? It's all new stonework here; at any moment a stone may be dislodged. But courage. Let us go. (*He takes a first step*)

HECTOR. Thank you, Ulysses.

ULYSSES. The first step is safely over. How many more?

HECTOR. Four hundred and sixty.

ULYSSES. Now the second! You know what made me decide to go, Hector?

HECTOR. Yes. Your noble nature.

ULYSSES. Not precisely. Andromache's eyelashes dance as my wife Penelope's do. *(Enter Andromache and Cassandra.)*

HECTOR. Were you there all the time, Andromache?

ANDROMACHE. Let me take your arm. I've no more strength.

HECTOR. Did you hear what we said?

ANDROMACHE. Yes. I am broken.

HECTOR. You see, we needn't despair.

ANDROMACHE. We needn't despair for ourselves, perhaps. But for the world, yes. That man is terrible. All the unhappiness of the world is in me.

HECTOR. A moment or two more, and Ulysses will be on board. You see how fast he is travelling. You can follow his progress from here. There he is, on a level with the fountains. What are you doing?

ANDROMACHE. I haven't the strength any longer to hear any more. I am covering up my ears. I won't take my hands away until we know what our fate is to be.

HECTOR. Find Helen, Cassandra!

(Ajax enters, more drunk than ever. He sees Andromache. Her back is towards him.)

CASSANDRA. Ulysses is waiting for you down at the harbour, Ajax. Helen will be brought to you there.

AJAX. Helen! To hell with Helen! This is the one I want to get my arms around.

CASSANDRA. Go away, Ajax. That is Hector's wife.

AJAX. Hector's wife! Bravo! I've always liked my friends' wives, my best friends' wives!

CASSANDRE. Ulysses is already half-way there. Hurry.

AJAX. Dont' worry, my dear. She's got her hands over her ears. I can say what I like, she can't hear me. If I touched her, now, if I kissed her, certainly! But words she can't hear, what's the matter with that?

CASSANDRA. Everything is the matter with that. Go away, Ajax!

(Ajax, while Cassandra tries to force him away from Andromache and Hector, slowly raises his javelin.)

AJAX. Do you think so? Then I might as well touch her. Might as well kiss her. But chastely, always chastely, with your best friends' wives! What's the most

chaste part of your wife, Hector, her neck? So much for her neck. Her ear has a pretty little look of chastity to me. So much for her ear. I'll tell you what I've always found the chastest thing about a woman . . . Let me alone, now; let me alone! She can't even hear when I kiss her . . . You're so cursed strong! All right, I'm going, I said I was going. Goodbye.

(He goes. Hector imperceptibly lowers his javelin. At this moment Demokos bursts in.)

DEMOKOS. What's this cowardice? You're giving Helen back? Trojans, to arms! They've betrayed us. Fall in! And your war-song is ready! Listen to your war-song!

HECTOR *(striking him)*. Have that for your war-song!

DEMOKOS *(falling)*. He has killed me!

HECTOR. The war isn't going to happen, Andromache!

(He tries to take Andromache's hands from her ears: she resists, her eyes fixed on Demokos. The curtain which had begun to fall is lifted little by little.)

ABNEOS. They have killed Demokos! Who killed Demokos?

DEMOKOS. Who killed me? Ajax! Kill him!

ABNEOS. Kill Ajax!

HECTOR. He's lying. I am the man who struck him.

DEMOKOS. No. It was Ajax.

ABNEOS. Ajax has killed Demokos. Catch him! Punish him!

HECTOR. I struck you, Demokos, admit it! Admit it, or I'll put an end to you!

DEMOKOS. No, my dear Hector, my good dear Hector. It was Ajax. Kill Ajax!

CASSANDRA. He is dying, just as he lived, croaking like a frog.

ABNEOS. There. They have taken Ajax. There. They have killed him!

HECTOR *(drawing Andromache's hands away from her ears)*. The war will happen. *(The Gates of War slowly open, to show Helen kissing Troilus.)*

CASSANDRA. The Trojan poet is dead. And now the Grecian poet will have his word.

THE CURTAIN FINALLY FALLS

JEAN ANOUILH's

The Lark

In the adaptation by LILLIAN HELLMAN

First presented by Kermit Bloomgarden at the Longacre Theatre, New York, on November 17, 1955, with the following cast:

WARWICK................ Christopher Plummer
CAUCHON...................... Boris Karloff
JOAN .... Julie Harris
JOAN'S FATHER .... Ward Costello
JOAN'S MOTHER.................. Lois Holmes
JOAN'S BROTHER .... John Reese
THE PROMOTOR............... Roger De Koven
THE INQUISITOR............ Joseph Wiseman
BROTHER LADVENU .... Michael Higgins
ROBERT DE BEAUDRICOURT....... Theodore Bikel
AGNES SOREL .... Ann Hillary
THE LITTLE QUEEN................. Joan Elan
THE DAUPHIN................. Paul Roebling

QUEEN YOLANDE .... Rita Vale
MONSIEUR DE LA TREMOUILLE..... Bruce Gordon
ARCHBISHOP OF REIMS......... Richard Nicholls
CAPTAIN LA HIRE............... Bruce Gordon
EXECUTIONER.................. Ralph Roberts
ENGLISH SOLDIER............... Edward Knight
SCRIBE .... Joe Bernard

LADIES OF THE COURT: Ruth Maynard, Elizabeth Lawrence
MONKS and SOLDIERS: Michael Price, Joe Bernard, Michael Conrad, William Lennard, Milton Katselas, Edward Grower

Directed by Joseph Anthony
Light-Setting by Jo Mielziner
Costumes by Alvin Colt
Music composed by Leonard Bernstein

ACT ONE

The music for the play was composed by Leonard Bernstein. It was sung and recorded by a group of seven men and women, without instruments, and with solos by a countertenor.

Before the curtain rises we hear the music of a psalm: the chorus is singing "Exaudi orationem meam, domine." When the curtain rises the music changes to a motet on the words "Qui tollis," from the Mass.

THE SCENE: *Another day in the trial of Joan. The stage is a series of platforms, different in size and in height. The cyclorama is gray in color and projections will be thrown on it to indicate a change of scene. At this moment we see the bars of a jail as they are projected on the cyclorama.*

AT RISE: *Joan is sitting on a stool. Cauchon is standing downstage near the Promoter. The Priests are about to take their places on the Judges' bench. The Inquisitor sits quietly on a stool near the Judges. Joan's family stand upstage; the royal family stand in a group. Village Women cross the stage carrying bundles of faggots and English Soldiers and Guards move into place. Beaudricourt and La Hire appear and take their places upstage. Warwick enters and moves through the crowd.*

———

WARWICK. Everybody here? Good. Let the trial begin at once. The quicker the judgment and the burning, the better for all of us.

CAUCHON. No, sire. The whole story must be played. Domremy, the Voices, Chinon—

WARWICK. I am not here to watch that children's story of the warrior virgin, strong and tender, dressed in white armor, white standard streaming in the wind. If they have time to waste, they can make the statues that way, in days to come. Different politics may well require different symbols. We might even have to make her a monument in London. Don't be shocked at that, sire. The politics of my government may well require it one day, and what's required, Englishmen supply. That's our secret, sire, and a very good one, indeed. (*Moves downstage to address the audience*) Well, let's worry about only this minute of time. I am Beauchamp, Earl of Warwick. I have a dirty virgin witch girl tucked away on a litter of straw in the depths of a prison here in Rouen. The girl has been an expensive nuisance. Your Duke of Burgundy sold her high. You like money in France, Monseigneur, all of you. That's the French secret, sire, and a very good one, indeed. (*He moves toward Joan*) And here she is. The famous Joan the Maid. Obviously, we paid too much. So put her on trial, and burn her, and be finished.

CAUCHON. No, sire. She must play out her whole life first. It's a short life. It won't take very long.

WARWICK (*moves to a stool near Cauchon*). If you insist. Englishmen are patient, and for the purposes of this trial I am all Englishmen. But certainly you don't intend to amuse yourselves by acting out all the old battles? I would find that very disagreeable. Nobody wishes to remember defeat.

CAUCHON. No, sire. We no longer have enough men to act out the old battles. (*Turns toward Joan*) Joan? (*Joan turns to Cauchon*) You may begin.

JOAN. Can I begin any place I want to?

CAUCHON. Yes.

JOAN. Then I'll start at the beginning. It's always nicer at the beginning. I'll begin with my father's house when I was very small. (*Her Mother, her Father and her Brothers appear on stage. She runs to join them*) I live here happy enough with my mother, my brothers, my father. (*We hear the music of a shepherd song and as she leaves the family group she dances her way downstage, clapping her hands to the music*) I'm in the meadow now, watching my sheep. I am not thinking of anything. It is the first time I hear the Voices. I wasn't thinking of anything. I know only that God is good and that He keeps me pure and safe in this little corner of the earth near Domremy. This one little piece of French earth that has not yet been destroyed by the English invaders. (*She makes childish thrusts with an imaginary sword, and stops suddenly as if someone has pulled her back*) Then, suddenly, someone behind me touched my shoulder. I know very well that no one is behind me. I turn and there is a great blinding light in the shadow of me. The Voice is grave and sweet and I was frightened. But I didn't tell anybody. I don't know why. Then came the second time. It was the noon Angelus. A light came over the sun and was stronger than the sun. There he was. I saw him. An angel in a beautiful clean robe that must have been ironed by somebody very careful. He had two great white wings. He didn't tell me his name that day, but later I found out he was Monseigneur the Blessed Saint Michael.

WARWICK (to Cauchon). We know all this. Is it necessary to let her go over that nonsense again?

CAUCHON. It is necessary, sire.

JOAN. Blessed Saint Michael, excuse me, but you are in the wrong village. I am Joan, an ignorant girl, my father's daughter—(Pauses, listens) I can't save France. I don't even know how to ride a horse. (Smiles) To you people the Sire de Beaudricourt is only a country squire, but to us he is master here. He would never take me to the Dauphin, I've never even bowed to him—(Turns to the court) Then the Blessed Saint Michael said Saint Catherine would come along with me, and if that wasn't enough Saint Marguerite would go, too. (She turns back as if to listen to Saint Michael) But when the army captains lose a battle—and they lose a great many—they can go to sleep at night. I could never send men to their death. Forgive me, Blessed Saint Michael, but I must go home now—(But she doesn't move. She is held back by a command) Oh, Blessed Saint Michael, have pity on me. Have pity, Messire. (The chorus sings "Alleluia, Alleluia" to the shepherd's tune. She listens, smiles, move back into the trial. Simply) Well, he didn't. And that was the day I was saddled with France. And my work on the farm.

(The Father who has been moving about near The Mother, suddenly grows angry.)

THE FATHER. What's she up to?

THE MOTHER. She's in the fields.

THE FATHER. So was I, in the fields, but I've come in. It's six o'clock! I ask you, what's she up to?

THE BROTHER. She's dreaming under the lady tree.

THE FATHER. What's anybody doing under a tree at this hour?

THE BROTHER. You ask her. She stares straight ahead. She looks as if she is waiting for something. It isn't the first time.

THE FATHER (angrily to the Brother). Why didn't you tell me? She is waiting for someone, not something. She has a lover.

THE MOTHER (softly). Joan is as clean as a baby.

THE FATHER. All girls are as clean as babies until that night when they aren't any more. I'll find her and if she is with someone, I'll beat her until—

JOAN. I was with someone, but my lover had two great white wings and through the rain he came so close to me that I thought I could touch his wings. He was very worried that day, he told me so. He said the Kingdom of France was in great misery and that God said I could wait no longer. There has been a mistake, I kept saying. The Blessed Saint Michael asked me if God made mistakes. You understand that I couldn't very well say yes?

THE PROMOTOR. Why didn't you make the Sign of the Cross?

JOAN. That question is not written in your charge against me.

THE PROMOTER. Why didn't you say to the archangel, "Vado retro Satanas?"

JOAN. I don't know any Latin, Messire. And that question is not written in your charge against me.

THE PROMOTER. Don't act the fool. The devil understands French. You could have said, "Go away, you filthy, stinking devil."

JOAN (angry). I don't talk that way to the Blessed Saint Michael, Messire!

THE PROMOTER. The Devil told you he was Saint Michael and you were fool enough to believe him.

JOAN. I believed him. He could not have been the Devil. He was so beautiful.

THE PROMOTER. The Devil is beautiful!

JOAN (shocked). Oh, Messire!

CAUCHON (to the Promoter). These theological subtleties are far above the understanding of this poor child. You shock her without reason.

JOAN (to the Promoter). You've lied, Canon! I am not as educated as you are, but I know the Devil *is* ugly and everything that is beautiful is the work of God. I have no doubts. I know.

THE PROMOTER. You know nothing. Evil has a lovely face when a lovely face is needed. In real life the Devil waits for a soft, sweet night of summer. Then he comes on a gentle wind in the form of a beautiful girl with bare breasts—

CAUCHON (sharply). Canon, let us not get mixed up in our private devils. Continue, Joan.

JOAN (to the Promoter). But if the Devil is beautiful, how can we know he is the Devil?

THE PROMOTER. Go to your priest. He will tell you.

JOAN. Can't I recognize him all by myself?

THE PROMOTER. No. Certainly not. No.

JOAN. But only the rich have their priests always with them. The poor can't be running back and forth.

THE PROMOTER (angry). I do not like the way you speak in this court. I warn you again—

CAUCHON. Enough, enough, Messire. Let her speak peacefully with her Voices. There is nothing to reproach her with so far.

JOAN. Then another time it was Saint Marguerite and Saint Catherine who came to me. (She turns to the Promoter) And they, too, were beautiful.

THE PROMOTER. Were they naked?

JOAN (laughs). Oh, Messire! Don't you think our Lord can afford to buy clothing for His Saints?

CAUCHON (to the Promoter). You make us all smile, Messire, with your questions. You are confusing the girl with the suggestion that good and evil is a question of what clothes are worn by what Angels and what Devils. (Turns to Joan) But it is not your place to correct the venerable Canon. You forget who you are and who we are. We are your priests, your masters, and your judges. Beware of your pride, Joan.

JOAN (softly). I know that I am proud. But I am a daughter of God. If He didn't want me to be proud, why did He send me His shining Archangel and His Saints all dressed in light? Why did He promise me that I should conquer all the men I have conquered? Why did He promise me a suit of beautiful white armor, the gift of my king? And a sword? And that I should lead brave soldiers into battle while riding a fine white horse? If He had left me alone, I would never have become proud.

CAUCHON. Take care of your words, Joan. You are accusing our Lord.

JOAN (makes the Sign of the Cross). Oh. God forbid. I say only that His Will be done even if it means making me proud and then damning me for it. That, too, is His Right.

THE PROMOTER (very angry). What are you saying? Could God wish to damn a human soul? How can you listen to her without shuddering, Messires? I see here the germ of a frightful heresy that could tear the Church—

(The Inquisitor rises. The Promoter stops speaking. The stage is silent. Ladvenu, a young priest, rises and goes to The Inquisitor. The Inquisitor whispers to him. Ladvenu moves to Cauchon, whispers to him.)

CAUCHON (looks toward The Inquisitor; very hesitant). Messire—(The Inquisitor stares at Cauchon. Cauchon hesitates, then turns toward Joan) Joan, listen well to what I must ask you. At this moment, are you in a State of Grace?

LADVENU. Messire, this is a fearful question for a simple girl who sincerely believes that God has chosen her. Do not hold her answer against her. She is in great danger and she is confused.

CAUCHON. Are you in a State of Grace?

JOAN (as if she knew this was a dangerous question). Which moment is that, Messire? Everything is so mixed up, I no longer know where I am. At the beginning when I heard my Voices, or at the end of the trial when I knew that my king and my friends had abandoned me? When I lost faith, when I recanted, or when, at the very last minute, I gave myself back to myself? When—

CAUCHON (softly, worried). Messire

demands an answer. His reasons must be grave. Joan, are you in a State of Grace?

JOAN. If I am not, God will help me in Grace. If I am, God will keep me in Grace.

(The Priests murmur among themselves. The Inquisitor, impassive, sits down.)

LADVENU (gently, warmly). Well spoken, Joan.

THE PROMOTER (sharply). And the Devil would have the same clever answer.

WARWICK (to Cauchon, pointing to The Inquisitor). Is that the gentleman about whom I have been told?

CAUCHON (softly). Yes.

WARWICK. When did he arrive?

CAUCHON. Three days ago. He has wished to be alone.

WARWICK. Why was I not told of his arrival?

CAUCHON. He is one of us, sire. We do not acknowledge your authority here.

WARWICK. Only when you count our money and eat our food. Never mind, the formalities do not matter to me. But time does and I hope his presence will not add to the confusion. I am almost as bewildered as the girl. All these questions must be very interesting to you gentlemen of the Church, but if we continue at this speed we'll never get to the trial and the girl will be dead of old age. Get to the burning and be done with it.

CAUCHON (angry). Sire! Who speaks of burning? We will try to save the girl—

WARWICK. Monseigneur, I allow you this charade because the object of my government is to tell the whole Christian world that the coronation of the idiot Charles was managed by a sorceress, a heretic, a mad girl, a whore camp follower. However you do that, please move with greater speed.

CAUCHON. And I remind you each day that this is a court of the Church. We are here to judge the charge of heresy. Our considerations are not yours.

WARWICK. My dear Bishop, I know that. But the fine points of ecclesiastic judgments may be a little too distinguished for my soldiers—and for the rest of the world. Propaganda is a soft weapon: hold it in your hands too long, and it will move about like a snake, and strike the other way. Whatever the girl is or has been, she must now be stripped and degraded. That is why we bought her high, and it is what we will insist upon. (Smiles) I'm coming to like her. I admire the way she stands up to all of you. And she rides beautifully— I've seen her. Rare to find a woman who rides that way. I'd like to have known her in other circumstances, in a pleasanter world. Hard for me to remember that she took France away from us, deprived us of our heritage. We know that God is on the side of the English. He proved himself at Agincourt. "God and my right," you know. But when this girl came along, and we began to lose, there were those who doubted our motto. That, of course, cannot be tolerated. "God and my right" is inscribed on all English armor, and we certainly have no intention of changing the armor. So get on with her story. The world will forget her soon enough. Where were we?

THE FATHER (comes forward). At the moment when I find her under the lady tree. (He goes to Joan) What are you doing? You were crying out to someone, but the bastard fled before I could catch him. Who was it? Who was it? Answer me. Answer me, or I'll beat you to salt mash.

JOAN. I was talking to the Blessed Saint Michael.

THE FATHER (hits Joan). That will teach you to lie to your father. You want to start whoring like the others. Well, you can tell your Blessed Saint Michael that if I catch you together I'll plunge my pitchfork into his belly and strangle you with my bare hands for the filthy rutting cat you are.

JOAN (softly). Father, it was Saint Michael who was talking to me.

THE FATHER. The priest will hear about this, and from me. I'll tell him straight out that not content with running after men, you have also dared to blaspheme.

JOAN. I swear to you before God that I am telling the truth. It's been happening for a long time and always at the noon or evening Angelus. The Saints appear to me. They speak to me. They answer me when I question them. And they all say the same thing.

THE FATHER. Why would the Saints speak to you, idiot? I am your father, why don't they speak to me? If they had anything to say they'd talk to me.

JOAN. Father, try to understand the trouble I'm in. For three years I've refused what they ask. But I don't think I can say no much longer. I think the moment has come when I must go.

THE FATHER. For forty years I've worked myself to death to raise my children like Christians, and this is my reward. A daughter who thinks she hears Voices.

JOAN. They say I can't wait any longer—

THE FATHER. *What* can't wait any longer?

JOHAN. They tell me France is at the last moment of danger. My Voices tell me I must save her.

THE FATHER. You?—You? You are crazy. Crazy. You are a fool! A fool and a crazy girl.

JOAN. I must do what my Voices tell me. I will go to the Sire de Beaudricourt and ask him to give me an armed escort to the Dauphin at Chinon. I'll talk to the Dauphin and make him fight. Then I will take the army to Orléans and we'll push the English into the sea.

THE FATHER. For ten years I have dreamed that you would disgrace us with men. Do you think I raised you, sacrificed everything for you, to have you run off to live with soldiers? I knew what you would be. But you won't—I'll kill you first.

(He begins to beat her and to kick her.)

JOAN *(screams)*. Stop! Stop! Oh, Father, stop!

LADVENU *(rises, horrified)*. Stop him. Stop him. He's hurting her.

CAUCHON. We cannot, Brother Ladvenu. We do not know Joan. You forget that we first meet her at the trial. We can only play our roles, good or bad, just as they were, each in his turn. And we will hurt her far more than he does. You know that. *(Turns to Warwick)* Ugly, isn't it, this family scene?

WARWICK. Why? In England we are in favor of strong punishment for children. It makes character. I was half beaten to death as a boy, but I am in excellent health.

THE FATHER *(he looks down at Joan who has fallen at his feet)*. Crazy little whore. Do you still want to save France? *(Then, shamefaced, he turns to the Judges)* Well, messieurs, what would you have done in my place if your daughter had been like that?

WARWICK. If we had known about this girl from the very beginning, we could have reached an agreement with her father. We tell people that our intelligence service is remarkable and we say it so often that everybody believes us. It should be their business not only to tell us what is happening, but what might happen. When a country virgin talked about saving France, I should have known about it. I tell myself now I would not have laughed.

(The Mother comes forward. She bends over Joan.)

THE FATHER *(to The Mother)*. The next time your daughter talks of running after soldiers, I'll put her in the river and with my own hands I'll hold her under.

(The Mother takes Joan in her arms.)

THE MOTHER. He hurt you bad.

JOAN. Yes.

THE MOTHER *(softly)*. He's your father.

JOAN. Yes. He is my father. Oh, Mama, somebody must understand. I can't do it alone.

THE MOTHER. Lean against me. You're big now. I can hardly hold you in my arms. Joan, your father is a good and honest man but—*(She whispers in Joan's ear)* I've saved a little from the house money. If you'd like one, I'll buy you a broidered kerchief at the very next fair.

JOAN. I don't need a kerchief. I won't ever be pretty, Mama.

THE MOTHER. We're all a little wild when we're young. Who is it, Joan? Don't have secrets from me. Is he from our village?

JOAN. I don't want to marry, Mama. That isn't what I mean.

THE MOTHER. Then what do you mean?

JOAN. Blessed Saint Michael says that I must put on man's clothes. He says that I must save France.

THE MOTHER. Joan, I speak to you in kindness, but I forbid you to tell me such nonsense. A man's clothes! I should just like to see you try it.

JOAN. But I'll have to, Mama, if I'm to ride horse with my soldiers. Saint Michael makes good sense.

THE MOTHER. Your soldiers? Your soldiers? You bad girl! I'd rather see you dead first. Now I'm talking like your father, and that I never want to do. *(She begins to cry)* Running after soldiers! What have I done to deserve a daughter like this? You will kill me.

JOAN. No, Mama, no. *(She cries out as her Mother moves off)* Monseigneur Saint Michael. It cannot be done. Nobody will ever understand. It is better for me to say no right now. *(Pauses, listens)* Then Saint Michael's voice grew soft, the way it does when he is angry. And he said that I must take the first step. He said that God trusted me and if a mountain of ice did rise ahead of me it was only because God was busy and trusted me to climb the mountain even if I tore my hands and broke my legs, and my face might run with blood—*(After a second, slowly, carefully)* Then I said that I would go. I said that I would go that day.

(Joan's Brother comes forward and stands looking at her.)

THE BROTHER. You haven't got the sense you were born with. If you give me something next time, I won't tell Papa I saw you with your lover.

JOAN. So it was you, you pig, you told them? Here's what I'll give you this time—*(She slaps him)* And the next time—*(She slaps him again, and begins to chase him. He runs from her)* and the time after that. *(Joan's voice changes and she moves slowly about not concerned with him any longer but speaking into space)* And so I went to my uncle Durand. And my uncle Durand went to the seigneur of the manor. And I walked a long way west and a little way south and there was the night I was shivering with rain—or with fear—and the day I was shivering with sun—or with fear—and then I walked to the west again and east. I was on my way to the first fool I had to deal with. And I had plenty of them to deal with.

(She moves upstage, bumps into two Soldiers as Beaudricourt comes on stage.)

BEAUDRICOURT. What is it? What's the matter? What does she want? What's the matter with these crazy fools? *(He grabs Joan and shakes her)* What's the matter with you, young woman? You've been carrying on like a bad girl. I've heard about you standing outside the doors ragging at the sentries until they fall asleep.

JOAN *(he holds her up. She dangles in front of his face)*. I want a horse. I want the dress of a man. I want an armed escort. You will give them orders to take me to Chinon to see the Dauphin.

BEAUDRICOURT. Of course. And I will also kick you in the place where it will do the most good.

JOAN. Kicks, blows. Whichever you like best. I'm used to them by now. I want a horse. I want the dress of a man. I want an armed escort.

BEAUDRICOURT. That's a new idea—a horse. You know who I am and what I usually want? Did the village girls tell you? When they come to ask a favor it usually has to do with a father or a brother who has poached my land. If the girl is pretty, I have a good heart, and we both pitch in. If the girl is ugly, well, usually I have a good heart, too, but not so good as the other way. I am known in this land for good-heartedness. But a horse is a nasty kind of bargain.

JOAN. I have been sent by Blessed Saint Michael.

BEAUDRICOURT *(puts her down hurriedly, makes the Sign of the Cross)*. Don't mix the Saints up in this kind of thing. That talk was good enough to get you past the sentries, but it's not good enough to get you a horse. A horse costs more than a woman. You're a country girl. You ought to know that. Are you a virgin?

JOAN. Yes, sire.

BEAUDRICOURT. Well, maybe we'll talk about a small horse. You have lovely eyes.

JOAN. I want more than a horse, sire.

BEAUDRICOURT *(laughs)*. You're greedy. But I like that sometimes. There are fools who get angry when the girl wants too much. But I say good things should cost a lot. That pleases me in a girl. You understand what I mean?

JOAN. No, sire.

BEAUDRICOURT. That's good. I don't like clear-thinking women in bed. Not in my bed. You understand what I mean?

JOAN. No, sire.

BEAUDRICOURT. Well, I don't like idiots, either. What is it you're up to? What else besides a horse?

JOAN. Just as I said before, sire. An armed escort as far as Chinon.

BEAUDRICOURT. Stop that crazy talk. I'm the master here. I can send you back where you came from with no better present than the lashes of a whip. I told you I like a girl to come high, but if she costs too much the opposite effect sets in —and I can't—well, I can't. You understand what I mean? (*Suddenly*) Why do you want to go to Chinon?

JOAN. As I said before, sire, I wish to find Monseigneur the Dauphin.

BEAUDRICOURT. Well, you *are* on a high road. Why not the Duke of Burgundy while you're at it? He's more powerful, and he likes the girls. But not our Dauphin. He runs from war and women. And hour with either would kill him. Why do you want to see such a fellow?

JOAN. I want an army, Messire. An army to march upon Orléans.

BEAUDRICOURT. If you're crazy, forget about me. (*Shouting*) Boudousse. Boudousse. (*A Soldier comes forward*) Throw some cold water on this girl and send her back to her father. Don't beat her. It's bad luck to beat a crazy woman.

JOAN. You won't beat me. You're a kind man, Messire. Very kind.

BEAUDRICOURT. Sometimes yes, sometimes no. But I don't like virgins whose heads come off at night—

JOAN. And you're very intelligent, which is sometimes even better than being kind. But when a man is intelligent *and* kind, then that's the very best combination on God's fine earth.

BEAUDRICOURT (*he waves the Guard away*). You're a strange girl. Want a little wine? Why do you think I'm intelligent?

JOAN. It shows in your face. You're handsome, Messire.

BEAUDRICOURT. Twenty years ago, I wouldn't have said no. I married two rich widows, God bless me. But not now. Of course, I've tried not to get old too fast, and there are men who get better looking with age—(*Smiles*) You know, it's very comic to be talking like this with a shepherd girl who drops out of the sky one bright morning. I am bored here. My officers are animals. I have nobody to talk to. I like a little philosophy now and then. I should like to know from your mouth what connection you see between beauty and intelligence? Usually people say that handsome men are stupid.

JOAN. Hunchbacks talk that way, and people with long noses, or those who will die of a bitter egg that grows in their head. God has the power to create a perfect man—(*She smiles at him*) And sometimes He uses His power.

BEAUDRICOURT. Well, you can look at it that way, of course. But you take me, for example. No, I'm not ugly, but sometimes I wonder if I'm intelligent. No, no, don't protest. I tell you there are times when I have problems that seem too much for me. They ask me to decide something, a tactical or administrative point. Then, all of a sudden, I don't know why, my head acts like it's gone some place else, and I don't even understand the words people are saying. Isn't that strange? (*After a second*) But I never show it. I roar out an order whatever happens. That's the main thing in an army. Make a decision, good or bad, just *make* it. Things will turn out almost the same, anyway. (*Softly, as if to himself*) Still, I wish I could have done better. This is a small village to die away your life. (*Points outside*) They think I'm a great man, but they never saw anybody else. Like every other man, I wanted to be brilliant and remarkable, but I end up hanging a few poor bastards who deserted from a broken army. I wanted to shake a nation—Ah, well. (*Looks at her*) Why do I tell you all this? You can't help me, and you're crazy.

JOAN. They told me you would speak this way.

BEAUDRICOURT. *They* told you?

JOAN. Listen to me, nice, good Robert, and don't shout any more. It's useless. I'm about to say something very important. You will be brilliant and remarkable. You will shake a nation because *I* will do it for you. Your name will go far outside this village—

BEAUDRICOURT *(puts his arms around her)*. What are you talking about?

JOAN *(she pulls away from him)*. Robert, don't think any more about my being a girl. That just confuses everything. You'll find plenty of girls who are prettier and will give more pleasure—*(Softly)* and will not ask as much. You don't want me.

BEAUDRICOURT. Well, I don't know. You're all right.

JOAN *(sharply)*. If you want me to help you, then help me. When I say the truth say it with me.

BEAUDRICOURT *(politely)*. But you're a pleasant-looking girl, and it's nice weather, and . . . *(Laughs)* No, I don't want you any more than that.

JOAN. Good. Now that we have got that out of the way, let's pretend that you've given me the clothes of a boy and we're sitting here like two comrades talking good sense.

BEAUDRICOURT *(fills a glass)*. All right. Have a little wine.

JOAN *(drinks her wine)*. Kind, sweet Robert. Great things are about to begin for you. *(As he starts to speak)* No, no. Listen. The English are everywhere, and everywhere they are our masters. Brittany and Anjou will go next. The English wait only to see which one will pay the higher tribute money. The Duke of Burgundy signs a bitter treaty and the English give him the Order of the Golden Fleece. They invented just such medals for foreign traitors. Our little monkey Dauphin Charles sits with his court in Bourges, shaking and jibbering. He knows nothing, his court knows nothing, and all falls to pieces around him. You know that. You know our army, our good army of brave boys, is tired and sick. They believe the English will always be stronger and that there's no sense to it any more. When an army thinks that way, the end is near. The Bastard Dunois is a good captain and intelligent. So intelligent that nobody will listen to him. So he forgets that he should be leading an army and drowns himself in wine, and tells stories of past battles to his whores. I'll put a stop to that, you can be sure—

BEAUDRICOURT *(softly)*. You'll put a stop to—

JOAN. Our best soldiers are like angry bulls. They always want to attack, to act fine for the history books. They are great champions of individual bravery. But they don't know how to use their cannon and they get people killed for nothing. That's what they did at Agincourt. Ah, when it comes to dying, they're all ready to volunteer. But what good is it to die? You think just as I do, my dear Robert: war isn't a tournament for fancy gentlemen. You must be smart to win a war. You must think, and be smart. *(Quickly)* But you who are so intelligent, knew all that when you were born.

BEAUDRICOURT. I've always said it. I've always said that nobody thinks any more. I used to be a thinker, but nobody paid any attention.

JOAN. They will, they will. Because you have just had an idea that will probably save all of us.

BEAUDRICOURT. I've had an idea?

JOAN. Well, you are about to have it. But don't let anything get in its way. Please sit quiet and don't, well, just—*(As he is about to move she holds him down)* You are the only man in France who at this minute can see the future. Sit still.

BEAUDRICOURT. What is it that I see?

JOAN. You know your soldiers. You know they will leave you soon. You know that to keep them you must give them faith. You have nothing else to give them now. A little bread, a little faith—good simple things to fight with.

BEAUDRICOURT. It's too late—

JOAN. A girl comes before you. Saint Michael and Saint Catherine and Saint Marguerite have told her to come. You will say it's not true. But I believe it *is* true, and that's what matters. A farm girl who says that God is on her side. You can't prove He isn't. You can't. Try it and see. The girl came a long, hard way, she got so far as you, and she has convinced you. Yes, I have. I have convinced you. And why have I convinced so intelligent a man? Because I tell the truth, and it takes a smart head to know the truth.

BEAUDRICOURT. Where is this idea you said I had?

JOAN. Coming, coming just this minute. You are saying to yourself, if she convinced me, why shouldn't she convince the Dauphin and Dunois and the Archbishop? After all they're only men like me, although a good deal less intelligent. *(Very fast)* All right, that's settled. But now you're saying to yourself when it comes to dying, soldiers are very intelligent, and so she'll have a harder time with them. No, she won't. She will say English heads are like all others: hit them hard enough, at the right time, and we'll march over them to Orléans. They need faith, your soldiers. They need somebody who believes it to say that God is on their side. Everybody says things like that. But *I* believe it—and that's the difference. Our soldiers will fight again, you know it, and because you know it you are the most remarkable man in France.

BEAUDRICOURT. You think so?

JOAN. The whole world will think so. But you must move fast. Like all great political men you are a realist. At this minute you are saying to yourself, "If the troops will believe this girl has come from God, what difference does it make whether she has or not? I will send her to Bourges tomorrow with the courier."

BEAUDRICOURT. The courier does go tomorrow. How did you know that? He goes with a secret packet—

JOAN *(laughs, delighted)*. Give me six good soldiers and a fine white horse. I want a *white* horse, please. I will do the rest. But give me a quiet white horse because I don't know how to ride.

BEAUDRICOURT *(laughs)*. You'll break your neck.

JOAN. It's up to Blessed Saint Michael to keep me in the saddle. *(He laughs. She doesn't like his laughter)* I will make you a bet, Robert. I'll bet you a man's dress that if you will have two horses brought now, and we both ride at a gallop, I won't fall off. If I stay on, then will you believe in me? All right?

BEAUDRICOURT *(laughs)*. All this thinking makes a man weary. I had other plans for this afternoon, as I told you, but any kind of exercise is good for me. Come on.

(He exits. Joan, smiling, looks toward Heaven. Then she runs after Beaudricourt. But she is stopped by a Soldier and suddenly realizes she is back in the trial. She sits quietly as the lights fade out on the Beaudricourt scene.)

WARWICK. She made that idiot believe he wasn't an idiot.

CAUCHON. It was a man-woman scene, a little coarse for my taste.

WARWICK. Coarse for *your* taste? The trick of making him believe what she put into his head is exactly what I do in my trade and what you do in yours. *(Suddenly)* Speaking of your trade, sire, forgive a brutal question but, just between ourselves, do you really have the faith?

CAUCHON *(simply)*. As a child has it. And that is why my judges and I will try to save Joan. To the bitter end we will try to save her. Our honor demands that— *(Warwick turns away. Cauchon, sharply)* You think of us as collaborators and therefore without honor. We believed that collaboration with you was the only reasonable solution—

WARWICK. And so it was. But when you say reasonable solution it is often more honorable to omit the word honor.

CAUCHON *(softly)*. I say honor. Our poor honor, the little that was left us, demanded that we fight for our beliefs.

WARWICK. While you lived on English money—

CAUCHON. Yes. And while eight hundred of your soldiers were at our gates. It was easy for free men to call us traitors, but we lived in occupied territory, dependent upon the will of your king to kill us or to feed us. We were men, and we wanted to live; we were priests, and we wanted to save Joan. Like most other men, we wanted everything. We played a shameful role.

WARWICK. Shameful? I don't know. You might have played a nobler part, perhaps, if you had decided to be martyrs and fight against us. My eight hundred men were quite ready to help.

CAUCHON. We had good reason to know about your soldiers. I remember no day without insults and threats. And yet we stood against you. Nine long months before we agreed to hand over a girl who had been deserted by everybody but us.

They can call us barbarians, but for all their noble principles I believe they would have surrendered her before we did.

WARWICK. You could have given us the girl on the first day. Nine long months of endless what?

CAUCHON. It was hard for us. God had been silent since Joan's arrest. He had not spoken to her or to us. Therefore, we had to do without his counsel. We were here to defend the House of God. During our years in the seminaries we learned how to defend it. Joan had no training in our seminaries and yet, abandoned, she defended God's House in her own way. Defended it with that strange conflict of insolence and humility, worldly sense and unworldly grandeur. *(Softly)* The piety was so simple and sweet—to the last moment of the last flame. We did not understand her in those days. We covered our eyes like old, fighting, childish men, and turned away so that we could not hear the cries of anguish. She was all alone at the end. God had not come to her. That is a terrible time for a religious nature, sire, and brings doubt and despair unknown to others. *(Cauchon rises and turns away)* But it is then and there that some men raise their heads, and when they do, it is a noble sight.

WARWICK. Yes, it is. But as a man of politics, I cannot afford the doctrine of man's individual magnificence. I might meet another man who felt the same way. And he might express his individual magnificence by cutting off *my* head.

CAUCHON *(softly, as if he hadn't heard Warwick)*. Sometimes, to console myself, I remember how beautiful were all those old priests who tried to protect the child, to save her from what can never now be mended—

WARWICK. Oh, you speak in large words, sire. Political language has no such words as "never now be mended." I have told you that the time will come when we will raise her a statue in London.

CAUCHON. And the time will come when our names will be known only for what we did to her; when men, forgiving their own sins, but angry with ours, will speak our names in a curse—

(The lights dim on Warwick and Cauchon and we hear the music of a court song. A throne is brought on stage and as the lights come up slowly on The Dauphin's Court, the cyclorama reflects the royal fleur-de-lis. The Dauphin, Charles, is lolling about on his throne playing at bilboquet. Agnes Sorel and The Little Queen are practicing a new dance. Yolande is moving about. Four Courtiers are playing at cards.)

THE LITTLE QUEEN *(she is having a hard time learning the dance steps)*. It's very hard.

AGNES. Everything is very hard for you, dear.

THE LITTLE QUEEN *(as they pass Charles)*. It's a new dance. Very fashionable. Influenced by the Orient, they say.

AGNES *(to Charles)*. Come. We'll teach you.

CHARLES. I won't be going to the ball.

AGNES. Well, *we* will be going. And we must dance better than anybody else and look better than anybody else. *(Stops, to Charles, points to her headdress)* And I'm not going in this old thing. I'm your mistress. Have a little pride. A mistress must be better dressed than anybody. You know that.

THE LITTLE QUEEN. And so must wives. I mean better dressed than other wives. The Queen of France in last year's shoddy. What do you think they will say, Charles?

CHARLES. They will say that poor little Queen married a King who hasn't a sou. They will be wrong. I have a sou.

(He throws a coin in the air. It falls and he begins to scramble on the floor for it.)

THE LITTLE QUEEN. I can hear them all the way to London. The Duchess of Bedford and the Duchess of Gloucester— *(Charles, on the floor, is about to find his sou as the Archbishop and La Tremouille come in. Charles jumps back in fear.)*

LA TREMOUILLE *(to Charles)*. You grow more like your father each day.

ARCHBISHOP. But his father had the decency to take to his bed.

CHARLES. Which father?

LA TREMOUILLE. You act so strangely, sire, that even I, who knew your mother, am convinced you are legitimate. *(Angrily, to Charles who is still on the floor)* Move. Move.

THE LITTLE QUEEN. Oh, please don't speak to him that way, Monsieur de la Tremouille.

ARCHBISHOP *(who has been glaring at the dancers).* You believe this is the proper time for dancing?

THE LITTLE QUEEN. But if the English take us prisoner, we have to know a little something. We can't disgrace our country—

(La Tremouille stares at her, exits.)

YOLANDE. What harm do they do, sire? They are young—and there isn't much ahead for them.

ARCHBISHOP. There isn't much ahead for any of us.

(He moves off.)

YOLANDE. Please get up, Charles. It is a sad thing to see you so frightened by so many men.

CHARLES. And why shouldn't I be frightened of La Tremouille and the Archbishop? I have been all my life. They could order every soldier in the place to cut me up and eat me.

AGNES. They're cheats, every woman in England. We set the styles—and they send spies to steal the latest models. But, fortunately, they're so ugly that nothing looks very well—*(Admires her own feet and hands)* with cows for feet and pigs for hands. We want new headdresses. Are you the King of France or aren't you?

CHARLES. I don't know if I am. Nobody knows. I told you all about that the first night you came to bed.

AGNES. The new headdress is two feet tall and has two horns coming from the side—

CHARLES. Sounds like a man. A very small married man.

THE LITTLE QUEEN. And they have a drape at the back—they will cause a revolution, Charles.

AGNES. The English ladies—the mistresses, I mean, of course—won't be able to sleep when they see us. And if they can't sleep neither will the Dukes. And if the Dukes can't sleep they won't feel well and they won't have time to march on us—

CHARLES. They won't march on us. Nobody wants this dull town. They're already in Orléans. So there isn't much sense counterattacking with a headdress.

THE LITTLE QUEEN. Oh, Charles, one has to have a little pleasure in life. And

Mama—*(Pointing to Yolande)* and the Archbishop and La Tremouille, and all the wise people, tell us that the end is here, anyway, and this will be the last state ball—

CHARLES. How much do they cost?

AGNES. I flirted with the man—*(Hastily)* in a nice way—and he's going to let us have them for six thousand francs.

CHARLES. Where would I get six thousand francs, you little idiot?

THE LITTLE QUEEN. Twelve thousand francs, Charles. I'm here.

CHARLES. That's enough to pay Dunois' army the six months' wages that I owe them. You are dreaming, my kittens. My dear mother-in-law, please speak to these children.

YOLANDE. No. I wish to speak to you.

CHARLES. For two days you've been following me about looking the way good women always look when they're about to give a lecture.

YOLANDE. Have I ever spoken against your interests? Have I ever shown myself concerned with anything but your welfare? I am the mother of your Queen, but I brought Agnes to you when I realized she would do you good.

THE LITTLE QUEEN. Please, Mama, don't brag about it.

YOLANDE. My child, Agnes is a charming girl and she knows her place. It was important that Charles make up his mind to become a man, and if he was to become a man he had to have a woman.

THE LITTLE QUEEN. I am a woman and his wife in the bargain.

YOLANDE. You are my dear little girl and I don't want to hurt you, but you're not very much of a woman. I know because I was just like you. I was honest and sensible, and that was all. Be the Queen to your Charles, keep his house, give him a Dauphin. But leave the rest to others. Love is not a business for honest women. We're no good at it. Charles is more virile since he knows Agnes. *(Worried)* You are more virile, aren't you, Charles?

AGNES *(too firmly).* Yes, indeed.

YOLANDE. I hope so. He doesn't act it with the Archbishop or La Tremouille.

AGNES. Things like that take a while. But he's much more virile. Doesn't read so much any more. *(To Charles)* And since it's all due to me the very least you can do is to give me the headdress. And one for the little Queen. *(Charles doesn't answer)* I feel ill. And if I feel ill it will certainly be for a whole week. And you'll be very bored without me. *(Eagerly, as she sees his face)* Sign a Treasury Bond and we'll worry afterwards. *(He nods. She turns to The Little Queen)* Come, my little Majesty. The pink one for you, the green one for me. *(To Charles, as they exit)* We'll make fools of those London ladies, you'll see. It'll be a great victory for France.

CHARLES *(to Yolande)*. A great victory for France. She talks like an army captain. I'm sick of such talk. France will be victorious, you'll be a great king—all the people who have wanted to make a king out of me. Even Agnes. She practices in bed. That's very funny. I must tell you about it some day. I am a poor frightened nothing with a lost kingdom and a broken army. When will they understand that?

YOLANDE. I understand it, Charles.

CHARLES *(softly, taken aback)*. Do you? You've never said that before.

YOLANDE. I say it now because I want you to see this girl. For three days I have had her brought here, waiting for you—

CHARLES. I am ridiculous enough without playing games with village louts who come to me on clouds carrying a basket of dreams.

YOLANDE. There is something strange about this girl, something remarkable. Or so everybody thinks, and that's what matters.

CHARLES. You know La Tremouille would never allow me to see the girl.

YOLANDE. Why not? It is time they understood that a peasant at their council table might do a little good. A measure of common sense from humble people might bring us all—

CHARLES *(sharply)*. To ruin. Men of the people have been at council tables, have become kings, and it was a time of massacre and mistake. At least I'm harmless. The day may come when Frenchmen will regret their little Charles.

At least, I have no large ideas about how to organize happiness and death. *(He throws his ball in the air.)*

YOLANDE. Please stop playing at bilboquet, Charles.

CHARLES. Let me alone. I like this game. When I miss the cup, the ball only falls on my nose, and that hurts nobody but me. But if I sit straight on the throne with the ball in one hand and the stick in the other, I might start taking myself seriously. Then the ball will fall on the nose of France, and the nose of France won't like it.

(The Archbishop and La Tremouille enter.)

LA TREMOUILLE. We have a new miracle every day. The girl walked to the village church to say her prayers. A drunken soldier yelled an insult at her. "You are wrong to curse," she said, "You will soon appear before our Lord." An hour later the soldier fell into a well and was drowned. The stumbling of a drunkard has turned the town into a roaring holiday. They are marching here now, shouting that God commands you to receive this girl.

CHARLES. He hasn't said a word to me.

LA TREMOUILLE. The day God speaks to you, sire, I will turn infidel.

ARCHBISHOP *(very angry)*. Put up that toy, your majesty. You will have the rest of your life to devote to it.

LA TREMOUILLE. Get ready to leave here.

CHARLES. Where will I go? Where will you go? To the English?

ARCHBISHOP. Even from you, sire, we will not accept such words.

(As La Tremouille angrily advances on Charles, Yolande moves between them.)

YOLANDE *(to Archbishop)*. Allow him to see the girl.

ARCHBISHOP. And throw open the palace to every charlatan, every bone setter, every faith healer in the land?

LA TREMOUILLE. What difference does it make any more? We have come to the end of our rope.

YOLANDE. If he sees the girl, it will give the people hope for a few days.

CHARLES. Oh, I am tired of hearing about the girl. Bring her in and have it ended. Maybe she has a little money and can play cards.

YOLANDE *(to La Tremouille).* We have nothing to lose, sire—

LA TREMOUILLE. When you deal with God you risk losing everything. If He has really sent this girl then He has decided to concern Himself with us. In that case, we are in even worse trouble than we thought. People who govern states should not attract God's attention. They should make themselves very small and pray that they will go unnoticed.

(Joan comes in. She stands small and frightened, staring at Charles, bowing respectfully to the Archbishop. As she moves toward the throne, one of the Courtiers laughs. Joan turns to stare, and the Courtier draws back as if he is frightened.)

CHARLES. What do you want? I'm a very busy man. It's time for my milk.

JOAN *(bows before him).* I am Joan the Maid. The King of Heaven has sent me here. I am to take you to Reims and have you anointed and crowned King of France.

CHARLES. My. Well, that is splendid, mademoiselle, but Reims is in the hands of the English, as far as I know. How shall we get there?

JOAN. We will fight our way there, noble Dauphin. First, we will take Orléans and then we will walk to Reims.

LA TREMOUILLE. I am commander of the army, madame. We have not been able to take Orléans.

JOAN *(carefully).* I will do it, sire. With the help of our Lord God who is my only commander.

LA TREMOUILLE. When did Orléans come to God's attention?

JOAN. I do not know the hour, but I know that he wishes us to take the city. After that, we will push the English into the sea.

LA TREMOUILLE. Is the Lord in such bad shape that he needs you to do his errands?

JOAN. He has said that he needs me.

ARCHBISHOP. Young woman—*(Joan kneels and kisses the hem of his robe)* If God wishes to save the Kingdom of France he has no need of armies.

JOAN. Monseigneur, God doesn't want a lazy Kingdom of France. We must put

up a good fight and then He will give us victory.

ARCHBISHOP *(to Charles).* The replies of this girl are, indeed, interesting and make a certain amount of good sense. But this is a delicate matter: a commission of learned doctors will now examine her. We will review their findings in council—

LA TREMOUILLE *(to Charles).* And will keep you informed of our decision. Go back to your book. She will not disturb you any more today. Come, Madame Henriette—

JOAN. My name is Joan.

LA TREMOUILLE. Forgive me. The last quack was called Henriette.

ARCHBISHOP. Come, my child—

CHARLES. No *(He motions to Joan)* You. Don't move. *(He turns toward La Tremouille, standing straight and stiff and holding Joan's hand to give himself courage)* Leave me alone with her. *(Giggles)* Your King commands you. *(La Tremouille and the Archbishop bow and leave. Charles holds his noble pose for an instant, then bursts into laughter)* <u>And they went.</u> It's the first time they ever obeyed me. *(Very worried)* You haven't come here to kill me? *(She smiles)* No. No, of course not. You have an honest face. I've lived so long with those pirates that I've almost forgotten what an honest face looks like. Are there other people who have honest faces?

JOAN *(gravely).* Many, sire.

CHARLES. I never see them. Brutes and whores, that's all I ever see. And the little Queen. She's nice, but she's stupid. And Agnes. She's not stupid—and she's not nice. *(He climbs on his throne, hangs his feet over one of the arms and sighs)* All right. Start boring me. Tell me that I ought to be a great King.

JOAN *(softly).* Yes, Charles.

CHARLES. Listen. If you want to make an impression on the Archbishop and the council, we'll have to stay in this room for at least an hour. If you talk to me of God and the Kingdom of France, I'll never live through the hour. Let's do something else. Do you know how to play at cards?

JOAN. I don't know what it is.

CHARLES. It is a nice game invented to amuse my Papa when he was ill. I'll teach you. *(He begins to hunt for the cards)* I hope they haven't stolen them. They steal everything from me around here and cards are expensive. Only the wealthiest princes can have them. I got mine from Papa. I'll never have the price of another pack. If those pigs have stolen them—No. Here they are. *(He finds them in his pocket)* My Papa was crazy. Went crazy young— in his thirties. Did you know that? Sometimes I am glad I am a bastard. At least I don't have to be so frightened of going crazy. Then sometimes I wish I were his son and knew that I was meant to be a king. It's confusing.

JOAN. Of the two, which would you prefer?

CHARLES. Well, on the days when I have a little courage, I'd risk going crazy. But on the days when I haven't any courage—that's from Sunday to Saturday —I would rather let everything go to hell and live in peace in some foreign land on whatever little money I have left.

JOAN. Today, Charles, is this one of the days when you have courage?

CHARLES. Today? *(He thinks a minute)* Yes, it seems to me I have a little bit today. Not much, but a little bit. I was sharp with the Archbishop, and—

JOAN. You will have courage every day. Beginning now.

CHARLES. You have a charm in a bottle or a basket?

JOAN. I have a charm.

CHARLES. You are a witch? You can tell me, you know, because I don't care. I swear to you that I won't repeat it. I have a horror of people being tortured. A long time ago, they made me witness the burning of a heretic at the stake. I vomited all night long.

JOAN. I am not a witch. But I have a charm.

CHARLES. Sell it to me without telling the others.

JOAN. I will give it to you, Charles. For nothing.

CHARLES. Then I don't want it. What you get free costs too much. *(He shuffles the cards)* I act like a fool so that people will let me alone. My Papa was so crazy they think I am, too. He was very crazy, did all kinds of strange things, some of

them very funny. One day he thought it would be nice to have a great funeral, but nobody happened to die just then so he decided to bury a man who'd been dead four years. It cost a fortune to dig him out and put him back, but it was fun. *(He laughs merrily, catches himself, stares at Joan)* But don't think you can catch me too easily. I know a little about the world.

JOAN. You know too much. You are too smart.

CHARLES. Yes. Because I must defend myself against these cutthroats. They've got large bones, I've got puny sticks. But my head's harder than theirs and I've clung to my throne by using it.

JOAN *(gently)*. I would like to defend you against them, Charles. I would give my life to do it.

CHARLES. Do you mean that?

JOAN. Yes. And I'm not afraid of anything.

CHARLES. You're lucky. Or you're a liar. Sit down and I'll teach you to play.

JOAN. All right. You teach me this game and I'll teach you another game.

CHARLES. What game do you know?

JOAN. How not to be too smart. *(Softly)* And how not to be afraid.

CHARLES *(laughs)*. You'll be here a lifetime, my girl. Now. See these cards? They have pictures painted on them. Kings, queens and knaves, just as in real life. Now which would you say was the most powerful, which one could take all the rest?

JOAN. The king.

CHARLES. Well, you're wrong. This large heart can take the king. It can put him to rout, break his heart, win all his money. This card is called—

JOAN. I know. It is called God. Because God is more powerful than kings.

CHARLES. Oh, leave God alone for a minute. It's called the ace. Are you running this game? God this and God that. You talk as if you dined with Him last night. Didn't anybody tell you that the English also say their prayers to God? Every man thinks God is on his side. The rich and powerful know He is. But we're not rich and powerful, you and I—and France.

JOAN. That isn't what God cares

about. He is angry with us because we have no courage left. God doesn't like frightened people.

CHARLES. Then He certainly doesn't like me. And if He doesn't like me, why should I like Him? He could have given me courage. I wanted it.

JOAN (sharply). Is God your nurse? Couldn't you have tried to do a little better? Even with those legs.

CHARLES. I am sorry to know that my legs have already come to your attention. It's because of my legs that Agnes can never really love me. That's sad, isn't it?

JOAN. No.

CHARLES. Why not?

JOAN. Because your head is ugly, too, and you can't be sad about everything. But what's inside your head isn't ugly, because God gave you sense. And what do you do with it? Play cards. Bounce a ball in the air. Play baby tricks with the Archbishop and act the fool for all to see. You have a son. But what have you made for him? Nothing. And when he's grown he, too, will have a right to say, "God didn't like me, so why should I like Him?" But when he says God he will mean you because every son thinks his father is God. And when he's old enough to know that, he will hate you for what you didn't give him.

CHARLES. Give him? What can I give him? I'm glad to be alive. I've told you the truth: I am afraid. I've always been and I always will be.

JOAN. And now I'll tell you the truth: I am also afraid. (With force) And why not? Only the stupid are not afraid. What is the matter with you? Don't you understand that it was far more dangerous for me to get here than it is for you to build a kingdom? I've been in danger every minute of the way, and every minute of the way I was frightened. I don't want to be beaten, I don't want pain, I don't want to die. I am scared.

CHARLES (softly). What do you do when you get scared?

JOAN. Act as if I wasn't. It's that simple. Try it. Say to yourself, yes, I am afraid. But it's nobody else's business, so go on, go on. And you do go on.

CHARLES (softly). Where do you go?

JOAN (slowly, carefully). To the English, outside Orléans. And when you get there and see the cannon and the archers, and you know you are outnumbered, you will say to yourself, all right, they are stronger than I am, and that frightens me, as well it should. But I'll march right through because I had sense enough to get frightened first.

CHARLES. March through a stronger army? That can't be done.

JOAN. Yes it can. If you have sense and courage. Do you want to know what happened in my village last year? They tell the story as a miracle now but it wasn't. The Bouchon boy went hunting. He's the best poacher in our village, and this day he was poaching on the master's grounds. The master kept a famous dog, trained to kill, and the dog found the Bouchon boy. The boy was caught and death faced him. So he threw a stone and the dog turned his head. That was sense. And while the dog turned his head the boy decided the only way was to stand and fight. That was courage. He strangled the dog. That was victory. See?

CHARLES. Didn't the dog bite him?

JOAN (as if to a stupid child). You're like the old people in the village—you really believe in miracles. Of course the dog bit him. But I told you the boy had sense, and sense saved his life. God gave man an inside to his head, and He naturally doesn't want to see it wasted. (Smiles) See? That's my secret. The witches' secret. What will you pay me for it now?

CHARLES. What do you want?

JOAN. The army of France. Believe in God and give me the army.

CHARLES (moves away from her). To-morrow. I'll have time to get ready—

JOAN (moves after him). No, right now. You are ready. Come on, Charlie.

CHARLES. Perhaps I am. Perhaps I've been waiting for you and didn't know— (Laughs nervously) Shall we send for the Archbishop and La Tremouille and tell them that I have decided to give the army to you? It would be fun to see their faces.

JOAN. Call them.

CHARLES (in a panic). No. I am frightened.

JOAN. Are you as afraid as you ever

can be, ever were or will be, then, now and in the future? Are you sick?

CHARLES (*holding his stomach*). I think so.

JOAN. Good. Good. Then the worst is over. By the time they get scared, you'll be all over yours. Now, if you're as sick as you can get, I'll call them (*She runs upstage and calls out*) Monseigneur the Archbishop. Monseigneur de la Tremouille. Please come to the Dauphin.

CHARLES (*almost happy*). I am very sick.

JOAN (*moves him gently to the throne and arranges his hands and feet*). God is smiling. He is saying to Himself, "Look at that little Charles. He is sicker than he's ever been in his life. But he has called in his enemies and will face them. My, such a thing is wonderful." (*With great force*) Hang on, Charles. We'll be in Orléans. We'll march right up.

(*The Archbishop and La Tremouille enter, followed by Yolande and the Courtiers.*)

ARCHBISHOP. You sent for us, Your Highness?

CHARLES (*very sharply*). I have made a decision. The Royal Army is now under the command of Joan the Virgin Maid, here present. (*Roars out*) I wish to hear no word from you. None.

(*They stare at Charles.*)

JOAN (*clapping her hands*). Good. Good, my Charles. You see how simple it is? You're getting better looking, Charles. (*Charles giggles. Then he suddenly stops the giggle and stares at Joan. She stares at him. She drops to her knees*) Oh, my God, I thank you.

CHARLES. There is no time to lose. We will need your blessing, sire. Give it to us. (*To La Tremouille*) Kneel down, sire. (*La Tremouille, Yolande and the Courtiers drop to their knees. As the Archbishop pronounces the blessing, we hear the chorus sing the "Benedictus." A Court Page gives a sword to The Dauphin. The Dauphin gives the sword to Joan. Warwick comes into the scene and moves downstage to address the audience.*)

WARWICK. In real life, it didn't work out exactly that way. As before, now, and forever, there were long discussions in the French fashion. The council met. Desperate, frightened, with nothing to lose, they decided to dress the girl in battle flags and let her go forth as a symbol of something or other. It worked well. A simple girl inspired simple people to get themselves killed for simple ideals.

(*Joan rises and moves away from The Dauphin. She puts her hand on the sword, and lowers her head in prayer.*)

CURTAIN

ACT TWO

Before the curtain rises we hear the music of a soldier's song. The Soldiers sing of Joan and her victories. As the curtain rises we see Joan, in full armor, move across the stage to the music. She carries her sword high above her head in a kind of hero's salute to a group of admiring Village Women. She marches off as Cauchon, The Inquisitor, and the Judges take their places. Warwick moves down to address the audience.

———

WARWICK. She was in the field. From that day laws of strategy no longer made any difference. We began to lose. They say that Joan worked no miracles at Orléans. They say that our plan of isolated fortresses was absurd, that they could have been taken by anyone who had courage enough to attack. But that is not true. Sir John Talbot was not a fool. He's a good soldier, as he proved long before that miserable business, and after it. By all military laws his fortified positions could not have been broken. And they could not have been broken except by— Well, by what? What shall we call it even now? The unknown, the unguessed —God, if that's the way you believe. The girl was a lark in the skies of France, high over the heads of her soldiers, singing a joyous, crazy song of courage. There she was, outlined against the sun, a target for everybody to shoot at, flying straight and happy into battle. To Frenchmen, she was the soul of France. She was to me, too. (*Smiles, to Cauchon*) Monseigneur, I like France. Of course, you have your fair share of fools and blackguards. (*Somebody coughs nervously. Warwick laughs*) But every once in a while a lark does appear in your sky and then everything stupid and evil is wiped out by the shadow of the lark. I like France very much.

CAUCHON. Your guns prove your affection.

WARWICK. They prove nothing. I love animals but I hunt with guns. *(Sharply)* Too difficult to explain to a man of your simple piety, Monseigneur. So let's get on with the trial. The lark has been captured. The King she crowned, the royal court she saved—for a minute, at least—are about to abandon their little girl. Their loyalty lasted through victory. When we took her prisoner, their luck ran out. They are returning as fast as they can to the old, stale political games. *(Charles and the Archbishop appear.)*

JOAN *(as she goes back to the trial)*. Charles. *(No answer)* Charles.

CHARLES *(he turns toward her, then turns away again. He speaks to the Archbishop)*. I didn't want to send the letter. I tell you I have a feeling that—

ARCHBISHOP. The letter was necessary, sire. We must be rid of the girl now. She is dangerous to us.

CHARLES. I didn't like the letter—

CAUCHON *(gently, to Joan)*. Yesterday Charles disavowed you in a letter sent to all his cities.

JOAN. Charles. *(No answer. To Cauchon)* Well. He is still my King. And he is your King.

CAUCHON. No, he is not my King. We are loyal subjects of Henry of Lancaster, King of England, King of France. Joan, we love France as much as you do, but we believe that English Henry will put an end to this terrible war. That is why we have taken him as king. The man you call king is, for us, a rebel, claiming a throne that does not belong to him, refusing a good peace because it does not suit his ambitions. He is a puppet man, and we do not wish him as master. *(Sharply)* But I only confuse you. This is not a political trial in which you state your beliefs and we state ours. We are here only to return a lost girl to the bosom of the Sainted Mother Church.

JOAN *(pointing to Charles)*. That puppet man is the king God gave you. He is a poor, skinny, miserable thing, but given a little time—

CHARLES *(to the Archbishop)*. I object as much to being defended in this fashion as I do to being attacked.

ARCHBISHOP *(maliciously)*. Let them speak, sire. Turn away. It will be over soon. They will speed up the trial now. They will burn her at the stake.

CHARLES *(softly, as if he were sick)*. I hate violence. It makes me sick—

ARCHBISHOP *(sharply)*. Count yourself a lucky man. If the English do not condemn her to death, we will have to do it.

CHARLES. I will never do that, Monseigneur. After all, the girl loved me. I will never do that.

ARCHBISHOP. No, sire, certainly not. We will do it for you. *(They move off.)*

CAUCHON *(to Joan)*. You are not stupid, Joan. You can understand what we think. You swear that you heard voices and you swear to the messages they sent you. But because we believe in another king, we cannot believe that it was God Who sent you to fight against us. We are priests but we are men. And man can not believe that God has turned against him.

JOAN. You'll have to believe it when we've beaten you.

CAUCHON. Ah, you answer like a foolish child.

JOAN. My Voices told me—

CAUCHON. How often have we heard those words? Do you think you are the only girl who has ever heard voices?

JOAN. No, I don't think that.

CAUCHON. Not the first and not the last. Every village priest has had his share of young girls in crisis. If the Church believed every sick child—*(Wearily)* You have good sense. You were commander in chief of the army.

JOAN *(with pride and sudden energy)*. I commanded brave men. *They* believed in me, and *they* followed me.

CAUCHON. Yes. And if on the morning of an attack one of your brave men had suddenly heard Voices that ordered him *not* to follow you, what would you have done with him?

(Joan laughs and there is sudden, loud laughter from offstage Soldiers.)

JOAN *(calls out toward the laughter)*. The

Seigneur Bishop is a priest. He has never been close to you, my soldiers. *(The laughter dies off. Amused, she turns back to Cauchon)* A good army fights, drinks, rapes—but they don't hear voices.

CAUCHON. A jest is not an answer. You know that a disobedient soldier in your army, in any army in this world, would be silenced. The Church Militant is also an army of this earth and we, its priests, do not believe in the Divine origin of *your* disobedience. Nobody believes in you now, Joan.

JOAN. The common people believe in me—

CAUCHON. They believe in anything. They will follow another leader to-morrow. You are alone, all alone.

JOAN. I think as I think. You have the right to punish me for it.

CAUCHON. You are strong and you are stubborn, but that is not a sign that God is on your side.

JOAN. When something is black I cannot say that it is white.

THE PROMOTER *(rises and speaks angrily to Joan)*. What spell did you cast upon the man you call your King? By what means did you force him to give his armies to you?

JOAN. I have told you. I cast no spell upon him.

THE PROMOTER. It is said that you gave him a piece of mandrake.

JOAN. I don't know what mandrake is.

THE PROMOTER. Your secret has a name. We want to know what it is.

JOAN *(sharply)*. I gave him courage. That is the only word I know for what was between us. When a girl says one word of good sense and people listen to her, that's proof that God is present and no strange spells or miracles are needed.

LADVENU *(softly)*. Now there is a good and humble answer, Monseigneur. An answer that cannot be held against her.

THE PROMOTER. I do not agree. She is saying that she does not believe in the miracles as they are taught in our Holy Book. *(To Joan)* You declare that you deny the act of Jesus at the Marriage of Cana? You declare that you deny the miracle raising of Lazarus from the dead?

JOAN. No, Messire. Our Seigneur changed the water into wine and retied the thread of Lazarus' life. But for Him Who is Master of life and death, that is no more miracle than if I were to make thread for my loom.

THE PROMOTER *(with great anger, to the Judges)*. Mark her words. Write them down. She says that Jesus made no miracles.

JOAN *(runs toward the Judges with great force)*. I say that true miracles are not tricks performed by gypsies in a village square. True miracles are created by men when they use the courage and intelligence that God gave them.

CAUCHON. You are saying to us, *to us*, that the real miracle of God on this earth is man. Man, who is naught but sin and error, impotent against his own wickedness—

JOAN. And man is also strength and courage and splendor in his most desperate minutes. I know man because I have seen him. He is a miracle.

LADVENU *(quickly, nervously)*. Monseigneur, Joan speaks an awkward language. But she speaks from the heart, and without guile. Perhaps when we press down upon her, we risk making her say here what she does not mean.

THE PROMOTER *(to Joan)*. Do you believe that man is the greatest miracle of God?

JOAN. Yes, Messire.

THE PROMOTER *(shouts)*. You blaspheme. Man is impurity and lust. The dark acts of his nights are the acts of a beast—

JOAN. Yes, Messire. And the same man who acts the beast will rise from a brothel bed and throw himself before a blade to save the soldier who walks beside him. Nobody knows why he does. He doesn't know. But he does it, and he dies, cleansed and shining. He has done both good and evil, and thus twice acted like a man. That makes God happy because God made him for just this contradiction. We are good and we are evil, and that is what was meant.

(There is indignant movement among the Judges. The Inquisitor rises, holds up his hand. Immediately there is silence. They have been waiting for him to speak.)

THE INQUISITOR. I have at no time spoken. *(To Joan)* I speak to you now. I represent here the Holy Inquisition of which I am the Vicar for France. I have arrived from the south of Spain, and have little knowledge of the French and English war. It does not concern me whether Charles or the Lancaster Henry rules over France. It does not concern me that the French Duke of Burgundy has joined the English, and thus Frenchman fights French brother. They are all children of the Church. Nor have I interest in defending the temporal integrity of the Church in these quarrels. *(Turns toward Cauchon)* We leave such matters to our bishops and our priests. *(Bows to Cauchon)* Nor time to be curious about the kindness and humanity which seem to move the judgment. *(Sharply, toward The Promoter)* Nor do we find interest in these endless dreams of the Devil that haunt the nights of the Promoter. The Holy Inquisition fights in the dark world of night, against an enemy it alone can recognize. *(Stops, moves toward Warwick)* We do not care that the princes of the earth have sometimes laughed at the vigilance with which we hunt the enemy, the time and thought that we give to the judgment of the enemy. The princes of the earth are sometimes hurrying and shallow men. They remove their enemies with a length of rope and, in the crudeness of their thinking, they believe the danger ended there. We hear the mocking laughter of such men and we forgive it. The Holy Inquisition concerns itself in matters unknown to temporal kings. Our enemy is a great enemy and has a great name. *(To Joan)* You know his name?

JOAN. No, Messire. I do not understand you.

THE INQUISITOR. You will understand me. Stand up. You will answer now to me. Are you a Christian?

JOAN. Yes, Messire.

THE INQUISITOR. The trees that shaded the village church threw shadows on the house of your father. The bells of the church brought you to prayer and sent you to work. The men we sent to your village all bring the same word: you were a pious girl.

JOAN. Yes, Messire.

THE INQUISITOR. You were a tender little girl. And you were a tender woman. You cried for the wounded in every battle—

JOAN. Yes. I cried for the wounded. They were French.

THE INQUISITOR. And you cried for the English. You stayed with a wounded English soldier who screamed through a night of pain. You held him until he died, calling him your child and giving him a hope of Heaven.

JOAN. You know that, Messire?

THE INQUISITOR. Yes. The Holy Inquisition knows much of you, Joan. Grave considerate talk was given to you. And they sent me here to judge you.

LADVENU. Messire Inquisitor, Joan has always acted with kindness and Christian charity, but this court has buried it in silence. I am happy to hear you remind them that—

THE INQUISITOR *(sternly)*. Silence, Brother Ladvenu. I ask you not to forget that the Holy Inquisition alone is qualified to distinguish between theological virtues and that troubled brew that man so boastfully calls the milk of human kindness. *(Turns to the Judges)* Ah, my masters. What strange matters concern you all. Your business is to defend the Faith. But you see the kind eyes of a young girl and you are overwhelmed.

LADVENU. Our Lord loved with charity and kindness, Messire. He said to a sinner, "Go in peace." He said—

THE INQUISITOR. Silence, I said to you, Brother Ladvenu. *(Softly, carefully)* You are young. I am told your learning is very great and that is why you were admitted to this trial. Therefore I am hopeful that experience will teach you not to translate the great words into the vulgar tongue, nor embroider the meaning to suit your heart. Be seated and be silent. *(He turns back to Joan)* You were very young when you first heard your Voices.

JOAN. Yes, Messire.

THE INQUISITOR. I am going to shock you: there is nothing very exceptional about the Voices you heard in those days. Our archives are full of such cases. There are many young visionaries. Girls frequently experience a crisis of mysticism. It passes. But with you—and your priest should have recognized it—the crisis was prolonged. The messages became precise and the Celestial Voices began to use most unusual words.

JOAN. Yes. My Voices told me to go and save the Kingdom of France.

THE INQUISITOR. A strange order to an ignorant peasant girl.

JOAN. Not so strange, Messire, because it turned out to be the truth.

THE INQUISITOR. I say a strange order to a girl who had seen nothing of war. The troubles of France could have been no more to you than tales told at twilight. And yet suddenly you went out into the great world of kings and battles, convinced that it was your mission to aid your brothers in their struggle to keep the land on which they were born, and which they imagine belongs to them.

JOAN. Our Lord could not want the English to kill us and to conquer us. He could not want us to live by their laws and wishes. When they have gone back across the sea, to their own land, I will not go and pick a quarrel with them. They can rest easy in their own house. I've always said that.

THE INQUISITOR (sternly). And I say your presumption is not suited to my taste.

LADVENU. She did not mean, Messire —she speaks in a youthful fashion.

CAUCHON (softly). Be still, Brother Ladvenu.

THE INQUISITOR (to Joan). It would have been more fitting for a pious girl to have spent her life in prayers and penitence and, in such manner, obtained from Heaven the promise that the English would be defeated.

JOAN. I did all that. But I think you must first strike and then pray. That's the way God wants it. I had to explain to Charles how to attack. And he believed me and Dunois believed me and La Hire—good men, wild bulls they were, and warriors. Ah, we had some fine battles together. It was good, in the dawn, riding boot to boot with friends—

THE PROMOTER. To the kill. Did your Voices instruct you to kill?

JOAN (angrily). I have never killed a man. But war is war.

CAUCHON. You love war, Joan.

JOAN (softly). Yes. And that is one of the sins from which God will have to absolve me. But I did not like pain or death. At night, on the battlefield, I would weep for the dead—

THE PROMOTER. You would weep at night for the dead but by morning you were shouting for a new battle.

JOAN (moves to him, with great force). I say God did not wish one Englishman to remain in France. That's not so hard to understand, is it? We had to do our work, that's all. You are wise men, you think too much. Your heads are filled with too much celestial science. You don't understand even the simplest things any more—things that my dullest soldier would understand without talk. Isn't that true, La Hire?

(She stumbles, moves away from the Judges, and falls to the ground. The lights dim on the trial and we hear again the whistling of the soldier's song. La Hire, in full armor, appears upstage and moves toward Joan.)

LA HIRE. The morning has come, Madame Joan.

(She sits up, shivers, stares at La Hire.)

JOAN. The night was cold, La Hire. (He sits beside her, warms her hands in his own. Joan looks toward the trial, then up, then back to La Hire, as if she were confused by the place and the time) Good La Hire. Great La Hire. You've really come to help me as I knew you would.

LA HIRE (he takes out an onion and begins to peel it). Come to help you? I was sleeping fifty feet from you, Madame Joan, watching over you as I always do. (She laughs and moves closer to him) Don't come too close. I stink of wine and onions.

JOAN. No, no. You smell fine.

LA HIRE. Usually you tell me I stink too much to be a Christian. You say I am a danger to the army because if the wind is behind me the English will know where we are.

JOAN. Oh, La Hire, I was so stupid in those days. You know how girls are. Nothing ever happens to them, they know nothing, but they pretend they know everything. But I am not so stupid any more. You smell good because you smell like a man.

LA HIRE. I can't stand a man who washes in the field because to me a man like that isn't a man. I was brought up on an onion in the morning. The rest can have their sausage. The smell is more distinguished, you tell me. I know you think a breakfast onion is a sin.

JOAN (laughs). A breakfast onion is not a sin. Nothing that is true is a sin, La Hire. I was a fool. I tormented you. But I didn't know anything then. I didn't. (Softly) Ah, you smell so good. Sweat, onions, wine. You have all the smells a man should have. And you curse, you kill, and you think of nothing but women.

LA HIRE. Me?

JOAN. You. But I tell you that with all your sins you are like a bright new coin in the hand of God.

LA HIRE. Well, I have had a bastard life and when I go into battle, I say my prayers. I say, "God, I hope You'll help me as I would help You if You faced those Goddamned"—

JOAN (shocked). La Hire!

LA HIRE (softly). To tell you the truth, I'm frightened of what will happen to me if I get killed.

JOAN. Paradise will happen to you. They are looking forward to having you with them.

LA HIRE. That gives me heart, Madame Joan. I've always wanted to go to Paradise. But if it's all full of saints and bishops, I might not be too happy—

JOAN. It's full of men like you. It's the others who are kept waiting at the gates— (Suddenly) The gates. The gates of Orléans. They're ahead of us—the day has come, La Hire. To horse, my boy, to horse. (She climbs on her stool. La Hire stands next to her. They hold imaginary reins in their hands as they ride imaginary horses) It's dawn, La Hire. The woods are still wet from the night, the trees are still dark and strange. It's fine to ride into battle with a good soldier by your side.

LA HIRE. Some people don't like it. Some people like to make a little garden out of life and walk down a path.

JOAN. But they never know what we know. (As if she were puzzled and ashamed)

Death has to be waiting at the end of the ride before you truly see the earth, and feel your heart, and love the world. (Suddenly, in a whisper) There are three English soldiers. (She looks back) We've outridden the others. We are alone.

LA HIRE. Get off your horse, Madame Joan. Lead him back. You have never used your sword.

JOAN. No. Don't meet them alone, La Hire—

LA HIRE (he draws his sword). I'll kill them . . . Goddamned English bastards. (Sword in hand, he disappears.)

JOAN (kneels in prayer). Dear God, he is as good as bread. I answer for him. He's my friend. (She turns toward the Judges, angry, defiant) The last word will not be spoken at this trial. La Hire will come to deliver me. He will bring three hundred lancers, I know them all, and they will take me from my prison—

CAUCHON. Yes. They came to deliver you, Joan.

JOAN (running to him). Where are they? I knew they would come—

CAUCHON. They came to the gates of the city. When they saw how many English soldiers were here, they turned and went away.

JOAN (shaken). Ah. They turned and went away. Without fighting? (Cauchon turns away) Yes. Of course. It was I who taught them to do just that. I would say to them, "Have a little sense. It doesn't cost a sou. Learn not to be brave when you are outnumbered, unless—(Violently) That's what they did. They went to get reinforcements for me—

CAUCHON. No—Your friends will not return, Joan.

JOAN. That's not true. "Learn not to be brave when you are outnumbered," I said, "unless you can't retreat. Then you must fight because there is no other way—" (Proudly) La Hire will return. Because there is no other way to save me now.

CAUCHON. La Hire sells himself to whichever prince has need. When he discovered that your Charles was tired of war and would sign any peace, he marched his men toward Germany. He looks for a new land on which to try his sword.

(Comes to her) You have been abandoned. It will sound strange to you, but the priests of this court are the only men who care for your soul and for your life. Humble yourself, Joan, and the Church will take your hand. In your heart, you are a child of the Church.

JOAN *(softly)*. Yes.

CAUCHON. Trust yourself to the Church. She will weigh your deeds and take from you the agony of self-judgment.

JOAN *(after a long silence)*. For that which is of the Faith, I turn to the Church, as I have always done. But what I am, I will not denounce. What I have done, I will not deny.

(There is a shocked silence. Then there is great movement in the courtroom, as if this were the answer that would bring the judgment. The Inquisitor rises. The Priests are suddenly silent. The Inquisitor slowly moves before the Priests, peering into their faces. The Priests draw back, frightened.)

THE INQUISITOR *(to one Priest)*. Not you. *(To another Priest)* Not you. *(To a third Priest)* Not you. *(Pauses before Cauchon, stares at him)* And not you, Bishop of Beauvais. I have spoken of the great enemy, but not even now do you know his name. You do not understand on whom you sit in judgment, nor the issues of the judgment. I have told you that the Holy Inquisition is not concerned with royal rank or merchant gold or peasant birth. To us, a scholar in his room is equal in importance to an emperor in his palace. Because *we* know the name of our enemy. His name is natural man. *(There is silence. Ladvenu moves forward)* Can you not see that this girl is the symbol of that which is most to be feared? She is the enemy. She is man as he stands against us. Look at her. Frightened, hungry, dirty, abandoned by all, and no longer even sure that those Voices in the air ever spoke to her at all. Does her misery make her a suppliant begging God for mercy and for light? No. She turns away from God. She dares to stand under torture, thrashing about like a proud beast in the stable of her dungeon. She raises her eyes, not to God, but to man's image of himself. I have need to remind you,

Master, that he who loves Man does not love God.

LADVENU *(with great force)*. It cannot be. Jesus Himself became a man.

THE INQUISITOR *(turns to Cauchon)*. Seigneur Bishop, I must ask you to send your young assessor from this courtroom. I will consider after this session whether he may return or whether I will bring charges against him. *(Shouts)* Against him, or against any other. *Any* other. I would bring charges against myself if God should let me lose my way.

CAUCHON *(softly)*. Leave us, Brother Ladvenu.

LADVENU. Messire Inquisitor, I owe you obedience. I will not speak again. But I will pray to our Lord Jesus that you remember the weakness of your small, sad, lonely—enemy.

(Ladvenu exits.)

THE INQUISITOR. Do you have need to question her further? To ask all the heavy words that are listed in your legal papers? What need to ask her why she still persists in wearing man's dress when it is contrary to the commandments? Why she dared the sin of living among men as a man? The deeds no longer matter. What she has done is of less importance than why she did it, the answers less important than the one answer. It is a fearful answer, "What I am, I will not . . ." You wish to say it again? Say it.

JOAN *(slowly, softly)*. What I am, I will not denounce. What I have done, I will not deny.

THE INQUISITOR *(carefully, as if he has taken the measure of an enemy)*. You have heard it. Down through the ages, from dungeon, from torture chamber, from the fire of the stake. Ask her and she will say with those others, "Take my life. I will give it because I will not deny what I have done." This is what they say, all of them, the insolent breed. The men who dare our God. Those who say no to us—*(He moves toward Joan. Cauchon rises)* Well, you and all like you shall be made to say yes. You put the Idea in peril, and that you will not be allowed to do. *(Turns to the Judges)* The girl is only a monstrous symbol of the faith decayed. Therefore I now demand her immediate punishment. I demand that she be excommunicated from the Church. I demand that she be returned to secular authority there to receive her punishment. I ask the secular arm to limit her sentence to this side of death and the mutilation of her members.

(Cauchon moves to The Inquisitor as if to stop the judgment.)

WARWICK *(to Cauchon)*. A passionate man and so sincere. I think he means simply to throw the dirty work to me. I am the secular authority here. Why didn't your French Charles have her burned? It was his job.

CHARLES *(very disturbed)*. I don't want to do it. I don't like killing.

(A large, masked figure appears.)

CAUCHON *(calls to the masked man)*. Master Executioner, is the wood for the stake dry and ready to burn?

EXECUTIONER. All is ready. Things will go according to custom. But I will not be able to help the girl this time.

CAUCHON. What do you mean help her, Master?

EXECUTIONER. We let the first flames rise high. Then I climb up behind the victims and strangle them the rest of the way. It's easier and quicker for everybody. But I have had special instructions this time to make the fire very high. And so it will take longer and I will not be able to reach her for the act of mercy.

CAUCHON *(moves to Joan)*. Did you hear that?

JOAN. I've remembered a dream from years ago. I woke screaming and ran to my mother—*(Screams as if in pain)* Ah.

CAUCHON *(desperately)*. Joan, for the last time I offer you the saving hand of your Mother Church. We wish to save you, but we can delay no longer. The crowd has been waiting since dawn. They eat their food, scold their children, make jokes, and grow impatient. You are famous and they have nothing better to do with their lives than bring garlands to the famous—or watch them burn.

JOAN *(as if she is still in the dream)*. I forgive them, Messire. I forgive you, too.

THE PROMOTER *(furiously)*. Monseigneur speaks to you like a father in order to save your miserable soul and you answer by forgiving him.

JOAN. Monseigneur speaks to me gently, he takes great pains to seduce me, but I do not know whether he means to save me or conquer me. In any case, he will be obliged to have me burned.

CAUCHON *(comes to her)*. For the last time I say: Confess your sins and return to us. We will save you.

JOAN *(she clings to his robe)*. I wish to return to the Church. I want the Holy Communion. I have asked for it over and over again. But they have refused to give it to me.

CAUCHON. After your confession, when you have begun your penance, we will give it to you. *(There is no answer. Very softly)* Are you not afraid to die?

JOAN. Yes. I am afraid. What difference does that make? I've always been so afraid of fire. *(Gasps)* I've remembered a dream—

CAUCHON *(pulls her to him)*. Joan, we cannot believe in the Divinity of your Voices. But if we are wrong—and certainly that thought has crossed our minds—

THE PROMOTER *(furious)*. No, I say no. Even to you, my Bishop of Beauvais—

CAUCHON *(to Joan)*. But if we are wrong then we will have committed a monstrous sin of ignorance and we will pay for it the rest of our eternal lives. But we are the priests of your Church. Trust our belief that we are right, as you trusted your good village priest. Place yourself in our hands. You will be at peace.

JOAN. I cannot follow what you say. I am tired. Oh, sire, I do not sleep at night. I come here and all is said so fast that I cannot understand. You torture me with such gentle words, and your voice is so kind. I would rather have you beat me—

CAUCHON. I talk to you thus because my pride is less than yours.

JOAN *(she moves away from him, as if she were sick and wanted to be alone)*. Pride? I have been a prisoner so long—I think my head is sick and old, and the bottom of me does not hold any more. Sometimes I don't know where I am and my dungeon seems a great beech tree. I am hungry, or I was, and I want a taste of country milk—

CAUCHON *(desperately, as if he were at*

the end). Look at me, Joan, keep your mind here. I am an old man. I have killed people in the defense of my beliefs. I am so close to death myself that I do not wish to kill again. I do not wish to kill a little girl. Be kind. *(Cries out)* Help me to save you.

JOAN *(very softly; broken now).* What do you want me to say? Please tell me in simple words.

CAUCHON. I am going to ask you three questions. Answer yes three times. That is all. *(With passion)* Help me, Joan.

JOAN. But could I sleep a few hours, sire?

CAUCHON. No! We cannot wait. Do you entrust yourself with humility to the Holy Roman and Apostolic Church, to our Holy Father, the Pope, and to his bishops? Will you rely upon them, and upon no one else, to be your judges? Do you make the complete and total act of submission? Do you ask to be returned to the bosom of the Church?

JOAN. Yes, but—*(The Inquisitor rises. Cauchon becomes nervous)* I don't want to say the opposite of what my Voices told me. I don't ever want to bear false witness against Charlie. I fought so hard for the glory of his consecration. Oh, that was a day when he was crowned. The sun was out—

CHARLES *(to Joan).* It was a nice day and I'll always remember it. But I'd rather not think it was a divine miracle. I'd rather people didn't think that God sent you to me. Because now that you're a prisoner, and thought to be a heretic and a sorceress, they think that God has abandoned me. I'm in bad enough trouble without that kind of gossip. Just forget about me and go your way.

(Joan bows her head.)

CAUCHON. Do you wish me to repeat the question? *(Joan does not answer. Cauchon is angry)* Are you mad? You understand now that we are your only protectors, that this is the last thing I can do for you? You cannot bargain and quibble like a peasant at a village fair. You are an impudent girl, and I now become angry with you. You should be on your knees to the Church.

JOAN *(falls to her knees).* Messire, deep in your heart do you believe that our Lord wishes me to submit to the judgment?

CAUCHON. I so believe.

JOAN *(softly).* Then I submit.

(There is great movement in the court. The Inquisitor rises; The Promoter moves to him.)

CAUCHON *(very tired now).* You promise to renounce forever the bearing of arms?

JOAN. But, Messire, there is still so much to do—

CAUCHON *(angrily).* Nothing more will ever be done by you.

WARWICK. That is true, Joan.

CHARLES. And if you're thinking of helping me again, please don't. I won't ever use you any more. It would be very dangerous for me.

JOAN *(broken now, almost as if she were asleep).* I renounce forever the bearing of arms.

CAUCHON *(in great haste).* Do you renounce forever the wearing of that brazen uniform?

JOAN. You have asked me that over and over again. The uniform doesn't matter. My Voices told me to put it on.

THE PROMOTER. It was the Devil who told you to put it on.

JOAN. Oh, Messire, put away the Devil for today. My Voices chose the uniform because my Voices have good sense. *(With great effort)* I had to ride with soldiers. It was necessary they not think of me as a girl. It was necessary they see in me nothing but a soldier like themselves. That is all the sense there was to it.

CAUCHON. But why have you persisted in wearing it in prison? You have been asked this question in many examinations and your refusal to answer has become of great significance to your judges.

JOAN. And I have asked over and over to be taken to a Church prison. Then I would take off my man's uniform.

THE PROMOTER *(to Cauchon).* Monseigneur, the girl is playing with us, as from the first. I do not understand what she says or why you—

JOAN *(angry).* One doesn't have to be an educated man to understand what I am saying.

THE PROMOTER *(turns to Judges).* She says that she submits to the Church. But

I tell you that as long as she refuses to put aside that Devil dress, I will exercise my rights as master judge of heretics and witchcraft. *(To Cauchon)* Strange pressures have been put upon all of us. I know not from where they come, but I tell even you—

JOAN. I have said that if you put me in a Church prison I will take off this uniform

THE PROMOTER. You will not bargain. Put aside that dress or, no matter who feels otherwise, you will be declared a sorceress.

JOAN *(softly, to Cauchon)*. I am not alone in prison. Two English soldier guards are in the cell with me night and day. The nights are long. I am in chains. I try hard not to sleep, but sometimes I am too tired—*(She stops, embarrassed)* In this uniform it is easier for me to defend myself.

CAUCHON *(in great anger)*. Have you had so to defend yourself since the beginning of this trial?

(Warwick moves to Joan.)

JOAN. Every night since I've been captured. I don't have much sleep. In the mornings, when I am brought before you, I am confused, and I don't understand your questions. I told you that. Sometimes I try to sleep here in the trial so that I will stay awake in the night—

CAUCHON. Why heaven't you told us this before?

JOAN. Because the soldiers told me they would be hanged if I said anything—

WARWICK *(very angry)*. They were right. *(To Cauchon)* Detestable bastards. It's disgusting. They've learned such things since they came to France. It may be all right in the French Army, but not in mine. *(Bows to Joan)* I am sorry, Madame. It will not happen again.

CAUCHON *(to Joan)*. The Church will protect you from now on. I promise you.

JOAN. Then I agree to put on woman's dress.

CAUCHON. Thank you, my child. That is all. *(He moves to The Inquisitor)* Messire Inquisitor, Brother Ladvenu drew up the Act of Renunciation. Will you permit me to recall him here? *(With bitterness)* The girl has said yes, this man has said yes.

THE PROMOTER *(to The Inquisitor)*.

Messire Inquisitor, you are going to allow this to happen?

THE INQUISITOR. If she said yes, she has fulfilled the only condition that concerns me.

THE PROMOTER *(turns to Cauchon)*. This trial has been conducted with an indulgence that is beyond my understanding. *(To The Inquisitor)* I am told that there are those here who eat from the English manger. I ask myself now if they have arranged to eat better from the French manger.

THE INQUISITOR *(rises, moves toward Joan)*. It is not a question of mangers, Messire Promoter. *I* ask myself how did it happen that this girl said yes when so many lesser ones did not bow the head. I had not believed it to be possible. *(Points to Cauchon)* And why was tenderness born in the heart of that old man who was her judge? He is at the end of a life worn out with compromise and debasement. Why now, here, for this girl, this dangerous girl, did his heart— *(He kneels, ignoring the others. As he prays, we hear only the words . . .)* Why, Oh Lord . . .? Why, Oh Lord . . .? Consecrate it in peace to Your Glory . . . Your Glory—

CAUCHON *(as Ladvenu enters)*. Please read the act.

LADVENU *(comes to Joan. With great tenderness)*. I have prayed for you, Joan. *(Reading)* "I, Joan, commonly called The Maid, confess having sinned through pride and malice in pretending to have received revelations from our Lord God. I confess I have blasphemed by wearing an immodest costume. I have incited men to kill through witchcraft and I here confess to it. I swear on the Holy Gospels I will not again wear this heretic's dress and I swear never to bear arms again. I declare that I place myself humbly at the mercy of our Holy Mother Church and our Holy Father, the Pope of Rome and His Bishops, so that they may judge my sins and my errors. I beseech Her to receive me in Her Bosom and I declare myself ready to submit to the sentence which She may inflict upon me. In faith of which, I have signed my name upon this Act of Renunciation of which I have full knowledge. *(Ladvenu hands the pen to Joan. She moves it in the air, as if she had not heard and did not understand. Ladvenu takes her hand and puts it on the paper)* I will help you.

CAUCHON *(as if he were a very old man)*. You have been saved. We, your judges, in mercy and mitigation, now condemn you to spend the remainder of your days in prison. There you will do penance for your sins. You will eat the bread of sorrow and drink the water of anguish until, through solitary contemplation, you repent. Under these conditions of penance, we declare you delivered of the danger of excommunication. You may go in peace. *(He makes the Sign of the Cross)* Take her away.

(Cauchon stumbles and is helped by Ladvenu. A Soldier pushes Joan away from the trial. The Judges rise and slowly move off. Cauchon moves past Warwick.)

WARWICK. There were several times, sire, when I thought I would have to interfere. My King must have what he paid for. But you were right and I was wrong. The making of a martyr is dangerous business. The pile of faggots, the invincible girl in the flames, might have been a triumph for the French spirit. But the apologies of a hero are sad and degrading. You did well, sire; you are a wise man.

CAUCHON *(with great bitterness)*. I did not mean to earn your praise.

(He moves off. The lights dim on the trial as Warwick moves off. Four Soldiers appear with spears, and their spears become the bars of Joan's jail cell. Charles appears and stands looking at Joan through the bars.)

CHARLES. I didn't want you to sacrifice yourself for me, Joan. I know you loved me, but I don't want people to love me. It makes for obligations. This filthy prison air is wet and stinks. Don't they ever clean these places? *(He peers into her cell, sees the water pail that sits beside her, and draws back)* Tell them to give you fresh water. My God, what goes on in this world. *(She does not answer him)* Don't you want to speak to me, Joan?

JOAN. Good-bye, Charlie.

CHARLES. You must stop calling me Charlie. Ever since my coronation I am careful to make everyone say sire.

JOAN. Sire.

CHARLES. I'll come and see you again. Good-bye.

(He moves off. Joan lies in silence. Then she tries to drink from the water pail, retches, and puts her hand over her mouth as if she were very sick.)

JOAN. Blessed Saint Michael. *(She makes a strange sound, shivers)* I am in prison. Come to me. Find me. *(Cries out)* I need you now. *(Very loudly)* I told you that I was afraid of fire, long before I ever knew—or did I always know? You want me to live? *(When there is no answer)* Why do I call for help? You must have good reason for not coming to me. *(She motions toward courtroom)* They think I dreamed it all. Maybe I did. But it's over now . . .

(Warwick comes slowly into the cell.)

WARWICK *(hesitantly)*. You are weeping?

JOAN. No, Monseigneur.

WARWICK. I am sorry to disturb you. I only came to say that I am glad you are saved. You behaved damned well. I, er, well, it's rather difficult to say in my language, but the plain fact is that I like you. And it amused me to watch you with the Inquisitor. Sinister man, isn't he? I detest these intellectual idealists more than anything in the world. What disgusting animals they are. He wanted only to see you humiliate yourself, no matter your state or your misery. And when you did, he was satisfied.

JOAN *(softly)*. He had reason to be satisfied.

WARWICK. Well, don't worry about him. It all worked out well. Martyrs are likely to stir the blood of simple people and set up too grand a monument to themselves. It's all very complex and dangerous. Tell me, are you a virgin?

JOAN. Yes.

WARWICK. I knew you were. A woman would not talk as you do. My fiancée in England is a very pure girl and she also talks like a boy. You are the greatest horsewoman I have ever seen. *(When there is no answer)* Ah, well. I am intruding on you. Don't hesitate to let me know if I can ever do anything for you. Good-bye, madame.

JOAN. Nobody else came to see me here. You are a kind man, Monseigneur.

WARWICK. Not at all. (*Motions toward courtroom*) It's that I don't like all those fellows who use words to make war. You and I killed because that was the way things turned out for us.

JOAN. Monseigneur, I have done wrong. And I don't know how or why I did it. (*Slowly, bitterly*) I swore against myself. That is a great sin, past all others—(*Desperately*) I still believe in all that I did, and yet I swore against it. God can't want that. What can be left for me?

WARWICK. Certainly they are not going to make you a gay life, not at first. But things work out and in time your nasty little Charles might even show you a speck of loyalty—

JOAN. Yes, when I am no longer dangerous, he might even give me a small pension and a servant's room at court.

WARWICK (*sharply*). Madame, there will be no court.

JOAN. And I will wear cast-off brocade and put jewels in my hair and grow old. I will be happy that few people remember my warrior days and I will grovel before those who speak of my past and pray them to be silent. And when I die, in a big fat bed, I will be remembered as a crazy girl who rode into battle for what she said she believed, and ate the dirt of lies when she was faced with punishment. That will be the best that I can have—if my little Charles remembers me at all. If he doesn't there will be a prison dungeon, and filth and darkness—(*Cries out*) What good is life either way?

WARWICK. It is good any way you can have it. We all try to save a little honor, of course, but the main thing is to be here—

JOAN (*rises, calls out, speaking to the Voices*). I was only born the day you first spoke to me. My life only began on the day you told me what I must do, my sword in hand. You are silent, dear my God, because you are sad to see me frightened and craven. And for what? A few years of unworthy life. (*She kneels. Softly, as if she is answering a message*) I

know. Yes, I know. I took the good days from You and refused the bad. I know. Dear my God forgive me, and keep me now to be myself. Forgive me and take me back for what I am. (*She rises. She is happy and cheerful*) Call your soldiers, Warwick. I deny my confession.

WARWICK. Joan. No nonsense, please. Things are all right as they are. I—

JOAN. Come.

(*She holds out her hand to him.*)

WARWICK. I don't want anything to do with your death.

JOAN (*smiles*). You have a funny gentleman's face. But you are kind. Come now. (*She calls out*) Soldiers! Englishmen! Give me back my warrior clothes. And when I have put them on, call back all the priests. (*Stops, puts her hands in prayer and speaks simply*) Please God, help me now.

(*The music of the "Sanctus" begins as the Judges, Cauchon, The Inquisitor, The Promoter Charles, the People of the Court, return to the stage. Two Soldiers bring a crude stake. Joan herself moves to the stake and the Soldiers lash her to it. Other Soldiers and Village Women pick up the bundles of faggots and carry them off stage. The Executioner appears with lighted torch and moves through the crowd.*)

JOAN (*as they are about to carry her off*). Please. Please. Give me a Cross.

THE PROMOTER. No Cross will be given to a witch.

AN ENGLISH SOLDIER (*he has taken two sticks of wood and made a Cross. Now he hands his Cross to Joan*). Here, my daughter. Here's your Cross. (*Very angry, to The Promoter*) She has a right to a Cross like anybody else.

(*Joan is carried off stage. The lights dim and we see flames—or the shadows of flames—as they are projected on the cyclorama. Ladvenu runs on stage with a Cross from the church and stands holding it high for Joan to see.*)

THE INQUISITOR (*calling to Executioner*). Be quick. Be quick. Let the smoke hide her. (*To Warwick*) In five minutes, Monseigneur, the world will be crying.

WARWICK. Yes.

THE INQUISITOR (*shouting to Executioner*). Be quick, master, be quick.

EXECUTIONER (*calling in to him*). All is ready, messire. The flames reach her now.

LADVENU *(calling out)*. Courage, Joan. We pray for you.

CAUCHON. May God forgive us all.
(Cauchon falls to his knees and begins the prayer for the dead. The prayers are murmured as the chorus chants a Requiem. The Soldiers and the Village People return to the stage: a Woman falls to the ground; a Soldier cries out; a Girl bends over as if in pain and a Soldier helps her to move on; the Court Ladies back away, hiding their faces from the burning; the Priests kneel in prayer.)

CHARLES *(in a whisper as he leaves).* What does she do? What does she say? Is it over?

THE INQUISITOR *(to Ladvenu)*. What does she do?

LADVENU. She is quiet.

THE INQUISITOR *(moves away)*. Is her head lowered?

LADVENU. No, messire. Her head is high.

THE INQUISITOR *(as if he were in pain)*. Ah. *(To Ladvenu)* She falters now?

LADVENU. No. It is a terrible and noble sight, messire. You should turn and see.

THE INQUISITOR *(moves off)*. I have seen it all before.
(The lights dim. Cauchon rises from his prayers. He stumbles and falls. Ladvenu and Warwick move to help him. He takes Ladvenu's arm, but moves away from Warwick, refusing his help. As the stage becomes dark, Cauchon, The Promoter, Ladvenu and Warwick move downstage and the light comes up on La Hire who stands above them. La Hire is in full armor, holding helmet and sword.)

LA HIRE. You were fools to burn Joan of Arc.

CAUCHON. We committed a sin, a monstrous sin.

WARWICK. Yes, it was a grave mistake. We made a lark into a giant bird who will travel the skies of the world long after our names are forgotten, or confused, or cursed down.

LA HIRE. I knew the girl and I loved her. You can't let it end this way. If you do, it will not be the true story of Joan.

LADVENU. That is right. The true story of Joan is not the hideous agony of a girl tied to a burning stake. She will stand forever for the glory that can be. Praise God.

LA HIRE. The true story of Joan is the story of her happiest day. Anybody with any sense knows that. Go back and act it out.
(The lights dim on the four men and come up on the Coronation of Charles in Reims Cathedral. The altar cloth is in place, the lighted candles are behind the altar, stained glass windows are projected on the cyclorama. The Archbishop appears, and the people of the royal court. Joan stands clothed in a fine white robe, ornamented with a fleur-de-lis.)

WARWICK *(moves into the coronation scene, stares bewildered as Charles, in coronation robes, carrying his crown, crosses to the altar)*. This could not have been her happiest day. To watch Holy Oil being poured on that mean, sly little head!

CHARLES *(turns to Warwick, amused)*. Oh, I didn't turn out so bad. I drove you out of the country. And I got myself some money before I died. I was as good as most.

WARWICK. So you were. But certainly the girl would never have ridden into battle, never have been willing to die because you were as good as most.

JOAN *(comes forward, smiling, happy)*. Oh, Warwick, I wasn't paying any attention to Charlie. I knew what Charlie was like. I wanted him crowned because I wanted my country back. And God gave it to us on this Coronation Day. Let's end with it, please, if nobody would mind.
(As the curtain falls the chorus sings the "Gloria" of the Mass.)

IVAN TURGENEV's

A Month in the Country

In the adaptation by EMLYN WILLIAMS

First presented by The Phoenix Theatre (T. Edward Hambleton and Norris Houghton), New York, on April 3, 1956, with the following cast:

SHAAF	Lou Gilbert	MATVEI	Stefan Gierasch
ANNA SEMYENOVNA YSLAEVA	Mary Morris	A FOOTMAN	Sorrell Booke
LIZAVETA BOGDANOVNA	Ann Hennessey	IGNATY ILLYICH SHPIGHELSKY	Luther Adler
NATALIA PETROVNA	Uta Hagen	VERA	Olga Bielinska
RAKITIN	Alexander Scourby	YSLAEV	Michael Strong
KOLIA	Tony Atkins	KATIA	Anne Meara
BELIAEV	Al Hedison	BOLSHINTSOV	Martin Wolfson

Directed by Michael Redgrave

————————————

ACT ONE

SCENE ONE

While the curtain is still down Vera is heard playing at the pianoforte in the ballroom: a mazurka of Chopin. A pause. The Curtain rises slowly.
The drawing-room of Yslaev's house on his estate in the country near Moscow, Russia; a summer afternoon. An almost triangular view of the room, with in the left wall ('left' and 'right' throughout refer to the audience's left and right) large French window opening on to the garden, and in the right wall (up a step and beyond pillars) folding doors (opening onstage) leading to the ballroom; a smaller window to the left of them; to the right of them, an entrance leading off right, presumably to the hall, the dining-room, and the stairs; to the right again, this side of the pillars and nearer the audience, a smaller door leading to the study. The room is beautifully furnished, the native Russian merging into great elegance of detail (markedly French in influence), revealing the taste of a well-bred young hostess. On the left, between the windows and the audience, a desk and desk-chair; a table; in the angle between the French windows and the pillars, a tall ornamented Russian stove; an armchair; a Récamier sofa; a footstool; a long stool; a mirror over the desk.
It is a beautiful summer afternoon, in the early forties of the last century.
At the table are seated Anna Semyenovna Yslaeva (Yslaev's mother), a fussy old lady who is used to her own way: Lizaveta Bogdanovna (her companion), thirty-seven, whose looks have long ago grown shabby through an incessant anxious desire to please her betters: and Shaaf, a middle-aged German tutor, ugly, slow and stupid. They are playing preference. At some distance from them are Natalia and Rakitin. She is a beautiful exquisite creature of twenty-nine, elegantly posed on the sofa; he is a fine-looking thoughtful man, of great breeding, a year or two older. He sits on the footstool, almost at her feet, a book open on his knees, looking at her; she has laid down her embroidery and is fanning herself.
A pause; the music begins again. For a space of time after the curtain rises, the only movement is the fingers of the card-players and the flutter of Natalia's fan, as she listens to the music. The music comes to an end. A pause.

———

SHAAF. Har-r-tz.
ANNA. Hearts again? If this goes on, my friend, you'll have the clothes off our backs——
SHAAF *(phlegmatically)*. Eight har-r-tz.
ANNA *(to Lizaveta)*. Did you ever know such a madcap? I declare, there's no playing with him——
LIZAVETA *(smiling and nodding)*. None at all ... *(Sniffing from a box)* So true——
ANNA. And you stop taking snuff, I've told you how bad it is for you.
LIZAVETA. Just this once ...
(A pause.)
NATALIA *(to Rakitin)*. Why have you stopped reading?
RAKITIN *(reading)*. 'Monte-Cristo se redressa haletant'... *(Looking up at her)* Are you interested?
NATALIA. No.
RAKITIN. Then why ask me to plough through——
NATALIA. It's perfectly simple why. The other day a woman said to me 'Have you read *Monte-Cristo*—my dear, you must, it's captivating!' I didn't say a word at the time, but now I shall be able to tell her I have read it, and that it isn't captivating at all. Do go on.
RAKITIN *(looking for his place in the book)*. 'Se redressa haletant, et——'
NATALIA. Have you seen Arkady today?
RAKITIN. Yes, ran into him working by the dam.
NATALIA. Was ever a woman blessed with such a pillar of industry for a husband
RAKITIN. He wanted to explain something to the workmen, and walked into the sand right up to his knees.
NATALIA. How like him ... He attack everything with too much enthusiasm—he tries too hard. And I consider that fault. Don't you agree?
RAKITIN. Yes, I do.
NATALIA. Oh, how boring of you .. You always agree with me. Read me more
SHAAF *(as Rakitin turns over pages)* Har-r-tz.

ANNA. What, again? Really, Shaaf, this is not to be borne! *(To Natalia)* Daughter-in-law, do you know what—daughter-in-law!

NATALIA *(paying attention with difficulty)*. Yes?

ANNA. What do you think, dear, our Prussian friend's beating us with the most monstrous tactics——

SHAAF. Und now aggin zeven har-r-tz. *(He has a strong German accent)*

ANNA *(rising and gathering up the cards)*. We're changing over to whist . . . *(To Natalia)* But where's our little treasure?

NATALIA. Kolia? Gone for a walk with his new tutor.

ANNA. Ah . . . Now whist—*(smartly flicking cards)*—Lizaveta Bogdanovna, you're my partner——

LIZAVETA. Oh, do you mean it—an honor——

RAKITIN *(to Natalia)*. Did you say something about a new tutor?

NATALIA. We acquired one while you were away, for general knowledge.

RAKITIN. Another old fogey?

NATALIA. No . . . My dear, I tell you what—you know how you love watching people, probing like a dentist into their innermost thoughts——

RAKITIN. Oh come——

NATALIA. I want you to focus your attention on him.

RAKITIN. The new tutor? Why?

NATALIA. Because I like him.

RAKITIN. Describe him to me.

NATALIA. Oh . . . well. Tall. Fair. Very young . . .

RAKITIN. Yes?

NATALIA. Very good eyes, that look straight at you, with an expression of great liveliness.

RAKITIN. Yes?

NATALIA. The whole face bears a marked air of vigor— something——

RAKITIN. Go on.

NATALIA. Something—forceful . . . but you'll see for yourself. There's one thing, though—his manner's a trifle gauche, and that's a grave defect in the eyes of a man of the world like you.

RAKITIN. I'm not in your good books today, I can see that——

NATALIA. Seriously, Rakitin, do have a look at him, it's my opinion he has the makings of a fine man. Though Heaven knows, it's early to say——

RAKITIN. You have whetted my curiosity.

NATALIA. I'm so glad . . . Shall we read?

RAKITIN *(reading)*. 'Se redressa haletant, et——'

NATALIA. But where's Vera? I haven't set eyes on her since this morning . . . *(As Rakitin shuts his book)* Ah . . . Tell me some news.

RAKITIN. What do you wish to hear? About my visit to the Krinitsins?

NATALIA. If you like. How are our newlyweds?

RAKITIN. Time lies heavy on their hands.

NATALIA. Already? Jamais! But how did you find out?

RAKITIN. Can one conceal boredom? Everything else, but boredom . . . no.

NATALIA *(looking at him)*. Can one conceal—everything else?

RAKITIN. I think so.

(A pause. She looks away.)

NATALIA. What did you do there?

RAKITIN. Nothing; I was bored too, and to be bored by one's friends is a calamity. One feels at ease and relaxed, one breathes an air of affection . . . and one is bored. To extinction. The heart aches stupidly, as if it were hungry.

NATALIA. A clever man like you must often find the world very dull——

RAKITIN *(quietly, with meaning)*. You're talking as if you had no idea what it felt like to live with a creature whom you love and who bores you.

NATALIA. 'Love' is a big word . . . You're a subtle creature, Rakitin, aren't you?

RAKITIN. Am I?

NATALIA. Oversubtle, in fact; it's your Achilles heel. You're as clever as a cartload of old professors. Sometimes, when you and I are talking, I feel we're just . . . making lace.

RAKITIN. Lace?

NATALIA. Have you ever watched women making lace? They sit in stuffy rooms, and never move an inch to the left or to the right. Lace is a lovely thing, but on a hot day I'd sooner have a drink of icy fresh water.

RAKITIN. Natalia Petrovna, you're annoyed with me.

NATALIA. Am I?

RAKITIN. I don't know quite why, but you are.

NATALIA. When men pride themselves on their subtlety, they have even less insight than when they don't . . . No, I'm not annoyed with you——

ANNA. At last! He's overreached himself—(rising)—played right into our hands! The rascal's overreached himself! My luck's turned, where's my purse—— (She crosses and rummages in the desk)

SHAAF (sulkily). It iss de fault von Lizaveta Bogdanovna.

LIZAVETA (annoyed). Oh, I protest! How was I to know that Anna Semyenovna had no hearts?

(During this, Rakitin rises, walks, then turns and surveys Natalia.)

SHAAF. In de future, vid Lizaveta Bogdanovna as my partner, I do not play. (He counts his winnings and writes figures in a pocket-book)

LIZAVETA. That suits me to a T, Herr Shaaf . . . Well, upon my word!

ANNA (calling). Shuffle the cards, Lizaveta Bogdanovna, and stop airing your views!

RAKITIN (to Natalia). The more I look at you today, the less I recognize you. You've changed, in some way——

NATALIA. Really? How interesting.

(Kolia runs in from the garden, and hurries to Anna Semyenovna. He is an attractive child of ten.)

KOLIA. Granny! Granny! (Covering her eyes with one hand) Guess what I've got!

ANNA. Now let me think—what can Granny's little treasure have for Granny! . . . (As Kolia uncovers her eyes and brings out a bow and arrows from behind his back) Oh, what a lovely toy! Now who made this for you?

KOLIA (pointing to the garden). He did! (Rakitin turns. Beliaev appears shyly at the windows. He is a slight personable youth of twenty-one, carefully but shabbily dressed; at the moment he is particularly coltish and self-conscious, but once he is at ease with people of his own age, all that breaks down and he becomes a high-spirited impressionable student. He carries books.)

ANNA. Really, it's beautifully put together—(rising and going back to the others)—and now to work——

KOLIA. D'you know what, Granny? I shot with it, twice, Granny, twice! I aimed at a tree, Granny, and I hit it! Both times, Granny! Both times——

NATALIA. Show me, Kolia.

KOLIA (running to her and giving her the bow to examine). Oh, Mamma, you should see the way he climbs trees, better than a squirrel—and he wants to teach me the way to, and he wants to teach me how to swim on my back . . . He's going to teach me everything there is, everything in the world, Mamma!

NATALIA (to Beliaev). It's so very kind of you to take such pains with him. I'm extremely obliged.

(Beliaev bows to her.)

KOLIA (running to Beliaev). Let's run as far as the stables, Alexei Nikolaich, shall we? And take some bread for Favorite!

BELIAEV. Shall we? That's a good idea——

ANNA (as Kolia runs out by the windows). Come and give Granny a kiss first, darling——

KOLIA (in the garden). Later, Granny, later——

(Beliaev smiles sheepishly at Rakitin and Natalia and follows Kolia into the garden.)

ANNA. What a little pet that child is, what a charmer! . . . (To Shaaf and Lizaveta Bogdanovna, insistently) Don't you agree?

LIZAVETA. An angel, no more no less——

SHAAF. Boodiful, boodiful—pass.

NATALIA (to Rakitin). Well, what did you think of him?

RAKITIN. Think of whom?

NATALIA. Why, the new tutor! You are provoking——

RAKITIN. Let me see, his eyes—yes it's a good face. He seems very shy doesn't he?

NATALIA. I tell you what, Rakitin Let's make a hobby of him!

RAKITIN. How do you mean?

NATALIA. Complete his education! It' a unique chance for sedate, sensibl people like us to exercise our virtues. You and I are eminently sensible, are we not?

RAKITIN. You find this boy interesting? He'd be flattered if he knew.

NATALIA. Ah, would he? I'm afraid, my dear, just because you and I study ourselves with the greatest industry, we bask in the belief that we know all about everybody else. But he isn't like us, not the least little bit.

RAKITIN. You're perfectly right. The soul of another man is a dark forest . . .

NATALIA (ironically). So true, so true . . .

RAKITIN. Why are you continually mocking me?

NATALIA. If one can't tease one's friends, whom can one tease? And you're my friend. (Pressing his hand) My old friend. As if you didn't know—ce que vous êtes pour moi.

RAKITIN. Natalia Petrovna, you play with me like a cat with a mouse!

NATALIA. Oh, do I?

ANNA. That means I've won twenty from you, Adam Ivanych—things are on the mend!

SHAAF. In de future, vid Lizaveta Bogdanovna as my partner, I do not play. (Matvei enters from the ballroom. He is a manservant, about forty.)

MATVEI (announcing). Ignaty Illyich Shpighelsky!

(Doctor Shpighelsky follows on his heels. He is a big, attractive florid man, with tremendous personality; behind his social manner—in which breezy exuberance alternates with portentous solemnity, the manner of a born comedian—he hides a sly, watchful and sardonic nature. It is clear from everybody's reaction to him that he is accepted as a great wag.)

THE DOCTOR. Stuff and nonsense, man, you don't announce a doctor, it'll be the undertaker next! (As Anna laughs, and Matvei goes back, closing the doors, stifling a smile) My undying regards to one and all, and all and one! (Kissing Anna's hand) And how is our charming duenna? Making her fortune?

ANNA. Fortune, the idea——

THE DOCTOR. The season's greetings

to Natalia Petrovna, and ditto—(to Rakitin)—to Mihail Alexandrovitch!

NATALIA. How are you, Doctor, are you well?

THE DOCTOR. 'How are you, Doctor, are you well'—now what a question, I ask you! What else can a physician do, but burst with health? No doctor worth his salt ever gets ill—he just dies. (Taking snuff)

NATALIA. Do sit down . . .

THE DOCTOR (sitting in the armchair). And what of your health, good lady?

NATALIA. Sound enough, Doctor, but I'm in a bad mood today. And that's a kind of disorder, isn't it?

THE DOCTOR (rising). Ah me, ah me, lackaday . . . (With mock seriousness, feeling her pulse) Do you know what's the matter with you, Natalia Petrovna?

NATALIA. No, what?

THE DOCTOR. Too serious-minded.

NATALIA (rapping him with her fan). Oh!

THE DOCTOR. There's nothing like a good laugh for bustling up the circulation. (Sitting again) Though a couple of my special pink drops won't do you any harm.

NATALIA. But I'm more than willing to laugh. Now, Doctor, you've a tongue like a rapier—which is what I like and respect you for—tell me something amusing—vite!

THE DOCTOR. At your service, peerless lady. Though I wasn't prepared to be held up for jokes at the point of a pistol—blindfold but unbowed, I walk the plank . . .

RAKITIN (sitting on the footstool). Ah . . .

THE DOCTOR. You know Verenitsin Platon-Vassilevitch?

NATALIA. I know whom you mean, yes——

THE DOCTOR. Well, he has a mad sister. 'Smatter o' fact, they're so dead alike that if she's mad he must be too, and if he's sane then she's no lunatic, but that's neither here nor there; all we know is that over every man jack of us there hovers the inscrutable—if rather grubby —finger of Fate; only the other day, with my own fair hands, I poured a basin of cold water over the lady, and when she was dried she was madder than ever—but still . . . Her brother has a daughter, a greeny-colored wench with pale little eyes, a red little nose and the chance of inheriting three hundred serfs from Auntie, which makes her perfect. Lunatics live for ever, so Auntie looks like being with us for quite a time, but one hopes for the best—anyway Papa claps her on the market, and various eligibles bob up: among them a certain Perekusov, thin as a rake and shy as a rabbit, but the highest principles. Papa fancies him, Miss fancies him, slap the young codger on the back, prod him in the belly, and publish the banns . . . But wait! Scene, the Grand Marshal's Ball, gaiety at its height; hey presto, jack-in-the-box-out-of-the-blue, Ardalion Protobekassov . . . *(clicking his heels)* . . . an officer!

NATALIA. Ahh . . .

THE DOCTOR. 'Mademoiselle, may I have the honor . . .' *(clicking his heels)* One polka. Two more polkas. *(Clicking his heels, smartly, twice)* Then we sit out, the military eyes start rolling like drums, and mademoiselle's head is turned as neat as a water-tap, swish . . . Tears, moans, breathe the word 'wedding' and she goes into a series of elegant fits. 'Bless my soul,' thinks Papa, 'well, if she wants the officer, I'll prove I'm her great-hearted father, anyway *he's* got money too.' So in the twinkling of a bed-post the officer is invited, does a pinch of courting, offers hand and heart. And then . . . what?

NATALIA. Happy ever after?

THE DOCTOR. That's what *you* think. Tears and fits again, a terrible rumpus. This time Papa's completely at sea. 'Now look here, my girl, which of 'em *do* you want?' And what d'you think her answer is?

RAKITIN. What?

THE DOCTOR. 'Papa, I've no idea . . . and yet my distress is profound. I am a woman who loves two men at the same time.'

(An awkward pause. He studies his finger-nails. Rakitin rises slowly.)

And there we are, that's the sort of thing goes on in these parts.

NATALIA *(as he takes snuff)*. I don't find it so staggering. Cannot one love two people at once?

RAKITIN. You think so?

NATALIA *(catching his eye, then rising and walking slowly to the windows)*. I don't know, though—perhaps it proves you don't really love either.

THE DOCTOR *(catching her eye)*. Exactly—hit the nail on the head.

ANNA *(rising)*. My legs have gone to sleep, but I've got my money back . . . Ah! *(To Shaaf)* You owe me seventy kopeks, I'm going to do the fleecing for a change . . . *(Walking towards the hall)* Forty winks before tea, that game's killed me—worth it, though—quick march, Liza, don't dawdle——

LIZAVETA *(rising, and scrabbling about on the card table)*. Coming—I'm filling your reticule——

ANNA. My legs, my legs . . .

(She goes out into the hall. Natalia comes down, sits at the desk, takes up a brush, and makes idle strokes on a watercolor propped on the desk.)

THE DOCTOR. Lizaveta Bogdanovna, snuff?

LIZAVETA *(simpering)*. I oughtn't to . . .

THE DOCTOR. Come, give that devil in you a chance!

LIZAVETA. Oh, Doctor . . .

ANNA'S VOICE *(in the hall, as Lizaveta takes a pinch)*. Liza!

LIZAVETA *(calling)*. Coming!

(She sneezes, and hurries into the hall. Shaaf collects the cards.)

THE DOCTOR *(to Rakitin, quietly)*. So you've no idea what is the matter with her today?

RAKITIN. Not the faintest.

THE DOCTOR. Well, if you don't know . . .

(Rakitin meets his eyes, goes up humming, and plays an idle game of patience; Shaaf is still writing in his pocket-book. The Doctor clears his throat and crosses to Natalia.)

THE DOCTOR *(with false bonhomie)*. Er —Natalia Petrovna! I have a little matter of business to go into with you . . .

NATALIA *(painting)*. Business? Monsieur le Diplomate, you make me quite nervous

THE DOCTOR. Actually, it's to do with a third party. A crony of mine.

NATALIA. Do I know him?

THE DOCTOR. You do indeed! He is no less than your neighbor.

NATALIA *(still painting)*. Old Bolshintsov? Yes?

THE DOCTOR. He has asked me to find out what your plans are for your ward. *(Natalia turns and stares at him.)*

NATALIA. For Vera Alexandrovna?

THE DOCTOR. Not to put too fine a point, this crony of mine——

NATALIA. You don't mean to say he wants to marry her?

THE DOCTOR. The whole thing in a nutshell.

NATALIA. You're being facetious, aren't you?

THE DOCTOR. I'm not, for a change.

NATALIA. But my dear man, she's a child! *(Laughing)* What a fantastic errand!

THE DOCTOR. Oh, I don't see why—my friend——

NATALIA. Of course one mustn't forget that almost before you're a doctor, you're a business man——

THE DOCTOR *(jovially)*. You slander me, dear lady——

NATALIA. Who is this *friend* of yours, Monsieur le Diplomate?

THE DOCTOR. Excuse me, you haven't given me any indication——

NATALIA. But really, Doctor, I've told you, she's a child——

(Vera and Kolia run in from the garden, from the left of the windows; Vera is a beautiful immature girl of seventeen, timid and highly strung.)

KOLIA *(running to Rakitin)*. Could we have some glue, do you think? Could we have some glue?

RAKITIN *(to Kolia)*. And what d'you want with glue, suddenly?

(Vera curtseys breathlessly to The Doctor, and sits.)

KOLIA. Oh, it's necessary, sir, absolutely essential—what d'you think my new tutor's making for me? A kite—so we must have some glue, mustn't we—may we?

RAKITIN *(about to ring the bell)*. In a winkling——

SHAAF. Erlauben Sie . . . Monsieur Kolia has not his Cherman lesson today prepared. *(Taking Kolia's hand)* Kommen Sie——

KOLIA *(imploring)*. Tomorrow—morgen, morgen—— *(Struggling)* No, Herr Shaaf—please——

NATALIA. Kolia!

RAKITIN *(to Natalia)*. It's rather a shame, they're making a kite, and he's being kidnapped for a German lesson——

SHAAF *(with dignity)*. Gnädige Frau—-

NATALIA *(severely, to Kolia)*. Kolia, you've had quite enough tearing around for one day——

KOLIA. But, maman——

NATALIA. Do you hear me?

KOLIA *(whispering, to Rakitin)*. Try and get us some glue, sir, will you, please? Cross my heart, sir? Please?

SHAAF. Kommen Sie—yonk vicked man—yonk vicked man——

(He pilots Kolia into the ballroom. Rakitin follows them. Vera rises and walks.)

NATALIA *(seeing her)*. Vera my dear, how flushed you are! I haven't seen you since this morning. What have you been doing all this time?

VERA. I've been with the new tutor.

NATALIA *(after a pause, looking at her)*. Really?

VERA. Oh, and Kolia . . .

NATALIA. Sit down, dear, you must be worn out.

THE DOCTOR *(as Vera obeys)*. But running about is good for one, at that age.

NATALIA. Oh . . . Ah well, Doctor, you know best . . . *(To Vera)* Tell me what you did in the garden.

(She crosses and sits in the armchair. The Doctor watches them.)

VERA. We played games, then he climbed a tree——

NATALIA. Kolia? Never——

VERA. No no, the—new tutor. He was chasing a squirrel and he climbed up and up, till he could shake the top—we felt quite frightened—then he made a bow-and-arrow for Kolia, —then he betted me that I couldn't play a mazurka, and I won, then we ran out again, and then—oh, I don't think I ought to tell you——

NATALIA. But I insist——

VERA. He crept up to one of your cows, made one leap, and landed on her back. She was so surprised she jumped five feet and spun round like a mad old top, and he laughed so much he fell off, and we laughed till we cried, then he said he'd make a kite, and that's why we came in.

NATALIA (*patting her cheek*). What a child . . . Don't you agree, Doctor?

THE DOCTOR. But I don't think it matters. On the contrary.

NATALIA. Don't you?

(*Vera looks at her, puzzled and disconcerted.*)

THE DOCTOR. Bother—I've suddenly remembered—your coachman's on the sick list, and I haven't looked at him yet —(*going*)—pray excuse me——

NATALIA. He looks as fit as a fiddle to me, rosy cheeks——

THE DOCTOR. Fever, dear lady, can be very deceptive.

(*He goes out into the hall as Rakitin returns from the ballroom.*)

NATALIA (*rising, to Vera*). Mon enfant, vous feriez bien de mettre une autre robe pour dîner.

VERA (*stammering*). What—(*rising*)— oh . . .

NATALIA (*suddenly, as Vera makes to go to the hall*). Come here.

(*Vera obeys; Natalia kisses her on the brow.*) What a child!

(*Vera smiles awkwardly, kisses her hand, and starts to go.*)

RAKITIN (*whispering to her*). I've sent the glue.

VERA. Thank you, Mihail Alexandrovitch, so much——

(*She sees Natalia looking at her, and hurries into the hall. Rakitin goes to Natalia; she holds out her hand, which he takes.*)

RAKITIN. Natalia Petrovna, what *is* the matter with you?

NATALIA. The sort of thing than can happen to anybody, surely. Like clouds trailing over the sky . . . (*After a pause*) Why are you looking at me like that?

RAKITIN (*simply*). Because when I look at you like this, I feel happy.

NATALIA (*smiling*). Ah . . . (*After a pause*) Open the study door, Michel, will you? It may make a breeze——

(*Rakitin rises and opens the study door.*) Welcome, O Zephyr-wind! The wild restless creature . . . (*Looking round*) Try and drive him out if you can!

RAKITIN. And now you've changed again. Soft and still, like a summer evening after a thunderstorm.

NATALIA. Ah . . . Has there been a thunderstorm?

RAKITIN. Not quite, but it was gathering.

NATALIA (*after a pause*). Do you know, Michel, you must be the kindest man in the world?

RAKITIN. But how dull that sounds——

NATALIA. I mean it, you're tolerant, you're affectionate, and you never never change. I owe so much to you; our feeling for each other is so sincere, so innocent . . . And yet . . .

RAKITIN. And yet what?

NATALIA. There's something not quite —natural about it, do you know what I mean? Oh, I know we have the right to look not only my husband in the face, but the whole world—and yet . . . (*Thoughtfully*) I suppose that's why I have this horrid desire to vent my bad temper, like a child with its nurse——

RAKITIN. With me as the nurse? A flattering comparison indeed——

NATALIA. Sometimes one takes pleasure in tormenting a creature one loves.

RAKITIN (*breathlessly*). A creature— one loves?

NATALIA. Of course, why should I pretend? I love you.

RAKITIN. Go on.

NATALIA. It comes over me sometimes, like a wave; 'I love him', I think to myself; and it's a wonderful peaceful feeling, warming my heart through and through . . . And yet . . .

RAKITIN. Another yet?

NATALIA. Well, you've never made me cry, have you? And it seems to me that if it *were* love . . .

RAKITIN. Natalia Petrovna, no more do you mind?

NATALIA. No more?

RAKITIN. I'm afraid the happiness I possess may melt into thin air.

NATALIA. Oh, it mustn't do that . .

RAKITIN. I'm in your power; you can twist me round your little finger.

(*They look at each other.*)

YSLAEV'S VOICE (*in the ballroom*). Is the new tutor back from the dam yet?

MATVEI'S VOICE (*in the ballroom*). haven't seen him come over, sir——

NATALIA (*rising, quickly*). Arkady's back—I don't want to see him——

RAKITIN. But my dear—your husband——

NATALIA. I know he's my husband, but I just don't want to see him——

(*She hurries into the study. Rakitin looks after her, puzzled. A pause. Yslaev enters from the ballroom. He is a prosperous landowner, seven years older than his wife; a kind pleasant man wrapped in his own affairs. He carries building plans.*)

YSLAEV. Ah, Michel—how are you today, my dear fellow?

RAKITIN. But we saw each other this morning!

YSLAEV. So we did, I beg your pardon . . . I've had a day, I can tell you, up to my neck——(*Crossing and sitting at the desk, comparing his plan with others in the desk*) D'you know, the oddest thing—the Russian peasant isn't at all a brainless fellow, shrewd as they make 'em—but you can tell him something in detail, explain it again, get it crystal clear . . . and you look at him and realize that not one word has sunk in, not one. The Russian——

RAKITIN. Still worrying about the dam?

YSLAEV. The Russian peasant is no fool, everybody knows that, but he hasn't got that—well, 'love of work', is the only way to put it—ah—(*putting aside the watercolors*)—where's my lady wife, bless her?

RAKITIN. She was in here a minute ago——

YSLAEV. Is it anywhere near tea? I've lost all sense of time; on my feet since dawn, it's appalling . . . (*As Rakitin smiles*) I amuse you, dear boy—but every man has his niche in life; and being a stolid sort of a fellow, I was born to be a farmer, and nothing more. Beliaev hasn't asked for me, has he?

RAKITIN. Beliaev?

YSLAEV. The new tutor, haven't you seen him? He's no fool, just ran into him in the drive and asked him if he'd see how the workmen are getting on with the new building——

(*Beliaev hurries in from the garden, from the right.*)

Well, my boy, how are they? Not doing a stroke, I bet?

BELIAEV. Oh yes, sir, at it hammer and tongs——

YSLAEV. *Are* they? Have they put down the second framework?

BELIAEV. They've started on the third. (*He is more at ease now he is alone with his own sex*)

YSLAEV. That's something, anyway. Thank you, my boy, very much——

(*Natalia returns from the study, with a large portfolio of paintings.*)

Ah, Natalia . . . how are you, my dear?

RAKITIN. But you're spending the whole day asking the same people about their health!

YSLAEV. I've told you, my dear fellow, it's overwork—snowed under! By the way, have I shown you my new winnowing machine?

NATALIA (*listlessly turning over pages*). No . . .

YSLAEV. But my dear, it's the most interesting thing you've ever seen! One flick of the wrist, and the wind whizzes round—a devil of a gale! (*Rising*) I tell you what—we'll just have time before tea—(*to Rakitin*)—care to see it?——

RAKITIN. If you like——

YSLAEV. Coming, Natalia?

NATALIA. I don't understand the first thing about winnowing——

YSLAEV. Back in a trice——

(*He and Rakitin go out into the garden, arm in arm, and disappear to the left. Beliaev hesitates and makes to follow them.*)

NATALIA. Are you going out again?

BELIAEV (*turning*). Me? I was just . . . going for a walk——

NATALIA. Do you want to?

BELIAEV. No, not—not particularly, I've been walking all day.

NATALIA. That's what I thought. So won't you sit down? (*As he looks at her, overcome with shyness*) As we haven't exchanged two words up till now, we can't say we've even properly met, can we? Won't you sit down?

BELIAEV (*bowing awkwardly and sitting*). That—that's very kind of you, madame.

NATALIA. You're afraid of me, aren't you?

BELIAEV *(overcome with shyness).* Oh, madame——

NATALIA. But when you get to know me, you won't be afraid of me any more. How old are you?

BELIAEV. Twenty-one.

NATALIA. Are your parents living?

BELIAEV. My father is, madame, yes.

NATALIA *(turning over pages).* Does he live in Moscow?

BELIAEV. No, madame, in the country.

NATALIA. Have you any brothers and sisters?

BELIAEV. One sister, younger than me.

NATALIA. What's her name?

BELIAEV. Natalia.

NATALIA *(looking up, eagerly).* Natalia! How very odd—my name's Natalia.

BELIAEV. Really, madame? *(Awkwardly)* How odd.

(A pause. She rises and places the portfolio on the table.)

NATALIA. And you're very fond of her?

BELIAEV *(rising, politely).* Yes.

NATALIA. Our Kolia's already very much attached to you.

BELIAEV. I'm so glad. I am naturally anxious to give every satisfaction.

NATALIA. Oh . . . You see, Alexei Nikolaich, my idea is for him to grow up —free. *(Sitting in the armchair)* Shall I tell you why?

BELIAEV. Madame?

NATALIA. Because I was brought up in a very different atmosphere. *(Motioning him to sit)* My father was excessively stern; the entire household was frightened of him. Even now I feel the influence of those years of constraint—I know that the first impression I give is often one of— coldness, perhaps . . . But I'm talking about myself—— were you kept under, as a child?

BELIAEV. I don't really know. Nobody bothered about me, either way.

NATALIA. But your father——?

BELIAEV. Oh, he was always out.

NATALIA. En voyage, you mean?

BELIAEV. No, he—he had his visiting.

NATALIA *(puzzled).* Paying calls?

BELIAEV. In a way, yes; he—*(blurting it out)*—he went round doing odd jobs.

NATALIA. Ah . . . I beg your pardon . . . *(Brushing the subject delicately aside)* Alexei

Nikolaich, was that you singing in the garden yesterday?

BELIAEV. Oh . . . *(Embarrassed)* The lake is so far from the house, I didn't think——

NATALIA. There's no need to apologize, you have a very pleasant voice . . . *(Suddenly rising)* Do you know, Alexei Nikolaich, I feel at ease with you? My chattering away so disgracefully should prove that! We are going to be friends, are we not?

(She holds out her hand. He takes it, hesitatingly, and after a moment of indecision, kisses it. She draws away her hand confused, as The Doctor enters from the hall and sees them. Beliaev crosses with exercise books and collects others from bookcase.)

(Embarrassed) Ah, Doctor——

THE DOCTOR *(overhearty).* Natalia Petrovna, I go into your kitchen for my patient, and there he sits the picture of health, wolfing pancakes and onions! How can a man pursue medicine and the innocent profits deriving therefrom, when that sort of cheating goes on?

NATALIA *(crossing to the mirror over the desk).* Doctor, vous êtes impayable . . . *(To Beliaev, as he makes to go out)* Oh, Alexei Nikolaich, I forgot to say——

VERA'S VOICE *(in the hall).* Alexei Nikolaich!

(Vera runs in from the hall.)

VERA *(calling).* Alexei—*(seeing Natalia)*—oh.

NATALIA. Gracious, child, what a tomboy!

VERA. Kolia wants his new tutor—I mean Kolia asked me about the kite——

NATALIA. I see. Mais on n'entre pas comme cela dans une chambre . . . *(She tidies her hair in the mirror.)*

VERA *(to Beliaev).* She did it!

BELIAEV. She didn't!

(They both burst out laughing. Natalia sees them in the mirror, while the Doctor watches all three.)

BELIAEV *(to Vera).* You're not making it up?

VERA. Cross my heart—she just fell straight off!

NATALIA *(into the mirror).* Who fell off?

VERA *(embarrassed).* Oh . . . It was our

swing—and Kolia's nurse took it into her head to——

(She catches Beliaev's eye and they both laugh again.)

NATALIA *(suddenly)*. Doctor!

THE DOCTOR. Madame!

NATALIA. Could I have a word with you?

THE DOCTOR *(hurrying down)*. À votre service, madame.

NATALIA *(to Vera)*. She didn't hurt herself, I hope?

VERA. Oh no—*(to Beliaev)*—but she looked so funny——

(Both laugh.)

NATALIA *(turning to them, severely)*. I don't think it was very wise, all the same.

(Both stand, like scolded children. Matvei enters from the hall.)

MATVEI *(announcing)*. Tea is served.

NATALIA. And the others?

MATVEI. All in the dining room.

(He goes back into the hall.)

NATALIA *(pointing to Beliaev)*. Vera, allez en avant avec Monsieur.

(Vera curtseys demurely to Beliaev, and they both follow Matvei.)

THE DOCTOR *(to Natalia)*. You wanted to tell me something?

NATALIA *(wiping her fingers on a paint-rag)*. Did I? Oh yes . . . We haven't yet properly discussed your suggestion, have we?

THE DOCTOR. My suggestion? About Vera here and my friend——?

NATALIA. About Vera, and your friend . . . Well, it was just to say that I'll think it over . . . Yes, I'll think it over.

(She walks, catches his eye, then goes out into the hall. The Curtain falls quickly, rising immediately on

SCENE TWO

A corner of the garden; late afternoon of the next day. All we see is a fragment of lofty wall overgrown with creeper, with before it a garden seat facing the audience and a narrow path running from left to right, the whole set very near the audience. The scene is bathed in a soft glow which deepens as the evening advances.

A pause. Matvei and Katia (a buxom, pretty servant-girl of twenty) stroll slowly from the left; she carries a basket, he a watering-can. He looks worried, she bored. They sit on the seat. A pause.

————

MATVEI. Put me out o' me misery, there's a good girl.

KATIA. Matvei Egorych, I don't know *what* to say—it is kind of you——

MATVEI. I'm older than you; it's no good me makin' out I'm not, because I am. But I'm in my prime, and if I may say so, a very good prime too. An' you know yourself what a respectable man I am, an' what more does a woman want than a respectable man?

KATIVA. Nothing more at all.

MATVEI. Well?

KATIA. Matvei Egorych, it *is* kind of you . . . but don't you think we ought to wait——

MATVEI. But, Katerina Vassilevna, excuse me—why? If you're afeared you might not be treated with respect, I can vouch for that—you'll have respect from me, Katerina Vassilevna, the like o' which no female ever yet got from a male, so 'elp me God; I've never had anything but good marks from the master and mistress, never a drop passes my lips, an' I'm a respectable man, what more does a woman want?

KATIA. Nothing more at all, it *is* kind of you——

MATVEI. I know it's kind of me, but what's the answer?

KATIA. Oh dear . . .

(Matvei rises, walks, then turns sharply on her.)

MATVEI. It's my 'umble opinion, Katerina Vassilevna, that you didn't always 'um an' 'aw like this.

KATIA *(confused)*. Not always? How do you mean?

MATVEI. It's only lately you've been at it.

KATIA *(blushing)*. I don't know what you're talking about—oh look, here comes that nasty German——

MATVEI. That bilious object, can't stomach 'im—we'll have to thrash it out later——

(He hurries off, to the right. Katia is about to run off to the left, when she runs into Shaaf, a fishing rod over one shoulder.)

SHAAF. Vither, o vither, my fair Katerina, ja?

KATIA. The housekeeper sent me to pick some red currants, in a great hurry——

SHAAF. Currant are gut fruit. You are currant fond, ja?

KATIA. I quite like them, thank you——

SHAAF. Me currant also fond, he he he! I am fond wid everyting dat you are fond wid. Currant pliss?

KATIA. Oh, I couldn't spare one—I'd catch it from the housekeeper——

SHAAF. I komme catch mit you. *(Pointing to the fishing rod)* What ist dies you call it? Fishing catch mit fishing-schtick? You underschtand fishing-schtick? You like fishes?

KATIA. I quite like them, thank you——

SHAAF. Also fishes me like, he he he. Do you know what I schpeak mit you now? A leedle sonk, a leedle sonk für Katerina . . . *(Singing, heavily)* 'Katerin-chen, Katerinchen, wie lieb' ich dich so sehr', which means one ting, one leedle ting . . . loff, loff, loff!

(He tries to put his arm round her.)

KATIA. Oh no, please—an old gentle-man like you, it doesn't look a bit nice—give over!—there's somebody coming—— *(She darts off to the right.)*

SHAAF *(muttering, sternly, his skittish manner gone)*. Shaaf, das ist dumm . . .

(Natalia enters from the left, arm in arm with Rakitin; she carries a parasol, he a magazine. She is much more restless than before.)

NATALIA. Ah, Adam Ivanych . . . where's Kolia?

SHAAF. Kolia ist in schkul-room mit Lizaveta Bogdanovna vitch titch him de bianoforte blay.

NATALIA. Good . . . Have you seen the new tutor?

SHAAF. No. He zay dat he choin me. *(He bows and shambles off to the left.)*

NATALIA *(after a pause, calling)*. Adam Ivanych, we'll come and keep you company while you blay mit your fishing-schtick—what do you say to that?

SHAAF'S VOICE. Boodiful lady, vot an honor, vot an honor——

RAKITIN *(aside, to Natalia)*. Now why on earth do you want to saddle us——

NATALIA. Come along, handsome stranger. Beau ténébreux . . . *(They drift out of sight, to the left. Katia appears cautiously from the right.)*

KATIA. That horrible old German, what a blessing, gives me the creeps . . . *(She sighs, dreamily, then sits on the seat, and hums snatches of a song.)*
(Singing)

> Must I love and have no lover
> While my heart it glows and burns
> Not with passion, but with Russian
> Melancholy sighs it yearns . . .

Matvei Egorych was right, what he said, about humming and hawing . . . oh dear . . .
(Singing)

> Not with madness but with sadness
> My heart its cruel lesson learns
> Not with madness——

(Beliaev and Vera enter from the right. He carries a kite. Katia sees them and stops singing.)

BELIAEV. Katia, why have you stopped? *(Singing)*

> Not with sadness but with madness
> My heart the art of kissing learns!

KATIA *(blushing, and giggling)*. Oh . . . we don't sing it with *those* words . . ,

BELIAEV. What are you picking—currants? I love currants.

KATIA *(handing him the basket)*. Take them all.

BELIAEV. All? I couldn't do that . . . Would you like some, Vera Alexandrovna? *(As he and Vera take a few)* Shall we sit here?

VERA. Shall we? *(Katia wanders off to the right. They munch for a moment.)*

BELIAEV. Now—*(showing the kite)*—this fellow's tail's got to be tied on. Will you give me a hand?

VERA. Delighted, sir——

BELIAEV *(as he and Vera sit on the seat)*. There . . . *(Arranging the kite over her knee)* Mind you hold it dead straight, or there'll be the devil to pay.

VERA *(laughing)*. I'll be careful. *(As he begins to tie on the tail)* But if you sit like that how can I watch you?

BELIAEV *(looking at her)*. Why do you want to watch me?

VERA. To see just how you're tying it on.

BELIAEV. Oh . . . One minute . . . *(Moving round so she can see, and calling)* Katia, where's that lusty treble? Pipe up! *(Katia is heard giggling, to the right.)*

VERA. Did you sometimes fly kites in Moscow?

BELIAEV. Good lord no. I had no time for kites in Moscow! Press with your finger, will you? . . . No, butter-fingers, like this . . . Do you really think that all we have to do in the great city is to fly kites?

VERA. Well, how *do* you spend your time in the great city?

BELIAEV. Oh . . . Studying.

VERA. I suppose—*(after a pause)*—you have hundreds of friends in Moscow?

BELIAEV. Oh yes . . . D'you know, I don't think this string's going to be strong enough——

VERA *(anxiously)*. Are you very attached to them?

BELIAEV. I should think I am! *(Intent on the kite)* Aren't you fond of your friends?

VERA. I haven't any.

BELIAEV. I mean girl friends.

VERA. Oh.

BELIAEV. Oh what?

(Katia's voice is heard, singing in snatches.)

VERA. They don't seem to have been very much in my thoughts lately.

BELIAEV. Anyway, how can you say you haven't any men friends? What about me?

VERA *(with a smile)*. Oh, you're different . . . *(After a pause)* Alexei Nikolaich, do you write poetry?

BELIAEV. No.

VERA. Oh. *(After a pause)* At the boarding school I went to, there was one girl who did.

BELIAEV. Wrote poetry? Good lord . . . *(Using his teeth to tighten the knot in the string)* Was it any good?

VERA. I don't really know. She read it out to us, and we all cried.

BELIAEV. Cried? Good lord, why?

VERA. Because we felt sorry for her.

BELIAEV. For writing such bad poetry?

VERA. Oh no, because it was so sad.

BELIAEV. Was your school in Moscow?

VERA. Madame Bolusse's. Natalia Petrovna took me away last year.

BELIAEV. Are you fond of Natalia Petrovna?

VERA. Oh, very. She's been so kind to me.

BELIAEV. Are you afraid of her as well? *(She looks at him; he grins at her.)*

VERA *(smiling)*. A little bit, yes . . .

BELIAEV *(after a pause)*. And who sent you to the school?

VERA. Her mother, she brought me up. I'm an orphan.

BELIAEV. An orphan? *(Putting down the kite)* Are you really?

VERA. Yes.

(Katia starts to sing again.)

BELIAEV. My mother died too. So I'm a sort of orphan as well.

VERA. Both orphans . . .

BELIAEV. It's not our fault, so there's no point in getting depressed about it, is there?

VERA. They say orphans make friends sooner than anybody.

BELIAEV. Do they?

(He looks into her eyes. Katia stops singing. A pause. He goes back to his work.) How long have I been here? Three, or four——

VERA. Twenty-eight days counting today.

BELIAEV. What a memory! A whole month, in the country . . . There, finished! Look at that tail, there's a swisher for you——

(Katia returns from the right, goes up to him with her basket.)

(Rising.) Now to get Kolia——

KATIA. Would you like some more currants, sir?

BELIAEV. No thank you, Katia.

KATIA *(disappointed)*. Oh . . .

(She walks slowly back to the right.)

BELIAEV. Where is Kolia, d'you know?

VERA. Over in the schoolroom with Lizaveta Bogdanovna.

BELIAEV. Keeping a child indoors in this weather——

VERA. Do you know she spoke very nicely about you yesterday?

BELIAEV. Lizaveta Bogdanovna? Did she?

VERA. Don't you like her?

BELIAEV. Never thought about it. *(Finishing off the kite)* She can take snuff till she's black in the face, I'm just not interested.
(A pause. Vera sighs.)
Why are you sighing?

VERA. I don't know. What a blue sky . . .

BELIAEV. Is that why you're sighing? Perhaps you're bored?

VERA. Bored? Oh no . . .

BELIAEV. You're not sickening for something, are you?

VERA. No, but . . . well.—Yesterday I was going up to fetch a book, and suddenly—imagine—I just sat on the stairs and burst into tears.

BELIAEV. Good lord.

VERA. What could it mean, do you think? Because I'm really quite happy.

BELIAEV *(turning to her)*. Shall I tell you what it is?

VERA. What?

BELIAEV. Growing pains.

VERA. Oh . . .

BELIAEV *(back to the kite)*. So that's why your eyes looked so swollen last night . . .

VERA. You noticed?

BELIAEV. Of course I noticed.
(She looks at him, he is looking at the kite. A pause. Katia is heard singing, very faintly, some way off. Vera listens.)

VERA *(thoughtfully)*. Alexei Nikolaich.

BELIAEV. Hmm?

VERA. Am I like her?

BELIAEV. Not a bit.

VERA *(disappointed)*. Oh.

BELIAEV. For one thing, you're better-looking.

VERA. Am I?
(He looks at her; an embarrassed pause.)

BELIAEV *(breaking it)*. Well, Vera Alexandrovna, what about young Kolia?

VERA. Why don't you call me Vérochka?

BELIAEV. Shall I? And what about your calling me Alexei?

VERA. Shall I? *(Starting)* Oh bother——

BELIAEV. What is it——

VERA *(in a subdued voice)*. Natalia Petrovna——

BELIAEV *(catching her tone)*. Let's go in to Kolia, shall we? He's bound to have finished his doh-ray-me by now——

VERA. Oh, do you think we ought?
(They both disappear to the right. Natalia and Rakitin re-enter from the left.)

NATALIA. Surely that was Vérochka scurrying along?

RAKITIN. Was it?

NATALIA. But they looked exactly as if they were running away from us!

RAKITIN. Perhaps they are.

NATALIA. Seriously, I don't think it at all *convenable* for her to be wandering in the garden all by herself with a young man, really I don't.

RAKITIN. I thought you said she was a child.

NATALIA. What? Of course she's a child—but still, it's not quite proper. I shall have to be cross with her.

RAKITIN. How old is she?

NATALIA. Seventeen . . . *(Sitting)* Where's the Doctor, he hasn't gone, has he?

RAKITIN *(sitting next to her)*. I rather think he has——

NATALIA. Oh, how provoking, why didn't you get him to stay? . . . Why a character like that should ever have disguised himself as a provincial apothecary, I can't imagine. He's *so* amusing.

RAKITIN. I had an idea you weren't in a laughing mood today.

NATALIA. Because I've taken against sentimentality? I have, I warn you—nothing, absolutely nothing, could touch me today, I've a heart of stone . . . But I wanted to see the Doctor, it *is* provoking of you——

RAKITIN. May I ask what about?

NATALIA. You may not, you already know every single thing I do, exactly why I do it—I have an uncontrollable desire to conceal something from you.

RAKITIN. Since I watch you so closely, shall I tell you one thing I have observed?
(A pause. She looks at him, then away.)

NATALIA. I am all ears.

RAKITIN. You won't be annoyed with me?

NATALIA. I should like to be, but I shan't succeed. Go on.

RAKITIN. For some time, Natalia Petrovna, you've been in a state of constant fretfulness.

NATALIA. Go on.

RAKITIN. Not ordinary short temper— but a fretting from within. You appear to be . . . in conflict with your own self. *(As Natalia traces a pattern in the dust with her parasol)* I've heard you sigh. Deep long breaths: the sighs of a creature immensely tired, who can never, never come to rest. *(A pause. Katia's voice, singing.)*

NATALIA. And what do you conclude from all that, Monsieur le Microscope?

RAKITIN. I conclude nothing. But it causes me concern——

NATALIA *(suddenly impatient)*. Oh, for Heaven's sake let's change the subject. *(A pause. Katia's voice dies away.)*

RAKITIN. You don't intend going for a drive today——

NATALIA *(suddenly)*. Tell me, what do you think of Bolshintsov?

RAKITIN. Our neighbor, you mean, Afanasy Ivanych?

NATALIA. Yes.

RAKITIN. Well, I never thought to hear you ask tenderly after a beef-witted old Jumbo like Bolshintsov. Though I must concede I can't think of anything worse against him.

NATALIA. Oh, he just came into my head. *(A pause.)*

RAKITIN. Look at the dark green of that oak, against the velvet blue of the sky . . . the deep glow of those colors . . . isn't it perfect? What a wealth of life and strength stand embodied in that tree! And then look at this slim young birch; her tiny leaves shimmer with a sort of liquid radiance, as if they were melting before our eyes . . . And yet, in her way, the birch is as lovely as the oak. *(A pause.)*

NATALIA. Rakitin, shall I tell you something?

RAKITIN. Do——

NATALIA. Something about you which I noticed ages ago—*(looking at him)*—I might even say 'observed' . . . You feel the beauties of Nature in a very rarefied way, and expatiate upon them most elegantly; so elegantly, indeed, that in return for the meticulous metaphors you shower upon her, I can imagine Nature saying, 'Really, it *is* good of that tall gentleman to say those kind things about me.' You court her as a scented marquis in red heels might court a rosy peasant girl. The only fly in the ointment, my dear, is that just as the girl would find every single compliment miles above her head, so Nature doesn't understand a word you say. And shall I tell you why? Because, thank Heaven, she is much coarser than you have any knowledge of; and she's coarse because she's healthy. Birch-trees don't melt or fade away, for the simple reason they're not highly-strung young ladies, they're birch-trees.

RAKITIN. What an onslaught! . . . I'm a morbid creature: I see.

NATALIA. Oh, you're not the only one. I don't think either of us is spiritually bursting with health.

RAKITIN. That's another thing I've observed.

NATALIA. What?

RAKITIN. Your trick of putting the nastiest things in the most innocent way. Instead of calling somebody an idiot, you turn to him with a smile and say 'Mon cher ami, you and I are fools.'

NATALIA. Well, if the word 'morbid' doesn't appeal to you, then I'll just say we're both old. As old as the hills.

RAKITIN. I don't feel particularly ancient.

NATALIA. Do you realize that not ten minutes ago, sharing the same garden seat, two creatures sat together who can truly claim to be young? *(A pause.)*

RAKITIN. You envy them their artless candor, their innocence—in short, their stupidity?

NATALIA. Do you think they're stupid? Oh, Rakitin, that's so like you! Anyway, what's the point of cleverness if it doesn't amuse?

(Katia enters from the right, carrying her basket.)

Ah, Katia! Have you been picking fruit, my dear?

KATIA. Yes, madame——

NATALIA. Let me look. *(Peering into the basket)* What gorgeous currants, how red they are——

KATIA. Aren't they, madame——

NATALIA. Not as red as your cheeks, though, Katia——

KATIA *(smiling and blushing)*. Oh, madame, do you think so——

NATALIA. I do indeed—*(suddenly weary)* —you may go, my dear . . .

(Katia curtseys and hurries off to the left.)

RAKITIN. Another callow creature who appeals to you.

NATALIA. Yes, she's young too. *(Rising, suddenly)* It's time Vérochka was in. Au revoir, mon ami.

(She opens her parasol and walks slowly away to the right. A pause.)

RAKITIN. She was right, Mihail Alexandrovich Rakitin—every minute of every day, you spend on the lookout for trivialities, and in the end you've turned into a triviality yourself. *(After a pause)* And yet . . . I cannot live without her; to part from Natalia Petrovna would be to leave life itself . . . What *is* this unrest of hers? Is she tired of me? I know too well the kind of love she bears me—but I had hopes that in time . . . What am I saying—she's a virtuous woman, and I am not a philanderer . . . *(smiling, wryly)* . . . worse luck . . . *(Walking up and down)* What a beautiful day! *(After a pause)* Meticulous metaphors, indeed . . . And why this sudden passion for simplicity? It all seems to go with that new tutor. She couldn't be . . . no, that's out of the question, she's just in a bad mood; Heaven knows, time will show. *(Sitting again)* . . . And it's not the first occasion in your life, my boy, that after a conference with yourself, you've had to throw all your theories overboard, fold your arms meekly and wait for events.

(He opens his magazine. Beliaev comes strolling back from the right.)

Ah, Alexei Nikolaich! Are you after a breath of fresh air too?

BELIAEV. Indeed I am, sir! What a lovely day!

RAKITIN. Won't you sit down?

BELIAEV. Thank you. *(He sits)*

RAKITIN *(after a pause)*. Did you see Natalia Petrovna?

BELIAEV. Yes, walking over to the schoolroom, with Vera.

RAKITIN. And how do you take to the rustic life?

BELIAEV. Oh, capitally, except for the shooting. That's pretty poor.

RAKITIN. Oh. Are you partial to shooting?

BELIAEV. Very. Are you, sir?

RAKITIN. I'm afraid not. I'm a deplorable shot; much too lazy.

BELIAEV. I'm lazy too, I'm afraid, but not where sport's concerned.

RAKITIN. And entertaining the ladies —are you lazy where that's concerned?

BELIAEV. You're laughing at me, sir . . . To tell you the honest truth, I'm rather afraid of them.

RAKITIN. The ladies? . . . Are you? But why should you think I was laughing at you?

BELIAEV. I don't know, I just did. It doesn't matter, sir, really . . . *(After a pause)* Could you tell me where I can get some gunpowder?

RAKITIN. Gunpowder? In the town, I should think, but very poor quality——

BELIAEV. That would do—it's not for shooting, it's for fireworks.

RAKITIN. Fireworks? You mean you can make them?

BELIAEV. Oh yes. I've already picked a spot, on the other side of the lake. As it's little Kolia's birthday tomorrow, I thought it would be just the thing.

RAKITIN. I'm sure Natalia Petrovna will be very touched by your kind thought. *(He has lingered a little over her name)*

BELIAEV. Oh, do you think so?

RAKITIN. She's taken a liking to you. Did you know?

BELIAEV. Has she really, sir? I'm so glad . . . Excuse me, sir, isn't that a Moscow magazine?

RAKITIN *(giving it to him)*. Do have it, I've finished——

BELIAEV. Oh, thank you, sir——

RAKITIN. It's a poetry review, I take it because they sometimes publish tolerably good verse.

BELIAEV. Oh. *(Putting down the magazine, disappointed)* Too bad.

RAKITIN. Why?

BELIAEV. I'm not very struck on poetry.

RAKITIN. Oh. What have you against it?

BELIAEV. I think it's rather affected. I like funny rhymes, of course, but that's different.

RAKITIN. It is, rather . . . You prefer novels?

BELIAEV. Oh yes, I like something that tells a story . . .

RAKITIN. Do you dabble in writing yourself?

BELIAEV. Lord no, I haven't any gifts for it and I know better than to try. I've got my work cut out trying to fathom what others get onto paper.

RAKITIN. Do you realize, Alexei Nikolaich, that very few young men have your common sense?

BELIAEV. Thank you, sir . . . *(After a pause)* I chose the lake because I know how to make Roman candles that'll burn on the water.

RAKITIN. Do you really? That must be a lovely sight . . . Alexei Nikolaich, do you speak French?

BELIAEV. I'm afraid I don't—my laziness again. I'd give a lot to master Georges Sand in the original—she's a woman of course, but damnably good reading. Thank the Lord other people aren't quite such loafers as I am.

RAKITIN. Now you're exaggerating—

BELIAEV. No, I'm not; you see, I know myself.

RAKITIN. I know something about you that you're not aware of.

BELIAEV. Oh? What is it?

RAKITIN. I know that what you look on as a fault in yourself—your naturalness—is the very thing which attracts people to you.

BELIAEV. Attracts people? Who, for example?

RAKITIN. Natalia Petrovna?

BELIAEV. Natalia Petrovna? Oddly enough, she's the one person with whom I don't feel in the least . . . natural, as you put it.

RAKITIN. Ah . . . indeed?

BELIAEV. And when all's said and done, surely the most important asset in a man isn't naturalness, but breeding? It's all very well for you, you've *got* breeding... Excuse me, sir—you're rather an odd character, aren't you?

RAKITIN. Am I?

(A pause.)

BELIAEV. Did you hear that? Sounded like a corn crake——

RAKITIN. Perhaps it was . . . *(As Beliaev rises quickly)* What is it?

BELIAEV. I'm going to the greenhouse for my shotgun——

(He makes to go off to the right, and meets Natalia.)

NATALIA. Alexei Nikolaich, where are you tearing off to?

BELIAEV. Oh . . . I was just . . .

RAKITIN. He heard a corn crake, and was fetching his gun.

NATALIA *(to Beliaev)*. Oh, don't do any shooting in the garden, do you mind? Let the poor bird live—besides, it would scare Kolia's Granny out of her skin!

BELIAEV *(confused)*. I beg pardon, madame, I'm sure . . .

NATALIA *(laughing)*. Alexei Nikolaich, what a thing to say! 'I beg pardon, madame, I'm sure', talking like a servant! Mihail Alexandrovich here and I will take you under our wing—c'est entendu—c'est entendu——

BELIAEV. It's very good of you——

NATALIA. First lesson—no diffidence. That's very important; it doesn't suit you at all . . . Oh yes, we'll take you in hand! You're a young man, while he and I— *(pointing her parasol at Rakitin)*—are old people. You get busy on my little Kolia, and we'll get busy on you!

BELIAEV. It's wonderfully kind of you——

NATALIA. C'est ça . . . What have you done with your kite?

BELIAEV. I left it in the schoolroom. I thought you didn't like it.

NATALIA *(embarrassed)*. Whatever made you think that? Because I told Vérochka—because I sent her in? *(With animation)* Do you know what we'll do? Kolia must have finished strumming by now, we'll go over and fetch him, and Vérochka, and the kite, and all go into a field and fly it! What do you say?

BELIAEV. It would be wonderful, Natalia Petrovna——

NATALIA. Splendid. Take my hand! *(As he hesitates, holding out first one hand, then the other)* Oh, how awkward you are —maladroit—come along—off we go!

(She and Beliaev hurry off, hand in hand, to the right. Rakitin looks after them.)

RAKITIN. I've never seen that expression on her face before. That smile, soft and yet crystal-clear, a look of—yes —a look of welcome . . . (*In a sudden outburst*) O God, spare me the pangs of jealousy! . . . Especially when it's as futile as this . . .

(*The Doctor strolls on from the left, followed by Bolshintsov, who lives up to the Doctor's description of him: near fifty, fat, good-natured, slow-witted, and extremely timid.*)

(*Jauntily.*) Well well, it's an ill wind——

THE DOCTOR. The lodge-keeper told us the whole family was in the garden—so here we are!

RAKITIN. But why didn't you come straight up the drive?

THE DOCTOR. As a matter of fact, Afanasy Ivanych here wanted to call in at the kitchen garden to have a look at the mushrooms.

BOLSHINTSOV (*puzzled*). But I——

THE DOCTOR (*to him*). Now we all know your passion for mushrooms . . .

RAKITIN. If you'd rather stay out of doors, I'll go and tell Natalia Petrovna where you are—I have to go over, anyway——

THE DOCTOR. Ah well, in that case we won't detain you. Please don't stand on ceremony——

RAKITIN. Thank you. Au revoir, gentlemen.

(*He bows and hurries off to the right.*)

THE DOCTOR. Au revoir. (*To Bolshintsov*) Now, Afanasy Ivanych, everything depends on——

BOLSHINTSOV (*agitated*). Ignaty Illyich, you could have knocked me down with a feather . . . Mushrooms!

THE DOCTOR. Did you expect me to tell him that you were so goggle-eyed with nerves you begged to go miles out of our way, just to gain time?

BOLSHINTSOV. But I don't think I've ever *seen* a mushroom. . . . It may be very slow of me, but I——

THE DOCTOR. It *is* very slow of you, my old dear, and you're leaving the whole thing to me, because I'm that much quicker . . . When I think you forced me here at the point of a blunderbuss——

BOLSHINTSOV. I know, my friend, but on my own property I feel ready for anything. But now I *am* here, I feel quite

giddy . . . Ignaty Illyich, you interviewed the older person—what *was* her exact answer, yes or no?

THE DOCTOR. Afanasy Ivanych, what is the span from your village to this august domain?

BOLSHINTSOV. Er—fifteen miles——

THE DOCTOR. During those fifteen miles, Afanasy Ivanych, you have asked me that identical question as regular as clockwork, three times to the mile. I have vouchsafed forty-five answers; and now prick up your ears, my old rabbit, for here comes the forty-sixth, and the last. (*Placing him on the seat and sitting beside him*) This is, word for word, what Natalia Petrovna said to me——

BOLSHINTSOV (*eagerly*). Yes?

THE DOCTOR (*quoting, slowly*). 'Doctor, on the——'

BOLSHINTSOV (*avidly*). Yes, I see——

THE DOCTOR (*irritated*). What d'you mean, you see, I haven't told you anything yet! She said, 'Doctor, on the one hand I '

BOLSHINTSOV (*holding out his hand*). 'On the one hand—yes——'

THE DOCTOR. 'On the one hand, I know very little about Monsieur Bolshintsov—'

BOLSHINTSOV. Monsieur? But I'm not a Frenchman——

THE DOCTOR. I know you're not, and so does she, but as I've told you forty-five times, she fancies you better in French. We'll have another shot . . . 'Doctor, I know very little about Monsieur Bolshintsov, but he looks kind.'

BOLSHINTSOV. 'Kind.' That's nice . . .

THE DOCTOR. 'On the other hand,' she went on——

BOLSHINTSOV (*holding out the other hand, thoughtfully*). The other hand, yes——

THE DOCTOR. 'On the other hand, I will not bring pressure to bear on Vérochka, but again on the other hand— (*as Bolshintsov holds out the first hand again*) . . . if he comes to win her respect, I shall place no obstacles.' In a word, Afanasy Ivanych, it's up to you to convince the young lady that marrying you would make her happy.

BOLSHINTSOV (*after thought*). It's a tall order.

THE DOCTOR. Of course it's a tall

order—but cut a dash, my old friend, cut a dash!

BOLSHINTSOV. Cut a dash, yes, that's it . . . But there is one thing, Ignaty Illyich; you may not believe me, but I have, from my tenderest years, made little contact with the fair sex.

THE DOCTOR. You stagger me.

BOLSHINTSOV. Well, they say it's the first step that counts, don't they—I wondered if you could think of a witty word or two to start the ball rolling? And as for paying you back——

THE DOCTOR. *Paying* me? *(Rising, and drawing himself up)* You do not labor, I trust, under the impression that I am bargaining with you?

BOLSHINTSOV *(rising)*. No no, but just to say that if you pull this off you can count on more than I said.

THE DOCTOR. Tch, tch, I have no wish to—*(sitting, and pulling Bolshintsov down with him)*—how d'you mean, more than you said?

BOLSHINTSOV. You know when your nag broke her leg and you said it was a disgrace for a doctor to be seen trudging about like a peasant?

THE DOCTOR. *And* I meant it, my friend—a doctor has as much right to do his rounds on horseback as any lord of the manor——

BOLSHINTSOV. Well, I'll not only replace your beast, I'll give you the team.

THE DOCTOR. The team? You mean—

BOLSHINTSOV. The three horses, and the wagonette with 'em.

THE DOCTOR *(his eyes shining)*. Wagonette . . . Now where was I . . . You have under you—three hundred serfs, is it?

BOLSHINTSOV. Three hundred and twenty.

THE DOCTOR. The most eligible bachelor in all the Russias . . . Always remembering, of course, that young female persons are partial to a good figure. Now yours, while eminently respectable in every way, is a drawback.

BOLSHINTSOV *(depressed)*. A drawback.

THE DOCTOR. But you have another source to draw from—the gushing spring, my dear Afanasy Illyich, of your virtues; and, of course, of your three hundred and twenty serfs . . . To cut a long story, I should simply say to the young person——

BOLSHINTSOV. Yes?

THE DOCTOR. 'Vera Alexandrovna!'

BOLSHINTSOV *(muttering, his eyes closed)*. 'Vera Alexandrovna . . .'

THE DOCTOR *(as Bolshintsov repeats after him, to himself)*. 'I am a simple, mild man, and not poor; I should be obliged if you would take a little more notice of me than heretofore, and having made inquiries, give me your answer.'

BOLSHINTSOV *(lost in admiration)*. That was a first-rate speech, Ignaty Illyich.

THE DOCTOR. Not bad, was it?

BOLSHINTSOV. Just one thing, my dear friend . . . You mentioned the word 'mild'—you called me 'a mild man'.

THE DOCTOR. Well, aren't you mild?

BOLSHINTSOV. Yes yes, of course . . . but still——

THE DOCTOR *(sternly)*. But still what?

BOLSHINTSOV *(after a pause)*. No, just tell her I'm a mild man.

THE DOCTOR. One more thing—you won't take offense?

BOLSHINTSOV. No no, my dear friend —out with it——

THE DOCTOR. You have a regrettable habit, Afanasy Illyich, of mispronouncing French words, and I think it would be safest not to use them.

BOLSHINTSOV. Oh dear.

THE DOCTOR. For instance, once when you meant to imply that a certain person was distinguished—'distinguée'—I heard you exclaim 'The lady looks distinky'. One knows what you mean, but one is not impressed. *(Looking)* And here they all are—— *(As Bolshintsov makes to go)* Now now, where are you off to? Mushrooms again?

BOLSHINTSOV *(smiling and blushing)*. Oh dear——

(Natalia returns from the right, followed by Vera, Beliaev, Kolia (carrying the kite), Rakitin, and Lizaveta Bogdanovna. Natalia is in high spirits.)

NATALIA *(to Bolshintsov and the Doctor)*. Ah, gentlemen! How are you, Doctor, an unexpected treat! Oh by the way, you won't forget our picnic tomorrow for Kolia's birthday, will you? And are you well, Afanasy Illyich?

BOLSHINTSOV *(raising his hat, perspiring and muttering, acutely embarrassed)*. Thank you, lady—thank you——

NATALIA. And to what do we owe this pleasure, Doctor?

THE DOCTOR. My friend here insisted on bringing me with him.

NATALIA. Oh ho! So you have to be dragged here, do you?

THE DOCTOR.   Dragged?   Good heavens——

NATALIA. Now I've got you into a muddle—hurrah!

THE DOCTOR *(as the others laugh)*. It's extremely kind of you to take it like that, Natalia Petrovna. And if I may pass such a remark, it is very pleasant to find you in such a gay mood.

NATALIA. You find it necessary to comment on it? Is it then so very rare?

THE DOCTOR. Good heavens no—good heavens——

NATALIA. Monsieur le Diplomate is getting into more and more of a tangle-

KOLIA *(eagerly)*. Maman, when do we fly the kite?

NATALIA. Any time you like, my pet. *(To Beliaev)* Come along, Alexei Nikolaich —*(as Vera runs impulsively forward)*— and you, Vera darling—we'll go into the field. *(To the others)* I don't think any of you would find it much fun, so I'll leave them in your charge, Lizaveta Bogdanovna.

RAKITIN *(as she starts to go)*. But Natalia Petrovna, why do you think we wouldn't be amused?

NATALIA. Because you're so clever . . . *(To Beliaev and Vera)* Ready, children? *(She hurries off to the left, taking Kolia by the hand, followed by Beliaev. Vera makes to follow; Bolshintsov tries to intercept her, but cannot get a word out. She stifles a giggle and follows the others. Rakitin looks after them, puzzled and unhappy; the Doctor takes his arm, slyly.)*

THE DOCTOR. Just look at the four of them, tearing up to the field! Let's go and see how they get on, shall we? Even though we are so clever! . . . *(Turning and seeing Bolshintsov standing alone, the picture of disconsolation, then calling)* Lizaveta Bogdanovna!

LIZAVETA *(eagerly)*. Doctor . . .

THE DOCTOR *(to Bolshintsov)*. Our good Afanasy Ivanych, would you offer your arm to this good lady?

BOLSHINTSOV. Only too pleased . . .

LIZAVETA. Mutual, I'm sure, mutual . . .

THE DOCTOR. Afanasy Ivanych, you two in front, what d'you think? *(Bolshintsov gives Lizaveta his arm, ceremoniously; they walk; the others watch them.)*

BOLSHINTSOV *(stiffly)*. The weather is very pleasant today, is it not, in a manner of speaking?

LIZAVETA. Isn't it just . . . *(They disappear to the left.)*

THE DOCTOR *(to Rakitin)*. Mihail Alexandrovich . . . *(As Rakitin laughs)* What are you laughing at?

RAKITIN. I suppose I'm tickled at our bringing up the rear like this.

THE DOCTOR *(as they cross, arm in arm)*. Ah, but don't forget, my dear friend, that the rear guard can only too easily become the advance guard. Shall I tell you how?

RAKITIN. How?

THE DOCTOR. By everybody turning round and going the other way. Ha ha . . . *(They follow the others. The Curtain falls quickly, rising immediately on*

SCENE THREE

The drawing-room, the next morning. Early sunlight. A coffee tray on the footstool before the sofa. Rakitin and the Doctor come in from the hall, arm in arm.

————

THE DOCTOR *(speaking as he enters)*. . . . And to cut a long story short, Mihail Alexandrovich—will you give an old friend a helping hand?

RAKITIN. But my dear Ignaty Illyich, I don't quite——

THE DOCTOR. Now see here, my dear old fellow, just for a moment, put yourself in my place. Mind you, I'm really a looker-on, as I'm only dabbling in this to please a bosom friend . . . *(Sitting on the sofa)* Oh dear, my soft old heart will be the ruin of me!

RAKITIN *(smiling)*. I wouldn't say you were anywhere near ruin at the moment—

THE DOCTOR *(laughing)*. Ah ha! Joking apart, old dear, Natalia Petrovna gave me permission to tell the old boy her answer.

And now that I have, she's gone into her sulks as if I'd done the wrong thing entirely; and he hangs round my coattails like a dear old sheep-dog.

RAKITIN (*sitting next to him, and pouring out coffee*). Doesn't it seem a pity, Ignaty Illyich, that you stuck your finger in this pie at all? Old Bolshintsov's a fool, now, isn't he?

THE DOCTOR. Of course he's a fool, but if we only allowed the clever ones to get married the race would die out! . . . Stuck my finger in the pie, indeed—a bosom friend begged me to put a word in —my finger was stuck in for me, voila! Could I refuse, with my soft heart?

RAKITIN. But nobody's blaming you— though we're all entitled to wonder why you're taking so much trouble.

THE DOCTOR. But because the old boy's a very old friend of mine!

RAKITIN. Is he really?

(*They catch each other's eye, and both laugh.*)

THE DOCTOR. There's no pulling wool over your eyes. The fact is, dear fellow, one of my horses has broken his leg.

RAKITIN. And your old friend is mending it for you?

THE DOCTOR. No.

RAKITIN. He's promised you a new horse?

THE DOCTOR. A team of three, and a wagonette.

RAKITIN. Ah . . . Now I see daylight!

THE DOCTOR. But I wouldn't like you to think I'd be a go-between if he wasn't of the highest character.

RAKITIN. No no——

THE DOCTOR. The whole thing, quite frankly, goes very much against the grain with me—snuff?

RAKITIN. No thank you——

THE DOCTOR (*sniffing*). If only I could squeeze a definite 'yes' or 'no' out of her . . . You see, the old boy's as innocent as a babe unborn; and besides, his intentions being of the highest order——

RAKITIN. And his horses . . .

THE DOCTOR. And his horses——

RAKITIN. But where do I come in?

THE DOCTOR. Do we not all know the esteem in which you are held by the lady in question—be an angel from heaven,

my dear old Mihail Alexandrovich, put in a word for me——

RAKITIN. Is it your honest opinion that he's a good match for this girl?

THE DOCTOR. If he isn't, then strike me dead where I stand. The first thing in a marriage is a stable character, and the old boy's more than stable, he—he's immovable. I think I hear Natalia Petrovna now—my dear old friend, my benefactor, remember—two chestnuts and a dream of a brown mare—will you do it for me?

RAKITIN (*smiling*). All right, I'll do my best——

THE DOCTOR. The Lord will bless you. Two chestnuts, and a brown!

(*He hurries into the ballroom as Natalia enters from the study. She sees Rakitin and stops.*)

NATALIA (*hesitating*). Oh . . . I thought you were in the garden.

RAKITIN. You look overjoyed to see me——

NATALIA. Oh, don't . . . Who was that?

RAKITIN. The Doctor.

NATALIA. That provincial Machiavelli . . He's still hovering, is he?

RAKITIN. He's staying on for the picnic to which you invited him. The provincial Machiavelli is out of favor today.

NATALIA. He's good value from time to time, but he's inclined to meddle, which I detest. (*Walking about*) Besides, with all his fawning, he's very impertinent, *and* a cynic . . . (*Sharply*) What was he trying on with you?

RAKITIN. He was telling me about your neighbor.

NATALIA (*sitting next to him*). Oh, that silly old thing.

RAKITIN. You've changed about him, too.

NATALIA. Today is not yesterday.

RAKITIN. It is, as far as I'm concerned, though, isn't it?

NATALIA. How do you mean?

RAKITIN (*handing her coffee*). You were unkind to me yesterday, and the same holds good today.

NATALIA. I know, my dear, I'm sorry . . . (*Suddenly gentle*) Whatever foolish thoughts may come into my head, there is nobody on whom I rely, as I rely on my Michel. *(Quietly)* There is nobody in the world whom I love, as I love you, *(After a pause)* You believe me, don't you? *(Vera begins to play on the pianoforte in the ballroom; Chopin.)*

RAKITIN. I believe you.

NATALIA. But I've come to think, my dear . . . that one can never—never really be responsible for one's actions; one can swear to nothing. We often fail to understand the past, how can we make pledges for what is to come? You can't put the future into chains.

RAKITIN. That's true enough.

NATALIA *(after a pause)*. Michel, I'm going to tell you something.

RAKITIN. Yes?

NATALIA. It will hurt you, but I know it would hurt you still more if I kept it from you . . . This young man . . .

RAKITIN. Yes?

NATALIA. I find he is constantly in my thoughts.

(A pause. The music trails away.)

RAKITIN *(quietly)*. I know.

NATALIA. You know? Michel, since when?

RAKITIN. Yesterday. In that field . . . If you could have seen yourself!

NATALIA. Did I look so strange?

RAKITIN. I should never have known it was you: your cheeks were flushed, your eyes shone like diamonds. And you looked at him with an attention so trusting, so brimful of happiness, and then the happiness broke into a smile . . . Even now, at the mere evocation your face is lighting up . . .

NATALIA *(as he averts his eyes)*. I don't mind anything you say, Michel, so long as you don't turn away from me . . . please . . . You're exaggerating now, you know; he was so wildly young, in that field—I caught it from him—it went to my head, and it'll pass off just like wine, in fact, it's not worth talking about. *(As he does not move)* I need your help, Michel . . . don't turn away from me—please . . .
(A pause.)

RAKITIN. I don't think you know yourself quite what is happening to you.

NATALIA. Don't I?

RAKITIN. One minute you say it's

hardly worth discussing, the next you're asking for help. People don't ask for help unless they're desperate. You need mine?

NATALIA. Yes, I do.

(He looks at her, realizing at last that his fears were well founded. A pause.)

RAKITIN *(bitterly)*. I see. I'm willing to live up to your expectations, Natalia Petrovna, but I must first recover my breath.

NATALIA. Recover . . . ? But—you don't think I might so far forget myself as to . . . You're not imagining——

RAKITIN. I imagine nothing. Shall we talk of something else? . . . *(After a pause)* About Vérochka? . . . The Doctor's still waiting for your answer.

NATALIA. You're angry with me.

RAKITIN. I'm sorry for you.

NATALIA. Sorry? *(Rising, and crossing, angrily)* Oh, Michel, this is too bad . . . *(As he does not answer, biting her lip)* The Doctor's waiting for my answer, did you say? But who asked him to meddle——

RAKITIN. He swore to me that you yourself had hinted——

NATALIA. Perhaps I did, I can't remember—what *does* it matter? The Doctor has so many irons in the fire, it can't be such a calamity if one of them falls out and singes his whiskers.

RAKITIN. He merely wants to know——

NATALIA. Michel, I can't bear this cold polite stare . . . please!

(A pause. Vera begins to play again, in the ballroom.)

I see, I made a mistake in being honest with you. You never suspected a thing, and now you're imagining Heaven knows what . . . *(After a pause, as he does not move, in a hard voice)* I shan't forget . . . *(Ingenuously)* Are you jealous?

RAKITIN. I have no right to be jealous, Natalia Petrovna, you know that . . . As for the other matter, Vera's in the ballroom now—shall I tell her you wish to see her?

NATALIA. This minute? Just as you like . . . *(As he rises to go)* Michel, for the last time . . . you said just now you're sorry for me . . . is this the way to show it?

RAKITIN *(coldly)*. Shall I tell her?

NATALIA (*angrily*). Yes, tell her, tell her . . .

(*Rakitin goes into the ballroom. Natalia stands a moment without moving.*)

Even *he* doesn't understand . . . And if I cannot turn to him, then who can . . . My husband? My poor Arkady, I've not given you one thought, not one . . .

(*The music stops. She looks round, and disposes herself in the armchair. Vera comes in from the ballroom, carrying a piece of music.*)

VERA (*timidly*). Did you want me, Natalia Petrovna?

NATALIA (*starting*). Ah, Vérochka!

VERA. Do you feel quite well?

NATALIA. Perfectly, it's a little close, that's all. Vera, I want to have a little talk with you.

VERA (*anxiously, putting down her music*). Oh?——

NATALIA. A serious talk. Sit down, my dear, will you? (*As Vera obeys*) Now . . . Vera, one thinks of you as still a child; but it's high time to give a thought to your future. You're an orphan, and not a rich one at that: sooner or later you are bound to tire of living on somebody else's property. Now how would you like suddenly to have control of your very own house?

VERA. I'm afraid I—I don't follow you, Natalia Petrovna——

NATALIA. You are being sought in marriage.

(*Vera stares at her. A pause.*)

You didn't expect this? I must confess I didn't either; you are still so young. I refuse to press you in the slightest—but I thought it my duty to let you know. (*As Vera suddenly covers her face with her hands*) Vera! My dear . . . What is it? (*Taking her hands*) But you're shaking like a leaf!

VERA. Natalia Petrovna, I'm in your power . . .

NATALIA. In my power? Vera, what do you take me for? (*Cajoling, as Vera kisses her hands*) In my power, indeed—will you please take that back, this minute? I command you! (*As Vera smiles through her tears*) That's better . . . (*Putting an arm round her, and drawing her nearer*) Vera, my child, I tell you what—you'll make believe I'm your elder sister—and we'll

straighten out these strange things together—what do you say?

VERA. If you would like me to— yes——

NATALIA. Good . . . Move closer— that's better . . . First of all—as you're my sister, this is your home; so there's no possible question of anybody pining to be rid of you—now is that understood?

VERA (*whispering*). Yes . . .

NATALIA. Now one fine day your sister comes to you and says 'What do you think, little one? Somebody is asking for your hand!' Well, what would be your first thought? That you're too young?

VERA. Just as you wish——

NATALIA. Now now—does a girl say 'just as you wish' to her sister?

VERA (*smiling*). Well, then, I'd just say 'I'm too young'.

NATALIA. Good; your sister would agree, the suitor would be given 'no' for an answer, fini . . . But suppose he was a very nice gentleman with means, prepared to bide his time, in the hope that one day . . . what then?

VERA. Who is this suitor?

NATALIA. Ah, you're curious. Can't you guess?

VERA. No.

NATALIA. Bolshintsov.

VERA. Afanasy Ivanych?

NATALIA. Afanasy Ivanych. It's true he's not very young, and not wildly prepossessing——

(*Vera begins to laugh, then stops and looks at Natalia.*)

VERA. You're joking . . .

NATALIA (*after a pause, smiling*). No, but I see the matter is closed. If you had burst into tears when he was mentioned, there might have been some hope for him; but you laughed. . . . (*Rising, smiling wryly*) The matter is closed.

VERA. I'm sorry, but you took me completely by surprise . . . Do people still get married at his age?

NATALIA. But how old do you take him for? He's on the right side of fifty!

VERA. I suppose he is, but he has *such* a peculiar face . . .

NATALIA. Bolshintsov, my dear, you are dead and buried, may you rest in peace . . . It was foolish of me to forget that little girls dream of marrying for love.

VERA. But, Natalia Petrovna . . . didn't *you* marry for love?

NATALIA *(after a pause)*. Yes, of course I did . . . Eh, bien, fini! Bolshintsov, you are dismissed . . . I must confess I never much fancied that puffy old moon-face next to your fresh young cheek. There! . . . *(Sitting again, next to Vera)* And you're not frightened of me any more?

VERA. No, not any more——

NATALIA. Well, then, Vérochka darling, just whisper quietly in my ear . . . you don't want to marry Bolshintsov because he's too old and far from an Adonis—but is that the only reason?

VERA *(after a pause)*. Natalia Petrovna, isn't it reason enough?

NATALIA. Undoubtedly, my dear . . . but you haven't answered my question. *(A pause.)*

VERA. There's no other reason.

NATALIA. Oh . . . Of course, that puts the matter on rather a different footing.

VERA. How do you mean, Natalia Petrovna?

NATALIA. I realize you can never fall in *love* with Bolshintsov; but he's an excellent man. And if there is nobody else . . . Isn't there *anybody* you're fond of?

VERA. Well, there's you, and little Kolia——

NATALIA *(with a hint of impatience)*. Vera, you must know what I mean . . . Out of the young men you've met . . . have you formed any attachment at all?

VERA. I quite like one or two, but——

NATALIA. For instance, don't I remember at the Krinitsins your dancing three times with a tall officer—what was his name——

VERA. With a long mustache? *(Smiling)* He giggled all the time.

NATALIA. Oh . . . *(After a pause)* What about our philosopher Rakitin?

VERA. Mihail Alexandrovich? I'm very fond of him, of course, who wouldn't be——

NATALIA. An elder brother, I see . . . *(Suddenly)* And the new tutor? *(A pause.)*

VERA. Alexei Nikolaich?

NATALIA. Alexei Nikolaich.

VERA. I like him very much.

(She has blushed; Natalia is watching her narrowly.)

NATALIA. He *is* nice, isn't he? Such a pity he's so bashful with everybody——

VERA *(innocently)*. Oh, he isn't bashful with me!

NATALIA. Isn't he?

VERA. I suppose it's because we're both orphans. I think he must appear shy to you because he's afraid of you. You see, he's had no chance to know you——

NATALIA. Afraid of me? How do you know?

VERA. He told me so.

NATALIA. He told you . . .

VERA. Don't you like him, Natalia Petrovna?

NATALIA. He seems very kind-hearted.

VERA. Oh, he is! If you only knew . . . *(Turning to her, enthusiastically)* The whole of this household loves him—he's so warm, once he's got over his shyness—the other day an old beggar-woman had to be taken to hospital—do you know he carried her the whole way? And one day he picked a flower for me off a cliff—he's as nimble as a reindeer. D'you remember yesterday, when he cleared that tremendous ditch? And he's always so good-tempered and gay——

NATALIA. That doesn't sound a bit like him—when he's with me, he——

VERA. But that's what I mean, Natalia Petrovna, it's because he doesn't know you! I'll tell him how truly kind you are——

NATALIA *(rising, ironically)*. Thank you, my dear——

VERA. You'll soon see the difference—because he listens to what I say, though I *am* younger than he is——

NATALIA. I never knew you two were such friends. You must be careful, Vera.

VERA. Careful?

NATALIA. I know he's a very pleasant young man, but at your age, it's not quite . . . People might think . . . *(As Vera blushes, and looks down)* Don't be impatient, my dear, will you, if I seem to be laying down the law? We older people regard it as our business to plague the young with our 'don't's' and 'mustn't's.' But, as you like him, and nothing more, there's no real need for me to say another word. *(Sitting next to her again)* Is there?

VERA *(raising her eyes, timidly)*. He . . .

NATALIA. Vera, is that the way to look at a sister? *(Caressing her)* If your *real* sister asked you very quietly, 'Vérochka, what *exactly* are your feelings towards So-and-so?' . . . what would you answer? *(As Vera looks at her, hesitating)* Those eyes are dying to tell me something . . . *(Vera suddenly presses her head to Natalia's breast. Natalia bites her lips.)* My poor Vera . . .

VERA *(without raising her head)*. Oh dear . . . I don't know what's the matter with me . . .

NATALIA. My poor sweet . . . *(As Vera presses herself closer to her)* And he . . . what of him?

VERA. I don't know . . .

NATALIA. Vera, what of him?

VERA. I don't know, I tell you . . . Sometimes I imagine . . .

NATALIA. You imagine what?

VERA *(her face hidden)*. That I see a look in his eyes . . . as if he thought of me—as a special person—perhaps . . . *(Disengaging herself, trying to be calm)* Oh, I don't know—

(She raises her head, and sees the expression on Natalia's face.)

What's the matter, Natalia Petrovna?

(Natalia is staring at her, as if she were a stranger.)

NATALIA. The matter? . . . *(Recovering)*. What did you say? Nothing——

VERA. But there *is* something the matter! *(Rising)* I'll ring——

NATALIA. No no—don't ring . . . *(louder)* . . . please! It's passed off already. You go back to your music—and we—we'll talk another time.

VERA. You're not angry with me, Natalia Petrovna?

NATALIA. Not in the least . . . I just want to be by myself.

(Vera tries to take her hand; Natalia turns away as if she had not noticed her gesture.)

VERA *(tears in her eyes)*. Natalia Petrovna . . .

NATALIA. Please . . .

(Vera goes slowly back into the ballroom. Natalia does not move.)

These children love each other . . . Well, it's a touching idea, and may Heaven bless them both. The way she came out with it . . . and I with no idea—*(laughing feverishly)*—ha! *(Rising, vehement)* But all is not lost—oh no . . . *(Stopping, and collecting herself)* But I don't know myself any more—what am I doing? *(After a pause, deliberately)* Shall I tell you, Natalia Petrovna? You're trying to marry a poor orphan girl to a foolish fond old man— you've gone as far as to use that wily old doctor as a go-between . . . Then there's your philosopher, and then your husband . . . what is happening—*(panic-stricken, her hands to her face)*—what is happening? *(After a pause, slowly)* Unhappy woman, for the first time in your life . . . you are in love.

(In the ballroom, Vera begins to play on the pianoforte; the same Chopin mazurka. Natalia listens, and walks slowly and dreamily out into the garden. The music echoes louder as the Curtain slowly falls.)

ACT TWO

SCENE ONE

The drawing-room, a few hours later; afternoon. Natalia is lying on the sofa, an untouched tray of food beside her. The blinds are down, and she is in a fitful sleep. A knock at the study door; a pause; another louder knock.

Natalia starts and wakes.

———

NATALIA *(calling)*. Come in . . .

(Katia enters, carrying a bottle of smelling-salts; she goes to Natalia, who takes the bottle and sniffs it. Katia takes the tray of food, curtseys, and goes back into the study, shutting the door behind her. Natalia rises and goes to the French windows. A pause.)

How has it happened? I still don't know . . . it's like—like a poison. One minute life was ordinary, the next—everything shattered and swept away . . . He's afraid of me, the same as everybody else, and as for any qualities I possess, how could he appreciate them? Rakitin was right, they're both stupid— how I hate that clever man! Control yourself . . . *(Deliberating)* Yes, I'm very much taken with him: very much indeed . . . *(After a pause)* He must go away . . . Love . . . so this is what it feels like . . . this— frightening enchantment . . . I'll go to Arkady—yes, my sweet trusting husband —all the others are strangers, and will remain strangers . . . But could she have made a mistake—it might be hero-worship, a sort of calf-love. I'll ask him myself . . . *(After a pause, reproachfully)* What is this, Natalia Petrovna, you refuse to give up hope? And what, pray, are you hoping for? O God, don't let me despise myself!

(She hides her head in her hands. Rakitin comes in from the garden. He is pale and disturbed. He sees her.)

RAKITIN. Natalia Petrovna . . .

(He raises the blinds; the room is flooded with sunlight.)

NATALIA *(raising her head)*. Yes, who is it? *(Seeing him)* Oh . . .

RAKITIN. We waited for you at the picnic—Kolia and everybody were bitterly disappointed——

NATALIA. I had a bad headache. I sent a message——

RAKITIN. I've come to ask you to forgive me.

NATALIA. Forgive you?

RAKITIN. I made a fool of myself this morning . . . You see, Natalia Petrovna, however modest a man's hopes . . . when they are suddenly snatched away, it's hard not to lose control, just for a moment. But I am myself again. *(After a pause, kneeling before her)* Please don't turn away, as I did— I am once more the Michel you've always known, the man who asks nothing better than to be your servant—you remember what you said? *(As she sits motionless, gazing at the floor)* 'There's nobody in the world . . .'— remember? Give me back your trust!

NATALIA *(absently)*. Yes . . . *(Collecting herself)* I'm sorry, I haven't heard a word you've been saying . . . Michel, what is the matter with me?

RAKITIN. You are in love.

(A pause.)

NATALIA *(slowly)*. But Michel, it's madness—can it happen so suddenly? . . . *(Brusquely)* She loves him, you know. They love each other . . . Michel, please —please tell me what to do!

RAKITIN. I will, on one condition: that you'll have complete faith in my dis-interested wish to help you.

NATALIA. I will—I will! Michel, I'm standing on the edge of a precipice. Save me!

RAKITIN. He must go away.

(A pause. She looks at him.)

Right away. I won't drag in—your hus-band, or your duty, because such senti-ments would not come well from me . . . but if these children love each other . . . imagine yourself standing between them.

NATALIA. He must go.

RAKITIN. For the sake of your hap-piness, both he and I . . . must go away for good.

NATALIA. You—go away too?

RAKITIN. It's the only way out.

NATALIA *(desperately)*. And then— what? What shall I have to live for?

RAKITIN. But—your husband, your son . . . What have you to live for, indeed! . . . *(As Natalia looks away, without answering)* Listen—I'll stay a day or two after he's gone, just to make sure that you——

NATALIA *(sombrely)*. I see.

RAKITIN. You see what?

NATALIA. That you are counting on a force of habit—which you call our old friendship—bringing me close to you again—am I right?

RAKITIN. Now you are insulting me. After your promise just now . . . when all I want on earth is for your good name to shine untarnished before the world——

NATALIA. My good name? But this is something new—why have you never mentioned it before?

(He shakes his head despairingly, and makes to go; she holds out her hand towards him.) Michel . . .

RAKITIN *(taking her in his arms, over-come)*. Natalia Petrovna——

NATALIA. Can anyone ever have been so unhappy . . . *(Leaning against his shoulder)* Help me, Michel—without you I am lost . . .

YSLAEV'S VOICE. Mind you, Mamma, it's always been my firm opinion——

(He enters from the hall, Anna Semyenovna on his arm. They both see Rakitin and Natalia, and stop in amazement. Natalia turns her

head, sees them, gives a distracted sob, and hurries into the study. Rakitin stands where he is, acutely embarrassed.)

ANNA. Well, upon my soul! What's the matter with Natalia Petrovna——

RAKITIN. Nothing, I tell you—really nothing——

ANNA. But my dear Mihail Alexandrovich, it couldn't be nothing! Well, upon my soul . . . *(Making for the study)* I'll go and ask her, point blank——

RAKITIN. No, I beg of you——

YSLAEV. But I should like to be enlightened—what's behind it all?

(Anna sits on the sofa, and glares at Rakitin.)

RAKITIN. There's nothing behind it, Arkady, I swear to you. I promise on my word of honor, that tomorrow morning I'll explain the whole thing.

YSLAEV. I—I'm right out of my depth —Natalia's never behaved like this before —it's quite fantastic——

ANNA. But she was crying! I could see the tears—and dashing out as if we were a couple of perfect strangers——

RAKITIN. Listen, dear people, both of you. Natalia Petrovna and I were in the throes of a discussion, and I must ask you —just for a moment—to leave us completely alone.

YSLAEV. Alone? But is there a secret between you?

RAKITIN. In a way, yes—but you shall know it.

YSLAEV *(after a pause)*. Very well, Mamma, we'll leave them to wind up this mysterious duologue in camera——

ANNA. But what on earth——

YSLAEV. Come along, Mamma, *please* don't let it be one of your obstinate days.

RAKITIN. I beg of you to rest assured—

YSLAEV *(coldly)*. I require no assurance, thank you.

ANNA. I repeat——

YSLAEV *(to Anna, sternly)*. Mamma . . .

(Anna rises, takes his arm and they both go into the ballroom. When he is sure they are out of earshot, Rakitin hurries to the study door.)

RAKITIN *(calling)*. Natalia Petrovna . . . *(Natalia comes back from the study; she is very pale.)*

NATALIA. What did they say?

RAKITIN. I said I'd explain the whole thing tomorrow, which means we have today anyway—*(as she sways, and he leads her to a chair)*—I'll think of something— you can see now, can't you, that we cannot go on like this? I'll have a word with him presently; I feel sure somehow that he's a boy with the right instincts, and he'll see at once——

NATALIA. A word with him? But what will you say?

RAKITIN. Why, that he and I must leave here at once.

(A pause.)

NATALIA. Rakitin, do let us be careful.

RAKITIN. Go on.

NATALIA. Are we not being a little rash? I lost my head for a minute, and made you lose yours—and all for nothing, we may discover——

RAKITIN. For nothing?

NATALIA. I mean it! What are we doing? It seems only a moment ago that this was a house of quiet and peace—and look at us now! Really, this nonsense has gone far enough, we're going to take life up where we left off—and as for this dramatic rencontre you're planning with my husband—don't bother, because I'll tell him myself all about our little teacup tempest, and we'll sit back together and laugh about it.

RAKITIN. Natalia Petrovna, this is dangerous talk indeed.

NATALIA. What do you mean?

RAKITIN. You're smiling, but you're deathly pale.

NATALIA. You don't think I've changed my mind about—about the young tutor leaving? Because I propose to dismiss him myself.

RAKITIN. Yourself?

NATALIA. He must have come back with the others—send him to me, will you?

RAKITIN. Now?

NATALIA. This minute. You see, I'm so completely recovered, I know I can do it.

RAKITIN. But what will you say to him? He confessed to me himself that he's always tongue-tied with you——

NATALIA *(sharply)*. You've already discussed me with him? . . . *(As he looks at her, a cold fixed look)* I'm sorry, Michel —send him to me, there's a dear; I'll give him his congé, and everything will be over and done with, like a bad dream.

RAKITIN. Very well.

NATALIA (as he goes to the ballroom door). Thank you, Michel——

RAKITIN (turning, in an outburst). Oh, please—at least spare me your gratitude... (He controls himself and hurries into the ballroom. A pause.)

NATALIA (touched). Michel, you're a truly generous creature... But have I ever really loved you?

RAKITIN'S VOICE (in the hall). Monsieur Beliaev! One moment...

(Natalia starts, crosses, and sits on the sofa in readiness for the interview.)

NATALIA. One last effort, and I shall be free. Freedom and peace... (shutting her eyes)... how I long for you both...

(Beliaev enters from the ballroom. He comes down, inquiringly, and looks at her. A pause.)

BELIAEV. Natalia Petrovna. (As she opens her eyes, and looks at him) You sent for me?

NATALIA. I should like an explanation.

BELIAEV. An explanation?

NATALIA (without looking at him, after a pause). I'm afraid... I'm dissatisfied with you.

BELIAEV (dumbfounded). Dissatisfied? (As she rises and wanders restlessly) If I have given any impression of neglecting my duties——

NATALIA. No, no, I've been more than pleased with the way you've been handling Kolia——

BELIAEV. Then—excuse me—what——

NATALIA. Please don't take it too much to heart. You're very young, and never having lived in a strange house before, you could hardly have foreseen ... Alexei Nikolaich, it's just this: Vérochka has made a clean breast to me of the whole thing.

(She looks at him. A pause.)

BELIAEV (bewildered). Vera Alexandrovna?

NATALIA. Yes.

BELIAEV. But... made a clean breast of what?

NATALIA. You mean to say you cannot guess?

BELIAEV. No.

NATALIA. Oh... Well, if you really don't know... then please forgive me—let's say no more about it... (Looking at him again, while he stares at her, still bewildered) Do you know that I'm not sure I believe you? Though I understand exactly why you should pretend——

BELIAEV. I'm sorry, Natalia Petrovna, but I have not the faintest idea to what you are referring.

NATALIA. Now come, you can't pretend that you haven't noticed!

BELIAEV. Noticed what?

NATALIA. That she is head over heels in love with you. She told me herself... Well?

BELIAEV. I... But—I've always behaved to Vera Alexandrovna——

NATALIA. I put the question to you as to a man of honor—what are your intentions?

BELIAEV. My—intentions?

NATALIA. Yes.

BELIAEV (acutely embarrassed). Natalia Petrovna, this—this is a bolt from the blue.

NATALIA (after a pause). I'm not doing this at all well... You think I'm angry with you—don't you? I'm not, I'm just ... concerned—understandably, I think. Shall we sit down?

(She sits. Beliaev hesitates, and sits next to her.)

Vera loves you—oh, I know that's not your fault, I'm quite ready to believe you had nothing to do with it... but you see, Alexei Nikolaich, I'm directly responsible for her future. At her age such upheavals do not last long, and now that I've told you, I know I can rely on you to change your attitude towards her.

BELIAEV. But Natalia Petrovna... in what way?

NATALIA. By avoiding her... (After a pause) Mind you, when I told you all that, I took it for granted that on your side there was nothing.

BELIAEV (perplexed). And if there had been?

NATALIA. If there had been... You're not rich, but you're young, you have a future, and if two people love each other...

BELIAEV. But——

NATALIA (hastily). Oh, please don't

think I'm trying to extort a confession from you . . . I must remind you, though, that Vera was under the impression that you were not entirely indifferent to her. *(A pause. Beliaev rises, acutely perplexed.)*

BELIAEV. As you have been frank with me, Natalia Petrovna, may I be frank with you?

NATALIA. By all means——

BELIAEV. I have a great affection for Vera Alexandrovna, but not—anything—anything more at all . . . and if, as you say, she is under the impression that I—that I am not indifferent to her, I must tell her the truth. But having told her, it would create too painful a situation . . . and it will be impossible for me to stay on here.

NATALIA *(after a pause)*. I see . . .

BELIAEV. I knew you would . . . I need not tell you how hard it will be for me to leave your house——

NATALIA. Will it?

BELIAEV. I shall always think of you with—with the deepest gratitude . . . *(After a pause)* Will you excuse me for now? I shall ask the honor of taking my formal leave of you, later on——

NATALIA. Just as you wish . . . *(As he turns to go)* But I must confess . . .

BELIAEV. Yes?

NATALIA. I didn't expect quite this. *(Rising)* All I intended was to remind you that Vera is still a child. I rather feel now that I've exaggerated—is it absolutely necessary for you to go?

BELIAEV. I'm sorry, but I don't see how I can stay.

NATALIA. I'm not in the habit of pressing people against their will, but I must confess to being a little displeased by this turn of events.

BELIAEV. Displeased? . . . Natalia Petrovna—*(hesitating)*—I—I'll stay.

NATALIA. Ah . . . *(After a pause)* You've changed your mind very quickly? *(Another pause, then spasmodically)* Perhaps you're right, perhaps you ought to go after all.

BELIAEV. Thank you. I am at your service. *(He bows and makes to go)*

NATALIA. One thing, though—you said you were going to explain something to Vera—I question the wisdom of that, very much.

BELIAEV. I bow to your wishes.

NATALIA *(as he goes)*. As for your going away, I'll let you know this evening. *(Beliaev inclines his head and goes out into the hall. A pause.)*

He does not love her! . . . Though I can't be proud of an interview that starts off dismissing him, and ends up begging him to stay. *(Going up, and sitting at the table)* And what right had I to tell him the poor girl's madly in love with him, I who dragged the confession out of her, and in such a heartless, cruel way—not even a confession, a half-avowal—*(covering her face with her hands)*—what have I done! . . . Perhaps he was beginning to fall in love with her? If he was, what right had I to trample such a flower into the mud. . . . But have I trampled it *right* in—perhaps he was deceiving me—after all, I did my best to deceive *him* . . . No, he's too highminded; not like me . . . When I think how crafty I tried to be with him, and how courageously he dealt with me; he was a man, suddenly . . . If he stays . . . I forgo any self-respect I ever had. *(Rising)* He leaves, or Natalia Petrovna—is lost. I'll write to him—before he has time to see her—he must go!
(She clasps her hands and walks swiftly up the stairs and into the hall.)

QUICK CURTAIN

SCENE TWO

A corner of the garden, a few hours later; evening. Fitful sunlight; storm-clouds have gathered.

A pause. Katia enters cautiously from the left, looks round, tiptoes quickly across and peers anxiously over to the right.

————

KATIA. I can't see him . . . bother! Then why did they tell me he was coming over to the greenhouse? I wish he'd hurry up, now's the time, while they're all at the schoolroom tea . . . *(Sighing, sitting on the seat)* Can it be true, this nasty tale that he's going away? . . . *(After another sigh)* Poor little thing . . . the way she begged and begged me! . . . Well, the least they can ask for is a last little chat together, the sweet pets . . . Mercy, what a hot day it's been . . . but it looks as if the rain might start any minute . . . *(Looking out, and stepping quickly back)* My goodness, they're not coming down here —yes they are—oh mercy me——

(She runs off right, as Lizaveta and the Doctor enter from the left.)

THE DOCTOR. Looks like another downpour—we'll shelter in this corner— what d'you say?

LIZAVETA. Oh—*(confused)*—I don't know, I'm sure——

THE DOCTOR. You must admit, Lizaveta Bogdanovna, that the clouds have picked the most awkward moment to gather. *(As they settle on the seat)* Just as we were getting to a—shall I say a soulful stage?

LIZAVETA. Soulful? *(With downcast eyes)* Oh, Ignaty Illyich . . .

THE DOCTOR. But now they're all over in the schoolroom, we can sit here and take up the sentimental cudgels where we left off . . .

LIZAVETA. Cudgels—the things you think of . . .

THE DOCTOR. Snuff?

LIZAVETA. Well, just this once . . .

THE DOCTOR *(as they both sniff)*. By the way, did you say the old tabby was in one of her tantrums today?

LIZAVETA. The master's mother? I should think she is. You know what happened this afternoon, don't you—oh no I mustn't, it's scandal——

THE DOCTOR. Oh yes you must, or I'll lock you up in a cupboard——

LIZAVETA. Oh, you are a terror! Well, she walked in here and found Natalia Petrovna with her professor as she calls him, with her head on his shoulder— crying!

THE DOCTOR. Crying? You don't say . . . But take it from me, Rakitin's not to be labelled as a dangerous customer.

LIZAVETA. How very very interesting —why, do you think?

THE DOCTOR. Much too good a conversationalist. Ordinary men may lose their heads and behave like beasts, but with those clever ones the whole thing gushes away down a wastepipe of talk. It's the quiet ones with eyes like live coals and a broad back of the neck—the world over, that spells red for danger . . . But shall we leave the riff-raff, bless 'em, and glance at our own affairs? Well?

LIZAVETA *(her eyes fluttering)*. Well, said the echo . . .

THE DOCTOR. Would you object to my inquiring why, when one puts to you a simple question, you raise and lower your eyeballs as if you were a mechanical doll?

LIZAVETA *(rattled)*. Oh—Doctor——

THE DOCTOR *(rising, and pacing)*. We're neither of us chickens, and all this simpering about the bush doesn't suit us in the least. What d'you say to a down-to-earth chat, in keeping with—with the length of our teeth?

LIZAVETA. O dear.

THE DOCTOR. To start with, we like each other; and in other ways surely, we're well suited. I must, in fairness, describe myself as not exactly of high descent——

LIZAVETA *(tolerantly)*. Ah, but a natural gentleman——

THE DOCTOR. But then of course you're not exactly blue blood yourself. I'm not rolling in money; if I were, I'd obviously be flying higher, but still . . . I've got a respectable enough practice; not all my patients die . . . And I may take it, I hope, that after fifteen years, the first careless rapture of being a governess is wearing off, and that you're also just about sick of waiting hand over fist on a female dragon, when you're not cheating at cards to make her think she's won. *(Sitting again)* Eh?

LIZAVETA. Oh dear . . .

THE DOCTOR. Then there's me. I can't say I'm tired of being a bachelor—on the contrary, suits me to a T; but I'm not getting any younger, and my cook is robbing me. So everything fits in nicely. . . . But there's one thing, Lizaveta Bogdanovna; you don't know me. I know you, of course, backwards.

LIZAVETA *(not sure whether she is on her head or her heels)*. Oh, Doctor, really?

THE DOCTOR. Backwards. And I can't say you're entirely free from faults.

LIZAVETA *(stiffly)*. Such as?

THE DOCTOR. For one thing, being a

spinster for so long has turned you a little bit sour.

LIZAVETA. Oh.

THE DOCTOR. But that would right itself in a jiffy—in the moral hands of a good husband, a wife is clay . . . But before the ting-a-ling of wedding bells, I'm more than anxious for you to know me, so you can't turn on me afterwards. I won't have any wool over your eyes— see what I mean? For example, it wouldn't surprise me if you took me for a cheerful man?

LIZAVETA. Cheerful? Oh, but of course—I've always known you were one to set the table in a roar——

THE DOCTOR. Exactly. Just because I play the fool, and tell the gentry funny stories, you label me like a shot as a sanguine character. Shall I tell you something? If those gentry weren't being damned useful to me, I wouldn't look at 'em twice. As it is, give me half a chance to poke fun at 'em to their faces without actually flicking 'em on the raw, and I'll take it. I get my own back—oh yes!

LIZAVETA. D'you include Natalia Petrovna?

THE DOCTOR (mimicking). 'Now Doctor, you've a tongue like a rapier, which is what I like and respect you for . . .' He he he, coo away, my dove, coo away! She's like all the others, that crinkle up their society faces at you in a permanent smile of hail-fellow-well-met, and all the time you can see their eyes writing the word 'peasant' flat across your phiz; say what you like, they've no use for us. And just because they drench themselves in eau-de-Cologne and drawl every syllable as if they were dropping it accidentally for you to pick up, they think you can't trip 'em by the heels. They're human just like us poor sinners, and what's more . . . (with meaning) . . . they're not saints themselves.

LIZAVETA. Ignaty Illyich, you take my breath away.

THE DOCTOR. I knew I would. Anyway, I must have proved to you that I'm not a sanguine character. Mind you, don't think because I play the fool that any of 'em has ever dared to snub me. They're even scared of me; they know I can bite. There was a big dinner once, and sitting a yard from me a landowner fellow—regular son of the soil suddenly up to his knees in filthy lucre; well, just for a joke, in front of the whole room, he took a radish and stuck it in my hair.

LIZAVETA. He didn't! Heavens, what did you do?

THE DOCTOR. Rose quietly to my full height, removed the offending vegetable from my person, bowed, and with the utmost cool courtesy challenged him to a duel.

LIZAVETA (thrilled and shocked). Oh! What did he do?

THE DOCTOR. Nearly had a stroke. Then in front of the whole room, the host made him ask my pardon; it had the most tremendous effect on everybody. Of course I'd known beforehand he was a martyr to gout and wouldn't fight anyway, but still . . . What I'm getting at, Lizaveta Bogdanovna, is that although I have an unconscionable amount of self-esteem, my life hasn't really come up to scratch. Nobody could call me well-read, and I'm not a good doctor—it's no use pretending I am, and if you ever fall ill, take a tip from one who knows, and don't call me in . . . I'm good enough for these provincial invalids, of course, but it ends there. And now my personal habits.

LIZAVETA (apprehensively). Personal habits—yes?

THE DOCTOR. In my own home I am extremely morose, abnormally silent, and highly exacting. Have I made myself clear?

LIZAVETA. Yes . . . oh yes . . .

THE DOCTOR. Though in fairness I must add that so long as my habits are observed and good hot food is served consistently before me, I keep my temper. What d'you say?

LIZAVETA. Ignaty Illyich, what can I say? Unless you've been slandering yourself on purpose——

THE DOCTOR (rising, and pacing). But you silly woman, I haven't been slandering myself at all! Kindly keep in mind that any other man would ha' died rather than breathe a word till after the wedding, when it'd be too late—no, I'm too proud to do that.

LIZAVETA *(looking at him)*. Proud?

THE DOCTOR. Yes, you can stare as much as you like—proud. To a stranger I'd bow to the ground for a sack of flour, saying to myself, 'What a fool, my friend, how you rise to the bait . . . *how* you rise!' *(Sitting again)* But to you, Lizaveta Bogdanovna—*(taking her hand)* my future spouse . . . I say what I think. At least, I don't say *everything* I think—I must be frank—but near enough not to mislead you. Well, that's me. A funny old stick, eh?

LIZAVETA. A little—ah—eccentric, perhaps——

THE DOCTOR. One of these days I'll tell you the story of my early life, and you'll be amazed that I've come through as well as I have . . . And now I'll give you a little time to chew the cud, what d'you say?

LIZAVETA. Oh . . .

THE DOCTOR. You shut yourself up somewhere, go carefully into the whole thing, and let me know. By the way, how old are you?

LIZAVETA *(knocked off her perch)*. Oh. Thirty.

THE DOCTOR. No you're not, you're forty.

LIZAVETA *(with spirit)*. No I'm not, I—I'm thirty-six.

THE DOCTOR. Well, thirty-six isn't thirty. That's another habit you'll have to get rid of, Lizaveta Bogdanovna. Anyway a married woman of thirty-six isn't old at all. You shouldn't take snuff either. *(Rising)* I think it's clearing up.

LIZAVETA *(rising)*. Yes, it seems to have blown over, doesn't it?

THE DOCTOR. So I may expect to hear from you in a day or two?

LIZAVETA *(suddenly practical)*. To-morrow.

THE DOCTOR. Good! I like that, Lizaveta Bogdanovna—common sense, nothing like it—oh, just one more thing.

LIZAVETA *(turning)*. Yes?

THE DOCTOR. I haven't kissed your hand, and I believe in these circumstances it's expected . . . *(She holds out her hand; he kisses it, while she blushes)* That's over . . . *(She takes his arm and they go out to the left. Katia emerges cautiously from the right.)*

KATIA. Mercy, what a spiteful man! And the *things* he said! . . . And now I've missed just what I came down here for. . . . *(Sitting on the seat)* And so Lizaveta Bogdanovna will be Mrs. Medicine—*(giggling)*—oh dear, it's so funny, I'm glad I'm not in her shoes . . . It's actually been raining over by the greenhouse . . . the grass looks as if it's had a wash. And what a lovely smell. Must be the wild cherry. *(Sentimentally)* Oh dear. . . . Here he is! . . .

(Beliaev appears from the left.)

(Calling cautiously) Alexei Nikolaich! *(Louder)* Alexei Nikolaich!

BELIAEV *(turning)*. Yes, who wants me? *(Coming up to the seat)* Oh, Katia, it's you!

KATIA. I want to tell you something.

BELIAEV. Tell me something? All right—*(sitting beside her)* Ecco! D'you know, Katia, you're looking damnably pretty today?

KATIA *(blushing and giggling)*. Oh go on . . .

BELIAEV. You are. *(Taking one from his pocket)* Peach?

KATIA. No thank you, really—you have it——

BELIAEV. Did I turn down the red currants you offered me yesterday? Come on, take it—I picked it for you.

KATIA. Oh, did you? . . . Thank you ever so much——

BELIAEV *(as she takes the peach)*. That's the style . . . Well, what was it you wanted to whisper in my ear?

KATIA. Oh . . . It's just that Vera Alexandrovna—that the young lady is very anxious to see you.

BELIAEV. Oh . . . *(His face falling)* Is she?

KATIA. She's over by the plum tree, waiting for me to fetch her—you wouldn't be disturbed down here, she said, with them all still at the birthday tea——

BELIAEV *(taken aback)*. Oh . . . I see . . .

KATIA. She's very fond of you. *(Sighing, deeply, then going)* I shan't be a minute—*(stopping, and turning)*—Alexei Nikolaich, is it true what they say?

BELIAEV. What?

KATIA. That you're leaving us?

BELIAEV. Leaving? I—who told you?

KATIA. So you're not going? *(Delighted)* Oh, gracious Heaven be thanked! *(Embarrassed, primly)* We'll be back presently. *(She runs off to the right. A pause.)*

BELIAEV. The most fantastic things are happening to me. Vera's a sweet little thing with the kindest of hearts, I'm sure, but . . . And what would be the meaning of a note like this—*(taking a scrap of paper from his pocket)*—from Natalia Petrovna? *(Reading)* 'Please make no decisions until I have seen you again.' What could *she* want to see me about? . . . *(After a pause, rising)* The stupidest thoughts will keep coming into my head. . . . Whatever it is, it's all damnably embarrassing. If somebody had told me three weeks ago that I . . . I . . . What I still can't make head or tail of, is that conversation I had with her . . . *(Sitting again)* Lord, I wish my heart would stop thumping like this . . .

(Vera enters from the right with Katia; she is very pale, and keeps her eyes averted. Beliaev jumps up.)

KATIA. Don't be frightened, miss—it'll be all right——

(She hurries back to the right. A pause.)

BELIAEV. Vera Alexandrovna, you wished to see me. Won't you sit down? *(Taking her hand, leading her to the seat, and sitting beside her)* But you've been crying!

VERA. You've been dismissed, haven't you?

BELIAEV. Who told you?

VERA. Natalia Petrovna herself. I had to talk to you, to—ask your pardon.

BELIAEV. Pardon? But what for?

VERA. If you only knew how this has upset me, Alexei Nikolaich—to be the cause of the whole thing—*(starting to cry, then controlling herself)*

BELIAEV. You the cause of it? But Vera Alexandrovna, nothing's settled, I assure you. It's quite possible I shall stay——

VERA. No, everything's settled, Alexei Nikolaich—everything's over. When you think how you are with me now, and only yesterday, in the garden . . . do you remember?

(A pause. She fights back her tears, rises, then turns to him.)

Alexei Nikolaich, is it true that you weren't exactly dismissed—that it was you who were anxious to go?

BELIAEV. Why?

VERA. Answer me!

BELIAEV. I—yes. You were right. She told me everything.

VERA *(faintly)*. That I . . . was in love with you?

BELIAEV *(stammering)*. Yes.

VERA *(quickly)*. It isn't true!

BELIAEV. But . . . if it isn't true . . . why should she——

VERA. At least—I didn't tell her—I don't remember . . . *(Her hands to her face)* Oh, how cruel of her . . . And is that why you wanted to leave?

BELIAEV. I ask you, Vera Alexandrovna, what else could I have done . . . *(He walks away in despair)*

VERA. He doesn't love me . . .

(She shakes her head, and covers her face again with her hands. He sits beside her.)

BELIAEV. Vera Alexandrovna, please . . . Give me your hand . . . *(Taking it)* I do love you, Vérochka, because it's impossible not to——

VERA. You . . . you mean——

BELIAEV. In the same way I love my sister—*(as she turns away)* I'm sorry—oh lord, I've never in my life been in a situation like this . . . I'd do anything rather than hurt you. . . . *(With resolution)* The best thing is not to pretend anything to you at all, don't you think so?

VERA. Yes yes——

BELIAEV. Well, I know that you—you've grown fond of me. But you see, Vérochka, I'm just twenty-one, and haven't a farthing to bless myself with——

(As Vera stifles a sob) I—oh lord, I don't know what to say to you——

VERA. But I haven't asked you to say anything—and suddenly to bring up your prospects—oh, it's so cruel——

BELIAEV. I'm sorry, Vérochka——

VERA. It isn't your fault, Alexei Nikolaich. I don't even blame her; she just lost her head.

BELIAEV *(puzzled)*. Lost her head?

(A pause.)

VERA. Yes. I'm not the only one who's given herself away. *(Turning to him)* She's in love with you.

BELIAEV *(after a pause, thinking he has not heard right)*. What did you say?

VERA. She's in love with you.

BELIAEV. Natalia Petrovna? . . . *(Staggered)* What—do you know what you're saying?

VERA. Yes. You see, today has made me years older . . . And she took it into her head to be jealous of me—*me!*

BELIAEV. I don't believe it.

VERA. Then why did she suddenly try and palm me off on to that old gentleman? If you could have seen her when I broke down and—and confessed . . . her face changed before my eyes. Yes, she's in love with you . . . .

BELIAEV *(after a pause)*. I still think you've made a mistake.

VERA *(wearily)*. I haven't, I haven't. . . . what have I ever done to her to torment me like that, unless it's to make her jealous? And now she's dismissed you, because she imagines that you and I . . . *(Hiding her head again)*

BELIAEV. But she hasn't even dismissed me, I've told you. Nothing at all is settled, yet.

VERA *(raising her head and looking at him)*. Nothing at all?

BELIAEV. Nothing . . . Why are you looking at me like that?

(Natalia enters from the left; she sees them both, and stops. They have not seen her.)

VERA. Because it's all perfectly clear to me now. She's come to her senses, and realized that she has nothing to fear from a gawky schoolgirl. And anyway perhaps *you're* in love with *her.*

BELIAEV. I?

VERA. You've turned quite red.

BELIAEV. Have I?

VERA. *Are* you in love with her? Or may you be, in time? *(After a pause)* You don't answer me.

BELIAEV. But what do you expect me to say——

VERA *(turning away)*. Oh, please stop talking to me as if I were five years old! And you *will* console me—I just can't bear it——

(She rises, makes to go out to the left, and finds herself face to face with Natalia. Beliaev turns, and springs to his feet. A pause.

Natalia comes forward, slowly; she is outwardly composed and icily dignified.)

NATALIA. I'm sorry to see, Vérochka, that you're becoming very headstrong. I've reminded you more than once—and you too, sir, appear to have forgotten that you gave me your word . . . You have deceived me. Vérochka, I'm just a little cross with you——

VERA. Don't you think it's time you dropped all this as well?

(Natalia looks at her in amazement.)

NATALIA. What do you mean?

VERA. I mean this talking to me as if I were still a child. From today on, I'm a woman . . . a woman like yourself.

NATALIA *(quickly)*. Vera——

VERA. He hasn't deceived you; he doesn't love me, you know. So you've no reason in the world to be jealous of me.

NATALIA *(shocked)*. Vera!

VERA. And will you please not throw any more dust in my eyes, because it just won't be any good . . . For the simple reason I'm no longer your ward, watched over by a tolerant and mocking elder sister—I'm your rival!

(A pause.)

NATALIA. You forget yourself.

VERA. And if I do, who is to blame? I dare talk to you like this, because I've nothing to hope for any more—you've seen to that . . . But I'm not going to pretend with you, as you did with me. I've told him.

(A pause.)

NATALIA. Told him—what?

VERA. Something I noticed. You hoped to worm everything out of me without giving anything away about yourself, didn't you?

NATALIA. Vera—I entreat you—you don't know what you're saying——

VERA. Then will you tell me I'm dreaming? That you don't love him? After all, he's made it perfectly plain that he doesn't love me . . .

(She bursts into tears and stumbles out to the left. A pause. It begins to grow dark. Beliaev makes to go, then turns.)

BELIAEV. Natalia Petrovna, is it any good my assuring you . . . *(He shakes his head, and makes to go again)*

NATALIA. She was right, it's no good

my pretending any more. The only possible way in which I can hope to regain your respect—and my own—is to be perfectly frank. Besides, as we shall never see each other again . . . this is the last time I shall ever speak to you. *(Going to him)* She was telling the truth. I love you.

(A pause.)

BELIAEV. You . . . Natalia Petrovna . . .

NATALIA *(with a strained and deliberate calm).* From the very first day, I loved you; though it was only yesterday that I was fully aware of it.

BELIAEV *(almost in a whisper).* Natalia Petrovna . . .

NATALIA *(crossing quickly).* One thing —please understand that it is pride, and pride only, that gives me the courage to tell you this; the farce of pretending revolted me to the marrow—*(sitting)*— and I have been desperately anxious to wipe from your mind this picture of a tyrannical, cunning creature—anxious that the memory of me which you take away, shall not be . . . too vile . . . I was jealous of her and I took advantage of my authority—it was all despicably unworthy of me, and we'll leave it at that. I have only one excuse, that I was in the power of something I knew nothing of. *(After a pause, with more emotion)* You have nothing to say. . . . But then I do understand why, I do: for a man to have to listen to a declaration of love from a woman to whom he is indifferent—there can be nothing more painful, I am even grateful for your silence. You must feel intensely uncomfortable even in my presence—you have my permission to leave it at once, without formality . . . It seems that we two were never destined to know each other. Good-by for ever.

(A pause. Beliaev tries to say something, fails, bows, makes to go, then turns.)

NATALIA. Well?

BELIAEV. I can't go.

(A pause.)

NATALIA. You . . . can't go?

BELIAEV. Not like this—how can I— how can I? . . . *(Controlling himself)* Natalia Petrovna . . . I—I—oh God, why can't I find the words to say it . . . I'm sorry, I don't know how to talk to

women . . . She was right, you know, I was afraid of you—and still am. I'm not exaggerating when I say that I looked upon you as a creature from another planet—a truly heavenly being . . . and yet, when you said——

NATALIA *(softly).* Go on.

BELIAEV. When you told me that you . . . love me . . . *(Sitting beside her with an exultant cry)* Natalia Petrovna, you love me! I can hear my heart beating, as I've never heard it before . . . *(With sudden feverish decision)* I cannot go away like this.

NATALIA *(as if to herself).* What have I done? *(After a pause, recovering)* I'm glad you told me all that, because it makes it clear that it was nothing in me personally which repelled you, only my position . . . I'm glad—it makes the parting easier.

(A pause. He rises.)

BELIAEV. It was madness just now, when I said 'I can't go', of course I must go . . . But you can have no idea of what is going on in my breast . . . I am seeing you for the first time, hearing your voice for the first time . . . *(He sits next to her; they look into each other's eyes)* Yes, I must go . . . if I don't, I—I can't answer for what might happen.

NATALIA. Yes, you must go . . . But can it be, that in spite of the way I've behaved, you still think of me . . . in such a way? If I'd known, I would have died rather than confess to you what I did——

BELIAEV. This time yesterday I myself could never have imagined—it was only just now, when suddenly——

NATALIA. Yes? *(Her eyes shining with happiness)* Suddenly——

BELIAEV. It was as if a hand were laid gently on my heart, a warm hand that pressed and pressed, until there was a burning in me that would scorch up my whole being . . .

NATALIA *(her eyes closed).* We have no right to forget that tomorrow you are leaving. That we are speaking to each other for the last time.

BELIAEV. Yes, the last time. And whatever happens, one memory will stay with me forever, how Natalia Petrovna came to love me . . .

NATALIA. But you told me just now

that you were still afraid of me . . . *(She looks into his eyes; her smile fades, she shudders, and puts her hand to her eyes)* But what am I saying . . . *(Recovering, trying to be practical)* Alexei Nikolaich, listen . . . I've no more strength to fight, and I count on your help. *(Rapidly, convincing herself)* It is for the best that all should end quickly, now; we have at least grown in this minute to know each other. Give me your hand, and good-by.

(He takes her hand.)

BELIAEV. I am parting from you, Natalia Petrovna, and my heart is so full that I have not a word to say. May Heaven give you—give you . . .

(He breaks off, overcome, and presses her hand to his lips.)

(In a stifled whisper.) Good-by——

(Rakitin appears from the left, and sees them.)

NATALIA. If you stay, my love . . . then Heaven must be our judge . . .

BELIAEV. Natalia . . .

RAKITIN. Natalia Petrovna.

(The others start, and look round at him. Beliaev bows, intensely embarrassed, and hurries awkwardly out to the right.)

RAKITIN. I'm sorry. I was walking past, and heard your voices.

NATALIA *(collecting herself)*. This seems the day for explanations, does it not? . . . Who sent you to look for me?

RAKITIN. Your husband.

NATALIA *(after a pause, rising)*. Shall we go back to the schoolroom?

(She makes to go past him.)

RAKITIN *(anxiously)*. May I ask—what decision you came to——

NATALIA. Decision? *(Affecting surprise)* I don't understand you.

(A pause. She faces his look.)

RAKITIN. You don't? Then I understand everything.

NATALIA. Oh, Rakitin, there you go again, hinting and hinting, really you are provoking! He and I thrashed the whole silly matter out, and anything you've ever discussed with me, is dead and forgotten. Puerile nonsense. Do you hear?

RAKITIN. But I haven't said a word, Natalia Petrovna. Except that I understand everything. How annoyed you must be with yourself.

NATALIA. What for?

RAKITIN. For your frankness to me this morning.

(She tries to turn away, hesitates, then looks at him.)

NATALIA *(uncertainly)*. Michel . . . you haven't yet spoken to him?

RAKITIN. Your husband?

NATALIA *(in an outburst, sitting on the seat)*. Please don't go on saying 'your husband', if his name's Arkady, then call him Arkady!

RAKITIN. I haven't yet had time to prepare my speech to him.

NATALIA. Oh, what a wretched business —it makes me positively ashamed that you should have to intrigue——

RAKITIN *(coldly)*. Please don't lose any sleep over that . . . A pity, though, that the young gentleman should turn out such a novice.

NATALIA. Novice?

RAKITIN. Taking to his heels like that; I've never seen a man quite so bursting with guilt. Give him time, though, and he'll soon pick up the rudiments . . . Shall we go?

(Yslaev appears from the left, followed by the Doctor.)

YSLAEV. You saw him go down this path, did you say?

THE DOCTOR. I certainly thought I did——

(Natalia draws back. Yslaev sees Rakitin.)

YSLAEV. Ah, you were right, my dear fellow—*(seeing Natalia)*. Oh . . . *(After a pause, with forced conviviality)* You're not still on this morning's talk, are you?

NATALIA. More or less, yes . . .

YSLAEV. It must be of world-shaking importance——

NATALIA. Oh, it is, cataclysmic!

YSLAEV *(after a pause)*. Tea's ready in the schoolroom. Shall we go across?

NATALIA *(rising, briskly, and taking his arm)*. What a good idea . . .

YSLAEV *(looking round)*. You know, Doctor, I was just looking at that schoolroom; when our Kolia grows up—to the credit of both his parents, one hopes— we've only got to set up a partition, and we'll have two gardeners' bedrooms— what d'you say?

THE DOCTOR. An excellent idea, first-rate——

(Yslaev crosses, Natalia on his arm; he has not looked once at Rakitin. He turns round.)

YSLAEV. Well, gentlemen? A cup of tea?

(He and Natalia go out to the left.)

THE DOCTOR *(to Rakitin)*. Will you grant me the honor of taking your arm? *(As they start to go)* It looks as if you and I are fated always to bring up the rear . . . ha!

RAKITIN *(in a sudden burst of temper)*. Allow me to inform you, Doctor, how much you get on my nerves!

(A pause. The Doctor, looks at him, startled, then recovers.)

THE DOCTOR. If you only knew, my friend, how much I get on my own.

(They follow the others out to the left.)

QUICK CURTAIN

SCENE THREE

The drawing-room, the next morning. Early sunlight.

Yslaev is seated at the desk, looking through papers. A pause. He begins to think, puts down the papers, then makes an effort to work again. He shakes his head, rises, pulls a bell rope and walks to the windows.

Matvei enters from the study, carrying a duster.

———

MATVEI. You rang, sir?

YSLAEV. Yes—er—send the bailiff to me, will you——

MATVEI. Very good, sir. *(Going, then remembering something)* Oh, excuse me, sir——

YSLAEV. Yes?

MATVEI. The workmen digging at the dam . . .

YSLAEV. What about them?

MATVEI. They're waiting to know what they are to do now.

YSLAEV. Oh. Tell them I shan't be a moment—say I've been delayed . . .

MATVEI. Very good, sir.

YSLAEV *(as Matvei bows and makes to go back)*. Is Monsieur Rakitin in the house?

MATVEI. I just saw him in the billiard-room, sir.

YSLAEV *(sitting back at the desk)*. Ask him if he would be so good as to take a glass of wine with me in here.

MATVEI *(after a slight pause)*. Yes, sir. *(He bows and goes into the ballroom, nearly running into Anna Semyenovna as she enters from the hall; she is in breakfast toilette and carries a cup of chocolate and a card-box. She is in a genuine state of agitation, but appears determined to let everyone know it. She looks at Yslaev, who does not stir. She moves across and deposits the card-box on the table; he looks up quickly, sees her and goes back to his papers. She sighs explosively, and sits on the stool; he still pays no attention to her.)*

ANNA. Arkasha . . .

YSLAEV *(turning)*. Oh, Mamma—I didn't see you . . . *(Rising, crossing, and kissing her on the brow, mechanically)* How are we this morning?

ANNA *(her voice quavering)*. Well, the Lord be thanked.

YSLAEV *(briskly)*. Good.

(He returns to his papers.)

ANNA *(with a deep sigh)*. As well as can be expected . . . Matters might be worse . . .

(Seeing that he takes no notice she draws a deeper breath, almost a sob. He turns to her.)

YSLAEV. Were you sighing, Mamma?

ANNA. Arkady Sergheich Yslaev, I am your mother.

YSLAEV *(back to his papers)*. Really, Mamma, that's no news to me——

ANNA. You're a great big man, Arkasha, grown up to Adam's estate—but I am the one who dangled you on my knee. It's a wonderful word, 'mother'.

YSLAEV. Mamma, do please explain what you're hinting at——

ANNA. My dear, you know perfectly well. Arkasha, you married an excellent wife——

YSLAEV *(drily)*. Did I? Good . . .

ANNA. Whose conduct up till *now* has been beyond reproach——

YSLAEV. You mean that Rakitin——

ANNA *(shocked)*. No no—God forbid —I don't mean that at all—no no——

YSLAEV. Do let me finish, Mamma . . . You mean that her relationship with Rakitin is not quite—as straightforward as it might be?

ANNA. Yes, I do. Arkady, has he given you any idea at all what those tears and those talks were about?

YSLAEV. I haven't asked him. *(Back to*

his papers) And he seems in no hurry to satisfy my curiosity.

ANNA. Then what d'you intend to do now?

YSLAEV. Nothing.

ANNA. Nothing? . . . *Well!* Of course, you're the master—and who am I to advise you, at your age; I'm only your mother, it's your bed, and you must lie on it . . . *(After a pause)* What I meant was, I should be only too pleased to clear the air with a little chat with them both——

YSLAEV *(rising, perturbed)*. Mamma, you'll do nothing of the sort—I mean—I can't have you worried. Now d'you promise me, faithfully?

ANNA. You can't say I haven't cautioned you; from now on I shan't lift a finger, I'll be like an oyster. Not another syllable.

(A pause. He sits again.)

YSLAEV. Are you driving out anywhere today——

ANNA. Still, I *must* give you one word of warning. True friends get scarcer every day, and my baby's too trusting, my baby judges everybody else by himself.

YSLAEV. Your baby's more than able to deal with his own life, Mamma——

ANNA. Ah well, an old woman like me—I'm probably out of my mind anyway, old women go out of their minds . . . *(Rising)* Then I was brought up on rather different principles, but of course all that's old-fashioned now. You go on working, I shan't lift a finger . . . *(At the steps)* I'll just turn into an oyster.

(She goes into the hall. A pause.)

YSLAEV. When you have an open wound, what makes people who really wish you well, prod into it first one finger, and then another?

(He holds his head, rises, crosses and pours out two glasses of wine. Rakitin comes in from the ballroom; he is very much on the defensive.) Ah good morning, Mihail Alexandrovich —a glass of wine?

RAKITIN. Thank you . . .

(They toast each other. A pause. Yslaev sits on the sofa.)

YSLAEV *(smiling)*. Michel, haven't you forgotten something?

RAKITIN. I?

YSLAEV. Your promise?

RAKITIN. My promise?

YSLAEV *(charging on)*. You remember —when Mother and I came in here— Natasha in tears—something about a secret—you remember?

RAKITIN. Can I have used the word 'secret'? *(Sitting beside him)* We had a talk, that was all——

YSLAEV. Michel, I can't bear to see you having to act such a shifty part. We've known each other since we were boys together—I've no talent for subterfuge, and you've never been anything but above-board with me. Will you allow me one question, if I give you my word that I shan't doubt the sincerity of your answer?

RAKITIN. Go on.

YSLAEV. Do you love my wife?

(A pause. They look at each other.)

I must make myself absolutely clear. Do you love her—with the sort of affection which it is hard to confess to her husband?

RAKITIN *(after a pause, quietly)*. Yes, Arkady, I do.

(A pause.)

YSLAEV *(taking his hand)*. Michel, your frankness does credit to the man of honor I have always known.

RAKITIN. Thank you.

YSLAEV. But the immediate problem is —what are we to do? *(Walking up and down)* I know Natasha, the range of her qualities—but I know the range of my own too, and I can't compete with you there, Michel——

RAKITIN. My dear friend——

YSLAEV. No no, I'm not in your class. You're brainier in every way, and immeasurably better company: there's no getting away from it, I'm a dull stick. I think Natasha's fond of me, but she's got eyes in her head—she was bound to be taken with you, I always appreciated that. . . . But I've always trusted you both, and so long as—er—nothing definite happened —oh, I wish I had your gift of the gab . . . But after us coming upon you yesterday— what *are* we to do? I'm a simple sort of fellow, but I've enough horse sense to realize that nobody should have the power to ruin other people's lives, and that there are times when to insist on one's rights, would be wicked. And I'm not saying that because I've read it somewhere—I've got it out of my conscience; freedom—every single soul should be free, that's always been my idea. Only this does need thinking over.

RAKITIN. I've already thought it over.

YSLAEV. You have?

RAKITIN. I'm leaving.

YSLAEV. Leaving? *(After a pause)* You think you should? For good, you mean?

RAKITIN. For good.

YSLAEV. That's—a big step to take, Michel . . . Perhaps you're right. There's no doubt that you—my very good friend —have become a menace to me. And when I said that just now about freedom, perhaps I was forgetting my own feelings, if she—you see, for me to be without Natasha, would be like being without . . . without . . . And then again, if your going away were to cure this unrest of hers—I haven't been imagining all that, have I?

RAKITIN *(bitterly)*. No, you haven't indeed . . .

(Matvei enters from the hall.)

MATVEI. Excuse me, sir, the bailiff is here.

YSLAEV. I shan't be a moment. *(As Matvei bows and goes back)* Michel, we'll miss you sorely, of course—you wouldn't be away long? That would be carrying things too far——

RAKITIN. I don't know—quite a time, I think——

YSLAEV. Now you're not going to turn me into Othello, are you? . . . Upon my soul, I don't think there can have ever been such a conversation between two friends, since the world began! *(Putting out his hand)* We can't part like this——

RAKITIN *(taking his hand)*. Will you let me know when I may come back?

YSLAEV. But which of our neighbors is going to take your place in our hearts? Poor old Bolshintsov?

RAKITIN *(lightly)*. There's—there's the new tutor, of course.

YSLAEV. The new tutor? Oh, a nice boy, but one can't mention him in the same breath with you.

RAKITIN *(sardonically)*. Oh, d'you think so?

(A knock at the ballroom door.)

YSLAEV *(calling)*. Just a minute! *(To Rakitin, hurriedly)* We take it as settled, then, my dear friend, that you're going away—just for a time—no hurry, you know, no hurry . . . Well, you've taken a weight off my mind . . . *(Moved)* My dear boy, God bless you . . .

(He embraces Rakitin impetuously, on both cheeks.)

YSLAEV *(calling)*. Come in!

(Beliaev enters from the ballroom. He looks smarter; his customary shyness can hardly hide glimpses of an excited buoyancy. He carries papers.)

Ah, it's you——

BELIAEV. I'm sorry, sir, I've made up Kolia's report, I hope I'm not interrupting——

YSLAEV. Not at all . . . Well, gentlemen, the devil finds work for idle hands, et cetera, I haven't looked at the dam this morning, this will never do. *(Taking his papers under his arm)* We shall meet again —*(calling)*—ready, Matvei! Matvei! All right . . .

(He goes out into the hall. Beliaev crosses to desk and arrays his papers.)

BELIAEV. How are you today, Mihail Alexandrovich?

RAKITIN. Surely that's a new coat you have on? And a buttonhole? . . .

BELIAEV *(blushing, and starting to pluck it out)*. Oh—if it's too much——

RAKITIN. But why, it's charming! . . . *(After a pause)* In case you want any messages run, I'm going into the town tomorrow, en route for Moscow.

BELIAEV *(turning)*. Moscow? Tomorrow?

RAKITIN. A matter of business has cropped up.

BELIAEV. Will you be away long?

RAKITIN. Possibly quite a time.

BELIAEV. May I ask—does Natalia Petrovna know?

RAKITIN. No, she doesn't. Why do you ask?

BELIAEV *(somewhat embarrassed)*. No particular reason.

RAKITIN. I don't see anybody else in the room?

BELIAEV *(turning round to him)*. What?
—no, there isn't— why——

RAKITIN. I thought there must be, for
us to be acting such a farce. *(As Beliaev
rises)* You mean to say you can't guess why
I'm going away?

BELIAEV *(on the defensive)*. No, I can't.

RAKITIN. Oh . . . well, I'll believe
you . . . Just before you came in then,
Arkady Sergheich and I had rather an
important talk, man to man, as a result of
which I have decided to take my departure: the reason being that he fancied
me to be in love with his wife.

BELIAEV *(after a pause, stiffly)*. Indeed...

RAKITIN. Now what would you do in
my place? *(After a pause)* His suspicions
were totally unfounded, of course, but it
didn't prevent him being tormented by
them, and I felt that for a friend's peace
of mind, an honorable man must be
prepared to sacrifice his own—his own
happiness. That is why I am going away.
(With meaning) If you were in my place
. . . you'd do the same, wouldn't you?
You'd go away?

BELIAEV *(after a pause)*. I suppose I
would, yes . . .

RAKITIN. I'm delighted to hear it. Of
course, there's a funny side to my de-
camping—it implies that I regard myself
as a menace. But I feel that a woman's
good name . . . Besides, haven't you
known women, innocent of heart and
pure as snow—real children in spite of
their intelligence—who by very reason
of that lack of guile, were the more apt to
yield to a sudden infatuation? . . . *(Suddenly)* After all that, do you still look
upon love as the greatest blessing on
earth?

BELIAEV *(with a non-committal laugh)*.
Not having yet fallen a victim, I'm not in
a position to say . . . but I've always
understood that to love a woman, and be
loved in return, is the—er—the nearest
a man can reach to perfect happiness.

RAKITIN. Long may you be soothed by
such pleasant lullabies! . . . Shall I tell
you what I think?

BELIAEV. Do.

RAKITIN. Just this. Once you surrender to it, all love—spurned or
returned—becomes a calamity. Mark my

words, my friend . . . the day will come
for you to know just how those flower-
like hands can torture, with what exquisite care they can tear your heart to
shreds; the day will come for you to
discover what a world of hate can smoul-
der underneath the most ardent passion.
When you find yourself longing for peace
of mind as a sick man pines for health—
for any insipid everyday peace—think of
me; when you stand shackled to a
woman's apron-string, and watch yourself envying, from the bottom of an
agonized heart, every carefree stranger on
the highway, while the shame of your
own slavery seeps into your vitals—the
slavery of paying the highest price for the
most miserable returns . . . think of me.
(A pause. Beliaev watches him, fascinated.)
(Collecting himself.) I mean, think of what
I've just said—I was . . . philosophizing.

BELIAEV *(soberly)*. With no motive?

RAKITIN *(drily)*. Exactly . . . So you
don't want anything in the town?

BELIAEV. Nothing, thank you. *(Rising)*
May I say how sorry I am you are going?
*(Natalia is seen walking in the garden from
the right, and stands in the French windows;
she is followed by Vera, who looks pale and
woebegone.)*

RAKITIN *(without seeing them)* May I say,
quite sincerely, how glad I am to have
made your acquaintance?

(They shake hands. Natalia watches them.)

NATALIA *(too lively)*. Well, gentlemen
what has your program been this morning

RAKITIN *(starting)*. Oh, good day—
nothing very exciting so far——

NATALIA *(coming in, followed by Vera, a
Beliaev bows, embarrassed)*. Vera and I have
been in the garden for hours—it's quite
heavenly out of doors today. I love the
smell of lime-trees, don't you? *(Sitting
We walked under them for ages, listenin
to the bees humming, it was perfect.

BELIAEV. No. *(Lamely)* I wasn't——

RAKITIN *(jauntily, to Natalia)*. So toda
it's your turn to pay tribute to the beauti
of Nature? *(After an awkward pause)* As
matter of fact, Alexei Nikolaich her
couldn't risk the garden this mornin
as he's sporting a new coat, hadn't yo
noticed?

BELIAEV *(stung)*. You mean that as

must be the only one I have, I couldn't have risked spoiling it?

RAKITIN *(confused).* Of course not. I was joking.

(An awkward pause. Vera sits and takes up some sewing.)

(Nonchalantly.) Oh, Natalia Petrovna—I knew there was something—it nearly slipped my mind. I'm leaving today.

NATALIA *(staring at him).* Leaving?

RAKITIN. I'm going to Moscow, on business.

NATALIA *(after a pause).* Well, hurry back, won't you . . . *(To Beliaev, suddenly)* Alexei Nikolaich, were those your drawings Kolia was showing me?

BELIAEV *(rising).* Oh—they're nothing much . . .

NATALIA. Nothing much, but they're charming! You have a distinct flair . . .

RAKITIN *(as Beliaev bows).* I observe that every day you discover new virtues in Monsieur Beliaev.

NATALIA. Do I? *(Coldly)* I'm so glad . . .

RAKITIN *(who has for the last few moments been on the rack).* Well, I must prepare for my journey—*(going)*—au revoir for the present——

NATALIA *(calling after him).* You'll come and say good-by, won't you—it won't slip your mind?

RAKITIN. No. It won't slip my mind.

BELIAEV *(suddenly, as Rakitin bows).* Mihail Alexandrovich, may I come and have a word with you?

RAKITIN. Certainly—by all means——

(He goes out into the ballroom. Beliaev bows awkwardly and follows him.)

NATALIA. Vera, don't be like this with me . . . *(As Vera does not respond in any way, rising impetuously, going to her, and kneeling, entreating, as Vera covers her face with her hands)* No, Vérochka—it's all my fault——

VERA *(through her sobs).* Don't kneel to me—I can't bear you to kneel to me——

NATALIA. I shall kneel to you until you say I'm forgiven . . . My dear, I know how hard it is for you, but is it any easier for me? The difference between us is that you've done nothing wrong to me, while I——

VERA *(in a hard voice).* There's another difference, Natalia Petrovna, that you haven't noticed. Today I find you gentle, and kind——

NATALIA. And do you know why? Because I realize how wicked I've been——

VERA *(suddenly).* You are gentle and kind today because you know that you are loved.

(A pause.)

NATALIA *(sombrely).* Will you believe me, when I tell you that you and I are as unfortunate as each other?

VERA. He loves you!

NATALIA. Vera, it's time we came back to reality. Do remember the position I'm in—the position we're both in. . . . When you think that our secret—entirely my fault, I know—that our secret is already known in this house by two men —Vera, instead of mortifying each other, shouldn't we be trying to rescue ourselves from an impossible situation? Have you forgotten who I am, my position in this house? . . . But you're not even listening to me.

VERA *(looking before her, tonelessly).* He loves you . . .

NATALIA. Vera, he'll be going away . . .

VERA *(in an outburst).* Leave me alone!

(Natalia looks at her, undecided what to do.)

YSLAEV'S VOICE *(calling, in the study).* Natasha, are you in the drawing-room?

NATALIA *(calling).* Yes? Did you want me?

YSLAEV'S VOICE *(calling).* I've got something to show you—the new plans of the dam, my dear—quick!

NATALIA. Coming——

(She goes into the study.)

VERA. He loves her. And I have to remain in her house . . . I can't bear it . . . *(She puts her hand to her eyes. The ballroom door opens and the Doctor's head appears slowly. He looks round cautiously, and steals across the room to Vera, who does not see him. He stands with his arms folded, grinning mischievously from ear to ear.)*

THE DOCTOR *(suddenly).* Boo!

VERA *(starting).* Oh . . . Oh, Doctor, it's you . . .

THE DOCTOR. What's the complaint

this morning? Delirium tremens, gout or St. Vitus's Dance?

VERA. I'm all right, really, thank you . . .

THE DOCTOR. Your pulse, young lady, stand and deliver . . . *(Feeling her wrist)* Hmm . . . Vivace, very vivace, one might say galloping . . . Now take my advice, as a professional man——

VERA *(looking at him, suddenly resolute)*. Ignaty Illyich, that gentleman, our neighbor . . . what was his name——

THE DOCTOR. Bolshintsov? Yes?

VERA. Is he really a nice man?

THE DOCTOR. A *nice man!* Young lady, there's only one word for my old Bolly— 'paragon'.

VERA. Has he a temper?

THE DOCTOR. A temper? My dear, I can only tell you— he's not a man, he's a mountain of dough; you just dump him on to the kitchen table, roll up your sleeves, and . . . *(making graphic gestures of kneading a pliable mass)*

VERA. You can answer for him?

THE DOCTOR. As I would for myself, hand on heart . . .

VERA *(after a pause)*. Then will you say . . . that I am willing to marry him.

THE DOCTOR. Willing to . . . *(With incredulous amazement)* No! *(Springing up)* No!!

VERA. But only if it's as soon as ever possible, do you understand?

THE DOCTOR. But tomorrow, if you like! Bravo, Vera Alexandrovna, bravo! *(Blowing ecstatic kisses to her) There's* spirit for you . . . He's waiting at the lodge gates—he'll have a fit—what a whirligig —have you *any* idea, Vera Alexandrovna, *how* much he worships you?

VERA *(brusquely)*. We'll take that for granted, Doctor, shall we——

THE DOCTOR. All right, my sugar plum, mum's the word—I'll take the short cut—on the wings o' the wind, I fly. Au revoir—bonne chance—enchanté! *(He kisses her hand tempestuously, and races out into the hall.)*

VERA. Anything in the world rather than stay here and watch her with him. Because she *is* happy, however much she may pretend to be wretched—the way

she tried to comfort me—*(rising)* I can't . . . bear it . . .

(Beliaev comes in from the ballroom, and nearly runs into her.)

BELIAEV *(quietly)*. Vera.

(She starts, and looks up at him. A pause.)

VERA. Yes?

BELIAEV. I'm glad you're by yourself. I've come to say good-by.

VERA. To say . . . good-by?

BELIAEV *(as she sits)*. I've just had a talk in there with Monsieur Rakitin, a serious talk—I can't give you any idea of the sting in his voice . . . He was right about my new coat, too—I deserved every word. Not only have I disturbed your peace of mind—I still don't know quite how—and Natalia Petrovna's . . . I've been the cause of old friendship breaking up . . . anyway, turning the heads of rich women and young girls is *not* my style. *(Sitting next to her)* When I've gone, everything will simmer down back to normal, you'll see—you'll forget me and wonder how on earth it ever came about——

VERA. Please don't break your heart over me. I shan't be staying here long myself.

BELIAEV. You won't? How d'you mean?

VERA. That's my secret.

BELIAEV *(rising)*. But that's what I mean, how can I *help* leaving this house, when I seem to have started a sort of fever that makes everybody want to disappear one after the other? Anyway, I feel acutely uncomfortable here—I keep thinking everybody's looking at me; I don't mind telling you, Vera Alexandrovna, I'm counting the minutes till I'm up on that dog-cart, bowling along the high road . . . It's a strange feeling, when your heart aches intolerably, and yet your head is as gay and light as if you were a sailor embarking on a long voyage beyond the seas. You know too well the perils ahead, you're sad at leaving your friends, and yet the waves call so joyously—the wind blows so fresh—that the blood starts dancing like mad through your veins. Yes, I must be off. Back to Moscow —all my old friends—I'll get straight to work——

VERA. You love her—and yet you're leaving——

BELIAEV. Can't you see, that all that's over and done with? It flared up and it went out, like a spark . . . Let's part friends, for Heaven's sake, shall we? . . . *(After a pause, awkwardly)* I shall never forget you, Vera—believe me, I've grown very fond of you . . . *(Embarrassed, taking a paper from his pocket)* Would you—would you be so kind as to give this note for me, to Natalia Petrovna?

VERA. A note?

BELIAEV. I—I don't feel able to say good-by to her.

VERA *(taking the note)*. But are you leaving straight away?

BELIAEV. This minute. I'm walking as far as Petroskoye, and waiting there for Monsieur Rakitin. You see, everything's in hand . . . And when you give that, would you just say—no, what's the point . . . *(Listening)* Somebody's coming —good-by . . .

(He hurries towards the hall, turns, looks towards the study, hesitates, and runs out into the hall. Natalia enters from the study, and looks at Vera.)

NATALIA. I heard his voice . . . *(Seeing her expression)* What's the matter?

(Vera hands her the note; Natalia looks from it to her.)

Vera, you're frightening me . . .

VERA. Read it.

(Natalia opens the note, and sinks to a chair. A pause. She stares before her.)

Natalia Petrovna . . .

NATALIA. But he said good-by to *you*. He was able to say good-by to *you* . . .

VERA. Only because he doesn't love me.

NATALIA. But he can't go like this—— *(rising abruptly)* he has no right—who gave him the idea of this ridiculous gesture —it's too slighting—how does he know that I wouldn't have had the courage . . . *(Sinking down again)* What am I to do— *(in a cry)*—what am I . . .

VERA *(walking slowly to the steps)*. Not a minute ago, you said yourself he would have to go . . . remember?

NATALIA. Well, he *is* going . . . and now you're glad. Because it makes us equal . . . *(Her voice breaks in a sob)*

VERA *(turning)*. Natalia Petrovna, you said to me just now——

NATALIA *(turning from her, almost in aversion)*. I don't want to hear . . .

VERA *(inflexibly)*. You said, 'Instead of mortifying each other, shouldn't we be saving ourselves?' We're saved now.

(She goes out into the hall. Natalia recovers.)

NATALIA. She was speaking the truth . . . we're saved. It's all over . . . all put beautifully to rights . . .

(Yslaev enters from the study with papers. Natalia rises abruptly and goes to the French windows. He crosses to the desk, then sees her.)

YSLAEV *(calling)*. Natasha!

(Natalia does not answer. He goes up to her.)

(Gently.) It's me, Natasha . . .

(She turns; he takes her hand; she attempts to smile at him.)

You're so pale, my dear. It worries me.

NATALIA. It's nothing, Arkady, really—

YSLAEV. Won't you lie down, my darling? Just to please me?

NATALIA. Very well . . .

(She takes a step and sways. He catches her.)

YSLAEV. There, you see? *(As she leans on him)* Shall I take you upstairs?

NATALIA *(trying to laugh)*. No, really, Arkady, I'm not as bad as all that! I just want some fresh air—just for a minute . . .

(She walks into the garden. Rakitin enters, from the ballroom.)

YSLAEV. Michel, what on earth possessed you to do it, when I'd begged you to wait—she was so upset when I came in here——

RAKITIN. To do what?

YSLAEV. To tell her you're leaving like that! *(A pause.)*

RAKITIN. You think that's what's upset her?

YSLAEV *(as Natalia turns, and comes into the room again)*. Are you going up now, my dear?

NATALIA. Yes. *(She crosses slowly towards the hall. They watch her)*

RAKITIN. Good-by, Natalia Petrovna. *(She stands, without turning round, then begins to go again.)*

YSLAEV. Natasha . . . *(as she stops)* . . . may one of his old friends remind you that here is one of the best of men?

(Natalia turns round, slowly; she looks from one to the other, as if she were dazed.)

NATALIA. Yes—he's the salt of the earth! *(With sudden vehemence)* You're both the salt of the earth . . . And yet . . . *(She puts her hand to her eyes and stumbles out into the hall. Yslaev walks to the French windows.)*

RAKITIN *(to himself)*. After four years of platonic devotion, what a touching farewell. Ah bien—*(viciously)*—it was high time to cut short a morbid and consumptive relationship . . . *(As Yslaev comes back to him)* Good-by, Arkady.

(Yslaev looks at him; there are tears in his eyes.)

YSLAEV. It's not easy. You see, I didn't expect it. Like a storm on a very fine day . . . Well, what we reap, we have sown—however, thank you for what you're doing. You are my friend.

RAKITIN *(in a frantic undertone)*. This is too much . . . *(Recovering)* Good-by.

(He is about to hurry out into the hall when he collides with the Doctor coming in.)

THE DOCTOR. What's happened? Somebody just said Natalia Petrovna's fainted——

YSLAEV. Nothing to worry about, Doctor, the heat, more likely than not——

THE DOCTOR. No doubt, no doubt . . . *(To Rakitin)* I hear you're going away?

RAKITIN *(patiently)*. Yes, on business.

THE DOCTOR *(slyly)*. Ah, business . . . fancy that now . . .

(Anna Semyenovna, Lizaveta Bogdanovna, Kolia and Shaaf pour in one after the other, from the ballroom.)

ANNA. What is it—what's happened— my poor dear Natasha—for Heaven's sake——

KOLIA. Where's Mamma? Why has she fainted? What makes a person faint? What's the matter with her?

YSLAEV. Nothing at all is the matter with her——

ANNA. But good gracious——⎤ *(All*
LIZAVETA. We were just told——⎬ *at*
SHAAF. Dies moment hier——⎦*once.)*

YSLAEV *(loud, peremptory)*. Quiet, all of you! . . . I've just seen Natalia Petrovna, and I repeat, there is nothing at all the matter with her—what's more to the point, is what's the matter with all of you?

ANNA. Really, Arkasha, there's no need to bite all our heads off just because we're a little concerned—pardonably, I think——

RAKITIN. Well, I must be off.

ANNA. Oh—are you going away?

RAKITIN *(resigned to still more explanations)*. Yes, I'm going away.

ANNA *(sweeping him from head to foot, with an all-embracing all-understanding look)*. Ah . . .

(She motions Lizaveta and Shaaf to the card-table and begins to arrange a game.)

KOLIA. Papa, why has my new tutor gone?

YSLAEV *(as Rakitin comes down to them)*. Gone? Beliaev? Where to?

KOLIA. I don't know. He just shook my hand, put his cap on and went—and it's time for my lesson, the best lesson of all——

YSLAEV. I expect you misunderstood, he'll be back in five minutes——

RAKITIN *(aside, to Yslaev)*. I'm afraid Kolia didn't misunderstand, Arkady. He won't be coming back.

(The others are making surreptitious attempts to overhear.)

YSLAEV. Now what does *this* mean?

RAKITIN. He's going away too. To Moscow.

YSLAEV. Is everybody in this house going stark staring mad?

RAKITIN. Between ourselves, Arkady, little Vérochka's fallen in love with him.

YSLAEV. With the tutor? *(Whistling)* Whew . . .

RAKITIN. And like an honorable man, he has decided it would be only tactful to take his departure. *(As Yslaev sits, with a gesture of bewilderment)* So now you understand——

YSLAEV. I don't understand anything at all, and my head's going round like a top. Everybody muttering what honorable men they are, and scurrying off north south east and west, like a lot of partridges!

ANNA *(coming to them)*. Now what is all this—something about a tutor, did I hear——

YSLAEV *(holding his head, in a shout)*. Nothing, Mamma, nothing, nothing!

KOLIA. But, Papa——

YSLAEV. Monsieur Shaaf——

SHAAF *(bustling forward, with alacrity)*. Mein Herr!

YSLAEV. Would you kindly give Kolia his German lesson now——

KOLIA *(bursting into tears)*. No, I want the other tutor! I want the other tutor— *(as Shaaf pilots him, screaming and kicking, into the ballroom)*—I want the other tutor . . .

(His voice dies away. A pause.)

YSLAEV *(to Rakitin)*. Michel, I'll come part of the way with you. I'll have Favorite saddled, and meet you at the dam. And Mamma, will you do something for me?

ANNA. My dear, any mortal thing to help——

YSLAEV. Keep away from Natasha, will you? And you too, Doctor, she's not at all well . . . *(Going into the study, calling)* Matvei! Matvei!

(Anna sits, bristling with wounded dignity. like an old hen. Lizaveta, her eyes round with amazement, takes up her stand behind her, like a shadow.)

THE DOCTOR *(to Rakitin, an uncontrollable twinkle in his eye)*. Mihail Alexandrovich, may I have the honor of driving you as far as the main road?

RAKITIN. Driving me? Have you got a horse?

THE DOCTOR *(beaming from ear to ear)*. Three horses, my dear friend, *and* a wagonette.

ANNA. What is all this——

RAKITIN *(bowing)*. Anna Semyenovna.

ANNA *(majestic, without rising)*. Good-by, Mihail Alexandrovich. *(Sepulchrally)* I wish you as pleasant a journey as can be expected.

RAKITIN. Thank you . . . Lizaveta Bogdanovna.

(He bows; Lizaveta drops a frightened curtsey. He hurries out abruptly into the hall.)

THE DOCTOR *(kissing Anna's hand)*. Au revoir, honored lady——

ANNA. Don't tell me you're going to Moscow too?

THE DOCTOR. No no, just as far as my own humble abode. My patients, you know, my patients . . . *(To Lizaveta)* Dear lady . . .

LIZAVETA *(her eyes fluttering)*. Doctor..

THE DOCTOR. Au revoir, but not good-by.

(He kisses her hand, peers to see that Anna is not looking, winks broadly at her, and hurries out into the hall.)

ANNA *(as Lizaveta sits opposite her, with knitting)*. Well, Lizaveta Bogdanovna... and what do *you* make of all this?

LIZAVETA. Anna Semyenovna, I am at a loss.

ANNA. Did you hear what *I* heard? That the tutor boy is leaving too?

LIZAVETA. No!

ANNA. But what is the world coming to? Ah well . . .

LIZAVETA *(her eyes modestly downcast)*. Anna Semyenovna.

ANNA. Yes, dear?

LIZAVETA. *I* may not be staying here much longer either . . .

(Anna sits back, staring at her in amazement.)

QUICK CURTAIN

SAM AND BELLA SPEWACK's

My Three Angels

Based on La Cuisine des Anges by ALBERT HUSSON

First produced by Saint-Subber, Rita Allen, and Archie Thomson at the Morosco Theatre, New York, on March 11, 1953, with the following cast:

FELIX DUCOTEL	Will Kuluva	JULES	Jerome Cowan
EMILIE DUCOTEL	Carmen Mathews	ALFRED	Darren McGavin
MARIE LOUISE DUCOTEL	Joan Chandler	HENRI TROCHARD	Henry Daniell
MME. PAROLE	Nan McFarland	PAUL	Robert Carroll
JOSEPH	Walter Slezak	LIEUTENANT	Eric Fleming
	ADOLPHE		

Directed by José Ferrer
Setting designed by Boris Aronson
Costumes by Lucinda Ballard

The action of the play takes place in the family Ducotel's living room back of a general store in Cayenne, French Guiana, December, 1910.

———

ACT ONE

The single set is a living room back of a general store in Cayenne, in French Guiana. The climate is hot and humid. The room reflects the tropics, but the furniture has obviously been imported from France and bespeaks another world. An arch in the center of the back wall, hung with bamboo curtains, opens into a corridor that leads into the shop. A bell rings when someone enters the shop and this can be heard in the living room. A double door in the upstage left wall leads to the family kitchen, and a door downstage of this leads to other rooms in the house.

Facing the audience upstage, left and right of the center arch, are two doors reached by three steps leading to two guest rooms, which figure prominently in the action. A bamboo gate, stage right, leads to the garden. A ladder is featured, to the right of the center arch. It reaches to an opening in the roof.

The rest of the ceiling is beamed and thatched.

In the center of the room is an oval dining table with three chairs, right, left and above the table. At right and left are armchairs. A bureau that is used for china, linen, books, papers and general catch-all is left of the center arch. Opposite the bureau hangs a hat rack and mirror. To the left of the garden gate is a commode stacked with unopened boxes and baskets. A similar stack of crates and baskets is heaped against the bamboo wall, right of the kitchen doors. An oil-lamp fixture hangs between the doors in the left wall, and on the side of the two bedroom doors hang two more such fixtures. A stand lamp is downstage of the garden gate. There are the usual pictures and decorations on the walls.

The thermometer-barometer hangs on a pole, stage right. Across the center arch is draped a piece of warm-colored material in contrast to the bamboo and raffia walls of the room.

———

TIME: Christmas Eve, 1910.

AT RISE: Felix Ducotel is sitting at the table, center, working at his ledgers, desultorily. He is in his late fifties, and is dressed for Paris rather than Cayenne. He wears a frock coat, boiled shirt, etc.

Felix Ducotel is a thoroughly amiable and impractical soul. We hear the bell of the shop door, but Felix does not. After a pause, the bell is heard again.

Emilie, his wife, enters from the kitchen after second bell, carrying a bowl of fresh green peas. She is patient with her husband, for she loves him.

EMILIE (Seeing that he has not responded to the bell, crosses to entrance to shop). I was sure I heard the bell, dear.

FELIX. No.

EMILIE. I was sure someone had come into the shop.

FELIX. Not a soul. Well, one hears bells at Christmas. I don't mean literally. There are bells in the air, so to speak. Sleigh bells, jingle bells. One remembers one's childhood. Father Christmas. The angels. The three wise men. (Mops his brow) Very hot for Christmas, of course. (Looks at thermometer) One hundred and five!

EMILIE. Must you wear that frock coat?

FELIX. My dear, I have a position to maintain—as a Frenchman, as a business man, as manager of a substantial establishment in . . .

EMILIE. In a colony of convicts! (Felix returns to table) Felix!

FELIX. What?

EMILIE. You don't think that bell means another sneak thief's been here?

FELIX. Why are you so suspicious? (He pinches her cheek) Always suspicious!

EMILIE. You ask me that here—in this colony of thieves! Desperate criminals wandering around free as air! (Hammering is heard) Three of them up there repairing our roof right now!

FELIX. My dear, they're perfectly honest.

EMILIE. Honest?

FELIX. They're not thieves! They're murderers.

(Harmonica playing is heard in the garden)

EMILIE (stunned). They are? Those three—on our roof?

FELIX. Most of them are, you know. At least so I've been told. They're excellent roofers, and considering the heat and humidity, extremely industrious.

EMILIE. Felix, did that boy ever pay you for the harmonica?

FELIX. What harmonica?

EMILIE. Felix!

FELIX. No. He's a very gifted boy.

(Harmonica playing is louder)

EMILIE. He's out there now. Go out and tell him he either pays or you take the harmonica.

FELIX *(firmly)*. Emilie, please! *(Placing the bowl of peas on the right end of table)* I'll handle this affair.

EMILIE. How?

FELIX. It's a matter of bookkeeping.

EMILIE. Bookkeeping?

FELIX. I'll put it down to overhead.

EMILIE. What?

FELIX. In any business enterprise, one must take account of local conditions. Here in Cayenne, we have musically frustrated natives. They're starved for music, for food, for life itself. They have no money. What can one do? One puts it down to overhead.

(Hammering is heard.)

EMILIE *(Indicating roof)*. Overhead! Those murderers are driving me mad—overhead!

FELIX. Overhead is a technical commercial expression.

(Hammering stops. He sighs. Bell rings.)

EMILIE. There's someone in the shop.

FELIX. Is there?

(Rises and moves toward shop. Mme. Parole enters. She carries an umbrella and a string shopping bag filled with parcels.)

MME. PAROLE. Merry Christmas!

(Emilie rises.)

FELIX. Merry Christmas, Mme. Parole.

MME. PAROLE. I only stopped by for a bottle of Chartreuse—for Ernest, you know.

FELIX *(begins searching through boxes)*. I'll get it.

MME. PAROLE *(places bag and umbrella on table)*. It's my yearly Christmas surprise for poor Ernest. He always gives me a box of biscuits. He eats them, of course, and I drink the Chartreuse.

(Hammering begins.)

FELIX *(searching)*. Let me see . . .

MME. PAROLE *(looking up)*. You still have your workmen. I must say I find convicts convenient. So cheap, and so

willing. I wouldn't have any other servants. No natives for me. Take my Louis. A treasure—a perfect treasure. Immaculate, and what a cook! He may be a little peculiar—shall we say effeminate. But my dear, it takes all kinds to make a world. He doesn't bother me. And he adores Ernest.

FELIX. I don't understand it. I had a case of Chartreuse here—right here . . .

MME. PAROLE *(taking bundle from shopping bag)*. Ernest gave me your mail. Two ships came in this morning.

EMILIE. Thank you. While we're waiting—Felix was just going over the accounts—weren't you, Felix? *(Indicates books)*

FELIX *(still searching, finds cognac bottle)*. Was I? Ah, yes.

EMILIE *(stifling her irritation)*. And he thought if you could possibly . . . It's quite a large bill . . .

MME. PAROLE. But, of course. You know how scatterbrained I am.

EMILIE. That's why I took the liberty of reminding you . . .

FELIX *(going to Mme. Parole)*. I'm terribly sorry, but we seem to be out of Chartreuse. I have some cognac.

MME. PAROLE. Cognac will do. *(Takes the bottle, puts it in shopping bag)* How much do I owe you? *(Searching in the bag)* Where's my purse? Oh! What a scatterbrain I am. I forgot! *(Getting up, preparing to leave)* Oh, well, it doesn't matter . . . charge it.

EMILIE. Well, how soon do you think you'll . . .

MME. PAROLE. By the way, how's the shop going? Better? Ernest says that you're too trusting, too careless. People take advantage. People are such beasts! Well, I must take a look at my bill one of these days. Good-bye. *(She exits into the shop)*

FELIX. What a scatterbrain!

EMILIE. As scatterbrained as a fox!

FELIX *(returning to his chair)*. I must get back to my books.

EMILIE. Books! Credit right and left, nobody pays, and sneak thieves take the rest. It's Cherbourg all over again. Thank goodness, we still have a little capital left. How much is left, Felix? *(Felix looks up)*

Of the money we brought from home?

FELIX. Oh, that capital. That's invested.

EMILIE. Invested?

FELIX. I forgot to tell you. There was a prospector through here with a very attractive proposition. A gold mine somewhere in the west. You wouldn't understand these affairs. Believe me, I'm being practical.

EMILIE. Then all I hope is that Marie Louise marries someone completely impractical.

FELIX. Marie Louise will marry for love, just as we did.

EMILIE. God help her!

FELIX. Do you regret it very much?

EMILIE. No.

FELIX. There you are. *(Rises, moves left, mopping his brow)* We have had our ups and downs, but it's not too bad here. The heat is a little trying, but as a practical business man I think of all the money I save in coal bills. The heat is free.

(Marie Louise enters from shop, carrying her hat, gloves and purse. She is tremendously excited.)

MARIE LOUISE. Mama, Paul's here. *(Going to armchair to leave hat, gloves, purse. Emilie turns to her)* He is on the *Mirabelle.* I knew he'd come for me. I knew it! I didn't dare breathe it, not even to you. But I knew he wouldn't wait a whole year, I knew it! Now do you believe me? Now do you think it is wrong to trust? Blindly, completely?

EMILIE. When you've simmered down, will you please tell me . . . Paul's here? Alone?

MARIE LOUISE *(picks up purse).* No, with his uncle. They're in quarantine. Papa, you've got to get them right out.

EMILIE *(still bewildered).* You've seen them?

MARIE LOUISE. How could I? I told you they're in quarantine. Uncle Henri sent word through M. Parole for you to get him right off the ship. Here's his note. *(Gives Felix the note taken from purse)* M. Parole gave it to me. I'll give Paul my room, and I suppose we'll have to give his uncle yours. I'm going to do Paul's room myself. I know just how he likes it. He's not fussy, just particular.

EMILIE. Felix . . . Did Henri write you he was coming?

FELIX. Well, not exactly . . .

EMILIE. Paul hasn't written *you,* has he, Marie Louise? It seems to me he hasn't written in months.

MARIE LOUISE. He wanted to surprise me. Paul always said letters are so banal. *(Picks up hat and gloves)* I'm going to get some flowers from the garden. Paul loves flowers.

EMILIE. Fresh sheets would be more to the point.

MARIE LOUISE. Yes. The embroidered ones. I won't tell Paul I embroidered them myself. He'll just *know.* Isn't it miraculous? Flowers in the garden for Christmas! Merry Christmas, Papa! Merry Christmas, Mama! Merry Christmas! *(Marie Louise exits to garden)*

EMILIE. My two children . . . One I gave birth to—one I married.

FELIX. This is a terrible shock . . . You don't know.

EMILIE. What don't I know? After all, Henri has many interests in many places. This shop's a bagatelle to him. He hasn't come down here to . . . Or has he? Felix, what don't I know?

FELIX *(disjointedly).* In some of his letters he threatened—unless I reorganized drastically—But how could I? With local conditions . . . He can afford to lose a little money the first year. Give a man a chance to get acclimated.

EMILIE. Felix . . .

FELIX. You'd think a man who swindled me out of a first-class department store —legally, I admit—a *cousin*—by marriage, I'll admit—but still a cousin—We grew up together as boys . . . *(Reads the note)* "I have two days to give you. I want to make a complete inventory and check your books. I shall then make the logical decision. Be good enough to get me off this damn ship at once."

EMILIE. Logical decision? Felix, is he going to close the shop?

FELIX. I don't know.

EMILIE. Or get someone else?

FELIX. I don't know.

EMILIE *(going to him, quietly).* Are your books in very bad shape, Felix? *(She indicates the books on the table)*

FELIX. Temporarily—only—temporarily—I really haven't checked . . .

EMILIE (*after a pause*). We can always go home.

FELIX. With what? And to what? At my age? God help us! (*Loud hammering*) What's that? (*Remembers the convicts*) Oh!

EMILIE. That's not God coming to the rescue. Just some of His wayward children who'll solve all our problems by murdering us in our beds tonight. (*Embracing him*) Oh, Felix, you should have been a poet.

FELIX. What am I going to do?

EMILIE. Do? Your going to do as he says. Go down and see the Health people and get him off the ship.

FELIX. I guess so . . .

(*Marie Louise enters from garden with flowers.*)

MARIE LOUISE. Papa, haven't you gone yet? Papa, they're waiting.

FELIX. I'm going. Thank God, come what may, I still have you, Emilie.

EMILIE. You still have me, Felix (*Felix exits into shop. Emilie goes to table and looks through bundle of letters*) Marie Louise, there's a letter here for you from Suzanne.

MARIE LOUISE (*takes letter*). It's always the same silly letter. In school she was always first with the bad news. Guess who's down with the mumps. (*Emilie picks up bowl of peas and letters, starts toward kitchen*) Guess who's going to be expelled. Guess who's pregnant.

EMILIE. Marie Louise! (*Exits to kitchen*)

MARIE LOUISE (*suddenly*). I wonder if she's written me about Paul. (*Opens letter and starts to read it*)

(*As Marie Louise sits down to read, three figures descend the ladder and stop. They wear pajamalike uniforms, with the appropriate numbers, straw hats and sandals. Joseph's number is 3011. Jules' number is 6817. Alfred's number is 4707. Joseph, like Jules, is in his forties. He's an ex-forger and ex-promoter. Jules killed a faithless wife, is fairly well educated, introspective. Alfred, in his twenties, is an ex-playboy who murdered for money. They watch her as she reads. She smiles. They smile. She chuckles. They chuckle silently. She rises, startled. They react. Then, suddenly, a gasp escapes her. She keels over.*)

The three convicts move to her. Joseph puts on his glasses and picks up the letter. Alfred is carrying a small cage made of a coconut shell and twigs; it has a leather handle. As he moves toward the girl, he leaves the cage on the table.)

JOSEPH. I wonder if this letter was poisoned.

JULES. Poisoned?

JOSEPH. I read somewhere poisoned letters were common in the days of the Borgias. The victim picked it up . . . Pouf!

JULES. Well, nothing's happened to you—yet.

JOSEPH. No.

JULES. Damn funny . . . There she was, reading away, smiling, chuckling and then—out like a light.

JOSEPH (*having glanced quickly through the letter*). Ah! Here's the poison (*Reads*) "Darling, Paul and I are engaged." Three exclamation points. Engaged, in capital letters. "Papa and M. Trochard arranged it just before Paul sailed with his darling uncle. Darling Marie Louise, I know how happy you'll be for us." Happy capitalized, two exclamation points. "After all, darling, a schoolgirl crush is not love, as we all know. And let's be frank. That's all there was between you and Paul, and honestly I don't mind. Not a bit." Two exclamation points.

(*Alfred goes to left of Joseph, staring at the girl.*)

"But I do want to save Paul embarrassment when he sees you. You know how kind"—capitalized—"how very kind he is." Want to hear any more?

JULES. No. (*Drinking in all the details of the room*).

JOSEPH (*examining envelope*). Suzanne Audibert . . . (*Alfred kneels to get a closer look at the girl*) Incidentally, she writes the day of her engagement her complexion cleared up completely. Putting two and two together . . . (*Feeling letter*) I should say—judging from the quality of the stationery— (*Sniffs it*) the general tone of the letter—I should say Suzanne Audibert is quite rich.

ALFRED. She's a bitch.

JOSEPH. Of course.

ALFRED. That Paul must be mad! To

turn this down. *(Staring at Marie Louise)* She's beautiful!

JOSEPH. Enough of that! In your position one doesn't admire a beautiful woman. Neither party stands to benefit.

ALFRED. I can look, can't I?

JOSEPH. Get me some water instead. *(Indicates kitchen)*

ALFRED. Right.

(Emilie enters as Alfred moves to kitchen. She backs away, frightened.)

EMILIE. Oh!

(Alfred exits to kitchen.)

JULES. Don't be afraid, Madame . . .

EMILIE *(seeing Marie Louise)*. Marie Louise! *(Goes to her)*

JULES. We were on that ladder when it happened.

EMILIE. Marie Louise, speak to me. When what happened?

JULES. She fainted.

JOSEPH. Nerves.

JULES. Shock.

JOSEPH. No wonder . . . Read this letter . . . *(Gives her the letter)* Here's the viperish paragraph. *(Alfred returns with glass of water)* Believe me, Madame, we sympathize with you. *(Sprinkles water on Marie Louise)* Uncle Henri's unexpected and unwelcome arrival. The fickle Paul! *(Emilie returns letter to Joseph. He hands glass to Alfred)* And she had such high hopes!

EMILIE *(staring at him)*. Did you hear everything up there? *(Indicates roof)*

JOSEPH. Everything.

EMILIE. Oh! *(Marie Louise moans. Joseph and Alfred move to ladder)* Poor darling.

JULES. She's coming around. When she opens her eyes, it *might* be a good idea if she sees you first. *(He moves up to join other two)* While we know a great deal about her, she doesn't know very much about us, and might be a little—shy.

EMILIE. Darling.

MARIE LOUISE *(sitting up)*. Where am . . . What happ . . . *(She sees men)* Oh!

EMILIE. Don't be afraid.

MARIE LOUISE *(getting up slowly)*. I'm not afraid. Nothing can frighten me now.

EMILIE. Marie Louise, my poor darling . . . I know what it means to you . . .

MARIE LOUISE. Please leave me alone. I don't want to talk about it. I don't want

to talk to anybody. I don't want to see anybody. I just want to die. *(She runs into her room)* I just want to die.

EMILIE. Marie Louise! *(Starts to follow her)*

JULES *(stopping her)*. I'd leave her alone. Youth always dallies with suicide. We who live on know better. Alfred . . .

(Alfred follows Marie Louise into her room.)

EMILIE. But . . .

JOSEPH. No danger. Everything's under control. Alfred's looking after her. He's quick as a cat.

EMILIE. She's so upset—so shocked . . . God knows what she might do . . .

JOSEPH. Alfred's problem!

(Alfred re-enters.)

ALFRED. She's in her room. Nothing to worry about. I checked. No poison. No weapons. *(Goes to table, puts down scissors and file)* I removed these. Scissors . . . nail file . . . no sedatives . . . no gas stove, of course . . . And if she jumps, her window is only three feet from the ground.

JOSEPH *(extending his hand)*. Well done.

ALFRED *(shaking hands)*. A pleasure . . . a real pleasure . . . *(Goes to door of Marie Louise's room)*

JULES. We disapprove of death. Especially for young and charming girls. She'll be all right. Time heals all wounds. We're authorities on the subject of time.

(Shop bell rings.)

EMILIE. Good Heavens. A customer. At a time like this. I suppose I'd better see . . . *(Starts toward shop)*.

JOSEPH *(stopping her)*. A customer is always welcome. May I? It'll be a treat for me. *(Exits into shop, leaving hat on bureau)*

EMILIE. He's not going to . . .

JULES. Wait on the customer? Of course. There's nothing he likes better. He can sell anything to anyone—and has. *(Emilie looks with uncertainty from the shop entrance to Alfred, then to Jules. There is an awkward pause.)*

JULES. We make you nervous, Madame?

EMILIE. No . . . It's just that . . .

JULES. You've never had convicts working for you before?

EMILIE. Never.

JULES. Our loss, Madame . . . Our loss . . .

(Places chair beside table for her. Alfred disappears quietly into Marie Louise's room, unnoticed by Emilie.)

EMILIE. You don't talk like a convict, somehow.

JULES. Well, I wasn't *born* in a cell. And on the other hand, I wasn't sent here for biting my nails.

EMILIE. Somehow you haven't the face of a . . . a . . .

JULES. A murderer? I agree. That's exactly what I said when I caught a glimpse of myself in the mirror after I'd . . .

EMILIE *(fascinated, despite herself)*. After you'd . . .

JULES. After I'd strangled my wife, Madame.

EMILIE. Oh!

JULES. She didn't think so, either, poor thing. If she'd thought I had the face of a fool, she would have been right. I was a fool, of course. When I realized it, it was too late. There she was stretched out on the carpet, her poor thin little neck all purple, her eyes staring—in astonishment, I'm sure.

EMILIE. My God!

JULES. Exactly what I said, Madame. I called out to Him, but He was busy elsewhere.

EMILIE. Was she—a bad woman? Did she make life miserable for you?

JULES. Never! Never in six years of happy marriage. It was my fault.

EMILIE. Oh!

JULES. I came home from a trip, one day—unexpectedly.

EMILIE. Unexpectedly?

JULES. *She* didn't expect me . . . *He* didn't expect me . . . As a matter of fact, I didn't even expect myself.

EMILIE. Well, you did have provocation, at least.

JULES. Crime of passion . . .

EMILIE. Well . . . yes . . .

JULES. I know. That's what the newspapers called it. My attorney was eloquent on the subject. But it was stupidity, Madame. Black stupidity, I should have sent her a telegram.

(Alfred enters.)

ALFRED. The patient is weeping.

EMILIE. I must go to her.

JULES. Why not let her weep?

(Joseph enters from shop before Emilie can move.)

JOSEPH. Madame, can you change this, please? Take out twenty-five francs.

EMILIE. What did you sell? *(Goes to bureau, takes a small cash box from drawer, brings it to table)*

JOSEPH. The painting . . . Madonna with Child . . . Artist unknown.

EMILIE. The painting? It's been here as long as we have. Who bought it?

JOSEPH. The postmaster.

EMILIE. He couldn't have. He's an atheist.

JOSEPH. He wanted a bedspread.

EMILIE. And you sold him the Madonna and Child? Why, that's a miracle.

JOSEPH. No, madame. I appealed to his cupidity. I asked one simple question. How do you know this isn't a Rembrandt? Besides, I couldn't find a bedspread. *(He takes the money and exits into shop)*

EMILIE *(to Jules)*. Are there very many like you in the . . .

JULES. In the Bastille? Oh, Madame, there are all kinds—a world like any other. All kinds.

EMILIE. Are you all so—busy? Selling paintings and looking after girls who've fainted?

JULES. No. Pleasant things like that don't often come our way.

(Joseph returns.)

JOSEPH. Ten francs extra, Madame. *(Gives it to her.)*

EMILIE. Extra?

JOSEPH. For the frame . . . A painting after all, consists of two items—the canvas and the frame. The canvas is an intangible. A matter of taste. Worth a fortune or zero. But the frame . . . Ah! That's real value. An investment.

EMILIE. I'm a little dizzy. *(Puts money in cash box, returns it to bureau drawer)*

JOSEPH *(spying the books on the table)*. Books! I have a passion for books. Account books. Jules, did I ever tell you about the night I had to doctor the books of a company that presumably owned three factories?

JULES. Tell Madame.

JOSEPH. They were air factories, Madame.

EMILIE. Air?

JOSEPH. Not compressed air. Just air. For invalids, convalescents. It was a marvelous idea.

EMILIE. I'm afraid I don't understand.

JOSEPH. Quite simple. As you know, doctors prescribe a change of air for their patients. Well, lots of people can't afford the Riviera or Switzerland. So we had factories at these resorts, where the air was bottled. Just as you bottle mineral water.

EMILIE. Oh!

JOSEPH. We had two kinds of bottles— big ones to change the air of an entire room and the handy pocket-size inhalators!

EMILIE. And people bought these bottles?

JOSEPH. We never put the product on the market. But we had a large group of stockholders.

JULES. A very large group, Madame. Until the judge ordered a change of air for *him*—and here he is!

JOSEPH. The judge, unfortunately, was one of our stockholders. Well, shall we run along? *(Goes to ladder)*

JULES. I guess so . . . *(To Alfred, who seems far away)* Alfred! *(Alfred starts)* Come on.

(Alfred picks up the coconut cage from table and passes Emilie.)

EMILIE. What have you got in there? *(He shows it to her)* Oh, a snake! What a horrible creature!

ALFRED. Why, that's Adolphe. He's our pal.

EMILIE. Is he poisonous?

JOSEPH *(moving to Alfred)*. Deadly.

JULES. We're very fond of Adolphe. Last year when we worked in the jungle, we used to be watched by a guard . . .

JOSEPH. Extremely unpleasant man and, unfortunately, incorruptible. Spurned all bribes. A combination of honesty and brutality, Madame, is unbearable.

JULES. He loved to treat us like slaves —while he lolled under the trees, in the shade. Well, one morning this little fellow dropped down from a branch right on to

his red neck. *(Snaps fingers)* Adolphe's a pal . . . Well, let's get going.

ALFRED *(suddenly, as they turn toward ladder)*. Wait a minute . . . *(He quickly hands Jules the cage and goes into Marie Louise's room)*

EMILIE. Where's he going?

JULES *(as he turns to her, he places the cage on the bureau)*. Perhaps you'd better go, too, Madame. I think your daughter may need you now. *(Emilie hurries into Marie Louise's room)* Alfred must have heard something. Did you?

JOSEPH. No.

JULES. I didn't hear a thing.

JOSEPH. Ah, youth! Keen ears—keen eyes. Of course, Alfred's the athletic type. *(With a glance toward the books on the table)* My exercises were always mental. *(Emilie returns.)*

EMILIE. I don't understand it. She's not in her room—her window's open . . .

JULES. And Alfred?

EMILIE. I didn't see him.

JOSEPH *(going to gate)*. Her window opens onto the garden.

EMILIE. Garden?

JULES *(suddenly)*. The river! Right off the garden.

(Emilie moves to go.)

EMILIE. I must stop her.

JOSEPH. She's been stopped.

EMILIE. By your friend?

JULES. Of course.

JOSEPH *(reporting from the lookout)*. She's arguing.

EMILIE. I'm going to her.

JOSEPH. Too late.

EMILIE. Too late?

JOSEPH. Alfred won the argument. *(He laughs)* He's convinced her.

EMILIE. Are you sure?

JOSEPH *(laughing as he goes to the table)*. Alfred has a striking eloquence. Your daughter, Madame, is no longer thinking of ending it all. In fact, your daughter is no longer thinking.

EMILIE. What?

JOSEPH. Knockout! *(Sits in chair at table, examining the books and papers)*

EMILIE. What? *(Starts toward gate. Jules stops her)*

JULES. Only thing to do, Madame. If she jumped in the river, what would

Alfred do? Jump, too. And then—she would struggle. He'd use the approved technique of knocking her out before he could swim back with her. The technique's just as effective ashore, and dryer. *(Alfred enters from the garden, carrying a limp Marie Louise.)*

ALFRED. All present and accounted for. *(His hair is mussed, his face scratched)*

EMILIE. Marie Louise!

ALFRED. She's all right, I assure you, Madame, as a sportsman. Pulse normal. I pulled my punch, of course.

JULES. Your efficiency is monotonous.

JOSEPH *(straightening up books, papers on table)*. I really don't approve of all this disorder.

EMILIE *(to Alfred)*. Oh! You're bleeding.

ALFRED. A scratch or two.

EMILIE. How could Marie Louise . . .

ALFRED. She wasn't herself. Madame.

EMILIE. Let me put some iodine on it. In this climate the slightest cut becomes infected.

(Exits to kitchen. Felix enters from shop, hangs up his hat, moves down in time to see Alfred carrying Marie Louise toward her room. Jules blocks his way.)

FELIX. Marie Louise! What are you doing with my daughter? Come back here! *(Goes toward shop, calling)* Police! Police! *(Alfred carries Marie Louise into her room)* Kill me, but spare them . . . That's all I ask. Police! Police!

EMILIE *(re-entering)*. No! No! Felix, not the police!

(Felix crosses back to Jules, trying to get around him.)

FELIX. Marie Louise, your father's coming to defend you . . . Courage . . . Courage . . .

(Alfred re-enters.)

EMILIE. You don't understand, Felix.

FELIX. What don't I understand?

EMILIE. He *had* to hit her.

FELIX. Hit whom?

EMILIE. Marie Louise.

FELIX. Why?

EMILIE. She scratched him. *(Goes to Alfred to treat the scratch)*

FELIX. Are you mad? *(Going to her)* Defending this—this—beast! Nursing him like a Florence Nightingale! *(Turns to see Joseph very busy with the papers, goes to him)* What are you doing with my papers?

JOSEPH. If you'll forgive me for saying so, I find unspeakable confusion. There's a place for everything and everything has its place!

FELIX. What? What the devil do you . . .

EMILIE *(goes to him, takes his arm)*. Please, Felix.

FELIX. But . . .

EMILIE *(to convicts as she pulls Felix toward Marie Louise's room)*. Don't go before my husband comes back. He'll want to thank you.

FELIX. Thank them?

EMILIE *(pushing him ahead of her)*. You don't know what we've been through. Just come along. I wonder if a hot compress . . .

(Felix exits.)

JOSEPH. Cold, Madame. As cold as the climate will permit.

EMILIE. Thank you. *(She exits)*

ALFRED *(dreamily)*. You know . . .

JULES. What?

ALFRED. That girl's light as a feather.

JULES. Forget her! Remember! We have one advantage—and only one—over other people. We can live without emotion. We can achieve serenity.

JOSEPH. You'd better achieve some serenity pretty damn quick.

JULES *(sitting)*. It seems to me I've been searching for serenity all my life. I never really wanted love. I wanted domesticity. Serenity again, you see.

JOSEPH. I have no passions—none—except . . . *(Shop door bell rings)* A customer! *(Rises, but hesitates)* Should I? *(His eyes glow)*

JULES. Oh, go on, enjoy yourself.

JOSEPH. Just this once.

JULES. Why not?

(Joseph exits to shop.)

ALFRED *(moving toward shop)*. He really gets a kick out of it.

JULES *(looking around)*. It's wonderful, isn't it?

ALFRED. What?

JULES. A home!

ALFRED: Oh. Yes.

JULES. Flowers . . .

ALFRED. Yes . . .

JULES. That chair . . . a picture . . . the evening paper. Her knitting . . .

(Emilie enters, followed by Felix.)

EMILIE. My husband has something to say to you.

(After a warning glance back at Felix, she exits into room. Jules rises.)

FELIX. My wife's just told me . . . I apologize for the misunderstanding . . . for my outburst . . . where's that other fellow?

(Joseph returns from the shop, carrying a white linen jacket over his arm.)

JOSEPH. The customer wants a larger size—14. This is a 12.

FELIX. I don't believe I have a 14.

JOSEPH. You don't. That's why I told him I'd get one back here—from stock.

FELIX. From stock? I have no clothing stock back here.

JOSEPH. I know that. I don't sell a piece of goods. I sell an idea. I'll just take this one right back to him. *(He exits into shop)*

FELIX. But . . . He's out of his mind. The man'll know it won't fit. He can see—feel it . . .

JULES. He won't see or feel anything. He won't get a chance to.

FELIX. But it's not fair—it's not ethical . . . Of course, I suppose you fellows aren't concerned with ethics, naturally. I mean—I don't want to hurt your feelings.

JULES. Not at all. No, some of us are downright crooked. Our world's just like yours. All kinds. The only difference is we were caught.

FELIX. Oh, yes. My wife told me, and I wanted to thank you. I'd like to repay you.

JULES. Not necessary.

ALFRED. Wouldn't dream of it. It was a labor of love.

(Jules looks at him.)

FELIX. Well, my wife thought . . . I'm not sure it's a practical idea . . . In fact, I'm not sure it's not . . .

ALFRED. What'd she have in mind?

FELIX. I know it's impossible. But she thought if you wanted to—and could spend the evening here—since it's Christmas Eve and all that . . .

JULES *(touched)*. That's very kind of her—very kind . . .

(Joseph enters, shows Felix the money.)

JOSEPH. Sold! Fits him like a glove when he doesn't button it. *(Goes to bureau, puts money in cash box)* Oh, yes, I sold him some cleaning fluid for the spots.

FELIX. There were spots? The coat was spotted?

JOSEPH. I made the spots myself. A little grease. The spots explain the bargain.

FELIX. Bargain?

JOSEPH. At the regular price of 27 francs, he wouldn't touch that jacket; but at the reduced price of 27 francs, he snapped it up.

JULES. Joseph, the gentleman has invited us to spend Christmas Eve here.

FELIX. Well, my wife thought . . .

JOSEPH. An enchanting prospect!

FELIX. Of course, I realize you can't . . .

JULES. Oh, but we can. We accept.

ALFRED. With thanks.

FELIX. But won't the authorities object? They'll miss you at roll call!

ALFRED. They'll forgive us!

JOSEPH. It can be arranged.

FELIX. It can? I must warn you— I haven't any spare beds . . .

JOSEPH. We're insomniacs.

JULES. Do you know what an armchair means to us?

JOSEPH *(quickly appraising the chair)*. Imitation Louis Sixteenth.

FELIX. And I must warn you. My wife hasn't prepared anything special. You know how expensive fowl is.

JOSEPH *(with a knowing look to Jules and Alfred)*. Christmas dinner without a turkey or at least a chicken? *(Shop doorbell rings)* Another customer! Business is brisk tonight. *(Starts toward shop)*

FELIX *(preceding him)*. If you don't mind . . .

JOSEPH. What?

FELIX. Allow me!

JOSEPH. By all means. *(Felix glares at him and exits into shop. A look of disappointment comes over Joseph)* I'll just coach from the sidelines. *(Exits into shop. Jules returns to his chair)*

ALFRED. Who gets the chicken?

JULES *(goes toward garden)*. I'll get it

ALFRED. I'll set the table. Pick a plump one.

JULES. One takes what one finds.
(He exits to the garden. Alfred begins setting the table. He takes the ledgers and papers to the bureau. Then he removes the brocaded cloth from the table, folds it, and places it on a tall basket standing near the bureau. Marie Louise enters from her room, carrying a small suitcase, hat, gloves, etc. She's obviously leaving. She stops as she sees him.)

MARIE LOUISE. Still here? *(She puts down hat and bag, and puts on gloves)*

ALFRED. How many for dinner tonight? Let's see. There's your father, mother, Uncle Henri, Paul, you . . . *(Gets dinner cloth from bureau, opens it onto table)*

MARIE LOUISE. I'm not having dinner. I'm leaving tonight.

ALFRED. You are?

MARIE LOUISE. Oh, don't worry, I won't try it again. I'm going to the Dominican convent first. Then, I'll see. *(Alfred gets plates from bureau, sets them)* The Mother Superior'll understand. My life is finished. *(Picks up bag and hat, starts toward shop)* At least, I can be of service to others.

ALFRED *(arranging plates)*. You want to sit next to Paul, of course . . .

MARIE LOUISE *(stops)*. I told you I won't be here. How dare you meddle in my affairs?

ALFRED. I asked a civil question. I don't get it. A man travels on a stinking ship for weeks to see you—and you run away from him. *(He gets silver from bureau drawer, sets places)* You're mad about this man. You don't want to live if you don't get him. He's here. He wants to see you . . .

MARIE LOUISE. See *me?*

ALFRED. Why did he come if he doesn't want to see you? You believe that Suzanne? A fellow doesn't travel four thousand miles just to prove he's a liar.

MARIE LOUISE. His uncle made him come.

ALFRED. Where's your trust? Your faith? How do you know there's a word of truth in what she says? And if there is—and a marriage has been arranged—how do you know he isn't coming here to explain, to make plans to *disarrange* it—get around his uncle, with your help, your support, your *love* . . .

MARIE LOUISE. Oh, no. *(Puts down hat)*

ALFRED. It's not impossible, is it?

MARIE LOUISE *(turns to him)*. Do you honestly think so?

ALFRED. Would he come all this way just to get his face slapped?

MARIE LOUISE. I wouldn't slap his face. He knows that. I don't go around slapping faces.

ALFRED. Oh, I don't know. *(Feels his scratch and gets cups and saucers from bureau, sets them)*

MARIE LOUISE. I'm terribly sorry—about that.

ALFRED. Forget it.

MARIE LOUISE. You really think . . . Of course, there may be something in what you say. He's come to explain—to. . .

ALFRED. Now shall I set a place for you?

MARIE LOUISE. Funny! I believe you because I *want* to believe you. And yet I *know* . . .

ALFRED. Give the fellow a chance! I'll tell you what. Heads you go, tails you stay. *(Picks up plate)* Let's toss a plate.

MARIE LOUISE. No, no, I'll stay. *(Puts down bag)*

ALFRED. Your mother almost lost a plate.

(Joseph enters from shop carrying a peignoir on a hanger and a nightcap. He goes to table, and to himself, counts to ten on his fingers. Then he hurries back into the shop to complete the sale. After his exit, Alfred gets glasses from bureau, sets them.)

MARIE LOUISE. Tell me . . .

ALFRED. Yes?

MARIE LOUISE. I know I shouldn't ask . . .

ALFRED. They all want to know. Why was I shipped here?

MARIE LOUISE. Was it a political crime?

ALFRED. Politics? Women? Yes. Horses? Yes. Politics? No! *(Gets the cruet from bureau, sets it in center of table)* I never was interested in politics. Anyway, I've never held with the anarchists. What's the point of shooting one scoundrel? Another will come along to take his place.

MARIE LOUISE. Were you . . .

ALFRED. Framed? No, I was guilty as hell. *(Gets napkins from bureau, sets them)*

MARIE LOUISE. You stole from somebody?

ALFRED. Yes.

MARIE LOUISE. You were hungry!

ALFRED. I'd just finished a magnificent dinner in Maxim's with a woman who . . . Well, I thought at the time she was the most beautiful woman I'd ever seen. We were *friends*. To keep her friendship—you'll pardon me—to keep *her*—I needed my stepfather's generosity. As long as my mother was alive, he was generous enough. I went to see him.

MARIE LOUISE. Yes . . .

ALFRED. I really went to see his safe. I knew he had negotiable securities, jewels, money . . .

MARIE LOUISE. Oh!

ALFRED. Unfortunately, he was a light sleeper. He suddenly appeared in the library. He was a very imposing figure, my stepfather. Legion of Honor. Very deep voice. Old soldier. He roused the servants, called for the police. I lost my head. I killed him.

MARIE LOUISE *(gasps)*. How could you?

ALFRED. With a poker, Mademoiselle. *(She is horrified. He goes to chair, picks up her hat and suitcase. Jules enters with a struggling chicken, which he keeps shoving under his pajama jacket. Alfred exits to her room.)*

MARIE LOUISE *(startled by the noise and fluttering of the chicken)*. Oh!

(Jules exits into kitchen as Felix enters from the shop.)

FELIX *(going toward her)*. My poor Marie Louise.

MARIE LOUISE. I'm all right now, Papa. Funny . . .

FELIX. What?

MARIE LOUISE. I can hope again.

FELIX. Of course. Of course.

MARIE LOUISE. He gave me hope.

FELIX. Who?

MARIE LOUISE. A murderer!

FELIX. Huh?

(Emilie enters.)

MARIE LOUISE *(going to her)*. Oh, Mama!

EMILIE. Yes, dear?

MARIE LOUISE *(embracing her parents)*.

We're going to have a lovely Christmas.

EMILIE. Of course, we are.

(Alfred enters, takes in the situation, goes to chair, and carries and places it at the table.)

MARIE LOUISE. We're going to be very festive—very gay. *(The family group move to the table)* I shall sit next to Paul. His uncle, of course, will sit over there . . . His uncle will grunt as he always does . . . Paul will be so tactful, as he always is . . . *(Alfred carries chair and places it at the table, then picks up footstool and places it against wall)* Then we'll drink lots and lots of wine—especially his uncle. And he'll turn mellow gradually and begin to laugh. We'll sing, and then we'll leave Paul alone with his uncle. And Paul'll say: You see, sir? Our love is steel. No one— no one can break it.

EMILIE. Yes . . .

FELIX. The only thing is . . .

MARIE LOUISE. What?

FELIX. They won't be here for dinner.

EMILIE. They won't? They have other plans? So much has happened I forgot to ask you if you'd got them out of Quarantine.

FELIX. Well, as a matter of fact, I didn't see the Health people. I—I thought it over. It occurred to me . . . Well, I just couldn't face it tonight . . . And they'll be comfortable on the ship.

EMILIE. Oh! Well, we'll get their rooms ready after dinner in any case. They're sure to be here by morning.

MARIE LOUISE. And I wanted to see Paul—tonight.

FELIX. You'll see him tomorrow. *(Alfred goes to table)*. You can dream about him tonight.

MARIE LOUISE. I've dreamt so long.

(Alfred picks up two settings, returns them to bureau.)

EMILIE. Well, with or without Paul, we still must have dinner, and I'd better see to it.

(The harmonica is heard from the garden. Emilie exits to kitchen as Jules enters. He goes below table, brushing chicken feathers from his hands, and exits into garden. Alfred goes to table and returns one of the chairs.)

FELIX *(as Alfred takes other chair from table)*. I may be selfish, but I know I'm not sorry to be alone in the bosom of my family. *(Sees Alfred as he is placing chair)* Well, practically alone. *(Alfred picks up chicken feathers from floor)* That reminds me—we ought to get the tree out. Young man . . .

ALFRED. Yes, sir?

FELIX. Can you open that box? *(Indicates a box on commode)*

ALFRED. Got a poker? *(Marie Louise starts)* No, a chisel would be better.

FELIX. Over there. In that drawer.

(Alfred goes to drawer, takes out chisel, begins to open box.)

ALFRED. Right! Here we go.

(Harmonica is heard.)

FELIX. I suppose I should do something about that harmonica, but it's Christmas Eve.

ALFRED *(takes out small, untrimmed tree)*. Here's our tree. They got this one young.

MARIE LOUISE. It's beautiful.

ALFRED. And here are the trimmings. *(Taking them from box.)*

MARIE LOUISE. It's France! It's home!

ALFRED. Uhuh.

MARIE LOUISE. That lovely pine fragrance we knew as children—in the forest near the sea . . .

ALFRED. Uhuh.

(Joseph enters from garden with another tree, larger and trimmed.)

JOSEPH. Oh, you *have* a tree!

FELIX. Where on earth did you get that?

JOSEPH. I'd better return it.

(Starts to exit, stops, swaps trees, exits to garden with the small tree. Jules enters from garden with an orchid and a camellia. Harmonica stops suddenly.)

EMILIE *(from kitchen)*. Felix, Felix. *(She enters)*

FELIX. Yes, my dear?

EMILIE. Felix, I found a chicken in the oven. Where did it come from?

JULES. Praise the Lord, from Whom all blessings flow.

EMILIE. Oh!

JULES *(handing it to Felix)*. An orchid for Madame . . .

EMILIE *(as Felix hands it to her)*. For me?

JULES. And a camellia for the young lady.

MARIE LOUISE. Why, thank you.

EMILIE. I've never seen a more beautiful orchid, except in the Governor's garden.

JULES. Neither have I.

(Goes to tree. He, Alfred and Marie Louise add more trimmings. Joseph enters from garden.)

JOSEPH. M. Ducotel, the young man out there has just paid for his harmonica.

FELIX. Paid?

EMILIE. How on earth did you . . .

FELIX. But, he has no money.

JOSEPH *(examines both)*. Of course not. We bartered. The young man wore a handsome gold ring. You get the handsome gold ring. *(Extends it to him)* Sometimes we don't sell. We barter.

FELIX. But how do I know he didn't steal the ring? After all, receiving stolen property . . .

JOSEPH. He made that ring himself—out of a gold nugget he found. He's always finding things—nuggets, watches, bicycles. How can you doubt his word of honor? Really! To besmirch the reputation of an altar boy! On Christmas Eve!

(He exits to garden. The harmonica is heard again.)

EMILIE. Felix, get a bottle of wine.

FELIX. Of course. *(He looks for wine, finds a bottle in basket)*

ALFRED *(indicating tree)*. Shall we put it on the table?

MARIE LOUISE. Let's!

JULES *(carrying it to table)*. Here—let me—Ah! A real tree! A real Christmas in a real home!

(Alfred takes cruet to bureau, picks up corkscrew, gets bottle of wine from Felix, opens it, then hands bottle to Jules. He places it on table.)

MARIE LOUISE. Careful now . . . *(Making room on table)*

JULES. We place it here—tenderly.

EMILIE. I've got to go back to the kitchen.

(Starts. Marie Louise gets the three-angel decoration from bureau, takes it to table.)

JULES *(stopping her)*. Oh, no, Madame. Tonight we are going to prepare, cook and serve your dinner. Tonight we are your servants. *(Places chair for her. She sits. Joseph enters from garden)* Beautiful! I've commissioned our young minstrel to play Christmas carols.

(Alfred brings wineglasses from bureau to table.)

JOSEPH *(seeing the wine, picks up the bottle, examines the label).* A Beaujolais! Not bad! May I?

MARIE LOUISE. Please.

JOSEPH *(pours a glass).* Color perfect. Bouquet exquisite. *(Tastes the wine)* Mmm! Ah . . . '97 . . . Bottled the same year I was! *(Hands Jules the bottle)* I once organized a winery that was the marvel of the trade. Chateau Joseph. We had no wines, no bottles, not even a cork. But the labels were museum pieces! The Prosecuting Attorney gave me a one-man show.

(Jules has poured for the others. Harmonica playing is quite loud now.)

MARIE LOUISE. Listen!

ALFRED. What?

MARIE LOUISE. He's playing: Three Angels.

JULES. So he is. That was my wife's favorite Christmas carol.

(The three convicts are standing together.)

MARIE LOUISE *(singing).* Three Angels came that night . . .

ALL *(joining).* That holy night . . .

MARIE LOUISE *(picks up the three-angel decoration, goes to front of table and places it on the top branch of tree).* And look! Look at the tree! We have three little angels on the tree, just as in the song. Only my angels are a little—shopworn—a little . . .

JOSEPH. A little unlucky, Mademoiselle. They were damaged by the long, rough journey here—bruised by unfeeling hands. Fallen angels, Mademoiselle.

MARIE LOUISE. I don't care. *(Lifting her glass, toasting the tree)* I'm going to drink to—to—my three angels.

JOSEPH—JULES—ALFRED: Thank you, Mademoiselle.

She turns to them. They toast her, and all drink as

THE CURTAIN FALLS

ACT TWO

AT RISE: *Several hours later.*

The table has been cleared. The boxes and baskets have been taken off the commode, and the decorated Christmas tree placed there.

Otherwise the room arrangement is the same as in the previous act.

Jules is sleeping in his armchair. Alfred is stretched out on the floor near the gate, the coconut cage near him.

Joseph is asleep in a chair, his head on the table. The lamps are turned low and the moonlight illuminates the room and the sleeping figures.

We hear thunderous knocking on the outside door of the shop. The knocking is repeated. Jules is the first to wake. He yawns and stretches, goes to the lamp on the left wall, turns it up. The knocking is heard for the third time, louder. He goes to Joseph and wakes him.

JULES. Someone's trying to get in. *(Turns lamp up)*

JOSEPH. Huh? Probably the Three Wise Men paying us the traditional visit.

(Knocking is heard again, still louder.)

JULES. Impatient, aren't they?

JOSEPH. I'll take a look.

(He goes into shop. Presently an angry voice is heard.)

HENRI *(off stage).* Are they deaf in there? Where the devil is everybody?

(Alfred wakes, gets up, joins Jules, puts cage on commode.)

JULES. Doesn't sound like the Three Wise Men to me.

(Joseph holds aside the bamboo curtains. Henri and Paul enter. They react to the two men in prison uniform. Paul carries two suitcases. Henri carries his portfolio.)

HENRI. What the devil . . . Convicts!

JULES. At your service, sir.

HENRI. It was so damn dark in the shop I didn't see . . . *(Puts hat and portfolio on table)*

PAUL. Neither did I, Uncle Henri.

JOSEPH *(enters after them and joins other two convicts).* Allow me to introduce myself. I'm 3011. *(Indicates number on his jacket)* My good friend 6817 . . .

JULES. Enchanted.

JOSEPH. And my esteemed colleague 4707.

ALFRED. How are you?

(Felix enters, wearing robe, as though he had dressed hurriedly.)

FELIX. I thought I heard the bell . . . Henri!

HENRI. Good evening. Or rather good morning.

FELIX (embracing them). My dear Henri . . . Welcome. Welcome. My dear Paul, welcome . . . (Paul puts bags on floor near ladder) I had no idea you'd come tonight. No idea, I assure you. Naturally we'd have waited up for you. (Henri sits near table. Paul places chair for him, then hangs their hats on pegs) Marie Louise was very anxious to see you, Paul . . . Expected your for Christmas dinner . . . Keenly disappointed.

HENRI. Was she? And were you . . .

FELIX. What, Henri?

HENRI. Keenly disappointed?

FELIX. Well . . .

HENRI. Did you get my note?

FELIX. Well . . .

HENRI. Don't lie.

FELIX. Henri, I never lie. You know that. I don't know how I manage it, but I never do.

HENRI. I asked you to use your influence with the Health officials. Did you?

FELIX. Well—Christmas Eve and—all that—You know how it is—I thought—you'd be better off on the ship.

HENRI. They said you hadn't been near them. And if I hadn't threatened to have them all fired, we'd still be on that garbage scow they call a ship.

PAUL. The heat was stifling.

HENRI (opens portfolio, arranges papers). A drunken cab driver was inflicted upon us. Even his horse was drunk! By great good fortune we managed to weave our way here without being killed. We are then greeted by your retinue of servants. (Indicates the three) I congratulate you upon your ménage!

FELIX. Ménage?

HENRI. Don't tell me they're not your servants. What are they? Your friends who are spending Christmas Eve with you?

FELIX. Well, as a matter of fact, they are—in a way.

JOSEPH (coming forward). The boss means a good servant is always a friend. A bad servant is bound to be an enemy. He'll not only ruin your digestion. He'll even squeal to the police. Believe me, I speak from bitter experience.

HENRI. Have our bags taken to our rooms.

FELIX. Certainly. Emilie has given you these rooms here. I hope you'll forgive the primitive quality of our hospitality. Marie Louise fixed her room for you herself, Paul. I'll take your bags. (He's about to pick up bags when Alfred forestalls him)

ALFRED. Allow me . . .

HENRI (to Paul). Paul, go with him and be sure and lock your door when you retire.

PAUL. Yes, sir. (Exits into room, followed by Alfred)

HENRI. I'm no more timid than the next man, but these fellows look dangerous. (Joseph smiles at Jules) I suppose you always go armed.

FELIX. No.

HENRI. Well, I intend to sleep with a revolver in my hand. (To convicts) Bear that in mind.

JULES. Yes, sir.

HENRY. You too!

JOSEPH. Yes, sir. We clean, oil and polish revolvers—part of our daily impeccable service.

HENRI. You won't get your hands on mine. (To Felix) The rest of our luggage is in the shop.

FELIX. I'll get them.

JOSEPH. Allow me. (Exits to shop)

JULES. Would you gentlemen care for something to eat?

HENRI. You're the cook, I suppose.

JULES. Yes, sir.

FELIX. He's very good. He did a chicken with almonds tonight that was superb.

HENRI. You dined well?

FELIX. Oh, very well.

HENRI. Congratulations! I had a nauseating dinner. Chicken with almonds! Business is suddenly booming, I take it.

JULES. Chickens cost nothing here.

HENRI. Bring me some fruit.

(Paul enters, carrying suit.)

JULES (starts toward kitchen). Very good, sir. (Turns to Paul) And you, sir, would you care for something to eat?

PAUL (hesitating). I'm famished. What have you got? (Places suit on chair)

HENRI. Whatever it is, have it brought to your room.

PAUL. Sir?

HENRI. I want to have a little talk with Felix.

PAUL. Yes, sir. I wouldn't mind some cold chicken.

JULES. Yes, sir. *(Exits to kitchen)*

HENRI. Good night, Paul.

PAUL. Good night, sir. *(Alfred enters)* You there . . . *(To Alfred, picking up suit, tossing it to him, then exits to room)* I have a suit for you to press.

(Joseph enters from shop with bag. Alfred exits with bag, after swapping the suit for the bag. Joseph continues to study Henri after throwing suit on chair.)

JOSEPH. Yes, sir?

HENRI. Get out!

JOSEPH. How can I resist such a cordial invitation? *(Exits to kitchen, followed by Alfred, who re-enters)*

HENRI *(staring after them)*. Assassins!

FELIX. They're really not bad fellows. For criminals, I mean.

HENRI. Now, let's get right down to it. I have very little time to give you. I have a factory to inspect and some mines. I have only two days here. Now . . .

FELIX. Henri, you're tired—it's awfully late—hardly the time to talk business . . .

HENRI. I'm not talking business—yet. I've sent Paul to bed so that you and I can straighten out this nonsense without a lot of silly chatter.

FELIX. Nonsense?

HENRI. I suppose you know Marie Louise had an affair with Paul before she left.

FELIX. Affair?

HENRI. At least I assume there was an affair. You are fortunate there were no consequences.

FELIX. Good God!

HENRI. At least I assume there were no consequences. You're not a grandfather. I take it.

FELIX. Do you mean to tell me . . . Are you implying . . .

HENRI. So there the matter rests. You may be an idiot, but even you must know I would never tolerate such a ridiculous marriage for Paul who is, at the moment, my legal heir. So if you're dreaming of a return to France via Marie Louise—wake up! I don't blame you for trying. I don't

blame Marie Louise. As a matter of fact, I find the matter amusing. Where the devil's my fruit?

(Marie Louise and Emilie enter. They have dressed hurriedly.)

FELIX *(miserably)*. Emilie, Henri's here.

EMILIE. How are you, Henri?

HENRI *(rises)*. Good to see you, Emilie. You, too, Marie Louise. *(He kisses their hands)* You look charming.

(Emilie joins Felix.)

MARIE LOUISE. Is Paul . . .

HENRI *(sits)*. Gone to bed.

MARIE LOUISE. Oh! Did you have a good trip?

HENRI *(sardonically)*. Delightful.

MARIE LOUISE. Was Paul seasick? He's such a poor sailor. I remember once he took me sailing, and it wasn't really rough at all, but pour Paul suffered so, we came right back. He was furious with himself.

HENRI. You little fool.

FELIX. But just a moment . . . The child merely . . .

EMILIE. There's no need to insult my daughter, Henri.

HENRI. I have no patience with fools, male or female. Paul's engaged. Damn good family and a damn good business. I couldn't buy old Audibert out. So I'm marrying him. The girl's a cow, but she'll give milk.

(Felix turns away in embarrassment. Henri returns to his papers.)

MARIE LOUISE. Oh!

EMILIE. If you'll excuse us, we're going to bed. Good night, Henri.

HENRI. Good night.

EMILIE. Come, Marie Louise.

MARIE LOUISE *(with dignity)*. Good night, M. Trochard.

HENRI. Good night, Marie Louise.

(Emilie and Marie Louise go out.)

FELIX *(as Henri makes no move)*. I must register my protest against your rudeness —your—your—insults—your—your arrogance! You had no right to upset Marie Louise—and her mother. Marie Louise is a very sensitive girl. A good girl. *(His voice breaks)*

HENRI. Dear, dear.

FELIX *(drawing himself up)*. It's very

late. If you'll excuse me, I'm going to bed. *(Starts)*

HENRI. I'm not excusing you *(Felix stops)* I'm not at all sleepy. Now that I've disposed of the affair Marie Louise, let's get down to business. How's it going?

FELIX. Well, I've spent the first year getting adjusted—acclimated. Getting used to local conditions, so to speak.

HENRI. And are you acclimated?

FELIX. I think you'll find the second year a great improvement. A great improvement. I know the obstacles, so to speak. I know the market . . .

HENRI. You do?

FELIX. Oh, yes.

HENRI. How much business did we do last month?

FELIX. Last month?

HENRI *(impatiently)*. November!

FELIX. November?

HENRI. November's always preceded December. Let's have the figures for November, if you don't mind?

FELIX. I don't remember.

HENRI. Where are the books? Look up the figures, man.

FELIX. I'm not sure what the figures are. I haven't added up the totals yet.

HENRI. It's the twenty-fourth of December—technically the twenty-fifth—and you haven't closed your books for November?

JOSEPH *(entering from kitchen, carrying large piece of cardboard and bamboo stick)*. Of course we have, sir.

(Felix turns in surprise.)

HENRI. What do you know about it?

JOSEPH. I'm the bookkeeper, sir.

HENRI. The bookkeeper! Congratulations. How much did you embezzle last month?

JOSEPH. Our gross receipts were thirty-two thousand, eight hundred and fifteen francs and forty-two centimes, sir. An advance over the preceding month of exactly eight thousand, five hundred and eighty-one francs and two centimes.

HENRI. An advance?

JOSEPH. Our figures for October were twenty-four thousand, three hundred and forty seven, and forty-eight centimes. *(Showing cardboard)* I am preparing a chart—a graph. You'll forgive the crude quality of cardboard and ink. Would you mind? *(Felix holds one end. Joseph uses pointer)* You will observe here that business declines steadily—in the first few months—due to new management—conservative clientele skeptical of anything new, et cetera—then observe that suddenly in August—with the reawakening of confidence—M'sieu's grasp of the affair, et cetera—the line rises, steadily up, up, up, up—I expect—and I am a cautious observer—a record breaker for December . . . Right up here. I'll need more cardboard. *(He indicates the line has run off the cardboard. He places the cardboard and pointer back of the bureau)*

HENRI. It's fantastic. A convict accountant. Charts, graphs. He knows more about the business than you do.

JOSEPH. The boss has more important things on his mind.

HENRI *(laughs)*. Did you hear that, Felix? You have more important things on your mind.

JOSEPH. He creates policy—guides, directs.

HENRI. Really? Tell me, Felix, it is still your policy to extend credit right and left?

FELIX. Well . . .

JOSEPH. Certainly not, sir. The boss always says that giving credit to a customer is like making him a gift of the merchandise.

HENRI. You said that, Felix.

FELIX. Well . . .

JOSEPH. The boss always says: I'm a business man, not a philanthropist. Let others play Santa Claus. I'll play safe. Hard as a rock, the boss. He has one God—cash on the line.

HENRI. Perhaps I never appreciated you Felix. But I doubt it.

FELIX. Just a moment . . .

HENRI. What about shortages?

JOSEPH. Inconceivable. The boss has an eye like a hawk.

HENRI. Losses due to thefts?

JOSEPH. Try it some time.

HENRI. What's that?

FELIX. As a matter of fact, I've just had some trouble about a case of Chartreuse—which did disapper mysteriously and . . .

JOSEPH. Pardon me, sir. The Chart

reuse was delivered by mistake to the Café de la Poste. I forgot to tell you. These bungling wholesalers! Call themselves merchants! No system, no organization. If you knew the difficulties the boss has to contend with!

HENRI. Well, we'll see when we take inventory tomorrow . . . *(Closing his portfolio)*

JOSEPH. Inventory—tomorrow? But, sir! You realize to morrow is Christmas! A holy day!

HENRI. Good. Then the shop will be closed, and we won't be disturbed.

FELIX. Can't we wait until the day after . . .

HENRI. The day after I'm devoting to somewhat more substantial matters. I've some mines to look into. *(Rising)* We'll go over everything tomorrow. I hope, for your sake, everything's in order. Where do I sleep?

FELIX *(pointing to room)*. In here, Henri.

HENRI *(going to room)*. Good. I rise at six. We can start at seven—promptly. Good night. *(He exits into room)*

FELIX *(to Joseph)*. Have you gone mad?

JOSEP. Sir?

FELIX. Fake charts—graphs—preposterous statements. I didn't have sense enough to stop you. Or the courage.

JOSEPH. The situation seemed to call for boldness—and a little exaggeration.

FELIX. It's not enough to pull figures out of the air—concoct stories about the Café de la Poste. I must produce books tomorrow—and the stock . . .

JOSEPH *(smiling)*. Oh, books! *(Goes to bureau, gets ledgers)*

FELIX. What do you mean: "Oh, books!"

JOSEPH *(bringing the ledgers to the table)*. We have all night to straighten those out.

FELIX. It'll take more than one night.

JOSEPH. You don't know my system of inspired accounting. *(Goes to bureau for inkwell and pens)* Trouble with most businessmen is they think mathematics is a science. With me, it's an art.

FELIX *(as it dawns on him)*. You mean . . .

JOSEPH. Sir, doctoring your books will be a delightful treat for me?

FELIX. I wouldn't dream of falsifying—any statements.

JOSEPH. Let me explain: Sir, in business, as in life itself, we have reality, and we have the *appearance* of reality. Now you're a painfully honest man. But your books make you look like a crook. All I want to do is to make your books reflect *you*—the real you. I want to paint your portrait.

FELIX. That's all very well, but . . .

JOSEPH. For example, you might have drunk the Chartreuse yourself or given your missing Swiss watches to some little native girl.

FELIX. I happen to be a devoted husband and father.

JOSEPH. Not in your books. In them you're a waster, a lecher, a scoundrel. I want to restore your character. And in presenting a picture of a prosperous establishment, I want to restore your confidence, your faith in yourself, your morale as a manager. Armed with my books, you'll go forth and make the books come true! And now—with your co-operation . . .

(He prepares to go work. Henri enters in his dressing gown.)

HENRI. I thought I'd find you still up.

FELIX *(startled, going to him)*. Can I get you anything, Henri?

HENRI. Just your books.

FELIX. My books?

HENRI. The accounts.

FELIX. Oh, yes—the accounts.

HENRI. Don't tell me you want to do a little work on them. I'll keep them in my room tonight. I want them just as they are now—in all their pristine purity.

FELIX. Henri, your suspicions are . . . are . . . *(He stops)*

JOSEPH *(assembling the books)*. I'm sure the gentleman will apologize in the morning, but if its the books he wants, sir, the books he shall have.

HENRI. Are they all there?

JOSEPH. Yes, sir. I'll put them in your room. *(At the door)* The fourth page is loose. *(Exits)*

HENRI. You don't seem to share your accountant's confidence?

FELIX. Well . . .

HENRI. Let's hope I can say I'm sorry in the morning.

(*As Henri reaches the door to exit, Joseph opens door. He fills the narrow doorway so that Henri cannot pass. Joseph turns sideways, but this does not create any more space. Realizing the impasse, Joseph backs in the room to allow Henri to exit. Then Joseph enters, closing door behind him.*)

JOSEPH (*admiringly*). Sharp as a razor, isn't he? I thought of dumping the books in water—making the ink run, the figures blur—but he'd have caught on. He's so damn suspicious. Besides, there was no water in there.

FELIX. I'm relieved.

JOSEPH. Relieved?

FELIX. Yes. Because I was tempted. I might have let you doctor the books. I would have lived to regret it.

JOSEPH. Regret?

FELIX. Oh, I know I'm ridiculous. But I still have honor left.

JOSEPH. There must be something that could be done.

FELIX. I forbid you to do anything.

JOSEPH (*impressively*). Do you realize, tomorrow morning at seven, a tornado will roar out of that room . . .

FELIX. I know.

JOSEPH. And you're not afraid!

FELIX. Of course, I'm afraid. If I were put upon a wild stallion, the fear of falling off would not make me a horseman. You see, I don't know how to ride. I'm an honest man. I don't say that boastfully. Nor apologetically. I state a fact. I don't know how to be anything else.

JOSEPH. Isn't that interesting? My dear sir, you're a phenomenon!

FELIX. You may laugh at me, but that's the way I am. I'm going to bed. I think I may even sleep. In fact, I'm sure I will. For an honest man I am a dreadful liar. How can I close my eyes tonight? What's to become of us? And Marie Louise— Paul didn't even ask for her. Good night.

(*Exits. In the pause that follows, Joseph devises a plan. After a look in the direction of the room that houses Henri, then toward Paul's room, he quickly puts on his glasses, goes to the bureau for writing paper, returns to the table and begins writing. Jules, carrying a plate with a chicken wing, followed by*

Alfred, enters from kitchen, headed toward Paul's room. Joseph interrupts them. They stop.)

JOSEPH. What have you got there?

JULES. I'm bringing the young man his cold chicken. (*Holds up chicken wing*)

JOSEPH. Pretty small portion.

JULES. All that's left. Alfred ate the leg just now. He wasn't hungry—just malicious.

(*A big grin from Alfred.*)

JOSEPH. We can't offend the young man with such measly hospitality. Besides, he shouldn't be thinking of food at a time like this.

(*Jules puts plate on table.*)

ALFRED. That's what I say! Here he is under the same roof with a girl who adores him, worships him . . .

JOSEPH. The situation is in hand.

JULES. What's up?

JOSEPH. *We* arrange a meeting. At once.

JULES. Huh?

JOSEPH. Too bad I haven't got a sample of the young man's handwriting.

JULES. Handwriting?

JOSEPH. So I'm printing it. (*Reads the note he has written*) "My dearling! My own! Come to me! I wait! I tremble! Oh, my adorable, my beloved! I shall always be your Paul." Alfred, give this to her. Her room is back of her parents' room. Be quiet as a cat.

ALFRED. Right. (*Takes note and exits.*)

JULES. She's not sleeping. I'll guarantee that.

JOSEPH. You get the young man.

(*Jules goes to door and knocks. Joseph returns paper to bureau. Paul emerges in robe.*)

PAUL. Yes?

JULES. Pardon me, sir. I'm awfully sorry, but there's no cold chicken left.

PAUL. Oh, what a nuisance!

JOSEPH. It wouldn't have been cold in any case. You know what our climate is like. We blow on all our food to cool it.

PAUL. Well, damn it, haven't you got anything else?

JOSEPH. We have warm centipede.

PAUL. What?

JULES. A native delicacy.

PAUL. I'd rather go to sleep hungry.

(*Starts to room. Jules stops him.*)

JULES. Sleep? You haven't seen *her* yet.

PAUL. What?

JOSEPH (*walking with him*). Do you think *she's* sleeping?

PAUL (*staring from one to the other*). Marie Louise?

JOSEPH. Who else?

JULES. She needs you, my boy. She needs you desperately. She loves you.

PAUL. What the devil?

JOSEPH. She waits! She trembles! She pants!

JULES. Be young, young man. There's so little time.

(*Alfred enters, followed by Marie Louise. He moves quickly out of the way, so that the girl is standing alone near the door.*)

JOSEPH. What a coincidence! Here she is!

(*Jules and Joseph join Alfred.*)

PAUL. Marie Louise . . .

MARIE LOUISE. Paul, dear, dear, Paul . . . (*She runs to him, throws her arms about him. Mission accomplished, the three convicts quietly go into garden*)

PAUL. I . . . Uh . . .

MARIE LOUISE. It's been so long . . .

PAUL. Marie Louise, my dear . . .

MARIE LOUISE. I couldn't sleep . . . I couldn't think . . .

PAUL. Neither could I, of course. It's been a wretched trip. Wretched. The God-awful heat—the filth—and Uncle Henri isn't the easiest traveling companion in the world.

MARIE LOUISE. Tell me everything.

PAUL. Everything? Well, where does one begin?

MARIE LOUISE (*sighing relief*). And to think I doubted you—for even a moment. That Suzanne . . .

PAUL. Oh, Suzanne . . . Well . . . Uh . . .

MARIE LOUISE. How could I have been so blind? Why couldn't I see for myself you wouldn't have come four thousand miles just to hurt me?

PAUL. If you only knew how I had to scheme and wangle to come at all!

MARIE LOUISE (*going to him*). How did you manage it?

PAUL. Persistence—patience—tact. It wasn't easy, but one manages when one

loves (*Holding her*) If you only knew how I ache for you, hunger for you . . .

MARIE LOUISE. Then marry me—now —here . . .

PAUL (*steps away with a look toward Henri's room*). Now? Here?

MARIE LOUISE. What does it matter what he thinks? What can he do? Fire you? Disinherit you? What does that mean?

PAUL (*turning away*). But my darling . . .

MARIE LOUISE (*moving close*). We're young. We'll get along somehow. I don't mind cooking and scrubbing—for you.

PAUL. I know, but . . .

MARIE LOUISE. And you'd find *something* to do. There are plantations. You can be a supervisor. Ride about in a pith helmet, looking very beautiful, and ordering people about.

PAUL. I don't know anything about plantations.

MARIE LOUISE. You'd learn.

PAUL. And this frightful heat.

MARIE LOUISE (*going to him*). There are the mines. They're cool. You could manage a mine.

PAUL. My dear Marie Louise, I'm thinking of you. Is it fair to condemn you to a life of—well, this sort of thing? You're entitled to a decent home, servants— Paris . . .

MARIE LOUISE. That'll come later. When you've become a huge success—at something—anything. I don't mind waiting. I don't mind waiting forever.

PAUL. But I do. I love you too much to condemn you to this wretched life here. No, my darling, it isn't as simple as you think. Oh, I've given it a lot of thought, believe me.

MARIE LOUISE. At home you had to fight him alone. Here you have me to help you.

PAUL. Exactly.

(*He kisses her. Henri's door opens. He carries one of the account books. He sees them, stops, closes door.*)

HENRI. Charming! (*The two separate quickly. Paul almost leaps*) Well, Paul, since you have so much excess energy, I suggest you expend it on something useful —these accounts. They're a mess. I want a report on them in the morning. Go to your room. *(Gives him book)*

MARIE LOUISE *(moving up to block his way)*. Paul, don't go!

PAUL. Sir, I wanted to explain . . .

HENRI. Didn't you hear me? Go to your room!

PAUL. Yes, sir. *(He goes toward room. Marie Louise is still standing where she blocked his way before. He cannot look at her. After a pause, he circles her and exits into his room)*

HENRI. Now you listen to me, young woman. *(She stops)* Apparently I didn't make myself clear earlier. For the rest of my stay—twenty-four hours precisely—I don't want you to exchange one single word alone with Paul. Is that clear?

MARIE LOUISE *(turns to him)*. That's what you want—yes. That's clear. What's also clear is you've frightened Paul—made him timid, abject, servile. How could you?

HENRI. You're wasting your time. I'm not going to let Paul make an ass of himself. He owes you nothing. It takes two to indulge in these little affairs. If your parents had taken proper care of you, it wouldn't have happened. *(Stops, eyes her shrewdly, curiously)* I take it you have had an affair.

(The three Angels appear at garden gate.)

MARIE LOUISE. That's not true!

HENRI. You resisted—bravely? Be that as it may . . .

MARIE LOUISE. I didn't want our love to be furtive—and cheap. I wanted everything—or nothing. I still do. Paul understands. It's difficult for him because he's a man, but he understands.

HENRI. Be that as it may—*(The Three Angels open gate and enter the room)* I suggest you turn your attentions elsewhere. You can find yourself a young man—or an older man. I suggest an older man with a little money in the bank whom you can hoodwink into an ironclad religious ceremony. On the other hand, if ceremonies don't interest you, but the comforts of life do, I should say your future was very bright. Very bright indeed. *(Now the three convicts move slowly forward)* You're young—pretty . . . You have a desirable air of innocence . . . *(As he turns away from her*

toward his room, he sees the men) What the devil do you want? *(Convicts do not move)* Are you all deaf? *(Silence. Finally, he turns to Marie Louise)* Well, I've nothing more to say to you, in any case. Good night. *(He exits into his room)*

MARIE LOUISE *(quickly going to them)*. There's something I must know—now. I can't sleep until I do.

JOSEPH. Yes?

MARIE LOUISE. I must see Paul—now. Tonight!

JOSEPH *(indicating bedroom)*. Go ahead!

MARIE LOUISE. I can't go to his room. I want you to tell him I'm waiting in the garden. Plaese hurry. *(She exits to garden)*

JULES *(to Alfred)*. Go get him.

JOSEPH. Wait a minute! I wonder if this is wise.

JULES *(sh ugs)*. Who knows? She wants him. She shall have him.

JOSEPH *(to Alfred)*. Go get him.

(Alfred goes into Paul's room.)

JOSEPH. I'm not sure she's going to be grateful to us for this.

JULES. Perhaps she's impatient to know the worst.

JOSEPH. The young man—and mind you, I'm pretty tolerant—is even more of a stinker than I thought.

JULES. Perhaps he's just cautious. Let's be fair. Caution is a virtue I've learned not to despise.

(Alfred enters with Paul. He pushes him forward. Paul is in his shirtsleeves. Alfred carries his jacket, stands blocking the door to his room.)

ALFRED. Come on.

PAUL. Where are you taking me?

ALFRED. Get going.

PAUL. What do you want?

JULES. We're concerned with your happiness, my boy.

PAUL. What?

JOSEPH. Someone is waiting for you in the garden.

JULES. Under the bougainvillea. Hurry.

PAUL. Marie Louise?

JULES. Correct.

PAUL *(looking from one to the other)*. I warn you! *(Looks about)* I'm going to call for help.

JOSEPH. Just because you're asked to meet a lovely girl in the garden on a gorgeous tropical night? Gentlemen, what has happened to France?

PAUL. I have work to do—the accounts . . .

JULES. Accounts? Can this be our youth?

PAUL. This is sheer insanity. *(Starts to room, but can't get by Alfred. He turns back)* What the devil are you interfering in my life for? This is grotesque!

JULES. You forget it's Christmas.

PAUL. What?

JOSEPH. You're our Christmas gift to the young lady.

PAUL. You're mad! What can I say to her?

JULES *(going to him)*. Whatever she wants to hear—that you love her.

JOSEPH. You *do* love her?

PAUL. Of course I love her. I've told her that.

JOSEPH. Tell it to her again.

JULES. Woman never get bored with repetition of the simple trite phrase: I love you. They supply their own variations on the theme.

JOSEPH. Exactly. Let her do most of the talking. Occasionally you may be called upon to say: "Yes, my love!" And occasionally you will say: "Always and forever." Since it's dark, she won't be able to see your face and know your lying.

PAUL. I'm not my own master. She doesn't understand that I *can't* marry her.

JOSEPH. Let's live for this night only. Let's leave the future—to the future. I suggest you kiss her . . .

ALFRED. What for?

JULES. It's customary!

JOSEPH. Kiss her frequently—and tenderly.

JULES *(moving close to him)*. Behave out there as if this were the most important, the most beautiful, the most cherished moment of your life.

PAUL. But Uncle Henri . . . Is he asleep? Awake? What if . . .

JOSEPH. We'll take care of Uncle Henri. Go! Think of *her* for once. We want to give the young lady an hour's happiness—and it seems to me we're giving you a pleasant interlude. You ought to be damn grateful.

PAUL *(finally)*. Very well, I'll go.

JOSEPH. Bravo!

(Alfred steps down, holds jacket for Paul to get into.)

PAUL *(smiles, puts on his charm)*. And I *am* grateful—*(Exits to garden. Jules goes to gate to watch Paul off stage)*

JOSEPH. We make progress.

JULES *(shrugs)*. It's what she wants.

ALFRED. Women!

JULES. Don't you think they ought to be chaperoned?

JOSEPH. Chaperoned?

JULES. She's overwrought—they have only this night—perhaps their last night —the garden—the moonlight . . .

ALFRED. I'll break every bone in his body. *(Exits to garden)*

JOSEPH. That is not the function of a chaperon!

(Follows Alfred out into the garden. Jules closes the gate, then slowly goes to his chair and stretches out in it. During this, church bells are heard chiming. After a pause he gets up and goes to the door of Henri's room, and peeks through keyhole. Emilie enters, to find Jules at Henri's door.)

EMILIE *(amazed)*. What are you doing?

JULES. Two o'clock and all's well. Our dear uncle sits with one hand clutching the bedpost as if it were a competitor's throat. With the other, he slashed at your husband's books with a pencil. He's broken three pencils in the past two minutes.

EMILIE. Where's Marie Louise? She's not in her room.

JULES. She's—around.

EMILIE. She's not in the garden with that young man, is she?

JULES. As a matter of fact, she is.

EMILIE. At this hour?!

JULES. Don't be afraid, Madame. They're being chaperoned.

EMILIE. Chaperoned?

JULES. Properly. My friends are out there.

EMILIE *(moving toward garden)*. Marie Louise!

JULES. Please, Madame, why spoil the happiness she's been dreaming about for so long?

EMILIE *(turning to him)*. She's only a child.

JULES. Only in your eyes. And if you must think of her as a child, then, Madame, remember it's Christmas. Children want toys for Christmas. Let her have her toy.

EMILIE. This is a very dangerous toy.

JULES. Why break her heart? No, it's better to let her have her toy, until in the natural course of events it gets broken, and she'll no longer care.

EMILIE. If I only knew what to do!

JULES. Believe me, I've given the matter considerable thought in the last few minutes. You see, Madame, I'm playing father to the child I never had.

EMILIE: Oh!

JULES (moving toward chair). I sit in this armchair, with my eyes closed, and imagine myself the head of this house.

EMILIE. Poor man.

JULES. We must see her through this trying moment, Madame. Patiently. One false step—and she's lost. Go to bed, Madame.

EMILIE. I won't sleep.

JULES. You must. You owe it to her. There's nothing you can do tonight, believe me. We're here.

EMILIE (staring at him). As I listen to you—look at you—I don't know whether I'm awake, or asleep and dreaming.

JULES. Good night, Madame. (Emilie exits. Jules closes his eyes. Alfred and Joseph enter. He opens his eyes) How's it going?

JOSEPH. Beautifully.

ALFRED (looking off stage to garden). He's a cold fish.

JOSEPH. On the contrary, I'll admit that at first it didn't sound promising.

JULES. And then . . .

ALFRED. He sat there—mumbling about his damn uncle.

JULES. And then?

JOSEPH. Then they were silent. They looked at the stars.

ALFRED. Not a word from him! Like a mute! Then he talked. Dribbled. He's quoting poetry right now. It took him all this time!

JOSEPH. Some men respond slowly. Be fair, be tolerant. (Jules goes to his chair, sits) I had the feeling that if the boy were free to think for himself, one could hope . . .

JULES. Really?

ALFRED. He's a spineless flounder.

JOSEPH. You're prejudiced. I tell you the boy wouldn't be half bad without his uncle. (Indicates Henri's room) One man capable of so much mischief.

ALFRED. Yeah.

JOSEPH. Ironical, isn't it? He's free and we're in prison. There's no justice.

JULES. Let's bring him to justice. The case of humanity versus Henri Trochard! Bring in the prisoner. (Alfred goes to chair, places it facing upstage, in the area between the table and the chair Jules is sitting in. Then he goes back to table. To Joseph) Proceed, Mr. Prosecuting Attorney.

JOSEPH. Stand up! Do you deny the evidence? Hurry up! I haven't got all year.

JULES. Please, this is a solemn occasion.

JOSEPH. I'm in a hurry! I need another conviction. I am ambitious. I mean to be Prime Minister some day, or at least Deputy Administrator of Outdoor Comfort Stations.

ALFRED. I object.

JULES. Sustained.

JOSEPH. Overruled.

JULES. I am the Judge.

JOSEPH. I'm in a hurry.

JULES. Mr. Defense Attorney.

JOSEPH. Gentlemen of the Jury—I say to you my client is no criminal. He is a patriot. He has contributed to the greater glory of our beloved country.

JULES. How?

JOSEPH. Who cares? Gentlemen of the Jury, I say to you my client is directly responsible for the tremendous increase in our country's birth rate. Consider how he overworks and underpays his many employees. After a fourteen-hour day, do the patronize they haunts of sin, the theatres, the concert halls, the cafés? No. They totter home to their wives and enjoy the only diversion left open to them. Vive la France.

JULES. Prisoner, stand up! A stupid jury which understands nothing of the nature of man nor of the world he lives in, has found you guilty as charged. (Henri's door opens and he enters, stares at them for a moment. He carries a sheaf of papers. He goes to Paul's room.)

HENRI. Paul . . . Paul . . . (*Tries the door, opens it, goes in. Jules returns the chair to place at table. Alfred goes to gate. Henri re-enters*) Where's my nephew?

JULES. Isn't he in his room?

HENRI. He is not. And you know he's not. Where is he?

JOSEPH. If you must know, he's in the garden, with the young lady. They make a charming couple. (*Henri moves toward garden. Alfred blocks his way*) They don't wish to be disturbed. This is their moment.

HENRI. Out of my way. I've had just about enough of your damned impertinence. (*Reaches in his pocket. Obviously doesn't find what he's looking for*)

JOSEPH. Alfred, the gentleman is looking for something.

ALFRED (*producing gun*). This, sir?

HENRI. Give me that. (*He snatches it. Alfred doesn't resist*)

ALFRED. I cleaned it.

JOSEPH. It was in dreadful shape. The barrel was filthy. Naturally we removed the cartridges. We had to . . . They were damp anyway.

JULES. The climate, you know.

JOSEPH. Frightful.

JULES. Very unhealthy.

JOSEPH. I'd never bottle this air. (*Henri meanwhile examines gun and confirms the facts. He puts gun back in pocket.*)

HENRI. You've got your nerve, you scoundrels!

JULES. You've no use for a revolver anyway.

JOSEPH. We're here. We'll protect you lovingly. We make ideal watchmen! We never sleep. Twenty-four-hour service!

HENRI. I'll have you all arrested in the morning.

(*Convicts laugh.*)

JOSEPH (*indicates Jules and Alfred*). I'm afraid you're much too late. They've been arrested permanently. I'm only in for a brief twenty years. Sounds long, but when one thinks geologically—historically—a mere flicker of time.

HENRI. Murderers!

ALFRED. Correct!

JOSEPH. Except for me. I was like yourself—a business man.

HENRI (*turns to him*). You're a thief.

JOSEPH. You're not very polite. I don't think I want to take inventory for you tomorrow!

HENRI. Don't worry. You won't.

JOSEPH. God knows I've taken inventory with all kinds of people. But one draws the line somewhere, and I draw the line at you.

HENRI. I'll settle your hash in the morning. They have ways of punishing scoundrels like you. I'll see to it that you pay for this outrage. I'll report you to the Governor—first thing in the morning. (*Exits into his room, slamming door. In the pause that follows, Joseph goes to his chair. Jules goes to Henri's door.*)

ALFRED. He's going to see the Governor in the morning.

JULES. Sixty days solitary . . .

JOSEPH. Or six months in that hellish jungle. (*Shudders*) I'm not normally a pessimist, but I say again: There's no justice.

ALFRED. No.

JULES. Sixty days solitary, if we're lucky.

JOSEPH. If only our dear uncle would disappear! Vanish!

JULES. Yeah.

ALFRED. He's human.

JOSEPH. I doubt it.

ALFRED. I still say he's human. Know what I mean?

JULES. Know what he means?

JOSEPH. Now, gentlemen, please, I'm not a man of violence. Anything physical is repugnant to me. Besides we may get caught.

ALFRED. Well?

JOSEPH. I want to live.

ALFRED. Why?

JOSEPH. I want to know what tomorrow will bring.

ALFRED. I know now.

JOSEPH. There are other tomorrows. Listen to me! I have a plan. If you help me escape . . .

JULES. Yes?

JOSEPH. I'll go to Cherbourg . . .

ALFRED. Well?

JOSEPH. I'll assume another name, another personality.

JULES. And then?

JOSEPH. I'll go to work for him and at the end of a year he'll go bankrupt and blow his brains out.

JULES. It doesn't sound very practical to me, your plan.

ALFRED. Always the promoter—escape —bankruptcy—a year. I'm a man of action.

JULES. Just a moment . . .

ALFRED. You're not weaseling out, too?

JULES. No.

ALFRED. Well, let's go.

JULES. Just a moment. Every man's entiled to a fair trial.

JOSEPH. He's already had his.

JULES. True.

(They think.)

JOSEPH. How? That is the question.

ALFRED. Simple.

JOSEPH. How?

ALFRED. Adolphe!

JOSEPH. Adolphe!

JULES. Of course.

JOSEPH. An inspiration! Quick, humanitarian and safe.

ALFRED. An accident.

JULES. Only too common in the tropics.

ALFRED. Here we go! *(Rises, picks up coconut cage from commode, goes below table to door of Henri's room)*

JOSEPH. An accident is about to be arranged.

JULES. Let justice be done.

ALFRED. Go, Adolphe! *(Opens the box against a crack in the door)* Right through the crack. Go Adolphe!

JOSEPH. Has he gone?

ALFRED *(looks into cage)*. Gone.

JULES *(with glee)*. I bet he's climbing right up the bed. Right up the post. Adolphe sees the hairy hand. The hand opens palm up, as if to say: I want mine. All right, says Adolphe. You can have it all. Keep the change.

JOSEP. Funny, I never thought of it.

JULES. What?

JOSEPH. A snake farm. There's a fortune in it! Think of the demand. Think of all the relatives in the world who want to get rid of other relatives.

JULES. Hear anything?

ALFRED. Not a sound. Trust Adolphe. He's a quiet worker.

JULES. As the presiding judge, I should note the exact time of execution.

JOSEPH. Let's not be bureaucratic. Shall I say a few flattering words about the deceased?

JULES. No.

JOSEPH. It's customary. *(Rises)* I was thinking of something like: He was a devoted bachelor and an uncle.

(Alfred, who has been peering through the keyhole, turns back.)

ALFRED. I can't tell if he's asleep or dead.

JOSEPH. I have an infallible test. Rattle a few coins.

ALFRED *(after another look)*. Hasn't moved.

JOSEPH. We shall know in the morning.

(During the following speech, Alfred goes to the lamp on the wall and turns it down. Then to the other lamps, turning them down. He then stretches out on the floor, prepared to sleep.)

JULES *(quietly as he gets up)*. Those who should be asleep are asleep. Those who should be dead are dead. *(Looking off stage)* Our young lovers are neither dead nor asleep. Just half way between, as they should be.

(He stretches out in his chair. As Alfred turns down the last lamp, Joseph, who has been sitting quietly, thinking, gets up and moves to bureau, where he picks up a stack of writing paper, inkwell and pens and brings these supplies to the table.)

JULES. What are you going to do?

JOSEPH. I'm going to write the last will and testament of Henri Trochard.

He puts on his glasses, sits and prepares for his new task as

THE CURTAIN FALLS

ACT THREE

AT RISE: *The next morning.*

Early morning sun is pouring into the room. Alfred is still asleep. Joseph is seated at table with collection of pens, inks, paper, and laboriously writing. Jules enters from kitchen with coffee, cheese and bread on a tray.

JULES (*placing tray on table*). How's it coming?

JOSEPH. The last will and testament of the deceased is practically ready. One more sentence and I'm finished.

JULES. One more sentence and we're all finished.

JOSEPH. Please! It's too early in the morning for your morbid fancies!

JULES (*pouring coffee for the three*). Anyway, you're enjoying the job.

JOSEPH (*showing letter*). Why not? This is my masterpiece! Here is the note from dear Uncle Henri. Here's *my* sample effort. Compare! Ink, handwriting! Perfection!

JULES. Don't ask me. I'm no expert. (*Takes his and Alfred's mugs, goes to Alfred, wakes him. Alfred sits up, drinks.*)

JOSEPH. I challenge the experts! There isn't a court in France that won't honor the deathbed request of our poor old uncle. (*Reads*) "My conscience has been bothering me grievously of late. I have a curious premonition of death, somehow. I am writing this shortly after midnight and ask that this constitute a codicil to my will. If anything should happen to me, I implore my nephew, Paul, to restore to Felix Ducotel, my cousin, the Gallery Moderne in Cherbourg, which I acquired by sharp practice. I could not face the judgment of Providence if this were not done. Paul, you are my heir, and I beg you to help a repentant and tortured sinner by making generous amends to my cousin, Felix. (*So moved by the following sentiments that a tear comes into his voice*) Please, Paul, respect my wishes. Be happy, Paul, as I was not. Be honest, Paul, as I was not . . . Henri Trochard."

JULES. Be happy! Be honest! Damn good advice to a young man starting out in life with a fortune. And easy to follow for a young man with a fortune.

JOSEP. I'm deeply moved by the old sinner's sudden repentance. It just goes to prove . . .

JULES. What?

JOSEPH. There's little good in the worst of us. After all, he had a conscience!

JULES. You gave him one. A beauty!

JOSEPH (*modestly*). It was nothing, really. Nothing at all. (*Dunks his bread in coffee, proceeds then with his work. Alfred, having finished his coffee, places mug on table, then goes to chair and picks up the coat of Paul's suit that has been there since the previous act*)

JULES. By the way . . . (*Dunking his bread in coffee*)

JOSEPH. Yes?

JULES. Before you finish his will . . .

JOSEPH. Only a codicil—technically.

JULES. Don't you think it would be a good idea to make sure the deceased—is dead?

JOSEPH. I have the utmost confidence in Adolphe. I'm sure everything went according to plan. Incidentally, we must get Adolphe back to his cozy little nest.

JULES. As soon as I finish my coffee, we'll take a look.

(*Alfred takes off his convict's coat and slips into Paul's jacket.*)

ALFRED. How do you like me?

JOSEPH. Splendid!

ALFRED (*going to mirror*). He's got a good tailor. I once had a wonderful tailor. I think I still owe him some money.

JOSEPH (*working*). Naturally! You were a gentleman!

ALFRED (*stroking cloth*). Feels good. Look at that lining. (*Strokes lining*) Feels like a woman's skin.

JULES. Why torture yourself?

ALFRED. No harm in pretending I'm human again.

JULES. You're an adolescent.

ALFRED. That's what my stepfather used to say! "Grow up!" he used to say. You know, I was thinking out there—it's all *his* fault.

JULES. Whose?

ALFRED. My stepfather's.

JULES. Because you smacked him over the head with a poker?

ALFRED. I wouldn't be just wearing Paul's jacket. I'd be in Paul's shoes. If it weren't for the old bastard.

JULES. I don't follow you.

ALFRED. Look! That night I dined with Jeannine at Maxim's. Suppose the old bastard were a different kind of old bastard. A real *father*. Someone like you. (*Indicates Jules*) I'd come up and see you. I'd say, "Good evening, sir."

JULES (*entering into spirit of the thing*).

What do you want now, you young scoundrel? More money?

ALFRED. How'd you guess, sir?

JULES. A girl, I suppose.

ALFRED. Yes, sir.

JULES. Sowing a few wild oats, eh?

ALFRED. Yes, sir.

JULES. Well, you're only young once. How much do you want?

ALFRED. Five thousand, sir.

JULES. Here you are, you rascal.

ALFRED. Thank you, sir.

JULES. And then?

ALFRED. I'd find out Jeannine was a tramp.

JULES. And then?

ALFRED. And then I'd go on a long journey to forget her. I'd try this place—that place—and then I'd wind up here. I'd walk into this shop. I'd see *her*. She'd see me. I'd wire you—my stepfather. "Have found *the* girl. We want your blessing."

JULES. Bless you, my children. Come home. All is forgiven.

ALFRED. Now do you see why it was all his fault?

JULES. Of course! The Judge should have given you the Legion of Honor and put the poker in the Louvre as a national monument.

(Alfred looks in mirror.)

MARIE LOUISE *(enters, dressed for church, carrying hat, gloves, prayer book).* Good morning. *(The men respond. She goes to table)* What are you writing?

JOSEPH *(covering his work).* My memoirs.

(Marie Louise stares at Alfred).

MARIE LOUISE. Oh, your jacket.

ALFRED. It's Paul's.

MARIE LOUISE. I know. Did he give it to you? You look very handsome.

ALFRED. I do?

MARIE LOUISE. Of course, Paul wears clothes with such—distinction. Such elegance.

ALFRED *(glumly).* Yes.

MARIE LOUISE. But you look very nice. What is your name? You know, I don't even know any of your names.

ALFRED. Alfred.

MARIE LOUISE. You look very nice,

Alfred. *(As she turns to Jules, Alfred walks away)* And you are—?

JULES. Papa Jules.

JOSEPH. I'm Uncle Joseph.

MARIE LOUISE. I'm going to Mass. Will you still be here when I get back?

ALFRED. Yes.

MARIA LOUISE *(to Alfred).* I want to thank you for—well—for everything you said yesterday. About Paul, I mean. You were right, you know. I was a fool to doubt him. Oh, I know he'll never love me as I love him. After all, I'm only a small part of his life. He has so many interests. But I don't mind. I want so little. Even his uncle must know that.

JOSEPH. His uncle knows everything now. I think you'll find he's acquired wisdom overnight. In fact, he's a changed man. *(Beams)*

MARIE LOUISE *(puzzled).* He is? How?

JULES. You'll be late for Mass.

MARIE LOUISE. Since you're so anxious to get me off to church, I'm going to say a little prayer to St. Anthony for all of you—and for myself. *(Exits into shop)*

JOSEPH. Done! *(Rising)* My masterpiece. My magnum opus! The codicil to Uncle Henri's will be discovered here. *(Puts it on bureau in a prominent position, and the writing materials in their place.)*

JULES. We have a will, but have we a corpus delicti? Suppose—now just suppose Adolphe missed him—or ignored him.

ALFRED. Adolphe wouldn't let his pals down.

JULES *(doubtfully).* I don't know.

JOSEPH. Shall we have a little bet?

ALFRED. I'm a sportsman.

JOSEPH. I'll hold the stakes.

JULES. Ten centimes our dear uncle's alive and snoring.

ALFRED *(giving coin to Joseph).* Take you.

JULES. Right.

(Joseph gets coin from Jules.)

ALFRED *(picks up cage at chair and goes toward Henri's room).* I'll go see.

JULES *(stopping him).* Just a minute. I don't trust you. If he's still alive, you might bash his head in just to win a bet. You go, Joseph.

JOSEPH *(sits facing table).* Me? I'r

squeamish. I don't like looking at dead people. It offends me esthetically.

JULES. Somebody's got to go.

JOSEPH. You go.

JULES. Oh, no. I'm the Judge. I never look at my victims. I like to sleep nights.

JOSEPH. Well, somebody . . .

(*Mme. Parole enters from the shop, wearing the same hat she wore in Act One, but a different dress. She carries an opened bottle of cognac and her purse.*)

MME. PAROLE. Well, making yourselves at home, aren't you?

JOSEPH. Sorry I didn't hear the bell. I'm M. Ducotel's new assistant. May I assist you?

MME. PAROLE. I want to see M. Trochard.

ALFRED and JULES. What?

JOSEPH. M. Trochard?

MME. PAROLE. Oh, don't stare at me so stupidly. I know he arrived last night. I want to tell him a few things about M. Felix Ducotel—the swindler! (*Showing the bottle*) Here, taste this cognac.

JOSEPH (*taking bottle*). You want me to . . . Thank you. Season's greetings. (*Gulps*)

MME. PAROLE. Delicious, isn't it?

JOSEPH. Well, you've got to remember the thousands of miles this bottle has traveled—and the climate. Travel broadens us all, including cognac.

MME. PAROLE. Really! How profound!

JOSEPH. I'll admit it has a little taste of—of . . .

MME. PAROLE (*exploding*). There's no taste at all. It's plain water.

JOSEPH. Water? Madame exaggerates.

MME. PAROLE. So I'm exaggerating, am I? Read that label!

JOSEPH. For window display purposes only.

MME. PAROLE. Of all the outrageous . . . Ruining my Christmas!

JOSEPH. This is the wrong label. You don't think a company in its right senses would send a sample bottle thousands of miles. For what? This is a sound cognac, Madame. I say that not only as a merchant, but as a connoisseur.

MME. PAROLE. Are you mad? Read that label.

JOSEPH. Do you believe everything you read?

MME. PAROLE. Assassin.

JOSEPH. Please, Madame, no personalities.

MME. PAROLE. I want to see M. Trochard.

JOSEPH. Somebody should see M. Trochard. (*Putting bottle on table*) It might as well be you. (*Indicates to the left*) Please. This way, Madame. (*She starts toward the kitchen. Alfred blocks her way at the same time as Joseph speaks*) No, no. Right in *here*. (*Points to Henri's room*)

MME. PAROLE (*doubtfully*). He's in there?

JOSEPH. Don't worry, Madame. It's not his bedroom. He's converted it into his office. M. Trochard is famous for converting everything into an office. Even his church pew on Sundays. (*She knocks*) Don't bother knocking. He may not hear you. Step right in, Madame.

MME. PAROLE. You're sure it's all right?

JOSEPH. Of course. After all, Madame, it's very important for you to see M. Trochard. The cognac is just an excuse. You've come because your husband is unhappy in the Customs Service and wants to be a merchant again. He wants to take over this shop. You want to help him get it.

MME. PAROLE. Of all the . . . (*She enters Henri's room*)

JOSEPH. We'll soon know.

JULES. This is one bet I hope to lose. (*Mme. Parole's suppressed shriek is heard. Alfred, with extended hand goes to Joseph, who pays off the bet. Mme. Parole enters from the room, dazed.*)

MME. PAROLE. He's dead!

JOSEPH (*apparently astonished*). What?

JULES. Did you say dead, Madame?

MME. PAROLE. I'm going to the police. If you scoundrels had anything to do with this, you'll pay for it.

JOSEPH. Madame, if you go to the police, we'll have to tell them—

MME. PAROLE. Tell them what?

JOSEPH. That we saw you coming out of his bedroom after your rendevous.

MME. PAROLE. Rendezvous?

JULES. Madame, what were you doing in his bedroom?

MME. PAROLE (indicating Joseph). He told me . . .

JOSEPH. It'll make a fascinating story. So romantic!

JULES. Shocking affair! Noted financier expires in ecstasy!

MME. PAROLE. But . . .

JOSEPH. A happy death. Madame, you have nothing to reproach yourself for. You gave yourself to him to help your husband. Your husband will understand. Your husband stayed up all last night on the ships working for you. And you stayed up all night here working for him.

MME. PAROLE. How dare you?

JOSEPH. Back of every successful man is a devoted wife! Yes, we have quite a story to tell the police. Shall we go along with you? (He backs toward shop entrance)

MME. PAROLE (weakly). I'm not going to the police. I'm going home.

JOSEPH. By the way, I just remembered. You have a bill. Quite a large bill. It's time you paid.

MME. PAROLE. I'll take care of it. (She tries to leave. He stops her)

JOSEPH. How about a little something on account. (Eyeing her bag) I'll bet you have a few hundred francs there. Yesterday was payday for the Customs and you have a model husband. Turns his pay right over to you.

MME PAROLE. I haven't any money with me. (As she backs away from him, she runs into Jules)

JOSEPH. I'll bet you have. Let's look together.

(As she turns to look at Jules, Joseph seizes her bag.)

MME. PAROLE. How dare you?

JOSEPH. What'd you say?

MME. PAROLE. (frightened). Nothing. (As Joseph is going through the contents of the bag) I need that money. I've some shopping to do . . .

JOSEPH. Don't tell me this is the only shop that gives you credit!

MME. PAROLE. Certainly not!

JOSEPH (fishing out bills). I was right. Here we are. Three hundred francs. Congratulations, Madame. (Hands her the bag) I'll credit them to your account.

MME. PAROLE. But . . .

JOSEPH. Don't forget your cognac. (Gives her bottle) Keep it well corked and at room temperature. I recommend you use a snifter. Warm it with your hands to bring out the bouquet. And sip—don't swill!

(Mme Parole exits, into shop, bewildered, frightened. Jules and Joseph chuckle. Joseph places the money in the cash box in the bureau drawer.)

JULES (to Alfred). You'd better get Adolphe.

ALFRED. Right.

JOSEPH. Use a towel on Adolphe.

ALFRED. I'll handle Adolphe. (Exits)

JULES. Godspeed.

JOSEPH (going toward Jules). I say this objectively—Despite his sudden repentance, I think the world will be a better place without our dear uncle.

JULES (hands him his mug). Still we face the old, old problem—Does the end justify the means?

JOSEPH (puts mug on table). Of course.

JULES. I wonder.

JOSEPH. My philosophy is simple. If I perpetrate an outrage, it's justifiable. It's moral! It's noble! If someone else does it—it's an outrage.

(Alfred enters from Henri's bedroom.)

ALFRED. I can't find Adolphe!

JULES (galvanized). What?

JOSEPH. Did you look in the bed?

ALFRED. Of course.

Jules. We've got to find him.

ALFRED. I looked everywhere. The window is shut tight. He may have crawled back in here.

(Jules quickly rises and looks under chair cushion, then under the chair.)

JOSEPH. We can't leave Adolphe loose. The poor little thing has no judgment when he bites. How can he differentiate between good and evil without us to guide him?

ALFRED (anxiously). Maybe Adolphe crawled off somewhere—sick—maybe he's dying . . .

JOSEPH. It's possible. Our dear Uncle was highly indigestible, even for a snake. (All three are looking as Paul enters. Joseph and Alfred are on their knees. Jules is searching to the left.)

PAUL. Where are my . . .

JOSEPH (*sees him, straightens up*). We were just looking for a collar button.

PAUL (*stares at Alfred*). What the devil are you doing with my jacket?

JOSEPH. The valet was just brushing it, sir.

PAUL. Does he have to wear it to brush it?

JOSEPH. It's a quaint local custom he's acquired. Alfred, take the gentleman's clothes to his room. And while you're there, I suggest you look for the collar button. (*He undulates his hand at Alfred as he exits*)

PAUL. What collar button? Mine?

JOSEPH. No. A native product.

PAUL. I can't wait to get out of this damn country. (*Exits, following Alfred*)

JOSEPH (*going to ladder and climbing it*). It just occured to me. We should look in the rafters. Adolphe likes trees— maybe he likes rafters. If he's strolled out into the garden, we're going to have a sweet job finding him. (*Emilie enters.*)

EMILIE. Looking for something?

JOSEPH. Yes, Madame—a collar button.

EMILIE. On the ceiling?

JOSEPH. Like other laws, the law of gravity doesn't always work. (*Climbing down the ladder*) If you will excuse me, I will continue my exploration in the Garden of Eden, looking hither and thither for the source of all our human wisdom. (*Exits to garden*)

EMILIE (*takes cup and saucer from bureau*). What a strange man! Is M. Trochard still asleep?

JULES (*nodding*). Dead—to the world. (*She starts to sit in chair. Jules quickly stops her, picks up the chair, examines it, taps it on the floor, then, sure Adolphe is not on it, places the chair for Emilie to sit. She does. Jules continues to look for Adolphe.*)

EMILIE (*pouring her coffee*). You'll be leaving us today, won't you?

JULES. Yes, Madame. We'll be off soon—all four of us, I hope.

EMILIE: Four?

JULES. Adolphe, our pet.

EMILIE (*shuddering*). Oh! (*After pause, during which she pours coffee for him*) It's been interesting—your visit here.

JULES (*turns to her*). It's been interesting for us, too. (*Picks up his mug*)

EMILIE. I want you to know—I don't know how to say this—but I want you to know that I don't blame you for what you did. (*Jules listens, puzzled*) That isn't what I meant to say. About your wife, I mean. It may console you a little to know that others, too, have these impulses— wild, almost uncontrollable impulses. I had such an impulse last night, as I was trying to fall off to sleep.

JULES. You? You wanted to kill somebody?

EMILIE. Henri—M. Trochard.

JULES (*moving closer*). Him? You wanted to kill him? (*He begins laughing*)

EMILIE. Oh, I know you think me ridiculous.

JULES. Not a bit.

EMILIE. It's absurd, of course.

JULES. Of course. Just how did *you* plan to exterminate M. Trochard?

EMILIE. My crime was all in my mind.

JULES (*smiles*). Of course. No, you could never do it, Madame—under any circumstances. Think it? Yes. Perhaps even plan it. But actually do it . . . (*Shakes his head*)

EMILIE. Felix wouldn't even let himself think it. Poor Felix.

JULES. Why poor Felix? He's happy. And you're not unhappy.

EMILIE. I suppose not. I know that in a few hours, many dreadful things may happen. We may be shipped back to France, penniless, with no prospects, nothing. God knows what we'll do. But somehow, I find myself echoing Felix: "Things will work out somehow. There's always hope."

JULES. He is right. Hope is everything. Even we have hope. We hope to escape, although we know we'll never do it. We hope for a pardon, although we know we'll never get it.

EMILIE. You know, sometimes I can't help wondering if I wouldn't have made a better wife for a man who wasn't a child—someone who didn't believe in fairy tales—who depended not on others, but on himself—and a little on me.

JULES. Men like that have no reason to marry.

EMILIE. You did.

JULES. Me? I believed in fairy tales, too—and when I stumbled on reality, I killed. You know what *I* was thinking when *I* finally fell off to sleep last night?

EMILIE. What?

JULES. I was thinking—if I had married a woman like you—well, I wouldn't be here.

EMILIE *(touched, excited)*. More coffee?

JULES. Thank you. *(Extends his mug)*

EMILIE. I'm beginning to wonder what is the matter with me this morning. I'm really feeling, thinking, saying—the most absurd—ridiculous . . .

JULES. Thank you for saying them.

EMILIE. I'm beginning to believe I'm the romantic—not Felix.

JULES. Yes . . .

EMILIE. I'm really not myself.

JULES. Thank you for this Christmas— it'll be a treasured memory. A man in my position doesn't store up many memories—and you—when you get back home to your Brittany—to the kind of home you should have—all this will be an amusing story for a dull dinner party.

EMILIE. I don't see a future of dinner parties, dull, or otherwise.

JULES. Remember: Hope! Things will work out somehow. *(Paul enters)* Perhaps *he'll* work them out.

(Emilie looks up, startled. Jules gets cup and saucer from bureau, pours coffee and takes cup to Paul.)

PAUL *(kisses her hand)*. Good morning, Madame.

EMILIE. Paul, it's nice to see you.

PAUL. I'm sorry I missed you last night.

EMILIE. That's quite all right.

PAUL. That's a strange valet you have.

EMILIE. Valet?

JULES. Alfred!

PAUL. He's standing on the bed in his muddy sandals and staring at the ceiling.

JULES. He's looking for native wild life. He's a great student of nature.

(Felix enters.)

FELIX. Where—Where is Henri?

(Jules hands Felix cup and saucer. He puts it on table. Emilie pours.)

EMILIE. He's still asleep.

PAUL. Asleep? *(Puts cup on table)* But that's impossible.

EMILIE. Why?

PAUL. He never sleeps this late. *(Looks at his watch)* He's always up at six-thirty. No matter where he is. No matter how late it is when we go to bed. I don't understand it. *(Goes to Henri's door)* I'm sure he'd want me to wake him. He said he had a heavy schedule. *(Knocks on door)*

FELIX. Well . . . Why not let him sleep?

PAUL. Then he'll think *I* overslept. I'd better go in and see. *(Paul exits into Henri's room)*

EMILIE. I hope nothing's happened.

JULES. Do you?

FELIX. Beautiful day. *(Looks at thermometer)* Only 104.

(Alfred enters, shakes his head. Jules signals him to wait quietly. There is a pause before Paul enters, dazed.)

FELIX. What's the matter?

PAUL *(moving away from door)*. My uncle—is—is—dead.

(Emilie rises.)

ALFRED. Dead as a mackerel. But where the hell is . . .

(Jules quiets him quickly, as he goes to table, busies himself with arranging the dishes, on the tray. Alfred exits to garden.)

EMILIE *(rises)*. Paul . . .

FELIX. Dead . . .

PAUL. His heart . . . It must have been his heart!

JULES. Did he have one?

EMILIE. Felix!

PAUL. I don't understand it. His doctors said he would live to be ninety!

JULES. He can sue his doctors for breach of contract.

FELIX. I'd better . . . *(Goes into Henri' room)*

EMILIE. I can't believe it!

PAUL. I don't understand it. *(Follow Felix into room)*

EMILIE. I must be dreaming.

JULES. You see, Madame, it isn' necessary to kill. Fate always arrange for the triumph of good over evil.

EMILIE *(stunned)*. He's dead!

JULES. Uhuh! No need for violence— no guilt—no self-reproach!

EMILIE. I can't help feeling a little—guilt. For even thinking . . .

JULES. In civilized countries, thinking is not a crime.

(Felix enters, followed by Paul.)

EMILIE. I'm so confused I no longer know where I am.

FELIX. It's so . . . It's terrible.

EMILIE. I think I'll go to my room.

JULES. A very good idea.

FELIX. Of course, darling. *(She exits)* I'll get a doctor to take care of the formalities. Paul, will you stay here, my boy? *(Joseph enters from garden with Alfred. Jules goes to them)* I'll be back as soon as I can . . .

JOSEPH. I've just heard the news. We've lost a great man.

FELIX. I would never have forgiven myself if I'd deceived him last night.

JOSEPH. You were right. Once more we see that virtue is its own reward.

FELIX. Extraordinary. To die so suddenly. *(Felix exits into shop)*

JOSEPH. The Lord giveth, the Lord taketh away.

(He and Alfred look about, still seeking Adolphe. Paul starts toward Henri'sroom. As he reaches the door he becomes aware that the three convicts have their eyes on him.)

PAUL *(mopping his brow elegantly)*. What a thing to happen. I can't believe it. This is dreadful!

JULES. May I offer my sympathy?

PAUL. Thank you.

JOSEPH. Your uncle's death must be a great loss to you. I speak emotionally—not financially.

PAUL. Oh, yes . . .

JOSEPH. A great loss. *(Makes his way to bureau where he has left the forged note)* Oh, there seems to be a note here for you.

PAUL. For me?

JOSEPH. Here it is. *(Taking it to him)*

PAUL. Thank you. *(Takes it. Stares at writing)* From Uncle Henri?

JOSEPH. I wouldn't know. *(Paul opens envelope. Joseph watches him warily, then casually)* I hope you didn't mind our little joke last night?

PAUL *(absently, staring at note)*. Little joke?

JOSEPH. The episode in the garden—under the bougainvillea—the bench . . .

PAUL. Oh, not at all. *(Stares at letter)* It was very pleasant—very . . . *(His voice trails off as he studies letter, then crumples it and is about to tear it up)*

JOSEPH *(seizing his hand)*. That's no way to treat a letter from your Uncle Henri—and he barely cold in his bed.

(Jules and Alfred move to table.)

PAUL. Let me go . . .

JOSEPH. All communications from the deceased must be preserved. Have you no respect for the law? *(Straightens out the letter)* All communications! No matter how trivial . . . *(Pretends to study it)* And this doesn't seem trivial at all. Not at all! *(Gasps)* A dying man's last request—his last gasp. A voice from the grave!

JULES. Really?

PAUL. I'm—so upset naturally that—I didn't understand it . . . I . . .

(He gets up to reach for the letter, but Joseph passes it to Jules.)

JOSEPH. It's clear. *(To Jules)* It's clear to you, isn't it?

JULES *(pretending to read)*. I have a curious premonition . . . to restore to Felix Ducotel, my cousin . . . Be happy as I was not. Be honest, as I was not . . . *(Hands letter to Joseph)*

JOSEPH *(Glaring at Paul)*. Your fiancée's father! Cheating *him!* Cheating the dead! Sir, you're a cad!

ALFRED. With all that money he's inheriting! He wants more—the swine!

PAUL. I have every intention of respecting my uncle's wishes.

JOSEPH. Now that we have this codicil to his will securely in our possession!

PAUL. I won't contest it, I assure you. I repeat: I respect my uncle's wishes. If the document is genuine!

JOSEPH. If? You doubt this document?

ALFRED. What about Marie Louise?

PAUL. What about her?

ALFRED. Are you marrying her?

PAUL. I don't see how that concerns you.

JOSEPH *(stopping Alfred from attacking Paul)*. We went to some considerable trouble last night to smooth the path of love.

PAUL *(after pause)*. In this, as in all other matters, I shall be guided by my uncle's wishes.

JOSEPH. You realize, of course, that you're now free to do as you please.

PAUL. Yes.

JULES. You're rich—your own master . . .

PAUL. Yes.

JOSEPH. But Suzanne Audibert, whose complexion cleared up miraculously, still attracts you?

PAUL (after pause). Yes!

JOSEPH. Gentlemen, a strange thing has happened. His uncle didn't die after all. He lives on—in him!

PAUL. I find this conversation distasteful—and impertinent. Once and for all . . . My relations with Marie Louise are my business, not yours. I'm not free to do as I please . . . Wealth is a responsibility.

JULES (going toward him). Get out! Before I forget myself!

PAUL. What?

ALFRED. I'd like to bash his head in.

PAUL. You can't intimidate me. I'll report you.

JULES (ominously). Your uncle wanted to report us.

ALFRED. Yeah.

JULES. We don't like being reported.

ALFRED. No.

PAUL. I believe the authorities have ways and means of punishing scoundrels like you. I was planning to call on the Governor with my uncle. Now I'll go alone, and tell him how his convicts behave. As for that—forgery . . .

JOSEPH. Forgery?

PAUL. Suddenly a note appears a moment after my uncle's death. Suddenly! Suddenly he's repentant. I'll tell you what I think. I think you concocted this little scheme. And if M. Ducotel was a party to this, and I suspect he was, you may tell him I shall demand an official inquiry. Handwriting experts. And you can also tell him I'm going to have his books audited. A man capable of forgery is capable of embezzlement! Now, with your permission, I'm going to pay my respects to the dead.

(Exits into Henri's room. There is a long silence, during which Jules moves to right of table, Joseph moves to above table, Alfred goes to door of Henri's room, glaring.)

JULES. Shall we hold another trial?

JOSEPH. Now, please, not two accidents!

ALFRED. Why not?

JOSEPH. We'll never get away with it. Besides we've lost our executioner.

ALFRED. I'll do this job myself.

JULES. No, Alfred. Don't lose your head.

JOSEPH. No! Very distasteful business —the guillotine.

ALFRED. He doesn't deserve to live.

JOSEPH. That isn't the issue. The issue is: Do we deserve to live? The answer, in my slightly prejudiced opinion, is: yes.

JULES. At least we want to—even in solitary.

ALFRED. I'll do it all by myself. You won't be involved.

JOSEPH. They won't believe you.

JULES. And even if they did—we don't want to lose you. We belong together— we three.

ALFRED. All our work down the drain!

JULES. We tried.

JOSEPH. We failed. We've learned that virtue is not its own reward.

JULES. And that good does not always triumph over evil!

JOSEPH. For us, Christmas is over. We pack away the tinsel—store the tree— sweep away the debris—and complain vaguely of indigestion.

(Paul enters quickly, holding his hand.)

PAUL. Call a doctor. Quick!

JULES. What's the matter?

PAUL. For Heaven's sake!

JOSEPH. What's wrong?

PAUL. I've just been bitten by a snake.

JOSEPH. What'd you say?

JULES. He said he'd just been bitten by a snake.

ALFRED (beaming). How? Where?

PAUL. What does it matter? It hurts. A doctor!

JOSEPH (going to him). Was it a little snake?

PAUL. Yes . . .

JOSEPH (quickly). On the floor?

PAUL. No.

JOSEPH (more quickly). On the bed?

PAUL. No!

JOSEPH. On the dresser?

PAUL. No!

JOSEPH. On the ceiling?

PAUL. No! In his trousers—in the pocket!

JOSEPH. What were you doing with your hand in your uncle's pocket?

JULES. He was taking inventory!

(*Alfred and Jules laugh. During the following, Paul's pain and discomfort increase.*)

JOSEPH. This is no laughing matter. The young man's shown admirable industry—and thrift. His uncle may have had cash stowed away in his pockets—possibly only a few sous—rich men generally pride themselves on never carrying cash so that others will always pay their dinner checks, their cab fares, their tips— but the young man overlooks nothing!

PAUL. I want a doctor!

JOSEPH. Why waste your money?

PAUL. I don't feel well.

(*Joseph, Jules and Alfred in a whispered conference.*)

JOSEPH. Damn nuisance to have him die in here.

JULES. Of course. Marie Louise'll be back soon. Imagine the shock. We've got to prepare her—and the family . . .

PAUL. What are you talking about? (*Starts toward shop entrance. Grabs on to ladder for support*) I want a doctor, I tell you.

JOSEPH. I have it. The garden! Let him die in the garden.

(*Alfred goes to door of Henri's room.*)

JULES. Good. We'll take him to the bench.

JOSEPH. Yes, the bench—the same bench as last night . . .

(*Joseph and Jules walk Paul to the gate.*)

PAUL. You're always sending me to that damn bench!

(*The three exit into garden. Alfred, with the coconut cage, goes into Henri's room. Marie Louise enters from the shop. She looks about. Alfred reappears. He hides the cage behind him.*)

MARIE LOUISE. Oh, you're still here.

ALFRED. Yes . . .

MARIE LOUISE. Where's Paul?

ALFRED. Oh, here and there . . .

MARIE LOUISE. Is he—very upset?

ALFRED. Well, yes. I should say that Paul is very upset.

MARIE LOUISE. I met Father coming out of church. He told me.

ALFRED. Told you?

MARIE LOUISE. Don't you know— about Uncle Henri?

ALFRED. Oh, that one! Yes.

MARIE LOUISE. How awful!

ALFRED. I don't see why you should go into mourning—considering.

MARIE LOUISE. You don't understand. I said: How awful—because I should feel sorry, and I don't. Why are you staring at me?

ALFRED. Staring? No. I was just thinking of what you just said. (*Joseph and Jules enter from garden*) You know, you might think you're losing something, when you're really not. Sometimes you can be in love with something that doesn't even exist.

MARIE LOUISE. Well . . . (*Looks to Joseph and Jules for help*)

MARIE LOUISE. What's happened? Where's Paul? Are you trying to hint he—he doesn't love me? Is that it? Now that he's free, he doesn't want me. Is that it?

JOSEPH. He wants—and loves you madly.

JULES. As much as you love him.

JOSEPH. He said something to us this morning that you should know.

MARIE LOUISE. What?

JOSEPH. He said: "Gentlemen," he said, "death has made me free to marry my adorable Marie Louise, and only death can part us now."

MARIE LOUISE. He said that?

JULES. Even more eloquently.

JOSEPH. If that's conceivable. He said—and these were his very words: "She doesn't realize how shy I am. How can I tell her nothing in this world matters as much to me as her love? Ambition? Wealth? Pouf!"

JULES (*snaps fingers*). "For her," he said, "I'd dig ditches . . ."

JOSEPH. "Or pick pockets . . ."

JULES. Yes.

MARIE LOUISE. This is amazing. He's so reserved—generally—and he confided in *you.*

JOSEPH. The shock of his uncle's death —you know. He had to talk to someone.

MARIE LOUISE. And I wasn't here. Where is he?

JULES. I think he's with your mother.

MARIE LOUISE. Excuse me . . . *(She exits)*

ALFRED *(puts the cage on bureau)*. What's the idea?

JULES. It's a civilized custom to praise the dead. It helps the living.

JOSEPH. We wanted to give her a memorial. She'll need one.

JULES. Time will heal the wound. Let her at least cherish a memory.

JOSEPH. She's young. Someone'll come along. Someone always does.

JULES. It won't be you, Alfred, unfortunately. It could have been. It'll be someone else.

JOSEPH. The bell will ring—and there he'll be.

JULES. She won't love him as much as the mythical Paul—but she'll love him enough.

(Shop doorbell rings. The three start. Joseph rises, moves to Alfred. But it is Felix who enters, hangs up hat.)

FELIX. What a time I've had. The doctor'll be along soon.

JOSEPH. Good. He has his work cut out for him.

FELIX. My wife still in her room?

JULES. Yes.

FELIX. I thought last night I'd be spending an entirely different kind of Christmas. Life is strange.

JULES. Isn't it?

FELIX *(cheerfully)*. Things work out somehow . . . *(Stops)* What am I saying? *(Guiltily)* I've got to see my wife. *(Exits)*

ALFRED. Well, back to the roof!

JULES. I guess so.

JOSEPH. It's too much to ask destiny to send along the young man we're waiting for at this precise moment. Still it would have been neater somehow. *(The shop bell rings. They look at each other, then step up toward the shop entrance, stop and wait. An extremely handsome young man in white naval uniform enters. They stare at him)* Yes?

LIEUTENANT. I beg your pardon, but there was no one in the shop. This is M. Ducotel's, isn't it?

JULES. It is.

LIEUTENANT. I suppose you work for him.

JOSEPH. We do.

LIEUTENANT. I've just landed, and I have a letter of introduction from friends in Cherbourg. May I see him?

JOSEPH. Forgive a question, sir. Are you married?

LIEUTENANT. I beg your pardon?

ALFRED. Well, are you?

LIEUTENANT. No. Why?

JULES. We were just wondering.

JOSEPH. You'll have to make certain allowances—have little patience—You've chosen a rather peculiar time to appear.

LIEUTENANT. Peculiar?

JOSEPH. There's been a death here . . .

JULES. Two, in fact . . .

LIEUTENANT. I'm sorry to hear that.

JOSEPH. You needn't be.

LIEUTENANT. Perhaps I could come back later.

JOSEPH. Oh, no, no. Don't move.

JULES. Life's too short. Have a chair.

LIEUTENANT. But . . .

JOSEPH. Sit down, sir.

(The Lieutenant moves toward the chair. Marie Louise enters and as she moves toward the garden comes face to face with the young man.)

MARIE LOUISE *(seeing stranger)*. Pardon me . . . *(Crosses to gate below table. The Lieutenant turns to watch her)* Why didn't you tell me Paul was in the garden? There he is. He's sitting out there on the bench. He looks as if he's fallen asleep. *(Turns to the three convicts)* waiting for me . . .

JOSEPH. It's nice to know someone's waiting for you. *(Looks at Lieutenant)*

MARIE LOUISE *(smiles)*. Yes. *(She exits to garden)*

LIEUTENANT. Was that Mademoiselle Ducotel?

JOSEPH. Uhuh.

LIEUTENANT. She's charming!

ALFRED *(turns to him)*. Yes, she is.

JOSEPH. You're charming, too.

LIEUTENANT. I beg your pardon?

JOSEPH. You even look intelligent, which is more than we'd hoped for.

(The harmonica is heard playing in the garden.)

LIEUTENANT. Well, now, really!

JULES. Sit down. Relax. Close your eyes. You've got nothing to do—except wait.

(Alfred picks up his hat at foot of ladder then goes to bureau.)

LIEUTENANT. If I closed my eyes, I'd be asleep in a minute. I was up all night on the ship.

JOSEPH. Well, then, sleep, sir. Sleep. *(Harmonica more distinct)* There's your lullaby.

(Lieutenant closes his eyes. Jules gets his hat from box, Joseph gets his from table under the mirror, and both move to ladder. When there, the three turn back for one last look at the sleeping Lieutenant. Felix enters, followed by Emilie.)

FELIX *(staring)*. Who's he?

JOSEPH. The future.

(Marie Louise's cry is heard.)

EMILIE. Marie Louise! *(Moves toward garden, exits, followed by Felix)*

JOSEPH. She's found happiness—and doesn't know it. She's only twenty, and she doesn't realize happiness wears many disguises. *(Looks at Lieutenant, who hasn't stirred)*

ALFRED *(picks up cage from bureau)*. Come, Adolphe.

JOSEPH *(staring up the ladder)*. Well, Your Honor, didn't we have a wonderful Christmas?

JULES. Yes, we did.

JOSEP. Let's do it again next year.

The three angels climb up the ladder as

THE CURTAIN FALLS

JEAN GIRAUDOUX's

Ondine

In the adaptation by MAURICE VALENCY

First presented by the Playwrights' Company at the Forty-Sixth Street Theatre, New York, on February 18, 1954, with the following cast:

AUGUSTE.....................John Alexander

EUGENIE..........................Edith King

RITTER HANS......................Mel Ferrer

ONDINE ....Audrey Hepburn

THE ONDINES, Dran Seitz, Tani Seitz, Sonia Torgeson

THE OLD ONE................Robert Middleton

THE LORD CHAMBERLAIN............Alan Hewitt

THE SUPERINTENDENT OF THE THEATRE Lloyd Gough

THE TRAINER OF SEALS..........James Lanphier

BERTHA........................Marian Seldes

BERTRAM ....Peter Brandon

VIOLANTE ....Anne Meacham

ANGELIQUE......................Gaye Jordan

VENUS ....Jan Sherwood

MATHO........................Barry O'Hara

SALAMMBO ....Lily Paget

A LORD ....William Le Massena

A LADY........................Stacy Graham

THE ILLUSIONIST (THE OLD ONE) Robert Middleton

THE KING...................William Podmore

A SERVANT.....................James Lanphier

THE FIRST FISHERMAN ....Lloyd Gough

THE SECOND FISHERMAN (THE OLD ONE)
Robert Middleton

THE FIRST JUDGE..................Alan Hewitt

THE SECOND JUDGE..........William Le Massena

THE EXECUTIONER..............Robert Crawley

THE KITCHEN MAID ....Stacy Graham

Directed by Alfred Lunt
Settings by Peter Larkin
Costumes by Richard Whorf
Lighting by Jean Rosenthal
Music by Virgil Thomson

ACT ONE

A fisherman's hut near a lake in the forest. The living room has a fireplace, a door that leads into the kitchen, and a door that leads out into the forest. The windows are shuttered. There is a table near the fireplace, with a bench next to it and a heavy wooden chair next to the fire, which is blazing. It is night. A storm is raging.

Two old people, Auguste and Eugenie, are in the room. Eugenie is setting the table. Auguste is at the window. He has opened the shutters and is peering out into the storm.

————

AUGUSTE. What can she be doing out there at this hour?

EUGENIE. Don't worry about her. She can see in the dark.

AUGUSTE. In this storm!

EUGENIE. She's quite safe. The rain doesn't wet her.

AUGUSTE. She's singing. Is it she that's singing? You think that's her voice?

EUGENIE. Whose else? There is no other house within twenty leagues.

AUGUSTE. Now it comes from the top of the waterfall and now from the middle of the lake.

EUGENIE. Because now she's on top of the waterfall and now in the middle of the lake.

AUGUSTE. It's all so simple, isn't it? But did you, by any chance, ever amuse yourself by diving down the waterfalls in the nude when you were her age?

EUGENIE. Yes. Once. They fished me out by the feet. Every girl tries just once to do what Ondine does fifty times a day. I jumped into the whirlpool once, and I tried to catch the waterfall once in a bowl, and once I tried to walk on the water. It seems very long ago.

AUGUSTE. You've spoiled her, Eugenie. A girl of sixteen has no business running around in the forest in the dark in a storm. A well brought-up girl does not insist on doing her sewing on the brink of a waterfall. She doesn't insist on saying her prayers under water. Where would we be today if you had been brought up like that?

EUGENIE. She's very helpful with the housework.

AUGUSTE. That brings up another question.

EUGENIE. Doesn't she wash the dishes? Doesn't she clean your boots?

AUGUSTE. I don't know. Does she?

EUGENIE. It's not clean, this dish?

AUGUSTE. That's not the point. Have you ever, in all her life, seen her cleaning or washing anything?

EUGENIE. What difference does it make whether or not I've seen her? She gets it done.

AUGUSTE. Yes. But explain this—three dishes or twelve, one shoe or eight, it takes her exactly the same time to do them. She takes them out; she's hardly gone a minute, and she's back. The dishcloth is dry. The shoe polish hasn't been used. But everything is clean, everything sparkles. And that affair of the golden plates on her birthday—did you ever get to the bottom of that? And her hands. Why are they never soiled, like anyone else's?

EUGENIE. Because she's not like anyone else. She's never been like anyone else.

AUGUSTE. Today she lifted the gate of the trout pond. All the trout are gone. All but the one I brought home for supper. Are you going to broil it? *(The windows spring open suddenly)* Who did that?

EUGENIE. The wind, Auguste.

AUGUSTE. I hope she doesn't start that performance again with the lightning, and those horrible heads that peer in at the window out of the storm. The old man with the crown—oh!

EUGENIE. I love the woman with the pearls. Well, bar the window if you're afraid.

(Auguste crosses to close the windows. There is a flash of lightning. The head of an old man with a crown and a streaming beard appears in the window frame.)

THE HEAD. No use, Auguste. No lock so strong, no bar so stout will serve to keep the old one out! *(He vanishes, laughing, in a clap of thunder)*

AUGUSTE. I'll show you if it's too late, Ondine. *(He closes the window. It immediately bursts open. There appears, in another lightning flash, a charming naiad's head with a necklace of pearls)*

THE NAIAD. Good evening, Eugenie!

(It vanishes)

EUGENIE. Ondine, you're annoying your father. It's time to come in.

AUGUSTE. Ondine, I'm going to count up to three. If you're not inside when I finish, I'll bolt the door. And you can sleep out.

(There is a roar of thunder.)

EUGENIE. You're not serious?

AUGUSTE. You'll see if I'm serious. Ondine, one!

(A roar of thunder.)

EUGENIE. Stop it, Auguste. It's deafening.

AUGUSTE. Am I doing it?

EUGENIE. Well, then, hurry. We all know you can count up to three.

AUGUSTE. Ondine, two!

(Thunder. Eugenie covers her ears.)

EUGENIE. Really, Auguste, I don't see the use—

AUGUSTE. Ondine, three!

EUGENIE *(waiting for the thunder)*. Well, well, finish, Auguste, finish—

(There is no thunder.)

AUGUSTE. I've finished. *(He bolts the door)* There. I'd like to see anyone come in now.

(The door springs open. They turn in terror. A knight in full armor stands on the threshold. He holds his helmet under his arm.)

RITTER HANS *(clicking his heels)*. Ritter Hans von Wittenstein zu Wittenstein.

AUGUSTE *(bows)*. My name is Auguste. I am a fisherman.

RITTER HANS. I took the liberty of putting my horse in your shed. The horse, as we know, is the most important part of the knight-errant. And the most sensitive.

AUGUSTE. I'll go and rub him down at once, my lord.

HANS. Thanks very much. I've already done it. I make it an invariable rule, away from home, to rub down my horse myself. In these parts, you rub horses down Swabian fashion, against the grain—the coat soon loses its luster. May I sit down?

AUGUSTE. The house is yours, my lord.

HANS *(sets down his helmet and puts by his sword)*. What a storm! The water has been running down my neck steadily since noon. Of course it doesn't stay. It runs out again through the blood gutters. But once it gets in, the damage is done. *(He sits down ponderously)* That's what we fear most, we knightserrant, the rain. The water. And, of course, a flea. Once a flea gets in here—

AUGUSTE. Would you care to remove your armor, my lord?

HANS. My dear Auguste, have you ever watched a lobster shed his carapace? Then you know it's not the affair of a moment. I will rest first. You said your name was Auguste, I believe?

AUGUSTE. And my wife, Eugenie.

HANS *(bows to Eugenie)*. Ah. Auguste and Eugenie. Charming names.

EUGENIE. Excuse them, my lord. They are not names for knights-errant.

HANS. Dear Eugenie, when a knight-errant has spent a month in the forest, searching in vain for Osmond and Pharamond, you cannot imagine his joy when he comes suddenly at dinner time upon Auguste and Eugenie.

EUGENIE. Thank you, my lord. It's ill-mannered, I know, to annoy a guest with questions, but perhaps you will forgive this one: are you hungry?

HANS. I am hungry. I am extremely hungry. It will give me great pleasure to share your meal.

EUGENIE. We have already supped, my lord. But there is a trout. Would you honor us by eating it?

HANS. With the greatest pleasure.

EUGENIE. Would you like it broiled or fried?

HANS. Poached, if you please.

(Auguste and Eugenie make a gesture of fear.)

EUGENIE. Poached? I really do them best *sautée, meunière*, with a little white butter. It's very good.

HANS. Since you ask my preference—

AUGUSTE. *Gratinée*, perhaps with fresh cream? Eugenie's specialty.

HANS. When we say poached—that's when the fish is thrown into the boiling water alive?

EUGENIE. Yes. Alive.

HANS. So that the fish retains all its tenderness because the heat takes it by surprise?

AUGUSTE. Surprise is the word, my lord.

HANS. Then that's it. I'll have it poached.

EUGENIE *(walks slowly to the kitchen. She turns at the door)*. Broiled, they're very nice, with a slice of lemon—

HANS. Poached, if you please. *(Eugenie goes into the kitchen. Hans makes himself comfortable in the chair by the fireside)* I'm happy to see, Auguste, that knights-errant are not unwelcome in these parts . . . ?

AUGUSTE. Much more welcome than armies, my lord. When the winter is over, the robins come; when the wars are over, the knights. A knight-errant is a sign of peace.

HANS. I love war.

AUGUSTE. Each to his taste, my lord.

HANS. Don't misunderstand me. *(Expansively)* If I love war, it's because by nature I'm a friendly person. I love company. Now in a war, you always have someone to talk to. If your comrades don't feel like chatting, there's always the enemy—you can always get yourself a prisoner. He shows you his wife's picture. You tell him about your sister. That's what I call living. But a knight-errant . . . ! Would you believe it, in all the time I've spent riding about this enchanted forest, I haven't so much as heard a human voice.

AUGUSTE. But isn't it true that knights-errant can understand the language of animals?

HANS. Ah, yes, that's true enough—they speak to us, the animals. And we understand them very well. But it's not quite what you think, the language of animals. For us every animal is a symbol, naturally, and its message is written indelibly on our souls. But that's it, you see, the animals write—they don't speak.

AUGUSTE. They don't speak?

HANS. They speak without speaking. What they say is important, of course. The stag speaks to us of nobility. The unicorn, of chastity. The lion, of courage. It's stimulating—but you don't call that a conversation.

AUGUSTE. But the birds . . . ?

HANS. To tell you the truth, Auguste, I'm a little disappointed in the birds. They chatter incessantly. But they're not good listeners. They're always preaching.

AUGUSTE. That surprises me. Especially with the lark. I should have thought that the lark would love to confide in one.

HANS. The knight's headgear does not permit him to converse with larks.

AUGUSTE. But what sent you, if I may ask, into the black forest?

HANS. What do you suppose? A woman.

AUGUSTE. I ask no more questions, my lord.

HANS. Please, Auguste! It's thirty days since I've said a word about her to a living soul. No, no, ask me questions. Ask me anything. Ask me her name.

AUGUSTE. My lord—I wouldn't dare.

HANS. Ask me. Ask me.

AUGUSTE. What is her name, my lord?

HANS. Bertha. Bertha! Tell me, fisherman, have you ever heard such a beautiful name? Bertha!

AUGUSTE. It's beautiful, my lord.

HANS. There are those who are called Angelique, Diane, Violante. Anybody can be called Angelique, Diane, Violante. But she alone deserves a name so solemn, vibrating, passionate: Bertha! *(Eugenie comes in with a loaf of bread)* And now, Eugenie, you will ask me is she beautiful?

EUGENIE. Is she beautiful?

AUGUSTE. We are speaking of Bertha, the Princess Bertha, Eugenie.

EUGENIE. Ah, yes, of course. And is she beautiful?

HANS. Eugenie, it is I who am entrusted with the purchase of horses for the king. You understand, then, my eye is sharp. No blemish, however slight, ever escapes me. The Angelique in question is not bad, but she has a ridge in her left thumbnail. Violante has a fleck of gold in her eye. Bertha is flawless.

AUGUSTE. That must be a lovely thing to see, a fleck of gold in a woman's eye.

EUGENIE. Stick to your fishing, Auguste.

HANS. A fleck of gold? Don't deceive yourself, my dear fellow. That might amuse you, a thing like that, two days at the most—

AUGUSTE. What is it like, exactly?

HANS. Well, it sparkles.

AUGUSTE. Like a grain of mica?

EUGENIE. Come, Auguste—you're getting on our nerves with your gold and your mica. Let the knight speak.

HANS. Yes, my dear Auguste, why this sudden partiality for Violante? Violante, when she joins with us in the hunt, crowns a white mare. And it's a pretty sight, a red-headed girl on a white mare, there's no denying it. And Violante, when she brings the queen the three-branched candlestick, always bears it high in both hands, like the celebrant approaching the altar. But Violante, when the old Duke takes her hand and tells her a spicy story, never laughs. She cries.

AUGUSTE. Violante cries?

HANS. I know. You are going to ask me what happens to these flecks of gold when they are drowned in tears—

EUGENIE. He's surely thinking of it, my lord. Once he gets his mind on anything . . . !

HANS. Yes, he will think of it till the day when he sees Bertha. For you shall certainly come to our wedding, both of you. You are invited. The condition Bertha made to our marriage was that I should come back alive after spending a month in the forest. And if I do come back, it will be thanks to you, my friends. And so, you shall see your Violante, fisherman, with her little red mouth and her pink ears and her little straight nose, you shall see what effect she makes next to my great dark angel! And now, fetch me my poached trout, Eugenie, or it will be overdone.

(The door opens slowly. Ondine appears on the threshold. She stands there motionless for a moment.)

AUGUSTE. Ondine!

ONDINE. How beautiful he is!

AUGUSTE. What did she say?

ONDINE. I said, how beautiful he is!

AUGUSTE. It is our daughter, my lord. She has no manners.

ONDINE. It's thrilling to know that men are so beautiful. My heart is racing.

AUGUSTE. Will you keep still?

ONDINE. I'm trembling from head to foot.

AUGUSTE. She's only sixteen, my lord.

ONDINE. I knew there must be some reason for being a girl. The reason is that men are so beautiful.

AUGUSTE. You are embarrassing our guest, Ondine.

ONDINE. I'm not embarrassing him. He likes me. What's your name?

AUGUSTE. That's not the way to speak to a knight, my child.

ONDINE *(coming closer)*. Look at his ear, Father. It's a perfect little shell. Do you expect me to treat it like a stranger? To whom do you belong, little shell? What is his name?

HANS. His name is Hans.

ONDINE. I should have guessed it. When people are happy and they open their mouths, they say Hans.

HANS. Hans von Wittenstein.

ONDINE. When there is sun in the morning, and the cloud of sadness lifts from your soul, when you sigh, you say Hans.

HANS. Hans von Wittenstein zu Wittenstein.

ONDINE. How lovely when a name makes its own echo! Why have you come, Hans? To take me away?

AUGUSTE. That will do, Ondine. Go to your room now.

ONDINE. Very well, take me. Take me with you.

(Eugenie comes in with the trout on a platter.)

EUGENIE. Here is your trout, my lord.

ONDINE. His trout!

HANS. It looks magnificent.

ONDINE. You dared to poach a trout, Mother?

EUGENIE. Be quiet. In any case, it's done.

ONDINE. Oh, my poor darling trout! You who loved the cold water! What have they done to you?

AUGUSTE. You're not going to make a scene before our guest, Ondine?

ONDINE. They caught you—and they quenched your life in boiling water!

HANS. It was I, my girl, who asked them to.

ONDINE. You? I should have known. When one looks closely at your face, it all becomes clear. You're not very bright, are you? No. You are stupid.

EUGENIE. She doesn't know what she's saying, my lord.

ONDINE. That's chivalry! That's courage! You run about looking for giants who don't exist, and when you come upon a little joyous creature springing in the clear water, you boil it alive.

HANS. And I eat it. And I find it delicious.

ONDINE. You shall see how delicious it is! *(She snatches up the dish and throws it out of the window)* Now eat it! *(She runs to the door.)*

AUGUSTE. Ondine!

EUGENIE. Where are you going, child?

ONDINE. There is someone out there who knows about men. So far I have refused to listen to him. Now that's over. I shall listen.

AUGUSTE. Ondine!

ONDINE. In a moment, I shall know. I shall know what they are, what they do, what they become. And so much the worse for you!

AUGUSTE. You're not going out.

(She springs aside.)

ONDINE. I already know that they lie, that their beauty is ugliness, that their courage is cowardice. And I already know that I hate them.

HANS. And they already know that they love you.

ONDINE *(stops at the door, without turning)*. What did he say?

HANS. Nothing.

ONDINE. Say it once more, just to see.

HANS. They already know that they love you.

ONDINE. I hate them! *(She runs out into the darkness.)*

HANS. My compliments. You've brought her up well.

AUGUSTE. God knows I scold her often enough.

HANS. You should beat her.

EUGENIE. Beat her? Try and catch her.

HANS. You should send her to bed without supper.

AUGUSTE. What good would that do? She's never hungry.

HANS. I'm starved.

AUGUSTE. That was the last of the trout, my lord. But we have smoked a ham. Eugenie will go down and cut you some slices.

HANS. Then she permits you to kill her poor darling pigs?

AUGUSTE. She has no interest in pigs.

HANS. That's a mercy.

(Eugenie goes out for the ham.)

AUGUSTE. You are annoyed with the girl, my lord.

HANS. I'm annoyed because I'm vain just as she said. When she said I was handsome, though I know I'm not handsome, I was pleased. And when she said I was a coward, though I know I'm no coward, I was hurt. I'm annoyed with myself.

AUGUSTE. You're very kind to take it so well.

HANS. Oh, I don't take it well at all. I'm furious.

(Eugenie comes in.)

EUGENIE. Where is the ham, Auguste? I can't find it.

AUGUSTE. The ham? Why, the ham is hanging in the cellar. Excuse me, my lord, I'll go and get it.

(He goes out with Eugenie. Hans turns to the fire and warms his hands. Ondine comes in noiselessly and stands just behind him. He doesn't hear her till she speaks.)

ONDINE. My name is Ondine.

HANS *(without turning)*. It's a pretty name.

ONDINE. Hans and Ondine. There are no more beautiful names in the world, are there?

HANS. Yes. Ondine and Hans.

ONDINE. Oh no. Hans first. He is the man. He commands. Ondine is the girl. She is always one step behind. She keeps quiet.

HANS. She keeps quiet? Now how the devil does she manage that?

ONDINE. Hans is always one step ahead. In the processions—before the king—before all the world, he goes first. He is the first to age. He is the first to die. It's terrible! But Ondine follows at once. She kills herself.

HANS. What are you talking about?

ONDINE. There is the little moment of agony to live through. The moment that comes after the death of Hans. But it is short.

HANS. At your age, luckily, it doesn't mean much to talk about death.

ONDINE. At my age? Is that what you think? Very well, try—*(She pulls his dagger from its sheath)* Here, kill yourself. You'll see if I am not dead the next moment.

HANS *(takes the dagger from her hand)*. I never felt less like killing myself.

ONDINE. Say you don't love me. You'll see if I don't die.

HANS. Fifteen minutes ago, you didn't even know I existed. And now you want to kill yourself on my account. I thought we had quarreled on account of the trout.

ONDINE. Oh, I can't be bothered with the trout. They're not very clever, the trout. If they don't like to be caught, all they have to do is to keep away from men. It's different with me. I want to be caught.

HANS. In spite of your mysterious friend outside?

ONDINE. I learned nothing from him that I didn't already know.

HANS. Naturally not. You asked the questions. You gave the answers.

ONDINE. Don't joke. He's very near. And he's very dangerous.

HANS. Who?

ONDINE. The Old One.

HANS. The Old One?

ONDINE. The King of the Sea. I'm afraid, Hans.

HANS *(smiles)*. You're afraid of what?

ONDINE. I'm afraid you will deceive me. That's what he said. He also said you were not handsome. But you are!

HANS. Do you know that you're beautiful?

ONDINE. No, I don't know it yet. I would prefer to be beautiful. But I can be beautiful only if you love me.

HANS. You're a little liar. You were just as beautiful a moment ago when you hated me. Is that all he told you?

ONDINE. He said that if ever I kissed you, I would be lost. That was silly of him. I hadn't even thought of it till then.

HANS. And now you are thinking of it?

ONDINE. Very much.

HANS. Well, there is no harm in thinking.

ONDINE. Oh no. It's good to think about it. Of course, in the end I shall do it. But first we shall wait a long time, as long as possible. We shall wait an hour. Then in after years we shall have this hour always to remember. The hour before you kissed me.

HANS. My little Ondine—

ONDINE. The hour before you said you loved me. Hans, I can't wait an hour. There isn't time. Tell me now.

HANS. You think that's something one says—just like that?

ONDINE. No? Well, then speak, command. What must I do? What is the appropriate posture? Do I sit in your lap, is that it?

HANS. In my lap in full armor?

ONDINE. Oh. Take it off quickly.

HANS. Do you know what you're saying? It takes me fifteen minutes to unbolt the shoulder-plates alone.

ONDINE. I have a way of removing armor.

(The armor falls to the floor.)

HANS. Well!

ONDINE. Sit down. *(He sits. She springs into his lap)*

HANS. You're mad, Ondine!

ONDINE. Yes. That's what he said.

HANS. And my arms—do you think they open to the first comer?

ONDINE. I have a way of opening arms—

(Hans opens his arms, with an expression of surprise.)

And of closing them.

(He closes them. A woman's voice is heard outside the window.)

THE VOICE. Ondine!

ONDINE *(turns furiously to the window)*. No! Go away. Nobody called you.

THE VOICE. Ondine! Be careful!

ONDINE. Do I meddle in your affairs? Did you consult me about your husband?

THE VOICE. Ondine!

ONDINE. A fine handsome husband you found yourself, wasn't it? A seal with nostrils like rabbit holes and no nose. He gave you a string of pearls and you were his. And not even matched pearls.

HANS. To whom are you speaking, Ondine?

ONDINE. Oh, one of the neighbors.

HANS. But I saw no other house in the forest. Do you have neighbors?

ONDINE. Thousands. And all jealous.

A SECOND VOICE. Ondine! Be careful!

ONDINE. Oh, you're a fine one to

speak! You were careful, weren't you? A narwhal dazzled you with his jet of water, and you gave yourself to him without a word.

THE SECOND VOICE. Ondine!

HANS. Their voices are charming.

ONDINE. My name is charming, not their voices. Kiss me, Hans. Kiss me.

A MAN'S VOICE. Ondine!

ONDINE. It's too late, Old One. Let me alone.

HANS. Is that the friend?

ONDINE. I'm sitting in his lap. He loves me.

THE MAN'S VOICE. Ondine!

ONDINE. It's too late, I say. It's finished. I'm already his mistress. Yes, his mistress. You don't understand? That's another word they have for wife.

(There is a noise at the kitchen door.)

HANS (pushing Ondine gently from his lap). That's your father, Ondine.

ONDINE. Oh. I didn't think I had taught you that?

HANS. What?

ONDINE. My way of opening arms.

(Auguste and Eugenie come in.)

EUGENIE. Your supper is almost ready, my lord.

AUGUSTE. I can't imagine who put the ham in the attic.

ONDINE. I did. So I could be alone with Hans.

AUGUSTE. Ondine! Have you no shame?

ONDINE. I've not wasted my time. He's going to marry me.

AUGUSTE. You might help your mother with the table instead of talking nonsense.

ONDINE. You're right. Give me the silver, Mother. From now on, it's I who will serve Hans.

AUGUSTE. I brought up a bottle of wine, my lord. If you permit, we shall drink a glass with you. The glasses, Ondine.

ONDINE. You will have to teach me everything, my lord Hans. From morning to night, I shall be your handmaid. In the morning I shall wake you . . .

HANS. You won't find that easy. I sleep very soundly.

ONDINE (sits down next to him and looks at him closely). Tell me, what does one do to awaken you?

(Eugenie comes out with a platter.)

EUGENIE. The glasses, Ondine.

ONDINE. Oh Mother, you set the table. Hans is teaching me how to awaken him. Let's see, Hans. Make believe you're asleep.

HANS. With this wonderful odor of cooking? Out of the question.

ONDINE. Wake up, little Hans. It's dawn. Take this kiss in your darkness and this in your day . . .

HANS (accepting a slice of ham). Thank you.

AUGUSTE. Pay no attention to the child, my lord. She doesn't know what she is saying.

ONDINE. I love you.

EUGENIE. She's young. She becomes attached. It's nothing.

ONDINE. I love you, Hans.

HANS (eating). This is what I call ham!

AUGUSTE. It's smoked with juniper.

HANS. Marvelous.

ONDINE. It was a mistake to awaken you, Hans. We should never awaken the man we love. In his sleep, he's ours completely. But the moment he opens his eyes, he escapes. Sleep again, little Hans—

HANS (accepting another slice). Yes, thank you. Simply wonderful.

ONDINE. You don't want to be loved, you want to be stuffed.

HANS. Everything in its place, my dear.

EUGENIE. Ah, you'd make a fine wife, you would!

ONDINE. I?

AUGUSTE. Silence, Ondine. I want to say a word. (He lifts his glass)

ONDINE. I shall certainly make a fine wife. You think you're a wife because you know how to cook a ham? That's not being a wife.

HANS. No? What else is it?

ONDINE. It's to be everything your husband is and everything he loves. It's to be the humblest part of him and the noblest. I shall be the shoes on your feet, my husband. I shall be the breath of your lungs. I shall be the hilt of your sword and the pommel of your saddle. I shall be your tears, your laughter and your dreams. What you are eating there, it's I.

HANS. It's seasoned to perfection.

ONDINE. Eat me, Hans. Eat me all.

(Auguste clears his throat.)

EUGENIE. Your father wishes to speak, Ondine. Quiet.

AUGUSTE *(lifting his glass again)*. Quiet! My lord, since you are doing us the honor of spending the night under our humble roof—

ONDINE. A hundred nights. A thousand nights—

AUGUSTE. Permit me to drink to the lady of your heart—

ONDINE. How nice of you, Father!

AUGUSTE. She who is even now trembling for your safety—

ONDINE. She's not trembling now. He's safe enough.

AUGUSTE. She whom you rightly call the most beautiful of women, although for my part, I am a little partial to Violante on account of—

EUGENIE. Yes, yes, we know. Go on.

AUGUSTE. I drink, then, to the most beautiful and noblest of women, to your dark angel, to your betrothed, the Princess Bertha.

ONDINE *(rising to her feet)*. What name did you say?

AUGUSTE. The name the knight told me.

ONDINE. Since when am I called Bertha?

EUGENIE. We were not speaking of you, dear.

AUGUSTE. The knight is going to marry the Princess Bertha, Ondine, as soon as he returns to court. Isn't that so, my lord?

ONDINE. It's not so at all!

HANS. My little Ondine—

ONDINE. Ah, he's emerging from the ham at last, that one. Well, speak, since your mouth is no longer full—is there a Bertha? Yes or no?

HANS. Let me explain—

ONDINE. Is there a Bertha? Yes or no?

HANS. Yes. There is a Bertha. No. There was a Bertha.

ONDINE. So it's true, what he told me about men! They're all deceivers. They draw you to them with a thousand tricks, they seat you in their laps, they pass their hands all over your body and kiss you till you can't breathe—and all the time they are thinking of a dark angel called Bertha!

HANS. I did nothing like that to you, Ondine!

ONDINE. You did. Don't you dare deny it. And you hurt me, too. *(She bites her arm)* Look at that, Father. See how he bit me? Let him deny it, if he dares!

HANS. You don't believe this nonsense, I hope?

ONDINE. I shall be the humblest part of you and the noblest, he said. I am your bare feet. I am the wine you drink. I am the bread you eat. Those were his words, Mother! And the things one has to do for him! One has to spend the whole morning waking him up. One has to kill oneself the moment he dies. Yes! And all the time, in their secret hearts, they are nursing the thought of a dark angel called Bertha!

HANS. Ondine, on my word—

ONDINE. I despise you! I detest you!

HANS. Nevertheless, you might listen to me—

ONDINE. I can see her from here, the dark angel, with her little shadowy mustache and her plucked eyebrows.

HANS. Now, Ondine, really . . . !

ONDINE. Don't come near me! Or I'll throw myself into the lake. *(She opens the door. It is raining heavily)* So her name is Bertha!

HANS. I think there is no longer any Bertha, Ondine.

ONDINE. Leave this house at once, or I shall never enter it again! *(She turns suddenly)* What did you say?

HANS. I said, I think there is no longer any Bertha, Ondine.

ONDINE. You lie! Farewell. *(She runs out into the rain)*

HANS. Ondine! *(He runs to the door)*

AUGUSTE. My lord, my lord—you'll get drenched! *(To Eugenie)* There's a pretty kettle of fish.

EUGENIE. Yes, there's a pretty kettle of fish.

AUGUSTE. I might as well tell him everything now.

EUGENIE. Yes, you might as well tell him everything now.

(Hans turns.)

HANS. She's not your daughter, is she?

EUGENIE. No, my lord.

AUGUSTE. We had a daughter. She was stolen from the cradle.

HANS. Who left Ondine with you?

AUGUSTE. We found her at the edge of the lake the day our daughter disappeared.

HANS. These things happen only in fairy tales.

AUGUSTE. Yes, my lord. But it happened to us.

HANS. Then it is you who must be asked for her hand?

AUGUSTE. She calls us her parents, my lord.

HANS. Then, my friends, I have the honor of asking you for the hand of your daughter.

AUGUSTE. My lord, are you in your right mind?

HANS. Do you think that little wine of yours would turn my head?

AUGUSTE. The wine? Oh, never. It's a little Moselle, very modest, very reliable.

HANS. I assure you, I have never been more sober in my life. I ask you for the hand of Ondine with nothing in mind but the hand of Ondine. I want to hold this hand in mine. I want it to lead me to church, to war, and when the time comes, to death.

AUGUSTE. But, my lord, you already have a hand for that. This would be a hand too many.

HANS. A hand? Whose hand?

AUGUSTE. The lady Bertha.

HANS. Bertha? Do you know Bertha? I know her. I know her, that is, now that I know Ondine—

AUGUSTE. But is not a knight, above all, required to be loyal?

HANS. To his quest, yes. And I shall be loyal, above all, to my quest. Because, you know, up to now, we knights have been fools, all of us. We've been exploited; they take us for imbeciles. When we kill a monster, we're expected to vanish gracefully. When we find a treasure, we give it away. Well, that's finished. From now on I shall try to profit a little by my exploits. I have found a treasure and I shall keep it. Whether or not I knew it, my quest was Ondine, and I have found Ondine, and I shall marry Ondine. And nobody else in this world.

EUGENIE. You are making a mistake, my lord.

HANS. Eugenie—there was once a knight and his quest was to find something wonderful. And one night in a forest on the edge of a lake, he found a girl called Ondine. In her hands, tin turned to gold and water to jewels. The rain did not wet her. Her eyes were full of joy and her manner was royal. And not only was she the most wonderful creature he had ever seen, but he knew also that she would bring him all the delight and tenderness and goodness he would ever know in this world. Whereupon he bowed to her and went off to marry a girl called Bertha. Tell me, Eugenie, what sort of knight was this?

AUGUSTE. You don't put the question properly, my lord.

HANS. I ask you what sort of knight this would be. You don't dare to answer, but you know as well as I do. He would be a sort of idiot, would he not?

EUGENIE. But, my lord, since you have given your word to another—

HANS. He would be an idiot!

EUGENIE. Speak, Auguste.

HANS. Yes, speak. If there is any reason why I should not have Ondine, tell it to me now.

AUGUSTE. My lord, you are asking us for the hand of Ondine. It's a great honor for us—but she's not ours to give.

HANS. You must have some idea who her parents may be?

AUGUSTE. With Ondine it's not a question of parents. If we had not adopted Ondine, she would have grown up just the same. Ondine is strange. You saw her tonight in the storm. You understand, my lord, it's not that she's in the storm. She is the storm. She's a beautiful child, my lord, there's no denying it. But there is more than beauty in Ondine. There is power.

HANS. It's because she's young.

EUGENIE. It's true, she's young—

AUGUSTE. When I first married you,

my poor Eugenie, you too were young. But your youth had no effect on the lake. You were beautiful. But the lake remained what it had always been, selfish and rude. And the floods were brutal and senseless as always, and the storm was a beast of prey. But since Ondine came to us, everything has changed. The water has become gentle.

HANS. It's because you're old.

AUGUSTE. It's true I'm no longer young. But a lake that counts into your net each day exactly the same twelve fish, a lake that never enters your boat, not even if it happens to have a hole in the bottom—I think you will agree that is a remarkably courteous lake.

HANS. Well, suppose it is. What do you suggest? That I apply to the lake for permission to marry?

AUGUSTE. I wouldn't joke about the lake. The lake has ears.

HANS. And what's it to me if the lake has ears? I have no designs on the lake.

AUGUSTE. We are speaking of Ondine, my lord. Ondine belongs to the lake. Ondine is the lake, my lord.

HANS. Then I shall gladly take the lake to my bosom, and with it all the water in the world. The rivers shall be my brothers, the sea my mother, and the ocean itself my father-in-law. I love the water.

AUGUSTE. Beware of the water, my lord!

HANS. But why, Auguste? Why?

AUGUSTE. That's all I know, my lord.

HANS. Give me Ondine, Auguste.

AUGUSTE. Give you Ondine! And who am I to give you Ondine? Where is she now, Ondine? Oh, I remember, naturally, having seen her once, the little Ondine. I remember her voice, her laughter, I remember she threw your trout out of the window, a twelve-inch trout, the only one I had left. But we shall never see her again, she will never again come to us except in tender little lightnings, in little storms; she will never again tell us she loves us except with the waves lapping at our feet, or the rain on our cheeks, or perhaps, suddenly one day with a great salt-water fish in my pike-weir. That wouldn't surprise me a bit.

EUGENIE. Auguste, you're tired. It's time you came to bed.

AUGUSTE. Do you remember the morning we found her, Eugenie?

EUGENIE. Permit us to retire, my lord.

AUGUSTE. There wasn't a mark on the sand, not a footprint—nothing—to show how the child got there. Only the wind and the sun and the lake staring at us fixedly with its eye—

EUGENIE. I will show you to your room.

HANS. Thank you. I shall sit here by the fire a little longer, if I may.

EUGENIE. Come, Auguste. Tomorrow we shall speak of Ondine.

AUGUSTE. If there is an Ondine. (He shakes his head)

EUGENIE. Good night, my lord.

HANS. Good night. Good night.

(Auguste and Eugenie go out. Hans sits down by the fire and closes his eyes for a moment. The wall of the hut slowly becomes transparent, and through it appear the lake and the forest. In the half-light there rises the figure of An Ondine, blond and nude.)

THE ONDINE. Take me, handsome knight.

HANS (looking up with a start). What?

THE ONDINE. Kiss me.

HANS. I beg pardon?

THE ONDINE. Take me. Kiss me.

HANS. What are you talking about?

THE ONDINE. Am I too bold, handsome knight? Do I frighten you?

HANS. Not in the least.

THE ONDINE. Would you rather I were clothed? Shall I put on a dress?

HANS. A dress? What for?

THE ONDINE. Come to me. Take me. I am yours.

(She vanishes. Another Ondine appears. She is dark and clothed.)

THE SECOND ONDINE. Don't look at me, handsome knight.

HANS. Why not?

THE SECOND ONDINE. Don't come near me. I'm not that sort. If you touch me, I'll scream.

HANS. Don't worry.

THE SECOND ONDINE. If you touch my hair, if you touch my breasts, if you kiss my lips, I swear, I'll kill myself. I will not take off my dress!

HANS. As you please.

THE SECOND ONDINE. Don't come out, handsome knight. Don't come near me. I am not for you, handsome knight.

(She vanishes. Hans shrugs his shoulders. The two Ondines appear together at opposite sides of the room.)

FIRST ONDINE. Take me.

SECOND ONDINE. Don't touch me.

FIRST ONDINE. I am yours.

SECOND ONDINE. Keep your distance.

FIRST ONDINE. I want you.

SECOND ONDINE. You frighten me.

ONDINE *(appears suddenly)*. Oh how silly you look, both of you!

(The two Ondines vanish.)

HANS *(takes Ondine in his arms)*. Little Ondine! What is this nonsense? Who are those women?

ONDINE. My friends. They don't want me to love you. They say anyone can have you for the asking. But they're wrong.

HANS. They're very nice, your friends. Are those the prettiest?

ONDINE. The cleverest. Kiss me, Hans.

FIRST ONDINE *(reappears)*. Kiss me, Hans—

ONDINE. Look at that fool! Oh, how silly a woman looks when she offers herself! Go away! Don't you know when you've lost? Hans—

SECOND ONDINE *(appears again next to the first)*. Hans—

ONDINE. Go away, I say! Hans—

A THIRD ONDINE *(appears next to the others)*. Hans—

ONDINE. It's not fair! No!

HANS. Let them speak, Ondine.

ONDINE. No. It's the Song of the Three Sisters. I'm afraid.

HANS. Afraid? Of them?

ONDINE. Cover your ears, Hans.

HANS. But I love music.

THE FIRST ONDINE *(sings)*.

Hans Wittenstein zu Wittenstein,
Without you life is but a fever.
Alles was ist mein ist dein,
Love me always, leave me never.

HANS. Bravo! That's charming.

ONDINE. In what way is that charming?

HANS. It's simple. It's direct. It's charming. The song of the sirens must have been about like that.

ONDINE. It was exactly like that. They

copied it. They're going to sing again. Don't listen.

THE THREE ONDINES *(sing)*.

Heed no more the west wind's
[urging,
Slack your sail and rest your oar.
Drift upon the current surging
Powerfully toward our shore.

HANS. The tune is not bad.

ONDINE. Don't listen, Hans.

THE THREE ONDINES *(sing)*

Sorrow once for all forsaking,
Take our laughter for your sighs.
These are yours but for the taking,
Tender breasts and wanton thighs.

ONDINE. If you think it's pleasant to hear others singing the things one feels and can't express . . .

THE THREE ONDINES *(sing)*

Come and take your fill of pleasure,
Taste delight and drink it deep.
We shall give you beyond measure
Joy and rest and love and sleep.

HANS. That's wonderful! Sing it again! Sing it again!

ONDINE. Don't you understand? They don't mean a word of it. They're just trying to take you away from me.

THE FIRST ONDINE. You've lost, Ondine, you've lost!

HANS. What have you lost?

ONDINE. Your song means nothing to him!

FIRST ONDINE. He holds you in his arms, Ondine, but he looks at me!

SECOND ONDINE. He speaks your name, Ondine, but he thinks of me!

THIRD ONDINE. He kisses your lips, Ondine, but he smiles at me!

THE THREE ONDINES. He deceives you! He deceives you! He deceives you!

HANS. What are they talking about?

ONDINE. He may look at you and smile at you and think of you as much as he pleases. He loves me. And I shall marry him.

THE FIRST ONDINE. Then you agree? You make the pact?

HANS. What pact?

ONDINE. Yes. I agree. I make the pact.

(The words are taken up mysteriously. They echo and re-echo from every quarter.)

THE FIRST ONDINE. I am to tell them?

ONDINE. Yes. Tell them. Tell them all.

Those who sit and those who swim, those who float in the sunlight and those who crawl in darkness on the ocean floor.

HANS. What the devil are you saying?

ONDINE. Tell them I said yes.

(The word "yes" is taken up by a thousand whispering voices.)

THE FIRST ONDINE. And the Old One? Shall we tell him also?

ONDINE. Tell him I hate him! Tell him he lies!

THE FIRST ONDINE. Yes?

ONDINE. Yes! Yes! Yes!

(Again the sound is taken up. The mysterious voices whisper through the darkness until the air is filled with echoes. There is a climax of sound, then silence. The Ondines vanish. The walls of the hut regain their solidity.)

HANS. What a fuss! What a racket!

ONDINE. Naturally. It's the family. *(Hans sits in the armchair. Ondine sits at his feet)* You're caught, my little Hans?

HANS. Body and soul.

ONDINE. You don't wish to struggle a little more? Just a little more?

HANS. I'm too happy to struggle.

ONDINE. So it takes twenty minutes to catch a man. It takes longer to catch a bass.

HANS. Don't flatter yourself. It took thirty years to catch me. All my life. Ever since I was a child, I've felt something drawing me toward this forest and this lake. It was you?

ONDINE. Yes. And now after thirty years, would it be too much if you told me at last that you love me?

HANS. I love you.

ONDINE. You say it easily. You've said it before.

HANS. I've said something like it that meant something else.

ONDINE. You've said it often?

HANS. I've said it to every woman I didn't love. And now at last I know what it means.

ONDINE. Why didn't you love them? Were they ugly?

HANS. No. They were beautiful. But they no longer exist.

ONDINE. Oh, Hans, I meant to give you everything in the world, and I begin by taking everything away. Some day you will hate me for it.

HANS. Never, Ondine.

ONDINE. Shall I ever see them, these women you don't love?

HANS. Of course.

ONDINE. Where?

HANS. Everywhere. In their castles. In their gardens. At the court.

ONDINE. At the court? I?

HANS. Of course. We leave in the morning.

ONDINE. Oh, Hans, am I to leave my lake so soon?

HANS. I want to show the world the most perfect thing it possesses. Did you know you were the most perfect thing the world possessed?

ONDINE. I suspected it. But will the world have eyes to see it?

HANS. When the world sees you, it will know. It's really very nice, Ondine, the world.

ONDINE. Tell me, Hans. In this world of yours, do lovers live together always?

HANS. Together? Of course.

ONDINE. No. You don't understand. When a man and a woman love each other are they ever separate?

HANS. Separate? Of course.

ONDINE. No, you still don't understand. Take the dogfish, for instance. Not that I'm especially fond of dogfish, mind you. But, once the dogfish couples with its mate, he never leaves her, never as long as he lives, did you know that? Through storm and calm they swim together, thousands and thousands of miles, side by side, two fingers apart, as if an invisible link held them together. They are no longer two. They become one.

HANS. Well?

ONDINE. Do lovers live like that in your world?

HANS. It would be a little difficult for lovers to live like that in our world, Ondine. In our world, each has his own life, his own room, his own friends—

ONDINE. What a horrible word that is, each.

HANS. Each has his work—his play—

ONDINE. But the dogfish too have their work and their play. They have to hunt, you know, in order to live. And sometimes they come upon a school of herrings which scatter before them in a thousand flashes, and they have a thousand reasons to lose each other, to swerve one to the right, the other to the left. But they never do. As long as they live, not even a sardine can come between them.

HANS. In our world, Ondine, a whale can come between a husband and wife twenty times a day, no matter how much they love each other.

ONDINE. I was afraid of that.

HANS. The man looks to his affairs; the woman to hers. They swim in different currents.

ONDINE. But the dogfish have to swim through different currents also. There are cold currents and warm currents. And sometimes the one likes the cold and the other the warm. And sometimes they swim into currents so powerful that they can divide a fleet, and yet they cannot divide these fish by the breadth of a nail.

HANS. That merely proves that men and fish are not the same.

ONDINE. And you and I, we are the same?

HANS. Oh yes, Ondine.

ONDINE. And you swear that you will never leave me, not even for a moment?

HANS. Yes, Ondine.

ONDINE. Because now that I love you, two steps away from you my loneliness begins.

HANS. I will never leave you, Ondine.

ONDINE. Hans, listen to me seriously. I know someone who can join us forever, someone very powerful. And if I ask him, he will solder us together with a band of flesh so that nothing but death can separate us. Would you like me to call him?

HANS. No, Ondine.

ONDINE. But, Hans, the more I think of it, the more I see there is no other way to keep lovers together in your world.

HANS. And your dogfish? Do they need to be soldered like that?

ONDINE. It's true. But they don't live among men. Let me call him. You'll see. It's a very practical arrangement.

HANS. No. Let's try this way first. Later, we'll see.

ONDINE. I know what you're thinking. Of course, she's right, you're thinking, the little Ondine, and naturally I shall be with her always, but once in a while,

for just a little moment perhaps I shall go and take a turn by myself, I shall go and visit my friend.

HANS. Or my horse.

ONDINE. Or your horse. When this angel falls asleep, you're thinking, this angel whom I shall never leave not even for a moment, then, at last, I shall have a chance to go and spend a good half hour with my horse.

HANS. As a matter of fact, I had better go and have a look at him now, don't you think? We're leaving at dawn, you know, and I ought to see if he's bedded properly. Besides I always tell him everything.

ONDINE. Ah yes. Well, tonight you shall tell him nothing.

HANS. But why, Ondine?

ONDINE. Because tonight you're going to sleep, my little Hans. (*And with a gesture, she throws sleep into his eyes*) Good night, my love.

(*He falls asleep.*)

THE FIRST ONDINE (*her voice seems very far away*). Good-bye, Ondine.

ONDINE. Look after my lake!

THE SECOND ONDINE. Good-bye, Ondine.

ONDINE. Take care of my stream!

THE KING OF THE SEA. Ondine!

ONDINE. Farewell, Old One.

THE KING OF THE SEA. Don't leave us, Ondine.

ONDINE. I have left you, Old One.

THE KING OF THE SEA. The world of men is not your world, Ondine. It will bring you sorrow.

ONDINE. It will bring me joy.

THE KING OF THE SEA. The man will deceive you. He will abandon you.

ONDINE. Never! Never!

THE KING OF THE SEA. And when he deceives you? When he abandons you? You will remember our pact?

ONDINE. I shall remember our pact.

THE KING OF THE SEA (*his voice recedes*). Remember, Ondine.

THE ONDINES (*their voices are like the murmur of water*). Remember, Ondine.

HANS (*turning in his sleep*). Remember, Ondine—

ONDINE. Oh dear, from this time on, how much I shall have to remember!

CURTAIN

ACT TWO

*The hall of honor of the king's palace. It is
a large vaulted loggia of Gothic design. The
roof is supported by columns. The upstage side
opens on the palace gardens, in which may be
seen three jets of water playing in marble
basins in the sunshine. To the left is a dais with
the king's throne, and above the throne a
mural depicting one of the labors of Hercules.
There are arched doorways.*

*The Lord Chamberlain and the Superin-
tendent of the Royal Theatres are engaged in a
conference. To one side stand respectfully the
Trainer of the Seals and the Illusionist.*

_____

THE CHAMBERLAIN. My dear Superintendent, this is a matter that will require
all your skill, and all your inventiveness.
The Knight of Wittenstein has at last been
persuaded to present his bride at court.
His Majesty has asked me to provide an
amusing interlude with which to grace
the occasion. But the reception is to take
place immediately.

THE SUPERINTENDENT. The time is
short, my Lord Chamberlain.

THE CHAMBERLAIN. It couldn't be
shorter. Well? As Superintendent of the
Royal Theatres, what do you propose?

THE SUPERINTENDENT. Salammbo.
*(At this word Matho and Salammbo appear
and begin at once to sing.)*

THE CHAMBERLAIN *(striking the floor with
his staff for silence).* But you played
Salammbo only last night for the Margrave's birthday. Besides, Salammbo is sad.

THE SUPERINTENDENT. It's sad. But it's
ready.

*(He signs to his actors who burst at once into
their duet.)*

THE CHAMBERLAIN *(stops them again).*
I don't see why it is any more ready than
Orpheus, which has only one character.
Or the *Interlude of Adam and Eve,* which
requires no costumes.

THE SUPERINTENDENT. Excellency, my
success in the theatre is based solely on
the discovery that each particular stage
has its likes and dislikes which it is useless
to combat.

THE CHAMBERLAIN. Time presses, my
good man.

THE SUPERINTENDENT. Each theatre,
Excellency, is built for one play and one
play only. The whole secret of management is to discover what play that is. It's
not easy, especially when the play is not
yet written. And so, a thousand disasters
—until that happy day when the play for
which it was intended comes to its proper
theatre and gives it its life, its soul, and,
if I may say so, its sex.

THE CHAMBERLAIN. Superintendent—

THE SUPERINTENDENT. For years I
managed a theatre which bumbled along
miserably with the classics until suddenly
one night it found its joy in a bawdy farce
with sailors. It was a female theatre. I
knew another which tolerated only
Othello. It was male. Last year I was forced
to close the Royal Ballet. Impossible to
determine its sex.

THE CHAMBERLAIN. And you believe
the Royal Auditorium—

THE SUPERINTENDENT. Exists only for
Salammbo, yes, your Excellency. At the
word *Salammbo,* the tightness of throat
with which the royal chorus is normally
afflicted suddenly relaxes, and the hall
resounds with voices full of resonance
and joy. *(Matho and Salammbo begin
singing, at first softly, crescendo to the end of
the speech)* I tell you, my Lord Chamberlain, sometimes when I play a German
opera, I notice one of my singers,
brimming with happiness, making magnificent gestures, sending out full-throated
tones which fill the audience with such
joy and comfort that it breaks into
spontaneous applause—Why? Because
among his fellow-actors, who are merely
grinding out their parts by rote, this
actor in the general confusion is blissfully
singing his role in *Salammbo.*

THE CHAMBERLAIN *(silencing the singers).*
No. It would hardly do to entertain a
newly married couple with a tragedy of
unhappy love. *Salammbo* is out of the
question. *(The Superintendent waves his
singers away. They go reluctantly. The
Chamberlain turns to the Trainer of Seals)*
Who are you?

THE TRAINER. I am the Trainer of
Seals, your Excellency.

THE CHAMBERLAIN. What do they do,
your seals?

THE TRAINER. They don't sing *Salammbo*.

THE CHAMBERLAIN. That's a pity. A chorus of seals singing *Salammbo* would constitute a very appropriate entertainment. Besides, I am told that your head seal has a beard that makes him look like his Majesty's father-in-law. Is that true?

THE TRAINER. I could shave him, Excellency.

THE CHAMBERLAIN. By a regrettable coincidence, his Majesty's father-in-law shaved his beard only yesterday. We had best avoid even the shadow of a scandal. And who are you?

THE ILLUSIONIST. I am an illusionist, Excellency.

THE CHAMBERLAIN. Where is your apparatus?

THE ILLUSIONIST. I am an illusionist without apparatus.

THE CHAMBERLAIN. Now what do you take us for? You don't produce claps of thunder and lightning without apparatus.

THE ILLUSIONIST. Yes.

(There is a clap of thunder and lightning.)

THE CHAMBERLAIN *(cowering with fear)*. Nonsense. You can't produce sudden clouds of smoke which leave the stage covered with flowers without apparatus? *(There is a sudden cloud of smoke, and flowers fall from the ceiling.)*

THE ILLUSIONIST. Yes.

THE CHAMBERLAIN. What stubbornness! You don't suddenly produce before the eyes of the Lord Chamberlain—

BERTRAM *(comes in)*. Your Excellency--

THE CHAMBERLAIN. Just a moment.— Venus completely nude—without apparatus.

THE ILLUSIONIST. Yes.

BERTRAM. Excellency— *(A nude Venus appears. Bertram bows)* Madame. *(Venus disappears.)*

THE CHAMBERLAIN. I've always wondered who these Venuses are that magicians produce out of thin air? Relatives?

THE ILLUSIONIST. Or Venus herself. It depends on the magician.

BERTRAM. Excellency, his Majesty is unavoidably detained by the African envoy. The reception is postponed for an hour.

THE CHAMBERLAIN. Excellent. That gives us time to think of something. *(To the Superintendent)* Have you thought of something?

THE SUPERINTENDENT. Yes, Excellency.

THE CHAMBERLAIN. Ah. Splendid. What?

THE SUPERINTENDENT. *Salammbo.*

(The two singers appear, only to be waved off peremptorily by the Chamberlain.)

THE CHAMBERLAIN *(to the Illusionist)*. And how do you propose to amuse his Majesty?

THE ILLUSIONIST. If your Excellency permits, I shall do what the occasion inspires.

THE CHAMBERLAIN. That's asking a great deal. After all, we have never seen your work.

THE ILLUSIONIST. I shall be happy, while we are waiting, to offer a little private entertainment by way of demonstration.

THE CHAMBERLAIN. Ah. Very good.

THE ILLUSIONIST. What would your Excellency like to see?

THE CHAMBERLAIN. I should very much like to see—

THE ILLUSIONIST. Splendid. I shall bring them together at once.

THE CHAMBERLAIN. You are also a mind-reader?

THE ILLUSIONIST. Yes. Excellency, I can, if you wish, bring together before your eyes a man and a woman who have been carefully avoiding each other for the past three months.

THE CHAMBERLAIN. Here? Now?

THE ILLUSIONIST. Here and now. If you will be so good as to conceal yourselves—

THE CHAMBERLAIN. But it's impossible, my dear fellow. Consider that the gentleman in question is at this very moment in the royal apartments supervising the last details of his wife's costume. A tornado could not draw him from her. The injured lady, on the other hand, is locked up in her room. She was sworn she will under no circumstances appear. These two cannot possibly meet.

THE ILLUSIONIST. Yes. But suppose that a dog were to steal the bride's glove and run out into the garden with it? And suppose that the lady's pet bullfinch should fly out of its cage and come to perch on the edge of the fountain?

THE CHAMBERLAIN. That will get you nowhere. It is the halberdier's high duty to divert all dogs from the royal apartments. And as for the bird—the king has just loosed a falcon in the garden. It is hovering over the bullfinch's cage.

THE ILLUSIONIST. Yes. But suppose that the halberdier slips on a banana peel? And suppose a gazelle distracts the falcon's attention?

THE CHAMBERLAIN. Bananas and gazelles are unknown in these parts.

THE ILLUSIONIST. Yes. But the African envoy peeled a banana while waiting for his morning audience. And among the gifts sent by his government, there was a gazelle which is at this moment feeding in the garden.

THE CHAMBERLAIN. Quite resourceful, you magicians.

THE ILLUSIONIST. Yes. Take your places. In a moment you shall see the Princess Bertha and the Knight of Wittenstein come together in this hall.

(Violante and Angelique come in from the garden. They hear the last words.)

VIOLANTE. Really?

ANGELIQUE. Really?

THE CHAMBERLAIN (beckoning to the ladies to join him behind a column). Sh! Come here.

BERTRAM. But, Excellency, why are we doing this evil thing?

THE CHAMBERLAIN. Sooner or later it would have to happen. That's life.

BERTRAM. Then why not let life take its course?

THE CHAMBERLAIN. My dear Bertram, you are young and you are a poet. When you have reached my age, you will understand that life is a very poorly constructed play. As a rule, the curtain goes up in the wrong places, the climaxes don't come off, the denouement is interminably postponed, so that those who should die at once of a broken heart die instead of a kidney ailment at an advanced age. If this excellent illusionist can make us see a life unfold for once with the concision and logic that a good play requires—(To the Illusionist) Can you?

THE ILLUSIONIST. Perhaps.

THE CHAMBERLAIN. Just one little scene, then. Just one little scene.

BERTRAM. But, Excellency, the poor girl—

THE CHAMBERLAIN. The girl has caused a knight to be false to his word. She deserves to suffer.

BERTRAM. But why should we . . . ?

THE CHAMBERLAIN. Don't excite yourself, my boy. Six months from now, in the normal course of events, Hans and Bertha would meet. Six months after that, they would kiss. A year after that, beyond a shadow of a doubt, they would—it's inevitable. And if we spare ourselves these delays, and bring their hands together at once; and, ten minutes later, their lips; and five minutes after that, whatever else is necessary—will we be changing their story, really, in any way? We shall just be giving it a little pace, a little tempo—Magician!—What's that noise?

THE TRAINER. The halberdier. He slipped on a banana peel.

THE CHAMBERLAIN. Splendid.

BERTRAM. Excellency, I beg of you, let's carry this no further. It's a mischievous thing. Left to themselves, perhaps these two would never meet again. (There is a scream from the garden) What's that scream?

THE SUPERINTENDENT. The gazelle. The falcon struck it.

THE CHAMBERLAIN. Perfect. You think you can bring off the whole thing at this pace, magician?

THE ILLUSIONIST. Perhaps.

(The bird appears, perched on the fountain.)

THE SUPERINTENDENT. The bird!

THE TRAINER (looking out into the garden). The dog!

VIOLANTE. The knight!

(Hans is seen running after the dog in the garden.)

THE SUPERINTENDENT. The lady!

(Bertha runs in and catches the bird.)

HANS. Ah! There you are, you rascal! At last I've caught you!

BERTRAM. Ah! There you are, you rascal! At last I've found you!

(Each goes off without seeing the other. The spectators poke their heads out of their hiding places. They hiss.)

BERTRAM *(sighs with relief)*. Thank heaven!

THE CHAMBERLAIN. What's this, magician? Are you making fun of us?

THE ILLUSIONIST. Sorry, sir. A fault in direction.

THE CHAMBERLAIN. Are they going to meet or are they not?

THE ILLUSIONIST. They are going to meet. And this time there will be no mistakes about it. I'll knock their heads together. *(The spectators hide once more)* Now!

(The dog runs across the garden, glove in mouth, with Hans in pursuit. The bird flies in and settles on the fountain. Bertha runs in from the right and catches it.)

BERTHA. Again! What a bad bird you are!

HANS. Again! What an obstinate beast! *(He enters the room with the glove in his hand, just as Bertha runs up with the bird. They collide. Hans takes her hands to keep her from falling. They recognize each other)* Oh! I beg your pardon, Bertha.

BERTHA. Oh! I'm sorry, Hans.

HANS. Did I hurt you?

BERTHA. Not a bit.

HANS. I'm a clumsy brute, Bertha.

BERTHA. Yes. You are. *(There is a moment of embarrassed silence. Then each turns and walks off slowly. Bertha stops)* Pleasant honeymoon?

HANS. Marvelous.

BERTHA. A blonde, I believe?

HANS. Blonde, like the sun.

BERTHA. Sunlit nights! I prefer the darkness.

HANS. Each to his taste.

BERTHA. It was dark that night under the oak tree. My poor Hans! You must have suffered!

HANS. Bertha!

BERTHA. I didn't suffer. I loved it.

HANS. Bertha, my wife is coming in at any moment.

BERTHA. I was happy that night in your arms. I thought it was for always.

HANS. And so it could have been, had you not insisted on sending me into the forest on a wild-goose chase. Why didn't you keep me with you, if you wanted me?

BERTHA. One takes off a ring sometimes to show to one's friends. Even an engagement ring.

HANS. I'm sorry. The ring didn't understand.

BERTHA. No. And so it rolled, as rings do, under the nearest bed.

HANS. I beg your pardon!

BERTHA. Forgive me. I shouldn't have mentioned a bed. Among peasants, you sleep in the straw, I believe? You pick it out of your hair the morning after. Is it fun?

HANS. One day you will see.

BERTHA. No, I don't think so. Black hair and straw don't go well together. That's for blondes.

HANS. You may be right. Although in love, these details don't seem to matter. But, of course, you've never had that experience.

BERTHA. You think?

HANS. When you're in love, you don't think of yourself so much. You think of the other. You will see one day. But when it happens to you, don't let your lover go.

BERTHA. No?

HANS. Don't send him into senseless danger and loneliness and boredom.

BERTHA. One would say you had a bad time in the black forest.

HANS. You are haughty. But when you meet the man you love, take my advice— pocket your pride, throw your arms around his neck and tell him, before all the world, that you love him.

BERTHA *(she throws her arms around his neck)*. I love you.

(She kisses him, then tries to run off. But he holds her by the hands.)

HANS. Bertha!

BERTHA. Let me go, Hans.

HANS. What game are you playing with me now, Bertha?

BERTHA. Be careful, Hans. I have a bird in my hand.

HANS. I love another woman, Bertha.

BERTHA. The bird!

HANS. You should have done that before, Bertha.

BERTHA. Hans, don't squeeze my hand so. You're going to kill it.

HANS. Let the bird go, Bertha.

BERTHA. No. Its little heart is beating

with fear. And just now I need this little heart next to mine.

HANS. What is it you want of me, Bertha?

BERTHA. Hans—Oh! *(Opening her hand and showing the bird)* There. You've killed it.

HANS. Oh, Bertha! *(Taking the bird)* Forgive me, Bertha. Forgive me.

(Bertha looks at him a long moment. He is completely contrite.)

BERTHA. Give it to me. I'll take the poor little thing away. *(She takes it from him)*

HANS. Forgive me.

BERTHA. I want nothing of you now, Hans. But once, I wanted something for you, and that was my mistake. I wanted glory—for the man I loved. The man I had chosen when I was a little girl, and whom I led one night under the oak tree on which long ago I had carved his name. I thought it was a woman's glory to lead her lover not only to his table and his bed, but to whatever in the world is hardest to find and most difficult to conquer. I was wrong.

HANS. No, Bertha. No, Bertha.

BERTHA. I am dark. I thought that in the darkness of the forest this man would see my face in every shadow. I am dark, I trusted my love to the darkness. How could I have known that in these shadows, he would come one night upon a head of gold?

HANS. How could anyone have known it?

BERTHA. That was my error. I have confessed it. And that's the end of it. I shall carve no more initials in the bark of trees. A man alone in a dream of glory— that's already foolish. But a woman alone in a dream of glory is completely ridiculous. So much the worse for me.

HANS. Forgive me, Bertha?

BERTHA. Farewell, Hans.

(She goes out, right. He goes out, left. The spectators appear, crying "Bravo!")

THE ILLUSIONIST. There it is, your Excellency. The scene that would have taken place, without my assistance, next winter. I have brought it about, as you see, here and now. It has happened.

BERTRAM. It is amply sufficient. We can stop here, can we not?

THE CHAMBERLAIN. No. No. No. No. I'm dying to see the next. The next, Magician, the next!

THE ILLUSIONIST. The next scene?

VIOLANTE. The next!

ANGELIQUE. The next!

THE ILLUSIONIST. At your service, ladies. Which one?

VIOLANTE. The one in which Hans unlaces the helmet of the knight he has killed and it is the Lady Bertha . . . ?

THE ILLUSIONIST. That scene is in another play, Mademoiselle.

THE SUPERINTENDENT. The scene in which the knight in the nick of time saves Bertha from the dragon . . . ?

THE TRAINER. The scene in which the knight, while twirling a ball on his nose—

THE ILLUSIONIST. Please!

THE CHAMBERLAIN. The scene in which Bertha and Hans first speak of Ondine.

THE ILLUSIONIST. Very well, Excellency. That takes place next spring.

THE CHAMBERLAIN. So much the better. I love the spring.

(He goes behind his column. The lights dim. Bertha and Hans come in slowly from opposite directions.)

HANS *(calls)*. Bertha.

BERTHA *(calls)*. Hans.

(They catch sight of each other.)

BERTHA. I was looking for you, Hans.

HANS. I was looking for you, Bertha.

(The Chamberlain comes out suddenly.)

THE CHAMBERLAIN. Magician! What does this mean? What have you done to me?

THE ILLUSIONIST. It is one of the inconveniences of my system. You have grown an eight months' beard. You see, it is now next spring.

THE CHAMBERLAIN. Ah—

(He disappears. The scene continues.)

BERTHA. Hans, must there be this awful cloud between us? Can't we be friends?

HANS. I wish we could be, Bertha. But—

BERTHA. I know. We can't be friends without Ondine. But it's your fault, Hans. You haven't let me see her since that awful day of the king's reception.

And that's eight months ago, and quite forgotten. Send her to me this evening, Hans. I am illuminating a manuscript of the *Aeneid* for the king. Ondine can draw in the initials, and I shall teach her the secret of the gold leaf.

HANS. Thanks, Bertha. But I doubt very much—

BERTHA. Ondine doesn't letter?

HANS. Ondine doesn't write.

BERTHA. How lucky she is! When you write, it takes away half the pleasure of reading. She has a charming voice. I'm sure she reads aloud beautifully?

HANS. Ondine doesn't read.

BERTHA. How I envy her! How wonderful among all these pedants to be able to give oneself up to the luxury of not reading. But she dances, I know—

HANS. Never.

BERTHA. You're joking, Hans! You don't mean to say that she neither reads, nor writes, nor dances?

HANS. Yes. And she doesn't recite. And she doesn't play the rote. Nor the harp, nor the lute. And she won't go hunting. She can't bear to see things killed.

BERTHA. But what then does she do, in heaven's name?

HANS. Oh, she swims. Occasionally.

BERTHA. That's nice. Though it's not by swimming that a girl advances her husband's interests at court. And yet, let's be just, Hans. After all, these accomplishments mean nothing. A pretty woman has the right to be ignorant of everything, provided she knows when to keep still.

HANS. It is this point precisely, Bertha, that worries me the most. Ondine does not know when to keep still. Quite the contrary. She says whatever comes into her head—and the things that come into that girl's head! Bertha, you know, the jousting season opens this week. And the thought of the phrases which will issue from Ondine as she watches these tournaments in which every step and pass-at-arms has its appropriate term—it makes me shudder.

BERTHA. She can learn.

HANS. I spent the morning trying to teach her the rudiments. Each time I give her a new term, she thanks me with a kiss. Now in the first position of the horseman alone there are thirty-three points to identify—

BERTHA. Thirty-six.

HANS. God, that's true! What am I thinking of? I tell you, I'm losing my wits, Bertha!

BERTHA. Send her to me, Hans. I'll see that she learns what she needs to know.

HANS. Thanks. But, what she needs to know above all is the special signs and prerogatives of the Wittenstein. And those are a family secret.

BERTHA. You forget, Hans. I was almost one of the Wittenstein. Ask me a question.

HANS. If you can answer this, I shall owe you a forfeit. What device does a Wittenstein bear on his shield when he enters the lists?

BERTHA. On a field azure, a squirrel passant, gules.

HANS. Does he bear this device into combat?

BERTHA. Never. At the moment he lowers his visor, his squire hands him a shield on which are emblazoned three lions rampant or, on a field sable. That is his device of war.

HANS. Bertha! You're incredible! And how does a Wittenstein approach the barrier?

BERTHA. Lance squared, charger collected, slow trot.

HANS. Ah, Bertha, what a lucky man the knight will be who marries you!
(*He kisses her hand. She snatches it away. They go off in opposite directions.*)

THE CHAMBERLAIN (*no beard*). Bravo! Bravo! Bravo! And how right he is! The Princess Bertha knows everything. She does everything. She is the ideal woman, beyond a doubt. You have us on pins and needles, Magician. The third scene! Quickly!

VIOLANTE. The scene in which Bertha sees Ondine dancing in the moonlight with her fairies.

THE ILLUSIONIST. You appear to be still a little confused, Mademoiselle.

THE CHAMBERLAIN. The first quarrel of Hans and Ondine.

BERTRAM. Couldn't we let that, at least, take care of itself?

THE CHAMBERLAIN. No, no. We'd never get to see it. Magician—

BERTRAM. But Excellency! His Majesty will be here in a moment.

THE CHAMBERLAIN. By heaven, that's true. I will just have time to give this young lady the customary words of advice before the reception begins. You're not planning to do anything more till I get back, Magician?

THE ILLUSIONIST. Just one tiny scene, perhaps.

THE CHAMBERLAIN. In connection with what?

THE ILLUSIONIST. In connection with nothing at all. Just a trifle to please an old fisherman whom I love. But your Excellency needn't leave.

THE CHAMBERLAIN. Oh no, I must. It is the Lord Chamberlain's duty to instruct all those who are presented at court. And in this particular case—

THE ILLUSIONIST. If your Excellency wishes, I can save you the trouble of going. Take your place and you shall see yourself speaking to her.

THE CHAMBERLAIN. You can't do it!

THE ILLUSIONIST. Nothing simpler.

THE CHAMBERLAIN (he backs away in astonishment until he is lost from sight). What an extraordinary illusion!

THE ILLUSIONIST. Yes. But first, the Lady Violante. (Violante steps forward. Auguste walks in from the garden. He looks in bewilderment at the Illusionist) The fleck of gold, Auguste.

AUGUSTE (he sees Violante). Are you the Lady Violante?

VIOLANTE. Yes. What do you wish?

AUGUSTE (looking into her eyes). I was right! It's marvelous!

THE VOICE OF EUGENIE. Auguste! Stick to your fishing!

(Auguste makes a gesture of resignation, bows and goes.)

THE ILLUSIONIST. Thank you, my lady. Here you come, your Excellency.

(Violante goes behind the column. The Chamberlain comes in leading Ondine by the hand.)

THE CHAMBERLAIN. Absolutely out of the question, dear lady!

ONDINE. But it would make me so happy—

THE CHAMBERLAIN. I regret deeply. To change the court reception, third class, into a water festival is entirely out of the question. The Minister of Finance would never hear of such a thing. Every time we turn the water into the pool, it costs us a fortune.

ONDINE. But this will cost you nothing.

THE CHAMBERLAIN. Please don't insist. There is absolutely no precedent for a court reception in the water.

ONDINE. But I am so much more at ease in the water.

THE CHAMBERLAIN. I am not.

ONDINE. You would be. You especially. Your palm is damp. In the water, it wouldn't show.

THE CHAMBERLAIN. I beg your pardon. My palm is not damp.

ONDINE. Oh, it is. Touch it and you will see.

THE CHAMBERLAIN. Madame, do you feel strong enough to listen for a moment to a word of advice which will help you to avoid a great deal of trouble in the future?

ONDINE. Oh yes.

THE CHAMBERLAIN. To listen without interrupting?

ONDINE. Oh, I shouldn't dream of interrupting.

THE CHAMBERLAIN. Splendid. Now, in the first place—the court is a sacred precinct—

ONDINE. Excuse me just one moment. (She goes to the place where Bertram is hidden and fetches him out) What is your name? You?

BERTRAM. Bertram.

ONDINE. You are the poet, are you not?

BERTRAM. So they say.

ONDINE. You are not beautiful.

BERTRAM. They say that too. But usually they whisper it.

ONDINE. Writing doesn't improve the appearance?

BERTRAM. Oh yes. I used to be much uglier.

(Ondine laughs and goes back to the Chamberlain. Bertram stands by.)

ONDINE. Excuse me.

THE CHAMBERLAIN *(controlling himself)*. As I was saying. The court is a sacred precinct in which it is necessary for a man at all times to control—his face and his tongue. Here, when a man is afraid, he seems brave. When he lies, he seems frank. It is quite appropriate also, if by chance one is telling the truth, to appear to be lying. It inspires confidence.

ONDINE. I see.

THE CHAMBERLAIN. Let us take the example that you in your innocence bring up. It is true, my palm perspires. Ever since I was a child it has caused me infinite embarrassment. But damp as my hand is, my arm is long. It reaches to the throne. To displease me is to put oneself in jeopardy—and it does not please me to hear any mention of my physical short-comings, to be precise, of my sole physical shortcoming. And now, lovely Ondine, tell me, as a sophisticated court-lady, how is my hand, damp or dry?

ONDINE. Damp. Like your feet.

THE CHAMBERLAIN. What?

ONDINE. Just a moment. Do you mind?

THE CHAMBERLAIN. I mind very much! *(Ondine crosses once more to the poet, who comes this time to meet her.)*

ONDINE. What was the first poem you ever wrote?

BERTRAM. The most beautiful.

ONDINE. The most beautiful of your poems?

BERTRAM. The most beautiful of all poems. It so far surpassed the others as you, Ondine, surpass all women.

ONDINE. Tell it to me quickly.

BERTRAM. I don't remember it. It came to me in a dream. When I awoke, it was gone.

ONDINE. You should have written it down sooner.

BERTRAM. I did. Even a little too soon. I was still dreaming when I wrote it. *(Ondine smiles and leaves him. She joins the Chamberlain who is fuming.)*

ONDINE. Yes, your Excellency?

THE CHAMBERLAIN *(with a prodigious effort)*. My lady, let us admit that the Lord Chamberlain's palm is damp, and let's admit that he admits it. But tell me this—would you tell his Majesty that his hand was damp?

ONDINE. Oh no!

THE CHAMBERLAIN. Ah, bravo! And why not?

ONDINE. Because it's not.

THE CHAMBERLAIN. But I put you a case where it is! Look here, my girl, suppose his Majesty should question you about the wart on his nose. And his Majesty, believe me, has a wart on his nose. And for heaven's sake don't make me shout. It is death to mention it. No one ever has. Now—suppose he asked you what his wart resembled?

ONDINE. Is it usual for a monarch who meets a lady for the first time to ask her what his wart resembles?

THE CHAMBERLAIN. My dear girl, I am putting you a hypothetical case. In the event that you had a wart on your nose—

ONDINE. I shall never have a wart on my nose.

THE CHAMBERLAIN. The girl is impossible!

ONDINE. Warts come from touching frogs. Did you know that?

THE CHAMBERLAIN. No.

BERTRAM *(coming forward)*. Madame, the Lord Chamberlain is merely trying to tell you that it is inconsiderate to remind people of their ugliness.

ONDINE. It is inconsiderate of them to be ugly. Why should they be ugly?

THE CHAMBERLAIN. Courtesy is an investment, my dear girl. When you grow old, in your turn, people will tell you, out of courtesy, that you look distinguished. When you grow ugly, they will say that you look interesting. And all this in return for a tiny payment on your part now.

ONDINE. I don't need to make it. I shall never grow old.

THE CHAMBERLAIN. What a child you are!

ONDINE. Yes. Excuse me a moment. *(She goes to Bertram)*

THE CHAMBERLAIN *(exasperated)*. Ondine!

ONDINE. I like you, Bertram.

BERTRAM. I'm delighted. But the Chamberlain is annoyed.

ONDINE. Oh dear. *(She goes back to the Chamberlain)* I'm sorry.

THE CHAMBERLAIN *(a bit stiffly)*. There is just time now for me to instruct you on the question that his Majesty asks of every debutante at court. It has to do with the sixth labor of Hercules. Hercules, as you know, is his Majesty's name—he is Hercules the Sixth. Now listen carefully.

ONDINE *(taking a little step toward Bertram)*. If I could just—

THE CHAMBERLAIN. Madame, his Majesty is almost here. When he asks you about the sixth labor of Hercules—*(A flourish of trumpets at some little distance)* Too late.

(Hans enters angrily.)

HANS. Excellency—

ONDINE. Don't interrupt, Hans. His Excellency is speaking.

HANS. What does this mean, Excellency? Have you put me below the Margrave of Salm?

THE CHAMBERLAIN. Yes, Knight.

HANS. I am entitled to the third rank below the king and the silver fork.

THE CHAMBERLAIN. You were. And even to the first, and even to the golden fork, if a certain project had materialized as we expected. But your present marriage assigns you to the fourteenth place and the pewter spoon.

HANS. The fourteenth place!

ONDINE. What difference does it make, Hans? I've been to the kitchen. I'm sure there's enough for all.

(Bertram laughs.)

HANS. And why are you laughing, Bertram?

BERTRAM. I am laughing because my heart is gay.

ONDINE. You don't wish to stop him from laughing, Hans?

HANS. He's laughing at you.

ONDINE. He's laughing at me because he likes me.

BERTRAM. That's very true, Madame.

HANS. My wife must provoke no laughter of any description.

THE CHAMBERLAIN. Gentlemen! Gentlemen!

ONDINE. He won't laugh if you don't like it. He has no desire to displease me. Have you, Bertram?

BERTRAM. My only wish is to please you, Madame.

ONDINE. Don't be angry with my husband, Bertram. It's flattering that he should be so scrupulous on my account. Don't you think so?

BERTRAM. We all envy him the privilege.

HANS *(belligerently)*. Thanks very much.

ONDINE. Don't show your nervousness, Hans. Be like me. I'm trembling. But an earthquake could not shake this smile from my lips.

(Meanwhile people have streamed in from all sides. The Illusionist comes up to Ondine.)

THE ILLUSIONIST. Ondine—

ONDINE. What are you doing here?

THE ILLUSIONIST. I am furnishing the entertainment. Pardon the intrusion.

ONDINE. Yes. On one condition. Go away.

THE ILLUSIONIST. If you like. But in a little while, you will call me back, Ondine.

(He walks off. There is another flourish of trumpets near at hand. The Chamberlain takes his place at the door. He strikes the floor with his staff three times.)

THE CHAMBERLAIN. His Majesty, the King!

(The King enters, bowing.)

THE KING. Hail, Knight von Wittenstein.

HANS. Your Majesty.

(The King mounts his throne.)

THE CHAMBERLAIN *(advancing with Ondine)*. Your Majesty, with your gracious permission, may I present the Lady von Wittenstein zu Wittenstein.

THE KING. Madame.

ONDINE. My name is Ondine.

(Bertha takes her place on the lower step of the dais. Ondine looks at no one else.)

THE CHAMBERLAIN *(whispers)*. You curtsey, madame.

(Ondine curtseys, with her eyes still on Bertha.)

THE KING. We receive you with pleasure, dear child, in this gallery which is called the Hall of Hercules. I love Hercules. Of all my many names, his is by far my favorite, and of course the one by which I am known. The resemblance between Hercules and myself has been noticed by everyone, ever since I was a little child, and I must confess that at work or at play I have tried to emulate him in everything. And speaking of work —you know, I presume, how many labors Hercules brought to a successful conclusion?

THE CHAMBERLAIN (whispers). Twelve.

ONDINE (without taking her eyes from Bertha's face). Twelve.

THE KING. Twelve. Exactly. The Lord Chamberlain prompts a little loudly, but your voice is delightful. It will be a little more difficult for him to whisper in your ear the complete description of the sixth labor, but he won't have to. If you lift your eyes, you will see it depicted on the wall. Look. Who is this woman who is trying to seduce Hercules, with a smile on her lips and a lie in her heart? Her name, my dear?

ONDINE. Bertha.

THE KING. I beg pardon?

ONDINE (taking a step toward Bertha). You shall never have him, Bertha!

BERTHA. What?

ONDINE. He will never be yours, Bertha. Never!

THE KING. Is the girl quite well?

THE CHAMBERLAIN. Madame, His Majesty is addressing you.

ONDINE. If you say a word to him, if you dare to touch him, I'll kill you!

HANS. Ondine!

BERTHA. The girl is mad!

ONDINE. Majesty, I'm frightened! I beg you, save us!

THE KING. Save you from what, my child?

HANS. Your Majesty, she's not used to the court.

ONDINE. You, be quiet. You don't see what's happening? Oh, King, isn't it a pity? You have a husband for whose sake you'd give up anything in the world. He's strong—he's brave—he's hand-some—

HANS. Ondine, for heaven's sake!

ONDINE. I know what I'm saying. You're stupid, but you're handsome. It's no secret—all the women know it. And they say, what a lucky thing it is for us that being so handsome, he's so stupid!

Because he's so handsome, how sweet it will be to take him in our arms. And how easy—since he's so stupid. Because he's so handsome, he will give us such joy as our husbands can never give us. And this, without the slightest danger to ourselves —since he's so stupid.

BERTRAM. Bravo!

ONDINE. I am right, am I not, Bertram?

HANS. Ondine, please! And you—what do you mean by saying, Bravo?

BERTRAM. When I say Bravo, Knight, I mean Bravo.

THE KING. That's quite enough, Count Bertram.

THE CHAMBERLAIN (intervening suavely). Your Majesty, I had hoped to offer by way of interlude, a little diversion—

BERTHA. His Majesty is sufficiently diverted. His adopted daughter has been insulted before all the court by a peasant!

HANS. Majesty, permit us to take our leave. I have an adorable wife, but she is not like other women. She is very innocent, and she says whatever comes into her head. I humbly beg your forgiveness.

ONDINE. You see, King? You see what's happening?

THE KING. Bertha is the soul of sweet-ness. She wants only to be your friend—

ONDINE. You're entirely mistaken!

HANS. Ondine!

ONDINE. You think it's sweet to kill a bird?

THE KING. Bird? What bird? Why should Bertha kill a bird?

ONDINE. To trouble Hans. To bring him to his knees. To make him beg her pardon.

BERTHA. The bird was in my hand, Majesty. He pressed my hand so hard that the bird was killed.

ONDINE. He did not. A woman's hand, no matter how soft, becomes a shell of iron when it protects a living thing. If the bird were in my hand, Your Majesty, Hercules himself could press with all his strength and never hurt it. But Bertha knows men. These knights whom dragons cannot frighten grow faint at the death of a bird. The bird was alive in her hand. She killed it.

HANS. It was I who pressed her hand.

ONDINE. It was she who killed it.

THE KING. Ondine, my dear, I want you to be Bertha's friend.

ONDINE. If you wish. On condition she stops shouting.

HANS. But she hasn't said a word, Ondine.

THE KING. She really hasn't.

ONDINE. Are you deaf? Don't you hear? She says that a week of this foolishness will cost me my husband, and a month will cost me my life, that all she needs to do is to wait and I shall vanish. That's what your soul of sweetness is saying. Oh, Hans, take me in your arms, here, now, before her eyes, or we are lost forever!

HANS. You forget where you are, Ondine.

ONDINE. The bird is alive, Hans. I wouldn't let it die.

BERTHA. She is out of her mind. The bird is dead.

ONDINE. Go and see if you don't believe me. You killed it. I brought it to life. Which of us is out of her mind?

THE KING. You brought the bird back to life, you say?

ONDINE. Yes, King. Now do you see what a hypocrite she is?

THE KING. Bertha is no hypocrite, Ondine.

ONDINE. She is. She calculates her every word. She flatters you constantly.

THE KING. Nonsense, my dear.

ONDINE. Has she ever dared to speak to you about—

THE KING. About my descent from Hercules on the sinister side? Do you think that makes me blush?

ONDINE. No. About the wart on your nose.

THE KING (rises). What? (General consternation. Violante faints and is carried out) Leave us, all of you.

THE CHAMBERLAIN. Clear the room! Clear the room!

(All leave, with the exception of the King and Ondine.)

THE KING. Ondine!

ONDINE (desperately). If you ask me what it resembles, it resembles a flower, a mountain. It resembles a cathedral.

Hercules had two in exactly the same place, one alongside of the other. They were called the Pillars of Hercules.

THE KING. Ondine!

ONDINE. He got them by touching the Hydra. He had to touch the Hydra, naturally, in order to strangle it. It was his fifth labor.

THE KING (sitting down again). My little Ondine, I like you very much. It's a rare pleasure to hear a voice like yours at court, even when this voice insists on discussing my wart—which, incidentally, I do inherit from Hercules, precisely as you say. But, for your own sake—tell me the truth.

ONDINE. Yes. Yes, I shall tell you the truth.

THE KING. Who are you?

ONDINE. I belong to the water. I am an Ondine.

THE KING. How old are you?

ONDINE. Sixteen. But I was born many ages ago. And I shall never die.

THE KING. What are you doing here? Does our world attract you?

ONDINE. From the water it seems so beautiful.

THE KING. And from the land?

ONDINE. There are ways to have water before one's eyes always.

THE KING. It is in order to make the world seem beautiful that you are weeping?

ONDINE. No. It's because they wish to take Hans away from me.

THE KING. And suppose they do. Would that be so great a misfortune?

ONDINE. Oh yes. If he deceives me he will die.

THE KING. Don't worry, my dear. Men have been known to survive under those conditions.

ONDINE. Not this one.

THE KING. And what makes you think that Hans will deceive you?

ONDINE. I don't know. But they knew it the moment they saw him. Isn't it strange? The lake had never known deceit, not even the sound of the word. Then one day there appeared on its banks a handsome man with a loyal face and an honest voice, and that very moment the word deceit thrilled through the depths.

THE KING. Poor Ondine!

ONDINE. It's because your world is inverted in ours. All the things that I trust in Hans—his straight look, his clear words—to the water they seem crooked and cunning. He said he would love me always—and the water said, he deceives you!

THE KING. The water speaks?

ONDINE. Everything in the universe speaks, even the fish. Each time I left the cottage that night, they spat the word at me. He is beautiful, I said. Yes, said the bass, he will deceive you. He is strong, I said. Yes, said the perch, he will deceive you. Are you fond of perch, by any chance?

THE KING. I have no particular feeling about them.

ONDINE. Spiteful little things! But I was proud of him. I decided to take the risk. I made the pact.

THE KING. The pact? What pact?

ONDINE. The king, my uncle, said to me, you agree that he shall die if he deceives you? What could I answer?

THE KING. But he hasn't deceived you—yet.

ONDINE. But he is a man. He will. And then he will die.

THE KING. A king's memory is short. Your uncle will forget.

ONDINE. No.

THE KING. But, after all, what power has your uncle over him? What danger is he in?

ONDINE. Whatever is wave or water is angry with him. If he goes near a well, the level rises. When it rains, the water drenches him to the skin. Wherever he goes, the water reaches after him.

THE KING. Will you take my advice, little Ondine?

ONDINE. Yes.

THE KING. Go away, my dear.

ONDINE. With Hans?

THE KING. Dive into the first river you come to, and vanish forever.

ONDINE. But he's so clumsy in the water.

THE KING. You have had three months of happiness with Hans. In our world, that is a lifetime. Go while there is time.

ONDINE. Without Hans?

THE KING. He's not for you. His soul is small.

ONDINE. I have no soul.

THE KING. Because you don't need one. You are a soul. But human souls are tiny. There is no man whose soul is great enough for you.

ONDINE. I wouldn't love him if there were. I have already seen men with great souls—they are completely wrapped up in them. No, the only men whom one can love are those who are just like other men, whose thoughts are the thoughts of other men, who are distinguished from other men only by being themselves and nothing more.

THE KING. You are describing Hans.

ONDINE. Yes. That is Hans.

THE KING. But don't you see, my dear, that Hans loves what is great in you only because he sees it small? You are the sunlight; he loves a blonde. You are grace itself; he loves a madcap. You are adventure; he loves an adventure. One day he will see his mistake—and at that moment, you will lose him.

ONDINE. He will never see it. If it were Bertram, he would see it. Not Hans.

THE KING. If you wish to save him, leave him.

ONDINE. But I cannot save him by leaving him. If I leave him, they will say he deceived me, and Hans will die. No, it's here that I must save him. Here.

THE KING. And how will you do that, my little Ondine?

ONDINE. I have the remedy. It came to me while I was quarreling with Bertha. Did you notice—each time I came between Hans and Bertha, I succeeded only in bringing them more closely together. The instant I said something against Bertha, he sprang to her defense. Very well, from now on I shall do exactly the opposite. I shall tell him twenty times a day how beautiful Bertha is, how right she is. Then she will be wrong. I shall manage so that they are always alone. Then they will no longer feel the slightest desire for each other. In that way, with Bertha always there, I shall have Hans completely to myself. Oh, how well I understand men! Don't I? *(The King rises and kisses her)* Oh, Your Majesty! What are you doing?

THE KING. The king thanks you, my child.

ONDINE. Thanks me? For what?

THE KING. For a lesson in true love.

ONDINE. My idea is good?

THE KING. Stupendous.

(Enter the Chamberlain.)

THE CHAMBERLAIN. Forgive me, Your Majesty. The court is in complete consternation. What is your will? Shall I tell them all to withdraw?

THE KING. By no means.

THE CHAMBERLAIN. The reception is to continue?

THE KING. Of course.

THE CHAMBERLAIN. And the interlude? You wish to see it?

THE KING. At once.

ONDINE. How wonderful! Now I shall be able to ask Bertha's pardon before everyone.

(The Chamberlain goes to the door and waves his staff. The Court comes in from all sides. Bertha takes her place, haughtily.)

THE KING. Princess Bertha, Ondine has something to say to you.

ONDINE. I ask your pardon, Bertha.

THE KING. Very nice, my child.

ONDINE. Yes. But she might answer me.

HANS. What?

ONDINE. I have asked her pardon, though I don't want it. She might at least answer me.

THE KING. Bertha, Ondine has acknowledged her error, whatever it was. I should like you to be friends.

BERTHA. Very well, Your Majesty. I pardon her.

ONDINE. Thank you, Bertha.

BERTHA. On condition that she admits publicly that I did not kill the bird.

ONDINE. I admit it publicly. She did not kill the bird. The bird is alive—you can hear it singing. But she tried to kill it.

BERTHA. You see, Your Majesty?

HANS. One doesn't speak like that to the royal princess, Ondine!

ONDINE. The royal princess? Would you like to know who she is, this royal princess? Shall I show you? Shall I?

HANS. Silence, Ondine.

ONDINE. I happen to know the father of this royal princess. He is not a king. He is a fisherman—

BERTHA. Hans!

HANS. Ondine. You've said enough. *(He takes Ondine by the wrist)* Come.

ONDINE *(resisting)*. Not yet, Hans!

HANS. Come, I say!

ONDINE. Old One! Old One! Help me!

(The Illusionist appears. He is followed by the Chamberlain.)

THE ILLUSIONIST. Your Majesty, the interlude.

THE KING *(as they seat themselves)*. Yes, Ondine, you have gone too far. Everyone knows there was a golden crown on Bertha's pillow when she was found.

ONDINE. The crown was mine!

(The lights go out, and come up immediately on a little set in the garden level. It depicts the fisherman's cottage on the edge of the lake. Two Ondines are dancing in the waterfall. An Ondine comes in with a child in its arms. The others join her as she puts the child into a basket which she covers with rich silks.)

THE ONDINE *(sings)*.

Wrap the child in silk and lace
So the princess of the sea
May be nurtured in her place
By Auguste and Eugenie.

(At this moment the burly tenor dressed a Matho and the robust soprano dressed a Salammbo advance to either side of the set and begin singing loudly. The Ondines stop in astonishment.)

MATHO *(sings)*. I am a soldier, that is all.

SALAMMBO *(sings)*. And I the niece of Hannibal.

(The Illusionist steps forward.)

THE ILLUSIONIST. Who are these people, Excellency? They have nothing to do with my show.

MATHO *(sings)*. I am a common mercenary.

SALAMMBO. I stand at the other pole.

MATHO. But I love this sacred person.

SALAMMBO. I adore this humble soul.

THE ILLUSIONIST. Where did they come from? What are they singing?

THE CHAMBERLAIN. *Salammbo.*

THE ILLUSIONIST. But they're spoiling the illusion. Tell them to stop.

THE CHAMBERLAIN. Impossible. Once they begin, nothing can stop them.

SALAMMBO *(sings)*. Take me, take me, and Carthage too.

THE ILLUSIONIST. Enough!

(He makes a gesture. The two singers continue singing and posturing, but without a sound. The Ondines resume.)

FIRST ONDINE *(sings)*.

Set the little creature down,
Whom we stole from Eugenie,
And beside her set the crown
Of the princess of the sea.

SECOND ONDINE *(sings)*.

Weep not, we shall not forsake you,
Helpless, human little thing,
Soon a knight will come and take you
To the palace of the king.

THIRD ONDINE *(sings)*.

But lest it ever be forgotten
Who she is and whence begotten,
On her skin I draw the sign
Of her father's hook and line.

(The Ondines turn toward Bertha and sing together.)

THE ONDINES.

Bertha, Bertha, if you dare,
show the world your shoulder bare!

(The lights go on suddenly; the fisherman's cottage and the Ondines vanish. Hubbub. Bertha is on her feet.)

ONDINE. Well, Bertha?

BERTHA. It's a lie!

ONDINE. Is it? *(She tears the dress from Bertha's shoulders. The sign is there)* You see?

(Bertha kneels before the King.)

MATHO and SALAMMBO *(suddenly audible, they walk off together, singing)*.

All is love beneath the stars,
Is love, is love, is love!

BERTHA. It's a lie! *(She kneels before the King)* It's a lie, Your Majesty.

(The King glances at her shoulder on which the mark is visible.)

THE KING. Is this true, Ondine?

ONDINE. Yes, King.

BERTHA *(desperately)*. Hans!

(Hans makes a protecting gesture.)

ONDINE. Old One! Where are they? *(The Illusionist lifts a hand. Auguste and Eugenie appear. They see Bertha)* Oh, my darlings!

THE KING. Bertha, it is your father.

Have you no word to say to him, to your mother? *(Bertha is silent)* As you please . . *(Auguste and Eugenie go. The King walks off. The court follows slowly)* But—*(He stops)*—until you have asked their pardon, I forbid you to show your face at court.

(He goes off, followed by the court. Bertha is left sobbing bitterly.)

ONDINE. Forgive me, Bertha. *(There is no answer)* You will see. The king will call you back in a moment. And they will all love you more than before. *(Bertha says nothing)* Ask her to come and stay with us, Hans.

HANS. Come with us.

(Bertha turns silently.)

ONDINE. Oh, how difficult it is to live among you, where what has happened can never again not have happened! How terrible to live where a word can never be unspoken and a gesture can never be unmade! But I will undo it all. You will see.

HANS. Come with us, Bertha. My castle is large. You shall live with us always, in the wing that looks out on the lake.

ONDINE. A lake? Your castle has a lake, Hans?

HANS. It has a lake. The other side faces the Rhine.

ONDINE. The Rhine?

(The Chamberlain comes in.)

THE CHAMBERLAIN. The king wishes to know whether the pardon has been asked.

ONDINE. It has been asked. From the heart.

THE CHAMBERLAIN. In that case, Princess—

ONDINE. Oh Hans, haven't you a castle in the plains, in the mountains far from the water?

THE CHAMBERLAIN. Princess Bertha, the king desires your presence. He forgives you.

ONDINE. You see?

HANS. Tell him we have asked you to come with us.

ONDINE. He already knows that.

(Bertha and the Chamberlain go out. Hans and Ondine cross in the direction of the garden.)

HANS *(as they pass the fountain)*. And

why all this fear of the water? What is it that threatens you from the water?

ONDINE. Me? Nothing.

HANS. If I sit down at the edge of a brook, you drag me away. If I walk near a pond, you come between us. What is it you fear?

ONDINE. Nothing, Hans.

HANS. Yes, Ondine, my castle is surrounded by water. And in the mornings, I shall bathe under my waterfall, and at noon I shall fish in my lake, and in the evening I shall swim in the Rhine. You don't frighten me with these tales about water. What's water? Can it see? Can it hear?

(As he passes, the jets of water rise high and threatening over their basins. The Illusionist appears.)

ONDINE. Yes, Hans.

(They go. The Chamberlain comes out from behind his column, and, a moment later, the Superintendent, the Trainer, Bertram and the Two Ladies come out of hiding.)

THE CHAMBERLAIN. Wonderful! Wonderful! *(To the Illusionist)* Very nice indeed.

THE SUPERINTENDENT. Wonderful!

VIOLANTE. But is all this really going to happen?

THE ILLUSIONIST. My dear, it has happened.

THE CHAMBERLAIN. And what happens next, Magician?

THE COURT. Yes. What next?

THE CHAMBERLAIN. Does he decide to marry Bertha?

THE COURT. Does he?

THE CHAMBERLAIN. Does he deceive Ondine?

THE COURT. Does he?

THE ILLUSIONIST. Naturally.

THE CHAMBERLAIN. When can we see that?

THE ILLUSIONIST. At once, if you like.

THE CHAMBERLAIN. Splendid. Let's see it. *(He goes behind his column)* Go on.

BERTRAM. No, Excellency. No.

THE CHAMBERLAIN. Yes, yes. Go on. Go on. But what's this? What's happened? *(He comes out)* I'm bald?

THE ILLUSIONIST. Five years have passed.

THE CHAMBERLAIN. My teeth are gone? I'm stuttering?

THE ILLUSIONIST. Shall I continue?

THE CHAMBERLAIN. No. No, for heaven's sake! An intermission! An intermission!

CURTAIN

ACT THREE

The courtyard of the castle of the Wittenstein. The yard is surrounded on three sides by the walls of the castle. Arched doorways lead into it. At one side there is a platform with a well.

It is the morning of the marriage of Bertha and Hans. There is a sound of church bells from the chapel. Hans, splendidly dressed, is sitting on the platform steps with his head in his hands. A servant enters.

THE SERVANT. My lord, the choir has filed into the chancel.

HANS. What did you say?

THE SERVANT. I refer to the choir which will sing at your wedding.

HANS. Do you have to use this pompous tone? Can't you talk like a human being? *(Bertha comes in. She too is dressed for a wedding.)*

THE SERVANT. Long life to the bride! To the Lady Bertha!

HANS. Oh. Go away!

BERTHA. But, Hans, why are you angry on the day of our wedding?

HANS. What? You too?

BERTHA. I had hoped that your face would be radiant with joy.

HANS. Stop it, stop it! Stop it!

BERTHA. Hans, really!

HANS. I'm lost, Bertha! I'm lost!

BERTHA. Hans, you frighten me. You're so strange today.

HANS. There is a tradition in our family, Bertha. Whenever misfortune threatens, the servants feel it before anyone else, and they begin to speak all at once in solemn language. On the day of misfortune, the kitchen-maids are filled with grandeur. The swineherds see what they never saw before. They speak of the curve of the stream; the shape of the flower fills them with awe; they exclaim with wonder at the honeycomb. They speak of nature, of the soul of man. They become poets. That day, misfortune strikes.

BERTHA. But the man wasn't speaking in poetry, Hans. There were no rhymes.

HANS. When I hear him speak in rhymes, I shall know that death is at hand.

BERTHA. Oh Hans, that's superstitious!

HANS. You think?

BERTHA. This is not the day of your death, Hans. It is the day of your wedding.

HANS *(he calls)*. Walter! *(The servant enters)* Where is the swineherd?

THE SERVANT. Under a spreading oak—

HANS. Hold your tongue.

THE SERVANT. On a grassy bank he lies—

HANS. Go fetch him. Quickly.

(The servant goes out. Bertha takes Hans in her arms.)

BERTHA. Oh Hans, my dear, I love you.

HANS. You're good to me, Bertha.

BERTHA. You are holding me in your arms, Hans, but you are not thinking of me. What are you thinking?

HANS. I was weak, Bertha. I should have made her confess. I should have made her suffer as she made me suffer.

BERTHA. Can't you put her out of your mind, Hans? Not even today?

HANS. Today less than any other. Oh, Bertha, you should have married a man full of joy and pride. And look at me! Oh, Bertha, how she lied to me, that woman!

BERTHA. She never lied to you, Hans. She was no woman. You married a creature of another world. You married an Ondine. You must forget her.

HANS. If she would only let me forget her! But that cry that awakened me the morning she left—"I have deceived you with Bertram!" Has it stopped echoing for even a moment? Does one hear anything else from the river, from the lake? Does the waterfall ever stop dinning it in my ears? Day and night, in the castle, in the city, from the fountains, from the wells—it's deafening! But why does she insist on proclaiming to the world that she deceived me with Bertram?

(An echo comes from the well.)

THE ECHO. Deceived you with Bertram. *(Another echo whispers from the right)* With Bertram. *(From the left)* With Bertram.

HANS. You hear? You hear?

BERTHA. Let's be just, Hans. You had already deceived her with me. And of course she knew it. It was only in revenge that she deceived you with Bertram.

THE ECHOES *(whisper back)*. Deceived you with Bertram. With Bertram.

HANS. Where is she now, Bertha? What is she doing? In the six months since she left, every huntsman, every fisherman in the region has been trying to find her. You would say she had vanished. And yet she's not far off. This morning at dawn they found a wreath of starfish and sea urchins on the chapel door. She put it there, of course. You know that.

BERTHA. Oh, my darling, who would have thought that you of all men would have seen anything in a girl like Ondine? When I sent you into the forest, I thought, this man will surely come back. He will look carefully, right and left, but he will never find an enchanted lake, nor the cave of a dragon, he will never glimpse among the trees at twilight the white forehead of a unicorn. He has nothing to do in that world. He will follow the human path. He will not lose his way.

HANS. I lost it.

BERTHA. Yes, but you found it again. It was in the fifth year of your marriage, that night in the winter when you told me it was me you had always loved, and I ran away from you, and you followed my tracks in the snow. They were deep and wide. They spoke plainly of my distress. They were not the tracks of a spirit. They were human tracks, and you found them, and once more you found your way. You carried me back in your arms that night.

HANS. Yes. Like Bertram when he carried away Ondine. *(The servant enters)* Where is the swineherd?

THE SERVANT. In the shadow of an oak, by the banks of a stream—

HANS. Well?

THE SERVANT. I called him, but he did not answer. He is gazing at the sky. He is looking at the clouds.

HANS. Never mind. Fetch me the kitchen-maid.

THE SERVANT. There is a fisherman to see you, my lord.

HANS. Get me the kitchen-maid at once, do you hear, no matter what she's gazing at.

THE SERVANT. Yes, my lord. The fisherman.

(The servant goes. The fisherman comes in.)

FIRST FISHERMAN. My lord! My lord!

HANS. Say it twice more and it's poetry.

FIRST FISHERMAN. We have her! She's caught.

HANS. Ondine?

FIRST FISHERMAN. Yes. Yes. An Ondine!

BERTHA. Are you sure?

HANS. Where did you catch her?

FIRST FISHERMAN. In the Rhine. In my net.

HANS. You're sure it's she?

FIRST FISHERMAN. Positive. Her hair was over her face, but her voice was marvelous, her skin like velvet. She's wonderfully formed, the little monster.

(The second fisherman appears.)

SECOND FISHERMAN. Prepare yourself. The judges are coming.

BERTHA. Judges?

HANS. What judges?

SECOND FISHERMAN. The Imperial and Episcopal judges who have jurisdiction over the supernatural.

BERTHA. So soon?

SECOND FISHERMAN. They were already holding assizes below in the city.

FIRST FISHERMAN. They came from Bingen, you see, to hang a werewolf. Now they will try the Ondine.

BERTHA. But why must they try her here?

FIRST FISHERMAN. Because an Ondine must be tried on a rock.

SECOND FISHERMAN. And besides, you are the complainant.

HANS. That's true.

BERTHA. Don't they know what day this is? Couldn't they try her another time?

SECOND FISHERMAN. My lady, the trial must be now.

HANS. They're right, Bertha. The trial must be now.

BERTHA. Hans—don't see her again, I beg you.

HANS. I shall never see her again. You heard what he said—he caught an Ondine in the Rhine. What I shall see won't even know me.

BERTHA. Don't look at her, Hans.

THE SERVANT (comes in). The judges, my lord.

HANS. Just a few minutes more, Bertha, and we shall be at peace.

THE FISHERMAN. The judges.

(The judges come in, puffing a little. They are followed by an ancient clerk with a great book.)

FIRST JUDGE. Marvelous! The exact altitude. Just above the realm of the water. Just below the realm of the air. It couldn't be better. (He bows to Bertha) My lady. Our felicitations.

SECOND JUDGE. Our compliments, my lord.

BERTHA. I shall be within call, Hans, if you want me. (Bertha goes out)

HANS. You come in the nick of time, gentlemen. But how did you know there was work for you here?

FIRST JUDGE. Our work gives us a degree of insight unknown to our colleagues in the civil and criminal law.

SECOND JUDGE. It is also more difficult.

(The servants arrange the court. The clerk sits down, opens his register and sharpens his quill.)

FIRST JUDGE. To determine the line that divides two vineyards is easy. But to fix the proper boundaries between humanity and the spirits, hoc opus, hic— excuse me—hic labor est.

SECOND JUDGE. But in the case at hand, our task appears to be easy.

FIRST JUDGE. It is the first time we have tried an Ondine who does not deny being an Ondine.

SECOND JUDGE. All the more reason to be careful.

FIRST JUDGE. Quite right, my dear colleague.

SECOND JUDGE. You have no idea of the subterfuges these creatures use to elude our investigations. The salamanders pretend to be Ondines. The Ondines pretend to be salamanders. (He sits down

FIRST JUDGE. Excuse me.

SECOND JUDGE. You remember, my dear colleague, that affair at Kreiznach, when we tried the pretended Dorothea, the alderman's cook? She gave us every reason to believe she was a salamander. But we didn't jump at conclusions. We put her to the torch to make sure. She burnt to a crisp.

FIRST JUDGE (*smiles reminiscently*). She was no more salamander than I am. (*He sits down*)

SECOND JUDGE. She was an Ondine.

FIRST JUDGE. We had a similar case last week, the matter of a certain Gertrude, a blonde barmaid of Tubingen. It was clearly established that in her presence the beer glasses filled by themselves and, what is even more miraculous, without heads of foam. You would have been certain she was an Ondine. We threw her into the water with her hands tied—

SECOND JUDGE. She immediately drowned.

FIRST JUDGE (*he shrugs*). A salamander.

HANS. Did you bring Ondine with you?

FIRST JUDGE. We have her in custody. But before we examine her, Knight, it would be extremely valuable for us to ascertain the exact nature of your complaint.

HANS. My complaint? My complaint is the complaint of all mankind. Is it so much after all that God has granted us, these few yards of air between hell and heaven? Is it so attractive, after all, this bit of life we have, with these hands that get dirty, these teeth that fall out, this hair that turns gray? Why must these creatures trespass on our little world? Gentlemen, on the morning of my marriage, I claim the right to be left in peace in a world that is free of these intrusions, these threats, these seductions, alone with myself, with my bride, alone at last.

FIRST JUDGE. That is a great deal to ask, Knight.

SECOND JUDGE. Yes. It may seem surrising that these creatures should derive ll their satisfaction from staring at us while we wash our feet, kiss our wives, or beat our children. But that is the undeniable fact. Around each human gesture, the meanest, the noblest, a host of grotesque presences with tails and horns is constantly dancing its round. What's to be done? We must resign ourselves.

HANS. Has there never been an age when they did not infest us?

SECOND JUDGE. An age? To my knowledge, Knight, there has never been a moment.

FIRST JUDGE. Yes, once there was a moment. One only. It was late August, near Augsburg, in the harvest season when the peasants were dancing. I had stretched out under an apple tree. I looked up into the sky. And suddenly I felt that the whole world was free of these shadows that beset it. Above my head I saw a lark soaring in the heavens— without its usual twin, the raven. Our Swabia spread to the Alps, green and blue, without my seeing over it the Swabia of the air, peopled with blue angels, nor below it the Swabia of hell, teeming with green devils. On the road there trotted a horseman with a lance unattended by the horseman with the scythe. By the river, in the sun, the mill wheel turned slowly, without dragging in its orbit that enormous shadowy wheel that grinds the souls of the damned. For that instant, the whole world was single-hearted, at work, at play, at peace— and yet I tasted for the first time a certain loneliness, the loneliness of humanity. But the next moment, the horseman was joined by Death, the clouds bristled as always with lances and brooms, and the customary fish-headed devils had joined the dancing couples. There they were, all back at their posts again just as before. Bring in the accused.

(*Ondine is led in by the executioner. She is nude, but draped around her body is the net in which she was caught. She is made to stand on a little elevation opposite the judges. A number of people come in to witness the trial.*)

SECOND JUDGE (*peering at her*). Her hands are not webbed, apparently. She is wearing a ring.

HANS. Remove it.

ONDINE. No!

(The executioner removes it by force and hands it to Hans.)

HANS. It is my wedding ring I shall need it presently.

FIRST JUDGE. Knight—

HANS. The necklace too. The locket has my picture in it.

ONDINE. No!

(The executioner takes it off.)

FIRST JUDGE. Knight, with all respect, I must ask you not to interfere with the conduct of this trial. Your anger is doubtless justified, but we must avoid even the semblance of confusion. We will proceed with the identification.

HANS. It is she.

FIRST JUDGE. Beyond a doubt. But we must follow the indicated procedure. Where is the fisherman who caught her? Summon the fisherman to the bar.

(The first fisherman takes the stand.)

FIRST FISHERMAN. It's the first time I ever caught one, your honor. This is my lucky day!

FIRST JUDGE. Congratulations. Now— what was she doing when you caught her?

FIRST FISHERMAN. I knew that some day I'd catch one. I have known it every morning for the last thirty years. How often have I said—today I'm going to catch one. But this morning, I was certain.

FIRST JUDGE. I asked you what she was doing.

FIRST FISHERMAN. And, mind you, I caught her alive. The one they caught at Regensburg, they bashed its head in with an oar. But I was careful. I just knocked her head against the side of the boat a few times to stun her. Then I dragged her in.

HANS. You ox. You hurt her head.

FIRST JUDGE. Answer my questions. Was she swimming when you caught her?

FIRST FISHERMAN. She was swimming. She was showing her breasts, her buttocks. She can stay under a full fifteen minutes. I timed her.

FIRST JUDGE. Was she singing?

FIRST FISHERMAN. She was making a little sound, like a moan. If it was a dog, you'd call it a yelp, a bark. I remember what she was barking. She was barking: I deceived you with Bertram.

FIRST JUDGE. You're talking nonsense. Since when can you understand a bark?

FIRST FISHERMAN. As a rule, I don't. To me a bark is a bark, as a rule. But this one I understood. And what it said was—

FIRST JUDGE. She had an odor of sulphur when you pulled her out?

FIRST FISHERMAN. She had an odor of algae, of pine.

SECOND JUDGE. That's not the same thing. Did she have an odor of algae or an odor of pine?

FIRST FISHERMAN. She had an odor of algae, of pine.

FIRST JUDGE. Never mind, my dear colleague.

FIRST FISHERMAN. She had an odor that said plainly: I deceived you with Bertram.

FIRST JUDGE. Since when do odors speak?

FIRST FISHERMAN. Odors don't speak. But this one said—

FIRST JUDGE. She struggled, I presume?

FIRST FISHERMAN. No. Not at all. You might say, she let herself be caught. But when I had her in the boat, she shuddered. It was a sort of movement of the shoulders that said, as clear as clear can be: I deceived you with—

HANS. Have you quite finished, you idiot?

FIRST JUDGE. You must excuse the man, Knight. These simple souls are always imagining things. That is the origin of folklore.

FIRST FISHERMAN. I swear by all that's holy that that's one of them. I'm sorry about the tail. She didn't have it when I caught her. There's a double reward for catching them alive?

FIRST JUDGE. You may collect after the trial. Very well, Fisherman. That's all.

FIRST FISHERMAN. And what about my net? Can I have my net back?

FIRST JUDGE. Your net is in evidence. It will be returned to you in due course.

SECOND JUDGE. Out you go.

(The fisherman goes out, grumbling.)

FIRST JUDGE. Proceed with the examination.

(The second judge extends a very long telescope and focuses it on Ondine.)

HANS. What are you doing?

SECOND JUDGE. I am going to examine the body of this girl—

HANS. No one is going to examine her body!

FIRST JUDGE. Calm your fears, Knight. My colleague is an experienced anatomist. It was he who personally established the physical integrity of the Electress Josepha in connection with the annulment of her marriage, and she commented especially on his tact.

HANS. I tell you, this is Ondine. That's enough.

SECOND JUDGE. Knight, I understand that it is painful for you to have me auscultate in public the body of someone who was once your wife. But I can, without touching her, study through the glass those parts which differentiate her species from the human race.

HANS. Never mind the glass. You can look at her from where you are.

SECOND JUDGE. To identify with the naked eye and from a distance the very subtle variations that distinguish an Ondine from a human being seems to me an extremely impractical operation. She could at least take off the net and walk a little. She could show us her legs?

HANS. She will do nothing of the sort.

FIRST JUDGE. It would perhaps be in better taste not to insist, my dear colleague. In any case, the evidence is sufficient. Is there anyone present who denies that this is an Ondine?

SECOND FISHERMAN (without moving). I deny it.

FIRST JUDGE. Who said that? Remove that man.

THE SERVANT. Don't kill her, your honor. She was good to us.

SECOND JUDGE (shrugs his shoulders). She was a good Ondine, that's all.

THE SERVANT. She loved us.

SECOND JUDGE. There are affectionate varieties even among turtles.

FIRST JUDGE. Since we hear no objection, we declare that the supernatural character of the accused has been established beyond a reasonable doubt. We proceed to the second part of the trial. Knight, do you accuse this creature, by reason of her illegal intrusion into our world, of having caused disorder and confusion in your domain?

HANS. I? Certainly not.

FIRST JUDGE. But you do accuse her of being a sorceress?

HANS. Ondine, a sorceress?

FIRST JUDGE. We are merely trying to define her crime, Knight.

SECOND FISHERMAN (stepping forward). Ondine, a sorceress?

FIRST JUDGE. Who is this man?

SECOND FISHERMAN. I am a witness.

ONDINE. He's lying!

FIRST JUDGE. Ah. In that case, you may speak.

SECOND FISHERMAN. This Ondine is no longer an Ondine. She has renounced her race and betrayed its interests. She has become a woman.

FIRST JUDGE. A sorceress.

SECOND FISHERMAN. This woman could call upon the earth and the heavens to do her bidding. The Rhine is her servant. But she gave up her power in favor of such human specialties as hay fever, headaches and cooking. Is that true, Knight, or is it false?

FIRST JUDGE. You accuse her, if I understand correctly, of having taken on a favorable appearance in order to ferret out the secrets of the human race?

HANS. Rubbish!

SECOND FISHERMAN. The human race has no secrets, your honor. It has only afflictions.

FIRST JUDGE. It also has treasures. Doubtless she stole your gold, Knight, your jewels?

HANS. She?

SECOND FISHERMAN. All the gold and the jewels of the world meant nothing to Ondine. Of the treasures of humanity, she preferred only the humblest—the stove, the kettle, the spoon. The elements loved Ondine, but she did not return their affection. She loved the fire because it was good for making omelettes, and the water because it made soup, and the wind because it dried the wash. Write this into your record, Judge—this Ondine was the most human being that ever lived. She was human by choice.

SECOND JUDGE. We are informed that the accused was in the habit of locking herself up for hours each day in order to practice her magic arts. What do you say to that?

SECOND FISHERMAN. It's true. And what was the result of her magic, you?

THE SERVANT. A meringue, your honor.

SECOND JUDGE. A meringue? What sort of meringue?

THE SERVANT. She worked for two months to discover the secret of a good meringue.

SECOND JUDGE. That is one of the deepest of human secrets. Did she succeed?

FIRST JUDGE. Fisherman, we thank you. We shall take account of these facts in considering our judgment. If these creatures envy us our pastry, our bric-a-brac, our ointments for eczema, it is hardly to be wondered at. It is only natural that they should recognize the pre-eminence of the human condition.

SECOND JUDGE. There's nothing in the world like a good meringue. You say she discovered the secret?

THE SERVANT. Her crust was pure magic, your honor.

SECOND JUDGE (to the first judge). You don't suppose that with a few turns on the rack we might perhaps induce her to—?

FIRST JUDGE. No, my dear colleague, no. (He clears his throat) We come now to the heart of the matter. At last, Knight, I understand the full import of your complaint. Ondine, you are accused of having cheated this knight of the joys of marriage. In place of the loving companion to which every man is entitled, you foisted upon this knight a wearisome existence with a woman who cared for nothing but her kitchen. In this way—and this is the greatest of the crimes against the human spirit—you have robbed him of love. Naturally. An Ondine is incapable of love.

HANS. Ondine incapable of love?

FIRST JUDGE. Really, Knight, it is becoming a trifle difficult to follow you. Of what, precisely, do you accuse this woman?

HANS. I accuse this woman of adoring me beyond human endurance. I accuse

her of thinking only of me, of dreaming only of me, of living only for me.

FIRST JUDGE. That is not a crime, exactly.

HANS. I was this woman's god, do you understand?

FIRST JUDGE. Now, now—

HANS. You don't believe me? Very well. Answer me, Ondine. Who was your god?

ONDINE. You.

HANS. You hear? She pushes love as far as blasphemy.

FIRST JUDGE. Oh, come, there's no need to complicate the issue. These creatures are not Christians. They cannot blaspheme. All she means is that she had a proper wifely reverence for you.

HANS. Who were your saints, Ondine?

ONDINE. You.

HANS. Who were your angels? Whose face did you see in the holy pictures in your Book of Hours?

ONDINE. Yours.

HANS. You see?

FIRST JUDGE. But where is all this leading us, Knight? We are here to try an Ondine, not to judge the nature of love.

HANS. Nevertheless, that is what you are required to judge. It is Love I am accusing. I accuse the highest love of being the foulest and the truest love of being the most false. This woman who lived only for me deceived me with Bertram.

FIRST JUDGE. You are heaping confusion on confusion, Knight. If what this woman says is true, she could not possibly have deceived you with anyone.

HANS. Answer, Ondine. Did you or did you not deceive me with Bertram?

ONDINE. With Bertram.

HANS. Swear it, then. Swear it before these judges.

ONDINE (rises to her feet). I swear it before these judges.

FIRST JUDGE. If she deceived you, we shall see soon enough. My dear colleague, put the three canonical questions. The first?

SECOND JUDGE. Ondine, when you see this man running, what do you do?

ONDINE. I lose my breath.

FIRST JUDGE. Hm.

SECOND JUDGE. And when he snores in his sleep—excuse me, Knight—what do you hear?

ONDINE. I hear the sound of singing.

FIRST JUDGE. So far her answers are correct. The third question, if you please.

SECOND JUDGE. When he tells an amusing story for the twentieth time in your presence, how does it seem to you?

ONDINE. Twenty times funnier than before.

FIRST JUDGE. And nevertheless you deceived him with Bertram?

ONDINE. I deceived him with Bertram.

SECOND FISHERMAN. You needn't shout, Ondine. I heard you.

ONDINE (whispers). I deceived him with Bertram.

HANS. There you have it.

FIRST JUDGE. Do you realize, young woman, what the punishment for adultery is? Do you realize that this is a crime that is never confessed, because the confession doubles the injury?

ONDINE. All the same—

SECOND FISHERMAN. You deceived him with Bertram?

ONDINE. Yes.

SECOND FISHERMAN. Answer me, now, Ondine. And see that you answer me truly. Where is Bertram now?

ONDINE. In Burgundy, where he is waiting for me to join him.

SECOND FISHERMAN. Where was it that you deceived your husband with Bertram?

ONDINE. In a forest.

SECOND FISHERMAN. In the morning? At noon?

ONDINE. At noon.

SECOND FISHERMAN. Was it cold? Was it warm?

ONDINE. It was icy. Bertram said: Our love will keep us warm. One doesn't forget such words.

SECOND FISHERMAN. Very good. And now, if you please, summon Bertram to the bar.

FIRST JUDGE. Bertram has been gone these six months, Fisherman. He is beyond the power of the law.

SECOND FISHERMAN. Its power seems limited. Here he is.

(Bertram comes in.)

HANS. Bertram!

FIRST JUDGE. Just a moment, Knight. You are the Count Bertram?

BERTRAM. Yes.

FIRST JUDGE. This woman says she deceived her husband with you.

BERTRAM. What?

FIRST JUDGE. Is it true?

BERTRAM. If she says it, it is true.

FIRST JUDGE. Where did it happen?

BERTRAM. In her room. In this castle.

FIRST JUDGE. In the morning? At night?

BERTRAM. At midnight.

FIRST JUDGE. Was it cold? Was it warm?

BERTRAM. The logs were blazing on the hearth. Ondine said: How hot it is, the way to hell! One doesn't forget such words.

SECOND FISHERMAN. Perfect. And now everything is clear.

ONDINE. And why is it so clear? Why should we remember these trifles? When people really love each other do you think they know whether it is warm or cold or noon or midnight?

SECOND FISHERMAN. Count Bertram, take this woman in your arms and kiss her lips.

BERTRAM. I take my orders only from her.

SECOND FISHERMAN. Ask him to kiss you, Ondine.

ONDINE. Before all these people? Never.

SECOND JUDGE. And yet you expect us to believe that you gave yourself to him?

ONDINE. Kiss me, Bertram.

BERTRAM. You really wish it?

ONDINE. Yes. I wish you to kiss me. Just for a moment. Just to prove that we can. And if I should shudder a little when you take me in your arms, Bertram, it's only because it's cold.

SECOND JUDGE. We are waiting, Ondine.

ONDINE. Couldn't I have something to cover myself with, at least?

SECOND JUDGE. No. As you are.

ONDINE. Very well. So much the better. I love to feel Bertram's hands on my body when he kisses me. Come, Bertram. But if I should scream a little, Bertram, when you take me in your arms, it's only because I'm frightened here before these people. Besides, I may not scream.

SECOND JUDGE. Make up your mind, Ondine.

ONDINE. Or if I should faint. But if I faint, Bertram, you may do whatever you please with me, whatever you please.

FIRST JUDGE. Well, Ondine?

ONDINE. Well, Bertram?

BERTRAM. Ondine! *(He takes her in his arms and kisses her)*

ONDINE. Hans! Hans!

SECOND FISHERMAN. There's your proof, gentlemen.

(The judges put on their hats.)

ONDINE. But you don't understand. If I say Hans when I kiss Bertram, it is only to deceive him the better. If I loved Bertram with no thought of Hans, would that be deceit? No, but every moment that I love Bertram, I think of Hans and I deceive him. With Bertram.

SECOND FISHERMAN. We understand. The trial is over. You may go, Count Bertram.

BERTRAM. Must I go, Ondine?

ONDINE. Farewell, Bertram.

BERTRAM. Farewell. *(Bertram goes)*

FIRST JUDGE. The court will now deliver its judgment.

SECOND JUDGE. Oyez! Oyez!

FIRST JUDGE. It is the judgment of this court that this Ondine has transgressed the boundaries of nature. However the evidence indicates that in so doing she brought with her nothing but kindness and love.

SECOND JUDGE. And even a little too much kindness and love.

FIRST JUDGE. Why she wished to make us believe that she deceived you with Bertram when in fact she did not, is a question beyond the scope of our inquiry. As she has done no great harm, it is our judgment that she shall be spared the humiliation of a public execution. She shall have her throat cut without witnesses this day directly after sunset. Until that time, we place her in the custody of the public executioner. *(Church bells begin to ring again)* What's that?

SECOND JUDGE. Wedding bells, my

dear colleague. The Knight is about to be married.

FIRST JUDGE. Ah, of course. The nuptial procession is forming in front of the chapel. Knight, permit us to join you in the hour of your happiness.

(The kitchen-maid walks up to Hans.)

HANS. Who is this?

FIRST JUDGE. Who?

HANS. This woman who walks toward me like a creature from the other world?

SECOND JUDGE. We don't know her.

FIRST JUDGE. She seems to be of this world.

THE SERVANT. It's the kitchen-maid, my lord. You asked me to fetch her.

HANS. How beautiful she is!

FIRST JUDGE. Beautiful?

HANS. How very beautiful!

SECOND JUDGE. We shall not contradict you. Will you precede us?

HANS. No, no. I have to hear first what she says. She alone knows the end of this story. Speak! Speak! We are listening.

SECOND JUDGE. Is he out of his mind?

FIRST JUDGE. He has every reason.

HANS. Speak! Speak!

THE KITCHEN-MAID.

My face is plain, my nature sour,
But, oh, my soul is like a flower.

HANS. That rhymes?

FIRST JUDGE. Rhymes? Not at all.

THE KITCHEN-MAID.

Had I been free to choose my lot,
My hands had never touched a pot.

HANS. You're not going to tell me these verses don't rhyme?

SECOND JUDGE. Verses?

FIRST JUDGE. What verses?

THE KITCHEN-MAID.

My clothes are poor, my face is plain,
And yet of high rank is my pain;
There is as much salt in my tears
As in those shed by emperors.
And when the butler vents his spleen,
It hurts as if I were a queen.
Oh, when we two come to your city,
And, kneeling, ask for grace and pity,
Both bearing on our brows the same
Affronts and thorns and marks of
                         [shame,
Will you know us one from the other,
My lord, my savior and my brother?

HANS. That's a poem, is it not? Would you call that a poem?

FIRST JUDGE. A poem? All I heard was a scullion complaining that she had been falsely accused of stealing a spoon.

SECOND JUDGE. She said her corns have been aching since November.

HANS. Is that a scythe she bears in her hand?

FIRST JUDGE. A scythe? No, that's a spindle.

SECOND JUDGE. It's a broom.

HANS. I thank you, kitchen-maid. When next you come, I shall be ready. Come, gentlemen.

(*The kitchen-maid goes out. The servant crosses the stage solemnly. He turns.*)

THE SERVANT. Your bride is in the chapel, my lord. The priest is waiting.

HANS. Go and say that I am coming.

(*The wedding bells begin to toll as for a funeral. They all go out, except the executioner, the second fisherman and Ondine.*)

THE EXECUTIONER (*taking hold of Ondine*). Now then, Mistress—

SECOND FISHERMAN. One moment, Executioner. (*With a gesture of his hand, he turns the executioner into an automaton and waves him off the stage*) The end is near, Ondine.

ONDINE. Don't kill him, Old One.

SECOND FISHERMAN. You haven't forgotten our pact?

ONDINE. Don't judge men by our standards, Old One. Men don't deceive their wives unless they love them. When they love them most they deceive them. It's a form of fidelity, their deceit.

SECOND FISHERMAN. Ah, Ondine, what a woman you are!

ONDINE. It's only because he wished to honor me that he deceived me. It was to show the world how pure I was, how true. I really don't see how else he could have done it.

SECOND FISHERMAN. You have always suffered from a lack of imagination.

ONDINE. When a man comes home in the evening with his eyes full of gratitude and his arms full of flowers, and he kisses our hands and calls us his savior and his angel—we all know what that means. It's scarcely an hour since he has deceived us.

And is there anything more beautiful in marriage?

SECOND FISHERMAN. He has made you suffer, my little Ondine.

ONDINE. Yes. I have suffered. But remember we are speaking of humans. Among humans you are not unhappy when you suffer. On the contrary. To seek out in a world full of joy the one thing that is certain to give you pain, and to hug that to your bosom with all your strength—that's the greatest human happiness. People think you're strange if you don't do it. Save him, Old One.

SECOND FISHERMAN. He is going to die. Ondine.

ONDINE. Old One!

SECOND FISHERMAN. What does it matter to you, Ondine? You have only a few minutes left of human memory. Your sisters will call you three times, and you will forget everything.

ONDINE. Save him! Save him!

SECOND FISHERMAN. If you wish, I will let him die at the same moment that you forget him. That seems humane.

ONDINE. He is so young. So strong.

SECOND FISHERMAN. You have strained his heart, Ondine.

ONDINE. I? How could I?

SECOND FISHERMAN. Since you show such interest in dogfish, perhaps you remember a couple who broke their hearts one day while swimming together peacefully in a calm sea. They had crossed the entire width of the ocean side by side in winter, through a tempest, without the slightest difficulty. And then one day in a blue gulf, they swam against a little wave. All the steel of the sea was in that ripple of water, and the effort was too much for them. For a week their eyes grew pale, their lips drooped. But there was nothing wrong with them, they said . . . but they were dying. And so it is with men, Ondine. What breaks the woodsman's heart, or the knight's, is not the great oak, nor the battle with the dragon: It is a slender reed, it is a child who loves him.—He has only a few minutes left to live.

ONDINE. But he has everything to live for now. His life is in order.

SECOND FISHERMAN. His brain is full of

those who are dying. When the kitchen-maid held forth just now on the price of eggs and cheese, you saw, it was all sheer poetry in his ears.

ONDINE. He has Bertha—

SECOND FISHERMAN. She is waiting for him in vain in the chapel. He is in the stable with his horse. His horse is speaking to him. Dear master, good-bye till we meet in the sky, his horse is saying. Today his horse has become a poet.

ONDINE. I can hear them singing in the chapel. He is being married.

SECOND FISHERMAN. What does this marriage mean to him now? The whole thing has slipped away from him like a ring too wide for the finger. He is wandering about by himself. He is talking to himself, he doesn't know what he's saying. It's a way men have of escaping when they come up suddenly against a reality. They become what is called mad. All at once they are logical. They don't compromise. They don't marry the woman they don't love. They reason simply and clearly like the plants and the water. Like us.

ONDINE. Listen to him. He is cursing me.

SECOND FISHERMAN. He loves you. He's mad. He's here.

(He goes. Hans comes in slowly and stands behind Ondine for a moment.)

HANS. My name is Hans.

ONDINE. It's a beautiful name.

HANS. Ondine and Hans. The most beautiful names in the world, are they not?

ONDINE. Yes. Hans and Ondine.

HANS. Oh, no. Ondine first. That's the title. Ondine. It will be called *Ondine*, this story in which I appear from time to time. And I don't play a very brilliant part in it, do I, because, as you said, once, I'm not very bright; I'm just the man in the story. I loved Ondine because she wanted me; I deceived her because I had to. I didn't count for much. I was born to live between the stable and the kennels —such was my fate, and I might have been happy there. But I strayed from the appointed path, and I was caught between nature and destiny. I was trapped.

ONDINE. Forgive me, Hans.

HANS. But why do you make this error, all of you? Was I the man for love? Lovers are of a different stamp—little threadbare professors full of fury, stockbrokers with heavy glasses; such men have the time and capacity for enjoyment and suffering. But you never choose such men, never. Instead you fall with all your weight on some poor general called Antony, or some poor knight called Hans, ordinary men of action for whom love is a torment and a poison. And then it's all up with them. Between the wars and the chase and the tourneys and the hospital, did I ever have a spare moment in my life? But you had to add also the poison in my veins, the flame in my eyes, the gall in my mouth! And then, oh God, how they shook me between them and bruised me, and flayed me between hell and heaven! It wasn't very just of you, Ondine.

ONDINE. Farewell, Hans.

HANS. And then, you see? One day they leave you. The day when suddenly everything becomes clear, the day you realize that you would die if they left you—that day they leave you. The day when you find them again, and with them, everything that gives life its meaning, that day, they look you in the eye with a limpid glance, and they say farewell.

ONDINE. I am going to forget everything, Hans.

HANS. And a real farewell, a farewell forever! Not like those lovers who part on the threshold of death, but are destined to meet again in another world, to jostle each other eternally in the same heaven. These part only in order never to part again—you don't call that a parting. But Ondine and I will never meet again. We part for eternity, we go to different worlds. We must do this properly, Ondine. It is the first real farewell that has even been said in this world.

ONDINE. Live, Hans. You too will forget.

HANS. Live! It's easy to say. If at least I could work up a little interest in living— but I'm too tired to make the effort. Since you left me, Ondine, all the things my body once did by itself, it does now only by special order. The grass doesn't look green to my eyes unless I order them to see it green. And it's not very gay, you know, when the grass is black. It's an exhausting piece of management I've undertaken. I have to supervise five senses, two hundred bones, a thousand muscles. A single moment of inattention, and I forget to breathe. He died, they will say, because it was a nuisance to breathe . . . *(He shakes his head)* He died for love. Why did you let the fisherman catch you, Ondine? What did you wish to tell me?

ONDINE. That an Ondine will mourn for you always.

HANS. No. No one will mourn for me. I am the last of my house. I shall leave no trace behind me. There will be only an Ondine, and she will have forgotten.

ONDINE. No, Hans. I have taken my precautions. You used to laugh at me because I always made the same movements in your house. You said I counted my steps. It was true. It was because I knew the day would come when I would have to go back. I was training myself. And now, in the depths of the Rhine or the ocean, without knowing why, I shall go on forever making the movements that I made when I lived with you. When I plunge to the bottom, I shall be going to the cellar—when I spring to the surface, I shall be going to the attic. I shall pass through doors in the water. I shall open windows. In this way I shall live a little with you always. Among the wild Ondines there will be one who will forever be your wife. Oh! What is it?

HANS. I forgot for a moment.

ONDINE. Forgot what?

HANS. To breathe. Go on. Ondine, go on.

ONDINE. Before I left, I took some of the things in our room. I threw them into the river. They seem strange to me in the water, these bits of wood and metal that speak to me of you, they float about aimlessly out of their element. It's because I'm not used to it yet: tomorrow they will seem as firm and stable as the currents in which they float. I shall not know what they mean, exactly, but I shall live among them, and it will be strange if I don't use them sometimes. I shall drink from your cup. I shall look into your mirror.

Sometimes perhaps your clock will strike. Timeless, I shall not understand this sound but I shall hear it. And so, in my way, though death and the infinite come between us, I shall be true to you always.

HANS. Thank you, Ondine. And I—

THE FIRST VOICE. Ondine!

HANS. They are calling you, Ondine.

ONDINE. They will call me three times. I shall remember until the last. Hans, let us not waste these moments! Ask me something quickly. What is it, Hans? What is it? You're pale.

HANS. I too am being called, Ondine.

ONDINE. Speak! Question me!

HANS. What did you say, Ondine, when you came out of the storm, the first time I saw you?

ONDINE. I said: How beautiful he is!

HANS. And when you saw me eating the trout?

ONDINE. I said: How stupid he is!

HANS. And when I said: It does no harm to think?

ONDINE. I said: In after years we shall have this hour to remember. The hour before you kissed me.

HANS. I can't wait now, Ondine. Kiss me now.

THE SECOND VOICE. Ondine!

ONDINE. It's all whirling about in my head! Speak, Hans, speak!

HANS. I can't speak and kiss you at the same time.

ONDINE. I'll be quiet.

(He kisses her. The kitchen-maid comes in with her broom.)

HANS. Look! Look! There she is!

ONDINE. Who?

HANS. Her face is plain, her nature sour. But oh, her soul is like a flower! *(He falls)*

ONDINE. Help! Help!

HANS. Ondine—

THE THIRD VOICE. Ondine!

(Hans dies. Ondine looks about in surprise.)

ONDINE. How did I get here? How strange! It's solid. It's empty. It's the earth?

(The Second Fisherman appears.)

SECOND FISHERMAN. It is the earth, Ondine. It's no place for you.

ONDINE. No—

(The Ondines are heard singing in the distance.)

SECOND FISHERMAN. Come, little one, let us leave it.

ONDINE. Oh yes. Let us leave it. *(She takes a few steps, then stops before the body of Hans which is lying on the platform steps)* Wait. Why is this handsome young man lying here? Who is he?

SECOND FISHERMAN. His name is Hans.

ONDINE. What a beautiful name! But why doesn't he move? Is there something wrong with him!

SECOND FISHERMAN. He is dead.

FIRST ONDINE. Come, Ondine.

ONDINE. Oh, I like him so much! Can you bring him back to life, Old One?

SECOND FISHERMAN. Impossible.

ONDINE. What a pity! How I should have loved him!

CURTAIN

JEAN GIRAUDOUX's

The Madwoman of Chaillot

In the adaptation by MAURICE VALENCY

First presented by Alfred de Liagre, Jr., at the Belasco Theatre, New York, on December 27, 1948, with the following cast:

THE WAITER.................... Ralph Smiley	THE SERGEANT................Richard Sanders
THE LITTLE MAN.................Harold Grau	THE SEWER-MAN .... James Westerfield
THE PROSPECTOR.............Vladimir Sokoloff	MME. CONSTANCE, *The Madwoman of Passy*
THE PRESIDENT.............,...Clarence Derwent	Estelle Winwood
THE BARON .... Le Roi Operti	MLLE. GABRIELLE, *The Madwoman of St. Sulpice*
THERESE....................Patricia Courtley	Nydia Westman
THE STREET SINGER .... Eugene Cibelli	MME. JOSEPHINE, *The Madwoman of La Concorde*
THE FLOWER GIRL............Millicent Brower	Doris Rich
THE RAGPICKER................John Carradine	THE PRESIDENTS.......... { Clarence Derwent / Jonathan Harris / Le Roi Operti
PAULETTE.....................Barbara Pond	
THE DEAF-MUTE...............Martin Kosleck	
IRMA...........................Leora Dana	THE PROSPECTORS .... { Vladimir Sokoloff / William Chambers / Maurice Brenner
THE SHOE-LACE PEDDLER.......Maurice Brenner	
THE BROKER .... Jonathan Harris	THE PRESS AGENTS .... { Archie Smith / Sandro Giglio / James Westerfield
THE STREET JUGGLER..............John Beahan	
DR. JADIN ....Sandro Giglio	THE LADIES.............. { Patricia Courtley / Barbara Pond / Sonia Sorel
COUNTESS AURELIA, *The Madwoman of Chaillot*	
Martita Hunt	
THE DOORMAN..............William Chambers	THE ADOLPHE BERTAUTS.... { Paul Byron / Harold Grau / William Chambers / Gilbert Smith
THE POLICEMAN................ Ralph Roberts	
PIERRE........................Alan Shayne	

Directed by Alfred de Liagre, Jr.
Settings and costumes designed by Christian Bérard

ACT ONE—The Café Terrace of *Chez Francis*.
ACT TWO—The Countess' Cellar—21 Rue de Chaillot.

© 1949, by MAURICE VALENCY
Reprinted by permission of RANDOM HOUSE, Inc.

ACT ONE

SCENE: *The café terrace at "Chez Francis," on the Place de l'Alma in Paris. The Alma is in the stately quarter of Paris known as Chaillot, between the Champs Élysées and the Seine, across the river from the Eiffel Tower.*

"Chez Francis" has several rows of tables set out under its awning, and, as it is lunch time, a good many of them are occupied. At a table, downstage, a somewhat obvious Blonde with ravishing legs is sipping a vermouth-cassis and trying hard to engage the attention of the Prospector, who sits at an adjacent table taking little sips of water and rolling them over his tongue with the air of a connoisseur. Downstage right, in front of the tables on the sidewalk, is the usual Paris bench, a stout and uncomfortable affair provided by the municipality for the benefit of those who prefer to sit without drinking. A Policeman lounges about, keeping the peace without unnecessary exertion.

TIME: *It is a little before noon in the Spring of next year.*

AT RISE: *The President and the Baron enter with importance, and are ushered to a front table by the Waiter.*

———

THE PRESIDENT. Baron, sit down. This is a historic occasion. It must be properly celebrated. The waiter is going to bring out my special port.

THE BARON. Splendid.

THE PRESIDENT *(offers his cigar case)*. Cigar? My private brand.

THE BARON. Thank you. You know, this all gives me the feeling of one of those enchanted mornings in the *Arabian Nights* when thieves foregather in the market place. Thieves—pashas . . .

(He sniffs the cigar judiciously, and begins lighting it.)

THE PRESIDENT *(chuckles)*. Tell me about yourself.

THE BARON. Well, where shall I begin? *(The Street Singer enters. He takes off a battered black felt with a flourish and begins singing an ancient mazurka.)*

STREET SINGER *(sings)*

Do you hear, Mademoiselle,
Those musicians of hell?

THE PRESIDENT. Waiter! Get rid of that man.

WAITER. He is singing *La Belle Polonaise*.

THE PRESIDENT. I didn't ask for the program. I asked you to get rid of him. *(The Waiter doesn't budge. The Singer goes by himself)* As you were saying, Baron . . . ?

THE BARON. Well, until I was fifty . . . *(The Flower Girl enters through the café door, center)* my life was relatively un-complicated. It consisted of selling off one by one the various estates left me by my father. Three years ago, I parted with my last farm. Two years ago, I lost my last mistress. And now—all that is left me is . . .

THE FLOWER GIRL *(to the Baron)*. Violets, sir?

THE PRESIDENT. Run along. *(The Flower Girl moves on.)*

THE BARON *(staring after her)*. So that, in short, all I have left now is my name.

THE PRESIDENT. Your name is precisely the name we need on our board of directors.

THE BARON *(with an inclination of his head)*. Very flattering.

THE PRESIDENT. You will understand when I tell you that mine has been a very different experience. I came up from the bottom. My mother spent most of her life bent over a washtub in order to send me to school. I'm eternally grateful to her, of course, but I must confess that I no longer remember her face. It was no doubt beautiful—but when I try to recall it, I see only the part she invariably showed me—her rear.

THE BARON. Very touching.

THE PRESIDENT. When I was thrown out of school for the fifth and last time, I decided to find out for myself what makes the world go round. I ran errands for an editor, a movie star, a financier . . . I began to understand a little what life is. Then, one day, in the subway, I saw a face . . . My rise in life dates from that day.

THE BARON. Really?

THE PRESIDENT. One look at that face, and I knew. One look at mine, and he knew. And so I made my first thousand—

passing a boxful of counterfeit notes. A year later, I saw another such face. It got me a nice berth in the narcotics business. Since then, all I do is to look out for such faces. And now here I am—president of eleven corporations, director of fifty-two companies, and, beginning today, chairman of the board of the international combine in which you have been so good as to accept a post.

(The Ragpicker passes, sees something under the President's table, and stoops to pick it up.) Looking for something?

THE RAGPICKER. Did you drop this?

THE PRESIDENT. I never drop anything.

THE RAGPICKER. Then this hundred-franc note isn't yours?

THE PRESIDENT. Give it here.

(The Ragpicker gives him the note, and goes out.)

THE BARON. Are you sure it's yours?

THE PRESIDENT. All hundred-franc notes, Baron, are mine.

THE BARON. Mr. President, there's something I've been wanting to ask you. What exactly is the purpose of our new company? Or is that an indiscreet question . . . ?

THE PRESIDENT. Indiscreet? Not a bit. Merely unusual. As far as I know, you're the first member of a board of directors ever to ask such a question.

THE BARON. Do we plan to exploit a commodity? A utility?

THE PRESIDENT. My dear sir, I haven't the faintest idea.

THE BARON. But if you don't know—who does?

THE PRESIDENT. Nobody. And at the moment, it's becoming just a trifle embarrassing. Yes, my dear Baron, since we are now close business associates, I must confess that for the time being we're in a little trouble.

THE BARON. I was afraid of that. The stock issue isn't going well?

THE PRESIDENT. No, no—on the contrary. The stock issue is going beautifully. Yesterday morning at ten o'clock we offered 500,000 shares to the general public. By 10:05 they were all snapped up at par. By 10:20, when the police finally arrived, our offices were a shambles . . . Windows smashed—doors torn

off their hinges—you never saw anything so beautiful in your life! And this morning our stock is being quoted over the counter at 124 with no sellers, and the orders are still pouring in.

THE BARON. But in that case—what is the trouble?

THE PRESIDENT. The trouble is we have a tremendous capital, and not the slightest idea of what to do with it.

THE BARON. You mean all those people are fighting to buy stock in a company that has no object?

THE PRESIDENT. My dear Baron, do you imagine that when a subscriber buys a share of stock, he has any idea of getting behind a counter or digging a ditch? A stock certificate is not a tool, like a shovel, or a commodity, like a pound of cheese. What we sell a customer is not a share in a business, but a view of the Elysian Fields. A financier is a creative artist. Our function is to stimulate the imagination. We are poets!

THE BARON. But in order to stimulate the imagination, don't you need some field of activity?

THE PRESIDENT. Not at all. What you need for that is a name. A name that will stir the pulse like a trumpet call, set the brain awhirl like a movie star, inspire reverence like a cathedral. *United General International Consolidated!* Of course that's been used. That's what a corporation needs.

THE BARON. And do we have such a name?

THE PRESIDENT. So far we have only a blank space. In that blank space a name must be printed. This name must be a masterpiece. And if I seem a little nervous today, it's because—somehow— I've racked my brains, but it hasn't come to me. Oho! Look at that! Just like the answer to a prayer . . . ! *(The Baron turns and stares in the direction of the Prospector)* You see? There's one. And what a beauty!

THE BARON. You mean that girl?

THE PRESIDENT. No, no, not the girl. That face. You see . . . ? The one that's drinking water.

THE BARON. You call that a face? That's a tombstone.

THE PRESIDENT. It's a milestone. It's a signpost. But is it pointing the way to steel, or wheat, or phosphates? That's what we have to find out. Ah! He sees me. He understands. He will be over.

THE BARON. And when he comes . . . ?

THE PRESIDENT. He will tell me what to do.

THE BARON. You mean business is done this way? You mean, you would trust a stranger with a matter of this importance?

THE PRESIDENT. Baron, I trust neither my wife, nor my daughter, nor my closest friend. My confidential secretary has no idea where I live. But a face like that I would trust with my inmost secrets. Though we have never laid eyes on each other before, that man and I know each other to the depths of our souls. He's no stranger—he's my brother, he's myself. You'll see. He'll be over in a minute. *(The Deaf-Mute enters and passes slowly among the tables, placing a small envelope before each customer. He comes to the President's table)* What is this anyway? A conspiracy? We don't want your envelopes. Take them away. *(The Deaf-Mute makes a short but pointed speech in sign language)* Waiter, what the devil's he saying?

WAITER. Only Irma understands him.

THE PRESIDENT. Irma? Who's Irma?

WAITER *(calls)*. Irma! It's the waitress inside, sir. Irma!

(Irma comes out. She is twenty. She has the face and figure of an angel.)

IRMA. Yes?

WAITER. These gentlemen would . . .

THE PRESIDENT. Tell this fellow to get out of here, for God's sake! *(The Deaf Mute makes another manual oration)* What's he trying to say, anyway?

IRMA. He says it's an exceptionally beautiful morning, sir . . .

THE PRESIDENT. Who asked him?

IRMA. But, he says, it was nicer before the gentleman stuck his face in it.

THE PRESIDENT. Call the manager!

(Irma shrugs. She goes back into the restaurant. The Deaf-Mute walks off, Left. Meanwhile a Shoelace Peddler has arrived.)

PEDDLER. Shoelaces? Postcards?

THE BARON. I think I could use a shoelace.

THE PRESIDENT. No, no . . .

PEDDLER. Black? Tan?

THE BARON *(showing his shoes)*. What would you recommend?

PEDDLER. Anybody's guess.

THE BARON. Well, give me one of each.

THE PRESIDENT *(putting a hand on the Baron's arm)*. Baron, although I am your chairman, I have no authority over your personal life—none, that is, except to fix the amount of your director's fees, and eventually to assign a motor car for your use. Therefore, I am asking you, as a personal favor to me, not to purchase anything from this fellow.

THE BARON. How can I resist so gracious a request? *(The Peddler shrugs, and passes on)* But I really don't understand . . . . What difference would it make?

THE PRESIDENT. Look here, Baron. Now that you're with us, you must understand that between this irresponsible riff-raff and us there is an impenetrable barrier. *We* have no dealings whatever with *them*.

THE BARON. But without us, the poor devil will starve.

THE PRESIDENT. No, he won't. He expects nothing from us. He has a clientele of his own. He sells shoelaces exclusively to those who have no shoes. Just as the necktie peddler sells only to those who wear no shirts. And that's why these street hawkers can afford to be insolent, disrespectful and independent. They don't need us. They have a world of their own. Ah! My broker. Splendid. He's beaming. *(The Broker walks up and grasps the President's hand with enthusiasm)*

BROKER. Mr. President! My heartiest congratulations! What a day! What a day! *(The Street Juggler appears, Right. He removes his coat, folds it carefully, and puts it on the bench. Then he opens a suitcase, from which he extracts a number of colored clubs.)*

THE PRESIDENT *(presenting the Broker)*. Baron Tommard, of our Board of Directors. My broker. *(The Broker bows. So does the Juggler. The Broker sits down and signals for a drink. The Juggler prepares to juggle)* What's happened?

BROKER. Listen to this. Ten o'clock this morning. The market opens. *(As he speaks, the Juggler provides a visual counterpart to the Broker's lines, his clubs rising and falling in rhythm to the words)* Half million shares issued at par, par value a hundred, quoted on the curb at 124 and we start buying at 126, 127, 129—and it's going up—up—up—*(The Juggler's clubs rise higher and higher)*—132—133—138—141—141—141—141 . . .

THE BARON. May I ask . . . ?

THE PRESIDENT. No, no—any explanation would only confuse you.

BROKER. Ten forty-five we start selling short on rumors of a Communist plot, market bearish . . . 141—138—133—132—and it's down—down—down—102—and we start buying back at 93. Eleven o'clock, rumors denied—95—98—101—106—124—141—and by 11:30 we've got it all back—net profit three and a half million francs.

THE PRESIDENT. Classical. Pure. *(The Juggler bows again. A Little Man leans over from a near-by table, listening intently, and trembling with excitement)* And how many shares do we reserve to each member of the board?

BROKER. Fifty, as agreed.

THE PRESIDENT. Bit stingy, don't you think?

BROKER. All right—three thousand.

THE PRESIDENT. That's a little better. *(To the Baron)* You get the idea?

THE BARON. I'm beginning to get it.

BROKER. And now we come to the exciting part . . . *(The Juggler prepares to juggle with balls of fire)* Listen carefully: With 35 percent of our funded capital under Section 32 I buy 50,000 United at 36 which I immediately reconvert into 32,000 National Amalgamated two's preferred which I set up as collateral on 150,000 General Consols which I deposit against a credit of fifteen billion to buy Eastern Hennequin which I immediately turn into Argentine wheat realizing 136 percent of the original investment which naturally accrues as capital gain and not as corporate income thus saving twelve millions in taxes, and at once convert the

25 percent cotton reserve into lignite, and as our people swing into action in London and New York, I beat up the price on raw silk from 26 to 92—114—203—306—*(The Juggler by now is juggling his fireballs in the sky. The balls no longer return to his hands)* 404 . . . *(The Little Man can stand no more. He rushes over and dumps a sackful of money on the table)*

LITTLE MAN. Here—take it—please, take it!

BROKER *(frigidly)*. Who is this man? What is this money?

LITTLE MAN. It's my life's savings. Every cent. I put it all in your hands.

BROKER. Can't you see we're busy?

LITTLE MAN. But I beg you . . . It's my only chance . . . Please don't turn me away.

BROKER. Oh, all right. *(He sweeps the money into his pocket)* Well?

LITTLE MAN. I thought—perhaps you'd give me a little receipt . . .

THE PRESIDENT. My dear man, people like us don't give receipts for money. We take them.

LITTLE MAN. Oh, pardon. Of course. I was confused. Here it is. *(Scribbles a receipt)* Thank you—thank you—thank you. *(He rushes off joyfully. The Street Singer reappears)*

STREET SINGER *(sings)*
Do you hear, Mademoiselle,
Those musicians of hell?

THE PRESIDENT. What, again? Why does he keep repeating those two lines like a parrot?

WAITER. What else can he do? He doesn't know any more and the song's been out of print for years.

THE BARON. Couldn't he sing a song he knows?

WAITER. He likes this one. He hopes if he keeps singing the beginning someone will turn up to teach him the end.

THE PRESIDENT. Tell him to move on. We don't know the song.

(The Professor strolls by, swinging his cane. He overhears.)

PROFESSOR *(stops and addresses the President politely)*. Nor do I, my dear sir. Nor do I. And yet, I'm in exactly the same predicament. I remember just two lines of my favorite song, as a child. A mazurka also, in case you're interested...

THE PRESIDENT. I'm not.

PROFESSOR. Why is it, I wonder, that one always forgets the words of a mazurka? I suppose they just get lost in that damnable rhythm. All I remember is: *(He sings)*

From England to Spain
I have drunk, it was bliss . . .

STREET SINGER *(walks over, and picks up the tune)*.

Red wine and champagne
And many a kiss.

PROFESSOR. Oh, God! It all comes back to me . . . ! *(He sings)*

Red lips and white hands I have
[known
Where the nightingales dwell . . .

THE PRESIDENT *(holding his hands to his ears)*. Please—please . . .

STREET SINGER

And to each one I've whispered,
["My own,"
And to each one, I've murmured:
["Farewell."

THE PRESIDENT. Farewell. Farewell.

STREET SINGER *and* PROFESSOR *(duo)*.

But there's one I shall never forget..

THE PRESIDENT. This isn't a café. It's a circus!

(The two go off, still singing: "There is one that's engraved in my heart." The Prospector gets up slowly and walks toward the President's table. He looks down without a word. There is a tense silence.)

PROSPECTOR. Well?

THE PRESIDENT. I need a name.

PROSPECTOR *(nods, with complete comprehension)*. I need fifty thousand.

THE PRESIDENT. For a corporation.

PROSPECTOR. For a woman.

THE PRESIDENT. Immediately.

PROSPECTOR. Before evening.

THE PRESIDENT. Something . . .

PROSPECTOR. Unusual?

THE PRESIDENT. Something . . .

PROSPECTOR. Provocative?

THE PRESIDENT. Something . . .

PROSPECTOR. Practical.

THE PRESIDENT. Yes.

PROSPECTOR. Fifty thousand. Cash.

THE PRESIDENT. I'm listening.

PROSPECTOR. *International Substrate of Paris, Inc.*

THE PRESIDENT *(snaps his fingers)*. That's it! *(To the Broker)* Pay him off. *(The Broker pays with the Little Man's money)* Now—what does it mean?

PROSPECTOR. It means what it says. I'm a prospector.

THE PRESIDENT *(rises)*. A prospector! Allow me to shake your hand. Baron. You are in the presence of one of nature's noblemen. Shake his hand. This is Baron Tommard. *(They shake hands)* It is this man, my dear Baron, who smells out in the bowels of the earth those deposits of metal or liquid on which can be founded the only social unit of which our age is capable—the corporation. Sit down, please. *(They all sit)* And now that we have a name . . .

PROSPECTOR. You need a property.

THE PRESIDENT. Precisely.

PROSPECTOR. I have one.

THE PRESIDENT. A claim?

PROSPECTOR. Terrific.

THE PRESIDENT. Foreign?

PROSPECTOR. French.

THE BARON. In Indo-China?

BROKER. Morocco?

THE PRESIDENT. In France?

PROSPECTOR *(matter of fact)*. In Paris.

THE PRESIDENT. In Paris? You've been prospecting in Paris?

THE BARON. For women, no doubt.

THE PRESIDENT. For art?

BROKER. For gold?

PROSPECTOR. Oil.

BROKER. He's crazy.

THE PRESIDENT. Sh! He's inspired.

PROSPECTOR. You think I'm crazy. Well, they thought Columbus was crazy.

THE BARON. Oil in Paris?

BROKER. But how is it possible?

PROSPECTOR. It's not only possible. It's certain.

THE PRESIDENT. Tell us.

PROSPECTOR. You don't know, my dear sir, what treasures Paris conceals Paris is the least prospected place in the world. We've gone over the rest of the planet with a fine-tooth comb. But has anyone ever thought of looking for oil in Paris? Nobody. Before me, that is.

THE PRESIDENT. Genius!

PROSPECTOR. No. Just a practical man I use my head.

THE BARON. But why has nobody ever thought of this before?

PROSPECTOR. The treasures of the earth, my dear sir, are not easy to find nor to get at. They are invariably guarded by dragons. Doubtless there is some reason for this. For once we've dug out and consumed the internal ballast of the planet, the chances are it will shoot off on some irresponsible tangent and smash itself up in the sky. Well, that's the risk we take. Anyway, that's not my business. A prospector has enough to worry about.

THE BARON. I know—snakes—tarantulas—fleas . . .

PROSPECTOR. Worse than that, sir. Civilization.

THE PRESIDENT. Does that annoy you?

PROSPECTOR. Civilization gets in our way all the time. In the first place, it covers the earth with cities and towns which are damned awkward to dig up when you want to see what's underneath. It's not only the real-estate people—you can always do business with them—it's human sentimentality. How do you do business with that?

THE PRESIDENT. I see what you mean.

PROSPECTOR. They say that where we pass, nothing ever grows again. What of it? Is a park any better than a coal mine? What's a mountain got that a slag pile hasn't? What would you rather have in your garden—an almond tree or an oil well?

THE PRESIDENT. Well . . .

PROSPECTOR. Exactly. But what's the use of arguing with these fools? Imagine the choicest place you ever saw for an excavation, and what do they put there? A playground for children! Civilization!

THE PRESIDENT. Just show us the point where you want to start digging. We'll do the rest. Even if it's in the middle of the Louvre. Where's the oil?

PROSPECTOR. Perhaps you think it's easy to make an accurate fix in an area like Paris where everything conspires to put you off the scent? Women—perfume —flowers—history. You can talk all you like about geology, but an oil deposit, gentlemen, has to be smelled out. I have a good nose. I go further. I have a phenomenal nose. But the minute I get the right whiff—the minute I'm on the scent —a fragrance rises from what I take to be the spiritual deposits of the past—and I'm completely at sea. Now take this very point, for example, this very spot.

THE BARON. You mean—right here in Chaillot?

PROSPECTOR. Right under here.

THE PRESIDENT. Good heavens!

(He looks under his chair.)

PROSPECTOR. It's taken me months to locate this spot.

THE BARON. But what in the world makes you think . . . ?

PROSPECTOR. Do you know this place, Baron?

THE BARON. Well, I've been sitting here for thirty years.

PROSPECTOR. Did you ever taste the water?

THE BARON. The water? Good God, no!

PROSPECTOR. It's plain to see that you are no prospector! A prospector, Baron, is addicted to water as a drunkard to wine. Water, gentlemen, is the one substance from which the earth can conceal nothing. It sucks out its innermost secrets and brings them to our very lips. Well— beginning at Notre Dame, where I first caught the scent of oil three months ago, I worked my way across Paris, glassful by glassful, sampling the water, until at last I came to this café. And here—just two days ago—I took a sip. My heart began to thump. Was it possible that I was deceived? I took another, a third, a fourth, a fifth. I was trembling like a leaf. But there was no mistake. Each time that I drank, my taste-buds thrilled to the most exquisite flavor known to a prospector— the flavor of— (With utmost lyricism) Petroleum!

THE PRESIDENT. Waiter! Some water and four glasses. Hurry. This round, gentlemen, is on me. And as a toast—I shall propose International Substrate of Paris, Incorporated. (The Waiter brings a decanter and the glasses. The President pours out the water amid profound silence. They taste it with the air of connoisseurs savoring something that has never before passed human lips. Then they look at each other doubtfully. The Prospector pours himself a second glass and drinks it off) Well . . .

BROKER. Ye-es . . .

THE BARON. Mm . . .

PROSPECTOR. Get it?

THE BARON. Tastes queer.

PROSPECTOR. That's it. To the unpracticed palate it tastes queer. But to the taste-buds of the expert—ah!

THE BARON. Still, there's one thing I don't quite understand . . .

PROSPECTOR. Yes?

THE BARON. This café doesn't have its own well, does it?

PROSPECTOR. Of course not. This is Paris water.

BROKER. Then why should it taste different here than anywhere else?

PROSPECTOR. Because, my dear sir, the pipes that carry this water pass deep through the earth, and the earth just here is soaked with oil, and this oil permeates the pores of the iron and flavors the water it carries. Ever so little, yes—but quite enough to betray its presence to the sensitive tongue of the specialist.

THE BARON. I see.

PROSPECTOR. I don't say everyone is capable of tasting it. No. But I—I can detect the presence of oil in water that has passed within fifteen miles of a deposit. Under special circumstances, twenty.

THE PRESIDENT. Phenomenal!

PROSPECTOR. And so here I am with the greatest discovery of the age on my hands—but the blasted authorities won't let me drill a single well unless I show them the oil! Now how can I show them the oil unless they let me dig? Completely stymied! Eh?

THE PRESIDENT. What? A man like you?

PROSPECTOR. That's what they think. That's what they want. Have you noticed the strange glamor of the women this morning? And the quality of the sunshine? And this extraordinary convocation of vagabonds buzzing about protectively like bees around a hive? Do you know why it is? Because they know. It's a plot to distract us, to turn us from our purpose. Well, let them try. I know there's oil here. And I'm going to dig it up, even if I . . . (He smiles) Shall I tell you my little plan?

THE PRESIDENT. By all means.

PROSPECTOR. Well . . . For heaven's sake, what's that?

(At this point, the Madwoman enters. She is dressed in the grand fashion of 1885, a taffeta skirt with an immense train—which she has gathered up by means of a clothespin—ancient button shoes, and a hat in the style of Marie Antoinette. She wears a lorgnette on a chain, and an enormous cameo pin at her throat. In her hand she carries a small basket. She walks in with great dignity, extracts a dinner bell from the bosom of her dress, and rings it sharply. Irma appears.)

COUNTESS. Are my bones ready, Irma?

IRMA. There won't be much today, Countess. We had broilers. Can you wait? While the gentleman inside finishes eating?

COUNTESS. And my gizzard?

IRMA. I'll try to get it away from him.

COUNTESS. If he eats my gizzard, save me the giblets. They will do for the tomcat that lives under the bridge. He likes a few giblets now and again.

IRMA. Yes, Countess.

(Irma goes back into the café. The Countess takes a few steps and stops in front of the President's table. She examines him with undisguised disapproval.)

THE PRESIDENT. Waiter. Ask that woman to move on.

WAITER. Sorry, sir. This is her café.

THE PRESIDENT. Is she the manager of the café?

WAITER. She's the Madwoman of Chaillot.

THE PRESIDENT. A Madwoman? She's mad?

WAITER. Who says she's mad?

THE PRESIDENT. You just said so yourself.

WAITER. Look, sir. You asked me who she was. And I told you. What's mad about her? She's the Madwoman of Chaillot.

THE PRESIDENT. Call a policeman.

(The Countess whistles through her fingers. At once, the Doorman runs out of the café. He has three scarves in his hands.)

COUNTESS. Have you found it? My feather boa?

DOORMAN. Not yet, Countess. Three scarves. But no boa.

COUNTESS. It's five years since I lost it. Surely you've had time to find it.

DOORMAN. Take one of these, Countess. Nobody's claimed them.

COUNTESS. A boa like that doesn't vanish, you know. A feather boa nine feet long!

DOORMAN. How about this blue one?

COUNTESS. With my pink ruffle and my green veil? You're joking! Let me see the yellow. (She tries it on) How does it look?

DOORMAN. Terrific.

(With a magnificent gesture, she flings the scarf about her, upsetting the President's glass and drenching his trousers with water. She stalks off without a glance at him.)

THE PRESIDENT. Waiter! I'm making a complaint.

WAITER. Against whom?

THE PRESIDENT. Against her! Against you! The whole gang of you! That singer! That shoelace peddler! That female lunatic! Or whatever you call her!

THE BARON. Calm yourself, Mr. President . . .

THE PRESIDENT. I'll do nothing of the sort! Baron, the first thing we have to do is to get rid of these people! Good heavens, look at them! Every size, shape, color and period of history imaginable. It's utter anarchy! I tell you, sir, the only safeguard of order and discipline in the modern world is a standardized worker with interchangeable parts. That would solve the entire problem of management. Here, the manager . . . And there—one composite drudge grunting and sweating all over the world. Just we two. Ah, how beautiful! How easy on the eyes! How restful for the conscience!

THE BARON. Yes, yes—of course.

THE PRESIDENT. Order. Symmetry. Balance. But instead of that, what? Here in Chaillot, the very citadel of management, these insolent phantoms of the past come to beard us with their raffish individualism—with the right of the voiceless to sing, of the dumb to make speeches, of trousers to have no seats and bosoms to have dinner bells!

THE BARON. But, after all, do these people matter?

THE PRESIDENT. My dear sir, wherever the poor are happy, and the servants are proud, and the mad are respected, our power is at an end. Look at that! That waiter! That madwoman! That flower girl! Do I get that sort of service? And suppose that I—president of twelve corporations and ten times a millionaire—were to stick a gladiolus in my button-hole and start yelling—(He tinkles his spoon in a glass violently, yelling) Are my bones ready, Irma?

THE BARON (reprovingly).

Mr. President . . .

(People at the adjoining tables turn and stare with raised eyebrows. The Waiter starts to come over.)

THE PRESIDENT. You see? Now.

PROSPECTOR. We were discussing my plan.

THE PRESIDENT. Ah yes, your plan. (He glances in the direction of the Madwoman's table) Careful—she's looking at us.

PROSPECTOR. Do you know what a bomb is?

THE PRESIDENT. I'm told they explode.

PROSPECTOR. Exactly. You see that white building across the river. Do you happen to know what that is?

THE PRESIDENT. I do not.

PROSPECTOR. That's the office of the City Architect. That man has stubbornly refused to give me a permit to drill for oil anywhere within the limits of the city of Paris. I've tried everything with him—influence, bribes, threats. He says I'm crazy. And now . . .

THE PRESIDENT. Oh, my God! What is this one trying to sell us?

(A little Old Man enters left, and doffs his hat politely. He is somewhat ostentatiously respectable—gloved, pomaded, and carefully dressed, with a white handkerchief peeping out of his breast pocket.)

DR. JADIN. Nothing but health, sir. Or rather the health of the feet. But remember—as the foot goes, so goes the man. May I present myself . . . ? Dr. Gaspard Jadin, French Navy, retired. Former specialist in the extraction of ticks and chiggers. At present specializing in the extraction of bunions and corns. In case of sudden emergency, Martial the waiter will furnish my home address. My office is here, second row, third table, week days, twelve to five. Thank you very much.

(He sits at his table.)

WAITER. Your vermouth, Doctor?

DR. JADIN. My vermouth. My vermouths. How are your gallstones today, Martial?

WAITER. Fine. Fine. They rattle like anything.

DR. JADIN. Splendid. *(He spies the Countess)* Good morning, Countess. How's the floating kidney? Still afloat? *(She nods graciously)* Splendid. Splendid. So long as it floats, it can't sink.

THE PRESIDENT. This is impossible! Let's go somewhere else.

PROSPECTOR. No. It's nearly noon.

THE PRESIDENT. Yes. It is. Five to twelve.

PROSPECTOR. In five minutes' time you're going to see that City Architect blown up, building and all—boom!

BROKER. Are you serious?

PROSPECTOR. That imbecile has no one to blame but himself. Yesterday noon, he got my ultimatum—he's had twenty-four hours to think it over. No permit? All right. Within two minutes my agent is going to drop a little package in his coal bin. And three minutes after that, precisely at noon . . .

THE BARON. You prospectors certainly use modern methods.

PROSPECTOR. The method may be modern. But the idea is old. To get at the treasure, it has always been necessary to slay the dragon. I guarantee that after this, the City Architect will be more reasonable. The new one, I mean.

THE PRESIDENT. Don't you think we're sitting a little close for comfort?

PROSPECTOR. Oh no, no. Don't worry. And, above all, don't stare. We may be watched. *(A clock strikes)* Why, that's noon. Something's wrong! Good God! What's this? *(A Policeman staggers in bearing a lifeless body on his shoulders in the manner prescribed as "The Fireman's Lift")* It's Pierre! My agent! *(He walks over with affected nonchalance)* I say, Officer, what's that you've got?

POLICEMAN. Drowned man.

(He puts him down on the bench.)

WAITER. He's not drowned. His clothes are dry. He's been slugged.

POLICEMAN. Slugged is also correct. He was just jumping off the bridge when I came along and pulled him back. I slugged him, naturally, so he wouldn't drag me under. Life Saving Manual, Rule 5: "In cases where there is danger of being dragged under, it is necessary to render the subject unconscious by means of a sharp blow." He's had that.

(He loosens the clothes and begins applying artificial respiration.)

PROSPECTOR. The stupid idiot! What the devil did he do with the bomb? That's what comes of employing amateurs!

THE PRESIDENT. You don't think he'll give you away?

PROSPECTOR. Don't worry. *(He walks over to the policeman)* Say, what do you think you're doing?

POLICEMAN. Lifesaving. Artificial respiration. First aid to the drowning.

PROSPECTOR. But he's not drowning.

POLICEMAN. But he thinks he is.

PROSPECTOR. You'll never bring him round that way, my friend. That's meant for people who drown in water. It's no good at all for those who drown without water.

POLICEMAN. What am I supposed do? I've just been sworn in. It's my first day on the beat. I can't afford to get in trouble. I've got to go by the book.

PROSPECTOR. Perfectly simple. Take him back to the bridge where you found him and throw him in. Then you can save his life and you'll get a medal. This way, you'll only get fined for slugging an innocent man.

POLICEMAN. What do you mean, innocent? He was just going to jump when I grabbed him.

PROSPECTOR. Have you any proof of that?

POLICEMAN. Well, I saw him.

PROSPECTOR. Written proof? Witnesses?

POLICEMAN. No, but . . .

PROSPECTOR. Then don't waste time arguing. You're in trouble. Quick—before anybody notices—throw him in and dive after him. It's the only way out.

POLICEMAN. But I don't swim.

THE PRESIDENT. You'll learn how on the way down. Before you were born, did you know how to breathe?

POLICEMAN (convinced). All right. Here we go.

(He starts lifting the body.)

DR. JADIN. One moment, please. I don't like to interfere, but it's my professional duty to point out that medical science has definitely established the fact of intra-uterine respiration. Consequently, this policeman, even before he was born, knew not only how to breathe but also how to cough, hiccup and belch.

THE PRESIDENT. Suppose he did—how does it concern you?

DR. JADIN. On the other hand, medical science has never established the fact of intra-uterine swimming or diving. Under the circumstances, we are forced to the opinion, Officer, that if you dive in you will probably drown.

POLICEMAN. You think so?

PROSPECTOR. Who asked you for an opinion?

THE PRESIDENT. Pay no attention to that quack, Officer.

DR. JADIN. Quack, sir?

PROSPECTOR. This is not a medical matter. It's a legal problem. The officer has made a grave error. He's new. We're trying to help him.

BROKER. He's probably afraid of the water.

POLICEMAN. Nothing of the sort. Officially, I'm afraid of nothing. But I always follow doctor's orders.

DR. JADIN. You see, Officer, when a child is born . . .

PROSPECTOR. Now, what does he care about when a child is born? He's got a dying man on his hands . . . Officer, if you want my advice . . .

POLICEMAN. It so happens, I care a lot about when a child is born. It's part of my duty to aid and assist any woman in childbirth or labor.

THE PRESIDENT. Can you imagine!

POLICEMAN. Is it true, Doctor, what they say, that when you have twins, the first born is considered to be the youngest?

DR. JADIN. Quite correct. And what's

more, if the twins happen to be born at midnight on December 31st, the older is a whole year younger. He does his military service a year later. That's why you have to keep your eyes open. And that's the reason why a queen always gives birth before witness . . .

POLICEMAN. God! The things a policeman is supposed to know! Doctor, what does it mean if, when I get up in the morning sometimes . . .

PROSPECTOR (nudging the President meaningfully). The old woman . . .

BROKER. Come on, Baron.

THE PRESIDENT. I think we'd better all run along.

PROSPECTOR. Leave him to me.

THE PRESIDENT. I'll see you later.

(The President steals off with the Broker and the Baron.)

POLICEMAN (still in conference with Dr. Jadin). But what's really worrying me, Doctor, is this—don't you think it's a bit risky for a man to marry after forty-five?

(The Broker runs in breathlessly.)

BROKER. Officer! Officer!

POLICEMAN. What's the trouble?

BROKER. Quick! Two women are calling for help—on the sidewalk—Avenue Wilson!

POLICEMAN. Two women at once? Standing up or lying down?

BROKER. You'd better go and see. Quick!

PROSPECTOR. You'd better take the Doctor with you.

POLICEMAN. Come along, Doctor, come along . . . (Pointing to Pierre) Tell him to wait till I get back. Come along, Doctor.

(He runs out, the Doctor following. The Prospector moves over toward Pierre, but Irma crosses in front of him and takes the boy's hand.)

IRMA. How beautiful he is! Is he dead, Martial?

WAITER (handing her a pocket mirror). Hold this mirror to his mouth. If it clouds over . . .

IRMA. It clouds over.

WAITER. He's alive.

(He holds out his hand for the mirror.)

IRMA. Just a sec— (She rubs it clean and looks at herself intently. Before handing it *back, she fixes her hair and applies her lip-stick. Meanwhile the Prospector tries to get around the other side, but the Countess' eagle eye drives him off. He shrugs his shoulders and exits with the Baron)* Oh, look—he's opened his eyes!

(Pierre opens his eyes, stares intently at Irma and closes them again with the expression of a man who is among the angels.)

PIERRE *(murmurs)*. Oh! How beautiful!

VOICE *(from within the café)*. Irma!

IRMA. Coming. Coming. *(She goes in, not without a certain reluctance. The Countess at once takes her place on the bench, and also the young man's hand. Pierre sits up suddenly, and finds himself staring, not at Irma, but into the very peculiar face of the Countess. His expression changes.)*

COUNTESS. You're looking at my iris? Isn't it beautiful?

PIERRE. Very. *(He drops back, exhausted.)*

COUNTESS. The Sergeant was good enough to say it becomes me. But I no longer trust his taste. Yesterday, the flower girl gave me a lily, and he said it didn't suit me.

PIERRE *(weakly)*. It's beautiful.

COUNTESS. He'll be very happy to know that you agree with him. He's really quite sensitive. *(She calls)* Sergeant!

PIERRE. No, please—don't call the police.

COUNTESS. But I must. I think I hurt his feelings.

PIERRE. Let me go, Madame.

COUNTESS. No, no. Stay where you are. Sergeant!

(Pierre struggles weakly to get up.)

PIERRE. Please let me go.

COUNTESS. I'll do nothing of the sort. When you let someone go, you never see him again. I let Charlotte Mazumet go. I never saw her again.

PIERRE. Oh, my head.

COUNTESS. I let Adolphe Bertaut go. And I was holding him. And I never saw him again.

PIERRE. Oh, God!

COUNTESS. Except once. Thirty years later. In the market. He had changed a great deal—he didn't know me. He sneaked a melon from right under my

nose, the only good one of the year. Ah, here we are. Sergeant!

(The Police Sergeant comes in with importance.)

SERGEANT. I'm in a hurry, Countess.

COUNTESS. With regard to the iris. This young man agrees with you. He says it suits me.

SERGEANT *(going)*. There's a man drowning in the Seine.

COUNTESS. He's not drowning in the Seine. He's drowning here. Because I'm holding him tight—as I should have held Adolphe Bertaut. But if I let him go, I'm sure he will go and drown in the Seine. He's a lot better looking than Adolphe Bertaut, wouldn't you say?

(Pierre sighs deeply.)

SERGEANT. How would I know?

COUNTESS. I've shown you his photograph. The one with the bicycle.

SERGEANT. Oh, yes. The one with the harelip.

COUNTESS. I've told you a hundred times! Adolphe Bertaut had no harelip. That was a scratch in the negative. *(The Sergeant takes out his notebook and pencil)* What are you doing?

SERGEANT. I am taking down the drowned man's name, given name and date of birth.

COUNTESS. You think that's going to stop him from jumping in the river? Don't be silly, Sergeant. Put that book away and try to console him.

SERGEANT. I should try and console him?

COUNTESS. When people want to die, it is your job as a guardian of the state to speak out in praise of life. Not mine.

SERGEANT. I should speak out in praise of life?

COUNTESS. I assume you have some motive for interfering with people's attempts to kill each other, and rob each other, and run each other over? If you believe that life has some value, tell him what it is. Go on.

SERGEANT. Well, all right. Now look, young man . . .

COUNTESS. His name is Roderick.

PIERRE. My name is not Roderick.

COUNTESS. Yes, it is. It's noon. At noon all men become Roderick.

SERGEANT. Except Adolphe Bertaut.

COUNTESS. In the days of Adolphe Bertaut, we were forced to change the men when we got tired of their names. Nowadays, we're more practical—each hour on the hour all names are automatically changed. The men remain the same. But you're not here to discuss Adolphe Bertaut, Sergeant. You're here to convince the young man that life is worth living.

PIERRE. It isn't.

SERGEANT. Quiet. Now then—what was the idea of jumping off the bridge, anyway?

COUNTESS. The idea was to land in the river. Roderick doesn't seem to be at all confused about that.

SERGEANT. Now how can I convince anybody that life is worth living if you keep interrupting all the time?

COUNTESS. I'll be quiet.

SERGEANT. First of all, Mr. Roderick, you have to realize that suicide is a crime against the state. And why is it a crime against the state? Because every time anybody commits suicide, that means one soldier less for the army, one taxpayer less for the . . .

COUNTESS. Sergeant, isn't there something about life that you really enjoy?

SERGEANT. That I enjoy?

COUNTESS. Well, surely, in all these years, you must have found something worth living for. Some secret pleasure, or passion. Don't blush. Tell him about it.

SERGEANT. Who's blushing? Well, naturally, yes—I have my passions—like everybody else. The fact is, since you ask me—I love—to play—casino. And if the gentleman would like to join me, by and by when I go off duty, we can sit down to a nice little game in the back room with a nice cold glass of beer. If he wants to kill an hour, that is.

COUNTESS. He doesn't want to kill an hour. He wants to kill himself. Well? Is that all the police force has to offer by way of earthly bliss?

SERGEANT. Huh? You mean— (He jerks a thumb in the direction of the pretty Blonde, who has just been joined by a Brunette of the same stamp) Paulette? (The young man groans)

COUNTESS. You're not earning your salary, Sergeant. I defy anybody to stop dying on your account.

SERGEANT. Go ahead, if you can do any better. But you won't find it easy.

COUNTESS. Oh, this is not a desperate case at all. A young man who has just fallen in love with someone who has fallen in love with him!

PIERRE. She hasn't. How could she?

COUNTESS. Oh, yes, she has. She was holding your hand, just as I'm holding it, when all of a sudden . . . Did you ever know Marshal Canrobert's niece?

SERGEANT. How could he know Marshal Canrobert's niece?

COUNTESS. Lots of people knew her— when she was alive. (Pierre begins to struggle energetically) No, no, Roderick—stop— stop!

SERGEANT. You see? You won't do any better than I did.

COUNTESS. No? Let's bet. I'll bet my iris against one of your gold buttons. Right?—Roderick, I know very well why you tried to drown yourself in the river.

PIERRE. You don't at all.

COUNTESS. It's because that Prospector wanted you to commit a horrible crime.

PIERRE. How did you know that?

COUNTESS. He stole my boa, and now he wants you to kill me.

PIERRE. Not exactly.

COUNTESS. It wouldn't be the first time they've tried it. But I'm not so easy to get rid of, my boy, oh, no . . . Because . . .

(The Doorman rides in on his bicycle. He winks at the Sergeant, who has now seated himself while the Waiter serves him a beer.)

DOORMAN. Take it easy, Sergeant.

SERGEANT. I'm busy saving a drowning man.

COUNTESS. They can't kill me because —I have no desire to die.

PIERRE. You're fortunate.

COUNTESS. To be alive is to be fortunate, Roderick. Of course, in the morning, when you first awake, it does not always seem so very gay. When you take your hair out of the drawer, and your teeth out of the glass, you are apt to feel a little out of place in this world. Especially if you've just been dreaming that you're a little girl on a pony looking for strawberries in the woods. But all you need to feel the call of life once more is a letter in your mail giving you your schedule for the day—your mending, your shopping, that letter to your grandmother that you never seem to get around to. And so, when you've washed your face in rosewater, and powdered it—not with this awful rice-powder they sell nowadays, which does nothing for the skin, but with a cake of pure white starch—and put on your pins, your rings, your brooches, bracelets, earrings and pearls—in short, when you are dressed for your morning coffee—and have had a good look at yourself—not in the glass, naturally—it lies—but in the side of the brass gong that once belonged to Admiral Courbet—then, Roderick, then you're armed, you're strong, you're ready—you can begin again.

(Pierre is listening now intently. There are tears in his eyes.)

PIERRE. Oh, Madame . . . ! Oh, Madame . . . !

COUNTESS. After that, everything is pure delight. First the morning paper. Not, of course, these current sheets full of lies and vulgarity. I always read the *Gaulois*, the issue of March 22, 1903. It's by far the best. It has some delightful scandal, some excellent fashion notes, and, of course, the last-minute bulletin on the death of Leonide Leblanc. She used to live next door, poor woman, and when I learn of her death every morning, it gives me quite a shock. I'd gladly lend you my copy, but it's in tatters.

SERGEANT. Couldn't we find him a copy in some library?

COUNTESS. I doubt it. And so, when you've taken your fruit salts—not in water, naturally—no matter what they say, it's water that gives you gas—but with a bit of spiced cake—then in sunlight or rain, Chaillot calls. It is time to dress for your morning walk. This takes much longer, of course—without a maid, impossible to do it under an hour, what with your corset, corset-cover and drawers all of which lace or button in the back. I asked Madame Lanvin, a while ago, to fit the drawers with zippers. She was quite

charming, but she declined. She thought it would spoil the style.

(The Deaf-Mute comes in.)

WAITER. I know a place where they put zippers on anything.

(The Ragpicker enters.)

COUNTESS. I think Lanvin knows best. But I really manage very well, Martial. What I do now is, I lace them up in front, then twist them around to the back. It's quite simple, really. Then you choose a lorgnette, and then the usual fruitless search for the feather boa that the prospector stole—I know it was he: he didn't dare look me in the eye—and then all you need is a rubber band to slip around your parasol—I lost the catch the day I struck the cat that was stalking the pigeon—it was worth it—ah, that day I earned my wages!

THE RAGPICKER. Countess, if you can use it, I found a nice umbrella catch the other day with a cat's eye in it.

COUNTESS. Thank you, Ragpicker. They say these eyes sometimes come to life and fill with tears. I'd be afraid . . .

PIERRE. Go on, Madame, go on . . .

COUNTESS. Ah! So life is beginning to interest you, is it? You see how beautiful it is?

PIERRE. What a fool I've been!

COUNTESS. Then, Roderick, I begin my rounds. I have my cats to feed, my dogs to pet, my plants to water. I have to see what the evil ones are up to in the district—those who hate people, those who hate plants, those who hate animals. I watch them sneaking off in the morning to put on their disguises—to the baths, to the beauty parlors, to the barbers. But they can't deceive me. And when they come out again with blonde hair and false whiskers, to pull up my flowers and poison my dogs, I'm there, and I'm ready. All you have to do to break their power is to cut across their path from the left. That isn't always easy. Vice moves swiftly. But I have a good long stride and I generally manage . . . Right, my friends?

(The Waiter and the Ragpicker nod their heads with evident approval) Yes, the flowers have been marvelous this year. And the butcher's dog on the Rue Bizet,

in spite of that wretch that tried to poison him, is friskier than ever . . .

SERGEANT. That dog had better look out. He has no license.

COUNTESS. He doesn't seem to feel the need for one.

THE RAGPICKER. The Duchess de la Rochefoucauld's whippet is getting awfully thin . . .

COUNTESS. What can I do? She bought that dog full grown from a kennel where they didn't know his right name. A dog without his right name is bound to get thin.

THE RAGPICKER. I've got a friend who knows a lot about dogs—an Arab . . .

COUNTESS. Ask him to call on the Duchess. She receives Thursdays, five to seven. You see, then, Roderick. That's life. Does it appeal to you now?

PIERRE. It seems marvelous.

COUNTESS. Ah! Sergeant. My button. *(The Sergeant gives her his button and goes off. At this point the Prospector enters)* That's only the morning. Wait till I tell you about the afternoon!

PROSPECTOR. All right, Pierre. Come along now.

PIERRE. I'm perfectly all right here.

PROSPECTOR. I said, come along now,

PIERRE *(to the Countess)*. I'd better go. Madame.

COUNTESS. No.

PIERRE. It's no use. Please let go my hand.

PROSPECTOR. Madame, will you oblige me by letting my friend go?

COUNTESS. I will not oblige you in any way.

PROSPECTOR. All right. Then I'll oblige you . . . !

(He tries to push her away. She catches up a soda water siphon and squirts it in his face.)

PIERRE. Countess . . .

COUNTESS. Stay where you are. This man isn't going to take you away. In the first place, I shall need you in a few minutes to take me home. I'm all alone here and I'm very easily frightened.

(The Prospector makes a second attempt to drag Pierre away. The Countess cracks him over the skull with the siphon. They join battle. The Countess whistles. The Doorman comes, then the other Vagabonds, and lastly the Police Sergeant.)

PROSPECTOR. Officer! Arrest this woman!

SERGEANT. What's the trouble here?

PROSPECTOR. She refuses to let this man go.

SERGEANT. Why should she?

PROSPECTOR. It's against the law for a woman to detain a man on the street.

IRMA. Suppose it's her son whom she's found again after twenty years?

THE RAGPICKER *(gallantly)*. Or her long-lost brother? The Countess is not so old.

PROSPECTOR. Officer, this is a clear case of disorderly conduct.

(The Deaf-Mute interrupts with frantic signals.)

COUNTESS. Irma, what is the Deaf-Mute saying?

IRMA *(interpreting)*. The young man is in danger of his life. He mustn't go with him.

PROSPECTOR. What does he know?

IRMA. He knows everything.

PROSPECTOR. Officer, I'll have to take your number.

COUNTESS. Take his number. It's 2133. It adds up to nine. It will bring you luck.

SERGEANT. Countess, between ourselves, what are you holding him for, anyway?

COUNTESS. I'm holding him because it's very pleasant to hold him. I've never really held anybody before, and I'm making the most of it. And because so long as *I* hold him, he's free.

PROSPECTOR. Pierre, I'm giving you fair warning . . .

COUNTESS. And I'm holding him because Irma wants me to hold him. Because if I let him go, it will break her heart.

IRMA. Oh, Countess!

SERGEANT *(to the Prospector)*. All right, you—move on. Nobody's holding you. You're blocking traffic. Move on.

PROSPECTOR *(menacingly)*. I have your number. *(And murderously, to Pierre)* You'll regret this, Pierre.

(Exit Prospector.)

PIERRE. Thank you, Countess.

COUNTESS. They're blackmailing you, are they? *(Pierre nods)* What have you done? Murdered somebody?

PIERRE. No.

COUNTESS. Stolen something?

PIERRE. No.

COUNTESS. What then?

PIERRE. I forged a signature.

COUNTESS. Whose signature?

PIERRE. My father's. To a note.

COUNTESS. And this man has the paper, I suppose?

PIERRE. He promised to tear it up, if I did what he wanted. But I couldn't do it.

COUNTESS. But the man is mad! Does he really want to destroy the whole neighborhood?

PIERRE. He wants to destroy the whole city.

COUNTESS (laughs). Fantastic.

PIERRE. It's not funny, Countess. He can do it. He's mad, but he's powerful, and he has friends. Their machines are already drawn up and waiting. In three months' time you may see the city covered by a forest of derricks and drills.

COUNTESS. But what are they looking for? Have they lost something?

PIERRE. They're looking for oil. They're convinced that Paris is sitting on a lake of oil.

COUNTESS. Suppose it is. What harm does it do?

PIERRE. They want to bring the oil to the surface, Countess.

COUNTESS (laughs). How silly! Is that a reason to destroy a city? What do they want with this oil?

PIERRE. They want to make war, Countess.

COUNTESS. Oh, dear, let's forget about these horrible men. The world is beautiful. It's happy. That's how God made it. No man can change it.

WAITER. Ah, Countess, if you only knew . . .

COUNTESS. If I only knew what?

WAITER. Shall we tell her now? Shall we tell her?

COUNTESS. What is it you are hiding from me?

THE RAGPICKER. Nothing, Countess. It's you who are hiding.

WAITER. You tell her. You've been a pitchman. You can talk.

ALL. Tell her. Tell her. Tell her.

COUNTESS. You're frightening me, my friends. Go on. I'm listening.

THE RAGPICKER. Countess, there was a time when old clothes were as good as new—in fact, they were better. Because when people wore clothes, they gave something to them. You may not believe it, but right this minute, the highest-priced shops in Paris are selling clothes that were thrown away thirty years ago. They're selling them for new. That's how good they were.

COUNTESS. Well?

THE RAGPICKER. Countess, there was a time when garbage was a pleasure. A garbage can was not what it is now. If it smelled a little strange, it was because it was a little confused—there was everything there—sardines, cologne, iodine, roses. An amateur might jump to a wrong conclusion. But to a professional—it was the smell of God's plenty.

COUNTESS. Well?

THE RAGPICKER. Countess, the world has changed.

COUNTESS. Nonsense. How could it change? People are the same, I hope.

THE RAGPICKER. No, Countess. The people are not the same. The people are different. There's been an invasion. An infiltration. From another planet. The world is not beautiful any more. It's not happy.

COUNTESS. Not happy? Is that true? Why didn't you tell me this before?

THE RAGPICKER. Because you live in a dream, Countess. And we don't like to disturb you.

COUNTESS. But how could it have happened?

THE RAGPICKER. Countess, there was a time when you could walk around Paris, and all the people you met were just like yourself. A little cleaner, maybe, or dirtier, perhaps, or angry, or smiling —but you knew them. They were you. Well, Countess, twenty years ago, one day, on the street, I saw a face in the crowd. A face, you might say, without a face. The eyes—empty. The expression— not human. Not a human face. It saw me staring, and when it looked back at me with its gelatine eyes, I shuddered. Because I knew that to make room for this one, one of us must have left the earth. A while after, I saw another. And another. And since then, I've seen hundreds come in—yes—thousands.

COUNTESS. Describe them to me.

THE RAGPICKER. You've seen them yourself, Countess. Their clothes don't wrinkle. Their hats don't come off. When they talk, they don't look at you. They don't perspire.

COUNTESS. Have they wives? Have they children?

THE RAGPICKER. They buy the models out of shop windows, furs and all. They animate them by a secret process. Then they marry them. Naturally, they don't have children.

COUNTESS. What work do they do?

THE RAGPICKER. They don't do any work. Whenever they meet, they whisper, and then they pass each other thousand-franc notes. You see them standing on the corner by the Stock Exchange. You see them at auctions—in the back. They never raise a finger—they just stand there. In theater lobbies, by the box office—they never go inside. They don't do anything, but wherever you see them, things are not the same. I remember well the time when a cabbage could sell itself just by being a cabbage. Nowadays it's no good being a cabbage—unless you have an agent and pay him a commission. Nothing is free any more to sell itself or give itself away. These days, Countess, every cabbage has its pimp.

COUNTESS. I can't believe that.

THE RAGPICKER. Countess, little by little, the pimps have taken over the world. They don't do anything, they don't make anything—they just stand there and take their cut. It makes a difference. Look at the shopkeepers. Do you ever see one smiling at a customer any more? Certainly not. Their smiles are strictly for the pimps. The butcher has to smile at the meat-pimp, the florist at the rose-pimp, the grocer at the fresh-fruit-and-vegetable pimp. It's all organized down to the slightest detail. A pimp for bird-seed. A pimp for fishfood. That's why the cost of living keeps going up all the time. You buy a glass of beer—it costs twice as much as it used to. Why? 10 percent for

the glass-pimp, 10 percent for the beer-pimp, 20 percent for the glass-of-beer-pimp—that's where our money goes. Personally, I prefer the old-fashioned type. Some of those men at least were loved by the women they sold. But what feelings can a pimp arouse in a leg of lamb? Pardon my language, Irma.

COUNTESS. It's all right. She doesn't understand it.

THE RAGPICKER. So now you know, Countess, why the world is no longer happy. We are the last of the free people of the earth. You saw them looking us over today. Tomorrow, the street-singer will start paying the song-pimp, and the garbage-pimp will be after me. I tell you, Countess, we're finished. It's the end of free enterprise in this world!

COUNTESS. Is this true, Roderick?

PIERRE. I'm afraid it's true.

COUNTESS. Did you know about this, Irma?

IRMA. All I know is the doorman says that faith is dead.

DOORMAN. I've stopped taking bets over the phone.

JUGGLER. The very air is different, Countess. You can't trust it any more. If I throw my torches up too high, they go out.

THE RAGPICKER. The sky-pimp puts them out.

FLOWER GIRL. My flowers don't last overnight now. They wilt.

JUGGLER. Have you noticed, the pigeons don't fly any more?

THE RAGPICKER. They can't afford to. They walk.

COUNTESS. They're a lot of fools and so are you! You should have told me at once! How can you bear to live in a world where there is unhappiness? Where a man is not his own master? Are you cowards? All we have to do is to get rid of these men.

PIERRE. How can we get rid of them? They're too strong.

(The Sergeant walks up again.)

COUNTESS (smiling). The Sergeant will help us.

SERGEANT. Who? Me?

IRMA. There are a great many of them, Countess. The Deaf-Mute knows them all. They employed him once, years ago, because he was deaf. *(The Deaf-Mute wigwags a short speech)* They fired him because he wasn't blind. *(Another flash of sign language)* They're all connected like the parts of a machine.

COUNTESS. So much the better. We shall drive the whole machine into a ditch.

SERGEANT. It's not that easy, Countess. You never catch these birds napping. They change before your very eyes. I remember when I was in the detectives... You catch a president, pfft! He turns into a trustee. You catch him as trustee, and pfft! he's not a trustee—he's an honorary vice-chairman. You catch a Senator dead to rights: he becomes Minister of Justice. You get after the Minister of Justice—he is Chief of Police. And there you are—no longer in the detectives.

PIERRE. He's right, Countess. They have all the power. And all the money. And they're greedy for more.

COUNTESS. They're greedy? Ah, then, my friends, they're lost. If they're greedy, they're stupid. If they're greedy—don't worry, I know exactly what to do. Roderick, by tonight you will be an honest man. And, Juggler, your torches will stay lit. And your beer will flow freely again, Martial. And the world will be saved. Let's get to work.

THE RAGPICKER. What are you going to do?

COUNTESS. Have you any kerosene in the house, Irma?

IRMA. Yes. Would you like some?

COUNTESS. I want just a little. In a dirty bottle. With a little mud. And some mange-cure, if you have it. *(To the Deaf-Mute)* Deaf-Mute! Take a letter. *(Irma interprets in sign language. To the Singer)* Singer, go and find Madame Constance. *(Irma and the Waiter go into the café.)*

SINGER. Yes, Countess.

COUNTESS. Ask her to be at my house by two o'clock. I'll be waiting for her in the cellar. You may tell her we have to discuss the future of humanity. That's sure to bring her.

SINGER. Yes, Countess.

COUNTESS. And ask her to bring Mademoiselle Gabrielle and Madame Josephine

with her. Do you know how to get in to speak to Madame Constance? You ring twice, and then meow three times like a cat. Do you know how to meow?

SINGER. I'm better at barking.

COUNTESS. Better practice meowing on the way. Incidentally, I think Madame Constance knows all the verses of your mazurka. Remind me to ask her.

SINGER. Yes, Countess.

(Exit.)

(Irma comes in. She is shaking the oily concoction in a little perfume vial, which she now hands the Countess.)

IRMA. Here you are, Countess.

COUNTESS. Thanks, Irma. *(She assumes a presidential manner)* Deaf-Mute! Ready? *(Irma interprets in sign language. The Waiter has brought out a portfolio of letter paper and placed it on a table. The Deaf-Mute sits down before it, and prepares to write.)*

IRMA *(speaking for the Deaf-Mute)*. I'm ready.

COUNTESS. My dear Mr.— What's his name?

(Irma wigwags the question to the Deaf-Mute, who answers in the same manner. It is all done so deftly that it is as if the Deaf-Mute were actually speaking.)

IRMA. They are all called Mr. President.

COUNTESS. My dear Mr. President: I have personally verified the existence of a spontaneous outcrop of oil in the cellar of Number 21 Rue de Chaillot, which is at present occupied by a dignified person of unstable mentality. *(The Countess grins knowingly)* This explains why, fortunately for us, the discovery has so long been kept secret. If you should wish to verify the existence of this outcrop for yourself, you may call at the above address at three p.m. today. I am herewith enclosing a sample so that you may judge the quality and consistency of the crude. Yours very truly. Roderick, can you sign the prospector's name?

PIERRE. You wish me to?

COUNTESS. One forgery wipes out the other.

(Pierre signs the letter. The Deaf-Mute types the address on an envelope.)

IRMA. Who is to deliver this?

COUNTESS. The Doorman, of course. On his bicycle. And as soon as you hav delivered it, run over to the prospector's office. Leave word that the President expects to see him at my house at three.

DOORMAN. Yes, Countess.

COUNTESS. I shall leave you now. I have many pressing things to do. Among others, I must press my red gown.

THE RAGPICKER. But this only takes care of two of them, Countess.

COUNTESS. Didn't the Deaf-Mute say they are all connected like the works of a machine?

IRMA. Yes.

COUNTESS. Then, if one comes, the rest will follow. And we shall have them all. My boa, please.

DOORMAN. The one that's stolen, Countess?

COUNTESS. Naturally. The one the prospector stole.

DOORMAN. It hasn't turned up yet, Countess. But someone has left an ermine collar.

COUNTESS. Real ermine?

DOORMAN. Looks like it.

COUNTESS. Ermine and iris were made for each other. Let me see it.

DOORMAN. Yes, Countess. *(Exit Doorman)*

COUNTESS. Roderick, you shall escort me. You still look pale. I have some old Chartreuse at home. I always take a glass each year. Last year I forgot. You shall have it.

PIERRE. If there is anything I can do, Countess . . . ?

COUNTESS. There is a great deal you can do. There are all the things that need to be done in a room that no man has been in for twenty years. You can untwist the cord on the blind and let in a little sunshine for a change. You can take the mirror off the wardrobe door, and deliver me once and for all from the old harpy that lives in the mirror. You can let the mouse out of the trap. I'm tired of feeding it. *(To her friends)* Each man to his post. See you later, my friends. *(The Doorman puts the ermine collar around her shoulders)* Thank you, my boy. It's rabbit. *(One o'clock strikes)* Your arm, Valentine.

PIERRE. Valentine?

COUNTESS. It's just struck one. At one, all men become Valentine.

PIERRE *(he offers his arm)*. Permit me.

COUNTESS. Or Valentino. It's obviously far from the same, isn't it, Irma? But they have that much choice.

(She sweeps out majestically with Pierre. The others disperse. All but Irma.)

IRMA *(clearing off the table)*. I hate ugliness. I love beauty. I hate meanness. I adore kindness. It may not seem so grand to some to be a waitress in Paris. I love it. A waitress meets all sorts of people. She observes life. I hate to be alone. I love people. But I have never said I love you to a man. Men try to make me say it. They put their arms around me—I pretend I don't see it. They pinch me—I pretend I don't feel it. They kiss me—I pretend I don't know it. They take me out in the evening and make me drink—but I'm careful, I never say it. If they don't like it, they can leave me alone. Because when I say I love you to Him, He will know just by looking in my eyes that many have held me and pinched me and kissed me, but I have never said I love you to anyone in the world before. Never. No. *(Looking off in the direction in which Pierre has gone, she whispers softly:)* I love you.

VOICE *(from within the café)*. Irma!

IRMA. Coming.

(Exits.)

CURTAIN

ACT TWO

SCENE: *The cellar of the Countess's house. An ancient vault set deep in the ground, with walls of solid masonry, part brick and part great ashlars, mossy and sweating. A staircase of medieval pattern is built into the thickness of the wall, and leads up to the street level from a landing halfway down. In the corners of the cellar are piled casks, packing cases, birdcages, and other odds and ends—the accumulation of centuries—the whole effect utterly fantastic.*

In the center of the vast underground room, some furniture has been arranged to give an impression of a sitting-room of the 1890's. There is a venerable chaise-longue piled with cushions that once were gay, three armchairs, a table with an oil lamp and a bowl of flowers, a shaggy rug. It is two p.m., the same day.

AT RISE: *The Countess is sitting over a bit of mending, in one of the armchairs. Irma appears on the landing and calls down.*

————

IRMA. Countess! The Sewer Man is here.

COUNTESS. Thank goodness, Irma. Send him down. *(The Sewer Man enters. He carries his hip-boots in his hand)* How do you do, Mr. Sewer Man? *(The Sewer Man bows)* But why do you have your boots in your hand instead of on your feet?

SEWER MAN. Etiquette, Countess. Etiquette.

COUNTESS. How very American! I'm told that Americans nowadays apologize for their gloves if they happen to take one's hand. As if the skin of a human were nicer to touch than the skin of a sheep! And particularly if they have sweaty hands . . . !

SEWER MAN. My feet never sweat, Countess.

COUNTESS. How very nice! But please don't stand on ceremony here. Put your boots on. Put them on.

SEWER MAN *(complying)*. Thanks very much, Countess.

COUNTESS *(while he draws on his boots)*. I'm sure you must have a very poor opinion of the upper world, from what you see of it. The way people throw their filth into your territory is absolutely scandalous! I burn all my refuse, and I scatter the ashes. All I ever throw in the drain is flowers. Did you happen to see a lily float by this morning? Mine. But perhaps you didn't notice?

SEWER MAN. We notice a lot more down there, Countess, than you might think. You'd be surprised the things we notice. There's lots of things come along that were obviously intended for us—little gifts, you might call them—sometimes a brand-new shaving brush—sometimes, *The Brothers Karamazov* . . . Thanks for the lily, Countess. A very sweet thought.

COUNTESS. Tomorrow you shall have this iris. But now, let's come to the point. I have two questions to ask you.

SEWER MAN. Yes, Countess?

COUNTESS. First—and this has nothing to do with our problem—it's just something that has been troubling me . . . Tell me, is it true that the sewer men of Paris have a king?

SEWER MAN. Oh, now, Countess, that's another of those fairy tales out of the Sunday supplements. It just seems those writers can't keep their minds off the sewers! It fascinates them. They keep thinking of us moving around in our underground canals like gondoliers in Venice, and it sends them into a fever of romance! The things they say about us! They say we have a race of girls down there who never see the light of day! It's completely fantastic! The girls naturally come out—every Christmas and Easter. And orgies by torchlight with gondolas and guitars! With troops of rats that dance as they follow the piper! What nonsense! The rats are not allowed to dance. No, no, no. Of course we have no king. Down in the sewers, you'll find nothing but good Republicans.

COUNTESS. And no queen?

SEWER MAN. No. We may run a beauty contest down there once in a while. Or crown a mermaid Queen of the May. But no queen what you'd call a queen. And, as for these swimming races they talk so much about . . . possibly once in a while—in the summer—in the dog days . . .

COUNTESS. I believe you. I believe you. And now tell me. Do you remember that night I found you here in my cellar—looking very pale and strange—you were half-dead as a matter of fact—and I gave you some brandy . . .

SEWER MAN. Yes, Countess.

COUNTESS. That night you promised if ever I should need it—you would tell me the secret of this room.

SEWER MAN. The secret of the moving stone?

COUNTESS. I need it now.

SEWER MAN. Only the King of the Sewer Men knows this secret.

COUNTESS. I'm sure of it. I know most secrets, of course. As a matter of fact, I have three magic words that will open any door that words can open. I have tried them all—in various tones of voice. They don't seem to work. And this is a matter of life and death.

SEWER MAN. Look, Countess.

(He locates a brick in the masonry, and pushes it. A huge block of stone slowly pivots and uncovers a trap from which a circular staircase winds into the bowels of the earth.)

COUNTESS. Good heavens! Where do those stairs lead?

SEWER MAN. Nowhere.

COUNTESS. But they must go some-where.

SEWER MAN. They just go down.

COUNTESS. Let's go and see.

SEWER MAN. No, Countess. Never again. That time you found me, I had a pretty close shave. I kept going down and around, and down and around for an hour, a year—I don't know. There's no end to it, Countess. Once you start you can't stop . . . Your head begins to turn—you're lost. No—once you start down, there's no coming up.

COUNTESS. You came up.

SEWER MAN. I—I am a special case. Besides, I had my tools, my ropes. And I stopped in time.

COUNTESS. You could have screamed—shouted.

SEWER MAN. You could fire off a cannon.

COUNTESS. Who could have built a thing like this?

SEWER MAN. Paris is old, you know. Paris is very old.

COUNTESS. You don't suppose, by any chance, there is oil down there?

SEWER MAN. There's only death down there.

COUNTESS. I should have preferred a little oil too—or a vein of gold—or emeralds. You're quite sure there is nothing?

SEWER MAN. Not even rats.

COUNTESS. How does one lower this stone?

SEWER MAN. Simple. To open, you press here. And to close it, you push there. *(He presses the brick. The stone descends)* Now there's two of us in the world that knows it.

COUNTESS. I won't remember long.

Is it all right if I repeat my magic words while I press it?

SEWER MAN. It's bound to help.

(Irma enters.)

IRMA. Countess, Madame Constance and Mademoiselle Gabrielle are here.

COUNTESS. Show them down, Irma. Thank you very much, Mr. Sewer Man.

SEWER MAN. Like that story about the steam laundry that's supposed to be running day and night in my sewer . . . I can assure you . . .

COUNTESS *(edging him toward the door)*. Thank you very much.

SEWER MAN. Pure imagination! They never work nights.

(He goes off, bowing graciously.)

(Constance, the Madwoman of Passy, and Gabrielle, the Madwoman of St. Sulpice, come down daintily. Constance is all in white. She wears an enormous hat graced with ostrich plumes, and a lavender veil. Gabrielle is costumed with the affected simplicity of the 1880's. She is atrociously made up in a remorseless parody of blushing innocence, and she minces down the stairs with macabre coyness.)

CONSTANCE. Aurelia! Don't tell us they've found your feather boa?

GABRIELLE. You don't mean Adolphe Bertaut has proposed at last! I knew he would.

COUNTESS. How are you, Constance? *(She shouts)* How are you, Gabrielle?

GABRIELLE. You needn't shout today, my dear. It's Wednesday. Wednesdays, I hear perfectly.

CONSTANCE. It's Thursday.

GABRIELLE. Oh, dear. Well, never mind. I'm going to make an exception just this once.

CONSTANCE *(to an imaginary dog who has stopped on the landing)*. Come along, Dickie. Come along. And stop barking. What a racket you're making! Come on, darling—we've come to see the longest boa and the handsomest man in Paris. Come on.

COUNTESS. Constance, it's not a question of my boa today. Nor of poor Adolphe. It's a question of the future of the human race.

CONSTANCE. You think it has a future?

COUNTESS. Please don't make silly

jokes. Sit down and listen to me. Today we must make a decision which may alter the fate of the world.

CONSTANCE. Couldn't we do it tomorrow? I want to wash my slippers. Now, Dickie—please!

COUNTESS. We haven't a moment to waste. Where is Josephine? Well, we'd best have our tea, and the moment Josephine comes . . .

GABRIELLE. Josephine is sitting on her bench in front of the palace waiting for President Wilson to come out. She says she's sorry, but she positively must see him today.

CONSTANCE. Dickie!

COUNTESS. What a pity! *(She gets the tea things from the side table, pours tea and serves cake and honey)* I wish she were here to help us. She has a first-class brain.

CONSTANCE. Go ahead, dear. We're listening. *(To Dickie)* What is it, Dickie? You want to sit in Aunt Aurelia's lap. All right, darling. Go on. Jump, Dickie.

COUNTESS. Constance, we love you, as you know. And we love Dickie. But this is a serious matter. So let's stop being childish for once.

CONSTANCE. And what does that mean, if you please?

COUNTESS. It means Dickie. You know perfectly well that we love him and fuss over him just as if he were still alive. He's a sacred memory and we wouldn't hurt his feelings for the world. But please don't plump him in my lap when I'm settling the future of mankind. His basket is in the corner—he knows where it is, and he can just go and sit in it.

CONSTANCE. So you're against Dickie too! You too!

COUNTESS. Constance! I'm not in the least against Dickie! I adore Dickie. But you know as well as I that Dickie is only a convention with us. It's a beautiful convention—but it doesn't have to bark all the time. Besides, it's you that spoil him. The time you went to visit your niece and left him with me, we got on marvelously together. He didn't bark, he didn't tear things, he didn't even eat. But when you're with him, one can pay attention to nothing else. I'm not going to take Dickie in my lap at a solemn

moment like this, no, not for anything in the world. And that's that!

GABRIELLE *(very sweetly)*. Constance, dear, I don't mind taking him in my lap. He loves to sit in my lap, don't you, darling?

CONSTANCE. Kindly stop putting on angelic airs, Gabrielle. I know you very well. You're much too sweet to be sincere. There's plenty of times that I make believe that Dickie is here, when really I've left him home, and you cuddle and pet him just the same.

GABRIELLE. I adore animals.

CONSTANCE. If you adore animals, you shouldn't pet them when they're not there. It's a form of hypocrisy.

COUNTESS. Now, Constance, Gabrielle has as much right as you . . .

CONSTANCE. Gabrielle has no right to do what she does. Do you know what she does? She invites *people* to come to tea with us. *People* whom we know nothing about. *People* who exist only in her imagination.

COUNTESS. You think that's not an existence?

GABRIELLE. I don't invite them at all. They come by themselves. What can I do?

CONSTANCE. You might introduce us.

COUNTESS. If you think they're only imaginary, there's no point in your meeting them, is there?

CONSTANCE. Of course they're imaginary. But who likes to have imaginary people staring at one? Especially strangers.

GABRIELLE. Oh, they're really very nice . . .

CONSTANCE. Tell me just one thing, Gabrielle—are they here now?

COUNTESS. Am I to be allowed to speak? Or is this going to be the same as the argument about inoculating Josephine's cat, when we didn't get to the subject at all?

CONSTANCE. Never! Never! Never! I'll never give my consent to that. *(To Dickie)* I'd never do a thing like that to you, Dickie sweet . . . Oh, no! Oh, no! *(She begins to weep softly.)*

COUNTESS. Good heavens! Now we have her in tears. What an impossible creature! With the fate of humanity hanging in the balance! All right, all right, stop crying. I'll take him in my lap. Come, Dickie, Dickie.

CONSTANCE. No. He won't go now. Oh, how can you be so cruel? Don't you suppose I know about Dickie? Don't you think I'd rather have him here alive and woolly and frisking around the way he used to? You have your Adolphe. Gabrielle has her birds. But I have only Dickie. Do you think I'd be so silly about him if it wasn't that it's only by pretending that he's here all the time that I get him to come sometimes, really? Next time I won't bring him!

COUNTESS. Now let's not get ourselves worked up over nothing. Come here, Dickie . . . Irma is going to take you for a nice walk. (She rings her bell) Irma! (Irma appears on the landing.)

CONSTANCE. No. He doesn't want to go. Besides, I didn't bring him today. So there!

COUNTESS. Very well, then. Irma, make sure the door is locked.

IRMA. Yes, Countess.

(Irma exits.)

CONSTANCE. What do you mean? Why locked? Who's coming?

COUNTESS. If you'd let me get a word in, you'd know by now. A terrible thing has happened. This morning, this very morning, exactly at noon . . .

CONSTANCE (thrilled). Oh, how exciting!

COUNTESS. Be quiet. This morning, exactly at noon, thanks to a young man who drowned himself in the Seine . . . Oh, yes, while I think of it—do you know a mazurka called La Belle Polonaise?

CONSTANCE. Yes, Aurelia.

COUNTESS. Could you sing it now? This very minute?

CONSTANCE. Yes, Aurelia.

COUNTESS. All of it?

CONSTANCE. Yes, Aurelia. But who's interrupting now, Aurelia?

COUNTESS. You're right. Well, this morning, exactly at noon, I discovered a horrible plot. There is a group of men who intend to tear down the whole city!

CONSTANCE. Is that all?

GABRIELLE. But I don't understand, Aurelia. Why should men want to tear down the city? It was they themselves who put it up.

COUNTESS. You are so innocent, my poor Gabrielle. There are people in the world who want to destroy everything. They have the fever of destruction. Even when they pretend that they're building, it is only in order to destroy. When they put up a new building, they quietly knock down two old ones. They build cities so that they can destroy the countryside. They destroy space with telephones and time with airplanes. Humanity is now dedicated to the task of universal destruction. I am speaking, of course, primarily of the male sex.

GABRIELLE (shocked). Oh . . . !

CONSTANCE. Aurelia! Must you talk sex in front of Gabrielle?

COUNTESS. There are two sexes.

CONSTANCE. Gabrielle is a virgin, Aurelia!

COUNTESS. Oh, she can't be as innocent as all that. She keeps canaries.

GABRIELLE. I think you're being very cruel about men, Aurelia. Men are big and beautiful, and as loyal as dogs. I preferred not to marry, it's true. But I hear excellent reports from friends who have had an opportunity to observe them closely.

COUNTESS. My poor darling! You are still living in a dream. But one day, you will wake up as I have, and then you will see what is happening in the world. The tide has turned, my dear. Men are changing back into beasts. They know it. They no longer try to hide it. There was once such a thing as manners. I remember a time when the hungriest was the one who took the longest to pick up his fork. The one with the broadest grin was the one who needed most to go to the . . . It was such fun to keep them grinning like that for hours. But now they no longer pretend. Just look at them—snuffling their soup like pigs, tearing their meat like tigers, crunching their lettuce like crocodiles! A man doesn't take your hand nowadays. He gives you his paw.

CONSTANCE. Would that trouble you so much if they turned into animals? Personally, I think it's a good idea.

GABRIELLE. Oh, I'd love to see them like that. They'd be sweet.

CONSTANCE. It might be the salvation of the human race.

COUNTESS (to Constance). You'd make a fine rabbit, wouldn't you?

CONSTANCE. I?

COUNTESS. Naturally. You don't think it's only the men who are changing? You change along with them. Husbands and wives together. We're all one race, you know.

CONSTANCE. You think so? And why would my poor husband have to be a rabbit if he were alive?

COUNTESS. Remember his front teeth? When he nibbled his celery?

CONSTANCE. I'm happy to say, I remember absolutely nothing about him. All I remember on that subject is the time that Father Lacordaire tried to kiss me in the park.

COUNTESS. Yes, yes, of course.

CONSTANCE. And what does that mean, if you please, "Yes, yes, of course"?

COUNTESS. Constance, just this once, look us in the eye and tell us truly—did that really happen or did you read about it in a book?

CONSTANCE. Now I'm being insulted!

COUNTESS. We promise you faithfully that we'll believe it all over again afterwards, won't we, Gabrielle? But tell us the truth this once.

CONSTANCE. How dare you question my memories? Suppose I said your pearls were false!

COUNTESS. They were.

CONSTANCE. I'm not asking what they were. I'm asking what they are. Are they false or are they real?

COUNTESS. Everyone knows that little by little, as one wears pearls, they become real.

CONSTANCE. And isn't it exactly the same with memories?

COUNTESS. Now do not let us waste time. I must go on.

CONSTANCE. I think Gabrielle is perfectly right about men. There are still plenty who haven't changed a bit. There's an old Senator who bows to Gabrielle every day when he passes her in front of the palace. And he takes off his hat each time.

GABRIELLE. That's perfectly true, Aurelia. He's always pushing an empty baby carriage, and he always stops and bows.

COUNTESS. Don't be taken in, Gabrielle. It's all make-believe. And all we can expect from these make-believe men is itself make-believe. They give us face-powder made of stones, sausages made of sawdust, shirts made of glass, stockings made of milk. It's all a vulgar pretence. And if that is the case, imagine what passes, these days, for virtue, sincerity, generosity and love! I warn you, Gabrielle, don't let this Senator with the empty baby carriage pull the wool over your eyes.

GABRIELLE. He's really the soul of courtesy. He seems very correct.

COUNTESS. Those are the worst. Gabrielle, beware! He'll make you put on black riding boots, while he dances the can-can around you, singing God knows what filth at the top of his voice. The very thought makes one's blood run cold!

GABRIELLE. You think that's what he has in mind?

COUNTESS. Of course. Men have lost all sense of decency. They are all equally disgusting. Just look at them in the evening, sitting at their tables in the café, working away in unison with their toothpicks, hour after hour, digging up roast beef, veal, onion . . .

CONSTANCE. They don't harm anyone that way.

COUNTESS. Then why do you barricade your door, and make your friends meow before you let them come up? Incidentally, we must make an interesting sight, Gabrielle and I, yowling together on your doorstep like a couple of tomcats!

CONSTANCE. There's no need at all for you to yowl together. One would be quite enough. And you know perfectly well why I have to do it. It's because there are murderers.

COUNTESS. I don't quite see what prevents murderers from meowing like anybody else. But why are there murderers?

CONSTANCE. Why? Because there are thieves.

COUNTESS. And why are there thieves? Why is there almost nothing but thieves?

CONSTANCE. Because they worship money. Because money is king.

COUNTESS. Ah—now we've come to it. Because we live in the reign of the Golden Calf. Did you realize that, Gabrielle? Men now publicly worship the Golden Calf!

GABRIELLE. How awful! Have the authorities been notified?

COUNTESS. The authorities do it themselves, Gabrielle.

GABRIELLE. Oh! Has anyone talked to the bishop?

COUNTESS. Nowadays only money talks to the bishop. And so you see why I asked you to come here today. The world has gone out of its mind. Unless we do something, humanity is doomed! Constance, have you any suggestions?

CONSTANCE. I know what I always do in a case like this . . .

COUNTESS. You write to the Prime Minister.

CONSTANCE. He always does what I tell him.

COUNTESS. Does he ever answer your letters?

CONSTANCE. He knows I prefer him not to. It might excite gossip. Besides, I don't always write. Sometimes I wire. The time I told him about the Archbishop's frigidaire, it was by wire. And they sent a new one the very next day.

COUNTESS. There was probably a commission in it for someone. And what do you suggest, Gabrielle?

CONSTANCE. Now, how can she tell you until she's consulted her voices?

GABRIELLE. I could go right home and consult them, and we could meet again after dinner.

COUNTESS. There's no time for that. Besides, your voices are not real voices.

GABRIELLE (furious). How dare you say a thing like that?

COUNTESS. Where do your voices come from? Still from your sewing-machine?

GABRIELLE. Not at all. They've passed into my hot-water bottle. And it's much

nicer that way. They don't chatter any more. They gurgle. But they haven't been a bit nice to me lately. Last night they kept telling me to let my canaries out. "Let them out. Let them out. Let them out."

CONSTANCE. Did you?

GABRIELLE. I opened the cage. They wouldn't go.

COUNTESS. I don't call that voices. Objects talk—everyone knows that. It's the principle of the phonograph. But to ask a hot-water bottle for advice is silly. What does a hot-water bottle know? No, all we have to consult here is our own judgment.

CONSTANCE. Very well then, tell us what you have decided. Since you're asking our opinion, you've doubtless made up your mind.

COUNTESS. Yes, I've thought the whole thing out. All I really needed to discover was the source of the infection. Today I found it.

CONSTANCE. Where?

COUNTESS. You'll see soon enough. I've baited a trap. In just a few minutes, the rats will be here.

GABRIELLE (in alarm). Rats!

COUNTESS. Don't be alarmed. They're still in human form.

GABRIELLE. Heavens! What are you going to do with them?

COUNTESS. That's just the question. Suppose I get these wicked men all here at once—in my cellar—have I the right to exterminate them?

GABRIELLE. To kill them?

(Countess nods.)

CONSTANCE. That's not a question for us. You'll have to ask Father Bridet.

COUNTESS. I have asked him. Yes. One day, in confession, I told him frankly that I had a secret desire to destroy all wicked people. He said: "By all means, my child. And when you're ready to go into action, I'll lend you the jawbone of an ass."

CONSTANCE. That's just talk. You get him to put that in writing.

GABRIELLE. What's your scheme, Aurelia?

COUNTESS. That's a secret.

CONSTANCE. It's not so easy to kill

them. Let's say you had a tank full of vitriol all ready for them. You could never get them to walk into it. There's nothing so stubborn as a man when you want him to do something.

COUNTESS. Leave that to me.

CONSTANCE. But if they're killed, they're bound to be missed, and then we'll be fined. They fine you for every little thing these days.

COUNTESS. They won't be missed.

GABRIELLE. I wish Josephine were here. Her sister's husband was a lawyer. She knows all about these things.

COUNTESS. Do you miss a cold when it's gone? Or the germs that caused it? When the world feels well again, do you think it will regret its illness? No, it will stretch itself joyfully, and it will smile—that's all.

CONSTANCE. Just a moment! Gabrielle, are they here now? Yes or no?

COUNTESS. What's the matter with you now?

CONSTANCE. I'm simply asking Gabrielle if her friends are in the room or not. I have a right to know.

GABRIELLE. I'm not allowed to say.

CONSTANCE. I know very well they are. I'm sure of it. Otherwise you wouldn't be making faces.

COUNTESS. May I ask what difference it makes to you if her friends are in the room?

CONSTANCE. Just this: If they're here, I'm not going to say another word! I'm certainly not going to commit myself in a matter involving the death sentence in the presence of third parties, whether they exist or not.

GABRIELLE. That's not being very nice to my guests, is it?

COUNTESS. Constance, you must be mad! Or are you so stupid as to think that just because we're alone, there's nobody with us? Do you consider us so boring or repulsive that of all the millions of beings, imaginary or otherwise, who are prowling about in space, there's not one who might possibly enjoy spending a little time with us? On the contrary, my dear—my house is full of guests always. They know that here they have a place in the universe where they can come. when they're lonely and be sure of a welcome. For my part, I'm delighted to have them.

GABRIELLE. Thank you, Aurelia.

CONSTANCE. You know perfectly well, Aurelia . . .

COUNTESS. I know perfectly well that at this moment the whole universe is listening to us—and that every word we say echoes to the remotest star. To pretend otherwise is the sheerest hypocrisy.

CONSTANCE. Then why do you insult me in front of everybody? I'm not mean. I'm shy. I feel timid about giving an opinion in front of such a crowd. Furthermore, if you think I'm so bad and so stupid, why did you invite me, in the first place?

COUNTESS. I'll tell you. And I'll tell you why, disagreeable as you are, I always give you the biggest piece of cake and my best honey. It's because when you come there's always someone with you—and I don't mean Dickie—I mean someone who resembles you like a sister, only she's young and lovely, and she sits modestly to one side and smiles at me tenderly all the time you're bickering and quarreling, and never says a word. That's the Constance to whom I give the cake that you gobble, and it's because of her that you're here today, and it's her vote that I'm asking you to cast in this crucial moment. And not yours, which is of no importance whatever.

CONSTANCE. I'm leaving.

COUNTESS. Be so good as to sit down. I can't let her go yet.

CONSTANCE (crossing toward the stairs). No. This is too much. I'm taking her with me.

(Irma enters.)

IRMA. Madame Josephine.

COUNTESS. Thank heaven!

GABRIELLE. We're saved.

(Josephine, the Madwoman of La Concorde, sweeps in majestically in a get-up somewhere between the regal and the priestly.)

JOSEPHINE. My dear friends, today once again, I waited for President Wilson—but he didn't come out.

COUNTESS. You'll have to wait quite a while longer before he does. He's been dead since 1924.

JOSEPHINE. I have plenty of time.

COUNTESS. In anyone else, Josephine, these extravagances might seem a little childish. But a person of your judgment doubtless has her reasons for wanting to talk to a man to whom no one would listen when he was alive. We have a legal problem for you. Suppose you had all the world's criminals here in this room. And suppose you had a way of getting rid of them forever. Would you have the right to do it?

JOSEPHINE. Why not?

COUNTESS. Exactly my point.

GABRIELLE. But, Josephine, so many people!

JOSEPHINE. *De minimis non curat lex!* The more there are, the more legal it is. It's impersonal. It's even military. It's the cardinal principle of battle—you get all your enemies in one place, and you kill them all together at one time. Because if you had to track them down one by one in their houses and offices, you'd get tired, and sooner or later you'd stop. I believe your idea is very practical, Aurelia. I can't imagine why we never thought of it before.

GABRIELLE. Well, if you think it's all right to do it . . .

JOSEPHINE. By all means. Your criminals have had a fair trial, I suppose?

COUNTESS. Trial?

JOSEPHINE. Certainly. You can't kill anybody without a trial. That's elementary. "No man shall be deprived of his life, liberty and property without due process of law."

COUNTESS. They deprive us of ours.

JOSEPHINE. That's not the point. You're not accused of anything. Every accused—man, woman or child—has the right to defend himself at the bar of justice. Even animals. Before the Deluge, you will recall, the Lord permitted Noah to speak in defense of his fellow mortals. He evidently stuttered. You know the result. On the other hand, Captain Dreyfus was not only innocent—he was defended by a marvelous orator. The result was precisely the same. So you see, in having a trial, you run no risk whatever.

COUNTESS. But if I give them the slightest cause for suspicion—I'll lose them.

JOSEPHINE. There's a simple procedure prescribed in such cases. You can summon the defendants by calling them three times—mentally, if you like. If they don't appear, the court may designate an attorney who will represent them. This attorney can then argue their case to the court, *in absentia*, and a judgment can then be rendered, *in contumacio*.

COUNTESS. But I don't know any attorneys. And we have only ten minutes.

GABRIELLE. Hurry, Josephine, hurry!

JOSEPHINE. In case of emergency, it is permissible for the court to order the first passer-by to act as attorney for the defense. A defense is like a baptism. Absolutely indispensable, but you don't have to know anything to do it. Ask Irma to get you somebody. Anybody.

COUNTESS. The Deaf-Mute?

JOSEPHINE. Well—that's getting it down a bit fine. That might be questionable on appeal.

COUNTESS *(calls)*. Irma! What about the Police Sergeant?

JOSEPHINE. He won't do. He's under oath to the state.

(Irma appears.)

IRMA. Yes, Countess?

COUNTESS. Who's out there, Irma?

IRMA. All our friends, Countess. There's the Ragpicker and . . .

COUNTESS. Send down the Ragpicker.

CONSTANCE. Do you think it's wise to have all those millionaires represented by a ragpicker?

JOSEPHINE. It's a first-rate choice. Criminals are always represented by their opposites. Murderers, by someone who obviously wouldn't hurt a fly. Rapists, by a member of the League for Decency. Experience shows it's the only way to get an acquittal.

COUNTESS. But we must not have an acquittal. That would mean the end of the world!

JOSEPHINE. Justice is justice, my dear. *(The Ragpicker comes down, with a stately air. Behind him, on the landing, appear the other Vagabonds.)*

THE RAGPICKER. Greetings, Countess. Greetings, ladies. My most sincere compliments.

COUNTESS. Has Irma told you . . . ?

THE RAGPICKER. She said something about a trial.

COUNTESS. You have been appointed attorney for the defense.

THE RAGPICKER. Terribly flattered, I'm sure.

COUNTESS. You realize, don't you, how much depends on the outcome of this trial?

JOSEPHINE. Do you know the defendants well enough to undertake the case?

THE RAGPICKER. I know them to the bottom of their souls. I go through their garbage every day.

CONSTANCE. And what do you find there?

THE RAGPICKER. Mostly flowers.

GABRIELLE. It's true, you know, the rich are always surrounded with flowers.

CONSTANCE. How beautiful!

COUNTESS. Are you trying to prejudice the court?

THE RAGPICKER. Oh no, Countess, no.

COUNTESS. We want a completely impartial defense.

THE RAGPICKER. Of course, Countess, of course. Permit me to make a suggestion.

COUNTESS. Will you preside, Josephine?

THE RAGPICKER. Instead of speaking as attorney, suppose you let me speak directly as defendant. It will be more convincing, and I can get into it more.

JOSEPHINE. Excellent idea. Motion granted.

COUNTESS. We don't want you to be too convincing, remember.

THE RAGPICKER. Impartial, Countess, impartial.

JOSEPHINE. Well? Have you prepared your case?

THE RAGPICKER. How rich am I?

JOSEPHINE. Millions. Billions.

THE RAGPICKER. How did I get them? Theft? Murder? Embezzlement?

COUNTESS. Most likely.

THE RAGPICKER. Do I have a wife? A mistress?

COUNTESS. Everything.

THE RAGPICKER. All right. I'm ready.

GABRIELLE. Will you have some tea?

THE RAGPICKER. Is that good?

CONSTANCE. Very good for the voice.

The Russians drink nothing but tea. And they talk like anything.

THE RAGPICKER. All right. Tea.

JOSEPHINE (to the Vagabonds). Come in. Come in. All of you. You may take places. The trial is public. (The Vagabonds dispose themselves on the steps and elsewhere) Your bell, if you please, Aurelia.

COUNTESS. But what if I should need to ring for Irma?

JOSEPHINE. Irma will sit here, next to me. If you need her, she can ring for herself. (To the Police Sergeant and the Policeman) Conduct the accused to the bar. (The officers conduct the Ragpicker to a bar improvised with a rocking chair and a packing case marked Fragile. The Ragpicker mounts the box. She rings the bell) The court is now in session. (All sit) Counsel for the defense, you may take the oath.

THE RAGPICKER. I swear to tell the truth, the whole truth, and nothing but the truth, so help me God.

JOSEPHINE. Nonsense! You're not a witness. You're an attorney. It's your duty to lie, conceal and distort everything, and slander everybody.

THE RAGPICKER. All right. I swear to lie, conceal and distort everything, and slander everybody.

(Josephine rings stridently.)

JOSEPHINE. Quiet! Begin.

THE RAGPICKER. May it please the honorable, august and elegant Court . . .

JOSEPHINE. Flattery will get you nowhere. That will do. The defense has been heard. Cross-examination.

COUNTESS. Mr. President . . .

THE RAGPICKER (bowing with dignity). Madame.

COUNTESS. Do you know what you are charged with?

THE RAGPICKER. I can't for the life of me imagine. My life is an open book. My ways are known to all. I am a pillar of the church and the sole support of the Opera. My hands are spotless.

COUNTESS. What an atrocious lie! Just look at them!

CONSTANCE. You don't have to insult the man. He's only lying to please you.

COUNTESS. Be quiet, Constance! You don't get the idea at all. (To the Ragpicker)

You are charged with the crime of worshipping money.

THE RAGPICKER. Worshipping money? Me?

JOSEPHINE. Do you plead guilty or not guilty? Which is it?

THE RAGPICKER. Why, Your Honor...

JOSEPHINE. Yes or no?

THE RAGPICKER. Yes or no? No! I don't worship money, Countess. Heavens, no! Money worships me. It adores me. It won't let me alone. It's damned embarrassing, I can tell you.

JOSEPHINE. Kindly watch your language.

COUNTESS. Defendant, tell the Court how you came by your money.

THE RAGPICKER. The first time money came to me, I was a mere boy, a little golden-haired child in the bosom of my dear family. It came to me suddenly in the guise of a gold brick which, in my innocence, I picked out of a garbage can one day while playing. I was horrified, as you can imagine. I immediately tried to get rid of it by swapping it for a little run-down one-track railroad which, to my consternation, at once sold itself for a hundred times its value. In a desperate effort to get rid of this money, I began to buy things. I bought the Northern Refineries, the Galeries Lafayette, and the Schneider-Creusot Munition Works. And now I'm stuck with them. It's a horrible fate—but I'm resigned to it. I don't ask for your sympathy, I don't ask for your pity—all I ask for is a little common human understanding . . .

(He begins to cry.)

COUNTESS. I object. This wretch is trying to play on the emotions of the Court.

JOSEPHINE. The Court has no emotions.

THE RAGPICKER. Everyone knows that the poor have no one but themselves to blame for their poverty. It's only just that they should suffer the consequences. But how is it the fault of the rich if they're rich?

COUNTESS. Dry your tears. You're deceiving nobody. If, as you say, you're ashamed of your money, why is it you hold onto it with such a death-grip?

THE RAGPICKER. Me?

STREET PEDDLER. You never part with a franc!

JUGGLER. You wouldn't even give the poor Deaf-Mute a sou!

THE RAGPICKER. Me, hold onto money? What slander! What injustice! What a thing to say to me in the presence of this honorable, august and elegant Court! I spend all my time trying to spend my money. If I have tan shoes, I buy black ones. If I have a bicycle, I buy a motor car. If I have a wife, I buy . . .

JOSEPHINE *(rings)*. Order!

THE RAGPICKER. I dispatch a plane to Java for a bouquet of flowers. I send a steamer to Egypt for a basket of figs. I send a special representative to New York to fetch me an ice-cream cone. And if it's not just exactly right, back it goes. But no matter what I do, I can't get rid of my money! If I play a hundred to one shot, the horse comes in by twenty lengths. If I throw a diamond in the Seine, it turns up in the trout they serve me for lunch. Ten diamonds—ten trout. Well, now, do you suppose I can get rid of forty millions by giving a sou to a deaf-mute? Is it even worth the effort?

CONSTANCE. He's right.

THE RAGPICKER. Ah! You see, my dear? At last, there is somebody who understands me! Somebody who is not only beautiful, but extraordinarily sensitive and intelligent.

COUNTESS. I object!

JOSEPHINE. Overruled!

THE RAGPICKER. I should be delighted to send you some flowers, Miss—directly I'm acquitted. What flowers do you prefer?

CONSTANCE. Roses.

THE RAGPICKER. You shall have a bale every morning for the next five years. Money means nothing to me.

CONSTANCE. And amaryllis.

THE RAGPICKER. I'll make a note of the name. *(In his best lyrical style)* The lady understands, ladies and gentlemen. The lady is no fool. She's been around and she knows what's what. If I gave the Deaf-Mute a franc, twenty francs, twenty million francs—I still wouldn't make a dent in the forty times a thousand million francs that I'm afflicted with! Right, little lady?

CONSTANCE. Right.

JOSEPHINE. Proceed.

THE RAGPICKER. Like on the Stock Exchange. If *you* buy a stock, it sinks at once like a plummet. But if *I* buy a stock, it turns around and soars like an eagle. If I buy it at 33 . . .

PEDDLER. It goes up to a thousand.

THE RAGPICKER. It goes to twenty thousand! That's how I bought my twelve chateaux, my twenty villas, my 234 farms. That's how I endow the Opera and keep my twelve ballerinas.

FLOWER GIRL. I hope every one of them deceives you every moment of the day!

THE RAGPICKER. How can they deceive me? Suppose they try to deceive me with the male chorus, the general director, the assistant electrician or the English horn—I own them all, body and soul. It would be like deceiving me with my big toe.

CONSTANCE. Don't listen, Gabrielle.

GABRIELLE. Listen to what?

THE RAGPICKER. No. I am incapable of jealousy. I have all the women—or I can have them, which is the same thing. I get the thin ones with caviar—the fat ones with pearls . . .

COUNTESS. So you think there are no women with morals?

THE RAGPICKER. I mix morals with mink—delicious combination. I drip pearls into protests. I adorn resistance with rubies. My touch is jeweled; my smile, a motor car. What woman can withstand me? I lift my little finger—and do they fall?—Like leaves in autumn—like tin cans from a second-story window.

CONSTANCE. That's going a little too far!

COUNTESS. You see where money leads.

THE RAGPICKER. Of course. When you have no money, nobody trusts you, nobody believes you, nobody likes you. Because to have money is to be virtuous, honest, beautiful and witty. And to be without is to be ugly and boring and stupid and useless.

COUNTESS. One last question. Suppose you find this oil you're looking for. What do you propose to do with it?

THE RAGPICKER. I propose to make war! I propose to conquer the world!

COUNTESS. You have heard the defense, such as it is. I demand a verdict of guilty.

THE RAGPICKER. What are you talking about? Guilty? I? I am never guilty!

JOSEPHINE. I order you to keep quiet.

THE RAGPICKER. I am never quiet!

JOSEPHINE. Quiet, in the name of the law!

THE RAGPICKER. I am the law. When I speak, that is the law. When I present my backside, it is etiquette to smile and to apply the lips respectfully. It is more than etiquette—it is a cherished national privilege, guaranteed by the Constitution.

JOSEPHINE. That's contempt of court. The trial is over.

COUNTESS. And the verdict?

ALL. Guilty!

JOSEPHINE. Guilty as charged.

COUNTESS. Then I have full authority to carry out the sentence?

ALL. Yes!

COUNTESS. I can do what I like with them?

ALL. Yes!

COUNTESS. I have the right to exterminate them?

ALL. Yes!

JOSEPHINE. Court adjourned!

COUNTESS (to the Ragpicker). Congratulations, Ragpicker. A marvelous defense. Absolutely impartial.

THE RAGPICKER. Had I known a little before, I could have done better. I could have prepared a little speech, like the time I used to sell the Miracle Spot Remover . . .

JOSEPHINE. No need for that. You did very well, extempore. The likeness was striking and the style reminiscent of Clemenceau. I predict a brilliant future for you. Good-bye, Aurelia. I'll take our little Gabrielle home.

CONSTANCE. I'm going to walk along the river. (To Dickie) Oh! So here you are. And your ear all bloody! Dickie! Have you been fighting again? Oh, dear . . . !

COUNTESS (to the Ragpicker). See that

she gets home all right, won't you? She loses everything on the way. And in the queerest places. Her prayer book in the butcher shop. And her corset in church.

THE RAGPICKER *(bowing and offering his arm)*. Permit me, Madame.

STREET SINGER. Oh, Countess—my mazurka. Remember?

COUNTESS. Oh, yes. Constance, wait a moment. *(To the Singer)* Well? Begin.

SINGER *(sings)*.

Do you hear, Mademoiselle,
Those musicians of hell?

CONSTANCE. Why, of course, it's *La Belle Polonaise* . . .

(She sings.)

From Poland to France
Comes this marvelous dance,
    So gracious,
    Audacious,
Will you foot it, perchance?

SINGER. I'm saved!

JOSEPHINE. *(reappearing at the head of the stairs)*.

Now my arm I entwine
Round these contours divine,
So pure, so impassioned,
Which Cupid has fashioned . . .

GABRIELLE *(reappearing also, she sings a quartet with the others)*.

Come, let's dance the mazurka, that
    [devilish measure,
'Tis a joy that's reserved to the gods
    [for their pleasure—
Let's gallop, let's hop,
With never a stop,
My blonde Polish miss,
Let our heads spin and turn
As the dance-floor we spurn—
There was never such pleasure as
    [this!

They all exit, dancing.)

IRMA. It's time for your afternoon nap.

COUNTESS. But suppose they come, Irma!

IRMA. I'll watch out for them.

COUNTESS. Thank you, Irma. I *am* tired. *(She smiles)* Did you ever see a trial end more happily in your life?

IRMA. Lie down and close your eyes a moment.

The Countess stretches out on the chaise-longue and shuts her eyes. Irma tiptoes out.

In a moment, Pierre comes down softly, the feather boa in his hands. He stands over the chaise-longue, looking tenderly down at the sleeping woman, then kneels beside her and takes her hand.)

COUNTESS *(without opening her eyes)*. Is it you, Adolphe Bertaut?

PIERRE. It's only Pierre.

COUNTESS. Don't lie to me, Adolphe Bertaut. These are your hands. Why do you complicate things always? Say that it's you.

PIERRE. Yes. It is I.

COUNTESS. Would it cost you so much to call me Aurelia?

PIERRE. It's I, Aurelia.

COUNTESS. Why did you leave me, Adolphe Bertaut? Was she so very lovely, this Georgette of yours?

PIERRE. No. You are a thousand times lovelier.

COUNTESS. But she was clever.

PIERRE. She was stupid.

COUNTESS. It was her soul, then, that drew you? When you looked into her eyes, you saw a vision of heaven, perhaps?

PIERRE. I saw nothing.

COUNTESS. That's how it is with men. They love you because you are beautiful and clever and soulful—and at the first opportunity they leave you for someone who is plain and dull and soulless. But why does it have to be like that, Adolphe Bertaut? Why?

PIERRE. Why, Aurelia?

COUNTESS. I know very well she wasn't rich. Because when I saw you that time at the grocer's, and you snatched the only good melon from right under my nose, your cuffs, my poor friend, were badly frayed . . .

PIERRE. Yes. She was poor.

COUNTESS. "Was" poor? Is she dead then? If it's because she's dead that you've come back to me—then no. Go away. I will not take their leavings from the dead. I refuse to inherit you . . .

PIERRE. She's quite well.

COUNTESS. Your hands are still the same, Adolphe Bertaut. Your touch is young and firm. Because it's the only part of you that has stayed with me. The rest of you is pretty far gone, I'm afraid. I can see why you'd rather not come near me when my eyes are open. It's thoughtful of you.

PIERRE. Yes. I've aged.

COUNTESS. Not I. I am young because I haven't had to live down my youth, like you. I have it with me still, as fresh and beautiful as ever. But when you walk now in the park at Colombes with Georgette, I'm sure . . .

PIERRE. There is no longer a park at Colombes.

COUNTESS. Is there a park still at St. Cloud? Is there a park at Versailles? I've never gone back to see. But I think, if they could move, those trees would have walked away in disgust the day you went there with Georgette . . .

PIERRE. They did. Not many are left.

COUNTESS. You take her also, I suppose, to hear *Denise?*

PIERRE. No one hears *Denise* any more.

COUNTESS. It was on the way home from *Denise*, Adolphe Bertaut, that I first took your arm. Because it was windy and it was late. I have never set foot in that street again. I go the other way round. It's not easy, in the winter, when there's ice. One is quite apt to fall. I often do.

PIERRE. Oh, my darling—forgive me.

COUNTESS. No, never. I will never forgive you. It was very bad taste to take her to the very places where we'd been together.

PIERRE. All the same, I swear, Aurelia . . .

COUNTESS. Don't swear. I know what you did. You gave her the same flowers. You bought her the same chocolates. But has she any left? No. I have all your flowers still. I have twelve chocolates. No, I will never forgive you as long as I live.

PIERRE. I always loved you, Aurelia.

COUNTESS. You "loved" me? Then you too are dead, Adolphe Bertaut?

PIERRE. No. I love you. I shall always love you, Aurelia.

COUNTESS. Yes. I know. That much I've always known. I knew it the moment you went away, Adolphe, and I knew that nothing could ever change it. Georgette is in his arms now—yes. But he loves me. Tonight he's taken Georgette to hear *Denise*—yes. But he loves me . . . I know

it. You never loved her. Do you think I believed for one moment that absurd story about her running off with the osteopath? Of course not. Since you didn't love her, obviously she stayed with you. And, after that, when she came back, and I heard about her going off with the surveyor—I knew that couldn't be true, either. You'll never get rid of her, Adolphe Bertaut—never. Because you don't love her.

PIERRE. I need your pity, Aurelia. I need your love. Don't forget me . . .

COUNTESS. Farewell, Adolphe Bertaut. Farewell. Let go my hand, and give it to little Pierre. *(Pierre lets go her hand, and after a moment takes it again. The Countess opens her eyes)* Pierre? Ah, it's you. Has he gone?

PIERRE. Yes, Countess.

COUNTESS. I didn't hear him go. Oh, he knows how to make a quick exit, that one. *(She sees the boa)* Good heavens! Wherever did you find it?

PIERRE. In the wardrobe, Countess. When I took off the mirror.

COUNTESS. Was there a purple felt shopping bag with it?

PIERRE. Yes, Countess.

COUNTESS. And a little child's sewing box?

PIERRE. No, Countess.

COUNTESS. Oh, they're frightened now. They're trembling for their lives. You see what they're up to? They're quietly putting back all the things they have stolen. I never open that wardrobe of course, on account of the old woman in the mirror. But I have sharp eyes. don't need to open it to see what's in it. Up to this morning, that wardrobe was empty. And now—you see? But, dear me how stupid they are! The one thing I really miss is my little sewing box. It's something they stole from me when I was a child. They haven't put it back? You're quite sure?

PIERRE. What was it like?

COUNTESS. Green cardboard with paper lace and gold stamping. I got it for Christmas when I was seven. They stole it the very next day. I cried my eyes out every time I thought of it—until I was eight.

PIERRE. It's not there, Countess.

COUNTESS. The thimble was gilt. I swore I'd never use any other. Look at my poor fingers . . .

PIERRE. They've kept the thimble too.

COUNTESS. Splendid! Then I'm under no obligation to be merciful. Put the boa around my neck, Pierre. I want them to see me wearing it. They'll think it's a real boa.

(Irma runs in excitedly.)

IRMA. Here they come, Countess! You were right—it's a procession. The street is full of limousines and taxis!

COUNTESS. I will receive them. *(As Pierre hesitates to leave her)* Don't worry. There's nothing to be frightened of. *(Pierre goes out)* Irma, did you remember to stir the kerosene into the water?

IRMA. Yes, Countess. Here it is.

COUNTESS *(looking critically at the bottle)*. You might as well pour in what's left of the tea. *(Irma shakes up the liquid)* Don't forget, I'm supposed to be deaf. I want to hear what they're thinking.

IRMA. Yes, Countess.

COUNTESS *(putting the finishing touches to her make-up)*. I don't have to be merciful —but, after all, I do want to be just . . . *(Irma goes up to the landing and exits. As soon as she is alone, the Countess presses the brick, and the trap door opens. There is a confused sound of auto horns in the street above, and the noise of an approaching crowd.)*

IRMA *(offstage)*. Yes, Mr. President. Come in, Mr. President. You're expected, Mr. President. This way, Mr. President. *(The Presidents come down, led by the President. They all look alike, are dressed alike, and all have long cigars)* The Countess is quite deaf, gentlemen. You'll have to shout. *(She announces)* The Presidents of the boards of directors!

THE PRESIDENT. I had a premonition, Madame, when I saw you this morning, that we should meet again. *(The Countess smiles vaguely. He continues, a tone louder)* I want to thank you for your trust. You may place yourself in our hands with complete confidence.

SECOND PRESIDENT. Louder. The old goat can't hear you.

THE PRESIDENT. I have a letter here, Madame, in which . . .

SECOND PRESIDENT. Louder. Louder.

THIRD PRESIDENT *(shouting)*. Is it true that you've located . . . ? *(The Countess stares at him blankly. He shouts at the top of his voice)* Oil? *(The Countess nods with a smile, and points down. The President produces a legal paper and a fountain pen)* Sign here.

COUNTESS. What is it? I haven't my glasses.

THE PRESIDENT. Your contract.

(He offers the pen.)

COUNTESS. Thank you.

SECOND PRESIDENT *(normal voice)*. What is it?

THIRD PRESIDENT. Waiver of all rights. *(He takes it back signed)* Thank you. *(He hands it to the Second President)* Witness. *(The Second President witnesses it. The President passes it on to the Third President)* Notarize. *(The paper is notarized. The President turns to the Countess and shouts)* My congratulations. And now, Madame— *(He produces a gold brick wrapped in tissue paper)* If you'll show us the well, this package is yours.

COUNTESS. What is it?

THE PRESIDENT. Pure gold. Twenty-four karat. For you.

COUNTESS. Thank you very much. *(She takes it)* It's heavy.

SECOND PRESIDENT. Are you going to give her that?

THE PRESIDENT. Don't worry. We'll pick it up again on the way out. *(He shouts at the Countess, pointing at the trap door)* Is this the way?

COUNTESS. That's the way.

(The Second President tries to slip in first. The President pulls him back.)

THE PRESIDENT. Just a minute, Mr. President. After me, if you don't mind. And watch those cigars. It's oil, you know.

(But as he is about to descend, the Countess steps forward.)

COUNTESS. Just one moment . . .

THE PRESIDENT. Yes?

COUNTESS. Did any of you happen to bring along a little sewing box?

THE PRESIDENT. Sewing box? *(He pulls back another impatient President)* Take it easy.

COUNTESS. Or a little gold thimble?

THE PRESIDENT. Not me.

THE PRESIDENTS. Not us.

COUNTESS. What a pity!

THE PRESIDENT. Can we go down now?

COUNTESS. Yes. You may go down now. Watch your step!

(They hurry down eagerly. When they have quite disappeared, Irma appears on the landing and announces the next echelon.)

IRMA. Countess, the Prospectors.

COUNTESS. Heavens! Are there more than one?

IRMA. There's a whole delegation.

COUNTESS. Send them down.

(The Prospector comes in, following his nose.)

IRMA. Come in, please.

THE PROSPECTOR *(sniffing the air like a bloodhound).* I smell something . . . Who's that?

IRMA. The Countess. She is very deaf.

THE PROSPECTOR. Good.

(The Prospectors also look alike. Sharp clothes, Western hats and long noses. They crowd down the stairs after the Prospector, sniffing in unison. The Prospector is especially talented. He casts about on the scent until it leads him to the decanter on the table. He pours himself a glass, drinks it off, and belches with much satisfaction. The others join him at once, and follow his example. They all belch in unison.)

THE PROSPECTORS. Oil?

THE PROSPECTOR. Oil!

COUNTESS. Oil.

THE PROSPECTOR. Traces? Puddles?

COUNTESS. Pools. Gushers.

SECOND PROSPECTOR. Characteristic odor? *(He sniffs)*

THE PROSPECTOR. Chanel Number 5. Nectar! Undoubtedly—the finest—rarest! *(He drinks)* Sixty gravity crude: straight gasoline! *(To the Countess)* How found? By blast? Drill?

COUNTESS. By finger.

THE PROSPECTOR *(whipping out a document).* Sign here, please.

COUNTESS. What is it?

THE PROSPECTOR. Agreement for dividing the profits . . .

(The Countess signs.)

SECOND PROSPECTOR *(to First Prospector).* What is it?

THE PROSPECTOR *(pocketing the paper).* Application to enter a lunatic asylum. Down there?

COUNTESS. Down there.

(The Prospectors go down, sniffing.)

(Irma enters.)

IRMA. The gentlemen of the press are here.

COUNTESS. The rest of the machine! Show them in.

IRMA. The Public Relations Counsellors! *(They enter, all shapes and sizes, all in blue pin-striped suits and black homburg hats)* The Countess is very deaf, gentlemen. You'll have to shout!

FIRST PRESS AGENT. You don't say—Delighted to make the acquaintance of so charming and beautiful a lady . . .

SECOND PRESS AGENT. Louder. She can't hear you.

FIRST PRESS AGENT. What a face! *(Shouts)* Madame, we are the press. You know our power. We fix all values. We set all standards. Your entire future depends on us.

COUNTESS. How do you do?

FIRST PRESS AGENT. What will we charge the old trull? The usual thirty?

SECOND PRESS AGENT. Forty.

THIRD PRESS AGENT. Sixty.

FIRST PRESS AGENT. All right—seventy-five. *(He fills in a form and offers it to the Countess)* Sign here, Countess. This contract really gives you a break

COUNTESS. That is the entrance.

FIRST PRESS AGENT. Entrance to what

COUNTESS. The oil well.

FIRST PRESS AGENT. Oh, we don't need to see that. Madame.

COUNTESS. Don't need to see it?

FIRST PRESS AGENT. No, no—we don' have to see it to write about it. We ca imagine it. An oil well is an oil well "That's oil we know on earth, and oil w need to know." *(He bows)*

COUNTESS. But if you don't see it, hov can you be sure the oil is there?

FIRST PRESS AGENT. If it's there, wel and good. If it's not, by the time we ge through, it will be. You underestimat the creative aspect of our profession Madame. *(The Countess shakes her head handing back the papers)* I warn you, if yo insist on rubbing our noses in this oil, will cost you 10 percent extra.

COUNTESS. It's worth it.

(She signs. They cross toward the trapdoor.)

SECOND PRESS AGENT *(descending)*. You see, Madame, we of the press can refuse a lady nothing.

THIRD PRESS AGENT. Especially, such a lady.

(Third Press Agent starts going down.)

SECOND PRESS AGENT *(going down. Gallantly)*. It's plain to see, Madame, that even fountains of oil have their nymphs ... I can use that somewhere. That's copy!

(The Press Agents go down. As he disappears, the First Press Agent steals the gold brick and blows a kiss gallantly to the Countess, who blows one back.)

(There is a high-pitched chatter offstage, and Irma comes in, trying hard to hold back Three Women who pay no attention to her whatever. These Women are tall, slender, and as soulless as if they were molded of wax. They march down the steps, erect and abstracted like animated window models, but chattering incessantly.)

IRMA. But, ladies, please—you have no business here—you are not expected. *(To the Countess)* There are some strange ladies coming ...

COUNTESS. Show them in, Irma. *(The Women come down, without taking the slightest interest in their surroundings)* Who are you?

FIRST WOMAN. Madame, we are the most powerful pressure group in the world.

SECOND WOMAN. We are the ultimate dynamic.

THIRD WOMAN. The mainspring of all combinations.

FIRST WOMAN. Nothing succeeds without our assistance. Is that the well, Madame?

COUNTESS. That is the well.

FIRST WOMAN. Put out your cigarettes, girls. We don't want any explosions. Not with my brand-new eyelashes.

(They go down, still chattering. The Countess crosses to the wall to close the trap. As she does so, there is a commotion on the landing.)

IRMA. Countess ...

(A Man rushes in breathlessly.)

MAN. Just a minute! Just a minute!

(He rushes for the trap door.)

COUNTESS. Wait! Who are you?

MAN. I'm in a hurry. Excuse me. It's my only chance!

(He rushes down.)

COUNTESS. But ... *(But he is gone. She shrugs her shoulders, and presses the brick. The trap closes. She rings the bell for Irma)* My gold brick! Why, they've stolen my gold brick! *(She moves toward the trap. It is now closed)* Well, let them take their god with them.

(Irma enters and sees with astonishment that the stage is empty of all but the Countess. Little by little, the scene is suffused with light, faint at first, but increasing as if the very walls were glowing with the quiet radiance of universal joy. Only around the closed trap a shadow lingers.)

IRMA. But what's happened? They've gone! They've vanished!

COUNTESS. They've evaporated, Irma. They were wicked. Wickedness evaporated.

(Pierre enters. He is followed by the Vagabonds, all of them. The new radiance of the world is now very perceptible. It glows from their faces.)

PIERRE. Oh, Countess ...

WAITER. Countess, everything's changed. Now you can breathe again. Now you can see.

PIERRE. The air is pure! The sky is clear!

IRMA. Life is beautiful again.

THE RAGPICKER *(rushes in)*. Countess—the pigeons! The pigeons are flying!

FLOWER GIRL. They don't have to walk any more.

THE RAGPICKER. They're flying ... The air is like crystal. And young grass is sprouting on the pavements.

COUNTESS. Is it possible?

IRMA *(interpreting for the Deaf-Mute)*. Now, Juggler, you can throw your fireballs up as high as you please—they won't go out.

SERGEANT. On the street, utter strangers are shaking hands, they don't know why, and offering each other almond bars!

COUNTESS. Oh, my friends ...

WAITER. Countess, we thank you ...

(They go on talking with happy and animated gestures, but we no longer hear them, for their words blend into a strain of unearthly music

which seems to thrill from the uttermost confines of the universe. And out of this music comes a voice.)

FIRST VOICE. Countess . . .

(Only the Countess hears it. She turns from the group of Vagabonds in wonder.)

SECOND VOICE. Countess . . .

THIRD VOICE. Countess . . .

(As she looks up in rapture, the First Voice speaks again.)

FIRST VOICE. Countess, we thank you. We are the friends of animals.

SECOND VOICE. We are the friends of people.

THIRD VOICE. We are the friends of friendship.

FIRST VOICE. You have freed us!

SECOND VOICE. From now on, there will be no hungry cats . . .

THIRD VOICE. And we shall tell the Duchess her dog's right name!

(The Voices fade off. And now another group of voices is heard.)

FIRST VOICE. Countess, we thank you. We are the friends of flowers.

SECOND VOICE. From now on, every plant in Paris will be watered . . .

THIRD VOICE. And the sewers will be fragrant with jasmine!

(These voices, too, are silent. For an instant, the stage is vibrant with music. Then the Deaf-Mute speaks, and his voice is the most beautiful of all.)

DEAF-MUTE. Sadness flies on the wings of the morning, and out of the heart of darkness comes the light.

(Suddenly a group of figures detaches itself from the shadows. These are exactly similar in face and figure and in dress. They are shabby in the fashion of 1900 and their cuffs are badly frayed. Each bears in his hand a ripe melon.)

FIRST ADOLPHE BERTAUT. Countess, we thank you. We, too, are freed at last. We are the Adolphe Bertauts of the world.

SECOND ADOLPHE BERTAUT. We are no longer timid.

THIRD ADOLPHE BERTAUT. We are no longer weak.

FIRST ADOLPHE BERTAUT. From this day on, we shall hold fast to what we love. For your sake, henceforth, we shall be handsome, and our cuffs forever immaculate and new. Countess, we bring you this melon and with it our hearts . . . ! *(They all kneel)* Will you do us the honor to be our wife?

COUNTESS *(sadly)*. Too late! Too late! *(She waves them aside. They take up their melons sadly and vanish. The voices of the Vagabonds are heard again, and the music dies)* Too late! Too late!

PIERRE. Too late, Countess?

IRMA. Too late for what?

COUNTESS. I say that it's too late for them. On the twenty-fourth of May, 1881, the most beautiful Easter in the memory of man, it was not too late. And on the fifth of September, 1887, the day they caught the trout and broiled it on the open fire by the brook at Villeneuve, it was not too late. And it was even not too late for them on the twenty-first of August, 1897, the day the Czar visited Paris with his guard. But they did nothing and they said nothing, and now—kiss each other, you two, this very instant!

IRMA. You mean . . . ?

PIERRE. You mean . . . ?

IRMA. But, Countess . . .

COUNTESS. It's three hours since you've met and known and loved each other. Kiss each other quickly. *(Pierre hesitates)* Look at him. He hesitates. He trembles. Happiness frightens him. . . . How like a man! Oh, Irma, kiss him, kiss him! If two people who love each other let a single instant wedge itself between them it grows—it becomes a month, a year, a century; it becomes too late. Kiss him, Irma, kiss him while there is time, or in a moment his hair will be white and there will be another madwoman in Paris! Oh make her kiss him, all of you! *(They kiss)* Bravo! Oh, if only you'd had the courage to do that thirty years ago, how different I would be today! Dear Deaf-Mute, be still—your words dazzle our eyes! And Irma is too busy to translate for you *(They kiss once more)* Well, there we are. The world is saved. And you see how simple it all was? Nothing is ever so wrong in this world that a sensible woman can't set it right in the course of an afternoon. Only, the next time, don't wait until things begin to look black. The minute you notice anything, tell me at once.

THE RAGPICKER. We will, Countess. We will.

COUNTESS *(puts on her hat. Her tone becomes businesslike)*. Irma. My bones. My gizzard.

IRMA. I have them ready, Countess.

COUNTESS. Good. *(She puts the bones into her basket and starts for the stairs)* Well, let's get on to more important things. Four o'clock. My poor cats must be starved. What a bore for them if humanity had to be saved every afternoon. They don't think much of it, as it is.

CURTAIN

JEAN–PAUL SARTRE's

No Exit

(Huis Clos)

Translated by STUART GILBERT

First presented* by Herman Levin and Oliver Smith at the Biltmore Theatre, New York, on November 26, 1946, with the following cast:

VALET (BELL BOY)* .... Peter Kass	ESTELLE .... Ruth Ford
GARCIN (CHADEAU)* ....Claude Dauphin	INEZ............................. Annabella

Huis Clos (No Exit) was presented for the first time at the Théâtre du Vieux-Columbier, Paris, in May, 1944.

-----

* In the adaptation by Paul Bowles

A PLAY IN ONE ACT

SCENE: *A drawing room in Second Empire style. A massive bronze ornament stands on the mantelpiece.*

————

GARCIN *(enters, accompanied by the Room-Valet, and glances around him).* Hm! So here we are?

VALET. Yes, Mr. Garcin.

GARCIN. And this is what it looks like?

VALET. Yes.

GARCIN. Second Empire furniture, I observe . . . Well, well, I dare say one gets used to it in time.

VALET. Some do. Some don't.

GARCIN. Are all the other rooms like this one?

VALET. How could they be? We cater for all sorts: Chinamen and Indians, for instance. What use would they have for a Second Empire chair?

GARCIN. And what use do you suppose *I* have for one? Do you know who I was? . . . Oh, well, it's no great matter. And, to tell the truth, I had quite a habit of living among furniture that I didn't relish, and in false positions. I'd even come to like it. A false position in a Louis-Philippe dining room—you know the style?—well, that had its points, you know. Bogus in bogus, so to speak.

VALET. And you'll find that living in a Second Empire drawing room has its points.

GARCIN. Really? . . . Yes, yes, I dare say . . . *(He takes another look around)* Still, I certainly didn't expect—this! You know what they tell us down there?

VALET. What about?

GARCIN. About *(makes a sweeping gesture)* this—er—residence.

VALET. Really, sir, how could you believe such cock-and-bull stories? Told by people who'd never set foot here. For, of course, if they had—

GARCIN. Quite so. *(Both laugh. Abruptly the laugh dies from Garcin's face)* But, I say, where are the instruments of torture?

VALET. The what?

GARCIN. The racks and red-hot pincers and all the other paraphernalia?

VALET. Ah, you must have your little joke, sir!

GARCIN. My little joke? Oh, I see. No, I wasn't joking. *(A short silence. He strolls round the room)* No mirrors, I notice. No windows. Only to be expected. And nothing breakable. *(Bursts out angrily)* But, damn it all, they might have left me my toothbrush!

VALET. That's good! So you haven't yet got over your—what-do-you-call-it? —sense of human dignity? Excuse me smiling.

GARCIN *(thumping ragefully the arm of an armchair).* I'll ask you to be more polite. I quite realize the position I'm in, but I won't tolerate . . .

VALET. Sorry, sir. No offense meant. But all our guests ask me the same questions. Silly questions, if you'll pardon me saying so. Where's the torture-chamber? That's the first thing they ask, all of them. They don't bother their heads about the bathroom requisites, that I can assure you. But after a bit, when they've got their nerve back, they start in about their toothbrushes and what-not. Good heavens, Mr. Garcin, can't you use your brains? What, I ask you, would be the point of brushing your teeth?

GARCIN *(more calmly).* Yes, of course you're right. *(He looks around again)* And why should one want to see oneself in a looking-glass? But that bronze contraption on the mantelpiece, that's another story. I suppose there will be times when I stare my eyes out at it. Stare my eyes out—see what I mean? . . . All right, let's put our cards on the table. I assure you I'm quite conscious of my position. Shall I tell you what it feels like? A man's drowning, choking, sinking by inches, till only his eyes are just above water. And what does he see? A bronze atrocity by—what's the fellow's name?—Barbedienne. A collector's piece. As in a nightmare. That's their idea, isn't it? . . . No, I suppose you're under orders not to answer questions; and I won't insist. But don't forget, my man, I've a good notion of what's coming to me, so don't you boast you've caught me off my guard. I'm facing the situation, facing it. *(He starts pacing the room again)* So that's that; no toothbrush. And no bed, either. One never sleeps, I take it?

VALET. That's so.

GARCIN. Just as I expected. *Why* should one sleep? A sort of drowsiness steals on you, tickles you behind the ears, and you feel your eyes closing—but why sleep? You lie down on the sofa and—in a flash, sleep flies away. Miles and miles away. So you rub your eyes, get up, and it starts all over again.

VALET. Romantic, that's what you are.

GARCIN. Will you keep quiet, please! . . . I won't make a scene, I shan't be sorry for myself, I'll face the situation, as I said just now. Face it fairly and squarely. I won't have it springing at me from behind, before I've time to size it up. And you call that being "romantic"! . . . So it comes to this; one doesn't need rest. Why bother about sleep if one isn't sleepy? That stands to reason, doesn't it? Wait a minute, there's a snag somewhere; something disagreeable. Why, now, should it be disagreeable? . . . Ah, I see; it's life without a break.

VALET. What do you mean by that?

GARCIN. What do I mean? *(Eyes the Valet suspiciously)* I thought as much. That's why there's something so beastly, so damn bad-mannered, in the way you stare at me. They're paralyzed.

VALET. What are you talking about?

GARCIN. Your eyelids. We move ours up and down. Blinking, we call it. It's like a small black shutter that clicks down and makes a break. Everything goes black; one's eyes are moistened. You can't imagine how restful, refreshing, it is. Four thousand little rests per hour. Four thousand little respites—just think! . . . So that's the idea. I'm to live without eyelids. Don't act the fool, you know what I mean. No eyelids, no sleep; it follows, doesn't it? I shall never sleep again. But then—how shall I endure my own company? Try to understand. You see, I'm fond of teasing, it's a second nature with me—and I'm used to teasing myself. Plaguing myself, if you prefer; I don't tease nicely. But I can't go on doing that without a break. Down there I had

my nights. I slept. I always had good nights. By way of compensation, I suppose. And happy little dreams. There was a green field. Just an ordinary field. I used to stroll in it . . . Is it daytime now?

VALET. Can't you see? The lights are on.

GARCIN. Ah yes, I've got it. It's *your* daytime. And outside?

VALET. Outside?

GARCIN. Damn it, you know what I mean. Beyond that wall.

VALET. There's a passage.

GARCIN. And at the end of the passage?

VALET. There's more rooms, more passages, and stairs.

GARCIN. And what lies beyond them?

VALET. That's all.

GARCIN. But surely you have a day off sometimes. Where do you go?

VALET. To my uncle's place. He's the head valet here. He has a room on the third floor.

GARCIN. I should have guessed as much. Where's the light-switch?

VALET. There isn't any.

GARCIN. What? Can't one turn off the light?

VALET. Oh, the management can cut off the current if they want to. But I can't remember their having done so on this floor. We have all the electricity we want.

GARCIN. So one has to live with one's eyes open all the time?

VALET. To *live*, did you say?

GARCIN. Don't let's quibble over words. With one's eyes open. Forever. Always broad daylight in my eyes—and in my head. *(Short silence)* And suppose I took that contraption on the mantelpiece and dropped it on the lamp—wouldn't it go out?

VALET. You can't move it. It's too heavy.

GARCIN *(seizing the bronze ornament and trying to lift it)*. You're right. It's too heavy.

(A short silence follows.)

VALET. Very well, sir, if you don't need me any more, I'll be off.

GARCIN. What? You're going? *(The Valet goes up to the door)* Wait. *(Valet looks round)* That's a bell, isn't it? *(Valet nods)* And if I ring, you're bound to come?

VALET. Well, yes, that's so—in a way. But you can never be sure about that bell. There's something wrong with the wiring, and it doesn't always work.

(Garcin goes to the bell-push and presses the button. A bell purrs outside.)

GARCIN. It's working all right.

VALET *(looking surprised)*. So it is. *(He, too, presses the button)* But I shouldn't count on it too much if I were you. It's— capricious. Well, I really must go now. *(Garcin makes a gesture to detain him)* Yes, sir?

GARCIN. No, never mind. *(He goes to the mantelpiece and picks up a paper-knife)* What's this?

VALET. Can't you see? An ordinary paper-knife.

GARCIN. Are there books here?

VALET. No.

GARCIN. Then what's the use of this? *(Valet shrugs his shoulders)* Very well. You can go. *(Valet goes out)*

(Garcin is by himself. He goes to the bronze ornament and strokes it reflectively. He sits down; then gets up, goes to the bell-push, and presses the button. The bell remains silent. He tries two or three times, without success. Then he tries to open the door, also without success. He calls the Valet several times, but gets no result. He beats the door with his fists, still calling. Suddenly he grows calm and sits down again. At the same moment the door opens and Inez enters, followed by the Valet.)

VALET. Did you call, sir?

GARCIN *(on the point of answering "Yes" —but then his eyes fall on Inez)*. No.

VALET *(turning to Inez)*. This is your room, madam. *(Inez says nothing)* If there's any information you require—? *(Inez still keeps silent, and the Valet looks slightly huffed)* Most of our guests have quite a lot to ask me. But I won't insist. Anyhow, as regards the toothbrush, and the electric bell, and that thing on the mantelshelf, this gentleman can tell you anything you want to know as well as I could. We've had a little chat, him and me. *(Valet goes out)*

Garcin refrains from looking at Inez, who is inspecting the room. Abruptly she turns to Garcin.)

INEZ. Where's Florence? *(Garcin does not reply)* Didn't you hear? I asked you about Florence. Where is she?

GARCIN. I haven't an idea.

INEZ. Ah, that's the way it works, is it? Torture by separation. Well, as far as I'm concerned, you won't get anywhere. Florence was a tiresome little fool, and I shan't miss her in the least.

GARCIN. I beg your pardon. Who do you suppose I am?

INEZ. You? Why, the torturer, of course.

GARCIN *(looks startled, then bursts out laughing)*. Well, that's a good one! Too comic for words. I the torturer! So you came in, had a look at me, and thought I was—er—one of the staff. Of course, it's that silly fellow's fault; he should have introduced us. A torturer indeed! I'm Joseph Garcin, journalist and man of letters by profession. And as we're both in the same boat, so to speak, might I ask you, Mrs.—?

INEZ *(testily)*. Not "Mrs." I'm unmarried.

GARCIN. Right. That's a start, anyway. Well, now that we've broken the ice, do you *really* think I look like a torturer? And, by the way, how does one recognize torturers when one sees them? Evidently you've ideas on the subject.

INEZ. They look frightened.

GARCIN. Frightened! But how ridiculous! Of whom should they be frightened? Of their victims?

INEZ. Laugh away, but I know what I'm talking about. I've often watched my face in the glass.

GARCIN. In the glass? *(He looks around him)* How beastly of them! They've removed everything in the least resembling a glass. *(Short silence)* Anyhow, I can assure you I'm not frightened. Not that I take my position lightly; I realize its gravity only too well. But I'm not afraid.

INEZ *(shrugging her shoulders)*. That's your affair. *(Silence)* Must you be here all the time, or do you take a stroll outside, now and then?

GARCIN. The door's locked.

INEZ. Oh! . . . That's too bad.

GARCIN. I can quite understand that it bores you having me here. And I, too—

well, quite frankly, I'd rather be alone. I want to think things out, you know; to set my life in order, and one does that better by oneself. But I'm sure we'll manage to pull along together somehow. I'm no talker, I don't move much; in fact I'm a peaceful sort of fellow. Only, if I may venture on a suggestion, we should make a point of being extremely courteous to each other. That will ease the situation for us both.

INEZ. I'm not polite.

GARCIN. Then I must be polite for two.

(A longish silence. Garcin is sitting on a sofa, while Inez paces up and down the room.)

INEZ *(fixing her eyes on him).* Your mouth!

GARCIN *(as if waking from a dream).* I beg your pardon.

INEZ. Can't you keep your mouth still? You keep twisting it about all the time. It's grotesque.

GARCIN. So sorry. I wasn't aware of it.

INEZ. That's just what I reproach you with. *(Garcin's mouth twitches)* There you are! You talk about politeness, and you don't even try to control your face. Remember you're not alone; you've no right to inflict the sight of your fear on me.

GARCIN *(getting up and going towards her).* How about you? Aren't you afraid?

INEZ. What would be the use? There was some point in being afraid *before;* while one still had hope.

GARCIN *(in a low voice).* There's no more hope—but it's still "before." We haven't yet begun to suffer.

INEZ. That's so. *(A short silence)* Well? What's going to happen?

GARCIN. I don't know. I'm waiting.

(Silence again. Garcin sits down and Inez resumes her pacing up and down the room. Garcin's mouth twitches; after a glance at Inez he buries his face in his hands. Enter Estelle with the Valet. Estelle looks at Garcin, whose face is still hidden by his hands.)

ESTELLE *(to Garcin).* No! Don't look up. I know what you're hiding with your hands. I know you've no face left. *(Garcin removes his hands)* What! *(A short pause. Then, in a tone of surprise)* But I don't know you!

GARCIN. I'm not the torturer, madam.

ESTELLE. I never thought you were. I—I thought someone was trying to play a rather nasty trick on me. *(To the Valet)* Is anyone else coming?

VALET. No, madam. No one else is coming.

ESTELLE. Oh! Then we're to stay by ourselves, the three of us, this gentleman, this lady, and myself. *(She starts laughing)*

GARCIN *(angrily).* There's nothing to laugh about.

ESTELLE *(still laughing).* It's those sofas. They're so hideous. And just look how they've been arranged. It makes me think of New Year's Day—when I used to visit that boring old aunt of mine, Aunt Mary. Her house is full of horrors like that . . . I suppose each of us has a sofa of his own. Is that one mine? *(To the Valet)* But you can't expect me to sit on that one. It would be too horrible for words. I'm in pale blue and it's vivid green.

INEZ. Would you prefer mine?

ESTELLE. That claret-colored one, you mean? That's very sweet of you, but really—no, I don't think it'd be so much better. What's the good of worrying, anyhow? We've got to take what comes to us, and I'll stick to the green one. *(Pauses)* The only one which might do, at a pinch, is that gentleman's. *(Another pause)*

INEZ. Did you hear, Mr. Garcin?

GARCIN *(with a slight start).* Oh—the sofa, you mean. So sorry. *(He rises)* Please take it, madam.

ESTELLE. Thanks. *(She takes off her coat and drops it on the sofa. A short silence)* Well, as we're to live together, I suppose we'd better introduce ourselves. My name's Rigault. Estelle Rigault. *(Garcin bows and is going to announce his name, but Inez steps in front of him)*

INEZ. And I'm Inez Serrano. Very pleased to meet you.

GARCIN *(bowing again).* Joseph Garcin.

VALET. Do you require me any longer?

ESTELLE. No, you can go. I'll ring when I want you.

(Exit Valet, with polite bows to everyone.)

INEZ. You're very pretty. I wish we'd had some flowers to welcome you with.

ESTELLE. Flowers? Yes, I loved flowers. Only they'd fade so quickly here, wouldn't they? It's so stuffy. Oh, well, the great thing is to keep as cheerful as we can, don't you agree? Of course, you, too, are—

INEZ. Yes. Last week. What about you?

ESTELLE. I'm—quite recent. Yesterday. As a matter of fact, the ceremony's not quite over. *(Her tone is natural enough, but she seems to be seeing what she describes)* The wind's blowing my sister's veil all over the place. She's trying her best to cry. Come, dear! Make another effort. That's better. Two tears, two little tears are twinkling under the black veil. Oh dear! What a sight Olga looks this morning! She's holding my sister's arm, helping her along. She's not crying, and I don't blame her; tears always mess one's face up, don't they? Olga was my bosom friend, you know.

INEZ. Did you suffer much?

ESTELLE. No. I was only half conscious, mostly.

INEZ. What was it?

ESTELLE. Pneumonia. *(In the same tone as before)* It's over now, they're leaving the cemetery. Good-by. Good-by. Quite a crowd they are. My husband's stayed at home. Prostrated with grief, poor man. *(To Inez)* How about you?

INEZ. The gas stove.

ESTELLE. And you, Mr. Garcin?

GARCIN. Twelve bullets through my chest. *(Estelle makes a horrified gesture)* Sorry! I fear I'm not good company among the dead.

ESTELLE. Please, please don't use that word. It's so—so crude. In terribly bad taste, really. It doesn't mean much, anyhow. Somehow I feel we've never been so much alive as now. If we've absolutely got to mention this—this state of things, I suggest we call ourselves—wait!—absentees. Have you been—been absent for long?

GARCIN. About a month.

ESTELLE. Where do you come from?

GARCIN. From Rio.

ESTELLE. I'm from Paris. Have you anyone left down there?

GARCIN. Yes, my wife. *(In the same tone as Estelle has been using)* She's waiting at the entrance of the barracks. She comes there every day. But they won't let her in. Now she's trying to peep between the bars. She doesn't yet know I'm—absent, but she suspects it. Now she's going away. She's wearing her black dress. So much the better, she won't need to change. She isn't crying, but she never did cry, anyhow. It's a bright sunny day and she's like a black shadow creeping down the empty street. Those big tragic eyes of hers—with that martyred look they always had. Oh, how she got on my nerves!

(A short silence. Garcin sits on the central sofa and buries his head in his hands.)

INEZ. Estelle!

ESTELLE. Please, Mr. Garcin!

GARCIN. What is it?

ESTELLE. You're sitting on my sofa.

GARCIN. I beg your pardon. *(He gets up)*

ESTELLE. You looked so—so far away. Sorry I disturbed you.

GARCIN. I was setting my life in order. *(Inez starts laughing)* You may laugh, but you'd do better to follow my example.

INEZ. No need. My life's in perfect order. It tidied itself up nicely of its own accord. So I needn't bother about it now.

GARCIN. Really? You imagine it's so simple as that. *(He runs his hand over his forehead)* Whew! How hot it is here! Do you mind if—? *(He begins taking off his coat)*

ESTELLE. How dare you! *(More gently)* No, please don't. I loathe men in their shirt-sleeves.

GARCIN *(putting on his coat again)*. All right. *(A short pause)* Of course, I used to spend my nights in the newspaper office, and it was a regular Black Hole, so we never kept our coats on. Stiflingly hot it could be. *(Short pause. In the same tone as previously)* Stifling, that it *is*. It's night now.

ESTELLE. That's so. Olga's undressing; it must be after midnight. How quickly the time passes, on earth!

INEZ. Yes, after midnight. They've sealed up my room. It's dark, pitch-dark, and empty.

GARCIN. They've slung their coats on

the backs of the chairs and rolled up their shirt-sleeves above the elbow. The air stinks of men and cigar-smoke. *(A short silence)* I used to like living among men in their shirt-sleeves.

ESTELLE *(aggressively)*. Well, in that case our tastes differ. That's all it proves. *(Turning to Inez)* What about you? Do you like men in their shirt-sleeves?

INEZ. Oh, I don't care much for men any way.

ESTELLE *(looking at the other two with a puzzled air)*. Really I can't imagine why they put us three together. It doesn't make sense.

INEZ *(stifling a laugh)*. What's that you said?

ESTELLE. I'm looking at you two and thinking that we're going to live together. . . . It's so absurd. I expected to meet old friends, or relatives.

INEZ. Yes, a charming old friend—with a hole in the middle of his face.

ESTELLE. Yes, him too. He danced the tango so divinely. Like a professional . . But why, why should we of all people be put together?

GARCIN. A pure fluke, I should say. They lodge folks as they can, in the order of their coming. *(To Inez)* Why are you laughing?

INEZ. Because you amuse me, with your "flukes." As if they left anything to chance! But I suppose you've got to reassure yourself somehow.

ESTELLE *(hesitantly)*. I wonder, now. Don't you think we may have met each other at some time in our lives?

INEZ. Never. I shouldn't have forgotten you.

ESTELLE. Or perhaps we have friends in common. I wonder if you know the Dubois-Seymours?

INEZ. Not likely.

ESTELLE. But *everyone* went to their parties.

INEZ. What's their job?

ESTELLE. Oh, they don't do anything. But they have a lovely house in the country, and hosts of people visit them.

INEZ. I didn't. I was a post-office clerk.

ESTELLE *(recoiling a little)*. Ah, yes . . . Of course, in that case—*(A pause)* And you, Mr. Garcin?

GARCIN. We've never met. I always lived in Rio.

ESTELLE. Then you must be right. It's mere chance that has brought us together.

INEZ. Mere chance? Then it's by chance this room is furnished as we see it. It's an accident that the sofa on the right is a livid green, and that one on the left's wine-red. Mere chance? Well, just try to shift the sofas and you'll see the difference quick enough. And that statue on the mantelpiece, do you think it's there by accident? And what about the heat here? How about that? *(A short silence)* I tell you they've thought it all out. Down to the last detail. Nothing was left to chance. This room was all set for us.

ESTELLE. But really! Everything here's so hideous; all in angles, so uncomfortable. I always loathed angles.

INEZ *(shrugging her shoulders)*. And do you think *I* lived in a Second Empire drawing-room?

ESTELLE. So it was all fixed up beforehand?

INEZ. Yes. And they've put us together deliberately.

ESTELLE. Then it's not mere chance that *you* precisely are sitting opposite me? But what can be the idea behind it?

INEZ. Ask me another! I only know they're waiting.

ESTELLE. I never could bear the idea of anyone's expecting something from me. It always made me want to do just the opposite.

INEZ. Well, do it. Do it if you can. You don't even know what they expect.

ESTELLE *(stamping her foot)*. It's outrageous! So something's coming to me from you two? *(She eyes each in turn)* Something nasty, I suppose. There are some faces that tell me everything at once. Yours don't convey anything.

GARCIN *(turning abruptly towards Inez)*. Look here! Why are we together? You've given us quite enough hints, you may as well come out with it.

INEZ *(in a surprised tone)*. But I know nothing, absolutely nothing about it. I'm as much in the dark as you are.

GARCIN. We've *got* to know. *(Ponders for a while)*

INEZ. If only each of us had the guts to tell—

GARCIN. Tell what?

INEZ. Estelle!

ESTELLE. Yes?

INEZ. What have you done? I mean, why have they sent you here?

ESTELLE (*quickly*). That's just it. I haven't a notion, not the foggiest. In fact, I'm wondering if there hasn't been some ghastly mistake. (*To Inez*) Don't smile. Just think of the number of people who—who become absentees every day. There must be thousands and thousands, and probably they're sorted out by—by understrappers, you know what I mean. Stupid employees who don't know their job. So they're bound to make mistakes sometimes ... Do stop smiling. (*To Garcin*) Why don't you speak? If they made a mistake in my case, they may have done the same about you. (*To Inez*) And you, too. Anyhow, isn't it better to think we've got here by mistake?

INEZ. Is that all you have to tell us?

ESTELLE. What else should I tell? I've nothing to hide. I lost my parents when I was a kid, and I had my young brother to bring up. We were terribly poor and when an old friend of my people asked me to marry him I said yes. He was very well off, and quite nice. My brother was a very delicate child and needed all sorts of attention, so really that was the right thing for me to do, don't you agree? My husband was old enough to be my father, but for six years we had a happy married life. Then two years ago I met the man I was fated to love. We knew it the moment we set eyes on each other. He asked me to run away with him, and I refused. Then I got pneumonia and it finished me. That's the whole story. No doubt, by certain standards, I did wrong to sacrifice my youth to a man nearly three times my age. (*To Garcin*) Do *you* think that could be called a sin?

GARCIN. Certainly not. (*A short silence*) And now, tell me, do you think it's a time to stand by one's principles?

ESTELLE. Of course not. Surely no one would blame a man for that!

GARCIN. Wait a bit! I ran a pacifist newspaper. Then war broke out. What was I to do? Everyone was watching me, wondering: 'Will he dare?' Well, I dared. I folded my arms and they shot me. Had I done anything wrong?

ESTELLE (*laying her hand on his arm*). Wrong? On the contrary. You were—

INEZ (*breaks in ironically*). —a hero! And how about your wife, Mr. Garcin?

GARCIN. That's simple. I'd rescued her from—from the gutter.

ESTELLE (*to Inez*). You see! You see!

INEZ. Yes, I see. (*A pause*) Look here! What's the point of play-acting, trying to throw dust in each other's eyes? We're all tarred with the same brush.

ESTELLE (*indignantly*). How dare you!

INEZ. Yes, we are criminals—murderers —all three of us. We're in hell, my pets; they never make mistakes, and people aren't damned for nothing.

ESTELLE. Stop! For heaven's sake—

INEZ. In hell! Damned souls—that's us, all three!

ESTELLE. Keep quiet! I forbid you to use such disgusting words.

INEZ. A damned soul—that's you, my little plaster saint. And ditto our friend there, the noble pacifist. We've had our hour of pleasure, haven't we? There have been people who burned their lives out for our sakes—and we chuckled over it. So now we have to pay the reckoning.

GARCIN (*raising his fist*). Will you keep your mouth shut, damn it!

INEZ (*confronting him fearlessly, but with a look of vast surprise*). Well, well! (*A pause*) Ah, I understand now. I know why they've put us three together.

GARCIN. I advise you to—to think twice before you say any more.

INEZ. Wait! You'll see how simple it is. Childishly simple. Obviously there aren't any physical torments—you agree, don't you? And yet we're in hell. And no one else will come here. We'll stay in this room together, the three of us, for ever and ever ... In short, there's someone absent here, the official torturer.

GARCIN (*sotto voce*). I'd noticed that.

INEZ. It's obvious what they're after— an economy of man-power—or devil-power, if you prefer. The same idea as in the cafeteria, where customers serve themselves.

ESTELLE. What ever do you mean?

INEZ. I mean that each of us will act as torturer of the two others.

(There is a short silence while they digest this information.)

GARCIN (gently). No, I shall never be your torturer. I wish neither of you any harm, and I've no concern with you. None at all. So the solution's easy enough; each of us stays put in his or her corner and takes no notice of the others. You here, you here, and I there. Like soldiers at our posts. Also, we mustn't speak. Not one word. That won't be difficult; each of us has plenty of material for self-communings. I think I could stay ten thousand years with only my thoughts for company.

ESTELLE. Have I got to keep silent, too?

GARCIN. Yes. And that way we—we'll work out our salvation. Looking into ourselves, never raising our heads. Agreed?

INEZ. Agreed.

ESTELLE (after some hesitation). I agree.

GARCIN. Then—good-by.

(He goes to his sofa and buries his head in his hands. There is a long silence; then Inez begins singing to herself.)

INEZ (singing).

What a crowd in Whitefriars Lane!
They've set trestles in a row,
With a scaffold and the knife,
And a pail of bran below.
Come, good folks, to Whitefriars Lane,
Come to see the merry show!

The headsman rose at crack of dawn,
He'd a long day's work in hand,
Chopping heads off generals,
Priests and peers and admirals,
All the highest in the land.
What a crowd in Whitefriars Lane!

See them standing in a line,
Ladies all dressed up so fine.
But their heads have got to go,
Heads and hats roll down below.
Come, good folks, to Whitefriars Lane,
Come to see the merry show!

(Meanwhile Estelle has been plying her powder-puff and lipstick. She looks round for a mirror, fumbles in her bag, then turns towards Garcin.)

ESTELLE. Excuse me, have you a glass? (Garcin does not answer) Any sort of glass, a pocket-mirror will do. (Garcin remains silent) Even if you won't speak to me, you might lend me a glass.

(His head still buried in his hands, Garcin ignores her.)

INEZ (eagerly). Don't worry. I've a glass in my bag. (She opens her bag. Angrily) It's gone! They must have taken it from me at the entrance.

ESTELLE. How tiresome!

(A short silence. Estelle shuts her eyes and sways, as if about to faint. Inez runs forward and holds her up.)

INEZ. What's the matter?

ESTELLE (opens her eyes and smiles). I feel so queer. (She pats herself) Don't you ever get taken that way? When I can't see myself I begin to wonder if I really and truly exist. I pat myself just to make sure, but it doesn't help much.

INEZ. You're lucky. I'm always conscious of myself—in my mind. Painfully conscious.

ESTELLE. Ah yes, in your mind. But everything that goes on in one's head is so vague, isn't it? It makes one want to sleep. (She is silent for a while) I've six big mirrors in my bedroom. There they are. I can see them. But they don't see me. They're reflecting the carpet, the settee, the window—but how empty it is, a glass in which I'm absent! When I talked to people I always made sure there was one near by in which I could see myself. I watched myself talking. And somehow it kept me alert, seeing myself as the others saw me . . . Oh dear! My lipstick! I'm sure I've put it on all crooked. No, I can't do without a looking-glass for ever and ever, I simply can't.

INEZ. Suppose I try to be your glass? Come and pay me a visit, dear. Here's a place for you on my sofa.

ESTELLE. But—(Points to Garcin)

INEZ. Oh, he doesn't count.

ESTELLE. But we're going to—to hurt each other. You said it yourself.

INEZ. Do I look as if I wanted to hurt you?

ESTELLE. One never can tell.

INEZ. Much more likely you'll hurt me. Still, what does it matter? If I've got suffer, it may as well be at your hands, your pretty hands. Sit down. Come closer. Closer. Look into my eyes. What do you see?

ESTELLE. Oh, I'm there! But so tiny I can't see myself properly.

INEZ. But *I* can. Every inch of you. Now ask me questions. I'll be as candid as any looking-glass.

(Estelle seems rather embarrassed and turns to Garcin, as if appealing to him for help.)

ESTELLE. Please, Mr. Garcin. Sure our chatter isn't boring you?

(Garcin makes no reply.)

INEZ. Don't worry about him. As I said, he doesn't count. We're by ourselves . . . Ask away.

ESTELLE. Are my lips all right?

INEZ. Show! No, they're a bit smudgy.

ESTELLE. I thought as much. Luckily *(throws a quick glance at Garcin)* no one's seen me. I'll try again.

INEZ. That's better. No. Follow the line of your lips. Wait! I'll guide your hand. There. That's quite good.

ESTELLE. As good as when I came in?

INEZ. Far better. Crueler. Your mouth looks quite diabolical that way.

ESTELLE. Good gracious! And you say you like it! How maddening, not being able to see for myself! You're quite sure, Miss Serrano, that it's all right now?

INEZ. Won't you call me Inez?

ESTELLE. Are you sure it looks all right?

INEZ. You're lovely, Estelle.

ESTELLE. But how can I rely upon your taste? Is it the same as *my* taste? Oh, how sickening it all is, enough to drive one crazy!

INEZ. I *have* your taste, my dear, because I like you so much. Look at me. No, straight. Now smile. I'm not so ugly, either. Am I not nicer than your glass?

ESTELLE. Oh, I don't know. You scare me rather. My reflection in the glass never did that; of course, I knew it so well. Like something I had tamed . . . I'm going to smile, and my smile will sink down into your pupils, and heaven knows what it will become.

INEZ. And why shouldn't you "tame" me? *(The women gaze at each other, Estelle with a sort of fearful fascination)* Listen! I want you to call me Inez. We must be great friends.

ESTELLE. I don't make friends with women very easily.

INEZ. Not with postal clerks, you mean? Hullo, what's that—that nasty red spot at the bottom of your cheek? A pimple?

ESTELLE. A pimple? Oh, how simply foul! Where?

INEZ. There . . . You know the way they catch larks—with a mirror? I'm your lark-mirror, my dear, and you can't escape me . . . There isn't any pimple, not a trace of one. So what about it? Suppose the mirror started telling lies? Or suppose I covered my eyes—as he is doing—and refused to look at you, all that loveliness of yours would be wasted on the desert air. No, don't be afraid, I can't help looking at you, I shan't turn my eyes away. And I'll be nice to you, ever so nice. Only you must be nice to me, too.

(A short silence.)

ESTELLE. Are you really—attracted by me?

INEZ. Very much indeed.

(Another short silence.)

ESTELLE *(indicating Garcin by a slight movement of her head)*. But I wish he'd notice me, too.

INEZ. Of course! Because he's a Man! *(To Garcin)* You've won. *(Garcin says nothing)* But look at her, damn it! *(Still no reply from Garcin)* Don't pretend. You haven't missed a word of what we've said.

GARCIN. Quite so; not a word. I stuck my fingers in my ears, but your voices thudded in my brain. Silly chatter. Now will you leave me in peace, you two? I'm not interested in you.

INEZ. Not in me, perhaps—but how about this child? Aren't you interested in her? Oh, I saw through your game; you got on your high horse just to impress her.

GARCIN. I asked you to leave me in peace. There's someone talking about me in the newspaper office and I want to listen. And, if it'll make you any happier, let me tell you that I've no use for the "child," as you call her.

ESTELLE. Thanks.

GARCIN. Oh, I didn't mean it rudely.

ESTELLE. You cad!

(*They confront each other in silence for some moments.*)

GARCIN. So that's that. (*Pause*) You know I begged you not to speak.

ESTELLE. It's *her* fault; she started. I didn't ask anything of her and she came and offered me her—her glass.

INEZ. So you say. But all the time you were making up to him, trying every trick to catch his attention.

ESTELLE. Well, why shouldn't I?

GARCIN. You're crazy, both of you. Don't you see where this is leading us? For pity's sake, keep your mouths shut. (*Pause*) Now let's all sit down again quite quietly; we'll look at the floor and each must try to forget the others are there.

(*A longish silence. Garcin sits down. The women return hesitantly to their places. Suddenly Inez swings round on him.*)

INEZ. To forget about the others? How utterly absurd! I *feel* you there, in every pore. Your silence clamors in my ears. You can nail up your mouth, cut your tongue out—but you can't prevent your *being there*. Can you stop thoughts? I hear them ticking away like a clock, tick-tock, tick-tock, and I'm certain you hear mine. It's all very well skulking on your sofa, but you're everywhere, and every sound comes to me soiled, because you've intercepted it on its way. Why, you've even stolen my face; you know it and I don't! And what about her, about Estelle? You've stolen her from me, too; if she and I were alone do you suppose she'd treat me as she does? No, take your hands from your face, I won't leave you in peace—that would suit your book too well. You'd go on sitting there, in a sort of trance, like a yogi, and even if I didn't see her I'd feel it in my bones—that she was making every sound, even the rustle of her dress, for your benefit, throwing you smiles you didn't see . . . Well, I won't stand for that, I prefer to choose my hell; I prefer to look you in the eyes and fight it out face to face.

GARCIN. Have it your own way. I suppose we were bound to come to this; they knew what they were about, and we're easy game. If they'd put me in a room with men—men can keep their mouths shut. But it's no use wanting the impossible. (*He goes to Estelle and lightly fondles her neck*) So I attract you, little girl? It seems you were making eyes at me?

ESTELLE. Don't touch me.

GARCIN. Why not? We might, anyhow, be natural . . . Do you know, I used to be mad about women? And some were fond of me. So we may as well stop posing, we've nothing to lose. Why trouble about politeness, and decorum, and the rest of it? We're between ourselves. And presently we shall be naked as—as new-born babes.

ESTELLE. Oh, let me be!

GARCIN. As new-born babes. Well, I'd warned you, anyhow. I asked so little of you, nothing but peace and a little silence. I'd put my fingers in my ears. Gomez was spouting away as usual, standing in the center of the room, with all the pressmen listening. In their shirt-sleeves. I tried to hear, but it wasn't too easy. Things on earth move so quickly, you know. Couldn't you have held your tongues? Now it's over, he's stopped talking, and what he thinks of me has gone back into his head. Well, we've got to see it through somehow . . . Naked as we were born. So much the better; I want to know whom I have to deal with.

INEZ. You know already. There's nothing more to learn.

GARCIN. You're wrong. So long as each of us hasn't made a clean breast of it—why they've damned him or her—we know nothing. Nothing that counts. You young lady, you shall begin. Why? Tell us why. If you are frank, if we bring our specters into the open, it may save us from disaster. So—out with it! Why?

ESTELLE. I tell you I haven't a notion. They wouldn't tell me why.

GARCIN. That's so. They wouldn't tell me, either. But I've a pretty good idea . . . Perhaps you're shy of speaking first? Right. I'll lead off. (*A short silence*) I'm not a very estimable person.

INEZ. No need to tell us that. We know you were a deserter.

GARCIN. Let that be. It's only a side issue. I'm here because I treated my wife abominably. That's all. For five years

Naturally, she's suffering still. There she is: the moment I mention her, I see her. It's Gomez who interests me, and it's she I see. Where's Gomez got to? For five years. There! They've given her back my things; she's sitting by the window, with my coat on her knees. The coat with the twelve bullet-holes. The blood's like rust; a brown ring round each hole. It's quite a museum-piece, that coat; scarred with history. And I used to wear it, fancy! ... Now, can't you shed a tear, my love? Surely you'll squeeze one out— at last? No? You can't manage it? ... Night after night I came home blind drunk, stinking of wine and women. She'd sat up for me, of course. But she never cried, never uttered a word of reproach. Only her eyes spoke. Big, tragic eyes. I don't regret anything. I must pay the price, but I shan't whine ... It's snowing in the street. Won't you cry, confound you? That woman was a born martyr, you know; a victim by vocation.

INEZ (almost tenderly). Why did you hurt her like that?

GARCIN. It was so easy. A word was enough to make her flinch. Like a sensitive-plant. But never, never a reproach. I'm fond of teasing. I watched and waited. But no, not a tear, not a protest. I'd picked her up out of the gutter, you understand ... Now she's stroking the coat. Her eyes are shut and she's feeling with her fingers for the bullet-holes. What are you after? What do you expect? I tell you I regret nothing. The truth is, she admired me too much. Does that mean anything to you?

INEZ. No. Nobody admired me.

GARCIN. So much the better. So much the better for you. I suppose all this strikes you as very vague. Well, here's something you can get your teeth into. I brought a half-caste girl to stay in our house. My wife slept upstairs; she must have heard—everything. She was an early riser and, as I and the girl stayed in bed late, she served us our morning coffee.

INEZ. You brute!

GARCIN. Yes, a brute, if you like. But a well-beloved brute. (A far-away look comes to his eyes) No, it's nothing. Only Gomez, and he's not talking about me ...

What were you saying? Yes, a brute. Certainly. Else why should I be here? (To Inez) Your turn.

INEZ. Well, I was what some people down there called "a damned bitch." Damned already. So it's no surprise, being here.

GARCIN. Is that all you have to say?

INEZ. No. There was that affair with Florence. A dead men's tale. With three corpses to it. He to start with; then she and I. So there's no one left, I've nothing to worry about; it was a clean sweep. Only that room. I see it now and then. Empty, with the doors locked ... No, they've just unlocked them. "To Let." It's to let; there's a notice on the door. That's—too ridiculous.

GARCIN. Three. Three deaths, you said?

INEZ. Three.

GARCIN. One man and two women?

INEZ. Yes.

GARCIN. Well, well. (A pause) Did he kill himself?

INEZ. He? No, he hadn't the guts for that. Still, he'd every reason; we led him a dog's life. As a matter of fact, he was run over by a tram. A silly sort of end ... I was living with them; he was my cousin.

GARCIN. Was Florence fair?

INEZ. Fair? (Glances at Estelle) You know, I don't regret a thing; still, I'm not so very keen on telling you the story.

GARCIN. That's all right ... So you got sick of him?

INEZ. Quite gradually. All sorts of little things got on my nerves. For instance, he made a noise when he was drinking—a sort of gurgle. Trifles like that. He was rather pathetic really. Vulnerable. Why are you smiling?

GARCIN. Because I, anyhow, am not vulnerable.

INEZ. Don't be too sure ... I crept inside her skin, she saw the world through my eyes. When she left him, I had her on my hands. We shared a bed-sitting-room at the other end of the town.

GARCIN. And then?

INEZ. Then that tram did its job. I used to remind her every day: "Yes, my pet, we killed him between us." (A pause) I'm rather cruel, really.

GARCIN. So am I.

INEZ. No, you're not cruel. It's something else.

GARCIN. What?

INEZ. I'll tell you later. When I say I'm cruel, I mean I can't get on without making people suffer. Like a live coal. A live coal in other's hearts. When I'm alone I flicker out. For six months I flamed away in her heart, till there was nothing but a cinder. One night she got up and turned on the gas while I was asleep. Then she crept back into bed. So now you know.

GARCIN. Well! Well!

INEZ. Yes? What's in your mind?

GARCIN. Nothing. Only that it's not a pretty story.

INEZ. Obviously. But what matter?

GARCIN. As you say, what matter? (To Estelle) Your turn. What have you done?

ESTELLE. As I told you, I haven't a notion. I rack my brain, but it's no use.

GARCIN. Right. Then we'll give you a hand. That fellow with the smashed face, who was he?

ESTELLE. Who—who do you mean?

INEZ. You know quite well. The man you were so scared of seeing when you came in.

ESTELLE. Oh, him! A friend of mine.

GARCIN. Why were you afraid of him?

ESTELLE. That's my business, Mr. Garcin.

INEZ. Did he shoot himself on your account?

ESTELLE. Of course not. How absurd you are!

GARCIN. Then why should you have been so scared? He blew his brains out, didn't he? That's how his face got smashed.

ESTELLE. Don't! Please don't go on.

GARCIN. Because of you. Because of you.

INEZ. He shot himself because of you.

ESTELLE. Leave me alone! It's—it's not fair, bullying me like that. I want to go! I want to go!

(She runs to the door and shakes it.)

GARCIN. Go if you can. Personally, I ask for nothing better. Unfortunately, the door's locked.

(Estelle presses the bell-push, but the bell does not ring. Inez and Garcin laugh. Estelle swings round on them, her back to the door.)

ESTELLE (in a muffled voice). You're hateful, both of you.

INEZ. Hateful? Yes, that's the word. Now get on with it. That fellow who killed himself on your account—you were his mistress, eh?

GARCIN. Of course she was. And he wanted to have her to himself alone. That's so, isn't it?

INEZ. He danced the tango like a professional, but he was poor as a church mouse—that's right, isn't it? (A short silence)

GARCIN. Was he poor or not? Give a straight answer.

ESTELLE. Yes, he was poor.

GARCIN. And then you had your reputation to keep up. One day he came and implored you to run away with him, and you laughed in his face.

INEZ. That's it. You laughed at him. And so he killed himself.

ESTELLE. Did you use to look at Florence in that way?

INEZ. Yes.

(A short pause, then Estelle bursts out laughing.)

ESTELLE. You've got it all wrong, you two. (She stiffens her shoulders, still leaning against the door, and faces them. Her voice grows shrill, truculent) He wanted me to have a baby. So there!

GARCIN. And you didn't want one?

ESTELLE. I certainly didn't. But the baby came, worse luck. I went to Switzerland for five months. No one knew anything. It was a girl. Roger was with me when she was born. It pleased him no end, having a daughter. It didn't please me!

GARCIN. And then?

ESTELLE. There was a balcony over looking the lake. I brought a big stone. He could see what I was up to and he kept on shouting: "Estelle, for God's sake don't!" I hated him then. He saw it all. He was leaning over the balcony and he saw the rings spreading on the water—

GARCIN. Yes? And then?

ESTELLE. That's all. I came back to Paris—and he did as he wished.

GARCIN. You mean he blew his brains out?

ESTELLE. It was absurd of him, really; my husband never suspected anything. *(A pause)* Oh, how I loathe you! *(She sobs tearlessly)*

GARCIN. Nothing doing. Tears don't flow in this place.

ESTELLE. I'm a coward. A coward! *(Pause)* If you knew how I hate you!

INEZ *(taking her in her arms)*. Poor child! *(To Garcin)* So the hearing's over. But there's no need to look like a hanging judge.

GARCIN. A hanging judge? *(He glances around him)* I'd give a lot to be able to see myself in a glass. *(Pause)* How hot it is! *(Unthinkingly he takes off his coat)* Oh, sorry! *(He starts putting it on again)*

ESTELLE. Don't bother. You can stay in your shirtsleeves. As things are—

GARCIN. Just so. *(He drops his coat on the sofa)* You mustn't be angry with me, Estelle.

ESTELLE. I'm not angry with you.

INEZ. And what about me? Are you angry with me?

ESTELLE. Yes.

(A short silence.)

INEZ. Well, Mr. Garcin, now you have us in the nude all right. Do you understand things any better for that?

GARCIN. I wonder. Yes, perhaps a trifle better. *(Timidly)* And now suppose we start trying to help each other.

INEZ. I don't need help.

GARCIN. Inez, they've laid their snare damned cunningly—like a cobweb. If you make any movement, if you raise your hand to fan yourself, Estelle and I feel a little tug. Alone, none of us can save himself or herself; we're linked together inextricably. So you can take your choice. *(A pause)* Hullo? What's happening?

INEZ. They've let it. The windows are wide open, a man is sitting on my bed. My bed, if you please! They've let it, let it! Step in, step in, make yourself at home, you brute! Ah, there's a woman, too. She's going up to him, putting her hands on his shoulders . . . Damn it, why don't they turn the lights on? It's getting dark. Now he's going to kiss her. But that's my room, *my* room! Pitch-dark

now. I can't see anything, but I hear them whispering, whispering. Is he going to make love to her on *my* bed? What's that she said? That it's noon and the sun is shining? I must be going blind. *(A pause)* Blacked out. I can't see or hear a thing. So I'm done with the earth, it seems. No more alibis for me! *(She shudders)* I feel so empty, desiccated—really dead at last. All of me's here, in this room. *(A pause)* What were you saying? Something about helping me, wasn't it?

GARCIN. Yes.

INEZ. Helping me to do what?

GARCIN. To defeat their devilish tricks.

INEZ. And what do you expect me to do, in return?

GARCIN. To help *me*. It only needs a little effort, Inez; just a spark of human feeling.

INEZ. Human feeling. That's beyond my range. I'm rotten to the core.

GARCIN. And how about me? *(A pause)* All the same, suppose we try?

INEZ. It's no use. I'm all dried up. I can't give and I can't receive. How could *I* help you? A dead twig, ready for the burning. *(She falls silent, gazing at Estelle, who has buried her head in her hands)* Florence was fair, a natural blonde.

GARCIN. Do you realize that this young woman's fated to be your torturer?

INEZ. Perhaps I've guessed it.

GARCIN. It's through her they'll get you. I, of course, I'm different—aloof. I take no notice of her. Suppose you had a try—

INEZ. Yes?

GARCIN. It's a trap. They're watching you, to see if you'll fall into it.

INEZ. I know. And you're another trap. Do you think they haven't foreknown every word you say? And of course there's a whole nest of pitfalls that we can't see. Everything here's a booby-trap. But what do I care? I'm a pitfall, too. For her, obviously. And perhaps I'll catch her.

GARCIN. You won't catch anything. We're chasing after each other, round and round in a vicious circle, like the horses on a roundabout. That's part of their plan, of course . . . Drop it, Inez. Open your hands and let go of everything.

Or else you'll bring disaster on all three of us.

INEZ. Do I look the sort of person who lets go? I know what's coming to me. I'm going to burn, and it's to last forever. Yes, I *know* everything. But do you think I'll let go? I'll catch her, she'll see you through my eyes, as Florence saw that other man. What's the good of trying to enlist my sympathy? I assure you I know everything, and I can't feel sorry even for myself. A trap! Don't I know it, and that I'm in a trap myself, up to the neck, and there's nothing to be done about it? And if it suits their book, so much the better!

GARCIN *(gripping her shoulders).* Well, *I,* anyhow, can feel sorry for you, too. Look at me, we're naked, naked right through, and I can see into your heart. That's one link between us. Do you think I'd want to hurt you? I don't regret anything, I'm dried up, too. But for you I can still feel pity.

INEZ *(who has let him keep his hands on her shoulders until now, shakes herself loose).* Don't. I hate being pawed about. And keep your pity for yourself. Don't forget, Garcin, that there are traps for you, too, in this room. All nicely set for you. You'd do better to watch your own interests. *(A pause)* But, if you will leave us in peace, this child and me, I'll see I don't do you any harm.

GARCIN *(gazes at her for a moment, then shrugs his shoulders).* Very well.

ESTELLE *(rasing her head).* Please, Garcin.

GARCIN. What do you want of me?

ESTELLE *(rises and goes up to him).* You can help *me,* anyhow.

GARCIN. If you want help, apply to her. *(Inez has come up and is standing behind Estelle, but without touching her. During the dialogue that follows she speaks almost in her ear. But Estelle keeps her eyes on Garcin, who observes her without speaking, and she addresses her answers to him, as if it were he who is questioning her.)*

ESTELLE. I implore you, Garcin—you gave me your promise, didn't you? Help me quick. I don't want to be left alone. Olga's taken him to a cabaret.

INEZ. Taken whom?

ESTELLE. Peter . . . Oh, now they're dancing together.

INEZ. Who's Peter?

ESTELLE. Such a silly boy. He called me his glancing stream—just fancy! He was terribly in love with me . . . She's persuaded him to come out with her tonight.

INEZ. Do you love him?

ESTELLE. They're sitting down now. She's puffing like a grampus. What a fool the girl is to insist on dancing! But I dare say she does it to reduce . . . No, of course I don't love him; he's only eighteen, and I'm not a baby-snatcher.

INEZ. Then why bother about them? What difference can it make?

ESTELLE. He belonged to me.

INEZ. Nothing on earth belongs to you any more.

ESTELLE. I tell you he was mine. All mine.

INEZ. Yes, he *was* yours—once. But now— Try to make him hear, try to touch him. Olga can touch him, talk to him as much as she likes. That's so, isn't it? She can squeeze his hands, rub herself against him—

ESTELLE. Yes, look! She's pressing her great fat chest against him, puffing and blowing in his face. But, my poor little lamb, can't you see how ridiculous she is? Why don't you laugh at her? Oh, once I'd have only had to glance at them and she'd have slunk away. Is there really nothing, nothing left of me?

INEZ. Nothing whatever. Nothing of you's left on earth—not even a shadow. All you own is here. Would you like that paper-knife? Or that ornament on the mantelpiece? That blue sofa's yours. And I, my dear, am yours forever.

ESTELLE. You mine! That's good! Well, which of you two would dare to call me his glancing stream, his crystal girl? You know too much about me, you know I'm rotten through and through . . . Peter dear, think of me, fix your thoughts on me, and save me. All the time you're thinking "my glancing stream, my crystal girl," I'm only half here, I'm only half wicked, and half of me is down there with you, clean and bright and crystal-clear as running water. . . Oh, just look at her face, all scarlet, like a tomato! No, it's absurd, we've laughed at her together, you and I, often and often . . . What's that tune?—I always loved it. Yes, the *St. Louis Blues* . . . All right, dance away, dance away. Garcin, I wish you could see her, you'd die of laughing. Only—she'll never know I *see* her. Yes, I see you, Olga, with your hair all anyhow, and you do look a dope, my dear. Oh, now you're treading on his toes. It's a scream! Hurry up! Quicker! Quicker! He's dragging her along, bundling her round and round—it's too ghastly! He always said I was so light, he loved to dance with me. *(She is dancing as she speaks)* I tell you, Olga, I can see you. No, she doesn't care, she's dancing through my gaze. What's that? What's that you said? "Our poor dear Estelle"? Oh, don't be such a humbug! You didn't even shed a tear at the funeral . . . And she has the nerve to talk to him about her poor dear friend Estelle! How dare she discuss me with Peter? Now then, keep time. She never could dance and talk at once. Oh, what's that? No, no. Don't tell him. Please, please don't tell him. You can keep him, do what you like with him, but please don't tell him about—that! *(She has stopped dancing)* All right, you can have him now. Isn't it *foul*, Garcin? She's told him everything, about Roger, my trip to Switzerland, the baby. "Poor Estelle wasn't exactly—" No, I wasn't exactly—True enough. He's looking grave, shaking his head, but he doesn't seem so very much surprised, not what one would expect. Keep him, then—I won't haggle with you over his long eyelashes, his pretty girlish face. They're yours for the asking. His glancing stream, his crystal. Well, the crystal's shattered into bits. "Poor Estelle!" Dance, dance, dance. On with it. But do keep time. One, two. One, two. How I'd love to go down to earth for just a moment, and dance with him again. *(She dances again for some moments)* The music's growing fainter. They've turned down the lights, as they do for a tango. Why are they playing so softly? Louder, please. I can't hear. It's so far away, so far away. I—I can't hear a sound. *(She stops dancing)* All

over. It's the end. The earth has left me. *(To Garcin)* Don't turn from me—please. Take me in your arms.

(Behind Estelle's back, Inez signs to Garcin to move away.)

INEZ *(commandingly)*. Now then, Garcin!

(Garcin moves back a step, and, glancing at Estelle, points to Inez.)

GARCIN. It's to her you should say that.

ESTELLE *(clinging to him)*. Don't turn away. You're a man, aren't you, and surely I'm not such a fright as all that! Everyone says I've lovely hair and, after all, a man killed himself on my account. You have to look at something, and there's nothing here to see except the sofas and that awful ornament and the table. Surely I'm better to look at than a lot of stupid furniture. Listen! I've dropped out of their hearts like a little sparrow fallen from its nest. So gather me up, dear, fold me to your heart—and you'll see how nice I can be.

GARCIN *(freeing himself from her, after a short struggle)*. I tell you it's to that lady you should speak.

ESTELLE. To her? But she doesn't count, she's a woman.

INEZ. Oh, I don't count? Is that what you think? But, my poor little fallen nestling, you've been sheltering in my heart for ages, though you didn't realize it. Don't be afraid; I'll keep looking at you for ever and ever, without a flutter of my eyelids, and you'll live in my gaze like a mote in a sunbeam.

ESTELLE. A sunbeam indeed! Don't talk such rubbish! You've tried that trick already, and you should know it doesn't work.

INEZ. Estelle! My glancing stream! My crystal!

ESTELLE. *Your* crystal? It's grotesque. Do you think you can fool me with that sort of talk? Everyone knows by now what I did to my baby. The crystal's shattered, but I don't care. I'm just a hollow dummy, all that's left of me is the outside—but it's not for you.

INEZ. Come to me, Estelle. You shall be whatever you like: a glancing stream, a muddy stream. And deep down in my eyes you'll see yourself just as you want to be.

ESTELLE. Oh, leave me in peace. You haven't any eyes. Oh, damn it, isn't there anything I can do to get rid of you? I've an idea. *(She spits in Inez's face)* There!

INEZ. Garcin, you shall pay for this. *(A pause. Garcin shrugs his shoulders and goes to Estelle.)*

GARCIN. So it's a man you need?

ESTELLE. Not *any* man. You.

GARCIN. No humbug now. Any man would do your business. As I happen to be here, you want me. Right! *(He grips her shoulders)* Mind, I'm not your sort at all, really; I'm not a young nincompoop and I don't dance the tango.

ESTELLE. I'll take you as you are. And perhaps I shall change you.

GARCIN. I doubt it. I shan't pay much attention; I've other things to think about.

ESTELLE. What things?

GARCIN. They wouldn't interest you.

ESTELLE. I'll sit on your sofa and wait for you to take some notice of me. I promise not to bother you at all.

INEZ *(with a shrill laugh)*. That's right, fawn on him, like the silly bitch you are. Grovel and cringe! And he hasn't even good looks to commend him!

ESTELLE *(to Garcin)*. Don't listen to her. She has no eyes, no ears. She's—nothing.

GARCIN. I'll give you what I can. It doesn't amount to much. I shan't love you; I know you too well.

ESTELLE. Do you want me, anyhow?

GARCIN. Yes.

ESTELLE. I ask no more.

GARCIN. In that case—*(He bends over her)*

INEZ. Estelle! Garcin! You must be going crazy. You're not alone. I'm here too.

GARCIN. Of course—but what does it matter?

INEZ. Under my eyes? You couldn't—couldn't do it.

ESTELLE. Why not? I often undressed with my maid looking on.

INEZ *(gripping Garcin's arm)*. Let her alone. Don't paw her with your dirty man's hands.

GARCIN *(thrusting her away roughly)*. Take care. I'm no gentleman, and I'd have no compunction about striking a woman.

INEZ. But you promised me; you promised. I'm only asking you to keep your word.

GARCIN. Why should I, considering you were the first to break our agreement? *(Inez turns her back on him and retreats to the far end of the room.)*

INEZ. Very well, have it your own way. I'm the weaker party, one against two. But don't forget I'm here, and watching. I shan't take my eyes off you, Garcin; when you're kissing her, you'll feel them boring into you. Yes, have it your own way, make love and get it over. We're in hell; my turn will come. *(During the following scene she watches them without speaking.)*

GARCIN *(coming back to Estelle and grasping her shoulders)*. Now then. Your lips. Give me your lips. *(A pause. He bends to kiss her, then abruptly straightens up)*

ESTELLE *(indignantly)*. Really! *(A pause)* Didn't I tell you not to pay any attention to her?

GARCIN. You've got it wrong. *(Short silence)* It's Gomez; he's back in the press-room. They've shut the windows; it must be winter down there. Six months since I— Well, I warned you I'd be absent-minded sometimes, didn't I? They're shivering, they've kept their coats on. Funny they should feel the cold like that, when I'm feeling so hot. Ah, this time he's talking about me.

ESTELLE. Is it going to last long? *(Short silence)* You might at least tell me what he's saying.

GARCIN. Nothing. Nothing worth repeating. He's a swine, that's all. *(He listens attentively)* A goddamned bloody swine. *(He turns to Estelle)* Let's come back to—to ourselves. Are you going to love me?

ESTELLE *(smiling)*. I wonder now!

GARCIN. Will you trust me?

ESTELLE. What a quaint thing to ask! Considering you'll be under my eyes all the time, and I don't think I've much to fear from Inez, so far as you're concerned.

GARCIN. Obviously. *(A pause. He takes*

his hands off Estelle's shoulders) I was thinking of another kind of trust. *(Listens)* Talk away, talk away, you swine. I'm not there to defend myself. *(To Estelle)* Estelle, you *must* give me your trust.

ESTELLE. Oh, what a nuisance you are! I'm giving you my mouth, my arms, my whole body—and everything could be so simple . . . My trust! I haven't any to give, I'm afraid, and you're making me terribly embarrassed. You must have something pretty ghastly on your conscience to make such a fuss about my trusting you.

GARCIN. They shot me.

ESTELLE. I know. Because you refused to fight. Well, why shouldn't you?

GARCIN. I—I didn't exactly refuse. *(In a far-away voice)* I must say he talks well, he makes out a good case against me, but he never says what I should have done instead. Should I have gone to the general and said: "General, I decline to fight"? A mug's game; they'd have promptly locked me up. But I wanted to show my colors, my true colors, do you understand? I wasn't going to be silenced. *(To Estelle)* So I—I took the train . . . They caught me at the frontier.

ESTELLE. Where were you trying to go?

GARCIN. To Mexico. I meant to launch a pacifist newspaper down there. *(A short silence)* Well, why don't you speak?

ESTELLE. What could I say? You acted quite rightly, as you didn't want to fight. *(Garcin makes a fretful gesture)* But, darling, how on earth can I guess what you want me to answer?

INEZ. Can't you guess? Well, *I* can. He wants you to tell him that he bolted like a lion. For "bolt" he did, and that's what's biting him.

GARCIN. "Bolted," "went away"— we won't quarrel over words.

ESTELLE. But you *had* to run away. If you'd stayed they'd have sent you to jail, wouldn't they?

GARCIN. Of course. *(A pause)* Well, Estelle, am I a coward?

ESTELLE. How can I say? Don't be so unreasonable, darling. I can't put myself

in your skin. You must decide that for yourself.

GARCIN *(wearily)*. I can't decide.

ESTELLE. Anyhow, you must remember. You must have had reasons for acting as you did.

GARCIN. I had.

ESTELLE. Well?

GARCIN. But were they the real reasons?

ESTELLE. You've a twisted mind, that's your trouble. Plaguing yourself over such trifles!

GARCIN. I'd thought it all out, and I wanted to make a stand. But was that my real motive?

INEZ. Exactly. That's the question. Was that your real motive? No doubt you argued it out with yourself, you weighed the pros and cons, you found good reasons for what you did. But fear and hatred and all the dirty little instincts one keeps dark —they're motives too. So carry on, Mr. Garcin, and try to be honest with yourself —for once.

GARCIN. Do I need you to tell me that? Day and night I paced my cell, from the window to the door, from the door to the window. I pried into my heart, I sleuthed myself like a detective. By the end of it I felt as if I'd given my whole life to introspection. But always I harked back to the one thing certain—that I had acted as I did, I'd taken that train to the frontier. But why? Why? Finally I thought: My death will settle it. If I face death courageously, I'll prove I am no coward.

INEZ. And how did you face death?

GARCIN. Miserably. Rottenly. *(Inez laughs)* Oh, it was only a physical lapse— that might happen to anyone; I'm not ashamed of it. Only everything's been left in suspense, forever. *(To Estelle)* Come here, Estelle. Look at me. I want to feel someone looking at me while they're talking about me on earth . . . I like green eyes.

INEZ. Green eyes! Just hark to him! And you, Estelle, do you like cowards?

ESTELLE. If you knew how little I care! Coward or hero, it's all one—provided he kisses well.

GARCIN. There they are, slumped in

their chairs, sucking at their cigars. Bored they look. Half-asleep. They're thinking: "Garcin's a coward." But only vaguely, dreamily. One's got to think of something. "That chap Garcin was a coward." That's what they've decided, those dear friends of mine. In six months' time they'll be saying: "Cowardly as that skunk Garcin." You're lucky, you two; no one on earth is giving you another thought. But I—I'm long in dying.

INEZ. What about your wife, Garcin?

GARCIN. Oh, didn't I tell you? She's dead.

INEZ. Dead?

GARCIN. Yes, she died just now. About two months ago.

INEZ. Of grief?

GARCIN. What else should she die of? So all is for the best, you see; the war's over, my wife's dead, and I've carved out my place in history.

(He gives a choking sob and passes his hand over his face. Estelle catches his arm.)

ESTELLE. My poor darling! Look at me. Please look. Touch me. Touch me. (She takes his hand and puts it on her neck) There! Keep your hand there. (Garcin makes a fretful movement) No, don't move. Why trouble about what those men are thinking? They'll die off one by one. Forget them. There's only me, now.

GARCIN. But they won't forget me, not they! They'll die, but others will come after them to carry on the legend. I've left my fate in their hands.

ESTELLE. You think too much, that's your trouble.

GARCIN. What else is there to do now? I was a man of action once . . . Oh, if only I could be with them again, for just one day—I'd fling their lie in their teeth. But I'm locked out; they're passing judgment on my life without troubling about me, and they're right, because I'm dead. Dead and done with. (Laughs) A back number.

(A short pause.)

ESTELLE (gently). Garcin.

GARCIN. Still there? Now listen! I want you to do me a service. No, don't shrink away. I know it must seem strange to you, having someone asking you for help; you're not used to that. But if you'll make the effort, if you'll only will it hard enough, I dare say we can really love each other. Look at it this way. A thousand of them are proclaiming I'm a coward; but what do numbers matter? If there's someone, just one person, to say quite positively I did not run away, that I'm not the sort who runs away, that I'm brave and decent and the rest of it—well, that one person's faith would save me. Will you have that faith in me? Then I shall love you and cherish you for ever. Estelle—will you?

ESTELLE (laughing). Oh, you dear silly man, do you think I could love a coward?

GARCIN. But just now you said—

ESTELLE. I was only teasing you. I like men, my dear, who're real men, with tough skin and strong hands. You haven't a coward's chin, or a coward's mouth, or a coward's voice, or a coward's hair. And it's for your mouth, your hair, your voice, I love you.

GARCIN. Do you mean this? Really mean it?

ESTELLE. Shall I swear it?

GARCIN. Then I snap my fingers at them all, those below and those in here. Estelle, we shall climb out of hell. (Inez gives a shrill laugh. He breaks off and stares at her) What's that?

INEZ (still laughing). But she doesn't mean a word of what she says. How can you be such a simpleton? "Estelle, am I a coward?" As if she cared a damn either way.

ESTELLE. Inez, how dare you? (To Garcin) Don't listen to her. If you want me to have faith in you, you must begin by trusting me.

INEZ. That's right! That's right! Trust away! She wants a man—that far you can trust her—she wants a man's arm round her waist, a man's smell, a man's eyes glowing with desire. And that's all she wants. She'd assure you you were God Almighty if she thought it would give you pleasure.

GARCIN. Estelle, is this true? Answer me. Is it true?

ESTELLE. What do you expect me to say? Don't you realize how maddening it is to have to answer questions one can't make head or tail of? *(She stamps her foot)* You do make things difficult . . . Anyhow, I'd love you just the same, even if you were a coward. Isn't that enough?

(A short pause.)

GARCIN *(to the two women).* You disgust me, both of you. *(He goes towards the door)*

ESTELLE. What are you up to?

GARCIN. I'm going.

INEZ *(quickly).* You won't get far. The door is locked.

GARCIN. I'll *make* them open it. *(He presses the bellpush. The bell does not ring)*

ESTELLE. Please! Please!

INEZ *(to Estelle).* Don't worry, my pet. The bell doesn't work.

GARCIN. I tell you they shall open. *(Drums on the door)* I can't endure it any longer, I'm through with you both. *(Estelle runs to him; he pushes her away)* Go away. You're even fouler than she. I won't let myself get bogged in your eyes. You're soft and slimy. Ugh! *(Bangs on the door again)* Like an octopus. Like a quagmire.

ESTELLE. I beg you, oh, I beg you not to leave me. I'll promise not to speak again, I won't trouble you in any way—but don't go. I daren't be left alone with Inez, now she's shown her claws.

GARCIN. Look after yourself. I never asked you to come here.

ESTELLE. Oh, how mean you are! Yes, it's quite true you're a coward.

INEZ *(going up to Estelle).* Well, my little sparrow fallen from the nest, I hope you're satisfied now. You spat in my face —playing up to him, of course—and we had a tiff on his account. But he's going, and a good riddance it will be. We two women will have the place to ourselves.

ESTELLE. You won't gain anything. If that door opens, I'm going, too.

INEZ. Where?

ESTELLE. I don't care where. As far from you as I can.

(Garcin has been drumming on the door while they talk.)

GARCIN. Open the door! Open, blast you! I'll endure anything, your red-hot tongs and molten lead, your racks and prongs and garrotes—all your fiendish gadgets, everything that burns and flays and tears—I'll put up with any torture you impose. Anything, anything would be better than this agony of mind, this creeping pain that gnaws and fumbles and caresses one and never hurts quite enough. *(He grips the door-knob and rattles it)* Now will you open? *(The door flies open with a jerk, nearly falling on the floor)* Ah! *(A long silence)*

INEZ. Well, Garcin? You're free to go.

GARCIN *(meditatively).* Now I wonder why that door opened.

INEZ. What are you waiting for? Hurry up and go.

GARCIN. I shall not go.

INEZ. And you, Estelle? *(Estelle does not move. Inez bursts out laughing)* So what? Which shall it be? Which of the three of us will leave? The barrier's down, why are we waiting? . . . But what a situation! It's a scream! We're—inseparables!

(Estelle springs at her from behind.)

ESTELLE. Inseparables? Garcin, come and lend a hand. Quickly. We'll push her out and slam the door on her. That'll teach her a lesson.

INEZ *(struggling with Estelle).* Estelle! I beg you, let me stay. I won't go, I won't go! Not into the passage.

GARCIN. Let go of her.

ESTELLE. You're crazy. She hates you.

GARCIN. It's because of her I'm staying here.

(Estelle releases Inez and stares dumb-foundedly at Garcin.)

INEZ. Because of me? *(Pause)* All right, shut the door. It's ten times hotter here since it opened. *(Garcin goes to the door and shuts it)* Because of me, you said?

GARCIN. Yes. *You,* anyhow, know what it means to be a coward.

INEZ. Yes, I know.

GARCIN. And you know what wickedness is, and shame, and fear. There were days when you peered into yourself, into the secret places of your heart, and what you saw there made you faint with horror. And then, next day, you didn't know what to make of it, you couldn't interpret the horror you had glimpsed the day before. Yes, you know what evil *costs.* And when you say I'm a coward, you know from experience what that means. Is that so?

INEZ. Yes.

GARCIN. So it's you whom I have to

convince; you are of my kind. Did you suppose I meant to go? No, I couldn't leave you here, gloating over my defeat, with all those thoughts about me running in your head.

INEZ. Do you really wish to convince me?

GARCIN. That's the one and only thing I wish for now. I can't hear them any longer, you know. Probably that means they're through with me. For good and all. The curtain's down, nothing of me is left on earth—not even the name of coward. So, Inez, we're alone. Only you two remain to give a thought to me. She —she doesn't count. It's you who matter; you who hate me. If you'll have faith in me I'm saved.

INEZ. It won't be easy. Have a look at me. I'm a hard-headed woman.

GARCIN. I'll give you all the time that's needed.

INEZ. Yes, we've lots of time in hand. *All* time.

GARCIN *(putting his hands on her shoulders)*. Listen! Each man has an aim in life, a leading motive; that's so, isn't it? Well, I didn't give a damn for wealth, or for love. I aimed at being a real man. A tough, as they say. I staked everything on the same horse. . . . Can one possibly be a coward when one's deliberately courted danger at every turn? And can one judge a life by a single action?

INEZ. Why not? For thirty years you dreamt you were a hero, and condoned a thousand petty lapses—because a hero, of course, can do no wrong. An easy method, obviously. Then a day came when you were up against it, the red light of real danger—and you took the train to Mexico.

GARCIN. I "dreamt," you say. It was no dream. When I chose the hardest path, I made my choice deliberately. A man is what he wills himself to be.

INEZ. Prove it. Prove it was no dream. It's what one does, and nothing else, that shows the stuff one's made of.

GARCIN. I died too soon. I wasn't allowed time to—to do my deeds.

INEZ. One always dies too soon—or too late. And yet one's whole life is complete at that moment, with a line

drawn neatly under it, ready for the summing up. You are—your life, and nothing else.

GARCIN. What a poisonous woman you are! With an answer for everything.

INEZ. Now then! Don't lose heart. It shouldn't be so hard, convincing me. Pull yourself together, man, rake up some arguments. *(Garcin shrugs his shoulders)* Ah, wasn't I right when I said you were vulnerable? Now you're going to pay the price, and what a price! You're a coward, Garcin, because I wish it. I wish it—do you hear?—I wish it. And yet, just look at me, see how weak I am, a mere breath on the air, a gaze observing you, a formless thought that thinks you. *(He walks towards her, opening his hands)* Ah, they're open now, those big hands, those coarse, man's hands! But what do you hope to do? You can't throttle thoughts with hands. So you've no choice, you must convince me, and you're at my mercy.

ESTELLE. Garcin!

GARCIN. What?

ESTELLE. Revenge yourself.

GARCIN. How?

ESTELLE. Kiss me, darling—then you'll hear her squeal.

GARCIN. That's true, Inez. I'm at your mercy, but you're at mine as well.

(He bends over Estelle. Inez gives a little cry.)

INEZ. Oh, you coward, you weakling, running to women to console you!

ESTELLE. That's right, Inez. Squeal away.

INEZ. What a lovely pair you make! If you could see his big paw splayed out on your back, rucking up your skin and creasing the silk. Be careful, though! He's perspiring, his hand will leave a blue stain on your dress.

ESTELLE. Squeal away, Inez, squeal away! . . . Hug me tight, darling; tighter still—that'll finish her off, and a good thing too!

INEZ. Yes, Garcin, she's right. Carry on with it, press her to you till you feel your bodies melting into each other; a lump of warm, throbbing flesh . . . Love's a grand solace, isn't it, my friend? Deep and dark as sleep. But I'll see you don't sleep.

(Garcin makes a slight movement.)

ESTELLE. Don't listen to her. Press your lips to my mouth. Oh, I'm yours, yours, yours.

INEZ. Well, what are you waiting for? Do as you're told. What a lovely scene: coward Garcin holding baby-killer Estelle in his manly arms! Make your stakes, everyone. Will coward Garcin kiss the lady, or won't he dare? What's the betting? I'm watching you, everybody's watching, I'm a crowd all by myself. Do you hear the crowd? Do you hear them muttering, Garcin? Mumbling and muttering. "Coward! Coward! Coward! Coward!"—that's what they're saying. . . . It's no use trying to escape, I'll never let you go. What do you hope to get from her silly lips? Forgetfulness? But I shan't forget you, not I! "It's I you must convince." So come to me. I'm waiting. Come along, now . . . Look how obedient he is, like a well-trained dog who comes when his mistress calls. You can't hold him, and you never will.

GARCIN. Will night never come?

INEZ. Never.

GARCIN. You will always see me?

INEZ. Always.

(Garcin moves away from Estelle and takes some steps across the room. He goes to the bronze ornament.)

GARCIN. This bronze. *(Strokes it thoughtfully)* Yes, now's the moment; I'm looking at this thing on the mantelpiece, and I understand that I'm in hell. I tell you, everything's been thought out beforehand. They knew I'd stand at the fireplace stroking this thing of bronze. with all those eyes intent on me.

Devouring me. *(He swings round abruptly)* What? Only two of you? I thought there were more; many more. *(Laughs)* So this is hell. I'd never have believed it. You remember all we were told about the torture-chambers, the fire and brimstone, the "burning marl." Old wives' tales! There's no need for red-hot pokers. Hell is—other people!

ESTELLE. My darling! Please—

GARCIN *(thrusting her away)*. No, let me be. She is between us. I cannot love you when she's watching.

ESTELLE. Right! In that case, I'll stop her watching. *(She picks up the paper-knife from the table, rushes at Inez, and stabs her several times)*

INEZ *(struggling and laughing)*. But, you crazy creature, what do you think you're doing? You know quite well I'm dead.

ESTELLE. Dead?

(She drops the knife. A pause. Inez picks up the knife and jabs herself with it regretfully.)

INEZ. Dead! Dead! Dead! Knives, poison, ropes—all useless. It has happened *already*, do you understand? Once and for all. So here we are, forever. *(Laughs)*

ESTELLE *(with a peal of laughter)*. Forever. My God, how funny! Forever.

GARCIN *(looks at the two women, and joins in the laughter)*. For ever, and ever, and ever.

(They slump onto their respective sofas. A long silence. Their laughter dies away and they gaze at each other.)

GARCIN. Well, well, let's get on with it . . .

CURTAIN

FRANZ WERFEL's

Jacobowsky and the Colonel

In the adaptation by S. N. BEHRMAN*

First produced by the Theatre Guild, in association with Jack H. Skirball, on March 14, 1944, at the Martin Beck Theatre, New York, with the following cast:

A YOUNG GIRL	Louise Dowdney	MARIANNE	Annabella
SLEEPING SHOPKEEPER	Harrison Winter	BRIGADIER	E. G. Marshall
THE TRAGIC GENTLEMAN	Herbert Yost	STREET SINGER	Joseph Kallini
OLD LADY FROM ARRAS	Jane Marbury	CHILD	Jules Leni
MADAME BOUFFIER	Hilda Vaughn	FIRST LIEUTENANT	Frank Overton
SOLLY	Harry Davis	GESTAPO OFFICIAL	Harold Vermilyea
SZYCKI	Peter Kass	WILHELM	Donald Lee
SZABUNIEWICZ	J. Edward Bromberg	MAX	Bob Merritt
S. L. JACOBOWSKY	Oscar Karlweis	PAPA CLAIRON	Harry Davis
AIR RAID WARDEN	Philip Collier	THE DICE PLAYER	Philip Coolidge
COLONEL TADEUSZ BOLESLAV STJERBINSKY		SENATOR BRISSON	Donald Cameron
	Louis Calhern	THE COMMISSAIRE	William Sanders
COSETTE	Kitty Mattern	GENDARME	Burton Tripp
A CHAUFFEUR	Coby Ruskin	SERGEANT DE VILLE	Edward Kreisler
MONSIEUR SEROUILLE	Donald Cameron		

Staged by Elia Kazan

Designed by Stewart Chaney

SCENES

ACT ONE

SCENE I.   The laundry of the Hôtel Mon Repos et de la Rose, serving as an air-raid shelter. Paris. Midnight, June 13th.

SCENE II.   In front of the hotel. Early morning, June 14th.

ACT TWO

SCENE I.   A lonely road at Saint-Cyrille near Sables d'Ollonne. June 16th.

SCENE II.   An open spot in the woods, near the city of Bayonne.

ACT THREE

SCENE I.   The "Au Père Clairon" waterfront café at Saint-Jean-de-Luz. Early evening, June 18th.

SCENE II.   Mole at Hendaye, Saint-Jean-de-Luz. Night, June 18th.

The action takes place from June 13th to June 18th, 1940, between Paris and the Atlantic coast of France.

* The American play based on the original play in German by Franz Werfel

ACT ONE

SCENE ONE

SCENE: *The subterranean laundry of the Hôtel Mon Repos et de la Rose. It is evening on the 13th of June, 1940. There has been an air-raid alert and the laundry of Madame Bouffier's fourth-class establishment is doing service as an air-raid shelter.*

AT RISE: *Madame Bouffier's guests have been aroused from their beds by the alert and are trying to find comfort among the functional oddments of the laundry: the pressing and drying machines, the washtubs, etc. Two of the big tin washtubs have been put together and on them is sleeping a stertorous guest. On a long, narrow table along the wall an exhausted soldier and his pretty young wife are doing the same. On the left on a narrow bench by the wall, completely covered with a gray service blanket, is Szabuniewicz, the Polish orderly of Colonel Stjerbinsky, fighting off bad dreams.*

The Tragic Gentleman, a faded figure out of Toulouse-Lautrec, all in black with a black cape over his shoulders and wide-brimmed felt hat, is sitting near the washtubs sardonically fending off his despair with an attitude of detachment.

From the shaded lamps an unearthly blue light bathes the sleepers in violet.

At right a flight of stairs leads up to the sidewalk, and at left another flight leads up into the interior of the hotel. In the distance we hear the buzzing of airplanes.

When the curtain goes up, those guests who are not asleep are listening to a radio announcement by the Prime Minister, Paul Reynaud.

During this speech the Old Lady from Arras comes down the stairs. She is over sixty, pale with fright and sleeplessness, but knits and twitters with a kind of nervous vigor. While the Prime Minister is speaking, she crosses the stage and sits left on her special chair which has a cushion on it. She pounds the cushion into what she conceives to be a comfortable submission and sits down to her knitting and listens to the radio announcement.

———

VOICE OF PRIME MINISTER RAYNAUD. . . . The situation is serious but not desperate. On the Somme our valiant troops are defending every inch of their native soil with the greatest bravery. However, the superiority of the enemy in men and material is so great that we must be prepared to expect . . .

(The radio groans off.)

YOUNG GIRL *(who is lying beside her sleeping husband).* Why did the radio go off?

TRAGIC GENTLEMAN. They are forbidden to broadcast during an air raid.

OLD LADY. Who was the gentleman on the radio?

TRAGIC GENTLEMAN. That was our Prime Minister, Monsieur Paul Reynaud, addressing the nation from Bordeaux.

OLD LADY *(very anxious).* But what did he say?

TRAGIC GENTLEMAN. He said the situation was serious but not hopeless, or maybe he said it was hopeless but not serious.

OLD LADY. Dear God, dear God, Monsieur Paul Reynaud is very far to the Left. My daughter is a schoolteacher, and she told me. Monsieur Léon Blum wouldn't have anyone work more than forty hours a week. And this is what it brings us to. The last war was better—I understood the last war. This war I don't understand at all. Why, my daughter says, why should we die for Danzig? *(Very militant)* She's right! Why should we?

(Madame Bouffier, the mistress of the establishment, bustles in. She is wonderfully gotten up: she wears a magenta dress with gold-fringe trimmings; her hair is a marvelously tinted pyramid. She is strident, not unkind, and acts as if her little hotel were Versailles. She carries a lantern, small notebook and pencil. She is followed by Solly, of whom she is fond and to whom she is tender. He is a white-faced, hunchbacked Jewish boy of eighteen. He also carries a lantern.)

MADAME BOUFFIER. Solly dear, you haven't drawn those curtains. We don't want to have the same trouble with the Chief Warden we had yesterday.

SOLLY. Yes, Madame Bouffier, at once. *(Solly hangs a lantern on the back wall as Madame Bouffier hangs hers on another hook.)*

MADAME BOUFFIER. And I'll check the

guests! *(Checking off a list of her guests)*
Well, is my little family all here?

OLD LADY *(full of self-pity)*. I'm here,
Heaven help me.

MADAME BOUFFIER *(chiding)*. You
should be used to air raids by this time,
Madame Arle. In my hotel the morale is
high. I am captain of the ship here, and I
want things to be bright and cheerful.
That's our way of defying the Germans.
*(In her tour around the room she lifts blanket
from Szabuniewicz' head, takes a peek at him
and re-covers him)*

OLD LADY *(decidedly not cheerful)*. But
this is the fourth night I've sat till dawn
in this wretched laundry.

MADAME BOUFFIER *(with professional
pride)*. No hotel in Paris has a more
distinguished laundry. You're lucky to
be in it, safe and cozy. *(Continues to check
her list)*

OLD LADY. I just can't believe what's
happened. You know I'm from out of
town—from Arras. A few days ago my
daughter said, 'Mama, this war is nonsense—it won't last a week.' My
daughter's a schoolteacher—and she
knows!

MADAME BOUFFIER. Some school-
teachers never learn anything they don't
teach. *(Checking her book)* Madame
Gravot—404?

YOUNG GIRL. Here.

MADAME BOUFFIER. And Monsieur
Gravot—404?

YOUNG GIRL *(caressing her young husband
lightly)*. He's asleep.

MADAME BOUFFIER. There! That com-
pletes my little family—except for 409
and 204. 409 is that Polish colonel and
204 is Monsieur Jacobowsky. Now where
is Monsieur Jacobowsky? I've just looked
in his room and he's not there. The Polish
colonel is probably asleep, but where is
Monsieur Jacobowsky?

TRAGIC GENTLEMAN. Is that important?

MADAME BOUFFIER. It is indeed important. It's important to our morale in
here. I prefer optimism to pessimism. I
prefer a sunny day to a cloudy day. Monsieur Jacobowsky has a nature like a sunny
day.

TRAGIC GENTLEMAN *(with mock sadness)*.
Monsieur Jacobowsky is your newest

paying guest, Madame Bouffier. I am your
oldest and yet you appear to prefer Monsieur Jacobowsky to me.

MADAME BOUFFIER. When you describe
yourself as a paying guest, Monsieur, you
employ poetic license.
*(In the distance the noise of a bomb. A fussy
and nervous little man in a meticulously pressed
suit comes into the shelter. He wears a pince-
nez and carries a brief case and cane. He
comes from the street door. As he comes in the
sound of ack-ack guns is heard. Then the
sound of planes dies out.)*

SZYCKI. I must see Colonel Stjerbinsky.

MADAME BOUFFIER. That's 409. He's
probably still in his room.

SZYCKI. During an air raid!

MADAME BOUFFIER. He doesn't take air
raids seriously. He sleeps through them.

SZYCKI. It's vital I see him.

MADAME BOUFFIER *(indicating Szabuniewicz)*. There's another Pole, his orderly,
also asleep. Won't he do?
*(Szycki goes to Szabuniewicz, kneels down be-
side him, prodding him.)*

SZYCKI. Szabuniewicz. Wake up!

SZABUNIEWICZ *(captured in a dreadful
dream, sprawls, kneeling, to the floor)*. Take
cover . . .

SZYCKI. Szabuniewicz!!

SZABUNIEWICZ. Take cover!

SZYCKI. You've been having a bad
dream, my friend. This is Szycki.
*(Szabuniewicz rises. He is rotund, sly, with
innocent round eyes, deeply Machiavellian.)*

SZABUNIEWICZ *(rubs his eyes)*. Dream
I chased by Messerschmitts.

SZYCKI. Where is the Colonel?

SZABUNIEWICZ *(evasive)*. He not here?

SZYCKI. Obviously he is not here.

SZABUNIEWICZ. Den he is somewhere
else. *(Folding his blanket)*

SZYCKI. He is never where you expect
to find him. He's never on time. He is
irregular—that's what he is—irregular!

SZABUNIEWICZ *(sits)*. Colonel irregular—that's what he is.

SZYCKI. And I risked my life to bring
him some material.

SZABUNIEWICZ. Give me. I give him.

SZYCKI. Impossible! My orders are to
put these documents in the Colonel's
hands . . .

SZABUNIEWICZ. Colonel's hands don't come till Colonel come.

SZYCKI (*furious*). You joking when time is of the essence! The Germans will be here any minute.

(*This statement puts the people in the cellar in a panic.*)

OLD LADY (*rises*). My God, what did he say? The Germans are here?

SOLLY. What did he say?

YOUNG GIRL. He said they are coming! The Germans are coming!

MADAME BOUFFIER (*piously*). May God inspire our generals, Marshal Pétain and General Weygand!

OLD LADY (*her voice rises in hysteria*). The Germans are in Paris. They're in Paris. Dear God! Dear God!

MADAME BOUFFIER. Quiet, Madame Arle. I'll have no panic here. Solly, bring in the gramophone from the salon.

YOUNG GIRL. Wonderful. Let's have a Chevalier record.

TRAGIC GENTLEMAN. Chevalier! He'll give the Germans their idea of Paris. God, how I hate that gigolo!

MADAME BOUFFIER. And, Solly dear, go up to Monsieur Jacobowsky's room. Maybe he has come back.

OLD LADY. If the Germans are in Paris, why do we stay here? Why don't we do something?

(*Monsieur Jacobowsky comes in through the doorway from the street. He is in his late forties, not tall but somehow not too short—a 'small medium.' He wears a well-cut lounge suit, which he bought in happier days and which has managed to retain, though it is somewhat shiny, an air of elegance. He has a neat bow tie, a neat voice and everything about him has the crisp edge of tidiness. You feel that in the life he deserted everything in his ménage both business and personal was in good order; that his extra shoes had a good polish; his correspondence was caught up; his desk clear and that when people crossed the threshold of his house to come to dinner they felt a glow of benevolence and the quickened anticipation of a happy evening. His cheerfulness is an emanation from a harried past; he knows that the worst will probably happen, so that our only chance is to improve the immediate present. This he is constantly trying to do in very small relation of life. He likes people and he wants them, if it is at all possible, to like him.*)

JACOBOWSKY. The Germans are not in Paris, Madame, believe me.

SOLLY. Monsieur Jacobowsky!

MADAME BOUFFIER. Oh! Here he is.

JACOBOWSKY. I have just been in the Rue Royale and I assure you there isn't a German in sight. In fact, there isn't even a Parisian in sight. I was the only one in sight.

MADAME BOUFFIER. The Rue Royale! Monsieur Jacobowsky! In the middle of an alert. Suppose something had happened—a falling building or a bomb . . .

JACOBOWSKY. So there would be one Jacobowsky more or less. The world has endured so much—it could endure that too.

YOUNG GIRL. Monsieur is a very courageous man.

JACOBOWSKY. Not at all, Madame. Only—at one period of my life I was an accountant—and about danger—I am statistical.

TRAGIC GENTLEMAN. No doubt you think that the bomb that will hit *you* has yet to be cast. It has been cast, believe me. At Krupp or Skoda.

JACOBOWSKY. Oh, I have no doubt. Krupp and Skoda think of me constantly. They cast their little bomb and they think : 'This one we'll send to our nice Jacobowsky.' But even Krupp has to yield to a powerful law—the law of probability. Listen : What is the population of Paris? Four million lives? Correct? Now what chance has Krupp, with all his precision work, of hitting one four-millionth of Paris? Practically non-existent. I tell you I feel sorry for him. So, moving under the immunity of this adorable law—I have brought you back some *marrons glacés*—first to our distinguished hostess. (*Offers Madame Bouffier the box*)

MADAME BOUFFIER. That's my dear Monsieur Jacobowsky—always thinking of others. (*Takes one*)

MAN ON THE WASHTUB (*he is trying to sleep*). All this shouting—I can't sleep! (*Jumps up—reversing his position, puts his head where his feet were before—and tries to sleep again*)

JACOBOWSKY (*drops his voice and tiptoes*

around). Please, Madame, allow me . . .
(To the Young Girl) Madame . . .

YOUNG GIRL *(in a whisper).* Thank you, Monsieur.

OLD LADY *(whispering).* Thank you, Monsieur.

JACOBOWSKY *(offering them to Solly).* Solly, friend, you must eat some of these. They'll warm you up.

(The Washtub Man sticks his hand out, the palm open. Jacobowsky pops a marron *into his hand.)*

YOUNG GIRL. Monsieur certainly knows what's delicious.

JACOBOWSKY. People say it's not good to eat between meals, but I would rather have a snack than a dinner.

MADAME BOUFFIER *(looks fondly at Jacobowsky).* Why is it that the best husbands are always unmarried?

JACOBOWSKY *(offering* marrons *to the Tragic Gentleman).* Monsieur.

TRAGIC GENTLEMAN. I hate *marrons glacés . . .*

JACOBOWSKY. They are quite fresh.

TRAGIC GENTLEMAN *(determined to be unhappy).* Especially when they are fresh.

MADAME BOUFFIER *(with sudden decision)* Monsieur Jacobowsky, you ought to get married.

JACOBOWSKY *(edging away).* I think maybe not, Madame Bouffier.

MADAME BOUFFIER *(advances).* Why not? Give me one good reason why not?

JACOBOWSKY *(retreats).* You see, Madame Bouffier, I myself am a worshipper of beauty but in my own person I am not quite dazzling. The indifference of the ladies has given me leisure for reading and philosophy. I am a quite well-read man, Madame Bouffier.

MADAME BOUFFIER. You won't know what life is till you get married.

JACOBOWSKY *(delicately).* Perhaps there are other ways of finding out. *(He goes over to the Old Lady)*

OLD LADY. Sweets are such a consolation in a situation like this.

JACOBOWSKY. Quite right, Madame— quite right.

OLD LADY *(waves her banner).* My daughter's a schoolteacher!

JACOBOWSKY *(sits beside her on stool).*

A noble profession. Aristotle was a schoolteacher.

OLD LADY. In Arras I left everything behind, even my daughter—and fled— fled in France itself! Who could ever imagine a thing like that? While I was doing it, I didn't believe I was doing it and even now, right this minute, I don't believe it.

JACOBOWSKY. Oh, you'll get used to flight. I did. I've spent all my life in a futile effort to become a citizen of some country. You know, I speak seven languages fluently. Wrong, but fluently. In the technique of flight I may say I am a virtuoso. Migration one: Poland to Germany. My poor mother took her five children, her candlesticks, her pillows and fled to Berlin. There I grew up. I was successful in business. I was a citizen, a patriot. I belonged. My mistake! Migration two: Berlin to Vienna! The City of Waltzes. *(Hums one or two bars)* But I soon found out that underneath the waltzes there was a counter-melody. Less charming, more ruthless. First thing you know I was embarked on migration three. Prague. Now Prague is a lovely city. Have you ever seen the lovely baroque architecture in Prague?

TRAGIC GENTLEMAN. I hate baroque!

JACOBOWSKY. I understand that, too. A lot of people very qualified don't like baroque. Still I hated to leave Prague. This time without an overcoat. It was a new experience. Very interesting. Migration four: Paris! City of Light. Here I breathed the air of freedom. I understood exactly how Heine felt when *he* got here I said to myself: "You are Heine—without the genius." But now I have the feeling that there is ahead of me still another migration. Well, I'm ready. You see, one gets used to it.

OLD LADY *(rises, fluffing her chair pillow)* But after all, Monsieur, between us there isn't any comparison. My family has lived in Arras for five centuries.

JACOBOWSKY *(impressed).* Five centuries! You don't mean it!

OLD LADY *(pounding her pillow).* And now the Boches may push us into the sea. My daughter is right. She always says "France needs a Hitler too!"

JACOBOWSKY (rises quietly). Don't worry, Madame, your daughter will probably get her wish—mustache, forelock and all.

MADAME BOUFFIER. I won't have such talk!

OLD LADY. Did I say something wrong?

MADAME BOUFFIER. Your daughter must be insane.

OLD LADY. She's not insane. She's a schoolteacher!

MADAME BOUFFIER. I won't hear such talk.

OLD LADY. Lots of people think so. (Police whistle off stage. The air raid warden enters explosively from the street. He is in high dudgeon.)

WARDEN. Are you of your mind, Madame Bouffier?

MADAME BOUFFIER. Certainly not! I am in full possession of my faculties.

WARDEN. It's always your hotel I have trouble with. It's your hotel that is putting all Paris in danger. Fourth floor, street side—second and third windows from the right. Lit up like a Christmas tree!

MADAME BOUFFIER. Fourth floor, street side? That's 409. That's the Polish colonel.

WARDEN. I don't care if he's the King of Poland. He's breaking the regulations and it's your responsibility!

MADAME BOUFFIER. I've told him ten times. He doesn't listen. When I tell him, he laughs.

WARDEN. He laughs, does he? He laughs! I'll teach him. I'll teach him to laugh. This is Paris, not Warsaw!

MADAME BOUFFIER (egging him on). Why don't you go up and tell him?

WARDEN. I will—I'll more than tell him. I'll teach him a lesson. I'll wipe up the floor with him.

MADAME BOUFFIER. This will be worth watching. Come along, Solly dear. (She and Solly follow the Warden upstairs)

THE WASHTUB MAN. Oh, my God, why won't they let me sleep . . . ? (He abandons the washtubs, wrapped in his blankets, and goes to a corner where he curls up on the floor)

SZABUNIEWICZ. Poor Warden. I pity or him.

SZYCKI. It will serve your Colonel

right—no matter what the Warden does to him.

SZABUNIEWICZ. I wonder what Colonel do to Warden. Colonel not alone and when he's not alone he wants strictly to be alone.

SZYCKI. So that's what he's doing!

SZABUNIEWICZ. Colonel has always time for romance.

SZYCKI. At a time like this!

SZABUNIEWICZ. Any time good for romance.

SZYCKI. And I have to entrust this mission to a man like that! I'll give him a piece of my mind.

SZABUNIEWICZ. You too—good! Piece of your mind what Colonel needs. Give him big piece.

(During this scene Jacobowsky has been sitting quietly reading a worn book which he has taken out of his pocket. The Tragic Gentleman comes up behind him, curious.)

TRAGIC GENTLEMAN. May I ask, sir, what you are reading?

JACOBOWSKY. The Ethics of Spinoza.

TRAGIC GENTLEMAN (laughs). Ethics! What an anachronism! In the age of the Nazis—Ethics!

JACOBOWSKY. I don't agree. The Nazis are the anachronism—not the ethics! Listen: (He reads from the book) "For the wise man, insofar as he is wise, is scarcely ever disturbed in spirit: he is conscious of himself, of God and things as a certain eternal necessity; he never ceases to be and always enjoys satisfaction of mind."

TRAGIC GENTLEMAN. "Satisfaction of mind!" Now! In this moment—when the locusts cover the earth!

JACOBOWSKY. This was not written for special emergencies, sir. It is for all eternity.

TRAGIC GENTLEMAN. And will this help you when the Germans catch you?

JACOBOWSKY. I think so. Did you ever spin a top? The top spins but the center is at rest.

(At this moment the Warden comes back, crestfallen.)

SZABUNIEWICZ (gloating). Well, did you wipe up the floor with him?

WARDEN (evidently bewildered by his contact with the Colonel). That colonel's crazy. No use talking to a crazy man!

What kind of a type is that? He's peculiar. I couldn't reach an understanding with him. What's the matter with him? He's dangerous. *(He stalks out through street door)*

(Madame Bouffier comes in, talking to the Colonel who is behind her.)

MADAME BOUFFIER. And I tell you, Colonel, even if you did fight for France your behavior is unpardonable. *(She comes down the little steps. A moment later the Colonel appears. He is magnificent in his uniform, tall, commanding, saturnine, electric with vitality, euphoric with a sense of his own immemorial authority in the scheme of things. His forehead is bandaged smartly. He follows Madame Bouffier down the steps into the laundry)*

COLONEL *(addressing his orderly)*. Szabuniewicz, prepare our departure from Paris.

SZABUNIEWICZ. Yes, Colonel.

COLONEL *(whispers a boudoir confidence)*. And, oh, Szabuniewicz, I part from this lovely creature who follows me. Disengage me from her—but—very gracious . . .

(Cosette, a pretty Frenchwoman of about thirty, comes in. She is a quite sensible person and generally unsentimental—except for the Colonel!)

COSETTE. Tadeusz, my darling, if you leave Paris, I go too . . .

COLONEL *(turns to her, rolling smoothly through the routines of gallantry)*. This I tell you. The madrigal of our farewell they have interrupt, but a rose for you will grow always in my heart. Our roads part —perhaps forever—but the memory of your sweet face . . .

MADAME BOUFFIER *(cutting in)*. It's all very well for you to be romantic but on account of you the police will padlock my hotel tomorrow.

COLONEL. No. No. They will not. They will lack the time. Tomorrow the police of Paris will be running errands for the Huns!

MADAME BOUFFIER *(startled)*. Do you mean, Colonel, that the Germans will meet with no further resistance?

COLONEL. This I know. The regiment I command is force of three thousand men.

On the Somme we defend a bridge and for every gun is only eight cartridges . . .

TRAGIC GENTLEMAN. Where was the French Army?

MADAME BOUFFIER *(echoes)*. What happened to our Army?

COLONEL. The German Stukas make black the sky and not one French plane to help us. That I know . . . On my right and on my left I see the French divisions— fine soldiers—want to fight—have nothing with which to fight—so they are obliged to run—and of my own three thousand Polish boys only is left fifteen. I am their father, and I lose my children—three thousand of them. This I know. This I see. This I feel—here . . . *(Slaps his heart)* Rather I would be with them, with my children that are gone.

JACOBOWSKY. Then, Colonel, it is your considered opinion that France is lost!

COLONEL. No. She is not lost, Monsieur. She is gift to the German. Charming gift to the German.

(Szabuniewicz has poured a drink from a pocket flask, which he gives to the Colonel. The Colonel drinks it.)

TRAGIC GENTLEMAN *(valedictory)*. Paris, farewell!

(At the vision of this disaster the Old Lady sways.)

OLD LADY *(about to faint)*. I don't feel very well. I don't feel . . .

JACOBOWSKY *(goes to her, grips her arm to sustain her)*. Courage, Madame. My poor mother, wise woman that she was, always used to say that no matter what happens in life there are always two possibilities. It is true. For example, right now it is a dark moment and yet even now there are two possibilities. The Germans—either they'll come to Paris or they'll jump to England. If they don' come to Paris, that's good. But if they should come to Paris, again there are two possibilities. Either we succeed in escaping, or we don't succeed. If we succeed, that's good, but if we don' there are always two possibilities. The Germans, either they'll put us in a good concentration camp or in a bad concentration camp. If in a good concentration camp that's good, but if they put us in bad concentration camp, there are still two . . .

TRAGIC GENTLEMAN (*catching him up*). Two fine possibilities. Jump in the river or be shot by the Boches. Paris, farewell! (*In spite of Jacobowsky's optimism, the Old Lady From Arras promptly faints. Some of the guests form a closely packed knot around her, trying to revive her. Cosette, in her personal coil, pleads with the Colonel.*)

COSETTE. And for us, Tadeusz, is there no longer any possibility for us?

COLONEL. My lovely friend, this is what I am about to tell you when they interrupt—since last I saw you I have fallen in love . . .

COSETTE. I knew it—the moment I saw you—I knew there was something. I knew it.

COLONEL. And for you my feeling is so tender, so precious, that I cannot give you less than myself for you deserve all.

COSETTE (*fatalistic*). I knew it . . . (*Szabuniewicz sidles up to the Colonel.*)

SZABUNIEWICZ. Please, Colonel.

COLONEL (*shouts*). What, Szabuniewicz?

SZABUNIEWICZ (*indicates Szycki; he enjoys the prospect of battle*). This gentleman here waiting for you. He angry. He says you are irregular.

COLONEL (*lofty*). What interest that to me?

SZABUNIEWICZ. Has very strong mind. Vants to give you piece.

COLONEL. I hope he has for me something less mediocre.

SZYCKI. I have the documents for which you wait.

COLONEL (*holds out imperious hand*). Then give.

SZYCKI (*hands him yellow oblong envelope*). Here it is.

COLONEL. Everything here?

SZYCKI. Everything in code. Addresses our men in Warsaw, Lodz and Cracow. Every plan and communication is there. You must get it to our government in London.

COLONEL. I bring it to London.

SZYCKI. In the Café of Papa Clairon in Saint-Jean-de-Luz you meet the man with the gray gloves.

COLONEL (*nods*). Gray gloves.

SZYCKI. He will give you passage on corvette with other of our people to London.

COLONEL. I meet him when?

SZYCKI. On the 18th in the afternoon.

COLONEL (*refuses to clutter his mind with tedious detail*). Szabuniewicz, how many days away is the 18th?

SZABUNIEWICZ (*promptly*). Six days.

COLONEL. I deliver the papers.

SZYCKI. I must impress upon you, sir, time is of the essence.

COLONEL. I must impress upon you, my desk bureaucrat, that you speak to one of Pilsudski's colonels. I deliver these papers my own method, my own way, my own time.

SZYCKI. The corvette won't wait for you. If you're not there on the afternoon of the 18th it sails without you.

COLONEL. Then let him sail. If necessary, I swim to London.

SZYCKI. I have obeyed my orders. The papers are in your hands. (*He starts to go*)

COLONEL (*shouts after him*). You go back to your bureau, give orders to your office boy, not to Tadeusz Boleslav Stjerbinsky. Szabuniewicz, we leave Paris now.

SZABUNIEWICZ. How?

COLONEL. I take plane.

SZABUNIEWICZ. The last plane leaved yesterday night.

COLONEL. Then I go by car.

SZABUNIEWICZ. Vice-consul go off yesterday night. He take all four cars.

COLONEL. Why that pig need four cars?

SZABUNIEWICZ. I don't know.

COLONEL. If no car, get me horse.

SZABUNIEWICZ. Horse!

COLONEL. Why not? In one day good horse cover so many kilometers as one medium tank. Pack my trunk, everything you see. (*As Szabuniewicz turns to obey*) Wait! Szabuniewicz, child—my rosary! Don't forget my rosary! (*Szabuniewicz goes upstairs.*)

MADAME BOUFFIER (*calls after him*). And don't forget not to put the light on!

COLONEL. Not to worry, Madame. My man find everything in the dark. (*The Colonel finds himself unexpectedly confronted by Jacobowsky. He stares at him.*)

JACOBOWSKY. Colonel, my name is

Jacobowsky—S. L. Jacobowsky—in a certain sense a countryman. I, too, was born in Poland.

COLONEL. *(turns away after a sharp glance).* About that—there is nothing I can do.

JACOBOWSKY *(as if he had been encouraged).* Inadvertently I heard you discuss with my other countryman means of locomotion. Do I understand, Colonel, that it is important for you to leave Paris?

COLONEL *(spinning around).* Monsieur, what your name was?

JACOBOWSKY. Jacobowsky, by your leave.

COLONEL. You eavesdrop on our conversation.

JACOBOWSKY. Eavesdrop? Why do I have to eavesdrop when I hear without eavesdropping? Now my suggestion is that possibly—we can get a car in which to leave Paris.

COLONEL. We?

JACOBOWSKY. The good Madame Bouffier here, she has spoken to me of a car for sale . . .

COLONEL. This no doubt very convenient for you but how does it concern me?

JACOBOWSKY. If the car were available we might take it together.

COLONEL. You persist in the use of this intimate pronoun "we". When I travel, I travel alone. When I travel with company it is company that I choose.

JACOBOWSKY. An admirable way to travel. And from my side, I would choose you gladly—because you are a strong man—you are a chivalrous man. Now I have to provide you with a reason why you should choose me. If you will forgive me for saying so, I am a resourceful man. Strength plus resourcefulness! Isn't it a good combination for an emergency like this? Tell me frankly, sir, your opinion.

COLONEL. I do not understand your mentality. *(He turns to Cosette, takes her in his arms)* When the alarm stop, my man will take you home.

COSETTE. But I don't want to go home. I want to stay with you. I want to stay with you forever.

COLONEL. My sweet child—this is not possible.

COSETTE *(bursts out).* Who is she—that you love?

COLONEL. And what will it avail you to know? How can I convey to you the tenderness I feel for you, the fragrance your image invokes in me . . . *(With an impulsive gesture he removes a decoration from his tunic, holds it out to her)* Do you know what this is, my child? It is the Grand Cross of the Order of St. George. It is yours!

COSETTE. I don't want your medal. I want you.

COLONEL. This is the best of me. When I received it, I wept. It is yours. *(Szabuniewicz returns.)*

SZABUNIEWICZ. Everything prepared to go, Colonel.

COLONEL. Szabuniewicz, you take my sweet friend here home safe . . . *(Szabuniewicz comes forward eagerly, a gleam in his eye.)*

SZABUNIEWICZ. Yes, Colonel.

COSETTE. I'd rather go alone, than you. *(Her eyes meet the Colonel's. She see it is hopeless)* I won't forget you—not in thousand years . . . *(She starts upstairs* Good-bye.

COLONEL. Farewell, Cosette. *(As she exits—in an ecstasy of romantic dramatization* In the cathedral of my soul a candle burn for you, a flame that will never go out. *(Cosette is gone. The Colonel looks Szabuniewicz, clucking appreciation of his ow gift for romantic rhetoric. Szabuniewicz clu back admiringly. Jacobowsky, now that t coast is clear, approaches the Colonel again*

JACOBOWSKY. Forgive me, sir, b may we resume our conversation?

COLONEL. Oh! You are Monsie Wolfsohn—no?

JACOBOWSKY. Yes, Jacobowsky— you don't mind. My mother always us to say, no matter how hopeless thin look, there are always two possibiliti

COLONEL *(flatly).* I disagree with yo mother.

JACOBOWSKY. I can prove it math matically.

COLONEL. Why you speak to mathematically? Hear me, Monsie Wolfsohn, for a true man is one po bility.

JACOBOWISKY. That's not enough. With one possibility I can't maneuver.

COLONEL. I repeat, Monsieur Wolfsohn, for a man of honor one possibility.

JACOBOWSKY. If that were true, I would be dead, I don't know how many times. Now—let us assume for the sake of argument—that we acquire this car . . .

COLONEL. Again you assume that we are engaged in a joint enterprise, and this is an exaggeration. I do not know you, Monsieur . . .

JACOBOWSKY (his voice rises a little desperately). I must tell you, sir, that this may be the last chance to get a car in Paris . . .

COLONEL. Then I go on horseback.

JACOBOWSKY. You will never be in Saint-Jean-de-Luz on the 18th if you travel on horseback.

COLONEL. Psiav Krev—you eavesdrop this too! (In a kind of despair) Szabuniewicz, disengage me from this fellow. (Szabuniewicz rushes to Jacobowsky and urges him away from the Colonel. At this moment the sirens howl. The alert is over. Solly and the Young Girl support the Old Lady from Arras, helping her out. This outgoing torrent carries along with it Jacobowsky, who, as he is swept away, cries out exhortations to the Colonel. Finally they all disappear. The Colonel and Szabuniewicz are left alone.)

COLONEL (to Szabuniewicz). Szabuniewicz, my sword! The effrontery of this fellow. Every rebuff he takes for an invitation.

SZABUNIEWICZ (buckling on the Colonel's sword—the opportunist). Still, if he should get a comfortable car . . .

COLONEL. Out of the question. You know I travel alone.

SZABUNIEWICZ. (temporizing—it would solve his problem if Jacobowsky got a car and the Colonel would take it). Yes, I know—I know.

COLONEL. Well—what are you waiting for?

SZABUNIEWICZ. I am formulating my plans.

COLONEL. Marianne awaits me at Saint-Cyrille.

SZABUNIEWICZ (aghast). Saint-Cyrille!

COLONEL. Saint-Cyrille.

SZABUNIEWICZ. But that is north!

COLONEL. Of course it's north. Did you think that I thought it was east, or west or south?

SZABUNIEWICZ. But that is where the Germans are!

COLONEL. Since when I fear the Germans? Marianne awaits me. No obstacle stops me—no German—no Germans. (Exalted by his own romantic Quixoticism he starts for the stairs, shouting aloud his affirmation) Marianne—I come—to you! (He is gone)

SZABUNIEWICZ (in a panic runs after him, importuning wildly). But, Colonel! Saint-Cyrille! Colonel, I beg you . . . Saint-Cyrille! Colonel!

CURTAIN

SCENE TWO

SCENE: The little square outside the Hôtel Mon Repos et de la Rose. It is very early in the morning; a vista of old Paris buildings, in the distance a church, all gleaming in the pearly iridescence of dawn. A crested and polished Renault limousine stands before the entrance to Madame Bouffier's hotel.

When the curtain goes up a Chauffeur in a violet uniform is expatiating to Jacobowsky on the miracles of this car. The chauffeur's uniform is impeccable. His face, however, is a study in stupidity and cunning.

————

CHAUFFEUR (with corrupt candor). I would ask Monsieur to consider nothing but the plain facts. Facts are facts, as they say. Now where are the Germans? At Meaux! Which way are they marching? This way! Tomorrow they'll be marching up the Champs Elysées. What an optimist I am! This evening!

JACOBOWSKY (his patience nearly gone). Come to the point, please . . .

CHAUFFEUR. The Germans will enter Paris from west-northwest. Whereas, here before you stands one of the most faithful autos in France, ready to drive you west-southwest.

JACOBOWSKY. Come to the point, if you please . . .

CHAUFFEUR. The point is you should thank your lucky stars that I came along

like this. There's not another car left in
Paris! Even the few taxis that are left are
hiding away since yesterday. Try to get a
cab, Monsieur. (*Jacobowsky starts to go.
The Chauffeur pulls him back*) Just try and
see what happens. And suppose you found
another car—where would you get the
gasoline? Where would that blood of
life come from to fill the hungry tank?
(*Abruptly*) Are you sick? Monsieur, you
know, you look sick.

JACOBOWSKY. Who looks well so early
in the morning? Well, it's possible I'm
nervous today.

CHAUFFEUR. Keep up your morale!
Swat your wife twice a day—that always
helps morale.

JACOBOWSKY. About this car . . .

CHAUFFEUR. This car comes from a
very distinguished stable. Guess which
one.

JACOBOWSKY. No guessing games,
please. No guessing games.

CHAUFFEUR (*playing his trump card*).
Rothschild!

JACOBOWSKY. The Baron Rothschild?
(*He whistles*)

CHAUFFEUR. Don't you recognize this
crest? Monsieur, in this car you will
travel like a king.

JACOBOWSKY. I don't want to be so
conspicious.

CHAUFFEUR. Just before he left, the
Baron shook hands with me. He said,
"Philbert, it is true that I am particularly
attached to this car . . ."

JACOBOWSKY. Come to the point.
What do you want? I have been listening
to you talk for twenty minutes. Your wife
and children are as familiar to me as my
own face. I know what you like to eat and
drink, what paper you read! But what do
you want for this car?

CHAUFFEUR (*not to be rushed*). The
rubber satisfies you, I take it?

JACOBOWSKY. It's rubber.

CHAUFFEUR. The tank is filled to the
brim with gasoline, I mentioned that?

JACOBOWSKY. You did.

CHAUFFEUR. And the Mobiloil?

JACOBOWSKY. You mentioned that too.

CHAUFFEUR. And that there are three
more cans in the back, free of charge?

JACOBOWSKY. You've told me three
times.

CHAUFFEUR. And you realize by now,
Monsieur, you're the luckiest man in
Paris?

JACOBOWSKY. Stop envying me and
tell me the price.

CHAUFFEUR. And on my side, I feel
almost certain the Baron would be happy
to have you as his successor. All in all,
adding all these facts together—there is
really nothing more to say.

JACOBOWSKY. Just the same I'm sure
you'll say it. Well?

CHAUFFEUR. Monsieur, this superb
vehicle will cost you a mere fleabite—
forty thousand francs.

JACOBOWSKY (*sways*). Don't lift me
till I fall . . .

CHAUFFEUR. Morale, Monsieur. Keep
it up!

(*But Jacobowsky washes his hands of the
negotiations. He starts away.*)

JACOBOWSKY. Thank you very much
for your trouble. Good-bye.

CHAUFFEUR (*follows him in a panic*).
Monsieur, I await your counterproposals
. . . Did I say forty? I really meant thirty.

JACOBOWSKY (*temporizes*). I want to
buy this car. You want to sell it. Fact?

CHAUFFEUR. Fact.

JACOBOWSKY. You told me the Germans will be here any minute. They will
requisition this car. Fact? Fact! You have
to sell it or dump it in the river. Fact?
Fact! Does it have a spare tire? No! And
look at the tires on the wheels . .
(*Kicking one*) That has seen a good thirty
thousand miles!

CHAUFFEUR. Not fifteen, Monsieur!

JACOBOWSKY (*riding over him*). And
under the hood— (*Lifts up hood of car*)
My God, what is going on in there! Black
and greasy! A regular Dante's Inferno in
there! (*He closes the hood*)

CHAUFFEUR. Excuse me, that motor
works like my own heart!

JACOBOWSKY. And how do I know you
haven't got a heart condition? All in all
this venerable monument isn't worth ten
thousand francs!

CHAUFFEUR (*aghast*). Monsieur!

JACOBOWSKY. Attention, Monsieur!
Are you *legally* authorized to sell this car?

I smell here a most irregular transaction —final price fifteen thousand! *(He counts out money)*

CHAUFFEUR. Monsieur. For the sake of my children . . .

JACOBOWSKY *(adds an extra banknote)*. For the sake of your children, sixteen thousand.

CHAUFFEUR. You are overreaching an soldier of Verdun . . .

JACOBOWSKY *(adds additional banknote)*. For the sake of Verdun, seventeen thousand. *(Gives Chauffeur money)*

CHAUFFEUR *(accepting the bills)*. Now you see how weak we Frenchmen are. The Nazis are right—that's our damned decadence for you! The ownership license . . . *(Gives him license)* As soon as you sign your name the Baron's limousine is yours. *(Handing him key)* Here is the ignition key . . .

JACOBOWSKY *(taking it)*. Ignition key? What do you do with the ignition key?

CHAUFFEUR *(surprised)*. Monsieur, in the lock, you . . . *(Jacobowsky tries to fit the ignition key in the keyhole of the door of the car)* You don't know what you do with the ignition key?

JACOBOWSKY. It now occurs to me that I don't know how to drive. At home I always had a driver.

CHAUFFEUR *(edging away)*. You'll find someone.

JACOBOWSKY. What are *you* doing today? I mean, would your wife permit you to leave Paris for a few days?

CHAUFFEUR. Out of the question, Monsieur. I have to sell two more cars before the Germans arrive.

JACOBOWSKY. Rothschild's too?

CHAUFFEUR *(pointing to the Tragic Gentleman, who has just come out of the hotel)*. Maybe he'll drive your car. *(Under his broad, capelike coat the Tragic Gentleman carries a modest piece of luggage. He takes a few deep breaths as if to fill his lungs with Paris air for the last time.)*

JACOBOWSKY. Good morning, sir. Can you drive a car?

TRAGIC GENTLEMAN. How does that concern you?

JACOBOWSKY. It seems to me you fill your lungs with the air of Paris as if for the last time.

TRAGIC GENTLEMAN *(sadly)*. Yes, I am leaving Paris.

JACOBOWSKY. Any conveyance?

TRAGIC GENTLEMAN. My legs.

JACOBOWSKY. Would you care to come with me? I have just bought a car. Now if you can drive, you could reach your destination much faster.

(Madame Bouffier comes in, stands on stoop, watching the scene.)

TRAGIC GENTLEMAN. Destination is a sixth sense, but only great men, artists and statesmen have it. I have no destination.

JACOBOWSKY. Wouldn't you rather ride to it?

TRAGIC GENTLEMAN. No. I shall continue on foot like everyone else. There, you hear them . . .

(In the distance the confused tramping of footsteps is now heard.)

JACOBOWSKY. *(pale)*. The Germans?

TRAGIC GENTLEMAN. No, the Parisians.

CHAUFFEUR *(lounging about out of curiosity; he has no cars to sell. He is simply lazy)*. Yes, that's the Parisians all right.

TRAGIC GENTLEMAN. Walking, walking, walking. They are marching to the stations but the stations are dead—no trains move out—so they turn about and walk through the long rows of suburbs—a thousand, ten thousand, one hundred thousand—all with bag and baggage. What is kept of life animates the legs and they walk and walk. Where we shall be when the Boches arrive only God and Saint Denis know! Listen! *(The sound of the rolling of shutters)* The last metal shutters rolling down to blind the shop windows. Lafayette and Potin and the smart little jewel boxes in the Rue de la Paix. When the Boches march in, Paris will be a dirty coffin, a coffin without a corpse. But I was born in Paris and to Paris I belong and I'm moving with the people of Paris out of Paris and I want to walk not drive—walk with all the others—with the moving boulevards, day after day—hour after hour. When your legs ache, the heart doesn't ache so much. *(He goes out. Jacobowsky gazes after him, spellbound. In his trance he muses aloud)*

JACOBOWSKY. He knows his destination—to be at one with the other Parisians; and my destination—like the Greeks of Xenophon—Thalassa! *(Madame Bouffier walks over to him. She is concerned and mystified. Jacobowsky explains to her)* Thalassa! That's what the ancient Greeks called the sea. Because on the sea there are ships and these ships sail to England and to America. *(He looks around in desperation and appeals to the Chauffeur again)* Won't you drive me to the sea?

CHAUFFEUR *(gaily)*. Impossible, Monsieur, my mother is dying.

(In the background an Old Man and a Little Boy walk by. The Old Man carries his belongings in a few bags and hums a street song. Other stragglers pass by.)

MADAME BOUFFIER *(as she looks at them)*. At last it's happening. Everyone is deserting me. Everyone is leaving Paris—and now you, too, my dear Monsieur Jacobowsky. My house is empty—only the mice and the water bugs and those two Poles are left. I have no courage any more. Just imagine, Monsieur Jacobowsky, at thirty-five I am a broken, old woman. *(Skeptical guffaw from the Chauffeur. Madame Bouffier is furious)* What are you laughing at, you scamp? Thirty-five in May. Do you want to see my birth certificate?

JACOBOWSKY *(consoling her)*. You have a young heart, Madame Bouffier.

MADAME BOUFFIER. Did you buy the car from this robber?

(Madame Bouffier and Chauffeur snarl at each other.)

JACOBOWSKY *(leading her out of controversy)*. Thank you for bringing him to me. Here is a warehouse list—old furniture I bought before the war—I had a dream of furnishing my own apartment. Take it. There are some nice things. Decorate your house with them.

MADAME BOUFFIER *(accepting warehouse list)*. I'll keep it for you. One day you'll find a beautiful woman who will love you and I'll give her your furniture.

JACOBOWSKY *(dismissing the possibility)*. A beautiful woman doesn't need my furniture. Where are my things?

MADAME BOUFFIER *(calling)*. Solly dear, Monsieur Jacobowsky's things!

JACOBOWSKY. It seems foolish, but I'm very much attached to those two Teheran rugs. They're museum pieces.

At least I'll take with me the illusion of a charming home.

(Solly enters staggering under the rugs.)

MADAME BOUFFIER *(indicating Chauffeur)*. Is he driving you south to the sea?

CHAUFFEUR. What would I do at the sea! I'm a Parisian!

JACOBOWSKY *(to Solly)*. Solly dear, I am worried about you. What will become of you if the Germans come?

SOLLY *(depositing his load in the car)*. I'd rather not think about it . . .

MADAME BOUFFIER *(with emotion)*. I make myself responsible for him—if I have to lock him in the cellar and stand guard.

(The Colonel's voice is heard off stage berating Szabuniewicz.)

COLONEL. Szabuniewicz, I have told you over and over again, you must provide transportation. Where is it?

(Szabuniewicz and Colonel Stjerbinsky now come out of the hotel. Szabuniewicz is carrying a bulging officer's knapsack and saddle bags. Under one arm the Colonel has a violin case.)

SZABUNIEWICZ. This question I fail to solve, Colonel.

COLONEL. Did you think we would remain in Paris forever? You should have thought about it, Szabuniewicz.

SZABUNIEWICZ. I think—but nothing comes. *(Drops baggage on the floor)*

COLONEL. I told you a car, a horse, a carriage—anything. Where are they?

SZABUNIEWICZ. Give me time, Colonel. I will solve it.

COLONEL. Time! There is no time. Time is of the . . . *(Automatically he finds himself repeating the hated phrase. He stops and at the same moment he takes in the Rothschild limousine)*

(Jacobowsky points dramatically to the car.)

JACOBOWSKY *(quietly)*. There she stands, Colonel.

COLONEL. What is to me—that she stands? Let her stand. *(To Szabuniewicz)* You say no car is left in Paris—here is car

SZABUNIEWICZ *(who is dying for the deal to go through—this will solve all his problems)*. Maybe I can negotiate . . .

JACOBOWSKY. Why negotiate? You are welcome to it. *(To Colonel)* You remember, perhaps, our conversation?

COLONEL. I remember no conversation.

JACOBOWSKY. Are you by any chance an automobilist?

COLONEL *(elegantly)*. I am cavalryist . . .

JACOBOWSKY *(pleasantly)*. But modern cavalry is generally motorized.

COLONEL *(with simple pride)*. In Poland —no!

JACOBOWSKY *(noticing violin case)*. You are a violinist?

COLONEL. I fiddle.

JACOBOWSKY. You are fond of chamber music?

COLONEL *(isolated)*. I fiddle solo.

JACOBOWSKY. Can you drive a car— solo?

COLONEL. If road is correct and straight I can drive. Curves I don't care to see.

JACOBOWSKY. Perhaps on the curves, we can compromise.

COLONEL *(with sudden recognition)*. I remember you now—you are Monsieur Leibowicz.

JACOBOWSKY *(pleased with his accuracy)*. Yes, Jacobowsky.

COLONEL. You are Pole?

JACOBOWSKY. I was born in Poland. It is the first of my native lands.

COLONEL *(interested)*. Where in Poland were you born?

JACOBOWSKY. In the village of Studno near Kasimisz.

COLONEL *(the recognition becomes almost intimate)*. So—Studno near Stanislau.

SZABUNIEWICZ *(helping along)*. Good locality!

COLONEL. My father had great estates there. Owned many villages. Your papa, a dealer in liquid spirits, no doubt?

JACOBOWSKY. Not spirits—spirit!— and not liquid. He taught the children Biblical history.

COLONEL. Good profession.

SZABUNIEWICZ *(all for the intellect)*. Very educational.

COLONEL *(mumbles an inventory to reassure himself)*. From the village of Studno near Kasimisz—father schoolteacher— understands music . . .

JACOBOWSKY *(feeling the moment has come for the coup de grace)*. Perhaps it might be interesting, sir, for us to travel together.

COLONEL. Interesting? How interesting?

JACOBOWSKY. Psychologically. You are—if I may make so bold—cast suddenly in a new role. Instead of being in the enviable position of persecuting other people, you are persecuted yourself. Now I'm used to that and I'll help you get used to it too.

COLONEL *(a bit put off)*. I need no help from you, Monsieur.

JACOBOWSKY. Probably not—but if you should want it, there I'll be.

COLONEL. If I consent drive your car, it is because it help me bring out from danger vital documents of our Polish motherland's fight for freedom.

JACOBOWSKY *(humoring him)*. Do not deny me the privilege of assisting in a patriotic act.

COLONEL *(struck by this)*. Ah! You would be patriot?

JACOBOWSKY *(firm)*. My deepest ambition.

COLONEL *(with a spasm of tolerance)*. Cannot deny man right to be patriot.

SZABUNIEWICZ *(godly)*. That would be sin.

COLONEL *(he has made the great decision. He turns to Jacobowsky)*. Monsieur, I will drive your car!

JACOBOWSKY *(overcome)*. Colonel! If it weren't for your rank, I'd embrace you. *(The Colonel stops any overtures with an upraised hand. Then he turns to inspect the car, sees Jacobowsky's rugs in the back seat.)*

COLONEL. First, come out from this car these rugs. *(He puts his violin in the back seat of the car)*

JACOBOWSKY. Excuse me, Colonel, these rugs mean very much to me.

COLONEL. Excuse me, please. I am one of Pilsudski's colonels! I not used to voyage in furniture truck. No, the backside must remain empty.

JACOBOWSKY. And why must the backside remain empty?

COLONEL. I am not used to give reasons.

SZABUNIEWICZ *(explaining)*. We travel light.

MADAME BOUFFIER *(intervenes)*. But it's his car . . .

COLONEL. Monsieur . . . *(To Szabuniewicz)* What's his name?

MADAME BOUFFIER *(shouting it)*. Jacobowsky!

COLONEL. Monsieur Jacobowsky. In this car you carry out not only your small self but you serve high purpose—maybe for first time in your life—no?

SZABUNIEWICZ. You help Poland.

JACOBOWSKY. Can't I help Poland and take my rugs too?

SZABUNIEWICZ *(whispers)*. Be careful—you'll irritate him.

COLONEL *(he is irritated)*. You see, Szabuniewicz, what means to take favor from certain people. *(He walks away, whispering imprecations to himself)*

SZABUNIEWICZ. You did irritate him!

JACOBOWSKY *(after a mournful pause)*. Solly dear, take the rugs out of the car. *(As Solly obeys)* Madame Bouffier, please keep these rugs as a further acknowledgment of my debt to you.

(Szabuniewicz keeps piling the Colonel's paraphernalia into the car.)

MADAME BOUFFIER *(outraged—to Jacobowsky)*. My dear, why do you stand for it?

JACOBOWSKY. There are two things a man shouldn't be angry at—what he can help and what he can't help.

(Madame Bouffier catches sight of the Colonel engaged in a violent controversy with himself.)

MADAME BOUFFIER. Look! He's talking to himself. The moment he stamped into my house I knew he was out of his mind.

JACOBOWSKY. You're wrong, Madame Bouffier. A man who talks to himself is usually lonely. I have the most charming conversations with myself.

SZABUNIEWICZ *(everything having been cleared, he opens the front door of the car)*. Take place, gentlemen—Boches is on the march.

(Colonel gets in the front seat, sits there stiffly. Jacobowsky comes forward with an automobile map.)

JACOBOWSKY. Our route is main boulevard, Place de la Bastille, Ivry, and down the Route Nationale west-south-west.

COLONEL. You are wrong, Yalofsky—

our way go down the Champs Elysées, Neuilly, Saint-Cloud and Route Nationale west-northwest.

JACOBOWSKY *(to Szabuniewicz, easily)*. I am sure the Colonel means west-south-west.

SZABUNIEWICZ *(with a malicious grin)*. No. Colonel means west-northwest.

JACOBOWSKY *(stunned as he sees the Colonel's set face)*. Northwest! *(Turns to Szabuniewicz)* Is there something wrong with my hearing?

SZABUNIEWICZ. Be careful—you'll irritate him.

JACOBOWSKY. Did he say northwest?

SZABUNIEWICZ. That's what he said. And that's where we go.

JACOBOWSKY. But northwest—there are the German divisions— *(To Madame Bouffier)* right into the arms of . . .

SZABUNIEWICZ *(warning him)*. Leave it to him.

(A silence. Jacobowsky struggles with this appalling fact. He advances toward the car and addresses the statue of the Colonel.)

JACOBOWSKY *(tentatively)*. Colonel dear—I don't ask for a shoe larger than my foot but, after all, it is my car, isn't it? *(Suddenly uncertain, he turns to the Chauffeur)* Did I buy this car from you or didn't I?

CHAUFFEUR. You bought it all right.

SZABUNIEWICZ *(increased warning)*. Be careful!

JACOBOWSKY. But it is *my* car.

MADAME BOUFFIER *(shouts)*. But it's his car.

JACOBOWSKY *(points to Chauffeur)*. There is the evidence

COLONEL *(rises in mighty anger)*. My car! What means that? On a stormy sea you say, "This lifeboat is my lifeboat?" The devil take you—to hell you go. *(He stamps out of the car and flings a command to Szabuniewicz)* Szabuniewicz! Horses! *(He goes off)*

(The lifeline is cut! The others stand frozen in silence. Szabuniewicz is the first to emerge.)

SZABUNIEWICZ. I told you to be careful—when he says northwest, he means northwest.

JACOBOWSKY. Evidently.

SZABUNIEWICZ. We go first to pick up lady.

JACOBOWSKY. Lady? What kind of lady?

SZABUNIEWICZ *(looking foxy)*. Lady-love.

MADAME BOUFFIER *(to Jacobowsky)*. My dear, can't you find another driver? *(The Colonel comes back. Locked in his indignation he stands apart, his arms crossed over his chest. He waits for the world to conciliate him. Jacobowsky looks at him.)*

JACOBOWSKY *(to Madame Bouffier)*. Just a minute . . . *(Clears his throat, whispers to Szabuniewicz)* Any lady who would interest the Colonel to such an extent where he risks his life and documents—well—she must be a very rare person.

SZABUNIEWICZ. Of course! *(A silence. Jacobowsky approaches the Colonel.)*

JACOBOWSKY. Any use to talk you about this?

COLONEL. No use!

SZABUNIEWICZ *(echoes)*. No use!

COLONEL *(the auctioneer's last announcement)*. Time is fleeting.

JACOBOWSKY *(helplessly, to Madame Bouffier)*. No use. *(He turns to Colonel and concedes all)* Colonel. You're right! You are a strategist. You have a plan. If you say west-northwest you have an idea in it—and I agree. Which direction you like, I agree. I agree. I agree. *(The Colonel clamps him on the shoulder as if bestowing an accolade for his good sense but the accolade quickly becomes a violent push. Jacobowsky finds himself in the Chauffeurs' lap. Meantime the Colonel has resumed his place in the car. Jacobowsky recovers his balance, runs to Madame Bouffier and Solly, embracing them.)*

JACOBOWSKY. Good-bye, dear Madame Bouffier. Good-bye, Solly friend. Good-bye in all seven languages.

MADAME BOUFFIER. Good luck. Good luck, dear friend. *Jacobowsky runs toward the car. The Colonel steps savagely on the accelerator, but the car does not react. He begins to swear.)*

COLONEL. What dirty thing is this? I give spurs to the villain but she don't move.

JACOBOWSKY *(shouts to the Chauffeur)*. The motor is a fake!

CHAUFFEUR. Would I be standing here if the motor was a fake? The battery needs recharging, that's all. There is a garage twenty meters away. Everybody out and push . . .

COLONEL *(scowling)*. Now, you see, Jacobowsky, what complications come with you?

SZABUNIEWICZ *(bitter)*. And is only now the beginning.

CHAUFFEUR *(his sleeves pushed up)*. Push, gentlemen, push. *(The Chauffeur, Jacobowsky, Szabuniewicz and Solly all start pushing the car from the rear fender. The Colonel sits at the wheel, his grandeur undimmed when suddenly he feels the need to invoke a higher power. He rises to his great height, addressing, without turning to look at them, the little strugglers at the rear of the car.)*

COLONEL. Stop! Nobody knows what lies before us. Therefore I think is wise to call upon the heaven before we start on the undertaking. *(Szabuniewicz jumps into an attitude of devotion, takes off his hat and puts his hand over his eyes. The Chauffeur also attempts to look otherworldly. Jacobowsky doesn't know quite what to do. The Colonel speaks severely)* This means also for you, Jacobowsky.

JACOBOWSKY. For me? *Twice* for me! I wept when I was born and every day shows me why. *(The Colonel himself stands still for a moment, then takes from the pocket of his tunic a Catholic prayer book and from it reads a prayer in Polish. He intones the words in a liturgical singsong and the sound of them, though strange, conveys somehow the resonant cadence of a great cathedral. He finishes the prayer, puts the prayer book back in his pocket, and in the same voice invokes the future)* I, Tadeusz Boleslav Stjerbinsky, go from Paris not to fly from the Hun but to overthrow him! *(Suddenly relapsing into the vernacular)* All right, push! *(The others resume their pushing with all their strength. The Colonel sits behind the wheel ready to guide the car)* Push! Push! *(They strain and push but the car is rooted to the spot)*

CHAUFFEUR *(from the tangle)*. The brake! Release the brake!

MADAME BOUFFIER. Release the brake, you big fool!

COLONEL *(bewildered for a moment)*.

What? Brake? *(Releases the brake)* Oh, the brake! Push! Forward!

(Now the car responds. It begins to roll forward. Szabuniewicz and the Chauffeur pushing strongly, Jacobowsky rather more doubtfully. Madame Bouffier, beside herself, begins to cry. She waves her handkerchief at Jacobowsky. He takes time off for a moment to wave back to her.)

MADAME BOUFFIER. God save Jacobowsky!

CURTAIN

ACT TWO

SCENE ONE

SCENE: *Saint-Cyrille. A lonely country road running along a garden wall. The wall is broken by a gate; the villa faintly visible through the gate beyond thick trees. Summer dusk. From time to time the roar of German planes.*

———

MARIANNE, *a lovely and vivacious young Frenchwoman, slim and girlish, is talking to her lawyer, Serouille, a crotchety old man.*

SEROUILLE *(importuning her).* You are young. You are strong. Life is still before you. I implore you—fly, run away, vanish —while there is still time—before the Germans come.

MARIANNE. I am surprised at you, Serouille, talking like that. That is defeatism.

SEROUILLE. It is realism.

MARIANNE. I sent for you to settle my boundary dispute with that pig of a neighbor, not to tell me to run away. Are you my lawyer—or are you hers?

SEROUILLE. Boundary dispute! Six feet of pasture and all rocky.

MARIANNE. But they are my six feet— not hers. I love them, every rock, every pebble. On this land I was born. Here my father and grandfather were born. Here I stay!

(An airplane zooms rather close. It makes a terrific racket.)

SEROUILLE *(looks up).* Messerschmitt. Admirable! How undeviating! Know just what they're about.

MARIANNE *(with hatred).* They trespass over my beautiful fields. How long will our government allow it? When will they be stopped?

SEROUILLE. Never.

MARIANNE. I am surprised at you, Monsieur Serouille. Can you conceive that France will no longer be France—can you?

SEROUILLE. I cannot conceive it but, alas! I know that it is true.

MARIANNE. But the whole world is with us—the whole world loves France. America! Poland!

SEROUILLE. That love, which so far has not materialized in planes, will not stop the Boches!

MARIANNE. How can you say that! The Poles—look how they fought!

SEROUILLE. But what good was it? The Poles they were done for six months ago. The Germans are a very few miles to the north. What are you waiting for?

MARIANNE. Right now I am waiting for the return of my lover—a noble Pole—Colonel Tadeusz Boleslav Stjerbinsky. Isn't it a lovely name?

SEROUILLE *(shakes his head).* He will not return.

MARIANNE. He will! Moreover he will return with men, with planes, with guns. He did not go to Paris for nothing.

SEROUILLE. I see there is nothing I can do.

MARIANNE. You can do what I engaged you to do. You can get me back that piece of land from that ugly, thieving Madame Vauclain.

SEROUILLE *(with a little laugh).* In forty-eight hours at most your land and her land will both belong to the Germans. Do you think the Boches will insist on clear title? They are not so meticulous.

MARIANNE. When our deliverance comes I shall not remind you that you have talked like this.

SEROUILLE *(turns to go).* I have done what I could.

MARIANNE *(calls after him).* And tell Vauclain if she goes to court it is she who will have to pay the costs!

SEROUILLE *(wearily).* I'll tell her.

MARIANNE. That'll teach her—the penny-pincher!

SEROUILLE. Yes. The world loves u

But the Nazis—*they* covet us! *(He goes out)*

(Left alone, Marianne stands dreamily looking out at her beloved fields, whitening in the bright moonlight. She is deeply stirred. Involuntarily her lips pronounce her lover's name. She hears herself murmuring.)

MARIANNE. Colonel Tadeusz Boleslav Stjerbinsky—Lover, Deliverer . . . *(She becomes conscious that she is saying it and then she speaks aloud in a firm tone)* Deliverer . . . *(She is in an entranced mood. The barking of her little dog breaks her out of it)* Oh, Coco! *(She runs through the gate and disappears in the garden)*

(For a second the scene is empty, only the disconsolate peep-peep of crickets audible. Gradually we hear the reluctant pounding and thrashing of an exhausted automobile motor. The sputtering approach can be followed as it comes closer and at last Jacoboswky's limousine appears, mud-bespattered, rattling, inching in by jerks. It runs into a heap of stones put up as a tank-obstruction. The car, its right to live impaired, halts with a sharp bump, the doors fly open. The first to tumble out is Jacobowsky. Szabuniewicz hurries around and looks at the freshly smashed mudguard. The Colonel, tall and leisurely, stands looking round with satisfaction.)

COLONEL. We arrive!

JACOBOWSKY *(rather short-tempered)*. Yes. But where?

COLONEL *(grandiose)*. At the object of my heart's desire.

JACOBOWSKY. Also twelve hours nearer the Germans!

SZABUNIEWICZ *(tapping the fender)*. Run into French tank-obstruction. Is enough to make laugh the Germans.

JACOBOWSKY. Are we running away from the Germans or do we have a rendezvous with them? Colonel, you will never know what these twelve hours have cost me!

COLONEL *(fixes him with a blue-eyed military stare)*. Cost you? Polish Government pay you back everything. Szabuniewicz, child, write down everything what we owe this *merchant*. Myself I have no head for figures.

SZABUNIEWICZ. Figures leave to me . . .

COLONEL. Therefore every time write down. Everything write down.

SZABUNIEWICZ *(taps his forehead)*. In my head is written!

COLONEL. Therefore, Polish Government, what it owe him?

JACOBOWSKY. Write down in your head the Polish Government in Exile owes me the following: Replacement One: a heart which has begun to flutter like a wounded bird; Replacement Two: one wrecked nervous system, plus body ditto. And, if the Germans catch me, one entire Jacobowsky.

COLONEL *(gruffly, drowning all in the computable)*. Szabuniewicz, what costs him this car?

SZABUNIEWICZ. Seventeen thousand francs.

COLONEL. Therefore for the car put down twenty thousand francs. Ten thousand add for gasoline and other slight specialties what we use. Also five thousand for two rugs was left behind.

SZABUNIEWICZ. Polish Government owe him now thirty-five thousand francs!

COLONEL *(haughtily)*. Now hear me, S. L. Jacobowsky! For this amount thirty-five thousand we toss the coin! Double or nothing. Give me coin! Top I win. Bottom you win. *(Takes coin from Jacobowsky. He tosses it into his palm, and reaches out his palm for Szabuniewicz to register the result. Szabuniewicz looks at coin and pockets it)*

SZABUNIEWICZ. Polish Government owe him now seventy thousand francs.

COLONEL *(lavishly)*. Write down!

SZABUNIEWICZ *(tapping his brow)*. Is written.

JACOBOWSKY *(looks up)*. Why—will you please tell me—why are we getting ourselves involved in all these intricate financial transactions when every second the Germans are getting closer?

COLONEL *(scornful)*. You are in a hurry it seem.

(Szabuniewicz fishes out from the car a cigar box containing the Colonel's toilet articles.)

JACOBOWSKY. And you are not in a hurry? This Messiah in the gray gloves who is waiting to save you in Saint-Jean-de Luz is not in a hurry? That corvette filled with Czechs and Poles is not in a hurry? *(Szabuniewicz is brushing the Colonel's uniform.)*

COLONEL. This corvette for us—not for you.

JACOBOWSKY. I know. But I want a sight of the ocean. Perhaps for me, too, a Moses will appear and will divide the Channel and let me walk across to England.

(Szabuniewicz starts polishing the Colonel's boots.)

COLONEL. Szabuniewicz, how many hours before our appointment at Saint-Jean-de-Luz?

SZABUNIEWICZ *(polishing away)*. Seventy-two.

COLONEL. Ample.

JACOBOWSKY. You don't think of breakdowns, the eternal problem of gasoline.

COLONEL. Is in your blood to get gasoline.

JACOBOWSKY. Colonel, I don't understand you. Really—I don't understand you. You seem to look down on the instinct of self-preservation.

COLONEL. In your case this ambition is trivial. *(He looks at Szabuniewicz to get appreciation for his little joke. Szabuniewicz responds. They both laugh. Szabuniewicz hands the Colonel a comb and holds a mirror while the Colonel combs his hair)* You do not realize that I, Stjerbinsky, under greater danger than little Jacobowsky. On my head the Germans have put price! *He returns the comb to Szabuniewicz)*

JACOBOWSKY. At the rate you're going, they'll collect it! Is this a time to stop for ladies?

COLONEL. Life of man is short but always time to think of ladies. For my spirit—this is the fuel. Without this fuel, I can no more live than this car without gasoline.

(Szabuniewicz gets perfume bottle from cigar box.)

JACOBOWSKY *(throws up his hands)*. Reason rebels!

COLONEL. Reason always rebel against life. What is reason? A dried-up little bureaucrat with a green eye-shade . . . *(Pointing to Marianne's house)* To that lady the Colonel give his word to return. I am return! Of equal importance my mission and my word. But this of course you don't understand. The concept of honor is not for you.

(Szabuniewicz dabs perfume on Colonel's hands.)

SZABUNIEWICZ. Promise of Spring.

(The Colonel inhales the scent with satisfaction.)

JACOBOWSKY. Isn't your concept of honor a little exclusive? Like a private park with a "No Trespass Sign," don't you think?

COLONEL. I do not think. I feel. I act. Food—I eat. Gun—I shoot. Horse—I ride. Woman—I love. Honor—I defend.

JACOBOWSKY. Admirable. A Renaissance figure as sure as the world is round.

COLONEL *(leans on car, truculent)*. Who say that?

JACOBOWSKY. Who says what?

COLONEL *(ready to make a fight for it)*. That she's round!

JACOBOWSKY. I don't insist. There is no doubt, Colonel, you have one of the finest minds of the fifteenth century. Unfortunately I live in the twentieth. I implore you, Colonel, see your lady and let's go.

SZABUNIEWICZ *(looking toward the house)*. Windows is dark . . .

COLONEL. Mademoiselle is sleeping probably.

SZABUNIEWICZ. I go knock.

JACOBOWSKY. Blow the horn.

COLONEL *(indignant)*. You wake lady with automobile horn? I break your hand for that! Szabuniewicz, child, my violin is in the car. Mademoiselle is sleeping. We wake her. We wake her sweet.

(Szabuniewicz has opened the violin case. The Colonel takes the violin with a flourish. Szabuniewicz puts the case back in the car.)

JACOBOWSKY *(unable to believe what he sees, fascinated)*. You pick this moment for a recital? *(As Szabuniewicz takes mouth organ out of his pocket and sits on the running board of the car and starts playing scales)* A regular orchestra!

SZABUNIEWICZ *(blinking his eyes like coquette)*. Sir, you not musical?

JACOBOWSKY. In Munich we had chamber music every Wednesday night. I played second fiddle.

COLONEL. You always play second fiddle.

JACOBOWSKY. What's wrong with

second? You need as much technique as to play first! Only I didn't have it!

COLONEL (*holds his violin lovingly*). On all the fronts she has been my companion.

JACOBOWSKY. Powerful instrument in the war of nerves. (*Colonel beats time for Szabuniewicz with his bow and then, his back to the audience, facing the house of his beloved, he goes into Drigo's "Serenade" while Szabuniewicz accompanies him on the mouth organ. All of this Jacobowsky watches incredulously. He presses his knuckles to his temples*) Is this real? The air is filled with German planes. The earth is crimson. Poland lies slain—and this last of her dead stands here fiddling in the moonlight! And I, the only son of Reba Jacobowsky, am lost, far from home, motoring to the guillotine in Rothschild's limousine! It is a grotesque dream I dream . . .

(*In the misty distance, Marianne appears. The Colonel hands his violin to Szabuniewicz; calls as if over an immeasurable distance.*)

COLONEL. Marianne . . .

MARIANNE (*answers*). Tadeusz . . .

COLONEL. I am return . . .

MARIANNE. I am here . . .

COLONEL. My arms wait to receive you . . .

(*By this time Marianne has come running through the garden gate into the Colonel's arms.*)

MARIANNE. I knew you would come back. I never faltered.

COLONEL (*enjoying himself hugely*). My journey is over. (*He kisses her*) My journey begins.

MARIANNE. Tadeusz.

COLONEL. My loved one.

(*They embrace.*)

MARIANNE. I fell asleep just now—I dreamt you were here—with guns, with planes—driving the Boches away. (*Szabuniewicz is playing a lively tune on the harmonica.*)

COLONEL (*grimly*). This I greatly fear was only a . . . (*Wrathfully to Szabuniewicz*) top damn all to hell this music! (*Szabuniewicz obeys despondently. He is more hurt than angry. The Colonel resumes his aria*) That, I fear, was only a dream.

MARIANNE (*sees plaster on Colonel's forehead*). But, darling! You are wounded. What did they do to you?

COLONEL. I no longer fight the Boches. I run from them. And you run with me.

MARIANNE (*aghast*). Run!

COLONEL. We must. To Bordeaux. To London!

MARIANNE. Then it's true. France is defeated.

COLONEL. For the moment.

MARIANNE. Everybody said it. And now you say it. You too!

COLONEL. I say it too!

MARIANNE (*dead voice*). Then it must be true. If you abandon us too—then it must be true. (*It takes a moment for her to assimilate this awful fact*) France—France is . . . (*Szabuniewicz steps forward to arrange something in back of car. Marrianne sees him*) Oh! Szabuniewicz . . .

SZABUNIEWICZ. At your service, honored lady.

MARIANNE (*sees Jacobowsky*). Who is that?

COLONEL. Not to be frightened, my life. It is only S. L. Jacobowsky.

JACOBOWSKY. The modest owner of this car, which bears us all to safety.

COLONEL (*stern*). You forget, Jacobowsky. This car requisition by Polish Government. And pay you well for it. (*To Marianne*) But very obliging person, my love. Takes care of everything—car, hotel rooms, *marrons glacés*, gasoline. What you will, Jacobowsky provides. Jacobowsky, gasoline! See?

JACOBOWSKY. Gasoline. It's easy to say. A pipeline to the sky.

COLONEL. If necessary.

JACOBOWSKY. Unfortunately, at the moment, the sky is in the possession of the Nazis!

COLONEL. Marianne, please to go and pack. Szabuniewicz and I—we help you.

MARIANNE. No, Tadeusz, my love.

COLONEL. No?

MARIANNE. I cannot leave.

COLONEL. But you must.

MARIANNE. I have never left France. I never shall.

COLONEL. But I ask you. I demand. It is necessary we do not part.

MARIANNE. We must. I love you. But to leave this land, I cannot do this.

COLONEL. I leave my land.

MARIANNE. I know. Other people do

it. They leave their countries lightly. I
cannot go. Go without me.
*(Jacobowsky intervenes, taps Colonel on
shoulder.)*

COLONEL. What you want?

JACOBOWSKY. I overheard your discussion.

COLONEL. Always you eavesdrop!

JACOBOWSKY *(to Marianne)*. The Colonel is a peculiar man. When he shouts
to me and I answer, he says I eavesdrop.
(Marianne smiles) Madame, if I may make
so bold, there are times when in order
to advance one must retreat. This is one
of those times.

MARIANNE. I cannot run away.

JACOBOWSKY. Right now the shortest
distance between this gate—and that
house—is Bordeaux, London and back.
Please believe me, Madame.

MARIANNE. Is it so hopeless?

JACOBOWSKY. For the moment. I am a
subtle man, and I have read much, but
the Colonel here has a faculty worth more
than all my subtleties. He will escape
with you, but he will also return with you
and he will fight for you.

COLONEL. I do not need you to speak
for me, Monsieur.

JACOBOWSKY *(briskly)*. It will save time.
You have the same idea I have but it takes
you too long to gather your thoughts.

COLONEL *(storms)*. I will not permit
you to . . .

JACOBOWSKY *(to Marianne)*. To come
back here he risked his life.

MARIANNE *(looks up at Colonel gratefully)*. Tadeusz . . .

JACOBOWSKY. What's more, he risked
mine. Did we do that for nothing?
Abandon your home, Madame, in order
to save your home.

MARIANNE. You are returning to fight
for France again?

JACOBOWSKY. Not I. He.

COLONEL *(to be just for once)*. He is not
a soldier, Marianne!

JACOBOWSKY. I fight in my own way.
Here I am a superfluous man, but even a
superfluous man wants to go on being
superfluous. Please, Madame, make up
your mind. Hurry! Join us.

MARIANNE *(amused, to Colonel)*. Your
friend is funny.

COLONEL. He is a traveling acquaintance,
merely.

MARIANNE. But amusing and sympathetic!

JACOBOWSKY. Madame, every minute
counts.

MARIANNE *(to Colonel)*. You will bring
me back?

COLONEL. I will bring you back.
(They kiss.)

MARIANNE *(in a flurry)*. Coco and
Mignon are in their baskets. They are very
frightened. I've got to shut off the gas and
water. I've got to pack my things.
Tadeusz, will you help me?

COLONEL. Szabuniewicz and I—we
both help you!

JACOBOWSKY *(adores her already)*. I'll
help you, too . . .

COLONEL. Mademoiselle has protector.
You get gasoline.

MARIANNE *(as she goes out through the
gate)*. If he gets gasoline, that's wonderful help. *(To Jacobowsky)* Good luck! *(She
hurries out, followed by Stjerblnsky and Szu-
buniewicz)*

COLONEL *(as he and Szabuniewicz follow
her)*. Fill up the tank!
(Left alone, with his chore, Jacobowsky sighs.)

JACOBOWSKY *(murmurs to himself)*. Fill
up the tank! Easy to say! Pipeline to the
sky! *(He does a little turn by himself in the
moonlight, his hands in his pockets, whistling
"La Donna è Mobile." Suddenly a plane
returns not far away and starts spitting
machine-gun bullets. Jacobowsky jumps into
the back of the car; obeying some reflex, though
the top is down and he is exposed to the
heavens, he bends, pulling his coat collar over
his head. The plane recedes. Cautiously he
straightens up, feeling his body all over. He
has not observed the entrance of a Brigadier
of the Gendarmerie on a bicycle. Now the
Brigadier dismounts. He wears a red cap and
service pouch)*

JACOBOWSKY *(very friendly, to the Brigadier)*. Good evening.

BRIGADIER *(businesslike)*. Good evening. Your identification, please.
*(Jacobowsky gets out of the car, starts fishing
out his documents, and hands the paper to
Brigadier.)*

JACOBOWSKY *(sighs)*. Ah! The one
fate you can't escape—your own identity

BRIGADIER (*more politely*). Literary man?

JACOBOWSKY. Only as a lover. Not a practitioner.

BRIGADIER. Your safe-conduct pass, please.

JACOBOWSKY (*mastering his anxiety*). Safe-conduct pass?

BRIGADIER. As a foreigner you have no right to fluctuate freely without the proper authorization.

JACOBOWSKY (*dryly*). But I'm fluctuating under compulsion, not freely. All of France is fluctuating now.

BRIGADIER. To be more specific, what are your personal plans, Monsieur?

JACOBOWSKY. My personal plans are so fluid I'm apt to drown in them.

BRIGADIER (*rattling off the rigmarole—tapping papers*). This paper gives your basic place of residence as Paris. If you desire to change your basic place of residence, you are required to submit to the Commissariat of Police of your precinct an application for stamped forms wherein you request the privilege of changing your residence. The Commissariat of Police will transmit your application to the Préfecture, which, after careful investigation and examination, will forward it to the Central Military Bureau of Circulation who will then decide in accordance with the prevailing situation in regard to transportation and communication whether you have the right to move to this spot to which you have already moved.

JACOBOWSKY. Sergeant, tell me—has the rumor by any chance reached you that Paris is about to fall to the Germans?

BRIGADIER. When it happens, that will be a mere fact. It will not alter the provisions of the law. You are accordingly required to proceed forthwith to Paris, Monsieur, and follow the legally prescribed course. Otherwise you are illegally, illicitly and surreptitiously standing on this highway. You are standing before me only de facto, not de jure.

JACOBOWSKY. That means arrest and shipping off to Paris?

BRIGADIER. In accordance with the regulations.

JACOBOWSKY. You know what the Boches will do with me if they catch me?

BRIGADIER. They won't eat you.

JACOBOWSKY. Especially me. For them I am caviar!

BRIGADIER. If they do execute you, at least you will have the satisfaction of knowing that you have not broken the regulations of France.

JACOBOWSKY. I shall die happy.

BRIGADIER. With a clear conscience. A good way to die . . .

JACOBOWSKY. Tell me, sir, unofficially . . .

BRIGADIER. I cannot give you an unofficial answer until nine o'clock, when I shall be off duty . . .

JACOBOWSKY (*looks at his watch*). Three to nine. What I was going to ask was . . . Officer, I have an irresistible compulsion to leave the soil of France. How should I go about it?

BRIGADIER. For the purpose of leaving France you require a visa de sortie. For this purpose you must apply to the nearest Sous-Préfecture, at Sable d'Olonne, for such a visa de sortie, first executing three questionnaires, each with one photograph, profile, showing right ear, and paying a fee of twenty-seven francs, seventy-five centimes. The Sous-Préfecture will communicate with the Préfecture of your basic place of residence, Paris, and will, by extended correspondence, compile a dossier of your case, which, after a few weeks, will be submitted to the Ministry of the Interior for further action. (*They consult their watches*) The Ministry of the Interior instructs a special commission to investigate whether you were worthy to set foot on French soil, and whether you are worthy to leave it. That takes a certain amount of time, but goes through with the greatest smoothness. There is, however, difficulty in your case. You must first return to Paris, and await your safe-conduct pass, permitting you to come here. Is that clear?

JACOBOWSKY. Crystal!

BRIGADIER. Monsieur is very intelligent. However, I must frankly tell you that even if you fulfill all the requirements I have just enumerated, your prospects are nil. After all, what consideration can you expect from a government which you have caused so much clerical work?

You'd better come along with me right now.

JACOBOWSKY *(look at watch)*. Nine o'clock!

BRIGADIER *(greatly relieved)*. Nine? Good—then I'm off duty. *(He and Jacobowsky both sit on bench, quite relaxed)* Now I can talk to you unofficially.

JACOBOWSKY. What would you do if you were me?

BRIGADIER. You want to go down the coast to Bayonne and beyond. Right?

JACOBOWSKY. Right.

BRIGADIER. Keep away from the shore roads to begin with. They are advancing fast along the coast.

JACOBOWSKY. Thank you very much, but I am unable to follow your counsel.

BRIGADIER. Why?

JACOBOWSKY. I have no gasoline—not a drop.

(Marianne comes in. She has two baskets containing Coco and Mignon. She is surprised to see the Brigadier.)

BRIGADIER. That's a pity.

JACOBOWSKY. Could you help me? Is there . . .?

BRIDAGIER *(sees Marianne, rises)*. Good evening, Ma'm'selle Roualet.

MARIANNE. Oh, good evening. Monsieur Jacobowsky—would you help me?

JACOBOWSKY *(goes to her, takes baskets)*. You remember my name?

MARIANNE. Why shouldn't I?

JACOBOWSKY. Some people have difficulty . . .

MARIANNE. Will you please—Coco and Mignon—they hate leaving home as much as I do.

JACOBOWSKY. I'll make them comfortable. I love animals. They accept you without reservation. *(He puts the baskets carefully in the back of the car)*

MARIANNE *(to Brigadier)*. This gentleman is taking us off in his car.

BRIGADIER *(to Jacobowsky)*. Why didn't you tell me?

MARIANNE. And a noble Polish officer —who will return one day to fight for France. Do you think it dreadful of me to leave?

BRIGADIER *(warmly)*. No, it is good you are going.

JACOBOWSKY *(calls across to the Brigadier, urgently)*. Gasoline—gasoline.

BRIGADIER *(stamping document)*. Take this stamped document. My colleague in Saint-Cyrille will furnish you with thirty gallons at the standard price. *(He hand him the stamped paper. Jacobowsky takes it)*

JACOBOWSKY *(moved)*. My friend. My dear friend. How is it possible to thank a man like you?

BRIGADIER *(gets back on his bicycle Crisply)*. Carry the greetings of Brigadier Jouet to England and to America.

JACOBOWSKY *(fervently)*. I shall. I shall

BRIGADIER *(to Marianne)*. Ma'm'selle Roualet, I bless you. I bless your journey I bless your mission.

JACOBOWSKY AND MARIANNE *(simul taneously)*. Amen.

BRIGADIER. If I were younger, I would go with you. But all I can do is put stamps on papers. Monsieur, I am happy to have given you what may be my las stamp for France. *(He pedals off into th dark)*

JACOBOWSKY *(overcome)*. You are goo fortune, Mademoiselle. You are mercy You are hope!

MARIANNE. If I thought I would not se these fields again . . .

JACOBOWSKY. You will see them.

MARIANNE *(torn)*. My poor country

JACOBOWSKY. It will be reborn. Ther will be a new France, a new world— because the old one is sick of its ow ineptitude.

MARIANNE. You are a comfort, Mo sieur.

JACOBOWSKY. You make me wish f youth that I might return and fight to

MARIANNE. Thank you, Monsieur.

JACOBOWSKY *(involuntarily)*. I sh dedicate myself to you.

MARIANNE *(rather amused)*. Thank yo Monsieur.

JACOBOWSKY. And to Coco and Mignon. Have you any other pets?

MARIANNE. Only the Colonel.

JACOBOWSKY. To him I am alrea dedicated.

MARIANNE *(laughing out loud)*. am I.

(Jacobowsky joins in her laughter. The Colo comes in carrying a little hatbox. He is s

*rised at the rapport there seems to have sprung
up between Marianne and Jacobowsky.)*

COLONEL. What you laughing at?

MARIANNE. Nothing.

COLONEL *(to Jacobowsky).* Why do *you*
laugh?

JACOBOWSKY. For no reason.

COLONEL. You get gasoline?

JACOBOWSKY *(softly).* Gasoline came
to us.

COLONEL. What does he talk—us?

JACOBOWSKY. A warm rain came down
from heaven and behold—it was gasoline.

MARIANNE *(sharing his mood).* Pipeline
from the sky!
(They both laugh again.)

COLONEL. Now what do you laugh at?

JACOBOWSKY. Nothing.

MARIANNE. Nothing.

*The Colonel is irritated by their evident
sympathy. This irritation breaks out into complaint as Szabuniewicz, loaded with Marianne's bundles, staggers in.)*

COLONEL. Marianne, is not possible
take all this stuff.

JACOBOWSKY. Why not?

COLONEL. Because is no room.

JACOBOWSKY. Room is elastic. Room
can be made to expand.

COLONEL *(to Szabuniewicz).* Less and
less I like this Jacobowsky!

SZABUNIEWICZ *(echoes).* Less and less.
*(He lifts large bag and is about to throw it
into the car)*

MARIANNE *(concerned for her pets).*
Mignon—Coco . . .

JACOBOWSKY *(goes over, puts bag in carefully).* They're in a safe place.

COLONEL *(bursts out).* Not to worry,
Marianne. Everyone safe. Dogs safe. You
safe. Szabuniewicz safe. I safe. All protect
by Monsieur Jacobowsky.

JACOBOWSKY. I do not undertake quite
so much, Colonel. Only these little
dogs—for them I am Goliath—a minia-
ture Goliath.

Marianne laughs).

COLONEL. What you laugh at?

MARIANNE. I don't know. He makes
me laugh. Why are you so bad-tempered?
*Szabuniewicz has already started packing
boxes in the car.)*

COLONEL *(roars).* Marianne, cannot
take all those packages!

SZABUNIEWICZ *(lifting hatbox).* He
travels light.

JACOBOWSKY. Plenty of room.

MARIANNE. Perhaps we can leave behind one bandbox.

JACOBOWSKY. I wouldn't hear of it.
*(He takes hatbox from Szabuniewicz and puts
it in car)*

COLONEL *(roars at him).* Who you not
to hear of anything?

JACOBOWSKY *(to Colonel).* Let me
explain, Colonel. You are great man but
as a refugee I am more experienced. Let
me tell you—nothing is so warming to
morale in difficult hours as to have a few
precious, familiar knickknacks with you.
It restores your identity—gives you a link
with the past, a bridge to what you were.
It's important, believe me, it's important,
and especially for a lady.

MARIANNE *(drawn to him).* You are *so*
understanding, Monsieur Jacobowsky.
*(The Colonel towers above them while Mari-
anne and Jacobowsky talk to each other.)*

JACOBOWSKY *(to Marianne under the
shadow of this tower).* It's experience,
Mademoiselle, simple experience.
(They both laugh again.)

COLONEL *(walks between them in a rage).*
All right! Take whole damn business,
only let's go. You make of this car a
furniture truck.

MARIANNE. We'll compromise. I'll
give up this hatbox.
(Szabuniewicz picks up the tiny hatbox.)

COLONEL *(sarcastic).* This will be great
help!

SZABUNIEWICZ *(seized with a bright idea,
whispers to Colonel).* Colonel, sew papers
in little hat.

COLONEL *(assimilating the idea slowly).*
What you say?

SZABUNIEWICZ. Hide documents in
little hat.

COLONEL *(straightens up. Announces
pridefully—any idea Szabuniewicz might have
belongs to him automatically).* Attention!
I have important idea! We take this
bandbox, Marianne. In your little hat you
sew my documents. Germans will never
look there for them. *(He is very owlish
about this)*

JACOBOWSKY. It is an inspiration!

MARIANNE *(bubbling)*. And it will make me feel so important.

COLONEL. Now at last we go! Marianne, the back seat. *(He gets in and sits at the wheel)* Szabuniewicz—beside me. *(Szabuniewicz complies.)*

MARIANNE *(barely fitting into a pile of luggage in the back seat, looks around to Jacobowsky)*. It's so crowded here. Where will you sit?

JACOBOWSKY *(darting forward)*. With great happiness at your feet. *(He gets in the back of the car, sitting on the floor at Marianne's feet, his own on the running board)*

COLONEL *(turning from the wheel)*. Szabuniewicz—change places with him.

MARIANNE *(as Szabuniewicz starts to comply; pats Jacobowsky)*. No. I like him here. He comforts me.

COLONEL *(to Szabuniewicz)*. Less and less I like this Jacobowsky.

SZABUNIEWICZ *(echoes)*. Less and less.

MARIANNE *(consoling Jacobowsky)*. Never mind! *(She smiles down at the ravished Jacobowsky, who looks up at her adoringly. Szabuniewicz bangs the front door. The fretting vehicle moves off)*

CURTAIN

SCENE TWO

SCENE: *An open spot in the woods near the city of Bayonne. An overcast summer day. In the background on the highway, somewhat elevated, stands Jacobowsky's car even more battered than before. In the middle distance a little stream winds through at which passing refugees stop to drink.*

AT RISE: *In the foreground on a little slope at the right Marianne sits on a small trunk at the foot of an immense haystack. At her feet is the Colonel's civilian coat, quite tattered. The Colonel is wearing civvies, corduroy trousers and an old shirt. It is the first time we have seen him without his uniform. Without it he is depressed. In these shabby misfits he feels himself deprived of his identity. He is moodily fighting melancholia.*

When the curtain goes up, Marianne has just finished sewing the Colonel's papers in her little hat. She holds up the hat, pleased at her own handiwork.

MARIANNE. There—I've sewn your precious papers in my hat. Who would ever think that in this frivolous little hat are the names of the future saviors of Poland? *(She puts the hat in the hatbox)* And now, I'll finish your poor coat! *(She picks up his coat and sews)*

COLONEL. Without my uniform—I feel like not a man!

MARIANNE *(gently, humoring him)*. Were you never without a uniform before?

COLONEL. Never!

MARIANNE. You weren't born in a uniform, were you?

COLONEL *(automatically)*. Yes. *(Amending his statement)* My father cavalry officer. My grandfather cavalry officer! We Stjerbinskys always in uniform.

MARIANNE. Even when you were a little boy?

COLONEL. When I am little boy I dress up! Always in my dreams I am in uniform.

MARIANNE *(with a look at the ragged coat)*. Well, this is a kind of uniform too, isn't it?

COLONEL. These filthy rags?

MARIANNE. There is a time to advance and a time to retreat . . .

COLONEL. That sounds like Monsieur Jacobowsky.

MARIANNE. What you are wearing now is the uniform of retreat.

COLONEL. Please, I beg you not to quote to me Monsieur Jacobowsky.

MARIANNE. Why not?

COLONEL. Because, if I have to govern myself with his mentality, I rather die.

MARIANNE. Monsieur Jacobowsky say it is easy to die. But to live require ingenuity . . . This uniform is part of the ingenuity. *(Patting the mended shoulder)* There! I have just sewed on your epaulettes! Look at this hole—sword thrust! This missing button—a sharpshooter! This lapel—what a fierce hand-to-hand encounter that was! Darling, for this uniform you could dream the most heroic exploits. In so many ways you are still little boy. Go on dreaming!

COLONEL. I cannot dream myself here in costume like this.

MARIANNE. We used to have a picture in our bedroom when I was a little girl—the Grande Armée returning through the snows of Russia. They were in rags, poor things. I used to shiver for them. Compared to what they wore this battle-scarred coat *(She holds up the poor garment)* is quite grand. In your uniform you were a symbol, darling. Wonderful, but a symbol. But in this you are a human being. I'm glad for once to have seen you in it. I love you in it.

COLONEL. This also sounds like Monsieur Jacobowsky.

MARIANNE. It's not very flattering of you to assume that I am an echo of Monsieur Jacobowsky. Am I so stupid?

COLONEL. When first I know you you do not talk like this.

MARIANNE. When I first knew you, it was so close and thrilling that, as I recall it, we didn't talk at all. There was no time between kisses.

COLONEL *(bitterly)*. But now there is plenty of time!

MARIANNE. Yes. The roads are so crowded—the waits so long, for meals, for a place to sleep, for a drop of gasoline.

COLONEL. And this time mainly you use to talk to Monsieur Jacobowsky!

MARIANNE. Yes. It passes the time.

COLONEL *(tensely)*. What you talk about?

MARIANNE. All sorts of things.

COLONEL. Sometimes I come upon you, you stop talking. Sudden you stop.

MARIANNE. Do we?

COLONEL. Why you stop?

MARIANNE. I don't know. I suppose because Monsieur Jacobowsky is afraid you won't be sympathetic or interested.

COLONEL. I don't ask why he stop—I ask why *you* stop.

MARIANNE. Do I?

COLONEL. Yes—you stop.

MARIANNE *(facing it)*. I suppose I must feel the same as Monsieur Jacobowsky feels—that you won't be sympathetic or interested.

COLONEL *(the damning evidence is now in his possession. He draws himself up accusingly)*. This is how I suspect. You no longer feel like me. You feel like Monsieur Jacobowsky.

MARIANNE. Isn't it possible to feel like you both?

COLONEL. No. Never. Impossible.

MARIANNE *(laughs)*. Darling!

COLONEL. You laugh at me.

MARIANNE. A little. In this hard journey—do you grudge me a little laugh?

COLONEL. But not at me. To this I am not used.

MARIANNE. All right, Tadeusz. If it will make you feel better, I will not laugh any more. There! *(The coat is finished. He puts it on. It hangs on him clumsily. She does her best to make it fit)* Shoulder better?

COLONEL. Shoulder better. Heart wounded!

MARIANNE. Poor heart. Poor heart. I'll mend that too.

COLONEL *(tragic)*. You don't mend. You break.

MARIANNE. Darling, because you catch me talking nonsense with poor little Monsieur Jacobowsky!

COLONEL *(fixed idea)*. If nonsense, then why you stop when I come?

MARIANNE. Perhaps it's because you're a hero. Too epic for nonsense.

COLONEL. This also sounds like Monsieur Jacobowsky.

MARIANNE *(with self-revelation, with surprise)*. Yes, it does! It's just like him!

COLONEL. He loves you, this Monsieur Jacobowsky.

MARIANNE *(walks to brook and sits down beside it)*. Ridiculous! What an idea! Do you think so? Perhaps he does—a little bit. Oh! It's touching.

COLONEL. You love him too.

MARIANNE. Now, Tadeusz, don't be silly.

COLONEL. Then what you see in him? Why you like him?

MARIANNE *(exploring her own mind)*. Why I like him?

COLONEL. You like him better than me!

MARIANNE *(scrupulously honest)*. In one way perhaps.

COLONEL *(triumphant)*. Ah, you admit! Why? Why?

MARIANNE *(resolute)*. I will tell you why. He makes me more—you make me less.

COLONEL *(scientifically)*. I think it necessary I kill this Monsieur Jacobowsky. I fight him.

MARIANNE. You're so absent-minded. You forget it's the Germans you're fighting. *(She wanders back to the trunk at the foot of the haystack and sits)*

COLONEL. Then what you want I do with him? Engage in arguments with him?

MARIANNE. Why not? Good for you.

COLONEL. I do not argue with people like Jacobowsky over the woman I love.

MARIANNE *(teasing him)*. Oh, it doesn't have to be about me. You can argue with him over all sorts of subjects—abstract subjects.

COLONEL. You make fun of me. This I do not tolerate.

MARIANNE. What shall I do with you!

COLONEL. Never did I believe that I, Stjerbinsky, would wear costume like this and have for rival S. L. Jacobowsky.

MARIANNE *(with gusto)*. Both good for you!

COLONEL. Ah! You admit!

MARIANNE. Admit what?

COLONEL. He *is* my rival.

MARIANNE. Not so much your rival, darling, as . .

COLONEL. As what?

MARIANNE. Your antidote! *(A silence)* The odd thing is, darling, Monsieur Jacobowsky adores you. *(She goes to Colonel, trying to win sympathy for Jacobowsky, pleading with him, but the Colonel's expression is impassive)* He's constantly telling me how wonderful you are. *(She keeps stealing glances at him but so far no change)* He envies you. He wants you to love him. He wants the whole world to love him.

COLONEL *(with satisfaction)*. In this he will never succeed.

MARIANNE. He knows that. Don't you find it touching? How cheerful he is. How gentle he is. Don't you find it—appealing? He wants so to be loved. I find it very—very . . .

COLONEL. Obviously you do!

MARIANNE. What shall I do then? Not speak to him? Ignore him? It's his car, after all. We're his guests.

COLONEL. Polish Government pay him in full—with profit.

MARIANNE. Then we're all guests of the Polish Government. Shall I be rude to a fellow guest?

(The Colonel looks at her. He decides on a new attack.)

COLONEL *(he sidles over to her, tries to be light and gay)*. Marianne?

MARIANNE. Yes, my dear.

COLONEL. You and I—why we don't talk about trivial things? Why we don't laugh together?

MARIANNE *(moved, but with a gleam. He sits beside her on the trunk)*. I'm willing.

COLONEL *(casting about for a delightful subject—finally)*. Do you know something about ballistics?

MARIANNE. Very little, but I'd love to learn.

COLONEL. You know, is very interesting science, ballistics. The trajectory of a cannon ball is a beautiful thing. My father used to draw me pictures when I am a boy of the trajectory the cannon balls make through space. He drew with different colored chalks. Like a rainbow they looked.

MARIANNE *(solemnly appreciative)*. It must have been beautiful.

COLONEL *(dejected)*. No good!

MARIANNE *(looks up at him)* What?

COLONEL. This subject, ballistics, not trivial enough.

MARIANNE. Let's try something else. *(Pause.)*

COLONEL. My great-great-great-grandmother when Napoleon came to Poland danced with him in Grand Ball in Warsaw.

MARIANNE. Was she beautiful?

COLONEL. Very beautiful. She danced with Napoleon!

MARIANNE. That's very interesting.

COLONEL. It's history. *(Pause.)*

MARIANNE. Have you her picture?

COLONEL *(wandering—he has a sense of defeat)*. Whose picture?

MARIANNE. Your grandmother's.

COLONEL. Oh, yes. In my home in Poland—but that home probably now destroyed by the Germans.

MARIANNE *(sadly)*. Like all our homes

COLONEL. Damn to hell. This subject is too tragic. It does not make you laugh like Monsieur Jacobowsky.

MARIANNE. Oh, darling, don't try to be like Monsieur Jacobowsky. You have your style—he has his. I love you both

COLONEL *(smarting with a sense of defe*

and snapping back to his own identity, rises).
My course is clear. We fight.

MARIANNE. Oh, my God!

COLONEL. No way out. We fight.

MARIANNE *(worried, rises).* Have you no other way of coping with a situation than to fight?

COLONEL. For a man of honor is no other way.

MARIANNE. I wish, in addition to being a man of honor . . .

COLONEL *(sharp).* Is not enough for you?

MARIANNE. I wish you had a little humor.

COLONEL. When I love I do not laugh.

MARIANNE. We French do. We manage both very well. Please, Tadeusz, be a darling and get off your high horse. Shake out of the stiff corset of your code. Relax a bit and admit the human race.

COLONEL *(worked up more and more).* This idea you also get from Jacobowsky!

MARIANNE *(furious, stamps her foot).* Don't keep saying that! I knew the alphabet before I met you *or* Monsieur Jacobowsky. You don't know me at all. What makes you think you know anything about me?

COLONEL. I realize now this ignorance. Monsieur Jacobowsky—he make me realize.

MARIANNE. Then you should be grateful to him.

COLONEL. I am. I will show my gratitude by allowing him to engage me on the field of honor.

MARIANNE. The field of honor! It's quite true—you're a medieval man, Tadeusz. *(Colonel opens his mouth for the refrain but she beats him to it, shouting)* Yes, that idea I got from Monsieur Jacobowsky! *(They glare at each other, openly hostile)* *(Szabuniewicz limps on dejectedly. He has been walking for quite a while. He leans against the haystack, exhausted, taking off his shoes meanwhile.)*

SZABUNIEWICZ. Is no food—nothing!

COLONEL *(working off his anger on Szabuniewicz, shouts at him).* I promise Madame you bring to eat, you!

SZABUNIEWICZ. In Bayonne city not even room to walk! All streets is full opp wid autos, wid no gasoline, like us. All hotel and café full opp. And the prices! The shops is wiped clean.—

(Some refugees drift by, loaded with bags and bundles. The Old Man and the Little Boy we have seen before stop at the brook. The Old Man fills a cup and gives the Little Boy a drink.)

MARIANNE. I'm so hungry! Well, so is all France. *(Watching the refugees as they walk down the road)* Where are they going? They walk, but where do they go?

COLONEL *(to Szabuniewicz).* Where is this Jacobowsky? You go forage with him. Where is he?

SZABUNIEWICZ. I look around—he is gone. *(Cocking one eye at the sky)* Soon it rain. My corn fall off with walking. I go in car and sleep.

COLONEL. You only good to sleep, you!

SZABUNIEWICZ. Good we all sleep! Dream we eat maybe! *(He waddles off toward the car, curls up on back seat and goes to sleep)*

(Between the Colonel and Marianne a moody pause. It is a bad moment. The Colonel sits on the trunk.)

COLONEL *(out of his despair).* Anything I endure but that you do not love me. This I cannot.

MARIANNE *(goes and kneels by Colonel).* Oh, I do love you, Tadeusz. It is only for you and with you that I would leave France for even one hour.

COLONEL *(straightens up).* Then I am able for anything. *(He kisses her)* My melancholy vanish like mist before the sun. *(He gets up, lifting her up with him)*

MARIANNE. There's no reason in the world for you to be sad. Be happy. Be happy in my love. *(She embraces him)*

COLONEL *(beams at her).* I struggle for you. I fight for you. I move mountains for you.

MARIANNE. And will you also be good to poor Monsieur Jacobowsky for me?

COLONEL *(his hands clench).* For you—yes.

MARIANNE. You give up this silly notion of fighting him?

COLONEL. For you—yes.

MARIANNE. That's my dear boy. *(She embraces and kisses Colonel)*

JACOBOWSKY *(breezes in; he is very gay)*. Hello!

COLONEL *(annoyed that the moment of his reconciliation should be broken into)*. Is here possible no privacy?

JACOBOWSKY *(he is lugging a bulging straw shopping bag. He is beaming)*. I met my brother-in-law's cousin! Would you think it—in Bayonne!

MARIANNE *(to Colonel, smiling)*. His family connections are something fabulous!

JACOBOWSKY. He used to be a conductor of the Gewandhaus Orchestra in Leipzig. Now he's a headwaiter in the leading café in Bayonne. He introduced me to the proprietor—and the proprietor —for a price—let me have some very interesting commodities. *(Shows bag)*

MARIANNE *(ecstatic)*. Food!

COLONEL *(resentful at Jacobowsky's success)*. You got something to eat?

JACOBOWSKY. Special. Very special. *(He holds up a chop)* For Coco!

MARIANNE. You remembered Coco!

JACOBOWSKY. As you love Coco—I love Coco. *(Gives her the chop)*

COLONEL. You have large heart it seems!

JACOBOWSKY. Now, Colonel, will you spread out that shawl and we will create the atmosphere of a picnic? *(Muttering to himself, the Colonel picks up a rolled rug that is lying in the grass and gives it to Marianne. She spreads it out. Jacobowsky throws down his hat and overcoat, inadvertently throwing his coat over Marianne's hatbox. Marianne sits on the shawl, Jacobowsky on the trunk, taking packages out of bag)* Just as I was walking out of the café after being told there was nothing, there he was—my brother-in-law's cousin. He fell on my neck and I fell on his. At home I never liked him. I hated his conducting. I once said: "He doesn't understand Mozart—no more than a headwaiter," and look, now he *is* a headwaiter!

MARIANNE *(gaily)*. Tadeusz, give Coco her little chop, will you?

(The Colonel, struggling to control himself, obeys. He takes the chop from her gingerly and goes back with it to the car. Jacobowsky keeps handing edibles to Marianne, who spreads them on the blanket.)

JACOBOWSKY *(as he puts them down one by one, he apostrophizes the delicacies)*. These, my dear Sigismund—that's my brother-in-law's cousin—this loaf of bread fresh from the oven—erases the memory of your *Don Giovanni* which you played like a pig.

(By this time the Colonel has reached the car and waked up Szabuniewicz.)

SZABUNIEWICZ *(grunting)*. What for you don't let me sleep?

COLONEL. I don't sleep, you don't sleep.

SZABUNIEWICZ. Go way, let me sleep.

JACOBOWSKY *(picking up pastry box)*. And these crisp brioches—your *Figaro*— which was even worse. Ah, Marianne, the God of War transmutes a bad conductor into a perfect headwaiter. Mars has a knack for vocational guidance.

(Marianne laughs.)

MARIANNE. And you, Monsieur Jacobowsky, what has Mars done for you?

JACOBOWSKY. He introduced me to you. Without him I should never have known you.

MARIANNE. That's a high price!

JACOBOWSKY. It's a bargain counter. I'd rather be in France escaping with you than getting a big welcome-home reception anywhere else.

(They become aware that the Colonel has returned and is lowering over them. They freeze up suddenly.)

MARIANNE. Oh, but . . .

COLONEL. Why do you stop talking?

MARIANNE. We don't.

COLONEL. You do. What were you saying, Monsieur Jacobowsky?

JACOBOWSKY *(blushing a little)*. I don't remember.

COLONEL *(menacing)*. You don't remember!

JACOBOWSKY. It was nothing at all.

COLONEL *(to Marianne)*. Marianne, what was he saying?

MARIANNE. It was nothing at all.

COLONEL. If it nothing at all why you don't go on saying nothing at all?

JACOBOWSKY. Before a man like you, savior of countries, we can't be trivial.

COLONEL. This explanation is not satisfactory. *(He confronts him, menacing)*

MARIANNE *(scared)*. Tadeusz!

JACOBOWSKY *(taking bottle from bag)*. Oh! I suppose you thought, Colonel, that I had forgotten you. Not at all. I thought you'd like this fine cognac . . . *(Presents him with a bottle of cognac)*

COLONEL *(looking at it)*. 1912—bad year. *(Gives Jacobowsky the bottle)* *(Szabuniewicz rouses himself and gets out of car.)*

JACOBOWSKY *(takes bottle back)*. A bad year but a good bottle. Sisgimund tried it. *(Smiles)* May I pour for you? *(He is about to pour the brandy into a paper cup when the Colonel stops him)*

COLONEL *(growling)*. Not from paper cup. Szabuniewicz, my silver cup. *(Takes bottle; to Jacobowsky)* You drink from paper cup. All right for you!

JACOBOWSKY. Today I'm drinking water . . . *(He goes to the brook)*

MARIANNE. Some water for me, too, please. I'm thirsty . . .
(Jacobowsky brings Marianne a drink of water.)

SZABUNIEWICZ *(gives silver cup to Colonel; sees the banquet)*. Who give eat? *(He makes for the food)*

JACOBOWSKY. Help yourself, my friend.

MARIANNE. I'll make a sandwich for you, Tadeusz . . .

COLONEL *(drinking)*. I not have hunger . . .

SZABUNIEWICZ *(picking up dried fish)*. Women and fish best in the middle.

COLONEL *(kicks him)*. Szabuniewicz, not to be impertinent. Don't forget your place.

SZABUNIEWICZ *(in full mutiny)*. When you not in uniform I man like you and I make jokes like anybody else—huh! *(He backs away before the menacing Colonel and sits on a little embankment upstage, eating hard-boiled eggs)*

COLONEL *(swallowing more cognac)*. Marianne, I apologize for this lout.

JACOBOWSKY. Don't drink too much, Colonel. Please.

COLONEL *(indignant)*. Who you to speak to me this way?

JACOBOWSKY. If you put out the candle, Chauffeur, we'll all be in the dark.

COLONEL *(swallows again)*. You got gasoline in pocket too?

JACOBOWSKY. I'm working on the problem.

COLONEL. Polish Government now owe you six hundred thousand francs. Double or nothing you not get gasoline today!

JACOBOWSKY *(trying to conciliate him with food)*. Try one of these hard-boiled eggs, my friend.

COLONEL *(his suppressed anger mounting)*. Jacobowsky, I resent you drink water.

JACOBOWSKY. Is that all about me you resent?

COLONEL. No!

MARIANNE. Tadeusz, please stop this!

COLONEL. Stop what . . . ?

MARIANNE. You owe Monsieur an apology!

COLONEL. I owe him!

MARIANNE. Yes, you do. I don't want any more nonsense about Monsieur Jacobowsky. Many women I am telling you would be very lucky to get him—especially in times like these!

COLONEL *(drawing himself up full)*. Very well. This so desirable gentleman—I challenge you!

JACOBOWSKY *(startled)*. Challenge!

COLONEL. Yes!

JACOBOWSKY. To what?

COLONEL. To a duel. To fight.

JACOBOWSKY. What for? *(Instinctively he draws to Marianne and she to him. He takes her hand in his)*

COLONEL *(enraged)*. Szabuniewicz—the pistols. *(To Jacobowsky)* Take your hand away from her!

MARIANNE *(holding onto Jacobowsky's hand)*. Not while you threaten!

COLONEL *(to Jacobowsky)*. Seducer by sobriety! Other men I can out-drink, out-fight—what I do with you?

JACOBOWSKY. Marianne, I should go away.

MARIANNE *(stamps her foot)*. I won't have this—you hear—I won't have it!

JACOBOWSKY. I have felt it coming. We must part.

COLONEL. No. We do not part. *(He drinks more cognac)*

JACOBOWSKY. He doesn't want me to stay—he doesn't want me to go!

SZABUNIEWICZ. It is the cognac.

Colonel always melancholy when he drink!

COLONEL (*storms*). Silence!
(*The outburst is so tremendous that Szabuniewicz chokes over his egg.*)

SZABUNIEWICZ (*still choking*). Swallop opp whole egg!

MARIANNE. Tadeusz, what's the matter?

COLONEL. Cognac make a man to see more clear. Jacobowsky, you afraid of me?

JACOBOWSKY. Yes. (*Turns to Marianne*) I heard in Bayonne the armistice has been signed in Wiesbaden. The Germans are going to occupy most of France. We have to think of gasoline, how to get to the coast. (*He sits on the trunk*)

COLONEL. Why do you fear me?

MARIANNE (*really frightened now*). Tadeusz, what's come over you?

(*Marianne stares at the Colonel hypnotized. Jacobowsky keeps looking from one to the other of these two suddenly strange people.*)

COLONEL (*in a spasm of self revelation*). He say, this Jacobowsky, he is afraid of me. I tell you truth—I am afraid of him.

JACOBOWSKY (*murmurs*). Thank you for the compliment!

COLONEL (*whirls on him*). Yes. I, Stjerbinsky, who have fought the Nzais on the Pruth and on the Somme and on the Vistula, I who have never known fear —now I know fear. I'm afraid of you, Jacobowsky. I am afraid of the thoughts you have that you make her share, the laughter that dries up when I approach. I am afraid of the silence you make between me and Marianne. Talk against you I cannot. But fight you I can. Fight you I must. To prove to myself that I do not fear, I fight. Because if I fear, I die.

JACOBOWSKY. But to prove this to yourself probably I'll have to die.

COLONEL. Perhaps you kill me, why not?

JACOBOWSKY. Why not? Then who will drive the car?

COLONEL (*shouts*). You are too practical.

JACOBOWSKY (*to Marianne*). Too practical! That's the trouble, Marianne, he is a fifteenth-century man but, unfortunately, I live in the twentieth.

COLONEL (*growls*). Twentieth century I do not like.

JACOBOWSKY. I don't like it either, but what can we do about it?

COLONEL. In twentieth century no poetry, no heroism, no honor. Twentieth century full with fleas and disinfectant, disinfectant and fleas. Everything sanitary, sterilized! Small rooms, good cheap manufacture, mouthwash, chromium fixture, umbrellas and those stuff! Everything in this damn century got to have sense! But where is style? Who gives elegance? These things I see no more! What is modern is small. You are small man, Jacobowsky. By fighting you I give you stature. What Nazis take away from you, I, Stjerbinsky, give you back—honor!

(*Jacobowsky rises.*)

MARIANNE. Tadeusz, you're crazy.

SZABUNIEWICZ (*murmurs*). She's right, Colonel.

COLONEL (*turns on him. Grabs him by collar*). I am your superior officer. When war is over and Poland triumphant— court-martial you!

SZABUNIEWICZ (*terrified*). Forgive me! Forgive me.

COLONEL. I forgive, but I do not forget. Get the pistols! (*Szabuniewicz goes to car, gets pistols. Colonel confronts Jacobowsky*) Jacobowsky, between us stands woman, Marianne—please go to the car. (*She stands silent, held as if in a spell*)

JACOBOWSKY (*with sudden determination —suddenly carried away*). And what if I kill you! Why not? In my veins flows the blood of great fighters—David, Saul . . And the truth is—yes—the truth is you are right, Colonel. I do love her! I am in love with her. I am happy to say the words for once. I am happy to hear the words for once. I love her! I love her! I love her! Pistols! (*He takes pistol from Szabuniewicz. To Marianne*) Marianne, will you forgive me if I kill him? (*Deflated suddenly, back to grim reality*) I still couldn't drive the car.

MARIANNE (*her thoughts expressing themselves aloud*). In the middle of the great war—this little war. What hope? (*Szabuniewicz helps Colonel take off his coat. The Colonel rolls up his sleeves, preparing for the fight.*)

JACOBOWSKY. Before we begin—Szabuniewicz is your second—who is mine?

MARIANNE *(involuntarily)*. I am!

JACOBOWSKY *(with a keen look at her, tapping the pistol to indicate his stratagem)*. Then I must survive! *(He motions Marianne to get in front of him. She does so. Behind her back, he empties the gun of its bullets. The Colonel's back is to them. Szabuniewicz is helping him to a drink)*

COLONEL *(giving instructions to Szabuniewicz)*. Szabuniewicz, you stand there. Count ten. We take ten paces away from each other. Give me another drink. *(Szabuniewicz complies.)*

JACOBOWSKY *(delicately)*. Colonel—don't drink so much. I don't want to fight you when you are not at your best. You're drunk, my friend.

COLONEL *(contemptuous)*. Drunk? One bottle? Water-drinker! *(Tosses empty cup to Szabuniewicz)*

JACOBOWSKY. Before we begin—one technicality—one little technicality.

COLONEL. What is this technicality?

JACOBOWSKY. In my knowledge of dueling—gained mainly from reading novels by Schnitzler—I have the impression that the man who is challenged, the challengee, has the choice of weapons. Correct?

COLONEL. Correct.

JACOBOWSKY. Then I pick swords.

COLONEL. Swords!

JACOBOWSKY. Swords. Sabres. Cutlasses. Anything you like.

COLONEL *(leans paternally on Jacobowsky's shoulder)*. My good man, I am the best swordsman in Poland. With swords I cut you to pieces. With pistols you have a chance.

JACOBOWSKY *(weighing his gun critically)*. I don't like this gun—it doesn't suit me.

COLONEL. Exactly same as mine.

JACOBOWSKY. Let me see. *(Jacobowsky takes the Colonel's gun, fingers it, weighs it. His face lights up)*. Ah! Much better! With this gun I feel I could work wonders!

COLONEL. Take him.

Jacobowsky gives Colonel the gun that he has emptied and then goes back to Marianne. The Colonel permits Szabuniewicz to pour him another drink.)

MARIANNE *(shielding Jacobowsky to give him a chance to repeat operation of emptying gun)*. I won't let you fight. I'll stand between you if you fight. Your bullets will pass through me.

(Szabuniewicz goes up center and stands commandingly, ready to umpire the duel.)

JACOBOWSKY *(to Marianne with bravura audacity)*. Marianne! Stand aside! *(He confronts the Colonel)* Colonel—prepare to meet your Maker. May God have mercy on your soul! *(They turn back to back)*

COLONEL. Ten paces.

JACOBOWSKY *(fiercely)*. Five paces!

COLONEL. Five paces. Szabuniewicz!

SZABUNIEWICZ. Ready—Gentlemen.

COLONEL. Ready.

SZABUNIEWICZ *(counts)*. One—two—three—four . . .

(So intent are they on the combat that before they know it the Germans are upon them: A German patrol has appeared on the highway. It is led by a First Lieutenant, accompanied by a Gestapo Man, who has not yet found time during the lightning advance of the Nazis to change his tourist's garb for a uniform. He wears a green hat with shaving-brush, anklets, Tyrolean socks, shorts, bright yellow jacket. He lisps. The Lieutenant approaches the group of fugitives, the Gestapo Man behind him.)

GESTAPO MAN *(with his lisp)*. Interething thpectacle. *(To soldier)* Ditharm them. *(The two soldiers collect the guns)* Highly interethting.

(Between the Lieutenant and the Gestapo Man is the blistering antagonism that the Regular Army feels for the interfering "psychological experts" who have become the Fuehrer's pets.)

LIEUTENANT *(short)*. What's this duel about? *(Jacobowsky looks from one to the other of the Germans and is inspired suddenly with a desperate improvisation. In dumbshow he points to the Colonel, and makes a gesture to his forehead indicating that the Colonel is crazy)* What?

JACOBOWSKY *(tapping his forehead)*. An obsession, sir.

GESTAPO MAN. Obthethion? What thort of obthethion?

JACOBOWSKY. May I explain?

LIEUTENANT *(pointing his gun at Jacobowsky)*. You'd better.

JACOBOWSKY. This poor man . . . *(He points to Colonel)*

LIEUTENANT. Yes? *(As Jacobowsky taps his forehead)* What's he doing at large?

JACOBOWSKY. You Germans freed him.

LIEUTENANT. What?

JACOBOWSKY. When your planes bombed the insane asylum at Nantes—by accident of course—Madame Deloupe here *(indicates Marianne)* with the help of this expert *(points to Szabuniewicz)* was able to find her poor husband half-buried in a swamp.

GESTAPO MAN *(morbid—turns to Colonel)*. What is your obthethion?

JACOBOWSKY. He can't speak. He believes that every man—in this instance me—has betrayed him with his wife. He insists on dueling. In the last four days, he has killed me six times. It's the only way to get him back to the insane asylum. The guns are empty as you can see.

(The Germans open guns. Gestapo Man looks in one, the Lieutenant in the other.)

GESTAPO MAN. Thith could only happen in Franth. Typically Frenth!

LIEUTENANT. Am I dealing with French citizens?

MARIANNE *(stepping forward)*. I am.

GESTAPO MAN *(interfering again, to the Lieutenant's annoyance)*. We have thtrict inthtructhionth to treat the populathion of the enemy countrieth with the motht polithed courtethy.

MARIANNE. And who are you, sir?

GESTAPO MAN. I am a touritht, whoth uniform ith on the way.

LIEUTENANT *(with a dirty look at him, taking over the leading role again)*. You need not be alarmed, Madame. Our action is not directed at the peaceable citizens of France, but at political evil-doers and certain members of the armed forces, particularly members of the so-called Czechish and Polish armies in France. You will, therefore, kindly authenticate yourselves? *(To Jacobowsky)* You, first. *(Jacobowsky presents his identification. The Gestapo Man snatches it out of his hand.)*

JACOBOWSKY. I am not a member of any armed forces.

GESTAPO MAN *(with contempt)*. Obviouthly. *(Leafing through the papers with relish)* Jacobowthky! Unmithtakable.

Former member of the German Reich, now denaturalithed . . . *(Sharply, handing papers to the Lieutenant)* Are you by any thanth a writer?

JACOBOWSKY. Business letters only.

GESTAPO MAN. A parathite on the body of humanity. How did you fall in with thethe people?

JACOBOWSKY. I undertook to help this lady recover her husband.

LIEUTENANT *(to Gestapo Man, returning papers to him)*. The papers are in order.

JACOBOWSKY *(reaches for papers)*. This is all? I may leave?

GESTAPO MAN. No, you may not leave. I'll keep your paperth.

JACOBOWSKY *(pale)*. But without papers I am . . .

GESTAPO MAN *(with a malicious grin)*. Without paperth you are exthactly what you are with paperth. Come to thee me at headquarterth tomorrow. I may return them. *(He folds the papers)* Nextht!

(Szabuniewicz takes passport out of his coat pocket.)

LIEUTENANT *(passing Szabuniewicz' papers to the Gestapo Man)*. Nationality?

SZABUNIEWICZ. Pole.

GESTAPO MAN. Aha. Pole! Bad to begin with. *(Gives passport back to Szabuniewicz after looking at it. Leafs through the pages of a black book he has been carrying under his arm)* Thabuniewith--eth--as in thwine! Let'th thee who we're looking for. *(Then)* Oh, yeth, Th— *(Reading)* Thaverthky, Ludomir, Lieutenant Colonel; Thpinith, Aloith, Captain; Thikorthky, Brigadier General; Thtjerbinthky Tadeuth, Bolethlav, Colonel, three crotheth. Thublow, Thaul. What nameth! Thtjerbinthky, Thublow . . . *(He laughs loudly. Szabuniewicz does so too, but with a look the Gestapo Man freezes him into silence. Closes the book)* Occupathion?

SZABUNIEWICZ *(at his slyest)*. Scientific, sirr. Trained foot-surgeon, masseur, barber and assistant asylum attendant.

GESTAPO MAN *(indicates Jacobowsky)* Hith athithtant?

SZABUNIEWICZ *(spits to please the Gestapo Man)*. No, sirr. My own.

GESTAPO MAN. Correct attitude!

LIEUTENANT *(to Marianne)*. Madame

MARIANNE. Madame Marianne Deloupe—by marriage.

LIEUTENANT (indicates Colonel). Your husband?

MARIANNE. Yes.

GESTAPO MAN. In our country which ith a virile thivilithathion we thterilithe fellowth like that.

MARIANNE. He wasn't always . . .

GESTAPO MAN. I want to thee thith Delupe'th paperth . . .

MARIANNE. Papers! Didn't you read what happened? When I found my husband he was lying in the mud in his hospital pajamas. In the town I washed him like a baby and bought him that suit. I'm going to nurse him myself in the sanitarium at Saint-Jean-de-Luz. (She indicates Szabuniewicz)

SZABUNIEWICZ (gravely). I affirm to it as an expert.

GESTAPO MAN (goes to Colonel, who is standing apart from all this—tauntingly). Well, my good man, how ith your domethtic life? Want to fight me a duel? (He starts toward Stjerbinsky, who falls back step by step, actually now with the eyes of a madman. Unable to control himself he lifts his arm to strike the German. The Gestapo Man whips out a gun on him)

MARIANNE (screaming, intervenes—to Gestapo Man). Don't speak to him! For God's sake! (Embraces and pats the Colonel, walking him away) It's nothing, my angel. These men won't hurt you. They have your welfare at heart. I'm here with you, your Marianne. Yes, yes, I'm right here with you.

GESTAPO MAN (calls Szabuniewicz). Here—you! Can't the man thpeak?

SZABUNIEWICZ (his eyes screwed up solemnly). He don't speak in fifteen years. But he very strong. Nearly killed the head official of the asylum.

(A pause. The Gestapo Man takes the Lieutenant aside. They whisper.)

GESTAPO MAN. What do you think of him?

LIEUTENANT (bored). That's your department.

GESTAPO MAN. Thomething about hith fathe that'th familiar to me. I've theen him or I've theen hith picture. I can't know till I get to head-quarterth.

LIEUTENANT. Let's take him along?

GESTAPO MAN (slyly). Might be wither to thee where he goeth. They're ethcaping fatht—the Thechth and Poleth —from Thaint-Jean-de-Luth. There'th a leak—a definite leak. I think I'll let thith fellow go—but on a leath. He will lead uth to the man we want.

LIEUTENANT (sharp). Suit yourself. (The Gestapo Man turns away, takes them all in in a slow circling look. The Lieutenant goes to Marianne. Pointedly—to Marianne) Madame, you will not be annoyed further. (Gestapo Man grins at her.)

GESTAPO MAN (lewdly). Our Army officerth are tho thivalrouth!

LIEUTENANT (to Szabuniewicz). Get this dangerous patient of yours to the nearest clinic at once!

JACOBOWSKY (solemnly). That's the trouble. Madame wants to do that but she has no gasoline. Could you help out with a few gallons?

(Lieutenant looks at Gestapo Man for permission. The Gestapo Man nods.)

LIEUTENANT. Certainly. Sergeant . . .

SERGEANT (on the highway). Sir!

LIEUTENANT (goes to Sergeant, exits as he talks, followed by two soldiers). Get a five-gallon tin of gasoline and put it in their car. (Disappears. We hear his voice off stage, grinding out orders) Right about—face! Half-right through the woods for further combing out.

(The Gestapo Man starts to go also. As he passes him, he flips Jacobowsky's papers in his face.)

GESTAPO MAN (tantalizing). I'll keep thethe for you at headquarterth. (He goes out)

(There is a silence. They all stand transfixed. For the moment they are saved; they cannot quite believe it. Sazbuniewicz runs up to the road, looking off to see whether the Germans are really gone.)

MARIANNE (to Jacobowsky, in a whisper). Monsieur, what do you hear?

JACOBOWSKY (listening intently). I hear the grass growing . . .

SZABUNIEWICZ (In an exalted whisper). Saved! Saved!

MARIANNE (cannot contain herself any longer. She rushes to Jacobowsky and kisses him on both cheeks). Saved!

(Jacobowsky sways a bit.)

SZABUNIEWICZ *(jocular)*. He faint!

MARIANNE *(anxious)*. Are you all right, Monsieur Jacobowsky?

JACOBOWSKY *(recovering)*. To escape the dragon and to be kissed by the princess—it's too much for one day.

SZABUNIEWICZ *(looking off)*. Sh! Sh!!

GERMAN SOLDIER. *(entering with tin of gasoline)*. Gasoline.

JACOBOWSKY *(casually)*. Put it down. Thank you. *(German obeys and exits. Jacobowsky takes charge again. To Marianne)* You heard what the Gestapo said. Hail and farewell!

MARIANNE. Farewell?

JACOBOWSKY. They're combing the world. Hurry before they comb you out!

MARIANNE. And leave you?

SZABUNIEWICZ. He speaks right. *(starts gathering up luggage, trunk, shawl, etc., and starts putting them into the car)*

MARIANNE. We can't leave you like this.

JACOBOWSKY. You must. I think it's a good idea the Colonel and I part while we're still friends!

MARIANNE. Come with us.

JACOBOWSKY. I can't. I have no papers. You go south to the sea. I go north to headquarters.

MARIANNE. What will become of you?

JACOBOWSKY *(minimizing the danger)*. I live on improvisation. Farewell.

MARIANNE. We'll meet again—I feel it.

JACOBOWSKY *(leading her to the car)*. In Existence Number Five—or Existence Number Six.

MARIANNE. Somewhere.

JACOBOWSKY *(gliding unconsciously into a groove of memory)*. In the cathedral of my heart a candle always will burn for you. *(At the sound of these familiar words the Colonel looks up slowly out of his morose brooding and stares at Jacobowsky)* Where did I hear that?

(By this time Marianne is in the car. Szabuniewicz makes a second trip to the improvised picnic. He picks up various articles, food, etc., which he bundles into the shawl.)

SZABUNIEWICZ. Everything packed. Soon begin to rain. Is necessary we go.

COLONEL *(goes to Jacobowsky, stiffly)*. Monsieur Jacobowsky, I thank you for saving my life. I will send to Polish Government in Exile for decoration for you.

JACOBOWSKY *(sees loaf of bread jutting out of Szabuniewicz's shawl)*. May I take this loaf of bread instead?

COLONEL. Certainly, sir.

JACOBOWSKY *(takes loaf of bread and waves it)*. Now I am armed for the future.

(The Colonel goes to the car, sits behind the wheel, closes the door. Szabuniewicz picks up the gasoline can and climbs over the back of the car, perching on the luggage. Marianne waves to Jacobowsky as the car starts away.)

JACOBOWSKY *(waving back)*. Bon voyage!

MARIANNE. Good luck and rendezvous in Existence Five!

JACOBOWSKY *(waving for dear life)*. I have a memory and I have a hope. Thank you for both.

MARIANNE. Good-by!

JACOBOWSKY. Good-by! *(Jacobowsky's wave subsides. He pauses for a moment. Loneliness descends on him. Finally he pulls himself out of it and walks down slowly to where his hat and raincoat are lying at the foot of the haystack. He bends to pick up his raincoat. Underneath the raincoat he is startled to see Marianne's hatbox. He drops the coat, picks up the hatbox, opens it, feverishly takes out Marianne's little hat and feels inside it. The papers are there)* My God, that schlemiel has forgotten his papers! *(He picks up the hat and the papers and runs back to the road after the automobile. But it is too late. The car has disappeared. He walks slowly back, the hat and the papers in his hands. He apostrophizes the papers)* Passport to death! What a joke that I, the only son of Reba Jacobowsky, have in my hand the future of Poland! *(He puts the paper back in the hat, sighs. He brushes the hat lightly against his cheek. His face lights up. He whispers to himself)* But I'll see you again, Marianne. I'll see you again. *(Meticulously he puts the hat into the hatbox. He ties up the hatbox. He picks up his raincoat and puts it over one arm. He picks up the loaf of bread and puts it under the other. Then he manages the hatbox. He starts walking toward the road, whistling the "Toreador Song" from Carmen. When he reaches the road, he is assailed by the temptation to go after his papers to go after possible safety, but it is only for a moment. He conquers. it. He turns and follows down the road in the direction in which the car has disappeared)*

ACT THREE

SCENE ONE

SCENE: *The waterfront café of Papa Clairon at Saint-Jean-de-Luz; a cramped little room feverishly lit by naked electric bulbs; at the left a bar; in the center a billiard table, small tables scattered about; in the back wall two doors inscribed in large letters, "Messieurs" and "Dames." At right a small staircase leads off stage to the street door. At left, behind the bar, a door to the private quarters of the establishment. Down right below the street door, a mechanical piano with a smoked, green-glass front that lights up and plays when a coin is put in.*

Papa Clairon, the proprietor, a gray-haired old man, is running about, serving his guests. At the bar sits the Dice Player, a gray-clad gentleman, very nonchalant, drinking Pernods one after the other and absorbedly shooting dice against himself. At one table sits the silent Man, his back to the audience, his head bowed. He and the Dice Player are the only ones not in motion.

When the curtain goes up, everybody is dancing to the music of the mechanical piano which is playing a soft, twangy, banjo-like rendition of an old waltz. Among the guests we recognize the Old Man and the Little Boy whom we have seen several times before. The Old Man is feeding the Little Boy a sandwich.

Down the steps from the street door comes the Tragic Gentleman. He has with him Senator Brisson, a distinguished old man with beautiful white hair and a rosy complexion. The two thread their way through the dancers to the billiard table, center.

TRAGIC GENTLEMAN *(observing the scene).* Danse Macabre! In their homes they are lonely. Terror lurks in closets! Here they drink. They dance. They hear the bad news. They think: "When we are together we are safe." This is an error. It only simplifies things for the Germans.

SENATOR *(affably).* What happiness to meet you, old friend, after all these years!

TRAGIC GENTLEMAN. Tell me, Senator, frankly, do I look as old to you as you do to me?

SENATOR *(almost too sympathetic).* You do look rather tired!

TRAGIC GENTLEMAN. I thought I would cure my heartache by walking. That was an illusion. Now my feet ache and my heart as well.

SENATOR. You used to be good at billiards. Let's have a game. It will distract you.

TRAGIC GENTLEMAN. Very well. I'll try that too.

(They take cues, chalk them.)

DICE PLAYER *(at the bar).* Cognac, please!

CLAIRON *(hurrying to him).* All right. All right. I have only two hands. *(As he passes the Senator the latter questions him)*

SENATOR. Who is that fellow at the bar?

CLAIRON *(whispers back).* Gestapo!

SENATOR. Ah! *(He transmits the information to the Tragic Gentleman)* Gestapo!

TRAGIC GENTLEMAN. Why do they need Gestapo when we have so many traitors of our own?

SENATOR. I beg you not to be violent against those who only are trying to accommodate themselves to the new situation. After all we—you and I—are intellectuals. We must be detached.

TRAGIC GENTLEMAN *(humorously).* Of all traitors the intellectuals are always the most logical! *(The Senator and the Tragic Gentleman are just starting to play when Jacobowsky hurries in. He wears his hat, overcoat and carries Marrianne's hatbox. The Tragic Gentleman recognizes him and calls over to him)* Well, well, the Santa Claus from the establishment of Madame Bouffier! The purveyor of *marrons glacés!* What brings you to this mouse trap?

JACOBOWSKY. The green cheese of hope.

TRAGIC GENTLEMAN. Cheese is rationed, my friend. And as for hope—it is an extinct commodity. May I introduce an old friend I just ran into? *(Introducing)* Senator Brisson—Monsieur Jacobowsky. *(They bow)* We were at the Sorbonne together. My friend is not only a Senator —he is also an intellectual.

JACOBOWSKY. Unusual combination in any country. *(He looks around the café)*

SENATOR *(amiably)*. Not in France, sir!

TRAGIC GENTLEMAN. You are looking for someone?

JACOBOWSKY. A demented man.

TRAGIC GENTLEMAN. Take your pick.

JACOBOWSKY. A demented man and a beautiful lady.

(Seated right at a table in the corner is the Dancing Couple, momentarily resting. They sit staring into space, not talking, rigid with liquor, stiff, ghastly, expressionless.)

TRAGIC GENTLEMAN. There!

JACOBOWSKY. There are many varieties, you know. I once took a course in abnormal psychology. I wanted to find out how to get along with certain relatives. *(Suddenly, out of his immobile trance, the male member of the Dancing Couple leaps up, makes a threatening gesture to his companion, bangs the table fiercely, then sits down abruptly)* Very interesting. Nervous type! Spasmodic! *(He has been eyeing the Dice Player who has started to hum)* That man at the bar, on the contrary, is not nervous at all. He is extraordinarily calm.

(The radio breaks in—the voice of Marshal Pétain.)

RADIO VOICE *(with much coughing and spluttering)*. . . . And I say the nation was not equal to its task . . .

SENATOR *(blissful)*. Ah, Pétain!

RADIO VOICE. Led to the abyss by political charlatans, feeble men and ideas, France resorted only hesitantly to arms . . . But France, though prostrate, is not defeated . . .

TRAGIC GENTLEMAN. The arch-defeatist denies defeat.

JACOBOWSKY. Who is that?

SENATOR *(solemnly)*. Our leader—the Marshal Pétain.

RADIO VOICE. In the architecture of the New Europe . . .

TRAGIC GENTLEMAN. Can no one silence that death rattle?

CLAIRON. I can! *(He snaps off the radio)*

SENATOR *(to Tragic Gentleman, gently chiding)*. Be careful, my dear friend . . . It is easy to be critical when you haven't the responsibility of power. After all, this gallant old man has to lead the nation out of our democratic chaos into the New Order.

TRAGIC GENTLEMAN *(recognizing at once the familiar cadence of appeasement)*. You too!

SENATOR *(with a side glance at the Dice Player)*. Your pessimism is unjustified, my dear friend. Things will right themselves. The German spirit is practical as well as mystical. It will unify Europe.

TRAGIC GENTLEMAN *(aware of what the Senator is doing)*. Talk louder. Perhaps he didn't hear you.

SENATOR. My old friend, you hurt my feelings. Please believe me—this bacillus of democracy imported from England and America—this infection . . .

JACOBOWSKY *(interrupting)*. Excuse me, but was the French Revolution an importation?

SENATOR. May I ask, sir, are you a citizen of France?

JACOBOWSKY. Unfortunately not.

SENATOR. On what passport do you travel?

JACOBOWSKY. I had a passport leading to nowhere but even that was confiscated by the New Order. They want to unify me out of existence.

SENATOR *(tolerantly)*. One could scarcely expect an objective opinion from a man in your position.

JACOBOWSKY. You are right, my dear Senator. I am nobody. I am a hunted man, but in this world a hunted man has one advantage. He can never be the hunter.

TRAGIC GENTLEMAN. But you, Senator, with a little German tuition, should make an excellent hunter. You will soon be hunting Jacobowsky. Perfect sport. No poaching laws, no penalties.

SENATOR *(to Tragic Gentleman)*. In this great convulsion of humanity what happens to Jacobowsky is none of our business. It shouldn't concern us *(Turns to Jacobowsky)* if you'll pardon my saying so . . .

(Jacobowsky makes an absolving bow.)

TRAGIC GENTLEMAN. If you'll pardon my saying so—it concerns us very much. You remember when the Hitler pestilence first broke out in Germany we all of us said, "What happens to Jacobowsky is none of our business." And when it spread from

Vienna to Prague we said the same thing. "It's none of our business." But if instead we, and the British and the Americans and the Poles, had said: "It is our business —Jacobowsky is a man too. We can't allow human beings to be treated so"—in six weeks with six divisions we could have exterminated this pestilence in Germany. In other words, my dear Senator, it was we who made Hitler. We are his blitz-krieg, his victory and his world domination. Now let's go on with the game. Your shot . . .

SENATOR *(wounded, puts up his cue).* No, thank you. I prefer not to . . .
(The Tragic Gentleman takes it philosophically. Jacobowsky goes to him.)

JACOBOWSKY. My dear friend, you remember the Polish Colonel from the establishment of Madame Bouffier?

TRAGIC GENTLEMAN. I remember him very well. And his man. Don Quixote and Sancho Panza.

(At this moment, when he hears Jacobowsky's reference to the Polish Colonel, the Dice Player at the bar, without altering his expression or his position, puts his hands in his pockets and takes out a pair of gray gloves and starts putting them on. Jacobowsky sees this.)

JACOBOWSKY *(eagerly).* Have you seen this Polish Colonel?

TRAGIC GENTLEMAN. No, I haven't.
(Jacobowsky leaves the Tragic Gentleman; goes to the Dice Player and starts importuning him with great tensity.)

JACOBOWSKY. I just had a very interesting experience. I have been traveling with a Polish officer.

DICE PLAYER *(ignores him; to Papa Clairon, who is now behind the bar).* Cognac.

JACOBOWSKY *(insists).* This Polish officer is an extraordinary fellow. We traveled together in a car requisitioned by the Polish Government in Exile . . .

DICE PLAYER. Cognac.

JACOBOWSKY. Interesting variation. I was saying we traveled together but our journey was interrupted . . . *(Dice Player puts dice away)* Who won?

DICE PLAYER. I did.

JACOBOWSKY. Congratulations! Victory over yourself! As I was saying, our journey was interrupted, but I cannot understand why the Colonel is still not here. What could have happened? Should not some effort be made? Don't you think some effort should be made?

DICE PLAYER. Excuse me. *(He walks away from the bar and goes into the Men's Room. Jacobowsky stands alone at the bar, discouraged. At this moment the Tragic Gentleman has come to the table near the bar where the Silent Man is sitting. The Tragic Gentleman looks at him, curious)*

TRAGIC GENTLEMAN. My friend here is so exhausted he sleeps sitting up. *(Looks more closely)* Sleeps?
(The Tragic Gentleman steps closer to the table and shakes the sleeping man by the shoulder. The sleeping man's elbows go out from under his chin and his face slides along the table; he has been dead for some time, an empty pillbox clenched in his fist. Everyone crowds around the table. One of the patrons overturns a chair in his haste. Jacobowsky turns to the table, deeply moved. Clairon pushes his way forward.)

CLAIRON. What's happened? He's dead. What's this? *(He takes pills from dead man's hand)*

SENATOR. He took some pills. Montaigne says . . .

JACOBOWSKY. Regardless of what Montaigne says, when you have a bad headache you take headache pills. Poor fellow. *(He takes the pills from Papa Clairon's hands and puts them in his pocket—almost enviously)* At any rate these pills gave him peace.
(A slatternly, gray-haired woman pokes her head in from the street door. She shouts a warning.)

TOWN WOMAN. They're coming in a truck. It's a raid! A raid!

TRAGIC GENTLEMAN. They're taking hostages. *(He starts to run out, stops as he sees the Nazis in the street)* Too late. They're here.

JACOBOWSKY. Excuse me, excuse me . . . *(He makes his way through the crowd and walks through the door marked "Dames")*

LITTLE BOY *(cries, terrified).* Grandpa!

OLD MAN. It's all right, Robert!
(Down the stairs the Commissaire speciale de police, a fat embarrassed man with a perspiring face, enters.)

COMMISSAIRE. All right in here. This

one first. *(Close behind him two French sol-diers stand guard at the doors)* No resistance from anyone and please don't make a disturbance! For your own good, don't lose your heads! If your papers are in order you have nothing to fear. Come along—the quicker, the better. One after another!

(The lisping Gestapo Man and the Lieutenant we have seen before come in with two Nazi soldiers. The Gestapo Man is now in the superb uniform of his order. He goes to the head of the billiard table and stands watching critically everything that goes on, allowing the Lieutenant to execute the details of the raid. The Dice Player comes back nonchalantly from the Men's Room and walks back to his old place at the bar, calmly removing his gray gloves as he does so. The Gestapo Man watches him carefully.)

COMMISSAIRE. Well, what are you waiting for? Go ahead!

(The arrests begin. Everybody is herded to the street door. One French soldier seizes the Old Man. Another holds back the Little Boy.)

OLD MAN. You can't take me. He has no one but me.

COMMISSAIRE *(to the German, helplessly)*. He says he has no one but him.

LIEUTENANT. If he can prove he's clear of this dirty sabotage he can come back to him. This dirty sabotage has got to stop and we'll stop it.

(The Old Man is led off—the Little Boy stands alone, his face in his hands. Tragic Gentleman goes to the Little Boy, holds him tenderly.)

LITTLE BOY *(mumbles)*.   Grandpa! Grandpa! Grandpa!

COMMISSAIRE *(to Little Boy)*. It's all right . . . It's all right.

TRAGIC GENTLEMAN *(holding child)*. You swine.

(The Tragic Gentleman stares at the collabo-rationist Commissaire, so angry he is unable to speak. The Lieutenant moves on to the Dancing Couple and orders them out.)

LIEUTENANT *(pushing the Tragic Gentle-man up to the street door)*. You're next for a haircut. Take him. *(The Lieutenant turns to Papa Clairon, who is back of the bar. To Commissaire)* What about this fellow?

COMMISSAIRE. I can vouch for him. Very respected innkeeper.

LIEUTENANT. Many of these respected innkeepers are hospitable to our enemies. *(Comes to Dice Player who goes on playing without looking up)* And who is this so concentrated gambler?

COMMISSAIRE *(pleadingly to Dice Player)*. Please don't make difficulties, Monsieur. *(Without looking up from his game, the Dice Player puts his passport on the bar. The Commissaire looks at it and explains to the Lieutenant)* Special diplomatic passport from the Armistice Commission at Wies-baden.

LIEUTENANT *(looks at passport, clicks to attention)*. Heil Hitler!

DICE PLAYER *(stands and salutes. An-swering in a bored voice)*. Heil Hitler! *(The Lieutenant turns from him, the Commis-saire following deferentially at his heels. The Lieutenant turns his attention to the Senator.)*

LIEUTENANT. Who is this artistic creature?

SENATOR. Commissaire, you know me. You must have seen my picture in the newspapers often. I spoke here twice last year. I am a Senator of France. *(Shows card case)*

COMMISSAIRE. He is a member of the Senate, he says.

LIEUTENANT. That institution no longer exists.

SENATOR. But you don't understand. I am sympathetic to the New Order. It can use me.

LIEUTENANT *(grins)*. Good! In the con-centration camp you can begin by indoc-trinating the other prisoners. Take him. *(The French soldiers force him out.)*

SENATOR *(protesting, as he is led off)*. But I'm a Senator of France. I'm a Senator! *(He is gone.)*

LIEUTENANT *(indicating the dead man)*. What's this one waiting for?

TRAGIC GENTLEMAN *(from the street door, where the soldiers are holding him)*. Dooms-day.

LIEUTENANT *(with threatening gesture)*. What?

TRAGIC GENTLEMAN. At least he is safe from you. He is dead.

(The soldiers take him out. The Lieutenant turns quickly and sees that it is true; then addresses the Commissaire.)

LIEUTENANT. Well, get along with it.

(At this moment the Gestapo Man intervenes for the first time. He lifts the dead man's head; lets it fall back.)

GESTAPO MAN. Take him too. *(Delicately he wipes his hands with a silk handkerchief which he takes from his sleeve, and then puts back)*

COMMISSAIRE *(a little surprised)*. With the rest of them?

GESTAPO MAN. Yeth. In the truck with the retht of them. Out the back way. *(The Lieutenant waves the order. The two French soldiers carry the body out left by the bar. To Commissaire)* Take a look in the wathroomth.

(The Commissaire goes into the men's washroom. The Gestapo Man is eying the Dice Player steadily. As if unaware of this the Dice Player crosses the room slowly and drops a coin in the piano. It starts its lugubrious strumming.)

CLAIRON *(to the Little Boy who is crying and mumbling "Grandpa, grandpa")*. Until they let your grandfather go, I'll take care of you.

COMMISSAIRE *(comes back from the Men's Room)*. Nobody in there. *(He goes out, following the others through the street door. Nobody is left on the stage except the Gestapo Man, Papa Clairon, the Little Boy and the Dice Player who is at the piano. In the melee of the exit, the Gestapo Man quietly and unobserved by anyone goes out through the door above the bar. The Dice Player stands at the piano, looking through the window above it to the street. We hear the sound of the raider's truck as it moves down the street. When he sees that is has gone, the Dice Player loses his nonchalance in an instant. He turns and runs across the room to the bar. Papa Clairon, rather trembly, is standing behind it.)*

DICE PLAYER. My things, please. Steady, old boy, your hand is shaking.

CLAIRON. It's been a busy day, Monsieur.

DICE PLAYER. Where is the anxious little man that was here?

CLAIRON *(pointing to the Ladies' Room)*. In there.

DICE PLAYER. He may now emerge. *(Papa Clairon goes to the door of the Ladies' Room and calls out.)*

CLAIRON. All clear in there.

JACOBOWSKY *(emerges, hatbox still in his hand)*. But is it clear out here?

CLAIRON. How did you get in there?

JACOBOWSKY. It wasn't locked.

DICE PLAYER *(grimly)*. You were lucky!

JACOBOWSKY. Not lucky. Scientific. I have learned that males, even policemen, have a reluctance to investigate a place reserved for ladies . . .

DICE PLAYER *(very sharp and fast)*. Now about this colonel of yours . . .

JACOBOWSKY *(looks doubtfully at Clairon)*. Yes?

DICE PLAYER. Papa Clairon is a friend.

JACOBOWSKY. Good! One needs friends!

DICE PLAYER. What happened to your man?

JACOBOWSKY. Probably ran out of gasoline!

DICE PLAYER. Unfortunate.

JACOBOWSKY. I'm sure he'll be here any minute.

DICE PLAYER. I'm afraid I can't wait.

JACOBOWSKY *(imploring)*. Please.

DICE PLAYER. Impossible. Listen. If he comes—would you mind giving him a message?

JACOBOWSKY. Yes.

DICE PLAYER. The Germans are watching the waterfront. We've had to change our plans.

JACOBOWSKY *(nods—echoes)*. Change plans.

DICE PLAYER. The corvette won't touch here. We'll pick him up at the Mole at Hendaye.

JACOBOWSKY *(nods—echoes)*. Hendaye.

DICE PLAYER. That's five miles south of here.

JACOBOWSKY. I'll tell him.

DICE PLAYER. Good. *(He turns to go)*

JACOBOWSKY *(calling after him)*. One second, please. On this corvette, will there possibly be a place for me?

DICE PLAYER. I'm sorry. Out of the question! *(He disappears up the stairs)*

JACOBOWSKY *(stunned; his last hope gone)*. That's a man of few words.

CLAIRON. Yes.

JACOBOWSKY *(unable to resist speculation)*. Why is it a man like that makes you believe in him more than a talkative man?

CLAIRON. I am not a philosopher. I think I'll shut up shop. *(He goes up the stairs to the little door which is not visible to the audience and we hear the sound as he locks it. He comes back in from the stairs and shuts off the piano)*

LITTLE BOY. Please don't lock the door.

CLAIRON. Why not?

LITTLE BOY. How will he get in?

CLAIRON. Who?

LITTLE BOY. My grandfather. I'm waiting for him.

CLAIRON. I'll find a place for you to sleep. *(He picks the Little Boy up in his arms and starts with him across the stage to the other door)*

JACOBOWSKY *(touched)*. I see you're a kind man, Papa Clairon.

(At this moment there is sharp knocking at the street door. Terrified, Jacobowsky flies back into the Ladies' Room. Clairon stands with the Little Boy in his arms. He doesn't know what to do. His legs wobble. From the other door the Gestapo Man comes in. He has a gun in his hand and he points it at Clairon. The knocking on the street door continues louder.)

GESTAPO MAN. Don't bother with that. I know who they are. Come in and chat with me. *(Papa Clairon puts the Little Boy down and goes out through the door above the bar. The Gestapo Man orders the Little Boy)* You open the door.

(The Little Boy runs up the stairs to obey. The Gestapo Man goes back through the door above the bar. For a moment the stage is deserted. Then the Little Boy comes back, followed by Marianne nnd the Colonel. The Colonel, very tense, looks around the café.)

COLONEL. Man with the gray gloves—I miss him!

LITTLE BOY *(piteously, to Marianne)*. Where's my grandfather?

MARIANNE. Your grandfather?

LITTLE BOY. They took my grandfather away. *(He whimpers)*

MARIANNE. You'll find your grandfather. *(She mothers the Little Boy)*

(Szabuniewicz enters, swaggers around.)

SZABUNIEWICZ. What kind of café is dis? Where's proprietor? I want whisky. *(Shouts)* Proprietor! *(Goes back of the bar)*

COLONEL. They probably arrest him too.

SZABUNIEWICZ *(lording it back of the bar)*. This is the dream of my childhood—to have café like this, all to myself. *(Holds up bottle)* Cognac, Madame?

MARIANNE. No, thank you.

COLONEL *(in an agony of self-abnegation)*. Too late. Always too late.

MARIANNE. Courage! Maybe he will come—later.

COLONEL. First I leave behind the papers. I go back for them. Too late. And then the car break down. I cannot start it—this cursed mechanical thing!

MARIANNE *(to bolster him)*. The papers were in my hatbox. It's my fault as well as yours. Anybody can make a mistake.

COLONEL. But not I!

SZABUNIEWICZ. Mistakes is human—even angels slip.

COLONEL *(giving himself no quarter)*. I am officer. These papers my responsibility. Everywhere I am too late just as in Poland we are too late when Germans come. History of my people is that we who rule them have failed them.

MARIANNE *(goes to him to comfort him)*. Darling.

COLONEL. No, Marianne. Please, I beg —don't pity me. I, Stjerbinsky, have been unfaithful to my own standards—which are of the highest. I hate myself. I despise myself. I am bitter with myself. *(He sits encompassed in despair)*

LITTLE BOY *(to Marianne)*. Did you see my grandfather?

MARIANNE. No, but he'll be back. *(Puts boy on her lap)*

SZABUNIEWICZ. English funny people, Colonel. Always appear unexpected. Man with gray gloves maybe any minute pop up.

COLONEL *(brooding)*. That little Jacobowsky—if he were here—what would he tell us to do?

MARIANNE. I wonder what's become of him?

SZABUNIEWICZ. Probably borrow from Germans passage money to America.

COLONEL *(borrows illumination from the vanished Jacobowsky)*. In every situation— no matter how dark—two possibilities.

MARIANNE *(laughs)*. This idea you got from Monsieur Jacobowsky!

COLONEL *(in the excitement of this, for*

him, unaccustomed speculation). Why not!

MARIANNE *(delighted).* Why not!

COLONEL *(threading uncertainly through the labyrinth).* These Germans—either they find the papers or they don't find the papers.

SZABUNIEWICZ *(assisting).* Right.

COLONEL. If they do not find the papers that's good. But if they do find the papers ... *(He pauses—the thread waving perilously in the air)*

MARIANNE. *(exhorting him to the finish line).* Yes, Tadeusz.

COLONEL. If they do find the papers ...

SZABUNIEWICZ *(breathless).* Yes, Colonel?

COLONEL. That's terrible. *(His flight collapses; so does he—back in his chair)*

MARIANNE *(smiles).* You don't talk quite like Monsieur Jacobowsky—not quite.

COLONEL. But I live like him—hunted! Someone knocks, I startle. Germans march across the square, I tremble. I hang on to life with one hand. I live like Jacobowsky ... Only he knows what to do and I don't.

(Jacobowsky comes in from Ladies' Room.)

SZABUNIEWICZ *(popeyed, waves hand before his eyes—he can't believe what he sees).* I drink too much cognac. Colonel, look ...

COLONEL *(turns, sees Jacobowsky, incredulous).* It looks like Monsieur Jacobowsky.

MARIANNE *(runs to him).* It is!

COLONEL. How did you get ...? Always you eavesdrop!

MARIANNE *(embracing him; she and the Colonel cluster around him).* How wonderful to see you! By this time we thought you would be on your way to America.

JACOBOWSKY. A fifth migration is too much to expect. My bank account with God is overdrawn already. I wanted, just for once, to see you in this little hat. *(He produces the hatbox)*

MARIANNE *(overcome).* My hat!

COLONEL. God be praised! My papers!

JACOBOWSKY. Here. Please take them. They give me heart palpitations. *(He hands the Colonel the box. The Colonel puts it on the bar)*

MARIANNE. Monsieur Jacobowsky—I embrace you.

COLONEL *(his arm around Jacobowsky's shoulder).* I embrace you, too.

SZABUNIEWICZ *(from behind the bar, quite fuddled).* I embrace.

(The three of them are standing close together, their arms around each other, laughing and happy at their reunion.)

MARIANNE. How did you get here? Oh, Monsieur Jacobowsky, we've missed you so. Haven't we, Tadeusz?

COLONEL *(unsure again).* Yes and no.

JACOBOWSKY *(to the Colonel).* I have a message for you, from the Messiah in the gray gloves.

(But before he can give him the message they are interrupted. The Gestapo Man has come in quietly and stands watching the three of them in their affectionate huddle.)

GESTAPO MAN. My friendth from the road. What a happy cointhidenth!

(The three of them stand stupefied. The Little Boy runs from his chair by the piano and stands beside Marianne, holding her hand. Marianne is the first to find voice.)

MARIANNE. We are on our way to the Asylum.

GESTAPO MAN. Granted. But thtill a cointhidenth!

(Two German soldiers come in from the inside room and post themselves at the stairway leading to the street. Papa Clairon comes in pushed on by the Lieutenant.)

CLAIRON. What have I done? What is there against me?

GESTAPO MAN *(genial, walking over to the piano).* We'll find out. *(Sits at the piano)* Oh! Ith thith piano adjuthtable?

CLAIRON. Yes, sir.

GESTAPO MAN. Adjutht it.

(Lieutenant pushes Clairon over to the piano. Clairon shifts a lever on it.)

GESTAPO MAN *(his fingers luxuriate over the keys).* I mith muthic tho while the Fuehrer thendth uth touring ... *(To the Lieutenant, indicating Clairon)* Take him away. *(Soldier pushes Clairon up the stairs)* Well, my dear Monthieur Jacobowthky, greetingth! *(He starts playing the piano, a lovely song of Schumann)*

JACOBOWSKY. Greetings!

GESTAPO MAN *(while he plays).* Why didn't you come to thee me at headquarterth to get your paperth back?

JACOBOWSKY. I was delayed.

GESTAPO MAN. Mutht have been thome-thing very vital to thtop you getting your paperth. You mutht be aware that without your paperth you have no identity at all?

JACOBOWSKY. In my case that's an advantage.

GESTAPO MAN (laughs). Very good. Very amuthing. (He plays on, lost in schwärmerei) Ithn't it exquithite? It maketh me thigh for home, for the dear German landthcape. (Recites)

"Im wunderschönen Monat Mai,
Als alle Knospen sprangen,
Da ist in meinem Herzen,
Die Liebe aufgegangen."

Ithn't that exquithite?

JACOBOWSKY. Pardon me—but those words are by Heine.

GESTAPO MAN. Of courth they are. But I am a liberal. Exthtremely liberal. (He stops playing suddenly, his esthetic mood vanished. He gets up, walks across the room and faces Marianne and the Colonel, huddled together at the foot of the bar. He confronts the Colonel) Well, my dumb friend, thtill jealouth?

MARIANNE. Please, sir, don't excite him.

(The Lieutenant goes out through the door above the bar.)

GESTAPO MAN. Why not? Why don't you get yourthelf a man? You're young and healthy. One of my boyth would oblige you. Though our Fuehrer hath well thaid you Frenth are white niggerth, in your cathe I'd be glad to overlook that. Ath I thay, I'm a liberal . . .

COLONEL (bursting out). This is not to endure!

GESTAPO MAN (turns, facing his soldier, triumphant at having made the Colonel drop his pose; throws his arms outward). Ah! He thpeakth!

COLONEL. Yes. I speak. (He becomes exhilarated, demoniac, inspired. He seizes the Gestapo Man in a great embrace, lifts him from the floor and, holding him before him like a shield, backs away toward the bar. The Nazi advances, pistol pointed. The Colonel's voice rings out triumphant) Shoot! Shoot us both! I die but he dies.

JACOBOWSKY (involuntary admiration, breathes out loud). Samson!

COLONEL (inspired). My shield—worm for shield! This is nature's use for worms! (To his little stupefied group) Get behind me. (They all get behind him. He shouts to the Nazi) Shoot! Shoot!

(The Nazi advances. He is covering them with his tommy gun, bewildered—doesn't know what to do.)

GESTAPO MAN. Let me go!

COLONEL. I want to die with you. This is the embrace of death!

GESTAPO MAN (struggling). Let me go!

COLONEL. To die like this is to live!

GESTAPO MAN (to Nazi soldier). Lower your gun—I'll let you go!

COLONEL. You are a lie and your words are a lie. (Lieutenant enters from the left—points his gun at Colonel. All jockey for position. Szabuniewicz, who is behind the Lieutenant when he comes in, knocks him down and pushes him off stage. There is a thud off stage) Marianne, get his gun. (She takes the Gestapo Man's gun from his pocket) Put it in his back. (She does so)

GESTAPO MAN (to the remaining Nazi, who is still covering them). Put down your gun. Put down your gun.

(German soldier puts gun on the billiard table.)

COLONEL. Szabuniewicz! (Szabunie-wicz comes back into the room) Put him in Ladies' Room.

SZABUNIEWICZ (doing so). I put! Go. Go—you! (He pushes Nazi soldier up and into the Ladies' Room)

COLONEL. Lock the door.

(Szabuniewicz does so and then takes Nazi's tommy gun from the billiard table and covers the Gestapo Man with it. The Colonel lets the Gestapo Man go and covers him too with his gun which he has taken from Marianne. The Gestapo Man straightens his tunic calmly and walks across toward the piano.)

COLONEL (to Marianne). Marianne, go to wait outside. Wait as if nothing is happening.

(Marianne takes the Little Boy and goes out with him.)

GESTAPO MAN. What do you mean to do now? (He moves up toward the stairs)

COLONEL. Don't move.

GESTAPO MAN. You have the gun, and am unarmed. Thall we negothiate?

COLONEL. Not with you.

GESTAPO MAN. I know you, Colone

Thtjerbinthky. You are a thurvival from a dead patht. Your code won't permit you to thoot an unarmed man.

COLONEL. You Nazis do it.

GESTAPO MAN. Ah! That'th different. We are not ditheathed by codeth. We have abolithed conthienth. That'th why your victorieth over uth don't latht—becauth when you win you are drugged by a thenth of guilt. Now my boyth—Wilhelm, Maxth—they don't under-thtand thivalry, but they do know how to kill. (His voice rises)

COLONEL. Keep your voice down.

GESTAPO MAN. All you have ith your code. If you break your code you are nothing—you are dethtroyed . . . (As if addressing two men behind the Colonel) Wilhelm—Maxth—in here quick.

(Obeying a reflex action, feeling that they are about to be attacked from behind, the Colonel and Szabuniewicz turn to face the unseen enemy. Szabuniewicz runs into the other room to see who is there. Immediately they turn, the Gestapo Man bolts for the door to the street. The Colonel swings around just in time and shoots him. The Gestapo Man falls dead.)

SZABUNIEWICZ (comes back into the room). No one in there, Colonel.

COLONEL. I have broken my code and it feels wonderful.

JACOBOWSKY. Now, Colonel, we are lost.

COLONEL (intoxicated with himself). On the contrary, this brings back the old days when I am in uniform. I am new found.

JACOBOWSKY. I think I am mislaid. I have a message for you from the Messiah in the gray gloves.

COLONEL. What did he say?

JACOBOWSKY. The corvette that takes you to England sails from Hendaye.

COLONEL. Hendaye. Good! We go! (Picks up hatbox) You come with us . . .

JACOBOWSKY. No use. I asked him. He said, "Out of the question."

COLONEL (completely restored to himself now; with Olympian authority). You come with us. From now on you take orders from me. I take you under my wing. Jacobowsky child, I adopt you! (He goes. Swept up by the torrent, Jacobowsky is carried along)

CURTAIN

SCENE TWO

SCENE: The Mole at Hendaye, late that evening.

A stone causeway juts out into the water, littered with barrels and boxes. On the left a few denuded, sepulchral poplars stand against the sky. On the right, Marianne sits on the steps of the causeway, the Little Boy she has picked up at Papa Clairon's asleep in her lap. It is a dark night with drifting clouds and fitful moonlight.

Szabuniewicz is standing guard over her. As the curtain rises, the silence is punctured with machine-gun shots.

SZABUNIEWICZ (pistol in his hand). German everywhere. On the hunt everywhere.

MARIANNE. And the Englishman—no sign?

SZABUNIEWICZ. Nowhere.

MARIANNE. Why don't you go, Szabuniewicz? I know you're impatient. Go.

SZABUNIEWICZ (faintly derisive). No. Colonel tells me to stay and guard you.

MARIANNE. I'll be all right . . .

SZABUNIEWICZ. I guard! On radio I hear new edict. Because someone kill Gestapo man all aliens and Jews got to be killed on sight.

MARIANNE (sighs). Poor Monsieur Jacobowsky!

SZABUNIEWICZ (peers at her closely). Why you don't say poor Colonel? Colonel alien too. (She looks at him, doesn't answer) Don't blame you. Colonel not man he was.

MARIANNE. Why do you say that?

SZABUNIEWICZ. Begin to think—very painful. (He makes a wry face. Marianne smiles) You like him this way? You do this to him.

MARIANNE. Not I, Szabuniewicz.

SZABUNIEWICZ. Who then?

MARIANNE (softly). It's being hunted. It's being helpless.

(Jacobowsky comes running in. He is pretty shaky.)

SZABUNIEWICZ. You find him? The man in the gray gloves?

(Jacobowsky shakes his head; passes a hand across his forehead.)

MARIANNE. What is it?

JACOBOWSKY. I was walking along the

road. I heard the tramp of feet. A platoon of Germans.

MARIANNE. Did they see you?

JACOBOWSKY. If they saw me—I wouldn't be here. Did you hear the new edict?

SZABUNIEWICZ. I hear.

JACOBOWSKY. No more than two persons allowed together in the streets. Should they detect a group of three, the third one will be shot. I am always the third.

MARIANNE (smiles at him). When the Colonel comes back, we'll be four. That will confuse them.

JACOBOWSKY. Where is the Colonel?

SZABUNIEWICZ (taking out pistol). I go find him. I come back. (He starts to go)

JACOBOWSKY. Wait! Have you got an extra one?

SZABUNIEWICZ. Pistol?

JACOBOWSKY. Yes. Pistol.

SZABUNIEWICZ. You want pistol?

JACOBOWSKY (firmly). Yes.

SZABUNIEWICZ. Here. (He gives him pistol, laughs. Takes second one from his pocket and goes. Jacobowsky pockets pistol)

JACOBOWSKY. They say we're adaptable. As this is an age of death from machines I must adapt myself to that also. (Looks down at the sleeping child) Asleep? (Siren screams crescendo off stage)

MARIANNE. Fast asleep.

JACOBOWSKY. He will awake to a world without many things, including his grandfather. (Jacobowsky looking off right anxiously) The moments are passing. No sign yet of the Messiah in the gray gloves. What can have happened to him?

MARIANNE. Tadeusz will find him.

JACOBOWSKY. I'm sure he will. The Colonel's a wonderful fellow.

MARIANNE (smiles). He will be—one day.

JACOBOWSKY (kneels beside her—after a moment). You love the Colonel?

MARIANNE. Yes.

JACOBOWSKY. One day you will marry him?

MARIANNE. I'm not sure I'll marry him.

JACOBOWSKY (probing delicately to touch his fate). But you'll always be in love with him? Of that you are sure?

MARIANNE (looks at him, wants to tell him the complete truth, firmly). Yes. (This is final. Jacobowsky receives the coup de grace, straightens up) But until he learns a little of what you know—I cannot marry him.

JACOBOWSKY. What I know! Useless knowledge.

MARIANNE. He must learn that the world is not made for him. He must learn what it is to suffer, to wait, to imagine, to endure. He is learning.

JACOBOWSKY (taps the pistol). I am learning, too.

MARIANNE. The world needs you both—why can't it use you both?

JACOBOWSKY (his irrepressible humor bubbling out). Yes. Between us—we're a hero! (They both laugh. He stops, apprehensive, looking around)

MARIANNE. What's the matter?

JACOBOWSKY. I was afraid the Colonel would come and find us laughing.

MARIANNE. Poor Tadeusz!

JACOBOWSKY. Still no sign of a boat! The ocean is as empty as on the third day of creation. Marianne, I have a feeling that in this ark that sails for England, there will be no place for me.

MARIANNE. There must be. If you stay here you will be tortured, killed.

JACOBOWSKY. Don't worry about me. I have this little box of headache pills . . . (Takes box from pocket) You can summon death at will. Gives you a curious independence.

(The Colonel comes in.)

MARIANNE. Tadeusz!

COLONEL (smiles good-humoredly; looks at them both). Why are you not laughing?

JACOBOWSKY. You see, Marianne! If he finds us laughing, he objects. If he finds us serious . . .

COLONEL. If I find you serious, that's worse. Man with gray gloves—he has not appear?

JACOBOWSKY. Not yet.

COLONEL. Damn all to hell, where is he? Where he hiding? (Anxiously to Marianne) You all right, Marianne?

MARIANNE. Yes, Tadeusz.

COLONEL. Button your coat, my love; the night is getting colder. (He draws her coat closer about her) Where's Szabuniewicz?

MARIANNE. He went to look for you.

COLONEL. Thousand curses—always he go to look for me and I cannot find him. The time passes. This cursed boat—she sail—she sail without us. These damn Germans everywhere. *(He sits on the steps beside Marianne)* Just now in the road while they pass, I have to hide in a ditch, like hunted animal. I . . .

MARIANNE *(sees he is very taut, puts her hand on his arm)*. But now it's all right. You're here. You're safe. It's all right.

COLONEL. No. It's how I feel when I lie in ditch. I feel—I think, I think . . .

MARIANNE. What did you think?

COLONEL *(forcing his thoughts into the open)*. I think. Formerly other people lie in ditch. I ride by, proud. I believe it is right that they should be in ditch and right that I should ride by.

MARIANNE *(excited by this development)*. And now?

COLONEL. Now I know: all over the world people lie in ditch because I, aristocrat Stjerbinsky, did not give damn. Now I know what it is to be Jacobowsky.

JACOBOWSKY *(quizzically)*. Then I feel sorry for you!

COLONEL *(truculent)*. What you say?

JACOBOWSKY. You think because you've been lying in a ditch for fifteen minutes you know what it is to be me! It's not so simple. You have to lie much longer, my dear Colonel. And the difference is this: when you get up you are still Colonel Stjerbinsky. When I get up—I am still S. L. Jacobowsky. The ditch follows me.

COLONEL *(rises, on his high horse again, turns to Marianne)*. I don't know that I care to travel with this fellow!

MARIANNE *(chiding)*. Tadeusz!

COLONEL. Don't understand this mentality. Don't like it.

MARIANNE. You know you won't sail without him.

COLONEL *(sheepishly)*. Well—I want him around to dislike him. *(To Jacobowsky)* Jacobowsky, I warn you, our duel is only postponed.

JACOBOWSKY *(goes to him, smiling)*. My dear friend and opposite, our duel is for all eternity.

(Szabuniewicz comes back.)

SZABUNIEWICZ *(salutes Colonel; triumphant)*. I find him!

JACOBOWSKY. Ah! The Gray Messiah!

DICE PLAYER *(comes in. He is a different person from what we saw before; crisp, commanding)*. Colonel Stjerbinsky? *(Both salute.)*

COLONEL. I have the documents.

DICE PLAYER. We have had to advance the time of sailing. The boat will be here in eight minutes. Ready? *(Szabuniewicz runs up on the pier left, looking for the boat.)*

COLONEL. Ready, Marianne? Ready, Jacobowsky? Ready?

DICE PLAYER *(dour)*. This bon-voyage party is really a charming notion, but I made an appointment with one, not with four. This is not a Cook's tour.

SZABUNIEWICZ. I don't go.

COLONEL. My man, Szabuniewicz, trustworthy fellow.

SZABUNIEWICZ *(from the pier)*. Very confidential.

COLONEL *(to Szabuniewicz)*. In name of Polish Government I appoint you listening post.

SZABUNIEWICZ. I listen. As masseur and attendant in insane asylum, I get contact to highest political circles.

DICE PLAYER *(indicates Marianne)*. And she?

COLONEL. My wife.

DICE PLAYER. It's very difficult . . . We're full . . .

COLONEL *(breaks in)*. Without my wife I don't go.

DICE PLAYER. Very well. For her I'll stretch a point. Two places.

COLONEL *(insists)*. Three places!

DICE PLAYER. I said two.

COLONEL. This Monsieur Jacobowsky —he goes with us.

DICE PLAYER. My congratulations. By what vessel?

COLONEL. With us on same vessel.

DICE PLAYER. Do you want me to throw my sailors overboard?

COLONEL *(the opacity of the landlubber)*. Who cares how many people go on a boat?

DICE PLAYER. You appear to be just as you were described to me. We English are fighting for our lives. We are removing only our own subjects and fighting men, as every experienced soldier is of the utmost value to us. But we can be quite brutal when we have to. On our last trip it was necessary to drive weeping woman and children off the boat. I don't care to repeat the experience.

COLONEL. Many kinds of fighting men. This Jacobowsky fight with his brain.

DICE PLAYER. Sorry. I'm not ferrying intellectuals.

COLONEL (grabs him as he turns to go). Damn all to hell! Listen to me. He is soldier like me. For days now we are in flight. With his property and with his own life he protect the cause of my people who bring him only bad before. Two times now, by clever turn of mind he rescue my life. He rescue papers. I ask you, as officer, can I leave this man to the Boches?

DICE PLAYER. That may indeed be a problem, but it is not mine. I'm sure you'll agree.

JACOBOWSKY. Quite right.

COLONEL. Jacobowsky, you keep out of this.

JACOBOWSKY. He happens to be right.

COLONEL. God, what things a man see when he does not command . . .

DICE PLAYER. I command them here. Take it or leave it.

COLONEL. Then you deliver the papers to Polish Government in Exile. I remain.

DICE PLAYER. Very well. Give them to me. (He puts out his hand for the papers)

JACOBOWSKY (intervenes). This fellow means business.

COLONEL. Damn all to hell I . . .

JACOBOWSKY. He's right. It will be better for all of us if I leave.

COLONEL. No—no . . .

JACOBOWSKY. Please, Colonel, forget the whole thing.

(Marianne gets up, goes to Colonel.)

COLONEL. I do not forget. If you do not go, I do not go.

MARIANNE (very tender; she is sure of him now—to the Colonel). Tadeusz, I am what you said—I am your wife. In my soul and in my body. Forever. I will wait for you, Tadeusz.

COLONEL. Wait?

MARIANNE. Till you return. Take Monsieur Jacobowsky in my place. When you return, I shall be waiting.

COLONEL. Marianne, without you, I don't go.

MARIANNE. Tadeusz, listen. Here I stand at the outermost tip of France. I cannot tear myself away. Behind me I feel the country's grief—the dreadful silence of the oppressed. How can I forsake my people to go into a foreign land, even for love? Soon you'll be fighting again. Shall I sit before your picture in a hotel room in London and do nothing? I must stay here and work for my people. Tadeusz, I know you understand me.

COLONEL. For days my heart tell me this. As we get closer to the sea I feel it more and more—that you would never leave France.

(She takes his head in her hands and kisses him. In the distance from the harbor we hear a low whistle. The Dice Player answers)

DICE PLAYER (looking off over the water). Cheerio, Jim . . . Jim, right! (To the Colonel) Two places. Have you decided?

MARIANNE. Yes. (To the Colonel) My love will reach out to you. It will whisper to you. In the day. In the night.

COLONEL (accepting the inevitable; to the Dice Player). My wife remains in France. This gentleman goes in her place.

(At this moment we hear the music of a German fife-and-drum corps in the distance, playing the Horst Wessel Lied.)

DICE PLAYER. That's impossible. For your wife . . .

SZABUNIEWICZ. What is that?

DICE PLAYER. The Boches are moving soldiers into the town. They are looking for us, rousing Frenchmen out of bed, taking hostages.

COLONEL. I cannot leave this man Jacobowsky here. There is no place for him any more on earth. Ten steps forward is the sea and ten steps back is death.

JACOBOWSKY. Please, Colonel, stop worrying about me. I'm used to facing death.

MARIANNE (to Colonel). He has some sleeping pills!

COLONEL (to Dice Player). You force this man to kill himself. Knowing this, I will not go. Knowing this, I cannot go.

JACOBOWSKY. Colonel, I beg you. I am

not afraid to die, but I am also not afraid to live. Marianne, look, my headache pills—I throw them away. Now are you convinced?

MARIANNE. But if they catch you? *(The music stops.)*

JACOBOWSKY. I promise you I will live as long as the circumstances permit. Colonel, you are endrangering your mission. Go! *(Hands him another little box which he takes from his pocket)* And take these.

COLONEL *(looking at the second box)*. What are these?

JACOBOWSKY. Seasick pills. I traded them yesterday for my French grammar.

DICE PLAYER *(giving up)*. Very well— the second place is his! *(We see the prow of a launch coming up alongside the pier.)*

COLONEL. His!

DICE PLAYER. Yes. I'm not convinced by your arguments, Colonel, but by his tenacity for life. Jacobowsky, England can use you in the Ministry of Propaganda.

COLONEL. You'll find him useful even on the boat!

JACOBOWSKY. I prayed for a Moses to open the Channel for me. You are Moses!

DICE PLAYER. You can come along but my name is Basil. *(He goes into the boat)*

JACOBOWSKY. Szabuniewicz, the money owed me by the Polish Government in Exile. You got it in your head?

SZABUNIEWICZ. I got.

JACOBOWSKY. Tear it up.

SZABUNIEWICZ. Is tore.

DICE PLAYER *(his head visible from the boat)*. All aboard. Come along, come along.

MARIANNE. Good-bye, Monsieur Ja-cobowsky. Thank you for giving me back the Colonel.

JACOBOWSKY. Thank you for your existence. Paris is the City of Light. You are its light. You are the light of France. *(He goes into the boat)*

COLONEL. Well, my love . . . *(Takes Marianne in his arms)*

MARIANNE. Between St. Cyrille and here we have gone through much.

COLONEL. It's strange, I leave you now, but for the first time I feel sure of you.

MARIANNE. Be sure. *(They kiss.)*

DICE PLAYER. Will you kindly curtail this grand opera before the Gestapo tunes in? *(The Colonel leaves Marianne and goes to the boat. On the way he has a brief farewell with Szabuniewicz.)*

COLONEL. Szabuniewicz, child! *(He kisses him on both cheeks and then goes into the boat, which moves off into the darkness. Szabuniewicz, disconsolate, sits on the steps of the causeway. To cheer himself up he takes out his harmonica and starts playing it. He plays "La Marseillaise." Marianne, the Little Boy clasped close to her, stands looking off into the darkness waving farewell)*

MARIANNE. Come back soon. I'll be waiting.

COLONEL'S VOICE. I come back.

JACOBOWSKY'S VOICE. Madame La France. Farewell and hail. *(Szabuniewicz is giving his all on the harmonica. Marianne admonishes him gently.)*

MARIANNE. Softly, Szabuniewicz, softly . . . *(Szabuniewicz obeys. "La Marseillaise" dims down very small but clear and defiant. Marianne holds the Little Boy closer to her. She looks off over the water, her expression resolute, her eyes full of tears.)*

CURTAIN

ANTON CHEKHOV's

The Sea Gull

In the translation by STARK YOUNG

The Alfred Lunt and Lynn Fontanne production, first presented by the Theatre Guild, Inc., at the Shubert Theatre, New York, on March 28, 1938, with the following cast:

IRINA NICOLAYEVNA ARCADINA, MADAME TREPLEFF .... Lynn Fontanne	MASHA (MARYA ILYINISHNA) .... Margaret Webster
CONSTANTINE GAVRILOVITCH TREPLEFF .... Richard Whorf	BORIS ALEXEYEVITCH TRIGORIN ...... Alfred Lunt
PETER NICOLAYEVITCH SORIN .. Sydney Greenstreet	EUGENE SERGEYEVITCH DORN ...... John Barclay
NINA MIKHAILOVNA ZARETCHNY ...... Uta Hagen	SEMYON SEMYONOVITCH MEDVEDENKO .... O. Z. Whitehead
ILYA AFANASYEVITCH SHAMREYEFF .. Harold Moffet	YAKOV .... Alan Hewitt
PAULINE ANDREYEVNA .... Edith King	COOK .... S. Thomas Gomez
	HOUSEMAIDS .... { Jacqueline Paige / Ernestine De Backer

Directed by Robert Milton
Settings and costumes by Robert Edmond Jones

The action is laid at Sorin's country place.
Between the Third and Fourth Acts two years elapse.

———————

ACT ONE

A section of the park on Sorin's estate. The wide avenue leading away from the spectators into the depths of the park toward the lake is closed by a platform hurriedly put together for private theatricals, so that the lake is not seen at all. To left and right of the platform there are bushes. A few chairs, a small table.

The sun has just set. On the platform behind the curtain are Yakov and other workmen; sounds of coughing and hammering are heard. Masha and Medvedenko enter on the Left, returning from a walk.

———

MEDVEDENKO. Why do you always wear black?

MASHA. I am in mourning for my life. I'm unhappy.

MEDVEDENKO. You unhappy? I can't understand it. Your health is good, and your father is not rich but he's well enough off. My life is much harder to bear than yours. I get twenty-three roubles a month, and that's all, and then out of that the pension fund has to be deducted, but I don't wear mourning.

(They sit down.)

MASHA. It isn't a question of money. Even a beggar can be happy.

MEDVEDENKO. Yes, theoretically he can, but not when you come right down to it. Look at me, with my mother, my two sisters and my little brother, and my salary twenty-three roubles in all. Well, people have to eat and drink, don't they? Have to have tea and sugar? Have tobacco? So it just goes round and round.

MASHA *(glancing towards the stage)*. The play will begin soon.

MEDVEDENKO. Yes. The acting will be done by Nina Zaretchny and the play was written by Constantine Gavrilovitch. They are in love with each other, and today their souls are mingled in a longing to create some image both can share and true to both. But my soul and your soul can't find any ground to meet on. You see how it is. I love you; I can't stay at home because I keep wishing so for you; and so every day I walk four miles here and four miles back and meet with nothing but indifference on your side. That's only

natural. I've got nothing, we're a big family. Who wants to marry a man who can't even feed himself?

MASHA. Fiddlesticks! *(She takes snuff)* Your love touches me, but I can't return it, that's all. *(Offers him snuff)* Help yourself.

MEDVEDENKO. I'd as soon not.

(A pause.)

MASHA. My, how close it is! It must be going to storm tonight. All you do is philosophize or talk about money. You think the worst misery we can have is poverty. But I think it's a thousand times easier to go ragged and beg for bread than— But you'd never understand that— *(Enter Sorin, leaning on his walking stick, and Trepleff.)*

SORIN. For some reason, who knows, my dear boy, the country's not my style. Naturally. You can't teach an old horse new tricks. Last night I went to bed at ten o'clock, and at nine this morning I awoke feeling as if my brain stuck to my skull, and so on. *(Laughing)* And then on top of all that I fell asleep after dinner just the same. And so now I'm a wreck, I'm still lost in a nightmare, and all the rest of it.

TREPLEFF. That's true, Uncle, you really ought to live in town. *(Sees Masha and Medvedenko)* Look, my friends, we'll call you when the play starts, but don't stay here now. I'll have to ask you to go.

SORIN *(to Masha)*. Marya Ilyinishna, won't you kindly ask your father to leave that dog unchained, to stop that howling? All last night again my sister couldn't sleep.

MASHA. You'll have to tell my father yourself. I shan't do it, so please don't ask me to. *(To Medvedenko)* Let's go.

MEDVEDENKO. Then you'll let us know before the play starts.

(Masha and Medvedenko go out.)

SORIN. That just means the dog will howl all night again. You see how 'tis; in the country I have never had what I wanted. It used to be I'd get leave for twenty-eight days, say, and come down here to recoup, and so on; but they plagued me so with one silly piece of nonsense after another that the very first day

I wanted to be out of it. *(Laughs)* I've always left here with relish. Well, now that I'm retired, I have nowhere to go and all the rest of it. Like it—like it not, I live—

YAKOV. We're going for a swim, Constantine Gavrilovitch.

TREPLEFF. So long as you are back in ten minutes. *(Looks at his watch)* We're about to begin.

YAKOV. Yes, sir.

TREPLEFF. Here's your theatre. The curtain, then the first wing, then the second wing, and still farther open space. No scenery at all. You see what the background is—it stretches to the lake and on to the horizon. And the curtain will go up at 8:30, just when the moon's rising.

SORIN. Magnificent!

TREPLEFF. If Nina's late, then, of course, the whole effect will be spoilt. It's time she were here now. But her father and stepmother watch her so she can hardly get out of the house, it's like escaping from prison. *(Straightening his uncle's tie)* Uncle, your hair and beard are rumpled up—oughtn't you to have them trimmed?

SORIN *(combing his beard)*. It's the tragedy of my life. I always look as if I'd been drunk, even when I was young I did —and so on. Women never have loved me. *(Sits down)* Why is my sister in such bad humor?

TREPLEFF. Why? Bored. *(Sits down by Sorin)* Jealous. She's set against me, against the performance and against my play, because Nina's going to act in it and she's not. She's never read my play but she hates it.

SORIN. You *(Laughing)* imagine things, really.

TREPLEFF. Yes, she's furious because even on this little stage it's Nina will have a success and not she. *(Looks at his watch)* A psychological case, my mother: She's undeniably talented, intelligent, capable of sobbing over a novel; she recites all of Nekrassov's poetry by heart; she nurses the sick like an angel; but you just try praising Duse to her; Oh, ho! You praise nobody but her, write about her, rave about her, go into ecstasies over her marvelous performance in "La Dame Aux Camélias" or in "The Fumes of Life." But all that is a drug she can't get in the country, so she's bored and cross. We are all her enemies—it's all our fault. And then she's superstitious—afraid of three candles or number thirteen. She's stingy. She's got seventy thousand roubles in an Odessa bank, I know that for a fact. But ask her for a loan, she'll burst into tears.

SORIN. You've got it into your head your play annoys your mother, and that upsets you, and so forth. Don't worry, your mother worships the ground you walk on.

TREPLEFF *(picking petals from a flower)*. Loves me—loves me not, loves me—loves me not, loves me—loves me not. *(Laughing)* You see, my mother doesn't love me, of course not. I should say not! What she wants is to live, and love, and wear pretty clothes; and here I am twenty-five years old and a perpetual reminder that she's no longer young. You see when I'm not there she's only thirty-two, and when I am she's forty-three—and for that she hates me. She knows too that I refuse to admit the theatre. She loves the theatre; it seems to her that she's working for humanity, for holy art. But to my thinking her theatre today is nothing but routine, convention. When the curtain goes up, and by artificial light in a room with three walls, these great geniuses, these priest of holy art, show how people eat, drink, make love, move about and wear their jackets; when they try to fish a moral out of these flat pictures and phrases, some sweet little bit anybody could understand and any fool take home; when in a thousand different dishes they serve me the same thing over and over, over and over, over and over—well, it's then I run and run like Maupassant from the Eiffel Tower and all that vulgarity about to bury him.

SORIN. But we can't do without the theatre.

TREPLEFF. We must have new forms! New forms we must have, and if we can't get them we'd better have nothing at all. *(He looks at his watch)* I love my mother—love her very much—but she leads senseless life, always making a fuss over this novelist, her name forever chucked about in the papers—it disgusts me. It's just the simple egotism of an ordinary mortal, I suppose, stirring me up sometimes that makes me wish I had somebody besides a famous actress for a mother, and fancy if she had been an ordinary woman I'd have been happier. Uncle, can you imagine anything more hopeless than my position is in her house? It used to be she'd entertain, all famous people—actors and authors—and among them all I was the only one who was nothing, and they put up with me only because I was her son. Who am I? What am I? I left the university in my third year, owing to circumstances, as they say, for which the editors are not responsible; I've no talent at all, not a kopeck on me; and according to my passport I am—a burgher of Kiev. My father, as you know, was a burgher of Kiev, though he was also a famous actor. So when these actors and writers of hers bestowed on me their gracious attentions, it seemed to me their eyes were measuring my insignificance. I guessed their thoughts and felt humiliated.

SORIN. By the by, listen, can you please tell me what sort of man this novelist is. You see I can't make him out. He never opens his mouth.

TREPLEFF. He's an intelligent man, he's simple, apt to be melancholy. Quite decent. He's well under forty yet but he's already celebrated, he's had more than enough of everything. As for his writings —well, we'll say charming, full of talent, but after Tolstoy or Zola, of course, a little of Trigorin goes a long way.

SORIN. My boy, I'm fond of writers, you know. Once there were two things I wanted passionately. To marry and to be an author. I never succeeded in doing either. It must be pleasant being a minor writer even, and all the rest of it.

TREPLEFF. I hear footsteps. (Embraces his uncle) I can't live without her. Just the sound of her footsteps is lovely. (Going to meet Nina Zaretchny as she enters) I'm insanely happy! My enchantress! My dream!

NINA. I'm not late, surely I'm not late.

TREPLEFF (kissing her hands). No, no, no.

NINA. All day I worried, was so frightened—I was so afraid father wouldn't let me come. But at last he's gone out. He went out just now with my stepmother. The sky has turned red, the moon will soon be up, and I raced the horse, raced him. (Laughs) But I'm so happy. (Warmly shaking Sorin's hand)

SORIN (laughing). You've been crying, I see by your little eyes. That's not fair.

NINA. That's so. You can see how out of breath I am. Do let's hurry. I've got to go in half an hour. I must. Don't ask me to stay, my father doesn't know I'm here.

TREPLEFF. It's time to begin anyhow— I'll go call them.

SORIN. I'll go. I'll go this minute. (Begins to sing "The Two Grenadiers," then stops) Once I started singing like that and a deputy who was standing by said, "Your Excellency has a very strong voice"— then he thought awhile and said, "Strong but unpleasant." (Exits, laughing)

NINA. My father and his wife won't let me come here; they say it's Bohemia. They are afraid I'll go on the stage. But I am drawn here to this lake like a sea gull. My heart is full of you.

TREPLEFF. We're alone.

NINA. Isn't that some one over there?

TREPLEFF. No, nobody. (Kisses her)

NINA. What kind of tree is that?

TREPLEFF. It's an elm.

NINA. Why does it look so dark?

TREPLEFF. Because it's evening and everything looks darker. Don't go away early, please don't.

NINA. I must.

TREPLEFF. But if I should follow you, Nina? I'll stand all night in the garden, looking up at your window.

NINA. Oh, no! You mustn't. The watchman would see you and Treasure doesn't know you yet, he'd bark.

TREPLEFF. I love you.

NINA. Ssh—!

TREPLEFF. Who's that?— You, Yakov?

YAKOV (from behind stage). Yes, sir.

TREPLEFF. You must get to your seats, it's time to begin. The moon's coming up.

YAKOV. Yes, sir.

TREPLEFF. Have you got that methylated spirit? Is the sulphur ready? (To Nina) You see when the red eyes appear there must be a smell of sulphur around.

You'd better go now, everything's ready. Do you feel nervous?

NINA. Yes, awfully. It's not that I'm afraid of your mother so much, it's Boris Trigorin terrifies me, acting before him, a famous author like him. Tell me, is he young?

TREPLEFF. Yes.

NINA. What marvelous stories he writes!

TREPLEFF (coldly). I don't know. I don't read them.

NINA. It's hard to act in your play. There are no living characters in it.

TREPLEFF. Living characters! I must represent life not as it is and not as it should be, but as it appears in my dreams.

NINA. In your play there's no action; it's all recitation. It seems to me a play must have some love in it.

(They go out by way of the stage. Enter Pauline Andreyevna and Dorn.)

PAULINE. It's getting damp, go back and put on your galoshes.

DORN. I'm hot.

PAULINE. You don't take any care of yourself and it's just contrariness. You're a doctor and know very well how bad damp air is for you, but you like to make me miserable. You sat out on that terrace all last evening on purpose.

DORN (sings low). Oh, never say that I—

PAULINE. You were so enchanted by Madame Arcadina's conversation you didn't even notice the cold. You may as well own up—she charms you.

DORN. I'm fifty-five.

PAULINE. Fiddlesticks! What's that for a man, it's not old. You're still young enough looking—women still like you.

DORN (gently). Tell me, what is it you want?

PAULINE. Before an actress you are all ready to kiss the ground. All of you!

DORN (sings low). Once more I stand before thee— If society does make a fuss over actors, treats them differently from, say shopkeepers—it's only right and natural. That's the pursuit of the ideal.

PAULINE. Women have always fallen in love with you and hung on your neck. Is that the pursuit of the ideal too?

DORN (shrugs his shoulders). Why? In the relations women have had with me there has been a great deal that was fine. What they chiefly loved in me was the fact that I was a first-class doctor for childbirths. Ten or fifteen years ago, you remember, I was the only decent ac- coucheur they had in all this part of the country. Besides, I've always been an honorable man.

PAULINE (clasping his hand). My dear!

DORN. Ssh—here they come!

(Enter Madame Arcadina on Sorin's arm, Trigorin, Shamreyeff, Medvedenko, and Masha.)

SHAMREYEFF. In '73 at the Poltava Fair—pure delight—I can assure you she was magnificent, ah, magnificent! Pure delight! But tell me if you know where Chadin, Paul Semyonovitch, the co- median, is now? Take his Raspluyeff—'twas better than Sadovsky's, I can assure you, most esteemed lady. But what's become of him?

ARCADINA. You keep asking me about someone before the flood—how should I know? (Sits down)

SHAMREYEFF. Ah (Sighs) Paulie Cha din! Nobody like that now. The stage i not what it was, Irina Nikolayevna, ah no In those days there were mighty oaks now we have nothing but stumps.

DORN. There are not many brillian talents nowadays, it's true, but the genera average of the acting is much higher.

SHAMREYEFF. I can't agree with yo there. However, that's a matter of taste De gustibus aut bene, aut nihil.

(Trepleff comes out from behind the stage.)

ARCADINA. My dear son, when does begin?

TREPLEFF. Please be patient. It's only moment.

ARCADINA (reciting from Hamlet). M son!

　　"Thou turn'st mine eyes into my ver
　　　　　　　　　　　　　　　[sou
　　And there I see such black an
　　　　　　　　　　　　　　　[grained spo
　　As will not leave their tinct."

TREPLEFF (paraphrasing from Hamlet Nay, but to live in wickedness, seek lo in the depths of sin— (Behind the stage horn blows) Ladies and gentlemen, w begin! I beg your attention. (A pause) begin. *(Tapping the floor with a stick. In a loud voice)* Harken ye mists, out of ancient time, that drift by night over the bosom of this lake, darken our eyes with sleep and in our dream show us what will be in 200,000 years.

SORIN. In 200,000 years nothing will be.

TREPLEFF. Then let them present to us that nothing.

ARCADINA. Let them. We are asleep. *(The curtain rises. Vista opens across the lake. Low on the horizon the moon hangs, reflected in the water. Nina Zaretchny all in white, seated on a rock.)*

NINA. Men and beasts, lions, eagles and partridges, antlered deer, mute fishes dwelling in the water, starfish and small creatures invisible to the eye—these and all life have run their sad course and are no more. Thousands of creatures have come and gone since there was life on the earth. Vainly now the pallid moon doth light her lamp. In the meadows the cranes wake and cry no longer; and the beetles' hum is silent in the linden groves. Cold, cold, cold. Empty, empty, empty! Terrible, terrible, terrible. *(A pause)* Living bodies have crumbled to dust, and Eternal Matter has changed them into stones and water and clouds and there is one soul of many souls. I am that soul of the world.— In me the soul of Alexander the Great, of Cæsar, of Shakespeare, of Napoleon and of the lowest worm. The mind of man and the brute's instinct mingle in me. I remember all, all, and in me lives each several life again. *(The will-o'-the-wisps appear.)*

ARCADINA *(in a stage whisper)*. We're in for something decadent.

TREPLEFF *(imploring and reproaching)*. Mother!

NINA. I am alone. Once in a hundred years I open my lips to speak, and in this void my sad echo is unheard. And you, pale fires, you do not hear me ... Before daybreak the putrid marsh begets you, and you wander until sunrise, but without thought, without will, without the throb of life. For fear life should spring in you the father of eternal matter, the Devil, causes every instant in you, as in stones and in water, an interchange of the atoms, and you are changing endlessly. I, only, the world's soul, remain unchanged and am eternal. *(A pause)* I am like a prisoner cast into a deep, empty well, and know not where I am nor what awaits me. One thing only is not hidden from me: in the stubborn, savage fight with the devil, the principle of material forces, I am destined to conquer; and when that has been, matter and spirit shall be made one in the shadow of my soul forever. And lo, the kingdom of universal will is at hand. But that cannot be before long centuries of the moon, the shining dog star, and the earth, have run to dust. And till that time horror shall be, horror, horror, horror? *(A pause; upon the background of the lake appear two red spots)* Behold, my mighty adversary, the Devil, approaches. I see his awful, blood-red eyes.

ARCADINA. I smell sulphur, is that necessary?

TREPLEFF. Yes, it is.

ARCADINA. Oh, I see *(Laughing)*—it's a stage effect!

TREPLEFF. Mother!

NINA. But without man he is lost—

PAULINE *(to Dorn)*. You're taking your hat off. Put it on, you'll catch cold.

ARCADINA. The doctor has taken off his hat to the Devil, the father of Eternal Matter?

TREPLEFF *(blazing up, in a loud voice)*. The play's over! That's enough! Curtain!

ARCADINA. Why are you angry?

TREPLEFF. That's enough. Curtain! Drop the curtain! *(Stamping his foot)* Curtain! *(The curtain falls)* You must excuse me! I don't know how it was but I forgot somehow that only a chosen few can write plays and act them. I was infringing on a monopoly— My—I— *(Instead of saying more he makes a gesture of having done with it and goes out to the Left)*

ARCADINA. What's the matter with him?

SORIN. Irina, my dear, you mustn't treat a young man's pride like that.

ARCADINA. Now what have I said?

SORIN. You've hurt his feelings.

ARCADINA. But he told us beforehand it was all in fun, that's the way I took it— of course.

SORIN. Just the same—

ARCADINA. And now it appears he's produced a masterpiece. Well, I declare! Evidently he had no intention of amusing us, not at all; he got up this performance and fumigated us with sulphur to demonstrate to us how plays should be written and what's worth acting in. I'm sick of him. Nobody could stand his everlasting digs and outbursts. He's an unruly, conceited boy.

SORIN. He was only hoping to give you some pleasure.

ARCADINA. Yes? I notice he didn't choose some familiar sort of play, but forced his own decadent raving on us. I can listen to raving. I don't mind listening to it, so long as I'm not asked to take it seriously; but this of his is not like that. Not at all, it's introducing us to a new epoch in art, inaugurating a new era in art. But to my mind it's not new forms or epochs, it's simply bad temper.

TRIGORIN. Everyone writes as he wants to and as he can.

ARCADINA. Well, let him write as he wants to and as he can, so long as he leaves me out of it.

DORN. Great Jove angry is no longer Jove.

ARCADINA. I'm not Jove, I'm a woman. *(Lighting a cigarette)* I'm not angry—I'm merely vexed to see a young man wasting his time so. I didn't mean to hurt him.

MEDVEDENKO. Nobody has any grounds for separating matter from spirit, for it may be this very spirit itself is a union of material atoms. *(Excitedly, to Trigorin)* You know, somebody ought to put in a play, and then act on the stage, how we poor schoolmasters live. It's a hard, hard life.

ARCADINA. That's so, but we shan't talk of plays or atoms. The evening is so lovely. Listen—they're singing! *(Pausing to listen)* How good it is!

PAULINE. It's on the other side of the lake.

(A pause.)

ARCADINA. Sit down by me here. *(To Trigorin)* You know, ten or fifteen years ago we had music on this lake every night almost. There were six big country houses then around the shore; and it was all laughter, noise, shooting and lovemaking

—making love without end. The *jeune premier* and the idol of all six houses was our friend here, I must present *(Nods toward Dorn)* Doctor Eugene Sergeyevitch. He's charming now, but then he was irresistible. Why did I hurt my poor boy's feelings? I'm worried about him. *(Calls)* Kostya! Son! Kostya!

MASHA. I'll go look for him.

ARCADINA. Would you, my dear?

MASHA *(calling)*. Ah-oo! Constantine. Ah-oo! *(She goes out)*

NINA *(coming from behind the stage)*. Evidently we're not going on, so I may as well come out. Good evening! *(Kisses Madame Arcadina and Pauline Andreyevna)*

SORIN. Bravo! Bravo!

ARCADINA. Bravo! Bravo! We were all enchanted. With such looks and such a lovely voice, it's a sin for you to stay here in the country. You have talent indeed. Do you hear? You owe it to yourself to go on the stage.

NINA. Oh, that's my dream. *(Sighing)* But it will never come true.

ARCADINA. Who can tell? Let me present Boris Alexeyevitch Trigorin.

NINA. Oh, I'm so glad— *(Much embarrassed)* I'm always reading your—

ARCADINA *(drawing Nina down beside her)*. Don't be shy, dear. He may be a famous author, but his heart's quite simple. Look, he's embarrassed too.

DORN. I suppose we may raise the curtain now. This way it's frightening.

SHAMREYEFF *(loudly)*. Yakov, my man, raise the curtain!

(The curtain is raised.)

NINA *(to Trigorin)*. It's a strange play, isn't it?

TRIGORIN. I didn't understand a word of it. However, I enjoyed watching it. You acted with so much sincerity, and the scenery was so lovely. *(A pause)* I dare say there are quantities of fish in this lake.

NINA. Yes.

TRIGORIN. I love fishing. I can think of no greater pleasure than to sit alone towards evening by the water and watch a float.

NINA. But, I'd have thought that for anyone who had tasted the joy of creation no other pleasures could exist.

ARCADINA *(laughing)*. Don't talk like

that. When people make him pretty speeches he simply crumples up.

SHAMREYEFF. I remember one evening at the Opera in Moscow when the celebrated Silva was singing, how delighted we were when he took low C. Imagine our surprise—it so happened the bass from our church choir was there and all at once we heard "Bravo Silva" from the gallery a whole octave lower—like this—"Bravo Silva." The audience was thunderstruck.

(A pause.)

DORN. The angel of silence is flying over us.

NINA. Oh, I must go. Good-by.

ARCADINA. Where to? Where so early? We won't allow it.

NINA. Papa is waiting for me.

ARCADINA. What a man, really! (Kissing her) Well, there's no help for it. It's too sad losing you.

NINA. If you only knew how I don't want to go.

ARCADINA. Somebody must see you home, child.

NINA (frightened). Oh, no, no.

SORIN (imploring her). Don't go.

NINA. I must, Peter Nicolayevitch.

SORIN. Stay an hour more, and so on. Come now, really!

NINA (hesitating with tears in her eyes). can't. (She shakes hands and hurries out)

ARCADINA. Now there's a really poor, unfortunate girl. They say her mother when she died willed the husband all her immense fortune, everything to the very last kopeck, and now this little girl is left with nothing, since her father has already willed everything he has to the second wife. That's shocking.

DORN. Yes, her papa is rather a beast, must grant him that.

SORIN (rubbing his hands to warm them). What do you say, we'd better go in too, it's getting damp. My legs ache.

ARCADINA. It's like having wooden legs, you can hardly walk on them. Come on, you poor old patriarch. (She takes his arm)

SHAMREYEFF (offering his arm to his wife). Madame?

SORIN. There's that dog howling again. (To Shamreyeff) Be good enough,

Ilya Afanasyevitch, to tell them to let that dog off the chain.

SHAMREYEFF. It can't be done, Peter Nikolayevitch, or we'll be having thieves in the barn, and the millet's there. (To Medvedenko walking beside him) Yes, a whole octave lower "Bravo Silva"! And not your concert singer, mind you, just ordinary church choir.

MEDVEDENKO. And what salary does a church singer get?

(All except Dorn go out.)

DORN (alone). I don't know—maybe I'm no judge, I may be going off my head, but I liked that play. There's something in it. When the girl spoke of the vast solitude, and afterward when the Devil's eyes appeared, I could feel my hands trembling. It was all so fresh and naïve. But here he comes. I want to say all the nice things I can to him.

(Enter Trepleff.)

TREPLEFF. They've all gone.

DORN. I'm here.

TREPLEFF. Masha's been hunting for me all over the park. Unbearable creature!

DORN. Constantine Gavrilovitch, I admired your play extremely. It's a curious kind of thing and I haven't heard the end, but still it made a deep impression on me. You've got great talent. You must keep on! (Constantine presses his hand and embraces him impulsively) Phew, what a nervous fellow! Tears in his eyes! What I wanted to say is you chose your subject from the realm of abstract ideas, and that's right—a work of art should express a great idea. There is no beauty without seriousness. My, you are pale!

TREPLEFF. So you think—I ought to go on?

DORN. Yes. But write only of what is profound and eternal. You know how I have lived my life, I have lived it with variety and choiceness; and I have enjoyed it; and I am content. But if ever I had felt the elevation of spirit that comes to artists in their creative moments I believe I should have despised this body and all its usages, and tried to soar above all earthly things.

TREPLEFF. Forgive me, where's Nina?

DORN. And another thing. In a work of art there must be a clear, definite idea.

You must know what your object is in
writing, for if you follow that picturesque
road without a definite aim, you will go
astray and your talent will be your ruin.

TREPLEFF (*impatiently*). Where is Nina?

DORN. She's gone home.

TREPLEFF (*in despair*). What shall I do?
I want to see her. I must see her. I'm
going—

(*Masha enters.*)

DORN. Calm yourself, my friend!

TREPLEFF. But all the same I'm going.
I must go.

MASHA. Constantine Gavrilovitch,
come indoors. Your mother wants you.
She's anxious.

TREPLEFF. Tell her I've gone—and
please—all of you let me alone! Don't
follow me around.

DORN. Come, come, come, boy, you
mustn't act like this—it won't do.

TREPLEFF (*in tears*). Good-by, Doctor
—and thank you— (*Exits*)

DORN (*sighing*). Ah, youth, youth—

MASHA. When there is nothing else left
to say, people always say, "Ah, youth,
youth." (*Takes a pinch of snuff*)

DORN (*takes snuff-box out of her hand and
flings it into the bushes*) It's disgusting. (*A
pause*) There in the house they seem to be
playing. We'd better go in.

MASHA. No, no, wait a minute.

DORN. What is it?

MASHA. Let me talk to you—I don't
love my father, I can't talk to him, but I
feel with all my heart that you are near
me— Help me—help me— (*Starts to sob*)
or I shall do something silly, I'll make my
life a mockery, ruin it—I can't keep on—

DORN. How? Help you how?

MASHA. I'm tortured. No one, no one
knows what I'm suffering— (*Laying her
head on his breast, softly*) I love Constantine.

DORN. How nervous they all are!
How nervous they all are! And so much
love! O magic lake! (*Tenderly*) What can
I do for you, child? What, what?

END OF ACT ONE

ACT TWO

*A croquet lawn. In the background on the
Right is the house with a large terrace; on the
Left is seen the lake, in which the blazing sun
is reflected. Flowerbeds. Noon. Hot. On one
side of the croquet lawn, in the shade of an old
linden tree, Madame Arcadina. Dorn and
Masha are sitting on a garden bench. Dorn
has an open book on his knees.*

———

ARCADINA (*to Masha*) Here, let's stand
up. (*They both stand up*) Side by side. You
are twenty-two and I am nearly twice
that. Doctor Dorn, tell us, which one of
us looks the younger?

DORN. You, of course.

ARCADINA. There you are—you see?
— And why is it? Because I work, I feel,
I'm always on the go, but you sit in the
same spot all the time, you're not living.
I make it a rule never to look ahead into
the future. I let myself think neither of
old age nor of death. What will be will be.

MASHA. But I feel as if I were a thousand, I trail my life along after me like an
endless train.— Often I have no wish to be
living at all. (*Sits down*) Of course that's
all nonsense. I ought to shake myself and
throw it all off.

DORN (*sings softly*). Tell her, pretty
flowers—

ARCADINA. Then I'm correct as an
Englishman. I'm always dressed and my
hair always *comme il faut*. Would I permit
myself to leave the house, even to come
out here in the garden, in a dressing-gown
or with my hair blowzy? Never, I should
say not! The reason I have kept my looks
is because I've never been a frump, never
let myself go, as some do. (*Arms akimbo
she walks up and down the croquet green*)
Here I am, light as a bird. Ready to play
a girl of fifteen any day.

DORN. Well, at any rate, I'll go on
with my reading. (*Takes up the book*) We
stopped at the corn merchants and the rats.

ARCADINA. And the rats. Go on. (*Sits*)
Let me have it, I'll read. It's my turn
anyhow. (*She takes the book and looks for
the place*) And the rats—here we are—
(*Reads*) "And certainly, for people of the
world to pamper the romantics and make
them at home in their houses is a
dangerous as for corn merchants to raise
rats in their granaries. And yet they are
beloved. And so when a woman has
picked out the author she wants to entrap

she besieges him with compliments, amenities and favors." Well, among the French that may be, but certainly here with us there's nothing of the kind, we've no set program. Here with us a woman before she ever sets out to capture an author is usually head over heels in love with him herself. To go no further, take me and Trigorin—

(Enter Sorin, leaning on a stick, with Nina at his side. Medvedenko follows him, pushing a wheel chair.)

SORIN *(caressingly, as if to a child)*. Yes? We're all joy, eh? We're happy to-day after all. *(To his sister)* We're all joy. Father and stepmother are gone to Tver, and we are free now for three whole days.

NINA *(sits down beside Arcadina and embraces her)*. I am so happy! I belong now to you.

SORIN *(sitting down in the wheel chair)*. She looks lovely today.

ARCADINA. Beautifully dressed, intriguing—that's a clever girl. *(She kisses Nina)* We mustn't praise her too much. It's bad luck. Where's Boris Alexeyevitch?

NINA. He's at the bath-house fishing.

ARCADINA. You'd think he'd be sick of it. *(She begins reading again)*

NINA. What is that you have?

ARCADINA. Maupassant's "On The Water," darling. *(Reads a few lines to herself)* Well, the rest is uninteresting and untrue. *(Shutting the book)* I'm troubled in my soul. Tell me, what's the matter with my son? Why is he so sad and morose? He spends day after day on the lake and I hardly ever see him any more.

MASHA. His heart's troubled. *(To Nina, timidly)* Please, Nina, read something out of his play, won't you?

NINA *(shrugging her shoulders)*. You really want me to? It's so uninteresting.

MASHA *(with restrained eagerness)*. When he recites anything his eyes shine and his face grows pale. He has a beautiful sad voice, and a manner like a poet's.

(Sound of Sorin's snoring.)

DORN. Pleasant dreams.

ARCADINA *(to Sorin)*. Petrusha!

SORIN. Eh?

ARCADINA. Are you asleep?

SORIN. Not at all.

(A pause.)

ARCADINA. You are not following any treatment for yourself, that's not right, brother.

SORIN. I'd be glad to follow a treatment, but the doctor won't give me any.

DORN. Take care of yourself at sixty!

SORIN. Even at sixty a man wants to live.

DORN *(impatiently)*. Bah! Take your valerian drops.

ARCADINA. I'd think it would do him good to take a cure at some springs.

DORN. Well—he might take it. He might not take it.

ARCADINA. Try and understand that!

DORN. Nothing to understand. It's all clear.

(A pause.)

MEDVEDENKO. Peter Nikolayevitch ought to give up smoking.

SORIN. Fiddlesticks!

DORN. No, it's not fiddlesticks! Wine and tobacco rob us of our personality. After a cigar or a vodka, you're not Peter Nikolayevitch, you're Peter Nikolayevitch plus somebody else; your ego splits up, and you begin to see yourself as a third person.

SORIN. Fine *(laughs)* for you to argue! You've lived your life, but what about me? I've served the Department of Justice twenty-eight years, but I've never lived, never seen anything, and all the rest of it, so naturally I want to have my life. You've had your fill and that's why you turn to philosophy. I want to live, and that's why I turn to sherry after dinner and smoking cigars, and so on. And that's that.

DORN. One must look seriously at life, but to go in for cures at sixty and regret the pleasures you missed in your youth, is, if you'll forgive me, frivolous.

MASHA *(gets up)*. It must be time for lunch. *(Walking slow and hobbling)* My foot's gone to sleep. *(Exits)*

DORN. She'll down a couple of glasses before lunch.

SORIN. The poor thing gets no happiness of her own.

DORN. Fiddlesticks, your Excellency.

SORIN. You argue like a man who's had his fill.

ARCADINA. Oh, what can be duller

than this darling country dullness is! Hot, quiet, nobody ever does anything, everybody philosophizes. It's good to be here with you, my friends, delightful listening to you, but—sitting in my hotel room, all by myself, studying my part—how much better!

NINA (ecstatically). Good! I understand you.

SORIN. Of course, in town's better. You sit in your study, the footman lets nobody in without announcing them, there's the telephone—on the street cabs and so on—

DORN (singing sotto voce). Tell her, my flowers—

(Enter Shamreyeff, behind him Pauline.)

SHAMREYEFF. Here they are. Good morning! (Kisses Madame Arcadina's hand, then Nina's) Very glad to see you looking so well. (To Madame Arcadina) My wife tells me you are thinking of driving into town with her today. Is that so?

ARCADINA. Yes, we are thinking of it.

SHAMREYEFF. Hm! That's magnificent, but what will you travel on, my most esteemed lady? Today around here we are hauling rye, all the hands are busy. And what horses would you take, may I ask?

ARCADINA. What horses? How should I know—what horses!

SORIN. There are carriage horses here!

SHAMREYEFF (flaring up). Carriage horses? But where do I get the harness? Where do I get the harness? It's amazing. It's incomprehensible! Most esteemed lady! Excuse me, I am on my knees before your talent, I'd gladly give ten years of my life for you, but I cannot let you have the horses!

ARCADINA. But what if I have to go? It's a fine business!

SHAMREYEFF. Most esteemed lady! You don't know what a farm means.

ARCADINA (flaring up). The same old story! In that case I'll start for Moscow today. Order me horses from the village, or I'll walk to the station.

SHAMREYEFF (flaring up). In that case I resign my position! Find yourself another steward! (Exits)

ARCADINA. Every summer it's like this, every summer here they insult me! I'll

never put my foot here again! (Goes out in the direction of the bath-house)

(Presently she is seen going into the house. Trigorin follows, with fishing rods and a pail.)

SORIN (flaring up). This is insolent! The devil knows what it is! I'm sick of it, and so on. Bring all the horses here this very minute!

NINA (to Pauline). To refuse Irina Nikolayevna, the famous actress! Any little wish of hers, the least whim, is worth more than all your farm. It's simply unbelievable!

PAULINE (in despair). What can I do? Put yourself in my shoes, what can I do?

SORIN (to Nina). Let's go find my sister. We'll all beg her not to leave us. Isn't that so? (Looking in the direction Shamreyeff went) You insufferable man! Tyrant!

NINA (prevents his getting up). Sit still, sit still. We'll wheel you. (She and Medvedenko push the wheel chair) Oh, how awful it is!

SORIN. Yes, yes, it's awful. But he won't leave, I'll speak to him right off.

(They go out. Dorn and Pauline remain.)

DORN. People are certainly tiresome. Really the thing to do, of course, is throw that husband of yours out by the neck; but it will all end by this old woman, Peter Nicolayevitch, and his sister begging him to pardon them. See if they don't.

PAULINE. He has put the carriage horses in the fields, too. And these misunderstandings happen every day. If you only knew how it all upsets me. It's making me ill; you see how I'm trembling I can't bear his coarseness. (Entreating) Eugene my darling, light of my eyes—take me with you. Our time is passing we're not young any longer; if—if only we could—for the rest of our lives a least—stop hiding, stop pretending.

(A pause.)

DORN. I am fifty-five, it's too late to change now.

PAULINE. I know, you refuse me because there are other women close to you. It's impossible for you to take them all with you. I understand. I apologize Forgive me, you are tired of me.

(Nina appears before the house picking a bunch of flowers.)

DORN. No, not all that.

PAULINE. I am miserable with jealousy. Of course you are a doctor. You can't escape women. I understand.

DORN *(to Nina, as she joins them)*. What's happening?

NINA. Irina Nikolayevna is crying and Peter Nikolayevitch having his asthma.

DORN *(rising)*. I must go and give them both some valerian drops.

NINA *(giving him the flowers)*. Won't you?

DORN. *Merci bien.* *(Goes toward the house)*

PAULINE. What pretty flowers! *(Nearing the house, in a low voice)* Give me those flowers! Give me those flowers!

(He hands her the flowers, she tears them to pieces and flings them away. They go into the house.)

NINA *(alone)*. How strange it is seeing a famous actress cry, and about such a little nothing! And isn't it strange that a famous author should sit all day long fishing? The darling of the public, his name in the papers every day, his photograph for sale in shop windows, his book translated into foreign languages, and he's delighted because he's caught two chub. I imagined famous people were proud and distant, and that they despised the crowd, and used their fame and the glamor of their names to revenge themselves on the world for putting birth and money first. But here I see them crying or fishing, playing cards, laughing or losing their tempers, like everybody else.

(Trepleff enters, without a hat, carrying a gun and a dead sea gull.)

TREPLEFF. Are you here alone?

NINA. Alone. *(Trepleff lays the sea gull at her feet)* What does that mean?

TREPLEFF. I was low enough today to kill this sea gull. I lay it at your feet.

NINA. What's the matter with you? *(Picks up sea gull and looks at it)*

TREPLEFF *(pause)*. It's the way I'll soon end my own life.

NINA. I don't recognize you.

TREPLEFF. Yes, ever since I stopped recognizing you. You've changed toward me. Your eyes are cold. You hate to have me near you.

NINA. You are so irritable lately, and you talk—it's as if you were talking in symbols. And this sea gull, I suppose that's a symbol, too. Forgive me, but I don't understand it. *(Lays the sea gull on the seat)* I'm too simple to understand you.

TREPLEFF. This began that evening when my play failed so stupidly. Women will never forgive failure. I've burnt it all, every scrap of it. If you only knew what I'm going through! Your growing cold to me is terrible, unbelievable; it's as if I had suddenly waked and found this lake dried up and sunk in the ground. You say you are too simple to understand me. Oh, what is there to understand? My play didn't catch your fancy, you despise my kind of imagination, you already consider me commonplace, insignificant, like so many others. *(Stamping his foot)* How well I understand it all, how I understand it. It's like a spike in my brain, may it be damned along with my pride, which is sucking my blood, sucking it like a snake. *(He sees Trigorin, who enters reading a book)* Here comes the real genius, he walks like Hamlet, and with a book too. *(Mimicking)* "Words, words, words." This sun has hardly reached you, and you are already smiling, your glance is melting in his rays. I won't stand in your way. *(He goes out)*

TRIGORIN *(making notes in a book)*. Takes snuff and drinks vodka, always wears black. The schoolmaster in love with her.

NINA. Good morning, Boris Alexeyevitch!

TRIGORIN. Good morning. It seems that things have taken a turn we hadn't expected, so we are leaving today. You and I aren't likely to meet again. I'm sorry. I don't often meet young women, young and charming. I've forgotten how one feels at eighteen or nineteen, I can't picture it very clearly, and so the girls I draw in my stories and novels are mostly wrong. I'd like to be in your shoes for just one hour, to see things through your eyes, and find out just what sort of a little person you are.

NINA. And how I'd like to be in your shoes!

TRIGORIN. Why?

NINA. To know how it feels being a famous genius. What's it like being famous? How does it make you feel?

TRIGORIN. How? Nohow, I should think. I'd never thought about it. *(Reflecting)* One of two things: either you exaggerate my fame, or else my fame hasn't made me feel it.

NINA. But if you read about yourself in the papers?

TRIGORIN. When they praise me I'm pleased; when they abuse me, I feel whipped for a day or so.

NINA. It's a marvelous world! If you only knew how I envy you! Look how different different people's lots are! Some have all they can do to drag through their dull, obscure lives; they are all just alike, all miserable; others—well, you for instance—have a bright, interesting life that means something. You are happy.

TRIGORIN. I? *(Shrugging his shoulders)* H'm—I hear you speak of fame and happiness, of a bright, interesting life, but for me that's all words, pretty words that —if you'll forgive my saying so—mean about the same to me as candied fruits, which I never eat. You are very young and very kind.

NINA. Your life is beautiful.

TRIGORIN. I don't see anything so very beautiful about it. *(Looks at his watch)* I must get to my writing. Excuse me, I'm busy— *(Laughs)* You've stepped on my pet corn, as they say, and here I am, beginning to get excited and a little cross. At any rate let's talk. Let's talk about my beautiful, bright life. Well, where shall we begin? *(After reflecting a moment)* You know, sometimes violent obsessions take hold of a man, some fixed idea pursues him, the moon for example, day and night he thinks of nothing but the moon. Well, I have just such a moon. Day and night one thought obsesses me: I must be writing, I must be writing, I must be— I've scarcely finished one novel when somehow I'm driven on to write another, then a third, and after the third a fourth. I write incessantly, and always at a breakneck speed, and that's the only way I can write. What's beautiful and bright about that, I ask you? Oh, what a wild life! Why

now even, I'm here talking to you, I'm excited, but every minute I remember that the story I haven't finished is there waiting for me. I see that cloud up there, it's shaped like a grand piano—instantly a mental note—I must remember to put that in my story—a cloud sailing by— grand piano. A whiff of heliotrope. Quickly I make note of it: cloying smell, widow's color—put that in next time I describe a summer evening. Every sentence, every word I say and you say, I lie in wait for it, snap it up for my literary storeroom—it might come in handy— As soon as I put my work down, I race off to the theatre or go fishing, hoping to find a rest, but not at all—a new idea for a story comes rolling around in my head like a cannon ball, and I'm back at my desk, and writing and writing and writing. And it's always like that, everlastingly. I have no rest from myself, and I feel that I am consuming my own life, that for the honey I'm giving to someone in the void, I rob my best flowers of their pollen, I tear up those flowers and trample on their roots. Do I seem mad? Do my friends seem to talk with me as they would to a sane man? "What are you writing at now? What shall we have next?" Over and over it's like that, till I think all this attention and praise is said only out of kindness to a sick man— deceive him, soothe him, and then any minute come stealing up behind and pack him off to the madhouse. And in those years, my young best years, when I was beginning, why then writing made my life a torment. A minor writer, especially when he's not successful, feels clumsy, he's all thumbs, the world has no need for him; his nerves are about to go; he can't resist hanging around people in the arts, where nobody knows him, or takes any notice of him, and he's afraid to look them straight in the eyes, like a man with a passion for gambling who hasn't any money to play with. I'd never seen my readers but for some reason or other I pictured them as hating me and mistrusting me, I had a deathly fear of the public, and when my first play was produced it seemed to me all the dark eyes in the audience were looking at it with hostility and all the light eyes with frigid indifference. Oh how awful that was! What torment it was!

NINA. But surely the inspiration you feel and the creation itself of something must give you a moment of high, sweet happiness, don't they?

TRIGORIN. Yes. When I'm writing I enjoy it and I enjoy reading my proofs, but the minute it comes out I detest it; I see it's not what I meant it to be; I was wrong to write it at all, and I'm vexed and sick at heart about it. *(Laughs)* Then the public reads it. "Yes, charming, clever— Charming but nothing like Tolstoy: A very fine thing, but Turgenev's 'Fathers and Sons' is finer." To my dying day that's what it will be, clever and charming, charming and clever—nothing more. And when I'm dead they'll be saying at my grave, "Here lies Trigorin, a delightful writer but not so good as Turgenev."

NINA. Excuse me, but I refuse to understand you. You are simply spoiled by success.

TRIGORIN. What success? I have never pleased myself. I don't like myself as a writer. The worst of it is that I am in a sort of daze and often don't understand what I write—I love this water here, the trees, the sky, I feel nature, it stirs in me a passion, an irresistible desire to write. But I am not only a landscape painter, I am a citizen too, I love my country, the people, I feel that if I am a writer I ought to speak also of the people, of their sufferings, of their future, speak of science, of the rights of man, and so forth, and I speak of everything, I hurry up, on all sides they are after me, are annoyed at me, I dash from side to side like a fox the hounds are baiting, I see life and science getting always farther and farther ahead as I fall always more and more behind, like a peasant, missing his train, and the upshot is I feel that I can write only landscape, and in all the rest I am false and false to the marrow of my bones.

NINA. You work too hard, and have no time and no wish to feel your own importance. You may be dissatisfied with yourself, of course, but other people think you are great and excellent. If I were such a writer as you are I'd give my whole life to the people, but I should feel that the only happiness for them would be in rising to me; and they should draw my chariot.

TRIGORIN. Well, in a chariot—Agamemnon am I, or what?

(They both smile.)

NINA. For the happiness of being an author or an actress I would bear any poverty, disillusionment, I'd have people hate me. I'd live in a garret and eat black bread, I'd endure my own dissatisfaction with myself and all my faults, but in return I should ask for fame—real resounding fame. *(Covers her face with her hands)* My head's swimming— Ouf!

ARCADINA *(from within the house)*. Boris Alexeyevitch!

TRIGORIN. She's calling me. I dare say, to come and pack. But I don't feel like going away. *(He glances at the lake)* Look, how beautiful it is! Marvelous!

NINA. Do you see over there that house and garden?

TRIGORIN. Yes.

NINA. It used to belong to my dear mother. I was born there. I've spent all my life by this lake and I know every little island on it.

TRIGORIN. It's all very charming. *(Seeing the sea gull)* What is that?

NINA. A sea gull. Constantine shot it.

TRIGORIN. It's a lovely bird. Really, I don't want to leave here. Do try and persuade Irina Nikolayevna to stay. *(Makes a note in his book)*

NINA. What is it you're writing?

TRIGORIN. Only a note. An idea struck me. *(Putting the notebook away)* An idea for a short story: a young girl, one like you, has lived all her life beside a lake; she loves the lake like a sea gull and is happy and free like a sea gull. But by chance a man comes, sees her, and out of nothing better to do, destroys her, like this sea gull here.

(A pause. Madame Arcadina appears at the window.)

ARCADINA. Boris Alexeyevitch, where are you?

TRIGORIN. Right away! *(Goes toward the house, looking back at Nina. Madame Arcadina remains at the window.)* What is it?

ARCADINA. We're staying.

(*Trigorin enters the house.*)

NINA (*coming forward, standing lost in thought*). It's a dream!

CURTAIN

ACT THREE

The dining-room in Sorin's house. On the Right and Left are doors. A sideboard. A medicine cupboard. In the middle of the room a table. A small trunk and hat-boxes, signs of preparations for leaving.

Trigorin is at lunch, Masha standing by the table.

———

MASHA. I tell you this because you're a writer. You might use it. I tell you the truth: if he had died when he shot himself I wouldn't live another minute. Just the same I'm getting braver; I've just made up my mind to tear this love out of my heart by the roots.

TRIGORIN. How will you do it?

MASHA. I'm going to get married. To Medvedenko.

TRIGORIN. Is that the schoolmaster?

MASHA. Yes.

TRIGORIN. I don't see why you must do that.

MASHA. Loving without hope, waiting the whole year long for something—but when I'm married I won't have any time for love, there'll be plenty of new things I'll have to do to make me forget the past. Anyhow it will be a change, you know. Shall we have another?

TRIGORIN. Haven't you had about enough?

MASHA. Ah! (*Pours two glasses*) Here! Don't look at me like that! Women drink oftener than you imagine. Not so many of them drink openly like me. Most of them hide it. Yes. And it's always vodka or cognac. (*Clinks glasses*) Your health. You're a decent sort, I'm sorry to be parting from you.

(*They drink.*)

TRIGORIN. I don't want to leave here myself.

MASHA. You should beg her to stay.

TRIGORIN. She'd never do that now. Her son is behaving himself very tactless-ly. First he tries shooting himself and now, they say, he's going to challenge me to a duel. But what for? He sulks, he snorts, he preaches new art forms—but there's room for all, the new and the old—why elbow?

MASHA. Well, and there's jealousy. However, that's not my business.

(*Pause. Yakov crosses Right to Left with a piece of luggage. Nina enters, stops near window.*)

MASHA. That schoolmaster of mine is none too clever, but he's a good man and he's poor, and he loves me dearly. I'm sorry for him, and I'm sorry for his old mother. Well, let me wish you every happiness. Think kindly of me. (*Warmly shakes his hand*) Let me thank you for your friendly interest. Send me your books, be sure to write in them. Only don't put "esteemed lady," but simply this: "To Marya, who not remembering her origin, does not know why she is living in this world." Good-by. (*Goes out*)

NINA (*holding out her hand closed to Trigorin*). Even or odd?

TRIGORIN. Even.

NINA (*sighing*). No. I had only one pea in my hand. I was trying my fortune: To be an actress or not. I wish somebody would advise me.

TRIGORIN. There's no advice in this sort of thing.

(*A pause.*)

NINA. We are going to part—I may never see you again. Won't you take this little medal to remember me? I've had it engraved with your initials and on the other side the title of your book: *Days and Nights*.

TRIGORIN. What a graceful thing to do! (*Kisses the medal*) It's a charming present.

NINA. Sometimes think of me.

TRIGORIN. I'll think of you. I'll think of you as I saw you that sunny day—do you remember—a week ago when you had on your white dress—we were talking —a white sea gull was lying on the bench beside us.

NINA (*pensive*). Yes, the sea gull. (*A pause*) Someone's coming—let me see you two minutes before you go, won' you? (*Goes out on the Left as Madame Arca dina and Sorin, in full dress, with a decoration, enter, then Yakov, busy with the packing)*

ARCADINA. Stay at home, old man. How could you be running about with your rheumatism? *(To Trigorin)* Who was it just went out? Nina?

TRIGORIN. Yes.

ARCADINA. *Pardon!* We intruded. *(Sits down)* I believe everything's packed. I'm exhausted.

TRIGORIN. *Days and Nights,* page 121, lines eleven and twelve.

YAKOV *(clearing the table)*. Shall I pack your fishing rods as well?

TRIGORIN. Yes, I'll want them again. But the books you can give away.

YAKOV. Yes, sir.

TRIGORIN *(to himself)*. Page 121, lines eleven and twelve. What's in those lines? *(To Arcadina)* Have you my works here in the house?

ARCADINA. Yes, in my brother's study, the corner bookcase.

TRIGORIN. Page 121. *(Exits)*

ARCADINA. Really, Petrusha, you'd better stay at home.

SORIN. You're going away. It's dreary for me here at home without you.

ARCADINA. But what's there in town?

SORIN. Nothing in particular, but all the same. *(Laughs)* There's the laying of the foundation stone for the town hall, and all that sort of thing. A man longs if only for an hour or so to get out of this gudgeon existence, and it's much too long I've been lying around like an old cigarette holder. I've ordered the horses around at one o'clock, we'll set off at the same time.

ARCADINA *(after a pause)*. Oh, stay here, don't be lonesome, don't take cold. Look after my son. Take care of him. Advise him. *(A pause)* Here I am leaving and so shall never know why Constantine tried to kill himself. I have a notion the main reason was jealousy, and the sooner I take Trigorin away from here the better.

SORIN. How should I explain it to you? There were other reasons beside jealousy. Here we have a man who is young, intelligent, living in the country in solitude, without money, without position, without a future. He has nothing to do. He is ashamed and afraid of his idleness. I

love him very much and he's attached to me, but he feels just the same that he's superfluous in this house, and a sort of dependent here, a poor relation. That's something we can understand, it's pride of course.

ARCADINA. I'm worried about him. *(Reflecting)* He might go into the service, perhaps.

SORIN *(whistling, then hesitatingly)*. It seems to me the best thing you could do would be to let him have a little money. In the first place he ought to be able to dress himself like other people, and so on. Look how he's worn that same old jacket these past three years; he runs around without an overcoat. *(Laughs)* Yes, and it wouldn't harm him to have a little fun —he might go abroad, perhaps—it wouldn't cost much.

ARCADINA. Perhaps I could manage a suit, but as for going abroad—no. Just at this moment I can't even manage the suit. *(Firmly)* I haven't any money! *(Sorin laughs)* I haven't. No.

SORIN *(whistling)*. Very well. Forgive me, my dear, don't be angry. You're a generous, noble woman.

ARCADINA *(weeping)*. I haven't any money.

SORIN. Of course if I had any money, I'd give him some myself, but I haven't anything, not a kopeck. *(Laughs)* My manager takes all my pension and spends it on agriculture, cattle-raising, bee-keeping, and my money goes for nothing. The bees die, the cows die, horses they never let me have.

ARCADINA. Yes, I have some money, but I'm an actress, my costumes alone are enough to ruin me.

SORIN. You are very good, my dear. I respect you. Yes— But there again something's coming over me— *(Staggers)* My head's swimming. *(Leans on table)* I feel faint, and so on.

ARCADINA *(alarmed)*. Petrusha! *(Trying to support him)* Petrusha, my darling! *(Calls)* Help me! Help!
(Enter Trepleff, his head bandaged, and Medvedenko.)

ARCADINA. He feels faint.

SORIN. It's nothing, it's nothing—

(Smiles and drinks water) It's gone already —and so on.

TREPLEFF *(to his mother)*. Don't be alarmed, Mother, it's not serious. It often happens now to my uncle. Uncle, you must lie down a little.

SORIN. A little, yes. All the same I'm going to town—I'm lying down a little and I'm going to town—that's clear. *(He goes, leaning on his stick)*

MEDVEDENKO *(gives him his arm)*. There's a riddle: in the morning it's on four legs, at noon on two, in the evening on three.

SORIN *(laughs)*. That's it. And on the back at night. Thank you, I can manage alone.

MEDVEDENKO My, what ceremony! *(He and Sorin go out)*

ARCADINA. How he frightened me!

TREPLEFF. It's not good for him to live in the country. He's low in his mind. Now, Mother, if you'd only have a burst of sudden generosity and lend him a thousand or fifteen hundred, he could spend a whole year in town.

ARCADINA. I haven't any money. I'm an actress, not a banker.

(A pause.)

TREPLEFF. Mother, change my bandage. You do it so well.

ARCADINA *(takes bottle of iodoform and a box of bandages from cupboard)*. And the doctor's late.

TREPLEFF. He promised to be here at ten, but it's already noon.

ARCADINA. Sit down. *(Takes off bandage)* You look as if you were in a turban. Some man who came by the kitchen yesterday asked what nationality you were. But it's almost entirely healed. What's left is nothing. *(Kisses him on the head)* While I'm away, you won't do any more click-click?

TREPLEFF. No, Mother. That was a moment when I was out of my head with despair, and couldn't control myself. It won't happen again. *(Kisses her fingers)* You have clever fingers. I remember long, long ago when you were still playing at the Imperial Theatre—there was a fight one day in our court, and a washerwoman who was one of the tenants got beaten almost to death. Do you remember? She was picked up unconscious—you nursed her, took medicines to her, bathed her children in the washtub. Don't you remember?

ARCADINA. No. *(Puts on fresh bandage)*

TREPLEFF. Two ballet dancers were living then in the same house we did, they used to come and drink coffee with you.

ARCADINA. That I remember.

TREPLEFF. They were very pious. *(A pause)* Lately, these last days, I have loved you as tenderly and fully as when I was a child. Except for you, there's nobody left me now. Only why, why do you subject yourself to the influence of that man?

ARCADINA. You don't understand him, Constantine. He's a very noble character.

TREPLEFF. Nevertheless, when he was told I was going to challenge him to a duel, nobility didn't keep him from playing the coward. He's leaving. Ignominious retreat!

ARCADINA. Such tosh! I myself beg him to leave here.

TREPLEFF. Noble character! Here we both are nearly quarreling over him, and right now very likely he's in the drawing-room or in the garden laughing at us—developing Nina, trying once and for all to convince her he's a genius.

ARCADINA. For you it's pleasure—saying disagreeable things to me. I respect that man and must ask you not to speak ill of him in my presence.

TREPLEFF. And I don't respect him. You want me too to think he's a genius, but, forgive me, I can't tell lies— his creations make me sick.

ARCADINA. That's envy. People who are not talented but pretend to be have nothing better to do than to disparage real talents. It must be a fine consolation!

TREPLEFF *(sarcastically)*. Real talents! *(Angrily)* I'm more talented than both of you put together, if it comes to that! *(Tears off the bandage)* You two, with your stale routine, have grabbed first place in art and think that only what you do is real or legitimate; the rest you'd like to stifle and keep down. I don't believe in you two. I don't believe in you or in him.

ARCADINA. Decadent!

TREPLEFF. Go back to your darling

theatre and act there in trashy, stupid plays!

ARCADINA. Never did I act in such plays. Leave me alone! You are not fit to write even wretched vaudeville. Kiev burgher! Sponge!

TREPLEFF. Miser!

ARCADINA. Beggar! (He sits down, cries softly) Nonentity! (Walks up and down) Don't cry! You mustn't cry! (Weeps. Kisses him on his forehead, his cheeks, his head) My dear child, forgive me! Forgive me, your wicked mother! Forgive miserable me!

TREPLEFF (embracing her). If you only knew! I've lost everything. She doesn't love me, now I can't write. All my hopes are gone.

ARCADINA. Don't despair. It will all pass. He's leaving right away. She'll love you again. (Dries his tears) That's enough. We've made it up now.

TREPLEFF (kissing her hands). Yes, Mother.

ARCADINA (tenderly). Make it up with him, too. You don't want a duel. You don't, do you?

TREPLEFF. Very well, only, Mother, don't let me see him. It's painful to me. It's beyond me. (Trigorin comes in) There he is. I'm going. (Quickly puts dressings away in cupboard) The doctor will do my bandage later.

TRIGORIN (looking through a book). Page 121—lines eleven and twelve. Here it is. (Reads) "If you ever, ever need my life, come and take it."

(Trepleff picks up the bandage from the floor and goes out.)

ARCADINA (looking at her watch). The horses will be here soon.

TRIGORIN (to himself). If you ever, ever need my life, come and take it.

ARCADINA. I hope you are all packed.

TRIGORIN (impatiently). Yes, yes— (In deep thought) Why is it I thought I felt sadness in that call from a pure soul, and my heart aches so with pity? If you ever, ever need my life, come and take it. (To Madame Arcadina) Let's stay just one more day. (She shakes her head)

TRIGORIN. Let's stay!

ARCADINA. Darling, I know what keeps you here. But have some self control. You're a little drunk, be sober.

TRIGORIN. You be sober, too, be understanding, reasonable, I beg you; look at all this like a true friend— (Presses her hand) You are capable of sacrificing. Be my friend, let me be free.

ARCADINA (excited). Are you so infatuated?

TRIGORIN. I am drawn to her! Perhaps this is just what I need.

ARCADINA. The love of some provincial girl? Oh, how little you know yourself!

TRIGORIN. Sometimes people talk but are asleep. That's how it is now—I'm talking to you but in my dream see her. I'm possessed by sweet, marvelous dreams. Let me go—

ARCADINA (trembling). No, no, I'm an ordinary woman like any other woman, you shouldn't talk to me like this. Don't torture me, Boris. It frightens me.

TRIGORIN. If you wanted to, you could be far from ordinary. There is a kind of love that's young, and beautiful, and is all poetry, and carries us away into a world of dreams; on earth it alone can ever give us happiness. Such a love I still have never known. In my youth there wasn't time, I was always around some editor's office, fighting off starvation. Now it's here, that love, it's come, it beckons me. What sense, then, is there in running away from it?

ARCADINA (angry). You've gone mad.

TRIGORIN. Well, let me!

ARCADINA. You've all conspired today just to torment me. (Weeps)

TRIGORIN (clutching at his breast). She doesn't understand. She doesn't want to understand.

ARCADINA. Am I so old or ugly that you don't mind talking to me about other women? (Embracing and kissing him) Oh, you madman! My beautiful, my marvel— you are the last chapter of my life. (Falls on knees) My joy, my pride, my blessedness! (Embracing his knees) If you forsake me for one hour even, I'll never survive it, I'll go out of my mind, my wonderful, magnificent one, my master.

TRIGORIN. Somebody might come in. (Helps her to rise)

ARCADINA. Let them, I am not ashamed of my love for you. (Kisses his hands) My treasure! You reckless boy, you want to be mad, but I won't have it, I won't let you. (Laughs) You are mine—you are mine. This brow is mine, and the eyes mine, and this beautiful silky hair, too, is mine. You are all mine. You are so talented, so intelligent, the best of all modern writers; you are the one and only hope of Russia—you have such sincerity, simplicity, healthy humor. In one stroke you go to the very heart of a character or a scene; your people are like life itself. Oh, it's impossible to read you without rapture! Do you think this is only incense? I'm flattering you? Come, look me in the eyes— Do I look like a liar? There you see, only I can appreciate you; only I tell you the truth, my lovely darling.—You are coming? Yes? You won't leave me?

TRIGORIN. I have no will of my own— I've never had a will of my own. Flabby, weak, always submitting! Is it possible that might please women? Take me, carry me away, only never let me be one step away from you.

ARCADINA (to herself). Now he's mine. (Casually, as if nothing had happened) However, if you like you may stay. I'll go by myself, and you come later, in a week. After all, where would you hurry to?

TRIGORIN. No, let's go together.

ARCADINA. As you like. Together, together then. (A pause. Trigorin writes in notebook) What are you writing?

TRIGORIN. This morning I heard a happy expression: "Virgin forest." It might be useful in a story. (Yawns) So, we're off. Once more the cars, stations, station buffets, stews and conversations! (Shamreyeff enters.)

SHAMREYEFF. I have the honor with deep regret to announce that the horses are ready. It's time, most esteemed lady, to be off to the station; the train arrives at five minutes after two. So will you do me the favor, Irina Nikolayevna, not to forget to inquire about this: Where's the actor Suzdaltsev now? Is he alive? Is he well? We used to drink together once upon a time. In "The Stolen Mail" he was inimitable. In the same company with him at Elisavetgrad, I remember, was the tragedian Izmailov, also a re-

markable personality. Don't hurry, most esteemed lady, there are five minutes still. Once in some melodrama they were playing conspirators, and when they were suddenly discovered, he had to say "we are caught in a trap," but Izmailov said, "We are traught in a clap." (Laughs) Clap! (Yakov is busy with luggage. Maid brings Arcadina's hat, coat, parasol, gloves. All help her put them on. The Cook peers through a door on Left, as if hesitating, then he comes in. Enter Pauline, Sorin and Medvedenko.)

PAULINE (with basket). Here are some plums for the journey. They are sweet ones. In case you'd like some little thing.

ARCADINA. You are very kind, Pauline Andreyevna.

PAULINE. Good-by, my dear: If anything has been not quite so, forgive it. (Cries)

ARCADINA (embracing her). Everything has been charming, everything's been charming. Only you mustn't cry.

PAULINE. Time goes so.

ARCADINA. There's nothing we can do about that.

SORIN (in a great coat with a cape, his hat on and his stick in his hand, crossing the stage). Sister, you'd better start if you don't want to be late. I'll go get in the carriage. (Exits)

MEDVEDENKO. And I'll walk to the station—to see you off. I'll step lively.

ARCADINA. Good-by, my friends. If we are alive and well next summer we'll meet again. (The Maid, Cook and Yakov kiss her hand) Don't forget me. (Gives Cook a rouble) Here's a rouble for the three of you.

COOK. We humbly thank you, Madam. Pleasant journey to you. Many thanks to you.

YAKOV. God bless you!

SHAMREYEFF. Make us happy with a letter. Good-by, Boris Alexeyevitch.

ARCADINA. Where's Constantine? Tell him I'm off now. I must say good-by to him. Well, remember me kindly. (To Yakov) I gave the cook a rouble. It's for the three of you.

(All go out. The stage is empty. Off-stage are heard the usual sounds when people are going away. The Maid comes back for the basket of plums from the table and goes out again.)

TRIGORIN *(returning)*. I forgot my stick. It's out there on the terrace, I think. *(As he starts to go out by the door on the Left, he meets Nina coming in)* Is it you? We are just going—

NINA. I felt we should meet again. *(Excited)* Boris Alexeyevitch, I've come to a decision, the die is cast. I am going on the stage. Tomorrow I shall not be here. I am leaving my father, deserting everything, beginning a new life. I'm off like you—for Moscow—we shall meet there.

TRIGORIN *(glancing around him)*. Stay at Hotel Slavyansky Bazaar. Let me know at once. Molchanovka, Groholsky House. I must hurry.

(A pause.)

NINA. One minute yet.

TRIGORIN *(in a low voice)*. You are so beautiful—Oh, how happy to think we'll be meeting soon. *(She puts her head on his breast)* I shall see those lovely eyes again, that ineffably beautiful, tender smile—those gentle features, their pure, angelic expression—my darling—

(A long kiss.)

CURTAIN

(Two years pass between the Third and Fourth Acts.)

ACT FOUR

One of the drawing-rooms in Sorin's house, turned by Constantine Trepleff into a study. On the Right and Left, doors leading into other parts of the house. Facing us, glass doors on-to the terrace. Besides the usual furniture of a drawing-room, there is a writing-table in the corner to the Right; near the door on the Left, a sofa, a book-case full of books, and books in the windows and on the chairs.

Evening. A single lamp with a shade is lighted. Semi-darkness. The sound from outside of trees rustling and the wind howling in the chimney. The night-watchman is knocking. Medvedenko and Masha come in.

———

MASHA. Constantine Gavrilovitch! Constantine Gavrilovitch! *(Looking around)* Nobody here. Every other minute all day long the old man keeps asking where's Kostya, where's Kostya? He can't live without him.

MEDVEDENKO. He's afraid to be alone. *(Listening)* What terrible weather! It's two days now.

MASHA *(turning up the lamp)*. Out on the lake there are waves. Tremendous.

MEDVEDENKO. The garden's black. We ought to have told them to pull down that stage. It stands all bare and hideous, like a skeleton, and the curtain flaps in the wind. When I passed there last night it seemed to me that in the wind I heard someone crying.

MASHA. Well, here— *(Pause)*

MEDVEDENKO. Masha, let's go home.

MASHA *(shakes her head)*. I'm going to stay here tonight.

MEDVEDENKO *(imploring)*. Masha, let's go. Our baby must be hungry.

MASHA. Nonsense. Matriona will feed it.

(A pause.)

MEDVEDENKO. It's hard on him. He's been three nights now without his mother.

MASHA. You're getting just too tiresome. In the old days you'd at least philosophize a little, but now it's all baby, home, baby, home—and that's all I can get out of you.

MEDVEDENKO. Let's go, Masha.

MASHA. Go yourself.

MEDVEDENKO. Your father won't let me have a horse.

MASHA. He will if you just ask him.

MEDVEDENKO. Very well, I'll try. Then you'll come tomorrow.

MASHA *(taking snuff)*. Well, tomorrow. Stop bothering me.

(Enter Trepleff and Pauline; Trepleff carries pillows and a blanket, Pauline sheets and pillow cases. They lay them on the sofa, then Trepleff goes and sits down at his desk.)

MASHA. Why's that, Mama?

PAULINE. Peter Nikolayevitch asked to sleep in Kostya's room.

MASHA. Let me— *(She makes the bed)*

PAULINE *(sighing)*. Old people, what children— *(Goes to the desk. Leaning on her elbows she gazes at the manuscript. A pause)*

MEDVEDENKO. So I'm going. Good-by, Masha. *(Kisses her hand)* Good-by, Mother. *(Tries to kiss her hand)*

PAULINE (*with annoyance*). Well, go if you're going.

MEDVEDENKO. Good-by, Constantine Gavrilovitch.

(*Trepleff without speaking gives him his hand. Medvedenko goes out.*)

PAULINE (*gazing at the manuscript*). Nobody ever thought or dreamed that some day, Kostya, you'd turn out to be a real author. But now, thank God, the magazines send you money for your stories. (*Passing her hand over his hair*) And you've grown handsome—dear, good Kostya, be kind to my little Masha.

MASHA (*making the bed*). Let him alone, Mama.

PAULINE. She's a sweet little thing. (*A pause*) A woman, Kostya, doesn't ask much—only kind looks. As I well know. (*Trepleff rises from the desk and without speaking goes out.*)

MASHA. You shouldn't have bothered him.

PAULINE. I feel sorry for you, Masha.

MASHA. Why should you?

PAULINE. My heart aches and aches for you. I see it all, I understand everything.

MASHA. It's all foolishness! Hopeless love—that's only in novels. No matter. Only you mustn't let yourself go, and be always waiting for something, waiting for fine weather by the sea. If love stirs in your heart, stamp it out. Now they've promised to transfer my husband to another district. As soon as we get there—I'll forget it all—I'll tear it out of my heart by the roots.

(*Two rooms off is heard a melancholy waltz.*)

PAULINE. Kostya is playing. That means he's feeling sad.

MASHA (*waltzes silently a few turns*). The great thing, Mama, is to be where I don't see him. If only my Semyon could get his transfer, I promise you I'd forget in a month. It's all nonsense.

(*Door on Left opens. Dorn and Medvedenko come in, wheeling Sorin in his chair.*)

MEDVEDENKO. I have six souls at home now. And flour at seventy kopecks.

DORN. So it just goes round and round.

MEDVEDENKO. It's easy for you to smile. You've got more money than the chickens could pick up.

DORN. Money! After practicing medicine thirty years, my friend, so driven day and night that I could never call my soul my own, I managed to save up at last two thousand rubles; and I've just spent all that on a trip abroad. I've got nothing at all.

MASHA (*to her husband*). Aren't you gone yet?

MEDVEDENKO (*apologizing*). How can I, when they won't let me have a horse?

MASHA (*under her breath angrily*). I wish I'd never lay eyes on you again.

(*Sorin's wheel-chair remains Left Center. Pauline, Masha and Dorn sit down beside him. Medvedenko stands to one side gloomily.*)

DORN. Look how many changes they have made here! The drawing-room is turned into a study.

MASHA. Constantine Gavrilovitch likes to work in here. He can go into the garden whenever he likes and think.

(*A watchman's rattle sounds.*)

SORIN. Where's my sister?

DORN. She went to the station to meet Trigorin. She'll be right back.

SORIN. If you thought you had to send for my sister, that shows I'm very ill. (*Reflecting*) Now that's odd, isn't it? I'm very ill, but they won't let me have any medicine around here.

DORN. And what would you like? Valerian drops? Soda? Quinine?

SORIN. So it's more philosophy, I suppose. Oh, what an affliction! (*He motions with his head toward the sofa*) Is that for me?

PAULINE. Yes, for you, Peter Nikolayevitch.

SORIN. Thank you.

DORN (*singing sotto voce*). The moon drifts in the sky tonight.

SORIN. Listen, I want to give Kostya a subject for a story. It should be called: "The Man Who Wanted To"—*L'homme qui a voulu.* In my youth long ago I wanted to become an author—and never became one; wanted to speak eloquently—and spoke execrably (*mimicking himself*) and so on and so forth, and all the rest of it, yes and no, and in the résumé would drag on, drag on, till the sweat broke out; wanted to marry—and never married; wanted always to live in town—and now am ending up my life in the country, and so on.

DORN. Wanted to become a State Counsellor—and became one.

SORIN (*laughing*). For that I never longed. That came to me of itself.

DORN. Come now, to be picking faults with life at sixty-two, you must confess, that's not magnanimous.

SORIN. How bullheaded you are! Can't you take it in? I want to live.

DORN. That's frivolous, it's the law of nature that every life must come to an end.

SORIN. You argue like a man who's had his fill. You've had your fill and so you're indifferent to living, it's all one to you. But at that even you will be afraid to die.

DORN. The fear of death—a brute fear. We must overcome it. The fear of death is reasonable only in those who believe in an eternal life, and shudder to think of the sins they have committed. But you in the first place don't believe, in the second place what sins have you? For twenty-five years you served as State Counsellor—and that's all.

SORIN (*laughing*). Twenty-eight.

(*Trepleff enters and sits on the stool beside Sorin. Masha never takes her eyes off his face.*)

DORN. We are keeping Constantine Gavrilovitch from his work.

TREPLEFF. No, it's nothing.

(*A pause.*)

MEDVEDENKO. Permit me to ask you, Doctor, what town in your travels did you most prefer?

DORN. Genoa.

TREPLEFF. Why Genoa?

DORN. Because of the marvelous street crowd. When you go out of your hotel in the evening you find the whole street surging with people. You let yourself drift among the crowd, zig-zagging back and forth, you live its life, its soul pours into you, until finally you begin to believe there might really be a world spirit after all, like that Nina Zaretchny acted in your play. By the way, where is Nina just now? Where is she and how is she?

TREPLEFF. Very well, I imagine.

DORN. I've been told she was leading rather an odd sort of life. How's that?

TREPLEFF. It's a long story, Doctor.

DORN. You can shorten it.

(*A pause.*)

TREPLEFF. She ran away from home and joined Trigorin. That you knew?

DORN. I know.

TREPLEFF. She had a child. The child died. Trigorin got tired of her, and went back to his old ties, as might be expected. He'd never broken these old ties anyhow, but flitted in that backboneless style of his from one to the other. As far as I could say from what I know, Nina's private life didn't quite work out.

DORN. And on the stage?

TREPLEFF. I believe even worse. She made her debut in Moscow at a summer theatre, and afterward a tour in the provinces. At that time I never let her out of my sight, and wherever she was I was. She always attempted big parts, but her acting was crude, without any taste, her gestures were clumsy. There were moments when she did some talented screaming, talented dying, but those were only moments.

DORN. It means, though, she has talent?

TREPLEFF. I could never make out. I imagine she has. I saw her, but she didn't want to see me, and her maid wouldn't let me in her rooms. I understood how she felt, and never insisted on seeing her. (*A pause*) What more is there to tell you? Afterward, when I'd come back home here, she wrote me some letters. They were clever, tender, interesting; she didn't complain, but I could see she was profoundly unhappy; there was not a word that didn't show her exhausted nerves. And she'd taken a strange fancy. She always signed herself the sea gull. In "The Mermaid" the miller says that he's a crow; the same way in all her letters she kept repeating she was a sea gull. Now she's here.

DORN. How do you mean, here?

TREPLEFF. In town, staying at the inn. She's already been here five days, living there in rooms. Masha drove in, but she never sees anybody. Semyon Semyonovitch declares that last night after dinner he saw her in the fields, a mile and a half from here.

MEDVEDENKO. Yes, I saw her. (*A pause*) Going in the opposite direction from here, toward town. I bowed to her,

asked why she had not been out to see us.
She said she'd come.

TREPLEFF. Well, she won't. *(A pause)*
Her father and stepmother don't want to
know her. They've set watchmen to keep
her off the grounds. *(Goes toward the desk
with Dorn)* How easy it is, Doctor, to be
a philosopher on paper, and how hard it
is in life!

SORIN. She was a beautiful girl.

DORN. How's that?

SORIN. I say she was a beautiful girl.
State Counsellor Sorin was downright in
love with her himself once for a while.

DORN. You old Lovelace!

(They hear Shamreyeff's laugh.)

PAULINE. I imagine they're back from
the station.

TREPLEFF. Yes, I hear Mother.

*(Enter Madame Arcadina and Trigorin,
Shamreyeff following.)*

SHAMREYEFF. We all get old and fade
with the elements, esteemed lady, but
you, most honored lady, are still young—
white dress, vivacity—grace.

ARCADINA. You still want to bring me
bad luck, you tiresome creature!

TRIGORIN *(to Sorin)*. Howdy do, Peter
Nikolayevitch. How is it you are still in-
disposed? That's not so good. *(Pleased at
seeing Masha)* Masha Ilyinishna!

MASHA. You know me? *(Grasps his
hand)*

TRIGORIN. Married?

MASHA. Long ago.

TRIGORIN. Are you happy? *(Bows to
Dorn and Medvedenko, then hesitatingly goes
to Trepleff)* Irina Nikolayevna tells me you
have forgotten the past and given up
being angry.

(Trepleff holds out his hand.)

ARCADINA *(to her son)*. Look, Boris
Alexeyevitch has brought you the magazine with your last story.

TREPLEFF *(taking the magazine. To
Trigorin)*. Thank you. You're very kind.
(They sit down.)

TRIGORIN. Your admirers send their
respects to you. In Petersburg and in
Moscow, everywhere, there's a great deal
of interest in your work, and they all ask
me about you. They ask: what is he like,
what age is he, is he dark or fair? For
some reason they all think you are no

longer young. And nobody knows your
real name, since you always publish under
a pseudonym. You're a mystery, like the
Man in the Iron Mask.

TREPLEFF. Will you be with us long?

TRIGORIN. No, tomorrow I think I'll
go to Moscow. I must. I'm in a hurry to
finish a story, and besides I've promised
to write something for an annual. In a
word it's the same old thing.

*(Madame Arcadina and Pauline have set up
a card table. Shamreyeff lights candles, arranges chairs, gets box of lotto from a cupboard.)*

TRIGORIN. The weather's given me a
poor welcome. The wind is ferocious.
Tomorrow morning if it dies down I'm
going out to the lake to fish. And I want
to look around the garden and the place
where—do you remember?—your play
was done. The idea for a story is all
worked out in my mind, I want only to
refresh my memory of the place where
it's laid.

MASHA. Papa, let my husband have a
horse! He must get home.

SHAMREYEFF *(mimics)*. A horse—
home. *(Sternly)* See for yourself: they are
just back from the station. They'll not go
out again.

MASHA. They're not the only horses—
*(Seeing that he says nothing, she makes an
impatient gesture)* Nobody can do anything
with you—

MEDVEDENKO. I can walk, Masha.
Truly—

PAULINE *(sighs)*. Walk, in such
weather! *(Sits down at card table)* Sit down,
friends.

MEDVEDENKO. It's only four miles. —
Good-by. *(Kisses wife's hand)* Good-by,
Mama. *(His mother-in-law puts out her hand
reluctantly)* I should not have troubled
anybody, but the little baby— *(Bowing to
them)* Good-by. *(He goes out as if
apologizing)*

SHAMREYEFF. He'll make it. He's not
a general.

PAULINE *(taps on table)*. Sit down,
friends. Let's not lose time, they'll be
calling us to supper soon.

*(Shamreyeff, Masha and Dorn sit at the card
table.)*

ARCADINA *(to Trigorin)*. When these

long autumn evenings draw on we pass the time out here with lotto. And look: the old lotto set we had when my mother used to play with us children. Don't you want to take a hand with us till supper time? *(She and Trigorin sit down at the table)* It's a tiresome game, but it does well enough when you're used to it. *(She deals three cards to each one.)*

TREPLEFF *(turns magazine pages)*. He's read his own story, but mine he hasn't even cut. *(He lays the magazine on the desk; on his way out, as he passes his mother, he kisses her on the head)*

ARCADINA. But you, Kostya?

TREPLEFF. Sorry, I don't care to. I'm going for a walk. *(Goes out)*

ARCADINA. Stake—ten kopecks. Put it down for me, Doctor.

DORN. Command me.

MASHA. Has everybody bet? I'll begin. Twenty-two.

ARCADINA. I have it.

MASHA. Three.

DORN. Here you are.

MASHA. Did you put down three? Eight! Eighty-one! Ten!

SHAMREYEFF. Not so fast.

ARCADINA. What a reception they gave me at Kharkoff! Can you believe it, my head's spinning yet.

MASHA. Thirty-four.

(A sad waltz is heard.)

ARCADINA. The students gave me an ovation, three baskets of flowers, two wreaths and look— *(She takes off a brooch and puts it on the table)*

SHAMREYEFF. Yes, that's the real—

MASHA. Fifty!

DORN. Fifty, you say?

ARCADINA. I had a superb costume. Say what you like, but really when it comes to dressing myself I am no fool.

PAULINE. Kostya is playing. The poor boy's sad.

SHAMREYEFF. In the papers they often abuse him.

MASHA. Seventy-seven.

ARCADINA. Who cares what they say?

TRIGORIN. He hasn't any luck. He still can't discover how to write a style of his own. There is something strange, vague, at times even like delirious raving. Not a single character that is alive.

MASHA. Eleven!

ARCADINA *(glancing at Sorin)*.— Petrusha, are you bored? *(A pause)* He's asleep.

DORN. He's asleep, the State Counsellor.

MASHA. Seven! Ninety!

TRIGORIN. Do you think if I lived in such a place as this and by this lake, I would write? I should overcome such a passion and devote my life to fishing.

MASHA. Twenty-eight!

TRIGORIN. To catch a perch or a bass —that's something like happiness!

DORN. Well, I believe in Constantine Gavrilovitch. He has something! He has something! He thinks in images, his stories are bright and full of color, I always feel them strongly. It's only a pity that he's got no definite purpose. He creates impressions, never more than that, but on mere impressions you don't go far. Irina Nikolayevna, are you glad your son is a writer?

ARCADINA. Imagine, I have not read him yet. There's never time.

MASHA. Twenty-six!

(Trepleff enters without saying anything, sits at his desk.)

SHAMREYEFF. And, Boris Alexeyevitch, we've still got something of yours here.

TRIGORIN. What's that?

SHAMREYEFF. Somehow or other Constantine Gavrilovitch shot a sea gull, and you asked me to have it stuffed for you.

TRIGORIN. I don't remember. *(Reflecting)* I don't remember.

MASHA. Sixty-six! One!

TREPLEFF *(throwing open the window, stands listening)*. How dark! I don't know why I feel so uneasy.

ARCADINA. Kostya, shut the window, there's a draught.

(Trepleff shuts window.)

MASHA. Ninety-eight.

TRIGORIN. I've made a game.

ARCADINA *(gaily)*. Bravo! Bravo!

SHAMREYEFF. Bravo!

ARCADINA. This man's lucky in everything, always. *(Rises)* And now let's go have a bite of something. Our celebrated author didn't have any dinner today. After supper we'll go on. Kostya, leave your manuscript, come have something to eat.

TREPLEFF. I don't want to, Mother, I've had enough.

ARCADINA. As you please. *(Wakes Sorin)* Petrusha, supper! *(Takes Shamreyeff's arm)* I'll tell you how they received me in Kharkoff.

(Pauline blows out candles on table. She and Dorn wheel Sorin's chair out of the room. All but Trepleff go out. He gets ready to write. Runs his eye over what's already written.)

TREPLEFF. I've talked so much about new forms, but now I feel that little by little I am slipping into mere routine myself. *(Reads)* "The placards on the wall proclaimed"—"pale face in a frame of dark hair"—frame—that's flat. *(Scratches out what he's written)* I'll begin again where the hero is awakened by the rain, and throw out all the rest. This description of a moonlight night is too long and too precious. Trigorin has worked out his own method, it's easy for him. With him a broken bottle-neck lying on the dam glitters in the moonlight and the mill wheel casts a black shadow—and there before you is the moonlit night; but with me it's the shimmering light, and the silent twinkling of the stars, and the far-off sound of a piano dying away in the still, sweet-scented air. It's painful. *(A pause)* Yes, I'm coming more and more to the conclusion that it's a matter not of old forms and not of new forms, but that a man writes, not thinking at all of what form to choose, writes because it comes pouring out from his soul. *(A tap at the window nearest the desk)* What's that? *(Looks out)* I don't see anything. *(Opens the door and peers into the garden)* Someone ran down the steps. *(Calls)* Who's there? *(Goes out. The sound of his steps along the veranda. A moment later returns with Nina)* Nina! Nina! *(She lays her head on his breast, with restrained sobbing)*

TREPLEFF *(moved)*. Nina! Nina! It's you—you. I had a presentment, all day my soul was tormented. *(Takes off her hat and cape)* Oh, my sweet, my darling, she has come! Let's not cry, let's not.

NINA. There's someone here.

TREPLEFF. No one.

NINA. Lock the doors. Someone migh come in.

TREPLEFF. Nobody's coming in.

NINA. I know Irina Nikolayevna is here Lock the doors.

TREPLEFF *(locks door on Right. Goes t door on Left)*. This one doesn't lock. I'l put a chair against it. *(Puts chair agains door)* Don't be afraid, nobody's comin in.

NINA *(as if studying his face)*. Let m look at you. *(Glancing around her)* It' warm, cozy— This used to be the draw ing-room. Am I very much changed?

TREPLEFF. Yes—you are thinner an your eyes are bigger. Nina, how strang it is I'm seeing you. Why wouldn't yo let me come to see you? Why didn't yo come sooner? I know you've been her now for nearly a week. I have been ever day there where you were, I stood unde your window like a beggar.

NINA. I was afraid you might hate me I dream every night that you look at m and don't recognize me. If you only knew Ever since I came I've been here walkin about—by the lake. I've been near you house often, and couldn't make up m mind to come in. Let's sit down. *(The sit)* Let's sit down and let's talk, talk It's pleasant here, warm, cozy— Yo hear—the wind? There's a place i Turgenev: "Happy is he who on such night is under his own roof, who has warm corner." I—a sea gull—no, that not it. *(Rubs her forehead)* What was saying? Yes—Turgenev. "And may th Lord help all homeless wanderers." It nothing. *(Sobs)*

TREPLEFF. Nina, again—Nina!

NINA. It's nothing. It will make m feel better. I've not cried for two years Last night I came to the garden to se whether our theatre was still there, an it's there still. I cried for the first time i two years, and my heart grew lighter an my soul was clearer. Look, I'm no crying now. *(Takes his hand)* You are a author, I—an actress. We have both bee drawn into the whirlpool. I used to be a happy as a child. I used to wake up in th morning singing. I loved you and dreame of being famous, and now? Tomorro early I must go to Yelets in the thir class—with peasants, and at Yelets the cultured merchants will plague me with attentions. Life's brutal!

TREPLEFF. Why Yelets?

NINA. I've taken an engagement there for the winter. It's time I was going.

TREPLEFF. Nina, I cursed you and hated you. I tore up all your letters, tore up your photograph, and yet I knew every minute that my heart was bound to yours forever. It's not in my power to stop loving you, Nina. Ever since I lost you and began to get my work published, my life has been unbearable—I am miserable —All of a sudden my youth was snatched from me, and now I feel as if I'd been living in the world for ninety years. I call out to you, I kiss the ground you walk on, I see your face wherever I look, the tender smile that shone on me those best years of my life.

NINA *(in despair)*. Why does he talk like that? Why does he talk like that?

TREPLEFF. I'm alone, not warmed by anybody's affection. I'm all chilled—it's cold like living in a cave. And no matter what I write it's dry, gloomy and harsh. Stay here, Nina, if you only would! and if you won't, then take me with you. *(Nina quickly puts on her hat and cape.)*

TREPLEFF. Nina, why? For God's sake, Nina. *(He is looking at her as she puts her things on. A pause)*

NINA. My horses are just out there. Don't see me off. I'll manage by myself. *(Sobbing)* Give me some water. *(He gives her a glass of water.)*

TREPLEFF. Where are you going now?

NINA. To town. *(A pause)* Is Irina Nikolayevna here?

TREPLEFF. Yes, Thursday my uncle was not well, we telegraphed her to come.

NINA. Why do you say you kiss the ground I walk on? I ought to be killed. *(Bends over desk)* I'm so tired. If I could rest—rest. I'm a sea gull. No, that's not it. I'm an actress. Well, no matter— *(Hears Arcadina and Trigorin laughing in the dining-room. She listens, runs to door on the left and peeps through the keyhole)* And he's here too. *(Goes to Trepleff)* Well, no matter. He didn't believe in the theatre, all my dreams he'd laugh at, and little by little I quit believing in it myself, and lost heart. And there was the strain of love, jealousy, constant anxiety about my little baby. I got to be small and trashy, and played without thinking. I didn't know what to do with my hands, couldn't stand properly on the stage, couldn't control my voice. You can't imagine the feeling when you are acting and know it's dull. I'm a sea gull. No, that's not it. Do you remember, you shot a sea gull? A man comes by chance, sees it, and out of nothing else to do, destroys it. That's not it— *(Puts her hand to her forehead)* What was I—? I was talking about the stage. Now I'm not like that. I'm a real actress, I act with delight, with rapture, I'm drunk when I'm on the stage, and feel that I am beautiful. And now, ever since I've been here, I've kept walking about, kept walking and thinking, thinking and believing my soul grows stronger every day. Now I know, I understand, Kostya, that in our work—acting or writing—what matters is not fame, not glory, not what I used to dream about, it's how to endure, to bear my cross, and have faith. I have faith and it all doesn't hurt me so much, and when I think of my calling I'm not afraid of life.

TREPLEFF *(sadly)*. You've found your way, you know where you are going, but I still move in a chaos of images and dreams, not knowing why or who it's for. I have no faith, and I don't know where my calling lies.

NINA *(listening)*. Ssh—I'm going. Good-by. When I'm a great actress, come and look at me. You promise? But now— *(Takes his hand)* It's late. I can hardly stand on my feet, I feel faint. I'd like something to eat.

TREPLEFF. Stay, I'll bring you some supper here.

NINA. No, no—I can manage by myself. The horses are just out there. So, she brought him along with her? But that's all one. When you see Trigorin— don't ever tell him anything. I love him. I love him even more than before. "An idea for a short story" I love, I love passionately, I love to desperation. How nice it used to be, Kostya! You remember? How gay and warm and pure our life was;

what things we felt, tender, delicate like flowers. Do you remember? "Men and beasts, lions, eagles and partridges, antlered deer, mute fishes dwelling in the water, starfish and small creatures invisible to the eye—these and all life have run their sad course and are no more. Thousands of creatures have come and gone since there was life on the earth. Vainly now the pallid moon doth light her lamp. In the meadows the cranes wake and cry no longer; and the beetles' hum is silent in the linden groves." *(Impulsively embraces Trepleff, and runs out by the terrace door.)*
(A pause.)

TREPLEFF. Too bad if any one meets her in the garden and tells Mother. That might upset Mother. *(He stands for two minutes tearing up all his manuscripts and throwing them under the desk, then unlocks door on Right, and goes out.)*

DORN *(trying to open the door on the Left)*. That's funny. This door seems to be locked. *(Enters and puts chair back in its place)* A regular hurdle race—
(Enter Madame Arcadina and Pauline, behind them Yakov with a tray and bottles; Masha, then Shamreyeff and Trigorin.)

ARCADINA. Put the claret and the beer for Boris Alexeyevitch here on the table. We'll play and drink. Let's sit down, friends.

PAULINE *(to Yakov)*. Bring the tea now, too. *(Lights the candles and sits down)*

SHAMREYEFF *(leading Trigorin to the cupboard)*. Here's the thing I was telling you about just now. By your order.

TRIGORIN *(looking at the sea gull)*. I don't remember. *(Reflecting)* I don't remember.
(Sound of a shot offstage Right. Everybody jumps.)

ARCADINA *(alarmed)*. What's that?

DORN. Nothing. It must be—in my medicine case—something blew up. Don't you worry. *(He goes out Right, in a moment returns)* So it was. A bottle of ether blew up. *(Sings)* Again I stand before thee.

ARCADINA *(sitting down at the table)*. Phew, I was frightened! It reminded me of how— *(Puts her hands over her face)* Everything's black before my eyes.

DORN *(turning through the magazine, to Trigorin)*. About two months ago in this magazine there was an article—a letter from America—and I wanted to ask you among other things— *(Puts his arm around Trigorin's waist and leads him toward the front of the stage)* since I'm very much interested in this question. *(Dropping his voice)* Get Irina Nikolayevna somewhere away from here. The fact is Constantine Gavrilovitch has shot himself.

CURTAIN

ANDRÉ OBEY's

Noah

In the adaptation by ARTHUR WILMURT

First presented by Jerome Mayer at the Longacre Theatre, New York, on February 13, 1935, with the following cast:

NOAH	Pierre Fresnay	THE BEAR	Charles Holden
MAMA	Margaret Arrow	THE LION	Richard Spater
SHEM	David Friedkin	THE MONKEY	Milton Feher
HAM	Harry Bellaver	THE ELEPHANT	Joseph Willis
JAPHET	Norman Lloyd	THE COW	Igene Stuart
NORMA	Fraye Gilbert	THE TIGER	Richard Fleming
SELLA	Cora Burlar	THE WOLF	Jane Churchill
ADA	Gertrude Flynn	THE LAMB	Georgia Graham
A MAN	Royal Beal		

Staged by Jerome Mayer
Settings by Cleon Throckmorton
Animals and Masks by Remo Bufano
Costumes, animals and scenery under the
personal supervision of Ludwig Bemelmans
Music composed and arranged by Louis Horst
Dances directed by Anna Sokolow and Louis Horst

SCENES
ACT ONE—A clearing

ACT TWO
SCENE I. The Ark. Forty days later.
SCENE II. The Ark.

ACT THREE
SCENE I. The Ark.
SCENE II. The top of Mt. Ararat.

ACT ONE

A glade. The Ark is at the Right, only the poop showing, with a ladder to the ground. Noah is taking measurements and singing a little song. He scratches his head and goes over the measurements again. Then he calls.

————

NOAH *(softly)*. Lord— *(Louder)* Lord — *(Very loud)* Lord.—Yes, Lord, it's me. Terribly sorry to bother you again, but— What? Yes, I know you've other things to think of, but after I've shoved off, won't it be a little late? Oh, no, Lord, no, no, no— Now, Lord, please don't think that— Oh, but look, of course I trust you! You could tell me to set sail on a plank—on a branch—on just a cabbage leaf. Why, you could tell me to put out to sea with nothing but my loincloth, even without my loincloth—complete-ly— Yes, yes, I beg your pardon. Your time is precious. Well, this is all I wanted to ask: Should I make a rudder? I say, a rudder— No, no. R as in Robert; U as in Hubert; D as in— That's it, a rudder. Ah, good—very good, very good. The winds, the current, the tides— What was that, Lord? The tempests? Oh, and while I have you, one other little question— Are you listening, Lord? Gone! He's in a temper— Well, you can't blame Him; He has so much to think of. All right; no rudder. *(He considers the ark)* The tides, the currents, the winds. *(He imitates the winds)* Psch!—Psch!— The tempests. *(He imitates the tempests)* Vloum! Ba da bloum!— That's going to be something— *(He makes a quick movement)*—magnifi-cent!— No, no, Lord, I'm not afraid. I know that you'll be with me. I was just trying to imagine— Oh, Lord, while you're there I'd like to ask— *(To the audience)* Chk! Gone again. You see how careful you have to be. *(He laughs)* He was listening all the time. Tempests—I'm going to put a few more nails in down here. *(He hammers and sings)*
When the boat goes well, all goes well.
When all goes well, the boat goes well.
(He admires his work.)
And when I think that a year ago I couldn't hammer a tack without mashing

a nail. That's pretty good, if I do say so myself. *(He climbs aboard the ark and stands there like a captain)* Larboard and star-board!—Cast off!—Close the portholes! —'Ware shoals!—Wait till the squall's over— Good!—Fine! Now I'm ready, completely ready, super-ready! *(He cries to heaven)* I am ready! *(Then quietly)* There. I'd like to know how this business is going to begin. *(He looks all around, at the trees, the bushes, and the sky)* The weather is magnificent; the heat—oppressive, and there's not a sign of a cloud. Well, that part of the program is His affair. *(Enter the Bear Left)* Well!—Now what does *he* want? *(Bear moves toward the ark)* Just a minute there! *(Bear makes a pass at the ark. Noah frightened)* Stop it! *(Bear stops)* Good. Sit down! *(Bear sits)* Lie down. *(Bear lies down on its back and waves its legs gently)* There, that's a good doggie. *(Enter the Lion Left)* What the devil! *(Lion puts its paw on the ark)* Stop that, you!— And lie down. *(Lion lies down beside the Bear)* Fine!—Splendid!—Now what do they want? And besides, why don't they fight? *(To the Animals)* Hey! Why aren't you fighting? Come on, there. Boo! Woof! *(The Bear and the Lion get up and sniff at each other sociably)* Who ever heard of wild animals acting like that? *(Enter the Monkey Left)* Another one!—It's a zoo— Sit down, you monkey. Now, look here, my pets, for a year I've been work-ing here every day. Not one of you has ever shown me the tip of his nose. Now that I've finished, are you out to make trouble for me? Go on, this doesn't concern you. *(He thinks it over)* Unless— But then, that changes everything— Lord! Lord! *(Between his teeth)* Naturally He isn't there! *(Enter the Elephant Left)* Get back there, Jumbo! *(Elephant salutes him)* Good morning, my fine fellow. Now, if I understand you, you want to get aboard, eh? *(The Animals move forward)* Stop! I didn't say you could!—Good. All right, I'll let you come aboard— Yes, don't see what I can— No, I don't see anything against it. *(He sighs deeply)* So the time has come! All right. Up with you. *(Enter the Cow, Left, gamboling)* Gentlthere, gently— And get in the rear. *(He taps Cow on the rump)* But wait a minute. Don't I know you? Aren't you that old cow from Mardocheus's herd? *(Cow moos gaily)* For heaven's sake! *(With feeling)* And He's chosen you! *(To the Bear)* Well, my friend, will you make up your mind? *(Bear sniffs the ground, but doesn't advance)* What's the matter, old boy? *(Noah puts on his spectacles and leans over the spot where the Bear is sniffing)* What? You're afraid of that insect? An ant! Ha, ha, ha! A bear afraid of an ant. Ha, ha, ha! *(But suddenly he strikes his brow)* But what a fool I am! That's not an ant, it's *the* ant! It got here first, and I never saw it. Lord! What marvels there are on the threshold of this new life. It will take a stout heart, a steady hand, and a clear eye! I think my heart is right, but my eyes are dim—my hand is trembling—my feet are heavy— Ah, well, if You've chosen me, perhaps it's because I am like her—the least wicked of the herd. Come, all aboard. Make yourselves at home. *(The Animals go into the ark)* Straight ahead, across the deck. Down the stairway to your left. You'll find your cabins ready. They may look like cages, but they'll be open always. *(He turns towards the forest Left)* Come one, come all! Hurry, you lazy ones, you slow-pokes, you crawlers, you who travel in droves and you who live alone, forked hoofs, hunchbacks! Hurry! Everyone! Everyone! *(He catches his breath)* Ah ha! Here comes the wolf and the lamb, side by side .*(The Wolf and the Lamb enter Left and go into the ark)* Here is the bullfrog and the bull— The fox and the raven. And the birds! What are they waiting for? Come, my little ones. Come! Come! *(The singing of the Birds begins)* Look. The hare and the tortoise! Come on. Come on. Hurrah! The hare wins! Things are getting back to normal! Ah, his will be the golden age!

(A great concert of Birds. Noah falls on his knees. A pause. Then the Tiger enters Left behind Noah. He goes to Noah and taps him on the shoulder. The Birds are suddenly still.)

NOAH *(terrified)*. Ooooo! *(He rises to see)* I know you wouldn't hurt me; it's just the surprise, you know. I'm not afraid— *(His teeth are chattering)* I'm not afraid of anything. Don't g-get that idea th-that *I* have gooseflesh. Come now, this will go away. *(Tiger creeps towards him)* Wait a minute. Maybe it won't, either— Perhaps, if I do this. *(He turns his back and covers his ears)* Go on, get up! Hurry! *(Tiger, with one bound, leaps aboard the ark)* Are you there? *(Roaring of animals from the ark)* Good! *(Noah turns around and wipes his brow)* Phew!

(Off Left is heard the voice of a boy. It is Japhet.)

JAPHET. Whoo-hoo! Papa!

NOAH. Ah, here come the children— Whoo-hoo!

JAPHET *(nearer)*. Whoo-hoo!

NOAH. Whoo-hoo!

SHEM *(off Left)*. Come on, now, Japhet. We agreed; no running. Follow the rules or I won't play.

JAPHET *(entering down Left. He is 17)*. I'm not running. H'lo, Pop! *(He goes to Noah in great strides)*

SHEM *(entering up Left. He is 21)*. You're running! Isn't he running, Father?

JAPHET *(throws himself into Noah's arms)*. Home! I told you my way was shorter.

SHEM. Well, of course, if you're going to run the whole way— Hello, Father.

NOAH *(embracing them both)*. Good morning, children. You both win; Japhet got here first, but he cheated a little. Well, my great big boys, did you have much trouble finding me?

JAPHET. So, Pop! This is where you've been coming every day. Come on, tell us about it.

NOAH. Just be calm a minute.

(Enter Ham up Left. He is 19.)

SHEM and JAPHET. We beat you!

HAM. All right, all right.

SHEM and JAPHET. We won!

HAM. Sure, sure. *(He goes to Noah)* Good morning, Father.

NOAH *(embracing him)*. Hello, Ham, my boy. *(To the three of them)* Where is your mother?

HAM. She's coming.

NOAH. One of you might have waited for her. *(Ham wanders over to the ark)*

JAPHET. She didn't want us to. She said she'd get along better alone. Then she can puff as much as she likes.

NOAH. You could go back a ways and meet her.

SHEM (lying on the ground). Aw, Father, it's so hot.

JAPHET. Come on, we'll take it slowly.

SHEM (getting up). It's terrible. (They go toward the back)

JAPHET (pointing to the ark). New house?

NOAH. Ssshh!

JAPHET. It's nice.

NOAH. Isn't it? (Shem and Japhet go out down Left. Ham is examining the ark, his hands behind his back. Noah goes to him and takes his arm) Well, son, what do you think of it?

HAM. That?

NOAH. Why, yes.

HAM. What is it?

NOAH. Can't you tell? Is it that shapeless?

HAM. Hm! It isn't easy. Come on, Father, what is it, exactly?

NOAH. It's—well, it's made of cypress. It's all cypress. And it's—it's coated with pitch, inside and out.

HAM. Like a boat?

NOAH. Like a—yes. Hm! And it's three hundred cubits long and fifty cubits wide and thirty cubits high—

HAM. But that's ten times too big for us.

Noah. It's—yes, it's pretty big. But does it—look like anything?

HAM. It's not bad—not bad, but why the devil build a house like a boat?

NOAH. Ah! It looks like a—?

HAM. Exactly.

NOAH. Listen. (His tone changes) Who knows what will happen? Suppose a great flood—

HAM (laughing). Here?

NOAH. Who knows? A—a tidal wave—

HAM. In these parts?

NOAH. A deluge— (A noise is heard offstage Left. To Ham) Ssshh!

(Enter Shem and Japhet down Left, carrying Mama on their crossed arms and singing:)

"Here is Mama.

Look at Mama.

See the escort that comes with Mama."

(Noah begins to laugh. Shem and Japhet seat Mama on the grass and dance around her.)

HAM. Oh, calm down a little! (They stop dancing)

NOAH. Hello, you poor Mama! (He kisses her)

MAMA (panting). Phew! Phew!

NOAH. Tired, eh?

MAMA. It's so terribly hot. (To Japhet) Oh, sonny, did you lock the door carefully?

JAPHET. Why—er—yes.

MAMA. You didn't at all.

JAPHET. Why—er—yes.

JAPHET. I did, but—I guess I left the key in the lock.

MAMA. We must get it out right away. Run down to the house—

JAPHET. Oh, say, he—!

MAMA. Go on, run!

NOAH. No, stay here! (To Mama) I beg your pardon, but—there's no use getting the key.

MAMA. No use!—What, with our neighbors?

NOAH (sits on the ramp of the ark). Well,—I don't know how to tell you. In my head I had planned a lot of nice pretty phrases— My poor dear wife, my beloved children, we're never going to back to our house—There! (A short pause)

THE THREE BOYS. What?

MAMA. For months I've felt things weren't going the way you liked. Why didn't you say anything? You know I always understand.

HAM. Father always liked to be mysterious.

NOAH. Don't be silly.

HAM. All right, but you must admit that we might have been consulted. People don't build houses out in the middle of a forest, miles from everybody and everything. Why, just to get provisions it'll take two hours, going and coming.

NOAH. Be quiet.

HAM. When Mother forgets the bread —and that does happen sometimes—

NOAH (laughing bitterly). The bread Ha, ha, ha! Bread—

HAM. We'll need it, won't we? Don' we eat any more?

NOAH. Be quiet, do you hear? Quiet

MAMA. Now stop it, both of you, sto

it! All right, dear, we're not going home any more. That's that. I gusses you've told us the worst.

JAPHET. And I don't see why that's so terrible. This house looks much nicer than the old one. Doesn't it, Shem?

SHEM *(practically asleep)*. Hmmmm?

JAPHET. You see, he isn't losing any sleep over it. *(Japhet and Mama have a good laugh)*

NOAH. You're so good. How good you both are.

MAMA. We love you very much, that's all. It isn't hard to love a man like you. Now finish your story and we'll go see our new house.

NOAH *(in a low voice)*. It isn't a house.

JAPHET and MAMA. What?

JAPHET *(nudging Shem)*. Listen to this, you.

NOAH. It's not a house.

SHEM. What is it?

NOAH. It's a ship.

MAMA and BOYS. A what!

NOAH. A ship.

JAPHET. It isn't.

HAM. Ridiculous!

SHEM *(sitting up)*. No fooling!

MAMA. A ship!

JAPHET. Didn't I tell you? Shem, what did I tell you? It's a boat. *(He runs up ramp)*

SHEM *(following him)*. Can we go on board?

NOAH. Not without me. Admire it from here.

HAM. That's right. Wait. *(Shem and Japhet go behind the ark)*

SHEM. What shall we call it?

MAMA. A ship—

HAM. What on earth for?

NOAH. Well—er—for going sailing.

HAM. Sailing! But on what?

NOAH. God will provide, my boy.

HAM. Oh, come now, Father. Let's be serious!

NOAH. We're going sailing. Yes— we're going on a little trip.

MAMA. But you hate trips.

NOAH. Oh, no, no! A person can change, you know. We'll be nice and quiet, just by ourselves. We won't see anyone. People are pretty unbearable these days, don't you think? Wicked!

Coarse! Hateful! A bit of solitude between the sea and the sky; it will give us new ideas. And when we get back— *(In a low voice)* When we get back—

HAM. So! In an arid land, where an unbelievable heat wave has dried up even the memory of water, a hundred miles from the sea, among shrunken streams and dried-up river beds, at the end of a long life as a farmer, you suddenly feel the call of the briny deep.

NOAH. No, it isn't that, exactly. I don't feel that at all.

MAMA *(tenderly)*. Tell us, Noah, confide in us. Your heart is heavy. I know it. Tell us about it.

HAM. Yes, for heaven's sake, tell us.

JAPHET *(off behind ark)*. Why, this is wonderful!

SHEM *(also off)*. You bet it is. This is great!

NOAH. Come on, let's go to them. *(He helps Mama to her feet)* It will do us good to hear them laugh.

HAM. But, Father—

JAPHET *(appears up Right, beaming)*. Papa! What's that gadget with the rope—!

NOAH. Gadget? Rope? Which one? There are plenty of gadgets and ropes.

JAPHET. The one with the two pulleys in front; a big one and a little one, for lifting machinery.

NOAH. Ah, yes.

JAPHET. Well, it's marvelous. Come and see it, Ham.

HAM. Do you mind, for a minute?

JAPHET. It's genius!

NOAH. Ah, well. A good little son can make genius come afresh.

SHEM *(appearing)*. Japhet, come and see the sliding panel. Father, you're an ace! Mama, your husband's an ace!

MAMA. I don't doubt it for a minute.

JAPHET. But, Papa, how did you ever invent that?

NOAH. I'll tell you. I'd noticed that when a woodcutter wanted to lift a tree-trunk— Have you ever noticed the way a woodcutter rolls up his rope— *(They all go out up Right)*

HAM *(following them)*. I never heard of anything like—

(A cat's meow is heard off Right. Their voices

die away. Enter, down Left, three girls: Ada, Sella and Norma.)

ADA. Come, girls, follow the cat. Don't lose it. I feel we must follow the cat.

SELLA. And *I* think it's getting us lost. We've never been so far into the forest.

NORMA. Besides, we've lost it.

ADA. Then we must look for it. We've got to find it. Hunt for it, sisters, hunt for it! *(She calls)* Kitty, Kitty!

SELLA and NORMA. Kitty, Kitty, Kitty! *(They make the little lip-noise which calls cats. Cat meows)*

ADA. There it is. Look at its little white tail sliding through the grass. Come on, come on.

NORMA. I can't go any further. The heat's killing me. *(They see the ark)*

ADA. Look! A woodcutters' house.

SELLA. Huh. What a funny-looking

NORMA. Ada, I'm afraid you've led house.

us into some nasty trouble.

ADA. We must go into that house.

SELLA *(frightened)*. Oh, no!

NORMA. No, no!

SELLA. Please, let's go back.

NORMA. Yes, let's try to find the road back to the village. *(Cat meows)*

ADA. Be quiet. Listen.

MAMA *(offstage up Right)*. Oh, look! The cat! Noah! Noah! Look at the cat! *(Gay voices)*

JAPHET. Kitty!

NOAH. Kitty!

SHEM. Well, if it isn't dear old Kitty!

ADA. What did I tell you? *(She calls)* Mrs. Noah!

THE THREE GIRLS. Mrs. Noah!

MAMA *(enters up Right)*. What's this? You here, my pretties? *(She calls to offstage)* Shem! Ham! Japhet! Come and see your friends. *(To the Girls)* What brought you here?

ADA *(wrapping her arms about Mama's neck)*. Oh, Mother. Dear little Mother!

MAMA. There, there. What's the matter?

SELLA. She's been excited all morning. *(Noah and Three Boys enter up Right.)*

NORMA. Yes. She couldn't stay still. She'd burst into tears for no reason at all.

SELLA. She never stopped talking about you.

NORMA. She wanted to go to your house. She wanted to see you. She insisted on seeing you.

ADA. Dear Mrs. Noah! *(To her sisters)* We've just escaped a great danger.

NOAH. How do you know, little one?

ADA. I—I feel it. *(She goes and kneels before Noah)* I'm *sure* of it. *(Noah lifts her up, gazes at her, presses her to him, and raises his eyes to Heaven. A short silence)*

THE THREE BOYS *(in a low voice, but joyously)*. Good morning!

JAPHET. Are you sailing with us?

SELLA and NORMA. What?

SHEM. You know, you'd make pretty little cabin-boys.

SELLA and NORMA. Pretty—*what?*

HAM. If we should have to draw lots to see who's to be eaten, I hope fate picks on Norma. She's so plump and white. I'll take a wing, please. *(Mama and the Boys laugh)*

NORMA. What are you talking about? *(More laughter)*

NOAH *(coming back to earth)*. Yes, you have just escaped a dreadful danger. *(A pause. Then joyously)* How could I have missed it? We have three lovely neighbors— Orphans, oddly enough. They share our life, they live it with us. We say our prayers together. We talk across the fence. We send each other tidbits from our dinners. And I—I forgot them. Imagine! Now, isn't it lucky that— But how did you happen to meet the cat?

ADA. She was over in your house—

MAMA. Oh, you've been to our house?

ADA. Yes.

SELLA. Yes. I must say there were a lot of people out in front.

NOAH. Aha.

NORMA. Oh, yes, a whole crowd. Men and women and children from the village And some men from other villages, too And they were all whispering and waving their arms.

NOAH. Yes, of course. It was time— Go on.

SELLA. All of a sudden Ada cried, "We must go over."

NORMA. She took each of us by the hand and led us outdoors.

SELLA. We went through the crowd—

NORMA. There we were at your door.

ADA. I pulled away a man who was listening with his ear glued to the panel. I went in—

MAMA. Japhet, the key!

ADA. Nobody was there.

SELLA. Except the cat.

ADA. Except the cat. She came and rubbed herself against my legs and meowed so it would break your heart.

MAMA. Poor Kitty!

ADA. We came out—

SELLA. That is, we wanted to get out, but the crowd was so thick—

NORMA. It was like a wall of faces across the door—

ADA. Then Kitty let out a great big wail; you know, the battle cry of cats.

JAPHET. Meow!!

SELLA. She arched her back—

NORMA. She spat like mad—

ADA. And the crowd backed up. (The Three Boys laugh) So we went through. We followed that cat and she led us into the forest.

THE THREE BOYS. Ah!

SELLA. Every hundred steps she turned around to see if we were following.

THE THREE BOYS. Oh!

NORMA. We lost her!

THE THREE BOYS. Woe!

ADA. We found her again!

THE THREE BOYS. Whee!

ADA, SELLA and NORMA. And here we are!!

THE TREE BOYS. Hurray! (General embraces)

HAM (to Noah). Now, are you going to explain?

NOAH (his voice vibrating). Yes!

ALL. Ah!

NOAH. I'll tell you everything. It's a great secret, a terrible secret. I has weighed on my tongue and on my heart for months—for a year— I had no right to unburden myself to you. But today—

JAPHET. Sshh!

NOAH. Eh?

JAPHET (in a low voice). Someone's hiding right over there.

ALL Where?

JAPHET. Sshh! There. (He points off Left) In the bushes. (Something whistles over the stage)

THE THREE BOYS. An arrow!

NOAH. Women to the rear! (Mama and the Girls retreat toward the ark. Another whistling)

THE THREE BOYS. Another!

NOAH. To the ship! (All move toward the ramp)

(A shout offstage. Then A Man, a sort of hunter, with a savage face, runs in from the Left, stops short in the Center of the stage, plants himself firmly, and points a spear at Noah.)

THE MAN. Stop!—Stop!—Stop! (To the Girls, who are moving up ramp) Well, you floozies, are you deaf? One move and I nail the old gent to the wall of his house.

JAPHET (Trying to drag his brothers). Get him!

MAMA. Don't budge!

MAN. Watch out, you little rooster!

NOAH. Quiet, Japhet, quiet. He'd hit you.

MAN. I sure will.

MAMA and the YOUNGSTERS. Bandit!

NOAH. Silence. (Mutterings from the Youngsters) Now, that's enough! (To the Man) Put your spear down; you'll tire yourself out. What do you want?

MAN. I seen you. I seen you. You sorcerer. Talking to the animals. Swiping a cow from Mardocheus. Playing with the bears and the lions and tigers, not to mention the elephants. I seen you. The whole village is going to know. I'll tell them. Sorcerer! Sorcerer!

THE THREE BOYS. Stop it!

MAN. You weren't in on it. All you have to do is shut up. What's more, the animals are in there. (He points to the ark) They've been scampering up here in droves. That's where they are—in there! (Mama and the Youngsters laugh. The Man rushes to the ark and beats on it with his fist. Roaring from the animals)

MAMA and YOUNGSTERS. (Frightened) Oh!

MAN. Hahaha! Who's laughing now? Ah, he's all very sweet and gentle but he does plenty of tricks when you ain't lookin'! He's bad. He's jealous. He never could make anything with his hands. He's a menace to the whole country.

MAMA. Be quiet!

MAN. You know what? This drought that's been frying us for three months, that nobody's never seen nothing like before, that'll knock us all dead with our mouths open this winter—that's him. He done it! He's the one!

NOAH. Aren't you a little bit out of your mind?

MAN. You done it! There! We all got together! We took a vote. And we all voted alike—unanimous—that it's all your fault.

NOAH. Oh, but—

MAN. Get this: I'm on what you call a mission. The head man says to me, "watch that old guy. He acts stupid but he knows all the tricks. Everything that's happened to us—he started them."

MAMA. Oh, Noah, if they think that, that's terrible!

NOAH. Ssshh! Ssshh!

MAN. You look in the air like this— (He imitates Noah praying) And right away it gets hotter, all the time hotter. I was watching you. I seen you doing your mugging. (He imitates Noah) I was lying on the ground, and it's hot like a grate.

THE YOUNGSTERS (in a low voice). Oh!

MAN. All right, now you got to pay for it. Yeah, you got to come with me. But I don't need all of you. The head'll do. (He leaps toward Noah. Mama and the Girls scream. The Boys line up in front of Noah)

NOAH. Sssh. (He steps in front of them All and smiles) What a beast! (A pause) The drought— (He half turns toward his family) He hoped it would open their eyes; that they'd say to themselves, "It isn't possible. It's a judgment from Heaven." I told them that myself. I sang it in every key. They laughed in my face. They spit on me. They threw stones at me.

MAMA and YOUNGSTERS. Yes.

NOAH. Didn't I tell them enough?

MAMA and YOUNGSTERS. Oh, yes.

NOAH. I really told them often enough?

MAMA and the YOUNGSTERS. Oh, yes, yes, yes.

NOAH (turning toward the Man). What a beast! To think they're all like you! Lazy! Lying! Wanton! Thieving! (Man sneers) And on top of that, sneering and drunk like that one!

MAN (blowing a berry, probably). Aw, you old fool. You old ass.

NOAH (walking up to him). Tell me, my good fellow, can you swim?

MAN. What?

NOAH. I asked if you could swim.

MAN. What's it to you?

NOAH. Come now, yes or no. Can you swim?

MAN. Sure.

NOAH. Can you swim a long time?

MAN. Absolutely!

NOAH. You'll have to swim a long time—a terribly long time. So long that it might be better if you couldn't swim at all. Then it would be over sooner.

MAN. Over?

NOAH. That's it: finished.

MAN. What's going to be finished?

NOAH. Everything! You! Your relatives! Your friends! The town! All the towns! This forest! All the trees and the animals, and the men—all in the water! Under the water! With your sins like stones around your necks.

MAN (bending double). Hahahahaha!

NOAH (bending double too). Hahahahaha!

MAN. Hahahahahaha!

NOAH. It's going to rain. Rain! More than that, it's going to—ah—rain! (The Man, the Youngsters and Mama raise their eyes to the sky)

MAN. Hahahahaha!

HAM (to Shem, under his breath). Ha Father got a fever? The sky was never so clear.

NOAH. A rain such as there's neve been before. A drenching, a bath, a water fall! A storm of water! A fury of water Tempests will scream endlessly throug the air. A great wind will yell night an day over the world, like an immense blac curtain ripped by lightning. Fish will pla in the trees. On the mountain top instead of flocks of eagles there will b schools of sharks. And the drowned wit their arms outstretched will roll over an over, down and down and down. He tol me so.

MAN. Who?

NOAH. God.

MAN. Who's that?

NOAH. God.

MAN. Oh, yeah?

NOAH *(louder)*. God.

MAN. Sure, sure.

NOAH *(very loud)*. Blessed God! *(Mama and Youngsters drop to their knees)*

MAN. Hahahaha! *(He stutters with glee)* God! Blessed God!—Dear, good, kind— *(He stops short. His hands go to his forehead. The light dims)*

NOAH. Hah! Did you feel that, my boy? You felt the first drop. *(Savagely)* Right on your head, between the eyes, like an arrow. A perfect shot. *(Mama and Youngsters rise, trembling)*

MAN. Oh, you think so? Well, it was a sparrow.

NOAH. And that? *(The Man's hand goes to the back of his neck)* I suppose that was a nightingale? And that? *(The Man's hand covers his eyes)* A robin, maybe? *(The Man stretches out his hands and quickly draws them in again)* And those. A brace of pigeons??

MAMA and YOUNGSTERS. Oh!

NOAH. Dance, my good man, dance! *(And the Man dances as if he were trying to avoid a cloud of arrows)* Fire, O Lord! Pierce this vile target through and through with all Your might!

MAMA and YOUNGSTERS *(every hand extended)* It's raining, raining, raining! *(Pantomime of Youngsters seeking the rain with every gesture around the Man, whose every gesture dodges the rain. The light is growing dim)*

NOAH. Strike those evil eyes. That prying nose. Those ears. Nail up that lewd mouth whose thread of insults You cut off as with a sword. Pierce the hands which were never raised to You. The feet that strayed. The glutton's belly. O God, split that wicked heart. Fire, fire, King of Archers!

MAN *(sinks down, still warding off the rain with both hands)*. Help! Help! It's burning— *(The light grows dimmer)*.

MAMA *(her hands stretched to the rain)*. It's cool like an evening breeze.

THE YOUNGSTERS *(their hands outstretched)*. Like an evening breeze.

MAMA. Like the blue of heaven.

THE YOUNGSTERS. Like the blue of heaven.

MAMA. Like the laughter of angels.

THE YOUNGSTERS. The laughter of angels.

MAN *(on his knees)*. Help! Help! Help! Help! *(Thunder rolls)*

NOAH. We're off! Into the Ark, my good crew! Heavy weather tonight! Go into our home. Into the bark of God! You first, Mama. Ada! Sella! Norma! Shem! Ham! Japhet! And sing, my children, all together! *(A clap of thunder)* *(The chorus is singing in unison. Noah goes up last. The storm rages. It is completely dark. The Animals timidly peer out of hatchways)*

MAN. Help me! Help me! Help me! *(The singing spreads through the ark)*

ACT TWO

SCENE ONE

The deck of the ark at dawn. Two cocks are crowing, one near, one far away. We hear Noah in the hold, coughing, yawning, whining, stretching, and finally jumping out of bed.

———

NOAH *(is heard)*. Everybody up! Six o'clock. Up everybody. *(Chorus of protests from Youngsters, who would rather sleep a while longer)* Come on, get up, lazybones. *(Cock crows)*

NORMA. How's the weather?

SHEM. How do you think? It's raining, of course.

SELLA. Did you hear the downpour in the night?

SHEM. Father, this cruise is a washout. *(Sound of feet on floor)*

NOAH. Who's cabin-boy today?

MAMA. Ada, isn't she?

ADA. Yes, Mother, I am.

NOAH. Sweep out the corners well, won't you, dear? And sprinkle a little water on the floor. The dust, you know— *(Sound of a broom sweeping)*

JAPHET *(is heard)*. Coffee, in the hold. Coffee, everybody! *(Cheers)* And it's good, I'm telling you.

NOAH. Not too much for Mama, eh. This weather has been hard on her. Let's be careful of Mama's heart.

NORMA. Pwhew! How hot it is!

SHEM. A good thing, too. It's the only thing on this trip that is hot. Otherwise we'd freeze.

ALL. Brrr! Brrr! (*Cock crows. The day is brightening*)

NOAH. Where's Ham?

ADA. He isn't here, sir.

NOAH. So I see. Where is he?

ADA. I don't know, sir.

NOAH. What on earth is he doing. We never know where he is.

JAPHET. Well, I'm going up on deck a minute and see what's happening.

SHEM. You're crazy. You'll be drowned.

MAMA. Bundle yourself up well, child. Wear your muffler and the coat with the hood.

JAPHET. Yes, Mama.

MAMA. Look out for those big waves. You never know when they're coming.

JAPHET. Sure, I will, Mama.

MAMA. Be careful not to slip on the deck.

JAPHET. Oh, I'm getting regular sea legs.

NOAH. Breakfast, children, breakfast. (*There is a noise in the mess hall, the noise of eating. It is broad daylight on deck. The sun is brilliant. Enter Japhet from hatch, with his hood up. A fanfare from the cocks.*)

JAPHET (*astounded at the clear sky*). No!!! (*He throws back his hood*) No!!! (*He pulls off his muffler and coat and appears half nude. With a huge sigh*) Aaah! Clear! At last! (*He goes to lean over the hatch from which he entered, but instead he straightens up and stretches toward the sun, his hands clasped above his head. Joyfully*) Aaah! (*With arms outstretched, he turns slowly around, gazing at the horizon. Passionately*) Oh! (*He is dazzled. He covers his eyes. Then he uncovers them and facing the audience, begins to laugh silently. After which he commences to run around the deck, stumbling, and singing in a little throaty voice*)

SHEM (*from below*) Hey! Hey there! Quiet down.

THE GIRLS. What's he doing?

THE OTHERS. He'll wreck the boat.

SHEM. He's gone crazy. Lunatic!

NOAH. Japhet! No foolishness, do you hear? The ceiling's coming down.

JAPHET (*stops and goes to the hatch to shout the news; but he controls himself and his voice is low and trembling*) Come here! Come up here, everybody.

NOAH (*anxiously*). What is it? What's the matter?

JAPHET. Come here!

NOAH. Come on. All hands on deck! Something's up!

(*Low rumblings from below. Japhet waits in the back, motionless, bursting with joy. The others, excepting Ham, come up through the hatch and the brilliant light strikes their faces. Each in turn gives a little, strangled cry and goes to join Japhet in silence. The cocks are singing at the top of their lungs.*)

NOAH (*lining them up*). Sshh. (*In a clear whisper*) Everybody on tiptoe. Walk on tiptoe. It's so beautiful—so new—so fragile—

ADA. Look! The deck is steaming—

SELLA. The planks are drying up.

NORMA. The sea is singing.

MAMA. The silence—

SHEM (*staring at the sun, sneezes thunderously*). At at at chou!

NOAH. Sshh! Now, where is Ham?

JAPHET. Aw, that's his loss.

NOAH (*having lined theim all up at the back, steps in front of them and cries in resounding voice*). For—the—Lord—God King of the Earth! (*He raises his arm*)

THE YOUNGSTERS. Hurray! Hurray! Hurray! (*Their capes fall*)

CHORUS OF ANIMALS (*from below*) Ouahh! Ouahh! Ouahh! (*The Youngsters laugh*).

NOAH. The Golden Age!—Just as said. (*A pause. He gazes at the sky, the water, the ark, then turns to the others, and cries, profoundly joyful*) My children, good morning!

THE YOUNGSTERS. Good morning Father!

NOAH. How are you?

THE YOUNGSTERS. Well!

NOAH. Good!

THE YOUNGSTERS. And how are you?

NOAH. Very well!

THE YOUNGSTERS. Splendid!

NOAH. Louder!

THE YOUNGSTERS. Splendid!

NOAH. Still louder!

THE YOUNGSTERS. Splendid!!!

NOAH (*delighted*). That's it. We must

shout, my darlings. We must exhale. Like this: Hah! *(He blows all the air out of his lungs)* We must cast out these forty days of darkness, these forty nights of fear. They've filled our lungs with soot, but we survived them. Exhale!

THE YOUNGSTERS. Hah!

NOAH. All together!

THE YOUNGSTERS *with* NOAH. Haaaaaah!

NOAH. There; we're cleaned out. Now we must learn everything all over. How to walk, how to talk, how to sleep! We've got to learn how to live. You know what? We must learn to be happy. The others all died because they couldn't laugh. That's right. Haha! Yes! *(He begins to laugh)* Hahahahaha!

THE YOUNGSTERS. Hahahahaha!

NOAH. Hahaha, hahaha!!!

THE YOUNGSTERS. Hahaha, hahaha!

NOAH *(exulting)*. I feel—so new! My body—all brand new! *(He strikes his chest)* In here there are doves. I feel them flying from my heart to God. Ah, I wish I could speak German, so my words would sound less flowing and more the way things are. Walk, children. Let's walk. *(They line up and walk in great strides towards the audience)* As you see, to the South we have a view of the ocean.

THE YOUNGSTERS *(interested)*. Aha!

NOAH *(walking Left)*. To the East we have a vast expanse of water, probably salt, of an appearance and character distinctly oceanic.

THE YOUNGSTERS. Well, well!

NOAH *(walking up)*. To the North we are right on the edge of—well—the sea.

THE YOUNGSTERS. Isn't it lovely?

NOAH. Lastly, to the West we see— and hear—the laughter upon laughter of the waves. *(Toward audience)* To sum up the entire situation: we are on the water.

THE YOUNGSTERS. We're at sea! Ha! Ha! Ha! Ha!

JAPHET. Faster! *(All walk more quickly)*

NOAH. Don't you think it's marvelous?

THE YOUNGSTERS. Marvelous!

JAPHET. Faster! *(Again they quicken the pace)*

NOAH. I don't believe Mama can keep up with this.

MAMA *(panting)*. Yes—I can! I'm so— so happy.

NOAH. No, no, get out of line, Mama. Just give us your good wishes.

MAMA *(dropping out)*. You're—so young—Noah!

NOAH. Ah! Faith, I'm as old as the world— I was born—this morning.

THE YOUNGSTERS. Come on. Faster, faster!

NOAH. On the sea, beneath the sky, between the two great elements which were in the beginning—

THE YOUNGSTERS *(impatient)*. Come on! Come on! Come on! Come on!

NOAH. I give up. *(He drops out and joins his wife)*. But you go ahead. Go on, go on!

THE BOYS. A-hi!—A-ha!—Ah-yah!— Ah-you!

THE GIRLS. You-ou-ou-ou!

NOAH *and* MAMA *(sitting on the sidelines, beat the measure with their hands)*. March! March! March—March—March!

THE YOUNGSTERS *(beside themselves with joy)*. Ha—ah—ah—ah.—Ha! *(They drop down in a circle. Norma in Center, arms up)*

ALL. The sun!!

(Suddenly Ham leaps up through the hatch, the Monkey after him. Animals are roaring in ark.)

HAM. What is all this? What's going on? Have you gone mad? What's got into you?

NOAH *(with a gesture)*. Look!

HAM. You've driven the animals crazy. As crazy as you are! They're running all over below, jumping around and screaming. Listen to them. *(Roars of animals from the hold)*

NOAH. They're happy. It's joy—

HAM. Someone left the bird cage open. The whole flock is preening itself down there. When I came up some of them got out. *(Pointing above)* There— See them? Now just try to catch them.

NOAH. Why, that's so. We can let out the birds. I never thought of that. When they're tired they'll come back all right. We can let them out. I really believe we ought to. Wouldn't you say so, Mama?

MAMA. Oh, yes, that would be nice.

NOAH. Release the birds.

THE THREE GIRLS. Yes, let's release

the birds. *(They get up together, link arms, and rush toward the hatch)*

HAM *(blocking the way)*. Oh, no, you don't, ladies! You're not going down there. I'm sorry, but I'm beginning to catch on. You want to upset everything, throw everything up in the air. And then you can suck your thumbs while your friends get the house back in shape. Not a chance, ladies. *(The Monkey sucks thumb)*

NOAH *(laughing)*. Fine! Wonderful! Bravo, monkey! *(To Ham)* Have you been training him long? *(Noah's laughter spreads to Mama, then to Shem and Japhet. But the Girls remain fixed, speechless, arms locked, lips tight shut)*

HAM *(furiously)*. Ladies, will you please go away? Come on, drop your arms. Split up, for goodness' sake. Take it easy. Make yourselves at home, ladies. Will you, for heaven's sake, stop clinging to each other?

NOAH *(to the heavens)*. Wonderful! Immense! It's immense! Sit down. Hahaha! Sit down, little ones. Don't take it so hard. *(The girls sit down, timidly smiling. Then, seeing the others laughing, they begin to laugh. Ham shrugs his shoulders and the Monkey copies him)*

HAM. To think I should find you here, on the other side of the earth, barely escaped from drowning, just as I always knew you; childish, gullible, giddy!

NOAH. That's why He saved us. Because He knew He'd always find us just the same; just as young; just as confident. Just as glad to be alive!

THE YOUNGSTERS. Yes, glad! Glad!

HAM. Wallowing in this rocky old shoe! Mumbling prayers!

NOAH. Ham, that's blasphemy—

A VOICE *(from above)*. Ha-am!

NOAH. Now, you see! *(All fall on their knees but Ham, who looks up)*

THE VOICE. Ha-am! Ha-am!

HAM. Hi, there, old boy. *(To the horrified others)* Oh, don't worry, it's only Polly. Polly, the parrot! See it, up on the mast? *(All get up, laughing)* Had your breakfast, Polly?

THE VOICE. Poor Pol. Poor Pol. Polly wants a cracker.

HAM *(to Noah)*. Didn't it ever occur to you that it might be a good idea to feed the birds before you let them out? Father, Father, Father. It's gotten so I wonder if you haven't mixed up what you think are orders from Heaven with what seem like good ideas to you.

MAMA. Ham, be still.

NOAH. Let him speak.

HAM. For instance, Father, where are we?

NOAH. Well—my boy, I don't know.

THE YOUNGSTERS. Nobody knows.

HAM. Where are we going?

THE YOUNGSTERS. We'll find out.

HAM. What are we doing?

THE YOUNGSTERS. Nothing.

HAM. Suppose I ask you this: What day is it?

THE YOUNGSTERS. That's easy!

HAM. All right, tell me. *(The rest are silent)* Well, well—it's not so easy, is it.

NOAH. This is—the first day.

HAM. Aha! They've lost track. They've lost their wits.

MAMA. It's Sunday, children. Every day will be Sunday.

NOAH. Good for you, Mama.

HAM. That's enough. They've lost their wits. How are you going to live without wits? There's no more time. You've lost track of time.

NOAH. What are you trying to start here, you rascal? *(Whirls Ham around to him)*

HAM. You're just castaways. Naked stripped! You're castaways. *(The chorus lower their heads in silence)*

NOAH. No, no, my boy. We mustn't let any sadness come to us here. If it should come, we must throw it overboard at once. Down to that rotting dung heap 'way down there. Thank God, there are fathoms of clean water between it and us. Isn't that right, children?

THE YOUNGSTERS. Oh, yes, Father!

SHEM. But—

THE YOUNGSTERS *(enthusiastically)*. Yes, yes, yes, yes!

SHEM. But—

HAM. That's it! That's just it! Yes—"but". Yes, yes, yes—but!!!

SHEM *(going up to Ham)*. Listen, old boy—

HAM *(backing up toward the hatch)*. Yes, old boy?

SHEM. Tell me, old boy—

HAM. I'm listening, old boy.

SHEM. Maybe *you* can tell us. Maybe *you* know what day it is?

NOAH. Such childishness!

HAM. Ah. There you have it! There you have it! *(Followed by the Monkey, who salutes him, he goes down the hatch, murmuring)* There you have it. *(Shem remains leaning over the hatch)*

NOAH. Come, Shem, come back and sit down. *(Shem, preoccupied, resumes his seat. Noah's gaiety a bit forced)* What, my hearties, there's nothing wrong?

THE YOUNGSTERS *(dully)*. No—no.

NOAH. Here's luck!

THE PARROT. What day is it? What day is it?

NOAH. That's a nuisance, that bird. *(To the Parrot)* Hey there, you! You're bothering us. Hahaha! *(He laughs alone, then signals Mama to help him out. Mama clears her throat)*

SHEM *(suddenly jumping to his feet)*. No —you can never make me believe that if we all thought hard, if we all tried, we couldn't remember what day it is. *(The Three Girls and Japhet get up excitedly)*

NOAH. That tale again. You certainly do stick to it. *(Peevishly)* All right, go ahead. Find out if you can. *(He gets up and paces the deck. The Three Girls, Shem and Japhet hold a low but heated discussion)* It scares you, eh? Eternity frightens you! You, you puny mortals. You morsels of men. *(To Mama)* They are, you know, Mama. They are not ready for this new timeless world.

JAPHET. Why don't you ask Him about it?

NOAH. Oh, certainly! That would be fine. I could ask Him the time, too, eh? I might ask Him for a light. You have a beautiful idea of God, you have. *(He laughs heartily. The Youngsters begin to laugh with him)*

JAPHET. You always tell us He is so simple.

NOAH. Certainly He is simple. He's more simple than you are. Time means nothing to eternal God and so it's no concern of ours.

THE YOUNGSTERS. But what day is it?

NOAH. You whelps. You kids. All right, we'll find the day for you. Come on.

THE YOUNGSTERS *(delighted)*. Ah!

NOAH. Come on, Mama. *(He helps her up)* We'll all play.

THE YOUNGSTERS. We're all going to play.

MAMA. Oh, it's a game?

NOAH. Of course it's a game. What do you think it is? We'll keep them amused and they'll forget the time. Let's see— How shall we do it? *(Chorus overjoyed)* Now! Pay attention. Mama, Monday. Enter into the spirit of Monday, Mama. *(He makes passes before her)* You— are—Monday! Ada, Tuesday. Japhet, Wednesday—

JAPHET. I feel more like Thursday.

NOAH. All right. *There's* a conscientious little day for you. Shem, you be Wednesday, eh?

SHEM. All right with me.

NOAH. Fine! Japhet, Thursday; Norma, Friday; and Sella, Saturday. Ah! There you are; everyone a day. You know this is important. Now, my week, let me see you.

SHEM. Wow! Old Monday looks pretty awful! *(Laughter)*

THE YOUNGSTERS. And Sunday?

NOAH. Wait a minute, it's very important, you know. Now, blindfold me and I'll try—and how I can try—to catch one of you. *But*, if I catch no one, it's Sunday!

SHEM. It's blindman's buff.

NOAH. Hey! Whoa there—quiet! It's inspired blindman's buff. This game is controlled by God.

THE YOUNGSTERS. Come on. Let's play; let's play.

NOAH. Scatter, all you days! Mama's going to blindfold me. *(The children scatter, screaming. Noah comes down front and joins Mama)*

MAMA *(tying the blindfold. Softly)*. You're sweet, Noah, you're so sweet.

NOAH *(kissing her)*. Go away, Mama. Everything's fine.

MAMA. They're so weak.

NOAH. Weak, but not wicked. Go on, now. Time to play. *(Turning around, blindfolded, toward the back)* Aha!

THE YOUNGSTERS. Look out, Mama!
Look out!

MAMA. Not yet, Noah— Don't come
yet!

NOAH. Hurry up!

MAMA (trotting toward the back). I'll
beat you.

THE YOUNGSTERS. Go! (Noah advances
with comic ominousness. The children scream)
Eeeeee!

NOAH.

Blindly but without delay
I'll write the calendar's first page,
For children have to know the day
Even in the Golden Age.

(Shouts, laughter, running, flights.)

SCENE TWO

The deck of the ark. Intense sunlight.
Downstage Shem is fishing. Ham is standing
near him. A little behind them Norma is
keeping watch.

———

HAM. Wasn't that a bite?

SHEM. No, it was a weed.

HAM. Pull in a little and see.

SHEM. It's a weed, I tell you.

HAM. Maybe there aren't any fish.

SHEM. There are fish, all right. But you
know what Father said, "Nothing can be
killed."

HAM. Let's see if I can stir them up.

SHEM. They just won't bite, that's all.

HAM. Oh, sure! They're wise, I suppose, specially educated fish!

SHEM. Go ahead and joke. I believe it.

HAM. Hahaha!

SHEM. Not so loud, you fool! (Turning
around) See anything, Norma?

NORMA. Not a thing. I'll tell you if
I do.

SHEM (to Ham). Do you know what
Father's doing?

HAM. He's down with the animals.
They're the only ones he cares about
these days. He understands them. He
talks to them. Hahaha!

NORMA. Ssst! (The boys turn around
with their backs to the railing and pretend to
chat innocently) False alarm.

HAM. Keep your eyes open now.

NORMA (tenderly). You know you can
count on me.

HAM (to Shem). Come on, boy.

SHEM (going back to his fishing). That
girl's crazy about you.

HAM. She's pretty nice— Come on,
Shem. Where are these fish? You
promised me one. Go ahead, strike at that
big one. He's a five pounder, I bet. Get
him by the nose. Strike! (Shem casts his
line) Ooops! If he'd only jumped. So
they're not biting, hm? Pull in, pull in.

SHEM (pulling in without getting anything). They're not biting, I tell you.
Even when they get on the hook, they
work loose again.

HAM. Try some more.

SHEM. I've tried enough. (He lays down
the line)

HAM. Once more. Go on, just once.
Think of Father's face if you presented
him with a fish from the celestial school.
Think of that, Shem.

SHEM (casting again). That would be
funny.

HAM. Oh, that should have gone
further.

NORMA (warning). Look out!

HAM (to Shem). Stay the way you are.
Lean over the rail. If it's he you can drop
the line.

(Ada and Sella enter from hatch.)

NORMA. It's nobody, just the little
girls.

HAM. Good. Come on, Shem, old boy,
one last real try. Give it everything you've
got!

NORMA. I want to see this. (She goes
and leans on Ham's shoulder. Ada and Sella
come down, whispering)

SELLA (low, to Ada). Did you hear
that? —"little girls—nobody."

ADA. Yes. That's what she thinks.

SELLA. Always chasing the men.

ADA. We can clean up the dishes and
wash clothes. That's all we're good for.

SELLA. Have you noticed? She doesn't
even make her own bed any more. Just
pulls the cover over it any old way.

ADA. All she does is pretty herself up.

HAM (half-turning). Don't whisper
like that, kids. You're bothering us.

SELLA. We're not kids.

HAM. Indeed? Ladies, then. Well

ladies, give us a rest, will you? *(Norma lets out a laugh)*

ADA *and* SELLA *(indignant)*. Oh! *(They draw away and continue their gossiping)*

HAM. Well, Shem? What's the matter? Things don't look so good, do they? Never mind, get a move on. You're a swell fisherman, you are. *(He pushes Shem to rail)*

SHEM. I tell you these fish aren't—

HAM. Oh, don't kid me! I've had enough of this sleight-of-hand. No more hocus-pocus, see! It's time we had some order around here. *(Violently)* Go on! Fish!

NORMA *(passionately)*. Oh, you darling! You're so wonderful when you want something. *(She kisses him)*

ADA *and* SELLA *(choking)*. Oh!

HAM *(freeing himself)*. Yes, sure— You keep watch, dear. *(To Shem)* Of course, this is all a surprise to me.

SELLA. Did you see that?

ADA. I should say I did.

SELLA. I'm going to tell Mr. Noah.

ADA. It would be better to tell Mrs. Noah first.

HAM. Are you brats beginning again? *(Ada and Sella are silent. Whirling Shem around)* Now, you listen to me! You've got to catch a fish. Get that? Just one, but I've got to have it. And right away, too!

SELLA. A what?

HAM. Shut up! *(His eyes travel over the frozen group)* I want to haul something out of the water *alive* and see it die before my eyes. See? *(To Shem)* Hop to it. *(Shem casts again and Ham watches the line with burning eyes. In a low voice)* This one settles it. Well, boy?—Well? Well?

SHEM. Maybe—

HAM. Be sure! Let him take a good bite and then hook him. If he fights, I'll jump into the water—

NORMA. Look out! Careful!

HAM. Damn! *(He turns around. Shem starts to follow suit, Ham pushing him against the rail)* Fish!

SHEM. Ah, no! Listen—

HAM. Fish, I tell you. Do it quietly. I'll take the blame. *(A little pause. Shem fishes, trembling)*

JAPHET *(enters from hatch)*. Oh, here you are!

HAM *(fairly shrieking)*. What do *you* want?

JAPHET. Nothing. I—I was just looking for you.

HAM. I thought you were officer-of-the-day.

JAPHET. I am, but I'm all done for today.

HAM. Well—do something over.

JAPHET. What?

HAM. The officer-of-the-day ought not to be trailing around the decks.

JAPHET. Who said so?

HAM. I did!

ADA. Ooooh!

HAM. Silence!

JAPHET. Oh!

HAM. You've all been doing what you pleased long enough. From now on, when I give an order—

SHEM *(dropping his line)*. A what?

NORMA. An order!

SHEM. Who's talking to you?

HAM. Oh, so you stick to him, do you?

SHEM. Not me. He and I have split up for good. I'm thinking of myself, that's all, and I'm not going to take any—

HAM. Go on and fish! Keep out of this!

JAPHET. Papa has told you a hundred times not to fish here.

SELLA. Ham made him.

NORMA *(up on box)*. Will you be quiet, you chippy! Babbler! Tattle-tale!

ADA. Oh, is that so? Lazybones! Flirt! You conceited little hussy!

MAMA *(enters from hatch, distracted)*. Children, your father's coming. *Now* what's the matter? My goodness, it's always the same. You can't be left alone a second.

SELLA *and* JAPHET. It's him.

NORMA. It isn't!

ADA *and* SHEM. It's him!

NORMA. It's her!

JAPHET. It's Ham!

NORMA. It's Ada!

SELLA *and* ADA. It's Norma!

JAPHET. It's Ham!

MAMA. Be quiet! Be quiet! Your father's coming. He's right behind me.

JAPHET. He wants to catch fish.

ADA. She kissed him.

SHEM. He said he was captain.

NORMA. Liar!

ADA and SELLA. Lazybones!

JAPHET, ADA and SELLA. Flirt!

MAMA. Oh, Lord, here he is!

NOAH (enters from hatch. Sudden silence. He comes downstage slowly, passing among the others without seeming to see them. He comes to the front, gazes at the sky and sea, and sighs) Not a breath— Not a ripple— Well—

HAM (advancing a step). Father—

NOAH (strongly). No! (A pause)

HAM. Just the same, Father—

NOAH (more strongly). No, I say!

MAMA (under her breath, to Ham. Be quiet, dear. Be nice. Give in. Father's worried. (A pause)

NORMA (simpering). Mr. Noah, excuse me, but—

NOAH (thunderously). No!! (He takes a step forward. The others retreat) Go away. (The others murmur) Not a word! Get out! Below, everybody! (The others have reached the hatch) Who is officer today?

JAPHET. I am, Papa.

NOAH. Send up the animals. It's their hour.

JAPHET. Yes, Papa.

NOAH. No violence, understand? No shouting, or cursing, or whipping them. Go. (The Youngsters go down. Mama is following them. In a sudden outburst) Mama!— Stay with me! I wasn't talking to you. You know that— Please stay with me.

MAMA. I'd better go with them— I'll have to cheer them up. (In a choking voice) It's—it's long for them, you know—this trip. They're not really bad, Noah. They're not wicked— (She goes away, sobbing) (Noah makes a great helpless gesture and sinks down on the box. He seems very old and tired. After a short pause the Bear enters from hatch, followed by the Lion. After sniffing about a little, they lie down at Noah's feet.)

NOAH. No, don't lie there. Walk around. You must take some exercise. (The Animals get up and place their heads on Noah's knees. Stroking them) Yes, you're good beasts— But don't worry about me— I'm tired, that's all. Go on, now. (The Lion wanders away. The Bear rises on its hind legs and tries to dance) No, Bruin, old boy. Don't do that. On all fours. It's so much better. (The Bear obeys and goes to join the Lion in the sunlight. The Tiger and the Monkey enter from hatch. Both stop by Noah) Leave me alone, mates. Go play with the others. (The four Animals, flank to flank, sit on their haunches and comtemplate Noah sorrowfully) Leo!—Sultan—Bruin—Jocko ——My friends, my friends— (Noah begins to cry. The four Animals toss their heads in sympathy. Suddenly the Monkey leaps to its feet, calls for attention, and starts to dance a horn-pipe, to amuse Noah. But the Bear goes to it, growling, and with a rap on its head, puts it back on all fours. The Lion and the Tiger approve) My friends— My friends! (The Cow comes in at a gallop. She nods to Noah. Tiger blocks her path to Noah. Drying his eyes) Good morning, Bossy, good morning. (In a trembling voice which strengthens as he proceeds) It's the children, you see. It's the children. (The Animals nod) And there's Mama. She's weakening, too. Mama's beginning to fail me! I never thought I'd live to see that. It's breaking me up—it's killing me. Here I am in the middle of six of seven question marks— I have to know all the answers. But I'm only an old farmer — All these things that are happening to me—they—you know—flatten me, bowl me over, don't you see? I don't know everything. They all keep asking me questions: "Why is this? How is that? What next? And after that?" If they were simply driven by the natural curiosity of youth—but they're all after just one thing: to catch me— Oh, my friends, I'm so afraid of Ham! (The Animals all growl together) Now, now, behave! —Yes, I'm afraid that it's Ham. (Animals growl) He's very bad to you, eh?—And to me, too, if you only knew. (Animals growl louder) There, there, be quiet— There, it's over— We won't talk about it any more. (He goes and strokes the Animals, who press around him) And then there's another thing. But this is just between us, eh? (He makes sure they are alone and then whispers) God isn't with us any more— Sh!—There! (The Animals, dismayed, lower their heads) Put yourselves in His place. Try to put yourselves humbly in His place. Every day, every hour hearing His

existence doubted. And often at times
when He is most apparent!—It used to be
all men. Now it's these children— All
the time asking for proofs, for miracles—
How can I give them proofs?—"If You
exist, change this button into mutton—"
"If You exist, take away my toothache—"
"If there was a God He wouldn't have
let me bang my head coming upstairs—"
Yes, comrades, one of the little girls had
the nerve to tell me that!—So, you see,
He's deserted us. Still, I must say I don't
see why He didn't do it long ago. He had
patience— Well, now it's gone, that's all.
You can't really blame Him. You couldn't
expect Him to be a saint— (The Tiger
raises head and bays anxiously) No, no,
never mind. He'll come back. He's sort
of on a vacation. For three weeks, maybe,
or a month. Well, all right, we'll wait
till He comes back, eh? (But the Tiger
and the other Animals are howling. A bit
nervous) Sh! Sh! Now, now— Yes, I
understand. I know what's the matter.
But we mustn't give up. (The Animals are
howling louder. The other Animals in the
hold begin to join in) Now, now! Look
out, you'll frighten Him up there. Call
to Him, yes. Let's raise our voices. I'm
willing. But not in fear. Not in anger.
Make it a song to please His ear. Lord!
Lord!— Lord!!

THE ANIMALS. Oouh— Oouh—
Oooogh!

NOAH. Once more, mates! But with-
out a shadow of fear, or doubt. Now!
All together. One voice! One soul!
Lord!—Lord!—Lord!—

THE ANIMALS. Oough!—oough!—
oough!

NOAH. There!—That's good. Have
with now. Quiet. Quiet down, everybody.
(The Animals become calm) There, there,
rest. I'm tired, children. Bruin's going
to let me have his back, and I'm going
to lie down with you. (He sits) Haaaah.
Here on the boundless, bottomless,
motionless waters we'll build a towering
monument of patience— That'll attract
His attention. Just as an oak attracts
lightning. (He is falling asleep) There,
now—There— He must see how much we
now—of everything in the world—that is
to slow— (A little silence. Then the song of

the Birds is heard) (Sleepily) The birds are
singing— They haven't sung for a long
time— God isn't far away, children— (He
falls asleep. The Animals lie down, lower their
heads on their paws and sleep. Silence. A breeze
rustles over the stage. The Animals wake up. A
stronger breeze passes, and the awning flutters
in it. The Animals raise their muzzles to
Heaven)

ACT THREE

SCENE ONE

Three short blasts of wind blow the curtain
up. The scene is the same. A strong wind is
blowing. Noah is standing, facing the
audience, his head in the air, overjoyed. He
blows a whistle.

———

NOAH. Bravo, wind! Hurrah for the
wind! Oh, God, I thank You for this
wind! (He begins to pace the deck excitedly.
A gale. Noah seizes a megaphone and goes
to the hatch and cries) All hands on deck!
All hands on deck! (He goes back to his
whistle)
(The Youngsters rush up through the hatch.)
JAPHET. What?
SHEM. What is it?
HAM. What do you want?
NORMA. What's the matter?
SELLA. What's up?
ADA. What's happening?
NOAH. Ah, children! Look! (He raises
his arms)
ADA (in a high voice). Are we sinking?
THE THREE GIRLS. Are we sinking?
NOAH. No, no—
THE YOUNGSTERS. Yes, yes!
NOAH. No no, we're not!
THE GIRLS. Yes, we are!
THE BOYS. We are! We are!
THE YOUNGSTERS. Help! He-e-l-l-l-p!
(Enter Mama. The girls run to her, wailing.)
THE GIRLS. Mama! Mama!
MAMA (feebly). More trouble— I
knew it— I told you so.
NOAH. No, no. Our troubles are over!
Look!
JAPHET (at Right, holding up a corner of
the awning which is flapping). Papa, papa!
It's blowing away.
THE BOYS (running to Noah). What shall

we do, Father? Tell us what to do?
(A gale)

NOAH. Get back there, Shem and Ham.

THE GIRLS. Mama! Look out!

HAM *(who has jumped on the other corner)*.
Pull! Use your strength. The pressure's
terrible. *(Cries from the women)*

NOAH. All together now, crew. The
wind's blowing everything away.

THE GIRLS. Quick! Quick!

NOAH. Ham! Japhet! Get back there.
Stow it!

JAPHET *and* HAM. Right!

NOAH. Pull!

JAPHET *and* HAM. Right!

NOAH. Shem, you too. Grab the end
of the big hawser. Pull, all together. It's
a sailor's knot—it ought to slip through
by itself. Heave! Heave! Heave—ho!

THE GIRLS. It doesn't work.

NOAH. Help them, girls. Don't stand
there shivering like a lot of wet hens.
(The girls go to help)

MAMA. They'll hurt themselves.

NOAH. Be still, Mama. *(To the
Youngsters)* Avast, you sea dogs! Heave—
ho! Heave—ho! How about it, Shem? Put
some strength into it, boy. You're not
playing the harp. Avast, there! All together!—That'll do it. All together!
Heave—ho! Heave—ho! There! *(The
rope gives way. The Youngsters fall all over
each other. Then they get up, laughing
childishly)* That's the way to be! Young
and happy! *(To Mama, low)* Laugh a little
too, will you? You're leaving everything
to me. *(To the Youngsters)* That's it! Now
roll it up right. As few twists as possible.
Careful, careful! There! Perfect. Hahaha.
(The Youngsters laugh too) Now we can see
better. *(Raising his megaphone prophetically
to Heaven)* This wind is good. It's a dry
wind. It's warm. It's lowering us. It's
lowering the water. Our trip's almost
over. The Earth—blessed old Mother
Earth, smothered so long! Now she's
shouldering her way back to the light.
*(The Youngsters get up together and lean over
the rail near Mama. Noah, smitten with
poetry)* Oh, Earth!—Earth!—Earth! *(His
eye falls on the deserted deck. He raises his
megaphone)* Hey! Hey, there! Where are
you?

MAMA. We're looking for land.

NOAH *(laughing)*. Hoho. You don't
lose any time, do you? *(He goes to them)*

SELLA. We're looking for it, but we
don't see any.

JAPHET. Aw, Pop, we don't ask for a
harbor or a beach—

ADA. Or even an island—

SHEM. All we want is a reef—not a
high one, either—just level with the water.

NORMA. At least we ought to be able
to see the bottom.

HAM. We ought to be able to see the
whole thing again, all at once. Everything
should be just as it used to be, right now.

THE YOUNGSTERS. Yes! Right now!

HAM. Listen to me. If God really has
the power—

NOAH. Are you going to disturb the
peace again? Leave me alone. Don't
bother God and me.

MAMA. But listen, Noah, you said—

NOAH. Tsk, tsk, even Mama. What's
made her change like this? Calm down
Order! Show some sense. First you're
wallowing in despair, then you blow sky
high. Shiver my timbers, can't you hold
your course?! *(The wind blows again)*

JAPHET. Say, do you see anything out
there?

NOAH. Where, child? *(They all gather
around Japhet)*

JAPHET. There! Way off on the
horizon!

THE YOUNGSTERS *(exploding)*. That blue
line?

NOAH. It's land! It's land! *(The
Youngsters run about madly)*

HAM. Father's eyesight certainly
improving.

SHEM. The wind's blowing us away
from it. Oh, it was silly not to make
rudder.

JAPHET *(running to the mast)*. I'm
going up!

SHEM *(climbing over the railing)*. I'm
going in! *(Sella holds him back)*

SELLA. Shem, look out.

ADA. Is it any nearer?

JAPHET. I can't tell. I can't
see it well enough.

NORMA. If we only had
some oars!

HAM. Don't be a fool,
Shem.

(Together

NOAH. Stop! Stop! Come here, everybody. Listen— (*The Youngsters come back regretfully*) Now listen. We don't need to budge. We'll send a scout on ahead.

THE YOUNGSTERS. Good—good. Who?

NOAH. One of the birds.

THE YOUNGSTERS. Why a bird?

NOAH. Because if he doesn't come back we'll know he's found enough land to sit upon.

THE YOUNGSTERS. Oh, yes! Which bird?

NOAH. The raven.

THE YOUNGSTERS. Good! Good! (*All the Youngsters but Ham rush into the hold*)

HAM. Why the raven?

NOAH. Because he's a great traveler and because when he goes we'll be rid of his black wings and his nasty voice.

MAMA. Yes, but will he go?

NOAH. We'll see, Mama. We'll see. (*The Youngsters return, Shem carrying the Raven*)

SELLA. Give it to me.

NORMA. I want it now.

JAPHET. Let me have it.

SHEM. I'm keeping it. I'm officer-of-the-day. I'll give it to the captain and no one else. (*He gives the bird to Noah*)

THE YOUNGSTERS. Let it go!

NOAH. Tell me, children, don't you think a nice little prayer would fit into the picture?

THE YOUNGSTERS. Later! Later!

NOAH (*laughing*). Well, well, you've learned patience at last, eh? I'm so glad. All right, then, here goes! One—two—three!—Go!

THE YOUNGSTERS. Go! (*Silence. All the raised heads follow the Raven in three great circles. The Raven's cry is heard. "Caw! Caw! Caw!" The wind blows*). Goodbye! Goodbye!

NOAH. It's silly, isn't it? But it does something to me.

THE YOUNGSTERS. Go on, it's wonderful. Look at it.

NORMA. Yes, look. The wind's taking it right up to the sky.

THE YOUNGSTERS. That's right. Straight up!

HAM. Straight into God's mouth.

NOAH. Now, now—

SHEM. Look out below! The wind's knocking it down. It's falling!

THE YOUNGSTERS. Falling!

JAPHET. No, no, no. It's caught itself.

NOAH. Bravo, there! Look at it! Look how high it's climbing. Right up the clouds. There's a mountain-climber for you. (*The wind stops*)

SELLA. I don't see it any more. Does anybody see it?

THE YOUNGSTERS. It's lost!

HAM. God probably ate it.

THE YOUNGSTERS. Oh! Oh! None of that!

ADA. There it is again!

THE YOUNGSTERS. Where? Where?

ADA. Where I'm pointing— Higher— Way up there. See that cloud like a camel's head? Well, just over that.

THE YOUNGSTERS. I see it! (*They stare at the zenith*)

MAMA. I don't see it any more. I'm dizzy. And there are spots in front of my eyes. (*A little pause*)

HAM. Well, how about it, boys and girls? I guess your bird's lost interest, hey? He's been hit on the head, if I'm not mistaken.

NOAH. He's gliding. You'll see. He's looking around, getting his bearings.

ADA. Mr. Noah, he's coming down.

NOAH. Oh, no, he isn't. It's just a manoeuvre. He's catching his breath.

THE YOUNGSTERS. He's coming down! He's coming down!

JAPHET. And full speed, too.

HAM. I'd say he was crashing.

THE YOUNGSTERS. Oh, oh, he's crashing!

SELLA. He's falling like a rubber ball.

SHEM. Like a stone!

MAMA. His wing is broken.

NORMA. He's going to crush himself on the deck.

NOAH. Oh, Lord, Lord! We've got to catch him. (*They All gather together, arms raised, hands outstretched. The heads all begin describing circles again*)

THE YOUNGSTERS. Here! Here! Here we are.

NOAH (*catching the Raven*). Here he is back again. His heart's pounding. He's trembling. He's all excited. (*He carries the Raven back into the hold, Mama following Noah)*

HAM. Ladies and gentlemen, we're lost.

(The sound of tramping animals begins. Dragging Mama with him, Noah rejoins the Youngsters upstage. He comes forward with them in a great, warm-hearted sweep, then abruptly stops them, his arms outstretched.)

NOAH *(leaning over the hatch)*. Listen. *(The Youngsters turn toward him sullenly. Noah goes to the mast)* Listen! *Grudgingly the Youngsters trail after him)* Listen! Listen to them all, down there, running off mile after mile in one spot. It's as if they felt the earth—as if it made them restless. Listen to them tramp! *(The heavy dull tread of the Animals is heard)*

THE YOUNGSTERS. Ah!

NOAH. Think of it! In that rumbling you can hear the elephant's great pads, the little white paws of Mama's cat, the claws of the lion, the hoofs of the buffalo, the tiny feet of the fly.

THE YOUNGSTERS. That's true.

NOAH. The earth is coming back. God told me so. I believe it. But I don't know for sure. I don't even feel it. My five senses, that I'm so proud of— Ha, ha, not one of them senses earth. I'm as senseless as a rock. Down there, they know everything. All of them. They're all certain, big and small. Isn't it amazing?

THE YOUNGSTERS. Yes, yes, quite.

NOAH. Ham, my boy, honestly, now, don't you think it's amazing?

HAM. Well, yes— *(The tramping stops)*

NOAH. Let yourself go a little, like us. Don't be calculating all the time. Try it: it will do you good. *(He raises his hands to Heaven passionately)* O God!—O God!— You are so—you are so—Godlike! *(In a broken voice)* Ada, my child, you're the youngest here. Go and get the most lovely of creatures, the purest one, the little white soul on wings. Bring us the dove.

THE YOUNGSTERS *(gently)*. The dove.

NOAH. She is so near to God—she is the scout that He would send.

(Ada goes down hatch. Silence. Noah stands motionless, facing front, his arms crossed, his eyes raised. About him wait the others, moved and a bit troubled.)

NORMA *(coughing)*. Hm. Hm.

THE YOUNGSTERS. Sh!

HAM *(softly)*. You'll spoil the effect.

NORMA *(softly)*. I'm excited!

THE YOUNGSTERS. Sshhh!

(Ada returns up hatch, pressing the Dove to her breast. She goes to give it to Noah.)

NOAH. No, let it go, yourself.

ADA. Oh, I'm not—

NOAH. We'll let it go just like this: perfectly, simply—without any ceremony— Bella, Bella, my little wing, my tiny angel— Up. Up! She's gone!

HAM. Yeah?

JAPHET. Where?

HAM *and* SHEM. Yeah?

THE GIRLS. There!

THE BOYS. Where?

NOAH. Over your heads. No, behind you! Now, straight ahead. Up there! Up there!

JAPHET. Where? *(All eyes search; every hand points)*

NOAH. I don't see it any more. *(He is still upstage, straining every nerve to search the sky)*

MAMA. I never saw it at all. *(She goes to the Youngsters)*

THE YOUNGSTERS. Neither did we.

NORMA. This is all very unpleasant. *(A pause. Everyone studies the sky)*

JAPHET *(pointing vaguely)*. Is that it?

HAM. He's sweet, that lad. The tactful son. *(The Youngsters sneer)*

NOAH *(from behind)*. Did you see something?

HAM. No, we're saying prayers!

NOAH. That's the idea.

MAMA. Ham, child, please! *(A pause)*

HAM. I bet he never sent the bird at all.

SHEM. I was just thinking the same thing.

THE YOUNGSTERS. Oh!

HAM. I knew it— He's a humbug. Worse than I thought! He's hidden the dove to make us think it's found land.

MAMA. Oh, no, Ham. No, no.

HAM. Ah, Mama!—I know your tricks. Go away. Go on now. Shem, he's an old fisherman!

SHEM. Sure, he knows how to dangle the bait.

HAM. Doesn't he, though. He stick

his hook in a cute little symbol and throws it up in the air for you. You can always jump for it. "This'll amuse 'em," he says. "While they're jumping around, I'll have some peace." Ha ha. Do you know what? He's put the pigeon in his pocket! *(The chorus laughs)*

NOAH *(from the back)*. Do you see it, children?

MAMA *(anxiously)*. No, Noah, but it's all right. They're just having a little fun.

NOAH. They're right. We mustn't lose patience. We're so near the end now. *(He comes to the others)* Ah, children, if you knew— Nothing can give you any idea of how good God has been to me. He's changed so much—and for the better. He's better than ever. He's come nearer. He's less far off. No less stupendous, of course, but less high, less— remote. He's joked a little. He pretended to be joking to hide His emotion. But you know I have a keen ear. His mighty voice was trembling. He was glad to find us again.

HAM. In other words, He's been kidding us.

NOAH. He simply left us for a little while, that's all.

HAM *(softly)*. He does it well, doesn't he?

MAMA. Ham, I swear he means it.

HAM. Think of that pigeon pecking at his shirt! *(The Youngsters titter suddenly)*

NOAH. Who's coughing?

HAM. Nobody. Mama sneezed.

NOAH *(getting up)*. She'll catch cold. She ought to go inside.

HAM *(to Mama)*. Say no.

MAMA. No, Noah.

HAM. Mama wants to see that land with her own eyes.

THE YOUNGSTERS *(softly, to Ham)*. That's talking.

NOAH. It may be a long time.

HAM. You've taught her to wait.

NOAH. Yes, yes, yes— *(He wanders upstage)*

THE YOUNGSTERS. That got him.

HAM *(to chorus)*. Just as soon as we went away, by an odd coincidence the bird would tumble out of Heaven—with a message from God on a ribbon in its beak.

THE YOUNGSTERS *and* MAMA. Haha, haha!

NOAH. What's the matter?

NORMA. Nothing. Ham was just telling us the habits of the carrier pigeon. *(Gales of laughter)*

NOAH *(going toward the stern of the ark)*. Bella! Bella!—my little one—

HAM. Here comes the big moment.

NOAH. How wicked it was—and how stupid, to let you out in that hurricane!

HAM. Watch him. He's going to throw it overboard. It'll land all right—on the bottom. *(Youngsters take a step toward Noah)*

NOAH. Be brave, Bella. I'm thinking of you. I'm fighting for you.

HAM. Come on. Get closer. *(Youngsters advance on Noah)*

NOAH. Don't look at the big waves.

HAM. And watch his hands. *(A gale of wind)*

NOAH. Pick out a good strong air current, get into it, and use it, my pet.

HAM. This is absurd. It's a shame!

MAMA. It's just that he's getting dreadful old. *(Another gust)*

NOAH. Ah! You think I'm very silly, eh?

HAM. Oh, no!

THE YOUNGSTERS. On the contrary. Very crafty.

HAM. Yes. Sly as an old fox!

NOAH. I love that little bird so. I'm so afraid something will happen to it.

HAM. It might smother, for instance.

THE YOUNGSTERS. Ha, ha, ha!

NOAH. Not smother, but drown.

HAM. I think it'll smother.

THE YOUNGSTERS. Hahaha!

NOAH. What are you laughing at?

HAM. What are you blushing for?

MAMA. Listen, Ham. Listen—

NOAH. Am I blushing?

HAM. Why did you put your hand on your chest?

THE YOUNGSTERS. Why? Yes, yes, why?

MAMA. Listen to me— *(Noah retreats before the Youngsters up the stairs to the cabin)*

NOAH. What is it? What on earth's the matter?

HAM. Why are you putting your hands in your pockets?

THE YOUNGSTERS. Yes, why?

NOAH. They're cold.

MAMA. Yes, they're cold. His poor hands. Oh, God, Ham is wrong! He's wrong!

HAM. What's that big lump under your cloak?

THE YOUNGSTERS. Open your cloak!

HAM. What are you hiding in your hat?

THE YOUNGSTERS. Take off your hat!

MAMA. Oh, God. My God, let me die rather than see this.

HAM. Look, the wind has stopped. It's calm as a pond again. And here we still are; mired, stuck; in water like oil. Your last prophecy has gone wrong, just like the others.

NOAH. Like the others—

HAM. Now what are you going to think up to make us patient? Eh?

THE YOUNGSTERS. Answer him!

HAM. What trick can you pull out of your hat this time?

THE YOUNGSTERS. Don't move! Don't move!

NORMA. He'll pull out the dove. Haha!

HAM. Hey there! What's that white thing you took out of your pocket?

NOAH. My handkerchief, you overgrown lout!

MAMA. To wipe his face—

HAM. Let's see.

THE YOUNGSTERS. Show it to us.

HAM. Give it to me!

NOAH. Well, but—

THE YOUNGSTERS. Give it up. (A tussle)

NORMA. He's changed the bird into a handkerchief! (Tumult)

NOAH. Don't shove like that. You'll push me overboard.

THE YOUNGSTERS. The bird! Where's the bird? (Mama is praying, her hands raised. Suddenly the Dove drops into them. She shrieks)

MAMA. Here it is! Here it is! Look here! (The Youngsters rush to her)

HAM. Let's see it— Well, I'll be— He found some way to toss it to her.

THE YOUNGSTERS. So she's in on it too! A crony!

MAMA. It fell straight from Heaven into my hands.

HAM. That's a lie! (Noah, having pulled himself together, throws himself into the Youngsters like a buffalo)

MAMA. I swear it.

HAM. It's a lie!

NOAH (slapping Ham with all his strength). Maybe you'll believe that. (Murmurs from the Youngsters) Who's next? (Silence. The Youngsters draw back in a semi-circle. Noah turns to Mama. She is on her knees, crying. She holds out the Dove) Come, Mama. There, there. Get up.

MAMA. No, no, please let me stay like this. Oh, Noah, I'm not worthy.

NOAH. Now, come, come. (He lifts her up) Ah, why can't we all be simple-hearted. (He strokes the Dove) It wasn't hard, was it, Bella, to do your little bit? And now, all's well. See how well she is, Mama— Warm—happy— She's cooing— she's cooing here in my hands. And what's this? What's she got in her beak? (Youngsters gather near) It's a leaf. Three little leaves. A little green twig.

THE YOUNGSTERS (softly). A green twig!

NOAH. What is it now, Mama? You know all the plants.

MAMA (drying her eyes). It's—an olive branch.

NOAH. An olive branch!

THE YOUNGSTERS. An olive branch!

NOAH. The trees are above water!

HAM (as if he couldn't believe it). Above water?

SHEM and JAPHET (slowly). Above water!

THE GIRLS (rapidly). Above water! Out of the water! (They stamp heavily) Out of the water!

THE YOUNGSTERS (more quickly). Out of the water! (They rush to the hatch, yelling) Out of the water! (They disappear below. A pause)

MAMA. It's happened—just as you said it would.

NOAH (without joy). Yes.

MAMA. Everything's happened just as you said.

NOAH. Yes.

MAMA. Just as you said.

NOAH. Yes, Mama.

MAMA. Just as you said— Just as you said.

NOAH. Yes, Mama, yes.

MAMA. Just as you said.

NOAH. Mama, please!

(The Youngsters come back up dressed madly; dancing, twisting, mad with joy.)

THE YOUNGSTERS.

Out! Out! Out! Out!
The trees are out of the water!
The trees are out of the water!
The trees are out of the water!

THE BOYS. Out of the water!

THE GIRLS. Out of the water!

ALL. The water! The water! We're out of the water!

NOAH *(supporting Mama, who is fainting. To the Youngsters).* Bunglers! Bunglers of everything! Bunglers of anything! Bunglers of years! And of seconds! Bunglers! Bunglers!

THE YOUNGSTERS *(dancing).*

We're out! Out! Out! Out!
The trees are out of the water!
The trees are out of the water!

NOAH. Wasters of joy—of youth—of happiness!

THE YOUNGSTERS. Out! Out! Out!

NOAH. Lord! Lord! Old friend!—It's madness! It's madness! Drown us all. Destroy us! And think no more about it!

THE YOUNGSTERS.

We're out, we're out, we're out!!!
Out! Out! Out! Out!

ACT THREE

SCENE TWO

SCENE: *The top of Mount Ararat. The ark is to the Left. Only the bow is visible, with a ladder to the ground.*

AT RISE: *Noah comes down the ladder, alone and silent. He descends the last rungs slowly; places one foot on the ground, then the other, and kneels.*

———

(A pause. Mama enters on the ark.)

MAMA. There. I'm ready. I fixed a basket for the cat. She'll be very comfortable. It's like a little house. *(Then she is gloomy)* But she won't want to stay in it. She scratched me. Then she jumped out of the basket. All the animals have driven

her wild again. Oh, children, children, what a pity, what a pity. *(She weeps)*

(Noah gets up and begins to scour about for dead wood to make a sacrifice to the Lord.)

MAMA *(consoled).* But I was forgetting. We've landed— We're home. How do we get down, children? Oh, oh, not to feel the ground rock under your feet any more. How lovely—isn't it lovely? *(She looks about. Noah has gone up Right and is building an altar)* But— Look, this isn't home. What a wilderness! It's so cold. So bare! And that horrible damp smell. Oh, my, oh, me! All these changes at my age. Always moving— Noah! Where are we? Where's the water? Where's the ocean? I'm afraid. I want the ocean. Noah! Noah! Noah! *(See sees Noah and leans toward him from the ark)* Wicked man! Mystery man! Weakling! Dolt! You think you can lead men, and you let everything lead you. You're a traitor! That's what you are! Traitor! Oh! *(She turns, wild-eyed, towards the deck)* Oh, I was busy setting a basket ready for the cat— Kitty! Kitty! Come here, dear, you're all I have left. *(She goes back into the ark)*

(Noah coughs. Suddenly all the Youngsters throw their bundles to the ground and jump off the ark.)

ALL. Ah!

THE BOYS. Aha!

THE GIRLS. Haha! *(They are all lined up before the ark)*

HAM. Ha! Old Earth!

THE BOYS. Good old Earth!

THE GIRLS. Dear old Earth!

JAPHET *(stepping out of line).* Look! I'm going to walk! Watch me walk! *(He takes a step)* What am I doing? *(Bourrée dance rhythm)*

ALL. Walking!

JAPHET *(slapping his chest).* What's this boy doing?

ALL. He's walking!

JAPHET. And what on?

ALL. On the ground!

NORMA *(getting out of line).* Look at me! Look at me! *(She pulls her skirt up to her knees)*

ADA and SELLA *(copying her).* Look at us.

NORMA *(tapping the ground)*. I'm stamping in the mud.

ADA *and* SELLA. We're stamping, too.

THE BOYS. Let's all stamp. *(They dance)* It's soggy! It's cold! But it's warming up under our feet. It's soft! It's so good!

ALL. One, two! One, two!

NORMA *(with a shrill laugh)*. Look! My feet are all black!

ALL. One, two! One, two!

HAM *(getting out of line)*. Be quiet!

ALL. One, two!

HAM. Be still! *(Music stops)*. *(Pause)* It helps me feel that now—at last—I'm free! *(All are silent. Stretching)* Aaah! Hey! Nobody. *(Louder)* Anybody here! *(Noah coughs)*

ALL. Silence!

HAM *(shouting)*. Ham! Me! I! *(He climbs a little hill Center)* Ham!

NORMA *(pulling her sisters)*. Let's go look!

ADA *and* SELLA *(They run upstage)*. Let's all look!

NORMA *(glaring at ark)*. Boo! Boo! That old wreck!

ADA. Rotten decks!

SELLA. Rusty nails!

ALL THREE. Boo! Boo! Boo! *(They spit on the ark)*

HAM *(from his height)*. Ham is on top of the world.

JAPHET *(climbing up)*. Here comes Japhet.

HAM. No, you don't.

SHEM. Shem's coming, too!

HAM. Not Japhet *or* Shem! *(Planting himself firmly, he keeps them off with both hands)*

NORMA *(upstage)*. We're on a mountain.

SELLA *and* ADA. A high mountain. *(The Three Girls separate. Meanwhile Shem and Japhet shout and attack the hill from opposite sides)*

HAP *(driving them off)* No! No! No, you don't.

SHEM *and* JAPHET *(slipping)*. Why not?

HAM. I climbed up first. I got here first. I'm the strongest.

SHEM. I'm the oldest.

JAPHET. Well, I'm the youngest. *(They come to blows. Noah turns and watches without saying anything)*

ADA. Look at the water! It's making thousands of little streams down the mountain.

SELLA. The animals are following them.

NORMA. Everything's going down. They're all going down.

ADA. There are plains already.

SELLA. There's a jungle, too.

NORMA. Already there are deserts. *(The boys are fighting)*

THE GIRLS *(running toward them)*. No!

JAPHET *(to Ham)*. Nigger! Black man!

HAM *(to Shem)*. Chink! Yellow skin!

SHEM *(to Japhet)*. Whitey! Pale face! *(They roll down the hill and start up again. But the girls cling to them)*

NORMA. No, no! Why fight over a little chunk of rock when the world is so wide.

SELLA. The world is all around us.

ADA. There it is! Down there!

THE THREE GIRLS. Down there! *(But the boys free themselves and go back to their fight)*

JAPHET *(to Shem)*. Chink! Slant-eyes!

HAM *(to Japhet)*. Lily-face! Whitey!

SHEM *(to Ham)*. Nigger! Dinge! *(They roll down the hill again. The girls pick them up and hold them fast)*

NORMA *(to Ham)*. Behind you, Ham! Look behind you. Southward! Southward! Look straight into the South. Come on. Come, my hunter. Follow the lion over the sands to the South.

SELLA *(to Shem.* We'll go after the tiger to the East. We'll ride an elephant among hundreds of kinds of monkeys. Come, my farmer.

ADA *(to Japhet)*. Come, my shepherd. Take up your pipes. We'll follow the cow and the sheep and the dog into the clouds of the West. Come, my shepherd. *(The three panting boys turn each in his own direction)*

THE GIRLS. Come on!

NORMA. All life has left the mountain. *(The boys start to follow the girls, then suddenly turn and embrace)*

THE BOYS. So long!

THE GIRLS. Come on!

(They run and gather up their bundles. Norma struggles up with hers and Ham's and puts them on her head. Shem loads his on his

*houlder. Japhet and Ada put theirs together
nd carry them between them.)

THE GIRLS. There we are.

THE BOYS. Right! *(They all look at the
*rk, then at Noah. Noah is on his knees
own Left)

ALL. Sshh! *(Softly)* Farewell.

*(They go away, Norma before Ham, Shem
*eading Sella; Japhet and Ada side by side
*nd disappear down the roads they have chosen.
*1 shepherd's Pipes are heard. A pause. Noah
*ets up and turns fearfully to the deserted
tage.)

NOAH. They've all gone down the
*mountain.— Every living thing. And I,
*ny children! I'm alive! What about *my*
ife? (He calls. Oboe offstage) Children!
*Children! You've left someone behind!—
*'ou've forgotten *me! (The pipes grow more
'istant) It isn't possible. It can't be that
*his vital spark doesn't catch a single eye.
*'hat not a head will turn again to me.
*At least you'll look back toward me,
*von't you? Now and then you'll throw
*ne a little backward glance. In your hearts
*ou can't—you can't be happy deep down
*n your hearts. There *is* a cord that can't
*e cut—that binds you still to me! There
*ust be! It must be wrenching at your
*owels—straining against you as you go—
*ugging you back—back to your old
*'apa—What?—What? Shem, my boy—
*aphet, my little man— Ham— Ham, my
*hild. (The pipes fade into the distance and
'hen cease) Ah, well. Well— It's gone—
*don't hear them any more. Help! Help!
*He makes little rushes, first after Japhet, then
*fter Ham, then after Shem, and finally
omes back Center) I can't follow them—
*can't go with them— Which one?
*Vhich one? They've tied me, bound me,
*hut me up in emptiness. I'm caught in
*he middle of nothing—Ah! (He throws
imself on the ground, groaning) Ah, there
*hey are! Now I can hear them again!—
*'heir footsteps— Their little footsteps,
*oing away. (He drags himself along the
round) Ah, tell me I still hold the reins
*f my three splendid teams—Shem and
*ella—Ham and Norma—Japhet and Ada!
*—Giddap! Giddap! (He clucks as if encour-
qing his teams) Ah, the reins are stretching.
*'hey're pulling away— They're going to
reak—(He kisses the ground) Oh, my

children, catch up my voice. It's running
to you through the ground, like three fresh
brooks. Take one last drink. *(He stops;
places his ear to the ground and then gets up.
His voice is cold and dead)* Finished—
Gone— Wiped out— All right! *(He sighs
and beats his breast)* Oh, my heart! My
blood! My lungs! You must work hard,
you must pound aloud to keep me
company. *(He surveys the scene, laughing
despairingly)* Ah! Ha, ha! I'll have to
raise an echo, a nice echo—so we can
talk together—I, and myself! *(He cries)*
Noah! Noah! Noah! *(He listens)* Not a
sound— *(Enter the Bear Right)* Well, if it
isn't Bruin. This *is a* surprise! You're a
godsend, that's what you are! I thought
you'd left me too— Well, I'm certainly
glad to see you again— I always said we
had a little weakness for each other. *(He
goes toward the Bear, who stands up)* Sure,
you understand. You understand a lot of
things. *(The Bear opens his arms)* What?
All right. We'll hug each other again.
(He goes into the Bear's arms) My partner,
my friend!— He's squeezing me so hard!
—Oof!—Here, you're cutting off my
wind!—Hey! Careful, old boy! Oof!—
You're choking me! Come on, now, let
go! Let go! *(They roll on the ground)*
Hey!—Hey! *(His voice is muffled in the
Bear's fur. Man and beast struggle in silence.
Throwing back his head)* Help! Help!
(Mama appears on the ark.)

NOAH. Help!

MAMA *(bursting into laughter)* Hahaha!

NOAH. Mama!

MAMA. Hahaha! *(Noah succeeds in getting free, gets his wind and rushes, shouting
at the Bear, who scampers away. Noah pants
and mops his brow)* That was funny! That
was so funny!

NOAH. It nearly killed me, Mama.

MAMA. Dancing together like that. A
real bear-dance. Ha, ha, ha. *(She roars with
laughter)*

NOAH *(raising his eyes to Heaven)*.
There's the vulture already. I'll need a
lot of courage.

MAMA *(squatting downstage, her chin in
her hands)*. Where are the children?

NOAH. They'll be back. They've gone
to look around a little down below. But

they'll be back. They'll come back in a few days.

MAMA. It's very strange that our friends don't take the time to come and see us.

NOAH. What friends, Mama?

MAMA. Well, our friends in the village. My personal friends! Of course, nobody liked you. But I had a lot of relatives. After a trip like this it seems as if they might come and call.

NOAH. But, Mama—

MAMA. What?—Has that been forbidden, too?

NOAH. No, no!—They'll be here—

MAMA (getting up). It's Him up there—

NOAH. Now, now. Don't say that.

MAMA. But I must say it. I'm not afraid to tell Him what I think. I'm not crazy, you know. (Mama sobs softly)

NOAH. There, there, there. I want you to help me pick a place for our new home. You know I'm going to build you a grand new house. There's plenty of wood here. You're going to have that great big wonderful kitchen you've always dreamed about.

MAMA (weeping). I'm cold. (Noah takes off his cloak and puts it around her) What's that falling on my hair?

NOAH. Maybe a little snow.

MAMA. Snow?

NOAH. Yes— Ah! How shall I start? (To Mama) Are you all right? (Mama makes no reply. She is falling asleep) Poor old comrade. She couldn't hold out— quite long enough. (Softly) It has been hard— (Louder, and shaken with sobs) It's true; it has been hard!—Ah! (Standing in the middle of the stage, in a leather apron, hands on hips, legs spread, he throws back his head) Well, You must admit that my faith in You is supremely patient— Do You hear me? Yes. I say that You have given me hard knocks. Maybe You've gone beyond what I call sportsmanship. You've taken me from my garden and cast me on a rock, alone, with a dozen ways of dying. But I'm not complaining—Haha-ha!—That'll be all right— You'll see. I'll find a way out. Yes, God, I'll get out. I warn You; I've given up trying to understand. But that doesn't matter. Not a bit. Go on, I'm following You! March on! March on! Only I ask You to come to me once in a while. Will You? Let me hear Your voice now and then or just let me feel Your breath or simply let me have Your light. Oh, Lord, shed Your light upon my daily job! Let me have the impression—the feeling—Your assurance— that You are satisfied, will You? We must be satisfied. Isn't that so? I am satisfied. (He shouts) I am satisfied. (He attacks the ark with his hatchet) I am satisfied! (He sings) When the boat goes well, all goes well. Are You satisfied? (The seven colors of the rainbow appear in the background) That's fine.

CURTAIN

STEFAN ZWEIG's

Volpone

Adapted from Ben Jonson's Volpone

Translated from the German by RUTH LANGNER

First presented by the Theatre Guild at the Guild Theatre, New York, on April 9, 1928, with the following cast:

FIRST SINGER	Lucian Tranto	CANINA *(the Bitch)*	Helen Westley
SECOND SINGER	Vincent Sherman	COLOMBA, *wife of Corvino (the Dove)*	
THIRD SINGER	William Edmonson		Margalo Gillmore
FOURTH SINGER	George Ballard	MAID TO COLOMBA	Mary Bell
FIRST GROOM	Louis Veda	CORBACCIO'S SERVANT	John C. Davis
SECOND GROOM	Mark Schweid	LEONE, *Captain of the Fleet (the Lion)*	McKay Morris
MOSCA *(the Gadfly)*	Alfred Lunt	CAPTAIN OF THE SBIRRI	Albert van Dekker
VOLPONE *(the Fox)*	Dudley Digges	JUDGE	Morris Carnovsky
SLAVE *(to Volpone)*	John Henry	CLERK OF THE COURT	Sanford Meisner
VOLTORE *(the Vulture)*	Philip Leigh	COURT ATTENDANTS {	Leonard Perry
CORVINO *(the Crow)*	Ernest Cossart		Vincent Sherman
CORBACCIO *(the Raven)*	Henry Travers	PRIEST	John C. Davis

Staged by Philip Moeller
Settings and Costumes by Lee Simonson

ACT ONE

SCENE ONE

SCENE: *Volpone's room in a Venetian palazzo, spacious and richly appointed. To the left a broad, luxurious couch—Volpone's sickbed, which can be cut off from the sight of the others in the room by a curtain which does not, however, conceal the occupant of the bed from the audience.*

TIME: *Early morning. The curtains are half-drawn, as is usual in a sickroom.*

AT RISE: *Mosca, a Venetian, young, slender, dressed in black, a gay, vivacious fellow, storms in at the side door, claps his hands together.*

———

MOSCA. Hey there! Holloa! Bring on breakfast, the master's got up!
(Grooms tumble all over each other as they hurry in.)
Over there to the bed! The master is tired, the poor man had another awful night, ah, what a terrible night! I fear, I fear, he will not hear the bells of Venice chime the hour many times again. But don't let him see you know; put on merry faces, be deaf when he complains—you know he can't stand sympathy—whisk about, be light and merry. And you, tune your mandolin and play him his favourite song . . . Come, be at it, act carefree and gay, disport yourselves lustily. Meanwhile I'll lead him in.
(Off into the adjoining room again.)

FIRST GROOM *(bringing the breakfast).* Do you believe Messer Volpone is truly so ill? I don't believe it! By the seven lions, I don't believe it! Only yesterday that Canina was here all night, and they cut such capers over my head all night that the ceiling creaked and I had to pull the covers up over my ears.

SECOND GROOM. Oh, that must have been his toady amusing himself with her. He guzzles his wine, he reaches into his purse, he smacks his lips over his dinners, why shouldn't he sleep with his women? I can well believe that Messer Volpone is ill. He is badly galled, and death's throne is the gall-bladder.

THIRD GROOM, THE MUSICIAN
(Has taken the proper pose and now sings to the mandolin.)

Oh gold makes fools of young and old,
A fool will try to hold his gold;
A fool will lend and let it lie,
Content with juicy usury.
A double fool will dissipate it
A fool will love, a fool will hate it!
Prayer or curse; both bad or worse.
Act you may, to your dismay
You'll find it's not the proper way.
Be cool; your money's cooler still.
Know you're a fool: gold has its will.

All proper gold is minted round
So it can roll and race around,
For, buried deep, or hid at home
It still makes off, it still will roam.
However swift and bound to try it
No man can catch and keep it quiet.
The stuff, once seized, is not enough,
You keep on running, spent and sore
To seize on more and more and more.
And when you're worn out by the race
A hundred new fools take your place.

Oh gold, red gold, rules young and old;
No king in state maintains, like gold,
Better, complete subservience
To keep men jigging to his dance.
God knows, since there has been a world
Gold's been the care 'round which it's
                          [whirled.
Forever and a day the same
Each place, each land, will play this game;
The same old trick, same idiot dance
Which makes poor fools of young and old
The dance for gold, the dance for gold.

VOLPONE *(a richly dressed, large man with a keen face, has entered meanwhile on Mosca's arm and drags himself painfully to the bed-couch).* Thank you, my good, true servants, and thanks to you, my singer. If it were only true that music heals the sick, only true! But what a night! I no longer thought to live to see the morning. Ah, I am weary, perhaps I can find rest here. Thank you for your care of me, my good fellows, and now leave me to myself.
(The Grooms bow themselves off.)

VOLPONE *(turning from the bed)*. Are they gone?

MOSCA *(at the door)*. There! Well bolted! And now let yourself take pleasure in life. Away with infirmity, out with gay humours!

VOLPONE *(jumping up to the window, tearing aside the curtains)*.
Ah sunlight, morning bright on the canals,
Come bathe my pale face in your shining
[gold.
There, strew it on my arms and hands, and
[let me
Suck it up greedily into each vein,
For gold is all; it is the elixir
Which thrills each mortal nerve with life
[renewed.
Oh, give yourself to me, most blessed
[metal
Streaming from Heaven down to this poor
[earth;
Give, give yourself to me!
*(Suddenly turning away and letting the cur-
tain fall.)*
But no, what need of you,
Your pallid gleam which every night-time
[quenches?
You're given to each trembling out-
[stretched hand,
You gild the poorest idiot's coppers with
[cheap gold,
And lend your gold, unthanked, to every
[man.
But sole possession is the only bliss.
Go lend your golden lie to other men.
I need you not; my own light glows for
[me.
*(Goes to his chest, which he opens, gazing
with quickened breath at the gold and treasure
heaped high within it.)*
But you, my own sun, beam on me;
Dear heav'n that's closed to all but its
[own lord,
Blaze out, blaze out, you golden-irised
[eye,
Your master kneels before you, lodestar
[of the world.
Gold, gold, my own dear sunlight, gold,
[my gold,
Fill these my hands and whisper minted
[melody.
Sparkle, my gems, and clasp me with your
[bracelets,

Dance in your necklets! Docile gold, I
[sense,
I feel, the godhead in your shining
[presence.
Oh riches, mighty god and lord of earth,
You all and nothing, you mute alphabet
Wherein lie all of this earth's words
[concealed,
Whoso has learned your use is lord of life,
For honor, love, and fame, and all desires
Can he create from out your golden sign,
Even the ultimate—likeness to your
[godhood.
*(He stands up, turns to Mosca who looks on
indifferently.)*
What, Mosca? Do you not greet my gold?
MOSCA. Oh sir, I pity it.
VOLPONE. Pity it? Why?
MOSCA. Because it's caught there in the chest.
VOLPONE. And you, what would you do? Set it free?
MOSCA. If I had the power, I'd give it wings—
VOLPONE. You fool! You'd set gold, the god that holds the earth in chains, at liberty? Why, you must tense your muscles to hold it, the slippery sprite, so it won't slip between your fingers; coddle it, so it does not run away; and how you have to hover it so that it will grow. And you, you'd set it free. May I ask what you, supposing I should give them to you, would do with these golden swallows, these curious birds of paradise?
MOSCA. What I'd do?—Let me think. First I'd think up all the things I'd ever wished for and then the round ducats would have to run about till they'd laid them all at my boots; I'd have them declaim the whole alphabet of pleasure for me, to use your figure. This—*(He reaches in and jingles a few coins)*—would be a night of love with Donna Maria; this—*(Reaches in again)*—would be a night, blue and sultry—with a crowd of fine fellows; this—*(Reaches in again)*— a brocaded robe such as the Emperor of France wears, to tease the women; and this—a poem by the Aretine, which lends me wit and spirit and makes my fame resound even to the Papal throne; this— my picture painted by Messer Titian: immortality; this—a hundred backs

crooked low before me; here, a dagger stuck in my enemy's bowels; this, and this, and this, a dozen toadies, merry wine-bibbing, lovable fellows, like myself; this—a pleasure trip to Turkey in a noble caravel; this, a title from the Pope; this . . .

VOLPONE. Wait, wait, you've already reached the bottom of your treasure-chest and are no more than a ridiculous, pitiable, poverty-poor fellow with two holey trousers legs like ninety dozen others who daily dawdle about the piazza waiting till an old woman takes them to bed with her or a Brother of Charity gives them a bowl of soup. Ah, Mosca, you clever puppy, what a fool you are, how little you have learned of me. Do you really think you have to let the ducats fly in order to have everything? No, you fool. Let them rest quietly side by side, let them twinkle! Then people will come of themselves to offer you everything; women will creep into your bed and men doff their hats, the merchants lend you money and the poets flatter you. Get this through your head at last: the magic of gold is so great its smell alone makes men drunk. They only need to sniff it and they come creeping here on their bellies, stretching their necks, their senses whirling; they only need to smell it—and you must let them get no more than the smell, these rogues—and they grow drunk and fall into your hands like moths into a flame. You've been my parasite eight weeks, you stupid pupil—have you seen one single golden beetle creep out of my treasure chest in that time?

MOSCA. Never, master! Indeed a whole new swarm has settled there.

VOLPONE. And do I live badly? Do you taste water in my Falernian, are my carpets thin, my silver compotes light, is there one stinking blister of poverty in all my house?

MOSCA. I hope I never live worse. You are as luxurious as an Armenian, as lustful as a stallion, take your pleasure in all luscious things, and don't forget the women.

VOLPONE. And do I exert myself? Do I chaffer on the Rialto, do I lend gold at interest, do I let the poor fellows in the sulphur works grow as yellow as that horrid element? Do the widows shriek "usurer" after me, and the labourers cry "slave-driver"? When I ride out in my gondola, is there a hollow moaning from the debtors' dungeons: "Mercy, mercy!"

MOSCA. On the contrary, everyone honours you; everyone waits upon you and clusters about you and races to be the first to reach you.

VOLPONE. And how do I do it, you spendthrift? With air—with a little puff of breath, with a few thin words, with a dry cough, and seven sighs. They fly away and the money, yes, my good warm money, stays with me.

MOSCA. You fool them to the top of their bent. I marvel at the way you can pull them here by the nose again and again.

VOLPONE. What, you gabbling defamer, I pull them here? Lies, lies! The gold pulls them here. I do nothing but say I am rich; already they bow their backs in reverence. Then I let them know I have no wife, no child; their very tongues hang out. And then I make a pretence at mortal illness; ah, then the water drips off their tongues and they begin to dance for my money. Ah, how they love me: Friend Volpone! Best beloved friend! How they flatter me; how they serve me; how they rub against my shins and wag their tails; I'd like to trample the life out of these cobras, these vipers, but they dance to the tune of my pipe. They bring presents, they give me a share of their profits, the men bring coin and the women their favours—who, I ask you, does a more thriving business here in Venice, and has a juicier sport to boot? What did it bring in yesterday?

MOSCA. Three barrels of wine, sent you by your neighbour, fresh off a ship from Cyprus; to your recovery, he said. A hundred ducats sent as your share of a venture by Merchant Battista; two bowls from Giovanni, the goldsmith; and a benefice from the Secretary which you can sell for a thousand ducats.

VOLPONE. All that for two short hours of coughing and speaking in a thin voice my heart full of juicy villainy. Ah, my Mosca, what is the gold of Ophir com pared to the stupidity of men, and their wretched greed, when you know how to work them! It warms the cockles of my heart to see them ogling my gold, yearning for me to die the while I suck the marrow from their bones. How pitiable are all these puppet-plays compared to one man, dancing and jigging with the pangs of greed clawing properly at his bowels; ah, he dances far better than your marionettes and sings more movingly than a eunuch; each day they invent new comedies to play before me till I writhe with laughter. I'm chuckling now at the thought of their onslaught. Did you spray out the news everywhere that I am miserable, dying?

MOSCA. Full-cheeked, like a trumpeter.

VOLPONE. Then the troops will soon be moving up. But I am ready to receive them; I'll mow down your hopes for you, chop off your greedy hands, and above all, you marauders, you freebooters, I'll plunder your baggage.

(A knock at the door.)

Hello, the advance guard already? Out of the feathers early—it looks as if you don't sleep well with Greed; they say she's an old woman, as old as the world. Spy out carefully, my boy, who it was had this itch that drove him out of bed so early.

(Mosca goes out and returns quickly.)

MOSCA. Master Voltore, the Notary. I told him that your couch was being changed and he was to wait. Now to clear away these dainties, and substitute this rhubarb, these tinctures and mixtures. So—here, put on your fur cloak, and now—*(Pleadingly)* infirmity and a thousand murrains on you.

VOLPONE *(putting on the fur cloak)*. Be sure to heat their ardour. Let them sizzle and fry. Stir up their gall and fish out their tongues so that the water drips on the floor. Tweak them soundly.

MOSCA. Like a torturer of the Holy Inquisition.

VOLPONE. Pillage them completely!

MOSCA. As soldiers do a town when they have lain before it in the mud eight months.

VOLPONE *(stretching himself out on the couch)*. So, now I'll lay me down and make them think I'm ready for extreme unction. But I'll anoint you, you rogues,

with mustard and nauseous herbs, so your humped backs burn you for years; you've met your master this time! *(To Mosca, who starts to fetch Voltore)* Wait—ah—I must have one more good laugh first—if not it will burst forth while they dance their sympathy. So! Ah—and now to draw the curtain! *(He draws the curtain which makes the bed-couch invisible to the others in the room)* Now let the comedy begin.

MOSCA *(leads in Voltore, a notary, dressed in black, an estimable old man, rather pathetic)*. How magnanimous of you, Master Notary, to sacrifice your time— oh, all Venice knows how precious that is!—to our poor master! But be assured that he knows how to value that honour; your name is always on his lips. How is my friend Voltore? always his first question: what is my friend Voltore doing? Ah, yes, when a man is so alone in death, no wife or children, utterly alone, he thinks of nothing but his friends. *(Suddenly, in a very low, confidential tone)* Did you bring the will with you so I can have him fill it out?

VOLTORE *(also in a low voice)*. I never forget. Here it is, all filled out, nothing missing but his signature . . .

MOSCA. He'll give us that, never fear.

VOLTORE . . . and here . . . you see . . . I've left a space where he'll inscribe the heir he's named, for you know if I had set it down with my own hand . . . the world is so full of malice, people might have thought I had egged him on to it myself, but if he signs and in his own handwriting designates his heir, no tribunal can contest this document.

MOSCA. Rely on me!

VOLTORE. But don't be too urgent . . . I know it often irritates dying men, if you remind them of death, and a will *is* an instrumentum mortis . . . so be careful, —not too pushing . . . Here is a golden goblet I brought with me . . . show it to him and say I sent it . . .

MOSCA. Ah, how well you know the human heart; yet is it any wonder, Illustrissimo? With your experience of the world! How pleased he will be—but see for yourself: I'll wake him up. *(He goes to the bed and lifts the curtain)* Messer

Volpone, Master Notary has come to ask after your health . . . the first, as always.

VOLPONE (weakly). Thanks . . . many thanks.

MOSCA. Just think, he brought a golden goblet to you that you might drink health from it.

VOLPONE. Oh, a noble friend . . . a great soul. Tell him I want to see him often . . .

MOSCA (to Voltore). You hear? Did I speak the truth?

VOLPONE. Bring him here . . . my eyes are dark . . . but hand still . . . grasp hand . . .

MOSCA (handing him the goblet). Take the globet first.

VOLTORE (coming nearer). How do you feel, my honoured friend?

VOLPONE. Gold . . . ah . . . heavy . . . heavy . . . good gold . . . Ah, good friend . . . still thinks of a dying man . . .

VOLTORE. If I could only buy you health Instead of gold.

MOSCA (aside). It will cost you a pretty penny yet to keep him healthy!

VOLPONE. How true, how true! What use is all my gold to me now? . . . three houses . . . four hundred thousand sequins . . . vessels . . . precious stones . . . what use are they to poor, deserted Volpone? . . . ah, you do not desert me . . . I have no one but you . . .

MOSCA (softly). Do you hear?

VOLPONE. I can't last long . . . May God forgive me my sins . . . Oh, I was too fond of money, now it weighs upon my soul . . . I have deceived people . . .

VOLTORE. You? Never! You are the very first gentleman of Venice.

VOLPONE. How good you are to me . . . But I will think of you . . . you shall see . . . But have them read masses for my poor soul . . . ah, weary, weary.

MOSCA (lets the curtain fall. To Voltore). You see? I spoke in good faith.

VOLTORE. Ah, if it's only true! If we've only reached there.

MOSCA. We have. As soon as he gets back a little strength, I'll hand him your goblet filled with wine and let him write in your name.

VOLTORE. You are a good lad.

MOSCA. Ah, you say that now. But tomorrow when my poor good master is dead, I'll be chased out of the house; you have a wife and a child, there'll be no more room for me! Oh, if you would only grant me a place as your door-keeper, as a groom, as a scullery-boy; only do not chase me out of your house, do not chase poor Mosca out!

VOLTORE. You shall be treated like my own child. Here—(He gives him gold)—this is an earnest of my word.

MOSCA (kisses his hand). Oh, generous master! I will bring you the inventory this very day so that you may know what you possess, and I'll see to it: the moment he breathes his last breath, I go roaring to you—

(A knock on the door.)

Oh my! There's someone knocking. It may be the doctor or the priest, or even some interfering rogue. You had better go so that they do not see you, they might say—what villainies cannot the minds of men invent!—that you had used undue influence upon the legator. Better go down these stairs and speak to no one in the house, for they are all cupboard-courtiers and lickspittles.

(Voltore exits hastily.)

VOLPONE (jumping up). You are a sweet rascal, my Mosca, an excellent parrot, an apt pupil of mine. Ugh, that limping, pompous law-mangler, he hides his greed well under that black robe of his, but you'll have to get a pair of golden bowls out of him as well as the goblet. Who's the thief outside?

MOSCA. Corvino.

VOLPONE. At least he isn't wrapped in a little mantle, he's a stark naked villain but I'll scourge his naked hide till it's the colour of a monkey's pelt. Flay him, Mosca, tear the nails out of his fingers he has a heavy hand, that fellow, and we've rooked him pretty thoroughly already. Set bravely to your work . . .

MOSCA. And you; cough bravely, make saucers of your eyes, groan like a bag pipe—it will pay! (Takes the goblet and puts it on a table. Addressing the goblet) Ge flourish there and multiply! (Goes to the door, leads in Corvino) Softly, softly, he's just dozed off.

CORVINO. I wish he'd go to sleep forever.

MOSCA. Gently, gently, how impatient you are! You know that he intends everything for you and that I husband your interests.

CORVINO. A bird in the hand is worth two in the bush. How soon will he be dead?

MOSCA. He groaned in pain all night and prayed to God to end his torture soon.

CORVINO. And so He ought! Hark you, Mosca, I have brought him an opiate here; the doctor said that on taking it he'd fall into a fine deep sleep . . .

MOSCA *(aside).* Aye, his last sleep.

CORVINO. Give it to poor Volpone in his wine if he is thirsty. Why should he be tortured?

MOSCA. That I could hardly do, Messer Corvino, for he has no faith in physic and holds doctors are a greater danger than disease; I've always wanted to get him a good doctor . . .

CORVINO. For God's sake, no doctors! Sometimes they actually help. *(Furious)* If a man's going to die, let him die; none of this long-drawn-out torture. It ought to be forbidden by the State! Damn these quacks who botch God's handiwork! Never think to call in one of those black Latin-gabblers now, at this late day; the will's all made . . .

MOSCA. Ah, that's the rub; I was about to run to you to encourage you to visit him. It is written, but not signed and sealed, and the name of the heir is not inscribed . . .

CORVINO. Heaven, thunder, and culverins, the will not yet signed! And now perhaps he'll croak! Get a doctor right away, he'll have to dose him up with powders and bring him back to consciousness—once at any rate! The will not signed—what villainy, death may yet snatch it from his hands. The will not signed, thunder and hell! Hold—I just saw Master Notary go down the stairs.

MOSCA. The Notary . . . yes, yes, the Notary. He's a curious beast; he never took thought for Messer Volpone before, yet of a sudden he is so concerned . . . He came of his own accord to draw the will for him, wrote it without any charge, and sealed it . . .

CORVINO. Free?! Why, he's the most miserly of villains. Ah, he wants a last grab at the treasure chest, the rare old skinflint!

MOSCA. Oh no, you are mistaken; see, he is a generous, whole-souled gentleman: look at the heavy golden goblet which he brought Messer Volpone today as a present.

CORVINO. Legacy-hunter!

MOSCA *(humbly).* That's not for me to know.

CORVINO *(angrily).* 'S light I know it! Ugh, he sniffs the carrion, that hyena, that erudite ghoul: every time they scent that smell, all these law-twisters come flapping round . . . And Volpone, did he chase him? What did he say?

MOSCA *(a little simple).* Ah, master, old people are so peculiar! He hasn't enough breath to stir his nostrils and instead of thinking of God and the judgment day, what do you suppose: he's delighted as a child with that goblet. "Heavy," he says, "heavy gold, good gold, good friend." His senses are confused, he thinks every man who gives him gifts his friend, though he were his father's murderer. No fool like an old fool, you know that.

CORVINO *(trembling with rage).* Damn it, they all give presents, these legacy-hunters, these scamps; they all have money. But if I have to go to debtors' prison, I'll outplay that law-twister—he's the most dangerous of the lot. *(To Mosca)* Did you think I brought nothing along for Volpone? I've given him a share in my business; tell him I'll keep on sharing with him: here are three hundred sequins for a start.

MOSCA. Ah, that's what I call true medicine. The only one to cheer him. I'll jingle it in his ears; if the old miser heard ducats jingling, I'm convinced he'd burst out of his coffin. Watch, I'll liven him up once more. *(Goes to the bed. Calls loudly)* Messer Volpone, your friend Corvino is here.

(Volpone does not stir. Mosca jingles the money.)

Here . . . sequins . . . gold . . . three

hundred sequins . . . Messer Corvino brought them to you.

(Volpone wakes up.)

VOLPONE. Ah, Corvino . . . three hundred sequins . . . three hundred, you say? . . . much, much money. *(He coughs)* Ah . . . good friend . . . noble friend. . . . Thank him.

MOSCA. Lord, he hasn't said "Good friend" to anybody yet. Quick, now, butter the ducats with a few sweet words.

CORVINO. Ah, Messer Volpone, what pain to see you suffer so. If my own blood would cure you, I'd give it gladly! My wife prays for you all day, and when I trade, I think of you and work for you alone. These few ducats are a mere beginning—you may trust in me.

VOLPONE *(touched)*. So much goodness . . . *(He coughs)* so much friendship for a poor sick man like me . . . *(He coughs)* See, I'm coughing my life away. Mosca, my kerchief! . . . *He coughs)*

MOSCA *(softly)*. He's almost in tears.

VOLPONE. But I will repay you for it . . . *(He coughs)* You'll say: He thought of me on . . . oh, oh . . . *(He coughs)* . . . his dying bed . . .

(A knock at the door. Corvino starts.)

CORVINO. Damn it, who's coming there! Everything going so well—two minutes more and I'd have shoved the pen into his hand. *(Paces up and down)*

A GROOM. Master Corbaccio is below. He cannot climb the stairs alone, the others are helping him up.

MOSCA. Bring him, in God's name!

CORVINO. What does that damned vulture, that eighty-year-old skeleton want here? He hasn't stirred a step for fifty years except for profit . . . What does he want here?

MOSCA. Ah, he's coming to appraise the jewels, your jewels; he'd still like to chaffer, even buy. Go now, Messer Corvino, or you will tire Messer Volpone and I must try to rein him in properly.

CORVINO. No, my dear Mosca, I won't budge an inch; I want to know what the skeleton's up to. D'you think I'll let that usurious vulture guzzle my liver? Ah, I'm staying, I'm staying.

VOLPONE *(from his bed—coughs pitifully, calls)*. Mosca!

MOSCA *(hurries to him and speaks softly)*. The villain won't go away and we have to pull a few golden tailfeathers out of the old crow.

VOLPONE. Chase him, he must go! He's spoiling our business; he's sweated, now pour cold water over him.

MOSCA. Watch me get rid of him. I'll lend him wings. He is as jealous as two Turks. I'll nip him in his tender spot. *(To Corvino)* And now, my honoured friend, a word on nobler subjects; how is your gallant wife, the toast of all Venice?

CORVINO *(unpleasantly moved)*. Who said she was gallant? How, the toast of Venice? What are you gabbling about?

MOSCA. Oh, the whole town knows the lovely Colomba: St. Mark's is never so full as on Friday mornings when she goes to hear the sermon. Never are so many cavaliers at worship there. My friends have often made my mouth water to admire her.

CORVINO *(stammering with rage)*. What right have you to look at her, you good-for-nothing! . . . At St. Mark's, did you say?

MOSCA. Every Friday, the whole town knows that; at the sermon . . .

CORVINO. At the sermon . . . ah, I'll teach her about sermons. . . The whole town . . . all Venice . . . Ah . . . I'll go see to this myself.

MOSCA. I'll go with you.

CORVINO *(shoving him aside)*. That's all I need, you good-for-nothing! I'll grind your bones to blood inside your body—stay here with your master . . . ah, I'll preach her a sermon myself.

(Corvino runs away, meeting Corbaccio in the doorway.)

Master Corbaccio, in the flesh! Ah, so you're not dead yet? They told me your legs were so lame you couldn't move and here you come dancing up the stairs; this must be a wonderful little business deal a little hundred per cent profit to make you leave your treasure chests alone for a whole hour. I wish you luck . . . I wish you luck.

CORBACCIO *(an ancient, tottering, lame old man with a bony face)*. Thanks . . . I'm alive . . . thanks . . . I know your mind . . . no better than your credit . . .

wouldn't lend ten copper soldi on it . . .

CORVINO. I don't need your loans. No man you've strangled in your usurious grip has ever got off living. Grab, go on grabbing money; but take care, some day you may slip.

CORBACCIO. No fear . . . my money's kept well guarded—like your wife.

CORVINO. 'Fore God, what has my wife to do with you?

CORBACCIO. What has my business to do with you?!

CORVINO. My wife . . . what are they all saying? *(To Corbaccio)* The devil break your neck! *(He rushes out)*

CORBACCIO *(to Mosca)*. An uncomfortable person. Much malice, little gold. What does *he* want here?

MOSCA *(wondering, innocent)*. What does he want? Why, to crib a legacy, of course. Why else come to a rich dying man between the doctor and the gravedigger?

CORBACCIO. I . . . he, he . . . he, he . . . I like to look at dying men. I've seen so many and I enjoy each one more. I'm seventy-five . . . I've buried four brothers, sisters, friends, enemies, and I'm still alive. I'll outlive them all. I've known many of them in the cradle, and seen 'em grow up and all at once they lie there blue, cold, dead . . . he, he . . . and old Corbaccio stands by feeling the warm breath in his mouth . . . blood in his fingers. I can work, walk, make money . . he, he. It does me good to see it happen over and over. I'll outlive 'em all . . . and now this one, too . . . he, he . . . he lived a merry life,—young, could have been my son,—and he's come to die already. I want to take a look at it . . . he, he . . . and how are things today?

MOSCA.. Bad, very bad.

CORBACCIO. Good, you mean . . . he, he . . . nearing the end . . . Pulse?

MOSCA. Thin as a fly's leg.

CORBACCIO. Good . . . Breath?

MOSCA. Whistles like an organ.

CORBACCIO *(rubbing his hands)*. Fine, fine . . . His tongue?

MOSCA. Thick, yellow, hard, shoe-leather.

CORBACCIO. Ah, excellent! . . . Sweat: hot or cold?

MOSCA. Cold as a serpent's tail.

CORBACCIO. He, he, then it's coming soon. I know . . . Seen it often . . . it will soon be jolly . . . No air, pumps . . . pumps . . . pumps . . . can't raise any more . . . blue then, pale . . . he, he . . . coming soon now . . . Then stiff, no feeling . . . ears dulled, lids yellow . . . he, he . . . I know . . . 'twill soon come to that.

MOSCA. Woe, he's there already, just as you described it. He lies like a log, does Messer Volpone, since this morning, just as you picture it, hears nothing, feels nothing, notices nothing . . . Look, if you don't believe me. *(Yells at Volpone)* Hey, you Levantine thief, not dead yet? Am I rid of you at last, you bawd, you miser, you rheumy braggart, you stinking billy-goat? *(To Corbaccio)* See, you could discharge a cannon in his ear, he'd hear nothing. Lay hold of him, he'd feel nothing.

CORBACCIO *(gloatingly to Volpone, prodding him with his cane)*. Here, stand up, carcass, face the old man . . . You're younger, you have better legs . . . stand up . . . he, he . . . Often you've mocked poor old Corbaccio for being miserly and grudging others everything . . . he, he . . . who's mocking now, you libertine, you windbag, you glutton . . . He'll outlast you all, will old Corbaccio. He has more breath in his money than you have. He'll plunder you all and lie on your coverlets and live in your houses . . . he, he, corpse . . . he, he . . . You can't laugh any more . . . you laughed first . . . he, he . . . but I laugh last . . . *(Lets the curtain fall. To Mosca)* Keep the will here ready on the table. I want my money back at once. I invested fourteen hundred sequins, three thousand with interest . . . he, he . . . but I knew I'd outlive him. . . . He doesn't make any unsafe investments . . . old Corbaccio . . . I had good security . . . he, he . . .

MOSCA *(scratching his head)*. The will . . . yes . . . but don't you know . . . Messer Volpone has invited the Notary again today. He wants some more—what did he call them?—codicils to his will.

CORBACCIO *(stammers excitedly)*. A new will? Why codicils? If I hadn't seen him will me twenty thousand sequins . . . seen with my own eyes . . . never have given him the money . . . only safe investments . . . It's my guarantee, how can he change it . . . after he's dead?

MOSCA. Look, the Notary gave him this goblet and Master Corvino three hundred sequins; he means to remember them in his will.

CORBACCIO. And take it out of me, I suppose? . . . This can't be!

MOSCA. You see, the poor fool measures friendship by presents! If you were bright you'd quickly give him even more, so I could manage a good strong codicil for you.

CORBACCIO. These spendthrifts.— (Fingering the goblet) Gold, solid gold . . . three hundred sequins . . . I have nothing more . . . I'm a poor man . . .

MOSCA. Perhaps this ring? . . .

CORBACCIO. Ring! . . . thirty carats . . . worth a thousand sequins . . . I paid a hundred and twenty myself . . . No, no . . . too much . . . too much.

MOSCA (flattering him softly). It's only for a few hours. The corpse will scarce be cold when I tear it off its finger!

CORBACCIO (starting toward Volpone). True; he's three-quarters dead already . . . Here, take it, show it to him if he wakes again . . . and when he dies then bring it back. Here . . . this is for you. (Gives him money) . . . Right back . . . right off his finger before anybody sees it . . . here, take it . . . (Fearfully) lovely ring, lovely, brilliant fire . . . Wait, wait . . . I'll exchange it . . . bring another with a flaw this afternoon . . . He can't tell the difference any more . . .

MOSCA. He takes no more heed than a millstone. But go now, or the others will notice.

CORBACCIO. Better he died now . . . upsets me . . . another thousand sequins . . . lovely ring . . . bad business, bad business.

(Exit Corbaccio murmuring.)

VOLPONE (sitting up in bed). Is he gone?

MOSCA. The devil of greed has flown off with him.

VOLPONE. Lock the door! (Jumping up as he throws off the covers) Ah, it was high

time that you chased them. I was splitting with laughter. Well done, my lad, you ought to be a barber, you lathered them well and shaved them clean. Cut their throats boldly at the artery and let their blood—we've done a good morning's work, more comfortable than robbing a church or arguing with chafferers. Let me see: that goblet of Messer Voltore's I'll fill with wine; come, my little ring, right onto my finger, so you don't get cold; and you, my merry sequins, jingle gay table-music for me—for now, Mosca, sweet youth, we will breakfast; we'll feast like Romans, drink like Germans, and laze like Spaniards. Ah, life is easy to live as long as the dear Lord lets these cabbage-heads grow as thick as thistles.

(Mosca has drawn up the table. They sit down.)

MOSCA. At last you allow yourself good humour and enjoyment. This is the first time today. I'm glad to be your toady.

VOLPONE. You know, my boy, that food does not taste good to me until I've salted my throat; peppery malice first or a juicy villainy gives me a proper appetite. What better drink than that you quaff from a goblet stolen of a stranger? Your health, Master Voltore! And don't you worry too much about mine. I'll make the lot of you seventy-seven times as ill as you think I am. Oh, I'll drop scorpions into your boots yet, I'll break out your teeth and fling your tongues to the dogs; you shall learn to know Volpone yet! (To Mosca) I haven't enjoyed my food as much in weeks; after all there's no better spice than envy. To my health, Messer Corvino, to my health, Messer Corbaccio!

MOSCA. This is the way I like to have you; this is the way I like to see you.

VOLPONE. Yes, my boy, I know you do not wish to see worms in my body either, the coffin-lid over my head. You drink hard with me, eat hard with me, whore with me, cheat with me. But it goes against my grain that they can't see me in my cups. These jackals, these body snatchers, these lying dogs, if I could only thwack them well until their bone snapped; ah the villains!

MOSCA. Drink, drink, heat yourself with wine and not with gall. You've always known that they were villains . . .

VOLPONE. But why aren't they honest rogues? Why don't they come in and say—(*He bows before the treasure chest*) "I love you, Volpone's gold. I want you, Volpone's gold." Why don't they come begging, why do they give me presents and cram my room with lies, these rogues, unconscionable rogues, these hell-hounds, these murderous flattering hypocrites, these . . . these . . .

MOSCA. But, master, you're enraging yourself again. We were going to make merry; wait, I'll have the musician play, and fetch us women . . .

VOLPONE (*growing more and more embittered*). No . . . I shan't feel right till I have swinged these jackals well. I was too good to them, too kind: I only nipped them, tickled them; they must be scourged and branded like galley-slaves. I must rattle that skeleton who snuffled me once more, if I rot for it, and give the other one a few dreams in exchange for his little sleeping-potion which will kindle a purgatorial fire in his kidneys! Mosca, lovely boy, consider what we still might do to them, think you . . .

MOSCA. First, I must rinse the taste of all those lies out of my mouth with wine. Give them a breathing-space just for today . . .

VOLPONE. No, I won't feel right until I know their throats are burning. Think hard, lad, you're a clever scamp, that's why I like you—here! Corbaccio's sequins, here . . . ten—no, twenty—golden ox-eyes for you, if you think of something; but mind you, it must burn like pepper . . .

MOSCA. Hello; twenty sequins! Wait, that's oiling the machinery up here! Let me see—Corbaccio, then, and Corvino . . . Corvino. Where can we get him? In his sorest spot, of course. Money—no, we've robbed him thoroughly already; but you yourself say he is as jealous as two Turks . . . Wait . . . how would it be if we befuddled him so well that he himself brought you his wife, so you could horn him . . .

VOLPONE. His wife? Impossible!

MOSCA. D'you think so? I'll manage it. That one is lusting so for your gold he'd sell his own father for a galley-slave; why shouldn't he lend you the lovely Colomba for a night? What do you wager he'll bring her to you and beg you to take her, almost shove her to your bed? . . .

VOLPONE. Magnificent, magnificent! Twenty sequins more if you can bring the rascal to it. And Corbaccio; some archtrickery against the skeleton to make it start out of its sockets . . .

MOSCA. Corbaccio? . . . let me think. There's no more money to be got out of him, he's as tough as cow's meat over his sequins . . . But wait . . . yes, I have it! . . . He thinks you deathly ill, he hopes to outlive you, this graveyard turnkey, this hollowed corpse; that's where we'd have to nip him. What would you think of my persuading him to write you down his heir in order that he may be yours: that way you pocket everything of his at one fell swoop, and his son, the big-mouthed Captain, can eat husks and dried herring.

VOLPONE. Let me embrace you! If you get it, I'll give you half and you yourself can support little toadies, as clever and agile as you are. Magnificent, magnificent! Juicy malice like this warms me more than brandy. Ah, people always talk of mischief as Turks do of wine: they despise it because they are too cowardly to taste of it; if they knew how it tickles the senses, how it gets into your feet and makes them want to dance . . . ah, wonderful, wonderful! But quick now, my boy, run quickly . . .

MOSCA. What, you don't mean this morning? Heaven knows we've scooped in enough today.

VOLPONE. No, no, right away—ah, I'm itching to see the yellow in their eyes and rouse their bile. Now, now! Ha! ha! I can already see it—the jealous fool pushing his wife into my bed; I'll fit his horns to him before his eyes. Magnificent, magnificent! I feel so damned good now that I could dance.

MOSCA. And I'm to hop about it once more. Have pity on me, pity on them!

VOLPONE. If ever I'd had pity, I'd have no money. Pitiful people end in almshouses, and you never drink such good wine in good people's houses as you do in mine. Go along; stretch your legs.

MOSCA (yawning). Oh ... off again ... lie again ... Oh ...

VOLPONE (furious). Go along, I told you! Go along; buzz, gadfly, or I'll prod you.

MOSCA (lazily). Oh, when will I ever get enough rest! God give you a sweeter bile or me a new patron.

(A knock at the door.)

VOLPONE. Who's that again? Look and see.

MOSCA (looking out). Right away, right away! I just have to give him his physic. (Comes back, grinning mockingly)

VOLPONE. Who is it?

MOSCA. Your most nobly born bride, Canina.

VOLPONE. My bride! ... that whore?

MOSCA. Ah, she wants to marry you just the same: she's done more for you than any of the others. She's slept three times with you for nothing and she hasn't done that since she was twelve.

VOLPONE. I don't want to see the brazen wench; send her away.

MOSCA. Try yourself to send away a female that's crazy to get married; ninety devils haven't the strength to do that.

VOLPONE. I don't want her, the harlot.

MOSCA. Oh, go on, get a little angry so that you know how rage must taste in other people's mouths. Here she is, up already; quickly to your bed.

VOLPONE. You rascal, you're having your joke on me. But she'll find that she's mistaken. I'll make believe I'm asleep and say no word until she goes. (He lies down on his bed, furious, and closes the curtains)

(Canina, a voluptuous, bedizened harlot, coaxingly confidential, enters hastily.)

CANINA. Good morning, little toady!

MOSCA. Good morning, little whore!

CANINA. How's our lord and master?

MOSCA. Rotten, rotten! He's sleeping now. Your coming's useless.

CANINA. Nonsense, I'll wait till he wakes up. People like me learn to be patient with men.

MOSCA (softly). I don't begrudge him this. (Aloud) But tell me, zealous priestess of Aphrodite, what got into your head that you insist on marrying this crabbed,

deathly ill old rascal? You are still rich, you have more gold than enough, three different gallants each night, and a brisker business than the Pope—what devil's driving you to exchange rings with a vinegar-face like him, who'll bore you to distraction?

CANINA. Ah, little toady, you don't understand what boredom is—at first I too thought that it must be a bore always to have the selfsame man. But you see, when you've had a different one each night for twelve years and they all want and say and do the same, why, that gets boring too, in time. I have enough of it. And so I thought to myself, try it with one man, the best would be a sick one; he'll leave you in peace at night and sleep with you all the same—I can't get used to sleeping alone—and he won't live long either, poor good Volpone. Why shouldn't I try it for once?

MOSCA. Not a bad thought!

CANINA. And then I can say this to you, little toady: I'm not quite right. Three months ago, you remember, when the victorious fleet came back from Cyprus and we had flattened the Turks, there was much excitement, so much patriotic enthusiasm, and we all lost our heads—well, I think I got just a mite over-enthusiastic and over-careless; in a few months the state will have another little sailor. And, you see, my grandmother was illegitimate, so was my mother, and so was I, too. This has to stop sometime. You understand me, don't you, and you'll help me to marry him ... you know ... just talk to him a little, won't you?

MOSCA. Why, of course.

CANINA. And you can toady a bit when I'm here. You're a good-looking boy, and if you help him with his wine, you can be useful to him with his wife as well. But you will urge him, won't you? For what should I do if he died first—he seemed quite healthy when he slept with me; but now, my God, what shall I do if he dies first?

MOSCA. You can get a hundred others

CANINA. I know of none.

MOSCA. I'll tell you of one; old Corbaccio is as rich as a magpie, as old as Methuselah, and still keen on women. I any case, go to him too, show him your jewels, that will liven him—then you have two irons in the fire . . .

CANINA. You're a sweet boy. I love you . . . believe me, you'd be the first one for whom I'd do it for nothing in twelve years. That's a wonderful idea; I'll run right from Volpone to Corbaccio Here's a kiss for you on account, and more if you want it . . .

MOSCA. Sorry, but I have to go! I have work to do. Urgent business, not so sweet as your lips.

CANINA. And am I to stay here all alone?

MOSCA. Sit down by him on the bed.

CANINA (approaching the bed). But he doesn't move. He has his back to me. He's asleep. Listen to him snore. Must I sit here and wait till he wakes up, the lazy thing? Oh, how he snores . . .

MOSCA (already in the doorway). Stay there, stay there. Get yourself accustomed now to keeping still while another person sleeps—get accustomed to it in advance— have at least a foretaste of marriage with a rich old man.

SCENE TWO

SCENE: *Corvino's house. A room simply furnished. Colomba, Corvino's wife, sits at the embroidery frame sewing. Corvino enters, sneaking in at the rear, and suddenly bursts out at Colomba.*

———

CORVINO. Where were you this morning?

COLOMBA (startled). Sweet Lord Jesus!

CORVINO. Ah ha! You start! You grow pale. (Seizes her) Where were you, you deceitful woman, with whom were you, you church wanton, you arch-harlot?

COLOMBA. For heaven's sake, where else should I have been but here in your house? . . .

CORVINO. Ha, ha, in my house! Why re you so pale then? Your fear has betrayed you.

COLOMBA. Why shouldn't I be afraid when you make at me like a tiger?

CORVINO. In the house, were you . . . you expect me to believe that?! Swear to me you were, this minute, or I'll strangle you . . . Swear to me there before the crucifix that you have not left the house to-day. Come! (He drags her there)

COLOMBA. But what is wrong with you? I'll gladly swear you by the dear Redeemer and His painful wounds, I'll swear you by the kind Madonna that I have not left the house to-day. (Crying) Do you believe me now?

CORVINO. Let the devil believe you! Once he lodges in your body you'll swear by heaven and earth, but there's no one can lie to me. (Seizes her) When did you last see Mosca?

COLOMBA. Oh, you're hurting me! I don't know any Mosca.

CORVINO. Don't know him, ha ha; go on; yes, lie some more! Don't know him! And how does he know you, my dove, call you beautiful, white, tell me that you go to church every Friday, and flirt during the sermon? And how that fellow winked; he knows even more.

COLOMBA. Jesus, I am belied. What did I do to that strange man that he should smirch my honour! May God forgive him! I sat here the whole morning, here by the window.

CORVINO (in a new access of rage). By the window—ah, open. (He closes it with a bang) Haven't I forbidden you a thousand times to show yourself at the window?

COLOMBA. It was so close in here, I opened it a little.

CORVINO. To show yourself to those louts, to coquette, to throw them glances, to flirt, to fish for notes. Ah, I know, mould likes to settle on honey; when a woman shows herself at the window they come dawdling past, clanking their swords and twanging their mandolins. And dawdling makes them passionate, and because they are bold they please the women. Why isn't there a gallows penalty for these padded highway robbers, these sneak-thieves of honour who loaf about our homes while honourable men are at work? I've forbidden you a hundred times to hang yourself out of the window. (Seizing her again) How many of them were there? Did you speak to one of them? Did they send procuresses to you? How long were you at the window?

COLOMBA. But, sir, I never glanced out the window. Please believe me! I sat here with my sewing, twelve feet away from the window, just as you found me.

CORVINO. The lies are rooted twelve hundred feet deep in you, but I'll wrench them out. My God, what can a man do; two eyes are too few to watch over one wife. Ah, if I had money, if this Volpone would only puff his final breath at last! A man must be rich, rich, for they steal poor men's wives. You must get money; then I'll have the windows walled up, buy me a house with a garden on the inside, where you can have a breath of air, and I'll hire grooms and eunuchs and spies, twenty eyes to my two, to watch over you, and then I'll be able to sleep in peace. Oh, that Volpone, if he'd only breathed his last breath! *(To Colomba)* Once more, if I find that window open, I'll beat your every bone to bits; be a harlot with your thoughts if you must be a harlot, but not with your eyes. I have honour and I won't let it be stolen from me!

COLOMBA. But, sir, why do you distrust me? No one can say a word of me . . .

CORVINO. He smiled . . . he grinned like a dog . . . and people must not grin when they talk of me . . .

(A knock at the door.)

COLOMBA. Shall I open?

CORVINO. Into your room with you; you rush impatiently to show yourself to every man. Get in there! Wait till I call you!

(Colomba, hurt, goes off by side door, Corvino opens the street door and Mosca enters.) Is he dead?

MOSCA. Quite the contrary!

CORVINO. What does that mean? Are you trying to hoax me?

MOSCA. He's alive, very much alive, in fact; I'm afraid the devil has taken your ducats.

CORVINO *(stammering)*. How . . . how's that possible? . . . I saw him today, myself; he didn't have enough breath in his throat to flutter a feather . . .

MOSCA. And now he's fine. He struts, he throws out his chest, he fairly crows, he's bursting with life. Just imagine, his speech was broken, his eyes already set, his face drawn longer than is its wont . . . then it occurs to the groom, that ass, to fetch a physician, a Jewish physician, and he has him swallow a secret remedy, mutters half the cabala in his ear and all at once—bang!—up jumps Messer Volpone. Shouts and laughs and acts as healthy as you or I.

CORVINO. Haven't I always said they ought to burn up those damned Jews and drive them out? They stick their noses into everything. Is he really well now?

MOSCA. Damned well, I tell you. He's licking his very chops with well-being; and just imagine, hardly has he stood up, taken a few steps, wiped the death sweat from his forehead, when he asks for— what do you think? —for a woman, right off . . . The old Jewish doctor took me to one side and murmured that it was dangerous; that his health was not firmly established after such a magic cure and that nothing weakened a man so much as the enjoyment of women and he might easily have a stroke of apoplexy—I think that's what they call it—but the old dobbin would give me no peace. He whickered like a stallion, saying he must have a woman this very day, and he's commanded me to fetch him one. A gentle, appetizing little woman.

CORVINO. Damnation! But if it harms him, why not? I've heard too that apoplexy often overcomes old men right in the very midst of things. Yes, get him one, by all means, an experienced, battle some one, who will make trouble for him.

MOSCA. You needn't run far in Venice to find one of that sort! But you know how miserly he is, he'd like to have one for nothing . . .

CORVINO. For nothing! He'll wait long for that.

MOSCA. You are mistaken . . . You don't know how greedy, how rabid for money people can be . . . Hardly did the merchant next door hear of it when he came running in to say he'd send his daughter today, nineteen and proud a young panther and one of the seven sure virgins of Venice . . . this very evening he said he'd bring her, gentle and docile, bathed and anointed—her own father; and then—that's why I came to warn you—good-bye to your inheritance . . . For you don't need to be told that women carry an argument more persuasive than Demosthenes, which devours more ducats than all the Dukes of Milan . . .

CORVINO (*dazedly*). The devil . . . the devil . . . This evening, you say . . . his daughter, his own daughter.

MOSCA (*watching him, seemingly indifferent*). Yes, yes, he's making a bold attempt to sweep the whole fortune into his strong-box at one fell swoop . . . there's no surer proof of friendship than he is giving . . . Well, I thought I ought get the news to you quickly. May the Lord enlighten us as to how to outwit this old fox.

CORVINO (*still dazed*). The devil . . . the devil . . . His daughter . . . the fortune . . . today . . . today . . . this evening . . .

MOSCA (*still quite at his ease*). You see, thought you ought to know. Well, God be with you, sir.

CORVINO (*hastily*). No! Wait! Stay! One moment . . . O God . . . Tell Messer Volpone . . . no . . . wait . . . tell . . . tell him . . .

MOSCA. Go on, stammer more quickly. All this is no good anyhow; he thinks of nothing but the women.

CORVINO. For the love of heaven . . . wait . . . didn't you say my wife . . . my wife . . .

MOSCA. Well, what about your wife?

CORVINO. She's pretty . . . she's young and you know very well I'm Volpone's friend, his best friend . . . not that merchant . . . Wouldn't it be my duty, really . . . I mean, to cure him . . . to . . . to . . .

MOSCA. To what?

CORVINO. To send her to him . . . I can do for my friend what this intruder means to do for a stranger . . . rather he than one of these noble young bravoes who'd test out all thirty-eight of the Aretine's etchings on her . . . Volpone

is a respectable man, he is my friend . . . tell him, so that he sees how much I am his friend, I'm bringing Colomba to him today.

MOSCA (*acting surprise, embraces him*). You'll do that? Oh, what a godlike thought! Unsurpassable! you are the craftiest of them all. A whole life of riches for one hour . . . and dead men tell no tales. Masterly! But hurry, hurry, so as to forestall the merchant!

CORVINO. I'm coming right away. Ha, you stealer of legacies, your little snip will find the doors are locked to her.

MOSCA. Or I'll be so generous as to take my master's place with her.

CORVINO. Go now, run ahead and tell him . . . yes, tell him I am very happy to hear of his recovery, and that my first thought was . . .

MOSCA. Yes, I know.

CORVINO. To offer him the dearest thing in my possession. To give him all . . .

MOSCA. In order to get all . . . I understand. You know I can juggle words. But don't come too soon. I still have to go to Corbaccio's to roast his bile for him. Ah, if you knew what fun it is to hoax these greedy legacy-hunters.

CORVINO. I believe you, it must be.

MOSCA. And the merriest part of the sport is that none of them knows what I'm doing.—In one hour then, with Colomba! You're the cleverest of them all. You'll rake in the shekels. Farewell. (*Exit quickly*)

CORVINO (*paces up and down moodily. Finally goes to the door of the other room, leads Colomba in very gently and lovingly.*) Ah, Colomba, you're crying. Have I hurt you, my little dove? . . . forgive me. It's only love when I torment you so, and these wicked people know how near to my heart you are, and they nag at me and egg me on and wound me until I rage like a fool. And all the time I truly know what a gentle, good little wife, what a cooing turtledove I have in you. Forgive me, Colomba, if I've tormented you.

COLOMBA. Oh, how wonderful to hear you speaking kindly to me again. How often I have prayed to the dear Virgin to cure you of your groundless jealouys.

CORVINO. I, jealous! You ought to see other men, who lock in their wives, have them spied on, and clamp them in an iron girdle when they go on their travels. I, jealous? Well, you shall see if I'm jealous. I'll cure you of that delusion. You shan't mock me . . . I will give both you and me proof of my great trust in you, my turtledove! Come dress yourself, put on your jewels, make yourself lovely . . . I want to show you that Corvino's not the jealous spouse for whom you take him. Come!

COLOMBA (anxiously). Where am I to go?

CORVINO. To my friend, to Volpone. You are to nurse him in his decrepitude . . . I entrust him to you. Ah, you shall see how magnanimous Corvino is, how little befuddled by mistrust and evil thoughts; I shall leave you alone in his house today, and then you can no longer charge me with jealousy.

COLOMBA. Oh, Holy Trinity, am I to stay alone with a strange man?

CORVINO. He is weak and ill, he is my friend . . . I trust you both. You will tend him on his sickbed . . .

COLOMBA. Alack, is he in bed? My mother told me I should never stay alone with a man in a room where there is a bed or a couch.

CORVINO. May the mother of all devils take your mother. I want you to go, let that suffice.

COLOMBA. But suppose he should attack my honour?

CORVINO. Your honour is my honour; if he wounds it I shall know how to acquit myself, never fear. Poor people have no honour. When I am rich I shall maintain servants, gondolas, horses, silver dishes, and a personal honour: it's a luxury for the rich. But the devil take this empty talk; on with your cloak—so, with your breast bared, your sleeves short! There, just a few flowers now, and I advise you to look friendly or you won't see me looking friendly at all . . . Now for Volpone!

(He drags his frightened wife forcibly out of the room.)

SCENE THREE

SCENE: Corbaccio's house. A simply furnished room, chests and strong-boxes of iron.

———

CORBACCIO (His spectacles pushed back on his forehead, speaks to a servant). You say she's a fine lady? What does she want of me then? She came in a sedan-chair, so she needs no money. Caution! I don't like uncertainties! Call her in.

(Servant leads in Canina.)

CANINA. Messer Corbaccio, I hope I haven't disturbed your nap.

CORBACCIO. No time to nap . . . business, business. How can I serve you?

CANINA. Will you allow me to sit down, I'm so tired . . . Ah, I'm tired of this earthly life; what is it all worth? 'Tis true I'm rich, but that can't make me happy. I am beautiful, they say, but beauty passes. Forgive me, sir, for mentioning these things . . . but I want to renounce all my jewels before I enter the nunnery as one of the Holy Sisters, and I want to buy myself a little nook in Paradise with the benefactions I can purchase if I sell them. And now they tell me that the jewellers of Venice are all robbers and cut-purses, and I should like to consult a respectable man first and have him appraise their worth, not a Levantine, not a Greek, not a Jew, none of those carrion crows of the Rialto, but an honourable Christian merchant; and I was recommended to come to you.

CORBACCIO. To me . . . surprising . . . like to know who that was . . . But, to serve you, I'll appraise them at a half per cent, but only appraise them . . don't imagine I will lend you on their full value or pay you at that rate . . . no, no . . . the best I can do is fifty per cent . .

CANINA. How clever, how just! How clear you make it all. Ah, experience! Only mature men are mellow. Here's a ring to begin with. (Lays her hand on his) Ah, what cold hands you have, you poor man. Oh, you've no fur cloak. I'll send you mine. Ah, it's easy to see no one takes care of you.

CORBACCIO (has slid his spectacles down on his nose. Feels her hand). Ah, soft warm . . . *(Pulling himself together, looking at the stone)* . . . fine stone . . . good stone . . . genuine . . . clean fire . . . Indian diamond.

CANINA *(humbly)*. It's only one of the little ones; tomorrow I'll show you the others.

CORBACCIO. Valuable . . . valuable . . . two thousand sequins as brother to brother . . .

CANINA *(acting astonishment)*. So much money; oh, Jesus, such a little ring . . . Look at this chain for me? *(She opens her dress, baring her bosom and coming quite close to him)*

CORBACCIO *(reeling, stammering)*. Gold . . . heavy gold.

CANINA. But look at the medallion. Pull it out. Come, little bird, out of your warm nest! *(She pulls the medallion out of her dress)*

CORBACCIO *(staring at her)*. Warm . . . ah, warm . . . white . . . ah, ah . . . *(He pulls open the kerchief around his neck and stares again)* Ah . . . lovely, lovely.

CANINA *(very close to him)*. What did you say, my dear? . . . d'you think it's lovely?

CORBACCIO *(pulling himself together)*. Three thousand sequins for the chain . . . eight thousand for the ornament. *(Nearing her again, lustfully)* May I put it back?

CANINA. Yes, put him back again, the little foundling, between the two nuns! *(Leans toward him. Corbaccio tremblingly replaces the medallion)* These are only trifles. I have much better ones at home. But I am selling everything; you must help me. What good is the trash, for life is joyless when one has no one at all, no husband, no child, no brother, no sister, only gold, cold gold . . .

CORBACCIO *(close to her)*. And have you no one? No dependents . . . no relations, poor relations?

CANINA. No one, no one! *(Piteously)*

CORBACCIO. And *you* want to go into nunnery?

CANINA. What else can I do? Many men have wanted me to marry them but don't like them, these young chaps with down on their cheeks, the braggarts; I now all of them are itching for my money.

And where shall I find serious men I can respect, reliable, experienced?

CORBACCIO *(clearing his throat)*. You can find them; only they're not running the streets . . . they're attending to business.

CANINA. Ah, what true words! Everything you say has point to it; a woman could lean on you. *(She comes confidingly closer)*

(A knock at the door.)

CORBACCIO *(furious)*. Deuce take it!—Who's that, now? Send them away . . . come back later with the security . . . important business . . .

THE SERVANT. Master, it is Mosca, and very urgent.

CORBACCIO. Mosca . . . ah, he's dead! . . . ah, haha . . . *(To Canina)* Excuse me . . . come tomorrow . . . important business.

CANINA. I was just going . . . See you soon again, you dear good man!

(She meets Mosca in doorway.)

MOSCA *(bows deeply)*. Ah, Eccellenza, what an honour! Your very most humble servant!

CANINA *(rustling by him elegantly)*. Send my greetings to your honourable master. *(Exit)*

CORBACCIO. Do you know the lady?

MOSCA. As men of my kind know fine ladies. She's hellishly rich and equally haughty; she hasn't a kind word to throw to a mere Venetian citizen . . .

CORBACCIO. Ha ha, is that so? . . . not to you greyhounds . . . ha, ha, quite right. But tell me . . . what's new?

MOSCA. Master, I have run my shoes ragged to keep you well informed; everything's at stake now. In two hours the Notary is coming, the Doctor has given me a powder to prick Volpone into life once more so that he can hold a pen. Everything's in order, all's ready . . . everything's at stake now . . .

CORBACCIO. But I've given him my ring already . . . my thousand sequin ring.

MOSCA. And the minute goldsmith Battista saw it, he hurried in with another rope of pearls and Corvino came dashing with five hundred sequins more.—Oh, they're racing like antelope now they know death is straddling him.

CORBACCIO. Rope of pearls . . . five hundreds equins . . . the spendthrifts . . . What shall I do? . . . Help me . . . what shall I do? . . . I have no more . . . I'm poor. Fourteen hundred sequins, three thousand with interest, and the ring; I can't give any more . . .

MOSCA. That is just the reason I ran over here. I had an idea . . . worth at least twenty sequins.

CORBACCIO. Tell me, tell me.

MOSCA. I said, it is worth at least twenty sequins.

CORBACCIO. I'll give 'em to you . . . Tell me, tell . . .

MOSCA. I thought if I had something which proved your friendship even more surely, I'd down all these fools at once. And that thing you must give me; it will cost you nothing.

CORBACCIO. Cost nothing . . . good . . . good . . .

MOSCA. Only ten sequins for the Notary so that he waits until I bring it to him . . .

CORBACCIO. Bring what?

MOSCA. Oh nothing, a sheet of paper. You see, you merely make a will naming Volpone your sole heir before the Notary . . .

CORBACCIO. Volpone? . . .

MOSCA. And I'll take it to him, puff out my cheeks, and say: look, this is a real friend, he disinherited his son for you; see how he loves you! And what will he do? He'll name you his sole heir!

CORBACCIO. I understand . . . good . . . very good . . . But disinherit my son . . .

MOSCA. Oh, but only for then hours. Volpone will be dead by then and you'll have made your son again as rich; why, you're doing this for him. You know you'll outlive Volpone.

CORBACCIO. I should say so . . . he, he . . . I should say so . . . Oh, excellent idea . . . and cheap . . . I'll hurry right off to the Notary. I'll bring the paper right away . . . right away. (Starts to hurry off)

MOSCA. You've forgotten something!

CORBACCIO. Forgotten?

MOSCA. The ten sequins for the Notary.

CORBACCIO (groaning). Much money . . . much money. Here, take it.

MOSCA. And the twenty for me . . .

CORBACCIO. Later . . . later . . . I'll give you thirty when he's dead . . . (He hobbles off hastily.)

MOSCA (calls after him mockingly). Rattle away, you dried-up skeleton! What fools money makes of men; they snuff at each other like dogs and stay in heat all their lives. Sells his son, this one, and the other his wife; they'd sell the Almighty, if they could lay hold of him, for money, money, money. Ah, money everywhere, there, (knocks on the treasure chest) money, stinking with sweat and blood, locked in, imprisoned, there,— (he raps on the cupboard) money again, freezing in the dark, not warming a soul, and it's the same next door, across the street, upstairs, downstairs, in all the public squares, the whole city, the whole world, everywhere gold, gold, buried, coffined, hidden, the lust of possession weighing down on it like a gravestone, and envy after it, frenzied, its mouth hanging open. Oh, you fools, you make a man want to knock your heads together and twirl you around till St. Vitus' dance takes you; even if I haven't your gold—I spit on it—I'll have my sport of you.

(Enter Leone, a captain, big, brusque, loud clanking his sword, exaggeratedly military He notices Mosca.)

LEONE. What are you doing here, you rogue?

MOSCA (mockingly polite). I haven't the honour of knowing you.

LEONE. But I know you, as you can see by the fact that I call you a rogue. You are Volpone's toady, his back-scratcher, his pander, his doormat, his cheeseparer his nose-rag. What are you doing here I suppose he kicked you out and now you're looking for a new berth with my father.

MOSCA. Ha, ha, your father? So you're Leone! A clever child . . . a smart little son, in sooth; he has a beard like a forest bellows like a bull, is forty years old, an still doesn't know his own father Doesn't know that you can get a cough out of a dead man, children by a eunuch quicker than a copper farthing out of Corbaccio's pocket!

LEONE. But you are after something here. Dogs of your breed do nothing for nothing; what do you want there?

MOSCA. Wouldn't you like to know? But you are right; I do nothing for nothing, therefore I shall say nothing, nothing in any case because you pay no respect to my calling—which, God knows, is as respectable as yours.

LEONE. What, you lickspittle, do you dare compare yourself to me, a Captain regularly appointed by the Republic of Venice?

MOSCA. We are appointed by God himself to see that money doesn't get mouldy, the world boring, or sour dough stay unleavened. If it weren't for us, purses would burst with gold, whores would have to do it for love, innkeepers would have to swill their own wine, and the rich stifle in their own lard; but we're the blood-letters, we see to it that money flows from the stupid to the clever, out of the treasure-chests into the street; if we didn't prod it awake now and then, we wasters, we toadies—the world would go to sleep. To each its task; God made wine to drink, horses to ride, the poor to exploit, women . . . well, you know what for, sheep to be shorn: and there you have our task, but you must have brains inside your head for that, not just a bunch of plumes waving over it.

LEONE. It strikes me you're getting rude.

MOSCA. I spare my politeness for the rich; you others get the rough side of my tongue.

LEONE. You're not so stupid! When I'm rich, I'll have a couple of your sort about. But you're not clever enough to get money out of me.

MOSCA *(disdainfully)*. Out of you? Child's play.

LEONE. Ha ha! Then play, my child. Here. *(He slaps his hands on his pockets)* Get the money out of here. Dance all your capers for me and see if so much as one of my ducats dances out of my pockets after you!

MOSCA. Well—for instance. Wouldn't you very much like to give me five hundred sequins, if I got you three hundred thousand?

LEONE. Get them for yourself, why don't you! Three hundred thousand are better than five hundred. You're a poor sharper; I know these peasant-catchers from the barracks—all about buried treasure. Ha ha, we've heard all that before, we soldiers . . .

MOSCA. Stick to the point. Will you give me five hundred on the day you get three hundred thousand?

LEONE. Ha—why not?

MOSCA. On your honour and your word as a soldier?

LEONE. On my oath. But you can't do it honestly. You're planning some villainy, aren't you?

MOSCA *(hurt)*. What a boorish question! Of course, some villainy—how else? Did you ever hear of a man's earning such lordly gains in an honourable way? Work all day, from early till late, and they shove two soldi into your hand, perhaps three, and you turn to carrion on a dung heap; if you could earn sums like that honourably, no one would be a mason any more, or a clerk. Villainy, of course.

LEONE. I suppose you want me to put somebody out of the way for you?

MOSCA. How brash! I don't need you at all. This is an entirely bloodless, bone-dry villainy; I only have to betray a secret to you. But you must swear not to act on it too soon.

LEONE. I swear it, although one shouldn't swear to villains of your sort.

MOSCA. Well, you believe that your father is rich, and that is true; these shabby chests don't deceive me, I smell the gold; I know he is the nabob of all usurers, the pope of all extortioners. But you believe that when the old man dies his wealth all goes to you . . .

LEONE. To whom else?

MOSCA. But there you are mistaken; he's not your father at all.

LEONE. What? Are you trying to traduce my mother?

MOSCA. Oh, he's your father—but you are no longer his son. He has disinherited you. He ran from here straight to a notary to make a legacy-hunter his heir.

LEONE. Another man? Disinherited me? What scoundrel did this?

MOSCA. How you jump to conclusions! I, of course—acting for my master, who is to be his heir. But, as you rightly remarked, I am a scamp and I am telling this to you to earn five hundred sequins.

LEONE. It's impossible; let him slide down the hill to hell then, the old skinflint, and I'll give him the first shove. It's impossible . . .

MOSCA. You underrate our art; ah, we've set some merry cuckoo-eggs to hatch in his brain-pan. My pet sport is tweaking misers' noses.

LEONE. But if you've lied and I cursed my father unjustly, I'll stick my dagger between your ribs.

MOSCA. Save your skewer for the Turks; I'll let you see and hear for yourself. Come, I'll lead you to Master Volpone's house, hide you in his room where you can overhear the whole thing, but don't lose your temper. You've promised me. Come along now.

LEONE. I'll come and quickly, too. One moment while I fetch my things. (He goes off into the adjoining room for a moment)

MOSCA. I do believe I did something rather villainous just then; I don't exactly know if I've sinned against Leone, or Volpone, or Corbaccio, but let them fight it out among them. What is it to me! I throw the salt into the soup: let them spoon it out; whenever a man makes a proper pirouette, chance, the unbidden dancer, joins him and turns right left and left right. A friendly premonition tells me they will do nothing very nice to each other, but each is right from his own point of view, and all of them amuse me. Come along, Leone, you will hear and see all kinds of things that aren't printed in your dream-book. Come along, come.

(Mosca exits with Leone.)

ACT TWO
SCENE ONE

SCENE: Volpone's Room. The same day.

———

MOSCA (peers in cautiously; to Leone). Come in, come in, but don't clank your spurs. Quiet and careful as a dancing-master. Behind this wall's a corridor; wait there and you can hear everything. But don't come out until I call. Stay quiet, now; your dear father's in a hurry, he'll not keep us waiting long. And don't rattle your butcher-knife like that, you're not out fighting the Turks, you're in a Christian house.

LEONE. I'm going, I'm going, but if you're hoodwinking me, I shouldn't like to be in your hide. I'll stab it as full of holes as a fish net and no tailor will mend it.

MOSCA. All right, all right, go brag to yourself in there, but do it quietly; Volpone has sharp ears.

LEONE. I'll cut them shorter for him if he has a part in this, I'll . . .

MOSCA. Gently, gently.

(Pushes him outside; alone.)

Now I'm rid of one fool, but as sure as my beard sprouts, the next one is already on the stair; where there's money, fools are never far to seek. Good Lord! I'm only afraid that in the stress of lies I'll tell the truth by mistake, there's such a hubbub going on behind my teeth. I really ought to tie up my own tongue; one grows foolish among all these fools.

(Volpone enters.)

VOLPONE. At last. Where were you so long: after the women again, dawdling on the Piazza while my ears were burning with impatience. Did you make them soft, pliant? Tell me, tell me all about it.

MOSCA. First, a cup of wine. Most excellent!—It's working, it's working. Both of them are hooked by the gill . . .

VOLPONE. Both! Fine, my bully boy, you're no gadfly, no, you're a fine stinging fly, a valiant horse-fly; you've sweet excellence at driving them all mad. Is he bringing the will? Is he bringing Colomba?

MOSCA. Sure as the morning brings the evening. Ah, I shook the old broomstick well, and out of the double-dyed Turk made a pander from whom all the old women could take lessons; they'll dance attendance instantly. And on top of that did another little extra stroke of business.

VOLPONE. What? What more?

MOSCA. A small surprise for you

Greek fire that I shan't set blazing until all's made smooth . . . By the Twelve Apostles, a most wonderful display of rockets with cannons and balloons is still locked in my chest, a surprise . . .

VOLPONE *(at the window, laughing loudly)*. Mosca, ah ha, he's bringing her already. Magnificent . . .

MOSCA *(softly)*. Damn it. Now Corvino is here before the old man and I told him to wait an hour.

VOLPONE. How this Corvino drags her along, how he pushes her. It seems the little woman's not exactly willing . . . God often grants the simple-minded premonitions . . . but he, ha, ha . . . Jove! the way he shoved her then, another two inches and she would have been in the canal . . . Charming, that little couple! He can't wait to receive his horns. I'll make a bee-line to fit them on for you and all Venice shall know of your antlers.

MOSCA. Now he's dragging her into the house. Away to bed with you, groan roundly, wail sorely . . .

VOLPONE. I'll soon have her groaning another tune in my little bed!

MOSCA. But mind you make no noise so that the servants hear nothing; they glue their ears to the keyhole enough as it is. Come now, dying music, a few nice death-rattles, heart-breaking coughs, and trembling hands too, when I raise the curtain. *(He steps to one side)*
(Enter Corvino, plushing Colomba ahead of him, thinking himself alone.)

CORVINO. Haven't you yowled your fill? What will people think . . . ?

COLOMBA *(crying)*. Yes, what *will* they think? I'm afraid of that strange man!

CORVINO. Nonsense, strange man! That's far past being a man, it's merely a wretched bundle of diseased infirmity, more dead than alive; you ought to pity him, you that are a medicine for him . . .

COLOMBA. But if he takes me . . . ?

CORVINO. Then he takes you. You've yapped and yawped enough. Down with that kerchief; no more tears; stand there looking sweet and gentle with your eyes lowered; not another word.

COLOMBA. Oh my, what will my mother say?

CORVINO. God forbid her knowing it; she'd spill it out into all the wash-tubs of Venice. Shut your mouth, you cackling hen, and don't you shame me!
(Mosca steps forth, bows.)

MOSCA. Greetings, Corvino . . . greetings, Monna Colomba, as beautiful as you are chaste, the treasure of Venice.

CORVINO. Silence, babbler!

COLOMBA *(anxiously)*. Is this he? But he looks young and he doesn't look at all sick to me.

CORVINO *(furious)*. You idiot's spew, that is his puppy, his lick-spittle . . . don't you dare think of speaking to him. Not a word, not a look. He has the devil in him. *(To Mosca)* Did you give my message to Volpone? How did he take it? How is he?

MOSCA. The effect of the medicine is wearing off and he lies there weak and tired again. But perhaps your wife will bring him back to life . . .

CORVINO. And then the apoplexy, God willing.

MOSCA. Ah, how thankful he was to you: thus did Isaac sacrifice his child, he said, and the tears ran down his cheeks like muscat grapes. He has signed and sealed you his heir; look, the wax is still moist. But listen for yourself. *(Loudly)* Messer Volpone, your friend Corvino has come . . .

VOLPONE. Ah . . . good friend . . .

MOSCA. . . . and he has brought his wife Colomba to nurse you.

VOLPONE. What a friend! . . . But it's too late . . . how make green the sere and yellow leaf? . . . How help men whom God requires in Heaven? . . . My strength, gone again . . . but see wife . . . show me the lovely remedy at least . . . see Colomba . . .

CORVINO *(to Colomba)*. Come! Can't you see he can't stir so much as a toe?

COLOMBA. Oh, the poor sick man, how I pity him.

CORVINO. Now you see stupid you were. *(To Volpone)* Here is my spouse, Colomba, whom I have brought to guard your slumbers.

COLOMBA. I'll pray to the Madonna to make you well again.

VOLPONE. Sweet child . . . gentle child . . . yes, stay, stay with me . . . O happy Corvino to have health and a gentle wife . . . I'm all alone, an old, dying man . . . have pity, don't desert me . . . don't leave me to die alone . . .

COLOMBA. No, I will stay with you . . . I will care for you, you poor creature, and frighten away these bad thoughts. (To Corvino).

How I pity this poor man!

MOSCA (softly, to Corvino). Let us go!

CORVINO. You stay, my turtledove, be gentle with him, and do not be frightened if a fever should come over him; now you understand that I merely pitied him; I'll soon be back. Farewell, dear friend, my wife will guard you. (Exit)

(Colomba starts to take a seat away from the bed.)

VOLPONE. No, stay, let me hold your hand. How it warms me, lovely young hand, warm young blood. Like King David when he was old and cold; this warmth comforts me.

COLOMBA. Yes, my grandmother in Fusina, when she was old and had the gout, always used to lay little dogs on her legs, and it never failed to help her. Wait, I'll bring a blanket and make you more comfortable . . .

VOLPONE. No blankets—your hand. So you wish me to regain my health?

COLOMBA. Of course I do; I'll say five Hail Marys now for you and three Our Fathers.

VOLPONE. Will you really?

COLOMBA. I said I would.

VOLPONE. Then my health will return immediately. There is a magic cure; if a virtuous woman lays her hand upon your heart and says three times, "Be well," then you arise from your bed fully cured.

COLOMBA. Holy Mary, I never heard of that.

VOLPONE. It's printed in the Decameron or some other holy book. Come, try it—you are virtuous. I can read it in your eyes, my little dove—lay your little hand on my heart, so—ah, good; and now say three times: "Be well again, Volpone!"

COLOMBA (anxiously). But how . . . be well again, Volpone!

VOLPONE. Yes, yes . . . now two more times!

COLOMBA. Be well again, Volpone! Be well again, Volpone.

(Volpone throws off all the covers and jumps up. Colomba starts back.)

A miracle! Madonna, a miracle!

VOLPONE. Ah, well again, well again . . . and by your grace . . .

COLOMBA. I cannot believe it . . . I must run straight to Corvino to tell him what has happened.

VOLPONE. No, stay here, he'll get to see his nine days' wonder soon enough! Ah, I feel young, lively, I could dance.

COLOMBA. Oh, kind sir, take care not to get chilled, right out of your warm bed; God forbid you get sick again

VOLPONE. Never again, as long as you are with me. Feel this hand! Come, is it weak, is it cold? (He puts his arm around her) These arms, have they no marrow, no strength? (He embraces her) These lips, are they not hot? (He kisses her)

COLOMBA. Oh God, what are you doing? . . . You're delirious . . . lie down, I beg of you . . . I'm so frightened . . .

VOLPONE. No fear, no fear, my little dove. I am as healthy as two porters, full of life and gaiety, an absolutely sound and lively man; you can feel that. (He embraces her again) There . . . does your Corvino hold you more tightly when he desires you? . . . does he take hold of you better . . . tell me, does he?

COLOMBO. Yes, yes, I believe you . . . Let me go again, dear sir, I beg of you.

VOLPONE. Never again. You roused me, cured me, and I must thank you. Yes, I'll thank you as well as ever man thanked woman, I'll thank you in the best, the most natural, the very oldest way . . . not just once, but twice, three times . . . come, my little dove, give me your little beak . . .

COLOMBA. For heaven's sake, what do you want? Let me go! Corvino! . . . where is my husband? . . . Corvino . . .

VOLPONE. He is far away and if he were in the next room he'd stuff his ears with cotton-wool. Do you think he doesn' know why I wanted you? He sold you, he bartered you, my little dove . . .

COLOMBA. Oh don't say such things . . . he cannot be so low . . .

VOLPONE. Yes, he's a scoundrel, isn't he? But come, let us revenge ourselves on him, make him grow a pair of horns. Come, Colomba, let's do it to him.

COLOMBA. Let me go! . . . I'll scream for help . . .

VOLPONE. Damn little prude! Scream if it pleases you, there's no one here and it's all locked and bolted. Come here, or I'll use force.

COLOMBA. Let me be . . . for heaven's sake . . . I'll scream . . .

VOLPONE. The devil; get along, you stupid calf. *(He seizes her and throws her on the bed)*

COLOMBA *(shrilly)*. Help, help!

LEONE *(Who has burst in the locked door at one blow, knocks down Volpone with his fist, so that he reels back onto the bed)*. There, you Levantine scamp! A good one on the ear will teach you to dishonour Venetian women and rob men's sons. I will cure your sickness! To the gallows with you. *(Rushes to the window and tears it open)* Halloa, call the sbirri here! Rape! The Levantine is trying to rape a Venetian lady. Bring the sbirri, call them now! *(To Volpone)* Your little game's played out! *(To Colomba, leading her to a chair)* Rest here, you have nothing more to fear.

MOSCA *(rushing in)*. You lout, what's gotten into you; didn't you swear to stay quiet?

LEONE. Stay quiet; yes, that would just suit you! But I will shout so you hear the roar over all the churches of Venice, I won't close my mouth while you are picking pockets and dishonouring women; the Levantine must go to the gallows, be garrotted, but first he's to be whipped, beaten, flayed, he shall have as many lashes as he has sequins . . .

CANINA *(rushes in)*. Is he dead? Oh, he has murdered him, my bridegroom.

LEONE. Your bridegroom? If I had all your bridegrooms in my regiment, I'd conquer India!

CANINA *(inspecting prostrate Volpone)*. Living! God be praised!

LEONE. For the gallows.

(Captain of the Sbirri enters hastily with two of his men.)

CAPTAIN. Someone here called for help . . .

LEONE. Against a dirty scoundrel! Come in, come in.

CANINA. Against that murderer.

MOSCA *(leaping into the conversation)*. Ah, gentlemen, nothing's happened, a misunderstanding, a regrettable misunderstanding, a little domestic upset, nothing worth mentioning . . . Do not trouble yourselves, gentlemen, I beg of you, everything is already settled.

LEONE. You stay! *(Presenting himself)* Leone. Captain of the Fleet. I called for help against this Levantine. He attempted rape upon a Venetian lady and I demand justice upon him.

CAPTAIN *(bowing)*. At your service, Captain. So that man there tried to use force on this woman? . . .
(He points to Canina.)

LEONE. Not that one, five sequins turn the trick with her; he laid lustful hands upon this lady, the wife of Citizen Corvino. I swear to it, upon my oath.

CAPTAIN *(to Colomba)*. Do you also swear to it?

COLOMBA *(crying)*. Oh, I'm ashamed, I'm ashamed.

CANINA. You ought to be. This is what comes of chasing into men's houses . . .

CAPTAIN *(to Mosca)*. And you also bear witness . . . ?

MOSCA. God forbid . . . I know nothing . . . I was asleep at the other end of the house . . . I know nothing . . .

CAPTAIN. Was no one else on the spot? *(Corvino has entered. Mosca goes to him quickly and speaks to him softly.)*

MOSCA. Act surprised! You know nothing.

CORVINO *(astonished, to Colomba)*. What, you still here, my little dove? I was awaiting you impatiently. Come right home . . .

CAPTAIN. Stay here! All of you, right here! No one moves till everything is cleared up; now that man lying there is the Levantine, isn't he? Away with him to the court and all of you come along; they'll settle it there.

LEONE. Yes, come away; there the sneak-thieves of Venice will look upon their master's face with a rope decoration around the neck soon, I hope. He robs men of their money, women of their honour, and he talked my father into disinheriting me.

(Corbaccio has just entered stumblingly, a paper in his hand. Leone rushes at him like a tiger and tears the document out of his hand.)

CORBACCIO. Help, help—ow!

CANINA. He's murdering his father, the brute . . . parricide, parricide!

LEONE *(scanning the document)*. Here, here, here's the proof. Now the Judge can see the scoundrelly trick. Here is written proof of his thievery. Volpone must hang, hang on the highest gallows in Venice . . . Oh you goat, you thief, you swine! Here, here, we have you now . . .

CAPTAIN. Do not excite yourself, Captain . . . the Procurator will mete justice out to each of them. Come along, all of you, to the tribunal!

LEONE. Come, Colomba.

(All of them except Mosca and Volpone go, accompanied by the Sbirri.)

CAPTAIN *(to Mosca)*. I mean you too, and most of all, him, the accused.

MOSCA. I know nothing at all and Messer Volpone can't walk a step; you can see that for yourself.

CAPTAIN. Then let him be carried to court. And if you dawdle about it I'll have you brought there in chains.

(Captain exits with all the others. A short pause.)

MOSCA *(to himself)*. A man shouldn't bring fireworks home, a fuse is sure to go off prematurely and burn his fingers. A pretty surprise I engineered with that lout, Leone; now he's gripped us both by the neck and I already feel something like a hempen neckerchief. *(To Volpone, who lies there huddled and trembling)* Oh, pull yourself together.

VOLPONE *(shuddering with cold and fear)*. I won't go, no, I won't go . . . They'll put me on the rack, drip melted lead on me . . . lower me into a well . . . I won't go before the tribunal . . . they'll take away my money, my life, my money . . . Oh, what a fool I am . . . I could strangle myself . . . Instead of enjoying my money, instead of taking my pleasure, I'm driven by some devil into tormenting this vermin . . . Why did I have to have this legacy from Corbaccio or take that moon-calf Colomba? I didn't have a grain of desire for her . . . just malice . . . just malice . . . just lighting a fire under them, and now it's burning in my own bowels . . . Oh, if I ever get out of this, I'll take my ease . . . endow churches . . . praise God . . . give doubly to the poor and do charity . . . Mosca, Mosca, help me, they will stretch me on the rack, they will hang me, I'm an alien, a Levantine, they'll have no mercy on me . . . Help me, Mosca, help me.

MOSCA. Courage, courage. Every trial is like a game of cards. If you've nimble fingers you can call the turn. Corbaccio and Corvino are hanging by the same rope as we; I'll sway them to our side. All it needs is a little gold to smooth the path. Courage—it would be a curious trial if an honourable man were found to be in the right.

VOLPONE. No . . . I won't go to court . . . I know there'll be an inquisition . . . the rack . . . the strappado . . . I once heard the broken joints cracking and grinding as they tightened the ropes, the thumb-screws, the pincers, the red-hot pincers, pulling out the nails . . . how it stunk of burning flesh! Ugh, ugh! . . . no, I won't go . . . Mosca, come . . . get together my money, there, those jewels pearls, diamonds . . . *(He grabs greedily at the contents of the chest)* Get a gondola a closed one . . . I have a ship at dock in Genoa with a full cargo; I'll sail home to Smyrna to my wife and children. I have a house there where I can live quietly . . Ah, no trial . . . only not the rack, no rack . . . say I jumped into the canal so they won't follow me, spread the rumour I am dead . . . No, not to court to be a laughing-stock for those scoundrels . . only not the rack. Ugh, the rack . . .

(He throws his cloak about him. Voltore enters.)

VOLTORE. What has happened? I hear at court . . .

MOSCA. Oh, Master Notary, your money is lost, rescue your money, th dogs are wolfing down your ducats. Leone has brought an accusation against us, and Volpone is to be beaten, hanged, and the State will grab your house and your gold if you don't help him out of it . . .

VOLPONE *(on his knees)*. Help me, Illustrissimo, you know all the dodges and subterfuges. I will make you my sole heir and give you half during my own life . . . Only not the rack, the strappado . . . help me . . . my only heir, I swear it, and half while I am living . . . there, there, there . . . all for you.

VOLTORE *(impressively)*. Rely on me . . . I will take your case, *turpis causa*, of course; but have no fear, it is our science to create confusion and muddy the waters. *(To Mosca)* But what induced you to let that lout, Leone, into the house?

MOSCA *(softly)*. I did it for your sake. Corbaccio disinherited him and named Volpone his heir in order to oust you. So I thought: I'll set his son on him; but the bellowing bull crashed out too soon . . . But you'll set things straight again, Illustrissimo, won't you?

VOLTORE. I know the law; there is no law which cannot be circumvented. Unfortunately, the judges in our Republic are not venal; too bad, too bad. But we'll have to dazzle so many arguments before their noses that they can't see straight and confuse right and left; leave it to an expert. *(To Volpone)* You, say not a word, remain silent. And you— *(To Mosca)* Fix him so he looks more dead than alive. I need to make the impression that Leone hurt him badly. Follow me soon, I shall hurry ahead to my witnesses; they must sound in harmony like organ pipes, so we can play *Te Deum Laudamus* upon them. *(He exits)*

VOLPONE *(still trembling)*. I'm afraid . . . I'm afraid . . . Do you think he will help me?

MOSCA. Of course, of course, he is stupid and crafty at the same time; the best combination for a lawyer. And then, too, he thinks he is figthing for his own money; that makes even a donkey clever. *(Goes to the table with the mixtures)* But no more dawdling now. You have to set leeches on yourself till you are as pale as a drowned corpse. Here . . . *(He*

reaches him a spoonful)* dog's-gall to turn your stomach and make you look green.

VOLPONE *(takes it—spits)*. Brrrrrr . . .

MOSCA. You see, that's the way gall tastes; remember, and drink Lacrimae Christi in future. Now for the leeches, a half dozen at once so that you look truly miserable; I'll run ahead to sweeten Corbaccio's and Corvino's throats a little, so that the lies slip out more easily. And you follow on the litter. Courage, now, courage! God helps those who have money, and it would be a curious court which did not finally adjudge a rich man innocent.
(Exit hastily.)

SCENE TWO

SCENE: *Audience Chamber of the Senate. Judge's table, chairs for the witnesses.*

———

VOLTORE *(in conversation Corvino)*. You know what to say then; your wife went to Volpone out of sympathy, without your urging her . . .

CORVINO. But won't that shame me? Won't they point their fingers and say my wife went to a strange man and I ignorant of everything?

VOLTORE. It's a long time since that circumstance shamed anyone in Venice. The only shame would be if you had sent her or taken a pander's fee for her. But you can swear, can you not, that you received nothing from Volpone?

CORVINO. Received? *(Enraged)* He made a poor man of me. I gave him money, rings, silver; he emptied all my pockets.

VOLTORE. That makes you a man of honour, a man of spotless honour. Don't worry. Now once more; in case they ask you . . . *(He goes with Corvino toward the background nad exits)*

MOSCA *(enters with Corbaccio from other side)*. I only say to you, beware of your son; he has sworn to force your treasure-chests, to strike you dead because you've disinherited him . . .

CORBACCIO. My chests . . . my gold . . .

MOSCA. Therefore, you must say it was only a jest, a harmless jest to please a dying man. You wished to sweeten Volpone's last days through the belief he would outlive you, so you showed him a worthless piece of paper . . . your real will was at home. But above all, make it clear Volpone knew nothing, not a thing, do you hear me? I was the only one, shove it all on me; I allowed myself a little trick on Leone—everybody knows what a joker I am.

CORBACCIO. But supposing—if I say it was only a joke—supposing Volpone disinherits me then? Fourteen hundred sequins, three thousand with interest, he's cost me . . . I want my gold, I want my gold back first . . .

MOSCA. He will leave everything, everything to you if you will only help him against your son . . . If he is condemned, everything is lost, your three thousand too . . . think of that, and he'll make you his heir!

CORBACCIO. Lost! . . . Condemned . . . no, I will speak three thousand sequins lost . . . what a bad business . . . No more wills, never again; I won't lend on anything but tangible security or a promissory note!

(The Judge enters in conversation with the Captain of the Sbirri; behind him Leone, Colomba, Canina and Sbirri.)

JUDGE *(to the Captain)*. Highly unusual, a complicated case; he's held to be a brave soldier, and respectable.

CAPTAIN. So is Colomba's reputation excellent.

JUDGE. But you say you found Volpone unable to move and the servants swore that he was ill?

CAPTAIN. The servants and the neighbuors.

JUDGE. Highly unusual, these seem strange twists! Well, let us begin. *(He sits at the judge's table)* Are all the witnesses here who were cited in the case against Volpone, accused by Leone. Captain of the Fleet, of attempted rape against a Venetian citizeness, and manifold deceits?

VOLTORE *(rising)*. They are, except that I will speak in behalf of that unfortunate, Volpone, if you will allow it since he cannot defend his honour which was unjustly threatened by, may God forgive

him, that hothead there, who in an access of dementia, a temporary insanity, wounded him so badly that his thread of life is a mere breath within him. He is in his doctors' care . . .

JUDGE. Bring him here in any case to answer to the accusation!

VOLTORE. I would gladly have avoided doing that, for the sight of him alone will move your pity. His still, pale lips cry innocence louder than any words; he will work upon your sympathies, the sight of his wretchedness will shatter you. If there were any shame left in his accuser he would be ashamed of his deed . . .

LEONE. How much did he promise you for each word? Three ducats, hey? But drool on, he'll rob you of your eye teeth, wash his dirty linen, you old washerwoman.

JUDGE *(to Leone)*. You have not the floor, wait until the court has recognized you. *(To the Captain of the Sbirri)* Before the accused appears, outline to me what took place . . .

CAPTAIN. I, and these men, *(Indicating the Sbirri)* we were sitting in the taproom of the Inn, as usual . . . I mean, in accordance with our duty, we were sitting amongst suspicious characters, listening to them as they drank to find out if they were talking against the Procurator and the Inquisition . . . and suddenly there's a horrible yell across the street. "What's the matter," thinks I, "maybe a man beating his wife or a couple of harlots quarrelling; let's sit quietly where we are," but then somebody screamed out of the window, "Rape, rape!" We jumped up, for we had never heard that it's necessary in Venice to take a woman by force, and we hurried hot-foot into the house, to find that man there . . .

JUDGE *(questioningly, indicating Leone)* Leone, Captain of the Fleet?

LEONE. At your service.

CAPTAIN. . . . fiddling with his dagger Unfortunately, there was no rape to be seen any more, only that woman there . .

JUDGE *(to Colomba)*. Colomba, wife of the merchant, Corvino? . . .

(Colomba nods, sobbing into her handkerchief.)

CAPTAIN. . . . She was crying but I couldn't make out whether violence had been done her or not; perhaps she was crying because violence had been done her or perhaps just because she was afraid that somebody wanted to do it . . .

LEONE. It would have been done her if I had not been there to knock the libertine down.

CAPTAIN. Yes, there was a man lying on the floor, twitching like a calf that's just been felled by the axe-blow . . .

VOLTORE. Volpone, the unhappy victim of this drunken villain . . .

CAPTAIN. . . . and this one here was skipping about too . . .

JUDGE *(rustling through his papers).* Mosca, Venetian; what rank?

LEONE. Cat's-paw, lick-spittle, pander, dishwater parasite and dung-beetle, the glove to his hand in all these dirty transactions . . .

JUDGE *(to Leone).* Moderate your tone and do not libel the witness.

MOSCA *(humbly).* I care for the poor sick gentleman!

CAPTAIN. He tried to butter us with a lot of words and I could see he was trying to get us away quickly.

VOLTORE. Away from the bed of a dying man; highly reasonable.

CAPTAIN. But then that one there came in . . .

JUDGE. Canina?

CANINA. Honoured to be recognized by you.

LEONE. A pretty honour! For five sequins anybody can get to know her.

JUDGE. What rank?

CANINA. Private.

LEONE. Ha, ha, private; the most public of the public; the Cloaca Maxima of Venice!

JUDGE *(angrily).* Silence!

CAPTAIN. Yes, she came running in and then those others came and yelled at each other and into my ears so that I got all mixed up. Then I thought: take 'em all along; and I brought them here.

JUDGE. I thank you! Strangely twisted, these, and most confused. Now your version, Leone, you are the accuser.

VOLTORE. He is the accused, Excellency. I accuse him before the Senate of libel, of breaking the peace, of assault and battery, yes, I am afraid—his poor victim is not yet present—I shall have to accuse him of murder.

LEONE. What, you parchment-louse— you accuse me, you hair-splitter, you lie-merchant, you mangy wig?!

JUDGE. You transgress against the dignity of the court.

VOLTORE. Did I not say so? a libeler, excused at the very best by drunkenness.

JUDGE *(speaking impatiently to Leone).* Get along, come to the point. Speak!

LEONE. I went to the house of this Levantine . . .

VOLTORE. Why? Had he invited you?

LEONE *(angrily).* I'd be ashamed to be invited by such a rogue. I went secretly . . .

VOLTORE. You hear, secretly. Note that in the records.

LEONE *(even more furious).* Silence, wig! . . . What was I saying . . . I came secretly, because that other scoundrel there . . .

VOLTORE. May I be allowed to observe that he calls everyone a scoundrel while only he is honourable.

LEONE. . . . had informed on my father—for money, of course, for money —and told me the old idiot had disinherited me.

VOLTORE. Your Excellency, hear what he calls his father, his own aged father; has such language ever been heard in a court before?

LEONE. God knows it's a cross to have a father who lets himself be persuaded by such a loafer into disinheriting his own child.

VOLTORE. He probably had his reasons, important reasons . . .

LEONE *(furious).* Be still! I hope you choke! *(To the Judge)* He mixes me all up! Well . . . while I was waiting to see what he was going to do, there was all this hue and cry and I hear an unwilling woman and a pander persuading her and then all's quiet again and suddenly I hear her crying out . . .

VOLTORE. In her ecstasy.

LEONE. Then I rush at him in the nick of time, he's already grabbed her and on to the bed with her . . .

VOLTORE. A deathly sick man, a healthy young woman.

LEONE. I smashed at him with all my force . . .

VOLTORE. The first true word that's passed his lips!

LEONE. . . . and cried for help.

JUDGE. Do you confirm this account of events, Colomba? Did Volpone try to do you violence?

COLOMBA. Oh God, oh God, let me go home—I have forgiven him, oh, I am ashamed, let me go home, your Honour . . .

JUDGE. Noble lady, I sympathize with your shame, but justice demands clarity. Did that Levantine practice any sort of violence on you?

COLOMBA. I don't know, your Grace.

JUDGE (angrily). Why don't you? Who should if you don't? I ask you again, did he lay hands upon you, did he touch you with licence?

COLOMBA. I touched him first—I had to lay my hand on his heart—and then the miracle occurred . . .

JUDGE. What miracle?

COLOMBA. He regained all his strength.

JUDGE (to the Captain of the Sbirri). I think she's simple. (To Colomba) Speak clearly. Did this Levantine lay violent hands upon you, like . . . like your husband when . . .

COLOMBA. My husband? Corvino? . . . No, that's different . . . then I do it of my own accord . . . he's my husband. (Crying) Oh, oh, I'm ashamed—let me go home, your Grace.

JUDGE. There's nothing to be done with her. You speak for her, Corvino. How did your wife come to Volpone's house?

CORVINO. Pity, sir. She had heard from me that my poor, good friend, Volpone, lay on his dying bed; she prayed long for him in the cathedral and then she came to fetch me where I sat the whole day long at his side . . .

LEONE. You're lying, you dragged her there, drove her to him!

CORVINO. Master, I know that man, a wine-guzzler, a beer-swiller . . .

VOLTORE. Defamer, that's what he is, a malicious defamer.

LEONE. And I swear by the flag of the Republic and the bones of St. Mark that he drove her to him, and she his own wife . . .

VOLTORE. The most jealous man in Venice . . .

CORVINO. He maligns me, Excellency, but I'll throw the lies in his teeth. I ask you here, Colomba, have I ever sent you to young men and allowed you to mingle with them?

COLOMBA. Oh Lord! Why, he is so jealous that he locks me in the room.

VOLTORE. You see, the lie is proven!

LEONE. Who's lying, you blockhead? I'll slash you to bits!

JUDGE. Leone, I am warning you for the last time; you are maligning witnesses groundlessly and not upholding the dignity of the court. Moreover your father stands by you . . .

VOLTORE. His father? He wanted to murder him! Sbirre, bear witness . . .

CAPTAIN. Yes, he went for him like a devil . . .

LEONE. Because I had to have this paper as a proof of their villainy. There —(He throws the will on the Judge's table)— there, if you won't take my word for it, is the unanswerable, crystal-clear proof of his villainy. Was there ever such thievery hatched under the sun or moon? —my own father disinherits me, his son, in favour of that Levantine filth. Go on, tell me . . . is that robbery . . . is that villainy?

MOSCA (has given Corbaccio a little push forward). Now, pipe your tune.

CORBACCIO (rises, clearing his throat with a dry little cough). Allow me . . . he, he . . . there's a mistake here . . . a worthless scrap of paper, absolutely worthless . . . I had heard my poor friend, Volpone, was about to die . . . I thought: cheer him up . . . give him confidence . . . let the poor sick man believe he will outlive me . . . practice this pious deception to give pleasure to a dying man . . .

MOSCA. And I, God forgive me, enjoyed the little joke of fooling Leone. He had poured defamatory words upon me, such as always drip from his mouth like rain from a water-spout, and thought to myself: make this young gallant jealous, fetch him to the house . . . It was a jest, Excellency, a mere jest, that will . . .

LEONE. A nice jest; you wished to pluck me, you highway robbers! I saw the little joke on Colomba!

(Volpone is carried in on a couch by servants. He is quite white and lies with closed eyes like a dead man.)

VOLTORE *(pathetically)*. Look upon the ravisher, Excellency, the grand voluptuary. Look on these sightless eyes, already sealed by death, that withered powerless hand, look at that face: does lust speak so harshly, does sensuality breathe so coldly, greed so bloodlessly, licence so feebly? Oh my friend, my poor noble friend, you are struggling with death and we are still struggling over your honour. Oh, to think you can no longer command the words to shatter your defamer, that you lie there motionless . . .

LEONE. Motionless, ha, ha! Allow me to tickle him a little with my dagger, Excellency, and I swear he will jump up and dance like a performing bear! I will work a miraculous cure on him. Wait, you cheat . . .

(He rushes toward the litter with his dagger drawn. The others throw themselves in his way.)

CANINA. He wants to murder him again!

JUDGE *(angrily to Leone)*. Back to your place, immediately, and put up your dagger. This is no tavern.

VOLTORE. Put him to the strappado, perhaps his poor limbs will twitch again during the torture, you torturer, to whom death itself cannot teach reverence. A cheat, is it not, these waxy cheeks, these bloodless hands; he has the look of a libertine, an impostor—they all use such voluptuous couches as this. But there is one more witness here, Canina, his bride. Cast aside all shame, the honour of a dying man is now at stake; bear witness, if ever he asked you to do anything out of the ordinary!

CASINA *(acting shamefaced)*. I blush at speaking before all these men . . .

LEONE. She blushes . . . ha, ha . . . Buy yourself better paint!

CANINA. Although I am betrothed, I was—how shall I put it —just a sisterly friend . . . He was very weak, especially at night . . . I can swear under oath that he never approached me as a man.

LEONE. You'd swear you were a virgin.

VOLTORE. With one voice they testify against his lie; the voice of God! Oh, we cannot give you health, you friend of friends, but your gravestone shall shimmer marble-white, your honour shall be cleansed of every smirch. I ask you all, have you ever known Volpone to be other than worthy of reverence?

MOSCA. He was the kindest master!

CORBACCIO. An excellent friend . . . kind . . . never borrowed money . . .

CORVINO. The truest of the true . . .

CANINA. Oh, what I am losing in him . . . ah, woe's me!

LEONE. He was a miserable rascal.

VOLTORE. You see; his lies are scattered to the four winds of heaven. Not a word has two feet to stand on! But hurry, Excellency, his pulses are already halting, his cheeks paling; pronounce judgment, Excellency, judgment, the judgment which will give him back his honour, give him the last thing in this mortal world before the priest puts him at peace with God. Let him die in honour, this honourable gentleman.

JUDGE *(stands up and puts on his cap)*. Since the accusation against Volpone, the Levantine, was based on the statement of one witness only, and whereas this witness's testimony was contradicted by several witnesses and whereas, moreover, the injured party accuses him of no unseemly conduct and her husband harbours no suspicion of her, and whereas, moreover, the infirmity of the accused makes the possibility of an act of violence seem improbable, and whereas all the witnesses, every one of them a citizen of Venice, including the very father of the accuser, testify to the excellent reputation of the said Volpone, he is adjudged the injured party and unconditionally dismissed without a stain upon his character. I trust that our unavoidable demand that his infirmities be brought before us will not harm his health and that he will excuse the request as being a necessary portion of our duties. But you, Captain, I warn you not to bring such careless accusations against honourable men in future. Four trustworthy witnesses swore . . .

LEONE (interrupting furiously). Trust-worthy witnesses? A rattail of perjury pieced together to switch at the truth; usurer, whore, legacy-hunter, pander, all in his pocket and his purse. My word—no . . . (He spits) . . . here . . . my spit is worth more than all their filthy testimony, their pre-arranged perjury, their harlot's speeches. He bought them all and pro-bably you in the bargain to save him from the gallows . . .

VOLTORE (clapping his hands together). Bought, the Judges of Venice!

LEONE (still more furiously). What is there you can't do with your money, you blood-suckers, you exploiters, you per-verters of justice! You buy women, judges, office, honour, righteousness, and respect . . . you're all tied to the same rope; you hook it in at the top and at the bottom you cut off poor people's breath with it. And we sacrifice our blood for you, we fools, instead of letting the Turks fall upon you to smoke you out and burn down this filthy house of shame. My word less than the stinking drool of these hypocrites? A man ought to hack at you with his sword and write your laws with his fist . . . you miscarriages of lies and bribery . . .

(Judge rings a wall bell. The Sbirri enter again.)

JUDGE. Seize this man. He has slandered honourable men, borne false witness, and libelled the Tribunal of Venice. By all that's right and just he should be lashed and his hands cut off but since he fights well for the Republic as a soldier and seems flushed with wine, I shall merely sentence him to the pillory until sunset as a warning to careless slanderers.

LEONE (turning to the Sbirri). What, am I to go to the pillory and not these scoundrels! Plague take you, may your homes burn, the jannisaries take your women, and powder explode this rotten decaying state! . . .

JUDGE. Lead him off quickly, or he will yell himself to the block . . .

(Leone is forcibly dragged away.)

CORVINO. An excellent judge, kind, just.

CANINA. Oh my, I shall run to smear honey about his dirty mouth when he's in the pillory so that all the wasps will settle on his snout.

JUDGE. And now, carry the poor in-valid away. I trust the excitement has not harmed him. The court is adjourned.

(Judge and Sbirri exit. They all crowd about Volpone, who lies there with his eyes closed.)

MOSCA. Oh, my kind master, your honour has been given back to you. Look up, regain your strength!

VOLTORE. Your innocence has con-quered.

CANINA. My spouse, look at me.

CORBACCIO. Friend Volpone . . . friend Volpone . . . I am with you.

CORVINO. I did everything for you, my honourable friend. I would have sacrificed my life for you . . . Oh, return to health.

COLUMBA. The poor man . . . how I pity him. I will pray for him.

VOLPONE (weakly). Thank you, my friends . . . so much love . . . so much kindness . . . how have I deserved it, I, a poor, unworthy man?

VOLTORE. Now all Venice recognizes your true virtue.

CANINA. My darling, my beloved, you are avenged.

CORVINO. That loud-mouthed blasphe-mer is paid for his crime.

(They all surround him and help to carry out Volpone, lifted high on his litter in a sort of apotheosis.)

MOSCA (wiping off the sweat from his brow). Now you've come, sweat,—you can breathe again at last. I was only sweating inwardly up to now. This has been a red-letter day; for to-day the Venetian Republic has given villainy its patent of nobility and the next convention of the Council will canonize Volpone, Saint Volpone! But after all, these heroic exploits are making me choke a bit and I'm truly sorry for that poor lout in the pillory. But what unnecessary stupidity to tell the truth; what would the world come to if everyone allowed himself to do that?

VOLTORE (*joins him*). Well, tell me; how did I speak? How do I manage the law?

MOSCA. You turn it upside down like a wheel—magnificent.

VOLTORE. But now, let's make an end of his hesitation and delay. I'm coming right over about the money! Have everything ready, I want to see it in black and white at last, that will: I have Volpone in the hollow of my hand and I won't let him go again so easily!

MOSCA. Come by all means, come, you are the sole heir!

(*Voltore exits.*)

CANINA (*from the other side*). Well, how did I testify? No woman ever swore so beautifully beside the point in court before. But now he will marry me surely, won't he, sweet lad?

MOSCA. As surely as I'm a man of honour—of course, of course.

(*Exit Canina.*)

CORBACCIO (*from the other side*). My poor son, the pillory . . . what a disgrace on my grey head . . . can't be repaid . . . but you've sworn to me, I inherit everything . . . no more beating about the bush . . . I want a certificate of possession, clear and definite . . . in my hand . . . valid . . . incontrovertible, sure . . . . Otherwise I'll complain to the court.

MOSCA. No fear . . . you're sure of it. Aren't you the sole heir? Come along . . . come to Volpone, he will give you everything.

(*Corbaccio hobbles off.*)

CORVINO (*from the other side*). We trapped that Leone well, but now, before Volpone shuffles off, I want my document. I want to see it, stamped and sealed, with my own eyes; be sure that I'm the heir. Tell Volpone to expect me in an hour; no more fiddling about, I've had enough. I'll draw my sword.

MOSCA. Have no fear, everything will be cleared up, for you are the heir, the only heir, you alone.

COURT ATTENDANT. Clear the room! Next case.

(*They all go except Mosca, sunk in thought.*)

MOSCA. Oh my God, what's to happen now? They're all coming with their bills and all for the same thing, one after the other and each one after the same! Voltore, Corbaccio, Corvino, all sawing at the same fiddle! And when they let Leone down from the pillory, I'd rather not meet him in a dark corner either. Oh God, what a noise they'll make, and my wits are slowly going lame, so that I no longer know how to evade them. Why are there no shops in Venice to buy good advice in; for I am not fond of going into churches and I won't have a lawyer until my foot is on the gallows stair.

COURT ATTENDANT (*taking hold of him*). Hey there! Next case!

MOSCA (*deep in thought, mechanically, without looking at him*). Yes, you are the heir, the only heir, you alone.

COURT ATTENDANT. What? Whose heir?

MOSCA (*starts up*). I beg your pardon. (*To himself*) I'm all confused, but is it any wonder? Waking and sleeping, it's always the same tune; die, heir, heir, die, gold, gold, gold. Even a parrot's tongue is not so leathery 't will talk things straight again for me over and over. I'm all confused, and besides I have a continual itch in my left ring-finger. I must ask some old witch, I think it means either that by this evening I'll be a rich man or that I'll jig it at the end of a rope. Well, just a bit more patience, a little bit more, and we shall know.

ACT THREE

SCENE: *Volpone's house. The same day. Afternoon. Volpone lying motionless on the bed.*

————

MOSCA (*enters hastily*). Ah, there you are already, Messer Volpone, safe and lordly, home from your triumphal ovation! First, a goblet of wine; my tongue is smarting with lies as Leone's back is smarting from the sun.—There. . . . But now, master of lies, up, up with you, we will sing the *Jubilate* as a duet and make the ducats dance to our tune.

VOLPONE (*groaning*). Oh me, I'm sick . . . tired . . . tired.

MOSCA. But master, the doors are locked, leave this masquerade of dying; you don't want to end by enacting the little dance of death for your Mosca? Hurrah, up on your legs, stretch your limbs. Let's drink and be merry and empty your glass to the Judges of Venice, the wisest tribunal on earth. Ha, ha, that was sport.

VOLPONE (getting up painfully). Sour sport for me. No, Mosca, you are mistaken, I am not acting, I still feel as sick as a dog, and my stomach is turning over and over. Truly, my knees are still tottery; those damned leeches sucked all the sap out of my veins. You call that sport, you fool; for you, perhaps, not for me. You can believe me, when that lout, Leone, was fiddling with his dagger to tickle my ribs my stomach rose up with one sweep and I wouldn't have needed any dog's-gall to turn cheese-colour. All my life long, I've never had a fear settle so in my intestines. There was more fright in me than in the whole army when the cannonading begins. It shot up from my heels to my throat so hard that my teeth rattled . . .

MOSCA. Yes, I was struck with the natural way you chattered them. The whole faculty of doctors would have sworn you were ready to jump out of this earthly vale of sorrows.

VOLPONE (shaking himself). What fear, what fear! A horrible invention, fear! It's worse than poverty.

MOSCA. But in exchange, you have legally been made a man of honour by the Court.

VOLPONE. 'S truth, I was astonished myself. I really ought to have the record copied and hung over the mirror. And every time I think I'm a scoundrel I'll look into it and lo! what shall I behold, signed and sealed by the Court? "Volpone, you are an honourable man."

MOSCA. But I didn't fix that easily: I had to groan myself free of a whole tapeworm of lies. And the three thieves, too, played well, they fiddled off their lies better than the viola-players in St. Samuel's.

VOLPONE. Ah, the scoundrels, the bandits!

MOSCA. Weren't they your cat's-paws? Didn't they help you bravely? Why do you call them scoundrels?

VOLPONE. Wasn't it the height of villainy for them to help me instead of leaving me in the stew? I scourge their hides, make holes in their pockets, and they help me in exchange: is that honourable, isn't it seven times more scoundrelly than a straightforward dagger-thrust in the back? Oh, you dogs, I'll make mad dogs of you yet.

MOSCA. I think the dog's-gall is still upsetting your stomach. Come, drink! Be merry, be gay.

VOLPONE (drinking). Ah, wonderful! Another one. (Jumps up) Now I feel myself again. Ah, the joy of standing on two healthy legs, an honourable man with a court certificate. (Goes to the treasure chest) Your father is back with you, my good little sequins, he'll stay with you and take good care of you. (Pacing up and down) I'm beginning to feel happy and warm again, I already feel the old Volpone stirring inside Volpone's corpse. Ah, the pleasure of feeling your strength and wit.

MOSCA. You will need it very soon, master of lies, they'll come flapping along very soon, vulture, hawk and crow, their claws stretched. They're all much excited, especially Voltore, about being made your heir.

VOLPONE. I'll get the wind up for him, the windbag.

MOSCA. But you swore you'd do it for him, you promised him a half of your fortune during your life.

VOLPONE. I promised him nothing. My fear promised him something, I no longer remember what.

MOSCA. All three are in a frenzy of distrust, tired of speeches, demanding your last testament, signed and sealed.

VOLPONE. They shall see and have it— all three. Good old Volpone is grateful to all of his friends and will give each one what he wants. I'll make each one a testament, gladly, three, thirteen, twenty-three, three hundred, each one costs only a half ounce of ink and a piece of sheepskin. Each one shall have a testament, signed and sealed, with him as sole heir, and each one can take it home and wait confidently till I die—that is, if he lives that long.

MOSCA. Magnificent! Of course none of them will show it to the others. We'll give each of them a poultice to fight the legacy-fever and then they'll leave us in peace. Magnificent. Where's the pen and ink?

VOLPONE. I'll write one out for each of them in my own hand and let them pay me the government taxes. One for dear Voltore, one for kind Corbaccio, one for the exceedingly affectionate Corvino; ah, I'll fox you! You can wait for me to die with your little documents tucked away in a drawer, but I fear that event will be delayed for a few years. Poor sick Volpone will quickly regain his red cheeks, grow more and more healthy, till you yourselves get green-sick and vomit gall.

MOSCA. But if, God forbid, some fatality should overtake you, they would really become your heirs.

VOLPONE. But all at the same time— that would be the merriest thing, Mosca —what a little dance there would be! Just think, no Duke could have a dirge like that. They would smash each other's skulls in. First, they'd come slinking, craftily, their bellies full of joy: "I am the heir"—and there will be the three of them in a row, gloating. Ah, how furiously they will race to court, all three sheep with their sheepskins. Ha, ha, I can see them going now, with their silly flat faces.

MOSCA. But, Messer Volpone, how can you see that? A coffin has no windows.

VOLPONE. 'S blood, that's true, it will gall me in my shroud that I can't live to see and experience my master-prank, those scoundrels all at each other's throats. God's wrath, here I've conceived the finest thought and just at the baptism, when they're smashing in each other's skulls, I'm to be away; damn it.

MOSCA. Don't curse. You promised yesterday to turn pious. But before you enter the monastery, be merry first for a while.

VOLPONE. But you know that I can't—

God punish me—be merry before I've skinned one fool; that warms me more than a woman and makes me merrier than wine; but it devours me like fever that I shan't see the cream of the joke! My best villainy will go for naught and I shall have to die without feeling the grandest thing in life, just like a woman who dies a virgin. Damn it, damn it, why can't I watch them wrangling above my cold nose—I'd like to sell myself to the devil, then I'd know he would give my ghost an hour's leave to experience that pleasure. Oh damn, damn! *(He paces up and down furiously)*

MOSCA. What a curious fellow you are —hardly out of hot water, and you're kindling another fire beneath the pot. May all the saints protect me from inheriting this man's gall.

VOLPONE *(suddenly chortling)*. I have it! Ha, ha, I have it. I will live to see it. Splendid, splendid, ah, that's the idea. Ha, ha.

MOSCA. What's nipping you? You're jumping like the father of all the fleas.

VOLPONE *(enchanted)*. Mosca, Mosca, what was in that wine? The devil must have dropped a divine thought into it: it's burning through all my veins. Ah, what royal sport! What an orgy of merriment awaits me. Listen: chase the servants into the streets to spread the news that I, Volpone, am dead. Stone cold, lifeless, rotting. I'll put you into my will as the heir, you read it to them, and meanwhile I stand there—behind the curtain, listening and watching: I want to see the slaver dripping from their mouths before it turns to vinegar on their lips. I want to see their faces grow longer and then, when they make for you and bark and scream—I'll jump out of my hole and make them run so hard the wind will blow their ears off: I'll thwack and belabour them in the flesh, the scoundrels. Ah, what sport to drive from one's bier and oust the heirs and legacy-hunters.

MOSCA. An excellent sport. Good for some other time: I'll write it down on the calendar; but not today.

VOLPONE *(obsessed)*. Today, this very day, now.

MOSCA. Be reasonable, you still have

sweat in your hair and dog's-gall in your bowels! Is the devil already driving you into new deviltry?

VOLPONE. I need it. I shan't feel right until I have it.

MOSCA. Madness! I advise you not to drive yourself crazy. Don't tread on their poison fangs.

VOLPONE. I want to stamp upon the worms so that they writhe as much with malice as I do with laughter. But now let's start—so. (He writes something into the will) I wrote your name down there: "My true servant, Mosca." Now the instrument of torture is ready but don't use it too quickly nor too rashly. I want to see them licking their chops, slowly, and slowly grinning before the hammer lands on their pates. Don't cheat me of the shadow of a change of mood; I want to see them grinning first and floating round my corpse. I want to see them squirm and wriggle with the hook in their gullets and grow impatient for the will; only then must they be frightened, tremble, lash their tails, grow dangerous, and lose their heads. Then I'll burst in with my whip and your head and your heart will dance to see how I lash their legs! How they'll yap and circle before they cringe out of the door!

MOSCA. Magnificent, sir . . . but do it by yourself. I've made the truce of God with all creatures today. I've had enough. My bowels are still trembling with fright! Play your little joke alone.

VOLPONE. How can I do it alone? I'm playing dead! Get on with you, gadfly, and buzz!

MOSCA. But I don't want to. (Shouting) I've had too much. I am no bloodhound, no ghoul, no gallows-bird . . . I came to you as a respectable toady to drink wine, to enjoy women, to laugh and cause others to laugh. I make the ducats cringe, but not people; leave them in peace, enjoy your gold and cool your bile; I won't play this game with you any longer. A cold wind blew through my hair today in court; I've had too much; my flesh must needs creep on the road that leads to the gallows. Seek out someone else for your little jests.

VOLPONE. Just this one more time; it's my last, best prank.

MOSCA. No. I don't want to. Thank you very much for your food and drink but I like my nice straight neck better than anything else and I don't want to joke a hempen kerchief around it.

VOLPONE. What, you banquet-louse, *you* say no to *me?* Have you forgotten that I freed you from the debtors' prison with two hundred sequins? I wanted a jester and now the idiot will not jest! Continue, or I send you back again! You fly, I'll mash you against the wall with your receipted bills. Will you or won't you?

MOSCA (bitterly). I must will! Am I to thank you? But I demand those receipts in return for this sport; then I'll be quits with you, and go my ways.

VOLPONE (giving him the receipts). Go to the devil, if you like; I don't need you any more, you bore me! I thought out this best trick of all by myself. And now let us start; call the servants! (Claps his hands and creeps back behind the curtain)
(The Servants enter and stand waiting.)

MOSCA (awkward—makes several starts). Run to . . . Master Voltore . . . Corbaccio . . . Corvino . . . Say . . . er . . . say . . . your master is in a bad way. He may die any minute . . . er . . . hurry now . . . er . . . em . . . hurry . . .
(The Servants exit.)

VOLPONE (sticking out his head). You scoundrel, why didn't you say that I was dead?

MOSCA. I wanted to give you more time. I feel queer; my throat closes and the lies won't skip out merrily any more I warn you again; this is slippery sport and you may fall and break your ribs.

VOLPONE. I must see those vipers dance, if I die of it.

MOSCA. If you die of it? . . . Do you know, Messer Volpone, who will be your heir then? I!

VOLPONE. You, gadfly? You fool!

MOSCA. Here it is, written into the document.

VOLPONE. And do you imagine I will let you keep it? Troth, you are dazed and dancing now like the other fools. But come, sit down at the table, inventory in hand; receive the fellows so and the more excited they grow, the calmer must you be. Drip it, drop by drop, into them, turn the skewer slowly, slowly in their bodies. First, lard their hopes well, stroke the bloated belly of their greed, and wait till they are all cosily together, devouring each other with their looks; I tell you: just let them sizzle and roast and bake till they are well-cooked for me—a dainty meal. Meanwhile, I shall listen here, behind the curtain, and steal a few merry looks at their solemn mourners' faces; but then, then, when they are nicely heated and frenzied, then I'll sink my teeth into them; I'll tear bits out of their flesh and crack their bones to suck the marrow! I'll send you home like tottering scarecrows . . . . Ah . . . ah . . . how good I feel. And you, if you play the game well, you get another fifty sequins. And then you can ride to hell.

MOSCA *(mockingly)*. Thank you very much but I'd meet too many of your sort here!

VOLPONE *(starting)*. I hear someone coming! Sit down and begin . . . I'll grab them by the throat when the time comes. *(He takes his place behind the curtain of the bed and looks on greedily, stretching all Mosca's words with gestures of his arm.) (Voltore enters more hastily than he has yet done. Mosca has seated himself at the table, apparently absorbed in the papers he is reading, making notes and speaking at the same time.)*

MOSCA. Seven Ispahan rugs.

VOLTORE. Is he dead?

MOSCA. A porphyry table . . . two marble chests . . .

VOLTORE. Is he dead? *(Shaking Mosca by the shoulder)* Honest Mosca, tell me, is he dead?

MOSCA. You see me checking the inventory, Illustrissimo.

VOLTORE. Give me the will!

MOSCA. It lies here ready . . . *(Writing)* . . four onyx bowls and six candelabra of tempered gold, curiously engraved . . . *(Corvino enters with his wife, Colomba.)*

CORVINO. . . . Here is the raven already. There must be carrion where these black mantles wave . . . he must be dead.

COLOMBA. Poor Master Volpone! He was still so healthy and strong . . .

MOSCA *(continues to write indifferently)*. Two caskets of ebony, locked and sealed, very heavy.

CORVINO *(to Voltore)*. Were you called here in your official capacity to witness the opening of the will?

VOLTORE *(superciliously)*. We shall see. . . . Are you here as a witness?

CORVINO. Ha, ha . . . just a witness? . . . have it your way.
(Corbaccio enters hastily.)

CORBACCIO. Told me downstairs, dead . . . he, he . . . I knew right off he'd never walk again . . . he, he . . . *(Walks about rapping on the treasure chests)* . . . sounds fine . . . sounds full . . . he, he . . . the best music . . . finer than in church.

CORVINO *(mockingly)*. Have you already come to buy and barter? You're probably mistaken!

CORBACCIO. Buying nothing . . . he, he . . . need nothing . . . have enough now . . . Where's the will . . . read will . . .

CORVINO. Open your ears wide so you don't hear wrong . . . our names sound alike, Corvino, Corbaccio . . . but read, Illustrissimo, read his last will.

VOLTORE *(solemnly)*. God forbid, it might be contested and everything must be done legally. First, we must have a witness here from the Court.

MOSCA *(frightened)*. A witness from the court? Don't bother with such formalities. Let us send the will over later . . . later . . . later.

VOLTORE. It wouldn't be legal.
(He rings. To the Servant who enters.) Call the Judge for this district and tell him the Notary begs him to act as witness. Absolutely legal, everything legal.

MOSCA *(has let the pen fall in his fright)*. The Judge? . . . the Judge? . . . here? . . the Judge? . . . It isn't necessary . . . there are two witnesses here already . . . honourable Venetians . . .

CORVINO. No, no, I agree with the Notary, absolutely; legal, everything legal.

CORBACCIO. Excellent . . . I insist on that . . .

MOSCA *(creeping to one side)*. Oh me, it's getting uncomfortable now; that wasn't written in Volpone's calendar. I'm going, I can't stand it, I have an antipathy for all officials, especially those who are almost brother to the hangman! This broth is getting too hot for me, Messer Volpone, drink it yourself, I'm not hungry.

(Slinks along the wall to the door.)

VOLTORE. Hey there, whither away, Mosca?

MOSCA. There are all sorts of chests and caskets still in the cellar. I want to go and see if they are locked.

VOLTORE. Later, later. No one leaves the room; against the law.

CORBACCIO. Everything legal . . . absolutely legal.

MOSCA. Damn it, how can I get out of here? Oh, things are getting hotter and hotter.

(Canina rushes in.)

CANINA. Mosca, dear boy! Is he dead! Is it true? Oh, what shall I do? What can I do? Help me! . . . tell me is he really dead? Quite dead?

MOSCA. I'm afraid . . . I'm afraid . . .

CANINA. Quite dead? Tell me . . . maybe he'll wake up again, just for five minutes . . . I have the Priest right here . . . perhaps he will wake up once more. Some people have strokes and regain their breath after you think them corpses. Lead me to him, I want to see for myself. I'm a good hand at telling if a man is dead or alive.

CORBACCIO. True, very true . . . some of them only look dead . . . better see, better see . . . always safety, a hundred per cent safety.

MOSCA. One look will convince you . . .

(Volpone has flung himself down and lies motionless. Mosca raises the curtain for a second and then lets it fall again.)

You see, quite cold and stiff.

CORBACCIO. Deceptive . . . better still to burn a candle at the soles of his feet.

CORVINO (drawing his dagger). Safe is safe . . . a little jab in the heart to make sure . . . it wouldn't hurt the dead man and would be a real service to one who was seemingly dead. Oh well, I'll do it in any case.

(He goes resolutely toward the curtain. Vol-pone has huddled together, trembling with fright.)

MOSCA (throws himself in Corvino's path). No, no . . . the servants might see the blood and say we had done away with him . . . leave the corpse in peace.

VOLTORE. Quite true; never touch a corpse before the coroner comes. Always the proper official first; always the right official for everything, life or death, death or burial.

(The Judge enters; they all crowd about him, except Mosca who crouches timidly in a corner.)

JUDGE (to Voltore). I was apprised of the demise of this unhappy Volpone . . . I trust that the excitement over the unjustified accusation brought by Leone had no part in it, for else Leone's punishment would have to be heightened in consequence.

VOLTORE. No, Excellency, matters may be left as they are; Messer Volpone had been an invalid for many months and death was a release.

JUDGE. As you think best. If I am properly informed, you summoned me to be present at the opening of his will.

VOLTORE. I thought it advisable you should be here to prevent the occurrence of complications and I beg you to unseal the document yourself.

MOSCA (aside—trembling). Oh God, where shall I hide?

JUDGE (taking the will). There are four witnesses here, all citizens of Venice. Is the death of the above mentioned Volpone confirmed by their affadavit as eye witnesses?

VOLTORE. We all witnessed it at the same time, so no doctor's certificate of death is needed.

JUDGE. Do you recognize this will as having been sealed with Volpone's seal?

VOLTORE. Mosca, do you testify that this is your Master's seal?

MOSCA. Yes, yes . . . I think . . . I'm not very experienced . . . I think it is . . (Aside) If I were only safe in Padua.

VOLTORE. I, Voltore, the Notary recognize this will as having been written by my hand and given to Volpone on his sick-bed; only the names of the legator and the legatee were left blank in ac cordance with the wishes of the deceased; you will find them inserted in the handwriting of the dead man.

JUDGE. I will now break the seal and read . . .

(Meanwhile Volpone has sat up behind the curtain and peers greedily between the folds of the curtain at their faces.)

(Mosca has stood up tremblingly, looking for a place to hide.)

JUDGE *(reads)*. "I, Volpone, a former merchant of Smyrna, Levantine, wifeless and childless, hereby make the following disposition of my property, being of sound mind although threatened by illness, and witness the same with my hand and seal. In memory of the true friendship which he has shown me, and the incontrovertible proofs of his love and affection . . ."

CORVINO *(nudges Colomba)*. You see . . .

JUDGE. ". . . and desiring to repay his friendship with proper gratitude, I name as my sole heir, to be the unconditional possessor of all my goods and gold, real and personal property, my beloved friend, the Venetian, Mosca . . ."

VOLTORE *(starting to his feet)*. Mosca! What does that mean?

CORVINO. Mosca . . . that scoundrel?

CORBACCIO. Mosca? . . .

CANINA. Mosca! How wonderful! Oh, you sweet darling boy!

JUDGE. I must beg for quiet. ". . . to my other true friends who also gave me countless proofs of their affection . . ."

CORVINO. Ah, after all!

JUDGE. ". . . I leave the assurance of my deep gratitude and the request that they remember me with undying love. Given at Venice under my own hand and seal, this day,—Volpone."

VOLTORE *(jumping up)*. This is treachery. He forged it,—Mosca, that bandit!

CORBACCIO. Traitors! . . . both traitors! . . . Where are my twenty thousand sequins?

CORVINO. Arch-villainy; this document is stolen, false, forged, invalid . . .

VOLTORE. It is invalid; I contest it.

JUDGE *(astonished)*. You just recognized this will as being valid. Did you not write it?

VOLTORE. But not for him.

CORVINO. There is treachery here. I swear, Excellency, that yesterday Volpone, himself, and that fellow assured me I was the sole heir.

CORBACCIO. No, no, me . . . this morning!

(Volpone hops from one leg to the other in his joy.)

JUDGE. Curious! Highly involved and most strangely twisted! Then, as I understand it, this Levantine promised each of you all his fortune?

VOLTORE. No, only me, me!

CORBACCIO. Lies! . . . me, too . . . there was an agreement between us.

CORVINO. No, only me, me!

JUDGE. Involved! Involved! *(To Voltore)* You know the law; have you any particular claims which would make such a disposition of his fortune to you seem probable?

VOLTORE. I was his friend, his best friend.

CORVINO. Lies . . . it was me . . . me . . . he always told me I was the one.

CORBACCIO. Me . . . me . . . "Good friend" . . . "best friend" . . .

CORVINO. I managed his affairs . . . I took care of him . . . I was closest to him . . . I made him presents . . .

CORBACCIO. Presents? Poor stuff! . . . wretched trash . . . I . . . I . . . I *(Stuttering with excitement)* gold . . . minted gold . . . golden sequins, I gave him . . . fourteen hundred sequins . . . a ring worth a thousand sequins . . .

CORVINO. You usurer . . . you talked your mouse-dung out of other people. But I . . . a thousand sequins . . . my silver bowls, my goblets . . . I sold a piece of land . . . you are rich . . . easy to give . . . I alone gave him everything . . . I alone did it for frienship's sake!

CORBACCIO. Not true . . . lies . . . lies . . . I gave everything too, willed it to him, disinherited my son . . . I have more rights than anyone . . . I . . . I . . .

CORVINO *(shoves him aside furiously)*. You? . . . get back into your coffin, skeleton! . . . I threw him all my bloody money. What? You want to compare yourself, my friendship with yours, you usurer? . . . I sacrificed everything, everything . . . I brought him my wife to restore his health . . .

JUDGE (*jumps up and bangs his fist on the table*). What are you saying? What was it slipped out just then? So Leone did tell the truth to-day and you duped me?!

(*He rings the bell and a Sbirre enters.*) Hurry straight to Leone and release him from the pillory; I order you in the name of the Court. What a blot upon the Tribunal if all this proves true; an innocent man, a brave soldier, in the pillory for no fault of his! You will answer for this!

(*Volpone, who has listened with malicious glee to the raging outbursts of the three legacy-hunters, has grown uneasy and listens, excited and trembling.*)

VOLTORE. Forgive me, Excellency . . . he bewildered all of us . . . I found him this morning in bed dying of fear and he begged me to speak for him . . . I thought I must help a dying man. I did not dream, Excellency, what a deceiver he was . . .

CORVINO. The scoundrel of scoundrels! . . . not enough for him to rob me of my money . . . he attacked my wife. . . . Oh, she was too modest to admit it . . . he plundered me like any highwayman. Your Excellency, I swear I am poor as a church mouse through him.

CORBACCIO. He plundered me . . . every week gold, jewels. And a hundred others . . . Battista the goldsmith, the secretary . . . whole streets-full. He promised everyone, but I had a note . . . he showed it to me; twenty thousand sequins . . . and now, all lies . . .

JUDGE. What a scoundrel! I have not often seen his like. It does not matter that he looted you donkeys . . . you probably pushed his hand into your pockets. But to rob a soldier of his reputation, a woman of her honour, a Court of its integrity . . . what a scoundrel! Death did this criminal a good service, for if he were still alive, I swear to you no one should be whipped like this Levantine cur before ever he went to the gallows.

(*Volpone has grown pale and hidden himself trembling on the bed.*)

But his body shall do penance for his crimes. I shall have the corpse hung in the public square and the tongue nailed to the gallows as a warning, a symbol of the manner in which deceit and profanation are punished in Venice. (*To Mosca*) You shall give the corpse to the Sbirri. He must gulp the wind a few days before he graces the potter's field.

CORVINO. I shall see him dance, the scoundrel, as he made me dance.

CORBACCIO. But money . . . my money . . . fourteen hundred sequins.

VOLTORE. And I'll tear up his will.

JUDGE. No, not that, Illustrissimo, it was written before sentence was pronounced on him; it is valid since it was legally drawn by you, as you yourself testified—unless you can show your handwriting was traced or forged. Then, of course, since this Volpone had no descendants, his fortune would go to the poor . . .

VOLTORE (*disappointed*). The poor!

CORBACCIO (*starting up*). The poor!

CORVINO (*horrified*). The poor!

CORBACCIO (*furious*). What use is money to the poor? There are too many of them; they'll only get poor again . . . I want my sequins, fourteen hundred three thousand with interest . . .

VOLTORE (*bitterly*). Rather the poor than Mosca . . .

CORVINO. Rather throw it to the dogs only not him!

JUDGE. But as long as no legal objection is raised, the testament remains in force and Mosca, the Venetian citizen the heir.

CORVINO. Sooner the devil!

CORBACCIO (*quite beside himself*). Fourteen hundred sequins ... three thousand . . . ring a thousand . . . four thousand and interest . . .

MOSCA (*leaps out nimbly*). Will your Excellency allow me a few words? Messer Volpone, the deceased Messer Volpone certainly was—one should speak no ill of the dead—he was the most complete scoundrel from head to heel that Venice has ever seen. I don't know if the Lord gave him a larger gall than other people but he took a scoundrelly pleasure—who can testify to that better than I?—in sinking his teeth like a dog into other people and in doing evil for the joy of it —the gall-bitter joy he must have in herited from Satan. I was forced to serve him but I warned him, and God alone knows how many tricks I spoiled for him, and how much salt of his I've watered; I could serve in the devil's kitchen today after what I learned of him, but you see, Excellency, death has a bony fist that breaks the strongest neck. As he lay on that bed with his legs already cold, before it finally got him, he called to me from his bed: Mosca, he gasped, I have acted badly to my friends, choked and tormented them, clawed them like a buzzard. Make it up to them! I will make you my heir, but make it up to them! Make good the evil I have done and give back all I stole from my friends; may they forgive me. Thus the sinner spoke, your Excellency; I clasped his icy hand upon it. And since I am the heir, I will make good all the damage which he did in his frenzied greed, to you, Voltore—if I am the heir —to you, Corbaccio, to you, Corvino—if I am the heir—I will pay back Leone; I will—if I am the heir—put ten thousand sequins in your Excellency's hand for the poor—we shall have masses read in all the churches of Venice for Volpone; I will—if I am the heir—return all the silver, gold and jewelry he stole—there will still be plenty left for me.

JUDGE. You are a splendid man, Mosca.

CORBACIO. But with interest . . . three thousand and the ring.

MOSCA. Certainly; and a second one for Colomba.

CORVINO. And my sequins back?

MOSCA. In full and more . . . if I am the heir.

CORVINO. But you are, no one disputes that.

CORBACCIO. All of us are witnesses to that; the will is perfectly legal and valid . . .

VOLTORE. I have no objection . . . it is all legal . . . you will give me everything, you say, that . . .?

MOSCA. Doubled, Illustrissimo.

VOLTORE. No objection . . . all legal. I testify that Mosca is Messer Volpone's sole heir.

JUDGE. Then no one raises an objection to Messer Volpone's disposition of his property?

VOLPONE. No one, Excellency.

JUDGE. Then bring your parchment; the Court will validate it. And make better use of your riches than Master Volpone.

MOSCA. Just one more request, most gracious sir! Spare the corpse dishonour. The unholy fool regretted and I will atone for his misdeeds—spare the corpse the gallows! Allow me to have it sunk quietly into the canal.

JUDGE. You are a good soul. Very well, do it, but be sure to put a stone around his neck instead of the rope; may the fishes of Venice have more pleasure out of him than its citizens.

CANINA. And I, my lad, am the only one to whom you will give nothing?

MOSCA. I'll buy you a husband; I know a Spanish toady with a name as long as the Grand Canal, seven Christian names and nine surnames, and no taste for women. I'll buy him for you. He'll leave you in peace day and night, and your child will be a nobleman.

CANINA. You are a sweet boy! And I'm telling you now; whenever and as often as you like . . .

(*Confused shouts from outside. Leone bursts through the door into the room. He has no coat, his shirt is torn open and his arms are half bare. He carries a dagger in his hand.*)

LEONE. Where is the scoundrel? I must tear him limb from limb. I must cut his hide to ribbons. I must sink my fingers into his guts. Where is he?

JUDGE. You've come too late, Leone; heaven has judged him and he lies lifeless.

LEONE (*raging*). Then his corpse—I must tear it to rags. I must, I must. I'll rip out his guts and throw them to the dogs. I want to drag his body to the pillory . . . Where is it . . . where?

(*Volpone has huddled together in the extremity of fear. His terror is no longer ridiculous but rather horrible.*)

JUDGE (*intercepts Leone*). Calm yourself.

LEONE. Calm? . . . I was dragged all through the city like a criminal through this scoundrel—roped to the pillory . . . the flies, the gnats, the sun . . . Ugh!

Horrible! ... the little brats came and pulled lice out of their hair and threw them at me. And the sun always hot upon my neck, always hotter, my own sour sweat running into my mouth, and I couldn't stop it ... and the more I retched, the more they laughed, those stinking women, and spit at me, me, a soldier! All through that scoundrel's fault! *(In an access of rage)* I must choke him once more. Let me go, let me go. I must dig my nails into his damned eyes! *(They all hold him back. He suddenly totters.)* Oh, tired, tired! I'm dying of thirst ... give me something to drink.
(Mosca brings wine and Leone drinks greedily.)
Ah ... ah ... what shame ... oh ... oh ... tired ...

MOSCA. Rest, Leone. I am having a bed prepared for you and a hot bath; get well rested so you can drain a thousand bumpers at Volpone's funeral feast.

LEONE *(wearily)*. Ah, you there too, you rogue? I really ought to grab you by the collar ... but I'm too tired ... yes, sleep, just a grain of sleep ... *(With his last strength)* But I'll take the dagger with me so I can mow him down when he meets me in my dreams ... Oh the scoundrel, the Levantine scoundrel!

MOSCA. Help him, Canina, lead him away.
(Leone is led into the neighbouring room by several of them.)
And now, my amiable masters, let me formally invite you all to our deceased Volpone's funeral feast! We'll not be too very sad, I promise you, at the banquet table; all his life he gave us no taste of anything except his bitter gall; we'll drink his sweet wine now, and waste his money to make up for it. Bring on your colleagues of the Court, Excellency. Corvino, bring your customers. Corbaccio, bring your clients. Let Volpone's house be flung wide to everyone in Venice for the feast, and his departed soul shall hear the plates rattling and the goblets clinking even in the other world. We will fetch musicians and seek out lovely women and whoever tells me he is my friend, I will believe him, and whoever laughs, I will love him, and whoever asks

anything of me, to him shall be given, for thank Heaven I have inherited Volpone's gold alone and not his gall. If he locked in his gold I, on the other hand, shall let it roll abroad; if he has tortured you, I will make you merry, for I have been toady and know how bitter the crumbs from a rich man's table can taste; take with both hands, as long as there is money in the house, and set no limit on your merriment. This evening, then, my friends, and we will laugh in chorus at all misers and fools who make life a burden to themselves. And have fine sport, remembering the sport which Master Volpone had with us; and most of all, his last and best sport, which we must thank for all this.

JUDGE. Yes, Volpone's best idea was to make you his heir.

VOLTORE. And his death his first honourable action.

CORVINO. Amen. A stone on his grave and no prayers for his poor soul. You are a fine lad, Mosca, and I have always pitied you for having to serve such a scoundrel.

CORBACCIO. You were always honourable ... you alone. ...

VOLTORE. Be assured of my sincere friendship.

MOSCA. I thank you, and believe as much of what you say as I wish to believe; so long as you are merry, you are dear to me, and God protect me from needing you, for I fear that my money will run away more swiftly than my own legs. But as long as it's there, be merry, and as long as you're merry I will call you friends. This evening, then, all of you come in black clothes so that folk may know we mourn for Volpone, but let your minds and moods wear motley. Farewell.
(They all go off, bowing, and gesturing farewell. Mosca remains alone, looking anxious at the curtain behind which Volpone has stood all this while with clenched fists.)

VOLPONE *(leaps out, waving his fists)*. Scoundrel!

MOSCA *(bowing)*. Merely your pupil.

VOLPONE. Thief, legacy-hunter!

MOSCA *(with false humility)*. Ever you

zealous scholar. But tell me, who are you anyway? . . . You have some resemblance to the deceased Volpone, that evil joker and fox who nipped his tail in his own trap. What are you doing here in my house?

VOLPONE. In your house—you thief?—off with you, toady.

MOSCA. Really—how so—why? I shall get on famously here with Volpone's sequins.

VOLPONE. And you think—you really think—I'll let you keep all this?

MOSCA. Never dreamed of it; I'll keep none of it, it shall all be free to go, flying in the wind. The toadies of Venice will help me, I know, to make your ducats dance. There's an end of misery now, my little fox! Now there's to be laughter and singing and music in the house, music made with your imprisoned gold.

VOLPONE *(raging mad)*. Bandit, I shall go to court.

MOSCA. Beware, beware, you might meet the gallows on the way; and, moreover, quiet, quiet, a little more quiet, a dear friend of yours called Leone is sleeping in the next room, and might like to have a word with you—I think you'll find it wiser not to wake him. He's going to live with me, now, is Leone—I shall beg him to, and if the fancy ever takes you to frequent this house as a ghost I shall call him, so be quiet and make yourself invisible while yet there's time . .

VOLPONE *(stares at the door in terror—then to Mosca, indicating the treasure chest)*. Give me the jewels, the pearls, and I'll go.

MOSCA. What? That would be an injustice to the testator; he taught me that not one golden beetle should be allowed to fly the chest.

VOLPONE *(trembling—greedy)*. Give me half—just half!

MOSCA. Did you share with anyone?

VOLPONE *(begging)*. A quarter—one quarter—and I go.

MOSCA. Not one sequin, not one lousy, mouldy sequin, not one little gem! not a seed pearl! You think you can fool me like the others? You yourself told me that there was a ship in Genoa you owned all of merchandise and a house in Smyrna

where your wife and child live; go greet them and tell them it is poor sport joking with Venetians. You have tickled my gall and others' long enough, invented sufficient jests; you could have lived easily and well but you wanted to make fools out of everyone else, and so were one yourself. Now I laugh, Volpone. Get along with you! Hurry, you thieving fox, or I'll get the whip!

VOLPONE. Rather be broken on the wheel, rather the gallows, than let you have the money. I stay, I stay.

MOSCA. Then stay if you want, and I'll get Leone.

(He goes to the door of the room into which Leone went and half opens it.)

Very well, I'll count—to three—to three! Then I call Leone.

VOLPONE *(grimly)*. I stay. The gallows will be a pleasure if I see you dangling next to me.

MOSCA. You won't get that far—Leone and his dagger will see to that! Now—I'm counting. One!

VOLPONE *(raging—furious)*. I'm staying! To spite you, I'm staying! My money—or I stay.

MOSCA. Two!

VOLPONE *(raging but less sure)*. Half—and I go!

MOSCA. Three!

VOLPONE *(trembling)*. Only the rings and the pearls.

MOSCA *(calls loudly through the open door)*. Le—

(Volpone starts at the loud call and whisks out of the door in an instant.)

MOSCA *(laughing and lightly finishing the cry with a mocking bow in the direction of the fleeing man.)* . . . Down the cudgels, Messer Volpone, the game is over.

(A pause—then Mosca turns resolutely to the chest and throws it open with one strong gesture.)

Up with you, Gold, you substance magical! Innately Nature's, yearning back to the all.

Well do I know your temper: flux
          [unbounded,
At no rash fool's behest to be impounded.
How could we hold you fast? an elvish
          [creature

That, under a thousand shifts of form and
[feature,
Courses the globe, and only lives while
[flowing—
From palm to palm itself with zest
[bestowing,
By never a doit the more, nor yet
[diminished,
Vanishing clean at a touch, but as suddenly
[replenished—
Stealing like very blood in every vein,
To fire men's hearts and make them act
[amain.

Then seize me too, that mine may be
[your merit!
Pour out, gush forth, intoxicating spirit;
O myriad-formed and -fingered, no
[resistance!
Join in the sport! I give you back
[existence,
That in your dance a sharer I may be.
Dance, then, my money, dance! I set you
[free;
No more your lord, nor owning you for
[mine,

Playmate, I sow you broadcast—gift
[divine!

(He turns around and claps his hands.)
Hey there, holloa!
(The Servants hurry in.)
Open the doors, the windows—let in air
and light and people. This place still
smells of fear, it's close with grasping,
greed and malicious words. Bring flowers,
light lights, stand at the doors to herald
in my guests. Music! music! music! and
not another word of gold. We will be
merry now, feast off Volpone's dishes,
drink of his wines, and laugh at everyone
who's mad and most at him who's mad
about money, and then go contentedly
home, each one to sleep with his own
wife! Come then, gaiety! Music! Music!
*(He strides to the door, meeting Leone as he
enters.)*
*(Musician enters behind Leone carrying his
mandolin and repeats the initial song, "Oh
gold makes fools of young and old.")*

CURTAIN

SIDNEY HOWARD's

The Late Christopher Bean

Based on RENÉ FAUCHOIS's *Prenez Garde à la Peinture*

First produced by Gilbert Miller at Ford's Opera House, Baltimore, on October 24, 1932. New York opening performance, Henry Miller's Theatre, October 31, 1932, with the following cast:

DR. HAGGETT.................Walter Connolly		WARREN CREAMER..............William Lawson	
SUSAN HAGGETT.................Adelaide Bean		TALLANT....................George Coulouris	
ABBY.........................Pauline Lord		ROSEN.....................Clarence Derwent	
MRS. HAGGETT...................Beulah Bondi		DAVENPORT...................Ernest Lawford	
ADA HAGGETT................Katherine Hirsch			

Directed by Gilbert Miller
Setting designed by Aline Bernstein

ACT ONE—Morning.

ACT TWO—Noon.

ACT THREE—Afternoon.

ACT ONE

SCENE: *The dining room of an old house, not far from Boston.*

Double doors in the rear wall, to the Left of Center, give on the entry, from which the stair ascends to the bedroom floor. The newel post of the stair and the front door are seen. When the front door is opened, a small porch with lattice-work and ivy vine is seen. To the Right of the double doors is a large fireplace and mantel in natural old pine. Fire logs and a pair of andirons are seen in the fireplace. The Right wall, downstage, contains the door to the "L," where the kitchen is located. To the Left of the Left Center double doors, the rear wall jogs down, then carries off Left. In this section of the rear wall is located a window, through which is seen an elm-shaded yard with trees, grass, bushes and flowers, and a picket fence. A large bay window is located in the Left wall and gives on the same view. The rear wall, from the Right joint to the joint where it jogs down, is in natural old pine. Above and on both sides of the fireplace, the wall is panelled. The remaining walls are covered with wall-paper.

The room is worthy of more tasteful furnishing than the Haggett family has given it. Mingled with the few old pieces is much of less merit and more recent date. Added to this again, and producing an atmosphere of some confusion both in the entry and in the room itself, are the desk and other furnishings of the doctor's office from which they have been moved in honor of painting and papering, evidences of which (in the form of a ladder, buckets, brushes and a sign on the front door which reads "Paint!") clutter the entry. Below the door down Right and against the wall is a highback chair. Above the door, against the wall, is a sideboard. To the Right of the fireplace is a wicker basket with firewood. To the Left of the fireplace is a small footstool. Just Right of the double doors, against the rear wall, is a wooden medical cabinet. Exactly Right Center is the dining table with four chairs placed about it. To the Left of the double doors is a small bench or stool. There is a large corner cabinet set in the corner where the wall jogs down. On the shelves of the cabinet are many ornaments. Below this cabinet is an armchair facing down Right. The dining table is balanced on the Left side of the room by the doctor's desk with the knee hole facing Right. A swivel chair is placed at the desk. Below the desk is a side chair facing Right. Above the bay window, set in the corner, is a low-back side chair. On the wall over the mantel is a framed oil painting of a bowl of buttercup flowers.

On the wall over the door down Right is a large framed etching. On the wall over the double doors is a framed oil painting study of a dog's head. A small framed photograph is hung on the wall above the bay windows. There are simple white pull-back curtains on all the windows and a pair of tapestry drapes on the bay window. The floor is entirely covered by a wellworn carpet of old-fashioned design, with rag rugs placed just beyond the threshold of the three doors.

The light out of doors is of early morning in October. The stage is empty. The door Right leading to kitchen is only partly open. The double doors Left Center to the entry are both open. After a moment of silence, the front door opens to admit Dr. Haggett, a stout, undistinguished rural medical man of fifty. He closes the door, then removes his hat and overcoat and places them on a table in the entry. Then—

———

DR. HAGGETT. Hannah!

MRS. HAGGETT *(from upstairs).* Tha' you, Milton?

DR. HAGGETT. Yes, it is.

MRS. HAGGETT *(as before).* Back already, are you?

DR. HAGGETT. Yes, I am. *(Enters the room*

MRS. HAGGETT *(as before).* Had you breakfast?

DR. HAGGETT. No, I haven't. *(Goes * desk to set his doctor's satchel on it)

MRS. HAGGETT *(as before, calling loudly)* Abby! *(Something on Dr. Haggett's hand annoys him. Smelling them, he gets a strip o gauze from a glass jar on desk and goes * medicine cabinet)* Abby!! *(Haggett oper drawer in cabinet; gets out a bottle; procee to clean his hands with contents, drying the with gauze)* Abby!!! Get Doctor Hagge his breakfast! He ain't had none! *(Susa Haggett, a pretty girl of nineteen, comes dow the stair)* Better help Abby get your Pa breakfast for him, Susie!

SUSAN *(enters room and crosses to abo table).* I will.

DR. HAGGETT *(throws piece of gauze into firelog carrier next to fireplace)* What ails Abby that she wants help to get my breakfast?

SUSAN. Oh, Abby's terrible upset!

DR. HAGGETT. What about? *(Sits Left of table)*

SUSAN. Why, Pa! About leaving us!

DR. HAGGETT. That's right! Today *is* Thursday! I clean forgot! There's been enough talk about it, too! *(Susan moves a few steps Right)* So Abby's leaving us after all these years! *(He is looking toward Right door as Abby enters, carrying a tin tray with coffee pot, cup and saucer, cream and sugar, napkins)*

ABBY *(wears a smile that decreases in plausibility as it increases in determination. She is the help of the Haggett family, a Yankee villager, aged vaguely between youth and maturity, of a wistful prettiness, simple and serious. Speaking as she crosses to above table and Right of him).* I got strong coffee hot and ready for you, Doctor Haggett. Think of you going all this time on an empty stomach. Did everything come out all right?

DR. HAGGETT. Yes. Boy, eight pounds, three ounces, come out.

ABBY *(setting coffee things out on table).* Well, that's just lovely! I expect the Jordans must be real pleased it's a boy! I expect most parents'd sooner have boys than girls, and I don't know as I blame em. You just sit there, Doctor Haggett, and Susie, you fix your Pa his coffee while I get the rest of his breakfast. *(Starts to move toward Right door. Susan goes to above the table and Right of Haggett. Abby points to the newspaper and telegram lying on table)* There's his Boston paper handy for him. And there's a telegram with it that just come. *(She has vanished again, carrying the empty tray, on the last word. Susan pours a cup of coffee)*

DR. HAGGETT. She appears to be making quite an effort for the last day. *(He reaches for the telegram and opens it.*

SUSAN. Well, Abby would! It's going to seem like losing one of the family, ain't it? *(Moves a step Right. The contents of the telegram bring forth a low exclamation from Haggett. Susan stops and turns to him)* Pa, what is it?

DR. HAGGETT. It's from New York.

SUSAN. No!

DR. HAGGETT. Yes, it is. *(He reads)* "An admirer of the late Christopher Bean will do himself the honor of calling on you at noon on Thursday." Signed, Maxwell Davenport.

SUSAN *(thoughtful).* Chris Bean. *(Goes to Right of table and sits)*

DR. HAGGETT. I haven't thought of Chris Bean for years.

SUSAN. Chris Bean who painted all them pictures——

DR. HAGEGTT. Guess he thought they was pictures when he wasn't too drunk to think! But who's Maxwell Davenport? Guess I ain't supposed to know him, but—— *(Puts telegram in his left coat pocket. He accepts coffee which Susan has poured for him)*

MRS. HAGGETT *(comes down the stairs. Like her husband, she is Yankee, and they are about of an age. Unlike him, however, she has assumed certain cityfied airs in dress and bearing which, so she feels, lift her above the standards c' her native village. Distastefully viewing the debris in the entrance as she descends).* Why ain't that painter-paper-hanger come round like he said he would to fetch his stuff away? *(While speaking she picks up the two paint cans containing brushes which are placed against Left Center door, and puts them down by step-ladder. Next, she picks up end of canvas trailing on the floor at foot of the ladder and tucks it under the ladder)* He was all finished up when he went home last night, and he gave me his word he'd be here first thing this morning. *(Enters room and crosses to above table)* Deliver me from any more painters in the house! Your sister Ada's lying up in her bed this minute with the sick headache this paint smell's given her. *(Sits above table)* When I think of the work's got to be done in this house today, moving your Pa's things back into his office and all!

ABBY *(returns from kitchen, bringing a tray containing balance of Haggett's breakfast. She sets the tray on the lower end of the sideboard; gets the dish of cereal)* Here you are, Doctor Haggett.

MRS. HAGGETT *(still plaintive).* And Abby leaving us this afternoon——

ABBY. I'd as soon you didn't speak about me leaving, if you got no objection, Mrs. Haggett. *(Abby crosses Right of Mrs. Haggett. She leans over table and places dish before Haggett. He eats his breakfast during the ensuing scene)*

MRS. HAGGETT. Well, you are leaving, ain't you?

ABBY. Yes, I am. But you know I don't want to, and I wouldn't neither only it's the will of God. *(Returns to sideboard and gets covered dish of wheatcakes)* And the only way I can get through with it is if nobody speaks to me about it. But if you keep reminding me, I—I—— *(Returns to table; places dish in front of Haggett. Goes Left of Mrs. Haggett, who looks up. Susan lays a warning hand on her mother's arm. Abby just manages to control herself. She smiles bravely, then goes to sideboard for plate of butter)* What I want is to hear about Mrs. Jordan's baby. She didn't get married none too soon, did she? *(Returns to table; places dish, then returns to sideboard)* I should think when a baby comes that quick after a wedding you'd pretty near have to brush the rice off it. *(Returns to table with syrup jug, which she places before Haggett; crosses in between Mrs. Haggett and Susan)* Was she in labor long?

DR. HAGGETT. Not so long.

ABBY *(continuing)*. Did she have just a terrible time? You look kind of washed out yourself, Doctor Haggett. Well, it couldn't have been more than four o'clock when they called you out. Seems like babies is always getting you up or keeping you up, don't it?

(Ada Haggett, a girl of twenty-six, who fancies her baby prettiness and babylike manner, comes down the stair slowly).

SUSAN *(puts her arm about Abby's waist)*. If you feel so bad about leaving us, Abby, why don't you stay?

ABBY. You're all so good to me! I don't want to go. It's the will of God.

DR. HAGGETT. The first time I ever heard of the will of God sending a woman off to live in Chicago. *(Ada enters room and goes to Left of medicine cabinet)*

ABBY. It couldn't have been nothing less to make my poor brother's wife take sick and die and leave him with four little children and no woman in the house. You know it wouldn't be my way to will a thing like that.

DR. HAGGETT. Well, don't let's be going over it again. You're leaving us. We're sorry to have you go. We'll save our tears till the time comes for you to take your train. What time is it?

ABBY. The five-o'clock to Boston.

SUSAN. We're going to miss you, Abby.

ABBY. And me? What about me leaving this place where I been so long? Fifteen years I been here!

DR. HAGGETT *(exasperated)*. Don't keep on going over it!

ABBY *(turns and crosses toward Right door)*. No, I don't want to go over it, either. I just can't stand— *(Exits Right)*

SUSAN. Poor Abby! *(Rises)* We'll never get another like her. *(Exits Right, closing door)*

DR. HAGGETT. Well, that wouldn't be such a bad idea.

MRS. HAGGETT. Want us to do without no help, I suppose!

DR. HAGGETT. Don't see why not. Three women in the house. I'll undertake to make *my* bed mornings.

ADA *(moves down a step)*. But, Pa. Have you thought what folks'd say?

DR. HAGGETT. What *would* they say.

MRS. HAGGETT. That Doctor Haggett's practice has fallen off so bad he can't afford to keep help.

DR. HAGGETT. You keep house, Hannah, and I'll keep my practice.

MRS. HAGGETT. You'd set back and let everything go to the dogs if it wasn't for me. How long was I after you to have that office and entry painted and papered?

DR. HAGGETT *(peace at any price)*. Yes, I know, Hannah.

MRS. HAGGETT *(continuing, her voice rising)*. Who was it, you or me, found we could sell that *old* wall-paper for more than enough to give you a nice clean office sick folks could enjoy?

DR. HAGGETT. Oh, I know! I know.

MRS. HAGGETT. Now you want to spoil the *whole* impression by making your wife and daughters do their own work.

DR. HAGGETT. I know, Hannah, I know. And if you could find some way to make my patients pay the *bills* they owe me——

MRS. HAGGETT. If folks won't pay you, don't take care of them. *(Begins to read the newspaper)*

DR. HAGGETT. And what would happen to my practice then?

MRS. HAGGETT. God Almighty! There just ain't no reasoning with him.

DR. HAGGETT. Doctors have to care for the sick even if they can't pay. It's the ones who can and don't, these days——

MRS. HAGGETT *(quietly)*. Ada, you better go upstairs. I see I got to talk private with your Pa. *(Ada goes into entry and starts upstairs; pauses on stair, listening. Haggett rises and crosses toward desk. As he does he takes his tobacco pouch and his pipe from his coat pocket and begins to fill the pipe)*

DR. HAGGETT. If you could find new help for the same as we pay Abby——

MRS. HAGGETT. The new one I found won't cost us much more.

DR. HAGGETT *(stops and turns to her)*. You haven't gone and got a new one already!

MRS. HAGGETT. Oh, yes, I have. Last week when I went to Boston.

DR. HAGGETT. Have you got help in Boston?

MRS. HAGGETT *(puts newspaper down on table)*. Can't you understand, Milton, that it's in bad times like these you got to keep up appearances most of all? *(He sits uncomfortably in his chair at desk. She rises and crosses down to just Right of him)* I ain't sorry to see Abby leaving. *(He lights his pipe)* She's been here long enough. Mebbe fine for her to feel she's one of the family and call the girls by their first names and all. But you know she hasn't got a mite of style or dash about her. The new one ain't like that. She's a real city maid that can answer the doorbell proper!

DR. HAGGETT *(looks up at her)*. How much more does she cost?

MRS. HAGGETT. If you'll stop to think of all the girls and me are saving, making every stitch of our clothes for Florida!

DR. HAGGETT *(sits back, his glance sharpening to a very fine point)*. Oh, you're still talking *Florida* this winter?

MRS. HAGGETT *(flustered)*. Why— wouldn't I—be?

DR. HAGGETT. Well, the girls and you ain't going to Florida, nor any other place, till times get better.

ADA *(bursts in from upstairs. As she enters)*. Did I hear Pa say we can't go to Florida? *(Slowly moves to Left of table)*

DR. HAGGETT. Yes, you did, Ada. And it ain't the first time neither. Maybe I do sit by and let your Ma paint and paper up my office, and *maybe* your Ma is going to have a maid from Boston—maybe. But as long as I can't collect the bills my patients owe me, there ain't no use of no more *Florida* talk. I take my stand on that.

MRS. HAGGETT. Well, I take my stand too, Milton Haggett, and I wouldn't be no mother if I give it up.

DR. HAGGETT. What's Florida got to do with being a mother?

MRS. HAGGETT. You may not care if your daughters get married or not, but I do.

ADA. *And so do they!*

DR. HAGGETT. You don't have to go to Florida to get married.

ADA. Maybe not, but the opportunities down there are exceptional.

DR. HAGGETT *(irritably)*. Stuff and nonsense.

MRS. HAGGETT. No, it ain't, Milton. Them Miami beaches is just alive with boys who don't give a thought to nothing but romance and getting married.

DR. HAGGETT. Most boys get them ideas most any place.

MRS. HAGGETT. Not in New England in the winter time. *(Goes to armchair and sits)*

DR. HAGGETT. The girls can wait for spring, then.

ADA *(to mother)*. Pa wants for me to grow up an old maid.

DR. HAGGETT *(getting a little testy)*. I don't want no such thing.

ADA *(to him)*. I'm pretty near an old maid already.

DR. HAGGETT. You're not more than a baby.

ADA. I'm twenty-four.

DR. HAGGETT. No, you're not. You're twenty-six.

ADA *(sits Left of table)*. That makes it all the worse!

DR. HAGGETT. Well, if you're in such

a hurry to get married, go down to the Post Office and put up a notice.

ADA *(turns to him)*. Pa!

MRS. HAGGETT. After all the advantages we gave our girls, would you want to see 'em married to village boys?

DR. HAGGETT. What's wrong with village boys? You married one.

MRS. HAGGETT. Well, I hadn't been to Miami then. *(A short pause)*

DR. HAGGETT. I thank you, Hannah. I thank you. But if Ada can do half as well as you've done——

ADA. There aint' no boys to speak of in this place. And what there is don't like me.

DR. HAGGETT. What is it makes Florida boys like you better? Is it because they seen you in your swimming suit? All right, give the boys here a chance. Invite 'em in, put on your swimming suit, and set by the fire. *(Susan enters Right; goes to chair Right of table)*

MRS. HAGGETT *(rises; crosses to chair above table)*. Well, your Pa's got the best of us again. There ain't no hope of Florida this winter. I'll have to make 'em take back my flowered foulard.

SUSAN *(cheerfully)*. Well, that's too bad. But I don't see as it matters. *(Sits)*

ADA. It does matter! It does! *(Mrs. Haggett sits)* Pa says I'm only a baby. But what he really wants is for me to grow up an old maid.

DR. HAGGETT *(rises; crosses Center)*. I don't want no—— *(Paces to and fro, muttering to himself)*

ADA *(her voice rising)*. If we stay here, Susie'll get married before me, because the boys here like her better than they like me, and if she gets married before me I'll just die. I'll die. I know I'll die. *(Sobbing, she lowers her head on table. Haggett stops his mutterings and pacings)*

MRS. HAGGETT *(rises, comes to above Ada and pats her on the shoulder)*. It's this forever having just enough and not one mite over for——

DR. HAGGETT *(sorrowfully)*. Greed, Hannah! Greed! *(Crosses up to Left Center doorway, then returns to Left of table)*

MRS. HAGGETT *(savagely)*. Maybe I am greedy! But it's only *fools* and *wastrels* who don't try to get all they can out of life.

(Abby enters Right, her eye cocked malevolently. She goes to sideboard and gets empty tray)

DR. HAGGETT. No man has never called me greedy for money, Hannah. And I hope no man ever does. I'll go upstairs now and shave. *(Goes out Left Center and upstairs)*

ABBY *(moves to above table and with her tray goes about gathering up Haggett's breakfast dishes)*. I declare, if folks ain't peculiar, though! There I was crying and carrying on over going away and you're doing the very same as me because you got to stay.

MRS. HAGGETT. I'll thank you, Abby, not to make observations and remarks.

ABBY. Mrs. Haggett, don't mind me. I'm only help, without a mite of style about me, and I call the girls by their first names like one of the family. And now you got a real city maid coming from Boston. And she knows how to answer the doorbell proper. *(She carries filled tray to lower end of sideboard)*

MRS. HAGGETT *(above and Left of table. Furious)*. You're a common, impudent girl, and I discharge you for listening at keyholes.

ABBY. You can't discharge me because I discharged myself already. I won't go till I'm good and ready.

MRS. HAGGETT. I'll take no more back talk from you, young lady. You'll go now.

ABBY. I'll go this afternoon.

(Warren Creamer, the village painter and paperhanger, has come into the entry from behind Right. He is a personable, self-satisfied youth in his early twenties)

WARREN *(in doorway)*. Morning, Mrs. Haggett.

MRS. HAGGETT. Oh! It's the paperhanger!

WARREN *(continuing)*. Morning, Ada. Morning, Susie.

MRS. HAGGETT *(as the girls return his greetings)*. I was just saying it was about time you showed up.

ABBY. Warren ain't so late you need fret about it. *(Mrs. Haggett swings on her again)*

WARREN *(placid)*. Weather's getting sharp. Guess winter must be coming. Had trouble starting the old truck this morning.

MRS. HAGGETT (*turns back from Abby with great dignity, then crosses up to Right of Warren and indicates his materials in entry*). Well, get your stuff on out of here. I'm sick of the smell of paint.

ABBY (*picks up the tray and starts for Right door*). There's plenty of things in this house smells worse than paint does. (*Exits; closes door*)

WARREN (*still calmly*). I come to get my stuff out, Mrs Haggett. And I brought you each a little present too.

ADA. Did you, Warren? What?

WARREN. Well, I brought each of you girls one of my pictures. (*He produces two small framed oil paintings of still life from under his arm, as he crosses to Left of table*)

SUSAN (*delighted*). Oh!

ADA. A picture of you, Warren?

WARREN. No, not of me. They're pictures I painted. (*Hands a picture to each of the girls*)

MRS. HAGGETT (*crosses round to Left of table, behind Ada and examines her picture*). It's a *dead fish!*

SUSAN (*leans over to see it*). Looks like salmon you caught last Sunday, Warren.

WARREN. That's what it is.

MRS. HAGGETT (*to Susan*). What's yours? (*Susan tilts picture for her to see*) A *dead duck!* Better swap round with your sister, Susie. Fish always makes Ada break out terrible.

ADA. Oh, not in pictures, Ma! (*Turns to Warren with a too-ingratiating smile*) And they're your *own* work, Warren?

WARREN. Yeah.

ADA. The *frames* too? (*Mrs. Haggett goes up a few steps*)

WARREN (*nodding*). They're first-rate painting. I thought maybe you'd like to hang 'em up over the sideboard. I thought they'd look kind of suitable.

MRS. HAGGETT. I wouldn't have no appetite if I had to look up at a dead fish and a dead duck.

ADA. No! Warren's right, Ma. They'd look just lovely! (*Turns her fatal flattery on Warren*) To think I never knowed you was a picture painter!

WARREN (*blandly*). Seems like all kinds of painting comes natural to me.

ADA (*same tactics*). I can see that. My! I adn't no idea you was so clever. I didn't know the boys here were like *you*, Warren.

WARREN. They ain't! (*Mrs. Haggett goes to desk; begins to arrange the papers, etc.*)

ADA. Why, you could paint real well, if you was to study. I'm only a baby, but I used to take painting lessons myself. Did you know that, Warren?

WARREN. No.

ADA. That flower-piece there on the wall is my work. (*Points to it. Abby returns from kitchen, goes to sideboard, gets vase of flowers, crosses to table and sets it there*) It took a prize, it looked so natural. I guess I could give you some pointers, if you'd like.

ABBY. What are you giving him pointers about, Ada? Is it about pictures? (*Sees the two paintings on the table*) Did you paint these, Warren? Let's see, Susie.

WARREN (*above table, Left of Abby*). They're what's called still life.

ABBY. Still life. That's a painting term, still life.

MRS. HAGGETT (*turns from desk*). What do you know about painting terms?

ABBY. Oh, I know. See this, Susie? (*She points*) Know how he did that? He didn't use his brush. No, he stuck his thumb in the paint and went like this— (*She indicates*) —and like this.

WARREN. That's right.

ABBY (*to Warren*). Oh, I know. I know.

ADA (*her mother's dignity*). Don't notice her, Ma. Let her go out in the kitchen and wash Pa's dishes and let Susie go out and help her. And you go up to Pa and leave Warren and me to hang the pictures together. (*Picks up pictures and starts to rise. Warren turns his back on her. Abby takes newspaper to mantel, then empties ashtray on medicine cabinet into fireplace. Mrs. Haggett starts for the stairs. Haggett comes downstairs in his shirtsleeves*)

DR. HAGGETT. I was trying to shave, but there's no hot water. Morning, Warren.

MRS. HAGGETT. Susie, you get the kettle for your Pa. (*Susan rises; starts to move toward kitchen*)

ABBY. Don't you trouble, Susie. I don't mind fetching for your Pa and you.

MRS. HAGGETT (*crosses above table toward*

ABBY. *Quickly*). No, but if it was me I suppose you'd tell me to shave in cold water. (*Abby sweeps into the kitchen, closing door. Mrs. Haggett goes to sideboard and puts napkins and table-runner in drawer*)

SUSAN (*quickly*). 'Tain't nothing, Pa. (*Picks up her painting, crosses below table, picks up Ada's painting, goes to Haggett and hands them to him*) Just Ma and Abby having one of their regular spats. Look at what Warren's painted for the dining room.

DR. HAGGETT (*examines the pictures without much pleasure. Between Susan and Warren*). Hmmm—— Hmmm——

WARREN (*right of him*). If you don't like this pair, I got plenty more I painted down at the shop. I guess I must have close on a hundred. (*Susan takes paintings and places them by corner cabinet, then stands below armchair*)

DR. HAGGETT. A hundred? You must have taken a good bit of time off regular painting to get that many pictures painted.

WARREN. I don't mind how much time I take for painting pictures. I'm too good to stay with paper-hanging.

MRS. HAGGETT (*a step to above chair Right of table*). You ain't fixing to be an artist, I hope?

WARREN You bet I am, and I'll be a good one, too!

MRS. HAGGETT (*with wise decision. Ada offers chair*). No, Ada. No. I guess I'll set right here. (*Does in chair Right of table*) I'd rather have a real painter in the family than a picture-painter.

WARREN (*a step Right*). I was thinking of painting the dooryard fence for you, Mrs. Haggett, but——

MRS. HAGGETT (*breaking in sharply*). Free?

WARREN. Yeah. But I got a better idea now. I'll paint you a portrait of the girls instead.

SUSAN (*left*). Oh, Warren, will you?

ADA (*seated chair Left of table. Turns and nods at Susan*). Does Susie have to be in it?

WARREN. Yeah. The both of you.

DR. HAGGETT. Warren, what's made you get so generous all of a sudden?

WARREN (*turns to Haggett*). I got to thinking over what good care you took of my Ma the time she died and how you ain't never been paid for that, and so——

MRS. HAGGETT. If you're that grateful, mebbe you'd let us have the job you just done in the office free.

WARREN. Well, I ain't that grateful.

MRS. HAGGETT. Could you paint the girls *and* the dooryard fence?

WARREN. If you'd buy the paint for the fence, I could.

MRS. HAGGETT. Couldn't you use the portrait paint on the fence?

WARREN. 'Tain't the same kind.

MRS. HAGGETT. Then I guess we'll let the fence wait for spring.

ADA. How about the portrait?

MRS. HAGGETT. I got no use for it, but I got nothing against it.

SUSAN. How will you paint us, Warren? (*He turns to them and sees that with Ada seated in an old chair and Susan behind her, the pair of them, both in color and composition, would make a picture*)

DR. HAGGETT (*moves a few steps up*) Now that's a question.

WARREN. Well, I don't know—I' have to think. Ada, you go over and sit in that chair by Susie. (*Ada goes to armchair and sits*)

DR. HAGGETT. If Ada was listening to a sea-shell and Susie looking on——

WARREN. No——

MRS. HAGGETT. Or both of them looking off into the future like.

DR. HAGGETT (*a step to Warren*). You ought to paint Mrs. Haggett with them. She don't take up much room.

WARREN (*decision*). I'll paint them just like they are.

ADA. Not in this dress! I got a lovely new one.

WARREN. I like that dress. I like the color. (*Has become thoroughly professional* Yours and Susie's and that old chair together. I like that fine. Just give me scrap of paper. Any old scrap and a pencil—— (*Looks about him, goes to desk and finds a large pad there. He takes an artist drawing pencil from his coat pocket as he returns to chair above table, watching the girls meanwhile*)

ADA (*rises. To Susan as she pulls her down into the chair*). You sit down and I'll stand behind. (*The girls exchange places, Ada arranging herself over the back of the chair)* I'm such a baby, Warren wouldn't want you towering over me, would you, Warren?

WARREN. Either way. *(Crosses to Ada and poses her)* There, that's all right. *(Returns to chair above table and sits)* Now, Mrs. Haggett, just to give you an idea of what I can do. *(To girls as he begins to sketch excitedly)* Don't move, now! *(Pause)*

MRS. HAGGETT. Won't you even let Ada hold a bunch of flowers?

ADA. It's Warren's picture, Ma. If he likes me the way I am——

DR. HAGGETT *(leans over Warrens' shoulder)*. Look, Hannah! You got to admit the boy's quick with his pencil. You can see which girl is which already.

MRS. HAGGETT *(rises and joins him)*. Which *is* which?

ADA. Does it look like me, Ma?

DR. HAGGETT. Give the boy time. You don't get likenesses as quick as that.

MRS. HAGGETT. What do you know about it?

DR. HAGGETT. Guess I know that much. Look at that, Hannah! *(Pulls Mrs. Haggett nearer)* You're quite an artist, Warren. You'll be painting patriotic pictures before you're through. Ever seen the pictures in the Boston State House? *(Mrs. Haggett reseats herself Right of table)* They got fine patriotic pictures there. *Warren stops sketching for a moment and squints over his pencil at girls in a typical artist's manner)* Figures life size! Frames thirty feet long! Pictures that make you proud to be an American! "Bunker Hill" and "The Spirit of '76"! I could give you ideas for pictures if you wanted, Warren. "The First Thanksgiving!" *Warren repeats the same business)* Now, that would be a good picture for a dining room. Look at that, will you, Hannah? Where ever did you learn such tricks, Warren?

WARREN *(still working)*. You remember that painter here named Chris Bean?

DR. HAGGETT. Chris Bean! Patient of mine! I had a telegram about him this morning. *(Fumbles for his coat pocket and finds that he is coatless)*

MRS. HAGGETT. About Chris Bean?

DR. HAGGETT. Yes. A man who calls himself an admirer of his.

MRS. HAGGETT. Wonder what he finds to admire him for? *(Abby enters with the kettle. Stops still by the sideboard as Warren speaks)*

WARREN. Chris started me off on a painting when I was a kid. He'd let me follow him wherever he went and sit beside him and draw the same things he did. He gave me lessons, all I ever had. I try to remember what he taught me and—— *(Abby has fairly yearned toward Warren)*

MRS. HAGGETT. Hope he didn't teach you to drink like he did!

ABBY *(stiffens)*. Well, if he—— *(Mrs. Haggett looks sharply at Abby)* Here's your hot-water kettle, Doctor Haggett. *(Crosses to above table and gives it to him)*

DR. HAGGETT. What do I want with—? That's so! I *was* shaving. Well, I better get back to it and get round to making my calls. *(Takes kettle and crosses toward Left Center door)* Thank you, Abby. *(Goes up the stair. Abby and Mrs. Haggett exchange a venomous glance as Abby turns back toward Right door)*.

ABBY. Oh, Mrs. Haggett, I forgot to tell you. The real city maid from Boston's out in the kitchen. I found her in back when I went to fetch the kettle. I don't hardly think she'll stay after what I told her about the place. *(She exits Right)*

MRS. HAGGETT *(rises; crosses to Right door)*. If Abby's gone and poisoned that new maid's mind! *(Exits Right)*

ADA *(crosses above table)*. You'll have to excuse me, Warren. This is important Oh, Ma! Do you think—— *(She follows Mother out, closing door)*

SUSAN *(rises and moves a step to him)*. Will you let me see?

WARREN *(rises; crosses to her)*. Sure, if you want to. *(She looks)* It's just rough.

SUSAN. Looks to me like it isn't quite fair to Ada.

WARREN. Well, as long as it's fair to you——

SUSAN *(a step Left)*. Oh, no, Warren! Be fair to Ada or you'll get Ma down on you.

WARREN. I paint pictures to suit myself, not your Ma. I don't care shucks for your Ma nor Ada neither. I guess you know why I'm painting this picture.

SUSAN (drawing back). You said you wanted to give Ma a present.

WARREN. All I want's an excuse to see you every day.

SUSAN. You've known me a long time to talk that way, Warren.

WARREN. Guess you know me long enough to know what I think about you.

SUSAN. Guess you'd better not say any more.

WARREN. You say you'll marry me and I won't .

SUSAN. Warren!

WARREN. What?

SUSAN. I wouldn't be any wife for you. Not if you're going to be an artist, I wouldn't.

WARREN. Why not? I'm a hard worker and I'm going to be a good artist.

SUAN. But I don't even know if I like art much.

WARREN. I'll teach you to like it.

SUSAN. You haven't even said you loved me.

WARREN. Do I have to say that?

SUSAN. Well, I think you ought to.

WARREN. Can't you take my word for it?

SUSAN. All right, Warren. Only there's one thing. We'd have to wait till Ada gets married first. (He turns and crosses to table; puts drawing there) We wouldn't have any peace if we didn't do that.

WARREN (turns to her). Guess I'd better kiss you.

SUSAN. Why?

WARREN. Well, I'm marrying you, not Ada, and I'm awful busy and I got no time to waste. And I guess being kissed'll make you stop your nonsense.

SUSAN. Well, mebbe it will.

WARREN. You ain't afraid?

SUSAN (smiles). No.

WARREN. All right, I'll do it, then. (Goes to her, Left Center; takes her in his arms rather stiffly; kisses her with little passion. The Right door opens and Ada appears)

ADA. Well, Warren, here I am back—— (A gasp. Then a step on) Pa! (Turns to kitchen) Ma! Come here this minute! (Susan breaks away to down Left)

DR. HAGGETT (off stage on stairs). What is it?

WARREN (quickly). It's Ada messing in other people's business.

ADA. Don't you dast speak to me.

MRS. HAGGETT (appears in Right door, closing it). Ada, don't you know I'm busy?

ADA (beside herself). I don't care if you are! There's things going on in here want 'tending to!

DR. HAGGETT (still in shirt-sleeves, and minus his collar, comes downstairs and enters room). What's come over this house of mine this morning?

ADA. There I was in the kitchen, Pa, with the new maid and Ma, and I come back and I caught him and Susie——

WARREN. Don't tell 'em what I was doing, Ada. (Stepping forward undismayed to Susan's side) I'd sooner show 'em. (Takes the terrified Susan in his arms again and again kisses her, this time with real passion. A gasp from Mrs. Haggett)

DR. HAGGETT (above chair Left of table). God bless my soul!

MRS. HAGGETT (crosses below table to Center. Furiously). You pack your stuff up and clear out of here.

WARREN (turns to her). All right. I don't mind. (To Susan) Coming with me, Susie? Susie and me are going to get married.

ADA (a step Left. A scream). Ma, if you let Susie get married ahead of me——

MRS. HAGGETT. Susie ain't going to marry no Warren Creamer. My daughter's too good to waste on any starving dead beat of an artist.

WARREN. You ain't talking about me Mrs. Haggett? I'm the best bet for marriage in this whole country. I'm going far and Susie's coming with me. I guess she's old enough to know her own mind.

SUSAN. Go along now, Warren. This won't help things any.

WARREN. I won't go unless you come with me.

MRS. HAGGETT (snorts as she crosses Left of Haggett). Milton, if he ain't out of this house before I count ten, I——

SUSAN. There won't be no need for throwing Warren out, Pa. Please go Warren. I'll see you later.

WARREN *(as steadily as ever)*. When?

SUSAN. I'll get word to you.

DR. HAGGETT *(crosses to Warren)*. Better go, Warren, and let things simmer down.

WARREN *(crosses to table)*. All right. Give me my drawing, and——

MRS. HAGGETT *(snatches the drawing off table just as Warren reaches for it, and crumples it. A general gasp)*. There'll be no more painting portraits in this house.

WARREN *(picks up his hat from table and puts it on; crosses into entry. Sullen)*. I'll go to keep the peace for Susie's sake. *(Opens the front door, then begins picking up his materials)* But she'd ought to come with me. Because we *are* going to get married. *(Takes a step into room)* And as for you, you're what they call a Philistine, Mrs. Haggett. Yes, a Philistine! I'll go now. But I'll show you yet. *(Turns and goes out through front door, slamming it. Susan bursts into tears)*

MRS. HAGGETT *(above table. Throws drawing toward fireplace)*. Well, I may be a Philistine, but I guess I nipped that romance in the bud. *(Susan sits in desk chair. Haggett goes to Right of her)*

DR. HAGGETT. Clear out, you two, and leave Susie and me alone. *(Ada looks at Susan)*

MRS. HAGGETT *(crosses above table to Right door)*. I said this was going to be a terrible upsetting morning, but I hadn't no idea how terrible—— *(Ada follows Mrs. Haggett into the kitchen; closes door. Susan continues sobbing. Haggett looks down on her)*

DR. HAGGETT *(patting her on shoulder)*. Don't take on, Susie.

SUSAN. He loves me, Pa, and I love him.

DR. HAGGETT. That's too bad. If he wasn't so hell-bent to be an artist——

SUSAN. What's wrong with artists?

DR. HAGGETT. Not a thing but the cost of food and lodging.

SUSAN. Not if he's a good one! And he ill be a good one.

(Tallant is seen passing by outside windows left.)

DR. HAGGETT. He's got conceit enough. But the best of 'em is poor providers, om all I hear, *and these days*——

SUSAN *(rises. Passionately, with her head on his shoulder)*. "These days!" That's all you ever say! "These days!" If it wasn't for these days you and Ma wouldn't have nothing against Warren, and Ma and Ada could go to Florida——

DR. HAGGETT. And I could get a little peace. *(The doorbell rings)* Here we are talking, and I ought to be making my calls. *(Both move toward the stair)* Come upstairs and wash your face, and I'll get my coat on. I'll have a talk with Warren and see what's what. *(Over his shoulder as Abby comes from Right through room into entry. Very concerned and solicitous)* If that's a patient, Abby, show him in here in the dining room and keep the others out. I'll be right down. *(Disappears with Susan upstairs)*

(Abby opens the front door to admit Tallant, a smooth, youngish and shabbily-dressed New Yorker.)

ABBY. Will you step in here? *(Tallant comes into the entry)* The Doctor'll be right down. *(She closes front door)*

TALLANT. Thank you. I'll wait, then. *(Enters to Left of medicine cabinet and casually glances about the room)*

ABBY *(crosses to behind armchair)*. You can have a chair. The waiting-room magazines got lost in the moving on account of the office being painted, but he won't keep you long. *(Is going below table toward kitchen. He smiles)*

TALLANT. You must be Abby. *(Very casually)*

ABBY *(surprised)*. I've never seen you before that I remember.

TALLANT *(places hat on top of medicine cabinet)*. No, this is the first time we've ever met.

ABBY *(stops at Center)*. How do you walk right in and call me by my name?

TALLANT *(crosses Left Center)*. Ever hear of mind readers?

ABBY *(continues on her way to kitchen)*. You're not one of them, are you?

TALLANT. Only in a small way.

ABBY. Whatever you are, you're fresh as paint. *(Exits Right, closing door)*

DR. HAGGETT *(comes downstairs, now fully dressed, and enters to Left of Tallant)*. Good morning, sir.

TALLANT. Is this Doctor Haggett?

DR. HAGGETT. Yes, it is. *(They shake hands)*

TALLANT *(over-elaborate)*. I'm very glad to meet you, Doctor Haggett.

DR. HAGGETT. Sit down, won't you? *(Gestures toward patients' chair below desk as he crosses to desk chair)* I'm sorry my office is out of commission.

TALLANT. Don't apologize, Doctor. I've come to see you because I feel—— *(Moves a step to him)*

DR. HAGGETT. A little bilious? You look it. *(Gestures again to chair below desk)* Can't fool me on a sluggish liver. *(Takes his place professionally at his desk)*

TALLANT. I daresay you're right, Doctor, but—

DR. HAGGETT *(turns to him. Indicates patients' chair)*. Sit down and put out your tongue. Headache? Nausea? Bowels all right?

TALLANT. You don't understand, Doctor. I'm not sick.

DR. HAGGETT *(sits up in surprise)*. Well, if you're not sick, what do you want with me?

TALLANT *(sits in armchair, Left Center)*. I was just coming to that, Doctor.

DR. HAGGETT *(rises. Impatiently)*. Might as well tell you I don't want no insurance.

TALLANT *(reassuring)*. I'm not here to sell *insurance*. I'm not here to sell *anything*. I'm here solely for the pleasure of making your acquaintance.

DR. HAGGETT *(surly)*. You don't tell me!

TALLANT. Oh, yes, I do! I happened to be motoring through your lovely State, enjoying the glory of its autumn foliage. *(Haggett shows signs of impatience)*. And as I came to this village I realized that I'd stumbled upon an opportunity to perform a duty I've postponed *too long*.

DR. HAGGETT. What's that?

TALLANT. The *payment* of a sacred *debt* I owe you, Doctor.

DR. HAGGETT *(re-seats himself. Astonished)*. What *debt* do you owe me?

TALLANT. A matter of ten years ago you had as a patient a man whom I called and still call my dearest friend.

DR. HAGGETT. Did I now!

TALLANT. A man known by a good Yankee name. An excellent Yankee name! Christopher Bean!

DR. HAGGETT *(enlightened)*. Oh, it's *you*, is it?

TALLANT *(startled)*. I beg your pardon!

DR. HAGGETT *(laughs)*. Funny, me taking you for a patient. But I wasn't expecting you for some hours yet.

TALLANT *(very much on his guard)*. You *were* expecting me?

DR. HAGGETT. Well, I got your telegram, Mr— *(Fumbling in his Right pocket for the wire)* Let's see, what was the name? *(He takes out telegram and unfold it)*

TALLANT *(rises, a step to him. Quickly)*. Is that the telegram? May I see it? They so often mix them up——

DR. HAGGETT *(looks up in surprise. Read. it carefully)*. That there seems clea~ enough. *(He hands it to Tallant)*

TALLANT *(as he reads it quickly)*. Oh yes. Quite! I forgot that I'd said "noon" *(Returns telegram to Haggett)* It took m~ less time to get here than I thought. *(Si~ again)* I hurried. *(He smiles, his affabilit~ restored)* I was afraid that you might g~ out on your rounds of visiting the sic~ and that I might miss you. And I was s~ eager, you see, so very eager——

DR. HAGGETT *(looking at the telegram)* You say here you're an admirer of Chr~ Bean's.

TALLANT. That's putting it prett~ mildly, Doctor Haggett.

DR. HAGGETT. I was just wondering ~ your Chris Bean's the same one I know~

TALLANT. Oh, I'm certain.

DR. HAGGETT. Well, I don't kno~ now. As my wife said when this telegra~ came: "Can't see what he finds to admi~ about Chris Bean!" *Not* that Chris wasn~ a likeable lad. I was fond of him.

TALLANT. Of course you were.

DR. HAGGETT. I just wanted to mak~ sure, though. *(Quickly)* Did the fello~ you're thinking of think he was a painte~

TALLANT *(surprised)*. You might put that way.

DR. HAGGETT. It's the same, the~ *(Places telegram on desk)*

TALLANT. Poor chap.

DR. HAGGETT *(confidentially)*. Oh, always humored him about his pictur~

You got to humor folks when they're sick as he was.

TALLANT. I know you did everything you could for him.

DR. HAGGETT. Well, I hope I done my duty for him. Of course, a case like his——This ain't no climate for tuberculosis. If he'd had the money to get himself out West he might have had some chance, if he'd quit drinking. But as it was, there wasn't much I could do.

TALLANT. We're all mortal, Doctor.

DR. HAGGETT. There's no denying that.

TALLANT. It delights me that you remember him with affection.

DR. HAGGETT. Oh, we ain't none of us forgot him. Why, we was speaking of him just a few minutes past. My wife, she took a real fancy to him. He kind of appealed to her, I guess, seeing as we ain't got no sons of our own only two daughters. And him coming to live here, sick like he was and an orphan without no family. She took him right to her heart, and gave him the old barn for his studio. He painted most everything round the place. They was terrible bad, though, them pictures of his. *(Laughs reminiscently)* Mebbe if he'd had some training——

TALLANT *(quickly)*. Oh, very like. *(Then, more seriously)* Recently, though, Doctor, only the other day in fact, as I was going through an old desk of mine, I came across some letters Chris wrote to me while he was living here. And in the last of them—it's disgraceful I should have neglected it all these years—he spoke of your kindness to him and his gratitude and asked if I couldn't help him pay what he owed you.

DR. HAGGETT *(very pleased)*. Well, that's like Chris. Never a penny to his name and forever borrowing! He didn't even own a hat.

TALLANT. Let me see—the sum came to——

DR. HAGGETT *(quite sincerely)*. I don't remember.

TALLANT *(firmly)*. Exactly a hundred dollars.

DR. HAGGETT. Mebbe so. Likely he asked me how much he owed me, and likely I told him if ever he had a hundred he could spare—— *(Rises)*

TALLANT. Allow me, Doctor. *(He rises and hands two fifty dollars bills to Haggett)*. A little late, but paid in full.

DR. HAGGETT *(amazed)*. Well, God Almighty!

TALLANT. And all my apologies for keeping you waiting.

DR. HAGGETT *(rises)*. My dear sir——

TALLANT. Well, the debt's paid at last. I shall go home to New York a happier man.

DR. HAGGETT *(completely flabbergasted as he turns to desk)*. I'll give you a receipt.

TALLANT *(protesting)*. Oh, Doctor, please!

DR. HAGGETT *(turns to Tallant)*. Would you allow me to shake you by the hand?

TALLANT. I should be honored, Doctor. *(They shake hands)*

DR. HAGGETT. Just a minute—— *(Crosses to below table and calls)* Hannah! Ada! Come back in here a minute! *(Turns back to Tallant)* I want you to meet my family, Mr. —Mr.—Davenport!

TALLANT. I'm sorry I left my cards at the hotel.

DR. HAGGETT. I don't need no visiting card of yours. *(Touching his heart)* Your name's engraved here, Mr. Davenport. *(Mrs. Haggett and Ada come in Right)* My wife. *(Mrs. Haggett crosses below table to Right of Tallant and shakes hands with him)* My daughter, Ada. My younger daughter Susan—she's not so well this morning. *(Ada crosses to below chair below table. To the two women as Tallant bows)* I called you in, though, to show you an honest man.

TALLANT *(Left of Mrs. Haggett)*. Don't be alarmed, please, ladies!

DR. HAGGETT. Mr. Davenport here, who sent me that telegram from New York, is a friend of your old friend, Chris Bean. And now, ten years after poor Chris's death, this loyal friend, this more than honest man, has paid me the little debt poor Chris owed me. A hundred dollars. Here! You see! *(Turns to Ada and hands her the money)* You take it, Ada. You take it down and put it in the bank. Such things don't happen every day.

MRS. HAGGETT (*profoundly impressed*). Well, I should say they don't!

DR. HAGGETT. Let this be an example and inspiration to both of you.

ADA. Yes, Pa.

MRS. HAGGETT. Oh, it will be. Indeed, it will be, Milton. Won't you rest yourself? (*Tallant to armchair. Mrs. Haggett sits Left of table. Ada sits below table*)

DR. HAGGETT (*crosses to desk chair*). And don't neither of you never forget the name of—the name of——

TALLANT (*sits armchair*). Davenport.

DR. HAGGETT. That's right. Davenport. (*He sits*)

TALLANT. You cover me with confusion, Doctor. I see nothing extraordinary in what I've done.

DR. HAGGETT. You ain't tried collecting doctors' bills these days. (*Picks up his cash book, makes entry in it and mutters gleefully*) A hundred dollars!

TALLANT. But I told you how much my friend meant to me. (*Long pause as all look solemn. The merest afterthought*) I'm just wondering if he didn't leave some of his pictures to remember him by. Of course you've told me what you thought of them. (*Mrs. Haggett looks down*) And Chris wrote how even the village boys laughed at him when they watched him painting——

DR. HAGGETT. It seems mean to say so now, but I'm afraid *they* did.

MRS. HAGGETT. We never let him see *us* laugh.

TALLANT (*to her*). They'd have a special sentimental value for me. You can understand.

DR. HAGGETT. There ain't nothing to be ashamed of in that.

TALLANT (*to him*). Then if you *have* any, do you think I might take them away with me? (*More specific*) His letters mention six or seven he left here.

DR. HAGGETT. Oh, there was all of six or seven.

MRS. HAGGETT. Milton, I believe there's one out in the chicken house, still.

TALLANT (*to her. Barely suppressed horror*). In the chicken house!

DR. HAGGETT. Hannah, you're right. There is. (*Apologetically to Tallant*) But I hate to think what condition it must be in.

TALLANT (*the least pause. Then, quickly*). I'd like to have it, Doctor. No matter what shape it's in, I'd like to have it. It *is* a souvenir, you know.

MRS. HAGGETT (*rises*). You come with me, Ada. We'll see if we can't get if for Mr. Davenport. (*Ada rises and follows her mother out off Right in the entry*)

DR. HAGGETT. I remember now. There was a leak in the chicken house tar-paper roof. I was looking round for something watertight, and I found that picture. Fine, solid, thick oil paint, you know, and there wasn't no reason to set much store by it.

TALLANT. No.

DR. HAGGETT (*rises*). Wait! (*Calling*) Abby! (*He turns back to Tallant*) I just thought of something else. (*Abby enters and crosses above table to up Center*) Run up in the attic and look in that corner behind the north dormer. Seems to me like a few years ago we put one of them pictures of *Chris Bean's* in there to stop up that leak, too.

ABBY (*starts guiltily and gulps*). What do you want with it, Doctor Haggett?

DR. HAGGETT. Mr. Davenport here wants it to take along home with him.

ABBY. Mr. Davenport does?

DR. HAGGETT. Mr. Davenport was Chris Bean's closest friend.

ABBY. Mr. Davenport was?

DR. HAGGETT. See if you can get that picture off without tearing it. Then bring it down here.

ABBY. For Mr. Davenport?

DR. HAGGETT. That's what I said.

ABBY. Yes, Doctor Haggett. (*Abby goes upstairs. Haggett reseats himself*)

TALLANT. I'm sorry to cause your household so much trouble.

DR. HAGGETT. A man like you ain't no trouble to us. I only hope we can find what you're after. (*Mrs. Haggett and Ada return, through entry. Tallant rises*)

ADA. Well, we got it.

MRS. HAGGETT (*extending a filthy square of canvas as she enters to Right of Tallant*) It's kind of dirty. But you know chicken houses! (*Ada crosses to above table*)

DR. HAGGETT (*rises*). Just let Abby ge

at it with some *soap* and a *scrubbing brush*——

TALLANT *(hastily)*. No! No! No! No! That won't be necessary!

MRS. HAGGETT. 'Twon't be no trouble.

TALLANT. Oh, no, please! I'd be afraid—— *(Takes canvas from Mrs. Haggett)* I mean I'd rather clean it up myself.

DR. HAGGETT. But you can't carry it off all nasty like that!

TALLANT. Don't you see, Doctor, what it will mean to me to bring the picture back to life? It will seem almost as though Chris himself—— *(There is a pause in honor of his emotion)*

MRS. HAGGETT. Oh, yes. *(She points toward wall, Left Center)* Did you think of Ada's picture there?

DR. HAGGETT. But Mr. Davenport don't want Ada's pictures.

ADA *(below fireplace)*. Of course he don't want pictures painted by little me. *(Tallant looks at her)* But Ma means I turned one of Chris Bean's pictures over to paint my flower piece on the back. *(Points to picture over fireplace. Tallant looks at it)*

DR. HAGGETT. I didn't know that. Now ain't that a pity, Mr. Davenport? *(Crosses up to below firepace. He turns to Tallant)* There's another we might have given you if Ada hadn't gone splotching. *(Haggett takes the picture from the wall and considers it)*

TALLANT *(puts old canvas on chair Left of table, then crosses up to Left of Haggett)*. Did you paint this, Miss Haggett?

ADA *(right of Haggett. Archly)*. If you can *call* it painting, I did.

TALLANT *(takes painting from Haggett)*. This lovely, living thing!

ADA. Oh, Mr. Davenport! I did take a few lessons once, but——

TALLANT. You did this little masterpiece on a few lessons?

ADA *(happily)*. It isn't no masterpiece, Mr. Davenport! At least *I* wouldn't think it was.

TALLANT. My dear Miss Haggett, don't underrate your gifts. The exquisite texture of those buttercups is not to be underrated.

ADA *(excited)*. Ma, do you hear what Mr. Davenport's saying?

TALLANT. Of course I didn't mean that you won't do better things in the future or that you won't go farther. But here, already, I, the connoisseur, sense the spark of *genius*.

DR. HAGGETT. Of genius!

TALLANT. I do indeed!

MRS. HAGGETT *(left Center)*. Now don't you go making our Ada into an artist. *(Tallant crosses down to Right of her, still holding painting. Haggett comes down to above chair Left of table)*

TALLANT *(to her)*. Of course I know you won't want to part with it, but if you'd let me buy it——

MRS. HAGGETT *(quickly)*. What's it worth?

TALLANT *(looking at it)*. That's hard to say. Her name's not known, of course, but I should think the better dealers of New York would sell a thing like this for—let me see—fifty dollars. *(Quickly)* Not that it isn't worth much more!

ADA *(right)*. Fifty dollars!

TALLANT *(quickly)*. Well, say, forty!

ADA. But I could do one like it every day.

TALLANT *(a step Right to table)*. Don't hesitate, then, Miss Haggett. Your fortune's made.

DR. HAGGETT *(crosses to Left of Mrs. Haggett. Oddly dubious)*. It strikes me kind of funny, you coming in here and paying Chris Bean's bill and then offering my daughter *forty* dollars——

MRS. HAGGETT. Fifty dollars.

DR. HAGGETT *(to her)*. He said forty.

MRS. HAGGETT. He said fifty first, and fifty's Ada's price.

TALLANT *(places picture on table)*. I will of course pay fifty dollars if you'll sell it. *(To Ada)* And you may be sure that orders for more will follow. *(Has again produced a roll of bills from his pocket and extracts several bills. Ada crosses below table, nearer him)*

DR. HAGGETT. I don't know as she ought to take it, Hannah.

ADA. But Pa! A young girl like me can spend fifty dollars even if we don't go South. *(Takes the money from Tallant)* Thank you.

TALLANT. Thank *you* for the very great

pleasure of discovering a new artist, Miss Haggett.

DR. HAGGETT (*somewhat ashamed*). She gets it all from me. I always did have a kind of weakness for *art*, even though I am a doctor.

ADA. And you got Chris Bean's picture on the other side of mine.

TALLANT (*false laugh. Picks up picture*) By Jove, so I have! Do you know—— (*Turns the picture over*) —in my enthusiasm for your work I'd quite forgotten—— (*We see that he is struck by its beauty*)

DR. HAGGETT (*a step down to below and Left of Tallant*). What do you think he was getting at that time?

ADA (*a step nearer*). Isn't that meant to be the old covered bridge up the back river?

MRS. HAGGETT (*pulls Haggett by arm so that he is in proper position to see picture*). Why don't you try looking at it right side up, Milton?

DR. HAGGETT. Looks the same to me either way. (*Then remembering. To Tallant*) I beg your pardon, Mr. Davenport. I shouldn't have said that about a dead man. (*They all look solemn*) Not with you feeling for him the way you do. (*Mrs. Haggett crosses to armchair and sits*)

ABBY (*comes downstairs and enters, still eyeing Tallant with suspicion. Above armchair*). I couldn't find a thing in the attic. There's no pictures up there of any kind.

DR. HAGGETT (*turns to her*). But I know darn well I—— (*Tallant drops the picture to his side*)

MRS. HAGGETT. Mebbe the mice have et it.

DR. HAGGETT (*a step to her*). It was on the left of the north dormer——

ABBY (*very steady*). There's nothing there now but some tin cracker boxes Mrs. Haggett's saving.

DR. HAGGETT. But I tell you I'm positive.

ABBY (*not to be shaken*). I've been over every inch of that attic, Doctor. I didn't find a thing but the old trundle bed used to be in the front room before you got the brass bed, and the trunk with your Ma's pewter in it and the other trunk——

DR. HAGGETT. I could have sworn! Well, it's too bad. That's all, Abby.

(*Turns to Tallant. Abby crosses to above desk*) I'm sorry, sir. I'd have liked to show you how much I appreciate what you've done, but there you are. No man can do better than his best. (*Abby draws back, her gaze fixed on Tallant*)

TALLANT. I'm more than satisfied with what I've *got*, Doctor Haggett. (*Turns and picks up roll of canvas from chair Left of table*) And I repeat I'm only sorry to have caused so much trouble—— (*The ladies brush his apologies aside with low exclamations. He bows*) Mrs. Haggett. Miss Haggett.

DR. HAGGETT (*crosses up to Left of Tallant and escorts him to the Left Center door*). Mr. Davenport, your call this morning is going to stand out as one of the happiest memories of my medical career!

TALLANT (*gets his hat from top of medical cabinet and puts it on*). Doctor, you and I are going to be much better acquainted. And it occurs to me that we might go into business together. (*Mrs. Haggett looks around at them*) Business which might be highly profitable to both.

DR. HAGGETT. I ain't got no capital.

TALLANT. It will require nothing more of you than—(*Laughs*) —friendly co-operation.

DR. HAGGETT (*smiles*). I got a plenty of that!

TALLANT (*they move up to front door*). Then we're rich men, Doctor Haggett, we're rich men! (*They shake hands, then Tallant exits by front door*)

MRS. HAGGETT (*rises*) Well! (*Crosses to above the table*) At this rate we'll mebbe get to Florida after all. (*Haggett returns to room and crosses to desk. Tallant is seen passing outside windows Left*)

DR. HAGGETT. Well, after this morning, I'm not so sure you won't. Wish knew what the business is he's got in mind——

ADA (*below and Right of table*). I don' care what it is if it makes us rich. (*Abby goes to window and watches Tallant*)

DR. HAGGETT (*sententiously*). Ada, that's no kind of talk for my daughter. If there's one thing I can't abide it's greed for money.

ADA. Let's get on to our marketing

Ma, before Pa gets started. *(He looks at her; turns away)*

MRS. HAGGETT. Yes, Ada, come upstairs and get your hat on. *(Starts upstairs with Ada)* If anything ever did happen to make us rich I wouldn't worry much what it was. *(Ada laughs. They disappear)*

DR. HAGGETT *(listens, standing beside his desk. He picks up his case and moves away Right a few steps, where he pauses and smiles dreamily. Suddenly he rouses himself and turns to Abby)* You seen my call book, Abby?

ABBY *(turns away from bay window, goes to desk, takes it out of drawer and gives it to him)*. Here it is, Doctor Haggett.

DR. HAGGETT *(glancing at the open page)*. I'll go out to the Jordans' farm again first. After that the rest of 'em's all in town. *(Puts it in his coat pocket)*

ABBY *(pointing to another pad on desk)* I got 'em all written down, Doctor Haggett.

DR. HAGGETT *(moves away Right a step)*. Then you know where to reach me if I'm wanted. *(Slips away again into his day-dream. Again he recalls himself, laughing apologetically)* There I go day-dreaming again. *(Crosses up Left Center)* That man Davenport's got me all off doctoring.

ABBY *(crosses to him)*. If I was you, Doctor Haggett, I'd watch him careful.

DR. HAGGETT. What makes you say that?

ABBY. Strikes me it's always a good idea to watch folks careful when they know as much as he does.

DR. HAGGETT *(testily)*. I declare, Abby, I think Mrs. Haggett's pretty near right about the way you meddle. Didn't I get a telegram from him this morning? *(Abby says nothing. He goes out into the entry, picks up hat and coat and leaves. He passes outside windows Left. Abby stands still; glances toward window and then at telegram lying on the desk; starts toward it and picks it up. Before she can read it, however, Mrs. Haggett and Ada come chattering downstairs, dressed for going out. Abby drops the telegram and quickly goes to armchair and moves it a trifle upstage)*

MRS. HAGGETT. I don't believe I'll take back that flowered foulard just yet, Ada.

ADA. Oh, I wouldn't, Ma. You heard Pa say we might get to Florida after all.

We might even get as far as California now! It's always been my dream. *(They go out front door, closing it. Abby then crosses to upstage end of desk and begins to arrange papers, books, etc., on desk, meanwhile watching Mrs. Haggett and Ada as they pass outside window Left. As they pass from sight, she again picks up the telegram. This time she reads it through, pronouncing each word inaudibly to herself. A clock strikes ten. Susan comes sobbing downstairs. Abby quickly drops telegram on desk. Susan, however, is too miserable to notice Abby, and runs sobbing and snivelling to the fireplace)*

ABBY. Susie! *(She crosses to below armchair)*

SUSAN *(picks up piece of paper by fireplace)* Oh, Abby, I never knowed I *could* be so miserable.

ABBY *(crosses to above Susan)*. Oh, folks can be awful miserable sometimes.

SUSAN *(sits Right chair and lovingly smooths out the drawing)*. But look at poor Warren's drawing, all mussed up!

ABBY. He'll make another. *(Susan looks at her)* Artists always do.

SUSAN. Abby, *you* ain't got nothing against *artists*, have you?

ABDY. Me? No! *(Crosses toward kitchen)* No! Not me—— *(Smiles to herself. The Curtain falls)*

ACT TWO

It is only a little later. The furniture is arranged exactly as in the preceding Act. There are dishes, cups and saucers, glasses and a plate of crackers on the sideboard. On the dining table is a bowl of flowers. Bright sunshine pours into the room through the windows. The Right door is closed but the Left Center entry doors are open.

As the Curtain rises, Abby crosses above the table, into the entry, and opens the front door to admit Tallant. She stands with her hand on the knob of the open door, eyeing him suspiciously.

————

ABBY. Doctor's still out making calls and Mrs. Haggett and Ada's out to market.

TALLANT *(comes into entry to Right of*

her). It was *you* I came back to see, Abby.

ABBY (*surprised*). Me? (*She eyes him more narrowly than ever, as she closes the door*)

TALLANT (*enters the room and places his hat on the medicine cabinet*). I'd like to talk to you if you can spare a moment.

ABBY (*follows to Left of him. Challengingly*). Whatever have you got to say to me? (*A pause, then he takes a step to her and puts his left hand on her right shoulder*)

TALLANT. "Thank you."

ABBY. What are you thanking me for?

TALLANT. For being kind once to a friend of mine. For giving him things that other women denied him. You gave him all the good things that have no name. All the warm, tender things he so sorely needed. (*She draws back a step. He drops his hand*)

ABBY (*really frightened*). What do you know about me?

TALLANT (*simply*). Only what he told me. Except for you, I was the best friend he ever had.

ABBY (*with swift, low intensity*). I never heard him name no Davenport. He used to talk lots about his friend Bert Davis. But I never heard of you.

TALLANT. *I'm* Davis.

ABBY (*gasps*). If you're Bert Davis, *what* are you calling yourself Davenport for?

TALLANT (*flowerly*). Davenport's my professional name. I needed a name people would remember, and Maxwell Davenport's———

ABBY (*scornfully*). If you *was* Bert Davis that wouldn't be why you changed.

TALLANT. If you know a better reason I'd like to hear it.

ABBY. Well, I do know Bert Davis got in trouble. Chris told me that he owed a lot more money than he could pay. So he skipped out of the place he was living in. Anyways, that's how Chris said it was.

TALLANT. You remember all that, do you?

ABBY. I haven't forgotten nothing Chris ever told me. (*She turns and goes to above desk*) You don't look like I expected Bert Davis to look, neither.

TALLANT (*flattering*). You look exactly as I expected you to, Abby, only younger and prettier. And I knew your name too. Don't forget that.

ABBY. Yes, that's so. (*She returns to Left of him*)

TALLANT. I don't deny I used to skip my rent. I've done it often and got in *plenty* of trouble. Wouldn't you expect that of a friend of Chris's? (*Both laugh*) I wouldn't have put it beyond Chris himself!

ABBY (*smiling*). Guess mebbe I was wrong to be so wary of you. (*She forgets her suspicions in her pleasure*) Did Chris really mention my name to you? I wouldn't have expected him to mention my name. That was nice of Chris.

TALLANT. Chris was fond of you.

ABBY. Did he say that, too?

TALLANT. Over and over. Weren't you fond of him?

ABBY. He was the only man that ever took me serious and talked to me. He didn't talk so much. But what he said was awful pithy. And to think of you being Bert Davis! It certainly is a pleasure to make your acquaintance. I never expected to meet up with you. Don't you think we better shake hands on it? (*They do*) Set down, Mr. Davis, and I'll set down with you. (*She sits in armchair. He sits Left of table*) Mrs. Haggett don't favor the help setting in the setting room, but she's cityfied that way. And she ain't home anyhow and what she don't know won't hurt her. (*Her eyes shine as they take him in*) Bert Davis! My, dont' that name bring things back, though?

TALLANT. What kind of things?

ABBY (*laughs*). Oh, this and that!

TALLANT. Chris wrote me that you were the *only one* who ever liked his painting, or got what he was after.

ABBY (*nodding with delight*). Oh, yes. I liked it! Oh, I had to learn to like it. But he taught me. Oh, he taught me lots. And there wasn't nothing about him I didn't like.

TALLANT (*lightly. Leaning forward*). If you liked his *pictures* so much, why didn't you take better care of them? Why did you let so many of them get lost?

ABBY (*draws back. Casually*). Now, I'd

rather not go into that if you got no objection.

TALLANT *(pause. Covering himself)*. He *taught* you things, you said?

ABBY. Oh, yes, he taught me. Not that he set up to be a teacher. But you couldn't be with him and not pick up a mite here and a mite there.

TALLANT. What did he teach you? I'd be interested to hear, if you remember.

ABBY *(only too eager to tell)*. Oh, I remember! It was mostly things to see, I guess. Like the rust color the marshes get this time of year when the sky gets the color of that old blue platter. *(She points to the platter on the cabinet shelf, adding proudly)* That's cobalt blue! That's a painting term, cobalt blue! *(She continues)* And he showed me the old red barn and the covered bridge that he was forever painting and I was used to all my life and never noticed. And he taught me that old chairs may be more than just old chairs to be thrown away. That some of 'em may be beautiful. He used to say them very words about the old doors in the brick houses up along the Common. That was when they began taking the old doors out and putting in new ones ordered from Sears-Roebuck. And did you know that old brick houses ain't red but mostly green and brown and that moonlight and snow ain't white at all but all kinds of colors and that elm trees is most— decorative when their leaves come off? He taught me. *(Her reminiscence becomes more personal)* He taught me that a man can get drunk and not be no different only just more so and that everybody's got more good qualities than bad. Oh, he taught me lots. And I ain't never forgotten none of it. I lived over and over that time he spent here. Over and over it ever since he died.

TALLANT *(a pause. Then, cautiously leading up to the point again)*. Did he leave you much to remember him by?

ABBY. I just now told you.

TALLANT. But I was thinking of more *substantial* things.

ABBY *(not understanding)*. Substantial— in what way?

TALLANT *(as though accepting a correction)*. You're right there. Abby. Our memories *are* the most substantial things we have. They're the only things no one can take from us. *Still*, there are other kinds—souvenirs——

ABBY *(almost to herself)*. I wonder if you're right about memories, though. I know nobody can't take 'em away from us. But what happens to 'em when we take 'em away from the place they belong in? Don't they kind of get left behind? *(Pulls her chair nearer him)* I been kind of worried about that question lately.

TALLANT. Why have you?

ABBY. Because I'm going away from here, Mr. Davis. I'm going to Chicago, this afternoon. My brother's wife died and left him with four small children, and I got to go. It's the will of God. But I don't want to go one bit. *(She laughs)* The Haggetts, they think that's on their account.

TALLANT. I shouldn't worry. You'll carry your memories with you wherever you go.

ABBY *(looks away)*. But I won't see the red barn no more, nor the brick houses, nor the covered bridge, nor the hill pasture, nor any of 'em!

TALLANT. The places he liked to paint.

ABBY. Yes. *(Leans forward)* I used to take him hot coffee while he was painting.

TALLANT. And you knitted a sweater for him.

ABBY. Did he write you about that sweater?

TALLANT. You *must* know he'd have written me everything.

ABBY. Everything about me?

TALLANT. I was his closest friend.

ABBY *(a pause, then)*. I was pretty once.

TALLANT *(playfully)*. You don't need to explain.

ABBY. I'm not ashamed. Only I'd sooner you wouldn't tell Doctor or Mrs. Haggett or the girls. You know how folks thought about him here—him being only an artist and all. And they never understood him. And they wouldn't have understood him no better for liking me. And I wanted to keep their good opinion and my place here with Doctor Haggett. But I'm not ashamed.

TALLANT. I wouldn't tell, Abby. I'd

respect your memories. But you must have things of his, too. Little sketches, for instance.

ABBY (*proudly*). I could show you something a lot better than sketches.

TALLANT. Oh? What would that be?

ABBY. He painted a picture of me life size. (*She holds her right hand up to indicate size of portrait*) It's hung over my bed all these years.

TALLANT. I should certainly like to see *that*, Abby. Abby, show me the portrait. Show it to me now.

ABBY (*rises*). I'll show it to you. It's that makes me feel worst about leaving here. (*She starts toward the kitchen*) You've got to come out to my room to see it. Out this way. (*He rises and follows her. She stops abruptly as she nears the door and turns to him*) I forgot!

TALLANT. Is somebody out there?

ABBY. That city maid who's come to take my place! I wouldn't have her see me take a man into my room where I lived fourteen years.

TALLANT (*smiles*). What harm would it do?

ABBY. She'd tell Mrs. Haggett.

TALLANT (*moves away Left a few steps*). Oh! Well, *I'd* rather the Haggetts didn't know about our talk. When can I see you again?

ABBY (*a step after him*). Where are you living?

TALLANT. *At the hotel.* Can you come there to see me?

ABBY. I'll get around after dinner.

TALLANT. And bring the portrait with you.

ABBY. What? That great big portrait?

TALLANT (*quickly*). Abby, if ever you need money—— I'm no rich man. You know that—— But I've been doing a little better these last few years, and as I say, if ever you *are* in need, I'd buy *anything* of Chris's you had to sell.

ABBY (*quickly*). Oh, I wouldn't sell nothing, Mr. Davis!

TALLANT. Not to a stranger, Abby. I know you wouldn't. But to his friend. In memory of him and the old days——

ABBY. Why, I couldn't take money for the things he left.

TALLANT. Think it over, Abby. (*He takes a step up and looks away*) I'm trying to get all his works together in one place, where they'll keep each other company.

ABBY. Is that what you're doing? (*He turns to her as she follows up a step*) Oh, I think that's just lovely of you. I couldn't sell you nothing, but I might give you——

TALLANT (*too quickly. Breathlessly*). What? The portrait?

ABBY (*startled*). Oh, I didn't mean that. I'd have to think a lot to part with that.

TALLANT (*pressing her*). Of course you would. But to his best friend!

ABBY. If it was anyone on earth but you—— (*She turns at the sound of a door closing off Right*) Here comes one of 'em through the kitchen now. (*Tallant goes up to medicine cabinet and gets his hat there as Abby crosses to Right door*)

TALLANT (*turns to her*). Abby, I'm counting on you.

ABBY. Yeah—— Better get along if you don't want 'em to see you. (*As he goes into entry Abby quickly crosses above table to him*) Mr. Davis! And don't tell nobody what you know about Chris and me. (*He pats her on her arm and exits front door. Abby re-enters room and goes to above desk*)

SUSAN (*comes quickly downstairs*). That wasn't Ma, was it?

ABBY (*startled*). No. It wasn't nobody worth mentioning. (*Warren Creamer enters Right*) Now, I haven't got no time for——

SUSAN (*sees Warren*). Watch the front, Abby! (*She goes quickly below table to Warren, who takes a few steps toward her. They embrace and kiss*)

ABBY. You're taking awful chances. You can't mix me up in this, my last day. What's he doing here? (*She moves to behind armchair*)

SUSAN. I seen him standing out by the red barn.

WARREN. I seen you wave. What was it you wanted?

ABBY. What do *you* want hanging 'round our barn? There'll be just a terrible row.

WARREN. I had something to tell her.

SUSAN. What? What was it, Warren?

WARREN. I just come to an important decision in my life.

ABBY (*advancing, interested, down to*

below and Left of them). You come to an important decision, Warren?

SUSAN *(turns to Abby)*. Watch the door, Abby.

ABBY. How can I watch the door when Warren gets me so interested?

WARREN. 'Tain't no affair of yours.

ABBY. I wouldn't *be* so interested if it was. *(She goes huffily up to window above desk)* If you don't want me to hear, though, I'll——

SUSAN. We ain't got no secrets from you, Abby. What is it, Warren?

WARREN. Harold Sherman's been after me to sell my stock and business so as he can have all the contracting 'round here. He only wants to pay me five hundred dollars——

SUSAN. Oh?

WARREN. —It ain't enough, but I made up my mind to take it! *(Abby turns and looks at them)*

SUSAN. Now, what do you want to go and do that for, Warren?

WARREN. So as I can get to New York and study art.

SUSAN. Oh, Warren! That's an awful rash step to take. *(Drops her head)* And that means you'll be going away from here.

WARREN. I wouldn't do it only on one condition.

SUSAN. What *is* the condition?

WARREN. You've got to come with me.

SUSAN. Warren, you know Ma'll never let me go. Didn't you hear the way she took on this morning?

WARREN. I wasn't figuring to let your Ma know nothing about it.

ABBY *(moves to above armchair)*. Warren Creamer! You ain't proposing to elope!

WARREN. If Susie likes me much as she says she does, she won't take no chances on letting me go off without her. *(Susan takes his hand)*.

ABBY. As if there hadn't been enough happening in this house this morning you bringing in this eloping talk and getting Susie all upset again!

WARREN. This ain't no talk. Her Ma got me good and mad this morning and I'm a-going to show her. And there ain't no use of me wasting no time about it.

SUSAN. Oh, Warren, I think you're wonderful! *(He smiles. She turns to Abby)* Don't you think so, Abby?

ABBY. He wants taking down, but I do kind of admire him for it. *(Abby moves to bay window, then back to above desk)*

WARREN. *You* give your clothes to Abby to take with her when she goes on the train to Boston tonight. Then I'll bring the truck here to fetch Abby's trunk. And you come along with me like you was seeing her off. Then I drive you out to the junction and put you on the train there. And then I meet the both of you in Boston and we get married. Guess there ain't much wrong with that scheme.

ABBY. Susie! If you listen to one more word of this, I'll tell your Ma.

SUSAN *(frightened)*. You wouldn't do that, Abby!

ABBY *(moves down to below armchair)*. Why wouldn't I? It's my bounden duty.

SUSAN *(pleading)*. You said you hadn't nothing against artists.

ABBY. Mebbe I haven't, but all the folks here have.

SUSAN. Haven't you never cared for any man, Abby?

ABBY. Do you think I'd be watching this front door now if I hadn't? *(Crosses to above table)*

WARREN. Say you'll help her, Abby.

ABBY. If I do it wouldn't be on your account, young man. When a girl gets in the state you got Susie in, she needs someone to look after her and see to it that she does get married and not just fly off the handle regardless. I've been in love! I know—— *(The doorbell rings. They freeze—all three)* Better get along now, Warren Creamer, before you get caught. *(Goes to the window above desk and looks out)*

WARREN *(a step Right)*. I'll have the truck at the door at four-thirty.

SUSAN *(moves to him)*. That early, Warren?

WARREN. That ain't too soon if Abby's taking the five-o'clock to Boston. *(The young people kiss again. Abby turns from window and sees them)*

ABBY. Susie! Stop doing that. *(To Susan)* You get upstairs and fix yourself. *(Susan runs into the entry and disappears upstairs)* If you let your Ma and Pa see you in this state——

WARREN. Four-thirty. (He exits Right, closing door)

ABBY (goes to front door). I'd like to know what's come over this house this morning. (She opens the door to admit Rosen, an oily and too affable Jewish gentleman of middle age)

ROSEN (outside). This is where Doctor Haggett lives, I believe.

ABBY. It's where he's been living for thirty tears.

ROSEN (a step inside). I wonder if I can see him for a minute?

ABBY. You could if he was here, but he ain't here.

ROSEN. Will he be long?

ABBY. I wouldn't think so very. The Haggett family's awful prompt to meals.

ROSEN. I'll come in and wait, then, if you'll allow me. (Hands her his hat and enters room)

ABBY. Watch out for the paint! (Closes front door and puts hat on hall table)

ROSEN. I'm used to paint. (Looks about the room. Abby enters and crosses to behind armchair and watches him. He turns and meets her gaze) You must be Abby.

ABBY (surprised). You don't know me!

ROSEN. No, but I've heard an awful lot about you.

ABBY (a step to him). What did you hear and where did you hear it?

ROSEN. Well, I heard you've got a kind nature and appreciate modern painting——

ABBY. That I appreciate—— (Goes to desk and sits) I'll see if I can't get the doctor on the telephone. He ought never to have left this house today! (She picks up Haggett's call book)

ROSEN. Don't hurry him, Abby. Let me enjoy myself. Well, I've seen the "old brick fronts" on the Common—— (She looks at him) ——and "the red barn" behind this house and now I've seen you. (Casually) Only I expected you to be wearing a gingham dress.

ABBY (questioning) A gingham dress?

ROSEN. You know, red and white checked gingham, the same as you used to wear.

ABBY. What do you know what I used to wear—— (Haggett, Mrs. Haggett and Ada enter front door. The two women continue on their way upstairs. Haggett places hat and

satchel on table in entry. Abby rises and crosses into entry to Left of him) Well, I'm not sorry to see you come home, Doctor. There's too much going on around here that I can't grasp I guess I'll get back to my kitchen and stay there! (She disappears into entry, passing off Right. Haggett looks after her, puzzled, then comes into the room, Left of Rosen)

ROSEN (a step up). So this is Doctor Haggett?

DR. HAGGETT (nods his head). What can I do for you?

ROSEN. My card. (Presents it. Haggett looks at it, then turns and crosses toward desk, gesturing meanwhile to chair below desk)

DR. HAGGETT. Won't you sit down, Mr. Rosen? (Rosen follows after him a few steps. Haggett stops and turns to him) A patient?

ROSEN (shakes his head). No, no, no. (Haggett then points to armchair and seats himself at his desk) Thank you. (He sits) Doctor Haggett, in the course of your professional career, you once had a patient, a young friend of mine. A painter— (Haggett pricks up his ears) A painter with whom I confess I had personal difficulties. Ten years ago his death left me with that regret we all feel in such cases. Recently I have come across some letters— (Haggett shifts his chair forward, staring at Rosen in amazement) Letters which he wrote to me while he lived under your care. They showed me how in a small way I might ease my conscience regarding him Doctor Haggett, my friend Christopher Bean died owing you one hundred dollars I have computed the interest on the unpaid bill at six percent, and the total for ten years comes to exactly one hundred and sixty dollars. Allow me to offer you my check for the sum. (He presents the check)

DR. HAGGETT (takes check—reads it then almost breathless) I thank you, sir.

ROSEN. Don't mention it. In paying this I fulfill a sacred duty to a poor devil whom I might have helped before he passed beyond all human aid. Of course know that we're all mortal, but I shall go back to New York feeling——

DR. HAGEGTT. A happier man?

ROSEN. You take the words out of my mouth, Doctor Haggett.

DR. HAGGETT. Mr. Rosen. I'm delighted to make your acquaintance and I see that artists make better paying patients than what I thought. *(As he pockets the check)* But there's a question occurs to me that I'd like to ask you.

ROSEN. Don't hesitate, Doctor Haggett! *Anything!*

DR. HAGGETT *(timorous)*. Are you, by any chance, on the point of inquiring if I haven't got *something* in the way of *pictures* poor Chris Bean left behind him that you can take away as souvenirs?

ROSEN *(protests)*. *No, no, no!* I don't do things that way. I don't come begging.

DR. HAGGETT *(with humility)*. I never said you did. I only asked you——

ROSEN *(gives him a look. Then lifting his hand so graciously)*. Well, if you'll allow me to be businesslike, I *was* on the point of asking you about any such pictures you may still have in your possession. *(Haggett sits up. (Rosen assumes a businesslike manner)* I assume, of course, that they are your property. The boy had no family and any pictures he left here, even those which he did not give you personally, may be considered security for that unpaid bill and so forfeit to you. Doctor Haggett, I'll give you a *thousand dollars* for the lot!

DR. HAGGETT *(stunned)*. A thousand dollars!

ROSEN. For the lot, understand.

DR. HAGGETT. *A thousand dollars!* For Chris Bean's pictures?

ROSEN. I can't go any higher. I hope you don't *exaggerate* their value.

DR. HAGGETT *(quite voiceless)*. A thou——

ROSEN. That is my offer. Take it or leave it. I consider it very generous.

DR. HAGGETT *(quickly)*. I'm not saying a word *against* your offer, Mr. Rosen. The only trouble is you ain't the first. There was a man here not two hours ago——

ROSEN *(leaning forward)*. With the same proposition?

DR. HAGGETT. No, not quite the same.

ROSEN. You didn't sell *him* your Christopher Bean pictures!

DR. HAGGETT. No. I gave 'em to him.

ROSEN. *What?!!*

DR. HAGGETT. There was one Chris painted of the old covered bridge—and there was another——

ROSEN *(rises. Breaks in. Clutching his brow, or the equivalent)*. You gave away "The Covered Bridge"! Doctor Haggett, you've been *swindled!*

DR. HAGGETT. You don't have to tell me that.

ROSEN. But how in God's name did you——

DR. HAGGETT. He sent me a telegram he was coming from New York.

ROSEN. What was his name?

DR. HAGGETT. I ain't much good at remembering names—— *(Fumbles through his pockets)* I ought to have his telegram some place, though. *(Sees telegram on desk and picks it up)* Here it is now. *(He reads)* "Maxwell Davenport." That was his name. Maxwell Davenport.

ROSEN *(staggered)*. Maxwell Davenport?

DR. HAGGETT. That's right. Yes.

ROSEN *(incredulous)*. You mean to say Maxwell Davenport let you *give* him——

DR. HAGGETT. I thought they wasn't no good. He *said* they wasn't.

ROSEN *(unable to believe his hearing)*. Davenport said that?

DR. HAGGETT. Yes! Davenport! Here— *(Rises and hands telegram to Rosen)* If you don't believe me! Do you know him?

ROSEN *(as he reads it)*. Do I know Davenport? Yes! Of course I know him. *(Moves away Right a step)* But I never would have believed such a thing of him. *(He sniffs the smell of powder)* Have you got witnesses?

DR. HAGGETT. I got my wife and daughter.

ROSEN *(grinning and confidential)*. Then I tell you, Doctor, this may not be so serious. *(Returns telegram to Haggett. They reseat themselves)* I think I see how we can fix Davenport. He's the art critic on the *New York Tribune*, the best we've got down in the big city and everybody's looking up to him. Now, he would hardly care to have it known what a dirty trick he played on you to get those pictures free when they're worth—a thousand dollars. So this is what *we* do. (*Rises and extracts papers from his pocket and explains. Haggett listening attentively*) I have here with me a bill of sale for what he took, all made out in advance by my lawyer. (*The doorbell rings*) You sign it and I give you my check for a thousand dollars. *Then* we get you and your wife and daughter and go down to the Court House and swear out an affidavit about every word that great art critic said. *Especially* that the pictures were no good. You leave the rest to me. (*Abby passes through the entry from Right and goes to the front door. Rosen laughs*) I think we can fix Mr. Davenport!

(*Abby admits Maxwell Davenport, an elderly and distinguished gentleman, carrying a coat on his arm.*)

DAVENPORT. Is Doctor Haggett in? He's expecting me. (*Steps into the entry. Abby shuts door. Davenport comes into room to Left of table. Haggett looks up, but Rosen silences him with a gesture and goes up Left. Abby enters to Right of Davenport*)

ABBY. He's got a gentleman with him. (*Indicates chair Left of table*) Won't you have a chair and rest yourself? (*Moves away to above table. Rosen recognizes Davenport, smiles and moves up to corner cabinet and stands with his back partly to Davenport*)

DAVENPORT (*at table*). Oh, thank you. That's very kind of you. Tell me, are you by any chance the famous *Abby*?

ABBY (*pause. Above table at the Right. Practically annihilated*). Does everybody from New York know me?

DAVENPORT. Then you *are*! What luck that you're still here! "*The Covered Bridge*," "*The Brick Houses*" on the Common, "*The Red Barn*," and now, Abby, *herself*!

ABBY (*crosses to behind chair Right of table*). Doctor Haggett, I can't stand no more folks who never saw me before in my life streaming in here and calling me by name. (*Crosses toward Right door*)

DAVENPORT. Don't be alarmed, please, Abby. (*She bursts out of the room in a panic; closes door. Davenport places his coat over the back of chair Left of table, turns and moves a few steps toward Haggett*) Is this Doctor Haggett?

DR. HAGGETT (*rises*). Yes, it is.

DAVENPORT. I'm Davenport.

MR. HAGGETT (*sharply*). Who?!!

DAVENPORT. Maxwell Davenport. I sent you a night letter yesterday from New York. Don't let me disturb you, though. (*Moves up a step as he indicates Rosen*) I'll wait outside.

DR. HAGGETT (*a step toward him*). No! No! No! Don't you go! (*Turns and crosses up to Rosen. Lowly*) Is *this* Davenport?

ROSEN (*nodding*). Yes. It's Davenport.

DR. HAGGETT. But it ain't the same!!!

ROSEN. What?!!!

DR. HAGGETT. It ain't the same, I tell you! And if this is Davenport, *who* was the other?

ROSEN (*quickly to Haggett as he calms him*). Don't say any more, Doctor Haggett! (*Confidentially*) Don't say another word! Wait till we find out where we stand. (*Pockets his papers hastily and turns, smirking*)

DAVENPORT. Rosen!! (*Rosen turns to face Davenport. Disgust*) May I ask what the devil you're doing here?

ROSEN (*crosses to Davenport*). Do you think you ought to swear at me, Mr. Davenport? You've got no cause to swear at me in public. *Print* what you like about me, but don't insult me to my face!

DAVENPORT. I might have known the scavengers would be gathering. (*Turns to Haggett, who makes a strong gesture*) I beg your pardon, Doctor, but this man, who exploits artists and treats their work like so much merchandise———

ROSEN. It's not the *artists* I exploit. It's the *customers*. And it's men like me who justify the existence of you art critics. Where would you be, writing about your *tactile* values, *limpid* shadows, your something or other highlights, if you didn't have *us* to create interest in art by building up prices?

DAVENPORT. You befoul the whole business of dealing in art with your tricks and forgeries, and— (*Rosen snorts; turns away a step. Haggett brushes him aside as he crosses up to Left of Davenport*)

DR. HAGGETT (*floundering*). Just a minute, please! This is my house and I got a right to know what's going on! (*Rosen returns to behind armchair*) You say you're Mr. Davenport. And Mr. Rosen says you are. All right, you must be. But will you please tell me what this is all about?

DAVENPORT. It's about one of the world's greatest injustices, Doctor Haggett, which I am doing my small part to set right. You once had for your patient a poor boy, a painter——

DR. HAGGETT. Yes, I know. Chris Bean.

DAVENPORT (surprised). Oh, I'm glad, Doctor, that you remember him. Now, this boy that I mention ——

DR. HAGGETT (breaks in. Points his finger on Davenport's chest). Died owing me a hundred dollars, and you come to pay it.

DAVENPORT. No, Doctor! No! Don't say that Bean owed any man anything. It is we—(Davenport taps Haggett on shoulder with his left hand)—all of us, who stand in everlasting debt to him. As the world always stands in debt to its men of genius.

DR. HAGGETT. Genius? Chris Bean a—— (Turns, moves toward desk, stops, turns and motions Davenport to be seated in armchair. Davenport sits. Haggett sits at desk)

DAVENPORT (then, more quietly). I've come to gather any details that I may find concerning his life here for a critical biography of him that I am writing.

DR. HAGGETT. You're writing a book about Chris Bean!

DAVENPORT. That is my occupation at the moment, yes.

DR. HAGGETT. Whatever gave you that idea?

DAVENPORT. Haven't you read of the sensation his pictures have been making in New York? (Rosen gives Davenport a look of annoyance. Haggett shakes his head dizzily) Haven't you seen the last Atlantic Monthly?

ROSEN (a step down, below armchair). That only came out yesterday, Mr. Davenport.

DAVENPORT. Quite! (Rosen moves to above desk and takes out cigarette case) Well, Doctor Haggett, art is long, and the world is often slow to recognize it. Only now, ten years after his death, has Christopher Bean had his first exhibition in New York. Only now do we realize that he was not merely the greatest American

painter, but one of the great masters of all times.

DR. HAGGETT. Our Chris Bean was?

DAVENPORT. Your Chris Bean, who painted and drank and—coughed his short life away here in this village. From which he wrote to his friend, Davis, alas, also dead, the exquisite group of letters published yesterday in the Atlantic Monthly. (Rosen takes out lighter and lights a cigarette)

DR. HAGGETT. Our Chris Bean! (A pause. Then turns to Rosen) So them's the letters you folks has been finding going through your desks! (Mrs. Haggett comes downstairs)

ROSEN. You guessed it, Doctor. (Haggett gives him an indignant look, turns and sees Mrs. Haggett)

DR. HAGGETT. Oh! Hannah, come in here! (Mrs. Haggett comes down to Right of Davenport, who rises) This is my wife, Mr. Davenport.

MRS. HAGGETT (stares at the name). Mr. Davenport?

DR. HAGGETT (quickly). No, don't say a word, Hannah. I'll explain later. And Mr. Rosen. (Turns to the company with fine, simple dignity) Mr. Davenport, we live a long way from New York. (Ada comes downstairs) I'm nothing but just a simple country doctor. I'll have to admit that much as I liked Chris Bean, I never would have expected him to get nowheres. (Ada slowly enters; crosses above table to Right of it)

DAVENPORT. I'm not exaggerating, Doctor, when I say that no painter of our times has got so far as he.

MRS. HAGGETT (is dumbfounded). Does this mean folks is paying money for Chris Bean's pictures?

DAVENPORT (to her). If only the dealers could find more to sell! There are so few they bring large prices even in these days.

ADA. As much as fifty dollars?

DAVENPORT. Not less than five, as much as ten thousand.

ADA. Dollars?!

MRS. HAGGETT. Each! (Ada sits above table)

DR. HAGGETT (to Rosen). And you offered me a measly thousand for the lot!

ROSEN. Remember, Doctor, I wasn't

the first and say no more. *(Haggett turns away, dazed)*

DAVENPORT. A very generous offer, for *Mr. Rosen.* I hope I arrived in time to stop his game.

MRS. HAGGETT *(a sudden scream of anguish).* God Almighty, I just remembered——

DR. HAGGETT. What?

MRS. HAGGETT. No, I won't say no more, neither. I don't feel well. *(Sits Left of table, staring in horror before her. Abby passes along entry from Right and enters the room)*

ABBY *(crosses down to above Haggett).* Here's another telegram, just come for you, Doctor Haggett.

DR. HAGGETT *(weakly).* Another telegram? *(Opens telegram. Abby goes into entry and disappears to Right)*

DAVENPORT. Now, really, Rosen, I think you might have gone higher than a thousand.

ROSEN *(pleasantly).* I'm not a rich man, Mr. Davenport. And my business is a small one.

DAVENPORT. Stick to your forgeries. They're more respectable than swindling *honest men* who aren't equipped to defend themselves. *(Turns to Haggett. Crisply)* Now, Doctor! I don't usually mix in buying and selling, but to protect you I will gladly put proper values on any *Christopher Beans* you may have.

DR. HAGGETT *(breaks in. Haggard as he looks from the telegram in his hand).* Would you mind explaining this telegram to me?

DAVENPORT. May I see it? *(Takes it. Then as he reads telegram)* Why, it's clear enough. The Metropolitan Museum— *(Looks at Haggett)*—that's in New York— offers you seven thousand five hundred dollars for the choice of your Christopher Bean canvases. *(Returns telegram to Haggett)*

DR. HAGGETT *(pause. Quietly).* Mr. Davenport, you see in me a desperate man.

DAVENPORT. Desperate, Doctor? The owner of pictures worth a fortune!

DR. HAGGETT. How do you know I got any such pictures?

DAVENPORT. From the *Atlantic Monthly.* Bean, in his letters, enumerates—*(Haggett looks up and winces)* —seven of the pictures he painted and left behind him here. "The Hill Pasture," "The Covered Bridge," "The Red Barn," "The Brick——"

DR. HAGGETT *(breaks in).* I guess I didn't take 'em as serious as I should have——

DAVENPORT. Don't reproach yourself, Doctor. You weren't the only one. *(Haggett draws in his breath and gives him an agonized look. Davenport, suddenly alarmed)* Doctor, for God's sake! You haven't let anything happen to them! *(Mrs. Haggett feels even worse)*

DR. HAGGETT *(rises. On the rack).* I must have 'em *somewheres.* There's two I can't account for just at the moment. But if he left *seven* I must have the rest. Did you ever hear of folks throwing away oil paintings? Valuable oil paintings? *(Sets his teeth grimly, rallying)* I'll have a look for 'em! I'll find 'em! And when I do, I'll pay 'em the honor they deserve. I'll hang 'em all up here in the dining room! And I don't know as I'm interested in selling 'em. Not now that I know what they're worth, I don't! At least—— *(With a glare toward Rosen)* At least, not for no small sums like I've *been offered!* *(Falls exhaustedly into his chair)* But now I'd like for you all to go away. And leave me to eat my dinner in peace, and talk matters over with my family. This is all kind of sudden. I got to think.

DAVENPORT *(still anxious).* But you'll let me come in again this afternoon?

DR. HAGGETT. What for?

DAVENPORT. Why, to get your recollections of Bean's life here. *(Turns and goes to chair where Mrs. Haggett is seated)*

DR. HAGGETT *(suffering).* After I've had my dinner.

DAVENSPORT *(tries to pick up his coat but Mrs. Haggett is seated on part of it).* Oh excuse me. *(She barely rises and does not look at him)* Thank you. *(As he moves toward Haggett he takes a copy of "The Atlantic Monthly" out of a pocket in his coat)* Let me leave this number of the *Atlantic* with you. You'll find Bean's letters in it. I brought it along for the list of pictures he mentions—*(Extends it to Haggett, then returns to Center)* —but you'll enjoy reading what he says about *you.*

DR. HAGGETT. Thanks. *(Lays the magazine on the desk)*

DAVENPORT (looks about, embarrassed). Well—good-by. (Exits front door)

ROSEN (the moment the front door closes, Rosen goes up to entry, then returns to above Haggett). Now about that man who was here before me. If you don't know his real name, what did he look like?

DR. HAGGETT. You get out too!

ROSEN (conciliatory). All right, Doctor. All right. (Goes into entry and gets his hat) But I'll be back. (Looks into room) And don't do anything final till you see me. (Goes; passes by outside window Left)

DR. HAGGETT (a pause). The one chance I ever had to make any money, and it's slipped through my fingers!

ADA (rises and goes up a step). I can't look at that spot on the wall where my picture was without just boiling.

MRS. HAGGETT. I'm going upstairs to my room to lay down. (Rises and starts for stairs wearily. Abby enters Right, closes door and crosses to Right of table. Takes flower vase to sideboard, returns to table and begins removing table-cover)

ABBY. Now that all them city folks is gone, I guess I better set the table for dinner.

MRS. HAGGETT (back to audience. Weakly). I don't want no dinner. (Abby folds the table-cover)

DR. HAGGETT (indignant). You don't! You don't! Who's to blame for this? (Abby looks up, astonished)

MRS. HAGGETT (turns to him). You can't blame me.

DR. HAGGETT. Which one of us was it took him in and gave him the old barn to paint in?

MRS. HAGGETT. You didn't have no more use for his pictures than I did.

ABBY (crosses to sideboard and opens drawer). I can't have you quarreling this way on my last day! (Puts cover in drawer)

DR. HAGGETT. Mrs. Haggett and I'll quarrel, if we want to, without any help from you, young lady.

ABBY (slams sideboard drawer shut). Doctor Haggett, you ain't never spoke to me like that before.

DR. HAGGETT (practically screaming). Get back in your kitchen. I can't stand no more talk. (Abby runs for her life, slamming right door)

ADA (by chair above table). Now, the important thing is for us not to lose our heads. There's only two things that matter. The first man wasn't Mr. Davenport. And since he wasn't, who was he?

MRS. HAGGETT (up Center). What's that matter? Your Pa gave the pictures to him.

ADA. It matters a lot. He got 'em out of Pa under false pretenses.

DR. HAGGETT (rises). That's right. He did.

MRS. HAGGETT. Then we can get 'em back.

DR. HAGGETT. If it wasn't for that fifty dollars he gave Ada.

ADA. That fifty dollars wasn't for the back side.

MRS. HAGGETT (crosses down to Right of him). You got to find him, Milton.

DR. HAGGETT. How? I don't even know what his real name is. All I know is he's gone back to New York a happier man. (Through his teeth) I'll find him somehow, though. And when I find him I'll give him a thrashing he'll remember.

MRS. HAGGETT. He's younger than you are. He'll give you the thrashing.

DR. HAGGETT (strides to and fro as he forms his plan). All right, then. I'll get a lawyer. (Crosses to desk and lifts phone) I'll get a lawyer after him and bring suit against him. (He pauses) Lawsuits cost money if you ain't sure of winning. (Drops phone) 'Tain't as though we minded parting with what he took.

MRS. HAGGETT. But he didn't know what it was worth.

DR. HAGGETT. And I called the both of you in to have a good look at an honest man. (Croaks hoarsely)

ADA. The wicked, sneaking, thieving, greedy scoundrel. It just makes me sick—that's what it does.

DR. HAGGETT (breaks in. Snatching at the straw of comfort). That's it, Ada. Our baby's said it. Hannah. It's the greed of it that turns my stomach. The greed! If Davenport ain't lying—I let that greedy crook snatch between ten and twenty thousand dollars out of my hands.

MRS. HAGGETT (crosses to him). Milton, he said he was going into business with you. Couldn't you tell him you won't have no more dealings with him unless he brings back the pictures?

ADA *(scornfully)*. Wasn't all that business talk jest to pull the *wool* over Pa's eyes?

MRS. HAGGETT *(breaks in. Returns to Left of table)*. Oh, the wicked, scheming, greedy——

ADA *(to Haggett)*. How many pictures did Chris Bean leave here? *(Mrs. Haggett's strange alarm revives)*

DR. HAGGETT. Davenport said seven.

ADA. And *you* said folks don't *throw away* oil paintings. Well, what's become of the other five?

DR. HAGGETT. That's right, Ada. *(To his wife)* Our baby's got more head than either of us. *(He calls)* Abby! Abby! Come in here! *(Abby enters Right)* Are you sure you made a thorough search of that attic?

ABBY *(in doorway. Frightened)*. Of the attic, Doctor Haggett?

DR. HAGGETT. Yes. When that first fellow came here this morning?

ABBY. Yes, Doctor Haggett.

DR. HAGGETT. And you didn't see *no* sign of no pictures up there?

ABBY. I didn't see no sign, Doctor Haggett.

DR. HAGGETT. Get out! *(Abby goes out Right as before; closes door)* Ada, you go look. *(Ada runs up the stairs. Haggett crosses up a step and calls again)* Susie!! Come down here, Susie!

MRS. HAGGETT. Now, what do you want with Susie? *(Sits Left of table)*

DR. HAGGETT *(moves down to his desk)*. We ain't asked Susie yet. She may know something.

SUSAN *(comes downstairs and enters to Upper Right. Frightened)*. What is it, Pa? What do you want?

DR. HAGGETT *(below armchair)*. Have you seen any old pictures of Chris Bean's laying around?

SUSAN *(relieved)*. Oh, is that all? *(Moves away toward above table)*.

DR. HAGGETT *(crosses to Left of her)*. "Is that all? Is it that *all?*" Don't talk like a fool!

SUSAN *(turns to him)*. Pa, what's come over you, hollering this way?

DR. HAGGETT. Answer my question.

SUSAN. Yes, of course I have.

MRS. HAGGETT. *What?!* *(Simultane-*
DR. HAGGETT. *Where!?* *ously)*

SUSAN. Last time I seen 'em they was in the barn. *(Mrs. Haggett seems on the point of fainting)*

DR. HAGGETT. In the *barn!*

SUSAN. Yes, Pa.

DR. HAGGETT. How many?

SUSAN. I don't know rightly. Eight or ten, I guess.

DR. HAGGETT. *Eight* or ten!

SUSAN. Yes, they was in the old box stall.

DR. HAGGETT. I'm in and out of that barn all day long. *(Moves away a few steps)* Taking the Ford out and putting it up again. *I* ain't seen no pictures! *(Returns to Susan)* When did you see 'em last?

SUSAN. I couldn't have been so long ago. *(Then guiltily)* I remember showing 'em to Warren Creamer.

DR. HAGGETT *(wildly excited)*. Aha! Then that's what's become of 'em. Warren Creamer's stole 'em.

SUSAN *(indignant)*. He ain't! He wouldn't!

DR. HAGGETT. They was in the barn. You showed 'em to Warren. They ain't there now and I'd have seen 'em. Warren *must* have stole 'em.

SUSAN. No!

DR. HAGGETT. *You* get your Warren over here this minute. No! Here! *I'll get* him. *(Crosses quickly to desk and sits)*

SUSAN *(follows quickly to Right of him)* Pa! Please!—— *(He snatches up the phone)*

MRS. HAGGETT *(suffocating)*. It ain't no use, Milton.

DR. HAGGETT. Why ain't it? *(Turns to her)*

MRS. HAGGETT. Warren didn't steal 'em.

DR. HAGGETT. How do you know he didn't?

MRS. HAGGETT *(pause)*. I burnt 'em.

DR. HAGGETT *(pause, as he looks at her speechless with horror. Rises)*. You what?

MRS. HAGGETT. I put 'em on the bonfire and burnt 'em.

DR. HAGGETT. All eight or ten?

MRS. HAGGETT. I'd have thought there was more.

DR. HAGGETT *(no longer able to control himself)*. You'd have thought there was more. At ten thousand and over for every one. You'd have thought there was more.

MRS. HAGGETT. You thought they were *terrible pictures too*, Milton.

DR. HAGGETT (*screaming*). *Don't keep on saying that!* (*Drops into his chair*) You ought to get down on your knees, Hannah, and beg forgiveness of both your children. (*After a moment his eye falls upon the "Atlantic Monthly" lying on his desk. He picks it up and begins to glance through it*)

ADA (*comes down the stairs and enters to Left of Mrs. Haggett*). Abby was right. There isn't a single picture in the attic.

MRS. HAGGETT. Your Pa knows that. There ain't none anywheres. (*Apologetic*) They took up so much room I burnt the lot.

ADA (*a pause*). *You never!* Then we'll have to get to work and get back that pair we gave away this morning! (*Haggett holds up his hand for attention. Ada turns to him*) Pa!—— (*Breaks off as she sees his outstretched hand. Susan moves nearer to Haggett*)

DR. HAGGETT (*reading aloud*). "Doctor H. takes conscientious care of me. He knows nothing of medicine but looks like a gargoyle and that amuses me."

SUSAN (*frightened*). What's he saying, Ma?

DR. HAGGETT. Doctor H. is me! That's what Chris Bean wrote about me in his letters. (*He continues reading*) "I beg him to let me do a portrait of him, but all my pleading avails me nothing. His notions of art belong to the lower animals."

MRS. HAGGETT. Mebbe if you'd let him paint your portrait you'd be better off now. You wouldn't have used no portrait of *yourself* to patch the chicken-house roof.

DR. HAGGETT (*loftily extending the magazine to Susan*). You can read the rest, Susie. Mebbe he says something kind about your Ma. (*Susan takes magazine and sits in armchair. Ada crosses to above chair and leans over Susan's shoulder*)

SUSAN (*reading*). "This angel of devotion is both sister and nurse to me, and more than both. I know that her care is adding months to my life, all the more because she, and only she, sees merit in what I paint. She is the single comfort I have found in my life here and in her own way she is beautiful."

MRS. HAGGETT (*Her smile broadens*). Well, I liked the boy and I encouraged him.

ADA (*reading over her sister's shoulder*). But, Ma! That ain't *you*. Its' *Abby!* (*Mrs. Haggett's smile fades. Ada reads on*) "When I go into the fields these chill autumn mornings, she brings me out hot coffee to drink."

MRS. HAGGETT. *Our* coffee.

DR. HAGGETT (*slowly*). It don't matter now.

MRS. HAGGETT. It matters to me that a man I took kindly to carried on behind my back with the help.

SUSAN. But Ma, it don't say that.

MRS. HAGGETT. It says she was beautiful. She never was.

DR. HAGGETT (*springing to his feet again*). Good God Almighty!

ADA. Pa!

SUSAN. What is it?

MRS. HAGGETT. You hadn't ought to screech that way, Milton!

(*Simultaneously*)

DR. HAGGETT. Chris Bean did paint one portrait while he was here. I remember he did.

ADA. Who did he paint it *of*?

DR. HAGGETT. Of Abby! (*Sensation*)

MRS. HAGGETT. That's so, he did!

ADA. It's a great *big* portrait.

DR. HAGGETT. What's become of it?

MRS. HAGGETT. She's had it hanging in her room ever since he died.

DR. HAGGETT. Ada, go in and see if it's still there. (*Ada crosses above table on her way to kitchen*)

SUSAN (*quickly*). But, *Pa*, if it is, it must belong to Abby. Ada, wait—— (*Ada stops above table and turns to them. Haggett goes to Susan and bends over her*)

DR. HAGGETT (*savagely*). Here we are, at the worst crisis of the Depression, with a fortune in the house and you try to tell me it belongs to Abby! Is Abby capable of knowing what that picture's worth?

MRS. HAGGETT (*angrily*). Susie! I'm surprised at you, after your Pa's just been swindled himself this morning!

ADA. I think it's about time Pa stood

up for his rights. *(Haggett paces up and down behind armchair)*

SUSAN. But that picture's Abby's rights.

DR. HAGGETT *(to Susan, loud and querulous)*. I ain't going to do nothing that ain't fair and square —*(Then quietly as he bends over her again)*—and don't talk so loud. Do you want Abby to hear?

SUSAN *(rises)*. Well, I *won't* stand by and see you take advantage of Abby. *(She flashes out into entry and upstairs. Haggett takes several steps after her as if to stop her)*

MRS. HAGGETT *(rises and crosses to him)*. Never mind her, Milton! We got one thing, and one thing only, to do now. And that is find out if Abby's planning to take that portrait to Chicago with her.

DR. HAGGETT. Call her in and ask her.

ADA. She'd get on to you.

DR. HAGGETT. That's right. Not that we got anything shameful to conceal, but she would get on to us.

MRS. HAGGETT. If it was me I wouldn't hesitate. I'd walk right into Abby's room and take that picture like it wasn't no account.

DR. HAGGETT *(crosses to swivel chair)*. There's a point of conscience here. I got to think. *(Sits)*

MRS. HAGGETT *(follows to Right of him)*. Shut your eyes, Milton. You know you always think best with your eyes shut. *(He has obeyed)* That's right. *(Slight pause)* Now—what?

DR. HAGGETT. Well, one way of looking at it the portrait is *our* property, too. Abby's no artist's model. She's our help. We was paying her thirty dollars a month and keep——

MRS. HAGGETT. We only paid her fifteen in those days——

DR. HAGGETT. The principle's the same. And the question is, did she have any *right* to let him paint it on the time we paid for?

MRS. HAGGETT. Your conscience is clear. Milton. There ain't no doubt but that portrait belongs to us. *(Crosses to Left of Ada)* Ada, go into Abby's room and get it.

ADA. But what will Abby say?

MRS. HAGGETT *(giving her imagination free rein)*. Wreck the room! Tear down the window curtains! Turn the bed over! Then your Pa can tell her a *burglar* must have got it.

DR. HAGGETT *(breaks in. Uncomfortably)*. I'm only a simple country doctor. I don't care for money. It's only for my loved ones I got to have it .

MRS. HAGGETT *(to him)*. We've got to get a move on! *(She pushes Ada ahead of her as they both go to Right door)* Go along, Ada. Take it out the back way and upstairs. *(Ada goes out Right. Mrs. Haggett closes door and crosses below table to Left of it)* Once we get it we'll hide it under your bed.

DR. HAGGETT *(to himself)*. If Abby feels bad I can give her a little something.

ADA *(returns; closes door)*. Abby's out there.

MRS. HAGGETT. How about the picture?

ADA. That's there too.

DR. HAGGETT *(rises)*. What's it like?

ADA. You know. Terrible!

DR. HAGGETT. Well, it's some comfort to know it's still all right.

MRS. HAGGETT. What's Abby doing?

ADA. Packing her trunk.

MRS. HAGGETT. Tell her she ought to be getting dinner ready.

ADA. But if she stays out there in the kitchen—

MRS. HAGGETT. Tell her to come in and set the table.

ADA. You call her. *(Ada moves to below sideboard. Haggett reseats himself. Mrs. Haggett looks at him for approval. He gestures for her to "go ahead")*

MRS. HAGGETT *(in her sweetest tones as she crosses below table to Right door)*. Abby! *(Opens door)* Abby! *(Closes door and turns to her husband)* You got to talk to her. *(Moves to Right of table. All Three watch Center door. Abby enters, still in a state of terror)*

DR. HAGGETT *(sits swivel chair. An heroic effort at play-acting)*. I'm sorry spoke so rough to you just now, Abby

ABBY *(crosses to below chair Right of table Eyeing him askance)*. Oh, that's all right

MRS. HAGGETT *(also play-acting)*. No Abby. Doctor Haggett couldn't rest til he'd apologized. *(Gets the tablecloth from drawer in the sideboard)*

ABBY *(eyeing her)*. It's all right.

MRS. HAGGETT (drops folded cloth on table). And you can go ahead now and set the table for dinner.

ABBY. Yeah. (Proceeds to spread the cloth. Mrs. Haggett nods to Ada, who slips into the kitchen, then Mrs. Haggett moves over to Right door, closes it and blocks it)

DR. HAGGETT (as before). It's nice of you to wait on us your last day, Abby.

ABBY. Oh, it's nothing.

MRS. HAGGETT (as before). Yes, it is, Abby. And we appreciate it. Doctor Haggett and me, with the new maid here and all.

ABBY. It's nothing. (Crosses to sideboard drawer and takes out napkins)

DR. HAGGETT. It wouldn't have seemed natural to have the new maid waiting on the table with you still in the house, Abby.

ABBY. No, I guess not. (Returns to table; places napkins on it)

ADA (returns. A whisper). Ma! The new maid's there!!

MRS. HAGGETT. Tell her to go out and take a walk around the village. (Ada turns to door) And Ada—— (Ada turns to her Mother) Never mind the burglar. (Ada exits Right; closes the door)

ABBY (left of table). What about a burglar——

MRS. HAGGETT (laughs). No, Abby, it's just a little joke between—you'll hear about it later. (Haggett laughs. Abby crosses below table toward kitchen) Where're you going, Abby?

ABBY. Just out to the kitchen to get the mustard pickles.

MRS. HAGGETT (blocking door. Pleasantly). Oh, I don't think we need mustard pickles for dinner. Do you think we do, Milton?

DR. HAGGETT. I'll be frank with you Abby, them mustard pickles don't seem to set good with me. (Abby starts again for the kitchen. He rises and moves to Center) Abby! (She stops and turns back again) Didn't you hear us, Abby? We said we didn't care for mustard pickles.

ABBY. I was going to get some watermelon preserves. You always liked my watermelon preserves.

MRS. HAGGETT (stumped). That's so, Milton! You always have liked them particular.

DR. HAGGETT (breaks in, likewise stumped). I know I have. And I can't think of a thing against 'em now.

MRS. HAGGETT (helpful). I thought you wanted to talk to Abby, Milton?

DR. HAGGETT. That's right, Hannah, I did.

ABBY (a step to him). What was it you wanted to talk to me about?

DR. HAGGETT (at a total loss). Well, about several things. Let me see, now. To begin with, I——

ADA (returns. A whisper). Ma!

MRS. HAGGETT. What is it?

ADA. She says she don't want to take a walk.

MRS. HAGGETT. Tell her either she takes a walk or goes back to Boston. (Ada exits Right; closes door)

ABBY (turns to Mrs. Haggett). Back to Boston?

DR. HAGGETT (quickly). I know what it was I wanted to talk about, Abby. It was about that new maid. What do you think of her?

ABBY. Oh, she's a nice girl.

DR. HAGGETT. Of course she's a nice girl. A very nice girl. Mrs. Haggett wouldn't have chosen anything else. (He becomes confidential) But, Abby—think now—think carefully. Will she give the same satisfaction you've given us.

ABBY. Now, that's real kind of you to say that, Doctor Haggett. Of course, in fairness you got to remember I had fifteen years to study your manners and ways. And I'm not saying she'll be on to the way you like your chowder nor things like that without being told. But she's a nice girl, and if she finds she likes the place enough——

MRS. HAGGETT. Don't you think she will, Abby?

ABBY. Well, mebbe she will and mebbe she won't, Mrs. Haggett. I'll get dinner on the table first and talk afterwards. (Again she starts for Right door. He takes a step after her, helplessly)

MRS. HAGGETT. But, Abby, you ain't even got the table set!

ABBY (brushing Mrs. Haggett aside). I know, but I can't stand here talking with my biscuits burning up. *(Goes into kitchen; closes door)*

MRS. HAGGETT. Why didn't you stop her?

DR. HAGGETT. How could I? Why didn't you stop her?

MRS. HAGGETT. You seen me try, didn't you? Now you'll just have to face it. It was a cowardly way to get round her, at that.

DR. HAGGETT. It was your idea. I never would have done it. *(Susan comes downstairs enters room to up Center and regards them distastefully)*

MRS. HAGGETT. Keep quiet! Listen! *(Listens at Right door)*

DR. HAGGETT. Can you hear anything?

MRS. HAGGETT. Not a sound!

DR. HAGGETT. Ada must be in the room now. She'll come out with the picture in her hands and Abby—— Hannah, go out there and do something——

MRS. HAGGETT. I can't! You go yourself! *(Phone rings. Haggett turns and moves Left a step).*

DR. HAGGETT. I got to answer.

MRS. HAGGETT. No, you don't. Susie, you answer that. *(He stops. Susan crosses toward desk. Just as she nears it Phone rings again)*

DR. HAGGETT *(to his wife).* Call her back in here. I'll talk to her some more.

MRS. HAGGETT. What have you got to talk to her about?

SUSAN *(into the phone).* Hello.

DR. HAGGETT. Let me think. *(Sits below table)* Don't hurry me. I'll think of something.

SUSAN *(into the phone).* Yes?

MRS. HAGGETT *(a step to him).* You can't take all day.

SUSAN. What?

MRS. HAGGETT *(continuing).* —Once she catches Ada——

DR. HAGGETT. I'll ask her not to leave.

SUSAN. This is Doctor Haggett's.

DR. HAGGETT *(continuing).* —That's what I'll do! I'll plead with her——!

MRS. HAGGETT. No! Than she might not leave. And if she doesn't *leave* it will be twice as hard.

DR. HAGGETT *(breaks in).* Call her.

I'll think of something. *(Ada returns, tottering; leaves door open)*

MRS. HAGGETT *(starts to call).* Ab——! *(Her voice catches as she sees Ada. Ada crosses to Right of Haggett. Mrs. Haggett rushes to door and closes it)*

SUSAN *(into phone).* Just a minute. I'll call him.

MRS. HAGGETT *(turns to Ada).* Did you get it?

ADA *(gasping, her hand on her heart).* No!

DR. HAGGETT. She didn't catch you?

SUSAN. Pa!

ADA. No. But if the biscuits hadn't been burning she would have caught me. I was just lifting it off the hook when I looked over my shoulder and there she stood with her head in the oven.

SUSAN. Pa! *(Haggett gestures for Susan to be quiet)*

MRS. HAGGETT. We'll just have to try again. *(Susan puts receiver down, and moves away Right a step)* We'll eat dinner quiet as if nothing happened. I'll send her out on an errand. Come on, Ada. We'll finish setting the table. *(She turns to upstage end of sideboard and begins taking silverware out of a drawer. Ada goes to lower end and gets a stack of soup plates)*

SUSAN. When you're done plotting and whispering over there, New York's calling Pa.

MRS. HAGGETT *(at sideboard. Turns).* New York—again!

SUSAN. I can't get the name. It sounds to me like Knoedler & Company.

DR. HAGGETT *(very agitated).* I won't speak to him! I won't speak to no more from New York! Tell him I'm out! Tell him I've gone away! Tell him—— *(Mrs. Haggett crosses and places silverware on table)*

SUSAN. You can tell your *own* lies, Pa! *(Moves to above armchair. Ada brings plates and glasses to table)*

DR. HAGGETT. All right, I will. *(Rises and crosses to desk; takes phone and sits)* A lot of help I get from you, young lady *(Mrs. Haggett and Ada continue setting the table mechanically, straining to hear every word)* Hello—— Yes. This is Doctor Haggett—— Who?—Go ahead—— Can' hear you—— What——? "The Covere

Bridge"? *(A pause) How* much? *(Mrs. Haggett and Ada pause and listen intently)* How much? *(Another pause. Then, dully)* I'll think it over. Call me tomorrow. *(Rings off, dazed)*

MRS. HAGGETT *(by chair Left of table. Stammering)* What—what is it, Milton?

DR. HAGGET *(weakly)*. He wants to pay me twelve thousand dollars for Chris Bean's picture of "*The Covered Bridge*" if it's in good condition—— *(A desperate echo)* In *good* condition! *(Then hysterically)* Can you beat that? In *good* condition.

MRS. HAGGETT *(leans on the table. Also hysterical)*. Twelve thousand! Twelve thou——!

ADA *(above table, also hysterical)*. That's the one I painted my picture on the back of and sold for *fifty dollars!*

DR. HAGGETT *(screaming)*. I know it is! *(Abby enters Right, carrying a soup tureen)*

ABBY. Well, I got dinner ready, folks. You can set down! *(She places the tureen at Mrs. Haggett's place on the Right side of the table. She then moves to the Right a few steps. The Haggetts fail to stir)* You can all set down. Dinner's ready—— *(She eyes them with surprise).*

(Finally the Haggetts move mechanically, as though under a spell, toward their respective places at the table. Mrs. Haggett goes below the table to her chair on the Right. Ada goes to her place below the table. Susan sits above table and Haggett sits Left of table. Susan is the only one who unrolls her napkin. Then she and Ada both lean forward on the table, staring down dejectedly. Mrs. Haggett removes the lid of the tureen and hands it to Abby, who has taken a position at the table between Mrs. Haggett and Susan. Abby takes the lid to the sideboard and places it there. She then returns to the same position at the table. Mrs. Haggett slowly serves the first bowl of soup and hands it to Abby, who solicitously places her other arm about Susans' shoulder and bends over to serve her. Susan, however, pushes the plate away. Then Abby hands it to Haggett, who has been following her every move with great concentration. Startled, he takes it very quickly. Mrs. Haggett hands the next bowl to Abby, who goes to Ada, who seems unaware of Abby's presence at her side. Abby, vexed at the strange behaviour of the Haggetts, slaps Ada roughly on the shoulder. Ada then sits

back and Abby places the bowl before her. However, neither Haggett nor Ada touch the soup. Mrs. Haggett does not serve herself but drops her head in her hands in despair. Abby looks at them queerly, then goes to the sideboard and gets a plate of crackers and returns to the table. More mystified than ever, she bends over and peers into Mrs. Haggett's face; looks at Haggett, who invokes the blessing)*

CURTAIN

ACT THREE

AT RISE: *The afternoon of the same day is well advanced. Furniture retains same arrangement as in the preceding Act. Sunshine of less brightness still pours into the room.*

Davenport is discovered standing at the fireplace with his back to the audience, waiting for Hagget's return. Susan comes downstairs and enters the room to up Center.

————

SUSAN. How do you do?

DAVENPORT *(turns)*. Oh, how do you do?

SUSAN. We haven't met, Mr. Davenport. I'm the other daughter, Susan. Ma said for me to apologize for keeping you waiting so long. Pa went out after dinner. We don't know where he is nor what's become of him.

DAVENPORT *(crosses to just Right of her)* I don't mind waiting and if your father's errand is what I hope it is, I pray it may prove successful.

SUSAN *(a step to him)*. Yes. Well, seeing as you aren't doing much at the moment I've got a kind of a funny *favor* to ask you.

DAVENPORT Please!

SUSAN *(quickly)*. You wouldn't tell Ma or Pa I asked it, would you?

DAVENPORT *(smiles)*. I can keep a secret.

SUSAN. I was thinking of eloping this afternoon.

DAVENPORT. My dear child!

SUSAN. Yeah. And it's just providential *you* turning up today because all I need's an *art critic.*

DAVENPORT. If you're counting on me to break the news to your parents——

SUSAN (quickly). Oh, nothing like that!

DAVENPORT. Suppose you explain more fully, then. There's always some reason for an elopement. Either that the man's married or that the girl's father and mother don't approve of him.

SUSAN. That's *my* reason. Why don't they?

DAVENPORT. Why don't they?

SUSAN. Because he's an artist and they got no use for artists.

DAVENPORT. Is he a *good* artist?

SUSAN (seriously). He thinks he is, but I'm not fit to judge. So I thought you'd mebbe run around and look at his pictures and tell me what you think.

DAVENPORT (sadly). You're a Yankee, too!

SUSAN. What do you mean by that?

DAVENPORT. Well, I naturally conclude that if his pictures don't measure up, you'll think twice before you marry him.

SUSAN (with determination). Oh, I'd have him anyways! I'd have him if he was the most terrible painter in the world! I just want to know the *worst* for my own information!

DAVENPORT. I see you belong to the *higher* type of Yankee.

SUSAN. I don't understand.

DAVENPORT. Fearless of both risk and reality.

SUSAN. No, I only want to know whether he ought to paint pictures or houses.

DAVENPORT (laughs). Let it pass. I warn you that if I don't like the pictures——

SUSAN. Don't tell him.

DAVENPORT. Are you wise to want to know the truth yourself?

SUSAN. I'll show you I'm not afraid. (Goes to above desk and picks up the two paintings brought in by Warren in Act I) I've got two of Warren's pictures here. (Moves a step down and Left) They're only little ones, so they don't do him justice. (Returns to Left of him) But you can tell me what you think right to my face. (Extends them for his inspection) This one's my dead duck and this one's my sister's salmon.

DAVENPORT (takes them). Let's see.

(He examines first one, then the other) Curious! Very curious!. (He turns to Susan) I'd certainly say a pupil of Christopher Bean's.

SUSAN. Yes, he was. When he was a little boy, thirteen years old. But he's been painting on his own ever since.

DAVENPORT. Oh, they've got their own individuality, too.

SUSAN. Does that mean they're bad?

DAVENPORT. No, no, it means they make me want to see *more* of his work. And to meet him. (Hands pictures back to her)

SUSAN. That's easy! (Replaces pictures above desk) I'll show you where! I'll take you! Will you come now? (Returns to him) You see, there isn't much time!

DAVENPORT. At what time *is* the elopement?

SUSAN. At four-thirty. So I can catch the Boston train with Abby.

DAVENPORT. Is Abby leaving too? (Haggett enters through the front door)

SUSAN. Yeah. Abby's going to Chicago, and—— (Puts out her hand to warn him) Shhh! Here's Pa! (Haggett enters room, haggard; gives them a look of agony; crosses to clair Left of table and sinks wearliy into it) Why, Pa! What's the matter? Where have you been?

DR. HAGGETT. I've been around. (A pause)

SUSAN. You look awful.

DR. HAGGETT. I feel awful.

DAVENPORT. Oh—yes——

SUSAN. I'm just taking Mr. Davenport out to see the village, Pa.

DR. HAGGETT. Yes, take him out.

SUSAN (to Davenport). You don object? (They turn and start for the fro door)

DAVENPORT. No, your young ma should certainly have things to tell me. must talk with Abby, too, before sh leaves. (They both get their coats and he from table in entry)

SUSAN (gaily). You'll have plenty time to see Abby. It's just across t street.

DAVENPORT. Which way, left or righ

SUSAN. This way, Mr. Davenpo (They exit front door and to Right. Mrs. H *gett comes in from the kitchen and crosses to below chair Right of table)*

MRS. HAGGETT. Well, Milton?

DR. HAGGETT. I been all over. Up to the hill pasture. Down to the covered bridge. Up to the *graveyard.*

MRS. HAGGETT. What'd you go *there* for?

DR. HAGGETT. Looking for that scoundrel who robbed me this morning.

MRS. HAGGETT. You didn't think he'd died and *buried* himself, did you?

DR. HAGGETT. He's still there. Painting somewhere.

MRS. HAGGETT. Painting?

DR. HAGGETT. I found out that much at the hotel. He checked in there this morning and he ain't checked out!

MRS. HAGGETT. Well, if the pictures are in his room, why didn't you get them?

DR. HAGGETT. He took 'em to the bank. They're in the vault. The bank wouldn't let me have 'em. Now he's gone out again. He's got his lunch and painting things with him. His name's Tallant.

MRS. HAGGETT. Tallant. With two "L's" or one?

DR. HAGGETT *(looks up to her).* Two *(He calls)* Abby! *(To his wife)* I've been running and running all afternoon. *(Abby enters Right. Mrs. Haggett crosses to above table).* Bring me a cracker and a glass of milk.

ABBY. Wouldn't you like something hot, Doctor Haggett?

DR. HAGGETT. I got no time for anything hot. *(Abby returns to the kitchen; closes the door)*

MRS. HAGGETT. There was three more telephone calls from New York while you was out. *(Crosses toward desk)* and there's seven more telegrams that come——

DR. HAGGETT *(testily, as he turns to her).* got no time for telegrams neither. *(Mrs. Haggett stops by lower end of desk.)* Look! *She turns to him. Pathetically he holds up his trembling hand)* This kind of thing is not good for no man of my age. This morning was a peaceful country doctor filled with gentle thoughts of a medical description and I coveted nothing, not even my collections. Look at me now. *(The shaking*

hand again)* Hannah, if a patient came in with an appendix now I'd miss it so far I'd put his eye out! *(Concludes desperately)* Once you get *started on* a thing like this, though— Once you let it get a *hold* on you——

MRS. HAGGETT *(crosses to back of him. Exasperated).* Oh, stick to business.

DR. HAGGETT. That's what I'm doing. *I* remembered Abby leaves at five o'clock, and we can't let her take that portrait with her. It's the *only* one we can be *sure* to get our hands on.

MRS. HAGGETT. You'll have to work on her, then. I ain't up to no more today.

DR. HAGGETT. That's just I come back home to do. Leave it to me. You started it, but I got to finish it. I got everything all thought out. *(Abby enters Right with glass of milk and a cracker; closes door)* I thank you, Abby. *(She crosses to above table; places glass before him)* That's just what I need.

ABBY. But I got a nice pork chop I could heat up for you.

DR. HAGGETT *(shudders).* Look! *(He shows Abby his hand. Mrs. Haggett goes up to window above desk and looks out)*

ABBY. I never seen you in such a state, Doctor Haggett. It's all them New York folks coming here.

DR. HAGGETT *(deep self-pity).* And they're all coming back any minute, too.

ABBY. Why do you bother with 'em, Doctor Haggett?

DR. HAGGETT. Can't avoid responsibilities in this life, Abby. *(With unaccountable intention)* Wouldn't mind so much if this room looked right. It's that *patch* over the fireplace where Ada's picture was. *Mrs. Haggett crosses to below armchair)*

ABBY *(a step up to fireplace).* I'll wash off where it's smoked.

DR. HAGGETT. No. There isn't time.

MRS. HAGGETT. You could hang one of Warren Creamer's pictures—— *(Points to pictures at upstage end of desk)*

DR. HAGGETT. No, Hannah! Warren's pictures ain't big enough for that. What we need is something to cover up the *whole* place. A *big* picture.

ABBY. Well, then, I—— *(Starts for kitchen. He stops her. She turns)*

DR. HAGGETT *(as though a thought struck*

him suddenly). Abby, ain't you got a picture Chris Bean painted of you before he died? *(Mrs. Haggett starts)*

ABBY. I got my portrait.

DR. HAGGETT. Well, if that isn't just the thing! We'll hang *that* there.

ABBY. Oh, Doctor Haggett!

DR. HAGGETT. Just till you go.

ABBY. I'd like very much to oblige. I certainly would like to oblige. But, Doctor—— *(Is covered with embarrassment)* Why, I couldn't have my picture hanging in there. It wouldn't look right.

DR. HAGGETT. Why wouldn't it?

ABBY. What'll people say if they come into your dining-room and seen a picture of me hanging there scraping carrots?

DR. HAGGETT. What do I care what people'd say? Ain't this a democracy? I'd rather have you there scraping carrots than half these society women who can't do nothing.

ABBY. But my portrait hasn't even got no frame, Doctor Haggett.

DR. HAGGETT. That don't matter, either. Anything to cover up that patch!

MRS. HAGGETT *(crosses to chair above table. Joining in persuasively).* Don't refuse him, Abby!

DR. HAGGETT *(piteously).* Look, Abby! *(Holds up his trembling hand again)*

ABBY. I never could say "no" to Doctor Haggett. *(Goes out Right; closes door. They catch each other's eyes)*

DR. HAGGETT. A much better way than stealing it would have been. This has got to be done. But it's got to be done *legitimate.*

MRS. HAGGETT. She ain't give it up to you yet.

DR. HAGGETT. She will—— Only you can't take more than one step at a time. I got it all thought out.

ABBY *(returns, carrying portrait; closes door; crosses to chair Right of table and props portrait against it. Back of portrait facing audience).* Well, here it is!

DR. HAGGETT *(rises).* That's very nice of you, Abby. I appreciate that.

ABBY. It'd look better if it had a frame.

DR. HAGGETT. There's no time for frames either.

MRS. HAGGETT *(to Haggett).* That pic-

ture of your Ma in the upstairs hall's about the size of this, and it's got a beautiful frame.

ABBY. Why don't you hang that up?

MRS. HAGGETT. No, she's been dead so long, she's just as happy in the upstairs hall. *(Haggett turns and goes up a few steps as though he were going for the frame)* You go and get it, Abby.

ABBY. But I wouldn't want for Doctor Haggett to take the frame off his Ma's picture.

DR. HAGGETT *(moves down again).* It gives me real pleasure, Abby, to show you this little mark of my esteem.

ABBY *(covered with confusion).* But my picture'll look too dressed up in that frame.

DR. HAGGETT *(with great dignity).* Abby, if I put my mothers' frame around your picture, it's not for you to say that it isn't fitting.

ABBY *(apologetically).* I didn't mean no offense, Doctor Haggett. I guess you know best. *(She crosses above table and goes upstairs. Mrs. Haggett looks at the portrait)*

DR. HAGGETT *(to himself.* I said I'd pay her something, and I will. I'll give her twenty-five dollars.

MRS. HAGGETT *(shakes her head in negation).* You'll *never* get your money back.

DR. HAGGETT *(moves to above table).* I ain't for you, who burnt up a fortune, to fret me for risking twenty-five dollars *(Looks at portrait)* I'll be frank with you though. If it hadn't been for them telegrams and telephone calls, I wouldn't be risking twenty-five cents on it.

MRS. HAGGETT *(bends over).* Look at that dab of red on the nose, will you. And the hands is blue.

DR. HAGGETT. Mebbe she just done the wash. *(Bends over to examine it closely)* What's that she's holding?

MRS. HAGGETT. A knife. She scraping carrots.

ABBY *(comes downstairs, carrying a large oldfashioned frame).* Well, here it is. I feel so embarrassed, Mrs. Haggett. *(Enters and moves toward Left side of table. Haggett turns and crosses to her)*

DR. HAGGETT. Oh, that's too heavy for you, Abby. *(Takes part of the frame and helps her place it face down on the table)*

MRS. HAGGETT *(inaudibly)*. I'll just clear these away—— *(She quickly takes the bowl of flowers and glass of milk to sideboard. Then she returns to Right side of table)*

DR. HAGGETT. Now! We'll see if it fits. *(Lifts the painting and places it face down into the frame. He then uses his fist to hammer stretcher into place. Both Abby and Mrs. Haggett crowd about him, aiding him)*

ABBY. Take care not to scratch yourself on them rusty nails.

DR. HAGGETT. Oh, that wouldn't matter now, Abby.

MRS. HAGGETT. Oh, it's too small.

DR. HAGGETT *(quiets her)*. No, Hannah, it's a little tight up there, maybe. That's funny! It was always *loose* on Ma. *(They finally get the painting set firmly in the frame)* Look! Now, wouldn't you say that frame had just been made for it? *(Picks up frame as he moves above table to Left of it and leans the frame against table, with back of picture to audience. He backs away a few steps)* Now we'll just have a look. *(The effect is admired, too warmly, by the Haggetts, ecstatically by Abby)*

ABBY *(left of him)*. Who'd ever have thought my portrait could look like that?

MRS. HAGGETT *(moves to Right of him)*. Wouldn't Chris Bean be proud to see it like that?

ABBY. I wish he could see it.

DR. HAGGETT. It's like you, Abby. There's no denying that.

ABBY *(proudly)*. All the time he was painting it he kept saying: "Abby, this is my masterpiece I'm painting now!"

MRS. HAGGETT *(sharp)*. Do you hear that, Milton?

DR. HAGGETT *(sharper)*. Are you sure he said that?

ABBY. Oh, yes——! And when it was all done he thanked me. He thanked me just like I'd done something for him! *(Voice choking)* Boys like him—— 'Tain't right for boys like him to die so young!

MRS. HAGGETT. Don't cry, Abby. You'll have me crying too. *(Goes to chair Right of table and sits)*

DR. HAGGETT. You'll have us all crying. *(Crosses up to entry and calls)* Ada! Come down here and see Abby's portrait! *(Crosses down to Left and below Abby)*

ABBY *(so gratefully)*. You're all so good to me! *(Ada appears on the stairs and enters to Right of Abby)*

DR. HAGGETT. We're fond of you, Abby. We're fond of you, Abby. Look Ada! Don't you think that makes a handsome effect?

ADA. I should say so——

DR. HAGGETT. We got *two* Abbies in here now. One of 'em standing here in flesh and blood and the other there in an oil painting. *(They all laugh)* Seems a pity to let the both of 'em leave us, don't it?

ABBY. Oh, Doctor Haggett! I don't know how to thank you. And I won't never forget——

DR. HAGGETT. If seeing the both don't give me an idea!

MRS. HAGGETT *(swallowing)*. I'll bet it's a good one, Milton.

ABBY. Doctor Haggett couldn't have nothing but good ideas.

DR. HAGGETT. Well, I'll let you have it just as it come to me. Since you're going away after all these years it'd be awful nice for you to leave your portrait behind you here with us.

ABBY *(unable to grasp)*. Leave it here for good! Go away without it!

DR. HAGGETT *(explaining quickly)*. Oh, I wouldn't ask you to make such a sacrifice without giving you something in return.

ABBY *(incredulous)*. How could you give me anything in return?

DR. HAGGETT *(on the spot again)*. Oh, I don't say I could give you anything equal to what the portrait would mean to *us*. But I guess twenty-five dollars would come in kind of handy in Chicago. *(Abby shakes her head)*

ADA. Make it *fifty*, Pa. *(Mrs. Haggett reaches out and grasps Ada's arm)*

DR. HAGGETT. All right, I *will* make it fifty. Yes, I will, Abby. It comes pretty hard to be handing out presents that size these days. I'll make it fifty. I guess you ain't got much to say against that!

ABBY *(embarrassed)*. No, Doctor Haggett, I ain't got nothing to say against it. It's real generous of you——

DR. HAGGETT *(turning to Mrs. Haggett)*. There, you see! It's settled.

MRS. HAGGETT. Milton, you're wonderful!

DR. HAGGETT (no relief like a guilty conscience put to rest). Everything open and above-board!

ABBY. Oh, but I couldn't never see my way to giving up my portrait. (Ada reacts to this)

DR. HAGGETT. Abby, you amaze me.

ABBY. Well, I'm funny that way about things I had so long.

DR. HAGGETT (gravely paternal). You'd better think twice, Abby, before you refuse what I must say is a generous offer.

ADA (quickly). How'd it be, Abby, if we had a nice photograph made of it, and gave that you to keep with you in Chicago?

MRS. HAGGETT (delighted). Now, ain't that a clever idea of Ada's, Milton? I declare I never would have thought of that myself.

ABBY (distracted). You got me too upset to know what to do. I hadn't no idea you was so fond of me.

MRS. HAGGETT. Abby!

ABBY. No, I hadn't, Mrs. Haggett. I knew Susie was, but I hadn't no idea about you and Ada and the Doctor. And it's awful hard for me to deny you, only——

DR. HAGGETT (so warmly). Then don't deny us, Abby. Say yes and shake hands on it.

ABBY (a slight pause). Oh! I know what we'll do. I'll get the photograph for you. I'll get it made in Chicago and send it back.

DR. HAGGETT (controlling his impatience). But don't you see, Abby, it's the——

ADA. The color and all makes it so much——

MRS. HAGGETT. No photograph'd ever give us the comforting feeling that we still had you with us.

} (Simultaneously)

ABBY. Would it really mean so much to all of you to have me hanging there in an oil painting?

MRS. HAGGETT. Would we want anyone we didn't love in our dining-room?

ABBY. But I got so used to looking at that portrait!

DR. HAGGETT. Why, Abby! That's no better than if you was to sit all day in front of a looking-glass.

ABBY. But it ain't me I see. It's—it's—it's the time when I was young. It's all how things used to be in the old days. It's—it's—I couldn't say it. I couldn't say it. (The doorbell rings)

MRS. HAGGETT (inaudibly). There's someone at the door.

ADA (a step Left). Don't disappoint us, Abby.

DR. HAGGETT. She won't. You know you won't, Abby. You'll say "yes." Think! Fifty dollars!

ABBY. Well, if you're all so set—— (The doorbell rings again) If you're so set on having it——

MRS. HAGGETT (smiles, to her Husband). Now our own dear Abby's speaking.

ABBY (to Mrs. Haggett). No. I still go to think.

DR. HAGGETT (silences his two women with a gesture). Of course you have, Abby. And I want you to think, and I know you won't reach no wrong decision. (The front door opens and Tallant appears, a painting dangling carefully from his right hand) You go set alone in your room for ten minutes. (A general gasp from the three Haggetts)

TALLANT (as he enters). No one answered the bell, but I took the liberty of—— (Puts picture, back to audience, against medicine cabinet. Places hat on top of cabinet)

ABBY (crosses to him). If you come for my portrait, I can't let you have it. (Tallant comes down Center; looks at portrait) I made up my mind I couldn't anyway and now it looks like I got to make other arrangements. So if you'll excuse me, Mr. Davis—— (Crosses above table and disappears quickly into kitchen; closes door)

ADA. Was you after Abby's portrait, well as what you got?

MRS. HAGGETT (breaks in quickly). You said you was Davenport. She called you Davis. Who in blazes are you?

DR. HAGGETT (breaks in). I didn't expect you to come here of your own free will, Mr. Tallant.

TALLANT (a step down to Haggett)

Would you ask the ladies to leave us alone together?

MRS. HAGGETT (*quickly*). Have you got secrets?

TALLANT (*to her*). Of the most delicate nature. (*Returns to his scrutiny of the portrait*)

DR. HAGGETT (*to his wife and daughter*). You can leave *me* to attend to him. (*Points to Tallant, then turns and crosses to desk*)

ADA (*crosses above table toward Left Center door*). Watch out, Pa! If he tries to get that, too, *shoot* him. (*Mrs. Haggett rises; crosses above table, behind Ada*)

MRS. HAGGETT. Just call out, Milton. We'll be listening.

TALLANT (*moves up to her*). I'm certain you will. But your husband and I are going to be friends now. (*Bows them into the entry. Ada and Mrs. Haggett go upstairs. Tallant closes the Left Center doors*)

DR. HAGGETT (*crosses up to Tallant*). Don't take much stock in that last remark, Mr. Tallant. You as good as stole a pile of money from me this morning.

TALLANT (*looking at picture*). I must ask you to be more careful with your language, Doctor Haggett.

DR. HAGGETT. What's your opinion of the trick you played on me?

TALLANT (*still looking at picture*). It was a simple business operation, carried through in the classic tradition of art collecting. Not a day passes but some collector finds some *rare* and *unappreciated* work of art——

DR. HAGGETT. Did you even *know* Chris Bean?

TALLANT (*turns and smiles at Haggett*). I never heard of him till a month ago.

DR. HAGGETT. Well, you certainly have got your nerve with you.

TALLANT (*a step down to Haggett*). Quite! But to come down to business—— How much have you told Davenport about the pictures Bean left here?

DR. HAGGETT. Didn't tell him nothing. I was still hoping I might find the rest.

TALLANT. You haven't succeeded?

DR. HAGGETT (*a groan*). They've been burnt! All but the two you got and that one there! (*Indicates the portrait*)

TALLANT (*goes up and looks at it. Admiring*). A masterpiece!

DR. HAGGETT. I'm glad you like it.

TALLANT. Oh, you and I can hardly hope to reach that height.

DR. HAGGETT. You and I? What are you driving at?

TALLANT (*returns to Left of Haggett*). Corot. (*Haggett does not see light*) The name means nothing to you?

DR. HAGGETT. Not a thing.

TALLANT. Corot was a French painter of landscapes. *He died in eighteen seventy-five*. The bulk of his painting has been done *since* then. (*Haggett is startled*) The same is true of the late Cezanne. He died in nineteen hundred and six. I know a dozen *excellent* Cezanne's, all painted in the last year. (*Goes for the picture he brought in with him*) I spoke this morning of a business partnership between us. Allow me—— (*He exhibits it*) "*The Hill Pasture*" by the late Christopher Bean. (*Haggett starts to take it from him*) Careful! Don't touch it! It's not dry yet! (*Haggett draws back*)

DR. HAGGETT. Where did you find it?

TALLANT. I *painted* it.

DR. HAGGETT. *What* are you?

TALLANT. A *forger*. (*Drops picture to his side. Light dawns on Haggett*). I see that you begin to understand. Those letters in the *Atlantic* tell us about the pictures Bean left here. The originals are lost. Thanks to *my* peculiar gifts, their loss needn't disturb us. (*Haggett gasps*) I assure *you*, Doctor Haggett, I am offering you a *gold* mine. We have an *absolute* corner on Christopher Bean. (*Haggett looks at him*) Because you cannot only vouch for *my* forgeries, but can also discredit my competitors. (*He turns and places the painting against the medicine cabinet, showing to audience. Then he returns to Haggett*) Have I made myself clear?

DR. HAGGETT (*A pause, then Haggett wrings his hands*) It's too risky! (*Turns and goes toward desk chair*)

TALLANT. Not at all. (*Follows down to Right of Haggett*)

DR. HAGGETT (*turns*). It's *criminal*!

TALLANT. Perhaps. But no picture-collecting sucker ever admits that he's been "stung," so——

DR. HAGGETT (*sits*). I don't like the sound of it. I was all right this morning before you come in. I was respected by the world and at peace with myself, and I wasn't tempted by nothing nor no man.

TALLANT. As I remarked this morning, we are all mortals, Doctor. You have a wife and two lovely daughters——

DR. HAGGETT (brightening). That's so. I have. And being tempted for your loved ones ain't as bad as if it was just on your own account. (An uneasy glance toward the portrait) How much would I get from this scheme of yours?

TALLANT. I thought twenty percent.

DR. HAGGETT. 'Tain't worth it.

TALLANT. I'll be liberal. Twenty-five.

DR. HAGGETT. Not a cent under fifty!

TALLANT (drawing himself up). If you persist in letting your greed come between you and——

DR. HAGGETT (rises). My greed! Mine! (A pause, then he adds craftily) You can't work this scheme of yours without my help. Because I'm in a position to discredit you!

TALLANT (holding out his hand). Doctor Haggett, it's done! (Haggett starts to take hand; stops, then takes it)

(Voices are audible in the entry. Rosen opens Left Center doors and enters living room to Left of table.)

MRS. HAGGETT (in entry). There's someone else in there but I guess you can go in——

DR. HAGGETT (shaking Tallant's hand). I better warn Hannah and Ada not to talk——

ROSEN (down Center to Tallant). You up here too?

TALLANT (smiling). I got here first, Rosen.

ROSEN. So it was you beat me to it! I might have known it!

DR. HAGGETT. You two acquainted with each other?

TALLANT. Mr. Rosen will be the selling end of our firm.

DR. HAGGETT (to his Wife and Ada, who are visible in the entry). Hannah! Shut that door and keep out! (Mrs. Haggett closes the Left Center doors)

TALLANT. We've just organized, Rosen. Coming in on the ground floor?

ROSEN. I'm not talking your kind of business today. I've come up here after the real thing, and I'm going to get it!

TALLANT (indicating Abby's portrait). There it is—if you can pay the price for it. (Rosen crosses up to portrait)

ROSEN. Aha! (Bends over to examine it) It isn't signed.

TALLANT. That's easily fixed.

ROSEN. Oh, one of yours, is it?

TALLANT (winks at Haggett). Thanks.

DR. HAGGETT. I should say not! It's——

TALLANT (turns to Haggett). Leave him be, Doctor! He's not one of the "suckers." I forge most of the pictures he sells.

ROSEN. I know you're good, Tallant, but I never knew you were this good!

TALLANT (crosses to below table. Delighted). You do recognize my brushwork then?

ROSEN (laughs). You can't fool me! (To Haggett) If it was real I'd buy it, but—— (He moves down to Center)

DR. HAGGETT. It is real!

ROSEN (pointing to Tallant). With him on the premises!

TALLANT. Word of honor!

ROSEN. Yours?

DR. HAGGETT. Mine!

TALLANT. There you are. (Rosen looks at the portrait) We'll take twenty thousand for it. (Haggett gasps. Rosen moves down a step)

ROSEN (amused). Now, isn't that good of you? Would you throw in the frame

TALLANT. You'll get twice twenty thousand in a year.

ROSEN. If it was genuine I might.

DR. HAGGETT. But I assure you, Mr Rosen, it is genuine. Only trouble is ain't in a position——

ROSEN. Excuse me for doubting your word, Doctor Haggett, but—— (Indicating Tallant. Tallant takes a step toward Rosen)

TALLANT (quickly). Come on, now Rosen. Admit you don't know. (Rosen crosses up to portrait and looks at it. Tallant laughs at him)

ROSEN (explodes). Well! Which is it Genuine or not?

(The Left Center door is opened and Davenport appears. He is speaking to Susan, who has come back with him and is on her way upstairs)

TALLANT (*laughs; indicates Davenport*). Here's Davenport back again. Ask *him*. (*Tallant moves away Right a few steps*)

DAVENPORT (*comes into room, to up Center*). Well, Doctor Haggett, have you found the missing treasures? (*Haggett gestures to the portrait. Davenport turns and sees it*) Ah! (*To Rosen, who is in front of portrait*) Allow me? (*Rosen takes a step Right*) And the man who painted this died miserably. Here is all womanhood. It's nobility! (*Drops down to one knee*) It's tenderness and it's strength. This is beautiful as only—only—— (*Rises*) Damn comparisons! The thing's beautiful. (*Backs up stage a step*)

ROSEN. That's *all* I need to hear. Doctor Haggett, I'll give you *seventy-five hundred* for it. (*Mrs. Haggett opens Right double Left Center door and enters to above armchair. Haggett drops down into armchair*)

DAVENPORT (*turns to Rosen, who is on his Right*). You're not buying it, Rosen?

ROSEN. Yes, I am, Mr. Davenport, and I'm glad to have you here to see me do it.

DAVENPORT. What do *you* want with it? (*Ada appears in the entry; enters to just Left of medicine cabinet*)

ROSEN (*exultant*). To show it in my gallery A one-man show! A one-picture show! For a whole month before *I* try to sell it. I'm going to bring all Duveen's customers over to Lexington Avenue.

DAVENPORT (*laughs*). Are you going to force me to respect you at last?

ROSEN. Yes, I am, Davenport. If it ruins me! (*Crosses above table to chair Right of table and sits*) Come on, now, Doctor! Be reasonable and I'll talk business. Davenport moves a step toward portrait and looks at it. Susan comes downstairs and enters Left of Ada)

DR. HAGGETT (*utterly distracted*). I——I—I'd like to sell it to you, but—— you see I ain't in a position——

SUSAN (*a few steps down*). Don't you do nothing you'd be ashamed of, Pa. (*Mrs. Haggett moves up a step and grasps Susan's arm*)

DR. HAGGETT. You get out of here. I don't have no child of mine criticizing me.

DAVENPORT. Doctor Haggett, please!

DR. HAGGETT. I can't talk business with womenfolks around.

ROSEN. Ten thousand, Doctor Haggett!

DR. HAGGETT. I tell you I ain't in a position to sell it yet.

MRS. HAGGETT (*crosses down a step and bends over him*). You ain't got much time Her train goes at five.

DR. HAGGETT. I know it does. Where is Abby?

MRS. HAGGETT (*points*). She's out there in the kitchen.

DR. HAGGETT (*he changes his mind and rises*). No, never mind her. (*To Tallant as he crosses to chair Left of table*) Might as well be hanged for a sheep as a lamb.

TALLANT. Leave this to *me*, partner. I'll handle it.

DR. HAGGETT. You shut up too. You got no part in this deal. (*Glances nervously toward Right door, then turns to Rosen and goes off the deep end; sits chair Left of table. Tallant goes up to below fireplace*) Ten thousand ain't enough.

ROSEN. Don't be foolish.

DR. HAGGETT. It ain't enough.

ROSEN. You've got to think of my expenses.

DR. HAGGETT. Don't care about 'em. Ten thousand ain't——

ROSEN. How do I know I'll ever be able to sell it?

DR. HAGGETT. I ain't so anxious to sell——

ADA (*in Left Center doorway*). Pa!

MRS. HAGGETT (*crosses to Left of him*). Remember you risked *fifty dollars* on it.

DR. HAGGETT. I ain't risked it yet. (*Mrs. Haggett a step down to look at kitchen door*)

ROSEN. Twelve thousand, then, but *that's* the top.

DR. HAGGETT. *No!*

ROSEN. How much *do* you want?

DR. HAGGETT (*another anxious glance toward Right door*). I ain't quite ready to sell this yet, but if I'm going to sell it you got to make it worth my while. (*Gulps*) I'd take forty thousand! (*A gasp from the Haggett ladies*)

ROSEN (*laughs*). You're crazy!

DR. HAGGETT. *Thirty-five.*

ROSEN. Even *that*, Mr. Davenport——

DAVENPORT *(above table).* A little high.

DR. HAGGETT. All right. *Thirty!*

MRS. HAGGETT *(behind Haggett).* Don't be easy, Milton.

DR. HAGGETT *(to her).* I won't go no lower— *(A nervous glance toward Right door. To Rosen)* And you got to be quick about it!!

ROSEN. *Fifteen!*

MRS. HAGGETT and ADA *(together).* No!

ROSEN. Seventeen and a half!

ALL THREE HAGGETTS. No!

DAVENPORT *(to Rosen).* You're dealing with a *united* family.

SUSAN *(a step to Davenport).* Not with *me,* Mr. Davenport! And I want to say that I got *no use* for any one trying to——

DR. HAGGETT *(beside himself).* Go up to your room. You'll get what's coming to you for mixing in matters you can't grasp!!

SUSAN. I don't care. I just can't *stand* to see Abby—— *(Goes upstairs indignantly)*

ADA *(looks at Susan and then turns to Davenport. Covering quickly).* My sister ain't right on account of falling on her head when she was a baby.

MRS. HAGGETT *(crosses up to Left of Ada).* She's a sentimental fool, that's all she is. *(Pushes Ada ahead of her, front of table, toward kitchen)* She just can't bear to part with this after having it 'round so long.

DR. HAGGETT. *I* can part with it, though. *(Looks at his watch)* Good God Almighty!

MRS. HAGGETT *(low to Ada).* Keep Abby out of here. *(Ada goes into kitchen, closing door. Mrs. Haggett turns and watches Haggett)*

DR. HAGGETT. *Thirty thousand,* Mr. Rosen! Take it or leave it.

ROSEN. Well, I certainly won't take it.

DAVENPORT *(to Rosen).* You've met your match this time.

ROSEN. *Twenty!*

DR. HAGGETT. *Thirty!*

ROSEN. *Cash in three days!*

DR. HAGGETT *(quickly).* Twenty-nine!

MRS. HAGGETT *(quickly as she totters a step Left).* Milton, don't slip!

ROSEN. *Twenty-three!* Half of it down and the balance tomorrow!

DR. HAGGETT. *Twenty-five* on the same terms.

ROSEN *(a slight pause. Pounds the table with his fist).* Done!

DAVENPORT *(above table).* Good work, Rosen!

DR. HAGGETT *(on the verge of collapse but still painfully conscious of that kitchen door).* Let's see the money.

ROSEN *(truculently).* Good God, give me time. *(Takes his checkbook, a fountain pen and the bills-of-sale out of his coat pocket. Ada returns Right; closes door)*

ADA. Ma!

MRS. HAGGETT. What is it?

ADA. The new maid from Boston——

MRS. HAGGETT. What about her?

ADA. She's going *back* to Boston.

MRS. HAGGETT. Let her go! We're going to get a *butler* now! *(The doorbell rings)* See who that is. If it's a patient, tell him your Pa has retired from doctoring. *(Ada goes above table and out Left Center answer)*

ROSEN *(breaks in).* Now, I had that bill-of-sale all ready made out for—— *(He looks at his checkbook)* Oh, I see—a thousand dollars. Well, I'll just have to alter it to fit. *(Writes. Haggett watches him, fascinated. Ada admits Warren Creamer by front door)*

ADA. What are you doing here, Warren? *(Warren enters to Left side Left Center door. Ada closes front door and enters to Right side Left Center door)*

WARREN. I've come for Abby's trunk.

DAVENPORT *(moves a few steps Left)* Ah, the boy marvel!

MRS. HAGGETT. Who? Warren?

WARREN. Hello, Mr. Davenport.

DAVENPORT *(moves to Center).* I've been looking at his pictures, Mrs. Haggett. You produce *talented* painters in this village.

MRS. HAGGETT *(incredulous).* Are his pictures good too? *(Her eyes shine. She quickly moves up toward the entry, brushing Davenport aside as she passes him. She calls out in her sweetest tones)* Susie! Warren's here *(Returns to below door, Right of Warren)* Come in, Warren. Don't be afraid. We kind of *changed* our minds abouts artists since this morning! *(Ada glares at Warren)*

WARREN *(still truculent).* Guess I'll

just get that trunk. *(He goes through the entry to Right. Susan hurries downstairs and follows him out)*

ROSEN *(to Haggett)*. Now, you sign here. *(He hands pen and bill-of-sale paper to Haggett, who glances toward the kitchen door and signs)* And here's the check. *(He delivers)*

MRS. HAGGETT *(crosses down to Left of him)*. Let's see it, Milton.

DR. HAGGETT. How do I know I get the balance tomorrow? *(Mrs. Haggett crosses to Right door, then returns to below table)*

ROSEN. My God, it's in writing, isn't it?

DR. HAGGETT. Well, so long as you get that picture on out of here before—— *(Another uneasy glance toward Right door)*

ROSEN *(rises; crosses above table to portrait)*. That's what I'm going to do. *(Begins removing the portrait from the frame)*

DR. HAGGETT *(rises)*. Hannah, watch that door— *(Abby enters, Right, dressed for her departure, and carrying a small suitcase. Mrs. Haggett gasps with dismay; crosses to Left Center. Haggett goes to Left of Abby)*

ABBY. Please excuse me for interrupting Doctor Haggett, but it's time for me to go—— *(Puts bag down, below sideboard)* And I had to tell you that much as I hate denying you what you asked, I made up my mind——

DR. HAGGETT *(breaks in)*. I knew it was all right, Abby. I knew it was. *(He fumbles bills out of his pocket)* And here's the fifty dollars I promised you! *(Forces the money into her hand)* God bless you, Abby! *(Is hurrying her toward Right door)*

ABBY *(wrenching free from Haggett)*. What's that man doing there with my portrait?

ROSEN *(blandly)*. Taking it to New York, Abby! To exhibit it! *(She slowly crosses below table to Left of it)* Where everybody will come to look at it! Could you let me have some string and wrapping paper?

ABBY. What right have you got to take it away?

ROSEN. Well, I never paid *more* for a sight in my life.

ABBY *(flatly)*. It belongs to me. *(Sensation. Pause. Then:)*

ROSEN. How's that? *(Tallant smirks)*

ABBY. It *belongs* to me.

DR. HAGGETT *(right of her)*. What's come over you, Abby? Did anyone ask you to come in like this? What are you after in here anyway?

ABBY. I come in to say goodbye and get my portrait, and I seen him fixing to go off with it——

DR. HAGGETT *(right of her)*. But you just sold it to *me*.

ABBY. *I never! I never!*

MRS. HAGGETT *(left Center)*. You got the money there in your hand, Abby.

DAVENPORT *(above table)*. Oh, Doctor Haggett! It can't be that you——

ABBY *(violently)*. Here! Take this money back! Go on, take it! *(He takes it)* You said you wanted my portrait to remember me by. *I* said I'd think about giving it to you. And I have thought. And I ain't never going to part with it. And now you're trying to sell it behind my back. I'd be ashamed. *(Haggett lowers his head)*

MRS. HAGGETT. Abby!

ABBY. I'd be ashamed. Of all the sharp, *underhanded* tricks!

DR. HAGGETT *(breaks in, explosively)*. This house is mine and everything in it's mine, and you're my paid help. *(Rosen replaces portrait to against table)*

DAVENPORT *(indignantly)*. Good God!

ABBY *(fortissimo)*. My portrait ain't yours.

DR. HAGGETT *(desperately)*. If you'd all step into the entry, Mr. Davenport, and leave me to explain things quickly to Abby! There won't be no more difficulty. Just five minutes, Hannah! *(General murmurs as Mrs. Haggett and Haggett urge the company out into entry)*

ROSEN *(protesting)*. Damn it, Doctor, I just gave you a check for——

DR. HAGGETT. Now don't you get upset, Mr. Rosen. There's just a little misunderstanding here. *(Closes the Left Center door upon them, mops his brow and turns to Abby. Abby moves to above portrait)* You ain't showing much gratitude for all we done for you, Abby, all these years. *(Crosses down to Left of her)*

ABBY *(at bay, low)*. I can't help that. I won't part with my portrait.

DR. HAGGETT. And I was just working up such a nice surprise for you.

ABBY. Well, I caught you at it. And I'd be *ashamed*.

DR. HAGGETT. You think I was trying to do something sneaky.

ABBY. *Sneaky* and *greedy!* I knew your wife and Ada was both greedy. But I never knew you was.

DR. HAGGETT (*hurt*). Oh, Abby, how could you say that of me? When I was only trying to make some money for you! I don't mean that fifty. That was just for fun. I was really going to give you a thousand dollars. *A thousand dollars.* Abby!

ABBY. And you were going to get it by selling my portrait?

DR. HAGGETT. People in your circumstance ain't got no right to own things that are worth so much money.

ABBY. *That may be!* But my portrait's all I got in the world. The boy who painted it—Well, I ain't ashamed to say it now, it's so long ago. I loved him and I still love him. And he died just after he finished painting it, so it was the last thing he ever painted. That's why it means so much to me. It means all the happiness I ever had. And you know that I ain't had so much, Doctor Haggett. Now I guess I better go and catch my train. (*Moves down to below the table*)

DR. HAGGETT (*follows and grasps her arm. She stops*). Abby, you're thinking only of yourself. How about your poor brother and his children? He's a poor man, Abby.

ABBY. I know he is.

DR. HAGGETT. And he ain't got work now.

ABBY. I know that.

DR. HAGGETT. You'll all be poor out there in Chicago.

ABBY. I can't help it, Doctor.

DR. HAGGETT. And his children. Wouldn't you like to give 'em advantages?

ABBY (*breaks in*). But I promised Chris Bean I'd never part with it. The last time I ever seen him I promised him that. He painted it for *me*.

DR. HAGGETT. Who's being *greedy* now?

Who would your brothers' children say was greedy?

ABBY. Don't keep after me. Let me go and catch——

DR. HAGGETT (*a gulp, then his tone changes*). Abby, there's something else you ain't thought of! That portrait don't even belong to you. (*Abby gasps. He drives on*) It was time I paid for, you wasted sitting for Chris Bean to paint it when you'd ought to have been working.

ABBY (*indignantly*). It ain't so! I worked every minute he was painting. Every minute! I remember how we used to set out in that barn, me working and him painting.

DR. HAGGETT. You used to take him out *our* coffee to drink.

ABBY. I *never*. You know how Mrs. Haggett always watched the coffee. That was *my own* breakfast coffee that I saved for him and took out to him. It was all I ever had to give him, my coffee was. There now! What more meanness can you think up?

DR. HAGGETT. I'll be honest with you. Honesty the best policy, after all. They want to pay me twenty-five thousand for your portrait.

ABBY (*stunned*). Twenty-five thou——

DR. HAGGETT. Divide with me, Abby (*Poignant*) Take half and give me half. If it wasn't for me you wouldn't have none of it.

ABBY (*decisively*). No!

DR. HAGGETT (*desperately*). Take more than half! Take *fifteen* thousand! Think what you could do for your brother' children with *fifteen* thousand.

ABBY (*backing away from him*). No! No I tell you.

DR. HAGGETT (*grasps her arm*). Take twenty thousand!

ABBY. *Let go of my dress.*

DR. HAGGETT. Greed, Abby, greed!

ABBY (*fortissimo*). It ain't greed! I wouldn't take a million. You ought to be ashamed!!!

DR. HAGGETT (*a despairing gesture*). I am. (*Turns, crosses to armchair and sits*)

ABBY (*long pause. Follows to Right of him*). Well, now will you let me go?

DR. HAGGETT. Yes, God help me, I'll have to let you go.

ABBY *(looks lovingly at the portrait).* He was so poor, Chris was. He never had no good coat nor nothing warm, only that one sweater I knitted for him. He never had no warm room to sleep in nights, nor nothing he needed, he was so poor. If he could have afforded to go away from here down South he needn't have died. I used to pray that we'd get an early thaw just for Chris's sake. How is it a man dies so poor when he painted pictures that's worth so much?

DR. HAGGETT. Because nobody had any use for his pictures while he was living.

ABBY. I always liked 'em. That's why I kept so many. *(Dr. Haggett has turned slowly).* No, only just because——— *(She crosses below table towards her suitcase)*

DR. HAGGETT *(rises, a step after her).* You kept so many?

ABBY *(stops below table; turns to him).* Yes, I kept them.

DR. HAGGETT *(crosses to her, wetting his dry lips feverishly)* How did you get them?

ABBY. Mrs. Haggett she put 'em on the bonfire but *I* took them off.

DR. HAGGETT. Where are they now?

ABBY. In my trunk. I rolled 'em up. But they're all right. *(Starts again for her bag)*

DR. HAGGETT *(all but voiceless).* How many are there?

ABBY *(stops again).* There's seventeen.

DR. HAGGETT *(gasps).* Seventeen, Abby? Did you say seventeen? *(Turns and crosses up toward Left Center door, shouting)* Hannah! Ada! Mr. Rosen! Come back in here! *(The Left Center door is opened from without and the others pour back into the room)*

MRS. HAGGETT *(enters and crosses to Haggett).* What is it, Milton?

ADA *(enters to up Center).* Pa!

ROSEN *(enters to Left of table).* Good God, what now?

DR. HAGGETT. Never mind the *portrait!* The *other* pictures have been *found. (Davenport enters to above Rosen)*

TALLANT *(enters to above Haggett).* No! *(Abby listens in confusion and alarm)*

DR. HAGGETT. The ones you burned Hannah! *(Hugs her).*

MRS. HAGGETT. *Milton!*

DR. HAGGETT. Only you *never* burned

'em. Abby's got 'em in her trunk. *There's seventeen of 'em.*

DAVENPORT. *Seventeen new* Christopher Beans! *(Abby moves up to below the fireplace. Warren comes into the entry from the Right carrying Abby's old leather trunk, tied up with rope. Susan following to steer it clear of the paint)*

MRS. HAGGETT. It's a *fortune,* Milton.

ADA. And it *ours!*

DR. HAGGETT *(breaking loose from his wife).* Put that trunk down and open it! *(Charges the entry)*

WARREN *(stops)* I just roped it up!

DR. HAGGETT. Unrope it! Got a knife, ain't you! *(Warren puts the trunk down, takes out a pocket knife and bends over the trunk. The others all move up closer to the trunk)*

ABBY *(crosses above table to Haggett).* You'll make me miss my train, Doctor Haggett.

ADA. Talking about *trains* at a time like this!

WARREN *(cutting the rope).* There!

DR. HAGGETT *(throws up the lid of the trunk).* Now, Abby, where are they?

ABBY *(goes up to trunk).* Better let me, Doctor Haggett. I don't like for folks to go messing in my trunk. *(Silence. She bends over the trunk and takes out a flattish roll of canvases from beneath several articles of wearing apparel)*

DR. HAGGETT. Ha! *(Snatches them from her and comes down to Rosen, who is by chair Left of table).* Now I'll talk business with you, Mr. Rosen.

ROSEN. Excuse me, Doctor Haggett, but I am the picture dealer. *(Takes pictures from Haggett, turns and crosses to desk. Sits in swivel chair; places paintings on desk and unrolls them. Haggett crosses to above desk. Mrs. Haggett follows to below desk. Ada goes above the desk to Left of it. Tallant moves to rear of armchair)*

ROSEN. Well, Doctor Haggett, I wasn't prepared for any such deal as this!

DAVENPORT. *Carefully* now! *(Crosses to Right of Haggett and peers over his shoulder* Don't harm them. *(As the roll opens out flat)* Ah!

DR. HAGGETT. What would you say it's worth, Mr. Davenport?

DAVENPORT. Well, now, I don't know——

ABBY (to Warren). Will you rope up my trunk for me again, please, Warren? (Warren ropes up the trunk, Susan assisting. Abby looks from the trunk to the group at the desk indeterminately)

DR. HAGGETT. You promised you'd tell me. Is it worth ten thousand?

DAVENPORT. Easily, I should say.

DR. HAGGETT (wildly excited). Do you hear that, Hannah! Easily ten thousand for the first one on the pile! And seventeen of 'em!

ADA (comes down a step and puts an arm about her mother). We're rich, Ma! We're rich! (Rosen turns over a new picture)

DAVENPORT. Oh!

MRS. HAGGETT (sits below desk). Seems like we must be, but it kind of gets my stomach. (During the following scene, Abby makes repeated attempts to interrupt the proceedings at desk but her every effort to attract their attention is drowned in another outburst from them. Their attitude is one of complete indifference to her presence and they pay no heed to her pitiful attempts to edge in)

ABBY (crosses down to Right of desk Right of Group). Were you aiming to sell those too, Doctor Haggenett?

DR. HAGGETT. What's that?

DAVENPORT (bends over the second canvas) "The Hill Pasture." It must be "The Hill Pasture"!

DR. HAGGETT. Certainly it's "The Hill Pasture"! (Tallant looks over Davenport's shoulder at the painting, shrugs his shoulder, and crosses to the medicine cabinet)

ABBY. I saved them—— (Stops as she sees Tallant pick up his forgery of "The Hill Pasture," put on hat, and go into entry)

DAVENPORT (as he sees another painting). Oh, look!

ABBY. ——I saved those from burning and I thought they are mine to keep!

ROSEN (to Haggett). Say, now, before we start talking business, I got to know if you really are the rightful owner this time. (Tallant goes out front door. Susan and Warren watch Tallant exit)

MRS. HAGGETT. Who would be if he aint'?

DR. HAGGETT. I got your word for it they're mine. And wasn't they left here against an unpaid bill?

DAVENPORT. Yes, Rosen, I expect they do belong to him.

ABBY. Oh!

DR. HAGGETT. There, you see!

ABBY. Well——

DAVENPORT. Let's look through the rest. (No one pays the slightest attention to Abby)

ROSEN. Well—as I say, I never tackled anything this big before. A corner in Christopher Bean.

ABBY. Goodbye, Doctor Haggett. I'll be going now.

DR. HAGGETT. That's what it is, Mr. Rosen! (He laughs) A corner!

ABBY. My train will be going, Doctor Haggett. That's why I——

DAVENPORT. I wouldn't be in any hurry to sell, Doctor. Not the lot, anyway.

ROSEN. I wasn't figuring on that, Mr. Davenport.

ABBY. Goodbye, Ada—— Goodbye, Mrs. Haggett——

ROSEN. Why, he may have a couple of hundred thousand in this pile.

ADA. Ma.

ROSEN (pounds top of desk with his fist). I don't know, though. I might get the deal financed. Would you give me time?

DR. HAGGETT. Don't know about giving time.

ABBY. Goodbye. I got to be going now—— Well— (Turns back to Warren with a pathetic little laugh) I guess I'll just go. I guess there ain't nothing else to do.

ROSEN (to himself). Schmidt might come in on this—and there's Goldstein. I might put him down for a—— (The group at the desk turn over another and another with low exclamations of delighted amazement)

ABBY. Will you take my trunk out Warren? (Warren nods to Susan, who exit front door. Warren picks up the trunk and goes out front door; leaves door open. Abby goes for her suitcase, picks it up and stands for moment looking about her down Left)

ROSEN. I tell you what, Doctor Haggett. Suppose you keep that check for thirty-day option?

DR. HAGGETT. Well, if you set a price on the lot now. But a good price, mine——

ROSEN. Let me figure up. (Davenpo

turns away from the group at the desk and sees Abby picking up the bag)

DR. HAGGETT *(laughs).* You go right ahead, Mr. Rosen, we're not going to stop your figuring. *(Rosen proceeds to do so, all the others watching over his shoulder. Abby returns to above the portrait)*

DAVENPORT. Oh, Abby! *(Goes to Left of her)* You're not going, are you? *(Stoops and puts bag down in front of portrait)*

ABBY. Yes, I'm going. I tried to say goodbye, but they're so busy.

DAVENPORT. Will you let me say just one word to you about your portrait? *(She turns away from him)* Oh, I'm not trying to take it from you. But, Abby, a work of art like that is a responsibility. It's *yours*, but only yours in trust for the future. Take it with you to Chicago by all means. But when you get there, don't keep it where it won't be safe. Lend it to the Chicago Art Institute. You could go and see it *every* day, you know. Would you do that, Abby?

ABBY. I'd think about it.

ROSEN *(looking up from his figures).* A hundred and eighty thousand.

DR. HAGGETT. You said two hundred!

ROSEN *(turns to Davenport).* I appeal to Mr. Davenport! *(Haggett also turns to face Davenport)*

DAVENPORT *(holding up his hand for silence. Mrs. Haggett looks up and rises).* Please, Abby! I know it's more that a work of art to you. I *know* the *bond* there must have existed between you and Chris Bean when he painted it.

MRS. HAGGETT *(a supercilious sniff).* Bond, huh! *Carryings on!* If you call that a bond!

ABBY *(looks at her, but turns back with her own dignity to answer Davenport).* Mr. Davenport, he was the only man ever asked me to marry him. *(Though her words are spoken shyly, they fall like lead upon the room's sudden attention)*

DR. HAGGETT *(pause. All but speechless).* You— *(He moves toward her)* You didn't marry him, though, Abby? *(Mrs. Haggett moves a step Right. Ada moves to below desk)*

ABBY. He was so sick. I couldn't refuse him nothing. *(The idea strikes all simultaneously)*

DAVENPORT *(pleased surprise).* Then

you're his *widow?* *(Rosen rolls up the paintings)*

ABBY. I know I am. *(Warren enters front door, gets the portrait and the suitcase, then exits. All of the following speeches are spoken simultaneously)*

DR. HAGGETT *(shaking his head).* She's got to prove it! She's got to prove it! She's got to prove it!

DAVENPORT *(to Doctor).* I believe she can! I certainly believe she can! *(To Abby)* And you never told! But, Abby! Why didn't you?——This is magnificent! And it's certainly turning out just like Chris Bean would have——

ROSEN *(to Mrs. Haggett).* In that case these pictures belong to *her!* My God; I can't do business this way! If they don't know the—— *(Mrs. Haggett tears the roll of painting out of his hands)* Well, I give it up.

MRS. HAGGETT *(clasping the paintings tightly in her arms).* Well, she doesn't get 'em away from me! Not over my dead body——

ADA. Ma! Does that mean Pa can't —Ma, answer me! Aren't these pictures ours to sell? Oh, it isn't fair! It just isn't fair! I don't think it's——

ABBY *(to Haggett).* Certainly I can. I got my marriage lines out in my—— *(Points towards the front door through which Warren has taken her trunk)* Do you want to see—— And my wedding ring on a—— *(Pulls out her wedding ring on a ribbon from her bosom)* Look! *(Haggett throws up his hands in defeat, turns and goes toward Mrs. Haggett. Abby follows down after him a few steps)* I wanted to hold folks' good opinion and my——But I don't care who knows it now, that I'm Mrs. Christopher Bean— That's who I am, just as much as Mrs. Haggett's Mrs.—— *(Haggett tears the roll of paintings away from his wife, turns and goes to Abby)* And I never carried on with—— *(He hands the paintings to her. The Curtain starts to fall)*

DR. HAGGETT. There!!!

ABBY. Oh, are you giving me back my—— *(She takes the roll of paintings, smiles her appreciation; turns and moves toward the front door. Davenport bows her out. Ada bursts into tears)*

THE CURTAIN IS DOWN

FERENC MOLNAR's

The Play's the Thing

In the adaptation by P. G. WODEHOUSE

The Play's the Thing was presented for the first time in any language in the Gilbert Miller production by the Charles Frohman Company at Irving M. Lesser's Great Neck Playhouse, Great Neck, N. Y., on October 21, 1926, and first presented in New York at Henry Miller's Theatre, on November 3, 1926, with the following cast:

SANDOR TURAI	Holbrook Blinn	ALMADY	Reginald Owen
MANSKY	Hubert Druce	JOHANN DWORNITSCHEK	Ralph Nairn
ALBERT ADAM	Edward Crandall	MELL	Claude Allister
ILONA SZABO	Catherine Dale Owen	LACKEYS	{ Stephan Kendal John Gerard

The adaptation by P. G. Wodehouse was first presented by Gilbert Miller, in association with James Russo and Michael Ellis, at the Booth Theatre, New York, on April 28, 1948, with the following cast:

SANDOR TURAI	: Louis Calhern	ILONA SZABO	Faye Emerson
MANSKY	Ernest Cossart	ALMADY	Arthur Margetson
ALBERT ADAM	Richard Hylton	MELL	Claude Allister
JOHANN DWORNITSCHEK	Francis Compton	LACKEYS	{ Ted Paterson Fred Wentler

Directed by Gilbert Miller
Setting by Oliver Messel

The entire action of the play takes place in a room
in a castle on the Italian Riviera.

ACT ONE—About 2:00 A.M.

ACT TWO—About 6:00 A.M.

ACT THREE—About 7:30 P.M.

ACT ONE

SCENE: *As the curtain rises a distant orchestra is heard playing Leoncavallo's "Mattinata." The stage is almost dark. The only light comes through two large French windows at the back. Through them we see the moonlit Mediterranean far below, the vague outlines of the precipitous coast, twinkling lights along quays and esplanades, and here and there the faint glow from some lighted window. A lighthouse blinks intermittently in the far distance. Within the dark room three darker shadows loom against the moonlit windows; the lighted ends of three cigarettes prick the blackness. There is a long pause. It is almost embarrassingly long. Just before one wonders if anything is ever going to happen a man's voice breaks the silence.*

THE MAN'S VOICE. When you stop talking, Sandor, for sixty consecutive seconds, there's something wrong. *(One of the shadowy forms is seen to rise and cross to the Right wall. We hear the click of an electric switch and instantly the stage is flooded with the warm glow of several electric sconces and candelabra lamps. The light reveals a room beautifully furnished in Italian Renaissance. At the back one shallow step leads up to a raised portion which runs the whole width of the room. Behind it are the French windows, now closed, with a balcony beyond them. To the Right a short flight of steps leads to a landing and a door to a bedroom suite. To the Left one step leads up to a door to the hall and the remainder of the castle. Occupying the Right wall of the lower portion of the room is a great fireplace with a corbelled chimney. A long table stands near it. At the Left is a grand piano. Below the piano in the Left wall is a door to another bedroom. All these doors are closed. Above the piano toward the Center is a small stand with a telephone on it. There are comfortable chairs here and there. The ceiling is beamed and carved. The whole room reflects wealth and beauty. The speaker, who has just lighted the room, is a large and portly man of middle age. His name is Mansky. He is in a dinner jacket, as are his two companions, Sandor Turai, seated in the Center, and Albert Adam, near the piano. Turai is also middle-aged, but younger-looking and less portly than Mansky. A glance shows him to be a man of consequence and dynamic personality. He is wearing a monocle. Albert Adam is a dreamy, handsome boy just over the threshold of manhood. The distant orchestra has stopped playing. Mansky reseats himself to the Right of Turai, and speaks again)* What's on your mind, Sandor?

TURAI. I was just thinking how extraordinarily difficult it is to begin a play. The eternal problem of how to introduce your principal characters.

ADAM. I suppose it must be hard.

TURAI. It is—devilish hard. Up goes the curtain, there is a hush all over the theatre, people come on the stage. Then what? It's an eternity—sometimes as much as a quarter of an hour before the audience finds out who's who and what they are all up to.

MANSKY. I never saw such a fellow. Can't you forget the theatre for a single minute?

TURAI. No. That's why I'm such a great dramatist.

MANSKY. You can't be happy for half an hour unless you're talking shop. Life isn't all theatre.

TURAI. Yes, it is—if you write plays. You know what Alphonse Daudet says in his "Memoirs"? When he stood by his father's deathbed, all he could think of was what a wonderful scene it would make for the stage.

MANSKY. It's silly to let your job become an obsession.

TURAI. Well, that's the theatre for you. And of all the brain-racking things in the world, beginning a play is the worst. Take this scene here, for instance. We three— Curtain goes up on three ordinary men in ordinary dinner jackets. How is anybody to know even that this room we're sitting in is a room in a castle? And how are they to know who we are? If this were a play we would have to start jabbering about a lot of thoroughly uninteresting things—to the accompaniment of slamming seats—until the audience gradually found out who we were.

MANSKY. Well? Why not?

TURAI. Think how much simpler it would be if we were to cut out all that stuff and just introduce ourselves? *(He rises and addresses the audience)* Ladies and gentlemen, good evening. We three arrived tonight to spend a couple of weeks at this castle. We've just left dinner where we did ourselves remarkably well with some excellent champagne. My name is Sandor Turai. I am a playwright. I have been a playwright for thirty years. I make a very good thing of it. I bow and step back leaving the stage to you.

(Turai steps back and Mansky steps forward and addresses the audience.)

MANSKY. Ladies and gentlemen, my name is Mansky.—I, too, am a playwright, and this gentleman's life-long collaborator. We are probably the best-known firm in the business.

TURAI. Come to Mansky and Turai for all comedies, farces and operettas. Satisfaction guaranteed.

MANSKY. I, too, make a very good thing out of it.

TURAI. Which brings us—

MANSKY. —to the remaining member of the trio.

(They indicate Adam, who rises and addresses the audience in similar fashion but with more diffidence and none of their assurance.)

ADAM. The last and least. I, ladies and gentlemen, am Albert Adam. I am twenty-five years old and I compose music.

TURAI. Very good music, too.

ADAM. I have done the score for the latest operetta by these two kind gentlemen. My first effort. They discovered me. Without them I am a complete nonentity. I have no parents, no reputation, and no money.

TURAI. But—he's young.

MANSKY. And gifted.

ADAM. And in love with the prima donna.

TURAI. You don't have to tell them that. An audience takes it for granted that the young composer is in love with the prima donna. That's tradition, isn't it?

ADAM. Thank Heaven.

TURAI. At any rate, here we are. Free at last from the dusty world of make-believe; out of the reach of thin-skinned actors and thick-skinned managers. What's more, there is nothing to worry us. Our operetta is finished and off our

minds. Moreover, it is summer. The weather is perfect, the night is gorgeous, the sea—

MANSKY. Yes? What's the matter with the sea?

TURAI. It's moist! And the world is the world. Now, there you are. Wouldn't that be the simplest way to begin a play?

MANSKY. Very crude. If that were all there was to it, any fool could write plays.

TURAI. A great many do. You should know that. But you can see how absurdly simple it is.

MANSKY. All right, all right. For heaven's sake, stop talking shop. I've had enough. Save it for tomorrow.

TURAI. At any rate, it's been a great day—and we must remember it—August the twentieth.

MANSKY. Friday.

TURAY. What of it?

MANSKY. I wish it wasn't.

TURAI. Don't be such an old woman.

MANSKY. No one should arrive anywhere on a Friday.

ADAM. What difference does it make—Friday, Saturday, Sunday—life's always wonderful.

TURAI. My unlucky day is Tuesday. Among other things *(indicates Mansky)*, he was born on a Tuesday. During, I believe, the Second Crusade—

MANSKY. Well, look at it for yourself. Here's today's little bag of bad luck. Midday—blowout—followed by violent thunderstorm. Set us back an hour. Early afternoon—ran over dog. More delay. And when we arrive, who is out? Our princely host. Who else? Everbody. All gone off on a picnic. Friday! And the beautiful, the one and only, our adorable prima donna, where is she? Also off on a picnic. Is she expected home tonight? No. When is she expected? No one knows. Friday!

TURAI. Oh, she'll be back.

MANSKY. Well, that won't spoil Friday's record because it's Saturday now.

ADAM. And I've got to wait a whole night before I can see her. It's cruel.

MANSKY. Just Friday.

TURAI. Well, now listen to me. I'll give you my version of the day's proceedings. Midday—capital lunch including some really drinkable coffee. During the meal, a few drops of rain. Result: perfect roads, no dust. We did injure a dog—but our Friday good luck held. The dog made a miraculous recovery and when last seen was sitting up taking nourishment. We arrived here a few hours late. But what a bit of good luck that was. Nobody in the house to expect tired men to make conversation. What's more, we dine on as fine a curried chicken as ever I tasted.

MANSKY. I loathe curry.

TURAI. You would! Now, in conclusion, let me give you the crowning piece of good fortune of this magical Friday. The room next to this is—Ilona's.

ADAM. What!

TURAI. Yes! Through that door is the room of the beautiful prima donna, the one and only. And I managed to get this suite for us. What a piece of good luck that was.

MANSKY. For him.

TURAI. No, no. For all of us. When a composer is happy, he writes song hits. When a prima donna is happy, she occasionally sings on key. And the librettists gather royalties from the resulting triumphs.

MANSKY. Sordid brute. You've no poetry in your soul.

TURAI. But I have a balance in my bank account, and that's far more important. As for Ilona being away, think what a piece of good luck that is. Think of the pleasant surprise she'll get. The little darling comes home from her picnic. All unsuspecting, she goes into her little room, she sinks upon her little bed—

MANSKY. Why on earth must everything always be so little?

TURAI. I never gave it a thought. Why not?

MANSKY. Damned sentimentalism. I know the house well. She has a *huge* room and an *enormous* bed.

TURAI. The point is she doesn't know we're here. That we've brought her the unfinished operetta—and that I am going to sing her the waltz song from Act Two.

MANSKY. God help her! Do you know it's past three? Let's go to bed. You can do your singing tomorrow.

TURAI. I've no objection to postponing the little surprise party. Suppose we wake her in the morning with the waltz.

ADAM. Suppose she finds out we're here?

TURAI. Oh, I've attended to that. I've particularly impressed on the butler that no one must know we're here until tomorrow morning. He's a very important man, that butler—practically runs this house.

ADAM. Then I'm going to have a bath.

TURAI. I don't follow his logic, do you? What has the importance of the butler to do with your having a bath?

ADAM. I hate logic. When you're tired and sleepy and looking forward so something particularly nice—well, it's wonderful to lie in a tub of lukewarm water with your eyes closed.

TURAI. Young! *(Laughs)* And an artist must pamper himself, eh? You're a lucky boy. You're going to escape the struggles that most young artists suffer before they reach the top. You've got a very clever man behind you—pushing you on.

MANSKY *(significantly)*. Yes. *Two* clever men.

TURAI. I beg your pardon? Oh! Of course, *two* clever men. So run along, my boy, and have your bath—and sleep and dream and love. And enjoy your youth in this not so beautiful world—what's left of it.

MANSKY. You ought to be ashamed of yourself. He should be learning by this time that life isn't all music and roses and happiness.

TURAI. Why be in such a hurry to teach him that?

MANSKY. I'm not in a hurry.

TURAI. Then why must he be in a hurry to learn it?

ADAM. Good night, Uncle Sandor.

TURAI. Good night, my boy. And don't forget who will presently be sleeping on the other side of that wall. Say! There's an idea for a scene. The lovers separated by the wall.

MANSKY. What lovers?

TURAI. Pyramus and Thisbe. "And thou, oh wall, oh sweet, oh lovely wall! Oh wicked wall, through whom I see no bliss!"

MANSKY. Shop again! Always shop!

ADAM. And what about you two?

TURAI. Oh, we're all right. Our room is on the far side of yours.

ADAM. Are you two sharing a room?

TURAI. We have to. Real collaborators never separate for a moment. Or the most priceless ideas might be lost forever. Besides, I talk in my sleep. I'm told that's when I say some of my best things. Mansky is a light sleeper, and wakes up and jots down whatever I say.

ADAM. Well, gentlemen—one last word before I go. I am very fond of both of you. I am finding life very beautiful. And I am very happy. (Exits upstairs, Right)

TURAI. Which startling announcement seems to call for a glass of very old brandy.

MANSKY. Make it two.

TURAI. Right. It's good to see the boy so happy. Now that I've reached the shady side of fifty, I find myself full of parental affection and nobody to lavish it on. His mother was a gentle, beautiful woman. They're still dancing down there on the terrace of the hotel. With that dark blue sky in the background and the colored lights on the water. Yes, the boy's right—life is beautiful.

MANSKY. Sandor.

TURAI. Yes?

MANSKY. I didn't like to tell you before.

TURAI. Tell me what?

MANSKY. Something rather unpleasant. A little piece of news. Rather unpleasant.

TURAI. You're an odd sort of fellow. Just when a man is feeling happy for five minutes, you have to come along and take the joy out of life.

MANSKY. It concerns you, too. It's rather unpleasant.

TURAI. Well, come on, old friend. Ruin my evening for me.

MANSKY. I was looking in the visitors' book downstairs, and I saw a certain name. Yes, it's rather unpleasant.

TURAI. Don't sit there making my flesh creep. What name did you see in the visitors' book?

MANSKY. Almady.

TURAI. The actor?

MANSKY. Yes.

TURAI. He's here?

MANSKY. He is.

TURAI. H'm. This is, as you say, rather unpleasant.

MANSKY. You realize what this means?

TURAI. It means that you're thoroughly happy.

MANSKY. Not at all. I may be a pessimist, but unfortunately, I'm a tender-hearted pessimist. When I am proved right, I do not enjoy the fact. The fact is that Mr. Almady is here.

TURAI. But how? He hasn't been invited here for ten years.

MANSKY. I suppose he fished for an invitation. He probably had his reasons.

TURAI. Does our young friend know anything about that business?

MANSKY. No! If he knew the part Mr. Almady has played in his fiancée's life, it would be a terrible shock to him.

TURAI. Well, how much of a part was it? When she was starting on the stage he gave her lessons in voice production. And then—well, it was just the usual business—the romantic leading actor and the little pupil. The sort of thing that lasts a couple of months at the outside. And, besides, it was all over and done with long ago.

MANSKY. Apparently it is not over and done with.

TURAI. Rot! Because by pure chance he happens to be in the same house?

MANSKY. It isn't pure chance. It's impure intention. Use your intelligence, man. Ilona was Almady's discovery—he took her out of the chorus and taught her all she knows.

TURAI. That's a thing of the past. Ilona's in love and she's engaged to be married. And you know how passionately an actress can be engaged to be married. I'm bound to say I'm not remarkably enthusiastic about this match, but if it makes the boy happy that's the main thing. My dear chap, you're crazy. She wouldn't be such a fool—with a worn-out elderly actor—a father with four children. She's got too much sense.

MANSKY. I never said a word about that. I merely said I had seen his name in the visitors' book. That means he is staying here. Is that pleasant? No. It is unpleasant. That was all I said. I now say something more. We ought to have wired Ilona that we were coming tonight.

TURAI. I admit it. You're right again. So be happy. Never surprise a woman. On several occasions in a longish life I have prepared a joyful surprise for a woman, and every time I was the one surprised. The telegraph was invented for no other purpose than that woman should not get surprises. *(There is a knock at the door)* Come in. *(A Footman enters from the hall. He is an elderly man in blue livery)* What do you want?

FOOTMAN. What do *you* want, sir? You rang, sir.

TURAI. Oh, yes, cognac.

FOOTMAN. Any particular brand, sir?

TURAI *(to Mansky)*. Do me a favor, old man, and go up and make sure Albert stays out of here. I want to have a few words with this fellow.

MANSKY. Don't drink both the brandies.

(Mansky goes out through door at Right.)

TURAI. What's your name?

FOOTMAN. Mine, sir?

TURAI. Yes, yours.

FOOTMAN. Johann Dwornitschek, sir.

TURAI. Johann?

FOOTMAN. Dwornitschek.

TURAI. Ah— Age?

DWORNITSCHEK. Fifty-two, sir.

TURAI. Born?

DWORNITSCHEK. Yes, sir.

TURAI. I should have said, where were you born?

DWORNITSCHEK. Podmokly. In Bohemia, sir.

TURAI. Nice place.

DWORNITSCHEK. No, sir.

TURAI. Ah—married?

DWORNITSCHEK. Yes, sir, thank you, sir.

TURAI. Wife living?

DWORNITSCHEK. Well, in a sense.— She ran away two years ago with a soldier, sir—thank you, sir.

TURAI. Don't thank me—thank the soldier. Now—Johann Dwornitschek. Here are more questions. That room next door there is Miss Ilona Szabo's?

DWORNITSCHEK. Yes, sir.

TURAI. Has she been out long?

DWORNITSCHEK. Yes, sir. They left at six o'clock this afternoon.

TURAI. They? Who's they?

DWORNITSCHEK. The entire house-party, sir, including the master. They were going to San Pietro, I think, sir.

TURAI. Is that far?

DWORNITSCHEK. The yacht would take them there in about an hour and a half, sir.

TURAI. When do you expect them back?

DWORNITSCHEK. Well, sir—they took a considerable quantity of liquor with them.

TURAI. My question was, "When do you expect them back?"

DWORNITSCHEK. That is the question I'm answering, sir. Hardly before tomorrow morning at the earliest.

TURAI. I see. Who's in the party?

DWORNITSCHEK. The core or center of it, if I may use the expression, sir—

TURAI. Certainly you may use the expression. It's a beautiful expression.

DWORNITSCHEK. Thank you, sir. The core or center of it is an American family, distant relatives of the master. Every time a holiday comes around, they insist on a picnic.

TURAI. What holiday is today?

DWORNITSCHEK. I don't know, sir. They have two every week here. They always go off at night in the big yacht. They're quite wild about the young lady. She sings for them on the yacht.

TURAI. Now, look here—do you know a Mr. Almady?

DWORNITSCHEK. Oh, yes, indeed, sir. I know Mr. Almady. I know Mr. Almady very well. He has been here three days.

TURAI. Here in the castle?

DWORNITSCHEK. Yes, sir, on this floor.

TURAI. And—he's a member of the yachting party?

DWORNITSCHEK. Yes, sir. Along with the young lady.

TURAI. What do you mean, *along* with the young lady?

DWORNITSCHEK. Well, sir, he escorted her to the boat. They're working together — like — like — as it were — partners. Mr. Almady gives recitations on the boat.

TURAI. My God! How did you find that out?

DWORNITSCHEK. They took me with them, sir, last Tuesday.

TURAI (Into each life some rain must fall). Tuesday?? Yes, it would be on a Tuesday.

DWORNITSCHEK. Yes, sir—Tuesday.

TURAI. Yes, I heard you. Thank you. That will be all.

DWORNITSCHEK. Excuse me, sir. Would it be taking a liberty if I inquired why—

TURAI. Why I began by asking you all those personal questions?

DWORNITSCHEK. Exactly, sir.

TURAI. Quite simple. It's a little matter of psychology. When you want a man to speak the truth, begin by making him tell you all about himself. It gives him a feeling of responsibility and makes him afraid to lie later on. That is from a little detective play by Mansky and Turai. You may take the tip as some slight return for your trouble.

DWORNITSCHEK. Thank you very much sir.

TURAI. Don't mention it.

DWORNITSCHEK. And which shall I bring you, sir?

TURAI. Which? What which?

DWORNITSCHEK. Which brand of cognac?

TURAI. Which brands have you?

DWORNITSCHEK. All the best brands, sir. Hennessy, Three Star Martel, Biscuit DuBouche— Excuse me, sir. I rather fancy that's the young lady coming back now. (They listen. From the adjoining room at the Left a soprano voice is heard singing casually but clearly a well-known aria from an operetta) Yes, sir. That's the young lady, all right.

TURAI. It is. It's she. Splendid! Then never mind the cognac. Champagne is clearly indicated. See that it's well iced and hurry it along.

DWORNITSCHEK. You wish it here, sir?

TURAI (going into room at Right). Of course. Of course.

DWORNITSCHEK. Very good, sir.

(Exit Dwornitschek.)

TURAI (in the room at Right). Hey! Stop that bath. You haven't time for baths now.

She's back! Sh! Hurry up. Quick, both of you. (The voices of Mansky and Adam are also heard) I tell you she is. She's in her room. Do be quick. I've ordered champagne. Here, I'll help you dress.

(The door at the Right is closed from the inside. From inside the adjoining room on the Left the singing continues until interrupted by Almady's voice raised in protest.)

ALMADY. What do you mean by this singing? I believe you're doing it just to annoy me.

ILONA. Well—it's pretty cool to come walking into my bedroom at this hour.

ALMADY. I came with you.

ILONA. Now, listen. Everything's over and ended. I'm engaged to be married and I intend to be a good little wife. You've no right to behave like this.

ALMADY. No right? I, who made you? I, with whom you have lived so many wonderful, unforgettable—

ILONA. Do go away, and leave me alone. Don't touch me. (A pause) Stop. I won't let you kiss me. Can't you understand my fiancé will be arriving any day now?

ALMADY. I'll kill him.

ILONA. You'll do nothing of the kind. (Almady sobs loudly) Oh, stop crying! The idea—a grown-up man, the father of four children.

ALMADY. But I love you so, Ilona. Don't you love me—still—just a little?

ILONA. You're nothing but a great big baby. All right, then you may kiss me. (A pause while they kiss) What are you doing? Don't take off your coat.

ALMADY. I want to say good-by.

ILONA. Well, you don't need to say it in your shirtsleeves. (Pause) Now run away and let me get some sleep. I'm worn out.

ALMADY. I'm only waiting till you're in bed. Is there anything to drink here?

ILONA. You'll find it in the ante-room (Pause. Shouting) Look in the sideboard And stay where you are till I've got m nightie on. Don't come in and don't look (There is a silence during which the door Right is opened and Turai, Adam and Mansky tipto in like three mischievous boys. They speak i whispers as they cross to the door to Ilona' bedroom.)

TURAI. Hush! She's gone to bed.

ADAM. Do you think she's asleep already?

TURAI. I doubt it. Come on. Get as close as you can get. *(They group themselves in a row as near the wall as the furniture will permit. Whispers)* Ready? Now—Ilona, Ilona—take the time from me. *(Raises his hand like a conductor; at the same moment Almady's voice is heard)*

ALMADY. I worship you—I adore you. *(The Three are riveted where they stand, transfixed with amazement.)*

ILONA. Are you starting all over again?

ALMADY. Yes, I am. All over again. I love you as the church steeple loves the cloud that settles above it and floats away with the first passing breeze. I can't go on living without you. Not a week, not a day, not an hour.

(The Three Men turn simultaneously.)

ILONA *(contemptuously)*. Just words.

ALMADY. It's the truth. I'm crazy about you. And you—you've used me up and squeezed me like a lemon, and now you want to throw me away.

ILONA. I don't want to throw you away, silly. Oh, come on, then. Come here and let me kiss your beautiful classic brow.

ADAM. She said—did you hear what he said?

ALMADY. That's not a kiss—that's a tip—Nothing but a paltry tip.

(Mansky sinks into chair.)

ILONA. Don't shout like that.

ALMADY. I will shout. I'm a squeezed lemon. That's what I am— *(Sobs)* —a lemon! The whole world shall know that I'm a lemon.

ILONA. Get off your knees. And, oh, please, do stop crying. You know how fond I am of you.

(Turai and Mansky clap their hands to their heads. Adam collapses on the piano stool.)

ALMADY. Those nights of love—those flaming wonderful nights! Have you forgotten them so completely?

ADAM. Why— That's Almady!

MANSKY. You can't be sure.

ILONA. Stop! Control yourself.

ALMADY. You ask me to control myself—when I look at *that*—at that perfect shape. The rose flush of that skin.

ILONA. Hands off!

ALMADY. My God! How round it is! How smooth, how velvety—and how fragrant.

(A pause.)

ILONA. Don't bite!

ALMADY. I must—I am so *hungry*—

TURAI *(to Adam and patting him on the shoulder)*. I think you had better go, old man. Go and turn in in our room.

ADAM *(bitterly)*. And I thought she was a Madonna. Holding her in his arms—stroking— *(Rising in sudden fury and rushing to the door)* —God, I could kill him!

TURAI. Steady, old man, steady.

(Adam covers his ears with his hands.)

ALMADY. Ah, well! I see I am nothing to you any more.

ILONA. Oh, for goodness' sake. I swear that no man has ever meant so much to me as you. From the top of your head to the soles of your feet you are a *man*! Who should know that better than I?

TURAI. Come, come, my boy—let's get out of this.

MANSKY *(goes to Adam)*. Come on, old chap. You're going to sleep in our room. *(Turai and Mansky lead him to stairway)*

ADAM. Sleep! *(He goes out at Right. Turai and Mansky are on the landing)*

ILONA. Oh! Don't look so pathetic.— Well, come here—kiss me.

MANSKY. I was right— We ought to have sent a telegram. *(He goes out)*

ALMADY. I want you to remember that kiss forever.

ILONA. It was your old kiss. Sweet and burning—like hot punch. But do be a dear and go away now. It was mad of you to come here. If my fiancé ever hears of this I'll kill myself. Oh, damn my idiotic sentimentality for getting me into this mess. You must leave here tomorrow on the first train. He'll be here any day now. *(Turai shifts uneasily)* Every day I've been expecting a telegram. *(Turai groans)* Get out, I tell you, get out!

ALMADY. If you insist, dear heart, so be it! Your word is law. I am going to bed now. Farewell, dear heart. But grant me one last kiss.

TURAI *(to himself)*. Damn all fools who don't know when they've had enough.

ILONA. Go *now*—

ALMADY. So be it. Good night, dear heart.

ILONA. Good night, you baby.

(Silence. A door is heard closing.)

TURAI *(to himself)*. At last! "Good night, dear heart!" *(After a moment he sits down in armchair. Pause. Mansky re-enters)*

MANSKY. This silence—what does it mean?

TURAI. This silence is a highly moral silence. The baritone hero has departed. And the fair heroine has deposited herself in bed.

MANSKY. After depositing *us* in the worst mess in my whole experience. Wasn't it awful?

TURAI. Awful? Well, how is he?

MANSKY. I got him to bed. Poor little Pyramus. A jolly wall that, isn't it? Church steeple! Lemon!! The damned fool.

TURAI. I can't look the boy in the face.

MANSKY. You managed to get this suite for us. Marvelous luck! Pyramus and Thisbe! "Oh, sweet wall!" Well, I hope you're satisfied.

TURAI. Oh, go to the devil.

MANSKY. I don't want to be unkind, but whichever way you look at it, you're to blame for this catastrophe. Why the deuce was it necessary to put the boy next to his lady-love? Friendship is friendship, but there are limits.

TURAI. I was merely trying to be sympathetic and helpful. I meant well.

MANSKY. Never mean "well." It's fatal. See what's happened as a result? Bride gone—love gone—waltz gone—operetta gone. All a total loss. On the other hand, the dog didn't die and the coffee was good. Well, Friday has certainly made a nice, clean, efficient job of it this time!

TURAI. What about the boy?

MANSKY. What about our operetta? The lady kissed the lemon's classic brow. After this, can you see her playing the part?

TURAI. To hell with all that. What about the boy? Did he say anything?

MANSKY *(gloomily)*. *One* of his remarks was: "I'll tear up the score and kill Ilona." The round and fragrant one. And the problem that presents itself to me is this: if he tears up his music and kills the prima donna, what sort of a first night shall we have?

TURAI *(thinks a moment, then with emphasis)*. We'll have a first night, I promise you that.

MANSKY. What, after all this?

TURAI. Yes, after all *this*. Don't worry, we'll have a first night all right.

MANSKY. With that music?

TURAI. With that music and that composer and that prima donna. And I'll tell you some other things. We'll have a hit, a wedding, and a happy ending.

MANSKY. Well, of all the optimists! It's just a suggestion, but wouldn't it be a good idea if you were to mention just what you propose to *do*. This is where Sandor Turai, famous for his happy endings, had better try to surpass himself. Get busy, my playwriting genius, and let's see how good you are.

TURAI. One can do but one's best. *(Mansky goes out at Right. A clock in the hall is heard to strike four. Turai takes a blank sheet of music from the piano. He paces up and down in deep thought, occasionally glancing toward Ilona's room. He jots down a few words. Mansky re-enters)* Well, how is he?

MANSKY. Lying in bed, staring at the ceiling. That's bad. He didn't even answer my question.

TURAI. What did you ask him?

MANSKY. I said: *(Plaintively)* "Feeling better now?"

TURAI. What did you expect him to answer to a damn fool question like that?

MANSKY. Well, have *you* solved the problem?

TURAI. If I have I'm not going to tell you. You've ruined enough good ideas of mine already with your collaboration. This time I mean to work alone. Without a partner. All I ask of you is a little information. There are a few *facts* I require.

MANSKY *(huffily)*. That's all I'm good for, is it?

TURAI. That's all. Where are Almady's wife and family now?

MANSKY. At Lake Balaton, I believe.

TURAI. Lake Balaton. Address?

MANSKY. Verona Cottage.

TURAI (*putting it down*). Verona Cottage. What's Ilona's mother's name?

MANSKY. Adele—Alma—something.

TURAI. Well, it begins with an "A."

MANSKY. Yes, I know that.

TURAI. Thank God! Mrs. A. Szabo. What's her address?

MANSKY. 70 Elizabeth Avenue, Fured.

TURAI. Would she be there now?

MANSKY (*petulantly*). Oh God! How should I know? But, listen— (*Points to Ilona's room*) My own humble suggestion would be to wake her up now and have a little chat.

TURAI. What about?

MANSKY (*starting across*). I'll rout her out.

TURAI. For God's sake, don't do that! The only thing a woman can do is deny everything. And what could she deny? Could she explain her half-hearted resistance? Of course, she might point out that it was nice of her to tell the man not to bite.

MANSKY. Women have lots of other tricks. Falling on their knees—fainting—bursting into tears—laughing hysterically —or just going *rigid* all over.

TURAI. That might work all right for you—or me. But that boy is twenty-five, so think again.

MANSKY. Then there's no solution to the problem.

TURAI. There's a solution to everything. One has only to find it.

MANSKY. By Jove! Rather a good line, that.

TURAI. Oh, I don't think—. Well, it's not bad. Jot it down. (*Mansky does so on his cuff*) The thing to do now is to be tactful and understanding with the boy. You go and sit by his bed until he falls asleep.

MANSKY. He won't sleep tonight.

TURAI. Give him something to make him sleep. He's got a big day ahead of him tomorrow. One false move and he'll find himself the center of a record scandal. That would break his heart. On his peace of mind, you know, depends—

MANSKY. Our success. Capacity business. A year's run.

TURAI. Beastly words.

MANSKY. And only yesterday—how beautiful they sounded.

TURAI. Look here. I'll take on this job. Leave everything to me. You know, it's a curious thing, but whenever you stop trying to help me, I can solve anything.

MANSKY (*bows stiffly and turns toward stairs*). Thank you, my dear fellow.

TURAI. Not at all.

MANSKY. Good night.

TURAI. Good night. See you tomorrow. Till then, don't leave him for an instant. That's official. I've enjoyed our little talk so much. Good night.

MANSKY. Good night. (*Goes out at Right. Turai goes to table, sits and jots down some more notes. There is a knock at door Left to hall*)

TURAI. Come in. (*Dwornitschek enters with cooler and champagne, four glasses on a tray*)

DWORNITSCHEK. The champagne, sir —just as you ordered.

TURAI (*motioning it away*). 'Mm, yes. But that was a long time ago. A very long time ago. Since then the world has changed quite a good deal. However, the motto of the Turai is: "Never refuse champagne"; so put it down. (*Dwornitschek places tray on the table and the cooler on the floor*)

DWORNITSCHEK. Will four glasses be sufficient, sir?

TURAI. Three more than sufficient. (*Dwornitschek leaves one glass on the tray before Turai, and places the other three on the table. There is a pause, Turai stares at him.*)

DWORNITSCHEK. Something in the expression of your eye, sir, tells me that you are trying to remember my name.

TURAI. Quite right. What is it?

DWORNITSCHEK. Dwornitschek, sir.

TURAI. Still Dwornitschek? Well, well! All right, Dwornitschek, you can go to bed.

DWORNITSCHEK. Is there anything special that you fancy for breakfast, sir?

TURAI. No. Just ham, eggs, cold chicken, smoked salmon, cold beef, bacon, butter, milk, honey, jam, rolls and tea.

DWORNITSCHEK. With lemon?

TURAI. No! With rum!

DWORNITSCHEK. Very good, sir.

TURAI. What are you waiting for?

DWORNITSCHEK. I was wondering if there were any more questions you desired to ask me, sir?

TURAI. No, thank you.

DWORNITSCHEK. Thank *you*, sir.

TURAI. No, no, thank you.

DWORNITSCHEK. I love being asked questions, sir. It shows that gentlemen take an interest.

TURAI. You mean in Dwornitschek, the servant, eh?

DWORNITSCHEK. Yes, sir. You are sure you have nothing more to ask, sir? It would be a treat for me.

TURAI. There's nothing more, thank you. My stock of knowledge for today is complete. I wish it weren't.

DWORNITSCHEK. Then I will bid you good night, sir.

TURAI. Good night— One moment! There is something I'd like. I'd like some writing paper, some telegraph forms, some ink and a pen.

DWORNITSCHEK. The writing materials are in the library, sir. But I can bring them to you here.

TURAI. No, thank you. I'll do my writing in the library. That's a good idea —no chance of being disturbed.

DWORNITSCHEK. I'll go and turn on the lights, sir.

TURAI. One moment. *(Points to champagne)* Might that come with us?

DWORNITSCHEK. Very good, sir.

TURAI. After you.

DWORNITSCHEK. Oh no, sir!

TURAI. I insist, my dear Dwornitschek —after you.

DWORNITSCHEK. At what hour do you desire breakfast, sir?

TURAI. What hour is it now?

DWORNITSCHEK. Quarter past four, sir.

TURAI. Then let us say at seven—or, no—make it six.

DWORNITSCHEK. Very good, sir. At six precisely.

TURAI. Look here, Dwornitschek,— when do you sleep?

DWORNITSCHEK. In the winter, sir!

CURTAIN

ACT TWO

SCENE: *As the Curtain rises a clock in the hall is heard to strike six. Golden sunlight pours in the windows. The Mediterranean is as blue as tradition has painted it. Sandor Turai, now jauntily attired in white flannels, is seated in the armchair at the Center, with the loose leaves of a manuscript before him. As the clock stops striking, the door at Left to the hall opened by Dwornitschek, who comes down to Turai bringing a newspaper on a salver. Dwornitschek is followed by two lackeys in livery, each carrying an enormous silver tray piled high with Turai's breakfast. During the dialogue that follows, the lackeys place the breakfast upon the long table at Right. This done, one of them stands at attention while the other goes up to the window, opens it, steps out on the balcony and lowers an awning which shuts off some of the now too brilliant sunlight*

———

DWORNITSCHEK. Good morning, sir.

TURAI. Good morning. What's this?

DWORNITSCHEK. Morning paper, sir.

TURAI. You've read it, of course?

DWORNITSCHEK. Oh yes, sir.

TURAI. Anything about me in it?

DWORNITSCHEK. No, sir.

TURAI. Then take it away. *(Dwornitschek gives salver with the newspaper to one of the lackeys and motions both off)*

DWORNITSCHEK. Let me see, sir, think it was ham, eggs, cold chicken smoked salmon, cold beef, bacon, butter milk, honey, jam and rolls that you ordered, was it not?

TURAI. Quite right.

DWORNITSCHEK. And tea with cold lemon.

TURAI. I loathe lemons.

DWORNITSCHEK. Yes, sir. Many people do. I once had an aunt—

TURAI. Suppose we don't talk about your aunt just for the moment.

DWORNITSCHEK. Very good, sir.

TURAI. Later on, perhaps.

DWORNITSCHEK. At any time that suits you, sir.

TURAI. You must make allowances for the artistic temperament, when I have been sitting up all night writing.

DWORNITSCHEK. I quite understand, sir.

(Turai has risen and crossed to the table, upon which he has put the manuscript. He now goes round to the Right side where his place is set and examines the breakfast with evident satisfaction. He lifts the covers from several silver dishes, looks at their contents with pleasure, and smiles at Dwornitschek with approval.)

TURAI. You're really a wonderful fellow. How on earth did you manage not to forget anything?

DWORNITSCHEK. It was a labor of love, sir. My heart is in that breakfast.

TURAI. Your heart, too? *(After he has taken a sip of tea)* Ah! that puts new life into a man.

DWORNITSCHEK. You must have had very little sleep, sir.

TURAI. Not much.

DWORNITSCHEK. I hadn't any.

TURAI. Yes, I remember you told me you were essentially a hibernating animal.

DWORNITSCHEK. Nobody else is stirring as yet. This is the time when I sometimes manage to lie down myself for a few moments.

TURAI. Then you will get some sleep, after all?

DWORNITSCHEK. Just forty winks, sir. That's the advantage of being by the sea. Gentlemen stay in bed till noon. Very different from the mountains.

TURAI. They get up early in the mountains, eh?

DWORNITSCHEK. At about five or four-thirty. They like to go climbing. But there's always a bright side, sir; they go to bed at nine.

TURAI. You know, you're broadening my mind tremendously. Every time I see you, I learn something new.

DWORNITSCHEK. If it's not a liberty, sir, I should like to say something.

TURAI. I'll bet it's something good. Go on.

DWORNITSCHEK. You ought to take more care of your health, sir. You don't get enough sleep.

TURAI. I don't?

DWORNITSCHEK. And you smoke too much, sir. I found at least fifty cigarette butts in the ash-tray in the library.

TURAI. Wrong. Thirty-seven.

DWORNITSCHEK. Too many, sir.

TURAI. What's your daily allowance?

DWORNITSCHEK. Fifteen, sir.

TURAI. You'll live to be a hundred.

DWORNITSCHEK. Thank you—is that a medical opinion, sir?

TURAI. No, just a hope. This weary world needs men like you.

DWORNITSCHEK. No, no, sir. Like *you*.

TURAI. Well, shall we say like both of us?

DWORNITSCHEK. Would it be a liberty, sir, if I expressed the opinion that you have a heart of gold?

TURAI. Not at all. Thank you very much.

DWORNITSCHEK. Thank *you*, sir.

TURAI. No, no. Thank *you*.

DWORNITSCHEK. It's the way you take an interest that touches a man, sir. I wish there was something I could do for *you*.

TURAI. At the moment, I think the best thing you can do for me is to leave me alone. And if anyone asks for me, tell them I'm sleeping and must not be disturbed. Understand?

DWORNITSCHEK. Oh, yes, indeed, sir. *(Dwornitschek starts to exit. Turai stops him. Turai pantomimes "Wait a minute. I must remember your name." He registers despair. Dwornitschek smiles indulgently and whispers)* Dwornitschek.

TURAI. Thank you.

DWORNITSCHEK. Thank *you*, sir.

(He goes out at the Left to hall. Turai rises, listens at staircase, then goes to the telephone and takes up the receiver.)

TURAI. Hello. Will you give me Miss Ilona Szabo's room? *(He waits. Telephone bell rings loudly in the room at Left. After a pause it rings again)*

ILONA *(sleepily)*. Yes???

TURAI. Hello.

ILONA. Hello!!!

TURAI *(softly)*. Hello.

ILONA. Who's that?

TURAI. The unfeeling brute who has aroused you from your slumber is known to the police as Sandor Turai.

ILONA *(changing in a flash, delighted)*. Sandor! Dear old Sandor!

TURAI. Well, and how's the prima donna?

ILONA. Where are you speaking from?

TURAI. Next door.

ILONA. What!

TURAI. I thought you'd be surprised. I'm in the next room.

ILONA. How on earth?—

TURAI. My dear little Ilona, let's postpone the explanations. I want to see you at once—immediately.

ILONA. You're frightening me. What is it?

TURAI (deliberately puts down receiver and speaks toward the wall). Don't be alarmed. Open the door, put something on, and come in. Or rather, put something on, open the door and come in.

ILONA. Do what? I can't hear you. There must be something wrong with this telephone.

TURAI (now at the door). I say: put something on, open the door, and come in. Can you hear me better now?

ILONA. Yes, I can hear beautifully now.

TURAI. Good.

ILONA. I'll be right in. (Enters) Sandor—what is it? I feel something terrible has happened. What's the matter?

TURAI. Sit down, my dear. You and I have got to do some quick talking.

ILONA. But what's happened? For heaven's sake, tell me!

TURAI. Sit down.

ILONA. Why?

TURAI. Because if you don't sit down now, you'll sit down later on when you hear what I've got to say—and you'll sit down hard. Better do it gracefully while you can. (He pushes her gently into the armchair)

ILONA. I don't understand.

TURAI. You will. My dear little Ilona, in spite of the fact that you are engaged to my young friend Adam, you are still carrying on an affair with Mr. Almady.

ILONA (with indignation). It's an outrageous lie.

TURAI. Good! I thought you were going to say it was none of my business.

ILONA. I couldn't say that, because you're Albert's guardian, guide, philosopher and friend and God knows what else. And you're a friend of mine and write plays for me. So I simply say that it's a lie.

TURAI. I'm glad you do, because it's an observation which I can answer. I've been in this room since last night and the walls in this new wing are as thin as paper.

ILONA (looks at walls. As the truth dawns upon her she is horrified). Good God!

TURAI. "Lemon." (Ilona hides her face.) "Lemon—Church steeple." Well, dear Ilona. Suppose we talk this over? Something's got to be done—and done quickly.

ILONA. If you heard, you heard what I said, too.

TURAI. Every word.

ILONA. Then you know that I told him to get out— and he's getting out today. At twelve o'clock. So if you don't say anything—and of course you won't—

TURAI. Not quite so fast, please. If the thing were as simple as that, you would never have known from me that I had overheard you. I regret to say matters are much more unpleasant.

ILONA (sinking back in chair). My God! You don't mean—?

TURAI. I see you've guessed.

ILONA. Did—did—I can't say it.

TURAI. I will say it for you. Yes, the boy did hear it, too.

ILONA. God!—He's here then?

TURAI. He is here.

ILONA. Where?

TURAI. Sh! He's up in Mansky's room—asleep. And last night he was in this room—awake.

ILONA. I'll take veronal, all there is in my bottle.

TURAI. That's not enough.

ILONA. Ten ounces?

TURAI. I was not referring to the veronal. I mean suicide is no solution.

ILONA. There isn't any solution that could survive. There are only two things I can possibly do—kill myself or deny the whole story.

TURAI. Deny the whole story? Do you suppose if it were just a question of telling lies, I would have troubled you? I'd have told them myself long ago.

ILONA. Then we come back to the veronal.

TURAI. Exactly. We come back to the veronal—and find it safely tucked away in its bottle.

ILONA. Well, what do you suggest?

TURAI. I have my plan. And all I ask of you is not to hinder it.

ILONA (*almost crying*). You know I worship Albert. If anybody knows that, you do. I've been a different woman since I met him. He looks on me as a saint. (*Turai gives her a quick ironic glance*) And he's right. I *have* turned into a saint since I began to love him. It was the only thing I wanted to do in life—to keep straight for his sake. I was so happy. (*She sinks into armchair crying*) I love him so.

TURAI. And yet you can't be true to him.

ILONA (*indignantly*). You've no right to say that. It was nothing but my damned sentimentality. You know very well that affair with that beast Almady didn't last a couple of months. First he gave me breathing lessons and taught me how to throw my voice—

TURAI (*with a significant glance*). Yes, he taught you that, all right.

ILONA. I'm just a victim of my kind heart. I thought I was rid of him, but he got himself invited here. And he's always bursting into tears. A woman hates to see a man cry. He stuck to me like a leech. But why on earth would I want to start in with him again? I give you my word, Sandor, that last night was simply—like the last dying vibrations of a high note.

TURAI. You'd have done better to stop vibrating a little earlier. Still, there it is. What we've got to do now is get you out of the mess.

ILONA (*runs across to Turai and throws herself on her knees, clasping him beseechingly*) Sandor! Sandor darling! Do you really think you *can?*

TURAI. Yes, I can. But don't think I'm doing it for your sake, my dear; not for the sake of your beautiful eyes. You deserve to be drawn and quartered. I'm doing it for that poor decent boy who still retains a few ideals in this unpleasant world. Yes, my dear Ilona, I think I must ask you to be a little ashamed of yourself.

ILONA (*bitterly*). Don't worry. (*Rises*) I am. What can I do?

TURAI (*goes to telephone*). I am just going to tell you. And you won't enjoy it. Still, good medicine's rarely pleasant.

(*Picks up receiver*) Hello. (*To Ilona*) What's the number of Almady's room?

ILONA (*apprehensively*). What do you want with him?

TURAI (*into the telephone*). Give me Mr. Almady's room, please. (*Pause*) Never mind about all that, my good man. I don't care what instructions he left—call him. And go on ringing till he answers. It's a matter of life and death.

ILONA. What are you doing?

TURAI (*into telephone*). Mr. Almady? Yes, yes, I know you gave instructions—Will you please be quiet for a moment?—This is Sandor Turai speaking. Here in the new wing—Last night, by car— Good morning—you were awake already! Capital! Would you mind coming here at once? Room number four— Yes, I mean now, right away— Yes, matter of life and death was what I said, but I made a slight error. I should have said a matter of death—yes, yes, this very minute—right. (*He hangs up the receiver. Ilona starts to go*) Where are you off to?

ILONA. Is Almady coming here?

TURAI. You will kindly stay just where you were.

ILONA (*looking toward Albert's bedroom*). He looked on me as a saint. He thought I was everything that was fine and pure. He called me his Madonna.

TURAI. You should have thought of that a long time ago.

ILONA. Tell me—what did Albert say?

TURAI. I wouldn't ask that if I were you.

ILONA. God! What was the plan you said you had?—Can't you speak?

TURAI. Patience.

ILONA. It's too cruel— Just because I hate hurting people's feelings— (*She breaks off as a knock sounds*)

TURAI. Come in.

(*Almady, who enters, is also in a state of nervous apprehension. He is attired in elaborate, not to say loud, house pajamas. A tall and but recently handsome man, now well into middle age, Almady is first, last and always the actor. He dramatizes every moment of his existence. He does not walk, he struts; he does not talk, he declaims.*)

ALMADY. Good morning. (*Sees Ilona, surprised*) Hullo, you here?

TURAI. Yes, she's here.

ALMADY. But what's the matter? Has something happened?

ILONA. Oh, do sit down.

TURAI. He'll sit down quite soon enough. I'm not afraid of his not sitting down.

ALMADY. You'll forgive me if I seem nervous—

TURAI. Glass of brandy?

ALMADY. Thank you. Never in the morning.

TURAI. Mr. Almady, you are a married man and the father of a family. And you are forcing your attentions on another man's fiancée.

ALMADY *(indignantly)*. It's an outrageous lie.

TURAI. Good. I thought you were going to say it was none of my business. You would have been quite right. But a lie—no, I'm afraid that won't do.

ALMADY *(aggressively)*. Mr. Turai, I would have you know—

TURAI. Shut up!

ALMADY *(outraged)*. "Shut up!"

TURAI *(significantly)*. "Lemon!" *(Almady sits down abruptly)* I told you he'd sit down. *(Almady looks at the Left wall)* Yes, quite right. It's as thin as paper.

ALMADY *(rises)*. Now come, Mr. Turai, between two gentlemen—

TURAI. I beg your pardon?

ALMADY. As one gentleman to another, I ask your discretion—

TURAI. Sit down.

ALMADY *(sitting down anxiously)*. Why? Is there something else coming?

TURAI. Yes, there is something else coming. Are you sitting down?

ALMADY. Yes.

TURAI. Then listen. I wasn't the only one who heard everything. Her fiancé was in this room with me at the time, and his hearing is excellent.

ALMADY *(strangling)*. Brandy!

TURAI *(pouring it out)*. In the morning? *(Gives Almady the brandy)*

ALMADY. I always take it in the morning. *(He gulps it down)*

ILONA. Well, what are you going to do now, you miserable idiot, you? You see what you've done. You've driven me to suicide. Oh, God! I shall die. I shall die!

ALMADY *(rising melodramatically)*. I'll die with you!

ILONA. I don't want you! I'm going to die alone.

ALMADY *(pompously)*. I am ready to give him satisfaction.

TURAI. That's the last straw. I'll tell you what you are going to do. You are going to do just as I order.

ALMADY *(starting up)*. Order?

TURAI. Sit down. *(Almady sits down)*

ILONA. Yes—order. *(To Turai—rapidly)* Tell us, please. Never mind how much he rants.

ALMADY. Rants! You dare to criticize my diction?

TURAI. Oh! Damn your diction! Just thank your stars that I'm going to get you out of this. A married man! Father of a family. With four children at home— four little lemons! One word from you, and this telegram, all ready and written, goes off to your wife.

(Almady looks again at wall and groans.)

ILONA. Look at him. Don't look at the wall. Last night was the time to have done that.

TURAI. In that room next door—last night—something occurred.

ILONA. Yes yes, *please*. We know what occurred.

TURAI. That is just what you don't know. You are now going to hear. What occurred was the rehearsal of a play. Do you grasp my meaning?

ILONA. In the middle of the night?

TURAI. In the middle of the night.

ALMADY. How do you mean—the rehearsal of a play?

TURAI. Your very loud remarks, so loud that they actually penetrated the wall, were dialogue from a play. Now, do you understand?

ILONA. I do. *(To Almady)* Don't you— idiot? It's the most marvelous, wonderful idea, you old darling— *(She is just about to embrace Turai, when she stops in consternation)*

TURAI. What's the matter?

ILONA. It's no good. He'd never believe it.

TURAI. Why wouldn't he believe it?

ILONA *(glances witheringly at Almady)*. Where on earth would you find a play with lines like those?

TURAI. Where? Here. *(Picks script up from table.)*

ILONA. What do you mean?

TURAI. Here you are. Here's the play. This is it.

ILONA. Who wrote it?

TURAI. I did. This morning—between four and six.

ILONA. What!!??

TURAI. After all, one is either a playwright or one isn't. Half of it I heard through the wall; the other half I wrote to fit. I feel this morning rather like an acrobat who for once has had the chance to use his skill to save a life. I don't suppose a play has ever been written with such altruistic motives. Well, there you are. There's the play. Read it, learn it—and play it.

ILONA. Play it!

TURAI. Naturally! How else can you make him believe that what you were saying last night was just dialogue? There will be a dress rehearsal this evening—then the performance.

ALMADY. Tonight? But where?

TURAI. At the concert, of course. After dinner in the ballroom. *(To Ilona)* You're already down for something, aren't you?

ILONA. A couple of songs. *(Looks at Almady contemptuously)* He's to recite some poems.

TURAI. Oh, my God. Then there'll be a slight change in the program. He's going to have to act.

ILONA. But how on earth can I learn all this by tonight?

TURAI. Well, really! You knew it well enough last night! *(Almady sighs deeply)* Why do you sigh?

ALMADY. Mr. Turai, that was a sigh of relief. You *know* my wife.

TURAI. Didn't I tell you it was a matter of death?

ILONA. Oh, but listen—what earthly reason could we have had for rehearsing at three o'clock in the morning?

TURAI. That's what I asked myself, and answered myself—quite simple. You had to play the thing tonight. You'd lost a lot of time at the picnic. Every moment was precious. And you were so conscientious that you insisted on rehearsing when you got home last night even though it was three o'clock in the morning.

ILONA. Well, we'd better get started. I'm a very slow study.

TURAI. One minute. Don't get excited. Who's supposed to be running this concert?

ILONA. The Count's secretary, Mr. Mell.

TURAI. We must notify him of this change in the program. *(Goes to telephone)* Hello—Give me Mr. Mell's room, please.

ILONA. But he'll be asleep.

TURAI. Oh, no, my dear. Not after this telephone bell has rung once or twice. *(He hands Ilona the receiver)* There you are—ladies first.

ILONA *(taking telephone)*. But what am I to say?

TURAI. Keep calm. I'll prompt you.

ILONA. Hello! Is that Mr. Mell? Yes, it is early, isn't it? *(She looks at Turai for directions)*

TURAI. Good morning.

ILONA *(into telephone)*. Good morning.

TURAI. How did you sleep?

ILONA *(her hand over the receiver)*. I can't say that. The poor man is furious.

TURAI. Use your own judgment.

ILONA *(into the telephone in her most seductive manner)*. Dear Mr. Mell! *(Coos)* I'm so dreadfully sorry to wake you up at this hour, but I wanted to tell you that there will be a little change in the program tonight. I'm sure the Count will be pleased. I'm sure you will be pleased. I'm sure the audience will be pleased.

TURAI. Unanimous.

ILONA *(into the telephone)*. Instead of working alone, I'm going to appear with Mr. Almady. Yes, Mr. Almady. In an extremely witty, charming, brilliant little duologue. *(Turai bows. Ilona listens at the telephone for a moment. Then she turns to Turai and asks, as if she were still speaking to Mell)* What kind of a play is it?

TURAI. French.

ILONA *(into the telephone)*. French. *(As before)* Who wrote it?

TURAI. Geraldy.

ILONA. Geraldy, I believe— *(Pause)* Oh, isn't that nice!

TURAI *(apprehensive)*. What's nice?

ILONA *(hand over receiver)*. He says he

knows every line that Geraldy ever wrote.

TURAI. Then it's by Sardou.

ILONA *(into the telephone)*. No, I'm sorry. I've just been looking at the script again. It's not by Geraldy; it's by Sardou.

TURAI. The Great Sardou.

ILONA *(into the telephone)*. The Great Sardou!— Indeed?

TURAI. How is he up on Sardou?

ILONA *(covering receiver)*. He says the only thing of Sardou's he knows is "Hedda Gabler."

TURAI. That's the man for us!

ILONA. That's the man for us!

TURAI. No, no, no!

ILONA. Goodbye, and thank you so much, Mr. Mell. You've been so sweet. —Oh, of course—as if we'd dream of having anybody but you as a prompter— The title?

TURAI. "A Tooth For a Tooth."

ILONA. "A Truth For a—

TURAI. No, no. Tooth, tooth!

ILONA. "A Tooth For a Tooth"— Yes, isn't it? Quite snappy. Well, good-by. *(Hangs up)* Why a French piece?

TURAI. So that nobody will know who wrote it. That's the beauty of French literature. There's so much of it. Besides, one has one's conscience, you know. I've stolen so much from the French in my time that it's only fair I should give them something for a change. Oh, Almady! So that no one will recognize my hand-writing, it will be necessary for you to copy out the script.

ALMADY. All of it?

TURAI. From beginning to end.

ALMADY. You think of everything.

TURAI. Two copies!

ILONA *(who has been looking through the script)*. Oh, but this isn't right!

TURAI. What isn't right?

ILONA. This line. You have me say, "Your kiss is revolting to me." What I really said was—

TURAI. "That was your old kiss. Sweet and burning like hot punch." I know. My memory is excellent. But fortunately we got the boy out the room before you got that far.

ALMADY. And may I be permitted to inquire *why* my kiss should be described as revolting?

TURAI. The line occurs in the second part of the play, where I was relying on my native inspiration.

ALMADY. You call my kiss revolting? I wish to know why.

TURAI. That is how I *see* it. I am the author of this play, and that is my opinion of your kiss.

ILONA. I do think you might have made some noise to warn us. Why couldn't you have coughed or something?

TURAI. Suppose I had, what should I have been able to do *now*? You overlook the fact that your very first words, my dear Ilona, left no room for misunder-standing. If I had stopped you then nothing could have averted the tragedy.

ALMADY. What a brain!

TURAI. You flatter me!

ILONA. No, he doesn't. He's right for once. Did this idea come to you the moment you heard us?

TURAI. No, I got it from you.

ILONA. From us?

TURAI. Yes, stupid of me, I admit. You see, I always assume the best of my fellow-men. And just for a minute I did think that you really were acting. Later on, I realized my mistake.

ILONA. You thought we were acting. Why?

TURAI. Because it all sounded so arti-ficial. No ring of conviction. I refer par-ticularly to the more erotic passages.

ILONA. I don't wonder. Considering I don't care one little bit for the man.

ALMADY. What's that?

ILONA. You heard.

ALMADY. You don't love me?

ILONA. No!

ALMADY. So you were lying!

ILONA. Yes.

ALMADY. Just to get rid of me?

ILONA. Yes. I hate the sight of you.

ALMADY *(sobs bitterly)*. Serpent!

ILONA. I'd like to murder you!

TURAI. Doesn't it tear your heart to hear a strong man weep?

ALMADY. What made you realize that we were not acting?

TURAI. The disgusting sloppy way you spoke to her. No author living would dare put such slush into the mouth of an actor who is supposed to be making love.

ALMADY. Slush?

TURAI. Utter slush!

ALMADY. Allow me to inform you—

TURAI. Shut up!

ALMADY. Oh, very well.

TURAI. My friends may be here any minute now. Please go and study your parts. (To Ilona, who has been turning over the leaves of the script) That's a bit you'll have to learn particularly well.

ILONA. Which?

TURAI. These lines here. This loathsome series of speeches—the ones we overheard last night. (Points) From there to there.

ILONA. Odd—I hardly remember—

TURAI. I do. Nor is your fiancé likely to have forgotten.

ILONA (reading). "I worship you. I adore you. I love you as the church steeple loves the cloud that settles on its summit." (Almady turns away, embarrassed) Just words!

ALMADY (takes script). "You have used me up and squeezed me like a lemon."

ILONA. Yes, now I remember—

ALMADY. It's all down, word for word. (Turai takes script)

TURAI. Yes, the passage is underlined in red ink. Three pages—here—from page sixteen. It goes on, "Come here and let me kiss that beautiful classic brow"—and then—this is the worst bit, here—his mad outburst of sensuality— (Reads rapidly) "When I look at that—at the perfect shape. The rose flush of that skin—just to stroke it!—"

ILONA. Yes, but I said—

TURAI. I know, I know. (Reads) "Hands off!" you said. But he evidently didn't obey you because he goes on, "My God! How round it is! How smooth! How velvety!" And then he must have gotten very close, indeed, because his next remark is "And how fragrant!" That's right, isn't it?

ALMADY. Quite right. It was fragrant.

ILONA. Yes, but I did try to—

TURAI. No, my dear, you did not. There was a complete silence until you were heard to exclaim, "You mustn't ite!" (Ilona rises; Almady turns away) Yes, I should think you would be ashamed of yourselves. All right, then; copy it, learn it, and play it. And if you ever studied parts in your lives, study these. I'll give you run-through here at seven-thirty— and Ilona—remember, we haven't seen each other for three months.

ILONA. All right, three months. (She exits)

ALMADY. A colossal brain!

TURAI (bows). Thank you.

(Almady follows Ilona off. Turai sits at table and resumes his interrupted breakfast. Throughout the following scene he goes on eating quietly, deliberately, and with apparent good appetite. Mansky enters dressed in white flannels. He is more doleful and dejected than ever.)

MANSKY. Have you been up long?

TURAI. I couldn't sleep. (Goes on eating) How is the infant?

MANSKY. Woke up a moment ago. I left him dressing.

TURAI You had breakfast yet?

MANSKY. Not a mouthful. Couldn't touch it. You seem to have no difficulty in putting it away.

TURAI (with mock sadness). One must keep up one's strength.

MANSKY. I'm amazed, and, if I may say so, a little shocked. Sitting there gorging as if nothing had happened. Can't you realize we're absolutely ruined? I'm positively ill thinking about it.

TURAI (mysteriously). Shall I let you into a secret, Mansky?

MANSKY (with excited anticipation). Yes. Tell me.

TURAI (with great deliberation). I am a man who weighs his words. I do not speak lightly. And I say to you solemnly, my friend— (Dramatic pause) —that this is the best bit of ham I've ever tasted.

MANSKY (furious). Bah! (Crosses to a mirror)

TURAI (continuing as before). Juicy— nutty—positively good. (Solicitously) Did the boy sleep at all?

MANSKY. He dropped off about daylight out of sheer exhaustion. (Looks in the glass) I'm pale.

TURAI. Say anything?

MANSKY. Not a word. Just stared at the ceiling. You know, that's bad.

TURAI. Ceilings aren't so bad. Walls are much worse.

MANSKY. What I can't understand is why a magnificent place like this should have walls like tissuepaper.

TURAI. Ah! These are deep waters.

MANSKY. Do stop eating!

TURAI. But I haven't finished.

MANSKY. Gobble—gobble—gobble! *(Looks in the glass)* My God, I am pale!

TURAI. Suits you. Intellectual pallor.

MANSKY. What about that solution you were hinting at last night?

TURAI. There were several possibilities. I considered them all thoroughly in the night watches—while you lay snoring in your bed. Oh, yes, I heard you while I was changing my clothes. *(Points to the table)* Telegrams, letters, all ready. Finally I hit on the best and simplest plan.

MANSKY. Which is?

TURAI. I'm going to do everything possible to make him break with her.

MANSKY. What for?

TURAI. Because that's the surest way of bringing them together. If he casts her off forever, in two weeks he'll be rushing after her and falling at her feet. The lady, after a little coaxing, will allow herself to melt. He will coax a little more. She will melt a little more. Finally she will melt altogether—and the curtain will fall on the lover's show embrace.

MANSKY *(with cumulative contempt)*. You thought of that in the night, did you?

TURAI. I did.

MANSKY. All by yourself?

TURAI. All by myself?

MANSKY. Well ! ! ! I've noticed all this past year that you've been slipping. I realize now that you've completely lost your grip. Our last show died the death simply because you would write psychology into it. And now you've become simply driveling. It's a great shock to me. Do you know what's happening? Little by little you're beginning to think—and that spells ruin for both of us. Haven't you grasped yet what a frightful knockdown blow last night's affair was to that boy?

TURAI. Sh! Here he is! *(Enter Adam. He is also in white flannels. Very solemn and miserable. Pause. He passes them without a word and goes to balcony)* Hullo! Not even a good morning?

ADAM. Oh, good morning.

(Turai rises; Mansky looks longingly at breakfast things.)

MANSKY *(to Adam with his best bedside manner)*. Had breakfast?

ADAM. No. *(Mansky goes to table and sits down; starts to eat)*

TURAI. Sleep?

ADAM. No.

TURAI. Nor did I. *(Adam looks at Left wall)* No. Nothing from there. Not another sound. He left and she went to sleep. *I* didn't on your account. *(To Mansky)* Hullo! Appetite picking up?

MANSKY *(starting guiltily and pushing his plate away)*. No. I can't swallow. Too nervous. I'm a wreck.

TURAI. Try the ham.

ADAM. I—my dear Uncle Sandor— I don't want to be a burden to you two any longer—now that my life has been blown to bits.

TURAI. Come, come, come!

ADAM. I mean it. I know what I'm talking about. There's a great crack in my heart, and—

TURAI. Come now, be a man. We had enough of that sort of talk last night. Tell me just what is it you want to do?

ADAM. Before anything else, I want to get away from this place.

TURAI. Quite reasonable. And then?

ADAM. Then I'll tear up the music I wrote for her— tear it into little bits and burn it.

TURAI. Right. And after that?

ADAM. Don't be so casual. You know I have nobody in the world but you—you two. If you hadn't been here, I'd have ended things long ago.

TURAI *(to Mansky, who has once more started on the breakfast)*. That's right Peck a bit.

MANSKY *(jumping up)*. No. It's no good. Absolutely can't swallow. I'm very sick man.

ADAM. You see? I'm to blame for that.

TURAI. Now listen to me, my boy. Sit down. *(Adam sits)* What has happened has happened. It's over, done with, a thing of the past. And I'm going to say something to you now which no young person will ever believe. You're twenty-five and you're gifted. The world's at your feet. And that world, let me remind you, contains a great many million women.

ADAM. What good are they to me? I only wanted this one. Can't we get away now—at once? I won't see her!

TURAI. Oh, yes you will! Everybody knows she's your fiancée. And you won't run away now. Mind you, I absolutely forbid any sort of reconciliation with her; but you will behave toward her quite naturally and nicely. I know it's going to hurt—it's a bitter pill to swallow. But, remember, today you're a man.

ADAM. Yes, you're right.

TURAI. Up with the head and out with the chin and damn everybody! That's the stuff. The day after tomorrow, when we leave, you shall write her a letter, and let yourself go as much as you like. And, no matter how it may hurt, you have finished with that woman forever.

ADAM (with an effort). Very well. And if it should hurt too much, don't be afraid that I'll go back to her. I'll always have pluck enough to put a bullet through my head.

MANSKY. There! See where you have got us to with your psychology.

TURAI (to Adam). You ought to be ashamed of yourself.

ADAM (smilingly). It's all right. It was silly of me to talk nonsense like that. I won't let you down. You shall be satisfied with me.

MANSKY. Good. Then you won't—er —tear anything up?

ADAM. No.

TURAI. You'll behave toward Ilona as if nothing had happened.

ADAM. Yes. Honor bright.

TURAI. I am satisfied.

MANSKY (sitting down to breakfast, a completely changed man). It's an enormous relief to me to see you getting hold of yourself again so capitally. (Eats rapidly) Bless my soul, yes, an enormous relief. I really feel a little better.

TURAI. I'm proud of you. (To Mansky) Haven't you finished breakfast yet?

MANSKY (delighted). I can swallow.

TURAI. So I notice.

MANSKY. Come and join me, my boy. You'll find your appetite steals back, little by little. (To Turai) He's suffering. He can't get over it.

TURAI. We must try to make him.

MANSKY. Come on, my boy—just a mouthful. Try a little of this excellent ham.

ADAM. I don't want any ham.

MANSKY. Well, a slice of chicken, then—and some nice hot tea with a drop of brandy.

ADAM. Oh, all right. (Sits down)

MANSKY (to Turai). Well, what's on your mind?

ADAM. After trying to cheer me up, are you going to be depressed yourself?

MANSKY. Do you know what I think's the matter with him? He's got another—

TURAI. You win. Another problem.

MANSKY. Theatre!

TURAI. As usual.

MANSKY. Good Lord!

TURAI. Last night I was thinking how hard it is to begin a play. Now I'm thinking how hard it is to finish a second act.

MANSKY. Oh, come and finish your breakfast.

TURAI. No, no. This is interesting. Take this situation of ours—just as we did last night. We've had a curious experience. We arrived here perfectly happy, and immediately got a terrible shock—a ghastly disillusionment. Oh, we've managed to survive it, and we've got ourselves in hand again. But, suppose all this had happened not in real life but on a stage. Suppose this were not a real room, but a painted set. Suppose we three were characters in a play who had just passed through the experiences that we have just passed through.

MANSKY. Well?

TURAI. Well, how would you end the act?

MANSKY. My dear fellow! It's ended already.

TURAI. Well, in a way, yes. But, at the last moment, just before the curtain actually falls, you need a new note of suspense. The act must end, and yet it mustn't quite end—if you know what I mean. Well, my distinguished collaborator, you've often told me how good you are. Try your hand at ending the second act of this dismal adventure of ours.

MANSKY. Simplicity itself. Now then. I'm all for the quiet curtain. One of those charming delicate things the French do so well. You know—sophisticated—lightly sentimental—the smile behind the tear. The three friends sit down to breakfast. Audiences always like to see actors eating. The storm has passed. The skies are still a little dark, but there is sunlight in the heart—and all that sort of thing. Let this sink in for a bit—everything very cozy and pleasant. *(Notices wineglass on table)* We each have a glass of wine. For a moment— silence—their thoughts are busy with what has passed. *(Pause)* Capital. And then— *(He raises his glass)* —you want a couple of smart lines, spoken with something of a flourish. *(Thinks)* Oh, well— My young friend, today you have become a man—

TURAI *(pointing to where he was sitting at the time)*. I said that.

MANSKY. For—always remember—

TURAI. Yes, that shows 'em it's coming.

MANSKY *(not heeding him)*. Always remember that in affairs of the heart it is not the first victory that makes us men, but the first defeat. *(Lifts his glass)* To Woman's Treachery, which has made our child a man! *(Raises his hand toward the Curtain)* Curtain. *(Curtain starts to come down. They put their glasses down on the table simultaneously, untasted)* How's that?

TURAI. Rotten! *(Stops Curtain with a motion. Curtain slowly goes up again)* Tame. Feeble. Nothing in the nature of a high spot. I'm not saying it isn't pretty and graceful. Charming even, but it lacks suspense. *(Pause. To Adam)* How would you do it?

ADAM. I? Feeling as I do now?

TURAI. Give us your idea.

ADAM *(with tremendous intensity)*. Very well, I'll give you my idea. We start from where Mansky gave that toast.

MANSKY. To Woman's—?

ADAM *(rises)*. Treachery. That's it. I'd say— "No. I won't drink any toast." *(Throws glass against the wall, smashing it to bits.)*

MANSKY *(approvingly)*. Effective.

ADAM *(rapidly losing control of himself and becoming hysterical)*. That woman was not just an incident in my life. She was my first great passion. I promised to act as if nothing had happened. I meant to keep that promise. But when I remember that I gave her my life and that she whispers words of love to another man— and—and kisses another man, that's such unbearable, burning torture, that the only right solution— *(Grabs small game carving knife from table)*

TURAI *(leaping forward)*. Hey! Stop that!

ADAM *(struggling with him)*. No! No!

MANSKY *(rushing forward)*. My God! You weren't really—

ADAM *(struggling)*. Let me go. I want to die. *(Turai has got knife away from him. He looks at it intently. Adam stands, pale and defiant)*

TURAI. What the devil do you think you're doing?

ADAM *(bitterly)*. Just—finishing the act. *(He sits down. Mansky follows him and sits down, too. Smiles wanly)* Curtain! *(Curtain starts to come down)*

TURAI *(stopping Curtain with a motion)* Very bad. *(Curtain goes up again)* My dear young fellow. You simply can't wipe out the young love interest at the end of the second act with a bread knife. That's crude. And there are the critics. *(Cringes)* The critics dislike bloodshed. If there is to be any slaughter, they prefer to attend to it themselves. No, no, my boy. What we need is suspense. Suspense—and a quick curtain.

MANSKY. And now, I suppose, you could show us how it really ought to be done?

TURAI *(goes to telephone)*. Hello. Will you give me Miss Ilona Szabo's room please. *(A bell sounds in Ilona's room)*

MANSKY. What on earth—?

ILONA. Hello.

TURAI. Hello, Ilona?

ILONA. Yes. Who is that speaking?

TURAI. Don't you recognize my voice? This is Sandor Turai.

ILONA. Oh, how wonderful! Are you here, then? Where are you speaking from?

TURAI. Yes. I'm right here in the

castle. Next door to you. Number four.

ILONA. What a perfectly delightful surprise.

TURAI. We came by car last night. All three of us.

ILONA. You don't mean Albert, too?

TURAI. Yes—and Mansky, if you think that worth mentioning. We're all three here in this room, and we've brought you the finished script of the operetta.

ILONA. Marvelous! That's something like a surprise!

TURAI. We were hesitating about waking you so early, but I particularly wanted to see you about something. Can you come in here for a minute? (*Replaces receiver and goes to door. Enter Ilona with assumed joy and excitement*)

ILONA. Well, this is wonderful of you all. (*She kisses Turai lightly and crosses quickly to Adam who kisses her hands*) What a surprise. Albert, darling! This *is* a surprise. Sandor! To think that it's—

TURAI. Three whole months—

ILONA. Three whole months since I've seen you. How brown you're looking. And younger than ever. Let me look at you. Wonderful! (*She crosses to Mansky and kisses him on each cheek*) And Mansky—how are you, Mansky dear? I think this is too sweet of you all. You don't know how I've been longing to see you. When did you get here?

TURAI (*very gravely*). Just a minute, Ilona. (*He looks through door into her room*) Why, Mr. Almady! Of all people! Won't you come in? (*Enter Almady*)

ALMADY (*nervously*). Good morning.

TURAI. Fancy finding *you* here after all these years.

ALMADY (*pompously*). Passing through. Just passing through. I only wanted to say how-d'you-do to the Count, but they wouldn't let me go. The—er—the shooting-party you know, and the concert. They insisted on my staying.

ILONA. I was so surprised to see him.

TURAI. Pardon me for disturbing you and possibly casting a slight gloom on what must have been a joyful reunion, but I have something rather important to say.

ILONA. What do you mean? Nothing—nothing unpleasant, I hope?

TURAI. Yes—extremely unpleasant. (*He motions them to sit down*) Well, then. We arrived here last night— (*Long pause*) And just now were sitting having breakfast—we three—. Weren't we?

ADAM (*puzzled*). Yes.

MANSKY. Well?

TURAI. Keep quite calm, please. We were sitting here, having breakfast—all three of us. (*He lowers his voice and speaks very earnestly*) I must entreat you all to hear what I am about to say quite calmy— Don't lose your heads—

ILONA. For God's sake—

ALMADY (*uneasily*). What is it?

TURAI (*holds up his hand*). Please! (*Dead silence*) What I am about to say—and I shall not detain you long now—must almost inevitably have a shattering effect on the lives—both the private and the professional lives—of all of us five people. I have asked myself—is it wise to speak? And I have answered myself—wise or not, it is unavoidable. Ilona—I have a question to ask you— (*Breaks off. Dead silence. Then very simply to Mansky*) How's that for suspense?

MANSKY. Yes. Yes. Well? What now?

TURAI. Nothing. That's all. (*Smiles*) Curtain! (*Curtain comes down while he offers Ilona his arm. The rest of the group breathe again and relax their tension*) We've just been having an argument about the proper way to end a second act.

THE CURTAIN IS DOWN

ACT THREE

SCENE: *As the Curtain rises it reveals the room lighted up by the electric sconces and candelabra. A large and elaborately painted screen in silver and green has been placed in front of the window. It is painted to suggest an orchard. The screen shuts out the view of the Mediterranean, but to the Left and Right of it we glimpse the lighted esplanade, and many more twinkling lights than in the first act, for it is early evening. There are two garden chairs in front of the screen in the raised portion of the room; otherwise the scene is unchanged. Mr. Mell, the Count's secretary, and the master of ceremonies, enters at Left from the hall. He is a fussy, pale young man with high pitched voice. He wears glasses and is in evening clothes. He is carrying a wicker table, and carrying it with difficulty and discomfort. He places it between the two wicker chairs in front of the screen and stands caressing his hands where the table has cut into them.*

————

MELL *(calls)*. Dwornitschek. *(To himself)* Where is that man? *(Calls)* Dwornitschek.

DWORNITSCHEK'S VOICE. Coming, sir, coming. *(Dwornitschek enters from the hall, followed by a lackey. They are both in formal, full dress livery of white with knee breeches, and powdered wigs. Dwornitschek carries a book, two letters, a scarf and a woman's hat. The lackey carries a tall brown hunting hat, whip, gauntlets and a large, luscious peach)*

MELL. Oh, there you are at last. Why are you so late?

DWORNITSCHEK. I fell downstairs, sir.

MELL. Well, that oughtn't to have taken you long. *(He fiddles with the screen)*

DWORNITSCHEK. You should have let *me* carry those things, Mr. Mell.

MELL. I couldn't wait. You are so slow.

DWORNITSCHEK. Slow but sure, sir. *(He puts things on table)* When I was a lad, my aunt used to say—

MELL. I don't want to hear about your aunt.

DWORNITSCHEK. No, sir. Very few people do.

MELL. Have you got all the properties?

DWORNITSCHEK. Props, sir, is the more professional expression.

MELL. I was using the more technical term— Well, properties or props, have you got them?

DWORNITSCHEK. Yes, sir. Book—

MELL. —Peach—

DWORNITSCHEK. —Scarf—

MELL. —Whip—

DWORNITSCHEK. —Two letters and a pair of gloves.

MELL. Good. *(Mops his forehead)* Oh, dear, what a headache I'm getting.

DWORNITSCHEK. What you need is an aspirin.

MELL. Have you an aspirin?

DWORNITSCHEK. No, sir.

MELL. You're a great help.

DWORNITSCHEK. Thank you, sir. If I might be allowed to say so, you let yourself get too nervous on these festive nights, sir. You *worry*.

MELL. How can I help worrying with all the responsibility there is on my shoulders?

DWORNITSCHEK. What I always say is—never worry too much today. Things may be worse tomorrow, and then you can worry twice as hard.

MELL. It does make me so nervous when people want to alter the program at the last moment. First Miss Szabo says she's going to sing, then she says she's going to act— *(He breaks off as Almady enters)* Good evening, sir, good evening. You are first in the field.

ALMADY *(grouchily)*. Good evening. The others will be here directly. They're dressing.

MELL. A wonderful shooting party today, sir. Capital sport, capital. There is nothing like a good brisk day out in the open with the guns. What a color it has given you.

ALMADY. I wasn't there.

MELL. Eh? Oh! Not there?

ALMADY. No. I've been in my room all day, writing.

MELL. Pardon my curiosity, but may one ask what you were writing?

ALMADY. No, one may not.

DWORNITSCHEK. I think the gentleman does not wish to say what he was writing, sir.

MELL. Oh, are you still there?

DWORNITSCHEK. Yes, sir. Still here.

MELL. Then go away.

DWORNITSCHEK. Really, I shouldn't worry, Mr. Mell. Look on the bright side, sir.

MELL. All very well for you. You have no responsibilities, and the guests give you big tips.

DWORNITSCHEK. That is the bright side, sir. *(He goes out followed by the lackey)*

MELL. A secretary's life is a dog's life, Mr. Almady. Work, work, work, from morning till night, and never a word of thanks. You are very silent, Mr. Almady.

ALMADY. I sometimes find it soothing to be silent. Try it yourself one of these days. I take it the concert begins directly after dinner?

MELL. Immediately following the serving of coffee.

ALMADY. And when does this—this play of ours come on?

MELL. It is the last item on the program. The place of honor.

ALMADY. Bah!

MELL. Sir?

ALMADY (absorbed in his part which he is studying). Nothing.

MELL. Miss Szabo tells me that no scenery is required but two elegant chairs and one elegant table.

ALMADY. Is that an elegant table?

MELL. Well, really no. But what can one expect in a garden? Oh—if only the scene had been an interior, there's some perfectly lovely furniture in the Count's room—genuine Louis the Fifteenth. A very elegant period, Louis the Fifteenth.

ALMADY. I don't care a damn. They're all the same to me. Louis the Fifteenth or Louis the Fourteenth or Louis the Seventeenth.

MELL. But there isn't a Louis the Seventeenth, and I've often wondered why. Why, I've wondered, should there be a Louis the Sixteenth and a Louis the Eighteenth, but not a Louis the Seventeenth?

ALMADY. Oh, God. Ask a furniture dealer.

MELL. I did. I'm always asking furniture dealers. But they only know as far as Louis the Sixteenth. That's where the Louis's stop for furniture dealers. Whenever I say Louis the Seventeenth they say you mean the Sixteenth, and I say no, I don't mean Louis the Sixteenth, I mean Louis the Seventeenth and— (Breaks off and mops his brow) I'm afraid I'm talking a great deal, sir.

ALMADY. Oh, you've noticed that?

MELL. The fact is, Mr. Almady, I'm all a-twitter.

ALMADY. What have you got to be nervous about?

MELL. I'm always like this on these big nights. You see I'm responsible for everything and it's terribly wearing on the nerves. I'm stage manager, property man and prompter. I turn the music, show the ladies to their seats, hand bouquets onto the stage—and I'm expected always to applaud at the right moment. I assure you I have often gone to bed after one of these entertainments with my hands so tender I could scarcely hold my toothbrush. You will pardon me for mentioning it, sir, but you don't seem quite your merry old self tonight.

ALMADY. I'm as cheerful as any man would be whose brain has been addled from studying an infernal part all day.

MELL. But I thought you said you had spent the day writing?

ALMADY. Yes, I—I always memorize a part by writing it out.

MELL. What energy! What enthusiasm! Have you a nice part?

ALMADY. No. Rotten.

MELL. Dear, dear, dear! You'll feel better when you hear the applause. We're great applauders here. We don't care how bad an actor is—

ALMADY (offended). Thank you.

MELL. I beg your pardon. I—I don't mean it like that. (Goes to door of Ilona's room and knocks) Miss Szabo, please. Miss Szabo, please. Beginners, please.

(Enter Ilona in evening dress. Enter Adam, Right, in dress clothes.)

ILONA. Well, we seem to be all here.

MELL. Good evening, Miss Szabo, good evening, good evening.

ILONA. Well, we may as well begin.

ALMADY. Wouldn't it be as well to wait for Mr. Turai? (Bitterly) Seeing that he is being so kind as to give us his invaluable assistance.

ILONA. He'll be here directly. Where is the prompter?

MELL. Present. Present.

ILONA. Here's the script.

MELL (goes to stage). I hope this extempore set meets with your approval? (Pointing to screen) A little idea quite my own.

ILONA. Charming. Albert—you seem —you seem—very quiet—this evening.

ADAM. Oh, no, not a bit. A little tired, that's all. We had rather a long motor drive and I didn't get much sleep last night—Please don't think—I'm afraid our friend the secretary is getting restive.

ILONA. What on earth is the matter?

MELL. I'm all a-twitter.

ILONA. Well, do simmer down. *(To Adam, who has sat down)* Surely you're not going to stay for this rehearsal?

ADAM. If you don't mind.

ILONA. Oh, I don't mind. But you'll be thoroughly bored. A silly little French piece. You'll be seeing it after dinner. I should have thought once would have been enough.

ADAM. Well, as a matter of fact, Mr. Turai asked me to stay and help out till he came. And I promised him I would.

ILONA. Just as you please. *(Very nervous)* Can't we begin? Are the props here?

MELL. Nothing is ever missing when I am the property man. There they all are—on the table.

ILONA *(takes the book and letter)*. Those are yours. *(Almady pockets the peach and the remaining letter)* Now then—let's start. The Countess—that's me—discovered alone. Seated in chair, reading book. *(Sits down. To Almady)* You're not on yet. *(Almady stalks off to the Left)*

MELL. Do we go on now?

ILONA. Don't ask so many questions. Yes, go on.

MELL. Curtain rises on a glorious garden. Period Louis the Fifteenth.

ILONA. You don't have to read *that*.

MELL *(doubtfully)*. I always *have*.

ILONA. You only have to give the actors the spoken lines.

MELL. Now, I never knew *that* before. Now, that's very interesting. *(He looks stupidly at script)*

ALMADY. What on earth's the matter now?

ILONA. I'm afraid Mr. Mell is not much of a prompter.

ADAM *(taking script from Mell)*. It's all right—let *me* hold the book.

ILONA. No.

ALMADY *(simultaneously)*. No, no.

ILONA. You mustn't.

ADAM. What do you mean?

ILONA. I won't have it—

ADAM. Why not?

MELL. No doubt Miss Szabo means that it is beneath the dignity of such an important person. Please give *me* the book.

ADAM. Do stop fussing. Can't you see you make them nervous.

MELL. Make *them* nervous? What about *my* nervousness?

ADAM. I tell you *I'll* hold the book. And you can do it for the performance. Does that satisfy you?

MELL *(deeply offended)*. Oh quite. Oh, perfectly—

ILONA *(to Adam)*. Now you've hurt the poor man's feelings. You've insulted him—

MELL. Madam, I'm a secretary. I spend all my time receiving insults.

ILONA. Oh? Well, let's begin. *(To Almady)* You're off. *(Again Almady stalks to Left)* Countess discovered seated in armchair, reading book. *(Takes up book. Almady is wearing the brown hat, gauntlets and carrying the riding whip)*

ADAM *(prompting)*. What a silly—

ILONA *(speaking her lines)*. What a silly story. *(Closes book)* Just like all novels.

ADAM. What *can* I do—

ILONA *(yawning)*. What *can* I do to kill time? The Count is always out riding. Paris seems very far away amidst these sleepy fields of Normandy.

ADAM. Hoof-beats heard off— *(Mell imitates hoof-beats by beating his thighs with his hands)*

ILONA. Hark! I hear him coming. Can this be my husband? Surely he went off on his horse to visit our old tenant honest Jacques Benoit. *(Mell makes the hoof-beats louder and louder. Almady comes into scene dramatically, ominously, but his entrance is completely ruined by Mell continuing the hoof-beats. Almady stamps his feet impatiently and at last Mell stops)*

ALMADY. So, madame!

ILONA. Why, what is the matter? Why do you frown, my dear Count?

ALMADY. Why do I frown? That madame, you will learn—and speedily, as sure as my name is Count—, Count—

ADAM *(prompting)*. Maurice du Verier—

ALMADY. As sure as my name is Count Maurice de Veyrier de la Grande Contumace Saint-Emilion.

ILONA. You frighten me, Maurice.

ALMADY. It is your guilty conscience that frightens you, madame.

ADAM. Traitress. *(Ilona starts and looks at him nervously. Adam rises)* Traitress! N doubt you supposed me a credulous imbecile whom it was simple to hoodwink. *(Enter Turai and Mansky, both in evening dress, from the Right. Ilona and Almady, confused by their guilt, for the moment, believe that Adam is accusing them)*

ALMADY *(very embarrassed)*. No doubt —you—I—

ADAM *(still prompting)*. You thought that any story would do for me? You imagined that I was fool enough to swallow anything.

TURAI *(coming down, horrified, thinking that Adam is making a scene)*. What ! ! ! !

ADAM. Shhh— *(Goes on prompting)* No doubt you supposed me a credulous fool—

TURAI. O-oh! *(Relieved; he grasps the situation. Takes the script from him)* Let me have that script.

ADAM. Why? Aren't I prompting well?

ILONA. No.

ALMADY *(simultaneously)*. No.

ADAM *(ruffled)*. Nothing like being frank.

MELL. Don't take it to heart. Even *I* wasn't good enough for them.

ADAM. Perhaps you'll tell me where I went wrong?

TURAI. Don't ask so many questions. *(Seats himself in Mell's place)* I'll take on his job.

MELL. Everybody is so rude.

TURAI. All right. From where you topped.

ALMADY *(glibly)*. Traitress, you have deceived me. I have long had my suspicions. I have now in my possession the proofs. No doubt you supposed me a credulous imbecile whom it was simple to hoodwink. You thought that any story would do for me. You imagined that I was a fool enough to swallow anything. Let me tell you, madame, that you are mistaken. For a long time I have suspected that there was something behind these rides of yours with our neighbor the Marquis Jean François Gelette de la Tour d'Argent. Day after day, for hours at a time, you have made a practice of riding with him on the road from Dunernois sur Saône to Saint-Sulpice de la Grande Carmentière—and slowly at that!

ILONA. It's a lie. Who told you?

ALMADY. Silence, woman! The proofs are in my pocket. Mon Dieu, is there no gratitude in this world? When I married you, who were you? A nobody. Your father, Brigadier-General Pierre Jean Bourmond de la Seconde-Chaumière-Rambouillet, fell in battle at Grande-Lagruyère Sur Marne, and you eked out a scanty living as a seamstress at your mother's home in the village of Sainte-Geneviève, in the Department of Seine et Oise. So, madame! And then what happened? I came. I gave you name, rank and wealth such as you had never dreamed of. You became Madame La Countess du Veyrier de la Grande Contumace Saint-Emilion. I bestowed upon you not only my estates in Pardubien-Grand-Amanoir, but also my two castles in Challenges-Debicourt de la Romanée and at Riva-lieux-Quandamouzières Sur Vantera-aux Alpes Maritimes. *(He stops, exhausted)*

TURAI. Don't stop. What's wrong? *(Almady takes off his hat and gloves, puts the whip down on the table, and, stepping out of character, comes down to Turai.)*

ALMADY. It's these damned French names. They're perfectly frightful.

TURAI. I don't see what we can do about it.

ALMADY. You surely don't need them all?

TURAI. They're in the script.

ALMADY. But I'll go mad trying to memorize them. Titles with six hyphens in them and names of places with a dozen "aux" and "de la's" and "surs." And, damn it, they're all in *my* part. *(Choking with fury)* It's deadly. At least let's leave out that second castle.

TURAI *(coldly)*. My dear fellow, have you no sense of dramatic construction? If he had given her only one castle, the audience would think her perfectly justified in deceiving him. If he had given her three, they would look on him as a purse-proud fool who didn't deserve a faithful wife. No, two is exactly the right number. You can't beat Sardou when it comes to technique. Go on, please.
(Almady goes up hopelessly and replaces his hat and gloves and takes up the whip.)

ALMADY. I made you a countess and a wealthy woman. And what return do I get? You betray me— yes, madame, betray me—with my best friend and nearest neighbor, the Marquis Jean François Gelette de la Tour d'Argent, lord of Perigord des Champignons and Saint-Sulpice de la Grande Parmentière. *(He breaks off and removes hat and gloves as before)* My God, it's enough to give a fellow apoplexy.

TURAI *(surprised)*. I beg your pardon? that doesn't seem to be in the script.

ALMADY. I'm sorry. I can't help it. It's these names.

TURAI. Well, I'm always open to suggestions. What would you like to call the gentleman?

ALMADY. Foch or Briand—or something short like that.

TURAI *(sarcastically)*. Perhaps—Vichy! Get on, please. *(Almady goes up stage)*

ILONA *(nervously)*. Oh, do let's get on. Count, you have said enough.

TURAI. So *he* seems to think.

ILONA. I will not endure these shameful accusations. You are insulting the woman who bears your name.

ALMADY *(again taking off hat and gloves and putting down the whip)*. It's a damned shame.

TURAI. What is?

ALMADY. I always have to say the whole infernal thing from beginning to end, and she just says "your name."

TURAI *(coldly)*. We're wasting time.

ALMADY. Another word, madame, and I produce the proof.

ILONA *(laughing)*. The proof? One is amused. One smiles.

ALMADY *(takes stage and turns)*. A smile which I will make to die upon your lips. Behold! The proof! *(He fuddles in his coat-tail pocket from which he belatedly takes the peach with sinister flourish)*

ILONA *(with insincere terror)*. Ah, gracious heaven! The peach!

ALMADY *(lays the peach on table)*. Yes, madame, the peach. The first peach that ripened on the lovingly cherished, early-blooming, richly-bearing, East Indian dwarf peach trees in my orchard at Simarineux de la Pomme d'Api, making a triumphant entry into the world days ahead of any other peach in the whole of France. *(He turns and glares at Turai*

resentfully) You know what a passionate fruit-grower I am. You know that I have tended this peach from its first budding, cared for it, watched over it, wrapped it abouth with my love, kept a diary about it, and awaited its ripening like the coming of a Messiah. And what happens? This afternoon I go out riding. I am proceeding at a gentle jog-trot— *(Mell imitates hoof-beats as before. Almady is incensed by his stupidity. Mell subsides, abashed, and Almady resumes)* I am proceeding at a gentle jog-trot from Duvernois Sur Saône to Saint-Sulpice de la Grande Parmentière— *(He breaks off with an anguished look at Turai)*

TURAI *(coldly)*. Along the highroad—

ALMADY. Along the highroad. And whom should I see there, tripping along, but Juliette, your maid. I speak to her. She betrays embarrassment at seeing me. She stammers and ties her apron-strings in a knot. I ask her where she is going. Terrified, she bursts into tears and whispers, "My lady sent me to the Marquis Jean François Gelette de la Tour d'Argent"—curse him!

TURAI. Right. This time that was in the script.

ALMADY. Why, I ask the girl, did your mistress send you to the Marquis? And then suddenly, happening to look closer I see that she is trying desperately to hide a little parcel from me. I take it from her I open it, and what do I see? *(Points to peach)* That peach! The king of peaches the apple of my eye—my pride and joy my first born, the supreme peach from the orchards of Simarineux de la Pomme d'Api—the last word in stoneless fruit which I have been guarding since birth like a baby sister. And, as if this were not enough, wrapped round that glorious specimen of its kind, I discover a letter *(He fuddles in his inside coatpocket, draws out a letter, sees it is the wrong one, replaces it hastily, and draws forth the proper one* This letter— *(He reads)* —"My beloved This is the first peach that has ripened in France this year. I send it to *you.* Eat it reverently." *(He holds the letter under his nose)* There!

ILONA. Are you trying to make me smell it?

ALMADY. I am. For even if you were shameless enough to deny your writing you cannot deny your perfume. Or are you proposing to deny it?

ILONA. No.

ALMADY. Ha! Then you admit it?

ILONA. Yes.

ALMADY. You sent him this peach?

ILONA. Yes.

ALMADY (*again takes off his hat and gloves*). It's simple rank injustice. I've got to say yardlong speeches at the top of my voice, and all her part consists of is little exclamations like "oh!" "no!" and "yes!"

TURAI. Yes—I noticed that mysef. These short crisp speeches are characteristic of Sardou's women! It can't be helped. Go on, please.

ALMADY (*goes back, puts on hat and gloves, more miserable than ever*). So! You accept from me everything, love, name, rank, riches, estates—two castles—and then you go about the place sending my cherished fruit to your lover!

ILONA (*rises; tragically*). No.

ALMADY. You have effrontery to pretend that the Marquis is not your lover?

ILONA. Yes.

ALMADY. You mean he is?

ILONA. No.

ALMADY. You mean he is *not*?

ILONA (*triumphantly*). Yes.

ALMADY (*with a theatrical laugh*). A likely story, madame. I am a fruit-grower, the leading amateur horticulturist in France and President of the Paris Peach Club. I know—I say, I know—that one does not give fruit like this save where one has first given—the heart. Madame, I despise you.

ILONA. You consider conduct like mine despicable?

ALMADY. I do.

ILONA. Good! Then I have one little question to ask you. In the early spring of the year there ripened in your orchard the first crop of whiteheart cherries. To whom did you send those cherries?

ALMADY (*turns away, embarrassed*). To my mother. The Dowager Countess de la Grande Contumace Saint-Emilion.

ILONA. Indeed? To your mother? Then permit me to show you something. You

are not the only one who has discovered an interesting letter. (*Takes letter from table*) Smell that! Do you recognize the perfume? (*Holds it under his nose*)

MELL. What a *sensation*! Sardou at his best. There's no one like him.

ILONA. The perfume is of Mademoiselle Emilienne, première danseuse at the Folies Bergères, whom you honor with your friendship and protection.

ALMADY. How—how did you get this?

ILONA. Never mind. Always remember letters are like spent arrows. You never can tell where they are going to drop.

MELL (*applauds vigorously*). An epigram.

ILONA. Read it, please.

ALMADY (*reading*). "My dearest. This morning that doddering old idiot of a count of mine—"

ILONA. You notice how your divinity writes of you? Go on.

ALMADY (*reading*). —"that doddering idiot of a count of mine sent me a basket of cherries. Did I tell you he was a famous fruit-grower? He says these are the first cherries that have ripened in France this year and he sends them to me as a token of his love. Drop in this evening, darling, and we'll eat the old fool's cherries together. Your loving Emilienne. P. S. Ring twice as usual!" (*He sobs*)

ILONA. You see, what you do to me, I do to you. An eye for an eye, *a tooth for a tooth*, a peach for a cherry.

ALMADY (*brokenly*). Yes. It's true.

ILONA. And now, leave my garden. This very afternoon I pack my boxes and go back to my mother. And if you will question my maid you will find that I told her to hang about till you came by—to blush and stammer —and finally to give you the letter *and* the peach. (*She breaks into stage laughter*) Ha, ha, ha! Oh, ha, ha, ha, ha, ha!

ALMADY. Well, I must face it. I've lost.

ILONA. You've lost me.

ALMADY (*kneeling*). Yvonne! Don't say that. See! I beg your forgiveness on my knees—overlook this one false step.

ILONA. The idea! A count and an *elderly* count—groveling like that. (*Almady gets up and turns away*) All the same, you have touched me. So I will forgive you. But you are not to get off without punishment. Firstly, I forbid you to eat this peach.

ALMADY. My God! Not that!

ILONA (firmly). Yes.

ALMADY. So be it.

ILONA. Secondly, you will permit me to go to Paris alone.

ALMADY (despairingly). Yvonne!

ILONA. Not a word. Either you trust me or you do not! If you do, I will return. If not, not.

ALMADY. Oh, heavens! And how long do you expect to stay in Paris?

ILONA. A week.

ALMADY (suddenly bursting out). No! I can't live without you. I worship you. I adore you. I love you as the church steeple loves the cloud that settles on its summit, only to be wafted away by the first passing breeze. I can't live without you. Not a week, not a day. Not an hour.

ILONA. Just words.

(At the words "church steeple" Mansky and Adam have exchanged a glance of utter astonishment.)

MANSKY (rises). But—but—but— Just one moment— What was that you said?

ILONA. I beg your pardon?

TURAI. Now, listen, please. We can't have these interruptions. Don't pull them up the moment they've got nicely into the swing of it.

MELL. I can't wait to see how it all ends. Will she leave him? Or will the memory of their past love prove too strong?

MANSKY (goes to Adam— Aside to him). This is devilish queer.

TURAI. Quiet, please. All right. Go on. Better go back to "Not a week! Not a day! Not an hour!"

ALMADY. Not a week! Not a day! Not an hour!

ILONA. Just words.

ALMADY. It's the truth. I'm crazy about you. And you—you have used me up and squeezed me like a lemon, and now you want to throw me away.

(At the word "lemon" Mansky and Adam again exchange glances. Mansky gets up, deeply agitated.)

MANSKY. Sandor—

TURAI. What is it?

MANSKY (to Ilona and Almady). You'll

excuse me? I have something very urgent to say to Mr. Turai. (He crosses to Turai and drags him over to the corner below the fire-place) Do you hear what they're saying?

TURAI (feigning non-comprehension).— How do you mean, do I hear what they're saying?

MANSKY. I mean—didn't those last lines sound familiar to you?

TURAI. That's right. Now you mention it. I did notice something, only I thought it was my fancy.

MANSKY (to Adam). Come here. I give you my word, Sandor. Those lines were syllable for syllable the ones we heard last night through the wall.

TURAI (looking at script). By Jove, you're right— This is uncanny.

MANSKY. Go on with the rehearsal, or they will be suspecting something. I want to hear some more.

(Mansky takes hold of Adam's arm. Adam is very excited. Both listen intently.)

TURAI. Well, let's get on. "Now you want to throw me away."

ILONA. I don't want to throw you away, silly. Oh, come on, then. Come here and let me kiss that beautiful classic brow.

MANSKY. Great heavens!

ILONA. What's the matter?

MANSKY (whispering). Listen, you two. They're saying word for word what we heard them say last night. Do you grasp now what they were doing last night Rehearsing! Simply going through their lines.

TURAI. I must admit this has come upon me as a complete surprise. Really, I'm quite shaken.

ADAM. Imitate me. If I can be perfectl calm, you can.

MANSKY (pointing to Turai). And h never recognized it!

ILONA. Mr. Turai! What's going on

ALMADY. Yes. What's all the discussio about?

TURAI. Well, it's like this. Mansk says— and I'm bound to say I agree wit him—that for the actual performanc tonight you will have to dig up a classi brow from somewhere.

ALMADY. Dig up a classic brow?

TURAI. You see, it's rather awkwar

The script says— "Kiss that beautiful classic brow."

ALMADY. Well?

TURAI. Well, you'll have to get one somewehere.

ALMADY (bitterly). You think my own would not be convincing?

MANSKY. My God, no!

ALMADY. It has been so described.

TURAI. In this play, yes. But, if you'll pardon my saying so, you wouldn't suggest that any woman of taste could say such a thing in real life?

ALMADY (bitterly). Very good. No doubt the property man will be able to supply me with a face. (Mell is appalled at the prospect of having to get a "face" but he dutifully makes a notation of it in his little book)

TURAI. Oh—my dear fellow.

(All go back to their places).

ADAM (impatiently). We're wasting time. Let's get on.

TURAI. Sh! Sh! We've only a few minutes more.

ADAM. No more interruptions.

MELL. Thank God!

ILONA. Where were we? Oh, yes. Come here and let me kiss that beautiful classic brow. (Kisses him on the forehead)

ALMADY. That's not a kiss. That's a tip.

MANSKY. Surely that line is a trifle vulgar.

TURAI. It's vulgar because it's spoken by a vulgar man.

MANSKY. The speaker is a count.

TURAI. But a dull-witted bounder, for all that. He's the sort of man who would say things like that. Don't you start trying to teach Sardou how to write dialogue.

ALMADY (furious). For God's sake, are we going to rehearse?

TURAI. Yes. Go on, please.

ALMADY. That's not a kiss. That's a tip.

ILONA. Don't shout like that.

ALMADY. I will shout. I'm a squeezed lemon. That's what I am—a lemon. (Falls sobbing at her feet. Mansky whispers something to Adam. Adam smiles happily and whispers back. They shake hands)

TURAI. Please—please— What's the matter?

MANSKY. Nothing. I was merely saying to Adam that I think that word "lemon" is all wrong.

TURAI. I think it's excellent. Absolutely in character. The speaker is a big lemon-and-peach man from Saint-Sulpice de la Grande Parmentière, and he naturally goes to the orchard for his similes. Try to realize that he's practically an imbecile with virtually no vocabulary. (Almady looks up from Ilona's lap and registers indignation. Prompting) "Please, please" — (To Ilona) From you, my dear. (To Almady) You're crying. (Almady sobs)

ILONA. Please, please. Don't cry. I can't bear it. You know how fond I am of you. (She goes to table where peach is)

ALMADY. Those nights of love—those flaming, wonderful nights! Have you forgotten them so completely? (He stands up, ands starts to touch the peach)

ILONA. Stop! Control yourself.

ALMADY (gazing at peach). You ask me to control myself—when I look at that? At that perfect shape The rose flush of that skin. (Starts to touch peach) Just to stroke it—

ILONA. Hands off.

ALMADY (snatching up the peach, holds it in one hand and with the other strokes it voluptuously). My God! How round it is! How smooth, how velvety— and how fragrant! (Raises it to his mouth)

ILONA. You mustn't bite it.

(She snatches his hand. Mansky gives a shriek and goes into fits of laughter. Adam stretches his arms out to Mansky and roars. Adam slaps Mansky on the back, Mansky laughing uninterruptedly. Almady turns away furiously, Ilona turns away, ashamed.)

MANSKY. Heavens! What fools we've been!

ADAM. Haven't we?

MELL (eagerly). Won't you tell me the joke?

ADAM. You wouldn't understand.

ILONA. What are you two so amused about?

TURAI (curtly). Come, come. We're wasting time. Let's get on.

MANSKY. Yes, get on. I want to hear this. Round, smooth, velvety and fragrant.

ADAM. And you mustn't bite.

ILONA. You mustn't bite it.

ALMADY. I must—I am so hungry.
(Adam and Mansky go on laughing. Mell laughs too, but with a puzzled look, as much as to say "I'm joining in, but I really don't understand.")

ALMADY. Ah, well! I see I am nothing to you any more.

ILONA. Oh, for goodness' sake! I swear that no man— *(Breaks off, unable to go on)*

TURAI *(prompting)*. No man who has ever come into my life—

ILONA. —has meant so much to me as you. From the top of your head to the soles of your feet you are a man.

TURAI. I think we might cut that last bit.

ALMADY. Why?

TURAI. Well, I mean to say— A little too explicit, don't you think? Rather too obvious a sexual implication. A wee bit coarse, perhaps, yes? We must consider the feelings of the audience. *(To Mell)* Will there be any young girls there tonight?

MELL. Oh, yes, indeed.

TURAI. Then we must cut it. They may bring their parents. Instead suppose we say "I love you, even though you are only a poor imitation of a man." *(Almady registers rage.)* Go on. *(To Almady)* "My God! I suffer—"

ALMADY *(bitterly)*. My God! I suffer like a sick horse. *(To Turai)* Look here, that ought to come out.

TURAI. Why?

ALMADY. How could anyone speak of himself so vulgarly?

TURAI. We went into all that just now. Just what a cattle-raiser would say.

ALMADY. But he's a fruit-raiser!

TURAI. Cattle, too. Cattle as a side line.

ILONA. Don't look so pathetic. Well, come here. Kiss me. You donkey.

ALMADY *(furiously to Turai)*. It's too much—horse and donkey.

ADAM *(aside to Mansky)*. This is were I went out. How funny it seems now.

TURAI *(looks at script)*. We're getting near the end now. They kiss here.
(Almady starts to kiss Ilona.)

ILONA *(pushing him away)*. Oh, never mind the kiss. Kiss over.

ALMADY *(offended)*. Just as you please.

I want you to remember that kiss forever.

ILONA. Your kiss is revolting to me.

ALMADY *(despairingly)*. Does that stay in?

TURAI. My dear fellow, we can't cut everything.

ALMADY. But a line like that's so damned personal. The audience will loathe me.

MANSKY. It beats me why on earth you ever chose a part like this.

TURAI *(with subtle mockery)*. Yes. It's no business of mine, but I must say I can't understand that, either. It doesn't help to cut lines here and there. It's the whole part. The character's a bounder and a fool.

MANSKY. The author must have loathed this fellow. You notice that, Sandor, don't you?

TURAI *(ironically)*. Of course, I noticed it.

ILONA. Do let's get to the end. Mademoiselle Emilienne describes you as an old fool.

TURAI *(prompting)*. "And so I am."

ALMADY. And so I am, Yvonne. *(Furious)* So I am.

MANSKY. You certainly are.

ILONA *(sincerely)*. It's disgusting that a man of your age should persecute a woman, and by playing on her sense of gratitude seek to obtain a love which she would never bestow as a free gift.

ADAM *(crossing down to Turai and whispering)*. Uncle Sandor, will you give me your word of honor that Ilona shall never know how shamefully I suspected her?

TURAI. Don't be childish.

ADAM. If ever she found out she'd never look at me again.

TURAI. I'll never tell her.

ILONA. Please don't interrupt any more.

ADAM *(bows elaborately and says with meaning)*. Forgive me.
(Ilona accepts his apology with an affectionate gesture, and when his back is turned it she who is mutely asking forgiveness.)

TURAI. Go on!

ILONA. Think of your wife. Think of your children.

ALMADY *(turns away)*. My children!

ILONA. What would your son say? Your son, a highly respected colonel in the Dragoons.

(This is too much. The actor in Almady is crushed. He comes down to Turai brokenly and speaks supplicatingly.)

ALMADY. Mr. Turai.

TURAI *(amiably)*. Yes?

ALMADY. It's just a suggestion, but couldn't we say lieutenant there?

TURAI. I'm afraid not. You see it was "general" in the text.

ALMADY *(wildly)*. My son a general?

ILONA *(to Turai)*. How far back can I go?

TURAI. At the most a major.

ILONA *(quickly)*. Very well. Your son, a highly respected major in the Dragoons.

ALMADY. You are right, Yvonne. The shock would kill him.

(Almady breaks off, evidently unwilling to speak his next line. But Turai prompts him relentlessly.)

TURAI. "A ridiculous old petticoat-chaser."

ALMADY *(speaking the lines almost sotto voce in a casual offhand manner)*. A ridiculous old petticoat-chaser, that's what I am. Bah!

TURAI. Oh, come, Mr. Almady. Not so tamely, please. More *life*. Once more.

ALMADY *(with petulance and irritation)*. A ridiculous old petticoat-chaser, that's what I am. Bah!

TURAI *(relentlessly)*. Still not quite strong enough. More gusto. More sincerity.

ALMADY *(shouts the line to relieve his fury)*. A RIDICULOUS OLD PETTICOAT-CHASER, THAT'S WHAT I AM. BAH!

TURAI *(coldly)*. Once more, please.

ALMADY *(shouting to the full limit of his vocal chords in wild desperation)*. A RIDICULOUS OLD PETTICOAT-CHASER, THAT'S WHAT I AM. BAH!

TURAI *(with approval)*. Fine—that's it. Now read it that way at the performance.

(Almady returns up stage, completely crushed and beaten.)

ALMADY *(genuinely)*. I promise you I shall never again make myself obnoxious to this woman who loves another man and is sick and tired of me. Never, never again.

ILONA *(briskly)*. Never again?

ALMADY *(briskly)*. Never again.

ILONA. Then, Maurice, I will be generous. I will not go to Paris, and you may eat the peach.

ALMADY *(hurls himself at the peach)*. My God! At last! *(Gnaws the peach)*

TURAI *(rising)*. Curtain.

MANSKY. The end?

TURAI. The end.

MANSKY. He really should have given his wife the peach. That would have made a much prettier finish.

TURAI. Oh, my dear fellow! Where's your sense of character? The man's selfish to the core. He'd never give his wife peaches.

MANSKY. A very unsympathetic part. Still, he played it well.

TURAI. It fitted him.

MELL *(dancing about in anguish, pointing to Almady, incoherent with agitation)*. Oh, Oh!

TURAI. What's the matter with you?

MELL. He's eating the peach! He's eating the peach! I never dreamed he was going to *eat* the peach. I shall have to dash out and get another. *(He rushes off to the hall)*

ILONA *(takes off scarf. To Adam, who stands overcome with happiness)*. Well, how do you like me in this part?

ADAM. Oh, darling, you were wonderful, simply wonderful. And, if you want to know what I think—this little comedy is worth all Shakespeare put together. *(He kisses her hands)*

MANSKY. Oh, no, no, no. The thing dates terribly. When did Sardou write it?

TURAI. I don't know. What period Sardou is this, Mr. Almady?

ALMADY. I should imagine it was his last work.

MANSKY. Then he must have been a very old man at the time. It's terrible. He probably wrote it just before he died.

TURAI. Or just after. *(To Ilona)* Can I have a minute? Just a few things I'd like to tell you about your part.

ILONA. Yes, yes, I shall be very grateful. *(To Mansky and Adam)* Go along. We shan't be a moment.

MANSKY. What beats me is why an actor who has always played heroes picked a part like that for himself. He must be terribly fond of acting.

(Mansky and Adam go out at Right.)

TURAI *(to Almady, who is sitting dejectedly).* You seem upset.

ALMADY *(miserably).* Not at all. *(He glares at Turai)*

TURAI. So you've decided to take the midnight express directly after the performance?

ALMADY. Yes.

TURAI. I think you're wise. A good, fruity train, highly spoken of by connoisseurs. Well, just to show you the sort of fellows we Turais are, I'll let you off the major. Ilona, you can say lieutenant.

ALMADY. Even lieutenant seems a little—

TURAI. Good God! We can't make him a drummer boy.

ALMADY *(picks up part).* Very well. So be it. I suppose I ought to be thankful for small mercies. *(Goes toward door to hall)*

TURAI. Where are you off to?

ALMADY. I'm going to have another go at those infernal French names. But in spite of everything—thank you.

(Almady bows and then goes out.)

ILONA. Sandor, you're an angel. Was it awfully difficult, writing that play?

TURAI. Oh, no. That damned peach stumped me for a while. Smooth, round, velvety and fragrant, and you mustn't bite. It wasn't easy to get 'round that. Believe me, there are very few things in this world that are round, smooth, velvety —and respectable.

ILONA *(turns head away).* Oh—he was talking about my shoulder.

TURAI *(with delicate irony and gazing at her shoulder, then kissing it).* Really? I thought it was your forehead.

ILONA. You're an old devil; that's what you are.

TURAI. Just what I expected. Now that it's all over, everybody else is a gentleman and I'm an old devil. But somehow I don't think I am. My little Ilona, I have saved a young man a bad heartache. It's a negative kindness, but is there a positive one that's better? Yes, on the whole, I think I'm fairly well satisfied with myself. And there's a little old woman looking at me from somewhere—probably from hell—and her eyes seem to be twinkling, as if she was satisfied, too. It's unfortunate, that you won't have me always on hand to—

(Re-enter Mansky and Adam)

MANSKY *(on the landing, to Adam).* Poor old Turai's feeling awfully sore about all this. He had a wonderful scheme for bringing you two together, based on what he calls psychology. And now he's furious because that won't be needed.

(Enter Dwornitschek from hall.)

ADAM. Sh! Ilona will hear you. Let's drop the subject.

DWORNITSCHEK. Dinner is served.

(Adam meets Ilona at Center. They embrace and kiss lovingly and go out to the hall arm in arm.)

MANSKY *(with self-satisfaction to Turai).* So, my friend, it comes down to this. There are many clever writers, but the most successful of them all is still old man life himself.

TURAI. That's because he doesn't have to collaborate with you.

(He takes Mansky's arm. As he passes Dwornitschek he stops and looks at him.)

DWORNITSCHEK *(smiling).* Dwornitschek, sir.

TURAI. Now, look here—that really is your name, isn't it?

DWORNITSCHEK. Oh, yes sir.

TURAI. I just wondered. Thank you.

(Turai and Mansky go out.)

DWORNITSCHEK. Thank you, sir.

THE CURTAIN FALLS

LUIGI PIRANDELLO's

As You Desire Me

In the translation by MARTA ABBA

First produced*by Lee Shubert at the Maxine Elliott Theatre, New York, on January 28, 1931, with the following cast:

MOTO	Goo Chong	SALESIO	Philip Leigh
MOP	Mary Miner	BRUNO PIERI	Peter Brandon
CARL SALTER	Douglass Dumbreville	MAID	Charlotte Orr
THE UNKNOWN ONE	Judith Anderson	INEZ	Katherine Warren
YOUNG MAN	Maurice Ramon	MASPERI	Mortimer Weldon
ANOTHER YOUNG MAN	Hugh Cairns, Jr.	ANOTHER WOMAN	Amy Jonap
BOFFI	José Ruben	DOCTOR	John O'Meara
LENA	Vera G. Hurst	NURSE	Charlotte Orr

Staged by Marcel Varneli

SCENES

ACT ONE—Carl Salter's apartment in Berlin.

ACT TWO—The villa of Bruno Pieri, not far from Milan.

ACT THREE—The same.

© 1956, by MARTA ABBA

* In the adaptation by Dmitri Ostrow.

ACT ONE

SCENE. *Living room in the house of Carl Salter, the writer. Decorated with bizarre luxury. Door in center leading to a wide vestibule. Beyond it, a glimpse of the outside door of the apartment. In the right wall is a large archway, through which a part of the rear wall of the study can be seen.*

It is night, and so the living room and study are lit by several lamps with different colored shades, which throw the bizarre decor into fantastic relief, and give the scene a feeling of mystery and secrecy.

AT RISE: *When the curtain rises, Mop is discovered, crouched in a big armchair; she is dressed in a strange suit of black silk pajamas, flowered with orchids. She is huddled up over the arm of the chair, with her face hidden. She looks as if she were sleeping. She is crying. Her hair is cut mannishly short, and her face, when she lifts it, has a strange look that makes one shudder; at the same time, there is something tragic about it that is deeply moving.*

A moment later Carl Salter enters from the archway, to the right. He is very excited and upset. He is about fifty, pale, full face, very light, bright eyes, puffy and with dark circles under them. He is going a trifle bald on top, but has a thick growth of short, iron-gray hair. He is cleanshaven and has thick, sensual lips. He wears an expensive dressing gown. His hands are in his pockets.

———

SALTER *(rushing in).* She's here! With the usual mob! I saw her from the window. *(He inadvertently takes his hand from his pocket—he is clutching a small revolver)*

MOP *(seeing it).* What have you got there?

SALTER *(quickly putting it back—annoyed).* Nothing. I warn you, if she brings them up, I forbid you to stay.

MOP. What do you expect me to do?

SALTER. I don't know. This has got to stop.

MOP. What do you mean, stop? Are you crazy?

SALTER. I'm not going to let them see me either. Listen at the door and see if she's coming up alone. *(Mop starts to go into the hallway,)* Wait! *(He holds her back. They listen.)* I hear her shouting.

(Sounds of confused voices come up the stairs from below.)

MOP. Perhaps she's saying good night to them.

SALTER. They're all drunk. And there was someone following them.

MOP. Give me that revolver!

SALTER. No, no. I'm not going to use it. I'm just—carrying it around—in my pocket.

MOP. Give it to me.

SALTER. Don't bother me. *(Voices heard nearer.)* Do you hear them?

MOP. Sounds like a quarrel. *(They run out into the lobby and open the outside door. As far as one can see through the door of the living room, is immediately filled with a violent irruption of four very stupid and more or less drunken young men in evening clothes. In the middle of them is the Strange Lady, and Boffi, who is trying to protect her. Mop and Salter mingle with the crowd, Mop trying to extricate the Strange Lady, and Salter endeavouring to repel the invaders.*

In the dim light and in the confusion one can discern that one of the young men is chubby and fresh-complexioned, another rather bald, another has bleached hair and seems more woman than man. All seem like battered marionettes, with the same wide, jerky and meaningless gesticulations. They are all shouting at once.

The Strange Lady is in her thirties, and very beautiful. She is a little intoxicated herself, and she cannot quite attain the expression she would like—that dark anger which reveals her contempt for everything and everybody; in this way she tries to compensate for the desperate abandon in which she could so easily lose her very soul, devastated as it has been by all the storms of a tempestuous life. Under an extremely elegant evening cloak, she wears one of the strange and splendid costumes which characterize her particular dance specialties.

Boffi seems a little out of place. He is a good looking man, obstinate and headstrong. He is convinced that life is nothing but a game, and is humorously determined not to be baffled by it. He has a Mephistophelian sort of face, but somehow amiable. He uses it as a kind of mask, partly in order to make an effect, and partly to preserve something simple and natural which lies beneath. He has a habit of jerking up his head as if he were suffocating, and has therefore contracted a sort of twitch in the muscles of his neck, which makes him from time throw his chin forward and pull down the corners of his mouth. Every time this happens he says, as if to himself: "Don't let's j-joke about it!")

(The following lines overlap each other.)

STRANGE LADY. No—that's enough, now! That's enough! I won't have any more! Get out! A joke's a joke.

FIRST YOUNG MAN. . . . one more dance among the wineglasses . . .

SECOND YOUNG MAN. . . . one last drink . . . "Bubbling Champagne" . . .

THIRD YOUNG MAN. . . . We'll all sing the chorus . . .

FOURTH *(chanting drunkenly).* Clo-o-o-o-dovee-o . . . clo-o-o-o-dovee-o . . .

FIRST. . . . all bored to death . . .

STRANGE LADY. Let me alone—let me alone!

BOFFI. Get out of here—get out! All right—fine, fine . . . But that's enough . . . You heard what she said!

SALTER. Get out . . . Leave my house!

FIRST YOUNG MAN. That's no way to treat us! We want a drink!

SECOND. Don't be silly. She invited us!

THIRD. At the end of the chorus—we all strip naked!

FOURTH. Clo-o-o-dovee-o . . . *(Someone punches him in the chest)* Beasts! You brute!

MOP. You ought to be ashamed. This is outrageous! *(Puts her arms round the Lady as if to draw her away into the room)* Come—come away.

STRANGE LADY *(freeing herself).* For God's sake, no! That is the last straw!

SALTER *(in the hallway, blocking the invasion with Boffi's help).* Gentlemen, if you don't go I will shoot.

BOFFI *(pushing them through the door).* Get out—get out! That's all, I tell you. Get out!

FIRST YOUNG MAN. Pet me a little, Elma darling.

SECOND YOUNG MAN. I'm your pekingese.

MOP. They make me sick. *(The door is slammed, the four take their departure, but are still heard shouting on the stairs, the third persistently chanting "Clo-o-Dovee" as he goes)*

SALTER. What did they want?

STRANGE LADY. The usual thing. Pigs! They made me drink so much.

SALTER. It's scandalous! All the tenants will start complaining.

STRANGE LADY. Throw me out—I've told you to.

MOP. No, Elma, no!

STRANGE LADY. He says it's scandalous.

SALTER. It would be all right if only you wouldn't go out with them.

STRANGE LADY. Just for that I will go out with them. I prefer to. *(Rushing toward the door)* I'm going to join them.

BOFFI *(stopping her).* Signora Lucia!

STRANGE LADY *(stops short).* But—who are you, if I may venture to ask?

SALTER. Yes, and why are you still here?

BOFFI. I've been taking care of this lady.

SALTER. You were following the others. I saw you.

STRANGE LADY. So many evenings—like a bodyguard—he's *always* near me.

MOP. And you don't know who he is?

BOFFI. Oh yes, the lady knows perfectly well who I am *(He twitches)* Don't let's j-joke about it! *(He calls her again, as if persuading her to yield.)* Signora Lucia!

MOP *(astonished).* Lucia?

STRANGE LADY. That's it—like that—in every kind of tone—"Signora Lucia" —"Signora Lucia"! Following me, passing close to me—

BOFFI. And she always turns round.

STRANGE LADY. Of course.

BOFFI. Because she *is* Signora Lucia.

MOP. No, no—

BOFFI. Yes! And every time she starts and goes pale—

STRANGE LADY. Well of course! When you hear someone calling you—

BOFFI *(correcting her).* Re-calling you—

STRANGE LADY. —at night, you can imagine. And that face of his—like a devil.

BOFFI. That's just a mask, Signora! No one is really a devil.

STRANGE LADY. It's your—role?

BOFFI. Exactly. It's the part I play, just as you play *your* little act—whatever it is—in the presence of this lady and gentleman; but actually you are Signora Lucia all the time.

MOP. But this is fantastic!

STRANGE LADY. He hasn't the faintest doubt of it, you see?

BOFFI. I'd stake my right arm.

SALTER. Perhaps you have an extra one at home?

BOFFI. No sir, this is the only one I have; and I'd stake it.

STRANGE LADY. That I am Signora Lucia?

BOFFI. Pieri.

STRANGE LADY. What did you say?

BOFFI. Don't pretend you don't know the name.

STRANGE LADY. No—I didn't hear you.

BOFFI *(to Salter—denunciatory and yet challenging)*. I said Pieri. And the lady's husband is here.

STRANGE LADY *(overcome—sitting down)*. My husband?

BOFFI. Yes, Signora. Bruno is here.

STRANGE LADY. What are you talking about? Here? Where?

SALTER. He's out of his mind.

BOFFI. I sent for him.

STRANGE LADY. You're crazy.

BOFFI. He arrived this evening.

SALTER. The lady's husband has been dead for four years.

STRANGE LADY *(to Salter—on an impulse —quickly)*. No! No, that's not true!

SALTER. Not true!

BOFFI. He's here—at the Eden Hotel—right up the street.

STRANGE LADY *(to Boffi excitedly)*. Let's stop joking about my husband. I have no husband. Who did you send for?

BOFFI. See how upset you are?

SALTER *(to her)*. Then he's still alive?

BOFFI *(answering for her)*. I tell you here, right up the street! If the lady would like . . . *(Looks around)* There must be a telephone . . .

(The Strange Lady suddenly bursts out laughing like a mad woman.)

SALTER. What is all this, for God's sake?

STRANGE LADY. Didn't you hear him? He says I have a husband—right up the street. I can even telephone him to come, when I want to.

SALTER *(to Boffi—to finish the matter)*. You can see for yourself, sir, that this is not the moment for either of us to carry this tomfoolery any further!

STRANGE LADY *(to Salter, joking, but a challenge too)*. Wait a moment. Suppose I really were—

SALTER. Who?

STRANGE LADY. Why, this Signora Lucia the gentleman is so sure he recognizes. What would *you* say?

SALTER. You heard what I said— tomfoolery.

STRANGE LADY. And what about you?

SALTER. Me?

STRANGE LADY. Yes. Do you think *you* know me better than *he* does?

SALTER. I? I know you better than you know yourself.

STRANGE LADY. That's a great achievement! It's been a long time since I wanted to know myself.

SALTER. Very convenient, if you don't want to answer for what you do.

STRANGE LADY. On the contrary, my dear; indispensable, if I am to endure what others do to me.

BOFFI. Magnificent!

SALTER *(rounding on him)*. What do you mean—magnificent?

BOFFI. The way she answered you. *(Adds with compassion)* And what life has done to her!

STRANGE LADY *(to Boffi)*. But think a minute. If I tried to know myself even a little, to be "somebody" to myself too— *(Turning to Salter)* There, this gentleman's "Signora Lucia," for example— *(Taking Boffi by the arm)* Tell me, do you think I could bear to go on living here with him? *(Leaving Boffi and turning to Mop)* Mop, tell what my name is!

MOP. Elma!

STRANGE LADY. Elma—you understand? An Arabic name. Do you know what it means? Water—water . . . *(She makes a motion with her hands—fluid— indicating the intangible nature of her kind of life. Then a change of tone)* But they made me drink so much wine! Five cocktails—champagne—God! *(To Mop)* Suppose you give me something to eat.

MOP. Of course. I'll get something. What would you like?

STRANGE LADY. I don't know. I'm burning up.

MOP. I'll go and see—

STRANGE LADY. Don't bother too much—

MOP. A sandwich or two?

STRANGE LADY. Anything—a crust of bread—just to get something inside of me and stop my head from going round and round.

MOP. Yes, of course. I'll go and get them. *(She runs out)*

SALTER *(to Boffi)*. Will you be kind enough to admit that you have made a mistake—and go?

STRANGE LADY. No, let him stay, he's an acquaintance of mine.

BOFFI. The lady knows that I have not made a mistake.

STRANGE LADY. Only don't telephone for my husband. I don't want that.

BOFFI *(resolutely)*. Signora, your husband—

SALTER *(breaking in)*. That's enough about her husband. *(Rounding on her)* You told me he has been dead for four years.

BOFFI *(quickly)*. She lied!

STRANGE LADY *(rises, goes over and grasps his hand)*. Thank you, sir, for that statement.   .

BOFFI. Ah, thank God!

SALTER. Then you lied to me?

STRANGE LADY. Yes. *(And turning to Boffi)* But wait a minute before you thank God. I thanked you for the satisfaction you gave me in affirming so strongly my right to lie, considering the life I lead. *(To Salter)* Do you want me to give you an account of all the lies I've told? Then give me an account of yours!

SALTER. I have never lied!

STRANGE LADY. You've never lied? Why, none of us do anything else!

SALTER. To you—never.

STRANGE LADY. Simply because you have sometimes been shameless enough to tell me—

SALTER *(cutting her short, violently)*. That's enough!

STRANGE LADY. You lie even to yourself—even in your disgusting confessions —because you're not really as terrible as all that. But console yourself; nobody is a complete liar. We just try to fool people —to fool ourselves too! Four years ago, my dear, "someone" may have died for me—even if it wasn't my husband; so, there may be some truth in my story—as there is in every story which is told. *(To Boffi)* But that doesn't mean that my husband is alive and here—at least for me. *(She is playing a game of mystery—improvising)* He is the husband—at most—of someone who no longer exits; a poor widower. That is to say, a man who, as a husband, is dead. Go on, tell us the story. It should be interesting, if he's come all the way here. And perhaps we shall learn the real truth about this Signora Lucia— who is supposed to be me. *(To Salter)* Listen, listen!

BOFFI *(coming forward—with decision)*. Let me have a word with you Signora— alone.

STRANGE LADY. Alone! Good heavens, no! Say it here—in front of him. I want him to know. *(She reclines)* There are no more secrets nowadays—no inhibitions.

SALTER. Like animals!

STRANGE LADY. Just so. But God knows at least animals are natural.

SALTER *(contemptuous)*. The wisdom of instinct!

STRANGE LADY. While mankind, my dear sir, is horrible. Nature is insane— bored to death, as Fritz would say; it is also very dirty. Unless our powers of reason can confine us in a strait jacket . . . Woe betide us! *(Mop comes back with a sandwich)* Ah—good! So you found one. *(She takes it and eats it)* Excuse me—I'm so hungry.

MOP. But look at your sleeve.

STRANGE LADY. Torn? It must have been those—

MOP. No, it's just come unstitched.

STRANGE LADY. Do you know, tonight I couldn't manage to knock the bottle over? I must have been too far away. *(She kicks off her slippers, runs over to Boffi—takes his top hat)* Excuse me . . . *(Opens the hat and puts it on floor. Draws up her skirt, balances on one foot, lifts the other, as if, in the dance, she were kicking over a bottle of champagne represented by the hat. She hums an accompaniment)* Tairirarari . . . tairirarari . . .

(Twice she lifts her foot, but her toe does not touch the hat) There—you see? I was too far away. *(Closes the hat and gives it back to Boffi)* Thanks. I'm sorry if her husband doesn't like it—but she's a dancer at the "Lari-Fari", a night club. Did you know that?

BOFFI. Everything you say convinces me, more than ever, that you are she. But how, may I ask, could I fail to recognize you—I, who have known you since you were a baby.

STRANGE LADY. Since I was a *baby?* Well, well! And haven't I changed at all since I was a baby?

BOFFI. Of course you've changed; everyone changes; but very little, considering all that must have happened to you.

STRANGE LADY *(after looking at him a moment)*. Do you know, you interest me enormously? Everything you can imagine has happened to me at some time or other. And even now—with these two here—*(points to Salter and Mop)* if you only knew!

SALTER *(who can't stand it any longer)*. That will do! Have you no shame?

MOP. No, she's right, poor darling— *(Runs over to embrace her)*

STRANGE LADY *(disgusted—slipping away quickly)*. Mop, for heaven's sake!

SALTER *(to Mop—furious—taking advantage of this movement of repulsion)*. Leave her alone! And stop fooling around in your pajamas. Go to bed.

MOP *(tragically—facing her father)*. It's you! You ought to be ashamed—not she!

STRANGE LADY *(restraining her—tired and exasperated.* For God's sake don't begin all over again!

SALTER. Go on, I tell you! Go to bed!

STRANGE LADY. Yes, go on, darling. Run and see if you can get me another sandwich, eh?

MOP. And will you come out there and eat it?

STRANGE LADY. Yes, on condition that you don't kiss me. You know I can't bear it.

(Salter laughs savagely.)

MOP. Coward!

STRANGE LADY *(to Salter—furious)*. Stop laughing like that. *(To Boffi)* This could only happen to me! Jealous of each other!

MOP *(imploring—hurt)*. No, Elma— don't say that!

STRANGE LADY. Oh, my dear—if only it weren't *true!* But look at him. *(Indicates Salter)*

SALTER. Take care! I can't stand this much longer.

STRANGE LADY *(taunting, cruel—turning to Boffi)*. His wife won't divorce him. She sent the daughter to get her father to leave me—and now the daughter won't leave me herself! *(To Mop)* Yes, my dear, I hate to say it—but you're worse than he is. He may be old, but at least . . . *(She means "he is a man")*

MOP *(comes forward, looks at her father, then turns to the Strange Lady)*. He has a revolver in his pocket, did you—did you know? I'm warning you.

STRANGE LADY *(looking at Salter coldly)*. A revolver?

SALTER *(takes the revolver from his pocket without a word and puts it on the table beside her, sneering)*. There it is—at your service.

STRANGE LADY *(smiling)*. Oh. Thank you. Is it loaded?

SALTER. It's loaded.

STRANGE LADY *(picks it up)*. For me or for you?

SALTER. For whom you like.

BOFFI *(as she lifts the weapon)*. Hey— look out! *(The nervous tic)* Don't let's j-joke about it!

STRANGE LADY *(lowers it and puts it back on the table. Turning to Boffi)*. You see Tragedy! *(She sits)*

SALTER *(restraining himself with difficulty)*. Leave him out of it. Talk to me Tonight we were to come to a decision Are you trying to pretend you've forgotten? Well, I haven't!

STRANGE LADY. What *kind* of a decision? This kind? *(Looks at revolver)*

SALTER. I'm ready for anything.

STRANGE LADY *(at this answer she jumps to her feet, pale but resolved, picks up the weapon and points it at Salter)*. Do you want me to kill you? I could do it—believe me! *(She relaxes, lowers it)* I'm so tired of it all . . . *(Goes to him)* Instead, shall give you—look—a kiss on the forehead—here. *(Kisses him)* You might say thank you. *(Hands him the revolver)* Take it, my dear, go ahead and kill me if you like.

MOP *(impulsively)*. No—no! He might really do it.

STRANGE LADY. Let him! After all, when you can't go on any longer—If he only had courage enough! *(Going back to her place, she turns to Boffi. In a voice of desolate sincerity, like weariness itself)* It's true, you know. I can't go on any longer. *(Then, as if she'd got back her breath)* I'm so hungry—you've no idea. I ask for bread; he gives me a revolver; you keep calling me Signora Lucia. This is the most ridiculous evening.

SALTER *(suddenly, going to Boffi)*. This is my house. I must ask you to leave.

BOFFI. I shall not leave. I am here because of the Signora, not because of you.

SALTER. She is in my house; she is my guest.

STRANGE LADY. That is true. But if I like I can surely entertain a gentleman who says he knows me.

BOFFI *(to Salter)*. And do you generally entertain your guests clutching a revolver?

SALTER *(replying to the Strange Lady)*. Not now. We have to come to an understanding—we two. *(Then to Boffi)* Will you kindly go?

BOFFI. Yes. But with the lady.

STRANGE LADY. Right—fine! I'll go with you.

SALTER. *(seizing her by the wrist)*. You're not leaving this house!

STRANGE LADY *(struggling to free her hand from his grip)*. If I want to go, can you stop me?

SALTER *(holding her)*. Yes, I'll stop you!

STRANGE LADY. By force?

SALTER. Yes, if you're going to grab hold of the first man who comes along!

BOFFI. I am not "the first man who comes along!"

STRANGE LADY. Let me go!

SALTER. No!

STRANGE LADY. I want to go with him.

BOFFI. Don't use violence on the lady. assure you I really do know her.

SALTER. You are an intruder here. The lady doesn't know you at all.

BOFFI. It's not that she doesn't know me; she doesn't want to know me. I am Boffi.

STRANGE LADY *(quickly)*. The photographer?

BOFFI *(triumphantly)*. You see, she knows me!

SALTER. Boffi? *(Suddenly realizing)*. Oh yes—you're the one who discovered..

BOFFI. The stereoscopic photograph. Precisely!

SALTER. Then of course—she knows of you—that's it! You came here for an exhibition—

MOP. And we were looking at the reproductions in the papers together. Remember?

STRANGE LADY *(resolves to see it through—with final resolution)*. It's not true! I do know him! I do know him! He's a friend of my husband's! *(She gets her hand free)* Let me go!

SALTER *(amazed)*. But up to now you've laughed at the whole thing!

STRANGE LADY. Because I didn't want to be recognized.

BOFFI. At last! But do you suppose, Signora, that your husband doesn't know?

STRANGE LADY. No! He couldn't know—he couldn't know!

BOFFI. He knows the whole story. He got together all the evidence—down there.

STRANGE LADY. There? Where?

BOFFI. In the villa. But unfortunately—

SALTER *(noting the Lady's bewilderment—contemptuously)*. Villa? What villa? Tell us! Tell us, what villa?

STRANGE LADY *(suddenly, proudly)*. Mine! *(Turns to Boffi)* Tell him—give him the evidence! Throw it in the face of this coward who found me in despair and took advantage of it for himself.

BOFFI. They heard your cries. The old gardener heard you—you know—Filippo. He died not long ago.

STRANGE LADY. Filippo! Yes!

BOFFI. How could you have defended yourself, alone in the villa? When we came back, we saw for ourselves all the horror, the ruin, that followed the invasion of our country.

STRANGE LADY *(her face lights up as if*

she remembered, miraculously, something which she had actually witnessed). Ah! The invasion. *(To Salter)* Do you hear? Do you hear?

SALTER *(checked in his anger—forced to agree).* Yes, you've spoken to me of the invasion—

STRANGE LADY. I am a Venetian.

BOFFI. We all experienced the savagery of the enemy. *(To Salter, haughtily—flinging an old wrong into the face of the enemy)* Bruno Pieri, a brave and gallant officer, came back with the victorious army to his own land. He found his villa a heap of ruins, and no trace of the bride to whom he'd been married for barely a year.

STRANGE LADY. Bruno!

BOFFI. His Cia—

STRANGE LADY. He called me Cia! He called me Cia!

BOFFI. He could imagine easily enough what the officers who had been quartered in his villa must have done to you. He almost went mad, Signora—for more than a year he was like a madman. You cannot imagine how he searched for you, those first few years. He supposed, of course, that the enemy army had dragged you with them in the wild haste of their retreat—

STRANGE LADY. They did! they did drag me with them—

SALTER *(to Boffi).* Wait a minute! *(Trying to remember)* I'm sure I've read that story somewhere—

BOFFI. Probably in the newspapers.

SALTER. That's it! Years ago . . .

BOFFI. Her husband gave the story to the papers, years ago.

STRANGE LADY. I certainly never read it.

SALTER *(to the Strange Lady).* You've made up the whole thing! *(To Boffi)* But I'm sure I know something more about it. Yes, some theories a friend of mine had—a doctor—a psychiatrist, in Vienna. *(To the Strange Lady, contemptuously)* You're trying to mix this story with your own life. You'd like to pretend it's your own!

BOFFI. But I tell you, she is the lady.

SALTER *(still more contemptuously).* You!

STRANGE LADY *(calmly).* He says so—

don't you hear him? He's known me since I was a baby.

BOFFI. And I cannot be mistaken.

STRANGE LADY. While you've known me only a few months.

SALTER *(shouting—in an outburst).* I have wrecked my life for you!

STRANGE LADY. For your insane passion—not for me.

SALTER. And who drove me to it? Who made me lose my head?

STRANGE LADY. You wanted to lose it when you first came to me.

SALTER. Because you tempted me.

STRANGE LADY. That's my profession, my dear—as a woman. Life has brought me to it. Didn't you hear what happened to me?

SALTER. Will you stop! You're just trying to profit by this gentleman's obstinacy, his mistake—

BOFFI. I have made no mistake.

STRANGE LADY. I'll profit by it all right. *(To Boffi)* Heaven itself sent you to me tonight! You're my saviour. Please —talk to me about my childhood. I was so different then. When I think about it now, it seems as if it were a dream.

BOFFI. But that's the way it seems to all of us—the days of our youth—Signora Cia.

STRANGE LADY. You call me Cia too? Does everybody call me Cia? I thought it was only he . . . What a pity!

SALTER *(unable to restrain himself any longer).* I tell you, you can't walk out on me like this! You trapped me—

STRANGE LADY. Trapped you?

SALTER. Yes!

STRANGE LADY. So you let yourself be trapped, did you? You should have been on your guard! Well, it's true, in a way. But you deceived me.

SALTER. I did?

STRANGE LADY. Yes! I thought you were just a fool; and you've become insufferable—insufferable!

SALTER. Have you no pity on me?

STRANGE LADY. I? You dare say that I took pity on you—indeed I did! And your daughter is witness . . . *(To Boffi)* He's a famous writer, you know—

SALTER *(interrupting).* I forbid you to talk about me.

STRANGE LADY. Then why do you bring up your wrecked life?

SALTER. Because you should be afraid if you are thinking of getting rid of me like this.

STRANGE LADY. Afraid?

SALTER. Yes, afraid!

STRANGE LADY. I have never known that kind of fear.

SALTER. You are going to know it now.

STRANGE LADY. Because you carry a revolver in your pocket? Look here: I go off with this gentleman—Cia, taking a walk, as she did when she was a child. You pull out the revolver and you kill me—as a joke. Shall we try it?

SALTER. Don't put me to the test.

STRANGE LADY. I am. (To Boffi, taking his arm) Come on.

(Salter takes out the revolver.)

BOFFI (throwing himself between them). No, Signora—not like that!

STRANGE LADY. I have been through the war! Let him kill me! He would have to kill himself afterwards—and he hasn't the courage!

SALTER. I have—you know very well that I have!

STRANGE LADY (to Boffi). Listen, I could have kicked him into a corner, like this—like a bundle of rags on the floor—

SALTER. I am not a fool!

STRANGE LADY. Indeed! (To Mop) Tell me, Mop: is it true or isn't it, that he broke with your mother because she was always reproving him for being too frivolous for a serious writer?

MOP. Yes, it's true.

STRANGE LADY. You wouldn't believe what an act he put on, it was disgusting; smirking and grinning at the people who came to call: "Excuse me, ladies and gentlemen, but I find it impossible to be serious in the presence of my wife, who —you can see for yourselves—watches over my reputation like a broody hen!"

SALTER (exasperated). I couldn't be serious—I couldn't be! (To Boffi) It's really appalling, my dear sir, how a stupid little thing like that—something one does without thinking—can become fixed and irrevocable. That is what I am, and I can't be anything else. I've been labeled forever. I am a fool!

STRANGE LADY. Can you deny that's how you behaved—like a fool—when I first met you, you and your gang?

SALTER (interrupting angrily). That was because inwardly I was tortured, my life was unbearable.

STRANGE LADY. But nowadays he chases out other people. Did you see him just now? Such righteous indignation! Now he scolds me for compromising his reputation. He has turned into his own wife! (Getting angry) So I was to make your life bearable, was I? With your daughter, who—Heavens above! (She covers her face with her hands—in disgust, exasperation, despair) Don't make me speak of it—don't.

MOP (running to her in dismay). No, no—Elma—I beg you!

STRANGE LADY (almost shouting at her). Get away! I want to tell it!

MOP. Tell what?

STRANGE LADY. What you've done to me.

MOP. I?

STRANGE LADY (incoherently). You—all of you—I can't stand it any longer. This is an insane life. It chokes me, it makes me sick. Wine, wine—crazy, grinning creatures —all hell let loose—mirrors, bottles, glasses—reeling, dizzy—people shouting, dancing—clinging naked bodies—all the vices jumbled together—nothing normal any more—nothing any more—only an obscene craving which cannot be satisfied—(Seizes Boffi's arm—points at Mop) Look—look at her! Is that the face of a normal human being? And look at him there—(at Salter) with that face like a corpse, and all the vices crawling like maggots behind his eyes. And I dressed up like this. And you, trying to look so diabolical. This house—or any other house—the whole town. It's all mad— crazy—mad! (She points to Mop again) She arrived here. I knew nothing about it. Every evening I'm at the Lari-Fari. Who knows what went on between her and her father? She had a scratch—here—from her forehead to her cheek. (Takes Mop's face and turns it so that Boffi can see) Take a good look; she has the scar still.

SALTER. It wasn't I!

MOP. I did it myself, but she won't believe me.

STRANGE LADY. I don't know anything about it. I wasn't here. I came home—drunk, of course. I kick over the bottles and then I drink what's in them—I do "Bubbling Champagne." (Showing her costume) You see? It's my most famous dance. And so, of course, I get drunk, every night. That night, I didn't even see who took me and put me to bed.

MOP (trembling—almost leaping at her). Elma, please—please—that's enough!

STRANGE LADY (pushing her away). No, let me alone. He had gone out—

MOP (still clinging to her). What do you mean? Are you crazy?

STRANGE LADY (pushes her into a chair where she lies with her face hidden). Oh yes, I know! You have to be mad to be able to shout things like that openly—in front of everybody! (To Boffi, pointing to Salter, who is smiling) Look at him—he's laughing! The way he laughed the next morning when he wanted to know—

SALTER. Because it's strange that you—

STRANGE LADY. That I should make so much of something which doesn't matter to you at all! Nothing matters here. (Pointing to his daugher, whose face is hidden) While she—look at her!

SALTER. It is remorse—because she has betrayed her mother who sent her here.

MOP (leaping to her feet, screaming). No! Because it isn't fair—it isn't fair.

STRANGE LADY (to Boffi). They proclaim their rights, you understand? You accuse them, and they scream that it isn't fair! I must get away from all this—away from everybody—from everybody—including myself—away. I can't live like this any more, I can't be this—this—

BOFFI. The choice is yours, Signora. You can still take up your life.

STRANGE LADY. My life? What life?

SALTER (with angry scorn). Why, your life as Signora Lucia—with your husband. Surely you haven't forgotten?

STRANGE LADY (to Salter, proudly, emphatically). I have not forgotten! (To Boffi—a change of tone) After ten years, this man is still looking for his wife?

SALTER. For his Cia!

BOFFI (to her, firmly). Yes, Signora.

(Defiantly to Salter) His Cia. (To her again) Still, after ten years, and in spite of great opposition from some who for their own reasons would have preferred her to remain dead.

SALTER (suddenly—diabolically). Who? Who would have preferred it? (To the Strange Lady) Come on, you ought to know. Tell us!

STRANGE LADY. I know nothing about it. I'm asking him a question: how can this man go on believing she is alive, if she's never come back to him?

BOFFI. Because he believes that, after all that must have happened to her—

STRANGE LADY. The woman he is looking for can no longer exist!

BOFFI. No, Signora! He presumes that you have not come back simply because you feared you could never be the same to him after what had happened.

STRANGE LADY. And does he believe, then, that she could truly still be the same?

BOFFI. Why not, Signora, if you choose to be?

STRANGE LADY. After ten years—the same? After all that must have happened to her—the same? He's mad! And the proof is that she has not come back to him.

BOFFI. But I'm telling you, that if you want to now, Signora—

STRANGE LADY. If I want? To flee from myself—yes, that I want; no longer to remember anything, anything at all, to put my whole life behind me. Here. Look: this body—to be only this body. You say that it is hers? That I am like her? I no longer feel myself. I don't want myself. I know nothing any longer and I don't even know myself. My heart beats and don't know it; I breathe and I do not know it; I no longer know I am alive. A body, a body without a name, waiting for someone to come and take it! Very well; if he can re-create me—if he can give a soul again to this body, which is his Cia's—let him take it. Let him take it and fill it with his memories—a beautiful life—a beautiful life, a new life——Oh, am in despair!

BOFFI. I'm going to call him, at once

SALTER. You will not call anyone to my house.

STRANGE LADY *(starts to run towards the writing table in the study).* I'll call him.

SALTER *(holding her back).* No, wait! I'll go. I'll call him—and we shall see. *(He runs into the study)*

STRANGE LADY *(bewildered).* Call? Call whom?

BOFFI. What is he going to do?

MOP *(who has turned to see what her father is doing in the other room, gives a scream of terror).* No! *(Runs towards him. A revolver shot rings out)*

MOP. Father—Father! Oh God! Oh God!

BOFFI *(running toward her).* He's fallen on the floor—

STRANGE LADY. He's killed himself! *(Their voices, anxious and excited, are heard from the other room as they crowd round Salter's body. He is wounded in the chest. They first look at him, then lift him up to lay him on a divan.)*

MOP. Through the heart! Through the heart!

BOFFI. No, no! He's not dead. His heart isn't touched.

MOP. Look—he's bleeding from the mouth.

BOFFI. He's pierced a lung.

STRANGE LADY. Lift him up—lift his head a little.

MOP. No, gently! I'll do it. Father—Father!

BOFFI. We must lift him up—carry him over to the divan there. Help me—help me!

MOP. Gently—gently!

BOFFI. Get on that side—that's it. Like this.

MOP. It's Mop, Father, your Mop! Here—here—this way—gently! Watch his head. A cushion—a cushion—

STRANGE LADY. We must call a doctor—quick!

BOFFI. I'll go—I'll go—

MOP. Speak, Father! Speak to me! What do you want to say? *(To the Strange Lady)* He's looking at you.

STRANGE LADY. It's not serious—it can't be serious! But the doctor—quickly!

MOP *(to Boffi).* Yes, the doctor. There's

one right here in the building. But listen —there's the bell. Someone's banging on the door.

(Ringing of bell and knocking are heard.)

BOFFI. Just a minute—I'm coming.

STRANGE LADY *(following Boffi).* The doctor's right here, on the floor below. *(Boffi has opened the door, and a huge, typically German Janitor comes in. He is dishevelled and very angry.)*

JANITOR. What's all this? What's all this? When are we going to get some peace in this house? Fooling around with firearms now, eh?

STRANGE LADY. Yes, look. He's over there—Mr. Salter—he's wounded.

JANITOR. Wounded? How? Did he do it himself?

BOFFI. Yes, through the lung. He shot himself. It's serious.

STRANGE LADY. Please go and call Dr. Schutz—at once.

JANITOR. Dr. Schutz is asleep at this time of night.

BOFFI. Then wake him up!

STRANGE LADY. Yes, please, please! We must have *help* for him *at once.*

JANITOR. I'm not waking anybody up. You people turn the whole house upside down. It's got to stop.

BOFFI. I'll go—I'll go and call him.

JANITOR *(catching hold of him and stopping him).* You're not going out of here, if there's a wounded man around.

BOFFI *(twisting free).* You're crazy!

JANITOR. It's you people who are crazy! Those are the apartment house rules. You people live under wraps— everything soft and padded and covered up. But there are walls, all the same, and staircases, and a house; and the house has its rules, and it's my job to see that they're kept. I shall report this, I warn you! Where's the casualty? In there? Is it serious?

BOFFI. Yes, of course it's serious. We must get help for him.

JANITOR. Well, if it's serious, I say that—

MOP *(coming from the other room).* Look, wouldn't it be better if we took him to a hospital. There's nobody here.

JANITOR. Right! Sure! Get him out

of here—get him to a hospital. I'll call an ambulance.

MOP. Yes, please—at once—call an ambulance. *(She goes back to her father, and the Janitor goes out grumbling.)*

BOFFI. But is there no one here? No maid or anything?

STRANGE LADY. That's the way we live. At night there's no one here. And the janitors own the place!

BOFFI. Come with me, Signora, now!

MOP *(calling from the study)*. Elma— Elma! Come here!

STRANGE LADY. No—where do you want me to go now?

BOFFI. Signora Lucia!

MOP *(appearing in the doorway)*. Elma!

STRANGE LADY. She calls me Elma— you hear?

BOFFI. Then I'm going to fetch him.

MOP. You can't think of leaving now.

BOFFI. After he's been threatening her all the evening?

MOP. Only because she wanted to leave.

BOFFI *(taking the Strange Lady's arm)*. I shall come back here with him, Signora Lucia; and I am sure that as soon as you see him—

MOP *(taking her other arm)*. Come, Elma, come! He's calling you—he wants you!

(Boffi shrugs, annoyed, and goes resolutely.)

STRANGE LADY *(to Mop)*. Go on. Go on. I'm coming.

MOP *(takes a step, then turns)*. You're not going to leave . . .?

STRANGE LADY. No, I'm coming, I'm coming. Don't leave him alone—go to him. *(Mop goes. Left alone, the Strange Lady puts her hands over her face; then she presses them to her temples, one on each side of her forehead, as if to support the weight of her head. She lifts it despairingly and closes her eyes as she says:)* A body without a name! Without a name!

CURTAIN

ACT TWO

SCENE: *A room on the ground floor of the Villa Pieri, open and full of sunlight.*

The rear wall gives onto a loggia, with a marble balustrade. The four slender columns which support the glass roof can be seen through the opening. Beyond the loggia there is a view of a beautiful, peaceful landscape with its clear colors and restful, sun-drenched greens. Toward the end of the act it is veiled with violet shadows.

At the right is a rather wide staircase leading to the floor above. Only the lower steps can be seen, covered with a rich, red stair carpet. At the left are large glass doors, leading to the garden in front of the villa.

The furnishing are luxurious and light— those of a comfortable lounge hall. On the rear wall, towards the right, hangs a large oval portrait in oils. It represents Signora Lucia Pieri, as she was when she married, the year before the outbreak of war. She is standing in a graceful attitude, and wears a fresh, youthful gown of the fashion of the period.

TIME: *Four months have elapsed since Act One. It is an April afternoon.*

AT RISE: *At the rise of the curtain Aunt Lena Cucchi is discovered, speaking to someone in the garden. Aunt Lena is in her sixties, plump but sturdy, with a slightly masculine head, covered with grey curls. She has heavy black eyebrows and wears round, tortoise-shell glasses. She is dressed in black, with a starched collar. Her manner is brisk and frank.*

LENA *(talking from the French window to someone outside)*. Yes, yes, come on up That's enough, I tell you! At last! Good heavens, what a bunch! You're spilling them! Oh, never mind, don't stop to pick them up. You must have stripped the entire garden.

(Uncle Salesio Nobile enters from the French windows, carrying a huge bunch of flowers He is a spare little old man, who would still be quite agile, were it not for his neck and back which are almost rigid. His hair and mustache are newly dyed; the latter looks like two little dabs of soot underneath his long, acquiline nose. Elegance is his chief care in life, and perhaps also his martyrdom. He is almost strangled by a collar at least four inches high He wears faultless formal dress.)

SALESIO. Look here, I'll explain—

LENA. Don't explain; put them down there. *(Points to the table)*

SALESIO *(doing so)*. No, dear cousin, you'll allow me, I *will* explain.

LENA. All right, go ahead and explain. In the meanwhile I'll arrange the flowers. *(She starts putting the flowers in vases in various places around the room)*

SALESIO. I definitely did *not* pick them for the benefit of our expected guests.

LENA. I don't care who you picked them for. You picked too many, that's all I have to say.

SALESIO. I'm explaining to you why—

LENA. Explain, explain! You spend your whole life explaining.

SALESIO. How can I help it? The lack of understanding—or rather, of any wish to understand—

LENA. I'm feeling pretty good today. Explain that! And you're feeling pretty bad.

SALESIO. I'm feeling very good.

LENA. No, dear cousin—bad.

SALESIO. *Very Good!*

LENA. *Very Bad!*

SALESIO. Well then, will you explain to me why I should be feeling so very bad?

LENA. If you really want me to explain, that simply means that you have no feeling of what you've done.

SALESIO. What've I done?

LENA. Oh, never mind, never mind. Leave it alone. Thank heavens it's all over at last. Today we'll go through those wretched legal agreements—

SALESIO. What do you mean "draw up agreements"! We have to sign affidavits.

LENA. Well, at least we're going to agree about something! Of course, if I had my way, I'd put you on an allowance —as a punishment, mind you. But now that Cia's back, I certainly wouldn't have you around here any more.

SALESIO. Fine, fine! As a reward for having deprived myself of everything for my niece's sake.

LENA. When you gave Cia the villa and the grounds as a dowry you certainly were not depriving yourself of everything. You were right then—it meant nothing at all to you.

SALESIO. And now that I have nothing left, I'm to be told to get out, eh? It's the punishment I deserve.

LENA. Don't misunderstand me. I mean, a punishment for not having

Bruno's faith—his unshakeable faith— that our Cia was not dead.

SALESIO. You didn't have much faith either, at one time. You told me so yourself.

LENA. I may have said so. But at least I didn't sign any legal applications to have her declared dead.

SALESIO. Huh. Simply because your signature wasn't necessary.

LENA. I'm telling you I never would have done it—never! And we wouldn't now find ourselves in the position—which is extremely disagreeable for all of us—of having to draw up agreements asking for an annulment. And when I think that you did the whole thing just because you wanted to get the villa and the estate away from Bruno—it's contemptible!

SALESIO. Contemptible . . . take them away . . . ha! As if they had ever been his!

LENA. Certainly his—his twice over! He rebuilt the villa from the ground up, restored the value of the property, yet you denied him the right—

SALESIO. He had no right!

LENA. Oh, I know all about that fine excuse Inez thought up about the State being responsible for the repairs, after a survey had been made. Whereas I, instead of going along with Inez' little scheme—

SALESIO. But good God! You forget that without Cia, Bruno wasn't even one of the family any more! While Inez, after all, was my own niece—my other niece— for whom I hadn't been able to do anything at the time of her marriage, because I myself was already a poor man.

LENA. And so you admit that you did it for Inez?

SALESIO. Pardon me. I also did it myself.

LENA. I should think it would have turned your stomach when you saw how implacable she was about having her sister declared dead.

SALESIO. It was the feud with Bruno which made her so implacable! It's strange. Bruno understood and made allowances for me—but not you!

LENA. No, not me; because I wasn't going to take sides. And I use my head! Bruno, yes—a stranger—I can understand that. And I—if I'd become poor, and wanted to recover possession of what I had once given my niece—oh yes, I can understand that too, up to a point. It isn't very nice, but it's human. Men are not very nice; which is so true that I have never wanted to have anything to do with one.

SALESIO. Huh! Well! I could say that no man has ever wanted to have anything to do with you either!

LENA. No man has ever wanted to have anything to do with me either—that's fair enough.

SALESIO. For you're a good woman, Lena, but ugly. Ugly! And you have an ugly disposition. You don't seem to realize that I am poor because of all I have given away.

LENA. My dear Salesio, that's just what I'm saying! Because you *are* now so poor —all right! You should be in possession here! But as for that niece of yours—that Inez, who has the nerve to come here today and face her sister—I'd punish her! I'd shout in her face: "No! The villa and the estate will never go to you now! I'd rather throw them to the dogs, you understand, and you can go whistle for them." (*She catches sight of the Strange Lady coming down the stairs*) But here's our Cia now! (*The appearance of the Strange Lady creates a sensation, because, with a care which is apparent even to those who know her best, she has dressed and adorned herself exactly like the large oval portrait that hangs on the wall*) But look! Good heavens! You've made yourself into her!

SALESIO. It's the picture come to life!

STRANGE LADY. I have come to compare myself with her (*indicating the portrait*). I have to play the comedy.

LENA. To play the comedy?

STRANGE LADY. They are coming, aren't they? Dead—after ten years—you never know. It's better to go back, to re-make oneself like the original. Only I . . . (*She makes a gesture indicating her distaste*) Never mind. Who else will be here besides—sister Inez?

LENA. Her husband.

STRANGE LADY. Livio? Silvio?

LENA. Silvio, Silvio!

STRANGE LADY. I don't know why, but I keep thinking—Livio.

SALESIO. He's a lawyer. Be careful!

LENA. Careful of what?

SALESIO. He's the one who took charge of the—

LENA. Oh, let's not think about that. He's polite—

SALESIO. Shrewd!

STRANGE LADY. I shall be glad to know him.

LENA. But you do know him—not as a brother-in-law, certainly. He was a friend of Bruno's.

STRANGE LADY. Oh, Bruno had so *many* friends. I hope I'm not expected to know them all, now that the doors have been opened . . . Who else is coming?

LENA. Well, your sister-in-law, Barbara, I suppose—if Bruno thought of sending for her.

SALESIO. She's nobody.

LENA. Nobody? She's always been—secretly—the worst enemy of them all.

STRANGE LADY. And Boffi? Will Boffi be here too?

LENA. I don't know whether he's in town.

STRANGLY LADY. He is, he is. I told Bruno to ask him too. I want Boffi. I want him. (*She looks at the portrait, then at herself*) Perfect, isn't it?

SALESIO. Just as if you had stepped out of the frame.

LENA. Yes, though I never did think that picture of you as a girl was particularly like you.

STRANGE LADY. No? But Bruno told me it had been painted from an enlarged photograph—

SALESIO. Of course—from a photograph.

STRANGE LADY. —And he had given the painter all the directions.

SALESIO. Now we can see if it's like you! Good Lord, it's the living image Just what I always said! Look at that!

LENA. I was talking about the eyes Excuse me—you don't mind... (*She takes the Strange Lady's face between her hands and peers at her eyes*) There—you see? Her are her real eyes, as I have always see them. They are these eyes—not those at all.

STRANGE LADY. You always saw these eyes in Cia?

LENA. Of course.

SALESIO. And they are not the same?

LENA. The same—good heavens! These are the same—not those. Almost green.

SALESIO. What do you mean, green? They're blue!

STRANGE LADY (to Lena). Green to you—(to Salesio) Blue to you (She draws Salesio over to the portrait) and to Bruno— Look, Uncle—gray, with black lashes. Then the painter added his own touch. "Cia's real eyes!" How can you be sure even with the proof of a portrait?

SALESIO. I can't possibly be mistaken. Your father and I were like brothers. You have his eyes.

LENA. His eyes! Inez—yes, she has her father's eyes. But not these. On the contrary, you have your mother's eyes. Believe me. We grew up together—cousins with the same name, poor dear Lena and I. Surely I ought to know! (Uncle Salesio laughs) All right, laugh—laugh!

STRANGE LADY. What is he laughing at?

LENA. Because, since we were girls, whenever the boys saw us two cousins together—

SALESIO. We used to call them the pretty Lena and the ugly Lena.

STRANGE LADY. No! Lena—ugly!

LENA. Darling! That's just how you always used to protest, ever since you were tiny: "No! Lena—ugly!" And when the pretty Lena died, this ugly one became a mother to you—

STRANGE LADY (disturbed). Lena— please. Don't go on.

LENA (as if acknowledging a promise she has made). All right, I won't—I won't! But that's a part of your life that ought not to grieve you.

SALESIO. Well it does—you can see. She told you not to go on.

LENA. I mean it can't grieve her because she was so small; she can't possibly remember. (By way of conclusion) You are the living image of your mother; she was just like you when she died.

SALESIO. She looks completely different to me!

LENA. Huh!

STRANGE LADY. This, Uncle, is the comedy, that I am going to play: how I look to you and how I look to Lena and how one recognizes a woman has who vanished for ten years and who must have been swept under by the whole Army of the enemy. You'll see—you'll see. (She sits down and gestures Lena and Salesio to do the same) Now, to begin with, I wish you would both explain to me, clearly, just what Bruno's position is, here, with regard to the villa and the estate.

SALESIO (astonished). His position? Don't you know?

STRANGE LADY (drily). I do not know.

SALESIO. But surely Bruno must have told you—

STRANGE LADY. He told me—I don't quite know—something about contested rights. But he seemed so upset and embarrassed. Perhaps because as I listened to him I felt . . .

LENA. I know; it really makes me feel quite sick too.

STRANGE LADY. No, Lena, it's not what you think. It was something else that upset me . . . He went off shrugging his shoulders: "Oh, well never mind! At any rate, you'll appear as if you knew nothing about it. It's better if they know that I haven't told you anything." But instead, I want to know everything, and clearly, and now.

SALESIO. But the situation is perfectly simple, now.

LENA. Now that you're back—

SALESIO. All litigation has been stopped—

LENA. In fact we were talking about it just this minute.

STRANGE LADY. All the same, the death-certificate has not yet been annulled, has it?

LENA. Don't worry about that. It will be annulled by the affidavits we're going to sign now.

SALESIO. It would have been annulled immediately, if you'd wanted, from the beginning—

STRANGE LADY (scornfully). From the beginning . . . (Restraining herself a moment) Don't make me speak of it. (She must give vent to what she feels) I wanted nothing, from the beginning—nothing of all this!

LENA. Yes, yes. We know. You should

at least have been spared this bitterness.

STRANGE LADY. If it were only bitterness!

LENA. But you know, there are certain claims involved.

STRANGE LADY. *Nothing* has been said to me.

LENA. You have claims too.

STRANGE LADY. I have no claims whatever.

SALESIO. Pardon me, but of course you have!

STRANGE LADY. No. No, no! If there are claims involved, I warn you right away that I'll have no part of it! Tell me—tell me! Because if that's the case—first of all I would go and take off these clothes. (*She points to her clothes*) It would be unworthy—unworthy!

LENA. Not at all. Why do you think that way?

STRANGE LADY. Because it is that way! The declaration of death is correct. It's correct!

SALESIO (*astounded*). Correct? How?

STRANGE LADY. Yes, correct! I said so to Boffi, back there! And I've said so to him! You spent ten years waiting for her. Did you see her come back? No. Why did she never come back? Is it difficult to imagine the reason? She was dead—dead—or as good as dead to all her former life here. Dead to every memory of that life, which she no longer wanted—is that clear?—*which she no longer wanted!* Even if she is still alive.

LENA. Yes, yes. You're right, my child. I understand. I understand perfectly.

SALESIO. And I too, Cia—I too. But since you *have* come back—

STRANGE LADY. But knowing nothing of all these claims and conflicts, nor that I should be forced to play this part, which I detest. I came for his sake—I did it only for him. And I made a condition beforehand that no one, no one should except me to recognize them; that no memories were to be awakened, either from my former life, or since. In the beginning I did not even want to see you two, who were living here with him.

SALESIO. Yes, and in fact we did go away for more than a month.

STRANGE LADY (*getting up—passionately*. He ought to have told me—he ought to have told me! I wouldn't have come.

LENA (*after a pause—timidly*). Perhaps he didn't like to tell you—out of delicacy—because your sister had—

SALESIO. After your disappearance—

LENA. Making excuses for her again!

SALESIO. I am not making excuses. I am explaining. She says so herself, didn't you hear? After ten years—

STRANGE LADY. She applied—and rightly—for a death certificate, in order to have the villa and the estate made over to her. Isn't that so?

LENA. No, not to her. So that they should revert to him (*points to Uncle Salesio*) because he gave them to you as a dowry.

SALESIO. Since there was no heir—

STRANGE LADY (*joyously, to Uncle Salesio*). Ah—then they revert to you? They're not Bruno's any more?

LENA. No, they are Bruno's—they are Bruno's!

STRANGE LADY. But there's the death certificate! And I was so happy about it back there because it freed me from the obligation. It seemed—I don't know—like salvation, for him too! (*Turns to sit again*). Tell me—how are they still Bruno's?

LENA. Because Bruno rightly opposed.

SALESIO. Rightly? Hardly that!

LENA. Rightly, yes!

SALESIO. No!

STRANGE LADY. But Lena, don't you understand how happy I should be if they had reverted to him —if he could still dispose of them, and give them to her?

LENA. No, no!

SALESIO. To her? No! What an idea!

STRANGE LADY. Yes, yes! To her, to her!

SALESIO. No! Leave me out of it—it has nothing to do with me any more. Your coming back made the whole thing pointless. Lena and I were just discussing—hypothetically of course—before you came down, whether the motive behind the dispute was justifiable or not. You can imagine what a state they were in—the villa and the whole property, after the war, a heap of ruins—everything completely devastated—

LENA. And as long as it remained in ruins, you understand, nobody so much as thought of having you declared dead! That idea only occurred to them after Bruno—

SALESIO. Oh, to hear you talk—

LENA. Do you mean to imply that it isn't true?

STRANGE LADY. Let him speak, Lena, let him speak. I want to know his opinion too.

SALESIO. You always had good sense enough for us all, Cia. Now, you should understand clearly—

STRANGE LADY. Yes, I want to understand—to understand clearly!

SALESIO. Very well, then. *(To Lena)* With your permission? *(To the Strange Lady again)* This is the crux of the whole thing; who was responsible for the reparation of the war damages?

LENA. The State! Tell him that, and make him happy! You see it's like this: your husband rebuilt the villa for you immediately, in the hope that you would return at any moment. But any rights that he claimed, in consequence of the work he had done, were denied by the opposite side. "Thanks," they said to him, "Reparations? They don't constitute any claim, because in time the State itself would have made them."

SALESIO. It was at this juncture—

LENA. That the news of your reappearance burst upon us like a bomb!

SALESIO. All litigation was stopped immediately, and everything settled down just as it was before.

LENA. You can imagine how they felt! They were so sure they had won. *(Pause. The Strange Lady is deep in thought.)*

STRANGE LADY. Then if my "reappearance," as you put it, had not occurred, Bruno would have lost everything?

SALESIO. Certainly. Everything.

LENA. When, after the necessary period of time, the death certificate had been granted.

STRANGE LADY. And Boffi knew all this when he came to Berlin?

LENA. Of course he knew! How could

he have helped knowing? It was an open scandal.

SALESIO. You can imagine! Round here they talked of nothing else.

LENA. Sentimental reasons on one side, and reasons of self-interest on the other—strong ones too, because the property, as you know, is considerable, and your husband's management had made it extremely valuable. His enemies laughed about it. It was easy enough for them to sneer at his "sentimental reasons." They maliciously implied that this noble behaviour of Bruno's was nothing but a cunning attempt to further his own interests.

STRANGE LADY. They even thought he might have found it convenient to plead sentimental reasons, as a matter of self-interest?

LENA. Oh, the spiteful tongues, the spiteful tongues!

SALESIO. They all got so worked up . . . *(Pause. The Strange Lady is becoming more and more overwhelmed by a dreadful suspicion.)*

STRANGE LADY. I understand . . . I understand.

LENA *(to distract her)*. But it's all over now! Let's not talk about it any more. Of course it disturbs you to see them again.

STRANGE LADY *(with a movement of disdain)*. No. Why should that matter to me? *(With a change of tone)* Something else disturbs me. Even then, that first time . . .

LENA *(timidly)*. What?

STRANGE LADY. Nothing, nothing!

LENA. But you see, there are certain formalities. You were supposed to be dead; you *must* reappear, alive.

STRANGE LADY *(without taking any notice of this)*. Boffi told me he had *sent* for Bruno the moment he thought he *recognized* me.

LENA. Yes. And you can imagine how he rushed off immediately!

STRANGE LADY. Because the question of the death certificate had come up, isn't that so? And, in consequence, the probability of his losing the case?

LENA. Good heavens, no! What are you thinking about?

STRANGE LADY. I am right, Lena; believe me, I am right!

LENA. No, you are not. He never believed that you were dead. He was the only one!

SALESIO. That's true!

LENA. He rushed off to get you. He guessed exactly what you have since told us; the very reasons why you hadn't wanted to come back!

STRANGE LADY (getting up—nervously). Do you know where he found me? I had to take someone to the hospital—in the middle of the night. His daughter was there too. He had tried to kill himself—

LENA. Because of you?

STRANGE LADY. Yes.

LENA. Good God! Was he crazy?

STRANGE LADY. He didn't want to let me go. He still writes to me. At the door, as I was following the stretcher bearers, I suddenly saw—

SALESIO. Bruno?

STRANGE LADY. Yes, Bruno. Boffi had gone and fetched him from the hotel and wanted to keep me from leaving. I shouted to him, "You're crazy!" I told him to let me go, because I had no husband, had never had any, and I didn't even know this gentleman he had brought to me.

SALESIO. And what about Bruno?

STRANGE LADY. I went straight out, following the wounded man, without giving him time to answer. When I came back, a couple of hours later, I found them both still there. Boffi must surely have told him that I . . . (To Lena) You can understand—in the presence of that madman, who had a gun in his pocket and who had already threatened me, I had given in, naturally, in order to escape, to find a way out. I had admitted—I don't know what—that I knew him, that I remembered Filippo the gardener, that I had been left alone in the villa . . . And now, when I saw them right there in front of me, and realized that they must have been discussing all this, I denied everything—everything! I told them why I had been compelled to say what I did, but that none of it was true; that I did not know him at all, I did not know either of them, and would they please go—go

away, and stop this silly farce of Boffi's, this stubborn insistence that he had recognized me.

SALESIO. But Bruno too he recognized you immediately!

STRANGE LADY. No. Bruno? No.

SALESIO (astonished). No?

STRANGE LADY. No, I tell you. He didn't. I'm quite sure of it. When he saw me for the first time, standing there in the doorway, he saw no such resemblance as Boffi had promised him. I'm certain of it. He must have been terribly disappointed. (To Lena) You know how it is; when you first meet someone, you detect a certain resemblance; you speak of it to someone else; they look, and they can't see it at all. We do not see with the same eyes. (To herself) Yes, but then why—that's what I keep asking myself—why, if he didn't see it at once . . . (To the others) There must have been some sort of resemblance, it was undeniable; I admitted it. I couldn't do anything else. I even admitted I was a Venetian—but not from around here, not from here; I even told them where I did come from. What I said and did finally convinced them both that it was only a likeness after all—a striking one, certainly, similarity of circumstance as well as of looks—but nothing more than that. I was not I, the lady he was searching for was not I. What more could I do? But then . . . I don't know . . . something . .

LENA. You were sorry?

STRANGE LADY. No. I was in such a state that . . . (Again half to herself) He oughtn't to use it now as a pretext. He oughtn't to try and profit by it. If he had used it, to further his own interests—

LENA. No, no. Why do you torture yourself like this? What do you mean?

STRANGE LADY. I was so tired—oh Lena, I was so tired—and desperate. Never before had I felt so desperate—lost, finished—so disgusted by my own life; I couldn't go on any more. I didn't know where to turn, what to do; the ghastly night when it seemed to me that life hung suspended over an abyss—abyss of agony . . .

LENA (deeply moved). My poor child

STRANGE LADY. He began to talk abo

his Cia—as she was, all she had meant for him that year she had been his—with such desolate sadness, that just listening to him . . . He seemed so alone—and I was so desolate myself, so hopeless—that I began to cry. I cried and cried—for myself, for my own wretchedness—never thinking that he would take it as a sign of remorse because of all I had denied. There was my body, in itself a further proof that I was his Cia; I let him embrace me, press me against his heart till I could hardly breathe. But I did it for no other reason; this alone was why I came with him. I made understand that I would come here—come back from the dead—only for him, only for him.

LENA. Yes, yes. The old life is ended—finished. I could read it so plainly in your eyes, as soon as I saw you.

STRANGE LADY. Did you recognize me too, immediately?

LENA. No, my dear girl, I must confess I didn't—not immediately.

STRANGE LADY. Not you, either!

SALESIO. No more did I. But that's easily explained. After all those years—

LENA. On the contrary! All those years! If I'd thought about it at all, I'd have been surprised that all those years seem to have left no mark on her at all. No, it was something—I don't know—your manner, the way you move, something even in your voice.

STRANGE LADY. Did you notice a difference in my voice?

LENA. Yes, it seemed to me—

STRANGE LADY. Boffi did too. He told me so afterwards. It was the only difference he did notice. (Pause) It's strange that he—(She means Bruno) must have noticed it too. He never spoke of it. (Rising—half to herself) So many things are beginning to fit together.

LENA. Ah, well, that's easily explained, Salesio would say. You were away for long, speaking a different language. And you've changed in yourself, above . . . You said to me: "Lena," just like that, in a small, weak voice, and I could tell from it—I could feel death itself in your voice, the death of everything you had once been, and that you had determined, deliberately, never to be again. I

realized that if I had reminded you of something, perhaps the very thing which had once been most alive in you, that you would be—well, like you are now: not wanting to remember any more, perhaps not able to remember.

STRANGE LADY. (absorbed in herself, not listening to Lena). I was just thinking—

SALESIO. You mustn't think of anything any more, from now on!

STRANGE LADY (as if to herself). Yes, that's it! He took advantage of it first by telling me that there was an excuse, a good excuse, for not seeing her . . .

LENA. Inez, you mean?

STRANGE LADY. No, I mean this double game he's been playing. At first I flatly refused to come here, knowing . . .

LENA. What Inez had done to you?

STRANGE LADY. No, no, I knew nothing about that. On the contrary, I'm saying that when he persuaded me to come, this was the pretext he found: *that I would not have to see her;* everyone would understand that I had a good reason for not seeing her. You see? But now he's using what Inez did—that death certificate she was in such a hurry about—to compel me to see her.

LENA. But you must remember that he never wanted this quarrel with your sister.

SALESIO. You've been shut up here for four months now.

STRANGE LADY. Perhaps that was deliberate too.

LENA. Deliberate?

STRANGE LADY. I'd stake my life on it!

SALESIO. What do you mean?

STRANGE LADY. What do I mean? (Restraining herself) Oh, it's perfect—this whole scheme of his—perfect! Even this business of seeming to be on tenterhooks—

SALESIO. No, no Cia! I assure you, you are unjust!

LENA. It seems unjust to me too.

STRANGE LADY. Because you cannot understand.

SALESIO. Then I tell you, you don't understand either—forgive my saying so —or else you don't want to understand. He has every reason to be on tenterhooks. He has respected your feelings too far.

You must take into consideration the fact that your reappearance after ten years has aroused a great deal of curiosity, and this curiosity has been brought to fever heat during these four months that you have been shut up here; what people are thinking—what they're saying—

STRANGE LADY. I can imagine—oh, I can imagine! (To Lena, with a wink) The "spiteful tongues"?

SALESIO. Yes. "First, the family quarrel," they say, "Then," they say, "her not wanting to see her own sister—her husband's relatives," they say—

STRANGE LADY. Everything they say is against me? And who knows what else! What more—about my other life! They must know everything. Boffi—

SALESIO. Boffi? No, no, on the contrary! He—

LENA. —Has always taken your part—always—I'm sure—

STRANGE LADY. But he must have told them—where he found me, what sort of life I led. And the more he refrained from actually saying, the more he must have let them guess—with a look or so, a gesture, that little 'tic' he has—that he knew plenty! They must have asked questions. Do they know I was a dancer? Are they saying that?

LENA. It's outrageous!

STRANGE LADY. No, it's not outrageous, Lena, it's true. I was a dancer—and worse. You can't possibly imagine all the things I've done. To be a dancer is an honorable profession—besides, I invented my own dances, wrote the music, designed my costumes. No, it's worse—much worse.

LENA. And—does he know?

STRANGE LADY. Bruno? Of course! But they've found out the worst too, haven't they, Uncle Salesio? They know it, don't they? They're saying it?

SALESIO. They say all sorts of things.

STRANGE LADY. Then they'll also say that he overlooked all this because I was useful to him here.

LENA. No, no!

STRANGE LADY. Be quiet.

LENA. Who could ever have said such a thing? Or even thought it?

STRANGE LADY. I! I am thinking it.

Tell me the truth, Uncle Salesio. Aren't they saying so?

SALESIO. Yes. They're saying so.

STRANGE LADY. You see?

LENA. Who said so?

SALESIO. Whoever it was—they've said so.

STRANGE LADY. I can well imagine all the gossip and suspicion about the two of us. Oh, it's all been spoiled now; it's all been degraded by this dirty entanglement of claims and counter claims.

LENA. Bruno's not to blame—

STRANGE LADY. I'm telling you how it seems to me now, all this; and if I thought he had done it for—

(The crunch of automobile tires on the gravel drive is heard from outside.)

SALESIO. There they are now!

STRANGE LADY (recovering her self possession—with a gesture of defiance). Yes At once. At once.

LENA. But why so early?

SALESIO (looking out into the garden) No, it's Bruno.

LENA. Ah, I thought—They said si o'clock.

SALESIO. There's Boffi too. Boffi's wit him.

LENA. You see? Bruno has brough him.

(Long pause.)

STRANGE LADY. What are they doing

LENA. Bruno's reading a letter.

STRANGE LADY. A letter?

SALESIO. Yes, the gatekeeper ju handed it to him.

LENA. What's happening? Boffi's goi away again with the letter.

STRANGE LADY. No. Uncle Salesi run and call him back. I want him come in.

SALESIO (going out into the garder Bruno—Boffi! Come here! Yes, you t Boffi! Come here!

(Bruno and Boffi come in, followed by Ur Salesio. Bruno is about thirty-five; he is p with anxiety, and looks nervous and up every look and movement betray his impatie and perturbation.)

BRUNO. Why do you want Boffi no Please let him go.

BOFFI. Good evening, Signora. I'd really better hurry.

BRUNO. Yes, go on—hurry. And stop them at any cost!

STRANGE LADY. What's the matter?

BOFFI. A letter just came—

STRANGE LADY. From him? Another one?

BOFFI. He's making the most of the fact that he's still alive! He's out for revenge.

STRANGE LADY. But what does he say?

BRUNO *(to Boffi—impatiently)*. Go on, go on for heaven's sake! There's no time to lose.

STRANGE LADY *(to Boffi)*. No, wait a minute! *(To Bruno)* I want to know. Give me that letter.

BRUNO. The letter's nothing! If it were only the letter. *(Turning to Aunt Lena and Uncle Salesio)* Lena, if you please —and you too, Uncle Salesio. *(Motions towards the stairs)*

LENA. Of course, yes, at once.

SALESIO. We're going—we're going! *(They both go upstairs.)*

STRANGE LADY. What is it? What's the matter?

BRUNO. Today of all days! It's becoming a persecution! It's unheard of!

STRANGE LADY. What does he write?

BRUNO. Write? He does more than write! He's left! He's on his way here!

STRANGE LADY. Here?

BOFFI. Yes, here, here! And he's not done either!

STRANGE LADY. Is his daughter coming too?

BRUNO. No. What daughter? To unmask you, he says!

STRANGE LADY. To unmask me?

BOFFI. It's the old story. You know how he threatened.

STRANGE LADY. Threatened what? I don't remember.

BOFFI. What he said about having read the papers—

STRANGE LADY. Oh, yes! The story—

BOFFI. You remember he spoke about doctor friend of his, in Vienna?

BRUNO. He went to Vienna! He writes from Vienna! *(Shows the letter without giving it to her)* There—look!

STRANGE LADY. He went to Vienna? What for?

BRUNO. It's incredible—absolutely incredible!

BOFFI. He's playing his last card! All or nothing!

STRANGE LADY. Yes, but what does he say in the letter?

BRUNO. I'm telling you, am I not? He says he'll be here this evening, with a woman from a sanitarium—an insane woman—and the doctor who takes care of her.

STRANGE LADY. Oh, yes—now I remember. And he's bringing her here?

BRUNO. Yes. Claiming he has proof.

STRANGE LADY *(staring at him)*. Proof? Proof of what?

BRUNO. Why, that she is the one— *that she is the one*—and not you!

BOFFI. And he's bringing her here?

BRUNO. He's bringing her here! Now do you understand?

STRANGE LADY *(impassive—still gazing at Bruno)*. Here? And why is he bringing her?

BRUNO. He's written several times— to you, to me. Perhaps we were wrong not to answer him.

STRANGE LADY. But he said nothing of this threat to me.

BRUNO. Well, he did to me. He even asked me to go to Vienna and see the patient.

STRANGE LADY *(astonished—on her guard)*. He did?

BRUNO *(irritated by her attitude)*. Yes, he did! And to talk to his friend the doctor, the one who's coming here with him now.

STRANGE LADY *(still staring at him, as if his attitude alone made any impression on her)*. Why did you never tell me about it?

BRUNO. Was I to tell you—you of all people—that I had been asked to go to Vienna to see another woman—

BOFFI. You should have answered him, though—you really should—if only to tell him he was crazy!

BRUNO. Even when I knew he was doing it simply to revenge himself on her?

STRANGE LADY *(emphasizing each syllable)*. I would have advised you to go.

BOFFI *(quickly)*. There, you see? I advised him to go, too!

BRUNO *(increasingly irritated)*. But for

what? To look at some poor half-wit, with a vacant, grinning face . . .?

STRANGE LADY. How do you know that?

BOFFI. He sent me a picture of her. Luckily it never occurred to him to appeal to the authorities.

STRANGE LADY. You have the picture?

BOFFI. Yes. I haven't got it with me. There was nothing to worry about in that, believe me. Not a thing. I was going to answer him, but he—(pointing to Bruno)—contrary to the demands—

STRANGE LADY. What demands?

BOFFI. The demands he made in his letter to me.

STRANGE LADY. I know nothing about it. I'm hearing all this for the first time. And yet I have a right to know. A picture —demands? What demands?

BOFFI. You understand, Signora, he had received no answer from Bruno; and he must certainly have suspected that since Bruno, as the husband, had already acknowledged you, it would be entirely against his interests to have another woman show up now. So he turned to me— and, I repeat, it's lucky he thought of sending the photograph to me, as a photographer, instead of taking it to the authorities. He sent it to me and demanded that I show it to the relatives, if any, of the missing woman, to see if they recognized it; and he also asked that some of the relatives should go—

BRUNO. He's simply hell-bent . . . . Such obstinacy!

BOFFI. I need hardly say that both Bruno and I were extremely perturbed by all this. You see, the picture was sent only a few days ago. Should we show it to the relatives? Right now, with all this business going on? That would be fine! Should we go to Vienna after all? I was even in favor of that—to put a stop to the whole thing at once by appearing in person—

BRUNO. Go to Vienna! That's easy to about. But how? In secret?

STRANGE LADY. In secret?

BRUNO. Were we to let everbody in on it, then? The slightest hint, and they know everything! That's all they do, watch us and talk about us!

STRANGE LADY. And so, you told me nothing; you didn't answer—you didn't go—

BRUNO. I'm telling you why!

STRANGE LADY. Like an ostrich, hiding its head in the sand!

BOFFI. Certainly, if you had gone you would have stopped them—

BRUNO. How was I to foresee that they would come here?

BOFFI. No, no—you couldn't; that was unforeseeable. And so quickly!

STRANGE LADY. What I want to know is, how did he manage to persuade the doctor—

BOFFI. He tells us that, in this letter which just came. It's obvious that he has money to burn. He has convinced his doctor friend, and they're all four on the way—he, the doctor, the patient, and a nurse. He has convinced the doctor that it's to the interest of everybody here to prevent the truth from coming out; also that the sight of familiar surroundings, or something, may re-awaken in this poor woman's mind—I don't know! And perhaps he quite likes the idea of a free trip to Italy!

BRUNO. But he's doing it for revenge

BOFFI. I mean the doctor! Of course . . . We know why he's doing it! But what proof can they possibly have . . . (A pause. All three wait for a moment un certain—in suspense. The Strange Lady studying Bruno. Then she asks him:)

STRANGE LADY. And you?

BRUNO. What about me?

STRANGE LADY. You seem so anxious— so frightened—

BRUNO. Not in the least. But I wish .

STRANGE LADY. What do you wish?

BRUNO. I wish—Well, what can wish, now? You tell me! I was just send ing Boffi to find out what train they' likely to come on . . .

STRANGE LADY. Oh. And then?

BRUNO. Really, what a peculi question! To prevent them from bursti in while the others are here, at events!

STRANGE LADY. Prevent them—wh for? They have already started, and soon or later they'll arrive! You seem to r as if—

BRUNO. As if what? I'm just worried!

STRANGE LADY. No, darling. You seem more as if you expected the roof to fall on your head or the ground to open under your feet.

BRUNO. Does it mean nothing to you to have them come bursting in, while all the others are here, with a lot of supposed evidence—which must be fairly impressive, I imagine, or the doctor would never have agreed to bring his patient.

STRANGE LADY. So you're afraid of the evidence, is that it?

BOFFI. No, Signora! Afraid that the others might take advantage of . . .

STRANGE LADY. Of what? The evidence?

BOFFI. Not only that, but of the doubts which this evidence might arouse . . .

STRANGE LADY. That I may not be the one, but she may be?

BRUNO. Not that there can be any real doubt, you understand; but simply because it might be convenient for them!

STRANGE LADY (ironically). You mean they would be happy to make use of these doubts, in their own interest?

BOFFI. Of course! Don't you believe that?

STRANGE LADY. But if you prevent it today, you can't prevent it tomorrow. It's a game they can always play, even if they do recognize me today. Tomorrow, if they decide to admit this evidence as valid—(To Bruno) You say it would be to their advantage? No. If they choose to accept her—excuse my contradicting you, Boffi—it would be much worse for them.

BRUNO. Why?

STRANGE LADY. Don't you understand? They would be accepting her on the basis of this evidence, and thereby admitting that it is indisputable. Whereas here am I, without any evidence—just myself—that's all. And if they choose, they can reject me at first sight.

BOFFI. I think it would be difficult.

STRANGE LADY. Well—if they want it that way—I have no evidence at all.

BOFFI. There is no need of any.

STRANGE LADY. No need? On the contrary, it's very easy indeed to doubt me, my dear Boffi! I myself could give you a hundred reasons for doubting me. I myself—and about myself! Seeing him like that—(She turns on Bruno with a motion of violent scorn) Just remember that whatever happens, you have nothing to lose!

BRUNO. I? What do you mean?

STRANGE LADY. I am speaking of what matters most to you now.

BRUNO. No, no, no! What matters most to me is the scandal that's bound to be started! Inevitably! We've already given rise to so much gossip by the way we've lived these past four months—

STRANGE LADY. Do you regret it?

BRUNO. No! But don't you see—

BOFFI. That's true!

STRANGE LADY. Keep calm, my dear Bruno; if the worst comes to the worst, you will have made a mistake, that's all.

BRUNO. A mistake? What do you mean?

STRANGE LADY. In thinking that I was the one, as Boffi did, as Lena and Uncle Salesio did! You see what good company you are in! You have nothing to lose, since it was I who deceived you, I, "the impostor." And Salter will shortly arrive and confirm it. (She laughs)

BRUNO. Yes! I suppose it's better to laugh after all!

STRANGE LADY. I suppose it is. But perhaps at this moment he[1] finds it a little difficult to laugh; because he knows very well that it was he who *wanted* to be mistaken, and not I who caused the mistake.

BRUNO. Are you out of your mind? What mistake are you talking about? Are you crazy? What mistake? In your being Cia?[2]

STRANGE LADY. Cia? Yes. That's all settled. Don't be afraid. (Points to the picture) That one. What more do you want? (Laughs again) You are my witness, Boffi, that I did everything I could to prevent him from being victimized by a possible—a suspected—an avowed, yes, avowed—impostor! But what does it matter? Here I am. I will answer for myself. But only for myself, mind you! Not for you—not any more. For I have been mistaken too, you know.

[1] Referring to Bruno—J.G.
[2] In my taking you to be Cia—J.G.

BRUNO. In what?

STRANGE LADY. In you. You don't know how much! (*Turning to Boffi*) Go along, Boffi, go along. I must talk to Bruno. But don't waste your efforts—it would be quite useless. Let them come, if possible while the others are here. It will be better that way—much better.

BRUNO. What do you propose to do?

STRANGE LADY. You shall see!

BRUNO. They will be here any minite!

STRANGE LADY. I am ready. Just a few words will be enough. Perhaps you won't be able to understand me. It doesn't matter. Don't be afraid of that "little game" of theirs. They won't play any game. I shall—I shall play it. I am ready! And for everybody. Even for me it will be a terrible game. (*To Boffi*) Go—go!

BOFFI. Then, if they arrive—shall I bring them here?

STRANGE LADY. Yes, bring them here—bring them here. Because it's useless—(*Sending him off quickly*) Go! (*As he leaves*) Useless, useless! Facts can never be disputed! Facts are down to earth! With your soul you can ascend for a moment, escape, arise above the worst that Fate has trust upon you! Yes, you soar, you recreate life within you; and then when you are filled to the brim with it—then—down you must come, to crash against the facts, which trample this life in you, soil it, defile it—friction, controversy, and self-interest . . . You know very well that I was ignorant of all these things. But it doesn't matter! I only want to tell you this—I have been here with you four months now. (*Takes him by the arm and faces him*) Look at me! Right into my eyes—deep within them! They have no longer seen for me, these eyes; they are no longer mine, not even to see myself! They have been like this—like this—in yours—always—so that there might be born in them, out of your eyes, my own image, as you saw me! The image of all things, of all life, as you have seen it! I came here; I gave myself to you utterly, utterly; I said to you: "Here I am, I am yours; there is nothing left in me of my own. Take me and make me, make me *as you desire me!*—Have you waited ten years for me? Think of them as nothing!

Here I am yours once again; but not for my own sake, nor for the sake of her past; no, no memory of hers any longer: give me yours, your memories, all you have preserved of her as she once was for you! And they shall come alive again in me, alive with all your life, with all your love, with all the first joys she gave you!" How many times have I said to you: "like this? . . . like this?"—delighting in the joy that was reborn in you out of my body, feeling it even as you!

BRUNO (*drunkenly*). Cia! Cia!

STRANGE LADY (*holding away from his embrace, drunken as he, but with the pride of having recreated herself like this*). Yes—I am Cia! I am Cia! I alone! I! I! Not she (*the portrait*) who was, and perhaps did not even know what she was—today like this, tomorrow what the accidents of life might make of her. To be? To be is nothing. To be is to become. And I have become her. But you—you have understood nothing at all.

BRUNO. Yes, yes I have understood

STRANGE LADY. What have you understood? If I have felt—if I have felt you hands searching—here—(*gestures toward her body*) I do not know—for some mark you thought you should have found—Didn't you find it? Because of that mark which you have not found, or for some other, I am not Cia—is that true? I cannot be Cia? It is gone—look!—I tell you it gone! What can you say to contradict me? I did not want it any more; and did all I could to make it go. Yes, yes tell you! Because I knew—I sensed—that always, in the old days, you used to feel fo it. Isn't that true?

BRUNO. Yes!

STRANGE LADY. You see? I knew! An to keep others from finding it, I got ri of it. But now, you are terrified that Ine as a sister[1], or even Lena—who wea spectacles, you know!—may want to fin that mark again, as legal evidence, befo the Courts, and that they may not willing to believe what I just told yo "Ah, so it's disappeared! But that serious! A mark like that! How can have disappeared?" Then they will a

[1] That is, "as a sister, who would have intim knowledge of my body."—J.G.

for expert scientific evidence. It may be, gentlemen, that this poor sick woman who is about to arrive—well, anything is possible—it may be that she actually has the mark! That she has it and I haven't! That would be the climax—the most overwhelming evidence of all! Poor Bruno, poor Bruno, so concerned about all these proofs and documents which might be brought to Court! Don't be alarmed. I am Cia—the new Cia. You want so many things! When I came here I wanted nothing—nothing—not even to live for myself, nor to breathe the air around me for myself, nor to touch a single thing, feeling that it belonged to me. I believed that you had waited ten years for your wife, loving her; and I gave her back to you alive, so that after all the horror and the shame, I might live again—a pure life. And this is so deeply true, that in the face of all the world, against all the evidence, even against you—yes, against you, if you are forced to disown me in order to save your financial interests, before everybody I shall have the courage to cry out that I am Cia—I—because *she*—*(the portrait)* can no longer be alive like that—except in me!

(The crunch of automobile tires is heard again from the driveway.)

BRUNO *(terrified)*. There they are! They've come!

STRANGE LADY. Leave it to me. You receive them. I cannot let them see me like this—not now. I'll be down directly. *(She starts up the steps)*

BRUNO *(imploring)*. Cia . . .

(She stops and turns—very calmly, as if asserting a fact that is no longer open to argument.)

STRANGE LADY. Yes—Cia.

CURTAIN

ACT THREE

Same scene as preceding act, twenty minutes later. Almost evening. From the open loggia, the room is flooded with the soft, violet glow of deepening twilight; one can see the landscape, between the pillars of the loggia, more peaceful than ever, with the tiny, clustered lights of a distant village, and other points of light scattered thinly over the countryside.

Inez, Barbara, Uncle Salesio, Bruno and Silvio Masperi are discovered.

Inez, although she is Cia's younger sister, seems older than the Strange Lady. She is dressed with elegance, and is wearing a hat. She has all the right things. She is beautiful. She has a husband. She has a fine reputation. She has a lovely home. She wants for nothing and she speaks evil of nobody, because only the envious do that, and she has no reason to envy anybody anything. What she has done, she has done because it was right to do it. Not against her sister. God only knows how she has grieved over her unhappy sister, first because of what happened to her, and afterwards when she believed her dead. But, having a daughter at home, and knowing that she was poor Uncle Salesio's only remaining niece, she had realized that he would never have given up the villa and the estate in order that a stranger might have the benefit of them; and that it was her duty—also, of course, to protect Uncle Salesio in his old age—to establish the right to regain possession of them. On the death of Cia, they must obviously revert to the family.

Barbara is an old maid of forty, thick-set, and with glossy black hair, touched with gray; she has the reserved and slightly belligerent manner of one who is always being imposed upon. When she makes a remark, she gives the impression of having said all there is to say. She never looks you straight in the eyes, and it is only too evident that she feels—who knows how deeply—the secret and dreadful torment of having been born ugly, and a woman.

Masperi is unfortunately disfigured by an upper lip which seems somehow to have been drawn back and fixed just under his nose, while his large, white teeth are thrust forward from under it. Otherwise, he would be a good-looking man, with an excellent appearance and personality and a fresh complexion which—heaven help us!—almost looks as if he were made up! He wears spectacles and, as he talks, constantly pushes them up on his nose with his finger and thumb. He always wishes to avoid unpleasantness; but in the world one has to know one's way around, and he has always known his. Naturally, one uses kid gloves! But his hands, inside the gloves, are certainly hard and firm.

*Just now he can hardly restrain his annoy-
ance, or conceal his impatience at the insult
offered to his wife and himself. He looks round
at the others, who are immobile but still filled
with expectation, after an interminable wait of
almost half an hour. The Strange Lady, having
said she would be down immediately, has not
yet reappeared.*

*This half hour of waiting seems to grow
longer and longer, especially since they have
waited four months already to be allowed to
pay this visit, although they should have been
invited at once.*

*The effect of this long-drawn-out waiting
should register when the curtain rises.*

Aunt Lena finally comes downstairs.

———

BRUNO. Well, what's she doing? Did
she say she was coming down?

LENA. Yes, she said "I'm coming."
But . . .

BRUNO. But?

LENA. She's up there with her dresses
spread about. She's opened the trunks—

BRUNO (*astonished*). The trunks?

LENA. She wanted to find something,
I suppose—or put something away—

INEZ. She isn't—she's not going away?

BRUNO. Of course she isn't! (*To Lena*)
Didn't you ask her why? (*To the others*)
She did say she wanted to change her
dress.

LENA. She has changed. And she looked
so nice as she was!

BRUNO. Well?

LENA. Well—what else can I say? She
seemed flushed—nervous. She practically
pushed me out of the door: "Go on
down," she said, "go on down and say
that I'm coming!"

SALESIO. Oh well then, she'll come!

BARBARA (*going over to the loggia*). What
a beautiful view this is. You can see the
whole countryside. Those lights—

MASPERI (*goes over to look*). Yes. And
what a peaceful evening . . . Er . . .
well . . . (*Pause*)

BRUNO (*in a low voice to Lena*). How
was she?

LENA. She's been crying—I'm sure
she had.

SALESIO. She's certainly very much

upset. But that's easily explained. The
idea of seeing you all again—

MASPERI. Ah, no—no—I beg your
pardon, that's all very well, but how
could the idea of seeing us—no! Unless,
of course, she's nursing a grievance against
her sister.

LENA. Of course not—what has her
sister got to do with it? Never pay attention to Salesio's explanations! (*To Uncle
Salesio*) I should think you ought to know
against *whom*—she talked about it quite
openly to you and me.

BRUNO (*very distinctly*). Her grievance
is against me.

MASPERI. Oh—well, if it's something
between you two . . .

BARBARA. Well, but—here we've been
waiting a quarter of an hour already . . .
(*Pause*)

INEZ. There shouldn't be any more
talk of grievances—

LENA (*to Inez*). There isn't any! She's
even gone so far as to say that what you
did was right. What more do you want?
She said she'd be happy if all the property
reverted to him (*indicating Uncle Salesio*),
because then he could dispose of it and
give it back to you!

SALESIO. Yes, she did.

LENA. Well then?

INEZ. But that has nothing to do with
it! Give it to me? Of course not!

LENA. I'm only trying to show you
how she feels about it.

SALESIO. Exactly so. She said that after
ten years it was right that you—

INEZ. I didn't do it for myself—you
know that, Uncle—but for you! And—
well, all right!—because I have a
daughter.

MASPERI. She must surely have understood that we never wanted to do anything
against her—

BRUNO (*speaking very clearly*). The
thing she doesn't seem to want to understand is what you have done against me.

MASPERI (*with a deprecating gesture*).
Oh . . . I trust we did not come here in
order to start arguing again!

BRUNO. No, no—

MASPERI (*trying to continue*). We're
waiting here—

BRUNO (*not giving him time to go on*)

She must make it clear, now, what she really does feel. For me too! I want it made clear to *me*. *(With an outburst of anger)* As if this were the time to fool around! I wish I were a thousand miles away! *(To Aunt Lena and Uncle Salesio)* She talked to you two—what has she got against me? Has she begun to suspect something?

LENA. Yes. You're quite right. She has.

SALESIO. She said that if she had known she was going to find herself in the middle of a business quarrel—

MASPERI. But why? Any quarrel there may have been ended with her return.

SALESIO. That's what we told her.

INEZ. I would have come at once—

BARBARA. And I too, if Bruno—

MASPERI. Certainly, if he hadn't give us to understand—

INEZ. That she didn't want to see anyone—me above all. I would have made her realize that never—never—did I . . . But what's the use? God alone knows the tears I have shed for her . . . *(She puts her handkerchief to her eyes with much emotion)*

MASPERI. Never mind! Never mind! Apparently she understood all that perfectly well. But now, it seems, there's something else!

BRUNO. I didn't say she didn't *want* to see anyone. I said she *couldn't*.

LENA. And she couldn't—really she couldn't! She couldn't even bear to see us two, at first! After all, you must remember what a terrible time she's been through, poor child!

SALESIO. And coming back here, all the horror of the past . . . She was only able to do it for love of him. She didn't want to come.

LENA. She was compelled to come. *(Bruno turns and glares at her. She repeats)* Of course! She said so. Compelled! *(Pause)*

BARBARA *(very precisely)*. But—what does she suspect? *(The bluntness of this question is followed by another pause.)*

MASPERI. Er—yes—what?

BRUNO *(there is nothing for it but to answer)*. She suspects that I compelled her to come because of the lawsuit with

you! It is true, she didn't want to come. And I think her suspicions were aroused simply because of what I said to her in order to persuade her, to help her to overcome—well, just that horror of the past that Uncle Salesio spoke of—not only that, but, even more, the horror of having to face you all . . . My good friends, you must consider the sort of life she's been forced to lead, after the hell and anguish she'd been through. She'd decided *never* to come back! *(To Inez)* The idea, above all, of seeing you—the sister who would undoubtedly bring back to her the whole image of her former life—you don't know what horror that aroused in her! And so I promised her that she would not have to see anyone. I said, "There's an excuse—a good excuse, for your not seeing her." I meant this quarrel about the estate. And I tell you, for her the whole business had no more importance than that; it was just an excuse for not seeing you. I was sure that when the first shock had passed and she was a little calmer—when she had settled back into her old life here—in time, anyway, she would have got over her reluctance.

INEZ. But I'd have helped her to get over it at once. I'd have told her—

BRUNO. Perhaps it wasn't so much you, as that she herself . . . At least, it seems to me . . . *(To Aunt Lena, bitterly)* Compelled, eh? Well, that's how I compelled her—if you can call it that. I never used any pressure. *(Growing more and more irritated)* Well, anyway, the situation finally had to be cleared up, didn't it? I felt I had to try and convince her that it had got to stop; that what had been simply a good excuse, up to now— *(turning back to Lena and Uncle Salesio)* especially if as you say, she herself has told you that she has nothing against you— *(to Inez)* So. Well. If she's willing herself to give it up—I mean—the excuse . . . *(he is in a perspiration of anxiety)* I don't know! *(Pause. Then he bursts out)* Why should I seem to be apologizing to you? Now, above all! It's maddening! *(He starts to walk up and down)* She suspects me! As if I were not the only one—the only one of you!—who always believed she wasn't dead! I was so sure of it that I didn't care—good God!—I wasn't afraid of spending all I had to rebuild this place for her! Will you tell me why I should have done that? Wouldn't I have been crazy to do it if I had anticipated that you would then walk in so charmingly and take it all away from me? And maybe I got a little annoyed too—piqued, anyway —I don't deny it. Not unnaturally, I should think! When I heard about it, I rushed to . . . I couldn't believe it—I had to put up a fight—I had to defend my own interests—that's not a crime, is it?—not to mention my feelings . . . *(He realizes himself that he is talking as if he were trying to justify himself and can only do it by making a kind of confession)* But one thing—one thing really shocks me . . . Once people begin to suspect—everything one has done before, quite thoughtlessly . . . It's dreadful to find that now—it really begins to look as if—in the light of this suspicion . . . *(Glaring angrily towards the stairs)* What on earth is she doing all this time?

INEZ. Yes, because if she doesn't want to come down—

BARBARA. It would seem quite useless for us to wait for her any longer!

LENA. Be patient! She wants time to calm herself down. I told you that—

BRUNO. Well, she might at least remember that at any moment they . . . *(He stops himself quickly; to Lena)* Lena, be kind enough to go up and ask her for me to think a minute about *where Boffi has gone and why!* She must be here! We've waited too long as it is. There's a limit—

LENA. All right, all right—I'll go! *(Goes towards the stairs)*

INEZ. And see how she feels too.

LENA. Yes, yes, yes. *(Goes up the stairs)*

INEZ. Because if she doesn't feel like it this evening—

BARBARA. Then, we'll go away again! *(Pause.)*

MASPERI. I'm sorry if a dispute which was settled, as far as we're concerned, the moment we heard of her arrival, should have caused a further dispute between you two.

BRUNO. But there's something else— something which . . . Perhaps that business between us is not quite as settled as you think!

MASPERI. What else?

BRUNO *(nods towards the stairs)*. She knows very well what it is! And she ought not to leave me like this! *(He starts to pace up and down again)* Please forgive me—I'm so upset. My God! I might have guessed something like this would happen! Don't bother about the facts! Simple! But if they're there—if they happen—you have to bother about them! And am I responsible, even though I had nothing to do with it?

(Lena is seen coming downstairs.)

INEZ. Lena's coming down!

BARBARA. Alone!

BRUNO. Well? What does she say?

LENA. Well—er—I don't quite know. She says it's "just because of that" that she hasn't come down yet!

BRUNO. What? "Just because of that?"

LENA. Yes.

BRUNO. Then does she want to wait—

LENA. Until Boffi comes back.

BRUNO. Oh! So that's what she said! Does she want to drive me completely crazy?

LENA *(with a shrug)*. What do you want to do about it? That's what she said.

BRUNO. I'll go up myself—I'll go up myself! *(He runs up the stairs)*

INEZ *(rising and crossing to Lena)*. What's happening here anyway? What's going on?

BARBARA. The moment we arrive to see her—

SALESIO. No, no. It must be something different—something quite different!

LENA. I think so too.

MASPERI. He hinted that much himself.

INEZ. But what could it be? He said that perhaps this business wasn't settled—

MASPERI. Exactly! The dispute between us. I don't know what he meant.

LENA. I think it was the letter.

INEZ. Letter?

SALESIO. Yes—I think so too. You can be sure it was!

INEZ. What letter?

LENA. A letter which they got only an hour or so ago—from abroad, I think.

SALESIO. They had a long talk about it—

LENA. It was from someone—I don't know exactly—something to do with what happened before.

SALESIO. They were terribly agitated— *(Through the loggia comes the dazzling beam of headlights; the horn of a car is heard, and the crunch of tires on the gravel drive.)* Ah—there he is now! That must be him!

LENA. Good, good! You'll see— she'll come down now. She was only waiting for him.

SALESIO. She said so to us—remember? That she wanted Boffi here.

LENA *(looking out through the French windows)*. Yes, there he is! *(She makes a movement of surprise and exclaims)* But—oh! He's not alone!

SALESIO *(also looking out)*. There are several of them.

MASPERI. Oh—who are they?

INEZ. Why—one of them seems to be an invalid—

LENA. So she does!

BARBARA. What does it mean?

SALESIO. They're helping her out—

MASPERI. They're lifting her down—

INEZ. Good God! What is all this?

BARBARA. What's it all about?

SALESIO. They look like foreigners.

LENA. Yes, so they are.

MASPERI. Look!

INEZ *(from behind)*. How horrible!

(The light in the room has become thin, clear, livid.

The Insane Woman comes in, followed by the Nurse and the Doctor, with Boffi and Salter behind them.

The Insane Woman is fat and flabby, with a waxen face and dishevelled hair; her eyes are vacant and staring; her mouth is fixed in a wide, foolish, empty smile; the smile does not change, even when she utters some sound or stammers out a few words, obviously without knowing what she is saying.

The Doctor and the Nurse are characteristically German in manner; and even Salter now seems very definitely German.)

THE INSANE WOMAN. Le—na . . . *(She utters the sounds breathily, with wide, loose lips; the two syllables are like a cadence: they no longer signify a particular name, but are simply a sound which she repeats like a perpetual refrain)*

LENA *(appalled)*. Oh, my God! What? Is she calling me?

INEZ. Who is she?

BOFFI *(coming in, with extreme anxiety)*. Where's Bruno? And the Signora?

INSANE WOMAN *(repeats)*. Le—na . . .

LENA *(looking at the others, in dismay)*. She *is* calling me!

SALTER. Are you one of the family? Is your name Lena?

LENA. Yes, I am the aunt . . .

SALTER *(to the Doctor)*. You hear? You hear? There is one of the family called Lena! Another proof! Another proof! Ah, now we're sure—we're sure of it! That was something we didn't know!

MASPERI *(stepping forward)*. Sure of what?

BOFFI. Don't take any notice of him. It's just a sound she repeats—over and over—she did it all the way here.

INSANE WOMAN. Le—na . . .

BARBARA. But she is saying Lena all the same!

BOFFI. Yes, but she's not calling anyone. And she smiles all the time, like that. *(Alluding to Bruno and the Strange Lady)* But where are they, for heavens' sake?

INEZ. Good God, are they mad?

MASPERI. What is the meaning of this? Why have you brought this lady here?

BOFFI. How can they possibly stay upstairs when—Call them, please!

SALTER *(to Boffi, indicating the others)*. Are these ladies and gentleman the other relatives?

BOFFI. Yes. This is the sister, Signora Inez Masperi.

SALTER. Ah, the sister! So there is a sister as well! A sister of hers? Well then, come here—quickly—

INEZ. Who is this gentleman?

BOFFI. Carl Salter, the writer.

SALTER. Look at her, Signora, look at her! There!

INEZ. I? What do you mean? Who?

BOFFI. He insists on believing—

SALTER *(to Inez)*. Is it possible it doesn't mean anything to you?

INEZ. No! Who? Good heavens, what should it mean to me?

BOFFI. That this woman is your sister!

MASPERI. What?

BARBARA. This woman?

INEZ. Cia? *(Together)*

LENA. Where? What are you talking about?

SALTER. Yes! Yes! This woman! Here!

SALESIO. He must be insane himself!

SALTER. I've brought her all this way—

INSANE WOMAN. Le—na . . .

SALTER *(pointing to her at the sound of her voice)*. There! Isn't that the proof? Can you possibly not realize that it's the proof? She's calling Lena!

DOCTOR. She's been calling Lena for years—all the time!

SALTER *(to Lena)*. You! You!

LENA. No, no. It isn't possible!

SALTER. Don't you recognize her? Look in her eyes! How can you help recognizing her?

LENA. What do you expect me to recognize? Whom should I recognize?

SALTER. My friend here—the doctor who has studied her for years—has documents, proofs—

MASPERI. What proofs? Show them to us!

BARBARA. But it's impossible!

MASPERI *(to Barbara)*. Let him speak, please. We are taken completely by surprise. What proofs?

LENA. But our Cia is upstairs!

SALTER. I know the lady upstairs—very well!

SALESIO. Well, this is a situation—

BARBARA. Unbelievable! Simply unbelievable!

MASPERI. Ladies and gentlemen, kindly let him speak! *(To Salter)* You know her?

SALTER. The lady upstairs? All too well!

LENA. Do you think you know her better than I do? I who was a mother to her!

SALTER *(pointing to the Insane Woman)*. To her—to her!

LENA. To her? What are you talking about?

MASPERI. If you think you have proofs and papers—

SALESIO. Proofs indeed! Do you seriously believe—

MASPERI. No, but there are ways of doing things! If they think they have definite evidence—

BOFFI *(ironically)*. Ah! Here it comes —here it comes!

SALESIO. It would be funny—if it weren't so tragic!

MASPERI. There are the proper authorities—

BOFFI. Even when you know the motive behind all this?

MASPERI. I don't know anything about the motive.

BOFFI. But I do, and Bruno does, and the Signora does! Where are they?

SALTER. You used the right word—revenge!

BOFFI *(to Masperi)*. You hear that?

SALTER. Only I call it punishment as well.

MASPERI. I do not know this gentleman—

SALESIO. Oh! The gentleman's motives are not of very great importance, after all! But if there are proofs and documents —out with them! Let's see them! Because we do not want anyone here to profit by his revenge—or punishment, or whatever it is!

BOFFI *(to Masperi)*. We foresaw this, you know!

MASPERI. Foresaw it—how? Who could possibly have foreseen a thing like this!

BOFFI. No, I mean that you would try to profit by it.

SALESIO. Nobody must be allowed to do that!

INEZ *(scornfully)*. Who said anything about "profiting"? You, too, Uncle! No! You shouldn't even say such things! *(To Salter)* Listen. We here—all of us—I her sister, her aunt, her uncle, her sister-in-law, and you too, Boffi—we all stand here, looking at this poor creature, and not one of us can recognize her.

SALTER. Because you have already recognized the lady upstairs.

INEZ. No. Not I.

SALTER. What? You haven't recognized her?

INEZ. I haven't seen her—not since she came. I am here now for the express purpose of seeing her.

SALTER. You didn't want to see her before?

INEZ. It wasn't I—it was she.

SALTER. Ah—so it was she! That makes it perfectly clear! Because with a sister she couldn't . . . a blood-relation as close as that . . . The very thought of it—such unbearable nearness, cheek against cheek —she was afraid you wouldn't feel the call of the blood! Here, Signora (*He points to the Insane Woman*) Here—try! See if you don't feel it—your own flesh and blood!

INEZ (*horrified*). No—no! In God's name, don't say that!

SALTER. If your pity could overcome your repugnance . . .? It is she. Look at her! Remember—ten years, all the agony, the war, the famine . . . I know the lady upstairs who pretends to be her. If you have found in her so great a likeness, look—at this one, carefully—try to see it. I tell you, under all the change, the ravages of time—the features are exactly the same!

INEZ. No, no!

LENA. What features?

SALESIO. What do you mean?

SALTER. Her eyes—if they were not so blank—

BOFFI. Not in the very least—the shape's entirely different. Perhaps the color's a little—

SALTER. She's been mad for nine years. She was found wearing a hussar's jacket—old and tattered, but still with a badge—

INEZ. What badge?

SALESIO. Where was she found?

SALTER. At Lintz.

MASPERI. What was the badge? You mean on the coat?

SALTER. The badge of the regiment to which the hussar had belonged. And that regiment had been stationed here—here! Right here!

MASPERI. You mean, during the invasion?

BOFFI. What does that prove? Some hussar who had been stationed here during the invasion may have come across her at Lintz, and given her the coat out of charity.

INSANE WOMAN. Le—na . . .

SALTER. And she keeps calling Lena, do you hear? Why? That name is the only thing that has stayed in her mind. (*To Lena*) But you who say you were a mother to her . . .

LENA (*with unexpected courage, overcoming the horror she feels—but to the horror of the others—she takes the head of the Insane Woman between her hands and calls*). Cia! Cia! Cia!

(*The Insane Woman remains impassive, with her silent, empty smile. They all look at her.*

Meanwhile the Strange Lady comes down the stairs, followed by Bruno. No one notices her. They suddenly find her among them, moving towards the Insane Woman, as Lena falls back from her, disillusioned. And it is a strange thing, after all that has happened— simply because the Insane Woman, whom no single one of them has recognized, is present— all those who have firmly believed in her before, Lena, Uncle Salesio and even Boffi himself, gaze at the Strange Lady in perplexity and doubt.

While everyone is staring at her in silence she says to Bruno.)

STRANGE LADY. You try and call her too.

SALTER. Ah, here ﾕ e i ﾟ)

STRANGE LADY (ﾟ ﾟ ﾟ ﾟ haughtily). Here I am.

INEZ (*in bewilderment, ﾟ ﾟ ﾟeling that she ought to overcome it*). Cia ﾟ

STRANGE LADY. Wait. Tﾟﾟ on the light. One can hardly see here. (*Uncle Salesio goes over to the door and turns on the lights.*)

INEZ (*looks at her in the light, and after a moment's hesitation says again*). Cia! (*Salter, in the face of the Strange Lady's great assurance, and hearing Inez call her twice, now comes to doubt himself, in the opposite sense to the others. He turns to Inez.*)

SALTER. You really believe . . .?

STRANGE LADY (*indicating Bruno*). I kept him upstairs, and I stayed up there myself, in order to give you time to make your impression. I recognize your brutality in this. Only someone like you would be capable of such an atrocity. Bring her over here . . . (*She comes close to the Insane Woman, and with a movement full of tenderness and delicacy, puts her hand under her chin, in order to look into the smiling face)*

INSANE WOMAN *(while the Strange Lady is gazing at her, still smiling vacantly, she emits her usual—).* Le—na . . .

STRANGE LADY. Lena? *(Subduing a shudder, she turns to Lena)*

SALTER *(quickly—pointing this out to the rest).* There—there—did you see? She heard her say Lena! She turned to look at her!

BOFFI *(breaking in).* No, no! That's all been explained!

STRANGE LADY. What has been explained?

LENA. She's not calling me—

BOFFI. It's just a sound she makes—a sound she keeps on repeating, all the time—

SALTER. The fact that she turned is enough for me!

STRANGE LADY. To prove, I take it, that I am not Cia?

SALTER. What's more, you just said to him: "You try and call her too."

STRANGE LADY. I knew you wouldn't believe me. But when I came in just now, I found *you (indicating Lena)* bending over her and calling: "Cia, Cia."

LENA *(abashed, trying to excuse herself).* But because . . . don't you see?

SALESIO *(simultaneously, pointing to Salter).* Because he insisted—

BOFFI *(also at the same time).* Hearing that "Le—na, Le—na . . ."

STRANGE LADY *(her voice dominates theirs).* Of course, of course! Naturally! *(To Lena)* And I see how you're looking at me now.

LENA *(confused).* How am I looking at you?

STRANGE LADY *(to Uncle Salesio).* You too.

SALESIO. I? No! No!

STRANGE LADY. And you yourself, Boffi.

BOFFI. Nothing of the sort! No one has recognized her!

SALESIO. We are all—*(Surprised and taken unawares, he doesn't know what to say. But they do not give him time.)*

BOFFI. And your sister herself! You can see that she . . .

STRANGE LADY. Yes. She called me Cia, twice.

BOFFI *(to Salter).* Did you hear? *(Then to Masperi)* And you must have heard too!

INEZ *(haughtily).* I have told you that no one here wants to take advantage—

BOFFI. No—I mean, if *anyone* could take advantage of *this*, it would be Bruno!

STRANGE LADY *(cutting in).* Ah, no! Not he! He's not going to take advantage of anything! Besides, don't you see? He's the most bewildered of all.

BRUNO *(pulling himself together).* Bewildered! I'm astounded at the presumption of this gentleman, who has dared to—Yes! he, indeed, has taken advantage.

STRANGE LADY. You can be sure, too, that he is not going to take any advantage *(looks at Salter)* either of me, or of this poor creature.

SALTER. I have felt obliged—

STRANGE LADY. To bring her here.

SALTER. To punish you—yes!

STRANGE LADY *(face to face with him).* To punish me?

SALTER. Yes—for what you've done. I was at death's door, because of you; and at that very moment, you elected to leave me, to come down here, to deceive these other people!

STRANGE LADY. I have deceived no one.

SALTER. Yes, you have! deceived them!

BRUNO *(on the point of leaping at him).* If you say that just once more—

STRANGE LADY *(restraining him quickly).* No! Quiet—quiet!

BOFFI. He asked for it!

STRANGE LADY. Leave it to me. *(She turns on Salter)* You mean I'm an impostor, eh? Have you proved it? How? Like this? Because of this atrocious thing you've been bold enough to do? *(Turning to the Doctor)* And you are the doctor who agreed to it?

DOCTOR. Yes, I agreed to it—the more readily because I had reason to think—

STRANGE LADY. Oh, yes—that's true. You thought it was to someone's interest here to suppress all doubt—though the doubt itself was hardly disinterested! I am happy to assure you that you have succeeded. The doubt has, in fact, arisen.

LENA. No, no!

BOFFI. When?

SALESIO. Who had any doubt?

STRANGE LADY *(almost shouting it)*. I am glad of it! *(In a different tone)* You deny it, but I took you by surprise—

SALESIO. But we didn't recognize her!

STRANGE LADY. It makes no difference.

BOFFI. Don't worry, Signora. I'll bet he doesn't believe it himself.

STRANGE LADY. It makes no difference. *(Slowly approaching Salter)* You can see for yourself what a strange sort of "impostor" I must be! I, myself, drew attention to the strange way you all looked at me when I came in. And take care, Boffi! It is only to reassure yourself against the doubt that you too began to feel—

BOFFI. I swear to you I have felt no doubt whatever!

STRANGE LADY. Oh yes, you have. It was to encourage yourself that you observed and pointed out to me that she *(indicates Inez)* twice called me Cia.

BOFFI. No! Because it's the truth! I beg your pardon, but what doubt do you think could possibly have arisen because of . . . *(He indicates the Insane Woman)*

STRANGE LADY. No. Because of me; even though you hadn't been able to recognize her. *The most natural of doubts;* as soon as I appeared unexpectedly and bewildered as you were already . . . ! *(Indicates Salter)* While he, on hearing me called Cia by someone who had not seen me until then, immediately had the opposite doubt. Naturally . . . Naturally. *(To Lena, who is crying quietly)* Don't cry. The utmost certainty may falter, when even a shadow of doubt arises and we can never again believe as before.

SALTER. Then you yourself admit that it is possible you are not Cia?

STRANGE LADY. I admit much more than that! I admit that Cia *may even be this woman,* if that's what they want to believe.

SALESIO. But we don't believe it!

SALTER *(pointing first to the Strange Lady and then to the Insane Woman)*. Just because she resembles her, and this one doesn't.

STRANGE LADY. No, no, not that. Not because I resemble her—indeed, I myself have told them that on the contrary, this resemblance through which you all thought you recognized me, is no proof— no proof at all. I even shouted at them: "How can you think it possible that one who has been swept under by the war— after ten years—should remain so much *the same?*" If anything, it would be proof that, on the contrary, it is not I!

MASPERI *(struck by this remark)*. Ah, quite so! Now, that—

STRANGE LADY *(turning on him)*. Isn't it true? A proof that it could not be I! *(To Salter again)* You see? There's someone who's only just realized it!

BRUNO. You seem to be doing everything you can to—

STRANGE LADY. But you agreed with it too.

BRUNO. I?

STRANGE LADY. Yes, you! You!

BRUNO. What are you talking about? When?

STRANGE LADY. When I first told you so; and you were shaken by it too, Boffi! Of course! It is only when you believe— or *when it is convenient to believe*—that you do not think—*or that you do not want to think*—of something as simple as this: That my being so much *the same*, is a proof against me; and that therefore—why not?—Cia could well be this poor creature, for the very reason that she *no longer resembles her at all.*

BRUNO. You take a malicious pleasure in saying things like that!

STRANGE LADY. I told you that I had to answer his challenge *(Indicates Salter)* that I am an impostor.

BRUNO. How? Like this? You yourself throwing doubt on yourself?

STRANGE LADY. Yes, like this! Because I want all of you—everybody—to doubt me, as he does, so that I may at least have the satisfaction of being the only one left to believe in myself! *(Motioning towards the Insane Woman)* You have not recognized her. Is that perhaps because she is unrecognizable? Because, to look at her, it does not seem likely? Because they have not produced enough evidence? No! No! It is simply because it does not yet seem to you possible to believe! That's all! More than one poor wretch has come back, years afterwards, like her—*(indi-*

cates the Insane Woman) almost featureless, unrecognizable, without memory; and sisters, wives, mothers—even mothers! —have fought over him! "He's mine!" —"No, he's mine!" Not because he looked like their dear *one* (for two sons, of two different mothers, could not look the same!), but because they believed it! They wanted to believe it! And there is no valid proof to the contrary, when you really *want* to believe. It is not he? And yet it is—for that mother—it is he! What does it matter! if that mother holds him to her breast, and with all the power of her love, makes him hers? Against all proof, she believes. Without any proof at all she still believes. Haven't you believed in me—without any proof either?

BOFFI. But that is because you are she, and there is no need of proof.

STRANGE LADY. That is not so. *(Turning quickly to Bruno who starts to protest)* Don't be afraid, darling. My trying to show that Cia may really be this woman is not against your interests. On the contrary. *(She points to the Insane Woman)* But there has been so much suspicion and mistrust. *(Indicates Salesio)* He has told me that, because I shut myself up here for four months without wanting to see anyone—

BRUNO. But everybody understood the reason!

STRANGE LADY *(winking at Lena)*. Except the "spiteful tongues" eh? *(To Bruno)* But it's not good that *you* should say so. *(To Masperi)* I see you are already trying to figure out—

MASPERI *(surprised)*. Not at all—I . . .

STRANGE LADY. No? But it's quite obvious! To figure out what I have just been saying! Think a little further—a little further and a little deeper! It's so easy to suspect—how shall I put it?— that some woman, simply taking advantage of a physical resemblance which others might perhaps have *found it convenient* to see in her—

BRUNO *(clearly and with emphasis)*. Convenient—for me.

STRANGE LADY *(quickly)*. What? Somebody did suspect that?

BRUNO. You did, yourself!

STRANGE LADY. Exactly! *(Then to Masperi)* As I was saying, it is so easy to

suspect that I may have been here, taking all the time I needed—*(winks at Uncle Salesio)*—four months—preparing to make myself into *her*, *(indicates the portrait)* saying, first, that I could not bear the sight of anyone! *(To Salter, with a wink)* And by good luck, eh?—there really was an excuse—an extremely convenient one for him! *(indicates Bruno)*

BRUNO *(quickly—to the relatives)*. There! What did I tell you?

STRANGE LADY. You may have told them, but now, you see, they're listening to what *I* have to say! *(To Salter)* A quarrel between them—business interests you know! *(To Inez and Masperi)* It was easy for me to pretend, in the beginning, that I wanted no memories of any kind— and woe betide Lena and Uncle Salesio if they showed signs of wanting to revive any! It was also easy for me to pretend that I had completely lost all memories; but in the meanwhile, eh? Little by little I could build them up. *(Goes over to Boffi. Pointing to Bruno)* He needed, didn't he, a certain length of time to restore the villa and repair all the devastation? Well, there had to be time for me, too, to reconstruct myself, stone upon stone, like the villa; and the pitiful memories of poor Cia—transplanted in me—time to make them grow again, to make them live and flower . . . *(Goes slowly towards Inez with outstretched arms)* till at last I should even be able to receive a sister, *(takes her hands)* quite at my ease—to talk, perhaps, of the times when we were children together, when we played together, orphans, the two of us, brought up by our aunt and uncle . . . *to make myself . . . to make myself . . .* to shape myself so closely that I could seem to be "the picture come to life," as Uncle Salesio said . . . the picture, copied even to the dress—

INEZ. Copied?

STRANGE LADY. Yes. I was all dressed to receive you just now—exactly like that portrait *(to Lena)* wasn't I? And I went upstairs to change, because it really seemed to me a little too much—*(There is a movement of embarrassment, doubt and dismay from the others)* Aha? Yes? So now you're beginning to suspect at last—if you hadn't already . . .

MASPERI (as if horrified). No—never!

INEZ. Who could ever have imagined—

BARBARA. —Such a thing!

STRANGE LADY (pointing to Bruno). He —he has been imagining such a thing!

BRUNO. I?

STRANGE LADY. Yes. And now he's terrified lest this suspicion—so easy to arouse, so easy for me to rouse myself— may turn out to be the truth!

BRUNO. How could it be the truth? Can you believe it—any of you?

STRANGE LADY. They believe it! They believe it! Because it is the truth—it is! The truth that is fact! The fact of the "impostor" that he believes I am! (indicating Salter)

BOFFI. But Signora! What are you saying?

SALESIO. How is it possible?

BRUNO. This is a vengeance on me, more savage than his!

STRANGE LADY. It is not mine. The facts avenge themselves, my dear, the facts avenge themselves! When you asked them to come here, didn't you want the facts? They have recognized me; but I cannot accept that—as fact. You alone should have recognized me—without self-interest! I certainly did not come here to defend a dowry! That, indeed, would have been a deception I should never have thought of—that I could never have practiced! Then, assuredly, I would have been the "impostor" he says I am! If it's useful to you—and without any thought of vengeance—why, then, believe! Look the facts in the face—and believe!

BRUNO. In what must I believe?

STRANGE LADY. In my "imposture"! What more do you want me to say?

BRUNO (exasperated—face to face with her). You're doing this to test me! You're doing all this simply to test me!

STRANGE LADY. No! No! Indeed, no.

BRUNO. Yes, I say! For that alone!

STRANGE LADY. On the other hand, this could be just another scheme of yours—

BRUNO. Scheme—?

STRANGE LADY. Deliberately to make them think I am doing this to test you!

BRUNO. No!

STRANGE LADY. No? Then believe!

I tell you the truth—you can all believe, believe the facts, believe him, (Salter) believe that he's right, completely right! Even about this poor creature! She should be—she could be Cia! It's true! Look at her! (She moves closer to the Insane Woman, and once again with the same delicacy and compassion, places her fingers under her chin)

INSANE WOMAN (hardly conscious of her touch, repeats). Le—na . . .

STRANGE LADY (to Lena). Lena do you hear? It's really you she's calling! Why don't you believe it?

INSANE WOMAN. Le—na!

STRANGE LADY. There! It is you! It's true! I didn't want to see you—I made you go away for more than a month—and when I did see you, I had nothing to say; she comes calling Lena—she has always called, Lena, Lena, and yet you don't want to believe her? Because she doesn't answer you? How could she possibly answer you? Don't you see? (She looks at the Insane Woman, an infinite sadness in her eyes) If she can call Lena, like that—with that smile—it means that no voice can ever reach her any more. (Addressing her) You are calling, who knows from what far-off-happy moment of your life, where you remain, eternally suspended . . . You can see nothing, any more . . . No one has anything to give you, any more . . . Pity? what use would that be to you? . . . All the care that could be given you— now . . .? Ah, but you are happy in that smile of yours—you have saved yourself— you are secure, untouchable—(To Salter) For whom did you bring her here? (To Lena, who has been drawn towards the scene in spite of herself, partly repentant) Ah! You have come closer . . .

LENA (dismayed—in a whisper). No . . . no . . .

STRANGE LADY (gently). Yes, stay— stay here . . . Perhaps also the sister . . . (Going to Salter) Meanwhile to him—I have something else to say. (Straight at him) You: as well being a bad man, you must be a bad writer.

SALTER. I? It's possible. Why?

STRANGE LADY. It must be all pretense for you—nothing else. You must be an impostor, in everything you write.

SALTER. In what I write?

STRANGE LADY. Your "contribution to literature." You can have put nothing into it, ever—neither heart nor blood, no vibration of the nerves, nor of the senses—

SALTER. Nothing?

STRANGE LADY. Nothing. You can never have felt compelled—because of a real torment, a real despair—to take revenge on life as it is, as it has been made for you by other people and through circumstance; to avenge yourself by creating a better life, more beautiful—as it should have been, as you would have wished it to be! And because you are like that, because you have known me—or part of me, such as I was for you—three months, you think that mine too must be an imposture like yours?

SALTER. Have you put your heart in it?

STRANGE LADY. Can you tell me why else I should have done it?

SALTER. To get rid of me.

STRANGE LADY. I could have got rid of you without deceiving anyone else.

SALTER. I thought you had just finished confessing the deception.

STRANGE LADY. Ah, good, good! You think I have deceived them?

SALTER. It's possible that you are confessing now for your own ends—

STRANGE LADY. What ends?

SALTER. Some personal advantage—

STRANGE LADY. Again! It seems that when you write you're simply playing a game, for profit—that's obvious. Would you like to see how one plays for nothing? I'm playing, now, for you alone—and there's no profit to be made by anyone. You talk of me as an impostor. That depends, Mr. Salter, on how far one can fall, under misfortune. One can fall very far—even to this! (Indicates the Insane Woman) If you are caught in the hands of a brutal enemy, fresh from the slaughter —if you are young, beautiful, trapped here alone, subjected to torture of the body, with every kind of shame and degradation, suffering an anguish of soul so terrible that you are driven mad— brought to this! so that it is impossible for the mind ever to return—yes! you could fall as low as this! But there are

other ways. You could suffer all the torture and the shame—just as fiercely, even to the point of madness—and yet still with a difference. For instance, you might find, out of your madness, a passion of vengeance against your own fate; you might feel yourself so utterly defiled, after the horror of what had happened, that you would shudder with revulsion at the very thought of going back to your former life—

SALTER (with a fierce laugh). So this is the game you play!

STRANGE LADY. Wait! To your former life, I said. To this villa, for instance, where—ah, God! fresh as a flower, eighteen years old—and pure, pure!— clinging to her—(She means Inez; without turning or looking at her, as if the present did not exist, and she saw her only in the past, that day when, at eighteen, she had come with her to the villa which her uncle had given her as a bridal dowry. Very slowly, as she goes on speaking, she moves backwards until she is touching Inez, and says the last words with her head against her breast)—clinging close, close, never wanting to leave her again, not because I did not love him, but because—that first night, so ignorant of everything—because of the words she spoke between her tears, she who knew no more than I: "They say, you know, that now he will have to see you!"

INEZ (very deeply moved, embraces her impulsively). Cia! Cia!

STRANGE LADY (holding away from her). No! Wait—wait!

BRUNO (triumphantly happy). That is something I didn't tell you!

STRANGE LADY (fixing her eyes on him— coldly). I could drive you mad. No one told me. (Bruno involuntarily turns to look at Lena; she adds quickly) No, not even Lena, no! Think! A thing as intimate as that—a secret confidence between two sisters! I spoke of it on purpose. No one could have told me of it—except she who really said it. (To Inez) Isn't it true?

INEZ. Yes! yes!

STRANGE LADY (turning quickly back to Bruno). You did not search well for you Cia. You rebuilt the villa at once; bu you never really searched among th scattered stones, the heaps of rubble, t see whether anything of her might still be left, something of her soul—some remembrance that was still alive—for her, not for you! Fortunately, I have found it.

BRUNO. What do you mean?

STRANGE LADY *(turns to Salter without answering Bruno)*. Is the story clear? You feel so utterly defiled that you can never again be clean; so you go off with the stupidest of all those officers—*(just as I have told you when I first met you—you go from one city to another, from one madhouse to another, in the chaos and confusion that follow the war; one evening, at the theatre, you see a famous dancer—you learn to dance; lights flame across your madness—applause—delirium —why should you deprive yourself of those gaudy trappings of madness? You can flaunt them through the public squares and down the streets—in the night clubs at three in the morning, among the clowns in evening dress—eh, Mr. Salter? just so long as one doesn't grow to be like you—morose and insufferable! And just until something happens —One night, when you least expect it, you suddenly find someone close to you— *(She turns towards Boffi)* sliding past you as swift as a devil—someone who calls to you, "Signora Lucia, Signora Lucia, your husband is here, right up the street; if you like, I'll go and call him!" *(Walking away, her hands to her face)* God knows, I believed that he was searching for someone who could no longer exist! Someone whom he knew he could only find alive in me, so that he could remake her not as she desired—for she no longer desired anything!—but as he desired her! Ah—madness—madness—*(She is speaking to her own dream as she seems to shake herself free of an illusion of madness; then she goes over to face Salter)* So you have come to punish me as an impostor? You are right! Do you know how far this imposture was destined to go? To the point of inducing recognition of me from three people— my sister, my brother-in-law, my husband's sister—three people whom I am seeing today for the first time in my life!

INEZ *(with profound astonishment)*. But Cia, what are you saying?

STRANGE LADY. That it is true: I had never been near this place until he brought me here.

BRUNO *(shouts at her, trembling with rage)*. You *know* that is not true.

STRANGE LADY. It is true—it is!

BRUNO. You want to make them believe it. You're saying . . .

STRANGE LADY. Yes. It pleased me to have you all go on believing I was Cia! But now—Cia's going away! She's going to be a dancer again.

BRUNO. What are you saying?

STRANGE LADY *(pointing to Salter)*. I'm going with him! I'm going back to dance! To dance!

BRUNO. You're not leaving this house!

STRANGE LADY. I told you that you had not searched well for your Cia! You see, darling, there was something you left stuffed away in a corner, unnoticed by anyone; it was a battered old sandalwood chest, with some traces of silver metalwork still left on the doors. Lena reminded me that Cia had always kept it, because it was her mother's. Do you know what I found in one of the drawers of this chest? A little notebook of Cia's, in which were written Inez' words on the day of the wedding: "They say, you know, that now he will have to see you!" That notebook is mine, and I am taking it with me! All the more because, strangely enough, the handwriting looks exactly like my own! *(She laughs, starts to rush out, then stops and adds)* Another thing! One more thing! Do not forget to have the sister look at this poor creature to see if she can find, on her thigh—

DOCTOR. Yes—a kind of mole—

STRANGE LADY. Red?—protruding? She really has it?

DOCTOR. Yes—protruding—but not red, black. And not really on her thigh—

STRANGE LADY. In the notebook it says: "red and protruding—on the thigh —like a small scarab." *(To Bruno)* You see? It must have turned black—it must have changed its place—but she has it! Another proof that it is she! Believe— believe me—it is she! Let's go, Salter! *(To Boffi)* Boffi, will you see about sending everything after me? *(To Salter)* Is the car outside? I'm coming—just as I am!

SALTER. Just as you are! Let's go!
(The two of them rush out towards the waiting car.)

DOCTOR *(running after them with the nurse)*. No, no—wait! What about us?

BRUNO *(bewildered, astounded, like the others)*. But—you can't . . . like this . . .

(He too runs into the garden followed by the others. The sound of their voices, confused and excited, can be heard outside. Only Aunt Lena and the Insane Woman are left, Lena a little apart, uncertain and bewildered.)

ISANE WOMAN. Le—na . . .

LENA *(as if she could not believe it—in a whisper)*. Cia . . .

CURTAIN

HERMAN HEIJERMAN's

The Good Hope

(A Drama of the Sea)

Translated from the Dutch by LILIAN SAUNDERS and CAROLINE HEIJERMANS-HOUWINK

First presented by the Civic Repertory Theatre (Eva Le Gallienne, Director),
New York, on October 18, 1927, with the following cast:

CLEMENTINE............Josephine Hutchinson	MARIETJE...............Beatrice de Neergaard
COBUS....................... Sayre Crawley	SIMON ....J. Edward Bromberg
DAANTJE.......................Robert Ross	SAART.......................Margaret Love
JELLE ....John Eldridge	MEES.......................Alan Campbell
BAREND .... Charles McCarthy	FIRST COASTGUARD ....Harold Moulton
KNIERTJE..................... Alma Kruger	SECOND COASTGUARD ....Walter Tupper Jones
JO.......................Eva Le Gallienne	TRUUS ....Leona Roberts
CLEMENS BOS ....Egon Brecher	KAPS........................Harry Sothern
GEERT....................Donald Cameron	MATHILDE......................Mary Ward

SCENES

The action takes place in a North Sea fishing village in Holland

ACT ONE—Kniertje's cottage.

ACT TWO—Same (two weeks later).

ACT THREE—Same (six weeks later).

ACT FOUR—Office of Clemens Bos (one week later).

ACT ONE

A bare, poorly furnished room in Kniertje's cottage. Right, two beds built into the wall and a door, leading outside. Left, a chest of drawers with holy images, photographs and small ornaments on it. Down stage, a fireplace. In the back a swinging door leading to the cooking shed . . . a cupboard with glass doors, a dove in a cage . . . a window with flower pots. It is afternoon.

———

CLEMENTINE *(a sketch book on her knee).* Now! Now! . . . Cobus!

COBUS *(waking with a start, smiling foolishly).* Héhéhé! I wasn't asleep . . . no . . . no.

CLEMENTINE. Your head more this way. Still more. What is the matter with you? You were posing so well just now. Your hand on your knee . . .

COBUS. Tja! When you sit still so long . . . you get to feeling funny.

CLEMENTINE *(impatiently).* And if you please . . . *if you please,* stop chewing.

COBUS. I . . . I ain't chewing . . . look for yourself.

CLEMENTINE. Keep your mouth shut, please.

DAANTJE *(coming in through the cooking shed).* Good day, everybody!

CLEMENTINE. Good day. Please go take a walk around the block.

DAANTJE. No, juffrouw . . . it's getting late. *(Looking at the drawing)* Well, now, I wouldn't recognize him yet.

CLEMENTINE *(smiling).* Ah?

DAANTJE *(setting his glasses straight).* See now . . . if I may make so free . . . his chin sets different . . . and his eyes don't suit me. But the nose . . . that's *him* . . . and . . . and his necktie, that's top notch . . . that you could swear to!

CLEMENTINE. So?

DAANTJE. And the bed with the curtains . . . that's wonderful. *(Takes a chew of tobacco)* Couldn't you use me sometime?

CLEMENTINE. Perhaps. *(To Cobus)* Your hand higher. Keep your mouth still.

COBUS. That's easy to say . . . but when you're used to chewing and you can't chew, then it's hard to hold your lips still. What do you say, Daantje?

DAANTJE. I say it's getting late. We eat at four o'clock and the matron is strict.

CLEMENTINE. That must be necessary with you old men.

DAANTJE. Peh! We haven't got a thing to say! *(Snaps his fingers)* Not that! The Old Folks Home makes me sick! Your grub handed to you with a snarl . . . like as if you were a beggar. Coffee this morning like . . . like the dregs of the rain barrel, and peas as hard as your corns!

CLEMENTINE. In your place . . . Keep your mouth still, Cobus . . . in your place I would thank God that I was taken care of in my old days.

COBUS. Tja—tja! You shouldn't complain . . .

DAANTJE. Thank God? Not me! I've earned It . . . a sailor all my life . . . worked hard . . . so many trips I can't count 'em . . . been shipwrecked . . . been starved . . . on the sea since I was ten years old . . . and the sea got my two sons. Listen now! Listen now! The matron is a stinker. I'd like to punch her in the snoot.

CLEMENTINE. Come, come! You're not in a pot-house here.

DAANTJE. That I am not. But it sticks in your craw. Last week I couldn't go out, because . . . with your permission . . . I spit outside of the box. Now, I ask you, would you spit outside of the box on purpose? An Old Folks Home is a jail. They stick you in there and then they wash their hands of you. I wish I had been gobbled up decently by the sharks while I was still at sea!

COBUS *(giggling).* Héhéhé! The sharks wouldn't like you, man. You're too tough.

DAANTJE. The sharks wouldn't like me? They would swallow a skeleton. Peh! I saw old Willem bitten in two by a shark before my eyes . . . so the blood spurted out of him! And he was skinny!

CLEMENTINE. Was old Willem eaten by a shark?

DAANTJE. By one? By six. The minute he fell overboard, they grabbed him. The water all around was red!

CLEMENTINE (*with an incredulous smile*). How terrible! And yet . . . I would like to have been there . . . to see a thing like that . . . that would be thrilling.

DAANTJE. Peh! You would like to have been there? We had to be there . . .

CLEMENTINE. Did he scream? (*Shuddering*)

DAANTJE. *Did* he?

COBUS. Tja! You wouldn't scream if you felt those teeth in your behind? . . . héhéhé! (*Violin is heard outside. Cobus jiggles up and down on his chair in time to the music*) Ta-de—da-de . . . da-da-da!

CLEMENTINE (*shutting her sketch book in vexation*). Now then. (*Getting up*) Tomorrow I hope you will be a little quieter.

COBUS (*stretching himself*). Stiff all over! (*Snapping his fingers, his legs shaking*) Ta-de-da-da-da-da-da—!

DAANTJE (*speaking through the window*). Pst! Nobody home.

JELLE. They expect me once a week.

DAANTJE. They've all gone down to the harbor.

CLEMENTINE. Here! (*Throws some money out of the window*)

JELLE (*stopping the music and groping in the dust for the coins*). Thank you very much.

COBUS. Behind the stone, stupid.

DAANTJE. No, further over there.

CLEMENTINE. I threw it the other way. What a donkey! Is he so blind?

COBUS. He has only half an eye, and with half an eye you can't see much. Behind you there.

JELLE. I can't see it.

DAANTJE (*seeing Barend from the window*). Pst! Hé, Barend!—help him a little.

CLEMENTINE. There is ten cents there somewhere.

BAREND (*through the window*). Why don't you give it to him in his paws? (*To Jelle*) Here.

JELLE. Thanks a thousand times, juffrouw. (*He walks away playing*)

COBUS. Did you hear that impudent boy?

CLEMENTINE (*as Barend enters*). Say, you big ape, were you talking to me?

BAREND (*embarrassed*). No, juffrouw, didn't know you were here. I thought . . .

COBUS. You mustn't think . . . you should only think how you can get to sea quick and earn bread for your mother.

BAREND. That's none of *your* business.

COBUS. Listen how big he talks to me . . . but other places he just stands with his mouth full of teeth. Héhéhé! *I'm* not afraid . . . *I* don't get a pain in my belly when I have to go to sea!

DAANTJE. Come along now. It has struck four.

CLEMENTINE. Tomorrow at ten o'clock, Cobus.

DAANTJE. Can't be done, juffrouw. We have to scrape stones tomorrow.

CLEMENTINE. Scrape stones? That's something new. What is it?

DAANTJE. Why now, that's grubbing the weeds up in the court yard.

CLEMENTINE. Tomorrow afternoon then.

COBUS. Tja . . . I'll be there. (*Taking a chew from Daantje's tobacco box*) 'Day, juffrouw. (*To Barend*) 'Day, mollycoddle! Héhéhé!

(*The two old men go out.*)

CLEMENTINE. They tease you all the time, don't they?

BAREND (*with an embarrassed laugh*). Yes, juffrouw.

CLEMENTINE. Have you been down to the beach? (*He nods.*) Find much?

BAREND. No, it was ebb tide last night, and then . . . then . . .

CLEMENTINE. Are you really afraid to go to sea, silly boy? (*He nods, smiling shyly.*) But everybody goes.

BAREND (*dully*). Yes, everybody goes.

CLEMENTINE. Well?

BAREND (*hesitating*). I'd rather stay on shore.

CLEMENTINE. *I* wouldn't try to make you go. How old are you?

BAREND. Last month I was rejected for army service.

CLEMENTINE. Past eighteen then. (*Barend nods.*) Why were you rejected?

BAREND. Because I . . . because I . . . I don't know why.

CLEMENTINE (*laughing*). Well, it's a good thing . . . a soldier that's afraid isn't much use.

BAREND (*flaring up*). On land I'm not

afraid . . . just let 'em get in my way . . . I'll put a knife through their ribs!

CLEMENTINE. Fine!

BAREND *(again embarrassed)*. Don't take it ill, juffrouw. *(The faint whistle of a steamboat is heard.)* That's the Anna. There's a dead man on board. The flag was half-mast.

CLEMENTINE. Another? That's the second this week. First the Agatha Maria . . .

BARAND. No, it was the Charlotte.

CLEMENTINE. Oh, yes, the Agatha was the week before. Do they know who it is on the Anna? *(He shakes his head.)* Didn't you ask? Weren't you curious?

BAREND. Ach, you get so used to it . . . and none of our people were on board. *(Gloomily)* Not father . . . nor Joseph . . . nor Hendrik . . . they . . . you know about that. And Geert . . . he's still in jail.

CLEMENTINE. Yes. What a disgrace he has brought on all of you.

BAREND *(indignantly)*. Disgrace! Disgrace!

CLEMENTINE. When will he be out?

BAREND. We don't know.

CLEMENTINE. You don't know?

BAREND. They gave him six months . . . but they take off the time before the trial and we don't know how long that was.

KNIERTJE *(through the window)*. 'Day, juffrouw.

CLEMENTINE. Good day.

KNIERTJE *(to Barend)*. How did the chickens get loose? Just look at that rooster! Get away, sallemander! Get away! Kischt! Jo! Jo!

BAREND. Let them alone. They'll go back of themselves.

KNIERTJE *(coming in)*. That's an everlasting torment, juffrouw. *(To Barend)* Come now, stir yourself! Stir yourself! We'll have another fuss with Arie.

BAREND *(indifferently)*. Then we'll have a fuss, that's all!

(He goes out lazily—one sees him chasing the chickens outside.)

KNIERTJE. That's all! Such a good for nothing lump of a boy was never born! Lazy brat. Are you going already, juffrouw?

CLEMENTINE. I want to find out what has happened on board the Anna.

KNIERTJE. Yes, I was on my way there, too, but it may be a long time before she's in and I have my belly full of waiting on the pier . . . if the pier could talk! Are you through with the picture of my brother?

CLEMENTINE. Tomorrow. I would like to sketch Barend too . . . as he came in just now with the basket of wood on his shoulders.

KNIERTJE. Barend? It's all the same to me.

CLEMENTINE. He doesn't seem to get much petting here.

KNIERTJE. Petting? I should say not! The sooner I get rid of him the better. *(Through the window)* Go after them now! Kischt! Kischt!

BAREND. The rooster is frightened at all that yelling.

KNIERTJE. Frightened? Then he takes after you! Kischt!

CLEMENTINE. Hahaha! Now he's sitting on Arie's roof.

JO *(coming in through the door . . . brown apron . . . digging irons in her dirty hands)*. 'Day, juffrouw.

KNIERTJE *(snappishly)*. The chickens are loose. The rooster is sitting up on Arie's roof.

JO *(gaily)*. Hahaha! He won't lay any eggs there.

KNIERTJE. Listen to her. And she knows how near we came to a fight the last time they got into Arie's potato field.

JO. I let them out myself, old grumbler. Truus dug her potatoes yesterday.

KNIERTJE. Why didn't you say so right away then.

JO. Now, then what have I done this time! Oh, juffrouw, she only feels natural when she has something to grumble about. At night when she's asleep she growls out loud. Last night she was cursing in her dreams. Hahaha! But go ahead! Snarl as you want to. You're a good old soul. *(To Barend, who enters)* Ach, you poor thing. Is the rooster on the roof? And he won't come down?

BAREND. Now, you . . . shut up!

JO. I bet if you make love to his little hens he'll be jealous and come skipping down of himself. Hahaha! See how white he gets. He's afraid of the rooster!

CLEMENTINE. Now, now!

JO. He ought to be a baker, hé, tante? With his little white feet in the rye meal. Hahaha!

BAREND. You . . . you can all go to the devil—

(Goes off in a rage.)

JO *(calling after him teasingly)*. Poor little thing!

CLEMENTINE. Now don't plague him so. Have you been digging potatoes?

JO. Since four o'clock this morning. Work wasted, tante . . . all withered and rotten.

KNIERTJE. Bad luck lodges with the poor. Rain and rain . . . nothing but rain. Everything had to rot . . . no help for it, and we start into the winter like that . . . the hard, hard winter . . . Ach, ach, ach!

JO. Now there you go, grumbling again. Please laugh a little. Am I so doleful? And—Geert may come any minute now . . .

KNIERTJE. Geert . . . and then what?

JO. Then what? Then . . . Then . . . why nothing. Be cheerful. You won't get one potato more by fussing and crying. Yes, I have to talk to her like that all day long. I caught a rabbit.

CLEMENTINE. In a trap?

JO. Just like that! *(Snaps her fingers)* The rascal wanted to eat off of us, poor as we are. Good enough! We should let ourselves be plundered! While I was busy digging, the spring went "snap" . . . he's a fat one, I tell you . . . forty cents at least.

CLEMENTINE. That's fine. I must go now.

BOS *(at the door)*. Hallo! *(To Clementine)* Are you taking up your lodging here? May I come in, Knier?

KNIERTJE *(amiably)*. Of course, meneer. If you please, meneer.

BOS. I have dirty boots, children.

KNIERTJE *(agreeably)*. That's nothing, meneer. Dry sand does no harm. Take a seat, meneer.

BOS. I won't say no to that. *(Lowers himself rheumatically into a chair)* Yes, Knier, my girl, we are getting older every day. Good day, Jo. *(Holds out his hand)*

JO. 'Day, meneer, You see . . . *(She shows her dirty hands laughing)*

BOS. Are you going to a ball with those little black gloves?

JO *(nods impudently—dances a step or two)*. The hornpipe and the schotsche drij.

BOS. Hahaha! You are a cheeky little black eyes! Now, let's have a look, Clementine.

CLEMENTINE *(impatiently)*. No. You don't know anything about such things.

BOS. Oh, thank you! Raise a daughter till she's grown up—have her taught drawing, but keep your nose out of it. Come! Don't act so childish! *(Takes hold of the drawing)*

CLEMENTINE. No. When it is finished.

BOS. Just a look.

CLEMENTINE *(pulling the drawing away)*. Now, father, don't bother me.

BOS. Always I get a scolding, hahaha!

BAREND *(coming in hesitatingly)*. 'Day, meneer.

BOS. Barendje, you come as if you were called.

BAREND. Me?

BOS. We have need of you, little fellow.

BAREND. Good, meneer.

BOS *(touching his lip)*. The deuce, something is beginning to grow here.

BAREND *(embarrassed)*. Yes, meneer.

BOS. You're getting to be a big fellow. How long have you been out of work now?

BAREND. Eight months.

KNIERTJE. He is lying. It is more than a year.

BAREND. That isn't true!

JO. It is so. Count it up yourself . . . November, December . . .

BOS. Now, now children! No quarreling! Life is too short. Well, Barendje, how would you like to sail on 47? What?

BAREND *(in alarm)*. The 47?

BOS. The Good Hope.

CLEMENTINE *(astonished)*. The Good Hope? Are you going to—

BOS *(sharply)*. Keep out of this! Keep out of this, I say!

CLEMENTINE. But just this morning . . . you said—

BOS (angrily). Clementine!

CLEMENTINE. But father . . .

BOS (stamping his foot heavily). Will you be good enough to get out of here!

CLEMENTINE (shrugging her shoulders). How absurd to get so angry about nothing! How petty! Good-by.

KNIERTJE. 'Day, juffrouw.

BOS (laughing). Exactly like her mother . . . a little cat. Yes, now and then I have to put my foot down, hahaha! Otherwise my wife and daughter would be running the fleet and I would sit in the kitchen peeling potatoes, hahaha! Not that I haven't done that often enough in my young years.

KNIERTJE. As if I didn't remember that . . .

BOS. Taters with fresh herring! (Smacks his lips) But that's all past long ago, long ago. With a fleet of eight luggers you have your mind on other things . . . (smiling) though I still like to look at a pair of pretty black eyes, little impudence! Will you let me say that? Not dangerous! Had my time . . . Hahaha!

KNIERTJE. Say anything you like . . .

BOS. And our little friend here?

KNIERTJE. Open your mouth, can't you?

BAREND. I'd rather . . .

KNIERTJE (snappishly). Rather . . . rather! . . .

JO. Hé, what a lout!

BOS. Children, no squabbling! My boy, you must decide for yourself. The crew is complete . . . all but one. Hengst is skipper . . . the second boy, the younker, the rope-shooter . . . all engaged . . . the skipper thought of you as head boy . . . now what do you say, little man?

BAREND (hesitating nervously). No . . . no, meneer.

KNIERTJE. Oh what a stubborn, dirty brat! I can't drive him on board with a whip!

JO. If I was a man . . .

BOS. Yes, but you're not a man . . . you're a pretty girl! Hahaha! We can't use such pretty little sailors. And why don't you want to go, little fellow? Afraid of seasickness? But you've already made one trip as younker and one as net-boy.

KNIERTJE. He's best as playboy, meneer!

JO. He'd rather loaf around and bum his living. The little milk-sop!

BOS. You are acting very foolishly, my boy. I sailed at your age with your grandfather . . . Oh, yes, then I would rather have sat by mother's pap-pot too, instead of handling live bait with hands like lumps of ice . . . and I would rather have bitten into a piece of bread and butter than bite off the heads of the bait . . . and your father . . .

BAREND (hoarsely). My father was drowned . . . and my brother Joseph . . . and my brother Hendrik . . . no, I won't go.

BOS (his manner friendly). Well, if that is the way he feels, it's better not to force him, Mother Kniertje. I can sympathize with him. My father didn't die in his bed either. But if you reason it out like that, the whole fishing business would go to pot . . .

KNIERTJE (angrily). It is enough to . . .

BOS. You don't catch fuddled herring by knocking them on the head . . .

JO (laughing). Fuddled herring! That's something I'd like to see!

BOS (laughing). She doesn't understand that, Knier. We know, eh?

KNIERTJE. Ach, ach . . . I don't think it's a thing to joke about, meneer. That wretched boy talks as if I had forgotten my husband, and the good Joseph, and . . . but I have not forgotten . . . no . . . (She ends by sobbing softly)

JO. Silly woman! Please! Tantetje dear! (To Barend) You coward! You booby! You whining fool!

BOS. Don't cry, Knier. You can't bring the dead to life by crying.

KNIERTJE. No, meneer. I know that, meneer. Next month it will be twelve years since the Clementine was lost—

BOS. Yes, the Clementine . . . in 1888.

KNIERTJE. In November, 1888. Barend was seven then. Would such an ape remember better than I would?

BAREND (nervously). I didn't say I did. I don't even remember my father's face . . . nor my brothers . . . but . . . but . . .

BOS. Well, then?

BAREND. I want another trade . . . not on the sea . . . no . . .

KNIERTJE. Another trade? Do you know anything else? You can't even read or write.

BAREND. Is that my fault?

KNIERTJE. No, it's mine. For three years I had the pension . . . the first year three gulden a week, the second year, two-fifty, the third, two-twenty-five. The other nine years I had to scratch for myself.

BOS. Do you forget me?

KNIERTJE. I shall always be thankful to you for your help, meneer. If I couldn't have worked for you and the pastor and got a little money and a few scraps to take home . . . I . . . I . . . and that dirty brat holds it against me that I . . .

BAREND. I don't hold anything against you . . . I . . . I will do anything . . . dig sand . . . plant grass on the dykes . . . salt down fish . . . I would like to be a carpenter, or a mason, or an errand boy . . .

JO. Or a burgermeester, or a policeman. Hahaha! And run around in the dark at night to catch little thieves. What a big man!

BOS *(laughing)*. Little impudence!

BAREND *(beside himself)*. You go to the devil! Have you ever heard me complain? Did I say a word when the salt ate the flesh off my hands and I couldn't sleep for the pain?

KNIERTJE. Be a mason! The boy is crazy. Be a carpenter! How many times masons have accidents! Every trade has something.

BOS. Yes, Barendje . . . risks of the trades . . . The miners, the engineers, the stokers, think how they . . . and how often, even at my age I climb the rigging! How often I row out to the lugger with waves breaking over our little boat! Foolishness, little man! You mustn't give up to it.

KNIERTJE. And we haven't any choice. God alone knows what the winter will be . . . all the potatoes are rotten, meneer.

BOS. Yes, it's so in the whole district. Well, youngster?

BAREND. No, meneer.

KNIERTJE. Then you can just get out of my house . . . lazy lubber!

BAREND *(dully)*. All right, mother.

KNIERTJE. March! *(Threateningly)* I could . . .

BOS. Come, come!

JO. If I had a son like that . . .

BOS. Better get yourself a sweetheart first.

JO *(merrily)*. I've got one! If I had a son like that I'd box his ears right and left! Bah! A coward! A sailor knows that sooner or later . . . but he just don't think about it. If Geert was like that . . . I know what I'd do. . . . Think, tante . . . *Geert!*

BOS. Geert?

JO. He'd stand up to the devil! . . . wouldn't he, tante? Well, now I'm going back to the potatoes. Goodby, meneer.

BOS. Say, Black-eyes, do you laugh all the time?

JO *(with a burst of laughter)*. No, I'm going to cry now. Good-by! *(Turning back at the door)* Tante, speak to him about Geert.

BOS. Geert . . . is that your son who . . .

KNIERTJE. Yes, meneer.

BOS. Six months for insubordination?

KNIERTJE. Yes, meneer . . . couldn't keep his hands to himself.

BOS. The stupid young fool.

KNIERTJE. I think they must have done something to him.

BOS. Nonsense. That's no excuse! Discipline would be thrown to the sharks if a sailor could hand out fisticuffs whenever something didn't please him.

KNIERTJE. That's true enough, meneer, but . . .

BOS. And is she sweet on that good-for-nothing?

KNIERTJE. She is crazy about him. And that's all right. He's a fine young fellow . . . just like his father . . . and strong! There stands his photograph. He was still wearing his uniform then . . . first class . . . now he is . . .

BOS. Reduced in rank?

KNIERTJE. Suspended from service! The sailor collar looked so beautiful on him! He was in India twice. It is hard . . . when he comes back next week . . . or in two weeks . . . or tomorrow . . . I don't know when . . . then I'll have him on my hands too. Although . . . although . . . that I must say for him . . . he won't let the grass grow under his feet. Such a giant can find a skipper anywhere.

BOS. Well, I'll tell you plainly, Knier . . . I'd rather not take him. There are too many such discontented rascals these days. Those that come from the Marines . . . it's the God-damned truth . . . they are red to the bone . . . and I won't have Reds around me. Am I right?

KNIERTJE. Of course, meneer. But my boy . . .

BOS. Now, now! . . . they're all alike. There was hunchbacked Jacob . . . the skipper had to throw him out too. Dissatisfied with everything . . . accused me of juggling my accounts . . . Yes, yes. He was crazy. Now he's trying what he can do in Maassluis. We don't stand such nonsense.

KNIERTJE. Can I send him directly to the skipper . . . or to the water-bailiff's office?

BOS. You must make him understand—

KNIERTJE. Yes, meneer.

BOS. If he comes in time he can go on the Good Hope. She's just off the dry docks . . . she'll bring a full cargo back . . . you know that.

KNIERTJE (happily). Yes, meneer.

BOS. Well, good-by. (A confusion of voices outside.) What is that?

KNIERTJE. People coming back from the harbor. The Anna has a dead man on board.

BOS. Pietersen's steam trawler? Too bad. Who is it?

KNIERTJE. I don't know. I'll go find out.

(The stage is empty. Outside there is a vague tumult of voices. Fishermen pass the window talking together. A church bell tolls. Geert slips in through the door, looks around, opens the cook shed door, peers through the window, throws down a bundle tied in a red handkerchief, and plumps himself down in a chair by the table, rests his head on his hand, muttering under his breath . . . gets up restlessly, finds a loaf of bread in the closet, cuts a slice and comes back to the table, chewing . . . lets the bread fall and stares in front of him. The church bell ceases.)

BAREND. Who is it? Geert!

GEERT (gruffly). Yes, it's me. Well, can't you give us your paw?

BAREND (grips his hand). Have you . . . have you seen mother?

GEERT. No, where is she?

BAREND. Mother . . . she . . . she . . .

GEERT. Why do you look at me that stupid way?

BAREND. You . . . you . . . have you been sick?

GEERT. Sick? I never get sick.

BAREND. You . . . you look so white.

GEERT. Why don't you say like a dead man! Give me the looking-glass. The devil . . . what a face! (Throws the mirror down angrily)

BAREND (anxiously). Was it so bad in prison?

GEERT. No . . . it was nice. They stuff you with beefsteak. Is there any gin in the house?

BAREND. No.

GEERT. Then go get some. If I don't get a drop soon, I'll keel over.

BAREND (timidly). I haven't got any money.

GEERT (fumbling in his pocket). I've got plenty. (Throws a handful of coins on the table) Earned that in prison. There . . .

BAREND. From the Red-head around the corner?

GEERT. What the devil do I care . . . just so you hurry. (Calling after him) Is . . . is mother well? (Barend nods) And Jo?

BAREND. She is digging potatoes.

GEERT. Have they got a grudge against me?

BAREND. What for?

GEERT. Because I . . . (Angrily) Don' stare at me like an idiot!

BAREND (embarrassed). I can't get use to your queer face.

GEERT. Queer face? Because I haven' got my goat beard! Did they make a row when I—(Gruffly) Well?

BAREND. I don't know.

GEERT. Go to hell! You don't know anything.

(A silence . . . Barend slips away.)

JO (coming in with the dead rabbit in h hand). Jezis! Geert! (She drops the rabbi *flies to him, throws her arms around his neck and bursts into tears)*

GEERT *(dully)*. Let up now! Stop that damned bawling! Stop it, I say!

JO. I am so happy! I am so happy, Geert, dear.

GEERT *(grimly)*. Now! Now!

JO. I can't help it! *(She cries harder)*

GEERT *(loosening her arms from his neck)*. Now then! Let up! My head can't stand all that racket!

JO *(startled)*. All that racket?

GEERT *(sullenly)*. Of course you don't understand . . . six months alone . . . all alone in your stinking black cell. *(Holding his hand before his eyes)* Pull down that curtain a little . . . the sun here is enough to drive you crazy!

JO. God . . . Geert!

GEERT. Please, now . . . that's better.

JO. Your beard? . . .

GEERT. My beard didn't please them. Look ugly, don't I? Look as if I had been buried and dug up, don't I?

JO *(between laughing and crying)*. No . . . no! Why do you say that? Nobody would notice . . . *(She begins crying softly again)*

GEERT. Well, the devil! Is that all you can say to me? *(She laughs nervously . . . he points to his temples)* Turned gray, eh?

JO. No, Geert.

GEERT. You lie! *(Kicking the mirror away)* I see it myself. The scoundrels, to shut a decent seaman up in a kennel— where you can't walk, where you can't talk, where you can't see . . . *(Strikes the table with his fist in a rage)*

BAREND. Here is the gin.

JO. The gin?

BAREND. For Geert.

GEERT. You keep out of this. *(Drinks greedily from the bottle)* That puts life into a fellow!

JO. Were you eating bread? Were you hungry?

GEERT. Yes. No. Yes. I don't know. *(Raises the bottle to his lips again)*

JO. Please Geert . . . not any more . . . you can't stand it.

GEERT. Not any more? *(Drinks)* Great! That's the best lining for your stomach. No kick yet! *(Drinks again)* Great! Don't look so wild, girl! I won't

get drunk. Bah! It stinks! Not used to it! Are there any provisions on board?

JO. Oh yes. Look at this. A fat fellow, eh? I caught it myself . . . not an hour ago.

GEERT. That will do for tomorrow. *(To Barend)* Here, take this and buy something . . . some ham and fresh meat . . .

BAREND. Meat?

JO. No, that's extravagant . . . if you want to buy meat, keep your money for Sunday.

GEERT. Sunday! Sunday! When I haven't had anything to eat for six months but black bread, horse beans and rotten fish! I'm too weak to set one foot before the other. Don't stand there jawing! Shut up! And a hunk of cheese . . . I'd like to eat myself into a colic. Hahaha! Shall I have another little drop?

(Barend goes off.)

JO. No.

GEERT. Then no little drop. Is there any tobacco?

JO. God, how glad I am that you are jolly . . . like yourself again! . . . Yes, there is tobacco in the jar.

GEERT. Fine! Great! Is that my old pipe?

JO. I kept it for you.

GEERT. And who have you been carrying on with while I was away?

JO *(gaily)*. With Uncle Cobus!

GEERT. What trash you women are. *(Takes a long pull at the pipe)* Half a year that I haven't had that taste in my mouth. *(Blows out a cloud of smoke)* That isn't tobacco . . . it's like hay! The gin stinks and the tobacco stinks . . .

JO. If you would eat something first . . . *(A pause.)*

GEERT *(putting down the pipe)*. Do you still sleep with tante?

JO. Right next to the pigpen. We've got little pigs.

GEERT *(laughing)*. And must I sleep up under the roof again?

JO. It's nice and warm there, boy.

KNIERTJE *(from outside)*. Why is the curtain down?

JO *(standing in front of Geert, her finger on her lips)*. Sst!

KNIERTJE *(coming in)*. What are you

doing? What happened to the looking-glass? Who is sitting there?

GEERT (standing up). Hello, old girl!

KNIERTJE (startled). God Almighty!

GEERT. No . . . it's me . . . Geert.

KNIERTJE. Oh, what a heart thumping I get from that!

GEERT. Hahaha! That's damn good! (Tries to hug her)

KNIERTJE. No . . . not yet . . . wait a minute . . .

GEERT (angrily). Wait a minute? What for?

KNIERTJE (reproachfully). What have you ever done in your life to make me happy?

JO (soothingly). Don't talk like that now.

GEERT. Are you going to begin on me right away? I've had enough to stand . . . if you do . . .

KNIERTJE. If I do? . . .

GEERT. I'll pick up my bundle and be off.

KNIERTJE (despairingly). And that's the way he comes home!

GEERT. Would you like me to sit on the sinner's bench? No thank you!

KNIERTJE (almost crying). The whole village has been talking about the disgrace . . . all the time you were gone . . . I couldn't go out on an errand without . . .

GEERT (harshly). Whoever has anything to say about me can say it to my face. I'm not a thief . . . nor a—

KNIERTJE. No, but you raised your hand against your betters.

GEERT (furiously). I ought to have wrung his neck!

KNIERTJE. Boy, boy . . . you'll bring misfortune on all of us!

GEERT (stamping back and forth). You too! Treated like a beast in prison and then bedeviled here! (Snatches up his bundle) I'm not in the humor to . . . to take anything from you. (Hesitates near the door, drops his bundle) Now! Don't cry, mother. Damn it!

JO. Please, tante dear . . .

KNIERTJE. Your father lies somewhere in the sea. He had plenty to put up with while he was alive . . . he would never have looked at you again . . .

GEERT. I'm glad I'm not like him. Not so submissive . . . A great honor to let yourself be walked on! I haven't got fish blood in my veins. Now then? Are we going to have more rain?

KNIERTJE (throwing her arms around his neck). If you would only come to yourself!

GEERT (rebelliously). I'd knock his teeth down his throat again tomorrow!

KNIERTJE. What was it that happened, Geert?

JO. Yes, now! Tell us all about it. Come and sit down quietly . . .

GEERT. I've been sitting long enough . . . hahaha! Let me walk up and down . . . so I'll get in the way of it again. (Lighting his pipe again) Bah!

JO. Why do you smoke it then, donkey!

GEERT. Better than nothing! . . . Now, if it hadn't been for you it would never have happened.

JO (laughing). Well, that's good!

GEERT. Good! . . . good! I had warned you against him . . .

JO. Against who? What are you talking about?

GEERT. Against that dirty dog . . . don't you remember that you danced with him in Red-head's saloon that night?

JO. Danced? Me?

GEERT. The night before we sailed.

JO. That cross-eyed quartermaster? I don't know what you mean . . . Was it him that you . . . But you told me to, yourself . . .

GEERT. Can you say "no" to your superior officer? . . . On board ship he told dirty lies . . . I heard him tell the skipper that he . . .

JO (angrily). What?

GEERT. That he . . . what the hell! He talked as if you were "first come, first served" with all the sailors!

JO. Me? The dirty liar?

GEERT. When he came below after the dog-watch I hammered him in the snoot with a belaying pin . . . five minutes later I was in irons . . . six days of that, because the detention cell was full . . . then fourteen days detention . . . then six months prison . . . and forbidden for ten years to serve in the Royal Marines! And that, God damn it, is the worst! I'd let both hands be chopped off to get back again . . . yes, to get back! . . . to be treated like a chattel again . . . to be cursed out like a tramp again, to be ground down like a slave again! . . .

KNIERTJE. Geert, Geert, don't say such things! In the Bible it is written . . .

GEERT. There's nothing written in the Bible for us!

KNIERTJE. Shame on you!

JO. Isn't he right?

KNIERTJE. If he had gone respectfully to the Commander . . .

GEERT. Hahaha! You ought to have been a sailor, mother! Hahaha! Respectfully! They were glad to get me into their clutches! While I was in the detention cell, they found newspapers among my things . . . newspapers that we weren't allowed to read . . . and pamphlets that we weren't allowed to read . . . that shut the door on me tight. Otherwise they would only have reduced my rank . . .

KNIERTJE. Papers that you weren't allowed to read? Why did you read them then?

GEERT. Why? You good old soul! When I look at your meek face, I hardly know how to tell you why. I can't hold it against you . . . you didn't know any better and I liked the fine uniform . . . but now that I have brains in my head I would like to warn everybody . . . A boy . . . to bind himself for fourteen years to murder!

KNIERTJE. To murder! Boy, don't say such frightful things!

GEERT. Yes, murder! I fought in the Atjeh campaign and got the Atjeh medal . . . for murder . . . ran poor fellows through with my bayonet so the blood spurted in my eyes! . . . *(Jerks his bundle open)* Where is that thing? *(Throws it violently out of the window)* There it goes! It has rattled on my chest long enough! *(Barend comes in and stands listening.)*

KNIERTJE. Geert, Geert! What has made you like this. I don't know you any more. Who . . .

GEERT. Who trapped a green youngster and bound him to serve in the Navy for fourteen years? Who trained him and drilled him and fitted him to that dog's life and then kicked him out of the only life he was fit for like the dog they had

made him! Who put him in irons because he took up for his girl! You ought to have seen them . . . those irons . . . you ought to have seen me walking in them, whimpering like an animal, chained to another animal with irons on his paws too . . . because he had been cheeky to the officer of the watch!

JO. Don't talk about it any more . . . you are so weak yet.

GEERT *(sunk in the grimness of his memories)*. The detention cell . . . that stinking black hole that makes a pigsty seem like a palace . . . a hole without light . . . a hole where you can't stand up straight . . . where you can't lie down! A hole where they throw you your bread and water . . . "Here, dog, eat" . . . ! There was a storm once . . . I thought I was going down to hell . . . that I'd never see any of you again . . . not you . . . nor you . . . nor you! down to hell in that stinking dark hole. No, let me talk it out . . . it does me good. Another mouthful! *(He drinks quickly)* From the detention cell to the court martial! . . . You don't have much chance there! "Hold your tongue!" "Stand up straight!" "Give your answer!" "Hold your tongue again!" Gold epaulettes sitting up in judgment over the trash that God has created to serve, to salute, to bow the head! . . .

KNIERTJE. Boy, boy! . . .

GEERT. Six months! Six months to reform me! To reform me with grub that I couldn't swallow . . . three months pasting paper bags, so hungry that when I got a chance I gobbled the sour paste . . . three months sorting peas . . . and . . . now you won't believe me but I hope to never see the sea again if I lie . . . at night, over the gas jet, I cooked the peas I had swiped during the day . . . in my slop pail! I ate them half raw . . . at least they filled my belly! All that to reform you . . . to reform you because you got mad and beat up a blackguard that called your girl a huzzy, and because you read papers that you weren't allowed to read.

KNIERTJE *(anxiously)*. That's really unjust.

GEERT. Unjust! How dare you say that! Fresh from the sea . . . flung into a cell . . . no wind, no water, no air! A little window with a grating high up in the wall, no bigger than a door in a bird cage . . . and the stink of the dirty bucket . . . the nights—the awful nights when you couldn't sleep . . . when you jumped up and paced like a crazy man, back and forth, back and forth . . . four steps each way . . . and the nights when you sat and prayed . . . prayed not to go mad . . . and cursed everything . . .everything! *(He lets his head fall on his hands and bursts into sobs)*

JO *(after a long silence).* Geert! *(Kniertje is crying. Barend stands stolidly.)*

GEERT. Now! Let's not . . . *(Speaks harshly to keep back his tears)* Give us a match. *(Smokes)* Now, mother! *(Saunters to the window)* Put your goodies down, Barend. *(Pulls up the curtain)* The God damned rooster is sitting on the roof. Halla! Will you believe now, that I would like to go to sea right away? Two days of the sea, the sea, the sea . . . and I'm as good as ever? Why is Truus going along crying? Truus!

KNIERTJE. Sst! Don't call her! The Anna has just come in without her husband. *(Some women, talking softly, walk past the window.)* The poor creature! Six children!

GEERT. Is Arie? . . . *(She nods)* That's a damned shame! *(Lets the window curtain fall, stands looking down thoughtfully)*

CURTAIN

ACT TWO

Two weeks later. Same scene as before.

———

JO *(setting the table as Simon and Marietje enter).* Hé!

MARIETJE. 'Day . . . They're not here yet?

SIMON. No, they're not here yet. *(Turns to go)*

JO. Are you going already?

SIMON. Well, that's to say . . .

MARIETJE. Jezis, father, stay a little while now.

SIMON. All right . . . I'll wait outside the door . . . I must . . . I must—

MARIETJE. You must nothing . . . please, now . . .

SIMON. Well, sallemanders, am I a child! *(He goes off mumbling to himself)*

MARIETJE. Fight against that, now! . . . and it begins early in the morning.

JO. Is he so bad again?

MARIETJE. You ought to have seen him yesterday . . . half the village was after him! Ach, ach! When mother was alive, he didn't dare. She slapped him in the face when he smelt of gin . . . suppose I tried that!

JO *(bursting into a laugh).* You say that as if . . . hahaha! . . . Mees ought to hear you.

MARIETJE. I've never seen Mees drink . . . and father never used to, you know. Well, I can't put a cork in his mouth . . . I can't lead him around with a string. *(Looking through the window)* There he goes, of course . . . straight to the Red-head. Disgusting old drunkard! How old is Kniertje today?

JO. Sixty-one. Spry for her age, isn't she? Sit down, and tell me now *(gaily)* when are you going to be married? *(They sit on the window bench.)*

MARIETJE. That depends on the trip. You see, we want it right away *(smiling hesitatingly)* because . . . because . . . now you understand . . . But first Mees had to send for his papers and that takes two weeks . . . and by that time he'll be far away on the sea. But five weeks . . . five little weeks, they will go by quick enough.

JO *(smiling to herself).* We'll be married in December.

MARIETJE. That will be about the same time. Are you . . . Are you too? . . . Come now, I've told you everything. *(Jo shrugs her shoulders and laughs.)*

KNIERTJE *(entering).* She laughs all the time. 'Day, Marietje.

MARIETJE *(kissing her).* A hundred years more!

KNIERTJE *(unpacking her basket).* God will protect me from that! A hundred years? I haven't got the money to keep me that long. *(Opening a twist of paper)* Here, you can try one of these . . . you too. Ginger snaps. No, not two . . . yo with the long grab-fingers. For each of the boys a half pound of ginger snaps and a half package of chewing tobacco, and a bag of cigars. Do you know what Barend is going to get now that he is acting like a man? Look here. *(Takes earrings from her pocket)*

JO. Now, you ought to give those to Geert.

KNIERTJE. No . . . I think it's so fine of the boy that he's cut through the knot at last, I want to give him some pleasure. For something, something should be given.

MARIETJE. Did you buy them?

KNIERTJE. Buy them? Do I buy things? Those are *old* earrings . . . I don't know how old. My husband used to wear them on Sundays when he was at home.

MARIETJE. There are little ships on them—and masts . . . and little sails . . . I wish I had them for a brooch.

JO. Why does that good-for-nothing get them? I should think that Geert, as the oldest . . .

KNIERTJE. Don't call him good-for-nothing any more. That's not right.

MARIETJE. There was a lot of coming and going before you got him to sign.

KNIERTJE. Yes, yes. But with his brother going along he is willing. And think how you would feel yourself . . . a boy that isn't strong . . . never has been strong . . . rejected for military service . . . and a boy that is always thinking about his father and brothers . . .

JO. Now I can't stand that! First you bawl him out and curse him out and now butter wouldn't melt in your mouth.

KNIERTJE. Never mind, now! No matter now what he's been . . . in an hour he'll be gone . . . in an hour. And you must never take leave of anyone in anger. Have a sweet drink, Marietje? We have fresh cookies and ginger nuts. All laid in for my birthday . . . though if I had known that they were sailing today . . . Set everything out, Jo. Saart will be here directly . . . and the boys can have a drink too.

COBUS *(coming in with Daantje)*. A glass of gin . . . glad we dropped in . . . why don't we begin? . . .

KNIERTJE. Cobus, throw your quid away outside.

COBUS. I should thank you . . . *(Wraps it in his red handkerchief—he and Daantje sit at the table—to Jo)* Now . . . now . . . you know what I want to say . . .

DAANTJE. And me the same . . . me the same.

JO. I don't need to ask you . . . *(She fills the glass in front of Cobus)*

COBUS. No, no . . . just go right ahead. Pour a little drop more.

JO. There now . . . it's running over.

COBUS. That's nothing. I won't waste a drop. *(Leans shakily over the table and drinks without lifting the glass)* Héhéhéhé!

DAANTJE. Ginger nuts? If you please. *(Yawns and stretches)*

MARIETJE *(yawning also, imitating him)*. Oh! What do you think of that!

DAANTJE. Peh! If you had my years . . . last night I hardly slept at all and this afternoon no nap . . .

JO. Crawl into bed there . . . hahaha!

COBUS. That he'd like to do with a young girl beside him to keep his feet warm.

MARIETJE. Take a hot water bottle instead, Daan.

COBUS. Now if I had my choice . . . *(Pinches Marietje's arm)*

KNIERTJE. Hold your tongue. You talk too much. The matron at the Home has to help him button his breeches and he wants . . .

JO. Hahaha! Oh, Uncle Cobus!

MARIETJE. Hahaha!

COBUS. Tja! They say in English, "A young man kisses the misses, and an old man misses the kisses." Do you understand that?

JO. Exactly. That means, "Woman, bring your cat into the house, it's going to rain." Hahaha! Hahaha!

SAART *(appearing at door)*. Good day. Congratulations to everybody.

COBUS. Come on in!

SAART. 'Day, Daantje, and 'day Cobus, and 'day, Marietje, and 'day, Jo. No, I won't sit down.

KNIERTJE. A drink?

SAART. No, I can't sit down. My pot is on the fire.

JO. Please, now.

SAART. No, I can't do it . . . my door is unlatched and the cat might knock over the oil stove. Just give it to me here . . . now . . . now! Many years yet, and may your boys . . . ach now—where are your boys?

KNIERTJE. Geert has gone to say good-by in the village and Barend has gone in the yawl with Mees to carry their mattresses and kit bags and oilskins on board. They'll be back here soon. They have to be on board at three o'clock.

SAART (emptying her glass). Hé, that burns your heart out! Say, were you at Leen's house yesterday?

KNIERTJE. No, I couldn't go.

SAART. They had everything there and lots of it! The bride took more than she could carry . . . three glasses of "Roses Without-Thorns," two of "Perfect Love," and at least four of "Maid-in-the-Bower!" How she stowed it away!

COBUS. How her sweet little lips must have smacked! Héhé! . . . Just give me an old-fashioned dram of brandy with syrup . . . eh, Daan?

DAANTJE (waking with a start). What?

KNIERTJE. He comes here to sleep. He acts as if he hadn't been to bed at all.

COBUS. To bed! Héhéhé!

DAANTJE (angrily). Now! Don't get so funny!

JO (giggling). Uncle Cobus! (Points to her nose)

COBUS (taking out his handkerchief). Ho, ho! Change in the weather!

KNIERTJE. Look out now! Don't drop your quid.

SAART. Old butt-snooper!

COBUS. Butt-snooper! You'll never guess how I got this quid. Not ten minutes ago I saw Bos . . . and he gave me . . . he gave me a little white roll . . . tissue paper with tobacco in it . . . what do you call those things?

MARIETJE. Cigarettes.

COBUS. Yes. Me smoke a thing like that . . . with nasty paper around it. That's a quid with a little shirt on.

SAART. And you're a gin-guzzler without any shirt on! No I can't sit down.

JO. I've filled the glasses up again.

SIMON (in the doorway, half drunk). 'Day, everybody.

KNIERTJE. 'Day, Simon. Just crowd in . . . always room for one more.

COBUS. A sweet drink?

MARIETJE (anxiously). No.

SIMON (obstinately). Why "no"?

MARIETJE. You've had enough.

SIMON. I've had nothing . . . salle-manders!

MARIETJE. Now the pleasure's all over.

KNIERTJE. Didn't you see Geert?

SIMON (muttering stupidly). Uh, uh . . . Geert . . .

COBUS. Give him another . . . just for good measure.

MARIETJE (angrily). No! No!

SIMON (stupidly). No? Well, I'll be damned! (Sits down, lights his cutty)

KNIERTJE. Is there much work at the docks, Simon?

SIMON. Yes, now . . . yes, now—listen— (Mumbles dully)

SAART. Well, I'll be off . . .

JO. Come now . . . that's neighborly! The boys will be here right away. Take a chair . . .

SAART. No . . . when I sit down I talk the time away . . . well, just half a glass then . . . no, no cookies.

GEERT (at the side door). It looks like all hands on deck here! Good day, all. Eh, Simon!

SIMON (mumbling). Uh . . . yes . . .

MARIETJE. Let him alone.

GEERT. The devil! Putting on airs with me! Only fifteen minutes more, people. Fill up the glasses, Jo. (Between Kniertje and Jo) Here you are, mother! Proost Santjes! Santjes, Jo . . . Santjes, Daantje

JO (pointing to Daantje). Hahaha! Asleep with a ginger nut in his hand!

KNIERTJE. Doesn't he feel well?

COBUS (mischievously). Sst! Sst! Last night . . . héhéhé . . . last night he wanted to get a drink of water . . . upset the pitcher all over his bed. (Giggling) And then he was afraid of the matron . . afraid she would think—(Giggling) So he got up . . . in his bare feet . . . and dried the sheets by the stove . . . héhéhé but the mattress was wet . . . dripping wet . . . and before it was dry . . . Sst! Sst! Don't let him know you heard it from me!

JO. Hahaha!

MARIETJE. Hahaha! Poor old Daan!

SAART. Nice to tell tales on your friend!

COBUS. Tell tales? I didn't tell the matron.

GEERT. And suppose you did tell her? Are you afraid of the matron? Are you eating charity bread? You've paid your money.

COBUS. Easy for you to talk! If they catch you in anything you can't go out for two weeks.

GEERT. Poor fellow! I hope I'll never live to be that old.

JO. Oh, isn't that nice! Not married yet and a widow already!

GEERT (gaily). How do you know you're *ever* going to get me? Hahaha! (Pointing to Daantje) Shall I give him a poke? I don't need a belaying pin for that. (He sings, beating time on the table with his fist . . . the others join in)

Sailing, sailing . . . don't let the
[bosun call you
Starboard watch, jump out of your
[bunks!
You can go swimming on the deck,
The rain falls fast and the wind has
[gone down
And it's sailing, sailing.
Sailing on the starboard watch!
[Hahaha!

DAANTJE (waking with a start). Now that could happen to any of you at my age!

GEERT. Hahaha! I'll never be old. Leaky ships must go to the bottom!

JO. Now, Geert!

SAART. He won't get old! If you had said that a while ago when you still looked like a flabby dishrag! . . . But now! . . . It did you good to sit in prison, young fellow!

COBUS. We can make a song about you pasting paper bags in prison . . . just like Domela[1] the Socialist! Héhéhé! (Sings in a piping voice)

My nevvy Geert pastes paper bags
Hi . . . ha . . . ho . . .
My nevvy Geert . . .

SAART. —Pastes paper bags.

THE OTHERS. Hi . . . ha . . . ho!—etc.

GEERT. What rowdies! (Laughing) They're making a joke of it!

·) Domela was a famous socialist about whom many songs were made.

KNIERTJE (anxiously). Please now, you mustn't act so wild . . . that brings bad luck.

JO. Ach! I expected that! It's your birthday, isn't it? Take a chair, now, Saart.

SAART. A chair? . . . where'll I get one?

MARIETJE. I can stand up.

SAART. No . . . I've got a seat. (Plants herself on half of Cobus's chair)

COBUS. You're pushing me off! You go sit on your thumb.

MARIETJE (to Simon who is huddled in a drunken stupor). Father!

SIMON (muttering thickly). They must— . . . they must . . . not . . . not . . . I told them . . . that's the truth—

MARIETJE. Come now!

GEERT. Let him scud under his own sails. The man isn't bothering anybody.

SIMON (gesturing aimlessly). You must . . . you must! . . .

MARIETJE (irritably). What do you mean? Must what? . . .

SIMON (mumbling). The ribs . . . the timbers . . . (Heavily) It's the truth . . .

GEERT, JO, COBUS, DAANTJE, SAART. Hahaha! Hahahaha!

MEES (from the side door). Sallusies!

KNIERTJE (anxiously). Are you alone? And . . . and . . . Barend?

MEES (good naturedly). Don't ask me.

KNIERTJE. But you went together with the bags and the mattresses . . .

MEES. A row with the skipper! What kind of a seaman is that!

JO. A row! Making trouble already?

MEES. I'm not going to talk about it . . . Afraid—afraid . . . always afraid! (To Marietje) Are you coming with me?

JO. No . . . first a drink . . . it's tante's birthday.

MEES. Well, think of that now! Well, well! Many more years, Kniertje!

KNIERTJE. You've made me uneasy.

JO (laughing). Uneasy?

KNIERTJE (angrily). Yes, uneasy. She's surprised at that? I've taken an advance from Bos.

GEERT. Don't be silly, mother . . . he's signed hard and fast . . .

COBUS. He's just gone to tell his girl good-by. (Jelle's violin is heard outside.) Ta-de-da-de-da-da! *(He jiggles about on his chair)*

SAART. Sit still, will you? You act as if you had fleas!

JELLE *(playing a polka at the window)*. If you please!

COBUS. Come on in, old man. *(Jelle stumbles into the room)*

JO. Ach, Jezis, the poor old man sees less every day!

JELLE *(as he plays)*. I come regularly once a week.

GEERT. That damned polka! Try another tune, old man.

JO. Play the . . . the . . . now what's the name of that? . . .

COBUS. Yes, that's a pretty tune . . . the one she says!

SAART. You know, Jelle . . . the . . . *(Sings)* "I know a song that charms the heart!"

MEES. Say, just give us . . . *(Jelle begins "La Marseillaise.")* That's the ticket! *(Sings)* "Allose-vodela-debieje . . . deboe-debie-deboelebie!"

COBUS. What's that you're singing?

MEES. That's French!

MARIETJE. Hahaha! That's dead-codfish French!

JO. Hahaha!

MEES. Laugh all you like! We lay in a French port once . . . everything fine there! When you said "pan" you got a piece of bread, and when you said "open the port" they opened the door . . . that's the truth.

GEERT. Hahaha! Play it again, Jelle. What the devil! . . . we've got our own words for it! *(Jelle begins again . . . Geert roars out the words)*

Up men, up brothers, all united!
Up burgers, join your strength to [ours!
Your woes, your griefs shall be [assuaged . . .

BOS *(shouting angrily through the window from where he has listened to the singing)*. What's all this here? *(Everybody is frightened into silence.)* Get yourselves on board, damn it . . . it's high time! *(Goes off raging)*

KNIERTJE *(after a long silence)*. Oh! Oh! How he frightened me! Hé! Hé!

JO. What was the matter with him?

MEES. I couldn't think where the voice came from . . .

SAART. How could you be so stupid . . . when you know that meneer Bos lives only two doors away . . . bellowing like a stuck pig!

MARIETJE. Jezis! How mad he was!

COBUS *(to Geert)*. Héhéhé! You won't last very long with him.

KNIERTJE. Why do you sing such low songs?

GEERT. Well, the devil! Am I in my own house, or not! If the old frog hadn't taken me by surprise, sticking his head in at the window all of a sudden, I'd have wiped up the floor with him! "Get yourself on board!" Play up, Jelle!
(Jelle begins.)

KNIERTJE. Ach, please, no, Geert . . . I'm afraid that if meneer Bos . . . *(Motions Jelle to stop)*

GEERT. This one is afraid to go to sea! . . . This one is afraid of the matron in the Home! . . . This one is afraid of a little ship-owner! Dictates to me in my own house! Orders me around as if I was his office boy.

SAART. Joking is joking . . . but if you was a ship owner you wouldn't like it either if one of your sailors sang socialist songs . . .

KNIERTJE. And when he knows how dependent I am.

GEERT *(passionately)*. Dependent! Don't be dependent! Is it an honor for you to do his cleaning? You ought to pay him for the privilege! . . . Say thank you when you scrub the floor he walks on . . . Go down on your knees to clean up his dirt! . . . Lick the mud off of his shoes! Dependent! Fifty cents twice week and the scraps they leave on their plates after they've stuffed themselves

JO. Don't get in such a temper, silly boy!

KNIERTJE. Oh, oh! What a scolding am going to get next Saturday! I . . . . . . May God protect me . . .

GEERT. May God protect you from bending your neck all your days! Here take this, Jelle! *(Sings)* Up, men! Up brothers, all united . . .

KNIERTJE *(puts her hand over his mouth)*. Please now, Geert!

JO. Hé! Why do you plague that old woman on her birthday!

(Jelle holds out his hand . . . they give him a few coins.)

COBUS. All my property is tied up in the bank.

JELLE. Many thanks to all. *(Goes off)*

MEES *(to Marietje)*. Now will you come with me?

GEERT. I'll wait a little while yet for Barend. What's your hurry? The boys will come by here anyway.

SAART *(to Geert)*. Don't you see what those two want? *(To Mees)* Good-by! . . . good luck!

MEES, MARIETJE. Good-by!

(There is much shaking of hands, good wishes . . . they go off.)

KNIERTJE. Half-past two . . . I'm getting worried.

SAART. Half-past two? Have I stayed that long? And my door on the latch! Lucky voyage, Geert! Good-by, Kniertje, old woman . . . good-by all! *(Goes out)*

BOS *(coming in brusquely)*. Well, are you planning to go back on me too?

GEERT *(roughly)*. Do you mean that for me?

BOS *(angrily)*. For you? Yes. Skipper Hengst has my orders, you understand.

GEERT *(nonchalant)*. Out of his head—

BOS *(furiously)*. The water-bailiff has been notified . . .

GEERT *(trying to control himself)*. To hell with you and the water-bailiff! *(Cobus and Daantje slip out, but stand listening at the window.)* Are you crazy! Who told you I wasn't coming on board?

KNIERTJE. He's all ready, meneer.

BOS. That other boy of yours, that Hengst took on as head boy . . . he's given us the slip.

KNIERTJE. Oh, good God!

BOS *(to Cobus and Daantje)*. Is this any of your business? *(They disappear.)* This house is getting disreputable . . . guzzling and brawling!

JO. It's tante's birthday.

GEERT. And if it wasn't mother's birthday, we'd do as we please anyway.

BOS. Be good enough to change your tone!

GEERT. My tone! . . . Get out of here!

KNIERTJE *(agitated)*. Ach, Geert dear!

Don't take it ill of him, meneer . . . He's angry and when you're angry you say things—

BOS. Unwarrantable things! You treat your employees decently and then . . . then you get dirt for your thanks! *(Threateningly)* If you are not on board in ten minutes, I'll have the Coast Guard drag you there!

GEERT. Drag me there! Who do you think you're talking to!

JO. Please, Geert . . . be still . . .

BOS. "Who do you think I'm talking to?" he says . . . he dares to say that! *(To Kniertje)* Ask me again to say a good word for a rowdy that's been kicked out of the Marines?

GEERT *(mockingly)*. Did you say a good word for me? Hahaha! You make me sick! You pay my wages . . . I do my work! And for the rest, the back of my hand to you!

BOS. You are an impudent, overgrown lout!

GEERT *(grimly)*. If I didn't hold back for mother's sake, I'd—

JO *(throwing her arms around his neck)*. Geert! Geert!

(A silence.)

BOS. And this in your house, Knier! *(At the door)* Understand what you are doing. I gave you the advance in good faith. Good day.

KNIERTJE. Ach meneer, ach, yes.

BOS. Have I ever treated you badly?

KNIERTJE. No, meneer . . . you and the pastor . . .

BOS. One of your sons won't work for me . . . the other . . . you'll come to a bad end, my young friend!

GEERT. Haul in your sails! On board I'm a sailor . . . here I'm the skipper. How ridiculous! A ship owner that won't have this and won't have that and pokes his nose in at the window when you sing something that don't suit him . . .

BOS. Go ahead and sing as far as I'm concerned . . . But would your father, who was a good man through and through, have dared to threaten his patron? You young people have no respect for gray hairs.

GEERT. Good enough! Respect for gray hairs! Yes! But only for gray hairs that have grown gray in poverty and hard work! . . .

BOS (*shrugging his shoulders*). Your mother has seen me as a child standing at the bait bucket . . . I've baited hooks in an east wind that was sharp enough to cut your ears off . . .

GEERT. Don't tell any more of those tales, meneer. You have worked yourself up very cleverly . . . you have become a man of money . . . and a petty tyrant. All right! You are no worse than the others . . . but in my own house you leave me alone! My father was a different sort from me . . . we are all going to be different . . . and perhaps if my sons live long enough . . . when they go, like I did twelve years ago, to ask if there is any news of their father and their brothers, they won't find the patron sitting snugly in his office, with a glass of grog by a warm stove and a well-filled money chest . . . and they won't be cursed because they come back so often with the same question . . . and they won't have the door slammed in their faces with the snarling words, "When there is any news you will be told!"

BOS (*roughly*). You lie! That I have never done!

GEERT. I won't waste words over that! . . . I only want you to know that I remember it. Gray hairs! My mother's hair is gray . . . my father's hair was gray . . . Jelle has gray hair too and *how* gray!

BOS. Big talk! Arguing without head or tail! And now I'll give you one bit of advice, my young friend, before you sail. . . . You have an old mother . . . you want to get married . . . you've been six months in prison . . . we won't talk about that . . . you have barked at me like an insolent dog in your own house . . . but if you try any funny business on board the Good Hope you will find out what ship discipline is . . .

GEERT. A year old child knows that.

BOS. When you have grown a little older and wiser, you will be ashamed of your impudence . . . the shipowner with his grog and his warm stove! . . .

GEERT (*mockingly*). And his money chest.

BOS (*angrily*). And his worries and

troubles, that you haven't any idea of. Who feeds you all?

GEERT. Who hauls the fish out of the sea? Who risks his life every hour in the day? Who goes around in watersoaked clothes for six weeks at a stretch, sleeping like beasts, two and two in a stall, with hands raw with salt water sores. Twelve of us are sailing on your ship in an hour. We get twenty-five per cent of the profits . . . you get seventy-five. We do the work . . . you sit comfortably at home. Your ship is insured, but we . . . we can go to hell if the ship sinks . . . we're not worth insuring!

(*Through the window one sees a crowd of fishermen going by . . . a Voice calls, "Are you coming with us, Geert?" . . . Bos is greeted respectfully.*)

GEERT. I'll follow you right away, boys.

BOS. A lucky voyage, fellows! Will you tell the skipper— no, you needn't tell him . . . I'll come myself. (*A silence*) I'll just take two minutes to tell you what I've tried to say three times. When you lie tonight in your stall . . . like a beast naturally . . . try to think a little of my risks . . . when the catch is bad . . . when the nets are lost or damaged . . . when the ship runs aground, and God knows what else! The hatches were swept away from the Jacoba not long ago, the Queen Wilhelmina had half her bulwarks torn away by a big wave! You don't take that into account . . . you don't have to pay for it. Three months ago the Expectation collided with a steamboat . . . without thinking of the ship, the fish, or the nets the crew took to the boats, leaving the ship adrift. Who thought of *my* interests? You can laugh, youngster, because you don't know the worries I have. Last week the crew of the Matilda smuggled gin and tobacco in their mattresses to sell to the English. Now the ship is held by the government. Do you pay the fine?

GEERT. Pluck feathers off a frog! Hahaha!

BOS. You don't have to worry about harbor charges, bait, towing rates, provisions, barrels, or salt. I don't make you pay for wear and tear. I fork over myself if a gaff or a boom is broken. I gave you

mother an advance and your brother
Barend has deserted . . .

KNIERTJE (anxiously). No, meneer, I
can't believe that.

BOS. Hengst telephoned me from the
harbor just now. I stopped to tell you
. . . otherwise I would not have come
back to be insulted by this son of yours!
(To Kniertje) And you . . . in the future
my wife will not need you. This house has
become a brothel!

KNIERTJE. Meneer, it isn't my fault.

GEERT. Must you take it out on the old
woman?

BOS. That's what you get when your
own son fouls the nest. After this trip you
can look for another employer.

GEERT (beside himself). And now, get
out! Get out! (He slams the door behind Bos)

KNIERTJE. What a birthday! What a
birthday!

JO. Don't hang your head like that,
tante! Geert was in the right.

KNIERTJE. In the right? What if he is in
the right! (Gets up)

GEERT (angrily). Are you going to run
after him?

KNIERTJE. No, I'm going to look for
Barend . . . Great God . . . If he has
deserted . . . if he has deserted he'll be
sent to prison too . . . both sons in . . .

GEERT. Won't you wish me a lucky
trip first . . . or don't you think that's
worth while?

KNIERTJE. My head is in a whirl. I'll
come down to the harbor . . . I'll come
there . . . (Goes out)

JO. I feel so sorry for her . . . the poor
thing.

GEERT. He's a dirty dog! . . .

JO. Where is your sou'wester? If we
have to look for that now! . . . You gave
it to him good! It was that drunken Simon
that made him so mad. Now don't look so
glum. Here's your sou'wester. (She picks a
geranium from a flower pot . . . puts it in his
button hole) There! And you keep it like
that! (On his knee) And think of me every
night, will you? (Jumping up) Are you
back so soon, tante!

KNIERTJE. Isn't Barend here?

GEERT. He's in my pocket. Hahaha!

KNIERTJE. Truus saw him sneaking
behind the house. Ach! Ach!

GEERT. We're going now. Will you
come along with us? If that little sneak
backs out it won't do a damn bit of good
for you to sit here.

KNIERTJE. No, no, no!

JO. Will you come later then?

KNIERTJE. Yes, yes. Don't forget your
package of tobacco and your cigars.

GEERT (gaily). If you come too late,
you'll never set eyes on me again. (They
go out)

BAREND (coming in and shutting the door
quickly behind him). Sst!

KNIERTJE. You miserable brat!

BAREND (shrinkingly). Sst.

KNIERTJE. Why "Sst!" I'll scream till
the whole village comes running if you
don't follow right away after Geert and
Jo.

BAREND (panting with agitation). If you
can call Geert back . . . don't let him go!
. . . don't let him go!

KNIERTJE. Have you gone crazy with
fear, you coward!

BAREND (shuddering). The Good Hope
is no good . . . no good! The hull is
rotten . . . the deck beams are rotten!

KNIERTJE. Don't stand there talking
nonsense to excuse yourself. Get down to
the ship!

BAREND (wildly). If you don't believe
me . . .

KNIERTJE. I won't even listen to you
. . . get out or I'll slap you in the face!

BAREND. Beat me then . . . beat me!
Oh God! Make Geert come back!
Mother! Simon knows . . . he worked on
the repairs . . . he warned me!

KNIERTJE. Simon! That drunken sot,
that can't put two words together! You
sickening brat! First sign on . . . then
run away! Stand up!

BAREND. No, not if you beat me to
death! I won't go on a ship that isn't seaworthy!

KNIERTJE. What do you know about it?
Isn't the ship just off dry docks!

BAREND. The seams couldn't be
caulked any more! Simon said . . .

KNIERTJE. Hold your tongue with your
Simon! Get out! Here . . . take your
tobacco . . .

BAREND (screaming). I won't go! I
won't go! You don't know . . . you

haven't seen . . . there was a foot of water in the hold the last trip!

KNIERTJE. The last trip? The last trip the Good Hope brought back fourteen tons of herring! Is she all at once unseaworthy just because *you* have to go on her!

BAREND. I looked in the hold . . . the barrels were floating— in water . . . you can see death hiding down there below!

KNIERTJE. There is bilge water in every ship. The barrels are floating? Don't talk to an old seaman's wife! Is Skipper Hengst a fool? Isn't Hengst going and Mees and Jacob and Gerrit and Nelis? . . . and your own brother, and little Pietje? Do you think you know better than old seamen? *(Violently)* Get up! I can't stand it to see you dragged on board by the Coast Guard.

BAREND *(imploringly)*. Oh, mother dear, mother dear! . . . don't make me go!

KNIERTJE. Oh God . . . how you have punished me in my children! Meneer Bos gave me an advance . . . the guard has been notified . . . I can't clean for meneer any more! *(Firmly)* Well, they'll have to drag you then. Oh, oh, that such a thing should happen in my family! *(She tries to push him out of the door)*

BAREND. Let go of me, mother . . . I don't know what I'm doing . . . I might . . .

KNIERTJE. Now he's brave enough! Raise your hand against me if you dare! . . . your old mother!

BAREND *(shaking his head crazily between his hands)*. Oh, oh, oh! If they drag me on board . . . you'll never see me again . . . you'll never see Geert again!

KNIERTJE. The ship is in God's hands. *(More kindly)* Come now, a boy of your age mustn't snivel like a child. I thought I would do you a pleasure by giving you your father's earrings. Come . . .

BAREND. Mother, dear . . . I don't dare . . . I don't dare! I'll be drowned! Hide me . . . hide me! . . .

KNIERTJE. Are you completely crazy, boy! If I believed one word of your nonsense I wouldn't let Geert go, would I? Sit still now, and I'll put the earrings in. Look! *(Talking as if to a child)* Solid silver . . . little ships on them and sails! Sit still! There's one! There's two. Go look in the glass.

BAREND. No, no!

KNIERTJE. Please now. You are making me sick . . . just for nothing. Please now, dear boy . . . I love you and your brother . . . You two are all I have in the world. Every night I will pray to the good God to bring you home safe and sound. Come now, Barend . . . *(Holds the mirror before him, wiping away her tears)* Look at your earrings now . . . See!

FIRST COAST-GUARD *(stepping in at the door)*. Skipper Hengst asked the waterbailiff . . . if you please, little fellow . . . we have no time to lose.

BAREND *(shrieking)*. I won't go! I won't go with you! The ship is rotten!

SECOND COAST-GUARD *(smiling good-naturedly)*. Then you ought not to have signed on, Barendje. Must we use force? Come now, little man . . . *(Slaps him pleasantly on the shoulder)*

BAREND *(clinging desperately to the door post)*. Don't touch me! Don't touch me!

THIRD COAST-GUARD. Must we put the handcuffs on, boy?

BAREND *(his teeth chattering with terror)*. Help me, mother! You'll never see me again! I'll drown! I'll drown in that dirty, rotten sea . . .

FIRST COAST-GUARD *(roughly)*. Come, come! Let go of the door! *(Takes hold of his wrist)*

BAREND *(holding on tighter)*. No! No! Cut my hands off! Oh God! Oh God! *(Crouches against the wall, wild with fear)*

KNIERTJE *(almost shrieking too)*. The boy is afraid!

FIRST COAST-GUARD. Make him let go

KNIERTJE *(sobbing)*. Please now, boy please now! God will take care of you.. *(She loosens Barend's hands)*

BAREND *(letting go of the door, moaning in despair)*. You'll never see me again . . never again!

FIRST COAST-GUARD. Out with you!

KNIERTJE. Oh, oh! *(A silence.)*

TRUUS *(looking through the window anxiously)*. What was that, Knier? . . .

KNIERTJE *(sobbing)*. Those brutes hav

taken Barend away . . . and now I don't dare go through the village to say good-by to Geert! Oh, the disgrace . . . the disgrace!

ACT THREE

Six weeks later. The same stage setting as before. Evening. A lamp burns. A glowing fire on the hearth throws a brilliant light over the whole scene. A fierce wind is howling and shrieking around the house.

JO *(reading in front of the bed where Kniertje is lying)*. This verse is beautiful . . . are you listening? "Prayer to Mary for the Dead."

Mother Mary, look in pity
On your children here below.
Fold your loving arms around them
Soothe them in their bitter woe.
At the throne of God on high
Beg for them his clemency.

(Peeping into the bed) Are you asleep, tante? Are you asleep? *(There is a knock . . . she tiptoes to the door, puts her fingers on her lips as Clementine and Kaps enter)* Softly, juffrouw!

CLEMENTINE. Shut the door quickly! What weather! What dog's weather! My eyes are full of sand. Is Kniertje sick?

JO. She just lay down a minute in her clothes . . . she don't feel just right . . . a cough and fever.

CLEMENTINE. I brought her a bowl of broth and six eggs . . . Now then, Kaps! Kaps!

KAPS. Well?

CLEMENTINE. Put them on the table! What a nuisance he is . . . as deaf as a post. *(In a loud voice)* Where did you put the eggs!

KAPS. I can hear you all right.

KNIERTJE *(from the bed)*. Is there someone here?

CLEMENTINE. It's Clementine.

KNIERTJE *(getting up)*. Has the wind gone down yet?

CLEMENTINE. I've brought you a bowl of veal broth . . . *(To Kaps)* Well, how's this? You have spilled half of it!

KAPS. It's not so easy to hold a bowl steady with the wind blowing your eyes full of sand . . .

CLEMENTINE. Where are the eggs? *(Kaps begins to take them out of his pocket)* One, two, three, four . . . Where are the other two?

KAPS *(feeling in his other pocket and taking out his hand dripping with egg yolk)*. What a mess! That happened when you stumbled against me. Just look at my keys . . . and my pocket book . . . and my handkerchief!

JO *(laughing)*. Make an omelet of them! Ha-ha-ha!

CLEMENTINE *(to Kaps)*. You may as well go home, Kaps!

KAPS. What?

CLEMENTINE. Go along home. I'll come back alone.

KAPS *(ill-naturedly)*. Good-night then! My God—my corkscrew! *(Goes off)*

CLEMENTINE. I can't understand why my father keeps such a bookkeeper . . . deaf . . . ill-natured . . . *(To Kniertje)* Does it taste good?

KNIERTJE. That it does, juffrouw! You must thank your mother for me.

CLEMENTINE. Indeed I will not! Father and mother are still angry. They haven't forgotten the trouble with your sons yet. May Jo come with me a minute to look at the sea! I've never seen it so high before.

JO. I'd like to go, juffrouw.

KNIERTJE. No, don't leave me alone . . . Is this weather to go to the beach! *(A crashing noise outside.)* Hé!

JO. What was that?

CLEMENTINE. I heard something break.

COBUS *(opens the door letting in a blast of wind)*. God protect me! That missed me by a hair.

JO. Are you hurt?

COBUS. I got a whack on my afterworks . . . a good strong one . . . suppose my head had been there! The tree by the pigpen is broken in two like a pipestem.

KNIERTJE. Did it come down on the shed?

COBUS. I think it did.

KNIERTJE. If only the whole thing hasn't caved in! . . . the wood is so old . . .

JO. Ach, now, no! Tante always expects the worse. *(In surprise)* Uncle

Cobus, what are you doing out in this awful weather and after eight o'clock.

COBUS. Getting a doctor for Daan.

CLEMENTINE. Is old Daan sick?

COBUS. Tja! Took to his bed all of a sudden . . . old age! . . . old age! . . . can't keep anything on his stomach . . . The beans and bacon grease he had for dinner he . . . with your permission . . . threw up right away.

CLEMENTINE. Do they give a sick old man like that beans and bacon grease?

COBUS. Tja! Should the matron roast a chicken or broil a beefsteak for him? She was furious that she had to beat up an egg for him this morning. This afternoon he was out of his head . . . talking about setting nets . . . lighting the beacon . . . about squalls from the north! "He's going fast," I says to the matron. "Just look out that it don't get you," says she. "Matron, the doctor must come," says I. "Attend to your own affairs," says she; "are you the matron or am I the matron?" "You're the matron," says I. "Well, then," says she, but right afterwards she said, "You'd better get the doctor." As if she couldn't have known that just as well at noon! I went for the doctor and the doctor is away. So I came to get Simon to drive me to the city in his dogcart.

CLEMENTINE. If drunken Simon is going to drive you, you have a good chance of rolling off the dyke.

COBUS. He isn't drunk tonight. Hé, what a wind! Listen! Listen now! The tiles will be flying off the roof soon. (A wild blast of wind drowns his voice)

CLEMENTINE. You say Daan is delirious?

COBUS. Yes . . . and a good thing for him, afraid as he was of dying.

CLEMENTINE. Everybody is afraid of dying, Cobus.

COBUS (with deep conviction). Everybody! No, it's just the way you take it. If tomorrow it's my turn . . . then I'll say, "We all have to go. God gives . . . God takes." Now this is something you ought to think about . . . and don't laugh! We take the fish and God takes us. On the fifth day He created the sea and the creatures therein, and He said, "Be fruitful!" and He blessed them. That was evening and that was morning and that

was the fifth day. And on the sixth day He created man, and said to him too, "Be fruitful!" and blessed him too. And that was again evening and again morning . . . and that was the sixth day. No, you mustn't laugh . . . there's no sense in laughing . . . you must reason it out. When I was at the fishing grounds or in the salting sheds sometimes I could hardly make up my mind to use the gutting knife . . . because when you push back a herring's head with your thumb, and the knife lifts out the insides, then that poor beast looks at you with such human eyes! . . . and you have to clean two quintals like that in an hour! And when you cut out the livers . . . a barrel of livers out of fourteen hundred codfish . . . that makes twenty-eight hundred eyes that look at you . . . just look at you . . . only look at you! Don't ask me how many fish I have killed . . . There weren't many that could lift out the bones and the fat livers like I did. Tja. Tja! And how afraid they all were! . . . afraid! They looked up at the clouds as if they were trying to say, "He blessed us just like he did you . . . how can this be?" I say . . . we take the fish and God takes us. We all have to go . . . men have to go . . . beasts have to go. And because we all have to go, it's just the same as if none of us had to go. It's as if you emptied a full barrel into an empty barrel. I would be afraid to stay alone in the empty barrel, but with all the rest in the full barrel, it's all right! It's foolish to be afraid . . . being afraid is like standing on your toes to look over the edge.

KNIERTJE. Is that any way to talk when it's night and the wind is howling so outside! You act as if you'd had a drop too much.

COBUS. A drink? Not even a bowl o coffee, woman! Where can Simon be?

KNIERTJE (listening). Was I right about the pigsty or not? Listen how that poor animal is going on! (Goes toward the door) I'll bet you what you like that the wall has fallen in.

JO. Let me go . . . don't you go outside.

KNIERTJE. Ach, leave me alone. (Goes out through the cooking shed)

JO. Stubborn, isn't she? I'll go help her. Pour yourself a bowl of coffee while we're gone.

CLEMENTINE. Oh, oh, what weather! What a gale! (Coming back to the table) I shall thank God when the Good Hope is safe in port.

COBUS. Tja! there is not one ship safe on the sea tonight . . . but the Good Hope is an old ship and old ships are the last to go down . . .

CLEMENTINE. You say that . . .

COBUS. No, everybody that has sailed says that . . . will you have a bowl, too, juffrouw?

CLEMENTINE. No . . . no thank you. (A silence) I shall pray God tonight to bring the Good Hope in safely.

COBUS. That is very kind of you, juffrouw . . . but the Jacoba is out, and the Matilda is out, and the Expectation is out . . . why should you pray for one ship?

CLEMENTINE. The Good Hope is so rotten! . . . They say . . . they say . . . (She hesitates)

COBUS (gulping his coffee). Who says that?

CLEMENTINE. Someone said . . . and I thought . . . that . . . it just came into my mind . . .

COBUS. Now you sit there talking nonsense—

CLEMENTINE. Oh, you are very polite!

COBUS. If the Good Hope was rotten, your father wouldn't—

CLEMENTINE (as Kniertje opens the door). Shut your big mouth . . . you'll make Kniertje uneasy!

KNIERTJE. A good thing that we went to look . . .

JO. The whole thing was blown down.

KNIERTJE. Oh my poor boys! How frightened Barend will be . . . and just on the homeward journey!

JO. Coffee, mother? . . . tante, I mean! . . . Isn't that crazy? I make that mistake all the time! Won't you have a bowl, juffrouw? The evening is so long and so dreary . . . yes?

SIMON. Good evening!

(Blast of wind blows in as he opens the door.)

KNIERTJE. Shut the door quick—for the lamp!

SIMON. Sallemanders! What a wind!

(To Marietje who follows him, sobbing) Shut up with your bawling!

KNIERTJE. Is anything the matter?

MARIETJE. When I think of Mees . . . in this storm . . .

KNIERTJE. Now, now! Look at Jo! Her sweetheart is out too. Be a good sailor's wife now! Stupid girl! Silly girl! Give her a bowl of coffee to put heart into her.

MARIETJE. It's going on for the sixth week . . .

COBUS. Don't cry before you're hurt. You haven't had anything to stand yet. Is the equipage at the door?

SIMON. I'm damned if I feel like going! If it wasn't for Daan . . .

JO. This will make you feel better, Simon.

SIMON (gulping a mouthful). Salle-manders, that's hot! (Drinks slowly) It happened to me like this once before with the dogcart . . . in just such a storm. That was for Katrien . . . she lay at the point of death. Twice the cart and I were turned upside down together . . . and when I got back with the doctor . . . Katrien was dead and the child was dead! Still, if you ask me, I'd rather be in my cart tonight than on the sea!

KNIERTJE. Yes! Yes!

JO. More coffee?

SIMON. No. Let's not waste our time. Ready, Cobus.

COBUS. If you'll drive careful, now! Good-night, all!

JO. Don't sit there so dumb! Let's talk about something pleasant, and then we won't think about anything . . .

MARIETJE (after a pause). Last night the wind was just as bad . . . and I had such a horrible dream . . . such an awful dream!

CLEMENTINE. Dreams always go by contraries, silly girl!

MARIETJE. I don't really know if it was a dream or not . . . there was a knock on my shutter . . . once . . . I lay still . . . then again . . . I got up, but there was nothing there, nothing . . . but when I laid down again, there was again a knock . . . like that! (She knocks on the table) And then I saw Mees . . . his face was as white as . . . God, oh God! And there was nothing, nothing but the wind!

KNIERTJE *(in deadly fear)*. Knocked three times? . . . three times!

MARIETJE. Like that . . . *(Knocks)* Exactly like that.

JO. You are a blockhead of a girl! . . . to give the old woman such a turn with your knocks!

(There is a knock at the door . . . everybody starts . . . Saart and Truus come in.)

SAART. How queer you all look. 'Day, juffrouw.

TRUUS. May we come in a minute?

JO. Hé, thank God that somebody has come!

SAART. It's wild outside! My neck and ears are full of sand! And cold! Throw on a couple of pieces of wood!

TRUUS. I couldn't stand it at home . . . the children are asleep . . . not a soul to talk to . . . and the wind howling around the house! . . . Two mooring posts have been blown away!

KNIERTJE *(taking up a stocking to darn)*. Two mooring posts!

SAART. Now talk about something else, will you?

JO. That's what I say too . . . why should we . . . milk and sugar? Eh?

SAART. Sugar? Have you got sugar? Of course! What a question!

JO. Well, Geert never takes sugar.

CLEMENTINE. Your little son behaved like a real sailor, Truus. I can see him now standing and waving his hand as they sailed away.

TRUUS *(knitting)*. He's a treasure of a boy . . . and not yet twelve years old . . . You should have seen him, two months ago, when the Anna came back without Arie! How that child acted! Like an angel! Like a grown man! In the evenings he sat up with me . . . and how he talked! That boy knows more than I do. If only the lamb hasn't been terribly seasick! . . .

SAART *(knitting)*. Now, you won't believe me, but if you wear red spectacles you'll never be seasick!

JO *(patching a pair of flannel drawers)*. Hahaha! Have you tried it? You are like the doctors . . . you make other people try your medicine!

SAART. I've slept many a night on board when my man was alive . . . I've made plenty of voyages . . .

JO. I'd like to have seen you in your oilskins!

CLEMENTINE. Have *you* been married, Saart?

SAART. Hé now! The young lady is spreading molasses on my mouth! I've got some looks left, girls . . . do you hear? Have I been married? . . . that I have! He was a good fellow . . . a fine fellow! Only when something didn't go to suit him . . . not to speak ill of him . . . he couldn't keep his paws to himself . . . he smashed everything to pieces! I still have a coffee kettle that he broke the handle off of . . . I wouldn't part with that for any money!

CLEMENTINE. Hahaha! I wouldn't like to risk offering you a gulden for it.

JO. Hé, she tells things so funny! Tell us about the Haarlemmer oil, Saart.

SAART. Yes . . . except for Haarlemmer oil, perhaps I wouldn't be a widow . . . a widow that can't marry again . . .

CLEMENTINE. That sounds interesting.

JO. Oh, you must hear her tell it! Come, drink up your coffee.

SAART. It sticks in my throat. What are you staring at, Knier? That's nothing but the wind. Now then! My husband was a funny fellow . . . you won't find another like him. You'd buy him a knife in a leather case . . . cost money, that . . . and when he came back from the trip five weeks later, you'd say, "Jacob, have you lost the knife?" then he'd say, "I don't know nothing about your knife. I didn't get any knife from you." That's all the good his head did him! But when he undressed . . . the first time in five weeks . . . and pulled off his sea boots . . . down fell the knife to the ground . . . He hadn't felt it all that time!

CLEMENTINE. Five weeks without taking off his rubber boots?

SAART. Or his clothes! And then I had to scrub him with soap and soda . . . no wash water in all that time . . . and thick with lice!

CLEMENTINE. Oh, how awful!

SAART. I wish I could get a cent a dozen for all the dirty bugs on board ship! That's thrown in with their wages! Hahaha!

CLEMENTINE. But what about the Haarlem oil?

SAART. Now then! One day in a storm a big wave threw him against the bulwarks just when one of the crew hauled the mizzen to port . . . and bam . . . his leg was smashed! And there they were! The skipper could make a poultice or cut a corn, but mend a broken leg . . . no! The mate wanted to lash it to a board, but Jacob wouldn't have that . . . he wanted Haarlemmer oil. Every day they had to rub Haarlemmer oil on his leg . . . and again Haarlemmer oil, and over and over Haarlemmer oil! . . . Ach, Jezis! . . . the poor fellow! When they got home, his leg was past help. You oughtn't to have made me tell it.

JO. You laughed at it yourself the last time.

SAART. Yes, yes. Well, you can't bring the dead to life. And if you stop to think it over it's a dirty shame that I can't marry again!

CLEMENTINE. Can't marry? Who prevents you?

SAART. Who? The fools that muddle up our laws! A year later the Caprice went down with mice and men . . . You'd sure think that if your man was dead . . . because Jacob had gone along with his leg and a half . . . you could marry another man. Not much! You've got to put three times in the paper a notice that your husband is missing and then if three times you don't get any sign of life from him you can get a new license.

TRUUS. I don't think I will ever marry again.

SAART. Why should you? You've been married twice already . . . if you haven't had enough of men by this time . . .

TRUUS. I wish I could tell things the way you do . . . No . . . it's too much anxiety! . . . I can't stand it. With my first it was a nightmare . . .

CLEMENTINE. Tell us about it, Truus. I could sit night after night listening to these stories of the sea.

KNIERTJE. Don't tell us anything about death and anxiety!

SAART. Hé, don't grumble so! (To Truus) Go on and tell it. (To Jo) Pour us some more coffee.

TRUUS (knitting quietly and speaking in a toneless voice). It was years ago . . . I lived in Vlaardingen then and I was a year married without children . . . Pietje is Arie's son . . . My man sailed to the herring grounds on the Magnet . . . and you know what happened. The Magnet went to the bottom somewhere . . but I didn't know it and wasn't thinking of such a thing . . .

JO (startled by a wild blast of wind). Sst! Be still a minute!

SAART. It's nothing . . . only the wind.

TRUUS. Now then . . . in Vlaardingen there is a tower, and on the tower is a lookout . . .

MARIETJE (knitting). They have that in Maassluis too . . .

TRUUS. And the lookout hoists a red ball when he sights a lugger or a trawler or a sloop in the distance . . . and when he sees what ship it is . . . and it's wonderful how he can recognize a ship by its masts, by its rigging, by its sails, by the cut of its bow . . . then he hoists the red ball and runs to tell the owner and the families of the crew. But he don't need to tell the families, because as soon as the ball is hoisted the children run through the streets crying, "The ball's up! The ball's up!" I did it too when I was young. Then the women go to the tower and wait below until the lookout comes down and if it is their ship they give him money.

CLEMENTINE. And then? . . .

TRUUS (staring into the fire). The Magnet with my first husband . . . I told you I had only been married a year . . . the Magnet stayed out seven weeks, eight weeks . . . with provisions for only six. And every time the children screamed, "The ball's up, Truus! The ball's up!" I ran like a crazy woman to the tower, and when the lookout came down I could have torn the words out of his mouth . . . but I couldn't even ask, "Is it the Magnet?" . . . only stare at him . . . and he would say, "No, it's the Concordia, or the Maria, or the Fidelity." And I would drag myself away, crying and praying to God that he would bring the Magnet in safely. And the Magnet never came . . . never came . . . That lasted for two months . . . two months . . . and then I had to believe it. *(Tonelessly)* The fish are dearly paid for!

CLEMENTINE *(fascinated)*. And Arie? What was it that happened to Arie?

JO. No, now . . . that happened such a little while ago.

TRUUS. Ach, child, I would like to talk about him to everybody and all day long. Such a splendid man . . . never a hard word from him . . . Never! In two hours he was dead . . . a blow from the windlass . . . never spoke again. If it had happened a week later they could have brought him home to me . . . I could have buried him here . . . but the sharks were already swimming around the ship . . . they smell it when there's a dead man on board.

KNIERTJE. Yes, that's true.

TRUUS. You'll never know what it is to be a fisherman's wife, juffrouw . . . but it's heartbreaking . . . heartbreaking . . . God . . . how heartbreaking, when the one you love is lashed to a board, wrapped in a piece of sailcloth with a stone inside . . . and then . . . three times around the main mast . . . "One, two, three . . . in God's name!" The fish are dearly paid for! *(She sobs softly)*

MARIETJE. It was that that made a drunkard of my father. When the Alert went down with Toontje, my little brother, and father brought home the wages that were coming to him as rope-caster . . . eighteen gulden . . . he acted as if he was crazy! . . . threw the money on the floor . . . and cursed . . . Cursed . . . I couldn't tell you what he said! And I . . . I was fourteen years old then . . . I picked up the money, crying . . . we had to have it . . . Eighteen gulden is a lot of money . . . a lot!

JO. Eighteen gulden for your child! . . . eighteen . . . *(A violent gust of wind startles them all.)* Be still a minute!

SAART. It's nothing at all. What makes you so easy frightened tonight?

JO. Frightened? I'm not frightened. Hahaha! Me . . . frightened!

KNIERTJE. Yes, yes! If the sea could speak . . .

CLEMENTINE. You tell us a story now, Kniertje. You have lived through so much.

KNIERTJE. Ach, juffrouw, life on the sea isn't a thing to make stories about. It is just work. The men work hard and the women work hard.

CLEMENTINE. But it must be so exciting!

KNIERTJE *(quietly)*. Just the thickness of a plank between you and eternity! *(A silence)* Yesterday evening I went past the burgemeester house. They were sitting at the table and boiled codfish with livers sent up a thick steam. The children were saying grace with folded hands. Then I thought . . . if I was wrong, may God forgive me . . . that it was not good of the burgemeester . . . not of the burgemeester . . . not of other people! For the wind blew so terribly, so terribly off the sea . . . and the fish came out of the same water where our dead . . . how shall I say that . . . where our dead . . . *(After a silence)* It isn't good to get such ideas . . . that is your living and you mustn't quarrel with your living.

TRUUS. Yes . . . she knows what she is talking about.

KNIERTJE. My husband was a fisherman . . . one in a thousand. When they dropped the lead he could tell by the sand they brought up just where they were. In the black nights he would say, "We are at fifty-six," and they would be at fifty-six. He felt it! What hasn't he gone through on the sea! Cut off from the ship by the fog . . . caught in a norther, fighting wind and water until the lugger sank under them . . . floating a day and a night on an overturned rowboat with another man who had gone raving crazy from a blow on the head . . . he never talked much about such things, they were just a part of his work. And in the end he went down on the Doggersbank in the Clementine . . . the boat your father named after you . . . he and my two oldest sons. That was twelve years ago. What happened to them I don't know . . . shall never know. Never a hatch nor a spar from the ship was washed ashore. Nothing. Nothing. At first it seemed as if it couldn't be true, but after so many years, you don't even remember their faces well any more. And for that you are thankful. It would be terrible if you should remember always. Now you have my story too. Every seaman's wife has such things in her family. Truus is right. The fish are dearly paid for. Are you crying, juffrouw?

CLEMENTINE *(bursting into tears)*. God! If only no ships go down tonight!

KNIERTJE. We are all in God's hands . . . and God is great and good.

CLEMENTINE. If only no ships go down tonight!

JO *(starting up wildly)*. Ships go down! Ships go down! You are enough to drive anyone crazy! *(Pounding her head with her fists)* One snivels . . . another bawls . . . I wish that I had sat by myself tonight!

CLEMENTINE *(alarmed)*. Jo, what is the matter?

JO *(passionately)*. Her husband . . . and her little brother . . . and my poor uncle! Such horrible stories! Instead of trying to cheer each other up! Why don't you ask *me* something? *(Screaming)* My father was drowned! . . . drowned! . . . drowned! And hundreds more have been drowned! And . . . and you are all horrible . . . horrible . . . horrible! *(Rushes out shutting the door violently behind her)*

MARIETJE. Shall I go after her?

KNIERTJE. No, child. Let her alone. She will come to herself outside. These two days of the storm have been too much for her. Are you going, juffrouw?

CLEMENTINE. It is late, Knier . . . and your niece . . . your niece forgot herself a little . . . no, I am not angry. Who will take me home?

SAART. If one goes, we'll all go. If we stick together we won't blow away. Good night, Knier.

MARIETJE. Good night, tante.

KNIERTJE. Thank you again, juffrouw, for the broth and the eggs.

TRUUS. Will you come to my house tomorrow for a bowl of coffee? Please now, say yes.

KNIERTJE. Well, perhaps. Good night, juffrouw. Good night, Marietje, good night, Saart. If you see Jo, send her in right away, will you? *(The wind shrieks, sweeping wildly around the house . . . she listens anxiously at the window . . . turns and gathers up the bowls . . . pushes a chair close to the fire . . . stares into the flames, her lips moving silently as she slips her rosary through her fingers . . . Jo comes in, drops into a chair by the window and unfastens her neckerchief nervously)* It's good that you are going to bed . . . you are all upset. How you talked! And that dear child that came through wind and weather to bring me broth and eggs!

JO *(roughly)*. Your sons are out in wind and weather for her and her father . . .

KNIERTJE. For us too . . .

JO. Yes, for us too . . . *(A silence)* The sea is so wild!

KNIERTJE. Did you go down to look?

JO. I couldn't stand up against the wind. The pier is under water . . . half the railing is washed away! *(A silence)* I'm half crazy from those dreadful stories!

KNIERTJE. I don't understand you tonight. You never acted like this when Geert went away with the Marines. Go to bed now and pray. Praying is the only comfort. A sailor's wife can't be weak. . . . After this storm there will be others . . . there are always storms . . . and there are other fishermen on the sea beside our boys! *(Her words sink into soft whispers . . . her old fingers touch the rosary gently)*

JO *(suddenly)*. We almost drove Barend away . . . I nagged at him till the last minute. *(Seeing that Kniertje is praying again she goes to the window, wringing her hands . . . pulls the curtain up hesitatingly, stares into the night . . . then cautiously opens a swinging pane. The wind swells the curtain out . . . the lamp flame dances . . . goes out. She closes the window quickly)*

KNIERTJE *(startled and angry)*. Now that's a crazy trick! Keep your paws off the window.

JO *(moaning)*. Oh! Oh! Oh!

KNIERTJE *(alarmed)*. Will you be quiet! Bring me the matches! Hurry up a little! They're by the soap dish. Have you got them? *(Jo lights the lamp, sobbing.)* I'm cold all over from that wind! *(Jo crouches by the fire, crying.)* Why do you sit like that?

JO *(shivering)*. I'm afraid.

KNIERTJE *(anxiously)*. You mustn't be afraid.

JO. If anything happens then . . . then . . .

KNIERTJE. Be sensible now and undress yourself for bed.

JO. I'm going to stay here all night.

KNIERTJE. I ask you now . . . how are you going to stand it . . . when you are married . . . when you're a mother yourself!

JO (wildly). You don't know what you're saying, tante . . . you don't know what you're saying! If Geert . . . (Breathes heavily) I haven't dared to tell you . . .

KNIERTJE. Is there something between you and Geert? . . . (Jo sobs harder.) That wasn't nice of you . . . to have secrets from me. Your sweetheart . . . your man . . . is my son. (A silence . . . the wind shrieks.) Don't cry any more . . . don't stare into the fire like that . . . I won't say any hard words to you . . . though it was wrong . . . of you and of him. Come sit beside me, and we will pray together.

JO (despairingly). I will not pray!

KNIERTJE. Not pray!

JO (distracted). If anything should happen . . .

KNIERTJE. Nothing will happen.

JO (wildly). If anything . . . anything . . . anything . . . then I'll never pray again . . . never! Then there is no God and no Mother Mary . . . then there is nothing . . . nothing!

KNIERTJE. Don't talk like that.

JO (wailing). What can you do with a child . . . when you haven't got a husband!

KNIERTJE. What are you saying?

JO (beating her head on the table). The wind . . . the wind . . . is driving me crazy . . . crazy . . .

(Kniertje opens her prayer book, touches Jo on the arm. Jo shakes her head, pushes the prayer book away, lets her head drop on the table again, sobbing passionately. The wind sweeps furiously around the house.)

KNIERTJE. Almighty God, I believe in your love with a confident faith . . . I believe . . . in your eternal compassion—

CURTAIN

ACT FOUR

One week later. The office of Clemens Bos. Right, down stage, the outside door, separated from the office by a railing. Between the door and the railing are two wooden benches. In the back, three windows looking out on the sea, dancing in the sunshine. In front of the middle window, a desk. Left down stage, a desk. Upstage left, a door leading to the dwelling. Between the desk and the door, a safe. On the walls, a blackboard with notices of wreckage, auctions . . . maps, a picture of a ship. In the center of the office a large round iron stove.

MATHILDE (entering from the dwelling rooms). Clemens!

KAPS (reading, his pipe in his mouth). "The following articles of wreakage . . . 2447 ribs, marked 'Kusta' . . . ten sails, marked 'M.G.S.'" . . .

MATHILDE. Be still a minute, Kaps. Bos!

KAPS. "Four deck timbers, two masts, five towing lines . . ."

BOS (impatiently). I have no time now.

MATHILDE. Then make time. I have drawn up the circular for the tower clock subscription. Please ring up the burgemeester.

BOS (taking up the telephone impatiently). Hello! Connect me with the burgemeester. Hurry up now. (Waits) This damn nonsense while I'm up to my ears in work! (Through the telephone, pleasantly) Are you there, burgemeester? My little wife asks . . .

MATHILDE. If mevrouw will come to the telephone a minute about the subscription.

BOS (disagreeably). Now, now! Make it short! (Pleasantly) Can mevrouw come to the telephone a minute? Exactly, burgemeester. The ladies . . . you understand. Hahaha! That's very good. (Sharply, to Mathilde) Now, what am I to say? Hurry!

MATHILDE. Here, read the circular to her. Then it can go to the printer.

BOS (furiously). All that? Are you crazy? Do you think I haven't got anything to do?

MATHILDE (with a look at Kaps). Think of appearances a little!

BOS. You go to hell! *(Pleasantly)* Yes, mevrouw, Good morning, mevrouw. My little wife? No, she can't come to the telephone. She doesn't know how to use it. *(To Mathilde)* Where is that rag? Quick now! *(Pleasantly)* My little wife has written out the subscription sheet for the tower clock . . . I'll read it to you. . . . Can you hear? "Ladies and Gentlemen!" What do you say? What do you say? You would like better, "Dear Fellow Citizens" . . . Yes, yes. Quite right. Can you hear me? "You have undoubtedly heard of the New Church" *(To Mathilde)* she says "no" . . . the stupid thing! Yes, mevrouw, I'm reading . . . "You have undoubtedly heard of the New Church. This church as you know has a high tower. This tower points to heaven, and that is good . . . that is fortunate, and indeed a necessary reminder for the people of this generation."

MATHILDE. Read more distinctly.

BOS. Hold your jaw! Pardon, I was speaking to my bookkeeper. Yes, yes! Hahaha! "But the tower can do something else, which is also good and also necessary . . . it can indicate the time to us, the children of these times. That it does not do. It has stood there since 1882 and has never given an answer to the question, 'What time is it?' It should do that. It was built for that purpose. The citizens wish it." Did you say something, mevrouw? No? "About three thousand gulden will be necessary. Who will help us?" What did you say, mevrouw? Of course you know the names. Yes, yes . . . very well drawn up. Yes, yes . . . all the ladies of the committee will naturally subscribe the same amount. A hundred gulden each. Yes, very good. Yes, my wife will be at home. Good-by, mevrouw. *(Hangs up the receiver ill-humoredly)* Damned nonsense! A hundred gulden thrown to the dogs! What difference does it make to you if there is a clock on that thing or not!

MATHILDE. I'll just let you stew in your own juice.

BOS. She'll be here in fifteen minutes in her carriage. Now, get out. *(Turns back to his desk)*

MATHILDE. Get out! Get out! If you drank less grog at night you wouldn't be in such a bad humor in the morning. Give me five gulden.

BOS. No. You took two gulden out of my pocket this morning while I was asleep . . . I can't keep up with you.

MATHILDE. Bah! . . . what a man! . . . to count his money before he goes to bed. I only took one gulden.

BOS. Get out!

MATHILDE. Don't give it to me then. When the burgemeester's wife comes I can treat her to a glass of gin. Three jugs of your nasty gin in the house and not a bottle of port or sherry! *(Bos throws her some money impatiently)* Well, am I your servant! Without me you wouldn't be able to throw money around like that. *(Goes off)*

KAPS *(reading)*. "Ijmuiden, December 24 . . . today five sloops came into port with 500 to 800 live haddock each, 1500 to 2100 dead haddock and a quantity of live codfish . . ."

BOS. Is that all you've got to do?

KAPS. "The live codfish brought seven and a quarter and the dead haddock brought thirteen and a half gulden a basket . . . flat fish and ray brought" . . .

BOS *(pounding on the desk)*. I know all that. Here, take this ledger. Turn to the Expectation's account. Set this down.

KAPS *(turning the pages)*. The Jacoba . . . the Queen Wilhelmina . . . the Matilda . . . the Good Hope . . . you can whistle for her! . . . here it is . . . the Expectation . . .

BOS. What is the gross sum?

KAPS. 144,347 gulden.

BOS. I thought so. How could you have been so ungodly stupid as to deduct four gulden and eighty-eight cents for the Widows and Orphans Fund? *(Getting up angrily)* If you're on the way to become a complete idiot, you blockhead . . . there's the door open for you. You make mistakes the whole goddamned time and always against us.

KAPS *(laughing confidentially)*. I might say something in my defense, meneer. I didn't get a tongue-lashing when . . . when . . .

BOS. That's enough now . . .

KAPS. And *that* was a mistake with a couple of big zero's behind it! héhéhé!

(Bos goes out impatiently. Kaps fills his pipe from Bos' tobacco jar, pokes the fire, looks up as Simon enters.)

SIMON. Isn't Bos here?

KAPS. Meneer Bos, eh? No.

SIMON. Is he out?

KAPS. Give me your message.

SIMON. I ask you if he is out.

KAPS. Yes.

SIMON. No news yet?

KAPS. No. Is that running to the office going to begin again? Meneer said he would tell you when he had any news.

SIMON. It will be nine weeks to-morrow.

KAPS. What of it? The Jacoba came in after fifty-nine days and brought in a hundred and ninety quintals.

SIMON. You know something.

KAPS. Are you full of gin this early?

SIMON. No, not a drop.

KAPS. Then it's time you were! I know something? Do I pull the ships in by a rope?

SIMON. I gave you warning when she still was in dry dock. . . . What did I say to you then?

KAPS. A lot of crazy talk trying to stick somebody for a drink.

SIMON. You lie! You were there and the juffrouw was there. . . . I said the whole ship was rotten . . . that the damn thing couldn't be patched up any more . . . that such a floating coffin . . .

KAPS. Yes, you said all that. I won't argue about that. But what of it? Are you so important that we have to listen to you even when you're dead drunk?

SIMON. That's a damn lie! I wasn't drunk!

KAPS. All right then, you weren't drunk. Are you such a little god that when you, the shipbuilder's assistant, say "no," my patron must take his ship and scrap it, even when the insurance company says "yes"?

SIMON. I gave you warning . . . and now I say . . . now I say . . . that if Mees, my daughter's sweetheart . . . if Mees . . . to say nothing of the others . . . there'll be murder done!

KAPS. How funny you are! Go get a few drinks inside of you then perhaps you can talk sense.

SIMON *(as Marietje comes through the door)*. You ought to have stayed outside. There's no news.

MARIETJE. No news yet?

SIMON. I tell you there'll be murder done! *(They go out)*

BOS *(coming back)*. Who was here?

KAPS. Simon and his daughter. Threatening you. Are you going out?

BOS. Threatening? Is the fellow crazy? I'll be back in ten minutes . . . Whoever comes will have to wait. *(Goes off)*

KAPS *(as the telephone rings)*. I can't understand you! I am the bookkeeper. Meneer will be back in ten minutes. You must ring up again. *(He turns as Saart comes in)*

SAART. 'Day, sweetheart.

KAPS. What do you want now!

SAART. I want you. Jezis, what a cold wind! Can I warm my hands a little?

KAPS. Keep back of the railing.

SAART. You go to the devil, sweetheart! Meneer Bos isn't here . . . he just went round the corner. I didn't come to ask about the Good Hope. *(Edges through the gate of the railing and warms her hands at the stove)*

KAPS. I wish you'd get back of the railing. *(Tries to push her out)*

SAART *(peering into his coat pocket)*. Look out! Haha! Don't break meneer's cigars, you old thief! Kaps, would you like to earn a gulden from me?

KAPS. That depends.

SAART. I've promised to marry Bol, the skipper.

KAPS. Congratulations.

SAART. He's lying here at the dock with a load of manure for the city. And now, how am I going to marry him?

KAPS. How? . . .

SAART. I can't marry yet because they don't know if my husband is dead.

KAPS. The legal time is . . . is . . .

SAART. I'm that smart myself.

KAPS. You must put a notice in the paper three times and if he doesn't come back . . . and he won't come back for there are no spooks in this world . . . then you can get a new license.

SAART. If you would just do that for us, Bol and I would be thankful to you always.

KAPS. Lawyers' work. You have to go to the city for that.

SAART. Jezis! What a lot of bother! When your good sense tells you! I haven't seen Jacob for three years! and the Caprice—

COBUS (pushing the door open trembling with agitation). You have news! You have news!

KAPS. News? What are you talking about?

COBUS (his voice shaking). You have some news of the Good Hope . . . of . . . of the boys?

KAPS. Nothing. (More kindly) What good does it do to wear out the floor of the office running here day after day? I can give you neither good news nor bad news . . . the bad you know yourself, anyway . . . sixty-five days out . . .

COBUS. The water-bailiff got a telegram . . . Ach, ach, ach, meneer Kaps . . . help us out of this uncertainty. My sister and my niece . . . are out of their heads with anxiety.

KAPS. On my word of honor, there is nothing. Are you going?

COBUS. There must be something . . . there must be something!

KAPS. Who told you there was news?

COBUS. The water-bailiff's clerk said . . . ach, dear God! (Goes off)

SAART. Perhaps he's right.

KAPS. Anything can happen.

SAART. Does meneer Bos still have hope?

KAPS. Hope? After nine weeks . . . that death ship . . . in such a storm! Provisions for only six weeks! I wouldn't give a penny for their chances. If they had run into an English port we would have had news.

CLEMENTINE (coming in from the street). Are there visitors in the house, Kaps? 'Day, Saart. Whose carriage is that outside?

KAPS (looking out of the window). The burgemeester . . . A committee meeting for the tower clock subscription. Another new span of horses! . . . I wish I had the money they cost!

CLEMENTINE (laying her sketch book on the desk). I saw Cobus walking down the street. Poor fellow! How old he has grown! I would hardly have recognized him. (Opening the sketch book) See! That's the way he looked three months ago. Jolly . . . lively! You can look too, Kaps.

KAPS. No, juffrouw, I haven't time.

SAART. He took Daantje's death very hard. You always saw those two together . . . always arguing about something. He hasn't a friend left in the Home now. It makes a lot of difference to him.

CLEMENTINE. Do you recognize the others?

SAART. I should say! That's Kniertje . . . that's Barend with the wood basket on his back . . . and that's . . .

(The telephone rings.)

KAPS. Meneer is out. Someone called up a little while ago.

CLEMENTINE (taking the telephone). Yes? Father isn't here. How long will he be gone, Kaps?

KAPS. Only a few minutes.

CLEMENTINE (startled). What do you say? A hatch marked 47? and . . . I don't understand you . . . (Screams and drops the receiver)

KAPS. What is it? What is it?

CLEMENTINE (terribly agitated). I can't listen any more . . . Oh, oh!

KAPS. Was that the water-bailiff?

CLEMENTINE. Barend's body has been washed ashore! Oh, God! . . . now it's all over!

SAART. Barend? Barend?

CLEMENTINE. A telegram from Nieuwediep . . . a hatch . . . and a body!

BOS. What's going on here? What are you crying about, girl?

KAPS. News of the Good Hope.

BOS. News?

KAPS. The water-bailiff is on the phone.

BOS. The water-bailiff? (Pushing Clementine away) Stand aside! Get out of my way! (To Saart) What are you gaping at?

SAART. I . . . I . . . (She hurries out)

BOS. Hello! Who is there? The water-bailiff? A telegram from Nieuwediep? I can't hear a word! (To Clementine) Stop that howling! A hatch, you say? Marked 47—Hell and damnation! And a body . . . in a state of decomposition? Barend Vermeer, signed on as head boy? Recognized by who? Who? Oh, the skipper of the Expectation. By his earrings? Yes, yes, silver earrings. That is sufficient then. It won't be necessary to send anyone from here to identify the body? Curse the luck! This village is cursed! Well, well . . . against God's will we are powerless. Yes, yes. I have been sure of it for some time. Thank you. Yes. I would like to have the official report as soon as possible. I will notify the underwriters. Good-by! *(Hangs up the receiver heavily)* That's a blow! A knockout blow! Twelve men!

KAPS. Barend, the son of old Kniertje? Washed ashore! Now, that's astonishing. I thought we'd never hear anything more of that ship . . . like the Clementine.

BOS *(angrily)*. Yes, yes, yes. *(To Clementine)* Will you be good enough to go inside there with your mother! What stupidity to talk before that woman . . . now inside of five minutes half the village will be here . . . Don't you hear me? You sit there, God help you, going on as if your sweetheart had been on board.

CLEMENTINE *(still sobbing)*. Why didn't you listen to Simon?

BOS. The fellow was drunk.

CLEMENTINE *(emphatically)*. He was not drunk!

BOS. He was! And if he wasn't, why do you stick your nose into things that are none of your business!

CLEMENTINE. I am guilty too . . .

BOS *(furiously)*. Guilty! Guilty! Have the novels you have read addled your brain? Guilty! Are you out of your head to use such words about a misfortune . . . a visitation . . .

CLEMENTINE. He said the ship was a floating coffin . . . and I heard . . . I heard you say that in any event it would be the last voyage of the Good Hope . . .

BOS *(beginning angrily, but ending argumentatively)*. That cursed boarding school . . . those damned boarding school notions! Run around the village as much as you like making a fool of yourself sketching the loafers and beggars you meet . . . but don't go blurting out things that you have no foundation for. What do you know about affairs here? A floating coffin! Did you hear him say that, Kaps?

KAPS *(uneasily)*. No, meneer, I heard nothing.

BOS. A floating coffin! An authority floating in gin! The Discovery and the Willem III and Pietersen's North Wind and the Jonge Jan . . . I can name a hundred . . . half the fishing fleet and half the freight boats are floating coffins . . .

CLEMENTINE. But, father . . .

BOS. . . . What do you need more than the yearly inspection of the ship by the underwriters? Do you think that when I call them up presently and say, "Gentlemen, you can plank down fourteen thousand gulden!" that they would pay that on a floating coffin? Your face should be burning with shame at the thought of the nonsense that you have been babbling! Nonsense? Nonsense, that might ruin my good name if I was not so well known by everybody!

CLEMENTINE. If I was a shipowner . . . and I heard . . .

BOS. May God protect the fishermen from a shipowner who draws little pictures and sheds tears over pretty poetry! I stand as father and protector to more than a hundred families. Business is business. Now, go to your mother. The burgemeester's wife is making a call.

KAPS. I have the list of the crew here. *(Begins to read)* Willem Hengst, thirty-seven years, married, four children.

BOS. Wait until she goes.

CLEMENTINE. I won't say another word.

KAPS *(continuing)*. Jacob Swart, thirty-five years, married, three children, Gerrit Plaas, twenty-five years, married, one child. Geert Vermeer, twenty-six years, unmarried. Nelis Boom, thirty-five years, married, seven children. Klaas Steen, twenty-five years, married. Salomon Bergen, twenty-five years, married, one child. Mari Stad, married. Mees Meijer, nineteen, unmarried. Jacob Boom, twenty years. Barend Vermeer, eighteen years, and Pietje Stappers, twelve years.

BOS *(shocked)*. Seven families.

CLEMENTINE. Sixteen children.

TRUUS *(throwing open the door, gasping for breath)*. Is there news? Is there any news of my little son? Ach, God! Ach, God! Have pity on me, meneer!

BOS. I'm sorry, mevrouw Stappers . . .

MARIETJE *(following on the heels of Truus).* It can't be! It can't be! You lie! It isn't possible.

BOS *(gently).* The beach-inspector at Nieuwediep telegraphed to the water-bailiff . . . the body of Barend Vermeer had been washed ashore . . . you know what that means . . . and a hatch from the Good Hope.

TRUUS *(violently).* Oh, Mother Mary, must I lose that child too! That lamb . . . not twelve years old! *(Moaning and sobbing)* Oh, Oh! Oh! Pietje! Pietje!

MARIETJE *(wild with grief).* Then . . . then . . . *(She bursts into hysterical laughter)* Hahaha! Hahaha!

BOS. Give her a glass of water.

MARIETJE *(dashing the glass from Clementine's hand).* Go away! Go away! *(Falling on her knees, grasping the railing with both hands)* Kill me too! Let me die too . . . in mercy . . . dear God! . . . dear God!

CLEMENTINE *(sobbing).* Please, Marietje . . . don't scream so . . . stand up . . .

TRUUS. On his first voyage . . . and how brave he stood there waving, when the ship . . . *(Sobs violently)*

BOS. It can't be helped, Truus. It is an act of God. There hasn't been such a storm in years. Think of Hengst with four children, and Jacob and Gerrit. And . . . though it will be no consolation to you now . . . I will pay you your little son's wages . . . today if you like. Go home now, and resign yourselves to the inevitable. *(Pointing to Marietje)* Take her with you . . . She's not fit to go alone.

MARIETJE. I won't go home . . . I want to die . . . to die! . . . to die!

CLEMENTINE *(lifting her up).* Cry it out, Marietje . . . cry it out, you poor lamb . . . *(They go out together.)*

BOS *(to Kaps, striding up and down angrily).* Why are you so stupid today? Are you too lazy to put pen to paper? No, I don't want any answer from you. Have you the Widows and Orphans Fund ledger at hand? Now? Now?

KAPS *(shuffling to the safe).* The compartment is locked. *(Bos throws him the keys.)* Thank you. *(Takes out the ledger and shuffles back to the desk)*

BOS *(turning over the leaves).* Ninety-five widows . . . fourteen old seamen and fishermen . . .

KAPS. Yes, we have been short of funds for a long time. It is time to send another petition to the public.

MATHILDE *(entering in a flurry).* Bos! What a catastrophe! The burgemeester's wife asks if you can come in to talk to her a moment. She sits there crying!

BOS. No. Enough bawling here. And no time!

MATHILDE. Ach! Ach! Kaps, here is the draft of the circular. Hurry with it please.

BOS. Mathilde! Talk to mevrouw right away about taking up a collection for the unfortunate victims.

MATHILDE. Yes, but Clemens . . . isn't that too much? Two subscriptions at the same time?

BOS. Leave it to me, then.
(They go off together.)

CLEMENTINE *(coming back crying softly).* Kaps! Kaps, I am so terribly unhappy! *(Goes over to him and sits down by the desk)* I'm heartsick!

KAPS. Absolutely without reason, juffrouw. Ships founder every day. Among so many the Good Hope hardly counts. I have here . . . where is it . . . where is it? The official statement for the month of October. In one month . . . in one month only . . . 105 sail ships went down and 30 steam ships. That's considered a small average . . . only fifteen hundred drowned. *(He points to the sea)* Yes, when you see it as it is today, so smooth, with the sea gulls floating on the waves . . . you can hardly believe that it has murdered so many people . . . *(While they are talking Cobus and Jo come in and sit down dejectedly on the bench outside the railing.)*

CLEMENTINE. Come in, Jo . . . come in!
(Jo shakes her head.)

COBUS *(trembling).* We have just come from the house . . . because Saart . . . just as I said! . . . just as I said . . .

BOS *(coming back from the dwelling rooms).* Come in, Jo . . . sit down. *(He pushes a chair near the stove)* You stay there, Cobus . . . I suppose you have already heard . . .

JO *(bursting into tears)*. About Barend, yes . . . but Geert . . . and it happens so often that they drift in rowboats . . .

BOS. No, I can't give you that hope . . . after all those days . . . and the body was in an advanced state of decomposition . . .

JO *(anxiously)*. Yes, yes. Then perhaps it isn't Barend. Who says that it is Barend?

BOS. Skipper Maatsuiker of the Expectation identified him . . . by the earrings.

JO. Maatsuiker? Maatsuiker? But suppose he made a mistake . . . there are other earrings. I came to ask you for some money, meneer, so I can go myself to Nieuwediep.

BOS. Come now, what foolishness!

JO *(crying)*. But Barend will have to be buried. . .

BOS. The Burgemeester of Nieuwediep will attend to that.

SIMON *(lurching in from the street, half drunk)*. I . . . I've just heard . . . just heard . . . *(Staggers toward Bos with convulsive gestures)*

BOS *(drawing back in fear)*. Get out of here, you drunken beast!

SIMON *(stammering)*. I . . . I'm not going to kill you . . . I have . . . have . . . haven't anything wicked in my mind . . .

BOS *(agitated)*. Call a guard, Kaps . . . this drunken fellow must . . .

SIMON *(holding himself up by the railing)*. No . . . stay there. I'll go myself . . . I . . . I . . . only wanted to say . . . that it's come out fine . . . with . . . with the Good Hope!

BOS. Get to hell out of here!

SIMON *(reeling, almost losing his balance)*. Don't come so close to me . . . you must never get too close to a man with a knife! Nooo! I don't mean anything wicked . . . I just want to say that I gave you warning . . . while . . . the ship was still in dry dock!

BOS. You lie, you drunken rascal!

SIMON *(more quietly)*. Now you must . . . just for the fun of it . . . you must . . . you must ask your bookkeeper . . . and your daughter . . . who were there . . .

BOS *(violently)*. That's a lie! You're not worth answering, you drunken sot! My dealings are with your employer, not

with you. Didn't you hear me, Kaps? The guard!

SIMON *(waving back and forth on his unsteady feet)*. My employer . . . he . . . he doesn't do the caulking! *(To Kaps, who has approached the railing)* Did I warn him? Were you there? Yes or no!

KAPS *(looking anxiously to Bos)*. No, I wasn't there . . . and if I was there, I didn't hear anything.

BOS *(to Clementine)*. And you now? Did this drunkard . . .

CLEMENTINE *(almost hysterical)*. Father!

BOS *(threateningly)*. You, as my daughter . . . *(Grimly)* give your answer.

CLEMENTINE *(agitated—in a low voice)*. I don't remember . . .

SIMON. That's mean . . . that's low . . . that's damned low! I said the ship was rotten . . . rotten . . .

BOS. A drunkard's ravings! You try to drag my daughter and my bookkeeper into it . . . and you see . . .

COBUS *(trembling)*. But . . . yes, now . . . I remember it too!

BOS. What the devil! Did you give me warning too?

COBUS. No . . . I don't say that. That would be a lie. But your daughter . . . your daughter, she said just now that she never heard that the ship was rotten . . . But the second night of the storm, when she was alone with me at my sister Kniertje's . . . then she said . . . that . . . that . . .

CLEMENTINE *(her voice shaking)*. Did I . . .

COBUS *(angrily)*. Yes. That you did. That very evening . . . and I said . . . these were my words, "Now, you sit there talking nonsense . . . because if your father knew that the Good Hope was rotten . . ."

CLEMENTINE. I—I—

JO *(springing up passionately, the words struggling furiously between clenched teeth)*. You . . . you lie! You began to cry! You were afraid the ship would sink! I was there! Truus was there! . . . Saart was there! Oh, you vipers! You vipers!

BOS *(pounding the desk with his fist)*. Vipers? Vipers? We who have given you your food year after year, you vermin! Haven't you the decency to believe us instead of this filthy rascal who stands there wabbling on his drunken legs?

JO (*raving*). Believe you? You? She lies and you lie! . . .

BOS. Out of my office!

JO (*beside herself*). You had Barend dragged on board by the Coast Guard . . . he knew the ship was rotten! Geert was too proud to be afraid! . . . Murderer! Murderer! (*Laughing hysterically*) No, no! You don't need to point to the door . . . we're going. If I stayed here any longer I'd spit in your face . . . spit in your face! . . .

COBUS (*holding her back*). Now! Now!

BOS (*after a silence*). Out of respect for your aunt, who is a decent woman, I will take it that you are overwrought . . . otherwise . . . otherwise . . . (*Firmly*) The Good Hope was seaworthy . . . perfectly seaworthy. (*A silence*) I am standing a big loss, even though the ship is insured. And even if that fellow *had* warned me, should I, as a businessman, trust the word of a sot who was thrown out of his job because he is unfit to handle his tools any longer?

SIMON (*stuttering*). I . . . I . . . I said to you and to him and to her . . . that a floating coffin like that . . . That's the truth now!

JO (*passionately*). Oh! Oh! Geert and Barend and Mees and all the others. (*Sinks into a chair sobbing*) Oh, God, how could you let it happen . . . how could you! . . . (*To Bos, after a silence*) Give me the money to go myself to Nieuwediep . . . then I'll say nothing more.

BOS (*grimly*). No. Not a red cent. A girl that has clapper-clawed me so impudently . . .

JO (*completely unnerved*). I didn't know what I was saying . . . and . . . and . . . I don't believe that you . . . that you! . . . then you would be more wicked than the devil!

BOS. The water-bailiff says that it isn't necessary to send anyone to Nieuwediep.

JO (*stumbling to the door*). Not necessary! Not necessary! what will become of me now! . . .

(*Cobus and Simon follow her out. Bos strides up and down. Kaps climbs on his stool and buries his head in his ledgers.*)

BOS (*to Clementine, stopping suddenly*). And if you ever set foot in my office again . . .

CLEMENTINE. No. Never again. (*A silence*) Father, I ask myself . . . can I ever respect you again? Can I ever respect myself again? (*Goes out*)

BOS. If anyone else comes, send them away . . . understand? Trash! Rabble! The whole pack isn't worth the snap of my finger! That damned drunken rag . . . stinking of gin! (*Jelle's violin is heard outside.*) And that . . . we have to have too! (*At the window*) Get out! No, not one penny. (*The music stops.*) I'm completely upset! (*He drops into his chair . . . sits a moment in thought, then turns to the telephone*) Hallo! Give me Dirksen . . . Dirksen, I say . . . the underwriter. Hallo! Are you there, Dirksen? It's all up with the Good Hope! A hatch with my number washed ashore and the body of one of the sailors. (*In a belligerent tone*) What do you mean? Well, I should say not! No question about it. Sixty-five days . . . the probability is so strong . . . (*Calming down*) Good . . . I'll wait for you in my office . . . but as soon as possible, eh! Yes . . . fourteen thousand gulden. Goodby. (*Hangs up the receiver*)

KNIERTJE (*comes in during the last words, her manner vague and bewildered . . . she sinks down on the bench crying quietly*). I . . . I . . .

BOS (*without seeing her, looking into the safe*). Have you moved the portfolio with the insurance policies? Confound you . . . you get everything out of place!

KAPS (*pointing from his stool*). The portfolio is higher up . . . behind the box of bonds.

BOS (*snarling*). Just hold your tongue! (*Turning with the portfolio in his hand, sees Kniertje*) Can't you knock?

KNIERTJE (*patiently*). I would like . . .

BOS (*unpleasantly*). You come five minutes too late. That girl that lives with you has just been raising such a row here that with a little more I would have telephoned for the guard! (*Gruffly*) Come in then. Shut the gate behind you.

KNIERTJE (*feebly*). Is it true? . . . is it true that . . . the pastor said . . . (*Bos nods sombrely*) Oh! Oh! (*Her eyes stare vacantly . . . her arms fall inert*)

BOS. For you . . . for you I feel sympathy. I have known you always as a decent woman . . . your husband was an honest man . . . but your children . . . it is a hard thing to say after the blow you have had . . . your sons and your niece have never been worth much. (*Kniertje's head sinks lower on her breast.*) Think of the years you worked for me . . . until your son Geert threatened me with his fist, mocked at my gray hairs, and almost threw me out of your house. And your other son . . . (*Stops in alarm*) Kniertje! Knier! (*He springs to his feet*) Kaps! Bring water! (*Bathing her wrists and her forehead*) Damn it! Damn it all!

KAPS. Shall I call mevrouw or the young lady?

BOS. No. Stay here. She's coming to. (*Kniertje sits motionless for a while staring with unseeing eyes, then begins to sob silently*)

KAPS. Knier . . .

KNIERTJE (*pathetically, her words broken by sobs*). He didn't want to go! He didn't want to go! . . . and with my own hands I tore his fingers loose from the doorpost.

BOS. You have nothing to reproach yourself with.

KNIERTJE (*despairingly*). Before he went I hung his father's earrings in his ears . . . decking him out like a lamb for the sacrifice . . .

BOS. Come now . . .

KNIERTJE. And my oldest son . . . I didn't go to tell him good-by! "If you are too late," those were his last words, "I'll never lay eyes on you again!" . . . never again . . . never again!

BOS. Be still! . . . in God's name, be still!

KNIERTJE. Twelve years ago . . . with the Clementine . . . I sat here like this . . . (*She sobs into her trembling old hands*)

BOS (*trying to master the emotion which is taking possession of him*). Be brave now, Kniertje . . . be brave . . .

MATHILDE (*bustling in*). Clemens, I . . . Ach, poor dear Knier! How sorry I am for you! It is terrible . . . it is frightful! . . . both your sons!

KNIERTJE (*staring*). My husband and four sons!

MATHILDE (*consolingly*). But don't be worried now! We are starting a subscription . . . the burgemeester's wife and I have written the notice and it goes into the paper tomorrow. Here, Kaps! (*Bos motions to Kniertje to go.*) Let her wait a minute, Clemens. I have a couple of cold chops . . . that will do her good . . . and . . . and . . . let's forget the past. You don't object if she comes again for the cleaning? We won't forget you, Knier . . . do you hear? Good-by. Be strong . . . (*She goes out*)

BOS. No, we won't forget you.

KNIERTJE (*in a toneless voice*). Now my only hope is the child . . .

BOS. The child?

KNIERTJE. The child of my niece . . . yes, that misfortune comes too . . . she will have a child by my son. (*Smiling feebly*) But no, that isn't a misfortune . . .

BOS. And you tell me that as if it was nothing! Did you allow such ungodliness under your own roof? Don't you know the rule of the Widow's and Orphan's Fund? . . . that no assistance can be given to anyone who leads an immoral life, or whose conduct, in our opinion, is not worthy.

KNIERTJE (*dully*). The gentlemen must decide themselves what they will do for me . . . the gentlemen . . .

BOS. There will be difficulties with the committee . . . the directors of the Fund . . . Well, I will do the best I can . . . I give you my word for that . . . but promise anything . . . that I can't do. There are seven new families that will expect assistance and sixteen new orphans. (*Getting up and shutting the safe*) Wait here a little longer . . . my wife wants to give you something to take home. (*Goes out*)

MATHILDE (*from behind the scenes*). Kaps! Kaps!

(*Kaps gets up, goes out and comes back with a covered dish and a small enameled pan.*)

KAPS (*good-naturedly*). You are to bring the dish back when you have time and you are to come for the cleaning again on Saturday.

(*Kniertje stares unseeingly . . . he puts the dishes in her lap and folds her limp hands around them then shuffles back to his desk. Kniertje sits dazed and motionless . . . her lips move wordlessly—at last she gets up and stumbles out of the office. The clumping of her wooden shoes is heard in the stillness.*)

CURTAIN

JOSEF AND KAREL CAPEK's

The World We Live In

(The Insect Comedy)

In the adaptation by OWEN DAVIS

First presented by William A. Brady at the Jolson Theatre, New York, on October 31, 1922, with the following cast:

THE VAGRANT	Robert Edeson
THE PROFESSOR	N. St. Clair Hales
APATURA IRIS	Beatrice Maude
APATURA CLYTHIA	Lola Adler
FELIX	Kenneth MacKenna
VICTOR	Rexford Kendrick
OTAKAR	Etienne Girardot
YOUNG BUTTERFLIES	Josine Carr, Elizabeth Jack, Selene Jackson, Martha Hatch
CHRYSALIS	Mary Blair
MALE BEETLE	Scott Cooper
FEMALE BEETLE	Jane Corcoran
ANOTHER MALE BEETLE	Paul Irving
ICHNEUMON FLY	Edgar Norton
ITS LARVA	Grace Dougherty
MALE CRICKET	Vinton Freedley
FEMALE CRICKET	Jill Middleton
PARASITE	Jasper Deeter
BAND OF PILLAGERS	William Evans, Frank Perry, Alvin Thomas
BLIND ANT	Paul Irving
DICTATOR	John Ward
HEAD OF GENERAL STAFF	N. St. Clair Hales

COMMANDER-IN-CHIEF OF YELLOW ANTS
Kenneth MacKenna

INVENTOR	James Difley
QUARTERMASTER	Orrin T. Burke
JOURNALIST	Robert Lawler
WAR WORKER	May Hopkins
BOND SALESMAN	Harold McGee
TELEGRAPHER	James Kinney
MESSENGER	Seldon Bennett

SOLDIERS OF THE ANT REALM — Howard Jones, Paul Westley, William Prince, George Placit, Evan Parry, Herbert Lorimer

ANT WORKMEN, SOLDIERS, CLERKS, MESSENGERS, WOUNDED, ARMY OF THE BLACK, ARMY OF THE YELLOW, *by many others.*

MOTHS Alice Bower, Helen Vivian, Helenka Adamowska, Laura Panne, Francine Dowd, Alice Aynesworth, Estelle Gray, Miriam Hudson, Mildred Henry

SNAILS	William McDermont, Jasper Deeter
WOODCUTTER	Henry Mortimer
A WOMAN	Susan Steele
A BABY	Ann Martin

Scenic production by Lee Simonson
from original designs by Josef Capek and M. Hilar,
director of the National Theatre, Prague

SCENES

PRELUDE—A Forest Glade.
ACT ONE—The Butterflies.
ACT TWO—The Maurauders.
ACT THREE—The Ants.
EPILOGUE—Life and Death.

There is a permanent circular incline across
the stage which is the background for Acts I,
II, III and Epilogue. This incline is about two
feet high at back and slopes gradually toward
the footlights. There are three traps, Right,
Center, and Left, on the incline which are
open in Ant Scene to represent entrances to the
ant hills. When the battle scene begins the ant
soldiers swarm through the traps and line up
on the platform at back Center of the incline.
On this platform are six set pieces of glass, two
feet by three feet and two inches thick.

For the dance of the Moths in the Life and
Death Scene the glass is lighted from below.

There is a platform built in at Center front
of the incline. This platform stands throughout.

The cyclorama is of heavy gauze and stands
throughout. This is lighted with Linnebach
lights and glass mediums as an appropriate
background for each setting.

PROLOGUE

As Curtain opens MUSIC soft and dies out as
Vagrant enters.

SCENE: A clearing in the forest. This
scene is in front of a gauze drop, well down
stage. There is a log at the Right.

AT RISE: Vagrant, a shabby fellow, drunk
and rather battered and worn in appearance,
enters at the Right. Trips and falls at Center.

Professor, a middle-aged man, enters Left.
Has followed a butterfly and looks eagerly
about to find it. In his hand he has a butterfly
net.

———

PROFESSOR. Hello!

VAGRANT (on his back at Center). Ha!
Ha! Ha! Here's a joke!

PROFESSOR (going to him). You're not
hurt?

VAGRANT. Ah, no—I just—sort of fell
down.

PROFESSOR. So I see.

VAGRANT. I do it sometimes when I get
tired of standing up. Ha! Ha! Ha! Ha!

PROFESSOR. Ha! Ha! Ha!

VAGRANT. I'm not drunk, you know.
Nothing like that. You saw how steadily
I fell, didn't you?

PROFESSOR. Oh, yes.

VAGRANT. Like a tree—like a hero!
You know what I was doing, don't you?
I was performing the fall of man.

PROFESSOR (shakes his head). Never a
very cheering spectacle.

VAGRANT. When I came in just now I
wasn't staggering, and why—because I
was sober.

PROFESSOR. Really I am very glad of
that.

VAGRANT. But I'm the only one that's
sober. Everything else in the whole world
is drunk, everything's staggering about,
whirling   around—and   around—and
around.

PROFESSOR. What is? (He looks about,
rather alarmed)

VAGRANT. The whole earth, the whole
universe. And the funny thing about it is
they're all whirling around me—— I
suppose you're standing there saying to
yourself—"Pah—he's a shabby thing to
play the part of the hub of the universe."

PROFESSOR. Are you that?

VAGRANT. I'm worse than that—at
this very moment I'm the center of the
harmony of the spheres—that's what I
am. The center of the harmony of the
spheres, the very center.

PROFESSOR. Rather a responsibility,
isn't it?

VAGRANT. Oh, I'll just fix that all
right. (He takes his battered old hat off and
looks at it) Here, old friend, you must
take my place. You must be the center
of the universe. (He throws his cap to some
distance away) Now, Universe, whirl
around my hat.

PROFESSOR. You settle large affairs so
simply that I suppose you have no
difficulty in settling smaller ones. We
are at some distance from the city. I have
a car over there. (He points) I am
wondering if I might offer to give you
a lift.

VAGRANT. To where?

PROFESSOR. To where you want to go.

VAGRANT. I'm there—— I've been
called a drunken lout today, back there
in your city. I came here to get away
from people—a man loses his self-respect
when he's called a drunken lout too often
and even here I meet you, and you think
I'm drunk. Even these flowers here that

I fell among think that. See how they shrink away from me? Look! (*He picks a wild flower and holds it up*) This flower scorns me, don't you, you pretty, dainty thing? But are you always so dainty, eh?— Sometimes they put your leaves on wounds.

PROFESSOR. I see that you know something of botany.

VAGRANT. Yes. At least, I did once. Just now I'm a bit confused.

PROFESSOR. Who are you?

VAGRANT. A man of understanding who knows enough to be a trifle puzzled in his mind. (*Crosses Right*)

PROFESSOR. You're sure that you are all right?

VAGRANT. I'm fine. I'm one of the world's lucky ones. (*Picks up hat*)

PROFESSOR. You're ill, I think. I'd like to help you.

VAGRANT. That's easier said than done. At least I've found it so. (*Crosses Center*)

PROFESSOR. May I try?

VAGRANT. No! I'm not what you are thinking—not a drunken lout—— I—I'm a gentleman. At least I was once, and a scholar, in a way. I remember once I took a prize in Latin, so now, naturally, there is no limit to my ambition, now there are many things that I can do.

PROFESSOR. What things?

VAGRANT. Well—let's count them up —as a result of my four years of Latin— and four more as a soldier—I can now—— (*He counts on his fingers*) Sweep the streets, empty out the slops, shovel manure, do anything that's too foul for another man to do. I am a gentleman, as you see, and a scholar, and a soldier. Now you know who I am?

PROFESSOR. What is your name?

VAGRANT. Just *man!* Everybody knows me. I'm just a man. Nobody calls me anything else. "Man," they say to me, "don't do that!" "Man, I'll have you arrested!" "Man, clean that up. Carry that out!" "Do this for me!" "Do that for me!" "Clear off, man, get out,— move on!"

PROFESSOR. I'm sorry for you.

VAGRANT. Me? Oh, no! I'm not offended at being a man. Suppose I should say to you, just by way of variety, "Man,

give me money," you'd be offended then, wouldn't you? That's different, eh? Well, don't you worry. I don't want your money.

PROFESSOR. I have already offered to help you, if you'd let me.

VAGRANT. And I've refused you, and now you are offended, aren't you? And I don't care a damn if you are, because you're just a man. What's a man anyway, any more than a butterfly, or a beetle, or an ant? They're all the same to me, man or insect. I'm not here to reform the universe. I don't want to put anybody right. All I want to do now is just look on, that's all. If I had roots, or a bulb in the earth, I'd look at the sky. All my life I'd just look up there, at the sky. To my dying day I'd look straight at the sky—but I'm a man—— (*He turns to the Professor*) And I must look at people.

PROFESSOR. Well, since I can't be of any service to you I'll go after my butterflies. (*Crosses Right*)

VAGRANT. Butterflies?

PROFESSOR (*turning to Vagrant*). I saw two splendid specimens, Apatura Iris and Apatura Clythia! The painted lady and the light blue butterfly. They were hovering over you as you lay there on the ground.

VAGRANT (*bitterly*). No doubt, they settle on everything unclean—on mud, on offal, on garbage—on anything that smells.

PROFESSOR (*kindly*). You have observation.

VAGRANT. And experience—of offal! I don't know much of butterflies.

PROFESSOR. If you know life you know them. They are very like us.

VAGRANT. Not like the life I know. They are always playing. (MUSIC)

PROFESSOR. My friend, you should watch their playing—it is simply the overture to mating. The male pursues the female, the bride allures, then slips away, the male follows—until a stranger comes and takes his place. The female stops only to make sure of being followed, then flits on, the lover after her, the eternal mating, the eternal round of sex!

VAGRANT. And you take it upon

yourself to end their love affairs? What for?

PROFESSOR. For my collection! They went this way, I think. *(Looks off Right)* Yes—— Oh, you beauty! This time I'll get you. *(He exits Right)*

VAGRANT. Eternal mating! Love's eternal contest! Perhaps it's because I'm drunk that I see so clearly. *(He looks about)* All about me everything's in pairs. Everything's two-fold. It's always pairing-time. Clouds, gnats, and trees, they all embrace and fondle. You birds up there— *(He looks at tree)* —I see you, you ants down there, I'm looking on. I see you all. And you—you back there in the shadow, I see you provoke and pursue, I see you struggling hotly and softly. Eternal mating! It's all right. *(He covers his eyes with his hands)* Kindly pardon me. I'm drunk but honest. I'll see nothing. I'll shout before I uncover my eyes. All strive to pair. In all this great forest I'm the only one in solitude. Well—why not—— *(He sits on fallen log Right)* I don't complain. I'm content with a spectator's seat to watch the comedy called Life. God knows I'm satisfied to just look on. I don't want to lift my hands again in love's hide and seek. If I know *Life*, this butterfly collector said, "I'd know the life of the insects all about me," but you see I don't know Life—Life so far hasn't taught me how to live, or how to die. Let's see Nature's answer to life's greatest riddle.

(MUSIC, which continues into First Act.)

ACT ONE

SCENE: *A circular room. Rayon silk drapes hanging from above. Pillows, etc. All butterfly colors to give a light and airy atmosphere. There is a couch Center in front of the platform.*

Felix enters Center, followed by Four Female Butterflies, gorgeous in their brilliant colorings, and they picture the words spoken by the Professor, "the male pursues the female, the bride allures then slips away, the male follows."

FELIX *(enters Center, followed by Yellow, White, Brown and Red, four young female butterflies)*. Iris—Iris! Iris! *(Down Center; crosses Left to pillows)*

YELLOW. Felix! Felix, dear. *(Following Felix)*

FELIX. Iris! Iris!

WHITE. Never mind that old thing, Felix. We are with you.

FELIX. But I want Iris, and she's gone. *(He throws himself down on pillows Left)*

BROWN. Never mind, dear.

RED. Don't be unhappy. *(Sits Left of Felix)*

WHITE. We are with you, Felix.

FELIX. I don't want you. I want Iris. You're children—you're so immature— so undeveloped—such callow fledglings— such impossible little flappers.

BROWN. Oh, Felix!

WHITE. Read us your poetry.

RED. Oh, it's so grand. So thrilling!

FELIX. I want to read my poetry to Iris. She inspires me—a poet must have his inspiration.

YELLOW. Are you writing poetry to her? *(Kneeling)*

FELIX. I am trying to. Iris—Iris—— It's hard to fit a rhyme to Iris.

BROWN. Oh, you couldn't—nobody could.

FELIX. I must. Let me see—Iris! Pure as fire is!

YELLOW. Oh!

BROWN. Isn't he wonderful?

WHITE *(much impressed)*. "Iris, pure as fire is."

FELIX. No, not really good, yet something like it. Where is she? Don't any of you know where she is?

WHITE. Flying about somewhere with Victor.

FELIX. Victor! Stupid idiot—Iris! *(He writes)* "Upon thy lips divine, thy smile of victory, Iris!"—Humph!—let's see— if she decides she loves Victor and refuses me, I might change this into an elegy in regular alexandrines! Ah, it's a poet's fate to suffer. *(Iris laughs outside)*

WHITE. There's Iris!

BROWN. And Victor!

FELIX. Victor—all her smiles are for him. *(Crosses Right)*

YELLOW. Poor Felix!

WHITE. How he suffers!

YELLOW. Isn't it just heart-breaking?

IRIS *(enters Right, followed by Victor)* Hush! You mustn't say such things.

VICTOR. But—— *(Pursuing her)*

IRIS. Hush, I say.

WHITE. Poor Iris, see how warm she is.

BROWN. Iris, dear—what *have* you been doing to yourself?

YELLOW. Isn't it terrible? What time does to one!

RED. Dear Iris! She *used* to be so pretty. *(The Four Female Butterflies giggle)*

IRIS. Go away. Fly off, you nasty little things. How dare you come around my flowers. Fly away, I say. *(The Four Female Butterflies exit Right, Center and Left)*

VICTOR. Listen to me, Iris.

IRIS. Hush! There's Felix. *(Downstage Left. Crosses Center)* Is that you over there by yourself, Felix—and so interestingly sad?

FELIX *(turning round)*. You, Iris? Ah, I didn't imagine——

IRIS. Why aren't you playing outside? Such lots of girls are out there.

FELIX. You know, Iris, that—that they don't interest me.

IRIS. Oh, poor fellow. Why not?

VICTOR *(contemptuously)*. He's too young. *(Falls on pillows Left)*

FELIX. No longer. I'm too old.

(MUSIC *stops*)

IRIS. Sit down beside me, Felix. Tell me. When did you love for the first time?

FELIX *(sits Right)*. I don't know now. It's too long ago. And even then it wasn't for the first time. I was a schoolboy——

VICTOR. Ah—you were still a caterpillar. A green caterpillar, devouring the leaves.

IRIS. Felix, was she dark? Was she beautiful?

FELIX. Beautiful as the day, as the azure, as——

IRIS. As what? Quickly!

FELIX *(boldly)*. As beautiful as you.

IRIS. Felix, dearest, did she love you?

FELIX. I don't know. I never spoke to her.

IRIS. Good Heavens, what did you do to her, then?

FELIX. I looked at her from afar——

VICTOR. Sitting on a green leaf——

FELIX. And wrote poems, letters, my first novel—

VICTOR. It's appalling the number of leaves a literary caterpillar uses up.

IRIS. You're horrid, Victor. Look, Felix has his eyes full of tears. Isn't that nice?

VICTOR. Tears? He's been fooling around wild onions. By the way, have you read the last poem that Felix wrote? *(Taking a book out of his coat)* It came out in the Spring Almanac.

IRIS. Quick, read it to me.

FELIX *(rising)*. No, I won't let you read it to her. It's bad. It's old. I've long since got past that stage.

IRIS. Sit down quietly, Felix.

VICTOR. It's called "Eternal Downfall."

FELIX *(sits Right of Iris)*. But I don't want you to read it to her.

VICTOR *(reads with emphasis)*

"When I plead with you, my dear,
Do not put me off with reasons.
Let us lie and watch the year,
Laughing at the timid seasons."

IRIS. That's witty, isn't it, Victor?

VICTOR *(reads on)*

"Winter fears the Spring's first call,
Spring avoids the Summer weather;
Autumn brings the flaming Fall;
So, love, let us fall together."

IRIS. Oh, how shocking! Felix, did you write such a thing? I'm afraid of you. How depraved you are!

FELIX. Have pity, Iris. It's such a bad poem.

IRIS. Why bad?

FELIX. It hasn't got the—the—real thing in it, the real feeling. *(Tenderly)* I could do so much better now.

IRIS. Aha! Victor, you'll find my fan in the garden. Would you mind getting it for me?

VICTOR *(offended)*. Oh, don't let me disturb you. *(Exits Center)* (MUSIC)

IRIS. Quick, Felix. Tell me the truth. You can tell me everything.

FELIX. Oh, Iris! *(Rising and going to pillows Right)* How basely he looks upon you, upon love, upon everything! How shamefully! How—how—how uncouthly! How can you put up with it? *(Reclining on pillows Right)*

IRIS. Poor Victor! He's so soothing. Now, Felix, talk about poetry. I'm so fond of poetry. *(Sits down among the pillows*

Left of Felix) "Do not put me off with reasons."

FELIX. Oh, Iris! I've long since got past what's in that poem.

IRIS. "So, love, let us fall together." If only it wasn't so coarse. I can put up with anything, anything, but it musn't have a horrid name. Felix, you should be delicate toward women. If you were to kiss me now, would you give that a horrid name, too?

FELIX. Iris, how could I dare to kiss you?

IRIS. Felix, you're a terrible fascinater. Tell me, who was your last conquest?

FELIX. Iris, you won't tell anybody? You really won't?

IRIS. No.

FELIX. Well, then—I haven't got one, not a conquest. I never had one.

IRIS. What?

FELIX. Not yet. Upon my honor.

IRIS. Oh, what a story! How many women have you told that to, you innocent creature? Felix, Felix, I see through you. What a dangerous man you are!

FELIX. Iris, you mustn't laugh at me. I've had terrible experiences—in my imagination. Awful disappointments! Loves without number, but only in my dreams! Dreams are the poet's life. I know all women, and haven't known one. Upon my honor, Iris!

IRIS. Then why do you say that you are tired of women?

FELIX. Oh, Iris, one always disparages the thing one loves the most.

IRIS. Brunettes?

FELIX. No; dreams! Eternal dreams!

IRIS. What are you thinking of now?

FELIX. Of you. Woman is a riddle.

IRIS. Solve her, then. But gently, Felix, please.

FELIX *(bending over her).* I cannot see into the depths of your eyes.

IRIS. You haven't really tried, my Felix.

FELIX. I—— Iris—really—— *(Leaning back again)*

IRIS. Felix, I'm in such a queer mood today. How stupid it is to be a woman. Today I should like to be a man, to conquer, to allure, to embrace—— Felix, I should be such a fearfully intense man.

I should—I—I should snatch everyone away wildly, savagely—— What a pity that you aren't a girl! Let's pretend, shall we? You will be Iris and I will be your Felix.

FELIX. No, Iris. That would be too venturesome to be Felix. That means desiring, desiring something——

IRIS *(in a faint voice).* Oh, Felix, everything!

FELIX. There is something much greater than to desire everything.

IRIS. And that is——

FELIX. To desire something impossible.

IRIS *(disappointedly standing up).* You're right. You're always right, poor Felix, but you're rather stupid. *(Crosses to platform Center and looks in mirror)* What can be keeping Victor so long? Would you mind calling him?

FELIX *(rising and crossing to her).* Iris, how have I offended you? Oh, I said too much?

IRIS. Too much? Oh, I wouldn't call it too much.

FELIX. To desire something impossible? Iris, I was mad to talk to you like that.

IRIS. Or, at least, impolite. Really, you know, it's appalling the trouble I'm taking with you. When we're in the company of ladies, we mustn't behave as if we were longing for something we're afraid to ask for.

FELIX. One must be afraid to ask for the unattainable.

IRIS *(looking in mirror).* Where is the unattainable? I don't know it.

FELIX *(pointing to the mirror).* There! Your image, Iris.

IRIS *(laughing).* My image? Have you fallen in love with my image? *(Bringing the mirror close to her face)* Look, my image has heard you. Embrace it. Kiss it, quickly.

FELIX. It is as unapproachable as you. *(Turning away)*

IRIS *(turning to him).* I am unapproachable? How do you know?

FELIX. If I did not know, I should not love you.

IRIS. Felix, what a pity that I am so unapproachable.

FELIX. Iris, there is no true love except in the unapproachable.

IRIS. Do you think so? "So, love, let us fall together." *(She laughs mockingly)*

FELIX. Don't repeat that poem.

IRIS. Make one for me, quickly. Something filled with love.

FELIX.

> "Oh, fragile and fluttering Iris,
> You sipped at the sweets of my soul,
> A dream that is dark as desire is
> My glory—my grandeur—my goal—
> Oh, pain that is priceless as passion,
> Oh, passion as perfect as pain,
> Let us burn in the blaze till we're
>   [ashen,
> Again and again and again—"

CLYTHIA *(behind the scene)*. Iris—Iris!

IRIS. Clythia is coming—and that booby of an Otakar—just as we—— *(Clythia enters Right, followed by Otakar, rather a clumsy and stupid male butterfly.)*

CLYTHIA. No! No! You mustn't. You really, really mustn't.   (MUSIC *stops*)

OTAKAR *(uneasily)*. Hush! They'll hear you!

CLYTHIA *(to Otakar, angry)*. Pooh! Don't be such a fool. *(She crosses to front of platform gaily)* Just fancy, Iris, Otakar says—— Why, Felix! *(As she sees Felix, crosses to Left, standing over him)* You here! Darling! *(She turns a bit coldly on Iris)* It's really so sweet of you to mother this poor boy.

IRIS. Ha! Ha! Ha! Something seems to have annoyed you, Clythia—and my dear, you do look so warm. *(Standing on couch.)*

CLYTHIA. This bad boy—— *(She taps Otakar playfully on shoulder)*—is always chasing me about. *(She runs in front of platform upstage to Right)*

OTAKAR *(running after her)*. Well, she keeps flying away and of course I have to follow her. It's a confounded nuisance, but what can a fellow do?

VICTOR *(entering up Center)*. Hello, here's quite a company here. *(Greets Clythia. Stands to Left of Iris)*

CLYTHIA. Oh, I'm so thirsty.

IRIS *(to Clythia)*. Your bodice is all torn. I'm afraid you're a clumsy man, Otakar. *(Down to Center; sits on couch)*

CLYTHIA. He's so strong. Oh, you don't know how strong he is.

OTAKAR. Never mind all that—— *(Confused)* I wish you'd be a little more discreet. Hello, what's wrong with Felix here?

IRIS. Oh, he's all right.

CLYTHIA. Poor fellow! He looks so sad. *(She crosses and stands beside him)* What is it, Felix—can't you tell me?

IRIS *(into group Left of Otakar)*. He just wrote something about me. Wait!

FELIX. Iris, I implore you.

IRIS *(she repeats the poem)*

> "Oh, pain that is priceless as passion,
> Oh, passion as perfect as pain—
> Let us burn in the blaze till we're
>   [ashen,
> Again and again and again—"

Felix is frightfully talented. None of you could make a rhyme to "Iris."

CLYTHIA. "Iris, than whom none slyer is."

FELIX *(rushing at her)*. Oh, ye gods, do stop it!

CLYTHIA. Ha, ha, ha! That's splendid. Iris—slyer is. *(They fly at each other)*

IRIS *(keeping her temper)*. Dearest, you have such strange ideas of poetry. But you'd never believe what beautiful poetry he was reading to me just as you came.

CLYTHIA *(yawning. Crosses to couch and sits)*. Do stop talking about literature. I'm so heartily sick of it. *(Followed by Otakar)*

VICTOR. Heartily? Fancy, poor Clythia imagines she's got a heart somewhere.

IRIS. Victor, you're awfully good company. I adore witty people. I could give you a kiss. See if you can catch me.
        (MUSIC)
(Iris runs out Right, followed by Victor.)

CLYTHIA. Oh, what a silly creature! What a perfect fright! What an awful figure! Felix! *(Crosses Left to Felix)*

FELIX. Yes? *(Rises)*

CLYTHIA. How ever could you fall in love with her?

FELIX. With whom?

CLYTHIA. With that old frump.

FELIX. Whom do you mean?

CLYTHIA. Iris, of course.

FELIX. I? What can you be thinking of—— That's all done with, long ago.

CLYTHIA. Is it really?

FELIX. An old story! *(He sighs)*

CLYTHIA *(to Center)*. Otakar darling, I am so afraid that dear Iris is angry at what I said. Do fly after her and tell her how sorry I am.

OTAKAR. But she has gone with Victor. Two is company, you know.

CLYTHIA *(looks at Felix)*. Yes, I know. *(Following Otakar)* Just hurry along, you stupid, and bring her back with you.

OTAKAR. But—— *(Turns and faces her)*

CLYTHIA *(angrily)*. Are you going to do as I say?

OTAKAR. Oh, yes, I suppose I must. *(Business of turning around all the way off. Otakar exits Right)*

CLYTHIA *(crossing back of platform to Left, then down to Center)*. Oh, dear how silly he is. *(She sits on couch)* You're sure, poor Felix, that Iris isn't breaking your heart?

FELIX. My heart! Ha! Ha! Ha!

CLYTHIA. I understand. Iris is so fearfully ignorant. Such awful feet! Oh, Felix, at your age you still have so many illusions about women.

FELIX. I? I assure you, Clythia—upon my honor, I've long since got past that stage.

CLYTHIA. No, Felix, you don't know women. Sit down beside me, will you? You've no idea of what they're like. Their opinions. Their minds. And their bodies. Ugh! You are so young——

FELIX. Oh, no! I'm not young, no. I've had so much experience. *(Sitting Right of her)*

CLYTHIA. You must be thoroughly young. That's the fashion now, to be young, to be a butterfly, to be a poet! Is there anything more beautiful in the whole world? Let's be friends, Felix, like two women together.

FELIX. Like two women?

CLYTHIA. Love means nothing to you. Love is so common. Ah, I'd like something quite special. Something out of the ordinary! Something new!

FELIX. A poem?

CLYTHIA. Yes, that would do. You see how I like you? I can even listen to your poetry.

FELIX *(jumps up, excitedly)*. Do you know, Clythia, that you inspire me—you really do. Listen! This is altogether a new note. *(He recites)*

"Crash!
You clash at the doors of my heart!
Your hair pours into my blood
Like a flood of yellow thunder.
Under the roaring, crumpled skies
Your eyes,
Two drunken nuns,
Are singing hymns to fever.
Your limbs are levers
Lifting the laughter of the world.
Hurl the light backward with
[abandon!
Command me, drive me with the
[whips of love!
Until your lips, brooding on mine,
Crow rude and rash.
Crash!"

CLYTHIA. What's that?

FELIX. A poem! Just the beginning!

CLYTHIA. And how does it go on from there?

FELIX. I don't know. I only know that it is to be my *masterpiece*. At last I have arrived. At last I am about to express myself. *(Bending over her)*

CLYTHIA. Go on. I'm waiting.

FELIX *(rises; crosses Left)*. I must have solitude.

CLYTHIA *(rising also, and follows him)*. But I thought I was your inspiration.

FELIX. Oh, I'll read it to you when it's finished. Please don't bother me now. Crash! *(Felix exits Left. Otakar flies in Right)*

OTAKAR. I couldn't find them. Hello! Where's Felix?

CLYTHIA *(crosses to front of platform)*. That silly poet! What does it matter where *he* is? Poets! Pah! I love a man.

OTAKAR *(crossing in front of platform beside her)*. That's my Clythia. Kiss me, dear.

CLYTHIA. Don't touch. *(She backs away up incline Left)*

OTAKAR. Clythia! *(He follows)* I love you! I love you! *(He catches her)*

CLYTHIA. Oh, you great, strong handsome thing!

OTAKAR. I'm mad about you.

CLYTHIA. I know. It's delightful the way your heart is beating. Say, "Ha." *(Puts her head on his chest)*

OTAKAR. Ha——
CLYTHIA. Again.
OTAKAR. Hm. Ha. *(He coughs)*
CLYTHIA *(taking her head up)*. How that rumbles in your chest. Like thunder! Otakar, you're fearfully strong, aren't you?
OTAKAR. Cly—Cly—Cly——
CLYTHIA *(crosses Right Center)*. What is it now?
OTAKAR. Be mine.
CLYTHIA. Don't be tiresome, please.
OTAKAR. I—I—— *(Pursuing her)*
CLYTHIA. So do I——
OTAKAR. Be mine. I adore you.
CLYTHIA *(running away)*. Not a bit of it. I should only spoil my figure.
OTAKAR *(pursuing her)*. I—I—I want—
CLYTHIA *(laughs and flies off)*. Wait, only wait. You mustn't be impatient. *(She exits Right and runs Left behind cyclorama)*
OTAKAR *(following her silhouette outside of cyclorama)*. Clytie! Clytie! Wait! Wait! *(Iris flies in Right, laughing; crosses down Center to front of platform. To Iris)* She flew away from me, Clythia did!
IRIS. Poor fellow! Ha! Ha! Ha! Did she run away from him? Too bad! Did the bad thing break his heart?
OTAKAR. I say! You're pretty, aren't you?
IRIS *(flies away from him up incline Right)*. Oh, shame on you—you bad man!
OTAKAR *(following her)*. It's your eyes. They make a fellow think of——
IRIS. Hush! Bad boy!
OTAKAR. Kiss me, Iris.
IRIS. Oh, no! *(She dodges him)*
OTAKAR. Iris! I love you. I love you so.
IRIS. Come, catch me, then. *(She exits Right. He follows)*
VAGRANT. Ha! Ha! Drawing room society. Eternal lives of eternal lovers, eternally unappeased. *(Clythia enters Left. Iris enters Right. Both going to back of platform.)*
IRIS. Something to drink, quickly. *(Drinks from flowers)* (MUSIC stops)
CLYTHIA. Where have you been?
IRIS. Outside. Oh, it's so warm. *(They both descend to front of platform and sit on couch Center)*
CLYTHIA. Where did you leave Victor?
IRIS. Wait, it'll make you laugh. He

kept running after me like mad, and suddenly, ha, ha, ha, a bird flew along and ate him up.
CLYTHIA. Never.
IRIS. As true as I'm sitting here! Oh, it did make me laugh. Ha! ha! ha!
CLYTHIA. Ha! ha! ha! *(Mockingly)* What's the matter with you?
IRIS. Ha! ha! ha! Oh, these men!
CLYTHIA. Do you mean Victor?
IRIS. No, Otakar! Victor was eaten by a bird. Just fancy, immediately afterwards, your Otakar came flying up. Oh, the look in his eyes, all on fire, and then, ha! ha! ha——!
CLYTHIA *(angrily)*. What then?
IRIS. He followed me all about. He kept saying, "How pretty you are! How I love you! Kiss me! Kiss me!"
CLYTHIA. He said that,—my Otakar?
IRIS. You're angry, aren't you? Ha! Ha! Ha! Otakar is a dear. He is really very nice.
CLYTHIA. He said he loved you? He called you pretty? You stole him from me! You robbed me!
IRIS. Oh! Ha! Ha! Ha!
CLYTHIA. Oh, I hate you—you shameless creature.
IRIS. Shameless! You call me shameless? That's good! You!
CLYTHIA. At least I took that silly poet away from you! I told him what you were!
IRIS. You've lied about me to Felix.
CLYTHIA. Worse, my dear! I told him the truth.
IRIS *(turning away)*. Oh——
CLYTHIA. You took my Otakar!
IRIS. You lied about me to Felix!
CLYTHIA. You vicious insect.
IRIS. You lying minx! *(They fly at each other. Clythia chases Iris away. Iris exits Right. Clythia following her to exit. As Vagrant starts to speak he attracts Clythia's attention and she descends toward him)*
VAGRANT. Big fleas have little fleas on their backs to bite them. Little fleas have lesser fleas. And so ad infinitum (MUSIC)
CLYTHIA *(standing Left of Vagrant)*. Are you a butterfly? *(Vagrant flits his cap at her. She flies away Left. Turning again toward him)* Aren't you a butterfly?
VAGRANT. I am a man.
CLYTHIA. What is that? Is it alive?

VAGRANT. Yes.

CLYTHIA *(flying up)*. Does it love?

VAGRANT. Yes. It's a butterfly.

CLYTHIA. How interesting you are. Why do you wear a black gown? *(Up close to Vagrant)*

VAGRANT. That's dirt.

CLYTHIA. Oh, how nice you smell.

VAGRANT. That's sweat and dust.

CLYTHIA. Your fragrance intoxicates me. It is so new! So thrilling!

VAGRANT *(throwing his cap at her)*. Shoo, you hussy.

CLYTHIA *(flying away Left)*. Catch me. Catch me.

VAGRANT. Flighty jade, worthless baggage——

CLYTHIA *(approaching him)*. Let me just smell. Let me just taste. You are so unusual. *(Hands stretched out toward Vagrant)*

VAGRANT. I've met the likes of you before, you minx. *(Catches hold of Clythia's hands)* Why did I love her? I caught hold of her insect hands like that, and begged her to smile at me, and then I let her go. I should have killed her. *(Lets her go)* Fly away, you wench. I don't want you.

CLYTHIA *(flies away)*. Ugh, how strange you are.

VAGRANT. Scented wanton, strumpet!

CLYTHIA *(coming close to him)*. Again, again. It's so lovely, so coarse, so violent!

VAGRANT. What, you pest, isn't that enough for you, you white-faced harridan?

CLYTHIA. I love you. Oh, I adore you.

VAGRANT *(flinching from her)*. Go, go, go. You're loathsome!

FELIX *(enters Center, followed by Iris and Four Female Butterflies, who enter Right, Center and Left)*. It's finished. My poem is finished. Listen, Clythia, this is my most modern note. My masterpiece. *(Crosses down Right toward Clythia)*

CLYTHIA *(running Left)*. Go away! Go away!

FELIX *(following her)*.
"Geometry of souls disputes the
    Roundness of your gesturing flesh."

CLYTHIA. Oh, you idiot!

FELIX. "Blind and weak and organized and resumed."

VAGRANT. Ha! Ha!

FELIX *(turning to Vagrant and going to*

him). Here's someone! I'll read it to you. "Let us elaborately sit into designs while vegetables lift up their powder puffs."

VAGRANT. Shoo, shoo, you pest!

CLYTHIA. Ah, stop it! Stop it! *(Iris and Four Female Butterflies fly down to Vagrant. He shoos them away)*

VAGRANT. Shoo! Shoo! *(Indicates Felix)* That's the one you're after.

FELIX *(crossing Left)*. "Tomatoes are uncouth but honest." *(Felix goes up incline Left, standing at Left of First Female Butterfly. He recites to her)*
"A green acre is so selfish and yet
                 [so pure."
(First Female Butterfly rebukes him. Felix crosses Right to Second Female Butterfly)
"Spread out for pink and purple
                [platitudes."
(Second Female Butterfly rebukes him. Felix crosses Right to Third Female Butterfly.)
"The moon is bitter diamonds in
               [a ditch."
(Third Female Butterfly rebukes him, and he crosses to Fourth.)
"While stars jump up and down
             [like angry gnats."
(Fourth Female Butterfly turns away.)
"A virgin caterpillar shrieks for
          [the embraces of the moon.
I am that caterpillar."

VAGRANT. Ha! Ha!

FELIX. 'Tis for her Clythia. *(He starts toward Clythia. Clythia, Iris and Four Female Butterflies laugh. Exeunt Clythia, Left, followed by Felix. Female Butterflies laugh and dance about the stage)*

VAGRANT. Butterflies. Just butterflies *(MUSIC rises to forte)*

THE MARAUDERS

ACT TWO

SCENE: *The scene represents a sand hillock, with a scanty growth of grass. On the Left side the lair of the Ichneumon Fly. On the Right side the desert cave of a Cricket. Vagrant lies asleep over Right. A Chrysalis fastened to a blade of grass up Left Center. The Chrysalis is attacked by a gang rapacious Insects. From the Left a small Beetle runs in. From the Right a Second One runs out, chases the First One off, and tries to snatch the Chrysalis away. From the Left a Third leaps forth, and chases the Second One away.*—MUSIC.

———

CHRYSALIS. I—I—I—— The whole earth is bursting. I am being born.

VAGRANT *(raising his head).* What's that? *(The Third Beetle exits Right)*

CHRYSALIS. Something great is at hand.

VAGRANT. That's good. *(Lays his head down. Pause)*

(A Male and Female Beetle enter Left, rolling a huge roll of manure. They roll it down incline Left to Center during these speeches.)

MALE BEETLE. What are you up to?

FEMALE BEETLE. I?

MALE BEETLE. You.

FEMALE BEETLE. I?

MALE BEETLE. You.

FEMALE BEETLE. I?

MALE BEETLE. You. Clumsy slattern.

FEMALE BEETLE. You wretch.

MALE BEETLE. Fathead.

FEMALE BEETLE. Dolt!

MALE BEETLE. Slut! Frump!

FEMALE BEETLE. Brute! Coward!

MALE BEETLE. Take care. Look out.

FEMALE BEETLE. Slowly.

MALE BEETLE. Lo—lo—ook out. Nothing's happened to it?

FEMALE BEETLE. Oh, dear, I do hope not. I'm all of a tremble.

MALE BEETLE. Ha, ha, that's our capital. Our nest egg. Our stock-in-trade. Our all.

FEMALE BEETLE. Oh, what a lovely little pile, what a treasure, what a beautiful little ball, what a precious little fortune.

MALE BEETLE. It's our only joy. To think how we've saved and scraped, toiled and moiled, denied ourselves, gone without this, stinted ourselves that—

FEMALE BEETLE. —And worked our legs off and drudged and plodded to get it together and——

MALE BEETLE. And seen it grow and added to it, bit by bit.

FEMALE BEETLE. Our very own.

MALE BEETLE. Our life.

FEMALE BEETLE. All our own work.

MALE BEETLE. Just sniff at it, old girl. Oh, how lovely! Just feel the weight of it. And it's ours.

FEMALE BEETLE. What a godsend. *(Fondling pile)*

MALE BEETLE. What a blessing. *(Fondling pile)*

THE CHRYSALIS. The fetters of the world are rended, now another life is coming! I am born. *(Vagrant raises his head)*

FEMALE BEETLE. Husband.

MALE BEETLE. What is it?

FEMALE BEETLE. Ha! Ha! Ha! Ha! Ha! I am so happy!

MALE BEETLE. Ha! Ha! Ha! Ha! Wife!

FEMALE BEETLE. What is it?

MALE BEETLE. Ha! Ha! Ha! It's fine to own something. Your property. The dream of your life. The fruit of your labors.

FEMALE BEETLE. Ha! Ha! Ha! Aren't you going off of your head with joy?

MALE BEETLE *(doubtfully).* W—e—l—l —yes?

FEMALE BEETLE. You don't seem very sure of it.

MALE BEETLE. Well, to tell you the truth, my dear, I am worried. As a matter of fact, I'm going off my head with worry.

FEMALE BEETLE. Worried! When we have won our treasure, the thing we've been looking forward to all our lives?

MALE BEETLE. We've won it—yes— but after all it's quite a small treasure.

FEMALE BEETLE. It's a fortune.

MALE BEETLE. Y—e—s? But it's only *one* fortune. Oh, dear, dear, now I must start out and get another. Nothing but work, work, work.

FEMALE BEETLE. Why another?

MALE BEETLE. You stupid creature, so that we can have two, of course.

FEMALE BEETLE. Ah, two. Quite right, of course we must have two.

MALE BEETLE. Ah, just fancy, two of them. At least two. Let's say even three. You know, everyone who's made one pile has to make another.

FEMALE BEETLE. So that we can have two.

MALE BEETLE. Or even three.

FEMALE BEETLE. Husband!

MALE BEETLE. Well, what is it?

FEMALE BEETLE. I'm scared. Suppose someone was to steal it from us.

MALE BEETLE. What?

FEMALE BEETLE. Our little pile. Our joy. Our all.

MALE BEETLE. Our pi—pile? My goodness! Don't frighten me.

FEMALE BEETLE. We—we—we can't roll it about with us till we've made another one. Oh, dear! I thought the hardest thing in the world was to make a fortune. Now it seems that it's even harder to keep it.

MALE BEETLE. I tell you what. We'll invest it. Invest it. We'll store it up. We'll bury it nicely. Wait a bit, in some hole, in some cranny. Out of harm's way, you know. It must be put aside.

FEMALE BEETLE. I only hope nobody'll find it.

MALE BEETLE. Eh? Not likely. What, steal it from us? Our little pile! Our treasure! Our little round nest egg!

FEMALE BEETLE. Our precious little store! Our life!

MALE BEETLE. Wait, stay here and watch—watch it. Keep an eye on it. (Starts off Left)

FEMALE BEETLE. Where are you off to now? (Following him)

MALE BEETLE. To look for a hole—a little hole—a deep hole—to bury it in. Our precious gold—out of harm's way. (Exit Left) Be careful.

FEMALE BEETLE (after hunting about, discovers a hole Left, the lair of Ichneumon Fly). Husband, husband, come here—— Wait a bit—— There's—Husband! He can't hear me. And I've found such a nice hole. Husband! He's gone. And I've found such a beautiful little hole. What a stupid he is. If only I could just have a look at it. No, I mustn't leave you, little pile. If I could—only peep. Little pile, dear little pile, wait a moment. I'll be back at once. I'll only have just a peep, and I'll be back again. (Runs to the back and turns around) Little pile, you'll be good and wait for me, won't you? I'll be back at once, little pile—— (Enters the lair of the Ichneumon Fly)

CHRYSALIS. Oh, to be born, to be born. The new world!

STRANGE BEETLE (runs in from Right, where he has been lurking. Starts to roll pile up Right). They've gone. (Looks about) Now's my chance.

VAGRANT. Here, don't knock me over.

STRANGE BEETLE. Out of my way, citizen. (Rolling pile up incline Right)

VAGRANT. What's that you're rolling along?

STRANGE BEETLE. Ha! Ha! Ha! That's my pile. Capital! Gold! Mine! My treasure!

VAGRANT (flinching). That gold of yours smells.

STRANGE BEETLE. Stupid! Gold doesn't smell. Roll along, pile. Off you go. Bestir yourself. Come on. Possession's nine points of the law. Ha! Ha! Ha! my boy.

VAGRANT. What's that?

STRANGE BEETLE. Ah, it's nice to own something. (Rolls the pile) My treasure. Your lovely nest egg. My jewel. My all. What a thing to possess. A little fortune to invest. To bury carefully. Lo—ok out. (Exits Right)

VAGRANT. To possess? Why not. Everyone likes something of his own.

FEMALE BEETLE (returns from lair). Oh, dear! Oh, dear! Someone's living there. A little larva. We can't put you there, pile. (Looks for pile) Where is my pile? Oh, where has my pile gone to? Where is our dear little pile?

VAGRANT. Why, just this minute——

FEMALE BEETLE (rushing upon him). Thief, thief! What have you done with my pile?

VAGRANT. I'm telling you, just this minute——

FEMALE BEETLE. You villain, give it here! Hand it back!

VAGRANT. Just this minute another beetle rolled it away.

FEMALE BEETLE. What beetle? Who?

VAGRANT. A pot-bellied fellow, a fat round, homely one.

FEMALE BEETLE. A surly chap with crooked feet, a vulgar, conceited creature

VAGRANT. Yes.

FEMALE BEETLE. That's my husband.

VAGRANT. And he said it was a fine thing to own something, and to bury something.

FEMALE BEETLE. That's him! He must have found another hole. (Calls) Darling

Where are you? Husband! *(Starts off Center, looking around for him)*

VAGRANT *(points Right)*. He rolled it out that way.

FEMALE BEETLE. The stupid fellow! Why didn't he wait for me? Husband! Wait! Wait! Wait for me! *(She exits up slope Right and off)*

VAGRANT. Well—at least these creatures are human, even if they are not fashionable. The desire for possession, even if it's for nothing but a ball of manure, is real enough.

CHRYSALIS. Make room! Make room for me. A wonderful thing is about to happen.

VAGRANT. What thing?

CHRYSALIS. I am being born.

VAGRANT *(dryly)*. Well—you deserve credit for it—after all, it's the most unusual thing most people ever do.

CHRYSALIS. I am being born.

VAGRANT. All things, I suppose, are fighting for their birth. Without that desire the Universe would perish. You want to be born—why, God knows—yet you struggle for it.

CHRYSALIS. Listen! Let the whole world listen! The moment is here when I—when I——

VAGRANT. What?

CHRYSALIS. Nothing. I don't know yet. I only know I want to do something great.

VAGRANT. Great! Good! Make yourself drunk with that desire. These beetles here with their pile won't understand you, but it's a big world with room in it for all ambitions.

CHRYSALIS. I must do something—something unbounded!

VAGRANT. That's fine, Chrysalis! I must see this great thing that you give forth—— Come—come— hurry up! Be born!

CHRYSALIS. The whole world will be astonished when I am delivered.

ICHNEUMON FLY *(enters Right with long quiet strides; carries Cricket into its lair)*. Look, larva. Daddy's bringing you something nice. *(Enters the hole)*

CHRYSALIS *(shouting)*. What pain! The pangs of birth! The earth is bursting, that it may set me free.

VAGRANT. Come, come, be born.

ICHNEUMON FLY *(returning from the hole)*. No, no, Daughter. You must eat. You mustn't come out. It wouldn't do at all. Daddy'll soon be here and he'll bring you something nice, eh? What would you like, you greedy little girl?

LARVA *(looking out of hole)*. Daddy, I feel bored here. *(She is of the neurotic female type)*

ICHNEUMON FLY. Ha! Ha! That's a nice thing. Come and give me a kiss. Papa'll bring you something tasty. What, you want another cricket? Ha! Ha! Not at all a bad idea of yours.

LARVA. I should like—I don't know.

ICHNEUMON FLY. Good heavens, how clever of you, Jarva. I must give you something for that. Ta-ta, my child. Daddy must go to work now and get something for his darling, for his pretty little baby. Go in now, my pet. Have a nice feed. *(Exit Larva lair Left. Ichneumon Fly, approaching the Vagrant with long strides, smells and starts back as Vagrant threatens)* Who are you?

VAGRANT. I?

ICHNEUMON FLY. Are you eatable?

VAGRANT. No—I don't think so.

ICHNEUMON FLY *(sniffing at him)*. You're not fresh enough. Who are you?

VAGRANT. A vagabond.

ICHNEUMON FLY *(bowing slightly)*. Have you any children?

VAGRANT. No, I don't think so.

ICHNEUMON FLY. Ah, did you see her?

VAGRANT. Who?

ICHNEUMON FLY. My larva. Charming, eh? A smart child. And how she grows. What an appetite she has. Ha! Ha! Children are a great joy, aren't they?

VAGRANT. Everyone says so.

ICHNEUMON FLY. Aren't they? When you have them, you do at least know who you're working for. If you have a child, then you must strive, work, struggle. That's real life, eh? Children want to grow, to eat, to feast, to play, don't they?

VAGRANT. Children want a lot.

ICHNEUMON FLY. Would you believe that I take her two or three crickets every day?

VAGRANT. Who to?

ICHNEUMON FLY. To my child. Charming, eh? And so clever! Do you think she eats them all up? No, only the softest bits, while they're still alive. Ha! Ha! A splendid child, eh?

VAGRANT. I should think so!

ICHNEUMON FLY (*crosses to Center*). I'm proud of her. Really proud. Just like her daddy, eh? She takes after me, you know. Ha! Ha! and I'm gossiping here instead of getting to work. Oh, the fuss and running about. But as long as we do it for somebody, what does it matter? Am I right?

VAGRANT. I suppose you are.

ICHNEUMON FLY (*striding toward Vagrant*). It's a pity you aren't eatable. Really it's a pity, you know. I must take her something, mustn't I? (*Goes Center and on stump. Fingering the Chrysalis*) What's this?

CHRYSALIS. I proclaim the rebirth of the world.

ICHNEUMON FLY (*sniffs at her*). You aren't ripe yet. No good, is it?

CHRYSALIS. I'll create something.

ICHNEUMON FLY (*gets down off stump and then crosses to Vagrant*). It's a worry to bring up children. A great worry, isn't it? To rear a family, just imagine. To feed those poor little mites. To provide for them, to secure their future, eh? It's no trifle, is it? Well, I must be off now. Good day to you. Pleased to have met you, sir. (*Calling to Larva*) Ta-ta, baby. I'll be back soon. (*Exit Right*)

VAGRANT. Here's a funny thing—he wants to provide for his family, natural enough—if a man doesn't do that they call him a lazy brute—so he goes out after live crickets—that seems all right—and yet even a cricket wants to live! Some things are hard to understand.

LARVA (*crawling out of lair*). Daddy, Daddy!

VAGRANT. So you're the larva? Let's have a look at you.

LARVA. How ugly you are.

VAGRANT. Why?

LARVA. I don't know. Oh, how bored I am. I should like—I should like——

VAGRANT. What else?

LARVA. I don't know. To tear something up, something alive—— Ah, it makes me writhe, the thought of it!

VAGRANT. What's the matter with you?

LARVA. There is something so hideously gross about one's body, isn't there? Life is so shocking, so vulgar! Oh, if one could only be dead and still conscious of one's superiority! (*Exit into lair*)

VAGRANT. To provide for a family like that. I can't make it out. To prey on all living things so that your own can live!

MALE BEETLE (*enters down incline Left*). Come along, old girl. I've found a hole. Where are you? (*To Vagrant*) Where's my pile? Where's my wife?

VAGRANT. Your wife? Do you mean that old harridan? That fat, ugly chatterbox——

MALE BEETLE. That's her. Where's my pile?

VAGRANT. That bad-tempered, dirty ragbag?

MALE BEETLE. That's her! What has she done with my pile?

VAGRANT. That evil-smelling ball?

MALE BEETLE. My treasure! My beautiful pile! I left my wife here with it.

VAGRANT. A beetle came soon after you had gone. I think your wife followed him.

MALE BEETLE. What do I care about my wife? What's happened to my pile? (*Looking around for pile, goes up incline Right*)

VAGRANT. That's what I'm trying to tell you. The beetle rolled it away.

MALE BEETLE. God in Heaven! Rolled my pile away! My hard-earned fortune! I'm done for—I'm ruined. I'm murdered. He took my fortune and left my wife behind.

VAGRANT. At least *she'll* come back to you.

MALE BEETLE. Oh, yes! Ha! Ha! *She'll* come back to me—no doubt of that—but my pile, my beautiful pile! Stop thief! Stop thief! I must have my pile. (*He runs off at Right*)

VAGRANT. Ha! Ha! We have life here—even mankind can do no more than these crawling beetles.

(*Male Cricket's voice heard outside.*)

MALE CRICKET (*enters Left with handbag down incline, followed by Female Cricket*) Look out, woman. Take care you don' stumble. Here we are. Here we are. This is where we live. This is our new little home. *(Stumbles off incline Left)* Oh, look out. You haven't hurt yourself, have you?

FEMALE CRICKET. No, Cricket. Don't be absurd.

MALE CRICKET. But darling, you must be careful. When you're expecting—— *(Points to cave Right)* And now look down the peephole. There. How do you like it?

FEMALE CRICKET. Oh, Cricket, how tired I am. How very, very tired I am!

MALE CRICKET. Sit down, sit down, darling, sit down. Take great care of yourself now. You know you must be careful, in your condition.

FEMALE CRICKET *(sits down)*. What a long way. And all that moving, too. No, Cricket, really it's not right of you to make me do it.

MALE CRICKET. Oh, darling, come, come. Look, Cricket, darling, look. *(Pointing to cave)*

FEMALE CRICKET. Now don't get angry, you horrid man.

MALE CRICKET. I won't say another word, really I won't. Fancy. Mrs. Cricket won't take care of herself, and in her state, too. What do you think of her? Ha! Ha! Ha! Isn't she a wicked little mother?

FEMALE CRICKET *(tearfully)*. You naughty man, how can you joke about it?

MALE CRICKET. But darling, when I'm so happy. Just fancy, all those little crickets, the noise, the chirping. Ha! Ha! Ha! Darling, I'm mad with joy.

FEMALE CRICKET. You—you—silly boy. Look, Daddy—— Ha! Ha! *(Looking down cave Right)*

MALE CRICKET. Ha! Ha! Ha! And how do you like it?

FEMALE CRICKET. It's nice. Is this our new house?

MALE CRICKET. Our little nest, our villa, our little show, our—Ha! Ha!—our residence.

FEMALE CRICKET. Will it be dry? Who built it?

MALE CRICKET. Why, goodness me, another cricket has been living there. *(Pointing down cave)*

FEMALE CRICKET. Fancy. And why has he moved?

MALE CRICKET. Ha! Ha! Ha! He moved away. He moved away. Don't you know where to? Have a guess?

FEMALE CRICKET. I don't know. Oh, dear, what a long time you are before you say anything. Do tell me, Cricket, quickly.

MALE CRICKET *(sitting Right of her)*. Well, then—yesterday a bird came and fastened him on to a thorn. Upon my soul, darling, from end to end. Just imagine, his feet were wriggling there— Ha! Ha!—he was still alive. So when I came along, I at once saw that it would suit us. So we're moving into his house. By Jove, what a piece of luck. Ha! Ha! What do you think of it?

FEMALE CRICKET. And he's still alive? Ugh, how horrible.

MALE CRICKET. Oh, but what a godsend for us. Tra la la, tra tra tra la la—tr—— Wait a bit. We'll hang up our doorplate. *(From a bag he takes out a plate with the inscription,* "CRICKET, MUSIC DEALER"*)* Where shall we hang it? *(Crosses to cave)* Up there? More to the right? More to the left?

FEMALE CRICKET. A little high. And you say that his feet are still wriggling?

MALE CRICKET. I'm telling you. *(He holds doorplate up)* Like that?

FEMALE CRICKET. Brr! Where is he?

MALE CRICKET. Would you like to see it?

FEMALE CRICKET. Yes, I would. No, I wouldn't. Is it horrible?

MALE CRICKET *(as he hangs doorplate)*. Yes. Ha! Ha! Ha! I should think so. Is it hanging properly?

FEMALE CRICKET. Yes. Cricket, I have such a queer feeling——

MALE CRICKET *(running up to her)*. Good heavens, perhaps it's—it's already——

FEMALE CRICKET. Oh, dear, I'm so frightened.

MALE CRICKET. But darling, why be frightened? Every lady——

FEMALE CRICKET. It's all very well for you to talk. *(Bursts into tears)* Cricket, will you always love me?

MALE CRICKET. Of course, darling. Dear me, don't cry. Come, come.

FEMALE CRICKET *(sobbing)*. Show me how his feet wriggled.

MALE CRICKET. Like this. *(Showing her in pantomine)*

FEMALE CRICKET. Ha! Ha! How funny that must be.

MALE CRICKET. Well, well, you see there's nothing to cry about. *(Sits Left of her)* We'll furnish this place beautifully. And as soon as we can manage it, we'll put up some——

FEMALE CRICKET. Curtains.

MALE CRICKET. Curtains as well. Ha! Ha! Ha! Curtains of course. How clever of you to think of it. Give me a kiss.

FEMALE CRICKET. Never mind that now. Go on, you're so silly.

MALE CRICKET. Of course I am. *(Jumps up; crosses Right)* Guess what I've bought?

FEMALE CRICKET. Curtains.

MALE CRICKET. No, something smaller. *(Searches in his pockets)* Where did I—— *(Goes to bag for rattle)*

FEMALE CRICKET. Quick, quick! Let me see. *(Male Cricket from bag takes a child's rattle and shakes it)* Oh, how sweet! Cricket, give it to me. Lend it to me, quickly. Oh, Daddy, I'm so pleased.

MALE CRICKET. Listen, then, darling— *(Shakes rattle)*

FEMALE CRICKET. Cricket, cricket!

MALE CRICKET *(crosses up to incline Left)*. Now I must run round a little. Let people know I'm here. Knock at the doors, bustle about, stir up trade, do a little advertising. *(On incline)* I must get some introductions, fix up orders, have a look round. Give me the rattle—I'll use it on my way.

FEMALE CRICKET. And what about me? What will amuse *me* while you are gone? *(Tearfully)* You won't leave me?

MALE CRICKET *(crosses to Center)*. Oh, you'll soon be making friends. This is really a very select neighborhood. Find some nice little mother cricket to talk to about babies and all that sort of thing, that will amuse you nicely until I get back. *(Crosses Left. Starts up incline)*

FEMALE CRICKET. You bad boy. You are really leaving me!

MALE CRICKET *(back and kisses her)*. Ha! Ha! Ha! Now, darling, be careful. It won't be long. Now, my pet, take care of yourself. Be prudent. No risks, you know, my dear. *(Crosses)* I'll be back

before you know it. *(After he exits up incline Left she calls, "Cricket, cricket." He answers. Repeat three times)*

FEMALE CRICKET. There was a born a little—— *Cricket!*— I feel so frightened.

VAGRANT. Don't be frightened. Small things are born easily.

FEMALE CRICKET. Who's there? *(Turns around; sees Vagrant)* Ugh, a beetle. You don't bite?

VAGRANT. No.

FEMALE CRICKET. And how are the children?

VAGRANT. *My* children?

FEMALE CRICKET. Yes, of course! Surely you have a family.

VAGRANT. No—I haven't a thing in the world but what you see, nothing behind me, or ahead of me— no one to hurt—no one to hurt me. As you may easily observe, I'm a very fortunate man.

FEMALE CRICKET. Oh, dear, haven't you any children? That's a pity. *(Calls)* Cricket, Cricket! Oh, he doesn't answer. And why did you never marry, Beetle?

VAGRANT. Selfishness, dear madam, selfishness. I ought to be ashamed of it. The egoist seeks comfort in his solitude. He doesn't waste his time either loving or hating—time is so short, you see, I save all of it I can and use it to think about myself.

FEMALE CRICKET. Yes, yes, you men— you're all alike. *(Calls)* Cricket, Cricket! *(Crosses Right; looks down cave)*

CHRYSALIS *(shouting)*. Within me I bear the future. I—I——

VAGRANT. Be born.

CHRYSALIS. I shall achieve something illustrious.

FEMALE BEETLE *(running in Right, down Center)*. Isn't my husband there? Where is the stupid man? Where is our pile?

FEMALE CRICKET *(back to stage Left)*. Your pile! What's a pile? Oh, Madam, can you play with it? Do let me see it.

FEMALE BEETLE. It's not to play with. It's our future, our nest egg, our all. My husband, the clumsy creature, has gone off with it.

FEMALE CRICKET. Oh, dear, perhaps he's run away from you. You know what they are, these men!

FEMALE BEETLE. I know what mine is.

Do you? Where is he now—your man?

FEMALE CRICKET. He's away on business. *(Calling off Left)* Cricket! Cricket!

FEMALE BEETLE. Fancy him leaving you all alone like that, poor thing. And you're expecting——

FEMALE CRICKET. Oh, dear—— *(She weeps)* Isn't it just terrible?

FEMALE BEETLE. So young, too. And aren't you making a pile?

FEMALE CRICKET. What for?

FEMALE BEETLE. A pile, that's for the family. That's the future. That's your whole life.

FEMALE CRICKET. Oh, no. My whole life is to have my own little house, my nest, a little place of my own. And curtains. And children, and to have my Cricket. My own home. That's all.

FEMALE BEETLE. How can you live without a pile?

FEMALE CRICKET. What would we do with it?

FEMALE BEETLE. Roll it about with you everywhere. I tell you, there's nothing like a pile for holding a man.

FEMALE CRICKET. Oh, no, a little house; that's the only way to hold a man.

FEMALE BEETLE. A pile, I tell you.

FEMALE CRICKET. A little house.

FEMALE BEETLE. Dear me, I should so much like to have a chat with you. You're so nice—but you do have such absurd ideas. *(Starts to exit Right)*

FEMALE CRICKET. And what about your children? Of course you have children?

FEMALE BEETLE. We had no time for children. We only thought of our pile. Oh! My pile, my pi—pi—pi-le. Pi-pi—— *(She exits up incline Right)*

FEMALE CRICKET *(crosses to Left in front of lair)*. Ugh, what a frump! And her husband's run away from her. Ha! Ha! Ha! I—I—have such a queer—Ha! Ha! Ha!—how his feet wriggle. Oh, my! How funny he was!

ICHNEUMON FLY *(enters Right. Crosses upstage and downstage Left. Parasite follows him on)*. Aha! *(Approaches her with long, quiet strides, pierces the Female Cricket with a dagger, and drags her to his lair)* A nice one! Ha! Ha! Ha! A fat one!

VAGRANT *(flinches)*. Oh—oh—— Murder!

ICHNEUMON FLY *(in the entrance to his lair)*. Look, Daughter. Come quick and have a look at what Daddy's bringing you.

VAGRANT. He's killed her. And I—I stood there like a log. I didn't make a move to stop it. She didn't even cry out and nobody shouted with horror. Nobody ran to help her.

PARASITE. Bravo, comrade, that's just my opinion too.

VAGRANT. To die like that, without a moment's warning!

PARASITE *(on incline Right)*. That's just what I say. I've been looking on for quite a while, but I couldn't do a thing like that. No, I couldn't. Everyone wants to live, don't they?

VAGRANT. Who are you?

PARASITE. I? Oh, nothing really. I'm a poor wreck. An orphan. They call me a parasite.

VAGRANT. How can anyone dare to kill like that?

PARASITE. That's exactly what I say. Do you think he needs it? Do you think he's hungry, like me? Not a bit of it. He kills to add to his store. He collects things. It's a scandal, isn't it? Isn't this a piece of injustice? Why has one got a store while another starves? Why has he got a dagger while I've only got these bare hands? Am I right?

VAGRANT. I should say so.

PARASITE. That's what I say. There's no equality. I say all things are born equal, or at least they should be. For instance, I don't kill anyone. My jaws are too tender. I haven't got the necessary attupt-appart—appurtenances. I'm merely hungry. Is that right?

VAGRANT. Right? I don't know, but it seems to me that it's wrong to kill. It's always wrong. Killing shouldn't be allowed.

PARASITE. My very words, comrade. Or, at any rate, collecting things shouldn't be allowed. You eat your fill and you've got enough. Collecting things is robbing them who can't collect things. Eat your fill and have done with it. Then there'd be enough for all, wouldn't there now?

VAGRANT. I don't know.

PARASITE. But I'm telling you.

ICHNEUMON FLY *(returning from his*

lair). Eat it up, Baby, eat it up. Choose what you like. Haven't you a nice Daddy, eh? (*Crosses Right; sees Parasite*)

PARASITE. Good day to you, sir. (*He trembles before the Ichneumon Fly*)

ICHNEUMON FLY (*crosses Right, up close to Parasite*). How are you? How are you? I wonder if you are eatable? (*Sniffs at him*)

PARASITE (*afraid*). Ha! Ha! You're joking, sir. Why me?

ICHNEUMON FLY. Get out, you filthy creature! You scamp! What do you want here? Clear off! (*Parasite cowers. To the Vagrant*) Good day, sir—— Well, did you see that? Did you see me bag that cricket?

VAGRANT. Yes.

ICHNEUMON FLY. A fine piece of work, eh? Ha! Ha! It's not everyone who could do that. Ah, my boy, for that you want— (*Taps his forehead*) —expert knowledge. Enterprise. I-ni-tiative. And foresight. And love for work. Efficiency! That's what I call it.

PARASITE (*approaching*). That's just what I say.

ICHNEUMON FLY (*attempting to stab Parasite*). My good sir, if you want to keep alive, you've got to fight your way. There's your future. There's your family. And then, you know, there's a certain amount of ambition. A strong personality is bound to assert itself. Am I right?

PARASITE. That's what I say, sir.

ICHNEUMON FLY. Of course, of course. Make your way in the world; use the talent that's in you. That's what I call a useful life.

PARASITE. Absolutely, sir.

ICHNEUMON FLY (*threatening Parasite*). Hold your tongue, you disgusting object. I'm not talking to you.

PARASITE. Just what I say, sir.

ICHNEUMON FLY. And how it cheers you up when you fulfill your duty like that. When you perform your job. When you feel that you're not living in vain. It's so elevating, isn't it? Well, good day to you, sir. I must be off again. My best respects. (*Starts off. Stops at lair*) Larva, au revoir. (*Upstage Left circles and exits Right*)

PARASITE. The old murderer. Believe me, it was all I could do not to fly at his throat. Yes, sir, I'd work too, if need be.

But why should I work when someone else has more than he can consume? I've got initiative too. Ha! Ha!—but here—— (*Pats his stomach*) I'm hungry, that's what I am, hungry. I tell you. A fine state of things, eh?

VAGRANT. I know what hunger means.

PARASITE. That's just what I say. Anything for a piece of meat, and a poor man's got nothing. It's against nature. Everyone should have what he can eat, eh? And nobody should have any more.

VAGRANT. Poor Cricket, poor Cricket, poor Cricket!

PARASITE. That's it. Everyone wants to live.

MALE CRICKET (*runs in Left, shaking a rattle*). Here I am, my pet, here, here, here. Where are you, darling? Guess what Hubby's bought you?

ICHNEUMON FLY (*appearing behind him*). Aha!

VAGRANT. Look out, look out!

PARASITE (*stopping him*). Don't interfere, mate. Don't get mixed up in it. What must be, must be.

MALE CRICKET. But, Mummy! Where are you, my little darling?

ICHNEUMON FLY (*with a great lunge pierces him and drags him in lair*). Daughter, larva, what is your kind Daddy bringing you now, eh?

VAGRANT. Oh, Almighty God! How can you allow it?

PARASITE. Just what I say. That's the third cricket he's had already and me nothing. And that's what the likes of us are expected to put up with.

ICHNEUMON FLY (*runs out from his lair*). No, no, Baby. I've got no time. Daddy must go back to work. Eat, eat, eat. Be quiet now. I'll be back in an hour. (*Runs off Left*)

PARASITE. I'm simply boiling over. The old scoundrel. (*Approaching the lair*) What injustice. What a disgrace. I'll show him, that I will. Just you wait! Has he gone? I must have a look. (*Enters the lair*)

VAGRANT. Murder, and more murder! Why can't I remember that they are only beetles? Why can't I remember that this is only a tiny drama between two blades of grass, nothing but insect war, nothing but beetle doings? I saw evil enough in the world, but there I saw something at least better than this insect crew! Man doesn't crave only to devour, he craves to create and build—he works—he saves, he collects his pile! No—no—that's the beetles again! Pah! I can't get them out of my head. A pile for the beetles, but surely for human beings there are mightier ambitions! To have a home, however small, to harm nobody, to have his children about him—to sit by his humble doorstep and watch his neighbor's feet wiggling as he lies impaled upon a thorn! —No—that's the crickets—— Why do I keep getting muddled? The silly joys of crickets would never content a man! Man wants more than just to eat his fill! Life calls for heroes, life calls for struggle! To win life's battles calls for a strong grip! A man must not be weak! If a man would live he must *rule*, if he would *eat*, then the must *kill!*—No—that's the Ichneumon Fly! God! I seem to hear it all about me, throughout the Universe feverish jowls are working! Chew, chew, chew! Bloodstained lips smack over still living victims! Life is the prey of life!

CHRYSALIS. I feel something great! Something great!

VAGRANT. What is great?

CHRYSALIS. To be born. To live. Help me to live.

VAGRANT. Chrysalis, Chrysalis! I will not desert you.   (MUSIC)

PARASITE *(is heard laughing and hiccoughing in lair of Ichneumon Fly. Rolling out of lair, enormously fat)*. Ha! Ha! Ha! The old miser! He had stores for that white-faced daughter of his. I'm all swelled up. I'm going to burst.

VAGRANT. What about the larva?

PARASITE. I gobbled her up too.

VAGRANT. And this is the World We Live In.   (MUSIC *rises to forte)*

PARASITE *(jumping around joyfully)*. Ha! Ha! Ha! Ha! Ha! Ha! Ha!

CURTAIN

ACT THREE

THE ANTS

SCENE: *Same as Prologue. —* MUSIC. *(The Vagrant sits on log in thought.)*

VAGRANT. I have seen enough! I have seen all creatures sucking like lice at the great body of creation in a fearful craving to increase their share! To increase it, as we humans do, by depriving others! I wonder if I am any different from these insects—— No—I am a cockroach who gathers from the dust the crumbs that others have left! That is my life—failure— fit for nothing—not even fit to be devoured!

CHRYSALIS. Make room! I'm being born. From my prison I'll set the whole world free!

VAGRANT *(rises fiercely)*. I'll leave this forest and go back to the city. I'll find the things that in human speech mean town, and district and county and stage——! And *Country!* The things that belong not to one, but to all of us—there's the whole difference—this insect greed of *self* knows only *self*, and doesn't know that there is anything beyond!

CHRYSALIS. Oh, this thirst! This awful thirst to do a great deed!

VAGRANT. That's it. Once a man's born he's got to pay for life.

CHRYSALIS. The hour draws near. Great things are about to happen.

VAGRANT. If a man's life is to be worth more than the lives of these bugs and beetles here, it's only because of what he can leave behind him—— It's a funny thing, but I never thought of that before, *the price we owe for life,* not to ourselves, to others.

CHRYSALIS. See what wings I have! What boundless wings!

VAGRANT. A new thought to take back with me—if I have strength enough to go back at all. *(He sinks down)* A new way to live my life, if I've any life left to live. My mind is clear enough, but my body's numb. I feel—— Ouch! What's that biting me? Ah! It's an ant! And there's another—— And a third. Good Lord! I've sat on an ant-heap. *(Stands up)* You fools, what are you crawling on to me for? Look at them running after me, look—one, two, three, four. And here's another one, two—three—four.

(GAUZE OPENS)

BLIND ANT *(front gauze flies and displays an ant-heap—full stage. The traps on the incline are open. The Blind Ant sits Center. He counts continuously. Ants carrying sacks and shovels are walking around in a circle. Three Ants are seen coming out of trap Left and crossing and descending into trap Right. Blind Ant, keeping time with his arm).* One, two, three, four—one, two, three, four.

VAGRANT. What's that? What are you counting, old boy?

BLIND ANT. One, two, three, four——

VAGRANT. What's this here? What's all this work and hurry about? Hi, what's this, a quarry, or a mine?

BLIND ANT. One, two, three, four——

VAGRANT. What's this place, I'm asking? Why is this blind creature counting? Ah, he's giving them the time. They all move in time as he counts. One, two, three, four. Like machines. Bah, it makes my head swim.

BLIND ANT. One, two, three, four——

FIRST ENGINEER *(he is afterwards Dictator. Running in Left and crossing down to Center).* Quicker, quicker. One, two, three, four.

BLIND ANT *(more quickly).* One, two, three, four—one, two, three, four. *(They all move more quickly)*

VAGRANT. What's that? I'm asking, sir, what's going on here?

FIRST ENGINEER *(starts walking back and forth across down stage, Right and Left).* Who's here?

VAGRANT. Myself.

FIRST ENGINEER. From which of the ants?

VAGRANT. From the humans.

FIRST ENGINEER. This is an ant-realm. What do you want here?

VAGRANT. I'm having a look.

FIRST ENGINEER. Are you trying to find work?

VAGRANT. To tell the truth I came here to avoid it.

SECOND ENGINEER *(he is afterwards Head of General Staff. Running in Left, down to Center).* A discovery! A discovery!

FIRST ENGINEER. What is it?

SECOND ENGINEER. Efficiency!—A new method of speeding up. Don't count one, two, three, four. Count one, two, four. That's shorter. Saves time, gets more out of the working man—if we can't make them work more hours we'll make 'em do more in an hour. Get the point? One,

two, four! Here, you blind fellow! Hello!

BLIND ANT. One, two, three, four.

SECOND ENGINEER. Wrong. One, two, four.

BLIND ANT. One, two, four—one, two, four! *(They all move more quickly)*

VAGRANT. Not so fast. It makes me feel giddy.

SECOND ENGINEER. Who are you? *(Starts walking back and forth Right and Left of down stage Left; turning Left at Center when he faces First Engineer, who is walking Right and Left of down stage Right)*

VAGRANT. A stranger.

SECOND ENGINEER. Where from?

FIRST ENGINEER. From the humans. Where is the humans' ant-heap?

VAGRANT. What?

FIRST ENGINEER. Where is the humans' ant-heap?

VAGRANT. Oh, yonder. And all about us. Everywhere.

SECOND ENGINEER *(yelping).* Everywhere! Fool!

FIRST ENGINEER. Are there many humans?

VAGRANT. Yes. They're called the masters of the world.

SECOND ENGINEER. Ha, ha! Masters of the world. Humph!

FIRST ENGINEER. *We're* the masters of the world.

SECOND ENGINEER. The Ant-Realm!

FIRST ENGINEER. The largest Ant-State.

SECOND ENGINEER. A world power.

FIRST ENGINEER. The largest democracy.

VAGRANT. What's that?

FIRST ENGINEER. All must obey.

SECOND ENGINEER. All have to work. All for Him.

FIRST ENGINEER. As He orders.

VAGRANT. Who?

FIRST ENGINEER. The Whole! The State! The Nation!

VAGRANT. Why, that's just like us. All for the Nation. That's democracy. Have you got democracy, too?

FIRST ENGINEER. No. We have the Whole.

VAGRANT. And who speaks for the Whole?

SECOND ENGINEER. He knows nothing

FIRST ENGINEER. The one who orders. The Whole only issues commands.

SECOND ENGINEER. He abides in the laws. He is nowhere else. The Whole is the voice of all—the will of the Community.

VAGRANT. And who rules the Community?

FIRST ENGINEER. Reason.

SECOND ENGINEER. Law.

FIRST ENGINEER. The interests of the Whole.

SECOND ENGINEER. That's it, that's it.

VAGRANT. I like that. That's very much what I've just been saying to myself. I'm nothing; you're nothing; all for the Whole.

FIRST ENGINEER. For its greatness.

SECOND ENGINEER. And against the enemies of the Whole!

VAGRANT. What's that? How can the Whole have enemies? Who are you against?

FIRST ENGINEER. Against all, against everybody but ourselves.

SECOND ENGINEER. We are surrounded by enemies.

FIRST ENGINEER. We defeated the Brown Ants.

SECOND ENGINEER. And starved out the Russets.

FIRST ENGINEER. And conquered the Grays. Only the Yellows are left. We must starve out the Yellows.

SECOND ENGINEER. We must starve out everybody.

VAGRANT. Why?

FIRST ENGINEER. In the interests of the Whole.

SECOND ENGINEER. The interests of the Whole are the highest.

FIRST ENGINEER. Interests of race.

SECOND ENGINEER. Industrial interests.

FIRST ENGINEER. Financial interests.

SECOND ENGINEER. World interests.

FIRST ENGINEER. Interests of the Whole.

SECOND ENGINEER. Yes, yes, that's it.

FIRST ENGINEER. The Whole has nothing but interests.

SECOND ENGINEER. Nobody may have as many interests as the Whole.

FIRST ENGINEER. Interests preserve the Whole.

SECOND ENGINEER. And wars nourish it.

VAGRANT. Aha, you're—you're the warlike ants.

SECOND ENGINEER. Tut, tut! He knows nothing.

FIRST ENGINEER. Our ants are the most peaceful ants in all the Universe.

SECOND ENGINEER. A nation of peace.

FIRST ENGINEER. A labor State.

SECOND ENGINEER. We only wish for world power——

FIRST ENGINEER. Because we wish for world peace.

SECOND ENGINEER. In the interests of our peaceable labor.

FIRST ENGINEER. And in the interests of progress.

SECOND ENGINEER. In the interests of our interests. When we rule over the world——

FIRST ENGINEER. We shall conquer time. We wish to rule over time.

VAGRANT. Over what?

FIRST ENGINEER. Time. Time is greater than space.

SECOND ENGINEER. Time has found no master yet.

FIRST ENGINEER. The master of time will be master of all.

VAGRANT. Slowly, for heaven's sake, slowly. Let me think.

FIRST ENGINEER. Speed is the master of time.

SECOND ENGINEER. The taming of time.

FIRST ENGINEER. He who commands speed will be ruler of time.

SECOND ENGINEER. One, two, four. One, two, four.

BLIND ANT (more quickly). One, two, four! One, two, four! (All move more quickly)

FIRST ENGINEER. We must quicken the pace.

SECOND ENGINEER. The pace of output.

FIRST ENGINEER. The pace of life.

SECOND ENGINEER. Every movement must be quickened.

FIRST ENGINEER. Shortened.

SECOND ENGINEER. Reckoned out.

FIRST ENGINEER. To an instant.

SECOND ENGINEER. To a hundredth of an instant.

FIRST ENGINEER. So as to save time.

SECOND ENGINEER. So as to increase output.

FIRST ENGINEER. Work has been proceeding too slowly. Too ponderously. We must force them to speed up.

SECOND ENGINEER. Unsparingly.

FIRST ENGINEER. For the good of the Whole.

VAGRANT. But what are they hurrying after like that?

FIRST ENGINEER. The interests of the Whole.

SECOND ENGINEER. A question of output. A question of power.

FIRST ENGINEER. There is peace. Peace is rivalry.

SECOND ENGINEER. We are waging the battle of peace by waging war.

BLIND ANT. One, two, four. One, two, four.

(An Ant Official approaches the Two Engineers from Left and reports something to them, and exits Left.)

VAGRANT. One, two, four. Quicker still. One, two, four. Flog this old slow time with the whip of speed, lash and hound it, make it rush forward more quickly, for speed is progress. The world wants to rush more hastily forward, wants to soar to its goal, even if it soars to ruin. Blind creature, count! One, two, four!

BLIND ANT. One, two, four!

FIRST ENGINEER. Quicker, quicker.

AN ANT *(collapsing under his load)*. Oh, I—can do no more!

SECOND ENGINEER. Tut, tut! What's that? Get up!

ANOTHER ANT *(bending over the one who has collapsed)*. Dead!

FIRST ENGINEER. One, two—— Carry him away, quickly. *(Two Ants lift up the Corpse)*

SECOND ENGINEER. What an honor! He fell on the field of speed.

FIRST ENGINEER. How are you lifting him? Too slowly. You're wasting time. Drop him. *(The Two Ants drop the Corpse)* Head and feet together. One, two, four. Wrong. Drop him. *(The Two Ants drop the Corpse)* Head and feet—one, two, four. *(The Two Ants pick up Corpse as directed and exit Right)* Take him away, quick march! One, two, four—one, two, four——

SECOND ENGINEER. One, two, four! Quicker!

VAGRANT. Anyhow, he died quick enough.

FIRST ENGINEER. To work, to work! He who has more must work more. *(They start walking Right and Left again)*

SECOND ENGINEER. He needs more.

FIRST ENGINEER. He has more to defend.

SECOND ENGINEER. And more to gain.

FIRST ENGINEER. We are a nation of peace. Peace means work.

SECOND ENGINEER. And work strength.

FIRST ENGINEER. And strength war.

SECOND ENGINEER. Yes, yes.

INVENTOR *(off Right)*. Look out, look out! Step aside! *(Enter Inventor from trap Right, groping)*

SECOND ENGINEER. Hello, our Inventor. Look! Look! He has invented something!

INVENTOR. Take care, take care, Don't knock against my head. It is huge. It is of glass. It is fragile. It is greater than I am. Keep out of the way. It would burst. It would be smashed bang. Look out. I'm carrying a head. Don't knock it. Step aside.

SECOND ENGINEER. Hello—how goes it?

INVENTOR. It's hurting. It's bursting. It's knocking against the walls of the world—bang! No, no, I can't get my two hands round it. No, no, I can't even carry it now. Look out, do you hear? Whew, whew, whew!

FIRST ENGINEER. What is it?

INVENTOR. A machine, a new machine. In my head. Do you hear it working? It's smashing my head. Oh, oh—a huge machine. Out of the way. Out of the way. I'm carrying a machine.

FIRST ENGINEER. What sort of a machine?

INVENTOR. A war-machine. An enormous one. The swiftest, most effective crusher of lives. The greatest progress. The acme of science. Whew, whew, whew, do you hear it? Ten thousand, a hundred thousand dead. Whew, whew, it keeps on working. Two hundred thousand dead. Whew, whew, whew, whew!

FIRST ENGINEER. A genius, eh?

INVENTOR. Oh, oh! What pain! My head's splitting. Out of the way, out of the way. Take care I don't knock against you. *(Exits Left)* Whew, whew, whew.

FIRST ENGINEER. A great intellect. The greatest of scientists.

SECOND ENGINEER. Nothing serves the State so much as science.

FIRST ENGINEER. Science is a great thing. There will be war.

VAGRANT. Why war?

FIRST ENGINEER. Because we shall have a new war-machine.

SECOND ENGINEER. Because we still need a new bit of the world.

FIRST ENGINEER. A bit of the world from the birch tree to the pine tree.

SECOND ENGINEER. And a road between two blades of grass

FIRST ENGINEER. The only open road to the South.

SECOND ENGINEER. A question of prestige.

FIRST ENGINEER. And trade.

SECOND ENGINEER. The greatest national idea.

FIRST ENGINEER. Either us or the Yellows.

SECOND ENGINEER. Never was war more honorable or more urgent——

FIRST ENGINEER. Than the one we must wage.

SECOND ENGINEER. We are prepared.

FIRST ENGINEER. We must only have a cause.

BLIND ANT. One, two, four. One, two, four.

(A gong is heard and the Engineers stop marching. Uniforms are thrown up through traps to Ants on stage, who put them on.)

FIRST ENGINEER. What's that?

VOICES. A messenger. A messenger.

MESSENGER *(runs in Left and down Right)*. Gentlemen! I am a messenger of the Southern army.

FIRST ENGINEER. Good.

MESSENGER. In accordance with orders, we crossed the frontier of the Yellows.

FIRST ENGINEER. What then?

MESSENGER. The Yellows captured me and took me to their Commander.

FIRST ENGINEER. And?

MESSENGER. Here is the Commander's letter.

FIRST ENGINEER. Show it to me! *(Takes the paper and reads)* "The Government of the Yellow Ants calls upon the Ant-Realm, within three minutes to withdraw his army lying between the birch tree and the pine tree on the road between two blades of grass."

SECOND ENGINEER. Listen, listen.

FIRST ENGINEER. "This territory comprises the historical, vital, industrial, sacred and military interests of our State, so that it rightfully belongs to us."

SECOND ENGINEER. An insult. We cannot tolerate it.

FIRST ENGINEER. "At the same time we are instructing our regiments to start advancing." *(Drops the paper)* War! War at last! The day—the day has come.

SECOND ENGINEER. They forced it on us. There is no choice!

FIRST ENGINEER. To arms!

ANOTHER MESSENGER *(entering Left)*. The Yellows are marching across our frontiers.

FIRST ENGINEER. To arms! To arms!

SECOND ENGINEER. Mobilization! To arms! *(First and Second Engineers exit Left)*

EVERYONE. To arms! To arms!

(Ants enter from traps Right, Center and Left and begin to mobilize, picking up bayonets, etc.)

BLIND ANT. One, two, four. One, two, four.

VAGRANT. To arms, to arms! The road between the blades of grass is threatened. Do you hear? The cranny from blade to blade, a span of earth from grass to grass, your sacred rights, the greatest interests of the State, the greatest problem in the world. All—all is at stake. Ants to arms! How could you live if another possessed the world between two husks? If another carried ant-baggage into a strange ant-heap. A hundred thousand lives for these two blades of grass are far too few. I was in the war—— Oh, yes—I know the game! That's a grand game for insects. Dig trenches, root yourself in clay. Hurrah! An attack in extended order. At the double over stacks of corpses, fix bayonets! Fifty thousand dead, to capture twenty paces of latrines! Hurrah! To arms! The interest of the Whole is at stake; the heritage of your history is in the balance—more—the freedom of your native land; nay, more—world power!

Nay, more—two blades of grass. Such a mighty cause can only be settled by the dead. To arms! To arms!

CHRYSALIS. The whole earth is quivering. I am being born.

(The Troops are lined up in ranks on platform at back, with metal helmets, machine guns, etc. Enter First Engineer with the badge of a Commander in Chief; his staff; the Second Engineer as Head of the General Staff, with Quartermaster and Telegraphers. They take their places on platform upstage Center. Telegraphers Right—First Engineer, Second Engineer and Quartermaster.)

VAGRANT. See what good training does. Attention! Sound the roll-call. Soldiers, your country is sending you to war, that you may fall. Remember you are being watched over by two blades of grass.

FIRST ENGINEER *(on platform)*. Soldiers! We find ourselves compelled to call you to the colors. A wicked enemy has treacherously attacked us, for the purpose of outwitting our pacific preparations. At this grave hour I am appointed Dictator.

HEAD OF GENERAL STAFF. Greet the Dictator. Shout, boys, or—— *(Soldiers cheer)*

FIRST ENGINEER *(now Dictator, saluting)*. Thank you. You have realized the demand of the moment. Soldiers, we are fighting for liberty and right.

HEAD OF GENERAL STAFF. —and for the greatness of the State.

DICTATOR. And for the greatness of the State. We shall wage war for civilization and military honor. Soldiers, I am with you to the last drop of blood.

HEAD OF GENERAL STAFF. Long live our great Commander! *(Soldiers all cheer)*

DICTATOR. I know my soldiers. They will fight until the final victory. Long live our gallant men, hurrah! *(Soldiers all cheer. To Head of General Staff)* First and Second Divisions attack. Fourth Division surround the pinewoods and break into the ant-heap of the Yellows. Women and embryos to be slaughtered. Third Division reserve. No quarter! *(Head of General Staff salutes)* May God assist us in this. Soldiers, forward!

HEAD OF GENERAL STAFF. One, two. War forced upon us. One, two. In the name of Justice. Give no quarter. For your hearths and homes! We are only defending ourselves. War for the world! For a greater native land. One, two. A cruel enemy. Will of the Nation! To battle! Strike hard! Historical claim! Brilliant spirit of the army! One, two. One, two. *(Fresh Troops continue to march past to the beating of the drums)*

DICTATOR. Good luck, Soldiers. I shall be behind you. Fifth Regiment. The conqueror of the pine cones. A mighty epoch! To victory! Conquer the world! Magnificent daring! Seventh Regiment, hurrah! Beat them, Soldiers. The Yellows are cowards. Burn and sack, heroes. Burn! Slaughter! Kill!

MESSENGER *(running in from the Left)*. The Yellows have invaded the stretch of country between the roots of the pine tree and the stone.

DICTATOR. Entirely according to plan. *(Messenger exits Left)* Faster, Soldiers. One, two. War forced upon us for honor and glory; needs of the State; noble conception of Justice; Soldiers, show your bravery; greatest moment in history! Quick march! Quick march! The battle is beginning. Second levy! *(Dictator inspects battlefield through a telescope)*

BLIND ANT. One, two, four—one, two, four.

CHRYSALIS *(shouting)*. The earth is bursting, listen to me. The depths of the world are toiling in pain for the birth that is mine.

DICTATOR. Second levy. Third levy. To arms! *(To the Quartermaster)* Issue a report.

QUARTERMASTER *(in a loud voice)*. The battle has begun at last amid favorable weather conditions. Our heroic men are fighting in magnificent spirits. *(New Troops march past to the beating of drums)*

DICTATOR. Quick march! One, two. One, two. Faster, boys!

SECOND MESSENGER *(running in Left)*. Our right wing is retreating. The Fifth Regiment is completely destroyed.

DICTATOR. According to plan. Sixth Regiment replace them. *(Messenger runs off Left)*

VAGRANT. Ha! Ha! According to plan. So it's all right, when Death himself serves on the staff as a general and carries out orders; I beg to report the Fifth Regiment is destroyed—according to plan! Oh, I know all about this, and I've seen it before. I've seen broad fields covered with corpses, slaughtered human flesh frozen in the snow; I've seen the Supreme Staff, and Death himself with a breast full of medals, survey the fallen, to see whether the rotting corpses are heaped, on the chart of the dead, according to plan.

A WOUNDED MAN *(screams. Enters Left and crossing Right. Exits Right).* The Fifth Regiment! Our regiment! We're all killed! Stop! Stop! *(The Telegraph instrument clatters)*

TELEGRAPHER *(reads dispatch).* Fifth Regiment destroyed. We await orders.

DICTATOR. Sixth take their places. *(To the Quartermaster)* Issue a report.

QUARTERMASTER *(in a loud voice).* The battle is developing successfully. The Fifth Regiment specially distinguished itself, heroically repelling all attacks, whereupon it was relieved by the Sixth.

DICTATOR. Bravo! I will decorate you with the great Order of Merit.

QUARTERMASTER. Thank you. I am only doing my duty.

JOURNALIST *(runs in Right to Center).* I am a journalist. Shall we announce a victory?

DICTATOR. Yes. Successful operations. Thanks to our plans prepared long ago. The admirable spirit of our forces. Irresistible advance. The enemy demoralized.

JOURNALIST. We will print everything.

DICTATOR. Good. We rely upon the co-operation of the Press. Don't forget the admirable spirit of our troops.

JOURNALIST. We will do our duty. *(Runs off Right)*

WAR WORKER *(with collecting-box, enters Right; comes down to front Center).* Help the wounded. All for the wounded. Gifts for the wounded. Give to the wounded. Help for the cripples. All for the cripples. Aid the cripples.

DICTATOR *(to Officer).* Second Division attack. It must break through. Whatever the sacrifice.

BOND SALESMAN *(enters Left with package of bonds; comes downstairs to front Center).*

Who'll buy bonds to run the war? Who'll give his money to make more war! Without money how can our Nation fight? Who'll give us money? *(Pantomime)*

WAR WORKER. For our heroes. Help your brothers. Help for the wounded.

VAGRANT. All for the wounded. War for the wounded. All for their wounds.

BOND SALESMAN. Who'll buy bonds to make a war? *(Exits Left)*

WAR WORKER. Help for the cripples. Give to the wounded.

VAGRANT *(tears off a button and puts it into the collecting-box).* All for the wounded. My last button for the war. *(He hands button to War Worker and she exits Right)*

TELEGRAPHER. The right wing of the Yellows is retreating.

DICTATOR. Pursue them. Finish them off. Don't be bothered with prisoners.

QUARTERMASTER *(in a loud voice).* The enemy retiring in confusion. Our regiments, in defiance of death, dogging his footsteps with splendid daring. *(Salutes and exits Left)*

DICTATOR. Fourth levy!

TELEGRAPHER. Sixth Regiment destroyed to the last man.

DICTATOR. According to plan. Tenth take their place. Fourth levy! *(New detachments of armed Troops march up)* At the double.

TELEGRAPHER. The Fourth Division has invested the pine trees and made a rear attack on the ant heap of the Yellows. The garrison is slaughtered.

DICTATOR. Raze it to the ground. Kill the women and embryos.

TELEGRAPHER. The enemy is overwhelmed. They have evacuated a foot of the reed patch.

DICTATOR. Great God, thou hast granted victory unto Justice. I appoint Thee, Colonel! *(He jumps up)* Third Division forward against the enemy! All reserves forward! Spare nobody! No prisoners! Forward! *(On his knees)* Righteous God of strength, Thou knowest that our holy cause is Thine! Thou knowest that in our victory lieth the victory of right and Justice over base and evil enemies, and in Thy divine will I bow my heart in humbleness! *(He jumps up)* After them! After them! Attack them! Hunt them down! Kill! Kill! Slaughter all! *(He kneels)* God, in this significant hour, I humbly bend my knee before Thee in gratitude for Thy splendid favors; before Thy august might I bow my head in reverence, Thy will, O Lord, be done! And, O God of infinite wisdom, I give thanks to Thee that under Thy favor the rule of the world is settled.

VAGRANT. Rule of the world! You wretched ant, you call this bit of clay and grass the world, do you? This miserable, dirty span of earth? Trample down all this ant-heap of yours, and you with it, and not a tree-top will rustle above you, you poor fool.

DICTATOR. Who are you?

VAGRANT. Now only a voice; yesterday perhaps a soldier in another ant-heap. What do you think of yourself, conqueror of the world? Do you feel great enough? Doesn't it seem to you that this heap of corpses is too small, upon which your glory is established, you poor wretch?

DICTATOR *(rises)*. No price is too great for victory! I proclaim myself Emperor. *(The Telegraph instrument clatters.)*

TELEGRAPHER. The Second Division is asking for reinforcements. Our troops fall exhausted.

DICTATOR. What? They must hold out. Drive them with whips.

TELEGRAPHER. The Third Division has been thrown into confusion.

AN ANT *(rushes across the stage Left to Right)*. We're running away.

DICTATOR. Fifth levy! All to arms!

ANOTHER ANT *(enters. Fleeing from Right)*. Stop! No, no! Back! Save yourselves!

DICTATOR. Fifth levy! The unfit to the front! Wounded to the front! All to the front!

A SOLDIER *(enters. Fleeing from the Left)*. They're beating us. Run.

TWO SOLDIERS *(running on from the Right)*. They've surrounded us. Escape.

A SOLDIER *(fleeing from the Left)*. To the West! Escape to the West!

SOLDIER *(enters. Fleeing from the Right)*. They've surrounded us from the West! Run to the East!

DICTATOR *(yells)*. Back to your places! To the front!

SOLDIER *(in a mad stampede)*. Out of it! The flames are spurting!

SOLDIER *(enters from Left)*. To the West! Save yourselves! Out of the way!

SOLDIER *(enters from Right)*. Escape, they're hunting us down! To the East!

SOLDIER *(enters from Left)*. To the West! Out of the way! They're here. *(The ranks of Soldiers are thrown into confusion and scuffle about and retreat)*

DICTATOR *(jumps upon them and strikes at them)*. Back! Cowards! You cattle! I am your Commander!

A TRAITOR. To hell with you and your commands! *(Stabs the Dictator)* Escape, comrades, escape!

HEAD OF GENERAL STAFF. They've taken the city. Put out the lights. *(The Yellows rush in—from both sides.)*

YELLOW COMMANDER. Hurrah, hurrah! The ant-heap is ours!

HEAD OF GENERAL STAFF. Fight, fight! Ah-h-h! *(Drops dead. Sound of turmoil and confusion among Troops as they fight)*

YELLOW COMMANDER. Into the passages after them. Spare nobody. Slaughter all the men. After them, Yellow Ants!

THE BLIND ANT. One, two, four.

YELLOW COMMANDER. Slaughter the women and embryos. Kill! Kill! Kill!

SHOUTS OF WOMEN. O-o-o-o-o!

THE BLIND ANT. One, two, four. One, two—!

YELLOW COMMANDER. After them! Murder! Murder them all! *(The din becomes more remote)* Light!

(The Yellows are forcing them to retreat. Corpses are heaped all about, Telegrapher lies murdered—also Dictator and Head of General Staff.)

YELLOW COMMANDER. We've won! We've won! The victory of Justice and Progress! Ours is the path between two blades of grass. The world belongs to us Yellows—— *(Throws the Blind Ant off stump. Blind Ant falls dead)* I proclaim myself Ruler of the Universe.

CHRYSALIS. Wait! Wait! I want to be born!

YELLOW COMMANDER *(kneels down and prays)*. Most righteous God, thou knowest that we fight only for Justice, our history, our national honor, our commercial interests——

VAGRANT *(rushes over to him and kicks him over and grinds him to pieces with his boot)*. Bah, you insect, you stupid insect!

CURTAIN

EPILOGUE

LIFE AND DEATH

SCENE: *The interior of a forest. Pitch-black night.*—MUSIC.

DISCOVERED: *The Vagrant sleeping in the foreground.*

____

VAGRANT *(dreaming and talking in his sleep)*. Enough, General! Enough! Hasn't there been blood enough?

(Wakes up. MUSIC stops) Where am I? This awful darkness—I can't—I can't see my hand before me. *(Stands up)* Why is it so dark? I can't see! I can't see! Who's speaking? Who's there? *(Shouts)* Who's there? *(Gropes about him)* Nothing—nothing—nothing— *(Shouts)* Is anything there? Is anything there at all? An abyss—everywhere this awful abyss! On which side does it begin to fall? If I had something to hold on to. There's nothing. There's nothing. Oh, God, I'm frightened. Where's the sky got to? If at least the sky were left. Or a single will-o'-the-wisp. A single human glimmer If—at least—some direction were left. Where am I? *(Kneels)* I'm frightened. Light! If only there were light!

VOICE OF YELLOW COMMANDER. There is light—light enough.

VAGRANT. A single human glimmer! Only one ray.

ANOTHER VOICE. This hunger! This thirst!

ANOTHER VOICE. I'm calling you. Come. I'm seeking you. I'm calling you. Come.

A THIN VOICE. A drink, a drink, drink!

VAGRANT. For God's sake! Only a tiny spark of light. What's that? Where am I?

VOICE OF MALE BEETLE *(far off)*. My little pile! Where is my little pile?

VAGRANT. Light!

A VOICE. This hunger! This thirst!

A DYING VOICE. Oh, this agony! This agony!

ANOTHER VOICE. Be mine! You darling! How I love you!

PARASITE'S VOICE. That's what I say.

VAGRANT. Light! What's here? Ah, a stone!

A VOICE. This thirst! This thirst!

ANOTHER VOICE. Mercy! Water—for God's sake—water!

VAGRANT. If I can only strike a small spark out of it—— *(Beats a stone against the stone)* A single spark of light. The least tiny spark. *(Sparks burst from the stone. The interior of the forest is lit up with a spectral radiance. Standing up)*

ALL VOICES. Then: Light!

VAGRANT. Light, thank God!

CHRYSALIS. Upon your knees. I—I, the chosen one—am entering the world.

ALL VOICES. Light.

VAGRANT. Where are you from with your transparent wings?

FIRST MOTH *(enters Left on back of platform, followed by a chorus of Moths Right and Left)*. Oh—oh—oh! Like a ray from the gloom has burst forth the radiant eternal, mighty life of the moths. Dance, my sisters. Oh—oh! From blending of rays our wings are woven. From star onto star, from glittering threads. We dance through life—*we*, the spirit of life, born from light; images of God, who—— *(Sinks down dead)*

SECOND MOTH *(enters Right. Comes forward and whirls round)* —who in us beholds Himself. Oh—oh—oh! Eternal, eternal is life.

VAGRANT *(towards her)*. How, then, is it eternal?

SECOND MOTH. To live, to encircle, to whirl. To us is given the mysterious task of eternally whirling; from our wings is showered the harmony of the spheres. Oh, what a duty and what a joy to be a moth—to live is to whirl and whirl to—to—oh—oh—oh! *(Whirl round)*

VAGRANT. Oh, what a duty and what creative joy——

SECOND MOTH. Unravel life. What else are we, we who are woven from daintiest fabrics, but the thought and the soul of

creation? We are transparent. We are life itself. Like sparks from God's furnace have we burst forth and we glorify——
(Falls down stage Right, dead)

VAGRANT. See, she is dead.

THIRD MOTH *(enters Left. Joins in circle of Moths)*. With us the whole world circles, its thanks and praises blending—it glorifies, it leaps and whirls about. Before thee, mighty, lovely, unending moth-gift of life! Breathless delight, eternal ecstasy. Hail to thee, life's roundelay. Eternal movement, movement without end—ah—— *(Falls dead)*

VAGRANT. Oh, life, life, you have cast a spell upon me, for even I, old, battered moth that I am, shout and cry. Oh, life—— Let us live, all of us. Look, each one desires to live. Each one defends himself, and each one fights on his own. See, if we all were to try it all together. If all of us who live could only join forces —against destruction, against death We all would join in such a fight as that. All moths and all mortals, and all thoughts, and works, and all the creatures in the water, and the ants, and grass, all units in this battle. But first we ourselves must unite, all of us who live, into one regiment; and you will lead us, oh, omnipotent life——

CHRYSALIS. Make room. Here I am. *(Bends its husk and leaps forth as a Moth upstage Center; sways over glass lights)*

VAGRANT. Chrysalis! Chrysalis! At last you have been born!

CHRYSALIS *(whirling on glass platform)*. Oh—oh—oh! I—proclaim sway over life. I enjoin creation. Live, for the rule of life over the universe has come. The whole of life surged up to bring me forth, and it burst in its throes. Harken! Oh, harken! I bear a mighty mission. I proclaim immense tidings! Silence, silence! I will utter great words! *(Chrysalis drops dead Center)*

VAGRANT *(crosses up to glass platform. Standing over Chrysalis)*. Rise up, moth. Why have you fallen? See, she's dead. Oh, the pity of it, of just one moment of life! *(Picks her up)* Do you hear, Chrysalis? What did you want to say? Speak! Why were you born to die like this? *(Carries it in his arms)* Dead. How pale it is, and

oh, God, how beautiful! Why must it die? What is this fearful lack of meaning? Moth! What does it mean? What does it mean to live? *(Lays her on the ground down stage Center)* Dead. *(Creeps along the ground and examines the dead Moths)* And you too are dead, you who danced? And you who sang? And you who were so young? These lips will utter no more sound. Dead. Do you hear, gray moth? If only it opened its eyes. Look, it is so good to live. All—hail—to—life! *(Crawls forward on his hands and knees)* Ugh! Who clutched at me? Who's hand was that? Who is here? Ugh! Stop! I feel a chill—— Who are you? *(Brandishes his hands in the void)* You with your cold and clutching hands? *(Stands)* Don't touch. Who are you? *(Defends himself)* Stop! Are you strangling me? Ha, ha, wait! I know who you are. You are—you are Death. So many times have I seen you. But I—will—not. Stop, skeleton, eyeless and loathsome. *(Struggles in the void)* Stop—stop! Have mercy!

(From the back Two Snails crawl in, Right and Left.)

FIRST SNAIL. Stop. Someone's making a noise.

SECOND SNAIL. You silly fool, come back.

VAGRANT *(struggling)*. That's for you, Death. I'll not give in without a fight. Ha, ha, ha, you felt that, eh? *(Rises to his knees)* Leave me alone. Don't smother so. Come now, I only want to live. Is that so much? *(Rises and waves his hands)* I won't give you my life, you old Death's-head, I won't! That's for you. *(Falls)* Oh, you're putting out your foot, too, are you? You'd trip me up! You coward! You coward Death! You won't fight fairly!

FIRST SNAIL. I say, Snail.

SECOND SNAIL. What?

FIRST SNAIL. He's struggling with Death.

SECOND SNAIL. We'll have a look, eh?

VAGRANT *(rising)*. Let me live. What will it matter to you? Only this time. At least till tomorrow. Let—only—breath— *(Struggles)* Stop, don't strangle, I don't want to die. I've had so little out of life. *(Shouts)* Ah! I don't want to die. *(Falls on his face)*

FIRST SNAIL. What fun, eh? To see him fight. Ha, ha, ha! To see him fight with Death!

SECOND SNAIL. I say, Snail.

FIRST SNAIL. What?

SECOND SNAIL. He's done for.

VAGRANT *(rises to his knees).* You strangle a man when he's down, do you, coward? Stop now, let me tell—all—I want—another moment—— *(Rises and staggers)* Let me—live. Only live. *(Shrieks)* No! Go away! There's still so much for me to live for—— *(Sinks on to his knees)* Now—when for the first time I know how to live. *(Falls dead, incline Right)*

FIRST SNAIL *(crawls slowly forward Center).* Well! It's all up with him!

SECOND SNAIL. What a blow! Oh, dear! Oh, dear! What misfortune!

FIRST SNAIL. What are you complaining about? It's nothing to do with us.

SECOND SNAIL. But you know that's what people say when someone dies.

FIRST SNAIL. Oh, yes. Well, we'll say it, too.

SECOND SNAIL. Oh, yes. That's the way of the world.

FIRST SNAIL. Oh, dear! It's such a pity.

SECOND SNAIL. That he is dead?

FIRST SNAIL. No, that there aren't fewer snails and more cabbages.

SECOND SNAIL. Ha, Snail, look, here's a lot of dead moths here.

FIRST SNAIL. That's a pity, too.

SECOND SNAIL. Oh, yes.

FIRST SNAIL. A pity they aren't good to eat.

SECOND SNAIL. Oh, yes. Well, we'll keep still, eh?

FIRST SNAIL. As long as we're alive.

SECOND SNAIL. That's about it. I say, Snail——

FIRST SNAIL. What?

SECOND SNAIL. Life's pleasant enough.

FIRST SNAIL. Rather. Nothing like life, you know.

SECOND SNAIL. Then we'll keep still and enjoy it. *(They start off Right and Left)*

FIRST SNAIL. That was a joke, eh? For a man to fight with Death.

SECOND SNAIL. Rather. As long as— we're—alive we're all right. *(Exeunt)*

WOODCUTTER *(front of gauze drop, same as Prologue. Enters Left with axe on his shoulder. Sees the Vagrant's corpse and bends over him).* What's that? Do you hear? *(Shakes him)* Old man! Come on, old fellow. Wake up. What's the matter with you? *(Stands up; takes off his hat)* He's dead. Poor man. *(Pause)* Anyhow—he's finished with everything.

WOMAN *(enters from Left. She is carrying a newborn child to be baptized).* Good day to you. What have you there on the ground?

WOODCUTTER. Good day. Someone's died here. It's a tramp.

WOMAN. Poor man. I hope it isn't bad luck to meet Death on the way to a christening.

WOODCUTTER. Taking the little one to be baptized, eh?

WOMAN. That's my sister's baby.

WOODCUTTER *(tickling the Baby under the chin).* Ks, ks, baby. Wait till you grow up.

WOMAN. If only he's better off than we are, that's all I ask for him.

WOODCUTTER. Oh, we can't complain. I'm satisfied so long as I can keep a steady job.

WOMAN. Yes, work is good—and there's pleasure enough between times, and this—*(She looks down at Baby)* —may be one of the lucky ones.

WOODCUTTER. Too bad about him, though—— *(He looks down at the Vagrant)*

WOMAN. It goes like that. One dies. Another is born. Good day to you.

WOODCUTTER. Good day.

(MUSIC swells to forte)

THE END

S. ANSKY's

The Dybbuk*

In the English version by HENRY G. ALSBERG

Adapted from the Habima Production

First presented at the Neighborhood Theatre, New York, December 15, 1925, with the following cast:

FIRST BATLON.....................Edgar Kent	SHLEMIEL........................ Benson Inge
SECOND BATLON.............. Junius Matthews	TSIPPE...........................Vera Allen
THIRD BATLON.................. George Bratt	NECHE .... Sadie Sussman
MEYER .... Harold West	RIVKE........................Blanche Talmud
MESSENGER..................... Ian Mclaren	DRAESL....................... Irene Lewisohn
CHANNON .... Albert Carroll	ELKE......................Helen Mack
CHENNOCH ....Otto Hulicius	KLIPPE .... Sophie Bernsohn
AN ELDERLY WOMAN................Vera Allen	NECHAME....................Grace Stickney
LEAH .... Mary Ellis	RACHEL ....Edith Segal
FRADE..........., ,.........Dorothy Sands	MUSICIAN .... Bernard Kugel
GITTEL ....Paula Trueman	BASSIA............................Lily Kubell
ASHER......................Lewis McMichael	NACHMON ...., ,... George Bratt
SENDER........................Marc Loebell	MENASHE .... Harold Minjer
FISHKE .... George Hoag	RABBI MENDEL............... Junius Matthews
LEYSER....................... George Heller	RABBI AZRAEL....................Edgar Kent
MOYSHEH..................... , ,.Otto Hulicius	MICHOEL .... Harold Minjer
ZEYDEL.....................Lewis McMichael	RABBI SAMSON .... Otto Hulicius

Staged by David Vardi (in association with Alice Lewisohn)

SCENES

ACT ONE—In the Synagogue at Brainitz.

ACT TWO—The Street between Sender's house and the Synagogue.

ACT THREE—In the house of Rabbi Azrael of Miropol.

ACT FOUR—The same.

* DYBBUK: a Hebrew word signifying an evil spirit or demon that takes possession of a person.

NOTE: The translation included in this volume is the work of HENRY G. ALSBERG and WINIFRED KATZIN.

ACT ONE

*Before the rise of the curtain, a low mys-
terious chanting is heard in the intense darkness, as if from far off.*

Why, from highest height,
To deepest depth below,
Has the soul fallen?
Within itself, the Fall
Contains the Resurrection.

*The curtain rises slowly, disclosing a wooden
synagogue of venerable age, its time-blackened
walls streaked as if with the tears of centuries.
Two wooden rafters support the roof. From
the center of the roof, directly above the bima[1],
hangs an ancient brass chandelier. The table
in the middle of the bima is covered with a
dark cloth. High up in the center wall, small
windows open into the women's gallery. A long
bench is against this wall, and in front of it
a wooden table, covered with books piled up
in confusion. Two yellow candle-stumps set in
small clay candlesticks are burning on the
table, but their light is almost entirely
obscured by the heaped-up volumes. Left of the
bench is a small door leading into a prayer-
cabinet. In the opposite corner, a closet filled
with books. In the center of the wall on the
right is the altar, with the Ark containing the
holy scrolls. To the right of this, the Cantor's
desk, upon which burns a thick memorial
candle of wax. On either side of the altar, a
window. A bench runs the entire length of the
wall, and in front of it are several small book-
rests. In the wall on the left is a large tile
stove, with a bench beside it. In front of the
bench, on a long table, are piled tomes. Water
container with tap. Towel pushed through a
ring in the wall. Wide door to the street, and
beyond this a chest over which, in a niche,
burns the Perpetual Light.
At a desk near the Cantor's, sits Chennoch,
absorbed in a book. Five or six students are at
the table along the front wall, half-reclining
in attitudes of great weariness; they are
engaged in the study of the Talmud, and their
voices rise in a low, dreamy chanting. Near
the bima Meyer is busy sorting the small bags
which contain prayer-shawls and phylacteries.*

*At the table on the left, sit the three Batlonim,[1]
chanting. Their attitudes and the expression
of their faces bestoken a state of pious ecstasy.
On the bench beside the stove, the Messenger
is lying at full length, with his knapsack for a
pillow. Channon, at the chest containing the
tomes, his hand resting upon its upper ledge,
stands lost in meditation.
It is evening. A mystic mood lies upon the
synagogue. Shadows lurk in the corners.
The First and Second Batlonim finish the
chant, "Why, from highest height," etc., and
then fall silent. There is a long pause.
Wrapped in dreams, all three Batlonim sit
silently at the table.*

———

FIRST BATLON *(in a narrative manner).*
Rabbi Dovidel of Talan, may his merits
hover over us, had a chair of gold which
bore the inscription: David, King of
Israel, who is living still. *(Pause)*

SECOND BATLON *(in the same manner).*
Rabbi Israel of Ruzhin, blessed be his
memory, kept royal state. An orchestra
of four and twenty musicians played to
him as he sat at table, and when he drove
abroad, it was behind a tandem of never
less than six magnificent horses.

THIRD BATLON *(excitedly).* And it is
told of Rabbi Schmool of Kaminka that he
went in slippers of gold. *(Rapturously)*
Golden slippers.

THE MESSENGER *(rising, and sitting upright on his bench, begins to speak in a low,
far-off voice).* The holy Rabbi Susi of
Anipol was as poor as a beggar all his life
long. Often he depended on alms for his
existence. He wore a peasant's blouse
with a rope for a belt. Yet his accomplishments were not inferior to those of
the Rabbis of Talan and Ruzhin.

FIRST BATLON *(annoyed).* Nothing of
the kind; excuse me, but you're breaking
in on us without any idea of what we're
really discussing. You don't suppose that
when we talk of the greatness of the Talan
and Ruzhin Rabbis, we mean their wealth,
do you? As though there aren't plenty of

[1] Pronounced bee'-ma—the tribune in the
center of a synagogue, railed round with a gate on
either side, where the holy scrolls are read.

[1] Pronounced bat'-lon (pl., batlon'-im)—a
professional prayerman.

men in the world whose riches make their importance! No, the point is that a deep and secret significance lies behind the golden chair and the orchestra of four and twenty musicians and the golden slippers.

THIRD BATLON. As though everyone doesn't know that!

SECOND BATLON. Everyone that isn't altogether blind, does. It is said that when the Rabbi of Apt first met the Sage of Ruzhin, he flung himself at the Sage's carriage-wheels to kiss them. And when asked the significance of that action, he shouted: "Fools! Can't you see that this is the chariot of the Lord Himself?"

THIRD BATLON (enraptured). Ay, ay, ay!

FIRST BATLON. Now the essence of the matter is this: The golden chair was no chair; the orchestra was no orchestra, and the horses no horses. They were merely the semblance of these things, a reflection, and their purpose was to provide a setting for greatness.

THE MESSENGER. True greatness needs no setting.

FIRST BATLON. You are mistaken. True greatness must have the setting which befits it.

SECOND BATLON (shrugging his shoulders). How can greatness and perfection such as theirs be measured at all?

FIRST BATLON. It is no matter for jesting. Did you ever hear the story of Rabbi Schmelke of Nikolsberg's whip? It's worth knowing. One day Rabbi Schmelke was called upon to settle a dispute between a poor man and a rich one who was on terms of friendship with the king and before whom, in consequence, everyone trembled. Rabbi Schmelke heard both sides of the case, and then gave his decision by which the poor man won. The rich man was furious and declared that he would not stand by the Rabbi's verdict. And the Rabbi calmly replied: "You shall do as I have said. When a Rabbi commands, his commands are obeyed." The rich man's anger increased and he began to shout: "I snap my fingers at you and your rabbinical authority." Thereupon Rabbi Schmelke drew himself up to his full height, and cried: "Do instantly as I have said, or I shall resort to my whip!"

This drove the rich man into a frenzy of rage, and he began to overwhelm the Rabbi with terrible insults. Then the Rabbi, perfectly calm, opens a drawer in his table—just a little way—and what should jump out of it but the Original Serpent, which coils about the neck of the rich man. Oh, oh, what a commotion follows! The rich man yells at the top of his voice, and throws himself into the most terrible contortions. "Rabbi! Rabbi! Forgive me! I'll do whatever you command—only call off your serpent." "Tell your children and your children's children to obey the Rabbi, and fear his whip," answered Rabbi Schmelke, and called the serpent off.

THIRD BATLON. Ha, ha, ha! There was a whip for you! (Pause)

SECOND BATLON (to First Batlon). You must have made a mistake, I think. The story couldn't have meant the Original Serpent . . .

THIRD BATLON. Why . . . what . . .

SECOND BATLON. It's quite simple. Schmelke of Nikolsberg could not possibly have used the Original Serpent, for that was Satan himself, the enemy of God —(May he have mercy upon us!) (He spits)

THIRD BATLON. Rabbi Schmelke knew what he was about—no doubt of that.

FIRST BATLON (insulted). I don't know what you're talking about. The incident I've just told you took place before a whole townful of people—dozens of them actually saw it with their own eyes. And here you come along and say it couldn't have happened. Just because you've got to have something to argue about, I suppose.

SECOND BATLON. Not at all. I only thought there couldn't be any spells or signs that the Serpent could be summoned by. (He spits)

MESSENGER. Only in one way can Satan be summoned, and that is by the utterance of the mighty double-name of God, the flame of which has power to weld together the loftiest mountain-crests and the deepest valleys below them. (Channon lifts his head and listens intently.)

THIRD BATLON (uneasily). But isn't there danger in speaking that great name?

MESSENGER *(meditatively)*. Danger? No. Only the heat of a too intense desire can cause the vessel to burst when the spark breaks into a flame.

FIRST BATLON. There's a wonder-worker in the village I come from. He's a terrific fellow, but he *can* work miracles. For instance, he can start a fire with one spell and put it out with another. He can see what's going on a hundred miles away. He can bring wine out of the wall by tapping it with his finger. And a great many other things besides. He told me himself that he knows spells that can create monsters and resurrect the dead. He can make himself invisible, too, and evoke evil spirits—even Satan himself. *(He spits.)* I have his own word for it.

CHANNON *(who has never moved from his place, but has listened attentively to all this discussion, now steps up to the table and gazes first into the face of the Messenger, then at the First Batlon. In a dreamy, remote voice)*. Where is he?

(The Messenger returns Channon's gaze with equal intensity, and thereafter never takes his eyes off him.)

FIRST BATLON *(astonished)*. Who?

CHANNON. The wonder-worker.

FIRST BATLON. Where could he be but in my own village? That is, if he's still alive.

CHANNON. Is it far?

FIRST BATLON. The village? Oh, very far. A long, long way down into the marsh-lands of Polesia.

CHANNON. How far?

FIRST BATLON. A good month, if not more. *(Pause)* What makes you ask? Do you want to see him? *(Channon does not answer)* Krasny's the name of the village. And the miracle-worker's name is Rabbi Elchannon.

CHANNON *(in astonishment—as if to himself)*. Elchannon? . . . El Channon! . . . that means the God of Channon.

FIRST BATLON *(to the other Batlonim)*. And he's a *real* one, I promise you. Why, one day in broad daylight he showed, by means of a spell, that . . .

SECOND BATLON *(interrupting)*. That'll do about such things. They aren't for this time of night, especially in a holy place. You may not mean it, but it might just

happen that you'll pronounce some spell or make some sign yourself (God forbid), and then there'll be a disaster . . . Accidents like that (God forbid) have been known to happen before.

(Channon goes slowly out, the others following him with their eyes. There is a pause.)

MESSENGER. Who is that youth?

FIRST BATLON. Just a young student in the *yeshiva*[1].

(Meyer closes the gates of the bima and crosses to the table.)

SECOND BATLON. A vessel beyond price —an Elui[2].

THIRD BATLON. A brain of steel. He has five hundred pages of the Talmud by heart, at his fingertips.

MESSENGER. Where is he from?

MEYER. Somewhere in Lithuania—in the *yeshiva* there, he was famous as their finest scholar. He was granted the degree of rabbi, and then, all of a sudden, he vanished. No more was heard of him for a whole year, and it was said that he was doing the great penance of the Golos[3]. When he returned—which was not long ago—he had changed entirely, and he has since been going about absorbed in deep meditation, from which nothing ever arouses him. He fasts from Sabbath to Sabbath and performs the holy ablutions continually. *(Whispering)* There is a rumor that he is studying the Kabala[4].

SECOND BATLON *(likewise)*. It has spread to the city, too. He has already been asked to give charms, but he always refuses.

THIRD BATLON. Who knows who he is? One of the Great Ones, maybe. Who can tell? It would be dangerous most likely to spy on him. *(Pause)*

SECOND BATLON *(peacefully)*. It's late —let's go to bed. *(To the First Batlon,

[1] A higher religious school.
[2] A scholar who has a remarkable memory and capacity for learning.
[3] The Exile of the Jews. According to religious tradition, the golos was imposed upon the race as a punishment. In the original Yiddish the "Penance of the golos" reads "Abrichten golos." The penitent, by wearing a hair-shirt and performing other acts of mortification of the flesh, and wandering through the world as a beggar, hoped to assist in the redemption of the race by shortening the period of exile from the Holy Land.
[4] System of Hebrew mysticism.

smiling) Pity your miracle-worker isn't here to tap us some wine out of the wall. I could do with a drop of brandy to cheer me up—I've not had a bite all day long.

FIRST BATLON. It's been practically a fast day for me, too. Since early morning prayers, a crust of oaten bread is the only thing I've had a chance to say grace over . . .

MEYER *(mysteriously, and in high glee).* Never mind—you just wait a bit, and very soon there'll be a deal of cheer going round. Sender's been after a bridegroom for his daughter. Only let him get the contract signed—it'll be a happy hour for him when *that's* done—and he'll be good for a grand spread.

SECOND BATLON. Bah! I don't believe he'll ever sign one. Three times he's been to get a bridegroom. Either it's the young man he doesn't like, or else the family that's not aristocratic enough, or it's the dowry. It's wicked to be as fastidious as all that.

MEYER. Sender has the right to pick and choose if he wants to (may he be protected from the evil eye). He's rich, and an aristocrat, and his only daughter has grown up a good and beautiful girl.

THIRD BATLON *(ravished).* I love Sender. He's a true Miropol Chassid[1]—there's some real spirit to *them.*

FIRST BATLON *(coldly).* Yes—he's a good Chassid. There's no denying that. But he might have done something very different with his only daughter.

THIRD BATLON. How do you mean?

FIRST BATLON. In the old days, when a man of wealth and fine family wanted a husband for his daughter, he didn't look for money or blue blood, but only for nobility of character. He went to the big *yeshiva* and gave the head a handsome gift to pick out for him the flower of the school for a son-in-law. Sender could have done this, too.

MESSENGER. He might even have found one in this *yeshiva* here.

FIRST BATLON *(surprised).* How do you know?

MESSENGER. I'm only supposing.

THIRD BATLON *(hastily).* Well, well— let's not gossip—particularly about one

[1] A Jewish sect.

of our own people. Marriages are all pre-arranged by destiny, anyhow.

(The street door is flung open, and an elderly Jewess hastens in, leading two small children.)

ELDERLY WOMAN *(rushes to the altar with the children).* Aie! Aie! Lord of the earth, help me! Come, children—let us open the Ark and throw ourselves upon the holy scrolls and not leave them until our tears have won your mother back from the valley of the shadow. *(She wrenches open the doors of the Ark and buries her head amongst the scrolls, intoning a wailing chant)* God of Abraham, Isaac, and Jacob, look down upon my misery. Look down upon the grief of these little ones, and do not take their mother away from the world, in the years of her youth. Holy scrolls! Do *you* intercede for the forlorn widow. Holy scrolls, beloved Mothers of Israel, go to the Almighty and beseech Him that He shall not uproot the lovely sapling, nor cast the young dove out of its nest, nor tear the gentle lamb away from the meadow. *(Hysterically)* I will pull down the worlds—I will tear the heavens apart—but from here I will not go until they give back to me the one who is the crown of my head.

MEYER *(crosses to her and speaks to her calmly).* Hannah Esther—wouldn't you like to have a *minyen*[1] sit down and say the psalms for you?

ELDERLY WOMAN *(withdraws from the altar and looks at Meyer at first uncomprehendingly. Then she begins to speak in agitation).* Yes—a *minyen* for psalms. But hurry—hurry—every second is precious. For two days already, God help her, she's been lying there without speaking, fighting with death.

MEYER. I'll have them sit down this minute. *(In the voice of a beggar)* But you'll have to give them something for their trouble, poor things.

ELDERLY WOMAN *(searching in her pocket).* Here's ten kopeks—but see they say the psalms for it.

MEYER. Ten kopeks . . . one kopek each . . . little enough, that is!

ELDERLY WOMAN *(not hearing).* Come children, let us run along to the other

[1] Ten or more adult males constituting a Jewish community.

prayer-houses. *(Hurries out with the children)*

MESSENGER *(to Third Batlon)*. This morning a woman came to the Ark for her daughter, who had been in the throes of labor for two days and had not yet given birth. And here comes another for hers, who has been wrestling for two days with death.

THIRD BATLON. Well, what of it?

MESSENGER *(deep in thought)*. When the soul of a human being not yet dead is about to enter a body not yet born, a struggle takes place. If the sick one dies, the child is born—if the sick one recovers, a child is born dead.

FIRST BATLON *(surprised)*. Ei, ei, ei! The blindness of people! Things happen all round them, but they have no eyes to see them with.

MEYER *(at the table)*. See, here's a treat from above! Let's get the psalms over, then we'll have a drop of something. And the Lord will have mercy on the sick woman and send her a quick recovery.

FIRST BATLON *(to the scholars sitting around the big table, half asleep)*. Who wants to say psalms, boys? There's a bit of oat bread for every one that does. *(The scholars get up)* Let's go in there.

(The three Batlonim, Meyer and the scholars, except Chennoch, pass into the adjoining prayer-room, whence the chanting of "Blessed be the man" presently emerges. The Messenger remains throughout beside the small table, immovable. His eyes never leave the Ark. There is a long pause. Then Channon comes in.)

CHANNON *(very weary, walks aimlessly across to the Ark, sunk in meditation. He seems surprised to find it open)*. Open? Who can have opened it? For whom has it opened in the middle of the night? *(He looks in)* The scrolls of the Law . . . there they stand like comrades, shoulder to shoulder, so calm . . . so silent. All secrets and symbols hidden in them. And all miracles—from the six days of creation, unto the end of all the generations of men. Yet how hard it is to wrest one secret or one symbol from them—how hard! *(He counts the scrolls)* One, two, three, four, five, six, seven, eight, nine. That makes the word Truth, according to the Minor

system. In each scroll there are four Trees of Life[1]. There again it comes—thirty-six. Not an hour passes but this number faces me in one manner or another. I do not know the meaning of it, but I have the intuition that within it lies the whole essence of the matter . . . Thirty-six is Leah. Three times thirty-six is Channon. . . . Le-ah—that makes Le-ha, which means Not God . . . not through God . . . *(He shudders)* A terrible thought . . . and yet it draws nearer . . . and nearer . . .

CHENNOCH *(looks up from his book, attentively at Channon)*. Channon! You go about dreaming all the time.

CHANNON *(moves away from the Ark, and slowly approaches Chennoch, standing before him, lost in thought)*. Nothing—nothing but secrets and symbols—and the right path is not to be found. *(Short pause)* Krasny is the name of the village . . . and the miracle-man's name is Rabbi Elchannon . . .

CHENNOCH. What's that you're saying?

CHANNON *(as if waking out of a trance)*. I? Nothing. I was only thinking.

CHENNOCH *(shaking his head)*. You've been meddling with the Kabala, Channon. Ever since you came back, you haven't had a book in your hand.

CHANNON *(not understanding)*. Not had a book in my hand? What book do you mean?

CHENNOCH. The Talmud of course—the Laws. You know very well . . .

CHANNON *(still in his dreams)*. Talmud? The Laws? Never had them in my hand? The Talmud is cold and dry . . . so are the Laws. *(Comes to himself suddenly. He speaks with animation)* Under the earth's surface, Chennoch, there is a world exactly the same as ours upon it, with fields and forests, seas and deserts, cities and villages. Storms rage over the deserts and over the seas upon which sail great ships. And over the dense forests, reverberating with the roll of thunder, eternal fear holds sway. Only in the absence of one thing does that world differ from ours. There is no sky, from which the sun pours down its burning heat and bolts of fire fall . . . So

[1] The handles at the top and bottom of each scroll.

S. ANSKY

it is with the Talmud. It is deep and glorious and vast. But it chains you to the earth—it forbids you to attempt the heights. *(With enthusiasm)* But the Kabala, the Kabala tears your soul away from earth and lifts you to the realms of the highest heights. Spreads all the heavens out before your eyes, and leads direct to Pardes[1], reaches out in the infinite, and raises a corner of the great curtain itself. *(Collapses)* My heart turns faint—I have no strength . . .

CHENNOCH *(solemnly)*. That is all true. But you forget that those ecstatic flights into the upper regions are fraught with the utmost peril, for it is there that you are likely to come to grief and hurl yourself into the deepest pit below. The Talmud raises the soul toward the heights by slow degrees, but keeps guard over it like a faithful sentinel, who neither sleeps nor dreams. The Talmud clothes the soul with an armor of steel and keeps it ever on the strait path so that it stray neither to the right nor to the left. But the Kabala . . . Remember what the Talmud says: *(He chants the following in the manner of Talmudic recitation)* Four reached Pardes. Ben Azzai, Ben Zoma, Acher and Rabbi Akiva. Ben Azzai looked within and died. Ben Zoma looked within and lost his reason. Acher renounced the fundamentals of all belief. Rabbi Akiva alone went in and came out again unscathed.

CHANNON. Don't try to frighten me with them. We don't know how they went, nor with what. They may have failed because they went to look and not to offer themselves as a sacrifice. But others went after them—that we know. Holy Ari and the holy Balshem[1]. They did not fail.

CHENNOCH. Are you comparing yourself to them?

CHANNON. To nobody. I go my own way.

CHENNOCH. What sort of way is that?

CHANNON. You wouldn't understand.

CHENNOCH. I wish to and I will. My soul too, is drawn toward the high planes.

CHANNON *(after a moment's reflection)*.

The service of our holy men consists in cleansing human souls, tearing away the sin that clings to them and raising them to the shining source whence they come. Their work is very difficult because sin is ever lurking at the door. No sooner is one soul cleansed than another comes in its place, more sin-corroded still. No sooner is one generation brought to repentance than the next one appears, more stiffnecked than the last. And as each generation grows weaker, its sins become stronger, and the holy men fewer and fewer.

CHENNOCH. Then, according to your philosophy, what ought to be done?

CHANNON *(quietly, but with absolute conviction)*. There is no need to wage war on sin. All that is necessary is to burn it away, as the goldsmith refines gold in his powerful flame; as the farmer winnows the grain from the chaff. So must sin be refined of its uncleanness, until only its holiness remains.

CHENNOCH *(astonished)*. Holiness in sin? How do you make that out?

CHANNON. Everything created by God contains a spark of holiness.

CHENNOCH. Sin was not created by God but by Satan.

CHANNON. And who created Satan? God. Since he is the antithesis of God, he is an aspect of God, and therefore must contain also a germ of holiness.

CHENNOCH *(crushed)*. Holiness in Satan? I can't . . . I don't understand . . . Let me think . . .
(His head sinks into his hands, propped up by both elbows on the desk. There is a pause.)

CHANNON *(stands beside him and in a trembling voice, bending down to reach his ear)*. Which sin is the strongest of all? Which one is the hardest to conquer? The sin of lust for a woman, isn't it?

CHENNOCH *(without raising his head)*. Yes.

CHANNON. And when you have cleansed this sin in a powerful flame, then this greatest uncleanness becomes the greatest holiness. It becomes "The Song of Songs." *(He holds his breath)* The Song of Songs. *(Drawing himself up, he begins to chant in a voice which, though subdued, is charged with rapture)* Behold thou art fair,

---

[1] Paradise.
[1] The founder of the Chassidic sect, know as the Basht.

my love. Thou hast dove's eyes within thy locks; they hair is as a flock of goats that appear from Mount Gilead. Thy teeth are like a flock of sheep that are even shorn, which came up from the washing; whereof every one bear twins and none barren among them.

(Meyer comes out of the prayer-room. A gentle knocking is heard at the street door, which is pushed hesitatingly open, and Leah enters. She has hold of Frade's hand, and behind them comes Gittel. They stop in the doorway. Meyer turns and sees them, and goes over the them, surprised, welcoming them obsequiously.)

MEYER. Look! Here comes Sender's daughter, little Leah!

LEAH *(shyly)*. You promised to show me the old embroidered curtains of the Ark—do you remember?

(Channon, hearing her voice, abruptly itnerrupts his song, and stares at her with all his eyes. As long as she remains in the synagogue, he alternately gazes at her thus, and closes his eyes in ecstasy.)

FRADE. Show her the curtains, Meyer —the old ones, and the most beautiful. Our dear Leah has said she will embroider a new one for the anniversary of her mother's death. She will work it with the purest gold upon the finest of velvet, just as they used to do in the olden days— little lions and eagles. And when it is hung over the Ark, her mother's pure spirit will rejoice in Eden.

(Leah looks timidly about her, and seeing Channon, lowers her eyes in embarrassment and keeps them so for the rest of the scene.)

MEYER. Oh, with the greatest pleasure. Why not, why not indeed? I'll bring the oldest and most beautiful curtains to show her—at once, this very minute. *(He goes to the chest near the street door and takes out the curtains)*

GITTEL *(taking Leah's hand)*. Aren't you afraid to be in the synagogue at night, Leah?

LEAH. I've never been here at night before, except on the Days of the Holy Scrolls. But that's a feast day and everything is bright and joyful then. How sad it is now, though—how sad!

FRADE. Dear children—a synagogue must be sad. The dead come here at midnight to pray, and when they go they leave their sorrows behind them.

GITTEL. Don't talk abouth the dead, Granny. It frightens me.

FRADE *(not hearing her)*. And each day at dawn, when the Almighty weeps for the destruction of the Holy Temple, His sacred tears fall in the synagogues. That is why the walls of all old synagogues look as if they have been wept over, and that is why it is forbidden to whitewash them and make them bright again. If you attempt to, they grow angry and throw their stones at you.

LEAH. How old it is—how old! It doesn't show so much from outside.

FRADE. Old it is, little daughter— very, very old. They even say it was found already built under the earth. Many a time this city has been destroyed, and many a time it has been laid in ashes. But this synagogue, never. Fire broke out once on the roof, but almost before it had begun to burn, innumerable doves came flocking down upon it and beat out the flames with their wings.

LEAH *(not hearing—speaking to herself)*. How sad it is! How lovely! I feel that I want never to go away from it again. I wish I could put my arms around those ancient, tear-stained walls and ask them why they are so sorrowful, and so wrapped in dreams . . . so silent and so sad. I wish . . . I don't know what I wish . . . But my heart is filled with tenderness and pity.

MEYER *(brings the curtains to the bima, and spreads one out to show)*. This is the oldest of all—a good two hundred years or more. It is never used except on Passover.

GITTEL *(enraptured)*. Leah, dear—just look. Isn't it gorgeous! Such stiff brown velvet, all embroidered in heavy gold. Two lions holding the shield of David above their heads. And trees on either side, with doves in their branches. You can't get such velvet nowadays, nor such gold either.

LEAH. The curtain is sad, too—I love it also. *(She smooths it out and kisses it)*

GITTEL *(takes Leah's hand and whispers)*. Look, Leah, dear! There's a student over there staring at you—so strangely!

LEAH *(keeping her eyes still more down-cast)*. That is Channon. He was a poor scholar, and he used to be a guest in our house.

GITTEL. It is as if he were calling to you with his eyes, he stares so. He would like to talk to you, but he is afraid to.

LEAH. I wish I knew why he is so pale and sad. He must surely have been ill.

GITTEL. He isn't sad really—his eyes are shining.

LEAH. They always are. He has wonderful eyes, and when he talks to me his breath comes short—and so does mine. It wouldn't be proper for a girl to talk to a strange young man.

FRADE *(to Meyer)*. Won't you let us kiss the holy scrolls? Surely! How could one be a guest in the house of God and leave without kissing His holy scrolls?

MEYER. By all means, by all means! Come!

(He goes ahead, followed by Gittel leading Frade, and Leah behind them. Meyer takes out a scroll and gives it to Frade to kiss.)

LEAH *(passing Channon, stops for a moment and says in a low voice)*. Good evening, Channon. You have come back?

CHANNON *(scarcely able to speak for agitation)*. Yes.

FRADE. Come, Leah, darling, kiss the holy scrolls. *(Leah goes to the Ark. Meyer hands her a scroll, which she takes in her arms and, pressing her lips against it, kisses passionately)* Now, now, child! That will do. A holy scroll must not be kissed too long. They are written in black fire upon white fire. *(In sudden alarm)* How late it is! How very late! Come, children, let us hurry home—come quickly.

(They hasten out. Meyer closes the Ark and follows them.)

CHANNON *(stands for a while with closed eyes; then resumes his chanting of the "Song of Songs" where he left off)*. Thy lips are like a thread of scarlet, and thy speech is comely. Thy temples are like a piece of pomegranate within thy locks.

CHENNOCH *(raises his head and looks at Channon)*. Channon, what are you singing? *(Channon stops singing and looks at Chennoch)* Your ear-locks are wet. You have been to the Mikva[1] again.

CHANNON. Yes.

CHENNOCH. When you perform the ablutions, do you also use spells and go through all the ceremonies prescribed by the book of Roziel?[1]

CHANNON. Yes.

CHENNOCH. You aren't afraid to?

CHANNON. No.

CHENNOCH. And you fast from Sabbath to Sabbath—isn't that hard for you?

CHANNON. It's harder for me to eat on the Sabbath than to fast the whole week. *(Pause)* I've lost all desire to eat.

CHENNOCH *(inviting confidence)*. What do you do all this for? What do you expect to gain by it?

CHANNON *(as if to himself)*. I wish . . . I wish to attain possession of a clear and sparkling diamond, and melt it down in tears and inhale it into my soul. I want to attain to the rays of the third plane of beauty. I want . . . *(Suddenly in violent perturbation)* Yes—there are still two barrels of golden pieces which I must get, for him who can count only gold pieces.

CHENNOCH *(appalled)*. Channon, be careful! You're on a slippery road. No holy powers will help you to achieve these things.

CHANNON *(challenging him)*. And if the *holy* powers will not, then?

CHENNOCH *(terrified)*. I'm afraid to talk to you! I'm afraid to be near you!

(He rushes out. Channon remains behind, his face full of defiance. Meyer comes back from the street. The First Batlon emerges from the prayer-room.)

FIRST BATLON. Eighteen psalms—that's enough and to spare! I suppose she doesn't expect to get the whole bookful for a kopek! You go and tell them, Meyer. Once they get started, there's no stopping them till they've said them all. *(Enter Asher in great excitement.)*

ASHER. I just met Baruch the tailor. He's come back from Klimovka—that's where Sender's been to meet the bridegroom's people. They haven't come to terms yet, it seems. Sender insisted that the bridegroom's father should board the couple for ten years, but he stood out for only five. So they all went back home again.

---

[1] Ritual bath.

[1] One of the books of the Kabala.

MEYER. That makes the fourth time.

FIRST BATLON. Heartbreaking, isn't it?

MESSENGER *(to Third Batlon, smiling)*. A little while ago you said yourself that all marriages were prearranged by destiny.

CHANNON *(straightening up and speaking in a voice of rapture)*. I have won again. *(He falls exhausted onto a bench, his face alight with joy.)*

MESSENGER *(taking a lantern out of his bag)*. Time to get ready for the road again.

MEYER. What's your hurry?

MESSENGER. I'm a messenger. Great ones and magnates employ me to carry import antcommunications and rare treasures for them. I am obliged to hurry— my time is not my own.

MEYER. You ought to wait until daybreak at least.

MESSENGER. That is still a long way off, and I have far to go. I shall start about midnight.

MEYER. It's pitch-dark outside.

MESSENGER. I shan't lose my way with this lantern.

(The scholars and Second Batlon come out of the prayer-room.)

SECOND BATLON. Good luck be with us. May the Lord send the sick woman a complete recovery.

ALL. Amen.

FIRST BATLON. Now let's go and get ten kopeks' worth of cakes and brandy.

MEYER. It's here already. *(Takes a bottle and cakes from under his coat)* Come on, let's drink a health!

(The door opens and Sender enters, coat unbuttoned, hat on the back of his head, thoroughly happy. Three or four men follow him in.)

MEYER AND THE THREE BATLONIM. Oh, Reb Sender—welcome, welcome . . .

SENDER. Happened to be passing. I really must go in, says I to myself, and see what our people are doing. *(Noticing the bottle in Meyer's hand)* I'll surely find them studying, says I, or deep in pious discussions. And what do I see? They're all deep in preparing for a celebration instead! Ha, ha, ha! Typical Miropol Chassidim!

FIRST BATLON. Will you have a drop with us, Reb Sender?

SENDER. No, blockhead. I won't. I'll stand treat myself—and splendid treat at that! Congratulate me—this is a happy day for me. I have betrothed my daughter.

(Channon, distraught, rises from his bench.)

ALL. Mazeltov! Mazeltov![1]

MEYER. Somebody just told us you hadn't been able to come to terms with the bridegroom's father, and so it had all fallen through.

THIRD BATLON. We were heartbroken to hear it.

SENDER. It nearly did, but at the last moment he gave in, and so the contract was signed. May good luck go with it.

CHANNON. Betrothed? Betrothed? How can that be? *(In despair)* So it was all of no avail—neither the fasts, nor the ablutions, nor the spells, nor the symbols. All in vain . . . So what remains? What is there still to do . . . by what means . . . *(He clutches the breast of his kaftan, and his face is illuminated with ecstasy)* Ah! The secret of the Double Name is revealed to me. Ah! I see him. I . . . I . . . I have won! *(He falls to the ground)*

MESSENGER *(opens his lantern)*. The wick has burnt down. A new one must be lighted. *(An ominous pause)*

SENDER. Meyer, why is it so dark in here? Let's have some light.

(Meyer lights another light.)

MESSENGER *(crosses quietly to Sender)*. Did you come to terms with the bridegroom's father?

SENDER *(surprised, and somewhat frightened, looks at him)*. I did.

MESSENGER. Sometimes it happens that the relatives promise, and then go back on their word. And litigation follows. It pays to be very careful in these matters.

SENDER *(in alarm)*. Who is this man? I don't know him.

MEYER. He is not from these parts. He is a Messenger.

SENDER. What does he want of me?

MEYER. I don't know.

SENDER *(more calmly)*. Asher, run over to my house and ask them to prepare some wine and preserves and something

[1] Good luck.

good to eat. Hurry up, now—run along. *(Asher hastens out)* We might as well stay here and talk a bit while they're getting things ready. Hasn't one of you some new parable of our Rabbi's? A saying, or a miracle, or a proverb . . . each of his looks is more precious than pearls.

FIRST BATLON *(to Meyer)*. Keep the bottle. It'll come in handy tomorrow. *(Meyer puts it away.)*

MESSENGER. I'll tell you one of his proverbs. One day a Chassid came to the Rabbi—he was rich, but a miser. The Rabbi took him by the hand and led him to the window. "Look out there," he said. And the rich man looked into the street. "What do you see?" asked the Rabbi. "People," answers the rich man. Again the Rabbi takes him by the hand, and this time leads him to the mirror. "What do you see now?" he says. "Now I see myself," answers the rich man. Then the Rabbi says: "Behold—in the window there is glass and in the mirror there is glass. But the glass of the mirror is covered with a little silver, and no sooner is the silver added than you cease to see others but see only yourself."

THIRD BATLON. Oh, oh, oh! Sweeter than honey!

FIRST BATLON. Holy words!

SENDER *(to the Messenger)*. You are tyring to score off me, eh?

MESSENGER. God forbid!

SECOND BATLON. Let's have a song! *(To the Third Batlon)* Sing the Rabbi's tune.

(The Third Batlon begins intoning a low mysterious Chassidic tune in which the rest join.)

SENDER *(rising)*. And now a dance, a round dance . . . Shall Sender give away his only daughter, and not celebrate it with a round dance? Nice Chassidim we'd be!

(Sender, the three Batlonim and Meyer put their arms on one another's shoulders and start turning in a ring, their eyes dim with ecstasy, chanting a weird, monotonous air. They revolve slowly, on the same spot. Then Sender breaks away from the circle.)

SENDER. Now a merry one. Come on —all together!

SECOND BATLON. Yes, come on, boys —let's all join in! *(Several of the scholars join them)* Chennoch, Channon, where are you? We're going to have a merry dance—come on!

SENDER *(somewhat perturbed)*. Ah, Channon . . . he's here, my little Channon, isn't he? Where is he, eh? Bring him here—I want him.

MEYER *(sees Channon on the floor)*. He's asleep on the floor.

SENDER. Wake him up then. Wake him up.

MEYER *(tries to rouse him. Frightened)*. I can't——

(They all crowd round Channon, and try to wake him.)

FIRST BATLON *(with a frightened cry)*. He's dead.

THIRD BATLON. The book of Roziel, the King—look—it's fallen out of his hand!

(Consternation.)

CURTAIN

ACT TWO

A square in Brainitz. Left, the old synagogue, built of wood and of ancient architecture. In front of it, somewhat to one side, a mound surmounted by a gravestone bearing the inscription, "Here lie a pure and holy bridegroom and bride, murdered to the glory of God in the year 5408. Peace be with them." An alley on one side of the synagogue, leading to a group of small houses which merge into the backdrop.

At the right, Sender's house, also built of wood, but of imposing size and adorned with a balcony and stoop. Past the house a wide double gate to the courtyard gives onto another alley with a row of small shops which also merge into the backdrop. On the drop to the right, past the shops, an inn, then the garden of a large estate and the owner's mansion. A wide road leading down to a river upon whose farther bank a cemetery is seen. To the left, a bridge over the river and a mill.

In the foreground, bathhouse and poorhouse. In the far distance, a forest. The double gates to Senders's courtyard stand wide open. Long tables have been set out in the yard, and jut out onto the square. The tables are spread with food which the poor, old and young, some of them crippled, are ravenously devouring. They are served continuously from the house, from great bowls of food and baskets with bread.

Before the shops and houses, women sit knitting, but their eyes hardly leave Sender's house. Men, old and young, leave the synagogue carrying their prayer-shawls and phylacteries, and go into the shops and houses. Some stand about talking in groups. Music is heard from the courtyard. Then dancing and the confused sound of voices.

It is evening. In the middle of the street, in front of the synagogue stands the Wedding Guest, a middle-aged Jew in a satin kaftan, his hands stuck into his belt. The Second Batlon is with him.

———

GUEST (gazing at the synagogue). A great synagogue you have here—a handsome building indeed—and spacious, too. The spirit of God is upon it. Very old, I should say.

SECOND BATLON. Very old it is. Our ancients say that not even their grandfathers could remember when it was built.

GUEST (seeing the grave). And what is that? (He reads the inscription) "Here lie a pure and holy bridegroom and bride, murdered to the glory of God in the year 5408." A bride and bridegroom— murdered to the glory of God?

SECOND BATLON. Yes—by that bandit Chamilouk[1]—may his name be wiped out forever—when he raided the city with his Cossacks and massacred half the Jews. He murdered that bride and groom as they were being led to the wedding-canopy. They were buried on the very spot, in one grave together. Ever since, it has been called the holy grave. (Whispering, as if he were telling a secret) At every marriage ceremony, the rabbi hears sighs from the grave, and it has become a time-honored custom for the people leaving the synagogue after a wedding to go and dance there, to cheer the dead bride and bridegroom where they lie.

GUEST. An excellent custom . . .

MEYER (coming out of Sender's house). Ah, such a feast for the poor. Never in all my born days have I seen the equal of this spread Sender's made for them.

GUEST. No wonder. He's giving away his only daughter.

MEYER (with enthusiasm). First a piece of fish; then a cut of roast, and a zimmis[1] to top it off. And cake and brandy before the meal began! . . . It must have cost him a fortune—more than can ever be reckoned up!

SECOND BATLON. Leave it to Sender to know his own buisness. When it comes to skimping an invited guest, you know where you are—let him snort all he likes, he can't do anything. But it's flying in the face of danger not to treat the poor right. There's no telling who a beggar's coat may be hiding. A beggar maybe, but maybe also some one quite different . . . a nister[2] . . . or one of the Thirty-Six[3].

MEYER. Why not the Prophet Elijah himself? He always appears as a beggar.

GUEST. It's not only the poor it pays to be careful with. You can't say for a certainty who any man might have been in his last existence, nor what he is doing on earth.

(From the alley on the right, the Messenger enters, with his knapsack on his shoulder.)

MEYER (to the Messenger). Sholom aleichem[4]—you have come back, I see.

MESSENGER. I have been sent to you again.

MEYER. You have come in good season, in time for a great wedding.

MESSENGER. I know—it is the talk of all the country round.

MEYER. Did you happen to pass the bridegroom's party on the way? They are late.

MESSENGER. The bridegroom will arrive in good time.

(He goes into the synagogue, and the Guest, Meyer, and the Second Batlon turn into Sender's courtyard. Leah appears beyond the tables, in her wedding-dress, dancing with one after another of the old women. The rest crowd

———

[1] Chmelnitzki the Cossack chieftain who led a great uprising in which thousands of Jews perished.

[1] A vegetable delicacy.
[2] A saint disguised.
[3] Thirty-Six men of virtue, on whose account God allows the world to continue.
[4] Peace be with you.

about her. Those with whom she has finished dancing pass into the square, and stand talking in groups.)

A POOR WOMAN *(with child holding onto her skirts. In a tone of satisfaction).* I danced with the bride.

LAME WOMAN. So did I. I took her round the waist and danced with her too. Hee, hee, hee!

A HUNCHBACK. How's that? The bride only dancing with the women? I'm going to take her by the waist myself, and swing her round and round. Ha, ha, ha!

(General laughter among the beggars. Frade, Gittel and Bassia come from the house onto the stoop.)

FRADE *(worried).* Oh, dear! Oh, dear! There's the darling still dancing with those people. She'll make herself dizzy if she doesn't stop. Go and tell her to come here, children.

GITTEL *(going to Leah).* Come away, Leah dear—you've danced enough now.

BASSIA. Yes—you'll be getting dizzy... *(They take Leah's hands and try to draw her away.)*

THE POOR WOMEN *(gather round Leah beseeching her in whining tones).* She hasn't danced with me yet . . . Aren't I as good as them? . . . I've been waiting an hour . . . Me . . . Me . . . It's my turn after Elka . . . She's been round ten times and more with that lame Yachna, and not one single turn with me . . . I've never got no luck!

MEYER *(comes out into the square and stands on the bench. In a high-pitched voice, he chants the following verse in the manner of a herald).*
Come in, come in, and feast your fill,
Rich Sender bids you straightway come!
Here's abundance and good will,
And ten kopeks for every one!

THE POOR *(run out jostling one another).* Ten kopeks! Ten kopeks!

(The square is left empty except for Frade, Leah, Gittel, Bassia and an old half-blind beggar woman.)

THE OLD WOMAN *(seizes Leah).* I don't want no alms . . . I only want you to dance with me. Just once—just one turn. That's all. I've not danced once these forty years . . . Oh, how I used to dance when I was a girl! How I did dance! *(Leah*

dances with her, but when she tries to release herself, the crone will not let her go, but begs for more and more) Again . . . again . . . *(They swing round faster still, the old woman now out of breath and hysterical)* More . . . more . . .

(Gittel has to force her into the courtyard. Then she comes back, and together with Bassia, they assist Leah to a bench. Sender's servants clear the tables and close the gate.)

FRADE. Oh, my darling, you're as white as a sheet. They've worn you out, so they have.

LEAH *(sits with closed eyes, her head leaning backward, and when she speaks, it is as though in a trance).* They seized me . . . they kept on turning and turning round me . . . so close . . . and clutched me to them with their cold, withered hands . . . my head swam . . . my heart turned faint. Then someone came and lifted me from the ground and carried me far away, very far away.

BASSIA *(in great anxiety).* Oh, Leah, look how they've crushed your dress— it's all dirty now. Whatever will you do?

LEAH *(in the same manner as before).* If the bride is left alone before the wedding, spirits come and carry her off.

FRADE *(alarmed).* What can have put such ideas into your head, my child? We may not mention the dark people—you know that. They're lurking in every tiny hole and corner and crevice. They see everything and hear everything—and they're forever on the alert to catch their unclean names on ours lips. Then out they spring on top of you. *(She spits three times)*

LEAH *(opens her eyes).* My spirits are not evil ones.

FRADE. Don't you believe them, my child. The minute you trust one of the dark people, he becomes unmanageable and begins to do mischief.

LEAH *(with utter conviction).* Granny— it isn't evil spirits that surround us, but souls of those who died before their time and come back again to see all that we do and hear all that we say.

FRADE. God help you, child, what is the meaning of all this? Souls? What souls? The souls of the pure and good fly up to heaven and stay there at rest in the bright garden of Eden.

LEAH. No, Granny—they are with us here. *(Her tone changes)* Grandmother, every one of us is born to a long life of many, many years. If he dies before his years are done, what becomes of the life he has not lived, do you think? What becomes of his joys and sorrows, and all the thoughts he had not time to think, and all the things he hadn't time to do? Where are the children he did not live long enough to bring into the world? Where does all that go to? Where? *(Lost in thought, she continues)* There was a lad here, Granny . . . his mind was full of wisdom and his soul was set on holy purpose. Long years stretched out before him. Then one day, without warning, his life is destroyed. And strangers bury him in strange earth. *(Desperately)* What has become of the rest of him? His speech that has been silenced? His prayers that have been cut off? . . . Grandmother—when a candle blows out we light it again and it goes on burning down to the end. So how can a human life which goes out before it has burnt down, remain put out forever? . . . How can it, Granny?

FRADE *(shaking her head)*. Daughter, you must not think about such things. He who lives above knows the reason for His actions. We are blind and know nothing.

(The Messenger approaches them unnoticed, and remains standing close behind them.)

LEAH *(not hearing her. With deep conviction)*. No, Granny. No human life goes to waste. If one of us dies before his time, his soul returns to the world to complete its span, to do the things left undone and experience the happiness and griefs he would have known. *(A pause)* Granny, do you remember you told us how the dead go trooping at midnight into the synagogue? They go to pray the prayers they would have prayed in life, had they not died too soon. *(A pause)* My mother died in her youth and had no time to live through all that lay in store for her. That is why I go today to the cemetery to ask her to join my father when he leads me under the wedding-canopy. She will be with me there, and after the ceremony we shall dance together. It is the same with all the souls who leave the world

before their time. They are here in our midst, unheard and invisible. Only if your desire is strong enough, you can see them, and hear their voices and learn their thoughts . . . I can. . . . *(Pointing to the grave)* The holy grave—I have known it ever since I was a child. And I know the bride and bridegroom buried there. I've seen them often and often, sometimes in dreams and sometimes when I am wide awake. They are as near to me as my own people . . . *(Deep in meditation)* They were on the way to their wedding, so young and lovely to see, with a long and beautiful life before them. But murderers set upon them with axes, and in a moment they both lay dead upon the ground. They were laid in one grave, so that they might be together for all time. *(She rises and goes to the grave, followed by Frade, Gittel and Bassia. Stretching out her arms, she says in a loud voice)* Holy bridegroom and bride, I invite you to my wedding. Be with me under the canopy.

(Gay march music is heard in the distance. Leah screams in terror and almost falls. Gittel catches her)

GITTEL. What is it, Leah dear? Don't be frightened. They must be greeting the bridegroom with music as he comes into the village.

BASSIA *(excited)*. I'm going to take a peep at him.

GITTEL. I, too. We'll run back, Leah, and tell you what he looks like. Shall we?

LEAH *(shaking her head)*. No.

BASSIA. She's only shy. Little stupid, there's nothing to be ashamed of . . . We won't give you away!

(Exit Bassia running, followed by Gittel.)

FRADE *(returning with Leah to the stoop)*. That is the custom, my child. The bride always sends her friend to see whether the groom is fair or dark, and . . .

MESSENGER *(approaching)*. Bride!

LEAH *(shivers as she turns toward him)*. Yes—what is it? *(She gazes fixedly at him)*

MESSENGER. The souls of the dead *do* return to earth, but not as disembodied spirits. Some must pass through many forms before they achieve purification. *(Leah listens with ever-increasing attention)* The souls of the wicked return in the forms of beasts, or birds, or fish—of plants even, and are powerless to purify themselves by their own efforts. They have to wait for the coming of some righteous sage to purge them of their sins and set them free. Others enter bodies of the newly born, and cleanse themselves by well-doing.

LEAH (in tremulous eagerness). Yes . . . yes . . .

MESSENGER. Besides these, there are vagrant souls which, finding neither rest nor harbor, pass into the bodies of the living, in the form of a Dybbuk, until they have attained purity.

(Exit the Messenger. Leah remains lost in astonishment, as Sender comes out of the house.)

SENDER. Why are you sitting here like this, little daughter?

FRADE. She entertained the beggars at their meal and danced with them afterwards. They tired her, so she is resting awhile now.

SENDER. Entertaining the poor, eh? That is a sweet and pious deed. (He looks up at the sky) It is getting very late but the bridegroom and his people have arrived at last. Is everything ready?

FRADE. She has still to go to the graveyard.

SENDER. Yes, go, my little one—go to Mamma. (He sighs) Let your tears fall on her grave and ask her to come to your wedding. Ask her to be with you, so that we may lead our only daughter under the canopy together. Say that I have fulfilled her dying wishes to devote my life to you and bring you up to be a true and virtuous daughter of Israel. This I have done, and am now about to give you in marriage to a learned and God-fearing young man, of good family.

(He wipes away his tears and with bowed head turns back into the house. A pause.)

LEAH. Granny, may I invite others at the graveyard besides mother?

FRADE. Only the near relations. You must ask your grandfather, Rabbi Ephraim, and your Aunt Mirele.

LEAH. There is some one else I want to ask—not a relation.

FRADE. No, daughter—that is forbidden. If you invite one stranger, the others might take offense and do you harm.

LEAH. He is not a stranger, Granny. He was in our house like one of ourselves.

FRADE (in a voice low with fear). Child, child—you fill me with fear . . . They say he died a bad, unnatural death. (Leah weeps silently) There, there, my little one, don't cry. You shall ask him if you must; granny will take the sin upon herself. (Bethinking herself) I don't know where they buried him, though, and it would never do to ask.

LEAH. I know where he is.

FRADE (surprised). You know? How?

LEAH. I saw his grave in a dream. (She closes her eyes in a trance). And I saw him, too. He told me his trouble and begged me to invite him to the wedding.

(Gittel and Bassia enter running.)

GITTEL AND BASSIA (together, in high excitement). We've seen him—we've seen him!

LEAH (in consternation). Whom— whom have you seen?

GITTEL. Why, the bridegroom, of course. And he's dark . . .

BASSIA. No, he isn't—he's fair . . .

GITTEL. Come, let's take another look and make sure . . . (They run off)

LEAH (rising). Come, Granny—let us go to the graveyard.

FRADE (sadly). Yes, my baby . . . Och, och, och!

(Leah takes a black shawl and puts it round her shoulders. With Frade at her side, she passes slowly down the alley to the right. The stage remains empty for a moment.)

(Music is heard approaching, as from the alley on the left come Nachmon, Rabbi Mendel and Menashe, a small, wizened youth who stares about him with wide, terrified eyes. They are followed by relatives, men and women, in holiday clothes. Sender comes out to meet them.)

SENDER (shakes Nachmon's hand warmly). Sholom aleichem, Nachmon. You are welcome. (They kiss. Sender shakes hands with Menashe and kisses him. He then shakes hands with the rest of the party). Have you had a good journey?

NACHMON. We have had a hard and bitter journey. First we missed the road and went astray in the fields. Then we plunged into a swamp which nearly swallowed us up. It was all we could do to pull ourselves out, and the thought flashed through my mind that the Evil Ones, God forbid, were at work to prevent our getting here at all. However, by the goodness of God we have still managed to arrive in time.

SENDER. You must be exhausted. Come in and rest.

NACHMON. There's no time to rest, we have still to settle the details of the marriage-contract, the transfer of the dowry—the wedding gifts—how long the couple should live in the bridegroom's father's house, and so forth . . .

SENDER. As you wish—I am entirely at your disposal. (Puts his arm around Nachmon's shoulders, and walks up and down the square with him, talking)

RABBI MENDEL (to Menashe). Remember now—you are to remain perfectly quiet at the table. Keep your eyes downcast, and make no movement of any sort. The moment the supper is over, the master of ceremonies will call out: "The bridegroom will now deliver his oration." Then you will rise immediately and stand on the bench. Begin intoning loudly—the louder the better. And you are not to be bashful—do you hear?

MENASHE. Yes, I hear. (In a frightened whisper) Rabbi, I'm afraid.

RABBI MENDEL (alarmed). Afraid— what of? Have you forgotten your oration?

MENASHE. No—it isn't that.

RABBI MENDEL. What then?

MENASHE (in anguish). I don't know myself. But no sooner had we left home than I was seized with terror. All the places we passed were strange to me— I've never in my life seen so many unfamiliar faces. I can't stand the way they look at me—I'm afraid of their eyes. (He shudders) Rabbi, nothing terrifies me so much as the eyes of strangers.

RABBI MENDEL. I'll pray that the evil eye be averted from you.

MENASHE. Rabbi, I'd like to stay alone, I'd like to creep into a corner somewhere. But here I'm surrounded by strangers. I have to talk to them, answer their questions; I feel as if I were being dragged to the gallows. (With mystic terror) Rabbi, above all, I'm frightened of her, the maiden.

RABBI MENDEL. Make up your mind to master your fears, and you will. Otherwise, God forbid, you may forget your oration. Let us go to the inn now, and I will hear you go over it again.

MENASHE (clutches at Mendel's hand). Rabbi—what's that grave there in the middle of the street?

(They read the inscription on the headstone in silence, and stand for a moment beside the grave; then with bowed heads pass down the alley to the left. Sender, Nachmon, and the Wedding Guest enter the house. The poor file out of the courtyard, with their bags on their shoulders and staves in their hands. They cross the square silently and vanish down the alley to the left. A few linger in the square.)

A TALL PALE WOMAN. Now the poor people's feast is over—like all the other things—just as if they'd never been.

LAME OLD WOMAN. They said there'd be a plate of soup for every one, but there wasn't.

A HUNCHBACK. And only little slices of white bread.

A MAN ON CRUTCHES. A rich man like him—as if it would have hurt him to give us a whole loaf each.

THE TALL WOMAN. They might have given us a bit of chicken. Just look, chicken and geese and turkeys for their rich guests.

A HALF-BLIND WOMAN. Oh, what does it matter? It all goes to the worms when we're dead. Och, och, och!

(They go slowly out. The stage is empty for a moment. Then the Messenger crosses from the left and enters the synagogue. Dusk is falling. The shopkeepers are closing for the night. In the synagogue and at Sender's house, lights are appearing. Sender, Gittel and Bassia come onto the stoop. They peer about.)

SENDER (worried.) Where is Leah? Where is old Frade? How is it they aren't back from the graveyard all this time? Can they have met with an accident, God forbid?

GITTEL AND BASSIA. We'll go and meet them.

(From the alley on the right, Frade and Leah come hurrying.)

FRADE. Hurry, child, hurry! Ei, ei—
how long we've been! Oh, why did I let
you have your way? I am so afraid something dreadful is going to happen, God
forbid!

SENDER. Oh, here they are. What can
have kept you all this time?

(Women come out of the house.)

WOMEN. Bring in the bride to pray before the candles.

(Leah is led into the house.)

FRADE *(whispering to Gittel and Bassia).*
She fainted. I'd a hard time bringing her
round. I'm shaking all over still.

BASSIA. That's because she's been fast-
ing . . . it weakens the heart.

GITTEL. Did she cry much at her mother's grave?

FRADE. Better not ask what happened
there. I'm still shaking all over . . .

*(A chair is set near the door and Leah is led
out. They seat her. Music. Nachmon, Menashe,
Rabbi Mendel and the guests approach from
the alley on the left. Menashe carries a cloth
over his outstretched hands, and crosses to
Leah in order to cover her face with it. The
Messenger comes out of the synagogue.)*

LEAH *(tears the cloth away, and springing
up, thrusts Menashe from her, crying out).*
No! YOU are not my bridegroom!

*(General consternation. They all crowd round
Leah.)*

SENDER *(overwhelmed).* Little daughter,
what is it, my darling? What has come
over you?

*(Leah breaks away from them and runs to
the grave, reaching out her arms.)*

LEAH. Holy bridegroom and bride,
protect me—save me! *(She falls. They
flock round her, and raise her from the ground.
She looks wildly about, and cries out, not in
her natural voice, but in the voice of a man)*
Ah! Ah! You buried me. But I have
come back—to my destined bride. I will
leave her no more! *(Nachmon crosses to
Leah, and she shrieks into his face)* Chamilouk!

NACHMAN *(trembling).* She has gone
mad.

MESSENGER. Into the bride has entered
a Dybbuk.

(Great tumult.)

CURTAIN

ACT THREE

*Miropol. A large room in the house of
Rabbi Azrael of Miropol. Right, door leading
to other rooms. In middle of wall, center, door
to street. On either side of this door, benches.
Windows. Left, a table almost the entire length
of the wall, covered with a white cloth. On
table, slices of white bread[1]. At the head of
table, a great armchair. Past the door right,
a small cupboard containing scrolls of the law.
Beside it, an altar. Opposite, a small table,
sofa and several chairs.*

*It is the Sabbath—evening prayers are just
over. Chassidim go to and fro in the room
while Elder Michoel places about the table
the pieces of white bread. The Messenger is
sitting beside the cupboard where the scrolls
are, surrounded by a group of Chassidim.
Others sit apart, reading. Two stand beside
the small table. A low chanting is heard from
an inner room: "God of Abraham, Isaac and
Jacob . . ." The two Chassidim speak.*

———

FIRST CHASSID. He has some wonderful
tales, the Stranger. It gives you the creeps
to listen to them—I'm afraid to, myself.

SECOND CHASSID. What are they about?

FIRST CHASSID. They're full of deep
meaning, but it's not easy to grasp what
the meaning is. For all *we* know, they
may have something to do with the
Bratslaver's creed[2].

SECOND CHASSID. There can't be anything very heretical in them if the older
Chassidim can listen to him.

(They join the group about the Messenger.)

THIRD CHASSID. Go on—tell us another . . .

MESSENGER. It is late. There is hardly
any time left.

FOURTH CHASSID. That's all right. The
Rabbi won't be here for a good while yet.

MESSENGER *(continuing his stories).*
Well, then. At the end of the earth stands
a high mountain; on the top of this mountain is a huge boulder, and out of the
boulder flows a stream of clear water. At

[1] Sabbath bread which is prayed over at the
close of the Sabbath.

[2] Nachmon Bratslaver, a descendant of Balshem,
the founder of Chassidism. Bratslaver was a famous
Rabbi, a poet and philosopher.

the opposite end of the earth is the heart of the world. Now each thing in the world has a heart, and the world itself has a great heart of its own. And the heart of the world keeps the clear stream ever in sight, gazing at it with insatiable longing and desire. But the heart of the world can make not even one step toward it, for the moment it stirs from its place, it loses sight of the mountain's summit and the crystal spring. And if, though for a single instant only, it lose sight of the spring, it loses in that same moment its life, and the heart of the world begins to die.

The crystal spring has no life-span of its own, but endures only so long as the heart of the world allows. And this is one day only.

Now at the close of day, the spring calls to the heart of the world in a song and is answered in a song from the heart. And the sound of their song passes over all the earth, and out of it shining threads come forth and fasten onto the hearts of all the world's creatures and from one heart to another. There is a righteous and benevolent man, who goes to and fro over all the earth's surface, gathering up the threads from all the hearts. These he weaves into Time, and when he has woven one whole day, he passes it over to the heart of the world, which passes it over to the crystal spring, and so the spring achieves another day of life.

THIRD CHASSID. The Rabbi is coming. (Silence falls. They all rise. Rabbi Azrael enters at door, left. He is a man of great age, dressed in a white kaftan and high fur cap. Very slowly and wearily, deep in thought, he crosses to the table, and sinks into the armchair at its head. Michoel takes his place at the Rabbi's right hand, and the Chassidim group themselves around the table, the elders sitting, the younger standing behind them. Michoel distributes white bread. Rabbi Azrael lifts his head, and in a low, quavering voice chants.)

RABBI AZRAEL. The feast of David, the King, the Messiah . . .

(The others make the response and say grace over the bread. They begin chanting in low tones, a sad, mysterious air without words. There is a pause. Rabbi Azrael sighs deeply, rests his head on both hands, and in that position remains seated, lost in

meditation. An atmosphere of suspense pervades the silence. At last, Rabbi Azrael again raises his head, and begins to intone) It is told of the holy Balshem—may his merits hover over us . . . (There is a momentary pause) One day there came to Meshibach a troupe of German acrobats who gave their performance in the streets of the town. They stretched a rope across the river and one of them walked along the rope to the opposite bank. From all sides the people came running to behold this ungodly marvel, and in the midst of the crowd of onlookers stood the holy Balshem himself. His disciples were greatly astonished, and asked him the meaning of his presence there. And the holy Balshem answered them thus: I went to see how a man might cross the chasm between two heights as this man did, and as I watched him I reflected that if mankind would submit their souls to such discipline as that to which he submitted his body, what deep abysses might they not cross upon the tenuous cord of life! (The Rabbi sighs deeply. In the pause that follows, the Chassidim exchange enraptured glances.)

FIRST CHASSID. Lofty as the world!

SECOND CHASSID. Wonder of wonders!

THIRD CHASSID. Glory of glories!

RABBI AZRAEL (to Michoel, whispering). There is a stranger here.

MICHOEL (looking round). He is a messenger, in the confidence of the Great Ones.

RABBI AZRAEL. What message does he bring?

MICHOEL. I don't know. Shall I tell him to go away?

RABBI AZRAEL. God forbid! A stranger must, on the contrary, be shown special honor. Give him a chair. (Pause) The world of God is great and holy. In all the world the holiest land is the Land of Israel. In the Land of Israel the holiest city is Jerusalem; in Jerusalem the holiest place was the Holy Temple, and the holiest spot in the Temple was the Holy of Holies. (He pauses) In the world there are seventy nations, and of them the holiest is Israel. The holiest of the people of Israel is the tribe of the Levites. The holiest of the Levites are the priests, and amongst the priests, the holiest is the High Priest. *(Pause)* The year has three hundred and fifty-four days. Of these the holidays are the holiest. Holier than the holidays are the Sabbaths and the holiest of the Sabbaths is Yom Kippur[1], Sabbath of Sabbaths. *(Pause)* There are in the world seventy tongues. The holiest of these is the holy tongue of Israel. The holiest of all things written in this tongue is the Holy Torah; of the Torah the holiest part is the Ten Commandments, and the holiest of all the words in the Ten Commandments is the Name of the Lord. *(Pause)* At a certain hour, on a certain day of the year, all these four supreme holinesses met together. This took place on the Day of Atonement, at the hour when the High Priest entered the Holy of Holies and there revealed the Divine Name. And as this hour was holy and terrible beyond words, so also was it the hour of utmost peril for the High Priest, and for the entire commonweal of Israel. For if, in that hour *(which God forbid)*, a sinful or a wayward thought had entered the mind of the High Priest, it would have brought the destruction of the world. *(Pause)* Wherever a man stand to lift his eyes to heaven, that place is a Holy of Holies. Every human being created by God in His own image and likeness is a High Priest. Each day of a man's life is the Day of Atonement; and every word he speaks from his heart is the name of the Lord. Therefore the sin of any man, whether of commission or of omission, brings the ruin of a whole world in its train. *(His voice becomes weaker and trembles)* Through many transmigrations, the human soul is drawn by pain and grief, as the child to its mother's breast, to the source of its being, the Exalted Throne above. But it happens sometimes that a soul which has attained to the final state of purification suddenly becomes the prey of evil forces which cause it to slip and fall. And the higher it had soared, the deeper it falls. And with the fall of such a soul as this, a world plunges to ruin. And darkness overwhelms the spheres. The ten spheres bewail the world that is lost. *(He pauses, and seems to awaken*

[1] The Day of Atonement.

to consciousness) My children, to-night we will shorten the seeing out of the Queen[1]. *(All except Michoel silently leave the room, the spell of the Rabbi's discourses still upon them.)*

MICHOEL *(approaches the table uncertainly)*. Rabbi . . . Rabbi, Sender of Brainitz is here.

RABBI AZRAEL *(mechanically repeating the words)*. Sender of Brainitz . . . I know.

MICHOEL. A terrible misfortune has befallen him. A Dybbuk—God's mercy be upon us—has entered into his daughter.

RABBI AZRAEL. A Dybbuk has . . . I know.

MICHOEL. He has brought her to you.

RABBI AZRAEL *(as if to himself)*. To me? . . . To me? . . . Why to me, when there *is* no me to come to? For I am myself no longer.

MICHOEL. But Rabbi—everybody comes to you—a world of people.

RABBI AZRAEL. As you say—a world of people. Yes, a blind world—blind sheep following a blind shepherd. If they had eyes to see with, they would seek guidance not from me, but from Him who alone can justly use the word "I," for He is, in all the world, the only "I."

MICHOEL. You are His representative Rabbi.

RABBI AZRAEL. So says the world. But as for me, I do not know. For forty years I have sat in the Rabbi's chair, and yet, to this very day I am not convinced that I am indeed the appointed deputy on earth of Him whose Name be praised. At times I am conscious of my nearness to the All. Then I am free of doubts, and feel the power within me—then I know I am master over the high worlds. But there are other times when that certainty abandons me, and then I am as small and feeble as a child, then I myself, and not those who come to me, need help.

MICHOEL. I know, Rabbi—I remember. Once you came to me at midnight, and asked me to recite the psalms with you. All the night long, we said them together, weeping.

RABBI AZRAEL. That was a long time

[1] The Sabbath is the Queen, whose going is celebrated with prayer.

ago—it is worse than ever now. *(His voice fails)* What do they want of me? I am old and weak. My body has earned its rest—my soul longs for solitude. Yet still they come thronging to me, all the misery and sorrow of the world. Each imploring word pierces my flesh like a thorn . . . No, I have no longer the strength . . . I cannot . . .

MICHOEL *(filled with fear)*. Rabbi, Rabbi! . . .

RABBI AZRAEL *(suddenly breaking into tears)*. I can't go on . . . I can't . . . *(He weeps)*

MICHOEL. Rabbi—do you forget the generations of righteous and holy men of God from whom you are descended? Your father, Rabbi Itzele, blessed be his name, your grandfather, our master and lord— our teacher, Rabbi Velvele the Great, who was a pupil of the holy Balshem himself . . .

RABBI AZRAEL *(regaining his self-control)*. No—I will not forget my forebears—my holy father who three times had a revelation direct from God; my uncle, Rabbi Meyer Baer, who upon the words of "Hear, O Israel" could ascend to Heaven at will; the great Velvele, my grandfather, who resurrected the dead . . . *(All his spirit has returned as he speaks to Michoel)* Michoel, do you know that my grandfather would drive out Dybbuks without either spells or incantations— with a single word of command, only one, he expelled them. In times of stress I always turn to him, and he sustains me. He will not forsake me now. Call in Sender.

(Michoel goes, and returns in a moment with Sender.)

SENDER *(tearfully, with outspread hands)*. Rabbi! Have mercy on me! Help me! Save my only daughter!

RABBI AZRAEL. How did this misfortune come upon you?

SENDER. Just as they were about to veil the bride, and . . .

RABBI AZRAEL. That is not what I asked. Tell me, what could have brought this thing to pass? A worm can enter a fruit only after it has begun to rot.

SENDER. Rabbi, my only daughter is a pious Jewish maiden. She is modest and

gentle—she has never disobeyed me.

RABBI AZRAEL. Children are sometimes punished for the sins of their parents.

SENDER. If I knew of any sin I had committed, I would do penance for it.

RABBI AZRAEL. Have you asked the Dybbuk who he was, and why he entered into your daughter?

SENDER. He refuses to answer. But we recognized him by his voice. He was a student in our *yeshiva* who died suddenly in the synagogue. That was months ago. He had been meddling in the Kabala and came to grief through it.

RABBI AZRAEL. What powers destroyed him?

SENDER. Evil ones, they say. An hour or two before his death, he had been telling a fellow-student that sin need not be fought against, for Satan too is holy at the core. He also tried the use of charms to obtain two barrels of gold.

RABBI AZRAEL. Did you know him?

SENDER. Yes. I was one of those in whose house he stayed.

RABBI AZRAEL *(bending his gaze intently upon Sender)*. You may have put some slight upon him or mistreated him. Try to remember.

SENDER. I don't know . . . I can't remember . . . *(Desperately)* Rabbi, I'm only human, after all . . . I . . .

RABBI AZRAEL. Bring in the maiden.

(Sender goes out and returns immediately with Frade, who supports Leah. Leah stops in the doorway and will go no further.)

SENDER *(weeping)*. Have pity on your father, my child—don't put him to shame before the Rabbi. Come inside.

FRADE. Go in, Leah dear—go in, little dove.

LEAH. I want to . . . but I can't . . .

RABBI AZRAEL. Maiden, I command you—come in! *(Leah advances into the room and crosses to the table)* Sit down!

LEAH *(does as the Rabbi tells her. Then suddenly springs up and cries out with a voice not her own)*. Let me be! I will not be here!

(She tries to escape, but is stopped by Sender and Frade.)

RABBI AZRAEL. Dybbuk! Who are you? I command you to answer.

LEAH *(in the voice of the Dybbuk)*. Miropol Rabbi—you know very well who I am. I do not wish the others to know.

RABBI AZRAEL. I do not ask your name —I ask: Who *are* you?

LEAH *(as before)*. I am one of those who sought other paths.

RABBI AZRAEL. He only seeks other paths who has lost the straight one.

LEAH *(as before)*. The straight one is too narrow.

RABBI AZRAEL. That has been said before by one who did not return. *(Pause)* Why did you enter into this maiden?

LEAH *(as before)*. I am her predestined bridegroom.

RABBI AZRAEL. According to our Holy Scriptures, a dead soul may not stay in the realms of the living.

LEAH *(as before)*. I have not died.

RABBI AZRAEL. You left our world, and so are forbidden to return until the blast of the great trumpet shall be heard. I command you therefore to leave the body of this maiden, in order that a living branch of the imperishable tree of Israel may not be blasted.

LEAH *(shrieks in the Dybbuk's voice)*. Miropol Rabbi—I know your almighty power. I know that angels and archangels obey your word. But me you cannot command. I have nowhere to go. Every road is barred against me and every gate is locked. On every side, the forces of evil lie in wait to seize me. *(In a trembling voice)* There is heaven, and there is earth —and all the countless worlds in space, yet in not one of these is there any place for me. And now that my soul has found refuge from the bitterness and terror of pursuit, you wish to drive me away. Have mercy! Do not send me away—don't force me to go!

RABBI AZRAEL. I am filled with profound pity for you, wandering soul! And I will use all my power to save you from the evil spirits. But the body of this maiden you must leave.

LEAH *(in the Dybbuk's voice, firmly)*. I refuse!

RABBI AZRAEL. Michoel. Summon a *minyen* from the synagogue. *(Michoel returns at once with ten Jews who take their places on one side of the room)* Holy Community, do you give me authority to cast

out of the body of a Jewish maiden, in your behalf and with your power, a spirit which refuses to leave her of its own free will?

THE TEN. Rabbi, we give you authority to cast out of the body of a Jewish maiden, in our behalf and in our name and with our power, a spirit which refuses to leave her of its own free will.

RABBI *(rises)*. Dybbuk! Soul of one who has left the world in which we live! In the name and with the power of a holy community of Jews, I, Azrael, son of Itzele, order you to depart out of the body of the maiden, Leah, daughter of Channah, and in departing, to do no injury either to her or to any other living being. If you do not obey me, I shall proceed against you with malediction and anathema, to the limit of my powers, and with the utmost might of my uplifted arm. But if you do as I command you, then I shall bend all my strength to drive away the fiends and evil spirits that surround you, and keep you safe from them.

LEAH *(shrieks in the voice of the Dybbuk)*. I'm not afraid of your anathema. I put no faith in your promises. The power is not in the world that can help me. The loftiest height of the world cannot compare with this resting-place that I have found, nor is there in the world an abysm so fathomless as that which waits to receive me if ever I leave my only refuge. I will not go.

RABBI AZRAEL. In the name of the Almighty, I adjure you for the last time. Leave the body of this maiden—If you do not, I shall utter the anathema against you and deliver you into the hands of the fiends of destruction. *(An ominous pause)*

LEAH *(in the voice of the Dybbuk)*. In the name of the Almighty, I am bound to my betrothed, and will remain with her to all eternity.

RABBI AZRAEL. Michoel, have white shrouds brought for all who are here. Bring seven trumpets . . . and seven black candles . . . Then seven holy scrolls from their place.

(A pause fraught with dire omen, during which Michoel goes out and returns with trumpets and black candles. The Messenger follows him with the shrouds.)

MESSENGER *(counting the shrouds)*. One

too many. *(He looks round the room)* Some one is missing, perhaps?

RABBI AZRAEL *(worried—as if recalling something)*. Before pronouncing the anathema against a Jewish soul, it is necessary to obtain the permission of the City Rabbi. Michoel, leave these things for the present. Here is my staff. Take it and go to the City Rabbi, and ask him to come without delay.

(Michoel puts the trumpets and candles aside and goes out with the Messenger, who still carries the shrouds over his arm.)

RABBI AZRAEL *(to the Ten)*. Wait outside until they come back. *(They leave the room. There is a pause. Rabbi Azrael turns to Sender)* Sender, where are the bridegroom and his people?

SENDER. They stayed in Brainitz over the Sabbath, at my house.

RABBI AZRAEL. Let a messenger ride over and tell them, in my name, to stay there and await my orders.

SENDER. I'll send at once.

RABBI AZRAEL. You may leave me now, and take the maiden into the next room.

LEAH *(wakes out of her trance, and speaks in her own voice, trembling)*. Granny— I'm frightened. What are they going to do to him? What are they going to do to me?

FRADE. There, there, my child— you've nothing to be frightened of. The Rabbi knows best. He couldn't harm any one. The Rabbi can't do wrong, my darling.

(Frade and Sender take Leah into the adjoining room.)

RABBI AZRAEL *(remains absorbed in his thoughts. Then he looks up)*. Even though it has been thus ordained in the high planes, I will reverse that destiny.

(Enter Rabbi Samson.)

RABBI SAMSON. A good week to you, Rabbi.

RABBI AZRAEL *(rises to meet him)*. A good week, a good year to you, Rabbi. Be seated. *(Rabbi Samson takes a seat)* I have troubled you to come here in a very grave matter. A Dybbuk *(the Lord of Mercy be with us)*, has entered into a daughter of Israel, and nothing will induce him to leave her. Only the last resort is left, to force him out by anathema, and this I ask

your permission to do. The salvation of a soul will thereby be added to your other merits.

RABBI SAMSON *(sighing)*. Anathema is cruel punishment enough for the living —it is far more so for the dead. But if, as you say, all other means have failed, and so godly a man as yourself believe it necessary, I give you my consent. I have a secret, however, which I must reveal to you, Rabbi, for it has a vital bearing on this affair.

RABBI AZRAEL. I am listening, Rabbi.

RABBI SAMSON. Rabbi, do you remember a young Chassid from Brainitz, Nissin ben Rifke by name, who used to come to you from time to time, about twenty years ago?

RABBI AZRAEL. Yes. He went away to some place a long way off and died there, still in his youth.

RABBI SAMSON. That is he. Well, that same Nissin ben Rifke appeared to me three times in my dreams last night, demanding that I summon Sender of Brainitz to trial before the Rabbinical Court.

RABBI AZRAEL. What was his charge against Sender?

RABBI SAMSON. He did not state it to me. He only kept saying that Sender had done him a mortal injury.

RABBI AZRAEL. A rabbi can obviously not prevent any Jew from summoning another to appear before the court, particularly when the complainant is dead and could appeal in the last resort to the Highest Tribunal of all . . . But how do these visitations of yours affect this Dybbuk?

RABBI SAMSON. In this manner . . . It has come to my ears that the youth who died and entered into the body of Sender's daughter as a Dybbuk, was Nissin ben Rifke's only son . . . There is also some rumor concerning a pact with Nissin ben Rifke which has not been kept.

RABBI AZRAEL *(after a moment's reflection)*. This being the case, I shall postpone the exorcising of the Dybbuk until tomorrow midday. In the morning after prayers, you shall summon the dead man to court, and God willing, we shall discover the reason for his visitations to you

And then, with your permission, I shall cast out the Dybbuk by anathema.

RABBI SAMSON. In view of the difficulty of a trial between a living man and a dead one, which is as rare as it is difficult, I beg that you will preside over the court, Rabbi, and conduct the proceedings.

RABBI AZRAEL. Very well . . . Michoel. *(Enter Michoel)* Bring in the maiden. *(Sender and Frade bring Leah into the room. She sits down before the Rabbi with her eyes closed)* Dybbuk! I give you respite until noon tomorrow. If at that hour you persist in your refusal to leave this maiden's body of your own accord, I shall, with the permission of the City Rabbi, tear you away from her with the utmost force of the *cherem*[1]. *(Sender and Frade lead Leah towards the door.)* Sender, you are to remain. *(Frade takes Leah out)* Sender, do you remember the bosom friend of your youth—Nissin ben Rifke?

SENDER *(frightened)*. Nissin ben Rifke? He died, didn't he?

RABBI AZRAEL. Know, then, that he appeared three times last night before the Rabbi of the City *(indicating Rabbi Samson)* as he slept. And Nissin ben Rifke demanded that you be summoned to stand trial by the Rabbinical Court for a wrong that you have done him.

SENDER *(stunned)*. Me? A trial? Is there no end to my misfortunes? What does he want of me? Rabbi, help me! What shall I do?

RABBI AZRAEL. I do not know the nature of his charge. But you must accept the summons.

SENDER. I will do whatever you say.

RABBI AZRAEL *(in a different tone)*. Let the swiftest horses be sent immediately to Brainitz, to fetch the bridegroom and his people. Have them here before midday tomorrow, in order that the wedding may take place as soon as the Dybbuk has been expelled. Have the canopy set up.

SENDER. Rabbi! What if they no longer wish to be connected with my family, and refuse to come?

(The Messenger appears in the doorway.)

RABBI AZRAEL *(with dignity)*. Tell them I have commanded them to come. Let

[1] The sentence of excommunication.

nothing prevent the bridegroom from arriving in time.

MESSENGER. The bridegroom will be here in time.

(The clock strikes twelve.)

CURTAIN

ACT FOUR

SAME SCENE AS ACT III. *Instead of the long table, left, a smaller one nearer to footlights. Rabbi Azrael, wrapped in his prayer-shawl and wearing the phylacteries, is in the armchair. The two Judges sit in ordinary chairs. Rabbi Samson stands beside the table and, at a distance, Michoel. They are finishing a prayer whereby an evil dream may be turned into good.*

———

RABBI AZRAEL, MICHOEL, AND THE TWO JUDGES. You beheld a good dream! You beheld a good dream! You beheld a good dream!

RABBI AZRAEL. We have found a solution of good to your dream.

RABBI SAMSON. I beheld a good dream —a good dream I beheld. I beheld a good dream.

RABBI AZRAEL. Will you now, Rabbi Samson, take your seat with the other judges? *(Rabbi Samson sits down next to Rabbi Azrael).* Let us now call upon this dead man to be present at the trial. First, however, I shall draw a holy circle beyond which he may not pass. Michoel, my staff . . . *(Michoel gives him the staff. Rabbi Azrael, then rises and, going to the corner left, describes a circle on the floor from left to right. He then returns to the table)* Michoel, take my staff and go to the graveyard. When you get there, go in with your eyes closed, guiding yourself with the staff. At the first grave it touches, stop. Knock with it three times upon this grave, and repeat what I shall tell you faithfully word for word: Pure dead, I am sent by Azrael, son of the great sage, Rabbi Itzele of Miropol, to beg you to pardon him for disturbing your peace, and to deliver his command that you inform the pure dead, Nissin ben Rifke, by means known to you as follows: That the just and righteous Rabbinical Court of Miropol summon him to be present immediately at a trial at which he shall appear in the same garb as that in which he was buried. Repeat these words three times; then turn and come back here. You will not look behind you, no matter what cries or calls or shrieks may pursue you, nor will you allow my staff to leave your hand even for one moment, otherwise you will place yourself in dire peril. Go and God will protect you, for no harm can come to him who is bound on a virtuous errand. But before you go, let two men come in and make a partition which shall separate the dead man from the living. *(Michoel, goes out. Two men enter with a sheet with which they screen the left-hand corner down to the floor. They then leave the room)* Let Sender come in. *(Sender appears)* Sender, have you carried out my instructions and sent horses for the bridegroom and his people?

SENDER. The swiftest horses were sent, but the bridegroom has not yet arrived.

RABBI AZRAEL. Have someone ride out to meet them and say they are to drive as fast as they can.

SENDER. Yes, Rabbi. *(Pause)*

RABBI AZRAEL. Sender, we have sent to inform the pure dead, Nissin ben Rifke, that the Rabbinical Court summon him to appear in his cause against you. Are you willing to accept our verdict?

SENDER. I am.

RABBI AZRAEL. Will you carry out our sentence?

SENDER. I will.

RABBI AZRAEL. Then step back and take your place upon the right.

SENDER. Rabbi, it begins to come back to me . . . It may be that the trial which Nissin ben Rifke has summoned me to concerns an agreement upon which we shook hands one day many years ago. But in that matter I am not to blame.

RABBI AZRAEL. You will have an opportunity to speak of this later on, after the complainant has made known his grievance. *(Pause)*. Very soon there is personally to appear in our midst, a man from the True World, in order to submit to our judgment a case between himself and a man of our Untrue World. *(Pause)* A trial such as this is proof that the laws set forth in the Holy Scriptures rule all worlds and all peoples, and unite both the living and the dead within their bonds. *(Pause)* A trial such as this is difficult and terrible. The eyes of all the worlds are turned towards it, and should this court deviate from the Law by so much as a hair's breadth, tumult would ensue in the Court on High. It is with fear and trembling, therefore, that we are to approach the trial at issue . . . with fear and trembling . . . *(He looks anxiously around him and as he does encounters the partition in the left-hand corner. He ceases to speak. There is a silence of awe)*

FIRST JUDGE *(in a frightened whisper to the Second Judge)*. I believe he's come.

SECOND JUDGE *(in the same tone)*. It seems so.

RABBI SAMSON. He is here.

RABBI AZRAEL. Pure dead Nissin ben Rifke! You are commanded by this just and righteous court to stay within the circle and partition assigned to you, and not to go beyond them. Pure dead Nissin ben Rifke, you are commanded by this just and righteous court to state your grievance and the redress you seek against the accused, Sender ben Henie.

(Awestruck pause. All listen as though turned to stone.)

FIRST JUDGE. I believe he is answering.

SECOND JUDGE. It seems so.

FIRST JUDGE. I hear a voice but no words.

SECOND JUDGE. And I words but no voice.

RABBI SAMSON *(to Sender)*. Sender ben Henie, the pure dead Nissin ben Rifke makes demand saying that in the years of your youth you and he were students in the same *yeshiva*, comrades, and that your soul and his were bound together in true friendship. You were both married in the same week, and when you met at the house of the Rabbi, during the Great Holidays, you made a solemn pact that if the wife of one of you should conceive and bear a boy and the other a girl, those two children should marry.

SENDER *(in a tremulous voice)*. It was so.

RABBI SAMSON. The pure dead Nissin ben Rifke makes further demand, saying that soon afterwards he left for a place very far away, where his wife bore him a son in the same hour as your wife gave you a daughter. Soon thereafter he was gathered to his fathers. *(Short pause)* In the True World, he found that his son had been blest with a noble and lofty soul, and was progressing upwards from plane to plane, and at this his paternal heart overflowed with joy and pride. He also found that his son, growing older, had become a wanderer from province to province, and from country to country, and from city to city, for the soul to which his soul had been predestined was drawing him ever onward. At last he came to the city in which you dwell, and you took him into your house. He sat at your table, and his soul bound itself to the soul of your daughter. But you were rich, while Nissin's son was poor, and so you turned your back on him and went seeking for your daughter a bridegroom of high estate and great possessions. *(Short pause)* Nissin then beheld his son grow desperate and become a wanderer once more, seeking now the New Paths. And sorrow and alarm filled his father's soul lest the dark powers, aware of the youth's extremity, spread their net for him. This they did, and caught him, and tore him from the world before his time. Thereafter the soul of Nissin ben Rifke's son roamed amidst the worlds until at last it entered as a Dybbuk into the body of his predestined. Nissin ben Rifke claims that the death of his son has severed him from both worlds, leaving him without name or memorial, since neither heir nor friend remains on earth to pray for his soul. His light has been extinguished forever—the crown of his head has rolled down into the abyss. Therefore, he begs the just and righteous court to pass sentence upon Sender according to the laws of our Holy Scriptures, for his shedding of the blood of Nissin's son and of his son's sons to the end of all generations.

(An awestruck pause. Sender is shaken with sobs.)

RABBI AZRAEL. Sender ben Henie, have you heard the complaint brought against you by the holy dead, Nissin ben Rifke? What have you to say in answer to it?

SENDER. I can't speak . . . I have no words to say . . . in justification. But I would ask you to beg my old comrade to forgive me this sin, because it was not committed in malice. Soon after we had shaken hands upon our pact, Nissin went away, and I did not know whether his wife had had a child, either boy or girl. Then I received news of his death, but none about his family. And gradually the whole affair of our agreement went out of my mind.

RABBI AZRAEL. Why did you not inquire about him? Why did you make no inquiry?

SENDER. It is customary for the bridegroom's father to make the first advances, not the bride's. I thought that if Nissin had had a son, he would have let me know. *(Pause)*.

RABBI SAMSON. Nissin ben Rifke asks why, when you received his son into your house and had him sit at your table, did you never ask him whence he came and of what family?

SENDER. I don't know . . . I don't remember . . . But I do swear that something urged me continually to take him for my son-in-law. That was why, whenever a match was proposed, I always made such hard conditions that the bridegroom's father would never agree to them. Three marriages fell through in this manner. But this time the bridegroom's people would not be put off. *(Pause)*

RABBI SAMSON. Nissin ben Rifke says that in your heart of hearts you were aware of his son's identity and therefore feared to ask him who he was. You were ambitious that your daughter should live in ease and riches, and for that reason thrust his son down into the abyss.

(Sender weeps silently, covering his face. There is a heavy pause. Michoel returns and gives the staff back to Rabbi Azrael.)

RABBI AZRAEL *(after a whispered conference with Rabbi Samson and the Judges, rises and takes the staff in his hand)*. This just and righteous court has heard both parties and delivers its verdict as follows: Whereas it is not known whether, at the time Nissin ben Rifke and Sender ben Henie shook hands upon their agreement, their wives had already conceived; and whereas, according to our Holy Scriptures, no agreement whatsoever which involves anything not yet in existence can be held valid in law, we may not therefore find that this agreement was binding upon Sender. Since, however, in the Upper World, the agreement was accepted as valid and never canceled; and since the belief was implanted in the heart of Nissin ben Rifke's son that the daughter of Sender ben Henie was his predestined bride; and whereas, Sender ben Henie's subsequent conduct brought calamity upon Nissin ben Rifke and his son; Now, therefore, be it decreed by this just and righteous court, that Sender give the half of his fortune in alms to the poor, and each year, for the remainder of his life, light the memorial candle for Nissin ben Rifke and his son as though they were his own kindred, and pray for their souls. *(Pause)* The just and righteous court now requests the holy dead, Nissin ben Rifke, to forgive Sender unreservedly, and to command his son in filial duty to leave the body of the maiden, Leah, daughter of Channah, in order that a branch of the fruitful tree of Israel may not be blighted. In return for these things, the Almighty will make manifest his grace to Nissin ben Rifke and to his lost son.

ALL. Amen!

RABBI AZRAEL. Pure dead Nissin ben Rifke, have you heard our judgment? Do you accept it? *(Pause)* Sender ben Henie, have you heard our judgment? Do you accept it?

SENDER. I accept.

RABBI AZRAEL. Pure dead Nissin ben Rifke, the trial between you and Sender ben Henie is now ended. Do you return therefore to your resting place, and in going we command you to do no harm to man nor other living creature whatsoever. *(Pause)* Michoel, water . . . And have the curtain taken away. *(Michoel calls in two men, who remove the sheet. Rabbi Azrael traces a circle in the same place as before, but from right to left. The men return with basin and ewer, and all wash their hands)* Sender, have the bridegroom and his people arrived?

SENDER. There has been no sign of them.

RABBI AZRAEL. Send another rider to meet them, and say they are to press on with all the speed their horses can make. Have the canopy raised and the musicians in readiness. Let the bride be dressed in her wedding-gown so that the moment the Dybbuk has been cast out you may lead her under the canopy. What is now about te be done—will be done.

(Sender goes out. Rabbi Azrael takes off his prayer-shawl and phylacteries, folding them up.)

RABBI SAMSON *(whispering to the Judges)*. Did you notice that the dead man did not forgive Sender?

JUDGES ONE AND TWO *(in low, frightened tones)*. Yes, we did.

RABBI SAMSON. Do you know the dead man did not accept the verdict?

JUDGES ONE AND TWO. Yes, we realized that.

RABBI SAMSON. He failed to say Amen to Rabbi Azrael's sentence—you felt that too, no doubt.

JUDGES ONE AND TWO. Yes, distinctly.

RABBI SAMSON. It is a very bad sign——

JUDGES ONE AND TWO. Extremely——

RABBI SAMSON. Rabbi Azrael is terribly agitated—look at him. See how his hands are trembling. *(Pause)* We have done our share—we can go now.

(The Judges slip out unobtrusively, and Rabbi Samson prepares to follow them.)

RABBI AZRAEL. Rabbi, please remain until the Dybbuk has been cast out—I should like you to perform the wedding ceremony. *(Rabbi Samson sighs and sits down again, with bowed head. An oppressive pause)* God of the Heavens, marvelously strange are Thy ways, and secret, yet the flame of Thy Divine Will illuminates with its reflection the path I tread. Nor shall I stray from the path forever, either to the right or the left. *(He raises his head)* Michoel, is everything prepared?

MICHOEL. Yes, Rabbi.

RABBI AZRAEL. Let the maiden be brought.

(Enter Sender and Frade with Leah, in her wedding-gown, a black cloak over her shoulders. They seat her on the sofa. Rabbi Samson takes his place behind Rabbi Azrael.)

RABBI AZRAEL. Dybbuk, in the name of the Rabbi of this city, who is present, in the name of a holy community of Jews, in the name of the great Sanhedrin of Jerusalem, I, Azrael ben Hadassah, do for the last time command you to depart out of the body of the maiden Leah, daughter of Channah.

LEAH (DYBBUK) *(firmly)*. I refuse!

RABBI AZRAEL. Michoel, call in people to witness the exorcism—bring the shrouds, the horns and the black candles. *(Michoel goes out and shortly returns with fifteen men, among them the Messenger. The shrouds, trumpets and candles are brought)* Bring out the scrolls. *(Michoel gives a scroll each to seven, and a trumpet each to seven others)* Stubborn spirit—inasmuch as you have dared to oppose our power, we deliver you into the hands of the Higher Spirits which will pull you out by force. Blow Tekiah![1]

(The horns are blown.)

LEAH (DYBBUK) *(leaves her seat and struggles violently as against invisible assailants).* Let me alone—you shall not pull me away—I won't go—I can't go——

RABBI AZRAEL. Since the Higher Spirits cannot overcome you, I surrender you to the Spirits of the Middle Plane, those which are neither good nor evil. I now invoke *their* power to drag you forth. Blow Shevarim[1].

(The horns are blown again.)

LEAH (DYBBUK) *(her strength beginning to fail).* Woe is me! The powers of all the worlds are arrayed against me. Spirits of terror wrench me and tear me without mercy—the souls of the great and righteous too have arisen against me. The soul of my own father is with them—commanding me to go——But until the last spark of strength has gone from me, so long shall I withstand them and remain where I am.

RABBI AZRAEL *(to himself).* It is clear that One of Great Power stands beside him. *(Pause)* Michoel, put away the scrolls. *(Michoel does so)* Hang a black curtain over the altar. *(This is done)* Light the black candles. *(This, too, is done)* Let every one now put on a shroud.

[1] Certain notes sounded on the Shofer, the sacred ram's horn.

(All, including the two Rabbis, do so. Rabbi Azrael stands with both arms upraised, an awe-inspiring figure) Rise up, O Lord, and let Thine enemies be scattered before Thee; as smoke is dispersed so let them be scattered . . . Sinful and obstinate soul, with the power of Almighty God and with the sanction of the Holy Scriptures, I, Azrael ben Hadassah, do with these words rend asunder every cord that binds you to the world of living creatures and to the body and soul of the maiden, Leah, daughter of Channah . . .

LEAH (DYBBUK) *(shrieking).* Ah! I am lost!

RABBI AZRAEL. . . . And do pronounce you ex-communicated from all Israel. Blow Teruah.

MESSENGER. The last spark has been swallowed up into the flame.

LEAH (DYBBUK) *(defeated).* Alas!—I can fight no more . . .

(They begin to sound the horns.)

RABBI AZRAEL *(hastily raising his hand to silence the horns).* Do you submit?

LEAH (DYBBUK) *(in a dead voice).* I submit——

RABBI AZRAEL. Do you promise to depart of your own free will, from the body of the maiden, Leah, daughter of Channah, and never return?

LEAH (DYBBUK) *(as before).* I promise——

RABBI AZRAEL. Dybbuk—by the same power and sanction which deputed me to place you under the ban of anathema, I now lift from you that ban. *(To Michoel)* Put out the candles—take down the black curtain. *(Michoel does so)* Put away the horns. *(Michoel collects them)* And dismiss the people—let them take off their shrouds before they go. *(Exeunt the fourteen with Messenger and Michoel. Rabbi Azrael prays with upraised arms)* Lord of the world, God of charity and mercy, look down upon the suffering of this homeless, tortured soul which the errors and misdeeds of others caused to stray into the bypaths. Regard not its wrongdoing, O Lord, but let the memory of its virtuous past and its present bitter torment and the merits of its forefathers rise like a soft, obscuring mist before Thy sight. Lord of the world—do Thou free its path of evil spirits, and admit it to everlasting peace within Thy mansions. Amen.

ALL. Amen.

LEAH (DYBBUK) (trembling violently). Say Kadish[1] for me! The hour of my going was predestined—and it has come!

RABBI AZRAEL. Sender, say Kadish.

(Sender begins the prayer as the clock strikes twelve.)

SENDER. Yisgadaal—ve yiskadesh—shmeh raboh![2]

LEAH (DYBBUK) (springs up). Aie! (Falls swooning upon the sofa)

RABBI AZRAEL. Bring the bride to the wedding-canopy.

MICHOEL (rushing in, greatly agitated). The last rider has just come back. He says a wheel has come off the wagon so that the bridegroom and his party must walk the rest of the way. But they are at the hill, so they will be here soon—they've been sighted already.

RABBI AZRAEL (profoundly astonished). What was to be, shall be. (To Sender) Let the old woman remain here with the bride. We will go—all of us—to meet the bridegroom.

(He traces a circle round Leah, from left to right, takes off his shroud, which he hangs up near the door, and goes out carrying his staff. Sender and Michoel follow him. A long pause.)

LEAH (waking—in a faint voice) Who is here with me? Granny—is that you? Oh! I feel so strange, Granny—so weary. Rock me in your arms.

FRADE (caressing her). No, little daughter—you mustn't feel that way. My little child must not be sad. Let the Black Cat be sad. My little one's heart must be as light as down, as light as a breath, as white as a snowflake. Holy angels should embrace her with their wings.

(Wedding Music is heard.)

LEAH (frightened and trembling, seizes Frade's hand for protection). Listen! They are beginning to dance round the holy grave to cheer up the dead bride and bridegroom.

FRADE. Be calm, my darling. No harm can come to you now—a mighty power is standing guard over you on every side.

[1] The prayer for the dead.
[2] Magnified and sanctified be His mighty Name!

Sixty giants, with drawn swords, protect you from evil encounter. The holy fathers and holy mothers ward off the evil eye. (Little by little she drifts into a chant)

Soon they'll lead you under the canopy—
A blessed hour—a happy hour—
Comes your mother—the good and
[virtuous—
From the Garden of Eden—the Garden of
[Eden.
Of gold and silver are her robes.

Angels twain go out to meet her, go out
[to meet her—
Take her hands—one the right hand, one
[the left hand.
"Channele—Channele mine,
Why do you come decked out so fine?"

So Channele answers the angel:

"Why should I not come robed in state?
Is this not a day of days?
For my bright crown, my only daughter,
Goes to her wedding and luck goes with
[her."

"Channele, as in robes of state you go,
Why is your face all wan and pale with
[woe?"
So Channele answers the angel:

"What should I do but sorrow, on this
day that my daughter's a bride,
For she's led to her wedding by strangers,
while I must stand mourning aside?"

Under the canopy stands the bride, and old and young bring her their greetings and good wishes.

And there stands the Prophet Elijah,
The great goblet of wine in his hand,
And the words of his holy blessing
Roll echoing over the land.

(Frade falls asleep. Long pause.)

LEAH (her eyes closed, sighs deeply—then wakes). Who sighed so deeply?

VOICE OF CHANNON. I.

LEAH. I hear your voice, but I cannot see you.

VOICE OF CHANNON. Because you are

within a magic circle which I may not enter.

LEAH. Your voice is as sweet as the lament of violins in the quiet night. Who are you? Tell me.

VOICE OF CHANNON. I have forgotten. I have no remembrance of myself but in your thoughts of me.

LEAH. I remember—now—the star that drew my heart towards its light—the tears that I have shed in the still midnight—the one who stood before me ever—in my dreams—was it you?

VOICE OF CHANNON. I——

LEAH. I remember—your hair, so soft and damp as if with tears—your sad and gentle eyes—your hands with the thin tapering fingers. Waking and sleeping I had no thought but of you. (Pause—sadly) You went away and darkness fell upon me—my soul withered in loneliness like the soul of a widow left desolate—the stranger came—and then—then you returned, and the dead heart wakened to life again, and out of sorrow joy blossomed like a flower . . . Why have you now once more forsaken me?

VOICE OF CHANNON. I broke down the barriers between us—I crossed the plains of death—I defied every law of past and present time and all the ages . . . I strove against the strong and mighty and against those who know no mercy. And as my last spark of strength left me, I left your body to return to your soul.

LEAH (tenderly). Come back to me, my bridegroom—my husband—I will carry you, dead, in my heart—and in our dreams at night we shall rock to sleep our little children who will never be born . . . (Weeps) And sew them little clothes, and sing them lullabies—(Sings, weeping)

Hush—hush, little children—
No cradle shall hold you—
In no clothes can we fold you.

Dead, that the living cannot mourn;
Untimely lost and never born . . .

(The music of a wedding-march is heard approaching.)

LEAH (trembling). They are coming to take me to a stranger under the canopy—come to me, my true bridegroom; come to me.

VOICE OF CHANNON. I have left your body—I will come to your soul.

(He appears against the wall, white-robed.)

LEAH (with joy). Come, my bridegroom. The barrier between us is no more. I see you. Come to me . . .

VOICE OF CHANNON (echo). Come to me.

LEAH (crying out with joy). I am coming . . .

VOICE OF CHANNON (echo). And I to you . . .

(Voices outside.)

VOICES. Lead the bride to the canopy. (Wedding-march is heard. Leah rises, dropping, as she does so, her black cloak onto the sofa, and in her white wedding-dress, to the strains of the music, she goes towards Channon, and at the spot where he has appeared their two forms merge into one.

Rabbi Azrael enters, carrying his staff, followed by the Messenger. They stand on the threshold. Behind them, Sender, Frade and the rest.)

LEAH (in a far-away voice). A great light flows about me . . . predestined bridegroom, I am united to you forever. Now we soar upward together higher and higher . . .

(The stage grows darker.)

RABBI AZRAEL (with lowered head). Too late!

MESSENGER. Blessed be a righteous judge.

(It is now completely dark. As if from a great distance, singing is heard, scarcely audible.)

Why, from highest height,
To deepest depth below,
Has the soul fallen?
Within itself, the Fall
Contains the Resurrection.

GEORG KAISER's

From Morn to Midnight

Translated from the German by ASHLEY DUKES

First presented by The Theatre Guild at the Garrick Theatre, New York, on May 21, 1922, with the following cast:

CASHIER	Frank Reicher	WAITER	Edgar Stehli
STOUT GENTLEMAN	Ernest Cossart	FIRST MASK	Clelia Benjamin
CLERK	Sears Taylor	SECOND MASK	Adele St. Maur
MESSENGER BOY	Francis Sadtler	THIRD MASK	Caroline Hancock
LADY	Helen Westley	FOURTH MASK	Annette Ponse
BANK MANAGER	Henry Travers	FIRST GUEST	Sears Taylor
MUFFLED GENTLEMAN	Allyn Joslyn	SECOND GUEST	Allyn Joslyn
SERVING MAID	Adele St. Maur	THIRD GUEST	Sam Rosen
PORTER	Charles Cheltenham	OFFICER OF SALVATION ARMY	Ernita Lascelles
THE LADY'S SON	Edgar Stehli	FIRST SOLDIER OF SALVATION ARMY	Philip Leigh
THE CASHIER'S MOTHER	Kathryn Wilson	FIRST PENITENT	Philip Loeb
HIS DAUGHTERS	{ Lelia May Aultman / Julia Cobb	SECOND SOLDIER SALVATION ARMY	Camille Pastorfield
HIS WIFE	Ernita Lascelles	SECOND PENITENT	Helen Westley
FIRST GENTLEMAN	Walton Butterfield	THIRD SOLDIER OF SALVATION ARMY	Henry Travers
SECOND GENTLEMAN	Philip Leigh	THIRD PENITENT	Ernest Cossart
THIRD GENTLEMAN	Herman Goodman	FOURTH SOLDIER OF SALVATION ARMY	William Crowell
FOURTH GENTLEMAN	Samuel Baron		
FIFTH GENTLEMAN	William Crowell	POLICEMAN	Stanley Howlett
SALVATION LASS	Helen Sheridan		

AND CROWD AT VELODROME AND SALVATION ARMY HALL:

Mary Beechwood, Peggy Vaughan, Albert Powers, Annette Ponse, Teddy Tolputt, Estelle Corcos, Barbara Kitson, Lester Nass, Kenneth Campbell, Genevieve Corbin, Sarah Fishman, Margaret Wernimont, Philip Loeb.

Staged by Frank Reicher
Settings designed by Lee Simonson

SCENES

I—The Interior of a Provincial Bank
II—The Writing Room of a Hotel
III—A Field in Deep Snow
IV—The Parlor in the Cashier's Home

v—The Steward's Box at a Velodrome during Bicycle Races
vi—A Private Supper Room in a Cabaret
vii—A Salvation Army Hall

In a Small Town and a City in Germany at the Present Time.

SCENE ONE

SCENE: *Interior of a provincial Bank. On the right, pigeon-holes and a door inscribed Manager. Another door in the middle: Strong Room. Entrance from the lower left. In front of the Cashier's cage on the left hand side is a cane sofa, and in front of it a small table with a waterbottle and glass.*

RISE: *The Cashier at the counter and the Clerk at a desk, both writing. On the cane sofa sits a Stout Gentleman, wheezing. In front of the counter stands a Messenger Boy, staring at the door, through which some one has just gone out.*

(Cashier raps on the counter. Messenger Boy turns, hands in a check. Cashier examines it, writes, takes a handful of silver from a drawer, counts it, pushes a small pile across the counter. Messenger Boy sweeps the money into a linen bag.)

———

STOUT GENTLEMAN *(rising).* Now the fat fellows take their turn. *(He pulls out a bag. Enter Lady, expensive furs; rustle of silk. Stout Gentleman stops short)*

LADY *(smiles involuntarily in his direction).* At last!

(Stout Gentleman makes a wry face. Cashier taps the counter impatiently. Lady looks at Stout Gentleman.)

STOUT GENTLEMAN *(giving place to her).* The fat fellows can wait.

(Lady bows distantly, comes to counter. Cashier taps as before.)

LADY *(opens her handbag, takes out a letter and hands it to Cashier).* A letter of credit. Three thousand, please. *(Cashier takes the envelope, turns it over, hands it back)* I beg your pardon. *(She pulls out the folded letter and offers it again. Cashier turns it over, hands it back)*

LADY *(unfolds the letter, hands it to him).* Three thousand, please.

(Cashier glances at it, puts it in front of the Clerk. Clerk takes the letter, rises, goes out by the door inscribed Manager.)

STOUT GENTLEMAN *(retiring to sofa).* I can wait. The fat fellows can always wait. *(Cashier begins counting silver.)*

LADY. In notes, if you don't mind. *(Cashier ignores her.)*

MANAGER *(youthful, plump, comes in with the letter in his hand).* Who is— *(He stops short on seeing the Lady. Clerk resumes work at his desk.)*

STOUT GENTLEMAN. Ahem! Good morning.

MANAGER *(glancing at him).* How goes it?

STOUT GENTLEMAN *(tapping his belly).* Oh, rounding out—rounding out!

MANAGER *(laughs shortly. Turning to Lady).* I understand you want to draw on us?

LADY. Three thousand marks.

MANAGER. I would pay you three— *(glancing at letter)*—three thousand with pleasure, but—

LADY. Is anything wrong with the letter?

MANAGER *(suave, important).* It's in the proper form. *(Reading the headlines)* "Not exceeding twelve thousand"—quite correct. *(Spelling out the address)* "B-A-N-C-O"—

LADY. My bank in Florence assured me—

MANAGER. Your bank in Florence is quite all right.

LADY. Then I don't see why—

MANAGER. I suppose you applied for this letter?

LADY. Of course.

MANAGER. Twelve thousand—payable at such cities—

LADY. As I should touch on my trip.

MANAGER. And you must have given your bank in Florence duplicate signatures.

LADY. Certainly. To be sent to the banks mentioned in the list to identify me.

MANAGER *(consults letter).* Ah! *(Looks up)* We have received no letter of advice. *(Stout Gentleman coughs; winks at the Manager.)*

LADY. That means I must wait until...

MANAGER. Well, we must have something to go upon!

(Muffled Gentleman, in fur cap and shawl, comes in and takes his place at the counter. He darts angry glances at the Lady.)

LADY. I was quite unprepared for this . . .

MANAGER *(with a clumsy laugh).* As you

see, Madame, we are even less prepared; in fact—not at all.

LADY. I need the money so badly . . .

(Stout Gentleman laughs aloud.)

MANAGER. Who doesn't? *(Stout Gentleman neighs with delight. Looking round for an audience)* Myself, for instance— *(To the impatient Muffled Customer)* You have more time than I—don't you see I'm busy with this Lady? Now, Madame, what do you expect me to do—pay you money on your—ah—

(Stout Gentleman titters.)

LADY *(quickly).* I'm staying at the Elephant.

(Stout Gentleman wheezes with laughter.)

MANAGER. I am very glad to know your address. I always lunch there.

LADY. Can't the proprietor vouch for me?

MANAGER. Has he already had the pleasure?

(Stout Gentleman rocks with delight.)

LADY. Well, I have my luggage with me . . .

MANAGER. Am I to examine it?

LADY. A most embarrassing position. I can't . . .

MANAGER. Then we're in the same boat. You can't—I can't—that's the situation.

(He returns the letter.)

LADY. What do you advise me to do?

MANAGER. This is a snug little town of ours—it has surroundings— The Elephant is a well-known house . . . you'll make pleasant acquaintances of one sort or another . . . and time will pass—days—nights—well you know?

LADY. I don't in the least mind passing a few days here.

MANAGER. Your fellow-guests will be delighted to contribute something for your entertainment.

LADY. But I must have three thousand today!

MANAGER *(to Stout Gentleman).* Will anybody here underwrite a lady from abroad for three thousand marks?

LADY. I couldn't think of accepting that. I shall be in my room at the hotel. When the letter of advice arrives, will you please notify me at once by telephone?

MANAGER. Personally, Madame, if you wish.

LADY. In whatever way is quickest.

(She folds up the letter, replaces it in the envelope, and puts both into her handbag) I shall call again in any case this afternoon.

MANAGER. At your service. *(Lady bows coldly, goes out. Muffled Gentleman moves up to counter, on which he leans, crackling his cheque impatiently. Manager ignoring him, looks merrily at the Stout Gentleman. Stout Gentleman sniffs the air. Laughs)* All the fragrance of Italy, eh? Straight from the perfume bottle. *(Stout Gentleman fans himself with his hand)* Warm, eh?

STOUT GENTLEMAN *(pours out water).* Three thousand is not bad. *(Drinks)* I guess three hundred wouldn't sound bad to her either.

MANAGER. Perhaps you would like to make a lower offer at the Elephant?—in her room?

STOUT GENTLEMAN. No use for fat fellows.

MANAGER. Our bellies protect our morals. *(Muffled Gentleman raps impatiently on the counter. Indifferently)* Well?

(He takes the cheque, smoothes it out, and hands it to the Cashier.)

(Messenger Boy stares after the departing Lady, then at the last speakers, finally stumbles over the Stout Gentleman on the sofa.)

STOUT GENTLEMAN *(robbing him of his wallet).* There, my boy, that's what comes of making eyes at pretty ladies. Now you've lost your money. *(Messenger Boy looks shyly at him)* How are you going to explain to your boss? *(Messenger Boy laughs)* Remember this for the rest of your life! *(Returning the wallet)* Your eyes run away and you bolt after them. You wouldn't be the first. *(Messenger Boy goes out)*

(Cashier has counted out some small silver.)

MANAGER. And they trust money to a young fool like that.

STOUT GENTLEMAN. Stupid!

MANAGER. People should be more careful. That boy will abscond the first chance he gets—a born embezzler. *(To Muffled Gentleman)* Is anything wrong? *(Muffled Gentleman examines every coin)* That's a twenty-five pfennig piece. Forty-five pfennigs altogether; that's all that's coming to you.

(Muffled Gentleman pockets his money with great ceremony; buttons his coat over the pocket.)

STOUT GENTLEMAN *(ironically)*. You ought to deposit your capital in the vault. *(Rising)* Now it's time for the fat fellows to unload.

(Muffled Gentleman turns away from counter, and goes out.)

MANAGER *(to Stout Gentleman, breezily)*. What are you bringing us this morning?

STOUT GENTLEMAN *(sets his attaché case on the counter and takes out a pocket-book)*. With all the confidence that your elegant clientele inspires. *(He offers his hand)*

MANAGER *(taking it)*. In any case we are immune to a pretty face when it comes to business.

STOUT GENTLEMAN *(counting out his money)*. How old was she, at a guess?

MANAGER. I haven't seen her without rouge—yet.

STOUT GENTLEMAN. What's she doing here?

MANAGER. We'll hear that tonight at the Elephant.

STOUT GENTLEMAN. But who's she after?

MANAGER. All of us, perhaps, before she gets through.

STOUT GENTLEMAN. What can she do with three thousand in this town?

MANAGER. Evidently she needs them.

STOUT GENTLEMAN. I wish her luck.

MANAGER. With what!

STOUT GENTLEMAN. Getting her three thousand if she can.

MANAGER. From me?

STOUT GENTLEMAN. It doesn't matter from whom! *(They laugh)*

MANAGER. I'm curious to see when that letter of advice from Florence will arrive.

STOUT GENTLEMAN. If it arrives!

MANAGER. Ah! If it arrives!

STOUT GENTLEMAN. We might make a collection for her benefit.

MANAGER. I dare say that's what she has in mind.

STOUT GENTLEMAN. You don't need to tell me.

MANAGER. Did you draw a winning number in the last lottery? *(They laugh)*

STOUT GENTLEMAN *(to Cashier)*. Take this. What's the difference if our money draws interest here or outside. Here— open an account for the Realty Construction Company.

MANAGER *(sharply, to Clerk)*. Account: "Realty Construction Company."

STOUT GENTLEMAN. There's more to come.

MANAGER. The more the merrier. We can use it just now.

STOUT GENTLEMAN. Sixty thousand marks, fifty thousand in paper, ten thousand in gold.

(Cashier begins counting.)

MANAGER *(after a pause)*. And how are you, otherwise?

STOUT GENTLEMAN *(to Cashier, who pauses to examine a note)*. Yes, that one's patched.

MANAGER. We'll accept it, of course. We shall soon be rid of it. I'll reserve it for our fair client from Florence. She wore patches too.

STOUT GENTLEMAN. But behind these you find—a thousand marks.

MANAGER. Face value.

STOUT GENTLEMAN *(laughing immoderately)*. Face value—that's good!

MANAGER. The face value! Here's your receipt. *(Choking with laughter)* Sixty— thousand—

STOUT GENTLEMAN *(takes it, reads)*. Sixty—thou—

MANAGER. Face.

STOUT GENTLEMAN. Value. *(They shake hands)*

MANAGER *(in tears)*. I'll see you to-night.

STOUT GENTLEMAN *(nods)*. The face— the face—value! *(He buttons his overcoat, and goes out laughing)*

(Manager wipes the tears from his pince-nez; Cashier fastens the notes together in bundles.)

MANAGER. This lady from Florence— who claims to come from Florence—has a vision like that ever visited you in your cage before? Furs—perfume! The fragrance lingers—you breathe adventure. Superbly staged. Italy . . . Enchantment —fairy-tale — Riviera — Mentone — Pordighera — Nice — Monte Carlo,— where oranges blossom, fraud blooms, too. Swindlers—down there every square foot of earth breeds them. They organize crusades. The gang disperses to the four winds—preferably small towns—off the beaten track. Then—apparitions—billowing silks—furs—women—modern sirens. Refrains from the sunny south—o bella Napoli! One glance and you're stripped to your undershirt—to the bare skin—to the naked, naked skin. *(He drums with a pencil on the Cashier's hand)* Depend upon it, this bank in Florence knows as much about the lady as the man in the moon. The whole affair is a swindle, carefully arranged. And the web was woven not in Florence, but in Monte Carlo. That's the place to keep in mind. Take my word for it, you've just seen one of the gadflies that thrive in the swamp of the Casino. We shall never see her again. The first attempt missed fire; she'll scarcely risk a second! I joke about it but I have a keen eye—when you're a banker —I really should have tipped off the police! Well, it doesn't concern me—besides, banks must be discreet. Keep your eye on the out-of-town papers—the police news. When you find something there about an adventuress, safe under lock and key—then we'll talk about it again. You'll see I was right—then we'll hear more of our Florentine lady than we'll ever see of her and her furs again. *(Exit)* *(Cashier seals up rolls of bank notes.)*

PORTER *(enters with letters, hands them to Clerk).* One registered letter. I want the receipt.
(Clerk stamps receipt form, hands it to Porter. Porter re-arranges glass and water-bottle on the table, and goes out. Clerk takes the letters into Manager's room, and returns.)
LADY *(re-enters; comes quickly to the counter).* I beg your pardon.
(Cashier stretches out his hand, without looking at her. Raps.)
LADY *(louder).* If you please! *(Cashier raps on the counter)* I don't want to trouble the Manager a second time. *(Cashier raps on the counter)* Please tell me—would it be possible for me to leave you the letter of credit for the whole sum, and to receive an advance of three thousand in part payment? *(Cashier raps impatiently)* I should be willing to deposit my diamonds

as security, if required. Any jeweler in the town will appraise them for you. *(She takes off a glove and pulls at her bracelet. Serving Maid comes in quickly, plumps down on sofa, and begins rummaging in her market-basket. Lady startled by the commotion, looks round. As she leans on the counter her hand sinks into the Cashier's. Cashier bends over the hand which lies in his own. His spectacles glitter, his glance travels slowly upward from her wrist. Serving Maid with a sigh of relief, discovers the check she is looking for. Lady nods kindly in her direction. Serving Maid replaces vegetables, etc., in her basket. Lady turning again to the counter, meets the eyes of the Cashier. Cashier smiles at her.)*
LADY *(drawing back her hand).* Of course I shall not ask the bank to do anything irregular. *(She puts the bracelet on her wrist; the clasp refuses to catch. Stretching out her arm to the Cashier)* Would you be so kind? I'm clumsy with the left hand. *(Cashier stares at her as if mesmerized. His spectacles, bright points of light, seem almost to be swallowed up in the cavity of his wide-open eyes. To Serving Maid)* You can help me, mademoiselle. *(Serving Maid does so)* Now the safety catch. *(With a little cry)* You're pinching my flesh. Ah, that's better. Thank you so much. *(She bows to the Cashier and goes out. Serving Maid coming to the counter, planks down her check. Cashier takes it in trembling hands, the slip of paper flutters and crackles; he fumbles under the counter, then counts out money)*
SERVING MAID *(looking at the pile of coins).* That isn't all mine. *(Cashier writes. Clerk becomes observant)*
SERVING MAID *(to Clerk).* But it's too much! *(Clerk looks at Cashier. Cashier rakes in part of the money)* Still too much! *(Cashier ignores her and continues writing. Serving Maid shaking her head, puts the money in her basket and goes out)*
CASHIER *(hoarsely).* Get me a glass of water! *(Clerk hurries from behind the counter; comes to table)* That's been standing. Fresh water—cold water—from the faucet. *(Clerk hurries out with glass. Cashier goes quickly to electric bell, and rings. Porter enters from the hall)* Get me fresh water.

PORTER. I'm not allowed to go so far from the door.

CASHIER *(hoarsely)*. For me. Not that slime. I want water from the faucet. *(Porter seizes water bottle and hurries out. Cashier quickly crams his pockets with bank notes. Then he takes his coat from a peg, throws it over his arm, and puts on his hat. He lifts a flap in the counter, passes through, and goes out)*

MANAGER *(absorbed in reading a letter, enters from his room)*. Here's the letter of advice from Florence, after all! *(Clerk enters with a glass of water. Porter enters with a full water bottle)*

MANAGER *(looking up)*. What the devil . . . ?

CURTAIN

SCENE TWO

SCENE: *Writing-room of a hotel. Glass door in background. On right, desk with telephone. On the left, sofa and armchair with table and newspapers.*

LADY *(writes. Son, in hat and coat, enters, carrying under his arm a large flat object wrapped in green baize. With surprise)*. Have you brought it with you?

SON. Hush! The wine dealer is downstairs. The old fool is afraid I'll run away with it.

LADY. But I thought this morning he was glad to get rid of it.

SON. Now he's suspicious.

LADY. You must have given yourself away.

SON. I did let him see I was pleased.

LADY *(smiling)*. That would open a blind man's eyes.

SON. Let it. But don't be afraid, Mother, the price is the same as it was this morning.

LADY. Is the man waiting for his money?

SON. Let him wait.

LADY. But, my dear boy, I must tell you—

SON *(kissing her)*. Hush, Mother. This is a great moment. You mustn't look until I say so. *(He takes off his hat and cloak, puts the picture on a chair and lifts the green baize covering)*

LADY. Ready?

SON *(in a low tone)*. Mother! *(Lady turns in her chair. Comes to her, puts his arm round her neck)* Well?

LADY. That was never meant to hang in a restaurant.

SON. It was turned to the wall. The old fellow had pasted his own photograph on the back of it.

LADY. Was that included in the price?

SON *(laughs)*. Tell me, what do you think of it?

LADY. I find it—very naïve.

SON. Marvelous, isn't it? Extraordinary considering it's a Cranach.

LADY. Do you really prize it as a picture?

SON. Of course! But just look at the peculiar conception—unique for Cranach. And a new treatment of this subject in the entire history of art. Where can you find anything like it—in the Pitti—the Uffizi—the Vatican? Even the Louvre has nothing to compare with it. Here we have without doubt the first and only erotic conception of Adam and Eve. The apple is still in the grass—the serpent leers from behind the indescribable green foliage—and that means that the drama is played in Paradise itself and not in the banishment. That's the original sin—the real fall! Cranach painted dozens of Adams and Eves—standing stiffly—always separated—with the apple bough between them. In those pictures Cranach says simply: they knew each other. But in this picture for the first time, he cries exultantly they loved each other. Here a German proves himself a master of an eroticism intensely southern in its feeling. *(In front of the picture)* And yet what restraint in this ecstasy! This line of the man's arm as it slants across the woman's hip. The horizontal line of her thighs and the opposing line of his—never weary the eyes. These flesh tones make their love a living thing—doesn't it affect you that way?

LADY. I find it as naïve as your picture.

SON. What does that mean?

LADY. Please hide it in your room.

SON. I won't get its full effect until we

get home. This Cranach in Florence. Of course, I'll have to postpone finishing my book. I must digest this first. A man must live with a thing like this before he dares write about it. Just now I am overwhelmed. Think of finding this picture here—on the first stage of our trip!

LADY. But you were almost certain that it must be in this neighborhood.

SON. I am dazed nevertheless. Isn't it amazing! I am lucky.

LADY. This is simply the result of your own careful research.

SON. But not without your generosity? Your help?

LADY. It makes me as happy as it does you.

SON. Your patience is endless. I tear you from your beautiful quiet life in Fiesole. You are an Italian, but I drag you through Germany in mid-winter. You live in sleeping cars or third-rate hotels; rub elbows with Tom, Dick, Harry!

LADY *(smiling—patting his cheek)*. Yes, I have had my fill of that.

SON. But now I promise you to hurry. I'm madly impatient to get this treasure safely home. Let's take the three o'clock train. Will you give me the three thousand marks?

LADY. I haven't them.

SON. But the owner is here, in the hotel.

LADY. The bank couldn't pay me. The letter of advice has somehow been delayed.

SON. I've promised him the money.

LADY. Then you must return the picture until the letter arrives.

SON. Can't we hurry it in any way?

LADY *(smiles)*. I've written a telegram; I'll have it sent now. You see, we traveled so quickly that—*(Waiter knocks at the door. Phone rings)* Yes?

WAITER. Someone from the bank.

LADY. Send him up. *(To Son)* They must be sending the money.

SON. Call me as soon as you've got it. I'd rather keep an eye on the old man.

LADY. I'll send for you.

SON. Then I'll wait downstairs. *(Pauses in front of picture. Lady closes her portfolio. Cashier is seen behind the glass* door, enters. Lady points to a chair, and starts to seat herself. Cashier stands)

LADY. I hope the bank— *(Cashier sees the picture, and starts violently)* My visit to the bank was closely connected with this picture.

CASHIER *(staring)*. You!

LADY. Do you find any point of resemblance?

CASHIER *(smiling)*. In the wrist!

LADY. Are you interested?

CASHIER. I should like to discover more.

LADY. Do such subjects interest you?

CASHIER *(looking straight at her)*. Yes— I understand them.

LADY. Are there any more to be found here? You would do me a great favor— that's more important than the money.

CASHIER. I have the money.

LADY. I fear at this rate my letter of credit will soon be exhausted.

CASHIER *(produces a roll of bank notes)*. This will be enough.

LADY. I can only draw twelve thousand in all.

CASHIER. Sixty thousand!

LADY. But—how did you—?

CASHIER. That's my business.

LADY. How am I to—?

CASHIER. We shall bolt.

LADY. Bolt? Where?

CASHIER. Abroad. Anywhere. Pack your trunk, if you've got one. You can start from the station; I'll walk to the next stop and board the train. We'll spend the first night in—a timetable! *(He finds it)*

LADY. Have you brought more than three thousand from the Bank?

CASHIER *(preoccupied with the timetable)*. I have sixty thousand in my pocket— fifty thousand in notes and ten thousand in gold.

LADY. And my part of that is—

CASHIER *(opens a roll of notes, and counts them with professional skill, then lays a bundle of them on the table)*. Your part. Take this. Put it away. We may be seen. The door has a glass panel. That's five hundred.

LADY. Five hundred?

CASHIER. More to come. All in good time. When we're in a safe place. Here we must be careful . . . hurry up—take it. No time for love-making. The wheel spins. An arm outstretched will be caught in the spokes. *(He springs to his feet)*

LADY. But I need three thousand.

CASHIER. If the police find them on you, you'll find yourself in jail!

LADY. What have the police to do with it?

CASHIER. You were in the Bank. Your presence filled the air. They'll suspect you; the link between us is clear as daylight.

LADY. I went to—your Bank.

CASHIER. As cool as a cucumber—

LADY. I demanded—

CASHIER. You tried to.

LADY. I tried—

CASHIER. You did. With your forged letter.

LADY *(taking a paper from her handbag)*. Isn't my letter genuine?

CASHIER. As false as your diamonds.

LADY. I offered them as a security. Why should my precious stones be paste?

CASHIER. Ladies of your kind only dazzle.

LADY. What do you think I am? I'm dark, it's true; a Southerner, a Tuscan.

CASHIER. From Monte Carlo.

LADY *(smiles)*. No, from Florence!

CASHIER *(his glance lighting upon the Son's hat and cloak)*. Ha! Have I come too late?

LADY. Too late?

CASHIER. Where is he? I'll bargain with him. He'll be willing. I have the means. How much shall I offer? How high do you put the indemnity? How much shall I cram into his pockets? I'll bid up to fifteen thousand. Is he asleep? Still rolling in bed? Where's your room? Twenty thousand—five thousand extra for instant withdrawal! *(Picking up hat and cloak)*

LADY *(in astonishment)*. The gentleman is sitting in the lounge.

CASHIER. Downstairs? Too risky! Too many people down there. Call him up; I'll settle with him here. Ring for him; let the Waiter hustle. Twenty thousand, cash down! *(He begins counting the money)*

LADY. Can my son speak for me?

CASHIER *(bounding back)*. Your— son ! ! !

LADY. I'm traveling with him. He's collecting material for a book on the history of art. That's what brought us from Florence to Germany.

CASHIER *(staring at her)*. Son?

LADY. Is that so appalling?

CASHIER. But—but—this picture—

LADY. A lucky find of his. My son is buying for three thousand marks; this was the amount needed so urgently. The owner is a wine dealer whom you will probably know by name . . .

CASHIER. Furs . . . silk . . . rustle— glitter. The air was heavy with perfume!

LADY. This is mid-winter. As far as I know, my way of dressing is not exceptional.

CASHIER. The forged letter—

LADY. I was about to wire to my bank.

CASHIER. Your bare wrist—on which you wanted me to put the bracelet—

LADY. We're all clumsy with the left hand.

CASHIER *(dully, to himself)*. And I— have stolen the money—

LADY *(diverted)*. Will that satisfy you and your police? My son is not utterly unknown in the art world.

CASHIER. Now—at this very moment— they've discovered everything! I asked for water to get the clerk out of the way —and again for water to get the porter away from the door. The notes are gone; I'm an embezzler. I mustn't be seen in the streets; I can't go to the railway station; the police are warned, sixty thousand! I must slip away across the fields—through the snow—before the whole town is on my track!

LADY *(shocked)*. Be quiet!

CASHIER. I took all the money. Your presence filled the Bank. Your scent hung on the air. You glistened and rustled— you put your naked hand in mine—your breath came warm across the counter— warm—

LADY *(silencing him)*. Please—I am a lady.

CASHIER. But now you must—

LADY *(controlling herself)*. Tell me, are you married? Yes? *(Violent gesture from Cashier)* Ah, that makes a difference.

Unless I am to consider the whole thing a joke, you gave way to a foolish impulse. Listen. You can make good the loss. You can go back to your Bank and plead a passing illness—a lapse of memory. I suppose you still have the full amount.

CASHIER. I've embezzled the money—

LADY *(abruptly)*. Then I can take no further interest in the matter.

CASHIER. I've robbed the bank.

LADY. You grow tedious, my dear sir.

CASHIER. And now you must—

LADY. The one thing I must do, is to—

CASHIER. After this you must—

LADY. Preposterous.

CASHIER. I've robbed for you. I've delivered myself into your hands, destroyed my livelihood. I've burned my bridges behind me. I'm a thief and a criminal. *(Burying his face in his hands)* Now you must! . . . After all that you must!

LADY *(turns)*. I shall call my son. Perhaps he—

CASHIER *(with a change of tone, springs nimbly to his feet. Grabbing her arm)*. Aha! Call him, would you? Rouse the hotel, give the alarm? A fine plan! Clumsy. I'm not so easily caught as that. Not in that trap. I have my wits about me, ladies and gentlemen. Yours are asleep. I'm always five miles ahead of you. Don't move. Stay where you are until I . . . *(He puts the money in his pocket)* . . . until I . . . *(He presses his hat over his eyes)* . . . until I . . . *(He wraps his coat closely about him)* . . . until I . . . *(Softly he opens the glass door and slips out. Lady rises, stands motionless)*

SON *(entering)*. The man from the Bank has just gone out. You're looking worried, Mother. Is the money—?

LADY. I found this interview trying. You know, my dear boy, how money matters get on my nerves.

SON. Is there still trouble about the payment?

LADY. Perhaps I ought to tell you—

SON. Must I give back the picture?

LADY. I'm not thinking of that—

SON. But that's the chief question!

LADY. I think I ought to notify the police.

SON. Police?

LADY. Send this telegram to my Bank. In future I must have proper documents that will satisfy everyone.

SON. Isn't your letter of credit enough?

LADY. Not quite. Go to the telegraph office for me. I don't want to send the porter.

SON. And when shall we have the three thousand marks? *(Telephone bell rings)*

LADY *(recoils)*. They're ringing me up already. *(At the instrument)* Oh! Has arrived? And I'm to call for it myself? Gladly. *(Change of tone)* I'm not in the least annoyed. Yes, of course. *(Change of tone)* Florence is a long way off. And then the Italian postoffice—I beg your pardon? Oh, via Berlin—a roundabout way. That explains it. Not in the least. Thank you. In ten minutes. Good-by. *(To Son)* All settled, my dear boy. Never mind the telegram. *(She tears up the form)* You shall have the picture. Your wine dealer can come along. He'll get his money at the Bank. Pack up your treasure. We go straight from the Bank to the station. *(Telephoning while the Son wraps up the picture)* The bill, please. Rooms 14 and 16. Yes, immediately. Please.

CURTAIN

SCENE THREE

SCENE: *Aslant a field deep in snow. Through a tangle of low-hanging branches, blue shadows are cast by the midday sun.*

CASHIER *(comes in backward, furtively)*. What a marvelous contraption a man is. The mechanism runs in his joints—silently. Suddenly faculties are stimulated, action results. My hands, for instance, when did they ever shovel snow? And now they dig through snowdrifts without the slightest trouble. My footprints are all blotted out. I have achieved a complete incognito. *(Pause)* Frost and damp breed chills. Before you know it you've got a fever and that weakens the will—a man loses control over his actions if he's in bed sick. He's easily tracked. *(Throws cuffs to ground)* Lie there! You'll be missed in the wash! Lamentations fill the kitchen! A pair of cuffs is missing! A catastrophy in the tubs! Chaos! *(Pause)* Strange! How keen my wits are! Here I work like mad to efface my tracks and then betray myself by two bits of dirty linen. It is always a trifle, an oversight—carelessness that betrays the criminal. *(Pause)* I wonder what's going to happen. I am keyed up to the highest pitch! I have every reason to expect momentous discoveries. The last few hours prove it. This morning a trusted employee—fortunes passing through my hands. The Construction Company makes a huge deposit. At noon an out-and-out scoundrel. Up to all the tricks. The details of flight carefully worked out. Turn the trick and run. Marvelous accomplishment—and only half the day gone. I am prepared for anything, I know I can play the game. I am on the march! There is no turning back. I march—so out with your trumps without any fuss. I have put sixty thousand on a single card—it must be trumps. I play too high to lose. No nonsense—cards on the table—do you understand? Now you'll have to, my beautiful lady. Your cue—my silken lady, give it to me, my resplendent lady—or the scene will fall flat. *(Pause)* Idiot—and you think you can act! Perform your natural duties—breed children and don't bother the prompter. Ah, I beg your pardon—you have a son— you are completely absolved. I withdraw my aspersions. Good-by, give my compliments to the manager of the bank. His very glances cover you with slime, but don't let that worry you. He's been robbed of sixty thousand. His roof rattles and leaks—never mind, never mind—the Construction Company will mend it for him. I release you from all obligations— you are dismissed—you can go! Stop! Permit me to thank you! What's that you say? Nothing to thank you for? Yes! There is. Not worth mentioning? You are joking. You are my sole creditor. How so? I owe you my life! Good God—I exaggerate? You have electrified me—set me free. One step toward you and I enter a land of miracles. And with this load in my breast pocket I pay cash for all favors.

And now fade away. You are outbid. Your means are too limited. Remember you have a son. Nothing will be knocked down to you. I'm paying cash down. *(Pause)* I have ready money. Come on— what's for sale? *(Pause)* Snow? Sunlight— stillness—. Blue snow at such a price. Outrageous, profiteering. I decline the offer. Your proposition is not *bona fide*. *(Pause)* But I must pay. I must spend, I've got the cash. Where are the goods that are worth the whole sum? Sixty thousand and the buyer to boot—flesh and bones— body and soul. Deal with me! Sell to me —I have the money, you have the goods— let us trade. *(The wind is blowing, the sun is overcast, distant thunder is heard)* The earth is in labor—spring gales at last! That's better! I knew my cry could not be in vain. My demand was urgent. Chaos is insulted and will not be put to shame by my colossal deed of this morning. I knew it. In a case like mine never let up. Go at them hard—pull down their cloaks and you'll see something. *(The tree has changed to the form of a skeleton, the wind and thunder die down)* Have you been sitting behind me all this time eavesdropping? Are you an agent of the police? Not in the ordinary narrow sense—but *(pause)* comprising all. Police of Fate? Are you the all-embracing answer to my emphatic question? Does your rather well ventilated appearance suggest the final truth —emptiness? That's somewhat scanty— very threadbare—in fact nothing! I reject the information as being too full of gaps. Your services are not required. You can shut your rag and bone shop. I am not taken in as easily as that. *(Pause)* This procedure would be exceedingly simple —it's true—you would spare me further entanglements. But I prefer complications. So farewell—if that is possible, to you in your condition! I still have things to do. When one is traveling one can't enter every house on the road—not even at the friendliest invitations. I still have many obligations to fulfill before evening. You can't possibly be the first—perhaps the last—but even then only as a last resort. I won't want to do it. But, as I said, as a last resort—that's debatable. Ring me up at midnight—ask Central for my number.

It will change from hour to hour. And excuse the coldness of my tone. We should be on friendlier terms, I know. We are closely bound. I really believe I carry you about with me now.

So, you see, we have come to a sort of understanding. That is a beginning which gives one confidence and backbone to face the future, whatever it is. I appreciate that fully. My most profound respects. *(After a peal of thunder and a last gust of wind the skeleton reverts to the tree. The sun comes out again)* There—I knew it wouldn't last.

CURTAIN

SCENE FOUR

SCENE: *Parlor in Cashier's house. In the window-boxes, blown geraniums. Table and chairs. Piano right. Mother (hard of hearing) sits near the window. First Daughter is embroidering at the table. Second Daughter is practicing the overture to* Tannhäuser. *Wife comes and goes on the Left. The clock ticks interminably.*

———

MOTHER. What's that you're playing?

FIRST DAUGHTER. The Overture to *Tannhäuser.*

MOTHER. "O Tannenbaum" is another pretty piece.

WIFE *(entering)*. It's time I began to fry the chops.

FIRST DAUGHTER. Oh, not yet, Mama.

WIFE. No, it's not time yet to fry the chops.

MOTHER. What are you embroidering now?

FIRST DAUGHTER. Father's slippers.

WIFE *(coming to Mother)*. Today we have chops for dinner.

MOTHER. Are you frying them now?

WIFE. Plenty of time. It's not twelve o'clock yet.

FIRST DAUGHTER. Not nearly twelve, Mama.

WIFE. No, not nearly twelve.

MOTHER. When he comes, it will be twelve.

WIFE. He hasn't come yet.

FIRST DAUGHTER. When Father comes, it will be twelve o'clock.

WIFE. Yes. *(Exit)*

SECOND DAUGHTER *(stops playing, listens)*. Is that Father?

FIRST DAUGHTER *(listens)*. Father?

WIFE *(enters)*. Is that my husband?

MOTHER. Is that my son?

SECOND DAUGHTER. Father!

FIRST DAUGHTER. Father!

WIFE. Husband!

MOTHER. Son!

(Cashier enters Right, hangs up hat and cloak. Pause.)

WIFE. Where do you come from?

CASHIER. From the cemetery.

MOTHER. Has somebody died suddenly?

CASHIER *(patting her on the back)*. You can have a sudden death, but not a sudden burial.

WIFE. Where have you come from?

CASHIER. From the grave. I burrowed through the clods with my forehead. See, here's a lump of ice. It was a great effort to get through—an extraordinary effort. I've dirtied my hands a little. You need a good grip to pull yourself up. You're buried deep. Life keeps on dumping dirt on you. Mountains of it—dust—ashes— the place is a rubbish heap. The dead lie at the usual depth—three yards. The living keep on sinking deeper and deeper.

WIFE. You're frozen from head to foot.

CASHIER. Thawed. Shaken by storms, like the spring. The wind whistled and roared; I tell you it stripped off my flesh until my bones were bare—a skeleton— bleached in a minute. A boneyard! At last the sun welded me together again. And here I am. Thus I've been renewed from the soles of my feet up.

MOTHER. Have you been out in the open?

CASHIER. In hideous dungeons, Mother. In bottomless pits beneath monstrous towers; deafened by clanking chains, blinded by darkness!

WIFE. The Bank must be closed. You've been celebrating with the manager. Has there been a happy event in his family?

CASHIER. He has his eye on a new mistress. Italian beauty—silks and furs—

where oranges bloom. Wrists like polished ivory. Black tresses—olive complexion. Diamonds. Real . . . all real. Tus . . . tus . . . the rest sounds like Canaan. Fetch me an atlas. Tus-Canaan. Is that right? Is there an island of that name? A mountain? A swamp? Geography can tell us everything. But he'll burn his fingers. She'll turn him down—brush him off like a bit of dirt. There he lies . . . sprawling on the carpet . . . legs in the air . . . our snug little manager!

WIFE. The Bank is not closed?

CASHIER. Never, Wife. Prisons are never closed. The procession is endless. An eternal pilgrimage. Like sheep rushing into the slaughter house. A seething mass. No escape—none—unless you jump over their backs.

MOTHER. Your coat's torn in the back.

CASHIER. And look at my hat! Fit for a tramp.

SECOND DAUGHTER. The lining's torn.

CASHIER. Look in my pockets. Left . . . right! (First Daughter and Second Daughter pulls out cuffs)

CASHIER. Inventory.

DAUGHTERS. Your cuffs.

CASHIER. But not the buttons. Hat—coat—torn—what can you expect—jumping over backs. They kick—they scratch—hurdles and fences—silence in the pen—order in the fold—equal rights for all. But one jump—don't hesitate—and you are out of the pen. One mighty deed and here I am! Behind me nothing and before me—What? (Sits. Pause) (Wife stares at him.)

MOTHER (half whispering). He's sick.

CASHIER (to one of the Daughters). Get my jacket. (To the other) My slippers. (To the first) My cap. (To the other) My pipe. (All are brought)

MOTHER. You oughtn't to smoke, when you've already been—

WIFE (motioning her to be silent). Shall I give you a light?

CASHIER (in jacket, slippers, and embroidered skull-cap, with pipe in hand, seats himself comfortably at the table). Light up!

WIFE (anxiously). Does it draw?

CASHIER (looking into pipe). I shall have to send it for a thorough cleaning. There must be some bits of stale tobacco in the stem. Sometimes way in . . . there are obstructions. It means I have to draw harder than is strictly necessary.

WIFE. Do you want me to take it now?

CASHIER. No, stay here. (Blowing great smoke-clouds) It will do. (To Second Daughter) Play something.

(Second Daughter at a sign from her mother, sits at piano and plays.)

CASHIER. What piece is that?

SECOND DAUGHTER. The Overture to Tannhäuser.

CASHIER (nods approval. To First Daughter). Sewing? Mending? Darning?

FIRST DAUGHTER. Embroidering your slippers.

CASHIER. Very practical. And you, Grandma?

MOTHER (feeling the universal dread). I was just having forty winks.

CASHIER. In peace and quiet.

MOTHER. Yes, my life is quiet now.

CASHIER (to Wife). And you, Wife?

WIFE. I was going to fry the chops.

CASHIER (nodding). Mmm—kitchen.

WIFE. I'll fry yours now.

CASHIER (nodding as before). Kitchen! (Exit Wife.)

CASHIER (to Daughters). Open the doors.

(Daughters exit Right and Left, returning immediately.)

WIFE (enters. Pause). Are you too warm in here? (She returns to her task)

CASHIER (looking around him). Grandmother at the window. Daughters—at the table embroidering . . . playing Wagner. Wife busy in the kitchen. Four walls . . . family life. Cozy . . . all of us together. Mother—son . . . child under one roof. The magic of familiar things. It spins a web. Room with a table. Piano. Kitchen . . . daily bread. Coffee in the morning . . . chops at noon. Bedroom . . . beds . . . in . . . out. More magic. In the end flat on your back . . . white and stiff. Table pushed against the wall . . . in the center a pine coffin . . . screw lid . . . silver mountings . . . but detachable . . . a bit of crepe on the lamp . . . piano unopened for a year.

(Second Daughter stops playing, and runs sobbing into the kitchen.)

WIFE *(enters)*. She is practicing the new piece.

MOTHER. Why doesn't she try something simpler?

(Cashier knocks out his pipe, begins putting on his hat and overcoat.)

WIFE. Are you going to the Bank? Are you going out on business?

CASHIER. Bank—business? No.

WIFE. Then where are you going?

CASHIER. That's the question, Wife. I've climbed down from windswept trees to find an answer. I came here first. Warm and cozy, this nest; I won't deny its good points; but it doesn't stand the final test. No! The answer is clear. This is not the end of my journey, just a signpost; the road leads further on. *(He is now fully dressed)*

WIFE *(distraught)*. Husband, how wild you look!

CASHIER. Like a tramp, as I told you. Never mind. Better a ragged wayfarer than an empty road!

WIFE. But, it's dinner-time.

MOTHER *(half rising)*. And you're going out, just before a meal?

CASHIER. I smell the pork chops. Full stomach, drowsy wits.

(Mother beats the air suddenly with her arms, and falls senseless.)

FIRST DAUGHTER. Grandma.

SECOND DAUGHTER. Grandma! Mother. *(Both fall on their knees, beside her. Wife stands motionless.)*

CASHIER *(going to Mother's chair)*. For once in his life a man goes out before his meal—and that kills her. *(He brushes the daughters aside and regards the body)* Grief? Mourning? Overflowing tears? Can they make me forget. Are these bonds so closely woven that when they break there's nothing left to me in life but grief?—Mother—son! *(He pulls the roll of banknotes out of his pocket and weighs it in his hand, then shakes his head and puts the money away)* Grief does not paralyze . . . the eyes are dry and the mind goes on. There's no time to lose, if my day is to be well spent. *(He lays his well-worn purse on the table)* Use it. There's money honestly earned. That may be worth remembering. Use it. *(He goes out on the left)*

(Wife stands motionless. Daughters bend over the dead Mother.)

BANK MANAGER *(coming from the Right)*. Is your husband at home? Has your husband been there? I have to bring you the painful news that he has absconded. We missed him some hours ago; since then we have been through his books. The sum involved is sixty thousand marks, deposited by the Realty Construction Company. So far, I've refrained from making the matter public, in the hope that he would come to his senses and return. This is my last attempt. You see I've made a personal call. Has your husband been here? *(He looks around him, and observes jacket, pipe, etc.)* It looks as though . . . *(His glance lights upon the group at the window. He nods)* I see! In that case . . . *(He shrugs his shoulders, puts on his hat)* I can only express my personal sympathy; be assured of that. The rest must take its course. *(Exit Manager)*

DAUGHTERS *(coming to Wife)*. Mother--

WIFE *(savagely)*. Don't screech into my ears! Who are you? What do you want? Brats—monkeys. What have you to do with me? *(Breaking down)* My husband has left me.

(Daughters stand shyly, holding hands.)

CURTAIN

SCENE FIVE

SCENE: *The steward's box of a velodrome during a cycle race meeting. Jewish gentlemen, stewards, come and go. They are all alike; little animated figures in dinner jackets, with silk hats tilted back and binoculars slung in leather cases. Whistling, catcalls and a restless hum from the crowded tiers of spectators unseen, off Right. Music. All the action takes place on the platform.*

FIRST GENTLEMAN *(entering)*. Is everything ready?

SECOND GENTLEMAN. See for yourself.

FIRST GENTLEMAN *(looking through glasses)*. The palms—

SECOND GENTLEMAN. What's the matter with the palms?

FIRST GENTLEMAN. I thought as much.

SECOND GENTLEMAN. But what's wrong with them?

FIRST GENTLEMAN. Who arranged them like that?

THIRD GENTLEMAN. Crazy.

SECOND GENTLEMAN. Upon my soul, you're right!

FIRST GENTLEMAN. Was nobody responsible for arranging them?

THIRD GENTLEMAN. Ridiculous. Simply ridiculous.

FIRST GENTLEMAN. Whoever it was, he's as blind as a bat!

THIRD GENTLEMAN. Or fast asleep.

SECOND GENTLEMAN. Asleep. But this is only the fourth night of the races.

FIRST GENTLEMAN. The palm-tubs must be pushed on one side.

SECOND GENTLEMAN. Will you see to it?

FIRST GENTLEMAN. Right against the wall. There must be a clear view of the whole track. *(Exit)*

THIRD GENTLEMAN. And of the royal box.

SECOND GENTLEMAN. I'll go with you. *(Exit)*

(Fourth Gentleman enters, fires a pistol-shot and withdraws. Fifth Gentleman enters with a red-lacquered megaphone.)

THIRD GENTLEMAN. How much is the prize?

FIFTH GENTLEMAN. Eighty marks. Fifty to the winner, thirty to the second.

FIRST GENTLEMAN *(re-entering)*. Three times round, no more. We're tiring them out.

FOURTH GENTLEMAN *(through megaphone)*. A prize is offered of eighty marks. The winner to receive fifty marks, the second thirty marks. *(Applause)*

(Second and Third Gentlemen return, one carrying a flag.)

FIRST GENTLEMAN. We can start them now.

SECOND GENTLEMAN. Not yet. No. 7 is shifting.

FIRST GENTLEMAN. Off!

(Second Gentleman lowers his flag. The race begins. Rising and falling volume of applause, with silent intervals.)

THIRD GENTLEMAN. The little fellows must win once in a while.

FOURTH GENTLEMAN. It's a good thing the favorites are holding back.

FIFTH GENTLEMAN. They'll have to work hard enough before the night's over.

THIRD GENTLEMAN. The riders are terribly excited.

FOURTH GENTLEMAN. And no wonder.

FIFTH GENTLEMAN. Depend upon it, the championship will be settled tonight.

THIRD GENTLEMAN. The Americans are still fresh.

FIFTH GENTLEMAN. Our lads will make them hustle.

FOURTH GENTLEMAN. Let's hope his Royal Highness will be pleased with the victory.

FIRST GENTLEMAN *(looking through glasses)*. The box is still empty. *(Outburst of applause)*

THIRD GENTLEMAN. The result!

FOURTH GENTLEMAN. Prizes in cash— fifty marks for No. 11, thirty marks for No. 4.

(Second Gentleman enters with Cashier. The latter is in evening clothes, with silk hat, patent shoes, gloves, cloak, his beard trimmed, his hair carefully brushed.)

CASHIER. Tell me what is this all about?

SECOND GENTLEMAN. I'll introduce you to the stewards.

CASHIER. My name doesn't matter.

SECOND GENTLEMAN. But you ought to meet the management.

CASHIER. I prefer to remain incognito.

SECOND GENTLEMAN. But you seem interested in these races.

CASHIER. I haven't the slightest idea what it's all about. What are they doing down there? I can see a round track with a bright moving line, like a snake. Now one comes in, another falls out. Why is that?

SECOND GENTLEMAN. They ride in pairs. While one partner is pedalling—

CASHIER. The other blockhead sleeps?

SECOND GENTLEMAN. He's being massaged.

CASHIER. And you call that a relay race?

SECOND GENTLEMAN. Certainly.

CASHIER. You might as well call it a relay rest.

FIRST GENTLEMAN *(approaching)*. Ahem

The enclosure is reserved for the management.

SECOND GENTLEMAN. This gentleman offers a prize of a thousand marks.

FIRST GENTLEMAN *(change of tone)*. Allow me to introduce myself.

CASHIER. On no account.

SECOND GENTLEMAN. The gentleman wishes to preserve his incognito.

CASHIER. Impenetrably.

SECOND GENTLEMAN. I was just explaining the sport to him.

CASHIER. Yes, don't you find it funny?

FIRST GENTLEMAN. How do you mean?

CASHIER. Why, this relay rest.

FOURTH GENTLEMAN. A prize of a thousand marks! For how many laps?

CASHIER. As many as you please.

FOURTH GENTLEMAN. How much shall we allot to the winner?

CASHIER. That's your affair.

FOURTH GENTLEMAN. Eight hundred and two hundred. *(Through megaphone)* An anonymous gentleman offers the following prizes for an open race of ten laps: eight hundred marks to the winner; two hundred marks to the second; one thousand marks in all. *(Loud applause)*

SECOND GENTLEMAN. But tell me, if you're not really interested in this sort of thing, why do you offer such a big prize?

CASHIER. Because it works like magic.

SECOND GENTLEMAN. On the pace of the riders, you mean?

CASHIER. Rubbish.

THIRD GENTLEMAN *(entering)*. Are you the gentleman who is offering a thousand marks?

CASHIER. In gold.

SECOND GENTLEMAN. That would take too long to count . . .

CASHIER. Watch me. *(He pulls out the money, moistens his finger and counts rapidly)* That makes less to carry.

SECOND GENTLEMAN. I see you're an expert.

CASHIER. A mere detail, sir. *(Handing him the money)* Accept payment.

SECOND GENTLEMAN. Received with thanks.

FIFTH GENTLEMAN *(approaching)*. Where is the gentleman? Allow me to introduce—

CASHIER. Certainly not!

THIRD GENTLEMAN *(with flag)*. I shall give the start. *(General movement from the stand)*

FIFTH GENTLEMAN. Now we shall see a tussle for the championship.

THIRD GENTLEMAN *(joining group)*. All the cracks are in the race.

FOURTH GENTLEMAN. Off! *(Outburst of applause)*

CASHIER *(taking first and second Gentlemen by the collar and turning them around)*. Now I'll answer your question for you. Look up!

SECOND GENTLEMAN. But you must keep your eye on the track, and watch how the race goes.

CASHIER. Childish, this sport. One rider must win because the other loses. Look up, I say! It's there, among the crowd, that the magic works. Look at them—three tiers—one above the other —packed like sardines—excitement rages. Down there in the boxes the better classes are still controlling themselves. They're only looking on but, oh, what looks—wide-eyed—staring. One row higher, their bodies sway and vibrate. You hear exclamations. Way up—no restraint! Fanatic—yells—bellowing nakedness—a gallery of passion. Just look at that group! Five times entwined; five heads dancing on one shoulder, five pairs of arms beating time across one howling breast! At the head of this monster is a single man. He's being crushed . . . mangled . . . thrust over the railing. His hat, crumpled, falls through the murky atmosphere . . . flutters into the middle balcony, lights upon a lady's bosom. There it rests daintily . . . so daintily! She'll never notice the hat; she'll go to bed with it; year in, year in, year out, she'll carry this hat upon her breast! *(The applause swells.)*

FIRST GENTLEMAN. The Dutchman is putting on speed.

CASHIER. The second balcony joins in. An alliance has been made; the hat has done the trick. The lady crushes it against the railing. Pretty lady, your bosom will show the marks of this! There's no help for it. It's foolish to struggle. You are pushed to the wall and you've got to give yourself, just as you are, without a murmur.

SECOND GENTLEMAN. Do you know the lady?

CASHIER. Look! Someone is being pushed out over the railing. He swings free, he loses his hold, he drops —he sails down into the boxes. What has become of him? Vanished! Swallowed, stifled, absorbed! A raindrop in a maelstrom!

FIRST GENTLEMAN. The fellow from Hamburg is making up ground.

CASHIER. The boxes are frantic. The falling man has set up contact. Restraint can go to the devil! Dinner jackets quiver. Shirt fronts begin to split. Studs fly in all directions. Lips are parted, jaws are rattling. Above and below—all distinctions are lost. One universal yell from every tier. Pandemonium. Climax.

SECOND GENTLEMAN (turning). He wins! He wins! The German wins! What do you say to that?

CASHIER. Stuff and nonsense.

SECOND GENTLEMAN. A marvelous spurt!

CASHIER. Marvelous trash!

FIRST GENTLEMAN (about to leave). We'll just make certain—

CASHIER (holding him back). Have you any doubts about it?

SECOND GENTLEMAN. The German was leading, but—

CASHIER. Never mind that, if you please. (Pointing to the audience) Up there you have the staggering fact. Watch the supreme effort, the lazy dizzy height of accomplishment. From boxes to gallery one seething flux, dissolving the individual, recreating-passion! Differences melt away, veils are torn away; passion rules! The trumpets blare and the walls come tumbling down. No restraint, no modesty, no motherhood, no childhood— nothing but passion! There's the real thing. That's worth the search. That justifies the price!

THIRD GENTLEMAN (entering). The ambulance column is working splendidly.

CASHIER. Is the man hurt who fell?

THIRD GENTLEMAN. Crushed flat.

CASHIER. When life is at fever heat some must die.

FOURTH GENTLEMAN (with megaphone). Result; eight hundred marks won by No. 2; two hundred marks won by No. 1. (Loud applause)

FIFTH GENTLEMAN. The men are tired out.

SECOND GENTLEMAN. You could see the pace dropping.

THIRD GENTLEMAN. They need a rest.

CASHIER. I've another prize to offer.

FIRST GENTLEMAN. Presently, sir.

CASHIER. No interruptions, no delays.

SECOND GENTLEMAN. We must give them a chance to breathe.

CASHIER. Bah! Don't talk to me of those fools! Look at the public, bursting with excitement. This power mustn't be wasted. We'll feed the flames; you shall see them leap into the sky. I offer fifty thousand marks.

SECOND GENTLEMAN. Do you mean it?

THIRD GENTLEMAN. How much did you say?

CASHIER. Fifty thousand. Everything.

THIRD GENTLEMAN. It's an unheard of sum—

CASHIER. The effect will be unheard of. Warn your ambulance men on every floor.

FIRST GENTLEMAN. We accept your offer. The contest shall begin when the box is occupied.

SECOND GENTLEMAN. Capital idea!

THIRD GENTLEMAN. Excellent!

FOURTH GENTLEMAN. This is a profitable visitor.

FIFTH GENTLEMAN (digging him in the rib). A paying guest.

CASHIER (to First Gentleman). What do you mean—when the box is occupied?

FIRST GENTLEMAN. We'll talk over the conditions in the committee room. I suggest thirty thousand to the winner; fifteen thousand to the second; five thousand to the third.

SECOND GENTLEMAN. Exactly.

THIRD GENTLEMAN (gloomily). Downright waste, I call it.

FIFTH GENTLEMAN. The sport's ruined for good and all.

FIRST GENTLEMAN (turning). As soon as the box is occupied.

(All go out, leaving Cashier alone. Enter Salvation Lass.)

SALVATION LASS. The War Cry! Ten pfennigs, sir.

CASHIER. Presently, presently.

SALVATION LASS. The War Cry, sir.

CASHIER. What trash are you trying to sell?

SALVATION LASS. The War Cry, sir.

CASHIER. You're too late. The battle's in full swing.

SALVATION LASS (shaking tin box). Ten pfennigs, sir.

CASHIER. So you expect to start a war for ten pfennigs?

SALVATION LASS. Ten pfennigs, sir.

CASHIER. I'm paying an indemnity of fifty thousand marks.

SALVATION LASS. Ten pfennigs.

CASHIER. Yours is a wretched scuffle. I only subscribe to pitched battles.

SALVATION LASS. Ten pfennigs.

CASHIER. I carry only gold.

SALVATION LASS. Ten pfennigs.

CASHIER. Gold—

SALVATION LASS. Ten—

CASHIER (seizing megaphone, bellows at her through it). Gold! Gold! Gold! (Salvation Lass goes out. Many Gentlemen enter)

FOURTH GENTLEMAN. Would you care to announce your offer yourself?

CASHIER. No, I'm a spectator. You stun them with the fifty thousand. (Handing him the megaphone)

FOURTH GENTLEMAN (through the megaphone). A new prize is offered by the same anonymous gentleman. (Cries of "Bravo!") The total sum is fifty thousand marks. Five thousand marks to the third, fifteen thousand to the second. The winner to receive thirty thousand marks. (Ecstasy)

CASHIER (stands apart, nodding his head). There we have it, the pinnacle. The summit. The climbing hope fulfilled. The roar of a spring gale. The breaking wave of a human tide. All bonds are burst. Up with the veils—down with the shams! Humanity—free humanity, high and low, untroubled by class, unfettered by manners. Unclean, but free. That's a reward for my impudence. (Pulling out a bundle of notes) I can pay with a good heart! (Sudden silence. The Gentlemen have taken off their silk hats and stand with bowed heads)

FOURTH GENTLEMAN (coming to Cashier). If you'll hand me the money, we can have the race for your prize immediately.

CASHIER. What's the meaning of this?

FOURTH GENTLEMAN. Of what, my dear sir?

CASHIER. Oh this sudden, unnatural silence.

FOURTH GENTLEMAN. Unnatural? Not at all. His Royal Highness has just entered his box.

CASHIER. Highness . . . the royal box . . . the house full.

FOURTH GENTLEMAN. Your generous patronage comes at the most opportune moment.

CASHIER. Thank you! I don't intend to waste my money.

FOURTH GENTLEMAN. What do you mean?

CASHIER. I find the sum too large . . . as a subscription to the society of back-benders!

FOURTH GENTLEMAN. But pray explain . . .

CASHIER. This fire that was raging a moment ago has been put out by the boot of his Highness. You take me for crazy, if you think I will throw one single penny under the snouts of these groveling dogs, these crooked lackeys! A kick where the bend is greatest, that's the prize they'll get from me.

FOURTH GENTLEMAN. But the prize has been announced. His Royal Highness is in his box. The audience is showing a proper respect. What do you mean?

CASHIER. If you don't understand my words, let deeds speak for me. (With violent blow he crushes the other's silk hat down upon his shoulders. Exit. Fourth Gentleman rushes after him, but is restrained by the others)

CURTAIN

SCENE SIX

SCENE: *Private supper room in a cabaret. Subdued dance music. A Waiter opens the door. The Cashier enters; evening clothes, coat, silk muffler, gold-headed bamboo cane.*

WAITER. Will this room suit you, sir?

CASHIER. It'll do.

(Waiter takes coat, etc. Cashier turns his back and looks into a mirror.)

WAITER. How many places shall I lay, sir?

CASHIER. Twenty-four. I'm expecting my grandma, my mother, my wife, and several aunts. The supper is to celebrate my daughter's confirmation. *(The Waiter stares at him. To the other's reflection in the mirror)* Ass! Two! What are these private rooms for?

WAITER. What brand would you prefer?

CASHIER. Leave that to me, my oily friend. I shall know which flower to pluck in the ballroom . . . round or slender, a bud or a full-blown rose. I shall not require your invaluable services. No doubt they are invaluable . . . or have you a fixed tariff for that too?

WAITER. What brand of champagne, if you please?

CASHIER. Ahem! Grand Marnier.

WAITER. That's the liqueur, sir.

CASHIER. Then I leave it to you.

WAITER. Two bottles of Pommery—extra dry. *(Producing menu card)* And for supper?

CASHIER. Pinnacles!

WAITER. Oeufs pochés Bergère? Poulet grillé? Steak de veau truffé? Parfait de foie gras en croûte? Salade coeur de laitue?

CASHIER. Pinnacles, pinnacles from soup to dessert.

WAITER. Pardon?

CASHIER *(tapping him on the nose)*. A pinnacle is the point of perfection . . . the summit of a work of art. So it must be with your pots and pans. The last word in delicacy. The menu of menus. Fit to garnish great events. It's your affair, my friend. I'm not the cook.

WAITER *(sets a large menu-card on the table)*. It will be served in twenty minutes. *(He rearranges glasses, etc. Heads with silken masks peep through the doorway)*

CASHIER *(sees them in the mirror. Shaking a warning finger at them)*. Wait, my moths! Presently I shall have you in the lamplight!

(The masks vanish, giggling. Waiter hangs a notice—"Reserved"—on the outside of the door, then withdraws and closes it behind him.)

CASHIER *(pushes back his silk hat, takes out a gold cigarette case, strikes a match, sings)*. "Tor . . . ea . . . dor, Tor . . . ea . . . dor . . ." Queer, how this stuff comes to your lips. A man's mind must be cram full of it . . . cram full. Everything. Toreador—Carmen—Caruso. I read all this somewhere . . . it stuck in my head. There it lies, piled up like a snowdrift. At this very moment I could give a history of the Bagdad railway. And how the Crown Prince of Roumania married the Czar's second daughter, Tatjana. Well, well, let them marry. The people need princes. *(Sings)* "Tat . . . tat . . . ja . . . na, Tat . . . ja . . . na . . ." *(Twirling his cane, exit)*

(Waiter enters with bottles on ice. Uncorks, pours out wine. Exit.)

CASHIER *(re-enters, driving before him a female Mask in a harlequin's red-and-yellow-quartered costume)*. Fly, moth! Fly, moth!

FIRST MASK *(running round the table)*. Fizz! *(She drinks both of the filled glasses)* Fizz!

CASHIER *(pouring out more wine)*. Liquid powder. Load your painted body.

FIRST MASK *(drinking)*. Fizz!

CASHIER. Battery mounted, action front.

FIRST MASK. Fizz!

CASHIER *(putting aside the bottles)*. Loaded *(Coming to her)* Ready to fire. *(The first Mask leans drunkenly towards him. Shaking her limp arm)* Look brighter, moth. *(First Mask does not respond)* You're dizzy, my bright butterfly. You've been licking the prickly yellow honey. Open your wings, enfold me, cover me up. I'm an outlaw; give me a hiding-place; open your wings.

FIRST MASK *(with a hiccough)*. Fizz!

CASHIER. No, my bird of paradise. You have your full load.

FIRST MASK. Fizz! *(Sinking onto sofa)*

CASHIER. Not another drop, or you'll be tipsy. Then what would you be worth?

FIRST MASK. Fizz!

CASHIER. How much are you worth? What have you to offer? *(Bending over her)*

FIRST MASK. Fizz!

CASHIER. I gave you that, but what can you give me? *(First Mask falls asleep)* Ha! You'd sleep here, would you? Little imp! But I've no time for the joke; I find it too tedious. *(He rises, fills a glass of wine and throws it in her face)* Good morning to you! The cocks are crowing!

FIRST MASK *(leaping to her feet)*. Swine!

CASHIER. A quaint name. Unfortunately I'm traveling incognito, and can't respond to the introduction. And so, my mask of the well-known snoutish family . . . get off my sofa!

FIRST MASK. I'll make you pay for this!

CASHIER. I've paid already. It was cheap at the price. *(Exit First Mask. Cashier drinks champagne; exits, singing. Waiter enters with caviar; collects empty glasses; exits. Cashier enters with two black Masks)*

SECOND MASK *(slamming the door)*. Reserved!

THIRD MASK *(at the table)*. Caviar!

SECOND MASK *(running to her)*. Caviar?

CASHIER. Black as your masks. Black as yourselves. Eat it up; gobble it, cram it down your throats. *(Seating himself between them)* Speak caviar. Sing wine. I've no use for your brains. *(He pours out champagne and fills their plates)* Not one word shall you utter. Not a syllable, not an exclamation. You shall be dumb as the fish that strewed this black spawn upon the Black Sea. You can giggle, you can bleat, but don't talk to me. You've nothing to say. You've nothing to shed but your finery . . . Be careful! I've settled one already! *(Masks look at one another, sniggering. Taking Second Mask by the arm)* What color are your eyes? Green . . . yellow? *(Turning to Third Mask)* And yours? Blue . . . red? A play of glances through the eyeholes. That promises well. Come, I'll offer a beauty prize! *(Masks laugh. To Second Mask)* You're the pretty one. You struggle hard, but wait! In a moment I'll tear down your curtain and look at the show. *(Second Mask breaks away from him. To Third Mask)* You have something to hide. Modesty's your lure. You dropped in here by chance. You were looking for adventure. Well, here's your adventurer. Off with your mask. *(Third Mask slips away from him)* This is the goal? I sit here trembling. You've stirred my

blood. Now let me pay. *(He pulls out a bundle of notes and divides it between them)* Pretty mask, this for your beauty. Pretty mask, this for your beauty. *(Holding his hand before his eyes)* One—two—three! *(Masks lift their dominoes. Looking at them, he laughs hoarsely)* Cover them—cover them up! *(He runs round the table)* Monsters—horrors! Out with you this minute—this very second,—or I'll . . . *(He lifts his cane)*

SECOND MASK. But you told us—

THIRD MASK. You wanted us—

CASHIER. I wanted to get at you! *(The Masks run out. Shaking himself, he drinks champagne)* Sluts! *(Exits, humming)* *(Waiter enters with fresh bottles, and exit.)*

CASHIER *(kicking the door open, entering with Fourth Mask, a Pierrette in a domino cloak reaching to her shoes. He leaves her standing in the middle of the room, and throws himself in chair)*. Dance! *(The Fourth Mask stands still)* Dance! Spin your bag of bones. Dance, dance! Brains are nothing. Beauty doesn't count. Dancing's the thing—twisting, whirling! Dance, dance, dance! *(Fourth Mask comes halting to the mirror. Waving her away)* No interruption, no delay. Dance! *(Fourth Mask stands motionless)* Why don't you leap in the air? Have you never heard of Dervishes? Dancing-men. Men while they dance, corpses when they cease. Death and dancing—sign posts on the road of life. And between them— *(The Salvation Lass enters)* Oh, Halleluja!

SALVATION LASS. The War Cry!

CASHIER. I know. Ten pfennigs. *(Salvation Lass holds out her box)* When do you expect me to jump into your box?

SALVATION LASS. The War Cry!

CASHIER. I suppose you do expect it?

SALVATION LASS. Ten pfennigs.

CASHIER. When will it be?

SALVATION LASS. Ten pfennigs.

CASHIER. So you mean to hang on to my coattails, do you? *(Salvation Lass shakes her box)* I'll shake you off! *(Salvation Lass shakes box. To Mask)* Dance!

SALVATION LASS. Oh! *(Exit)* *(Fourth Mask comes to table.)*

CASHIER. Why were you sitting in a corner of the ballroom, instead of dancing in the middle of the floor? That made me look at you. All the others went whirling by, and you were motionless. Why do you wear a long cloak, when they are dressed like slender boys?

FOURTH MASK. I don't dance.

CASHIER. You don't dance like the others.

FOURTH MASK. I can't dance.

CASHIER. Not to music, perhaps; not keeping time. You're right; that's too slow. But you can do other dances. You hide something under your cloak—your own particular spring, not to be cramped by step and measure! You have a quicker movement—a nimbler leap. (*Pushing everything off the table*) Here's your stage. Jump onto it. A boundless riot in this narrow circle. Jump now. One bound from the carpet. One effortless leap—on the springs that are rooted in your joints. Jump. Put spurs to your heels. Arch your knees. Let your dress float free over the dancing limbs!

FOURTH MASK (*sits on the edge of the table*). I can't dance.

CASHIER. You arouse my curiosity. Do you know what price I can pay? (*Showing her a roll of bank notes*) All that!

FOURTH MASK (*takes his hand and passes it down her leg*). You see—I can't.

CASHIER (*leaping to his feet*). A wooden leg! (*He seizes a champagne cooler and upsets it over her*) I'll water it for you! We'll make the buds sprout!

FOURTH MASK. I'll teach you a lesson.

CASHIER. I'm out to learn!

FOURTH MASK. Just wait! (*Exit*)

(*Cashier puts a bank note on the table, takes cloak and stick. Exit. Guests in evening dress enter.*)

FIRST GUEST. Where is the fellow?

SECOND GUEST. Let's have a closer look at him.

FIRST GUEST. A blackguard who entices away our girls—

SECOND GUEST. Stuffs them with caviar—

THIRD GUEST. Drenches them in champagne—

SECOND GUEST. And then insults them!

FIRST GUEST. We'll find out his price—

SECOND GUEST. Where is he?

THIRD GUEST. Given us the slip!

FIRST GUEST. He smelt trouble!

SECOND GUEST. The place was too hot for him.

THIRD GUEST (*finding the bank note*). A thousand!

SECOND GUEST. Good God!

FIRST GUEST. He must stink of money.

SECOND GUEST. That's to pay the bill.

THIRD GUEST. He's bolted. We'll do a vanishing trick too. (*He pockets the money*)

FIRST GUEST. That's the indemnity for our girls.

SECOND GUEST. Now let's give them the slip.

THIRD GUEST. They're all drunk.

FIRST GUEST. They'll only dirty our shirt-fronts for us.

SECOND GUEST. Let's go to the district for a week.

THIRD GUEST. Bravo! While the money lasts! Look out, here comes the waiter! (*Waiter entering with full tray, halts dismayed.*)

FIRST GUEST. Are you looking for anyone?

SECOND GUEST. You might find him under the table. (*Laughter*)

WAITER (*in an outburst*). The champagne—the supper—the private room—nothing paid for. Five bottles of Pommery, two portions of caviar, two special suppers—I have to stand for everything. I've a wife and children. I've been four months out of a place, on account of a weak chest. You won't see me ruined, gentlemen?

THIRD GUEST. What has your chest to do with us? We all have wives and children.

SECOND GUEST. Did we do you? What are you talking about?

FIRST GUEST. What sort of a place is this? Where are we? It's a common den of swindlers. And you lure people into a place like this? We're respectable people who pay for their drinks. Eh! What! Eh!

THIRD GUEST (*after changing the doorkey to the outer side*). Look under the table, there. Now we've paid you, too! (*He gives the Waiter, who turns round, a push which sends him sprawling. Waiter staggers, falls. Gentlemen exeunt*)

WAITER *(rises, runs to the door, finds it locked. Beating his fists on the panels.* Let me out! Let me out! You needn't pay me! I'm going—into the river!

CURTAIN

SCENE SEVEN

SCENE: *Salvation Army hall, seen in depth. The background is formed by a black curtain. In front of this stands the low platform on which is the penitent form. In the body of the hall, the benches are crowded. A great hanging lamp, with a tangle of wires for electric lighting, is above the audience. In the foreground on the Left, is the entrance. Music: "Jesus Lover of My Soul," played on an organ, and sung by the audience. From a corner, applause and laughter centering in one man. Salvation Lass goes to this corner and sits near the disturber. She takes his hand in hers and whispers to him.*

———

VOICE *(from the other side).* Move up closer. Be careful, Bill! Ha, ha! Move there!
(Salvation Lass, goes to the speaker, a young workman.)
WORKMAN. What are you after?
SALVATION LASS *(looks at him, shaking her head gravely).* Merriment.
OFFICER *(woman of thirty, coming to the front of the platform).* I've a question to ask you all.
SOME *(cry).* Hush! *(Or whistle for silence)*
OTHERS. Speech. None of your jaw!... Music!...
VOICES. Begin! Stop!
OFFICER. Tell me . . . why are you sitting crowded there?
VOICE. Why not?
OFFICER. You're packed like herrings in a barrel. You're fighting for places . . . shoving one another off the forms. Yet one bench stands empty.
VOICE. Nothing doing!
OFFICER. Why do you sit squeezing and crowding there? Can't you see it's a nasty habit? Who knows his next-door neighbor? You rub shoulders with him, you press your knees against his, and for all you know he may be rotting. You look into his face— and perhaps his mind is full of murderous thoughts. I know there are sick men and criminals in this hall. So I give you warning! Mind your next-door neighbor! Beware of him! Those benches groan under sick men and criminals!
WOMAN'S VOICE. Next to me?
SECOND VOICE. Or me?
OFFICER. I give you this word of advice; steer clear of your neighbor! In this asphalt city, disease and crime are everywhere. Which of you is without a scab? Your skin may be smooth and white, but your looks give you away. You have no eyes to see, but your eyes are wide open to betray you. You haven't escaped the great plague; the germs are too powerful. You've been sitting too long near bad neighbors. Come up here, come away from those benches, if you would not be as your neighbors are in this city of asphalt. This is the last warning. Repent. Repent. Come up here, come to the penitent form. Come to the penitent form, come to the penitent form.
(Music, "Jesus Lover of My Soul." Salvation Lass leads in Cashier, in evening dress, who arouses some notice. Salvation Lass finds Cashier a place among the crowd, stands next to him and explains the procedure. Cashier looks around him amused. Music ceases, ironical applause.)
OFFICER *(coming forward again).* One of our comrades will tell you how he found his way to the penitent bench.
(First Soldier of Salvation Army, a young man, steps onto the platform.)
VOICE. So that's the mug! *(Some laughter)*
FIRST SOLDIER. I want to tell you of my sin. I led a life without giving a thought to my soul. I cared only for my body. I built up my body like a strong wall; the soul was quite hidden behind it. I sought for glory with my body, and made broader the shadow in which my soul withered away. My sin was sport. I practiced it without a moment's pause; vain of the quickness of my feet on the pedals; and the ring of the applause among the spectators. I sent out many a challenge; I won many a prize. My name was printed on

every billboard; my picture was in all the papers. I was in the running for the world championship . . . At last my soul spoke to me. Its patience was ended. I met with an accident. The injury was not fatal. My soul wanted to leave me time for repentence. My soul left me strength enough to rise from those benches where you sit, and to climb up here to the penitent form. There my soul could speak to me in peace. What it told me I can't tell you now. It's all too wonderful, and my words are too weak to describe it. You must come yourselves, and hear the voice speak within you! *(He steps in)* *(A Man laughs obscenely.)*

SEVERAL *(cry)*. Hush!

SALVATION LASS *(to Cashier, in a low voice)*. Do you hear him?

CASHIER. Let me alone. *(Music plays and ceases)*

OFFICER *(coming forward)*. You've heard our comrade's testimony. Can you win anything nobler than your own? And it's quite easy, for the soul is there within you. You've only to give it peace . . . once, just once. The soul wants to sit with you for one quiet hour. Its favorite seat is on this bench. There must be one among you who sinned like our comrade here. Our comrade will help him. The way has been opened up. So come. Come to the penitent bench. Come to the penitent bench. Come to the penitent bench. *(Silence)*

(The First Penitent, a young man of powerful build, with one arm in a sling, rises in a corner of the hall and makes his way through the crowd, smiling nervously. He mounts the platform. A Man laughs obscenely.)

ANOTHER *(indignantly)*. Where is that dirty lout!

(The Man rises abashed, and makes his way toward the door.)

OTHERS. That's the fellow!

(Salvation Lass, hurries to him and leads him back to the place.)

VOICE *(facetiously)*. Oh, let me go, Angelina!

SEVERAL OTHERS. Bravo!

FIRST PENITENT *(on the platform)*. In this city of asphalt there's a hall. Inside the hall is a cycle-track. This was my sin. I was a rider too. I was a rider in the relay

races this week. On the second night I met with a collision. I was thrown; my arm was broken. The races are hurrying on, but I am at rest. All my life I have been riding without a thought. Now! I want to think of everything. *(Loudly)* I want to think of my sins at the penitent bench. *(Led by a Soldier, he sinks onto the bench; Soldier remains at his side)*

OFFICER. A soul has been won! *(Music plays and ceases)*

SALVATION LASS *(to Cashier)*. Do you see him?

CASHIER. My affair. My affair.

SALVATION LASS. What are you muttering?

CASHIER. The relay races.

SALVATION LASS. Are you ready?

CASHIER. Hold your tongue.

OFFICER *(stepping forward)*. Another comrade will testify.

(A Man hisses.)

OTHERS. Be quiet there!

SECOND SOLDIER *(girl mounts the platform)*. Whose sin is my sin? I'll tell you of my sin without shame. I had a wretched home, if you could call it a home. The man, a drunkard, was not my father. The woman—who was my mother—went with smart gentlemen. She gave me all the money I wanted; her bully gave me all the blows—I didn't want. *(Laughter)* No one thought of me; least of all did I think of myself. So I became a lost woman. I was blind in those days. I couldn't see that the miserable life at home was only meant to make me think of my soul and dedicate myself to its salvation. One night I learned the truth. I had a gentleman with me, and he asked me to darken the room. I turned out the gas, though I wasn't used to such ways. Presently I understood why he had asked me; for, I realized that I had with me only the trunk of a man whose legs had been cut off. He didn't want me to know that he had wooden legs, and that he had taken them off in the dark. Then horror took hold of me, and wouldn't let me go. I began to hate my body; it was only my soul that I could love. And now this soul of mine is my delight. It's so perfect, so beautiful; it's the bonniest thing I know. I know too much of it to tell you here. If you ask your souls, they'll tell you all—all! (She steps down. Silence)

OFFICER (coming forward). You've heard our sister testify. Her soul offered itself to her, and she did not refuse. Now she tells you her story with joyful lips. Isn't a soul offering itself now, at this moment, to one of you? Let it come closer. Let it speak; here on this bench it will be undisturbed. Come to the penitent bench. Come to the penitent bench. (Movement in the hall. Some turn round)

SECOND PENITENT (elderly prostitute, begins to speak as she comes forward). What do you think of me, ladies and gentlemen? I was just tired to death of streetwalking, and dropped in by chance for a rest. I'm not shy—oh, dear no! I don't know this hall; it's my first time here. Just dropped in by chance, as you might say. (Speaking from the platform) But you make a great mistake, ladies and gentlemen, if you think I should wait to be asked a second time! Not this child, thank you—oh, dear no! Take a good look at me, from tip to toe; it's your last chance; enjoy the treat while you can! It's quite all right; never mind me; I'm not a bit shy; look me up and down. Thank you, my soul's not for disposal. I've never sold that. You could offer me as much as you pleased, but my soul was always my own. I'm obliged to you for your compliments, ladies and gentlemen. You won't run up against me in the streets again. I've got no time to spare for you. My soul leaves me no peace. (A Soldier leads her to the penitent form)

OFFICER. A soul has been won! (Music. Jubilation of the Soldiers. Music ceases)

SALVATION LASS (to Cashier). Do you hear all?

CASHIER. That's my affair. My affair.

SALVATION LASS. What are you muttering about?

CASHIER. The wooden leg. The wooden leg.

SALVATION LASS. Are you ready?

CASHIER. Not yet. Not yet.

A MAN (standing upright in the middle of the hall). Tell me my sin. I want to hear my sin!

OFFICER (coming forward). Our comrade here will tell you.

VOICES (excitedly). Sit down! Keep quiet; give him a chance.

THIRD SOLDIER (elderly man). Let me tell you my story. It's an everyday story.

VOICE. Then why tell it?

THIRD SOLDIER. That's how it came to be my sin. I had a snug home, a contented family, a comfortable job. Everything was just—everyday. In the evening, when I sat smoking my pipe at the table, under the lamp, with my wife and children round about me, I felt satisfied enough. I never felt the need of a change. Yet the change came, I forget what started it; perhaps I never knew. The soul knocks quietly at your door. It knows the right hour and uses it.

SECOND PENITENT. Halleluja.

THIRD SOLDIER. However that might be, I couldn't pass the warning by. I stood out at first in a sluggish sort of way, but the soul was stronger. More and more I felt its power. All my born days I'd been set upon comfort; now I knew that nothing could satisfy me fully but the soul.

SOLDIERS. Halleluja.

THIRD SOLDIER. I don't look for comfort any longer at the table under the lamp, with a pipe in my mouth; I find it here alone at the penitent bench. That's my everyday story. (He stands back. Music plays and is interrupted by Third Penitent)

THIRD PENITENT (elbowing his way up). My sin! My sin! (From the platform) I'm the father of a family!

VOICE. Congratulations!

THIRD PENITENT. I have two daughters. I have a wife. My mother is still with us. We live in four rooms. It's quite snug and cozy in our house. One of my daughters plays the piano, the other does embroideries. My wife cooks. My old mother waters the geraniums in the window-boxes. It's cozy in our house. Coziness itself. It's fine in our house. It's grand . . . first-rate . . . It's a model—a pattern of a home. (With a change of voice) Our house is loathsome . . . horrible . . . horrible . . . mean . . . paltry through and through. It stinks of paltriness in every room; with the piano-playing, the cooking, the embroidery, the watering-pots. (Breaking out)

I have a soul! I have a soul! I have a soul!
(He stumbles to the penitent bench)

SOLDIERS. Halleluja.

OFFICER. A soul has been won!

SALVATION LASS *(to Cashier)*. Do you see him?

CASHIER. My daughters. My wife. My mother.

SALVATION LASS. What do you keep mumbling?

CASHIER. My affair. My affair.

SALVATION LASS. Are you ready?

CASHIER. Not yet. Not yet.

(Jubilant music. Loud uproar in the hall.)

MAN *(standing upright, and stretching out hands)*. What's my sin? What's my sin? I want to know my sin? Tell me my sin.

OFFICER *(coming forward)*. Our comrade will tell you. *(Deep silence)*

FOURTH SOLDIER *(middle-aged, comes forward)*. My soul had a hard struggle to win the victory. It had to take me by the throat and shake me like a rat. It was rougher still with me. It sent me to jail. I'd stolen the money that was entrusted to me; I'd absconded with a big sum. They caught me; I was tried and sentenced. In my prison cell I found the rest my soul had been looking for. At the last it could speak to me in peace. At last I could hear its voice. Those days in the lonely cell became the happiest in my life. When my time was finished I could not part from my soul.

SOLDIERS. Halleluja.

FOURTH SOLDIER. I looked for a quiet place where we two could meet. I found it here on the penitent form; I find it here still, each evening that I feel the need of a happy hour! *(Standing aside)*

OFFICER *(coming forward)*. Our comrade has told you of his happy hours at the penitent form. Who is there among you who wants to escape from this sin? Here he will find peace! Come to the penitent bench!

MAN *(standing up, shouting and gesticulating)*. Nobody's sin! That's nobody's sin! I want to hear mine! My sin! My sin! *(Many join in)* My sin! My sin! My sin!

CASHIER. My sin!

SALVATION LASS *(above the uproar)*. What are you shouting?

CASHIER. The bank. The money.

SALVATION LASS *(shaking him)*. Are you ready?

CASHIER. Yes, now I'm ready!

SALVATION LASS *(taking his arm)*. I'll lead you up there. I'll stand by you—always at your side. *(Turning to the crowd, ecstatically)* A soul is going to speak. I looked for this soul. I found this soul! *(The tumult ebbs into a quiet hum)*

CASHIER *(on the platform, Salvation Lass by his side)*. I've been on the road since this morning. I was driven out on this search. There was no chance of turning back. The earth gave way behind me, all bridges were broken. I had to march forward on a road that led me here. I won't weary you with the halting-places that wearied me. None of them were worth my break with the old life; none of them repaid me. I marched on with a searching eye, a sure touch, a clear head. I passed them all by, stage after stage; they dwindled and vanished in the distance. It wasn't this, it wasn't that, or the next—or the fourth or the fifth! What is the goal, what is the prize, that's worth the whole stake? This hall, humming with crowded benches, ringing with melody! This hall! Here, from bench to bench, the spirit thunders fulfillment! Here glow the twin crucibles; confession and repentance! Molten and free from dross, the soul stands like a glittering tower, strong and bright. You cry fulfillment for these benches. *(Pause)* I'll tell you my story.

SALVATION LASS. Speak, I'm with you. I'll stand by you.

CASHIER. I've been all day on the road. I confess; I'm a bank cashier. I embezzled the money that was entrusted me. A good round sum; sixty thousand marks! I fled with it into your city of asphalt. By this time, they're on my track; perhaps they've offered a big reward. I'm not in hiding any more. I confess! You can buy nothing worth having, even with all the money of all the banks in the world. You get less than you pay, every time. The more you spend, the less the goods are worth. The money corrupts them: the money veils the truth. Money's the meanest of the paltry swindles in this world! *(Pulling rolls of bank notes out of his breast pocket)* This hall is a burning oven; it glows with your contempt for all mean things. I throw the money to you; it shall be torn and stamped under foot. So much less deceit in the world! So much trash consumed. I'll go through your benches and give myself up to the first policeman; after confession, comes atonement. So the cup is filled!

(With gloved hands he scatters bank notes broadcast into the hall. The money flutters down; all hands are stretched upward; a scrimmage ensues. The crowd is tangled into a fighting skein. The Soldiers leap from the platform; benches are overturned, blows of fisticuffs resound above the shouting. At last, the cramped mass rolls to the door and out into the street. The Salvation Lass, who has taken no part in the struggle, stands alone on the steps.)

CASHIER *(smiling at her).* You are standing by me. You are with me still! *(Picking up an abandoned drum and a stick)* On we go. *(Roll of drum)* The crowd is left behind. *(Roll of drum)* The yelping pack outrun. Vast emptiness. Elbow room! Room! Room! Room! *(Drum)* A maid remains . . . upright, steadfast! Maiden and man. The old garden is reopened. The sky is clear. A voice cries from the silent tree tops. It is well. *(Drum)* Maiden and man . . . eternal constancy. Maiden and man . . . fullness in the void. Maiden and man . . . the beginning and the end. Maiden and man . . . the seed and the flower. Maiden and man . . . sense and aim and goal! *(Rapid drumtaps, then a long roll. Salvation Lass draws back to tne door, and slips out. Cashier beats a tattoo)*

SALVATION LASS *(throws the door open. To Policeman).* There he is! I've shown him to you! I've earned the reward.

CASHIER *(letting fall the drumstick in the middle of a beat).* Here above you, I stand. Two are too many. Space holds but one. Space is loneliness. Loneliness is space.

Coldness is sunshine. Sunshine is coldness. Fever heat burns you. Fever heat freezes you. Fields are deserted. Ice overgrows them. Who can escape? Where is the door?

POLICEMAN. Is this the only entrance? *(Salvation Lass nods. Cashier feels in his pocket.)*

POLICEMAN. He's got a hand in his pocket. Switch off that light. We're a target for him!

(Salvation Lass obeys. All the lights of the hanging lamp are put out. Lights from the left illuminate the tangle of wires, forming a skeleton in outline.)

CASHIER *(feeling with his left hand in his breast pocket, grasps with his right a trumpet, and blows a fanfare toward the lamp).* Ah!— Discovered. Scorned in the snow this morning—welcomed now in the tangled wires. I salute you. *(Trumpet)* The road is behind me. Panting, I climb the steep curves that lead upward. My forces are spent. I've spared myself nothing. I've made the path hard, where it might have been easy. This morning in the snow when we met, you and I, you should have been more pressing in your invitation. One spark of enlightenment would have helped me and spared me all trouble. It doesn't take much of a brain to see that— Why did I hesitate? Why take the road? Whither am I bound? From first to last you sit there, naked bone. From morn to midnight, I rage in a circle . . . and now your beckoning finger points the way . . . whither? *(He shoots the answer into his breast)*

POLICEMAN. Switch on the light.

(Salvation Lass does so. The Cashier has fallen back, with arms outstretched, tumbling headlong down the steps. His husky gasp is like an "Ecce," his heavy sigh is like a "Homo." One second later all the lamps explode with a loud report.)

POLICEMAN. There must be a short circuit in the main. *(Darkness)*

CURTAIN

JACINTO BENAVENTE's

The Passion Flower

(La Malquerida)

Translated from the Spanish by JOHN GARRETT UNDERHILL

First presented at the Greenwich Village Theatre, New York, January 13, 1920, with the following cast:

RAIMUNDA................... Nance O'Neil
ACACIA...................... Edna Walton
DOÑA ISABEL .... Clara Bracey
MILAGROS.................. Gertrude Gustin
FIDELA .... Alba Anchoriz
ENGRACIA................... Helen Rapport
BERNABEA.................... Aldeah Wise
GASPARA..................... Ridler Davies

JULIANA................ Mrs. Charles G. Craig
ESTEBAN.................... Charles Waldron
TÍO EUSEBIO................... Robert Fisher
FAUSTINO...................... Edwin Beryl
RUBIO .... Harold Hartsell
BERNABÉ.................... Charles Angelo
NORBERT .... J. Harper Macauley

SCENES

ACT ONE—Living room in Raimunda's home.

ACT TWO—Entrance hall to Raimunda's home.

ACT THREE—Same as Act Two.

The action takes place in Castile at the present day.

From *Plays*, First Series, by JACINTO BENAVENTE, translated by JOHN GARRETT UNDERHILL.

© 1917, 1945, by JOHN GARRETT UNDERHILL.

Reprinted by permission of the publishers, CHARLES SCRIBNER'S SONS.

ACT ONE

A room in a rich farmer's house, situated on the outskirts of a pueblo, or small town.

As the curtain rises, Raimunda, Acacia, Doña Isabel, Milagros, Fidela, Engracia, are bidding farewell to Gaspara, Bernabea, and four or five other women and young girls who are taking leave. While the others stand, Doña Isabel remains seated.

———

GASPARA. God be with you! Good-by, Raimunda.

BERNABEA. God be with you, Doña Isabel—and you, too, Acacia, and your mother. May everything turn out for the best.

RAIMUNDA. Thanks. May we all live to see it. Go down with them, Acacia.

ALL. Good-by! Good-by!

(The women and girls retire, keeping up an animated chatter. Acacia accompanies them.)

DOÑA ISABEL. Bernabea is a nice girl.

ENGRACIA. It is only a year since she got over that trouble. No one would ever believe it to look at her now.

DOÑA ISABEL. I hear that she is going to be married.

FIDELA. Yes, come next fiesta—God willing and San Roque.

DOÑA ISABEL. I am always the last person in the village to pick up gossip. When you have nothing but trouble at home, naturally you lose interest in what is taking place outside.

ENGRACIA. How is your husband?

DOÑA ISABEL. He varies—up and down. The rest of us are thoroughly worn out. We are not able to leave the house, not even to attend mass upon Sundays. I am used to it myself, but it is hard on my daughter.

ENGRACIA. I think you make a mistake to keep her at home so much. This is a great year for weddings.

DOÑA ISABEL. But not for her. I am afraid that we shall never be able to find a man who measures up to her expectations.

FIDELA. All the same, it never struck me that she was born to be a nun. Some day she will happen on the right one.

DOÑA ISABEL. How are you pleased with this match, Raimunda? I must say you

don't seem altogether cheerful about it.

RAIMUNDA. A wedding is always something of an experiment.

ENGRACIA. If you aren't satisfied, I am sure I don't know who could ever be. Your daughter has had the pick of the entire village.

FIDELA. She's not likely to want for anything, either. We all know how well they will both be provided for, which is not a thing you can afford to overlook.

RAIMUNDA. Milagros, run downstairs and enjoy yourself with Acacia and the boys. I hate to see you sitting there all alone in a corner.

DOÑA ISABEL. Yes, do go down.—The child is as innocent as the day that God made her.

MILAGROS. Excuse me.

RAIMUNDA. We might all take another glass and some *bizcochos*.

DOÑA ISABEL. Thanks, I have had enough.

RAIMUNDA. No, no, come, everybody. This is nothing.

DOÑA ISABEL. Acacia doesn't seem as happy as you might expect, either, considering that her engagement was only announced today.

RAIMUNDA. She is as innocent, too, as God made her. I never saw anyone like her; she is so silent. She distracts me. For weeks together she has not one word to say. Then there are times when she begins to talk, and her tongue runs until it fairly takes your breath away. It is a terrible thing to hear.

ENGRACIA. Naturally, you have spoiled her. After you lost the three boys she was all that you had, and you were too careful. Her father would have plucked the birds out of the air if she had asked for them, and you were no better. When he died—God rest his soul—then the child was jealous of you. She didn't like it when you married again, and she has never gotten over that grudge either.

RAIMUNDA. But what was I to do? I didn't want to marry again. I should never have thought of it if my brothers hadn't turned out the way that they did. If we had not had a man in the house to look after us, my daughter and I would have been in the street before this, and you know it.

DOÑA ISABEL. Yes, this world is no place for single women. You were left a widow very young.

RAIMUNDA. But I can't see why my daughter should be jealous. I am her mother, yet it would be hard to say which of us loves or spoils her the most. Esteban has never treated her like a stepdaughter.

DOÑA ISABEL. No wonder; you had no children of your own.

RAIMUNDA. He never comes nor goes without bringing her a present. He never thinks of such a thing with me—although, of course, I have no feeling. She is my daughter; it only makes me love him more to see how fond he is of her. You won't believe it when I tell you, but she would never let him kiss her even when she was a child, much less now. I have seldom had to lay my hand on her, but whenever I have, it was on that account.

FIDELA. Nobody can make me believe, just the same, that your daughter isn't in love with her cousin.

RAIMUNDA. Norbert? She turned him off herself between night and morning, and that was the end of it. That is another thing I can't understand. We never could find out what did happen between them.

FIDELA. Nor anybody else. Nobody has ever been able to explain it. There must have been some reason, but what it was is a mystery.

ENGRACIA. Well, she never seemed to regret it, which is more than I can say for him. She never looked at him again, but he hasn't changed. When he heard that Faustino was coming over with his father today to settle the matter and arrange things, he turned on his heel, took his gun, and went straight up to Los Berrocales. People who saw him said that you would have thought that it had broken his heart.

RAIMUNDA. Neither Esteban nor I influenced her in the least. She broke with Norbert herself, just as they were ready to publish the banns. Everybody knows it. Then she consented to see Faustino. He always had a fancy for her. His father is a great friend of Esteban's—they belong to the same party and always work

together. They have known each other for a long time. Whenever we went to Encinar for the Feast of the Virgin—or for any other fiesta—or if they were the ones who came here, it was easy to see that the boy was nervous. When she was around he didn't know what to do. He knew that there was something between her and her cousin, but he never said one word until the break came, whatever the reason was, which we don't know—no, not one; but as soon as they heard that she was done with her cousin, Faustino's father spoke to Esteban, and Esteban spoke to me, and I spoke to my daughter, and she seemed to be pleased; so now they are going to be married. That is all there is to it. If she is not satisfied, then God have mercy on her soul, because we are only doing it to please her. She has had her own way in everything.

DOÑA ISABEL. Then she ought to be happy. Why not? The boy is a fine fellow. Everybody says so.

ENGRACIA. Yes, we all feel as if he belonged in the village. He lives so near by, and his family is so well known that nobody ever thinks of them as strangers.

FIDELA. Tío Eusebio owns more land here than at Encinar.

ENGRACIA. Certainly, if you stop to count. He inherited everything from his Uncle Manolito, and when the town lands were sold, two years ago, they went to him.

DOÑA ISABEL. The family is the richest in the neighborhood.

FIDELA. Undoubtedly. There may be four brothers, but each of them will come into a fortune.

ENGRACIA. Your daughter is not going barefoot, either.

RAIMUNDA. No, she is an only child and will inherit everything. Esteban has taken good care of the farm which she had from her father; he could not have done more if she had been his own child. (The Angelus sounds.)

DOÑA ISABEL. The Angelus! (The women mumble the words of the prayer) It is time for us to be going, Raimunda. Telesforo expects his supper early—if the nibble of nothing which he takes can be called supper.

ENGRACIA. It is time for us all to go.

FIDELA. We were all thinking the same thing.

RAIMUNDA. But won't you stay to supper? I don't urge Doña Isabel—I know she ought not to leave her husband. He is impatient to see her back.

ENGRACIA. Yes. We all have husbands to look after. Thanks just the same.

DOÑA ISABEL. I suppose the young man stays to supper?

RAIMUNDA. No, he is going home with his father to Encinar. They cannot spend the night. There is no moon, so they should have been on the road long ago. It is getting late and the days are growing shorter. Before you know it, it is black night.

ENGRACIA. I hear them coming up now to say good-by.

RAIMUNDA. I thought so.

(Acacia, Milagros, Esteban, Tío Eusebio, and Faustino enter.)

ESTEBAN. Raimunda, here are Tío Eusebio and Faustino to say good-by.

EUSEBIO. We must be off before dark. The roads are in terrible shape after the heavy rains.

ESTEBAN. There are some bad stretches.

DOÑA ISABEL. Well, what has the boy to say for himself? I suppose he doesn't remember me. It is five years since I have seen him.

EUSEBIO. Don't you remember Doña Isabel?

FAUSTINO. I do, *sí, señor.* I was afraid she didn't remember me.

DOÑA ISABEL. No fear of that! My husband was *alcalde* at the time, when you gave us that awful fright, running after the bull. If you had been killed, I don't know what would have happened. I didn't enjoy it. God help San Roque!—it would have put an end to his fiesta. We certainly thought you were dead.

ENGRACIA. Julian, Eudosia's husband, was caught that year too.

FAUSTINO. I remember; *sí, señora.*

EUSEBIO. He remembers perfectly, because I gave him a sound thrashing when he got home—which he deserved.

FAUSTINO. I was a boy at the time.

DOÑA ISABEL. Yes—the boy of it! However, you have picked out the finest

girl in the village, and she will have no reason to regret her choice either. But we must be going. You have business of your own to attend to.

ESTEBAN. No, they have attended to everything already.

DOÑA ISABEL. Good night, then. Come, Milagros.

ACACIA. I want her to stay to supper, but she is afraid to ask you. Do let her stay, Doña Isabel!

RAIMUNDA. Yes, do. Bernabé and Juliana will see her home afterward, and Esteban can go along, too, if necessary.

DOÑA ISABEL. No, we will send for her. You can stay, to please Acacia.

RAIMUNDA. They have so many things to talk over.

DOÑA ISABEL. God be with you. Adiós, Tío Eusebio and Esteban.

EUSEBIO. Adiós, Doña Isabel. My best sympathy to your husband.

DOÑA ISABEL. Which he appreciates, coming from you.

ENGRACIA. Good-by! A safe return!

FIDELA. God be with you!

(The women go out.)

EUSEBIO. Doña Isabel looks remarkably young. She must be my age at least. Well, "To have and to hold is to prepare to grow old," as the proverb has it. Doña Isabel was one of the best of them in her day, and in her day there were plenty.

ESTEBAN. Sit down, Tío Eusebio. What is your hurry?

EUSEBIO. No, don't tempt me; it's time to go. Night is coming on. Don't bother about us. We have the hands along and shan't need you.

ESTEBAN. No, the walk will do me good. I'll see you to the *arroyo* at least.

(Raimunda, Acacia, and Milagros re-enter.)

EUSEBIO. If you young folks have anything to say, now is the time for you to say it.

ACACIA. No, we have settled everything.

EUSEBIO. So you think.

RAIMUNDA. Come, come! Don't you try to embarrass my daughter, Tío Eusebio.

ACACIA. Thanks for everything.

EUSEBIO. What? Is that a way to thank me?

ACACIA. It was a lovely present.

EUSEBIO. The showiest thing we could find.

RAIMUNDA. Entirely too much so for a farmer's daughter.

EUSEBIO. Too much? Not a bit of it! If I'd had my way, it would have had more jewels in it than the Holy Monstrance at Toledo. Give your mother-in-law a good hug.

RAIMUNDA. Yes, come, boy. I must learn to love you or I shall never forgive you for taking her away. My heart goes with her.

ESTEBAN. Now don't begin to cry! Come, Acacia! You don't want to pass yourself off for a Magdalen.

MILAGROS. Raimunda! Acacia! *(Bursts into tears also)*

ESTEBAN. That's right—all together! Come, come!

EUSEBIO. Don't be foolish! Tears are for the dead. You are only going to be married. Try to be happy and enjoy yourselves; everybody is willing. Adiós and good night!

RAIMUNDA. Adiós, Tío Eusebio. Tell Julia that I don't know whether I shall ever be able to forgive her for not coming over today.

EUSEBIO. You know how bad her sight is. We'd have had to hitch up the cart, and it was up at Los Berrocales. We are beginning to slaughter.

RAIMUNDA. Tell her how sorry I am. May she be better soon.

EUSEBIO. Thanks to you.

RAIMUNDA. Now you had better be going. It is getting dark. *(To Esteban)* Don't be long.

EUSEBIO. I tell him not to come.

ESTEBAN. Nonsense! It isn't any trouble. I'll go as far as the *arroyo*. Don't wait supper for me.

RAIMUNDA. No, we will wait. We're not anxious to eat alone tonight. Milagros won't mind if we are late.

MILAGROS. It makes no difference to me.

EUSEBIO. God be with you all! Good-by!

RAIMUNDA. No, we are coming down to see you out.

FAUSTINO. I . . . I have something to say to Acacia first . . .

EUSEBIO. It will have to wait until tomorrow. You have had the whole day to yourselves.

FAUSTINO. Yes, but with so many people around, I had no chance . . .

EUSEBIO. Before we were through I knew we were going to get some of this nonsense.

FAUSTINO. It isn't nonsense. Only I promised mother before we started to give Acacia this scapulary. The nuns in the convent made it on purpose for her.

ACACIA. How lovely!

MILAGROS. Oh! The Blessed Virgin of Carmen—with spangles all over!

RAIMUNDA. Very pretty. My daughter was always devoted to the Virgin. Thank your mother for us. We appreciate it.

FAUSTINO. It has been blessed.

EUSEBIO. Good! Now you have got that off your mind. I wonder what your mother would have thought if we'd taken it home again with us? I never saw such a boy! I wasn't so backward in my day. I am sure I don't know whom he does take after.

(All go out. For a moment the stage remains deserted. Meanwhile it continues to grow darker. Presently Raimunda, Acacia, and Milagros reappear.)

RAIMUNDA. They have made a long day of it. It is night before they start. How do you feel, my dear? Are you happy?

ACACIA. You can see for yourself.

RAIMUNDA. I can, can I? That is exactly what I want to do: see for myself. Nobody can ever tell how you feel.

ACACIA. I am tired out.

RAIMUNDA. It has certainly been a long day. I haven't had a minute's rest since five o'clock in the morning.

MILAGROS. Everybody has been here to congratulate you.

RAIMUNDA. The whole village, you might say, beginning with the priest, who was among the first. We paid him for a mass, and gave him ten loaves of bread besides for the poor. In our happiness it is only right to remember others who are not so fortunate. Praise God, we want for nothing! Where are the matches?

ACACIA. Here they are, mother.

RAIMUNDA. Light the lamp, dear. It makes me feel sad to sit in the dark. *(Calling)* Juliana! Juliana! I wonder where she is?

JULIANA *(downstairs)*. What do you want?

RAIMUNDA. Bring up the broom and dustpan.

JULIANA *(downstairs)*. In a minute.

RAIMUNDA. I had better change my skirt while I think of it. Nobody will be in now; it's so late.

ACACIA. I might take off my dress.

RAIMUNDA. What for? There is nothing for you to do. You have been busy all day. *(Juliana enters.)*

JULIANA. Show me that dust——

RAIMUNDA. Stand the broom in the corner and take these things away. Mind you scour them until they are clean; then put them back in the cupboard. Be careful with those glasses! They are our best.

JULIANA. Could I eat a cake?

RAIMUNDA. Of course you can!—though I don't see how you manage to hold so much.

JULIANA. I haven't touched a thing this whole day, God help me! I am my mother's own daughter. Haven't I passed cake and wine to the entire village? Everybody has been here today. That shows you what people think of this house—yes, and what they think of Tío Eusebio and his family. Wait till you see the wedding! I know somebody who is going to give her a new gold piece, and somebody who is going to give her a silk embroidered quilt that has flowers all over it, so lifelike that the first thing she will want to do is pick them off of it. That will be a great day for her, praise God! Not one of us but will laugh and cry then, and I will be the first—after her mother; she will be first because it is her right, but you know me. I love you all in this house. Besides, you make me think of my dead daughter. She looked just like you do when she died, and we buried her.

RAIMUNDA. Never mind that, Juliana. Go along and don't dig up any more of your troubles. We have enough of our own already.

JULIANA. God grant that I may never be a trouble to you! But everything goes topsy-turvy with me today, around and around, and every which way. The more you enjoy yourself the sadder it makes you feel. God forbid that I should ever drag in this child's poor dead father, who rests in heaven now, God bless him! But I wish he could have seen her today! He was fond of her.

RAIMUNDA. That will do, Juliana! That will do.

JULIANA. Don't talk like that to me, Raimunda. It's like a blow in the face, like beating a faithful hound. That's what I have been to you and your daughter and your house—a faithful hound, that has eaten your bread, God willing, in season and out—yes, and kept her self-respect while she was about it, and you know it. *(Goes out)*

RAIMUNDA. Juliana!—She is right, though. She has always been like a faithful hound—faithful and loyal to us and our house. *(She begins to sweep)*

ACACIA. Mother——

RAIMUNDA. Did you speak?

ACACIA. Will you let me have the key to this chest of drawers? I want to show Milagros some of my things.

RAIMUNDA. Yes, here it is; take the bunch. Sit down and rest while I go and keep an eye on the supper. *(She takes the broom and goes out)*

(Acacia and Milagros seat themselves on the floor before the chest of drawers and open the lower drawer or compartment.)

ACACIA. These earrings were a present from—well, from Esteban, since my mother isn't here. She always wants me to call him father.

MILAGROS. Don't you know that he loves you?

ACACIA. Yes, but you can have only one father and mother. He brought me these handkerchiefs, too, from Toledo. The nuns embroidered the initials. See all these postcards—aren't they pretty?

MILAGROS. What lovely ladies!

ACACIA. Yes, they're actresses from Madrid, or from Paris in France. Look at these boys—He brought me this box, too; it had candy in it.

MILAGROS. I don't see how you can say then . . .

ACACIA. I don't say anything. I know

he loves me, but I'd rather have been left alone with my mother.

MILAGROS. You don't mean to tell me that your mother loves you any less on his account?

ACACIA. I don't know. She's wrapped up in him. How do I know, if she had to choose between me and that man . . .

MILAGROS. I think it's wicked to talk like that. Suppose your mother hadn't married again, what would she do now when you get married? She would have no one to live with.

ACACIA. You don't suppose that I would ever have gotten married, do you, if I had been living alone with my mother?

MILAGROS. Of course you would! What difference would it make?

ACACIA. Could I be as happy anywhere else as living here alone with my mother?

MILAGROS. Don't be foolish. Everybody knows what a nice stepfather you have. If he hadn't been good there would have been talk, and I would have heard it. So would you and your mother.

ACACIA. I don't say that he isn't good. But all the same I wouldn't have married if my mother hadn't married again.

MILAGROS. Do you know what I think?

ACACIA. What?

MILAGROS. People are right when they say that you don't love Faustino. The one that you love is Norbert.

ACACIA. That's a lie! How could I love him?—after the way that he treated me.

MILAGROS. Everybody says that you were the one who turned him off.

ACACIA. I did, did I? Yes, I suppose it was my fault! Anyway, we won't talk about it. What do they know? I love Faustino better than I ever did Norbert.

MILAGROS. I hope you do. Otherwise you oughtn't to marry him. Did you hear that Norbert left the village this morning? He didn't want to be around.

ACACIA. What does he care? Why today more than any other? It is nothing to him. Here is the last letter he wrote me—after everything was over. I never mean to see him again; I don't know what I am keeping it for. It would be more sensible to tear it up. (She tears the letter into small pieces) There! That ends it.

MILAGROS. What is the matter with you? You are all excited.

ACACIA. It's what he says. Now I am going to burn the pieces.

MILAGROS. Look out! The lamp will explode.

ACACIA (opening the window). To the road with you! I'll scatter the ashes . . . The wind blows them away . . . It is over now, and I am glad of it. Did you ever see such a dark night?

MILAGROS (following her to the window). It is black as pitch—no moon, no stars . . .

ACACIA. What was that?

MILAGROS. Somebody slammed a door.

ACACIA. It sounded to me like a shot.

MILAGROS. Nonsense! Who would be out shooting at this hour? Unless there is a fire somewhere . . . No, I don't see any glow in the sky.

ACACIA. I am frightened. Yes, I am——

MILAGROS. Don't be silly!

ACACIA (running suddenly to the door). Mother! Mother!

RAIMUNDA (downstairs). What is it?

ACACIA. Did you hear anything?

RAIMUNDA (downstairs). Yes. I sent Juliana to find out. It's all right.

ACACIA. Oh, mother!

RAIMUNDA. Don't be afraid! I am coming up.

ACACIA. It was a shot! I know it was a shot!

MILAGROS. Suppose it was? What of it?

ACACIA. God help us! (Raimunda enters)

RAIMUNDA. Did it frighten you? Nothing is the matter.

ACACIA. Mother, you are frightened yourself.

RAIMUNDA. Because you are. Naturally, I was frightened at first—your father hasn't come back. But it is silly. Nothing could have happened. What was that? Do you hear? Someone is downstairs. God help us!

ACACIA. Mother! Mother!

MILAGROS. What do they say? What are they talking about?

RAIMUNDA. Stay where you are. I am going down.

ACACIA. Mother, don't you go!

RAIMUNDA. I can't make out what they say . . . I am too excited . . . Oh,

Esteban, my heart! May no harm have come to you! *(She rushes out)*

MILAGROS. There is a crowd downstairs. They are coming in. I can't make out what they say . . .

ACACIA. Something has happened! Something awful! I knew it all the time.

MILAGROS. So did I, only I didn't want to frighten you.

ACACIA. What do you think?

MILAGROS. Don't ask me! Don't ask!

RAIMUNDA *(downstairs)*. Holy Virgin! God save us! Terrible, terrible! Oh, his poor mother when she hears that her poor boy is dead—murdered! I can't believe it! What a terrible thing for us all!

ACACIA. What does she say? Did you hear? Mother! Mother! Mother!

RAIMUNDA. Acacia! Daughter! Don't you come down! Don't come down! I am coming up.

(Raimunda, Fidela, Engracia, and a number of other women enter.)

ACACIA. What's the matter? What has happened? Someone is dead, isn't he? Someone is dead?

RAIMUNDA. My poor child! Faustino! Faustino!

ACACIA. What?

RAIMUNDA. Murdered! Shot dead as he left the village!

ACACIA. Mother! *Ay!* But who did it? Who did it?

RAIMUNDA. Nobody knows. It was too dark; they couldn't see. Everyone thinks it was Norbert—so as to fill the cup of disgrace which we must drain in this house!

ENGRACIA. It couldn't have been any one else.

WOMEN. It was Norbert! It was Norbert!

FIDELA. Here come the constables.

ENGRACIA. Have they caught him?

RAIMUNDA. And here is your father. *(Esteban enters)* Esteban, my soul! Who did it? Do you know?

ESTEBAN. How do I know? I saw what the rest did. Don't leave the house, do you hear? I don't want to have you running around the village.

RAIMUNDA. But how is his father? Think of his poor mother when they carry her boy home to her dead— murdered! And he left her alive, happy, and well only this morning!

ENGRACIA. Hanging is too good for the wretch that did it!

FIDELA. They ought to have killed him on the spot! Such a thing never happened before in this village.

RAIMUNDA. Esteban, don't let them take the body away. I must see him—and so must my daughter. He was to have been her husband.

ESTEBAN. Keep cool! There is plenty of time. I don't want you to leave the house, do you hear? It's in the hands of the law now; the doctor and priest were too late. I must hurry back; we all have depositions to make. *(He retires)*

RAIMUNDA. Your father is right. What can we do?—except commend his soul to God, who was his Maker. I can't get his poor mother out of my head! Don't take it so hard, Acacia. It frightens me to see you so still. It is worse than if you cried your heart out. Who would ever have believed this morning that such a thing could be? But it is! A curse has fallen upon us!

ENGRACIA. The shot went straight through his heart.

FIDELA. He fell off his horse, like a log.

RAIMUNDA. What a shame, what a disgrace to the village! I blush to think that the murderer was born in this place, that he was one of us, and walked about here with all that evil in his heart! He is one of our own family, to make it worse!

GASPARA. But we aren't sure of that.

RAIMUNDA. Who else could it be? Everybody says so.

ENGRACIA. Everybody says it was Norbert.

FIDELA. It couldn't have been any one but Norbert!

RAIMUNDA. Light the candles, Milagros, before the image of the Virgin. Let us tell her a rosary, since we can do no more than pray for the dead.

GASPARA. God rest his soul!

ENGRACIA. He died without confession.

FIDELA. From purgatory, good Lord, deliver us.

ALL. God rest his soul!

RAIMUNDA *(to Milagros)*. You begin the rosary; I cannot pray. I am thinking of his mother's broken heart!
(The women begin to tell the rosary.)

ACT TWO

Entrance hall of a farmhouse. There is a large door at the rear, on either side of which is a window, having an iron grating. A door on the Left, and another on the Right.
Esteban is seated at a small table, taking lunch. Raimunda waits upon him, seated also. Juliana comes and goes, assisting with the service. Acacia sits in a low chair near one of the windows, sewing. A basket of clothes stands beside her.

———

RAIMUNDA. Don't you like it?

ESTEBAN. Of course I do.

RAIMUNDA. You haven't eaten anything. Do you want us to cook something else?

ESTEBAN. Don't bother me, my dear. I have had plenty.

RAIMUNDA. You don't expect me to believe that. *(Calling)* Juliana! Bring the salad!—Something is the matter with you.

ESTEBAN. Don't be silly.

RAIMUNDA. Don't you suppose that I know you by this time? You ought never to have gone to the village. You've heard talk. We came out here to the grove to get rid of it all, to be away from the excitement, and it was a good thing, too, that we did. Now you go back to the village and don't say one word to me about it. What did you want to do that for?

ESTEBAN. I wanted to see Norbert and his father.

RAIMUNDA. Yes, but you could have sent for them and have had them come out here. You ought to have spared yourself; then you wouldn't have heard all this talk. I know how they are talking in the village.

JULIANA. Yes, and that is all the good it does us to stay out here and shut ourselves up from everybody, because everybody that goes anywhere in the neighborhood passes through this grove, and then they stop, and smell around, and

meddle in what is none of their business.

ESTEBAN. Yes, and you meddle with every one of them.

JULIANA. No, señor; don't you make any mistake. I meddle with nobody. Didn't I scold Bernabea only yesterday for talking more than she had any right to with some men from Encinar who were coming down the road? If anyone asks questions send them to me, because I've learned what to do from my mother, who had good reason to know: When questioned much, answer little, and be sure you make it just the opposite.

RAIMUNDA. Hold your tongue! And get out. *(Juliana retires)* What do they say in the village?

ESTEBAN. Nothing. Tío Eusebio and his boys swear they are going to kill Norbert. They refuse to accept the decision of the court; he got off too easily. They are coming over someday, and then there will be trouble. You hear both sides in the village. Some think that Tío Eusebio is right, that it must have been Norbert; others think it wasn't Norbert. They say that the court let him go because he was innocent, and he proved it.

RAIMUNDA. That is what I think. No one could contradict his deposition; not even Faustino's father could find any flaws in it, nor the hands. You couldn't yourself, and you were with them.

ESTEBAN. Tío Eusebio and I had stopped to light our cigars. We were laughing like two fools because I had my lighter, and it wouldn't light; so Tío Eusebio got out his tinder and flint and said to me, laughing: "Here, get a light, and don't waste your time with that newfangled machine. All it is good for is to help fools waste their money. I still make out with this." That was what blinded us. We were fooling over the light when the shot was fired. We started up and could see nothing. Then, when we saw that he had dropped dead, we stood stock-still, as dead as he was. They could have finished us, too, while they were about it, and we would never have known it.

(Acacia gets up suddenly and starts to go out.)

RAIMUNDA. Where are you going, my dear? Don't be nervous.

ACACIA. You never talk about anything else. I don't see how you can stand it. Hasn't he told us how it happened over and over again? Do we have to hear the same thing all the time?

ESTEBAN. She is right. If I had my way, I'd never mention it again; it's your mother.

ACACIA. I even dream about it at night. I never used to be nervous when I was alone or in the dark, but now I am frightened to death, even in broad daylight.

RAIMUNDA. You are not the only one, either. I get no rest, day nor night. I never used to be afraid. I thought nothing of passing the cemetery after dark, not even on All Soul's Eve, but now the least thing makes me jump, no matter what—noise, silence. To tell the truth, as long as we thought it was Norbert, although he was one of the family, and it would have been a shame and a disgrace to us all, at the same time it couldn't be helped; there was nothing to do but resign oneself—and I had resigned myself. After all, it had an explanation. But now, if it wasn't Norbert, if nobody knows who it was, and nobody can explain why it was that that poor boy was shot—I can't be easy in my mind. If it wasn't Norbert, who could have wished him any harm? Maybe it was revenge, some enemy of his father's, or of yours— how do we know but that the shot was intended for you, and since it was night and pitch-dark, they made a mistake, and what they didn't do then they will another time, and . . . I can't stand this suspense! I get no rest! Every time that you go out of the house and show yourself on the road, it seems to me that I will go crazy. Today, when you were late, I was just starting for the village myself.

ACACIA. She was out on the road already.

RAIMUNDA. Yes, only I saw you and Rubio from the top of the hill, so I turned and ran back before you passed the mill, so you wouldn't be angry. I know it is foolish, but now I want to be with you all the time, wherever you go—I can't bear to be separated from you for one moment. Otherwise I can't be happy. This isn't living.

ESTEBAN. I don't believe anybody wishes me any harm. I never wronged any man. I go wherever I please, without so much as giving it a thought, day or night.

RAIMUNDA. I used to feel the same; there is nobody who could wish us harm. We have helped so many. But all that you need is one enemy, one envious, evil mind. How do we know but that we have some enemy without our suspecting it? A second shot might come from the same quarter as the first. Norbert is free because they couldn't prove that he was guilty; and I am glad of it. Why shouldn't I be glad when he is my own sister's son— my favorite sister's? I could never have believed that Norbert could have done such a thing as murder a man in the dark! But is this to be the end of it? What is the law doing now? Why don't they investigate, why doesn't someone speak? Somebody must know, somebody must have seen whoever it was that was there that day, hovering along the road. When everything is all right, everybody knows who is passing, and what is going on— who comes and who goes—you hear it all without asking; but when you want to know, then nobody knows, nobody has seen anything.

ESTEBAN. I can't see why that is so strange. When a man is going about his business, he has nothing to conceal; but when his intentions are evil, naturally the first thing he does is to hide himself.

RAIMUNDA. Who do you think that it was?

ESTEBAN. I? To tell the truth, I thought it was Norbert, the same as you. If it wasn't Norbert, I don't know who it was.

RAIMUNDA. I suppose you won't like it, but I'll tell you what I have made up my mind to do.

ESTEBAN. What?

RAIMUNDA. Talk to Norbert. Bernabé has gone to find him. I expect him any minute.

ACACIA. Norbert? What do you want to talk to him for?

ESTEBAN. That is what I say. What does he know about it?

RAIMUNDA. How can I tell? But I know he won't lie to me. By the memory of his mother, I will make him tell me the truth. If he did it, he knows I will never tell. I can't stand this any longer. I shake all over.

ESTEBAN. Do you suppose that Norbert is going to tell you if he was the one who did it?

RAIMUNDA. After I talk to him I shall know.

ESTEBAN. Well, have your own way. It will only make more talk and hard feeling, especially since Tío Eusebio is coming over today. If they meet . . .

RAIMUNDA. They won't meet on the road, because they come from different directions. After they are here the house is big enough. We can take care of them both.

(Juliana enters.)

JULIANA. Master . . .

ESTEBAN. Why are you always bothering me?

JULIANA. Tío Eusebio is coming down the road. Maybe you don't want to see him; I thought you might like to know . . .

ESTEBAN. Why shouldn't I want to see him? Didn't I tell you he was coming?— Now bring in the other one!

RAIMUNDA. Yes, he can't come too soon to please me.

ESTEBAN. Who told you that I didn't want to see Tío Eusebio?

JULIANA. Oh, don't blame it on me! It wasn't my fault. Rubio says don't want to see him because he is mad at you. You didn't side with him in court, and that's the reason that Norbert went free.

ESTEBAN. I'll teach Rubio it's none of his business whom I side with.

JULIANA. Yes, and there are other things you might teach him while you are about it. Have I nothing to do but wait on that man? God help me, he has had more to drink today than is good for him. And that isn't talk, either.

RAIMUNDA. This is the last straw! Where is he?

ESTEBAN. No, leave him to me.

RAIMUNDA. Everything goes wrong in this house. Everybody takes advantage of you as soon as anything is the matter. You don't need to turn your back—it's instinct. They know when you can't take care of yourself.

JULIANA. I'll not take that from you, Raimunda, if you mean me.

RAIMUNDA. You know who I mean. Take it any way you like.

JULIANA. Señor, señor! What curse has fallen on this house? We are all poisoned, snared, our feet are caught in some evil vine; we are changed. One takes it out on the other, and everybody is against me. God help me, I say, and give me the strength to endure it!

RAIMUNDA. Yes, and give me the strength to endure you.

JULIANA. Yes, me! It is all my fault.

RAIMUNDA. Look at me, will you? Do I have to tell you to your face to get out? That's all I want from you.

JULIANA. Yes, you want me to shut up like a tomb. Well, I'll shut up, God help me! Señor! Let me out! Don't talk to me! *(Goes out)*

ESTEBAN. Here comes Tío Eusebio.

ACACIA. I am going. He breaks down and cries whenever he sees me. He doesn't know what he is doing, but it's always the wrong thing. Does he think he is the only one who has lost anything?

RAIMUNDA. I am sure I have cried as much as his mother has. Tío Eusebio is not the same man; he forgets. But never mind. You are right not to see him.

ACACIA. I have finished the shirts, mother. I'll iron them as soon as I have time.

ESTEBAN. Were you sewing for me?

ACACIA. You can see for yourself.

RAIMUNDA. I don't know how we'd get on if she didn't sew. I am not good for anything. I don't know whether I am alive or dead, God help me! But she can work. She gets through with it somehow. *(She caresses Acacia affectionately as she passes out)* God bless you, Acacia, my child! *(Acacia goes out)* It is a terrible responsibility to be a mother. For a long time I was afraid that she was going to get married and leave me. Now, what wouldn't I give to see her married?

(Tío Eusebio enters.)

EUSEBIO. Hello! Where is everybody?

ESTEBAN. Come in, Tío Eusebio.

EUSEBIO. Good morning to both.

RAIMUNDA. Good morning, Tío Eusebio.

ESTEBAN. Where are your horses? I'll have them put up.

EUSEBIO. My man will tend to that.

ESTEBAN. Sit down. Come, a glass of that wine he likes so much, Raimunda.

EUSEBIO. No, no, thank you. I am not feeling well. Wine doesn't agree with me.

ESTEBAN. This wine will do you good. It's a tonic.

RAIMUNDA. Suit yourself. How are you, Tío Eusebio? How is Julia?

EUSEBIO. Julia? What do you expect? I am going to lose her just as I did the boy; I can see it.

RAIMUNDA. God forbid! Hasn't she four sons yet to live for?

EUSEBIO. Yes, the more worry! That is what is killing her—worry. Nobody knows what will happen next. Our hearts are broken. We were sure that we would get justice; but now we are bitter. Everybody said it would be like this, but we didn't believe it. The murderer is alive—you pass him on the street; he goes home to his house, shuts the door, and laughs at us. It only proves what I knew all the time. There is no such thing in this world as justice, unless a man takes it with his own hands, which is what they will drive us to do now. That is why I wanted to see you yesterday. If my boys come into the village, send them home. Don't let them stay around. Arrest them—anything rather than another tragedy in our house; although I don't want to see his murderer go free—the murderer of my boy—unless God avenges him, as he must, by God!—or else there is no justice in heaven.

RAIMUNDA. Don't turn against God, Tío Eusebio. Though the hand of justice never fall upon him after the foul murder he has done, yet there is not one of us that would be in his place. He is alone with his conscience. I would not have what he has on his soul upon mine, for all the blessings of this world. We have lived good lives, we have done evil to no man, yet all our days are purgatory and torment. He must have hell in his heart after what he has done—of that we can be sure—as sure as of the day of our death.

EUSEBIO. That is cold comfort to me. How does it help me prevent my boys from taking the law into their own hands? Justice has not been done—and it should have been done. Now they are the ones who will go to jail for it! They will make good their threats too. Your ought to hear them. Even the little fellow, who is only twelve, doubles up his fists like a man, and swears that whoever killed his brother will have to reckon with him, come what may. I sit there and cry like a child. I needn't tell you how his mother feels. And all the while I have it in my heart to say: Go, my sons! Stone him until he is dead! Cut him to pieces like a hound! Drag his carcass home to me through the mire—what offal there is left of it! Instead I swallow it all and look grave, and tell them that it is wrong even to think of such a thing—it would kill their mother, it would ruin all of us!

RAIMUNDA. You are unreasonable, Tío Eusebio. Norbert is innocent; the law says so. No one could bring the least proof against him; he proved where he was, and what he was doing all that day, one hour after the other. He and his men were up at Los Berrocales. Don Faustino, the doctor, saw him there and talked with him at the very hour it took place, and he is from Encinar. You know yourself no man can be in two places at the same time. You might think that his own people had been told to say what they did, although it isn't an easy thing for so many to agree on a lie; but Don Faustino is a friend of yours; he is in your debt. And others who would naturally have been on your side said the same. Only one shepherd from Los Berrocales would testify that he had seen a man at that hour, and that was a great way off; but he had no idea who it was. From his clothes and the way that he carried himself he was sure that it could not have been Norbert.

EUSEBIO. If it wasn't, I say nothing. Does it make it any better for us that he hired someone else to do it? There can't be any doubt; there is no other explanation. I have no enemies who would do such a thing. I never harmed any man; I help everyone, whether they are our own people or not. I make it easy. If I were to sue for one-half the damage that is done me every day, it would take all of my time. I will die a poor man. They killed Faustino because he was going to marry Acacia. That is all there is to it. Nobody could have had any such reason but Norbert. If everybody had told what they knew, the trial would have ended right there. But the ones who knew most said the least; they said nothing.

RAIMUNDA. Do you mean us?

EUSEBIO. I don't say who I mean.

RAIMUNDA. It is plain enough; you don't have to mention names nor point your finger. Do you mean to say that we keep quiet because Norbert is one of our family?

EUSEBIO. Do you mean to say that Acacia doesn't know more about this thing than she is willing to admit?

RAIMUNDA. No, sir, she knows no more about it than you do. You have made up your mind that it was Norbert because you want to make yourself believe that nobody else has anything against you. We are none of us saints, Tío Eusebio. You may have done a great deal of good in your time, but you must also have done some evil; you think that nobody remembers, but maybe the ones who have suffered don't think the same. If Norbert had been in love with my daughter to that extent, he would have shown it before now. Your son didn't take her away from him, remember that. Faustino never said one word until after she was done with Norbert, and she turned him off because she knew he was going with another girl. He never so much as took the trouble to excuse himself, so that when you come down to it, he was the one who left her. That is no reason why anyone should commit murder. You can see it yourself.

EUSEBIO. Then why did everybody say that it couldn't have been anyone else? You said so yourself; everybody said so.

RAIMUNDA. Yes, because at first he was the only one we could think of. But when you look at it calmly, it is foolish to say that he is the only one who could have done it. You insinuate that we have something to conceal. Once for all, let me tell you, we are more anxious than you are to have the truth known, to have this thing out and be done with it. You

have lost a son, but I have a daughter who is alive, and she has nothing to gain, either, by this mystery.

EUSEBIO. No, she hasn't. Much less when she keeps her mouth shut. And you haven't anything to gain. You don't know what Norbert and his father say about this house so as to divert suspicion from themselves? If I believed what they said...

RAIMUNDA. About us? What do they say? (To Esteban) You have been in the village. What do they say?

ESTEBAN. Nobody cares what they say.

EUSEBIO. No, I don't believe one word that comes from them. I am only telling you how they repay the kindness you do them by taking their part.

RAIMUNDA. So you are on that tack again? Tío Eusebio, I have to stop and force myself to think what it must mean to lose a child, or I would lose control of myself. I am a mother, God knows, yet you come here and insult my daughter. You insult all of us.

ESTEBAN. Wife! Enough of this. What is the use? Tío Eusebio . . .

EUSEBIO. I insult nobody. I only repeat what other people say. You suppress the truth because he is one of the family. The whole village is the same. What you are afraid of is the disgrace. People here may think that it was not Norbert, but in Encinar, let me tell you, they think that it was. If justice isn't done—and done quick—blood will be spilled between these villages, and nobody can stop it, either. You know what young blood is.

RAIMUNDA. Yes, and you are the one who stirs it up. You respect neither God nor man. Why, didn't you just admit that Norbert couldn't have done it unless he had hired someone to commit the murder? Nonsense! It isn't so easy to hire a man to commit murder. What had a boy like Norbert to give, anyway?—Unless you want us to believe that his father had a hand in it.

EUSEBIO. Bah! Rogues come cheap. How about the Valderrobles? They live here. Didn't they kill two goatherds for three and a half duros?

RAIMUNDA. How long was it before they were found out? They fought over the half duro. When you hire a man to do a deed like that, you put yourself in his power; you become his slave for the rest of your life. There may be people who can afford to do such things, but they must be rich, they must have power. Not a boy like Norbert!

EUSEBIO. Every family has a faithful servant who will do what he is told.

RAIMUNDA. No doubt yours has. No doubt you have had occasion to use him too; you know so much about it.

EUSEBIO. Take care what you say!

RAIMUNDA. Take care yourself!

ESTEBAN. Raimunda! Enough of this. What is the use of all this talk?

EUSEBIO. Well, you hear what she says. How about you?

ESTEBAN. If we dwell on this forever, we shall all of us go mad.

EUSEBIO. Yes. You heard what I said.

RAIMUNDA. If you mean by that you don't intend to let this matter drop until you have found the murderer of your boy, it is only right and proper, and I respect you for it. But that is no reason why you should come here and insult us. Once for all, you may want justice, but I want it more than you do. I pray to God for it every day, I pray him on my knees not to let the murderer go free—and I should pray to him just the same if I had a boy—if it had been my own boy that did it! (Rubio appears in the doorway)

RUBIO. How about me, master?

ESTEBAN. Well, Rubio?

RUBIO. Don't look at me like that; I'm not drunk. We started out before lunch, that was all. I had an invitation and took a drop; it went against me. I'm sorry you feel that way about it.

RAIMUNDA. What is the matter with him? Juliana was right.

RUBIO. Tell Juliana to mind her business, will you? I just wanted to tell the master.

ESTEBAN. Rubio! You can tell me later whatever you like. Tío Eusebio is here. Don't you see? We are busy.

RUBIO. Tío Eusebio? So he is. What does he want?

RAIMUNDA. Is it any of your business what he wants? Get out! Go along and sleep it off. You don't know what you are talking about.

RUBIO. I know, señora. Don't say that to me.

ESTEBAN. Rubio!

RUBIO. Juliana's a fool; I don't drink. It was my money, anyhow. I'm no thief. What I have is my own; and my wife is my own, too. She owes nobody anything, eh, master?

ESTEBAN. Rubio! Go along! Get to bed, and don't show yourself again until you have had a good sleep. What is the matter with you? What will Tío Eusebio think?

RUBIO. I don't know. I don't take anything, understand—from anybody. (Goes out)

RAIMUNDA. What was it that you were just saying about servants, Tío Eusebio? This man has us with our hearts in our throats, yet he is nothing to us. Suppose we had trusted him with some secret? What is the matter with Rubio, anyway? Is he going to get drunk every day? He was never like this before. You ought not to put up with it.

ESTEBAN. Don't you see? He isn't used to it. That is the reason he is upset by a thimbleful. Somebody invited him into the tavern while I was tending to my business. I gave him a piece of my mind and sent him to bed, but he hasn't slept it off yet. He is drunk. That is all there is to it.

EUSEBIO. Perfectly natural. Is that all?

ESTEBAN. Drop in again, Tío Eusebio.

EUSEBIO. Thanks. I am sorry this happened—after I took the trouble to come.

RAIMUNDA. Nonsense! Nothing has happened. We have no hard feeling.

EUSEBIO. No, and I hope you won't have any. Remember what I've been through. My heart is broken—it's not scratched. It won't heal either until God claims another one of his own. How long do you expect to stay in the grove?

ESTEBAN. Till Sunday. We have nothing to keep us. We only wanted to be out of the village. Now that Norbert is home, it is nothing but talk, talk, talk.

EUSEBIO. That's right—nothing but talk. If you see my boys around, look out! I don't want them to get into any trouble, which afterward we might have cause to regret.

ESTEBAN. Don't you worry. They won't get into any while I am around. Blame it on me if they do.

EUSEBIO. They're working down by the river now. They'll be all right unless somebody happens along and stirs them up. God be with you, I say. Adiós! Where is Acacia?

RAIMUNDA. I told her not to come down, so as to spare your feelings. It is hard on her, too; it brings back everything.

EUSEBIO. That's so. It must.

ESTEBAN. I'll send for your horses.

EUSEBIO. No, I can call myself.—Francisco!—Here he comes. Take care of yourselves. God be with you!

(They move toward the door.)

RAIMUNDA. God be with you, Tío Eusebio. Tell Julia not to worry. I think of her every day. I have prayed more for her than I have for the boy—God has forgiven him by this time. Surely he never did anything to deserve such a bad end! My heart bleeds for him.

(Esteban and Tío Eusebio have passed out while she is speaking. Bernabé enters.)

BERNABÉ. Señora!

RAIMUNDA. Is Norbert here? Could you find him?

BERNABÉ. Yes, I brought him along so as to save time. He wanted to see you himself.

RAIMUNDA. Didn't you meet Tío Eusebio?

BERNABÉ. No, we saw him coming up from the river when we were a long way off, so we turned and went in by the great corral. Norbert is hiding there until Tío Eusebio starts back to Encinar.

RAIMUNDA. There he goes up the road now.

BERNABÉ. Yes—under the great cross.

RAIMUNDA. Tell Norbert. No—wait! What do they say in the village?

BERNABÉ. No good, señora. The law is going to have its hands full before it gets to the bottom of this.

RAIMUNDA. Does anybody think it was Norbert?

BERNABÉ. You would get your head broke if you said it was. When he came back yesterday, half the town was out to meet him. Everybody was sitting by the roadside. They took him up on their shoulders and carried him home. The women all cried, and the men hugged him. I thought his father would die for joy.

RAIMUNDA. He never did it. Poor Norbert!

BERNABÉ. They say the men are coming over from Encinar to kill him; everybody here carries a club and goes armed.

RAIMUNDA. Mother of God! Did anything go wrong with the master while he was in the village this morning? What did you hear?

BERNABÉ. So they have been talking to you?

RAIMUNDA. No. That is—yes; I know.

BERNABÉ. Rubio was in the tavern and began to say things, so I ran for the master, and he came and ordered him out. He was insolent to the master. He was drunk.

RAIMUNDA. Do you remember what he said? I mean Rubio.

BERNABÉ. Oh! His tongue ran away with him. He was drunk. Do you know what I think? If I were you, I wouldn't go back to the village for two or three days.

RAIMUNDA. No, certainly not. If I had my way we would never go back. I am filled with a loathing for it all so great that I want to rush out, and down that long road, and then on and up over those mountains to the other side, and after that I don't know where I would hide myself. I feel as if some one were running after me, after me, always after me, with more than death in his heart. But the master . . . Where is the master?

BERNABÉ. Seeing to Rubio.

RAIMUNDA. Tell Norbert to come in. I can't wait.

(Bernabé goes out. Norbert enters.)

NORBERT. Aunt Raimunda!

RAIMUNDA. Norbert, my boy! Give me a hug.

NORBERT. I am so glad you sent for me. I've been treated like a dog. It's a good thing that my mother is dead and in heaven. I am glad she never lived to see this day. Next to my father, there is nobody in the world I think so much of as I do of you.

RAIMUNDA. I could never have believed

that you did it—not though everybody said so.

NORBERT. I know it; you were the first to take my part. Where is Acacia?

RAIMUNDA. In her room. We have our fill of trouble in this house.

NORBERT. Who says I killed Faustino? If I hadn't proved, as I did prove, where I was all that day, if I'd done as I meant at first and taken my gun and gone off to hunt alone by myself, and then couldn't have proved where I was, because nobody had seen me, I would have spent the rest of my life in prison. They would have had me.

RAIMUNDA. Are you crying?

NORBERT. No, I am not crying; but I cried when I found myself in that prison. If anybody had ever told me that I would ever go to prison, I would never have believed it; I'd have laughed in his face. But that isn't the worst. Tío Eusebio and his boys have sworn to kill me. They will never believe that I am innocent; they know I murdered Faustino. They are as sure of it as I am that my mother lies under the ground!

RAIMUNDA. Because nobody knows who did it. Nobody can find out anything. Don't you see? They will never rest at that. Do you suspect anyone?

NORBERT. I more than suspect.

RAIMUNDA. Then why didn't you say so? You were in court. You had the opportunity.

NORBERT. If I hadn't cleared myself I would have told. But what was the use? I am a dead man now if I speak. They will do the same thing to me.

RAIMUNDA. Eh? Will they? What do you mean? Was it revenge? But who did it? Tell me what you think. I must know, because Tío Eusebio and Esteban have always had the same friends; they have always stood together, for better or for worse, whichever it was. Their enemies would naturally be the same. No, I can get no rest. This vengeance was intended for us just as much as it was for Tío Eusebio; it was to prevent a closer union of our families. Maybe they won't stop at that, either. Someday they will do the same to my husband!

NORBERT. I wouldn't worry about Uncle Esteban.

RAIMUNDA. Why, what do you mean? Do you think? . . .

NORBERT. I don't think.

RAIMUNDA. Then tell me what you know. Somehow I believe you are not the only one who knows it. You think what the rest think—it must be the same—what everybody knows.

NORBERT. Well, they didn't get it out of me; that is one thing you can be sure of. Besides, how could they know? It's gossip, that's all—not worth that! Talk in the village! They will never get it out of me.

RAIMUNDA. Norbert, by the soul of your sainted mother in heaven, tell me what it is!

NORBERT. For God's sake, I can't talk! I was afraid to open my mouth in court. Now, if I say a word, I am a dead man. A dead man!

RAIMUNDA. But who would kill you?

NORBERT. Who killed Faustino?

RAIMUNDA. But who did kill Faustino? Someone was paid to do it, is that it? Rubio said something in the wine-shop this morning.

NORBERT. Who told you?

RAIMUNDA. Esteban went in and dragged him out; it was the only way he could stop him.

NORBERT. He didn't want to be compromised.

RAIMUNDA. What is that? He didn't want to be compromised? Was Rubio saying that he . . .

NORBERT. That he was the real master of this house.

RAIMUNDA. The master of this house? Because it was Rubio . . .

NORBERT. Rubio.

RAIMUNDA. Who killed Faustino?

NORBERT. Sí, señora.

RAIMUNDA. Rubio! I knew it all the time. But does anybody else know? That is the question. Do they know it in the village?

NORBERT. He gives himself away; he has money—bills, banknotes—wherever he goes. He turned on them this morning while they were singing that song. That was why they had to call Uncle Esteban, and he kicked him out of the wine-shop.

RAIMUNDA. That song? Oh, yes! That song—I remember. It goes . . . How does it go?

NORBERT.
"Who loves the maid that dwells by
[the Mill
Shall love in evil hour;
Because she loves with the love that
[she loves,
Call her the Passion Flower."

RAIMUNDA. We are the ones who dwell by the Mill; that is what they call us. It is here—our house. And the maid that dwells by the Mill must be Acacia, my daughter. This song that everybody sings . . . They call her the Passion Flower? That is it, isn't it? But who loves her in an evil way? How could anybody love her? You loved her, Faustino loved her; but who else ever loved her? Why do they call her the Passion Flower? Look me in the eye! Why did you give her up if you really loved her? Why? I want you to tell me; you have got to tell me. You cannot tell me anything worse than what I already know.

NORBERT. Do you want them to kill me? To ruin all of us? I have never said one word—not even when they had me in prison would I say one word! I don't know how it got out—Rubio told, or my father. He is the only one who ever had it from me. He wanted to put the law on them, but I said no. They would have killed him; they would have killed me!

RAIMUNDA. Stop! Don't you talk! I see it now. I see it all. The Passion Flower! La Malquerida! Come here to me! Tell me everything. Before they kill you, by God, they will have to kill me! It cannot go on like this. Somebody must pay for it. Tío Eusebio and his boys will never rest till they have justice. If they can't get it in any other way, they will take it out of you—revenge! You can't escape. Faustino was murdered so as to prevent him from marrying Acacia. You left her for the same reason—for fear that they would kill you. Was that it? Tell me the truth!

NORBERT. They told me to leave her because she was promised to Faustino; she had been for a long time. They said they had an understanding with Tío

Eusebio, and if I didn't make the best of it, then I could take the worst of it. But if I ever opened my mouth . . .

RAIMUNDA. They would kill you? Was that it? But you . . .

NORBERT. I believed it—I was afraid— I didn't know what to do. Then I began to run after another girl, who was nothing to me, so as to break off with Acacia. Afterward, when I found out that not a word of it was true, that neither Tío Eusebio nor Faustino had ever spoken to Uncle Esteban. . . . Then, when they killed Faustino I knew why they killed him. It was because he dared lay eyes on Acacia. There was nothing they could tell him. They couldn't scare him off. Tío Eusebio wasn't a man to stand by and see his son refused. They couldn't refuse, so they agreed to it, and went through with it until the end came, and they killed him. They killed him because I was here to take the blame. Who else could have done it? Of course it was I! I loved Acacia—I was jealous. That was the plot. Praise God, some saint surely watched over me that day! But now the crime has come home to him. It lies like lead on his conscience. He betrays himself . . .

RAIMUNDA. Is it possible that such a thing could be? I must have been blind not to see. What veil hung over my eyes? Why, it is all as clear as day! How could I have been so blind?

NORBERT. What are you doing?

RAIMUNDA. I don't know—I don't know where I am—something so awful, so vast is passing through my mind that it seems as if it were nothing. I can only remember one thing of all that you have told me—that song—La Malquerida! The Passion Flower! I want you to teach me the music. We can sing it together, and dance—dance and drop dead!—Acacia! Acacia! Acacia!

NORBERT. No, don't you call her! Don't take it like this! It wasn't her fault! (Acacia enters.)

ACACIA. Did you call, mother?— Norbert!

RAIMUNDA. Come here! Look at me— straight in the eye.

ACACIA. What is the matter with you, mother?

RAIMUNDA. No, it was not your fault.

ACACIA. But what have they been doing? What did you tell her?

RAIMUNDA. What every one else knows already—*La Malquerida!* The Passion Flower! Your honor is a scorn and a byword. It is bandied about in men's mouths!

ACACIA. My honor? Never! No one can say that.

RAIMUNDA. Don't you deny it! Tell me what you know. Why was it that you never called him father? Why was it?

ACACIA. Because a child has only one father, you know that. This man could never be my father. I hated, I despised him from the day that he entered this house, and brought hell along after him!

RAIMUNDA. Well, you are going to call him now, and you are going to call him what I tell you; you are going to call him father. Do you hear? Your father! I tell you to call your father.

ACACIA. Do you want me to go to the cemetery and call him? If that isn't what you want, I have no father. This man— this man is your husband; you love him, but all that he is to me is this man! This man! That is all he can ever be! Leave me alone if you know what is good for you— you think you are so smart. Let the law take its course. I don't care. If he has sinned, he can pay for it.

RAIMUNDA. Do you mean for Faustino's murder? Yes—go on! Go on! What else? Out with it!

ACACIA. No, mother, no! For if I had consented, Faustino would never have been murdered! Do you think I don't know how to guard my honor?

RAIMUNDA. Then what have you been so silent about? Why didn't you come to me?

ACACIA. Would you have taken my word against this man, when you were mad for him? And you must have been mad not to see! He would eat me up with his eyes while you sat there; he followed me around the house like a cat. What more do you want? I hated him so, I had such a horror of him that I prayed to God that he would make himself even more of a beast than he was, so that it would open your eyes, if anything could have opened

your eyes, and let you see what manner of man he was who had robbed me of your love, for you have loved him, you have loved him so much—more than you ever loved my father!

RAIMUNDA. No! That isn't true!

ACACIA. I wanted you to hate him as I hate him, as my father in heaven hates him! I have heard his voice from the skies.

RAIMUNDA. Silence! For shame! Come here to your mother. You are all that I have left in the world. And thank God that I can still protect you!

(Bernabé enters.)

BERNABÉ. Señora! Señora!

RAIMUNDA. What brings you running in such a hurry? No good, we may be sure.

BERNABÉ. Don't let Norbert leave the house! Don't let him out of your sight!

RAIMUNDA. How?

BERNABÉ. Tío Eusebio's boys are waiting outside with their men to kill him.

NORBERT. What did I tell you? You wouldn't believe it. They are here—they want to kill me! And they will kill me. Yes, they will!

RAIMUNDA. Not unless they kill us all first! Somebody has sent for them.

BERNABÉ. Yes, Rubio. I saw him running along the river bank where Tío Eusebio's boys were at work.

NORBERT. Didn't I tell you? They want to kill me, so as to save themselves. Then nothing will ever come out. Tío Eusebio's boys will think they have the man who murdered their brother. They will kill me, Aunt Raimunda! Yes, they will! They are too many for one; I can't defend myself. I haven't even a knife. I don't dare to carry a gun—I might kill someone. I'd rather die than be locked up in that cell again. Save me, Aunt Raimunda! I don't want to die. It wasn't my fault! They hunt me like a wolf.

RAIMUNDA. Don't be afraid. If they kill you, it will be over my dead body. Go in there with Bernabé and take that gun, do you hear? They won't dare to come in. If they do, shoot to kill! When I call, shoot—no matter who it may be! Do you understand? No matter who it may be! Don't shut the door. *(To Acacia)* You stand here by me. Esteban! Esteban! Esteban!

ACACIA. What are you going to do? (*Esteban enters.*)

ESTEBAN. Did you call?

RAIMUNDA. Yes, I want to speak to you. Norbert is here in our house. Tío Eusebio's boys are waiting outside. You sent for them to kill him—because you are not man enough to do it yourself.

ESTEBAN (*making a movement to draw a weapon*). Raimunda!

ACACIA. Mother!

RAIMUNDA. No, don't you do it! Call Rubio and let him make an end of us all! He will have to make an end of us all to cover your guilt. Murderer! Assassin!

ESTEBAN. You are crazy!

RAIMUNDA. I was crazy! I was crazy the day that you first entered this house—my house—like a thief, to rob me of all I held dear!

ESTEBAN. What are you talking about?

RAIMUNDA. I am not talking; other people are talking. Soon the law will speak. If you don't want that, do as I tell you, or I will cry out—I will rouse the house. You brought them here—take them away again, you cowards that lie in wait for innocent men, to stab them in the back! Norbert leaves this house, but he leaves with me. If they kill him, they kill me. I am here to protect him, and I will protect my daughter—I, alone, against you, against all the assassins you can hire! Go! Here come my people . . . Don't you touch me! Hide yourself in the uttermost recesses of those mountains, in caves where the wild beasts dwell. Now I know! You have nothing to hope for from me. Oh, I was alone with my child!—and you came. You knew that she was my child; there she stands—*La Malquerida!* The Passion Flower! Well! I am still here to guard her from you, to tell you that her father still lives in heaven —and to shoot you through the heart if you make one step to lay your hand on her!

ACT THREE

The scene is the same as in the Second Act. Raimunda stands at the door, peering anxiously out over the countryside. After a moment Juliana enters.

JULIANA. Raimunda!

RAIMUNDA. What do you want? Is he worse?

JULIANA. No, don't be nervous.

RAIMUNDA. How is he? Why did you leave him?

JULIANA. He's asleep. Acacia is with him; she can hear if he calls. You are the one I am worried about. Thank God, he's not dead. Do you expect to go all day without eating?

RAIMUNDA. Let me alone; don't bother me.

JULIANA. What are you doing out here? Come on in and sit with us.

RAIMUNDA. I was looking for Bernabé.

JULIANA. He can't be back so soon if he brings the men to take Norbert away. If the constables come with him . . .

RAIMUNDA. Constables? Constables in this house? Ah, Juliana, surely a curse has fallen upon us all!

JULIANA. Come on in, and don't be looking out of the door all the time. It's not Bernabé that you are looking for; it's the other one—it's your husband. When all is said and done, he is your husband.

RAIMUNDA. Yes, the habits of a lifetime cannot be changed in one day. Although I know what I know, and that it must always be so, although if I saw him coming it would be to curse him, although I must loathe him for the rest of my life, yet here I stand looking out of the door and scanning every rock and cranny upon those mountains only for a sight of him! It seems to me as if I were waiting for him as I used to do, to see him come happy and smiling, and then turn and walk into the house with him arm in arm like two lovers, and sit down here at the table to eat, and go over everything that we had done during the day. Sometimes we would laugh, sometimes we would argue, but always it was so dear, as if we had been fonder of each other than any one else who had ever lived in the world. Now it is all over; nothing remains. The peace of God has fled forever from this house!

JULIANA. You cannot believe what you see with your eyes. If you hadn't told me yourself, if I didn't know how you felt, how you were, I would never have believed it. Faustino is dead, God help him; we can leave it. There might be more of the sort, too, for all I care; but this devil that has gotten into him with Acacia, it doesn't seem possible, I can't believe it—although I must believe it. There is no other explanation of the mystery.

RAIMUNDA. Did you ever notice anything?

JULIANA. Nothing. When he first came to the house, it was to make love to you, and I needn't tell you how I felt. I was fond of your first husband; there never was a better nor juster man in the world, so I looked on him with disfavor. God have mercy on me, but if I had seen anything, what reason would I have had for keeping quiet? Of course, when you come to think, he gave her presents—and there were a good many of them, too—but we never thought anything of that. She was so haughty with him. They never had one good talk together from the day you were married. She was only a runt then anyway. She insulted him out of pure spite. Nobody could do anything with her. If you struck her, it made no difference. I'll say this while I am about it: if she had been nice to him when she was little, he might have looked on her as his own daughter. Then we would never have been where we are now.

RAIMUNDA. Are you trying to excuse him?

JULIANA. Excuse him? There can be no excuse for such a thing. It was enough that she was your daughter. What I say is that the girl was like a stranger to him from the beginning, although she was your own child. If she had treated him like a father, as she ought—it would have been different; he isn't a bad man. A bad man is bad through and through. When you were first married, I've seem him sit by himself and cry at the way the girl ran from him, as if he had had the plague.

RAIMUNDA. You are right. The only trouble we ever had was with the child.

JULIANA. After she was grown there wasn't a girl in the village that was her equal for looks. Nobody knows that better than you do. But she shrank from him as if he had been the devil. There she was all

the time—right before his eyes! No wonder if he had an evil thought; none of us are above them.

RAIMUNDA. I don't say he might not have had an evil thought, although he ought never to have had such a thought. But you put an evil thought out of your mind unless you are evil. He must have had more than an evil thought to do what he did, to murder a man in cold blood to prevent my daughter from marrying and going away—away from him; his mind must have been evil, like the criminal's, waiting to break out, with all the evil of the world in his heart. I am more anxious than anybody to believe that it is not so bad, but the more I think, the more I see that there can be no excuse for it. When I remember what has been hanging over my daughter all these years, that any moment—because a man who will do murder will do anything. If he had ever laid hands on her I would have killed them both, as sure as my name is Raimunda—him, because he had been guilty of such a crime, and her because she did not let him kill her before she would consent to it.

(Bernabé enters.)

JULIANA. Here comes Bernabé.

RAIMUNDA. Are you alone?

BERNABÉ. Yes, they are deciding in the village what is best to be done. I was afraid to stay any longer.

RAIMUNDA. You were right. This is not life. What do they say now?

BERNABÉ. Do you want to go mad? Forget it. Pay no attention to what they say.

RAIMUNDA. Are they coming to take Norbert away?

BERNABÉ. His father will tend to that. The doctor won't let them put him in the cart for fear it will make him worse. He'll have to be carried on a stretcher. The judge and the prosecutor are coming to take his story, so they don't want a relapse. He was unconscious yesterday and couldn't testify. Everybody has his own idea; no two agree. Not a soul went to the fields today. The men stand around the streets in groups; the women talk in the houses and run to and fro. Nobody stops to eat. Not a meal has been served today, dinner or supper either, on the hour.

RAIMUNDA. Didn't you tell them that Norbert's wounds aren't serious?

BERNABÉ. What difference does that make? Now they can't do anything. Yesterday, when they thought Tío Eusebio's boys had fallen on him with the master, and he was going to die, the thing was simple; but today they hear he is better. How do they know but that he will soon be well again? Even Norbert's best friends say that it's a great pity that the wound wasn't serious. If he was wounded at all, it might better have been serious. Then Tío Eusebio's boys could have been made to pay for it, and they would have had their revenge, but now, if he gets well, the law will get into it, and then nobody will be satisfied.

JULIANA. They are so fond of Norbert, are they, that they wish he was dead? The idiots!

BERNABÉ. That is the way they are. I told them they could thank you for it, because you were the one who called the master, and the master threw himself between them and knocked up their guns, so they couldn't kill him.

RAIMUNDA. Did you tell them that?

BERNABÉ. Every mother's son that asked me. I said the first because it was true, and I said the rest—because you don't know what they are saying in the village, nor how they feel about what is going on in this house.

RAIMUNDA. No! I don't want to hear! Where is the master? Have you seen him? Do you know where he is?

BERNABÉ. He and Rubio were up at Los Berrocales this morning with the goatherds from Encinar. They spent the night in a hut on the uplands. I don't like this going away. It's not right, if I know what is good for him. It looks as if he was afraid. This is no time to have people think what isn't so. Norbert's father talks too much. This morning he tried to persuade Tío Eusebio that his sons had no cause to shoot his boy.

RAIMUNDA. Is Tío Eusebio in the village?

BERNABÉ. He came with his boys. They arrested them this morning, tied them together by the elbows, and brought them over from Encinar. Their father followed on foot and brought the little fellow with him, holding his hand all the way. They cried with every step that they took. There wasn't a man in the village but cried, too, when he saw them, even the strongest, no matter if he had never cried before.

RAIMUNDA. And his mother is alone at home, and here I am! What do you men know?

(Acacia enters.)

ACACIA. Mother——

RAIMUNDA. Well? What is it?

ACACIA. Norbert wants you. He is awake now. He wants some water. He is thirsty; I was afraid to give him any for fear it wasn't right.

RAIMUNDA. The doctor says he can have all the orange-juice he can drink. Here's the jar. Does he suffer much?

ACACIA. No, not now.

RAIMUNDA (to Bernabé). Did you get the things for the doctor?

BERNABÉ. Yes, they're in the saddle-bags. I'll bring them in. (Goes out)

ACACIA. He is calling, mother. Do you hear?

RAIMUNDA. Coming, Norbert, my boy. (Goes out)

ACACIA. Has that man come back?

JULIANA. No. He took his gun and rushed out like one mad as soon as it was over. Rubio ran after him.

ACACIA. Have they caught him?

JULIANA. You'll hear soon enough when they do. They'll have to bring charges against him first.

ACACIA. But doesn't everybody know? They heard what my mother said.

JULIANA. No, nobody heard except me and Bernabé, and he won't tell what isn't good for him; he is honest and loyal to this house. They heard your mother shout, that was all. They thought it was because Norbert was here, and Tío Eusebio's boys were waiting outside to kill him. Nobody will say a word when the judge comes unless your mother tells us to open our mouths.

ACACIA. Do you mean that my mother isn't going to let you tell the truth? Won't she tell what she knows?

JULIANA. Is that what you want? So you want to disgrace this house, do you, and yourself? Then every man will think what he likes; some will believe that you are innocent, and some will never believe it. A woman's honor is not a thing to be bandied about in men's mouths, not when it is none of their business.

ACACIA. My honor? I can take care of my honor. Let the others do the same. Now I shan't marry. I am glad it happened, because I shall never marry. I only agreed to it to get rid of him.

JULIANA. Acacia, I don't want to hear you—not another word. Surely the devil must be in you!

ACACIA. Yes, he is, and he has always been, since I first learned to hate that man!

JULIANA. Yes, and who is to say that wasn't where the trouble began? You had no cause to hate him. Mind you, nobody blamed your mother more than I did when she married again; but all the same, I saw what a devil you were to this man when you were a little child, and how much it meant to him—which you were too young to know.

ACACIA. How much did it mean to me to see my mother always hanging around his neck? Do you suppose I liked it, sitting here and seeing her love him? I was always in the way.

JULIANA. You have no right to talk like that. You were always first with your mother, and you might have been with him.

ACACIA. Might have been? Never! Because I was, and I am.

JULIANA. But not like you mean, though you seem proud of it; in the way you should have been. He never would have loved you as he did if you had loved him as a daughter.

ACACIA. How could I love him? Didn't he turn me even against my own mother?

JULIANA. What do you mean? Turn you against your own mother?

ACACIA. Yes. Do you suppose I can love her now as I ought, as I should have loved her if that man had never entered this house? I remember once when I was a little girl, I spent all one night with a knife under my pillow, and I lay awake all night. The only thought that I had in my mind that night was to kill him.

JULIANA. Jesús, my child! What is that? Suppose you had? Suppose you had gotten up, and had dared, and had killed him?

ACACIA. I don't know who I might have killed next.

JULIANA. Holy Virgin! Jesús! Not another word. Don't you talk! You are beyond the pale of God's mercy. Do you know what I think? It was all your fault.

ACACIA. All my fault?

JULIANA. Yes, yours! It was your fault! And I'll go further: if you hated him as much as you say you do, then he would have been the only one you would have hated—yes, the only one! Jesús! It's a good thing that your mother doesn't know!

ACACIA. Know what?

JULIANA. That he wasn't the one you were jealous of. It was her! You were in love with him and you didn't know it.

ACACIA. In love with him?

JULIANA. Yes, hate turned to love. Nobody can hate like that. A hate like that always grows out of a great love.

ACACIA. Do you mean to say that I was in love with that man? Do you know what you are telling me?

JULIANA. I am not telling you anything.

ACACIA. No. What you will do now is run and tell my mother.

JULIANA. Is that what you are afraid of? I thought so. Now you are the one who is telling. You needn't worry, though. I'll not tell. She has enough on her mind, poor soul. God help us!

(Bernabé enters.)

BERNABÉ. Here comes the master!

JULIANA. Did you see him?

BERNABÉ. Yes. You wouldn't know him. He looks as if he had stepped from the grave.

ACACIA. Let me out!

JULIANA. Yes, let us all out—and shut your mouth, do you hear? What is done is done. Your mother must never know.

(The women go out)

(Esteban and Rubio enter, their guns over their shoulders.)

BERNABÉ. Can—can I do anything?

ESTEBAN. Nothing, Bernabé.

BERNABÉ. I'll tell the mistress.

ESTEBAN. No, don't tell her; they'll find us.

RUBIO. How about his wounds, eh?

BERNABÉ. Better. The doctor sent for these things. I'll take them in—unless you need me. *(Goes out)*

ESTEBAN. Here I am. What do you want me to do?

RUBIO. What do I want you to do? This is your house; you belong here. A man's house is his castle. Running away, being afraid to face it, is to confess. It will ruin us both.

ESTEBAN. Here I am; you have had your way. Now this woman will come and accuse me and raise the house. The judge will be here, and he will bring Tío Eusebio. What then?

RUBIO. Why didn't you let Tío Eusebio's boys handle it themselves? They would have finished it. Now he is only wounded. He will squeal, and so will his father; so will all the women. They are the ones I am afraid of. They will talk. Nobody can prove who shot Faustino. You were with his father; nobody saw me. I have a good pair of legs. I was with some friends two leagues away a few minutes before, and I set the clock ahead. When I left the house I took good care to have them notice it.

ESTEBAN. Yes, we would have been safe if that had been all. But you talked; you gave yourself away.

RUBIO. You ought to have killed me. That was the first time in my life that I ever was afraid. I never expected they would let Norbert go. I told you that we ought to go into court and have Acacia testify that Norbert had sworn he was going to kill Faustino, but you wouldn't listen. Do you mean to tell me that you couldn't have made her do it? We could have got others, too, to say the same. Then it would have been easy; they would never have let him go. I know I made a fool of myself, but when I saw that Norbert was free, that the law—yes, and Tío Eusebio—would never stop there, that they would look somewhere else, then I was afraid for the first time. I wanted to forget. So I began to drink, which I never do, and I talked. You ought to have killed me then; you had grounds for it. They

were talking already in the village; that was what scared me. When I heard that song—it put the blame here. Norbert and his father suspect. After what happened before, they have their eyes open. That is the talk that has got to be stopped, no matter what comes of it. That is the danger—the crime will be known by the cause. Nothing else counts. So long as nobody knows why he was killed, nobody will ever find out who killed him either.

ESTEBAN. But why? Why was he killed? What was the use of killing anybody?

RUBIO. I don't know. Don't ask me. Weren't you talking all the time? "If another man gets her, look out! Something happens." Then you told me she was going to be married. "I can't scare this one off; it's all over, he will take her away. I can't think . . ." Didn't you come to me in the morning early again and again, before it was light, and wake me up and say: "Get up, Rubio; I haven't closed my eyes all night. I must get out. To the fields! I must walk!" And then we'd take our guns and go out and walk for hours, side by side, without speaking a word. At last, when the fit has passed, and we'd put a few shots in the air so that nobody could say that we did no hunting when we went out to hunt, I'd tell you that we scared away the game; but you said we frightened evil thoughts: and down we'd sit on some hummock and then you would burst out laughing like one mad, as if some weight had been lifted from your soul, and you'd catch me around the neck and talk, and talk, and talk—you didn't know how you talked, nor what you said, nor why, nor whether it had any sense at all; but it always came to the same thing: "I am mad, crazy, a wild man! I cannot live like this. I want to die. I don't know what devil has gotten into me. This is torment, hell!" And then you'd shuffle the words again, over and over, but it was always the same, you were dying—death! And you talked death so long that one day death heard—and he came. And you know it.

ESTEBAN. Stop! Why do you have to talk?

RUBIO. Take care, master! Don't you touch me! I know what was in your mind when we were coming down the mountain. Make no mistake. You lagged behind. Another minute and your gun would have been at your shoulder. But don't you do it, master, don't you try! We'll stick together. I know how you feel; you're sick. You never want to see me again. If that would help, I'd get out. What did I care, anyway? It was nothing to me. Whatever I got you gave me afterward. It was your idea. I never asked. I don't need money. I don't drink, I don't smoke. All I want is to rove over the mountains, to do what I like, to be free. I want to be my own master. You trusted me, and I was proud of it. I know how you feel. We are like brothers. I'll take the blame. You needn't worry. They can grind me to powder but I'll never say a word. I'll tell them I did it—it was I—because—it's none of their business—just because. I don't care what they give me: they can make it ten years, fifteen. What's the difference? Then you fix it; you have influence. Only don't let them make it too much. Get busy; cut it down. Others have done the same. In four or five years everything will have blown over. Only I don't want you to forget. When I come out we will be brothers, the same as before. We can work together; we can do what we please. Only I mean to be my own master, to have power, to feel power in my hands! Nobody can stand alone. We'll be brothers. Hush! Someone is coming—the mistress!

(*Raimunda enters, carrying a water jar. She sees Esteban and Rubio and stops short, dazed. After hesitating for a moment she proceeds to fill the jar from a pitcher.*)

RUBIO. Señora!

RAIMUNDA. Get out of my house! Don't you come near me! What are you doing here? I never want to see you again.

RUBIO. Oh! You are going to see me again—and hear me.

RAIMUNDA. What do you mean? This is my house.

RUBIO. Just a word. Soon we will all be in court. We had better fix it beforehand. Because a few fools open their mouths is no reason why a good man should go to prison.

RAIMUNDA. More than one will go. You don't expect to get out of it?

RUBIO. I don't know. Only one will go, but that one will be I.

RAIMUNDA. It will?

RUBIO. But when I shut my mouth I don't want other people to talk. Take it from me: what you think is not so. Norbert and his father are back of these lies; they are the ones who do all the lying. They made up that song, too. It's a lie, and they know it.

RAIMUNDA. Is that so? You have agreed then on your story? Well, I don't believe one word of it. Gossip and songs are nothing to me. I believe nothing but the truth, the truth that I know—and I know it so well that I have known it all along. I guessed it from the beginning. I might have thought—but no, I never thought anything of you. He, he might have confessed; it would have been only fair. He might have known that I would hold my tongue, not for him, but for this house—which was my father's house—for my daughter, for my own sake. But why should I keep still when everybody knows it, and the very stones shout? They sing it from the housetops.

RUBIO. So long as you keep still, the rest can sing all they want to.

RAIMUNDA. Keep still? To save you? I could scream at the very sight of you! I could raise the village!

RUBIO. Don't be a fool! What's the use?

RAIMUNDA. Of course you weren't a fool when you murdered a man. And you nearly murdered another—in this house—or had him murdered.

RUBIO. I wouldn't have been a fool if I had.

RAIMUNDA. You are a coward! You are a murderer!

RUBIO. Your wife is speaking to you, master.

ESTEBAN. Rubio!

RUBIO. You see he can hear.

RAIMUNDA. Yes, hang your head before this man. What a humiliation! You are his slave for the rest of your life. Could any fate be more horrible? Now this house has a master. Thank God, he cannot be less jealous of its honor than you!

ESTEBAN. Raimunda!

RAIMUNDA. When I talk, you interrupt. You are not afraid of me.

ESTEBAN. If I had been man enough, I would have put a bullet through my head, and have been done with it.

RUBIO. Oh, master!

ESTEBAN. No! Stop there! That's all I'll take from you. Get out! What are you waiting for? Do you want me to beg you on my knees?

RAIMUNDA. Oh!

RUBIO. No, master. I am going. (To Raimunda) If it hadn't been for me, there wouldn't have been any murder, but you might have lost a child. Now, you have another. The blood made him faint; a bad turn, that was all. But he's better. I am a good doctor. Sometime you can thank me for it. Don't forget. I'll show you how. (Goes out)

ESTEBAN. Don't cry any more. I can't bear to see you cry. I am not worth all these tears. I ought never to have come back; I ought to have starved amid the brambles and thickets—they should have hunted me down like a wolf. I would not have raised my hand. Don't reproach me! Over and over again I have said to myself more than you can say. I have called myself murderer, assassin, times without number. Let me go. This is no longer my home. Turn me out! I am only waiting for them to take me. I don't go out on the road and give myself up, because I am too weak; my heart sinks; I am at the end of my tether. If you don't want me, tell me to go, and I will creep onto the highway and throw myself down in the fields, like carrion which you cast from your door.

RAIMUNDA. Yes, give yourself up! Bring shame and ruin on this house, drag my daughter's honor in the dust and mire of the village! I should have been the law to you; you ought to have thought of me. Do you suppose that I believe in these tears because this is the first time I ever saw you cry? Better you had cried your eyes out the day that wicked thought first entered your mind, rather than have turned them where you had no right. Now you cry—but what am I to do? Look at me. Nobody knows what I have been through. It could not be worse. I

want to forget, but I must think—think how I can hide the shame which has fallen on this house, keep it out of men's sight, prevent a man from being dragged from this house to prison—a man I brought into it to be a father to my child! This was my father's house; here my brothers lived with the fear of God in their hearts, and from it they went to serve their king, or to marry, or to till other fields by their labor. When they re-entered these doors it was with the same honor with which they went forth. Don't cry; don't hang your head. Hold it high, as I do. In a few minutes the officers will be here to trap us all. Though the house burn, and they are in it, they shall not smell the smoke. Dry your eyes; you have wept blood. Take a sip of water—I wish it was poison. Don't drink so fast; you are overheated. The thorns have torn your skin. You deserved knives. Let me wash you off; it makes my blood creep to look at you.

ESTEBAN. Raimunda! Wife! Pity me! You don't know. Don't talk to me. No, I am the one who must talk—I must confess as I shall confess at the hour of my doom! You don't know how I have struggled. I have wrestled all these years as with another man who was stronger than I, night and day, who was dragging me where I did not want to go.

RAIMUNDA. But when—when did that evil thought first enter your mind? When was that unhappy hour?

ESTEBAN. I don't know. It came upon me like a blight, all at once; it was there. All of us think some evil in our lives, but the thought passes away, it does no harm; it is gone. When I was a boy, one day my father beat me. Quick as a flash it came to me: "I wish he was dead!" But no sooner thought, than I was ashamed—I was ashamed to think that I had ever had such a thought. My heart stood still within me for fear that God had heard, that he would take him away. From that day I loved him more, and when he died, years afterward, I grieved as much for that thought as I did for his death, although I was a grown man. And this might have been the same; but this did not go away. It became more fixed the more I struggled to shake it off. You can't say that I did not love you. I loved you more every day! You can't say that I cast my eyes on other women—and I had no thought of her. But when I felt her by me my blood took fire. When we sat down to eat, I was afraid to look up. Wherever I turned she was there, before me—always! At night, when we were in bed, and I was lying close by you in the midnight silence of the house, all I could feel was her. I could hear her breathe as if her lips had been at my ear. I wept for spite, for bitterness! I prayed to God, I scourged myself. I could have killed myself—and her! Words cannot tell the horror I went through. The few times that we were alone, I ran from her like a wild man. If I had stayed I don't know what might have happened: I might have kissed her, I might have dug my knife into her!

RAIMUNDA. Yes, you were mad—and you did not know it. It could only have ended in death. Why didn't we find some man for her? She could have married. You ought not to have kept her from Norbert.

ESTEBAN. It was not her marrying, it was her going away. I could not live without the feel of her; I craved her day and night. All her hate, her spite, her turning away—which she always did—cut me to the heart; then, I came to depend upon it. I could not live without it; it was part of my life. That is what it was—I didn't realize it myself, because it always seemed to me as if it could not be—such things could not really be. I was afraid to face it. But now, I have confessed it to you. It is true! It is true! I can never forgive myself, not even though you might forgive me.

RAIMUNDA. The evil cannot be cured by forgiveness; if I should forgive you, it will not take the evil away. When I first heard of it, it seemed to me that no punishment could be too severe. Now, I don't know. To do what you did, you must have been all evil. But you were always kind and good, in season and out, to my daughter, when she was a child, when she was grown—and to me. I have seen it with my own eyes. You were good to all the servants from the day that you entered this house, to the men, to

everybody who came near. You have been faithful and loyal, and worked hard for the honor of this house. A man cannot be good so long and become all bad in one day. Yet these things are; I know it. It chills my heart. When my mother was alive—God rest her soul!—we always laughed because she used to say that many a deed had been foretold in this world that afterward took place exactly as it had been foretold. We never believed it, but now I know it is true. The dead do not leave us when they die, though we lay them in the ground. They walk by the side of those that they loved in this life, of those that they hated with a hate that was stronger than death. They are with us, day and night. We do not see them, but they whisper in our ears. They put thoughts into our minds which are evil and wicked and strange, which we never can believe could be part of ourselves.

ESTEBAN. Do you mean? . . .

RAIMUNDA. Vengeance! This is vengeance from the other world. My daughter's father will not forgive me in heaven; he will never accept a second father for his child. There are some things which we cannot explain in this life. A good man like you cannot, all of a sudden, cease to be good; for you were good . . .

ESTEBAN. I was—I was always. When you say it, you don't know what happiness, what boundless joy it is to me!

RAIMUNDA. Hush! Not so loud! I hear someone in the other part of the house. It is Norbert's father and his friends. They are going to take him away. If it had been the judge he would have come to this door. Stay here; I'll find out. Go in and wash; change your shirt. Don't let any one see you like this. You look . . .

ESTEBAN. Like a murderer, eh? Say it.

RAIMUNDA. No, no, Esteban! We mustn't dwell on these things. We must stop this talk; that is first. Then we can think. Acacia can go to the nuns for a few days at Encinar. They are fond of her; they always ask how she is. Then I can write to my sister-in-law, Eugenia; she likes her. She can go to Andrada and live with her. She might marry, who knows? There are fine boys there—the town is rich—and she is the best match in our village. Then she could come back and have her children, and we would be grandfather and grandmother, and grow old with them around us, and be happy once more in this house. If only . . .

ESTEBAN. What?

RAIMUNDA. If only . . .

ESTEBAN. The dead man.

RAIMUNDA. Yes. He will always be here, between us.

ESTEBAN. Always. The rest we can forget. *(Goes into the room. Acacia enters)*

RAIMUNDA. Acacia! Were you there?

ACACIA. Yes. Why not? Can't you see? Norbert's father is here with the men.

RAIMUNDA. What are they doing?

ACACIA. They seem more reasonable; they were surprised to find him better. Now they are waiting for the judge. He is down at Sotillo examining the men. He will come here as soon as he is done.

RAIMUNDA. I'll keep an eye on them.

ACACIA. I have something to say to you first, mother.

RAIMUNDA. You? Something to say? What is the matter with you? I am frightened. You never say anything.

ACACIA. I heard what you mean to do with me.

RAIMUNDA. You were listening at the keyhole, were you?

ACACIA. Yes, because it was my duty to hear. I had to know what you were doing with this man. It seems that I am the one who is in the way in this house. I have done nothing wrong, so I have to take the blame, while you stay here and enjoy yourself with your husband. You forgive him and turn me out, so that you can be alone together!

RAIMUNDA. What are you talking about? Who is turning you out? Who ever put that idea into your head?

ACACIA. I heard what you said. You want to send me to the convent at Encinar and shut me up, I suppose, for the rest of my life.

RAIMUNDA. How can you say such a thing? Didn't you tell me yourself that you wanted to go there and stay for a few days with the nuns? Didn't I refuse to let you go for fear that you would never come back, if you once saw the inside of the

cloister? How often have you begged me to let you go to your Aunt Eugenia? Now, when it would be a good thing for us all, for the good of the family, which is your family—I tell you that we must hold our heads high—now what do you want me to do? Do you expect me to give up my husband—the man it was your duty to love as a father?

ACACIA. You are as bad as Juliana. I suppose it was all my fault?

RAIMUNDA. I don't say that. But he never looked on you as a daughter because you were never a daughter to him.

ACACIA. I suppose I flaunted myself in his face? I suppose I made him kill Faustino?

RAIMUNDA. Not so loud! Somebody might hear!

ACACIA. Well, this time you won't find it so easy to have your way. You want to save this man and hush it up, but I am going to tell what I know to the judge, to everybody. I have only my honor to think of, not that of a man who hasn't any, who never had any—who is a criminal!

RAIMUNDA. Silence! Not so loud! It freezes my heart to hear you. You hate him—and I had almost forgiven him!

ACACIA. Yes, I do hate him. I always did hate him, and he knows it. If he doesn't want me to speak, to denounce him, let him kill me. I can die—that is what I can do—die. Let him kill me! then, perhaps, once for all, you might learn to hate him.

RAIMUNDA. Hush, I say!—Here he comes. *(Esteban enters)* Esteban!

ESTEBAN. She is right. She is not the one who ought to go. Only I don't want her to give me up. I will do it myself. I am strong now. I will go out on the road to meet them. Let me go, Raimunda. You have your child. You forgive me, but she never will. She hated me from the beginning.

RAIMUNDA. No, Esteban, don't you go! Esteban, my life!

ESTEBAN. No, let me go, or I will call Norbert's father. I will tell him . . .

RAIMUNDA *(to Acacia)*. Now you see what you have done. It was your fault. Esteban! Esteban!

ACACIA. Mother, don't let him go!

RAIMUNDA. Ah!

ESTEBAN. No, she wants to betray me. Why did you hate me like this? You never once called me father. You don't know how I loved you!

ACACIA. Mother, mother——

ESTEBAN. *La Malquerida!* The Passion Flower! I hang my head. But once—once how I could have loved you!

RAIMUNDA. For once, call him father.

ESTEBAN. She will never forgive me.

RAIMUNDA. But she must! Throw your arms about his neck. Call him father. Even the dead will forgive us then, and be happy in our happiness.

ESTEBAN. Daughter!

ACACIA. Esteban . . . My God! Esteban!

ESTEBAN. Ah!

RAIMUNDA. But you don't call him father. Has she fainted? Ah! Lip to lip, and you clutch her in your arms! Let go, let go! Now I see why you won't call him father. Now I see that it was your fault—and I curse you!

ACACIA. Yes, it was. Kill me! It is true, it is true! He is the only man I ever loved.

ESTEBAN. Ah!

RAIMUNDA. What do you say? What is that? I will kill you—yes, and be damned with it!

ESTEBAN. Stand back!

ACACIA. Save me!

ESTEBAN. Stand back, I say!

RAIMUNDA. Ah! Now I see! It is plain to me now. And it is just as well! What is one murder to me? We can all die. Here! Come, everybody! The murderer! I have the murderer! Take this wicked woman, for she is not my child!

ACACIA. Run! Get away!

ESTEBAN. Yes, together—to hell! For I am damned for love of you. Come! They can hunt us like wild beasts among the rocks. To love you and hold you, I will be as the wild beasts, that know neither father nor mother!

RAIMUNDA. Help! Help! Come quick! The murderer! The murderer!

(Rubio, Bernabé and Juliana appear simultaneously at different doors, followed by others from the village.)

ESTEBAN. Out of my way! Take care who crosses me!

RAIMUNDA. Stay where you are! The murderer!

ESTEBAN. Out of my way, I tell you!

RAIMUNDA. Over my dead body!

ESTEBAN. Yes—— *(Raising his gun he shoots Raimunda)*

RAIMUNDA. Ah!

JULIANA. God in heaven!—Raimunda!

RUBIO. What have you done?

A MAN. Kill him!

ESTEBAN. Yes, kill me! I don't defend myself.

BERNABÉ. No! Put the law on him!

JULIANA. It was this man, this wretched man!—Raimunda!—He has killed her—Raimunda! Don't you hear?

RAIMUNDA. Yes, Juliana. Don't let me die without confession. I am dying now. This blood . . . No matter—Acacia! Acacia!

JULIANA. Acacia!—Where is she?

ACACIA. Mother, mother!

RAIMUNDA. Ah! Then you are not crying for him? It consoles me.

ACACIA. No, mother! You are my mother!

JULIANA. She is dying! Quick—Raimunda!

ACACIA. Mother, mother!

RAIMUNDA. This man cannot harm you now. You are saved. Blessed be the blood that saves, the blood of our Lord Jesus Christ!

LEO TOLSTOY's

Redemption

(The Living Corpse)

First presented by Arthur Hopkins at the Plymouth Theatre, New York, on October 3, 1918, with the following cast:

ELIZAVETA PROTOSOVA (Lisa).... Maude Hanaford

SOPHIA KARENINA .... Zeffie Tilbury

IVAN MAKAROVICH .... Jacob Kingsbury

NASTASIA IVANOVNA.............. Helen Westley

PETRUSHKOV .... E. J. Ballantine

VOZNESENSKY................. Ernest Hopkinson

PETRUSHKIN..................... Arthur Clare

MISHA (1st act)................. Helen Gaskill

MISHA (2nd act) .... Louis Bartlett

ANNA PAVLOVA   .... Beatrice Moreland

SASHA..................... Margaret Fareleigh

AFREMOV .... John Reynolds

MASHA .... Mona Hungerford

ARTEMYEV .... Thomas Mitchell

A YOUNG LAWYER .... William J. McClure

A MAID...................... Ruza Wenclaw

A NURSE.................... Gladys Fairbanks

FEDOR VASILYEVICH PROTOSOV (FEDYA)
John Barrymore

VICTOR MICHAILOVICH KARENIN ... Manart Kippen

PRINCE SERGHEI ABRESKOV (PRINCE SERGIUS)
Russ Whytal

IVAN PETROVICH ALEXANDROV ... Hubert Druce

THE EXAMINING MAGISTRATE..... Charles Kennedy

HIS SECRETARY................ Eugene Lincoln

Staged by Arthur Hopkins

ACT ONE

SCENE ONE

The scene is the Protosovs' flat in Moscow. The scene represents a small dining room. Anna Pavlovna, a stout, gray-haired lady, tightly laced, is sitting alone at the tea-table on which is a samovar.

Enter Nurse carrying a tea-pot.

———

NURSE *(enters and goes toward the table at Center)*. Please, Madam, may I have some water?

ANNA PAVLOVNA *(sitting Right of the table)*. Certainly. How is the baby now?

NURSE. Oh, restless, fretting all the time. There's nothing worse than for a lady to nurse her child. She has her worries and the baby suffers for them. What sort of milk could she have, not sleeping all night, and crying and crying? *(Sasha enters and strolls toward the table at the Center.)*

ANNA PAVLOVNA. But I thought she was more calm now?

NURSE. Fine calm! It makes me sick to look at her. She's just been writing something and crying all the time.

SASHA *(to nurse)*. Lisa's looking for you. *(Sits in chair at the table.)*

NURSE. I'm going. *(She leaves)*

ANNA PAVLOVNA. Nurse says she's always crying. Why can't she try and calm herself a little?

SASHA. Well, really, Mother, you're amazing. How can you expect her to behave as if nothing had happened when she's just left her husband and taken her baby with her?

ANNA PAVLOVNA. Well, I don't exactly, but that's all over. If I approve of my daughter's having left her husband, if I'm ever glad, well, you may be quite sure he deserved it. She has no reason to be miserable—on the contrary, she ought to be delighted at being freed from such a wretch.

SASHA. Mother! Why do you go on like this? It's not the truth and you know it. He's not a wretch, he's wonderful. Yes, in spite of all his weakness.

ANNA PAVLOVNA. I suppose you'd like her to wait till he'd spent every kopek they had, and smile sweetly when he brought his gypsy mistresses home with him.

SASHA. He hasn't any mistresses.

ANNA PAVLOVNA. There you go again. Why, the man's simply bewitched you, but I can see through him, and he knows it. If I'd been Lisa, I'd left him a year ago.

SASHA. Oh, how easily you speak of these serious things.

ANNA PAVLOVNA. Not easily, not easily at all. Do you suppose it's agreeable for me to have my daughter admit her marriage a failure? But anything's better than for her to throw away her life in a lie. Thank God, she's made up her mind to finish with him for good.

SASHA. Maybe it won't be for good.

ANNA PAVLOVNA. It would be if only he'd give her a divorce.

SASHA. To what end?

ANNA PAVLOVNA. Because she's young and has the right to look for happiness.

SASHA. It's awful to listen to you. How could she love someone else?

ANNA PAVLOVNA. Why not? There are thousands better than your Fedya, and they'd be only too happy to marry Lisa.

SASHA. Oh, it's not nice of you. I feel, I can tell, you're thinking about Victor Karenin.

ANNA PAVLOVNA. Why not? He loved her for ten years, and she him, I believe.

SASHA. Yes, but she doesn't love him as a husband. They grew up together; they've just been friends.

ANNA PAVLOVNA. Ah, those friendships! How should you know what keeps them warm! If only they were both free! *(Enter a Maid.)* Well?

MAID. The porter's just come back with an answer to the note.

ANNA PAVLOVNA. What note?

MAID. The note Elizaveta Protosova sent to Victor Karenin.

ANNA PAVLOVNA. Well? What answer?

MAID. Victor Karenin told the porter he'd be here directly.

ANNA PAVLOVNA. Very well. *(The Maid goes out.)*

Why do you suppose she sent for him? Do you know?

SASHA. Maybe I do and maybe I don't.

ANNA PAVLOVNA. You're always so full of secrets.

SASHA. Ask Lisa, she'll tell you.

ANNA PAVLOVNA. Just as I thought! She sent for him at once.

SASHA. Yes, but maybe not for the reason you think.

ANNA PAVLOVNA. Then what for?

SASHA. Why, Mother, Lisa cares just about as much for Victor Karenin as she does for her old nurse.

ANNA PAVLOVNA. You'll see. She wants consolation, a special sort of consolation.

SASHA. Really, it shows you don't know Lisa at all to talk like this.

ANNA PAVLOVNA. You'll see.

SASHA. Yes, I shall see.

ANNA PAVLOVNA (alone to herself). And I am very glad. I'm very, very glad.

MAID (entering). Victor Karenin.

ANNA PAVLOVNA. Show him here and tell your mistress.

(The Maid shows in Karenin and exits.)

KARENIN (shaking hands with Anna Pavlovna). Elizaveta Andreyevna sent me a note to come at once. I should have been here tonight anyway. How is she? Well, I hope.

ANNA PAVLOVNA. Not very. The baby has been upset again. However, she'll be here in a minute. Will you have some tea?

KARENIN. No, thank you.

(He sits down.)

ANNA PAVLOVNA. Tell me, do you know that he and she——

KARENIN. Yes, I was here two days ago when she got this letter. Is she positive now about their separating?

ANNA PAVLOVNA. Oh, absolutely. It would be impossible to begin it all over again.

KARENIN. Yes. To cut into living things and then draw back the knife is terrible. But are you sure she knows her mind?

ANNA PAVLOVNA. I should think so. To come to this decision has caused her much pain. But now it's final, and he understands perfectly that his behavior

has made it impossible for him to come back on any terms.

KARENIN. Why?

ANNA PAVLOVNA. After breaking every oath he swore to decency, how could he come back? And so why shouldn't he give her her freedom?

KARENIN. What freedom is there for a woman still married?

ANNA PAVLOVNA. Divorce. He promised her a divorce and we shall insist upon it.

KARENIN. But your daughter was so in love with him?

ANNA PAVLOVNA. Her love has been tried out of existence. Remember she had everything to contend with: drunkenness, gambling, infidelity—what was there to go on loving in such a person?

KARENIN. Love can do anything.

ANNA PAVLOVNA. How can one love a rag torn by every wind? Their affairs were in dreadful shape; their estate mortgaged; no money anywhere. Finally his uncle sends them two thousand rubles to pay the interest on the estate. He takes it, disappears, leaves Lisa home and the baby sick—when suddenly she gets a note asking her to send him his linen.

KARENIN. I know.

(Enter Lisa at the Right. Karenin crosses to her.)

I'm sorry to have been a little detained.

(He shakes hands with Lisa.)

LISA. Oh, thank you so much for coming. I have a great favor to ask of you. Something I couldn't ask of anybody else.

KARENIN. I'll do everything I can.

(Lisa moves away a few steps down Right.)

LISA. You know all about this. (She sits down in a chair)

KARENIN. Yes, I know.

ANNA PAVLOVNA. Well, I think I'll leave you two young people to yourselves. (To Sasha) Come along, dear, you and I will be just in the way.

(Anna Pavlovna and Sasha go out.)

LISA. Fedya wrote to me saying it was all over between us. (She begins to cry) That hurt me so, bewildered me so, that—well, I agreed to separate. I wrote to him saying I was willing to give him up if he wanted me to.

KARENIN. And now you're sorry?

LISA (nodding). I feel I oughtn't to

have said yes. I can't. Anything is better than not to see him again. Victor dear, I want you to give him this letter and tell him what I've told you, and—and bring him back to me.

(She gives Victor a letter.)

KARENIN. I'll do what I can.

(He takes letter, turns away and sits down.)

LISA. Tell him I will forget everything if only he will come back. I thought of mailing this, only I know him: he'd have a good impulse, first thwarted by someone, someone who would finally make him act against himself. *(A pause)* Are you—are you surprised I asked you?

KARENIN. No. *(He hesitates)* But—well, candidly, yes. I am rather surprised.

LISA. But you are not angry?

KARENIN. You know I couldn't be angry with you.

LISA. I ask you because I know you're so fond of him.

KARENIN. Of him—and of you too. Thank you for trusting me. I'll do all I can.

LISA. I know you will. Now I'm going to tell you everything. I went today to Afremov's, to find out where he was. They told me he was living with the gypsies. Of course that's what I was afraid of. I know he'll be swept off his feet if he isn't stopped in time. So you'll go, won't you?

KARENIN. Where's the place?

LISA. It's that big tenement where the gypsy orchestra lives, on the left bank below the bridge. I went there myself. I went as far as the door, and was just going to send up the letter, but somehow I was afraid. I don't know why. And then I thought of you. Tell him, tell him I've forgotten everything and that I'm here waiting for him to come home. *(Crosses to Karenin—a little pause)* Do it out of love for him, Victor, and out of friendship for me.

KARENIN *(after another pause)*. I'll do all I can.

(He bows to her and goes out. Enter Sasha, going toward the table.)

SASHA. Has the letter gone? *(Lisa nods)* He had no objections to taking it himself? *(Lisa shakes head.)*

SASHA. Why did you ask him? I don't understand it.

LISA. Who else was there?

SASHA. But you know he's in love with you.

LISA. Oh, that's all past. *(Going over to the table)* Do you think Fedya will come back?

SASHA. I'm sure he will, but——

(Enter Anna Pavlovna.)

ANNA PAVLOVNA. Where's Victor Karenin?

LISA. Gone.

ANNA PAVLOVNA. Gone?

LISA. I've asked him to do something for me.

ANNA PAVLOVNA. What was it? Another secret?

LISA. No, not a secret. I simply asked him to take a letter to Fedya.

ANNA PAVLOVNA. To Fedor Protosov?

LISA. Oh, to Fedya, Fedya.

ANNA PAVLOVNA. Then it's not going to be over?

LISA. I can't let him leave me.

ANNA PAVLOVNA. Oh, so we shall commence all over again.

LISA. I'll do anything you like, but I can't give him up.

ANNA PAVLOVNA. You don't mean you want him to come back?

LISA. Yes, yes.

ANNA PAVLOVNA. Let that reptile into the house again!

LISA. Please don't talk like that. He's my husband.

ANNA PAVLOVNA. Was your husband.

LISA. No. He's still my husband.

ANNA PAVLOVNA. Spendthrift. Drunkard. Reprobate. And you'll not part from him!

LISA. Oh, Mother, why do you keep on hurting me! You seem to enjoy it.

ANNA PAVLOVNA. Hurt you, do I? Enjoy it, do I? Very well, then, if that's the case, I'd better go. *(A pause)* I see I'm in your way. You *want* me to go. Well, all I can say is I can't make you out. I suppose you're being "modern" and all that. But to me, it's just plain disgusting. First, you make up your mind to separate from your husband, and then you up and send for another man who's in love with you——

LISA. Mother, *he's* not.

ANNA PAVLOVNA. You know Karenin

proposed to you, and he's the man you pick out to bring back your husband. I suppose you do it just to make him jealous.

LISA. Oh, Mother, stop it. Leave me alone.

ANNA PAVLOVNA. That's right. Send off your mother. Open the door to that awful husband. Well, I can't stand by and see you do it. I'll go. I'm going. And God be with you and your extraordinary ways. *(She goes out with suppressed rage.)*

LISA *(sinking into a chair)*. That's the last straw.

SASHA. Oh, she'll come back. We'll make her understand. *(Going to the door and following after her mother)* Now, Mother darling, listen—listen—— *(She goes out after her)*

CURTAIN

SCENE TWO

A room at the gypsies', dark but beautifully lit. The actual room is scarcely seen, and although at first it appears squalid, there are flaring touches of Byzantine luxury. Gypsies are singing. Fedya is lying on the sofa, his eyes closed, coat off. An Officer sits at the table, on which there are bottles of champagne and glasses. Beside him sits a musician taking down the song.

———

AFREMOV *(standing)*. Asleep?

FEDYA *(on the couch, raising his hand warningly)*. Sh! Don't talk! Now let's have "No More at Evening".

GYPSY LEADER. Impossible, Fedor Protosov. Masha must have her solo first.

FEDYA. Afterwards. Now let's have "No More at Evening".

(The Gypsies sing.)

GYPSY WOMAN *(when they finish singing, turning to Musician who is sitting at the table at the Right, with his back to audience)*. Have you got it?

MUSICIAN. It's *impossible* to take it down correctly. They change the tune each *time*, and they seem to have a different scale, too. *(He calls a gypsy woman)* Is this it?

(He hums a bar or two.)

GYPSY WOMAN *(clapping her hands)*. Splendid! Wonderful! How can you do it?

FEDYA *(rising. Goes to the table back of the couch and pours out glass of wine)*. He'll never get it. And even if he did and shovelled it into an opera, he'd make it seem absolutely meaningless.

AFREMOV. Now we'll have "The Fatal Hour".

(The Gypsies sing quartette. During this song, Fedya is standing, keeping time with the wine glass from which he has drunk. When they finish he returns to the couch and falls into Masha's arms.)

FEDYA. God! That's it! That's it! That's wonderful. What lovely things that music says. And where does it all come from, what does it all mean? (Another pause) To think that men can touch eternity like that, and then—nothing— nothing at all.

MUSICIAN. Yes, it's very original. *(Taking notes)*

FEDYA. Original be damned. It's real.

MUSICIAN. It's all very simple, except the rhythm. That's very strange.

FEDYA. Oh, Masha, Masha! You turn my soul inside out.

(The Gypsies hum a song softly.)

MASHA *(sitting on couch with Fedya)*. Do I? But what was it I asked you for?

FEDYA. What? Oh, money. Voilà, mademoiselle.

(He takes money from his trousers pocket. Masha laughs, takes the money, counts it swiftly, and hides it in her dress.)

FEDYA. Look at this strange creature. When she sings she rushes me into the sky and all she asks for is money, little presents of money for throwing open the Gates of Paradise. You don't know yourself, at all, do you?

MASHA. What's the use of me wondering about myself? I know when I'm in love, and I know that I sing best when my love is singing.

FEDYA. Do you love me?

MASHA *(murmuring)*. I love you.

FEDYA. But I am a married man, and you belong to this gypsy troupe. They wouldn't let you leave it, and——

MASHA *(interrupting)*. The troupe's one thing, and my heart's another. I love those I love, and I hate those I hate.

FEDYA. Oh, you must be happy to be like that.

MASHA. I'm always happy when handsome gentlemen come and say nice things to me. *(The Gypsies stop singing)* *(A gypsy entering speaks to Fedya.)*

GYPSY. Someone asking for you.

FEDYA. Who?

GYPSY. Don't know. He's rich, though. Fur coat.

FEDYA. Fur coat? O my God, show him in.

AFREMOV. Who the devil wants to see you here?

FEDYA *(carelessly)*. God knows, I don't. *(He begins to hum a song)* *(Karenin comes in, looking around the room.)* *(Exclaiming)* Ha! Victor! You're the last man in the world I expected to break into this enchanting milieu. Take off your coat, and they'll sing for you.

KARENIN. Je voudrais vous parler sans témoins.

(Masha rises and joins the group at the Right).

FEDYA. Oh . . . What about?

KARENIN. Je viens de chez vous. Votre femme m'a chargé de cette lettre, et puis——

(Fedya takes the letter, opens it, reads. He frowns, then smiles affectionately at Karenin.)

FEDYA. You know what's in this letter, Victor?

(He is smiling gently all the time.)

KARENIN *(looking at Fedya rather severely)*. Yes, I know. But really, Fedya, you're in no——

FEDYA *(interrupting)*. Please, please don't think I'm drunk and don't realize what I'm saying. Of course I'm drunk, but I see everything very clearly. Now go ahead. What were you told to tell me?

KARENIN *(is standing at Left Center, shrugging his shoulders)*. Your wife asked me to find you and to tell you she's waiting for you. She wants you to forget everything and come back.

(Pause.)

KARENIN *(stiffly)*. Elizaveta Protosova sent for me and suggested that I——

FEDYA *(as he hesitates)*. Yes.

KARENIN *(finishing rather lamely)*. But I ask you not so much for her as for myself——Fedya, come *home*.

FEDYA *(looking up at him, smiling rather whimsically)*. You're a much finer person than I am, Victor. Of course, that's not saying much. I'm not very much good, am I? *(Laughing gently)* But that's exactly why I'm not going to do what you want me to. It's not the only reason, though. The real reason is that I just simply can't. How could I?

KARENIN *(persuasively)*. Come along to my rooms Fedya, and I'll tell her you'll be back tomorrow.

FEDYA *(wistfully)*. Tomorrows can't change what we are. She'll still be she, and I will still be I tomorrow. *(Goes to the table and drinks)* No, it's better to have the tooth out in one pull. Didn't I say that if I broke my word she was to leave me? Well, I've broken it, and that's enough.

KARENIN. Yes. For you, but not for her.

FEDYA *(politely insolent)*. You know . . . it's rather odd, that you, of all men, should take so much trouble to keep our marriage from going to pieces.

KARENIN *(revolted)*. Good God, Fedya! You don't think——

(Masha crosses over to Fedya.)

FEDYA *(interrupting him with a return of his former friendliness)*. Come now, my dear Victor, you shall hear them sing.

MASHA *(whispering to Fedya)*. What's his name? We must honor him with a song.

FEDYA *(laughing)*. O good God, yes! Honor him by all means. His name is Victor Michaelovitch. *(Saluting Karenin)* Victor, my lord! son of Michael!

(The gypsies sing a song of greeting and laudation. As they begin to sing, Masha and Fedya sit on the couch at the Left.)

KARENIN *(in an imploring tone when the song is finished)*. Fedya!

(Exits quietly.)

FEDYA *(to Masha)*. Where's the fur coat? Gone, eh? All right. May the devil go with it. Do you know who that was?

MASHA. I heard his name.

FEDYA. Ah, he's a splendid fellow. He came to take me home to my wife. You see she loves even a fool like me, *(caressing her hair)* and look what I'm doing.

MASHA. You should go back to her and be very sorry.

FEDYA. Do you think I should? *(He kisses her)* Well, I think I shouldn't.

MASHA. Of course, you needn't go back to her if you don't love her. Love is all that counts.

FEDYA *(smiling)*. How do you know that?

MASHA *(looking at him timidly)*. I don't know, but I do.

FEDYA. Now, let's have "No More at Evening". *(As the gypsies sing, Masha lies on her back across his lap, looking up into his face, which she draws down to her, and they kiss until the music begins to cease)* That's wonderful! Divine! If I could only lie this way forever, with my arms around the heart of joy, and sleep . . . and die . . . *(He closes his eyes; his voice trails away)*

CURTAIN

SCENE THREE

Sophia Karenina's boudoir. Sophia Karenina, Victor's mother, is reading a book. She is a great lady, over fifty, but tries to look younger. She likes to interlard her conversation with French words. A servant enters.

SERVANT *(enters, announcing)*. Prince Sergius Abreskov.

SOPHIA KARENINA *(on the sofa over to the Left)*. Show him in, please.

(She turns and picks up hand mirror from table back of couch, arranging her hair.)

PRINCE SERGIUS *(entering)*. J'espère que je ne force pas la consigne.

(Crossing to the sofa, he kisses her hand. He is a charming old diplomat of seventy.)

SOPHIA KARENINA. Ah, you know well que vous êtes toujours le bien venu . . . Tell me, you have received my letter?

PRINCE SERGIUS. I did. Me voilà.

SOPHIA KARENINA *(distressed)*. Oh, my dear friend, I begin to lose hope. She's bewitched him, positively bewitched him. Il est ensorcelé. I never knew he could be so obstinate, so heartless, and so indifferent to me. He's changed completely since that woman left her husband.

PRINCE SERGIUS. How do matters actually stand?

SOPHIA KARENINA. Well, he's made up his mind to marry her at any cost.

PRINCE SERGIUS. And her husband?

SOPHIA KARENINA. He agrees to a divorce.

PRINCE SERGIUS. Really?

SOPHIA KARENINA. And Victor is willing to put up with all the sordidness, the vulgarity of the divorce court, the lawyers, evidences of guilt . . . tout ça est dégoûtant. I can't understand his sensitive nature not being repelled by it.

PRINCE SERGIUS *(smiling)*. He's in love, and when a man's really in love——

SOPHIA KARENINA *(interrupting)*. In our time love could remain pure, coloring one's whole life with a romantic friendship. Such love I understand and value.

PRINCE SERGIUS *(sighing)*. However, the present generation refuses to live on dreams. *(He coughs delicately)* La possession de l'âme ne leur suffit plus. So what is the alternative? But tell me more of Victor.

SOPHIA KARENINA. There's not very much to say. He seems bewitched, hardly my son. Did you know I'd called upon her? Victor pressed me so it was impossible to refuse. But Dieu merci, I found her out. So I merely left my card, and now she has asked me if I could receive her today, and I am expecting her *(she glances at her watch)* any moment now. I am doing all this to please Victor, but conceive my feelings. I know you always can. Really, really, I need your help.

PRINCE SERGIUS *(bowing)*. Thank you for the honor you do me.

SOPHIA KARENINA. You realize this visit decides Victor's fate. I must refuse my consent, or——But that's impossible.

PRINCE SERGIUS. Have you met her?

SOPHIA KARENINA. I've never seen her, but I'm afraid of her. No good woman leaves her husband, especially when there's nothing obviously intolerable about him. Why, I've seen Protosov often with Victor, and found him even quite charming.

PRINCE SERGIUS *(murmuring)*. So I've heard. So I've heard.

SOPHIA KARENINA *(continuing)*. She should bear her cross without complaint. And Victor must cease trying to persuade himself that his happiness lies in defying his principles. What I don't understand is how Victor, with his religious views, can think of marrying a divorced woman. I've heard him say over and over again—once quite lately—that divorce is totally inconsistent with true Christianity. If she's been able to fascinate him to that point, I *am* afraid of her.—But how stupid of me to talk all the time! Have you spoken to him at all? What does he say? And don't you thoroughly agree with me?

PRINCE SERGIUS. Yes, I've spoken to Victor. I think he really loves her, has grown accustomed to the idea of loving her, pour ainsi dire. *(Shaking his head)* I don't believe he could ever now care for another woman.

SOPHIA KARENINA *(sighing)*. And Varia Casanzeva would have made him such a charming wife. She's so devoted already.

PRINCE SERGIUS *(smiling)*. I am afraid I hardly see her in the present . . . tableau. *(Earnestly)* Why not submit to Victor's wish and help him?

SOPHIA KARENINA. To marry a divorcée? And afterwards have him running into his wife's husband? How can you calmly suggest that a mother accept such a situation for her son?

PRINCE SERGIUS. But, chère amie, why not approve of the inevitable? And you might console yourself by regarding the dangers he'll avoid by marrying this gentle, lovely woman. After all, suppose he conceived a passion for someone——
(He suggests the word "disreputable".)

SOPHIA KARENINA. How can a good woman leave her husband?

PRINCE SERGIUS. Ah, that's not like you. You're unkind and you're harsh. Her husband is the sort of man—well, he's his own worst enemy. A weakling, a ne'er-do-well—he's spent all his money and hers too. She has a child. Do you think you can condemn her for leaving him? As a matter of fact she didn't leave him, he left her.

SOPHIA KARENINA *(faintly)*. Oh what a mud-pen I'm slipping into!

PRINCE SERGIUS *(amused)*. Could your religion aid you?

SOPHIA KARENINA *(smelling her salts)*. In this instance, religion would require of me the impossible. C'est plus fort que moi.

PRINCE SERGIUS. Fedya himself—you know what a charming, clever creature he is when he's in his senses—he advised to her leave him.
(Enter Victor, who kisses his mother's hand and greets Prince Sergius.)

KARENIN. Ah, Prince Sergius! *(Shakes hands with Prince—formally)* Maman, I've come to tell you that Elizaveta Protosova will be here directly. There's only one thing I ask you: do you still refuse your consent to my marriage——

SOPHIA KARENINA *(interrupting)*. And I most assuredly do.

KARENIN *(continuing, with a frown)*. In that case all I ask is for you not to speak to her about it.

SOPHIA KARENINA. I don't suppose we shall even mention the subject. I certainly shan't.

KARENIN *(standing at the head of the sofa)*. If you don't, she won't. *(Pleadingly)* Mother dear, I just want you to know her.

SOPHIA KARENINA. One thing I can't understand. How is it you want to marry Lisa Protosova, a woman with a living husband, and at the same time believe divorce is a crime against Christianity?

KARENIN. Oh, Maman, that's cruel of you. Life is far too complex to be managed by a few formulas. Why are you so bitter about it all?

SOPHIA KARENINA *(honestly)*. I love you. I want you to be happy.

KARENIN *(imploringly to Prince Sergius)*. Sergius Abreskov!

PRINCE SERGIUS *(to Sophia Karenina)*. Naturally you want him happy. But it's difficult for our hearts, wearied from the weight of years, to feel the pulse of youth and sympathize, especially is it difficult for you, my friend, who have schooled yourself to view Victor's happiness in a single way . . .

SOPHIA KARENINA. Oh, you're all against me. Do as you like. Vous êtes majeur. *(Sniffing into her pocket handkerchief)* But you'll kill me.

KARENIN *(deeply distressed)*. Ah, Mother,

please. It's worse than cruel to say things like that.

PRINCE SERGIUS *(smiling to Victor)*. Come, come, Victor, you know your mother speaks more severely than she could ever act.

SOPHIA KARENINA. I shall tell her exactly what I think and feel, and I hope I can do it without offending her.

PRINCE SERGIUS. I am sure of it.

(Enter a Footman.)
Here she is.

KARENIN. I'll go. *(Goes to back of sofa)*

FOOTMAN *(announcing)*. Elizaveta Andreyevna Protosova.

KARENIN *(warningly)*. Now, Mother.
(He goes out Left. Prince Sergius rises.)

SOPHIA KARENINA *(majestically)*. Show her in. *(To Prince Sergius)* Please remain.

PRINCE SERGIUS. I thought you might prefer a tête-à-tête?

SOPHIA KARENINA. No, no. I rather dread it. And if I want to be left alone in the room with her, I'll drop my handkerchief. Ça dépendra.

PRINCE SERGIUS. I'm sure you're going to like her immensely.

SOPHIA KARENINA. Oh you're all against me. *(Lisa enters and Sophia rises)* How do you do? I was so sorry not to find you at home and it is most kind of you to come to see me.

LISA. I never expected the honor of your visit, and I am so grateful that you permit me to come and see you.

SOPHIA KARENINA. You know Prince Sergius Abreskov?

PRINCE SERGIUS *(heartily)*. Yes, I have had the pleasure. *(Crossing to her, he shakes hands)* My niece Nellie has spoken often of you to me.

LISA. Yes, we were great friends. *(She glances shyly around her)* And still are. *(To Sophia)* I never hoped that you would wish to see me.

SOPHIA KARENINA. I knew your husband quite well. He was a great friend of Victor's and used frequently to visit us in Tambov, *(politely)* where you were married, I believe.

LISA *(looking down)*. Yes.

SOPHIA KARENINA. But when you returned to Moscow we were deprived of the pleasure of his visit.

LISA. Yes, then he stopped going anywhere.

SOPHIA KARENINA. Ah, that explains our missing him.
(Awkward pause.)

PRINCE SERGIUS *(to Lisa)*. The last time I'd the pleasure of seeing you was in those tableaux at the Dennishovs. You were charming in your part.

LISA. How good of you to think so! Yes, I remember perfectly.
(Another awkward silence.)
(To Sophia Karenina), Sophia Karenina, please forgive me if what I am going to say offends you, but I don't know how to cover up what's in my heart. I came here today because Victor Karenin said— because he said that— because he—I mean because you wanted to see me. *(With a catch in her voice)* It's rather difficult—but you're so sweet.

PRINCE SERGIUS *(sympathetic)*. There, there, my dear child, I assure you there's nothing in the world to———*(He breaks off when he sees Sophia Karenina pointing impatiently to the floor. She has dropped her handkerchief)* Permit me. *(He picks it up, presenting it to her with a smile and a bow; then looks casually at his watch)* Ah, five o'clock already. *(To Sophia Karenina)* Madame, in your salon pleasure destroys the memory of time. You will excuse me. *(He kisses her hand)*

SOPHIA KARENINA *(smiling)*. Au revoir, mon ami.

PRINCE SERGIUS *(bowing and shaking hands with Lisa)*. Elizaveta Protosova, au revoir. *(He goes out)*

SOPHIA KARENINA. Now listen, my child. Please believe how truly sorry for you I am and that you are most sympathetique to me. But I love my son alone in this world, and I know his soul as I do my own. He's very proud—oh I don't mean of his position and money—but of his high ideals, his purity. It may sound strange to you, but you must believe me when I tell you that at heart he is as pure as a young girl.

LISA. I know.

SOPHIA KARENINA. He's never loved a woman before. You're the first. I don't say I'm not a little jealous. I am. But that's something we mothers have to face.

Oh, but your son's still a baby, you don't know. I was ready to give him up, though—but I wanted his wife to be as pure as himself.

LISA *(flushing hotly)*. And I, am I not—

SOPHIA KARENINA *(interrupting her kindly)*. Forgive me, my dear. I know it's not your fault and that you've been most unhappy. And also I know my son. He will bear anything, and he'll bear it without saying a word, but his hurt pride will suffer and bring you infinite remorse. You must know how strongly he has always felt that the bond of marriage is indissoluble.

LISA. Yes. I've thought of all that.

SOPHIA KARENINA. Lisa, my dear, you're a wise woman and you're a good woman too. If you love him, you must want his happiness more than you want your own. You can't want to cripple him so that he'll be sorry all his life—yes, sorry even though he never says a word.

LISA. I've thought about it so much. I've thought about it and I've talked to him about it. But what can I do when he says he can't live without me? I said to him only the other day, "Victor, let's just be friends. Don't spoil your life. Don't ruin yourself by trying to help me". And do you know what he did? He laughed.

SOPHIA KARENINA. Of course he would, at the time.

LISA. If you could persuade him not to marry me, you know I'll agree, don't you? I just want him to be happy. I don't care about myself. Only please help me. Please don't hate me. Let's do all we can for him, because, after all, we both love him.

SOPHIA KARENINA. Yes, I know. And I think I love you too. I really do. *(She kisses her, and Lisa begins to cry)* Oh, it's all so dreadful. If only he had fallen in love with you before you were married!

LISA *(sobbing)*. He—he says he did—but he had to be loyal to his friend.

SOPHIA KARENINA. Alas, it's all very heart-breaking. But let us love each other, and God will help us to find what we are seeking.

KARENIN *(entering)*. Mother darling. I've heard what you just said. I knew you'd love her. And now everything must come right.

SOPHIA KARENINA *(hastily)*. But nothing's decided. All I can say is, had things been different, I should have been very glad. *(Tenderly)* So very glad. *(She kisses Lisa)*

KARENIN *(smiling)*. Please don't change. That's all I ask.

CURTAIN

SCENE FOUR

A plainly furnished room, bed, table and stove. Fedya is seated on the bed alone, writing.

At rise Masha is heard outside calling "Fedya! Fedya!" Masha enters, crosses to Fedya, and embraces him.

———

FEDYA. Ah, thank Heaven you've come. I was wasting away in boredom.

MASHA. Then why didn't you come over to us? *(Sees wine glass on the chair near the bed)* So, you've been drinking again? And after all your promises!

FEDYA *(embarrassed)*. I didn't come over because I had no money.

MASHA. Oh, why is it I love you so.

FEDYA. Masha!

MASHA *(imitating him)*. Masha! Masha! What's that mean? If you loved me, by now you'd have your divorce. You say you don't love your wife. *(Fedya winces)* But you stick to her like grim death.

FEDYA *(interrupting her)*. You know why I don't want to.

MASHA. Nonsense. They're right when they say you're no good. It's your mind that you can never make up comfortably causing you all the worry.

FEDYA. You know perfectly well that the only joy I've got in life is being in love with you.

MASHA. Oh, it's always "My joy," "Your love." Where's your love and my joy?

FEDYA *(a little wearily)*. Well, Masha, after all, you've got all I can give, the best I've ever had to give, perhaps, because you're so strong, so beautiful, that sometimes you've made me know how to make you glad. So why torture yourself?

MASHA (*kneels and puts her arms around his neck*). I won't if you're sure you love me.

FEDYA (*coming closer to her*). My beautiful young Masha.

MASHA (*tearfully, searching his face*). You do love me?

FEDYA. Of course, of course.

MASHA. Only me, only me?

FEDYA (*kissing her*). Darling, only you.

MASHA (*with a return to brightness*). Now read me what you've written.

FEDYA. It may bore you.

MASHA (*reproachfully*). How could it?

FEDYA (*reads*). "The snow was flooded in moonlight and the birch trees wavered their stark shadows across it like supplicating arms. Suddenly I heard the soft padded sound of snow falling upon snow, to slowly perceive a figure, the slender figure of a young child attempting to arouse itself almost at my feet—I——" (*Enter Ivan and Nastasia. They are two old gypsies, Masha's parents.*)

NASTASIA (*stepping up to Masha*). So here you are—you cursed little stray sheep. No disrespect to you, sir. (*To Masha*) You black-hearted, ungrateful little snake. How dare you treat us like this, how dare you, eh?

IVAN (*to Fedya*). It's not right, sir, what you've done, bringing to her ruin our only child. It's against God's law.

NASTASIA (*to Masha*). Come and get out of here with me. You thought you'd skip, didn't you? And what was I supposed to tell the troupe while you dangled around here with this tramp? What can you get out of him, tell me that? Did you know he hasn't got a kopek to his name, didn't you?

(*During scene with the parents, Fedya sits dumbly on the bed, bewildered. He puts his forehead against Masha's face and clings to her like a child.*)

MASHA (*sullenly*). I haven't done anything wrong. I love this gentleman, that's all. I didn't leave the troupe either. I'll go on singing just the same.

IVAN. If you talk any more, I'll pull your hair all out for you, you loose little beast, you. (*To Fedya, reproachfully*) And you, sir, when we were so fond of you—why, often and often we used to sing for you for nothing and this is how you pay us back.

NASTASIA (*rocking herself to and fro*). You've ruined our daughter, our very own, our only one, our best beloved, our diamond, our precious one. (*With sudden fury*) You've stamped her into the dirt, you have. Where's your fear of God?

FEDYA. Nastasia, Nastasia, you've made a mistake. Your daughter is like a sister to me. I haven't harmed her at all. I love her, that's true. But how can I help it?

IVAN. Well, why didn't you love her when you had some money? If you'd paid us ten thousand rubles, you could have owned her, body and soul. That's what respectable gentlemen do. But you—you throw away every kopek you've got and then you steal her like you'd steal a sack of meal. You ought to be ashamed, sir.

MASHA (*rising, puts her arm around his neck*). He didn't steal me. I went to him myself, and if you take me away now, I'll come right back. If you take me away a thousand times, I'll come back to him. I love him and that's enough. My love will break through anything—through anything. Through anything in the whole damn world.

NASTASIA (*trying to soothe her*). Now, Mashenka darling, don't get cross. You know you haven't behaved well to your poor old parents. There, there, come along with us now.

(*With greedy fingers that pretend to caress, Nastasia seizes her savagely and suddenly at the end of this speech and draws her to the door. Masha cries out "Fedya! Fedya!" as she goes out.*)

IVAN (*alongside*). You open your mouth again and I'll smash you dumb. (*To Fedya*) Good-by, your worship. (*They all go out to the Right*)

(*Fedya sits as though stupefied. The gypsies exit noisily. There is a pause. He drinks; then Prince Sergius appears, very quiet and dignified, at the door.*)

PRINCE SERGIUS. Excuse me. I'm afraid I'm intruding upon a rather painful scene.

FEDYA *(getting up)*. With whom have I the honor——*(recognizing the Prince)* Ah, Prince Sergius, how do you do?
(They shake hands.)

PRINCE SERGIUS *(in a distinguished manner)*. I repeat that I am afraid to be most inopportune. I would rather not have heard, but since I have, it's my duty to say so. When I arrived I knocked several times, but I presume you could not have heard through such uproar.

FEDYA. Do sit down. *(The Prince sits in a chair to the Right)* Thanks for telling me you heard. *(Sits on bed)* It gives me a chance to explain it all. Forgive me for saying your opinion of me can't concern me, but I want to tell you that the way her parents talked to that young girl, that gypsy singer, was absolutely unjust. She's as pure as your own mother. My relations with her are simply friendly ones. Possible there is a ray of poetry in them, but that could hardly degrade her. However, what can I do for you?

PRINCE SERGIUS. Well, to begin——

FEDYA *(interrupting)*. Excuse me, Prince, but my present social position hardly warrants a visit from you. *(Smiling)*

PRINCE SERGIUS. I know that, but I ask you to believe that your changed position does not influence me in what I am about to tell you.

FEDYA *(interrogatively)*. Then?

PRINCE SERGIUS. To be as brief as possible, Victor Karenin, the son of my old friend, Sophia Karenina, and she herself, have asked me to discover from you personally what your present relations are with your wife, and what intentions you have regarding them.

FEDYA. My relations with my wife—I should say my former wife—are several.

PRINCE SERGIUS. As I thought, and for this reason accepted my somewhat difficult mission.

FEDYA *(quickly)*. I wish to say first of all that the fault was entirely mine. She is, just as she always was, absolutely stainless, faultless.

PRINCE SERGIUS. Victor Karenin and especially his mother are anxious to know your exact intentions regarding the future.

FEDYA. I've got no intentions. I've given her full freedom. I know she loves Victor Karenin, let her. Personally, I think he is a bore, but he is a good bore. So they'll probably be very happy together, at least in the ordinary sense and que le bon Dieu les bénisse.

PRINCE SERGIUS. Yes, but we——

FEDYA *(rising, goes left, and leans on the table)*. Please don't think I'm jealous. If I just said Victor was dull, I take it back. He's splendid, very decent, in fact the opposite of myself, and he's loved her since her childhood *(slowly)* and maybe she loved him even when we were married. After all, that happens, and the strongest love is perhaps unconscious love. Yes, I think she's always loved him far, far down beneath what she would admit to herself, and this feeling of mine has been a black shadow across our married life. But—I—I really don't suppose I ought to be talking to you like this, ought I?

PRINCE SERGIUS. Please go on. My only object in coming was to understand this situation completely, and I begin to see how the shadow—as you charmingly express it—could have been——

FEDYA *(looking strangely ahead of him)*. Yes, no brightness could suck up that shadow. And so I suppose I never was satisfied with what my wife gave me, and I looked for every kind of distraction, sick at heart because I did so. I see it more and more clearly since we've been apart. Oh, but I sound as if I were defending myself. God knows I don't want to do that. No, I was a shocking bad husband. I say was, because now I don't consider myself her husband at all. She's perfectly free. There, does that satisfy you?

PRINCE SERGIUS. Yes, but you know how strictly orthodox Victor and his family are. Of course I don't agree with them—perhaps I have broader views— *(with a shrug)* but I understand how they feel. They consider that any union without a church marriage is—well, to put it mildly, unthinkable.

FEDYA. Yes, I know he's very stu—I mean strict. *(With a slight smile)* "Conservative" is the word, isn't it? But what in God's name *(crossing to Center)* do they want, a divorce? I told them long ago I was perfectly willing. But the business of hiring a street-woman and taking her to a shady hotel and arranging to be caught by competent witnesses—ugh—it's all so— so loathsome.

(He shudders; and, after a pause, sits on bed.)

PRINCE SERGIUS. I know. I know. I assure you, I can sympathize with such a repugnance, but how can one avoid it? You see, it's the only way out. But, my dear boy, you mustn't think I don't sympathize with you. It's a horrible situation for a sensitive man and I quite understand how you must hate it.

FEDYA. Thank you, Prince Sergius. I always knew you were kind and just. Now tell me what to do. Put yourself in my place. I don't pretend to be any better than I really am. I am a blackguard, but there are some things that even I can't do. *(With a smile and helpless gesture)* I can't tell lies.

PRINCE SERGIUS *(after a pause)*. I must confess that you bewilder me. You with your gifts and charm and really au fond—a wonderful sense of what's right. How could you have permitted yourself to plunge into such tawdry distractions? How could you have forgotten so far what you owed to yourself? Tell me, why did you let your life fall into this ruin?

FEDYA *(suppressing emotion)*. I've led this sort of life for ten years and you're the first real person to show me sympathy. Of corse, I've been pitied by the degraded ones but never before by a sensible, kind man like you. Thanks more than it's possible to say. *(He seems to forget his train of thought and suddenly to recall it)* Ah, yes, my ruin. Well, first, drink, not because it tasted well, but because everything I did disappointed me so, made me so ashamed of myself. I feel ashamed now, while I talk to you. Whenever I drank, shame was drowned in the first glass, and sadness. Then music, not opera or Beethoven, but gypsy music; the passion of it poured energy into my body, while those dark bewitching eyes looked into the bottom of my soul. *(He sighs)* And the more alluring it all was, the more shame I felt afterwards.

PRINCE SERGIUS *(after a pause)*. But what about your career?

FEDYA. My career? This seems to be it.

Once I was a director of a bank. There was something terribly lacking between what I felt and what I could do. *(Abruptly)* But enough, enough of myself. It makes me rather nervous to think about myself. *(He rises)*

PRINCE SERGIUS. What answer am I to take back?

FEDYA *(very nervous)*. Oh, tell them I'm quite at their disposal. *(Walking up and down)* They want to marry, and there mustn't be anything in their way; is that it? *(Stops walking very suddenly)* There mustn't be anything in their way—is that it?

PRINCE SERGIUS *(after a pause, while Fedya sits on the table at the Left)*. Yes. When do you—when do you think— you'll—you'll have it ready? The evidence?

FEDYA *(turning and looking at the Prince, and suppressing a slight, strained smile)*. Will a fortnight do?

PRINCE SERGIUS *(rising)*. Yes, I am sure it will. *(Rises and crosses to Fedya)* May I say that you give them your word?

FEDYA *(with some impatience)*. Yes. Yes. *(Prince Sergius offers his hand)* Good-by, Prince Sergius. And again thanks.

(Exit Prince Sergius. Fedya sits down in an attitude of deep thought.)

Why not? Why not? And it's good not to be ashamed——

CURTAIN

SCENE FIVE

A private room in a cheap restaurant. Fedya is shown in by a shabby waiter.

————

WAITER. This way, sir. No one will disturb you here. Here's the writing paper.

FEDYA *(as waiter starts to exit)*. Bring me a bottle of champagne.

WAITER. Yes, sir. *(He goes out)*

(Fedya sits at the table Left Center and begins to write. Ivan Petrovich appears in the doorway at the Right.)

IVAN. I'll come in, shall I?

FEDYA *(sitting Left of the table; very serious)*. If you want to, but I'm awfully busy, and——(*seeing he has already entered*) Oh, all right, do come in.

IVAN PETROVICH. You're going to write an answer to their demand. I'll help you. I'll tell you what to say. Speak out. Say what you mean. It's straight from the shoulder. That's my system. (*Picks up box that Fedya has placed on table—opens it and takes out a revolver*) Hullo! What's this? Going to shoot yourself. Of course, why not? I understand. They want to humiliate you, and you show them where the courage is—put a bullet through your head and heap coals of fire on theirs. I understand perfectly. (*The waiter enters with champagne on tray, pours a glass for Fedya, then exits. Petrovich takes up the glass of wine and starts to drink. Fedya looks up from his writing*) I understand everything and everybody, because I'm a genius.

FEDYA. So you are, but——

IVAN PETROVICH (*filling and lifting his glass*). Here's to your immortal journey. May it be swift and pleasant. Oh, I see it from your point of view. So why should I stop you? Life and death are the same to genius. I'm dead during life and I live after death. You kill yourself in order to make a few people miss you, but I—but I—am going to kill myself to make the whole *world* know what it lost. I won't hesitate or think about it. I'll just take the revolver—one, two—and all is over—um. But I am premature. My hour is not yet struck. (*He puts the revolver down*) But I shall write nothing. The world will have to understand all by itself. (*Fedya continues to write*) The world, what is it but a mass of preposterous creatures, who crawl around through life, understanding nothing—nothing at all—do you hear me? (*Fedya looks up, rather exasperated*) Oh, I'm not talking to you. All this is between me and the cosmos. (*Pours himself out another drink*) After all, what does humanity most lack? Appreciation for its geniuses. As it is, we're persecuted, tortured, racked, through a lifetime of perpetual agony, into the asylum or the grave. But no longer will I be their bauble. Humanity, hypocrite that you are—to hell with you. (*He drinks*)

FEDYA (*having finished his letter*). Oh, go away, please.

IVAN PETROVICH. Away? (*With a gesture*) Away? Me? (*With profound resolve*) So be it. (*He leans over the table and faces Fedya*) I shall away. I'll not deter you from accomplishing what I also shall commit—all in its proper moment, however. Only I *should* like to say this——

FEDYA. Later. Later. But now, listen, old man, give this to the head waiter. (*Handing him some money*) You understand?

IVAN PETROVICH. Yes, but for God's sake wait for me to come back. (*Moves away*) I've something rare to tell you, something you'll never hear in the next world—at least not till I get there—— Look here, shall I give him all this money?

FEDYA. No, just what I owe him.

(*Exit Ivan Petrovich, whistling. Fedya sighs with a sense of relief, takes the revolver, cocks it, stands at mirror on wall up Right, and puts it close to his temple. Then shivers, and lets his hand drop.*)

I can't do it. I can't do it.

(*Pause. Masha is heard singing. Masha bursts into the room.*)

MASHA (*breathless*). I've been everywhere looking for you. To Popov's, Afremov's, then I guessed you'd be here. (*Crosses to him. Sees revolver, turns, faces him quickly, concealing it with her body, stands very tense and taut, looking at him*) Oh, you fool! You hideous fool! Did you think you'd——

FEDYA (*still completely unnerved*). Awful! It's been awful! I tried——(*With a gesture of despair*) I couldn't——

(*Crosses to the table and leans against it.*)

MASHA (*puts her hand to her face as if terribly hurt*). As if *I* didn't exist. (*Crosses over to the table and puts down revolver*) As if I weren't in your life at all. Oh, how godless you are! (*Brokenly*) Tell me, tell me, what about all my love for you?

FEDYA (*as if suddenly aware of a great fatigue*). I wanted to set them free. I promised to—and when the time came I couldn't.

MASHA. And what about *me*? What about me?

FEDYA. I thought you'd be free, too. Surely my torturing you can't make you happy.

MASHA. Oh, I can look out for myself.

Maybe I'd rather be unhappy, miserable, wretched with you every minute than even *think* of living without you.

FEDYA *(half to himself)*. If I'd finished just now, you would have cried bitterly perhaps, my Masha, but you would have lived past it.

MASHA. Oh, damn you, don't be so sure I'd cry at all. Can't you even be sorry for me?

(She tries to conceal her tears.)

FEDYA. Oh God, I only wanted to make everybody happier.

MASHA. Yourself happier, you mean.

FEDYA *(smiling)*. Would I have been happier to be dead now?

MASHA *(sulkily)*. I suppose *you* would. *(Suddenly in a tender voice, crossing to him)* But, Fedya, do you *know* what you want? Tell me, what *do* you want?

FEDYA. I want so many things.

MASHA *(impatiently and clinging to him)*. But what? What?

FEDYA. First of all, I want to set them free. How can I lie? How can I crawl through the muck and filth of a divorce? I can't. *(Moves to end of table and stands there facing front)* But I must set them free somehow. They're such good people, my wife and Victor. I can't bear having them suffer.

MASHA *(scornfully)*. Where's the good in her if she left you?

FEDYA. She didn't. I left her.

MASHA. She made you *think* she'd be happier without you. But go on—— *(Impatiently)* Blame yourself, what else.

FEDYA. There's you, Masha. Young, lovely, awfully dear to me. If I stay alive, ah, where will you be?

MASHA. Don't bother about me. You can't hurt me.

FEDYA *(sighing)*. But the big reason, the biggest reason of all, is *myself*. I'm just lost. Your father is right, my dear. I'm no good.

MASHA *(crossing to him, at once tenderly and savagely)*. I won't unfasten myself from you. I'll stick to you, no matter where you take me, no matter what you do. You're alive, terribly alive, and I love you. Fedya, drop all this horror.

FEDYA. How can I?

MASHA *(trying to project the very essence*

of her vitality into him). Oh, you can, you can.

FEDYA *(slowly)*. When I look at you, I feel as though I could do anything.

MASHA *(proudly, foundly)*. My love, my love. You can do anything, get anywhere you want to. *(Fedya moves away impatiently. She sees letter)* So you have been writing to them—to tell them you'll kill yourself. You just told them you'd kill yourself, is that it? But you didn't say anything about a revolver. Oh, Fedya—listen to me. Do you remember the day we all went to the picnic to the White Lakes with Mama and Afremov and the young Cossack officer? And you buried the bottles of wine in the sand to keep them cool while we went in bathing? Do you remember how you took my hands and drew me out beyond the waves till the water was quite silent and flashing almost up to our throats, and then suddenly it seemed as if there were nothing under our feet? We tried to get back. We couldn't and you shouted out, "Afremov," and if he hadn't been almost beside us and pulled us in—and how cross he was with you for forgetting that you couldn't swim, and after, how wonderful it was to stretch out safely on the sands in the sunlight. Oh, how nice everyone was to us that day and you kept on being so sorry for forgetting you couldn't swim! And, Fedya, don't you see? Of course, she must know you can't swim. Oh, it's all getting as clear as daylight. You will send her this beautiful letter. Your clothes will be found on the river bank—but instead of being in the river you will be far away with me— Fedya, don't you see, don't you see? You will be dead to her, but alive for me. *(Embraces Fedya)*

CURTAIN

SCENE SIX

The Protosovs' drawing-room. Karenin and Lisa.
————

KARENIN *(sitting on the chair at the Right)*. He's promised me definitely, and I'm sure he'll keep to it.

LISA. I'm rather ashamed to confess it, but since I found out about this—this gypsy, I feel completely free of him. Of course, I am not in the least jealous, but knowing this makes me see that I owe him nothing more. Am I clear to you, I wonder?

KARENIN (coming closer to her). Yes, dear, I think I'll always understand you.

LISA (smiling). Don't interrupt me, but let me speak as I think. The thing that tortured me most was I seemed to love both of you at once, and that made me seem so indecent to myself.

KARENIN (incredulously amused). You indecent?

LISA (continuing). But since I've found out that there's another woman, that he doesn't need me any more, I feel free, quite free of him. And now I can say truthfully, I love you. Because everything is clear in my soul. My only worry is the divorce, and all the waiting to be gone through before we can—— Ah, that's torturing.

KARENIN. Dearest, everything will be settled soon. After all, he's promised, and I've asked my secretary to go to him with the petition and not to leave until he's signed it. Really, sometimes, if I didn't know him as I do, I'd think he was trying on purpose to discomfort us.

LISA. No. No. It's only the same weakness and honesty fighting together in him. He doesn't want to lie. However, I'm sorry you sent him money.

KARENIN. If I hadn't, it might have delayed things.

LISA. I know, but money seems so ugly.

KARENIN (slightly ruffled). I hardly think it's necessary to be so delicate with Fedya.

LISA. Perhaps, perhaps. (Smiling) But don't you think we are becoming very selfish?

KARENIN. Maybe. But it's all your fault, dear. After all, this hopelessness and waiting, to think of being happy at last! I suppose happiness does make us selfish.

LISA. Don't believe you're alone in your happiness or selfishness. I am so filled with joy it makes me almost afraid.

Misha's all right, your mother loves me, and above all, you are here, close to me, loving me as I love you.

KARENIN (bending over her and searching her eyes). You're sure you've no regret?

LISA. From the day I found out about that gypsy woman, my mind underwent a change that has set me free.

KARENIN (kissing her hands). You're sure?

LISA (passionately). Darling, I've only one desire now, and that is to have you forget the past and love as I do.

(Her little boy toddles in from the Right; he sees them and stops.)

Come here, my sweetheart.

(He goes to her and she takes him on her knees.)

KARENIN. What strange contradictory instincts and desires make up our beings!

LISA. Why?

KARENIN (slowly). I don't know. When I came back from abroad, knew I'd lost you, I was unhappy, terribly. Yet, it was enough for me to learn that you at least remembered me. Afterward, when we became friends, and you were kind to me, and into our friendship wavered a spark of something more than friendship, ah, I was almost happy! Only one thing tormented me: fear that such a feeling wronged Fedya. Afterwards when Fedya tortured you so, I saw I could help. Then a certain definite hope sprang up in me. And later, when he became impossible and you decided to leave him, and I showed you my heart for the first time, and you didn't say no, but went away in tears—then I was happy through and through. Then came the possibility of joining our lives. Mamma loved you. You told me you loved me, that Fedya was gone out of your heart, out of your life forever, and there was only, only me . . . Ah, Lisa, for what more could I ask! Yet the past tortured me. Awful fancies would flush up into my happiness, turning it all into hatred for your past.

LISA (interrupting reproachfully). Victor!

KARENIN. Forgive me, Lisa. I only tell you this because I don't want to hide a single thought from you. I want you to know how bad I am, and what a weakness I've got to fight down. But don't worry,

I'll get past it. It's all right, dear. *(He bends over, kissing the child on the head)* And I love him, too.

LISA. Dearest, I'm so happy. Everything has happened in my heart to make it as you'd wish.

KARENIN. All?

LISA. All, beloved, or I never could say so.

(Enter the Nurse.)

NURSE. Your secretary has come back.

(Lisa and Karenin exchange glances.)

LISA. Show him in here, nurse, and take Misha, will you?

NURSE. Come along, my pet. It's time for your rest. *(She goes out with the little boy)*

KARENIN *(gets up, and walks to the door)*. This will be Fedya's answer.

LISA *(kissing Karenin)*. At last, at last we shall know when. *(She kisses him)*

(Enter Voznesensky.)

KARENIN. Well?

SECRETARY. He's not there, sir.

KARENIN. Not there? He's not signed the petition, then?

SECRETARY. No. But here is a letter addressed to you and Elizaveta Protosova. *(Takes letter from his pocket and gives it to Karenin.)*

KARENIN *(interrupting angrily)*. More excuses, more excuses. It's perfectly outrageous. How without conscience he is. Really, he has lost every claim to——

LISA. But read the letter, dear; see what he says.

(Karenin opens the letter.)

SECRETARY. Shall you need me, sir?

KARENIN. No. That's all. Thank you. *(The Secretary goes out. Karenin reads the letter in growing astonishment and concern. Lisa watches his face.)*

(Reading). "Lisa, Victor, I write you both without using terms of endearment, since I can't feel them, nor can I conquer a sense of bitterness and reproach, self-reproach principally, when I think of you together in your love. I know, in spite of being the husband, I was also the barrier, preventing you from coming earlier to one another. C'est moi qui suis l'intrus. I stood in your way, I worried you to death. Yet I can't help feeling bitterly,

coldly, toward you. In one way I love both of you, especially Lisa Lizenska, but in reality I am more than cold toward you. Yes, it's unjust, isn't it, but to change is impossible."

LISA. What's all that for?

KARENIN *(standing Left of the table in the Center, continuing)*. "However, to the point. I am going to fulfill your wishes in perhaps a little different way from what you desire. To lie, to act a degrading comedy, to bribe women of the streets for evidence—the ugliness of it all disgusts me. I am a bad man, but this despicable thing I am utterly unable to do. My solution is after all the simplest. You must marry to be happy. I am the obstacle, consequently that obstacle must be removed."

LISA. Victor!

KARENIN *(reading)*. Must be removed? "By the time this letter reaches you, I shall no longer exist. All I ask you is to be happy, and whenever you think of me, think tender thoughts. God bless you both. Good-by. Fedya."

LISA. He's killed himself!

KARENIN *(going hurriedly upstage Left and calling off-stage)*. My secretary! Call back my secretary!

LISA. Fedya! Fedya, darling!

KARENIN. Lisa!

LISA. It's not true! It's not true that I've stopped loving him! He's the only man in all the world I love! And now I've killed him! I've killed him as surely as if I'd murdered him with my own two hands!

KARENIN. Lisa, for God's sake!

LISA. Stop it! Don't come near me! Don't be angry with me, Victor. You see I, too, cannot lie!

CURTAIN

ACT TWO

SCENE ONE

A dirty, ill-lighted underground dive; people are lying around drinking, sleeping, playing cards and making love. Near the front a small table at which Fedya sits; he is in rags and has fallen very low. By his side is Petrushkov, a delicate spiritual man, with long yellow hair and beard. Both are rather drunk.

Candle light is the only lighting in this scene.

———

PETRUSHKOV. I know. I know. Well, that's real love. So what happened then?

FEDYA *(pensively)*. You might perhaps expect a girl of our own class, tenderly brought up, to be capable of sacrificing for the man she loved, but this girl was a gypsy, reared in greed, yet she gave me the purest sort of self-sacrificing love. She'd have done anything for nothing. Such contrasts are amazing.

PETRUSHKOV. I see. In painting we call that value. Only to realize bright red fully when there is green around it. But that's not the point. What happened?

FEDYA. Oh, we parted. I felt it wasn't right to go on taking, taking where I couldn't give. So one night we were having dinner in a little restaurant, I told her we'd have to say good-by. My heart was so wrung all the time I could hardly help crying.

PETRUSHKOV. And she?

FEDYA. Oh, she was awfully unhappy, but she knew I was right. So we kissed each other a long while, and she went back to her gypsy troupe—— *(Slowly)* Maybe she was glad to go——

PETRUSHKOV. I wonder.

FEDYA. Yes. The single good act of my soul was not ruining that girl.

PETRUSHKOV. Was it from pity?

FEDYA. I sorry for *her?* Oh, never. Quite the contrary. I worshipped her unclouded sincerity, the energy of her clear, strong will, and God in Heaven, how she sang. And probably she is singing now, for someone else. Yes, I always looked up at her from beneath, as you do at some radiance in the sky. I loved her really. And now it's a tender beautiful memory.

PETRUSHKOV. I understand. It was ideal, and you left it like that.

FEDYA *(ruminatingly)*. And I've been attracted often, you know. Once I was in love with a grande dame, bestially in love, dog-like. Well, she gave me a rendezvous, and I didn't, couldn't, keep it, because suddenly I thought of her husband, and it made me feel sick. And you know, it's queer, that now, when I look back, instead of being glad that I was decent, I am as sorry as if I had sinned. But with Masha it's so different; I'm filled with joy that I've never soiled the brightness of my feeling for her. *(He points his finger at the floor)* I may go much further down.

PETRUSHKOV *(interrupting)*. I know so well what you mean. But where is she now?

FEDYA. I don't know. I don't want to know. All that belongs to another life, and I couldn't bear to mix that life and this life.

(A Police Officer enters. He kicks a man who is lying on the floor—walks down stage, looks at Fedya and Petrushkov, then exits.)

PETRUSHKOV. Your life's wonderful. I believe you're a real idealist.

FEDYA. No. It's awfully simple. You know among our class—I mean the class I was born in—there are only three courses: the first, to go into the civil service or join the army and make money to squander over your sensual appetites. And all that was appalling to me—perhaps because I couldn't do it. The second thing is to live to clear out, to destroy what is foul, to make way for the beautiful. But for that you've got to be a hero, and I'm not a hero. And the third is to forget it all—overwhelm it with music, drown it with wine. That's what *I* did. And look *(he spreads his arms out)* where my singing led me to. *(He drinks)*

PETRUSHKOV. And what about family life? The sanctity of the home and all that—I would have been awfully happy if I'd had a decent wife. As it was, she ruined me.

FEDYA. I beg your pardon. Did you say marriage? Oh, yes, of course. Well, I've been married, too. Oh, my wife was quite an ideal woman. I don't know why I should say was, by the way, because she's still living. But there's something— I don't know; it's rather difficult to explain—— But you know how pouring champagne into a glass makes it froth up into a million iridescent little bubbles? Well, there was none of that in our married life. There was no fizz in it, no sparkle, no taste, phew! The days were all one color—flat and stale and gray as the devil. And that's why I wanted to get away and forget. You can't forget unless you play. So trying to play I crawled in every sort of muck there is. And you know, it's a funny thing, but we love people for the good we do them, and we hate them for the harm. That's why I hated Lisa. That's why she seemed to love me.

PETRUSHKOV. Why do you say seemed?

FEDYA (wistfully). Oh, she couldn't creep into the center of my being like Masha. But that's not what I mean. Before the baby was born, and afterwards, when she was nursing him, I used to stay away for days and days, and come back drunk, drunk, and love her less and less each time, because I was wronging her so terribly. (Excitedly) Yes. That's it, I never realized it before. The reason why I loved Masha was because I did her good, not harm. But I crucified my wife, and her contortions filled me almost with hatred. (Fedya drinks)

PETRUSHKOV. I think I understand. Now in my case——

(Artemyev enters, approaches with a cockade on his cap, dyed mustache, and shabby, but carefully mended clothes.)

ARTEMYEV (stands Left of the table). Good appetite, gentlemen! (Bowing to Fedya) I see you've made the acquaintance of our great artist.

FEDYA (coolly). Yes, I have.

ARTEMYEV (to Petrushkov). Have you finished your portrait?

PETRUSHKOV. No, they didn't give me the commission, after all.

ARTEMYEV (sitting down on end of table). I'm not in your way, am I?

(Fedya and Petrushkov don't answer.)

PETRUSHKOV. This gentleman was telling me about his life.

ARTEMYEV. Oh, secrets? Then I won't disturb you. Pardon me for interrupting. (To himself as he moves away) Damn swine! (He goes to the next table, sits down and in the dim candlelight he can just be seen listening to the conversation.)

FEDYA. I don't like that man.

PETRUSHKOV. I think he's offended.

FEDYA. Let him be. I can't stand him. If he'd stayed I shouldn't have said a word. Now, it's different with you. You make me feel all comfortable, you know. Well, what was I saying?

PETRUSHKOV. You were talking about your wife. How did you happen to separate?

FEDYA. Oh, that? (A pause) It's a rather curious story. My wife's married.

PETRUSHKOV. Oh, I see! You're divorced.

FEDYA. No. (Smiling) She's a widow.

PETRUSHKOV. A widow? What do you mean?

FEDYA. I mean exactly what I say. She's a widow. I don't exist.

PETRUSHKOV (puzzled). What?

FEDYA (smiling drunkenly). I'm dead. You're talking to a corpse.

(Artemyev leans towards them and listens intently.)

Funny, I seem to be able to say anything to you. And it's so long ago, so long ago. And what is it after all to you but a story? Well, when I got to the climax of torturing my wife, when I'd squandered everything I had or could get, and become utterly rotten, then, there appeared a protector.

PETRUSHKOV. The usual thing, I suppose?

FEDYA. Don't think anything filthy about it. He was just her friend, mine too, a very good, decent fellow; in fact the opposite of myself. He'd know my wife since she was a child, and I suppose he'd loved her since then. He used to come to our house a lot. First I was very glad he did, then I began to see they were falling in love with each other, and then —an odd thing began to happen to me at night. Do you know when she lay there asleep beside me (he laughs shrilly) I would hear him, pushing open the door, crawling into the room, coming to me on his hands and knees, grovelling, whining, begging me (he is almost shouting) for her, for her, imagine it! And I, I had to get up and give my place to him. (He covers his eyes with his hands in a convulsive moment) Phew! Then I'd come to myself.

PETRUSHKOV. God! It must have been horrible.

FEDYA (wearily). Well, later on I left her—and after a while, they asked me for a divorce. I couldn't bear all the lying there was to be got through. Believe me it was easier to think of killing myself. And so I tried to commit suicide, and I tried and I couldn't. Then a kind friend came along and said, "Now, don't be foolish!" And she arranged the whole business for me. I sent my wife a farewell letter—and the next day my clothes and pocketbook were found on the bank of the river. Everybody knew I couldn't swim. (Pause) You understand, don't you?

PETRUSHKOV. Yes, but what about the body? They didn't find that?

FEDYA (smiling drunkenly). Oh yes, they did! You just listen! About a week afterwards some horror was dragged out of the water. My wife was called in to identify it. It was in pretty bad shape, you know. She took one glance. "Is that your husband?" they asked her. And she said, "Yes." Well, that settled it! I was buried, they were married, and they're living very happily right here in this city. I'm living here, too! We're all living here together! Yesterday I walked right by their house. The windows were lit and somebody's shadow went across the blind. (A pause) Of course there're times when I feel like hell about it, but they don't last. The worst is when there's no money to buy drinks with. (He drinks)

ARTEMYEV (rising and approaching them). Excuse me, but you know I've been listening to that story of yours? It's a very good story, and what's more a very useful one. You say you don't like being without money, but really there's no need of your ever finding yourself in that position.

FEDYA (interrupting). Look here, I wasn't talking to you and I don't need your advice!

ARTEMYEV. But I'm going to give it to you just the same. Now you're a corpse. Well, suppose you come to life again!

FEDYA. What?

ARTEMYEV. Then your wife and that fellow she's so happy with—they'd be arrested for bigamy. The best they'd get would be ten years in Siberia. *Now* you see where you can have a steady income, don't you?

FEDYA (furiously). Stop talking and get out of here!

ARTEMYEV. The best way is to write them a letter. If you don't know how I'll do it for you. Just give me their address and afterwards when the ruble notes commence to drop in, how grateful you'll be!

FEDYA. Get out! Get out, I say! I haven't told you anything!

ARTEMYEV. Oh, yes, you have! Here's my witness! This waiter heard you saying you were a corpse!

FEDYA (beside himself). You damn blackmailing beast——

ARTEMYEV. Oh, I'm a beast, am I? We'll see about that! (Fedya rises to go, Artemyev seizes him) Police! Police! (Fedya struggles frantically to escape) (The Police enter and drag him away.)

CURTAIN

SCENE TWO

In the country. A veranda covered by a gay awning; sunlight; flowers; Sophia Karenina, Lisa, her little boy and nurse.

———

LISA (standing in the door. To the little boy, smiling). Who do you think is on his way from the station?

MISHA (excitedly). Who? Who?

LISA. Papa.

MISHA (rapturously). Papa's coming! Papa's coming! (Exits through the center door.)

LISA (contentedly, to Sophia Karenina). How much he loves Victor! As if he were his real father!

SOPHIA KARENINA (on the sofa, knitting —back to audience). Tant mieux. Do you think he ever remembers his father?

LISA (sighing). I can't tell. Of course I've never said anything to him. What's the use of confusing his little head? Yet sometimes I feel as though I ought. What do you think, Mamma?

SOPHIA KARENINA. I think it's a matter

of feeling. If you can trust your heart, let it guide you. What extraordinary adjustments death brings about! I confess I used to think very unkindly of Fedya, when he seemed a barrier to all this. *(She makes a gesture with her hand)* But now I think of him as that nice boy who was my son's friend, and a man who was capable of sacrificing himself for those he loved. *(She knits)* I hope Victor hasn't forgotten to bring me some wool.

LISA. Here he comes. *(Lisa runs to the edge of the veranda)* There's some one with him—a lady in a bonnet! Oh, it's mother! How splendid! I haven't seen her for an age!

(Enter Anna Pavlovna.)

ANNA PAVLOVNA *(kissing Lisa)*. My darling. *(To Sophia Karenina)* How do you do? Victor met me and insisted on my coming down.

(Sits on the bench beside Sophia.)

SOPHIA KARENINA. This is perfectly charming!

(Enter Victor and Misha.)

ANNA PAVLOVNA. I did want to see Lisa and the boy. So now, if you don't turn me out, I'll stay till the evening train.

KARENIN *(kissing his wife, his mother and the boy)*. Congratulate me— everybody —I've a bit of luck. I don't have to go to town again for two days. Isn't that wonderful?

LISA. Two days! That's glorious! We'll drive over to the Hermitage tomorrow and show it to mother.

ANNA PAVLOVNA *(holding the boy)*. He's so like his father, isn't he? I do hope he hasn't inherited his father's disposition.

SOPHIA KARENINA. After all, Fedya's heart was in the right place.

LISA. Victor thinks if he'd only been brought up more carefully everything would have been different.

ANNA PAVLOVNA. Well, I'm not so sure about that, but I do feel sorry for him. I can't think of him without wanting to cry.

LISA. I know. That's how Victor and I feel. All the bitterness is gone. There's nothing left but a very tender memory.

ANNA PAVLOVNA *(sighing)*. I'm sure of it.

LISA. Isn't it funny? It all seemed so hopeless back there, and now see how beautifully everything's come out!

SOPHIA KARENINA. Oh, by the way, Victor, did you get my wool?

KARENIN. I certainly did. *(Bringing a bag and taking out parcels)* Here's the wool, here's the eau-de-cologne, here are the letters—one on "Government Service" for you, Lisa—— *(Hands her the letter. Lisa opens it, then strolls toward the Right, reading it, suddenly stops)* Well, Anna Pavlovna, I know you want to make yourself beautiful! I must tidy up, too. It's almost dinner time. Lisa, you've put your mother in the Blue Room, haven't you?

(Lisa is pale. She holds the letter with trembling hands and reads it, Karenin observing her.)

What's the matter, Lisa? What is it?

LISA. He's alive. He's alive. My God! I shall never be free from him. *(Victor crosses to Lisa)* What does this mean? What's going to happen to us?

KARENIN *(taking the letter and reading)*. I don't believe it.

SOPHIA KARENINA. What is it? *(Rising)* What's the matter? Why don't you tell us?

KARENIN. He's alive! They're accusing us of bigamy! It's a summons for Lisa to go before the Examining Magistrate.

ANNA PAVLOVNA. No—no! It can't be!

SOPHIA KARENINA. Oh, that horrible man!

KARENIN. So it was all a lie!

LISA *(with a cry of rage)*. Oh! I hate him so! Victor!—Fedya!——My God! I don't know what I'm saying. I don't know what I'm saying.

(She sinks in chair, down Right.)

ANNA PAVLOVNA *(rising)*. He's not really *alive?*

CURTAIN

SCENE THREE

The room of the examining magistrate, who sits at a table talking to Melnikov, a smartly dressed, languid, man-about-town.

At a side-table a Clerk is sorting papers.

MAGISTRATE. Oh, I never said so. It's her own notion. And now she is reproaching me with it.

MELNIKOV. She's not reproaching you, only her feelings are awfully hurt.

MAGISTRATE. Are they? Oh, well, tell her I'll come to supper after the performance. But you'd better wait on. I've rather an interesting case. *(To the Clerk)* Here, you, show them in.

CLERK. Both? Excellency.

MAGISTRATE. No, only Madame Karenina.

(The Clerk goes out Left.)

CLERK *(calling off-stage)*. Madame Protosova, Madame Protosova.

MAGISTRATE. Or, to dot my i's, Madame Protosova.

MELNIKOV *(starting to go out)*. Ah, it's the Karenin case.

MAGISTRATE. Yes, and an ugly one. I'm just beginning the investigation. But I assure you it's a first-rate scandal already. Must you go? Well, see you at supper. Good-by.

(Melnikov goes out at the Right. Then the Clerk shows in Lisa, who wears a black dress and veil.)

MAGISTRATE. Please sit down, won't you? *(He points to a chair Left Center, and Lisa sits down)* I am extremely sorry that it's necessary to ask you questions. *(Lisa appears very much agitated. The Magistrate appears unconcerned and is reading a newspaper as he speaks.)* But please be calm. You needn't answer them unless you wish. Only in the interest of everyone concerned, I advise you to help me reach the entire truth.

LISA. I've nothing to conceal.

MAGISTRATE *(looking at the papers)*. Let's see. Your name, station, religion. I've got all that. You are accused of contracting a marriage with another man, knowing your first husband to be alive.

LISA. But I did not know it.

MAGISTRATE *(continuing)*. And also you are accused of having persuaded with bribes your first husband to commit a fraud, a pretended suicide, in order to rid yourself of him.

LISA. All that's not true.

MAGISTRATE. Then permit me to ask you these questions: Did you or did you not send him 1200 rubles in July of last year?

LISA. That was his own money obtained from selling his things, which I sent to him during our separation, while I was waiting for my divorce.

MAGISTRATE. Just so. Very well. When the police asked you to identify the corpse, how were you sure it was your husband's?

LISA. Oh, I was so terribly distressed that I couldn't bear to look at the body. Besides, I felt so sure it was he, and when they asked me, I just said yes.

MAGISTRATE. Very good indeed. I can well understand your distraction, and permit me to observe, Madame, that although servants of the law, we remain human beings, and I beg you to be assured that I sympathize with your situation. You were bound to a spendthrift, a drunkard, a man whose dissipation caused you infinite misery.

LISA *(interrupting)*. Please, I loved him.

MAGISTRATE *(tolerantly)*. Of course. Yet naturally you desired to be free, and you took this simple course without counting the consequence, which is considered a crime, or bigamy. I understand you, and so will both judges and jury. And it's for this reason, Madame, I urge you to disclose the entire truth.

LISA. I've nothing to disclose. I never have lied. *(She begins to cry)* Do you want me any longer?

MAGISTRATE. Yes. I must ask you to remain a few minutes longer. No more questions, however. *(To the Clerk)* Show in Victor Karenin. *(To Lisa)* I think you'll find that a comfortable chair. *(He sits down)*

(Enter Karenin, stern and solemn.) Please sit down.

KARENIN. Thank you. *(He remains standing)* What do you want from me?

MAGISTRATE. I have to take your deposition.

KARENIN. In what capacity?

MAGISTRATE *(smiling)*. In my capacity of investigating magistrate. You are here, you know, because you are charged with a crime.

KARENIN. Really? What crime?

MAGISTRATE. Bigamy, since you've

married a woman already married. But I'll put the questions to you in their proper order. Sure you'll not sit down?

KARENIN. Quite sure.

MAGISTRATE (*writing*). Your name?

KARENIN. Victor Karenin.

MAGISTRATE. Rank?

KARENIN. Chamberlain of the Imperial Court.

MAGISTRATE. Your age?

KARENIN. Thirty-eight.

MAGISTRATE. Religion?

KARENIN. Orthodox, and I've never been tried before of any charge. (*Pause*) What else?

MAGISTRATE. Did you know that Fedor Protosov was alive when you married his wife?

KARENIN. No, we were both convinced that he was drowned.

MAGISTRATE. All right. And why did you send 1200 rubles to him a few days before he simulated death on July 17th?

KARENIN. That money was given me by my wife.

MAGISTRATE (*interrupting him*). Excuse me, you mean by *Madame* Protosova.

KARENIN. By my wife to send to her husband. She considered this money his property, and having broken off all relations with him, felt it unjust to withhold it. What else do you want?

MAGISTRATE. I don't want anything, except to do my official duty, and to aid you in doing yours, through causing you to tell me the whole truth, in order that your innocence be proved. You'd certainly better not conceal things which are sure to be found out, since Protosov is in such a weakened condition, physically and mentally, that he is certain to come out with the entire truth as soon as he gets into court, so from your point of view I advise . . .

KARENIN. Please don't advise me, but remain within the limits of your official capacity. Are we at liberty to leave? (*He goes to Lisa who takes his arm.*)

MAGISTRATE. Sorry, but it's necessary to detain you. (*Karenin looks around in astonishment*) No, I've no intention of arresting you, although it might be a quicker way of reaching the truth. I merely want to take Protosov's deposition

in your presence, to confront him with you, that you may facilitate your chances by proving his statements to be false. Kindly sit down. (*To Clerk*) Show in Fedor Protosov.

(*There is a pause. The Clerk shows in Fedya in rags, a total wreck. He enters slowly, dragging his feet. He catches sight of his wife, who is bowed in grief. For a moment he is about to take her in his arms—he hesitates— then stands before the Magistrate.*)

MAGISTRATE. I shall ask you to answer some questions.

FEDYA (*rises, confronting the Magistrate*). Ask them.

MAGISTRATE. Your name?

FEDYA. You know it.

MAGISTRATE (*rapping on his desk*). Answer my questions exactly, please.

FEDYA (*shrugs*). Fedor Protosov.

MAGISTRATE. Your rank, age, religion?

FEDYA (*silent for a moment*). Aren't you ashamed to ask me these absurd questions? Ask me what you need to know, only that.

MAGISTRATE. I shall ask you to take care how you express yourself.

FEDYA. Well, since you're not ashamed. My rank, graduate of the University of Moscow; age 40; religion orthodox. What else?

MAGISTRATE. Did Victor Karenin and Elizaveta Andreyevna know you were alive when you left your clothes on the bank of the river and disappeared?

FEDYA. Of course not. I really wished to commit suicide. But—however, why should I tell you? The fact's enough. They knew nothing of it.

MAGISTRATE. You gave a somewhat different account to the police officer. How do you explain that?

FEDYA. Which police officer? Oh yes, the one who arrested me in that dive. I was drunk, and I lied to him—about what, I don't remember. But I'm not drunk now and I'm telling you the whole truth. They knew nothing; they thought I was dead, and I was glad of it. Everything would have stayed all right except for that damned beast Artemyev. So if anyone's guilty, it's I.

MAGISTRATE. I perceive you wish to be generous. Unfortunately the law demands the truth. Come, why did you receive money from them?

(Fedya remains silent.)

Why don't you answer me? Do you realize that it will be stated in your deposition that the accused refused to answer these questions, and that will harm *(he includes Lisa and Victor in a gesture)* all of you?

(Fedya continues to be silent.)

Aren't you ashamed of your stubborn refusal to aid these others and yourself by telling the entire truth?

FEDYA *(breaking out passionately)*. The truth—— Oh, God! what do you know about the truth? Your business is crawling up into a little power, that you may use it by tantalizing, morally and physically, people a thousand times better than you. You sit there in your smug authority torturing people.

MAGISTRATE. I must ask you——

FEDYA *(interrupts him)*. Don't ask me for I'll speak as I feel. *(Turning to the Clerk)* And you write it down. So for once some human words will get into a deposition.

(Raising his voice, which ascends to a climax during this speech.)

There were three human beings alive: I, he, and she.

(He turns to his wife a gesture indicating his love for her. He pauses, then proceeds.)

We all bore towards one another a most complex relation. We were all engaged in a spiritual struggle beyond your comprehension: the struggle between anguish and peace; between falsehood and truth. Suddenly this struggle ended in a way that set us free. Everybody was at peace. They loved my memory, and I was happy even in my downfall, because I'd done what should have been done, and cleared away my weak life from interfering with their strong good lives. And yet we're all alive. When suddenly a bastard adventurer appears, who demands that I abet his filthy scheme. I drive him off as I would a diseased dog, but he finds you, the defender of public justice, the appointed guardian of morality, to listen to him. And you, who receive on the 20th of each month a few kopeks' gratuity for your wretched business, you get into your

uniform, and in good spirits proceed to torture—bully people whose threshold you're not clean enough to pass. Then when you've had your fill of showing off your wretched power, oh, then you are satisfied, and sit and smile there in your damned complacent dignity. And . . .

MAGISTRATE *(raising his voice, and rising excitedly)*. Be silent or I'll have you turned out.

FEDYA. God! Who should *I* be afraid of! I'm dead, dead, and away out of your power. *(Suddenly overcome with the horror of the situation)* What can you do to me? How can you punish me—a corpse? *(He beats his breast)*

MAGISTRATE. Be silent! *(To the Clerk)* Take him out!

(Fedya turns, seeing his wife, he falls on his knees before her . . . kisses the hem of her dress, crying bitterly. Then he slowly rises, pulls himself together with a great effort and goes out.)

CURTAIN

SCENE FOUR

A corridor in the lower courts; in the background a door opposite which stands a Guard; to the Right is another door through which the Prisoners are conducted to the court. Ivan Petrovich in rags enters at the Left, goes to this last door, trying to pass through it.

———

GUARD *(at the door)*. Where do you think you're going, shoving in like that?

IVAN PETROVICH. Why shouldn't I? The law says these sessions are public.

GUARD. You can't get by and that's enough.

IVAN PETROVICH *(in pity)*. Wretched peasant, you have no idea to whom you are speaking.

GUARD. Be silent!

(Enter a Young Lawyer from the Right.)

LAWYER *(to Petrovich)*. Are you here on business?

IVAN PETROVICH. No. I'm the public. But this wretched peasant won't let me pass.

LAWYER. There's no room for the public at this trial.

IVAN PETROVICH. Perhaps, but I am above the general rule.

LAWYER. Well, you wait outside; they'll adjourn presently.

(He is just going into courtroom through door at the Right Center when Prince Sergius enters from the Left and stops him.)

PRINCE SERGIUS. How does the case stand?

LAWYER. The defense has just begun. Petrushkin is speaking now.

PRINCE SERGIUS. Are the Karenins bearing up well?

LAWYER. Yes, with extraordinary dignity. They look as if they were the judges instead of the accused. That's felt all the way through, and Petrushkin is taking advantage of it.

PRINCE SERGIUS. What of Protosov?

LAWYER. He's frightfully unnerved, trembling all over, but that's natural considering the sort of life he's led. Yes, he's all on edge, and he's interrupted both judge and jury several times already.

PRINCE SERGIUS. How do you think it will end?

LAWYER. Hard to say. The jury are mixed. At any rate I don't think they'll find the Karenins guilty of premeditation. Do you want to go in?

PRINCE SERGIUS. I should very much like to.

LAWYER. Excuse me, you're Prince Sergius Abreskov, aren't you? (To the Prince) There's an empty chair just at the left.

(The guard lets Prince Sergius pass.)

IVAN PETROVICH. Prince! Bah! I am an aristocrat of the soul, and that's a higher title.

LAWYER. Excuse me.

(And he exits down Right Center into the courtroom. Petrushkov, Fedya's companion in the dive, enters approaching Ivan Petrovich.)

PETRUSHKOV. Oh, there you are. Well, how're things going?

IVAN PETROVICH. The speeches for the defense have begun, but this ignorant rascal won't let us in. Curse his damned petty soul.

GUARD. Silence! Where do you think you are?

(Door of the court opens, and there is a rush of lawyers and the general public into the corridor.)

A LADY. Oh, it's simply wonderful! When he spoke I felt as if my heart were breaking.

AN OFFICER. It's all far better than a novel. But I don't see how she could ever have loved him. Such a sinister, horrible figure.

(The other door opens over at the Left; the accused comes out.)

THE LADY (this group is down Right). Hush! There he is. See how wild he looks.

FEDYA (seeing Ivan Petrovich). Did you bring it?

(Goes to Petrovich.)

PETROVICH. There.

(He hands Fedya something; Fedya hides it in his pocket.)

FEDYA (seeing Petrushkov). How foolish! How vulgar and how boring all this is, isn't it?

(Men and women enter through door at the Left and stand watching. Enter Petrushkin, from center door, Fedya's counsel, a stout man with red cheeks; very animated.)

PETRUSHKIN (rubbing his hands). Well, well, my friend. It's going along splendidly. Only remember, don't go and spoil things for me in your last speech.

FEDYA (takes him by the arm). Tell me, what'll the worst be?

PETRUSHKIN. I've already told you. Exile to Siberia.

FEDYA. Who'll be exiled to Siberia?

PETRUSHKIN. You and your wife, naturally.

FEDYA. And at the best?

PETRUSHKIN. Religious pardon and the annulment of the second marriage.

FEDYA. You mean—that we should be bound again— to one another——

PETRUSHKIN. Yes. Only try to collect yourself. Keep up your courage. After all, there's no occasion for alarm.

FEDYA. There couldn't be any other sentence, you're sure?

PETRUSHKIN. None other. None other.

(Exits. Fedya stands motionless.)

GUARD (crosses and exits Left, calling). Pass on. Pass on. No loitering in the corridor.

(Victor and Lisa enter from the door at the

Left. The sound of a pistol shot stops them.)

FEDYA *(He turns his back to the audience, and from beneath his ragged coat shoots himself in the heart. There is a muffled explosion, smoke. He crumples up in a heap on the floor. All the people in the passage rush to him. He speaks in a very low voice).* This time—it's well done . . . Lisa . . .

(People come crowding in from all the doors, judges, etc. Lisa rushes to Fedya, Karenin, Ivan Petrovich and Prince Sergius follow.)

LISA. Fedya! . . . Fedya! . . . What have you done? Oh why! . . . why! . . .

FEDYA. Forgive me—— No other way—— Not for you—but for myself——

LISA. You will live. You must live.

FEDYA. No—no—— Good-by——
(He seems to smile, then he mutters just under his breath) Masha.
(In the distance the gypsies are heard singing "No More at Evening", they continue to sing until the curtain falls.)
You're too late——
(Suddenly he raises his head from Lisa's knees, and, as if he saw something in front of him, he whispers.)
Ah . . . Happiness! . . .
(His head falls from Lisa's knees to the ground. She still clings to it, in grief and horror. He dies.)

CURTAIN